Immigration Consequences of Criminal Activity

A Guide to Representing Foreign-Born Defendants

Sixth Edition

AILA PUBLICATIONS

AILA'S OCCUPATIONAL GUIDEBOOKS
Immigration Options for Artists and Entertainers
Immigration Options for Physicians
Immigration Options for Nurses & Allied Health Care Professionals
Immigration Options for Religious Workers
Immigration Options for Academics and Researchers
Immigration Options for Investors and Entrepreneurs

STATUTES, REGULATIONS, AGENCY MATERIALS & CASE LAW
Code of Federal Regulations
Immigration & Nationality Act

CORE CURRICULUM
Navigating the Fundamentals of Immigration Law
AILA's Guide to Immigration Law for Paralegals

TOOLBOX SERIES
AILA's Immigration Practice Toolbox
AILA's Litigation Toolbox
AILA's Immigration Forms Toolbox

AILA'S FOCUS SERIES
EB-2 & EB-3 Degree Equivalency
by Ronald Wada

Waivers Under the INA
by Julie Ferguson

Private Bills & Pardons in Immigration
by Anna Gallagher

The Child Status Protection Act
by Charles Wheeler

Immigration Practice Under AC21
by A. James Vazquez-Azpiri & Eleanor Pelta

ONLINE RESEARCH TOOLS
AILALink

TREATISES & PRIMERS
Kurzban's Immigration Law Sourcebook
by Ira J. Kurzban

Business Immigration: Law & Practice
by Daryl Buffenstein and Bo Cooper

AILA's Asylum Primer
by Dree Collopy

Immigration Consequences of Criminal Activity
by Mary E. Kramer

Representing Clients in Immigration Court
by CLINIC

Provisional Waivers: A Practitioner's Guide
by CLINIC

Essentials of Immigration Law
by Richard A. Boswell

Litigating Immigration Cases in Federal Court
by Robert Pauw

Immigration Law & the Family
by Charles Wheeler

Immigration Law & the Transgender Client
by Transgender Law Center & Immigration Equality

Immigration Law & the Military
by Margaret D. Stock

SPECIFIC TOPICS
The Waivers Book: Advanced Issues in Immigration Practice
AILA's Guide to U.S. Citizenship & Naturalization Law
The Entrepreneurial Lawyer: How to Run a Successful Immigration Practice
The Diplomatic Visas Handbook
Immigration Practice Pointers
The International Adoption Sourcebook

PERIODICALS
Inside Immigration: Monograph Series

Sixth Edition

Immigration Consequences of Criminal Activity

A Guide to Representing Foreign-Born Defendants

Mary E. Kramer

AMERICAN IMMIGRATION LAWYERS ASSOCIATION

Website for Corrections and Updates

Corrections and other updates to AILA publications
can be found online at: *www.aila.org/BookUpdates*.

If you have any corrections or updates to the information in this book,
please let us know by sending a note to the address below, or e-mail us at
books@aila.org.

This publication is designed to provide accurate and authoritative information in regard to the subject matter covered. It is distributed with the understanding that the publisher is not engaged in rendering legal, accounting, or other professional service. If legal advice or other expert assistance is required, the services of a competent professional should be sought.

—from a Declaration of Principles jointly adopted by a Committee of the American Bar Association and a Committee of Publishers

Copyright © 2003–2015 by the American Immigration Lawyers Association

All rights reserved. No part of this publication may be reproduced or transmitted in any form or by any means, electronic or mechanical, including photocopy, recording, or any information storage retrieval system, without written permission from the publisher. No copyright claimed on U.S. government material.

Requests for permission to make electronic or print copies of any part of this work should be mailed to American Immigration Lawyers Association, 1331 G St. NW, Suite #300, Washington, DC 20005, or e-mailed to *books@aila.org*.

Printed in the United States of America

ISBN 978-1-57370-385-7
Stock No. 53-85

In 2003, when the first edition of this book was published, I had the idea of dedicating my work to people in ICE detention. But a good friend told me I was crazy: "Don't dedicate the book to criminals and detainees; dedicate the book to your family." I did so, and in the four subsequent editions, I have steadfastly dedicated my writing to members of my family. I love my family. But this year, this sixth edition is dedicated to the men, women, and children who are languishing unnecessarily in immigration detention centers, away from their families, waiting for that final hearing or their appeal to come through. Most of you are detained for political clout, to justify DHS budgets, or to line the pockets of the private prison industry. It breaks my heart. So to those of you who are serving no prison sentence, but are detained anyway: I hear you, I see you, I think of you. My work—this edition—is dedicated to you.

PREFACE

Simply arriving at your destination without knowing the route taken means you won't find your way back the next time.

Welcome to the sixth edition of *Immigration Consequences of Criminal Activity*. The 2015 version presents a revamped format that I believe will be easier to use. Previously, some friends told me that chapter five, which had incorporated methodology and all classifications of crime (from aggravated felony to moral turpitude and beyond) was too large and cumbersome to navigate. So this year, I have abandoned the behemoth approach to analysis of all crimes and opted for separate chapters for methodology, moral turpitude, aggravated felonies, and then all other types of crime. I believe that breaking up the topics makes the book easier to use.

It has been an exciting couple of years in the world of criminal and immigration law. In 2013, the U.S. Supreme Court recalibrated the categorical approach with its decision in *Descamps v. U.S.* The Board of Immigration Appeals took up its marching orders and vacated *Matter of Lanferman*. Then, Attorney General Eric Holder vacated *Matter of Silva-Trevino*. Still, a circuit-court split already has developed regarding how to identify "divisibility" in a statute, such that a modified categorical approach applies. The point is, just as attorneys embark on an exciting new paradigm of analyzing criminal statutes in the context of immigration law, we find the earth below us still moving: Litigation continues to be fluid and it is vitally important that everyone, well, keep up.

There is something in this book for everyone. The first two chapters are a great introduction for criminal lawyers, new immigration attorneys, law students, and even office paralegal staff. Preparing applications, the final chapter, is also a good introduction for young attorneys, students, and staff. Criminal attorneys will certainly benefit from the chapter on successful plea bargaining and cooperating witness benefits. The experienced immigration attorney will note that I have included updated case law, new memos and motions, and cutting-edge analysis. I am particularly proud of chapter five, "Methodology," because I believe I have successfully broken down the *Descamps* precedent and the impending circuit split, with a focus on key terms and their application. Although there are now 13 instead of 10 chapters, the additions are for organization and readability, not to increase length.

The way to use this book is to allow the sequence of chapters to guide you through a real-life client's case. First, determine if there is a "conviction." Second, understand and be aware of the possibility of detention—always a client's main concern. Third, classify the crime according to the correct methodology to determine whether it involves moral turpitude, is an aggravated felony, a controlled substance offense, a firearm crime, etc. Fourth, assuming the crime falls into an immigration law classification, determine the immigration law consequence(s) based on the individual client's personal status. Fifth, assuming there is a consequence, determine the appropriate relief or resolution.

For the non–American citizen client fortunate enough to have a criminal defense attorney, chapter eleven includes effective plea bargaining tips and strategies. Chapter twelve is an explanation of cooperating witness benefits, which are parole, "S", "T", and "U" status. Finally, the last chapter contains practical advice on how to prepare and file an application or motion. Throughout the book there are useful sample motions, memoranda, and unpublished decisions that have been selected because of their strong analysis and the way they illustrate the proper application of the law.

So what are some of the emerging issues covered in this edition? Chapter two contains updated motions to vacate based on ineffective assistance of counsel *a la Padilla v. Kentucky*. Chapter four includes an update on detention litigation, including the "when released" and "prolonged detention" line of cases. Chapter five teaches the vocabulary: categorical to circumstance-specific to means versus elements—it's all there. And it is vital information. Chapters six, seven, and eight analyze and classify crimes such as burglary, theft, assault, fraud, controlled substances, and firearms. I have updated the case law and offered my perspective on the validity of the decisions. At every turn, I have sought to highlight the correct analysis so that—rather than providing a quick and easy answer—I show the reader *how* the deciding court *arrived* at that answer. Simply arriving at your destination without knowing the route taken means you won't find your way back the next time. I do not want my reader to be lost, but to know and understand the route every single time. That is why I have poured over the case law, shared my best tips and strategies, and even provided winning motions and memos. We are on this journey together. Enjoy.

Mary E. Kramer
June 2015

SUMMARY TABLE OF CONTENTS
IMMIGRATION CONSEQUENCES OF CRIMINAL ACTIVITY, SIXTH ED.

Dedication v
Preface vii
Acknowledgments xv
Glossary of Acronyms xvii
Detailed Table of Contents xix
Table of Decisions 677
Subject-Matter Index 695

Chapter One: An Overview of Basic Immigration Terms and the Immigration Law System 1
Who (or What) Is Your Client? An Introduction to Statuses 1
Other Useful Terms 13
Authority over Immigration Law Enforcement: A Look at the Government Agencies 14
The Agencies at Work: Removal Proceedings 20
Federal Judicial Review 27
Tips and Tools of the Trade 34
Sources of Legal Authority 38

Appendices

1A: Contact Information for Immigration Courts 39
1B: Structure of CBP 40
1C: Structure of ICE 41
1D: Structure of USCIS 42
1E: Sample Notice to Appear 43
1F: FBI Rap Sheet Request 46
1G: Appointment Confirmation Letter 48
1H: Client Information Sheet 49

Chapter Two: The Definition of "Conviction" According to Immigration Law 51
The Statutory Definition of "Conviction" 51

Proof of Convictions.. 81
Suspensions of Sentence.. 82

Appendices

2A: Motion to Vacate Plea, Judgment, and Sentence... 84
2B: *Padilla* Motion to Vacate Plea, Judgment, and Sentence 90

Chapter Three: Consequences of Criminal Activity: Removal from the United States.. 97

Inadmissibility 98
Deportability.. 104
Expedited Removal of Certain Aggravated Felons 107
Detention.. 110
Re-entering After Removal: Criminal Prosecution and Reinstatement of Removal... 111
How the Government Locates Your Client 115

Appendices

3A: Memorandum of Law in Support of Motion to Terminate................................ 121
3B: Motion to Terminate Based on Improper Designation as Arriving Alien 128

Chapter Four: Consequences of Criminal Activity: Detention Inside the United States.. 133

Mandatory Detention 133
Other Detention Issues... 153
    Detention After a Removal Order... 158

Appendices

4A: Custody Rule Invoked (Terminates the Transitional Period Custody Rules).... 164
4B: Section 309 of the IIRAIRA – the Transition Rule for 1996 Amendments to the INA 166
4C: Section 303(b) of the IIRAIRA – Effective Date of INA §236(c) Mandatory Detention.. 169
4D: Memorandum on INA §236(c)'s "Custody" Requirement and the Use of Alternatives to Detention to Meet the Statute's Requirements................................ 171
4E: Memorandum of Law in Support of Bond Motion – Joseph Motion Arguing Financial Loss to a Victim Did Not Exceed $10,000 for Purposes of INA §101(a)(43)(M) 176

SUMMARY TABLE OF CONTENTS xi

Chapter Five: Methodology: Classifying Crimes Under the Immigration and Nationality Act 181
Proper Classification of Crimes and the Methodology 181
Analyses and Terms 182
Divisibility after *Descamps*: Circuit Court Developments 197
Divisibility after *Descamps*: Board of Immigration Appeals 205
Chapter Review: A Review of Pertinent Terms 214
Appendices
5A: Unpublished BIA Decision, *Matter of Forvilus* 217
5B: Unpublished IJ Decision Terminating Arriving Alien Status, Not a CIMT 226
5C: Unpublished IJ Decision Finding 18 USC §1860 not a CIMT 232
5D: Immigration Attorney/Client Checklist for Analyzing a Case with a Crime 235

Chapter Six: Crimes Involving Moral Turpitude 363
The Concept of Crimes Involving Moral Turpitude 239
Specific Offenses and Whether They Involve Moral Turpitude 245
Crimes of Violence 253

Chapter Seven: Aggravated Felonies 263
The INA Definition of Aggravated Felony 263
The Definition of "Crime of Violence" 290
Contesting "Loss" Findings; Understanding "Relevant Conduct" 313
"Aggravated Felony"—Must It Be a Felony? 318
Attempts and Conspiracies 320

Chapter Eight: Classifications Beyond Moral Turpitude and Aggravated Felony 323
Controlled Substance Offenses 323
Firearms Offenses 333
Money Laundering 335
Crimes of Domestic Violence 336
Alien Smuggling 343
Crimes Involving Failure to Register; Visa and Passport Fraud 347
Export Law; National Security Violations 351
Public Safety and National Security 353
Failure to Register as a Sex Offender 354

Appendices

8A: Respondent's Motion to Dismiss Charges 356
8B: Unpublished BIA Decision on Drug Paraphernalia and *Pickering* Vacatur Standard 369

Chapter Nine: Consequences of Specific Criminal Activity 375
Consequences of Crimes Involving Moral Turpitude 376
Consequences of an Aggravated Felony Conviction 390
Consequences of a Controlled Substance Conviction 394
Consequences of a Firearms Offense 401
Consequences for Money Laundering Offenses 405
Consequences of a Domestic Violence Conviction 410
Consequences of Alien Smuggling 415
Falsification of Documents, and Visa and Passport Fraud 419
Consequences of Export Law Violations 425

Appendix

9A: Crimes and Possible Consequences Chart 429

Chapter Ten: Immigration Defense: Waivers and Other Relief 431
Adjustment of Status 432
Waivers Under INA §212(h) 441
INA §209(c) Waiver for Refugees and Asylees 459
Asylum and Withholding of Removal 461
Cancellation of Removal 466
The Waiver That Keeps Giving: INA §212(c) (repealed 1996) 476
Voluntary Departure 495
Is Your Client an American Citizen? An Introduction to Derivative and Acquired Citizenship 499
Naturalization as a Defense to Deportation 503
Relief from Alien Smuggling Charges 507
Nonimmigrant Visa Waiver Under INA §212(d)(3) 510
Defending the Criminal Charge of Re-entry After Removal 514

Appendices

10A: Unpublished BIA Decision re: Sua Sponte Motion to Reopen for §212(c) After Removal Order, Conviction by Trial 524

10B: Brief Excerpt – Addressing Difference In "Particularly Serious Crime Analysis" from Asylum to Withholding 526

10C: Motion to Pretermit Waiver Application Under INA §212(h) 529

10D: Sample Memorandum in Support of INA §212(h) Eligibility 534

10E: Unpublished BIA Decision re: Cancellation of Removal, Waiver of Inadmissibility Under INA §212(h) 540

10F: Sample Motion to Terminate Removal Proceedings 544

10G: Sample Memorandum in Support of INA §240A(a) Eligibility for Cancellation of Removal 549

10H: Sample Statement in Support of Naturalization Eligibility 556

Chapter Eleven: Immigration Defense: Fashioning a Plea to Avoid Adverse Immigration Consequences 561

Avoiding Adverse Immigration Consequences 562

Avoiding a Conviction of a Crime Involving Moral Turpitude 566

Avoiding the Aggravated Felony Conviction 572

Avoiding Deportability for Domestic Violence Offenses 580

Creating Eligibility for Relief 581

Appendix

11A: Sample Memorandum for Fashioning a Plea 588

Chapter Twelve: Visas for Cooperating Witnesses 599

"S" Status 600

"T" Status 609

"U" Status 614

Appendices

12A: Form I-854, Inter-Agency Alien Witness and Informant Record 625

12B: Freedom of Information Act Request 631

Chapter Thirteen: Preparing and Presenting Applications That Waive a Criminal Conviction 639

Venues: Consulate, USCIS, ICE, and Immigration Court 640

The Universal List: Evidence in Support of a Waiver 644

Adjustment of Status 648

INA §212(h) Waivers—15-Year, Hardship, and Battered Spouse or Child 651

Refugee Waiver Under INA §209(c) 652

Waiver Under the Pre-AEDPA INA §212(c) (repealed in 1996) 654

Cancellation of Removal—INA §240A(a) 655
Special Rule Cancellation of Removal 656
Waiver Under INA §212(d)(3)(A) 657
Memoranda of Law and Witness Lists 659
Applications Filed After an Order of Removal 663
Appendix
13A: Sample Respondent's Pretrial Statement 668

ACKNOWLEDGMENTS

As I sit down to write this, I am overwhelmed by the support I have received from so many people—not just this year, but over the years. This is the sixth edition in a 12-year time period. I want to thank Amy Novick and Randy Auerbach, my original publishers at AILA, for believing in me. The book's template still contains the name Stephanie Browning as the "creator"; I remember working nights, weekends, and holidays with Stephanie to create a basic theme and structure we've stuck with over the years. The staff at AILA National has been so loyal and supportive of this book, and today I thank Grace Woods, Robert Deasy, and Crystal Williams for their belief and dedication to this ongoing effort to educate and support our AILA members and students of the law. Their commitment to this publication demonstrates the value AILA National places on educating immigration attorneys in the law.

This book could not have been written without the invaluable assistance of friends and other professionals. I thank attorney Jordan Dollar, a friend and colleague on the Catholic Legal Services Board, who proofread the important new chapter on methodology. Attorney Sui Chung wrote a piece for the detention chapter on the "when released" litigation. Sui Chung, along with Professor Michael Vastine, also contributed research on the *Padilla* litigation and provided the motions to vacate that you'll find as appendix items. Over the past several years, Sui and Michael have become great supportive friends with whom I collaborate often on legal research, speaking, and advocacy. I acknowledge and thank them. The sections on "U" and "T" status in the cooperating witness visas chapter are largely the hard work of attorney Callan Garcia, a talented and tireless advocate, and I thank him for his research and writing. And my own mother, Elizabeth Kramer, not a lawyer, but a great editor, has had a hand at proofreading my work, so I thank my mom. In years' past, attorneys Britney Horstman, David Kubiliun, Linda Osberg-Braun, Pedro Pavon, and Gerald Seipp have edited or provided material for this book; and since one edition builds on another, I thank them and remember their assistance always. I also want to acknowledge attorney Randy McGrorty for his support and encouragement when I felt overwhelmed by writing this book and running a law practice. *Thanks to all of you.*

My own office staff devoted time both in and out of the office to this book. My associate, Ilaria Cacopardo, organized and modified motions and memos that are now in the appendices, and she updated the chapter on waivers and relief. Of note, Ilaria also has worked hard on our own office cases and met with clients while I took time off to research and write. She never complained about the extra responsibilities, and I appreciate her support and dedication so very much. Jennifer Vargas, law student and law clerk *extraordinaire*, updated the final chapter on the nuts and bolts of filing applications. She proofread several chapters and organized appendix items, working nights and weekends to assist me with all manner of logistics. Jennifer will be an incredible lawyer soon, and I have so enjoyed watching her progress. Always upbeat and energetic, Sophia Carballosa is another law clerk in my office. Sophia went through the tedious tasks of cite checking, proofreading, modifying motions and memos (to protect the confidentiality of the innocent and not-so-innocent) and organizing appendix items. Sophia was the primary recipient of my brainstorming (surges of inspiration) at all hours of the night or day and helped organized my thoughts and progress. Sophia is a tenacious hard-working professional who will one day make a very fine lawyer. And through it all, my husband and office manager supervises the daily business operations of the office so that the rest of us can practice law. So *thank you* to Ilaria, Jennifer, Sophia, and Jose—my office family: this book is as much yours as mine (and, of course, AILA's).

Mary Johnson, AILA's Marketing Associate Director, deserves my ongoing gratitude for her creative marketing and distribution of this book. She is a pleasure to work with, and this book is the fortunate beneficiary of her artistic and professional talents. I also thank attorney Richard Link for his second turn at editing and other contributions to the publication. I appreciate his efforts and hard work.

Finally, a heartfelt thanks goes out to Ms. Tatia Gordon-Troy. Tatia was my publisher for several years at AILA National and supervised the editing and publication of this book. Having recently transitioned into the private sector, Tatia had no further responsibility to this publication. However, when I reached out to Tatia and asked if she could assist, she displayed an incredible dedication to the book, and a personal loyalty to me, ultimately working simply crazy hours at night and on weekends to edit, format, and pull together this sixth edition. So I thank Tatia for standing by me and this book—and our readers—and for once again sharing her amazing talent for good legal writing and publication savvy with the community. *Thank you, Tatia.*

Mary E. Kramer
June 2015

GLOSSARY OF ACRONYMS

AEDPA	Antiterrorism and Effective Death Penalty Act of 1996, Pub. L. No. 104-132, 110 Stat. 1214
ACCA	Armed Criminal Career Act
BIA	Board of Immigration Appeals
CAT	Convention against Torture
CBP	U.S. Customs and Border Protection
CIMT	Crime Involving Moral Turpitude
DHS	Department of Homeland Security
DOJ	Department of Justice
DOS	Department of State
ERO	Enforcement and Removal Operations (part of ICE)
EOIR	Executive Office for Immigration Review
ICE	U.S. Immigration and Customs Enforcement
IIRAIRA	Illegal Immigration Reform and Immigrant Responsibility Act of 1996, Division C of the Omnibus Appropriations Act of 1996 (H.R. 3610), Pub. L. No. 104-208, 110 Stat. 3009
IJ	Immigration Judge
IMMACT90	Immigration Act of 1990, Pub. L. No. 101-649, 104 Stat. 4978
INA	Immigration and Nationality Act of 1952 (INA), Pub. L. No. 82-414, 66 Stat. 163
IV	Immigrant Visa
ISAP	Intensive Supervision Appearance Program
LEA	Law Enforcement Agency
LPR	Lawful Permanent Resident
NACARA	Nicaraguan and Central American Relief Act, Pub. L. No. 105-139, 111 Stat. 2644
NIV	Nonimmigrant Visa
NTA	Notice to Appear
OSC	Order to Show Cause
TRO	Temporary Restraining Order
USA PATRIOT Act	Uniting and Strengthening America by Providing Appropriate Tools Required to Intercept and Obstruct Terrorism Act of 2001, Pub. L. 107-56, 115 Stat. 272
USCIS	U.S. Citizenship and Immigration Services

VAWA	Violence Against Women Act of 1994, Pub. L. No. 103-322, 108 Stat. 1902-1955 (codified as 8 USC §§1151, 1154, 1186a note, 1254, 2245)
VTVPA	Victims of Trafficking and Violence Protection Act of 2000, Pub. L. No. 106-386, 114 Stat. 1464

Detailed Table of Contents
Immigration Consequences of Criminal Activity, Sixth Ed.

Dedication v
Preface vii
Acknowledgments xv
Glossary of Acronyms xvii
Table of Decisions 677
Subject-Matter Index 695

Chapter One: An Overview of Basic Immigration Terms and the Immigration Law System 1
Who (or What) Is Your Client? An Introduction to Statuses 1
    Citizenship and Naturalization 2
    The Lawful Permanent Resident ("Green-Card" Holder) 3
    The Nonimmigrant Visa Holder 4
        Persons from the Caribbean, Canada, and Mexico who do not need visas—tourists and temporary workers 4
        The Visa Waiver Program (tourists without visas) 5
    Other Protective Categories 5
        Refugees and asylees 5
        Withholding of removal 6
        Protection under the Convention Against Torture 7
        Temporary protected status 8
        Parole 8
        Deferred action 9
        Order of supervision 11
    No Status: Present Without Inspection or Admission, or Overstay 12
Other Useful Terms 13
    Notice to Appear 13
    Form I-94 13
    Visa 13
    Employment Authorization Document 13

Authority over Immigration Law Enforcement: A Look at the Government Agencies 14
    The U.S. Department of Homeland Security: USCIS, ICE, and CBP 14
        An arrest at the border 15
        An arrest upon termination of sentence 16
        Arrest while out in the community 16
    The U.S. Department of State 17
    The Executive Office for Immigration Review 17
    The Board of Immigration Appeals 18
    Attorney General Review 19
    The Administrative Appeals Office 19
The Agencies at Work: Removal Proceedings 20
    Notice to Appear 20
    Course of Proceedings 22
    The Burden of Proof 23
    Applications for Relief 24
    Appeal to the Board of Immigration Appeals 24
    Travel While a BIA Appeal Is Pending 26
    Review in Federal Court 27
Federal Judicial Review 27
    The REAL ID Act 29
    Jurisdiction 30
        No review of discretionary determinations 30
    Petitions for Review to the Courts of Appeals 31
    Petitions for Habeas Corpus to the Federal District Courts 32
Tips and Tools of the Trade 34
    1. Federal Bureau of Investigation (FBI) rap sheet 34
    2. Accurint 35
    3. PACER 35
    4. FOIA requests 36
    5. Polygraph examinations 36
    6. Westlaw, LEXIS, AILALink, AILA.org, and Fastcase 36
    7. Psychological and medical evaluations 37
    8. Country-condition experts 37
    9. Country-condition sources of information (websites) 37

Detailed Table of Contents

    10. Confirmation-of-appointment letters 37
    11. Intake sheets.. 37
Sources of Legal Authority 38
    Recent Legislation 38

Appendices
1A: Contact Information for Immigration Courts..................................... 39
1B: Structure of CBP 40
1C: Structure of ICE 41
1D: Structure of USCIS 42
1E: Sample Notice to Appear 43
1F: FBI Rap Sheet Request... 46
1G: Appointment Confirmation Letter 48
1H: Client Information Sheet.. 49

Chapter Two: The Definition of "Conviction" According to Immigration Law 51

The Statutory Definition of "Conviction" 51
    The "Beyond a Reasonable Doubt" Standard and Municipal Court Proceedings.. 52
    Court Martials 53
    Finality 53
    Withholds or Deferrals of Adjudication 54
        A withhold with no penalty 55
    Pretrial Intervention or Diversion 56
        Admissions to the prosecutor do not qualify 56
    Expungements and Record Sealings.. 57
        First offender/youthful offender provisions................................. 57
            The Ninth Circuit's treatment of FFOA dispositions and their state counterparts.. 58
            The other federal circuits 60
        Does an expungement under the FFOA result in a "conviction?"................. 61
    Pardons 62
        The effect of a pardon on a ground of inadmissibility.................. 63
        Pardon must be full and unconditional 64
        Foreign pardons 64
    Post-conviction Relief on the Merits: *Matter of Pickering*................. 64

The burden of proof in Pickering-type cases 67
Motions to reopen 68
BIA decisions after *Pickering* 69
The federal courts' approach to *Pickering* 70
    Vacatur found effective in eliminating the conviction 70
    Vacatur found ineffective for immigration purposes 71
    Vacatur ineffective for naturalization purposes 75
    Vacatur granted after removal order executed 75
Ineffective Assistance of Counsel 75
Post-conviction Relief Modifying the Sentence Imposed 76
Acts of Juvenile Delinquency 77
    Other juvenile acts 79
Foreign Convictions 80
Proof of Convictions 81
Suspensions of Sentence 82

Appendices
2A: Motion to Vacate Plea, Judgment, and Sentence 84
2B: *Padilla* Motion to Vacate Plea, Judgment, and Sentence 90

Chapter Three: Consequences of Criminal Activity: Removal from the United States 97
Inadmissibility 98
The Applications of INA §212(a)(2)(A) 98
    Knocking at the door 98
    Applicants for admission 99
    When an LPR seeks admission 99
    The *Fleuti* Doctrine 99
Supreme Court Finds IIRAIRA Amendment to §101(a)(13)(C) *Not* Retroactive 101
    Adjustment of status 102
    Visa applicants at American consular posts abroad 103
    Change of status 103
    Parolees 103
    Persons physically present in violation of the law 103
    Temporary protected status 104
    Naturalization and "good moral character" 104

Deportability	104
INA §237(a)	104
Deportability vs. Inadmissibility	105
Expedited Removal of Certain Aggravated Felons	107
Relief from Expedited Removal	110
Detention	110
Mandatory Detention	110
Re-entering After Removal: Criminal Prosecution and Reinstatement of Removal	111
Re-entry of Removed Aliens	111
Challenging the underlying order	111
Reinstatement of Removal	112
Limited exception for certain nationality-based benefits	113
U.S. Supreme Court upholds retroactive application of §241(a)(5)	114
How the Government Locates Your Client	115
The Sure Ways	115
Serving time in state or federal detention, both pre– and post-trial	115
Filing an immigration application	117
Frequently, But Not Always	118
While reporting to a probation or parole officer	118
When re-entering the United States after a trip abroad	118
Local Law Enforcement and the Enforcement of Immigration Laws	119
Local police	119

Appendices

3A: Memorandum of Law in Support of Motion to Terminate	121
3B: Motion to Terminate Based on Improper Designation as Arriving Alien	128

Chapter Four: Consequences of Criminal Activity: Detention Inside the United States 133

Mandatory Detention	133
Cooperating Witnesses	136
Demore v. Kim	136
Legal Challenges to Mandatory Detention Following *Demore*	137
Bond Hearings Before the IJ	139
Numerical Limitations and Jurisdiction	140
Matter of Aguilar-Aquino	141

    Matter of Joseph 142
    Jurisdiction over Custody Issues 145
        Arriving aliens 145
        Federal court review 146
        Deportable respondents and those who enter without inspection 147
    The "Release from Custody" Requirement 147
        "When released" litigation 148
        Does a sentence of imprisonment have to be imposed? 150
    Detention for Offense Not Charged on NTA 152
    Releases on or Before October 8, 1998 153
Other Detention Issues 153
    Non–Mandatory Detention Cases: The Standard 154
        The automatic stay 154
    Detention After a Removal Order 158
        Detention during judicial review of final removal order 160
        Alternatives to detention 161

Appendices

4A: Custody Rule Invoked (Terminates the Transitional Period Custody Rules) 164
4B: Section 309 of the IIRAIRA – the Transition Rule for 1996 Amendments to the INA 166
4C: Section 303(b) of the IIRAIRA – Effective Date of INA §236(c) Mandatory Detention 169
4D: Memorandum on INA §236(c)'s "Custody" Requirement and the Use of Alternatives to Detention to Meet the Statute's Requirements 171
4E: Memorandum of Law in Support of Bond Motion – Joseph Motion Arguing Financial Loss to a Victim Did Not Exceed $10,000 for Purposes of INA §101(a)(43)(M) 176

Chapter Five: Methodology: Classifying Crimes Under the Immigration and Nationality Act 181
Proper Classification of Crimes and the Methodology 181
Analyses and Terms 182
    U.S. Supreme Court Recalibrates the Categorical Approach:
Descamps v. U.S. 183
        Categorical Approach: An Elements Approach 183
        Taylor v. U.S. 184
    The Modified Categorical Approach: Divisible Statutes 185

Missing Element Statutes	186
Identifying the Minimal (Least Culpable) Conduct	188
Non-elemental Facts and the Circumstance-Specific Approach	189
Nijhawan v. Holder	190
The Realistic Probability Test: *Gonzales v. Duenas-Alvarez*	191
Re-emergence of the Categorical Approach	194
Moncrieffe v. Holder	194
Descamps v. U.S.	195
Divisibility	196
Means vs. Elements	197
Divisibility after *Descamps*: Circuit Court Developments	197
Alternative Statutory Phrases: Tenth Circuit on Conspiracy Statute	199
Alternative Statutory Provisions: Ninth Circuit on Controlled-Substance Schedules	200
Alternative Statutory Provisions: Fifth Circuit on General Export Statute	200
Facts-Based Approach: Third Circuit and Simple Assault	201
Essential Elements Only: Ninth Circuit on Felony Gang Enhancement	201
Essential Elements Only: Ninth Circuit on Disjunctive Burglary Statute	202
Essential Elements Only: Fourth Circuit on Disjunctive Larceny Statute	203
Essential Elements Only: Eleventh Circuit Throwing a Deadly Missile	203
Conclusion: Know the Circuit	204
Divisibility after *Descamps*: Board of Immigration Appeals	205
The Realistic Probability Test	207
Matter of Chairez II: Alternative Statutory Phrases	207
Matter of Silva-Trevino: Vacated in April 2015	208
The AG's Previous Methodology for Determining Moral Turpitude	209
Realistic probability test	210
Moral Turpitude as a "Non-elemental Fact"	210
After *Silva-Trevino*: The Federal Courts' Response	211
BIA attempts to limit *Silva-Trevino*	213
The Attorney General's 2015 vacatur	213
Chapter Review: A Review of Pertinent Terms	214
Appendices	
5A: Unpublished BIA Decision, *Matter of Forvilus*	217
5B: Unpublished IJ Decision Terminating Arriving Alien Status, Not a CIMT	226

5C: Unpublished IJ Decision Finding 18 USC §1860 not a CIMT 232
5D: Immigration Attorney/Client Checklist for Analyzing a Case with a Crime 235

Chapter Six: Crimes Involving Moral Turpitude 363
The Concept of Crimes Involving Moral Turpitude 239
    Felonies and Misdemeanors 240
        The elements of the criminal statute control 241
        The question of intent 241
        Divisible statutes and the record of conviction 244
Specific Offenses and Whether They Involve Moral Turpitude 245
    Theft and Larceny 245
    Burglary 249
    Fraud 250
    False Statements 251
    Obstruction of Justice; Misprision 252
Crimes of Violence 253
        Crimes involving moral turpitude 254
        Crimes not involving moral turpitude 256
        Not clear if moral turpitude exists 257
    Gang Enhancement 257
    Failure to Register as a Sex Offender 258
    Crimes Involving Children 259
    Driving Under the Influence 260
    Controlled Substance Offenses 261
    Firearms Offenses 261
    Immigration Law Violations 261

Chapter Seven: Aggravated Felonies 263
The INA Definition of Aggravated Felony 263
    Murder 265
    Sexual Abuse of a Minor 266
    Statutory Rape–Type Cases 267
    Drug Trafficking Crimes 269
        Federal controlled-substance law 269
            First-time simple possession not an aggravated felony—except for flunitrazepam 270

Detailed Table of Contents

- Recidivist simple possession statutes ... 270
- State controlled-substance convictions ... 270
  - Misdemeanor trafficking? ... 271
  - Offenses involving the element of illicit trafficking ... 271
- Divisible statutes ... 272
- Distribution Without Remuneration: *Moncrieffe v. Holder* ... 273
- Prescription Drugs ... 278
- Purchase of a Controlled Substance ... 278
- State Simple-Possession Offenses: A Mixed Approach ... 279
  - The "hypothetical felony" approach ... 280
  - The "guidelines" approach ... 281
  - Dueling circuits ... 282
  - The Supreme Court's decision in *Lopez v. Gonzales* ... 283
- The Federal Recidivist Statute ... 284
  - The Supreme Court's decision in *Carachuri-Rosendo* ... 285
  - The BIA's response to *Carachuri-Rosendo* ... 286
    - Charging phase vs. sentencing phase ... 288
    - Is there a "conviction"? ... 289
- Attempts and Conspiracies ... 290
- The Definition of "Crime of Violence" ... 290
  - Mens Rea: The Levels of Intent ... 291
  - The Supreme Court's interpretation of crime of violence ... 292
    - Recklessness and the use of force ... 294
    - Force versus contact ... 295
  - The Board's Analysis in Matter of *Chairez I* and *II* ... 299
  - Particular Offenses ... 300
    - Not crimes of violence ... 300
    - Crimes of violence ... 301
  - Firearms Offenses ... 304
    - Whether a state firearms offense is "described in" a federal statute ... 306
  - Theft and Burglary Crimes ... 307
    - Aiding and abetting ... 307
    - Burglary ... 309
    - Possession of stolen property ... 310
  - Alien Smuggling ... 311

  Offenses That Depend on the Sentence Imposed 311
    Commercial bribery; obstruction of justice 311
  Offenses That Depend on the Amount of Funds Involved 312
 Contesting "Loss" Findings; Understanding "Relevant Conduct" 313
  Offenses That Depend on "Commercial Advantage" 317
"Aggravated Felony"—Must It Be a Felony? 318
  Misdemeanor Crimes of Violence 318
  Misdemeanor Sexual Abuse of a Minor 319
Attempts and Conspiracies 320

Chapter Eight: Classifications Beyond Moral Turpitude and Aggravated Felony 323

Controlled Substance Offenses 323
 The Definition of "Controlled Substance Offense" 323
  Personal-use exception 326
  Drugs, but Not Controlled Substances 326
  Solicitation Offenses 328
  Paraphernalia 329
  Possession must be accompanied by "intent to use" 330
  Simulated or imitation controlled substances 331
 "Reason to Believe" 331
 Drug Abusers and Addicts 332
Firearms Offenses 333
 "Firearm" and "Destructive Device" Defined 333
  Firearm must be an element 334
  Firearms offense not a ground of inadmissibility 335
 No "Reason to Believe" or "Admission of the Essential Elements" Standards Apply 335
Money Laundering 335
 "Reason to Believe" 336
Crimes of Domestic Violence 336
 Offenses Included as Ground of Deportability 337
 "Crime of Domestic Violence" Defined 337
 The Domestic Violence Victim 339
  Defining the "victim"; applying the categorical approach 339
 Child Abuse 340

Detailed Table of Contents

Violations of Protection Orders 342
    Applies to convictions after September 30, 1996 343
    Domestic Violence Offense as a Crime Involving Moral Turpitude 343
Alien Smuggling 343
    Limited Exceptions for Smuggling an Immediate Family Member 345
    Alien Smuggling Defined 345
    The Crime of Alien Smuggling 345
Crimes Involving Failure to Register; Visa and Passport Fraud 347
    Failure to Register 348
    Visa and Passport Fraud 349
        Visa fraud as a crime involving moral turpitude and an aggravated felony 350
        Immigration document fraud 351
        Passport fraud 351
Export Law; National Security Violations 351
    Export Law Violations: A Matter of National Security 351
Public Safety and National Security 353
Failure to Register as a Sex Offender 354
    The Adam Walsh Act 354

Appendices
8A: Respondent's Motion to Dismiss Charges 356
8B: Unpublished BIA Decision on Drug Paraphernalia and *Pickering* Vacatur Standard 369

Chapter Nine: Consequences of Specific Criminal Activity 375
Consequences of Crimes Involving Moral Turpitude 376
    Inadmissibility, Including Adjustment of Status and Visa Eligibility 376
        Admission of the essential elements 377
        Petty offense and youthful offender exceptions 378
        Political offense exception 378
    Deportability/Removability 380
        Defining "admission" 380
        Multiple criminal convictions 381
    Mandatory Detention 382
    Voluntary Departure 383
        Pre-commencement or early stage of removal proceedings 383

Voluntary departure at conclusion of removal proceedings 383
Asylum, Withholding of Removal, and Convention Against Torture 384
 Asylum 384
  Withholding of removal 385
   Political offense exception 385
  Convention Against Torture 386
 Naturalization 387
  Revocation of naturalization (de-naturalization) 388
  Criminal prosecution for knowing illegal procurement of citizenship 389
  A defense attorney's obligations 389
Consequences of an Aggravated Felony Conviction 390
 Inadmissibility, Including Adjustment of Status and Visa Eligibility 390
 Deportability/Removability 390
 Mandatory Detention 390
 Voluntary Departure 390
  Summary of caveat eligibility for individual with aggravated felony conviction seeking voluntary departure: 391
 Asylum and Withholding of Removal 391
  Judicial review of the "particularly serious crime" determination 393
   Political offense exception 393
 Convention Against Torture 393
 Naturalization 394
  Revocation of naturalization (denaturalization) 394
Consequences of a Controlled Substance Conviction 394
 Inadmissibility, Including Adjustment of Status and Visa Eligibility 394
  "Reason to believe" 395
 Deportability/Removability 396
  The personal use exception 396
   Does the personal use exception extend to paraphernalia? 396
  Compare deportability with inadmissibility 397
 Mandatory Detention 398
 Voluntary Departure 398
  Pre-commencement or early stage of removal proceedings 398
 Conclusion of Proceedings 399
 Asylum and Withholding of Removal 399

Detailed Table of Contents

    Naturalization 400
        Revocation of naturalization (denaturalization) 400
Consequences of a Firearms Offense 401
    Inadmissibility, Including Adjustment of Status and Visa Eligibility 401
    Deportability/Removability 401
        Cross-reference with the aggravated felony definition 401
    Mandatory Detention 403
    Voluntary Departure 403
        Pre-commencement or early stage of removal proceedings 403
        Conclusion of proceedings 403
    Asylum and Withholding of Removal 404
    Naturalization 404
        Revocation of naturalization (denaturalization) 405
Consequences for Money Laundering Offenses 405
    Inadmissibility, Including Adjustment of Status and Visa Eligibility 405
        State money-laundering offenses 406
        Moral turpitude 406
    Deportability/Removability 407
    Mandatory Detention 407
    Voluntary Departure 408
        Pre-commencement or early stage of removal proceedings 408
        Conclusion of proceedings 408
    Asylum and Withholding of Removal 409
    Naturalization 409
        Revocation of naturalization (denaturalization) 410
Consequences of a Domestic Violence Conviction 410
    The Definition 410
    Inadmissibility, Including Adjustment of Status and Visa Eligibility 410
        Cross-reference to crimes involving moral turpitude 410
    Deportability/Removability 411
    Mandatory Detention 413
    Voluntary Departure 414
        Pre-commencement or early stage of removal proceedings 414
        Conclusion of proceedings 414
    Asylum and Withholding of Removal 414

Naturalization 415
    Revocation of naturalization (denaturalization) 415
Consequences of Alien Smuggling 415
    Inadmissibility, Including Adjustment of Status and Visa Eligibility 415
    Deportability/Removability 416
        Cross-reference with the aggravated felony definition 416
    Mandatory Detention 416
    Voluntary Departure 417
        Pre-commencement or early stage of removal proceedings 417
        Conclusion of proceedings 417
    Asylum and Withholding of Removal 417
    Naturalization 418
        Revocation of naturalization (denaturalization) 418
Falsification of Documents, and Visa and Passport Fraud 419
    Inadmissibility, Including Adjustment of Status and Visa Eligibility 419
        Visa fraud 419
        Possession vs. use 420
        Civil or criminal document fraud violations under INA §274C 421
    Deportability/Removability 421
        Registration and Visa Fraud 421
        Civil or criminal document fraud violations under INA §274C 422
    Mandatory Detention 422
    Voluntary Departure 422
        Pre-commencement or preliminary stage of removal proceedings 422
        Conclusion of proceedings 423
    Asylum and Withholding of Removal 423
    Naturalization 424
        Revocation of naturalization (denaturalization) 425
Consequences of Export Law Violations 425
    Inadmissibility, Including Adjustment of Status and Visa Eligibility 425
    Deportability/Removability 426
    Mandatory Detention 426
    Voluntary Departure 427
        Pre-commencement or early stage of removal proceedings 427
        Conclusion of proceedings 427

Asylum and Withholding of Removal 428
Naturalization 428

Appendix
9A: Crimes and Possible Consequences Chart 429

Chapter Ten: Immigration Defense: Waivers and Other Relief 431
Adjustment of Status... 432
    Available to Permanent and Non–Permanent Residents 435
    Discretionary Benefit... 435
    Jurisdiction.. 436
    Aggravated Felony Offenses 438
    Firearms Offenses... 438
    Domestic Violence Offenses 439
    Visa and Registration Offenses 440
    Export Violations.. 440
Waivers Under INA §212(h) 441
    The 15-Year Waiver 443
    The Extreme Hardship Waiver 443
    The Battered Spouse and Child Waiver... 444
    Special Rules for Lawful Permanent Residents................................. 444
        LPRs with aggravated felony and other convictions 444
        Retroactivity of the amendment.. 445
        Important circuit case law: defining "admission"...................... 445
            The analysis: understanding "admission"............................. 446
            The analysis: understanding the criminal bar's language 447
        Matter of Alyazji 448
            The analysis: what about entry without inspection?............... 448
            The response: BIA 449
            The next move: DHS argues subsequent re-entries are "admissions" 449
        LPRs with nonaggravated felony convictions 451
    Defining Lawful Continual Residence 451
    Tolling of Seven-Year Period: Initiation of Removal Proceedings................. 452
    Arriving Aliens or Those Adjusting Status.. 452
        BIA abandons *Matter of Sanchez* 454

- Limited Availability of INA §212(h) for Persons Convicted of Violent or Dangerous Crimes 455
- INA §209(c) Waiver for Refugees and Asylees 459
  - Compare with the INA §212(h) Waiver 459
  - Use of INA §209(c) by Certain Lawful Permanent Residents to Avoid Removal 460
- Asylum and Withholding of Removal 461
  - Asylum 462
  - Withholding of or Restriction on Removal Under the INA 463
    - Defining the "particularly serious crime" 464
  - Withholding and Deferral Under the Convention Against Torture 466
- Cancellation of Removal 466
  - Continuous Residence Versus Lawful Permanent Resident Status 467
  - Residence Cannot Be Imputed to Minor Children Living Abroad 467
  - Defining "Admission" 467
    - Offense need not be charged in removal proceedings to stop the time 470
  - The Requirement of a Lawful Admission 471
  - Individuals Who Are Ineligible for Cancellation 472
    - Combining waivers 472
  - Special Rule for Battered Spouses 473
  - Special Rule Cancellation of Removal: NACARA §203 474
- The Waiver That Keeps Giving: INA §212(c) (repealed 1996) 476
  - Overview of Eligibility Criteria for §212(c) Waiver 476
  - Introduction 477
  - Advance Permission to Return to Unrelinquished Domicile 479
  - Case Law Expands Eligibility to Those in Deportation Track 479
  - The Immigration Act of 1990 480
  - The Antiterrorism and Effective Death Penalty Act of 1996 480
  - The U.S. Supreme Court Decision: *INS v. St. Cyr* 481
  - The 2004 Regulation 482
    - Eligibility cut-off dates 482
    - Individuals in exclusion proceedings 484
    - IIRAIRA definition of aggravated felony retroactive: the summer of 1996 485
      - Persons convicted by trial 487

Utilizing the waiver to cure post-1996 convictions (persons already in deportation proceedings) 487
INA §212(c) Eligibility Criteria 488
   Persons who served five years in prison for aggravated felony 489
   Persons wrongfully removed prior to *St. Cyr, Judulang* or *Abdelghany* 489
      Re-entry after pretermission of §212(c) application and deportation 491
      Gabryelsky filings: adjustment of status combined with INA §212(c) 492
Combining INA §212(c) and Cancellation of Removal 493
Affirmative Applications for §212(c) 494
Naturalization After a Waiver Under INA §212(c) 494
Voluntary Departure 495
   Precommencement or preliminary stage of proceedings 496
   Voluntary Departure at Conclusion of Proceedings 498
Is Your Client an American Citizen? An Introduction to Derivative and Acquired Citizenship 499
   Watch for Effective Dates 500
   Acquired Citizenship at Birth 500
   Derivative Citizenship After Birth 501
      Individual who turned 18 before February 27, 2001 502
Naturalization as a Defense to Deportation 503
   Termination of Removal Proceedings for Naturalization 503
   Soldiers and Veterans 504
Relief from Alien Smuggling Charges 507
   Relief from Deportability and Inadmissibility, Absent a Conviction 507
      Waiver for smuggling immediate family members 507
      Cancellation of removal 507
   Relief from a Conviction for Alien Smuggling (An Aggravated Felony) 508
      Adjustment of status 508
      INA §212(h) waiver 508
      Cancellation of removal 509
      INA §212(c) waiver 509
      Asylum and withholding of removal 509
      Naturalization 509
Nonimmigrant Visa Waiver Under INA §212(d)(3) 510
   Introduction: "My son's been deported for an aggravated felony; can he ever come back?" 510

Jurisdiction 510
    Applications at the consulate 510
    Applications at a port of entry 511
    Separate permission to re-enter after deportation or removal (Form I-212) not required 513
    Does not waive security or terrorism grounds of inadmissibility 513
  Factors for Consideration 514
Defending the Criminal Charge of Re-entry After Removal 514
    Collaterally attacking the underlying removal order 516

Appendices

10A: Unpublished BIA Decision re: Sua Sponte Motion to Reopen for §212(c) After Removal Order, Conviction by Trial 524

10B: Brief Excerpt – Addressing Difference In "Particularly Serious Crime Analysis" from Asylum to Withholding 526

10C: Motion to Pretermit Waiver Application Under INA §212(h) 529

10D: Sample Memorandum in Support of INA §212(h) Eligibility 534

10E: Unpublished BIA Decision re: Cancellation of Removal, Waiver of Inadmissibility Under INA §212(h) 540

10F: Sample Motion to Terminate Removal Proceedings 544

10G: Sample Memorandum in Support of INA §240A(a) Eligibility for Cancellation of Removal 549

10H: Sample Statement in Support of Naturalization Eligibility 556

Chapter Eleven: Immigration Defense: Fashioning a Plea to Avoid Adverse Immigration Consequences 561

Avoiding Adverse Immigration Consequences 562
  Avoiding a Conviction Through Pretrial Diversion 562
    Beware of admissions to the crime 563
  Federal First Offender Act Treatment; 18 USC §3607 563
  Keep the Case in Juvenile Court 564
  The Petty Offense Exception 565
    Section 237's version of the petty offense exception 566
Avoiding a Conviction of a Crime Involving Moral Turpitude 566
  Why It Is Important (A Quick Rundown on Consequences) 566
    Eligibility for permanent resident status 566
    Mandatory detention 566
    Naturalization 567

Detailed Table of Contents

What Is "Moral Turpitude?" 567
    Fraud crimes 567
    Theft offenses 567
    Burglary 568
        Working with a divisible statute: control the conviction record 569
        Alternative pleas 569
    Crimes of violence 569
    DUIs (operating under the influence) 569
  Avoid Multiple Counts 569
  Summary Examples of Successful Plea Bargaining to Avoid a Crime
  Involving Moral Turpitude 571
Avoiding the Aggravated Felony Conviction 572
  Why It Is Important (A Quick Rundown on Consequences) 572
    Limited eligibility for relief from removal and mandatory detention 572
    Barred from asylum 572
    No naturalization for convictions entered after November 29, 1990 572
  Avoiding an Aggravated Felony—Keep the Sentence Under One Year 572
  Avoiding Loss to a Victim in Excess of $10,000 573
  Avoiding Crime of Violence by Pleading to a Non–Specific Intent Crime 574
  Avoiding Alien Smuggling/Aggravated Felony Conviction 575
  Summary Examples of Effective Plea Bargaining to Avoid Aggravated
  Felony 575
Avoiding Deportability for Domestic Violence Offenses 580
Creating Eligibility for Relief 581
  INA §212(h) 581
    Less than 30 grams of marijuana 581
    Avoid the aggravated felony conviction 581
  Cancellation of Removal 582
    Avoid offenses that toll the seven years of legal residence 582
    Avoid the aggravated felony conviction 582
  Withholding of Removal and Asylum 582
  Naturalization eligibility 583
  Creating a Good Record Through the Plea Agreement and Plea Colloquy 583
    Defense and immigration counsel must work as a team 584
  Plea Agreements to Avoid (Bad Plea Deals) 585

        False statements and currency transactions 585
        Possession, paraphernalia, and purchase 585
        Aggravated assault and probation only... 586
        Multiple counts 586
        365 days in jail... 586
        Five-year prison sentence 586

Appendix

11A: Sample Memorandum for Fashioning a Plea... 588

Chapter Twelve: Visas for Cooperating Witnesses 599

"S" Status... 600
        The Statute 601
        The Regulations 602
        Conditions of Status... 603
        Adjustment to Permanent Resident Status Under "S" 604
            The statute.. 604
            The regulations 605
            Special requirements for family members... 605
        Miscellaneous Tips and Advice About "S" Status 606

"T" Status... 609
        The Statute 609
        The Regulations 609
            "Severe form of trafficking" defined... 610
            "Extreme hardship" defined 610
        Application Procedure 610
            Effect of pending immigration proceedings 612
            Applicants with final orders of removal 612
            Annual cap on number of admissions... 612
            Revocation of status... 612
        Family Members.. 612
            Duration of nonimmigrant status and application for permanent residency 613

"U" Status... 614
        The Statute 615
            "Criminal activity" defined.. 615
        The Regulation... 616

Filing 617
Qualifying family members 618
Persons in removal proceedings 619
Age-out protection 621
Permanent Resident Status: A Change in Focus 622
Family Members Not Already in U Status 624
Jurisdiction 624

Appendices
12A: Form I-854, Inter-Agency Alien Witness and Informant Record 625
12B: Freedom of Information Act Request 631

Chapter Thirteen: Preparing and Presenting Applications That Waive a Criminal Conviction 639

Venues: Consulate, USCIS, ICE, and Immigration Court 640
Rules Regarding Biometrics Prior to Relief at Immigration Court 642
The Universal List: Evidence in Support of a Waiver 644
Evidence Relating to the Applicant 645
Evidence Relating to Family Members 647
Adjustment of Status 648
Forms, Fees, and Attachments 648
When Filing with the Court 650
Adjustment Is Discretionary 650
INA §212(h) Waivers—15-Year, Hardship, and Battered Spouse or Child 651
Form and Fee 651
When Filing with the Immigration Court 651
Emphasis on Hardship to Family Members 651
Discretion Must Be Warranted, Notwithstanding Hardship 652
Refugee Waiver Under INA §209(c) 652
Waiver Under the Pre-AEDPA INA §212(c) (repealed in 1996) 654
Form and Fee 654
When Filing with the Immigration Court 654
Emphasis on Unrelinquished Domicile; All Equities Are Relevant 654
Cannot have served five years in prison for an aggravated felony or felonies 655
A balancing of the equities 655

Cancellation of Removal—INA §240A(a) 655
    Form and Fee 655
    Emphasis on Residency Requirements; All Equities Apply 656
        A balancing of the equities 656
Special Rule Cancellation of Removal 656
    Form and Fee 656
    Supporting Documents 657
Waiver Under INA §212(d)(3)(A) 657
    Form and Fee 657
    Information Required 657
    Contacting LegalNet for Assistance When Consul Declines to Accept Waiver 658
Memoranda of Law and Witness Lists 659
    Before USCIS or American Consulate 659
    Pretrial Statements to the Immigration Court 660
    Witnesses 661
        Witness list 661
        Choosing witnesses 662
        Working with witnesses 662
        Details: The time and place of hearing, the need for an interpreter 662
    Conclusion 663
Applications Filed After an Order of Removal 663
    Stay of Deportation: Form I-246 663
        Criteria 664
    Application for Permission to Reapply for Admission into the United States After Deportation or Removal 665
        Criteria 667

Appendix
13A: Sample Respondent's Pretrial Statement 668

APPENDICES

Appendix—Chapter One
1A: Contact Information for Immigration Courts 39
1B: Structure of CBP 40
1C: Structure of ICE 41

DETAILED TABLE OF CONTENTS xli

1D: Structure of USCIS 42
1E: Sample Notice to Appear 43
1F: FBI Rap Sheet Request... 46
1G: Appointment Confirmation Letter 48
1H: Client Information Sheet... 49

Appendix—Chapter Two
2A: Motion to Vacate Plea, Judgment, and Sentence................................ 84
2B: *Padilla* Motion to Vacate Plea, Judgment, and Sentence 90

Appendix—Chapter Three
3A: Memorandum of Law in Support of Motion to Terminate.............. 121
3B: Motion to Terminate Based on Improper Designation as Arriving Alien 128

Appendix—Chapter Four
4A: Custody Rule Invoked (Terminates the Transitional Period Custody Rules).... 164
4B: Section 309 of the IIRAIRA – the Transition Rule for 1996 Amendments to the INA 166
4C: Section 303(b) of the IIRAIRA – Effective Date of INA §236(c) Mandatory Detention... 169
4D: Memorandum on INA §236(c)'s "Custody" Requirement and the Use of Alternatives to Detention to Meet the Statute's Requirements............................... 171
4E: Memorandum of Law in Support of Bond Motion – Joseph Motion Arguing Financial Loss to a Victim Did Not Exceed $10,000 for Purposes of INA §101(a)(43)(M) 176

Appendix—Chapter Five
5A: Unpublished BIA Decision, *Matter of Forvilus* 217
5B: Unpublished IJ Decision Terminating Arriving Alien Status, Not a CIMT 226
5C: Unpublished IJ Decision Finding 18 USC §1860 not a CIMT 232
5D: Immigration Attorney/Client Checklist for Analyzing a Case with a Crime..... 235

Appendix—Chapter Eight
8A: Sample Motion to Dismiss CIMT and RTB Charges 356
8B: Unpublished BIA Decision on Drug Paraphernalia and Pickering Vacatur Standard 369

Appendix—Chapter Nine
9A: Crimes and Possible Consequences Chart 429

Appendix—Chapter Ten

10A: Unpublished BIA Decision re: Sua Sponte Motion to Reopen for §212(c) After Removal Order, Conviction by Trial 524

10B: Brief Excerpt – Addressing Difference In "Particularly Serious Crime Analysis" from Asylum to Withholding 526

10C: Motion to Pretermit Waiver Application Under INA §212(h) 529

10D: Sample Memorandum in Support of INA §212(h) Eligibility 534

10E: Unpublished BIA Decision re: Cancellation of Removal, Waiver of Inadmissibility Under INA §212(h) 540

10F: Sample Motion to Terminate Removal Proceedings 544

10G: Sample Memorandum in Support of INA §240A(a) Eligibility for Cancellation of Removal 549

10H: Sample Statement in Support of Naturalization Eligibility 556

Appendix—Chapter Eleven

11A: Sample Memorandum for Fashioning a Plea 588

Appendix—Chapter Twelve

12A: Sample Form I-854 625

12B: Freedom of Information Act Request 631

Appendix—Chapter Thirteen

13A: Sample Respondent's Pretrial Statement 668

ABOUT AILA

The American Immigration Lawyers Association (AILA) is a national bar association of more than 14,000 attorneys who practice immigration law and/or work as teaching professionals. AILA member attorneys represent tens of thousands of U.S. families who have applied for permanent residence for their spouses, children, and other close relatives for lawful entry and residence in the United States. AILA members also represent thousands of U.S. businesses and industries who sponsor highly skilled foreign workers seeking to enter the United States on a temporary or permanent basis. In addition, AILA members represent foreign students, entertainers, athletes, and asylum-seekers, often on a pro bono basis. Founded in 1946, AILA is a nonpartisan, not-for-profit organization that provides its members with continuing legal education, publications, information, professional services, and expertise through its 39 chapters and over 50 national committees. AILA is an affiliated organization of the American Bar Association and is represented in the ABA House of Delegates.

American Immigration Lawyers Association
www.aila.org

Case Update

Just as this book was going to press, the U.S. Supreme Court delivered its decision in *Mellouli v. Lynch* (June 1, 2015), reversing the Eighth Circuit U.S Court of Appeals. You'll find a detailed discussion of the facts of the case and analysis in chapters seven and eight. The Court ruled that, for removal purposes, INA §237(a)(2)(B)(i) limits the meaning of "controlled substance" to those defined in 21 USC §802, and the government must connect an element of an immigrant's conviction to a drug in §802 to trigger removal.

CHAPTER ONE

AN OVERVIEW OF BASIC IMMIGRATION TERMS AND THE IMMIGRATION LAW SYSTEM

Who (or What) Is Your Client? An Introduction to Statuses 1
Other Useful Terms 13
Authority over Immigration Law Enforcement: A Look at the Government Agencies 14
The Agencies at Work: Removal Proceedings 20
Federal Judicial Review 27
Tips and Tools of the Trade 34
Sources of Legal Authority 38

Appendices
   1A: Contact Information for Immigration Courts, Offices of Chief Counsel, and Detention
      Centers 39
   1B: Structure of CBP 40
   1C: Structure of ICE 41
   1D: Structure of USCIS 42
   1E: Sample Notice to Appear 43
   1F: FBI Rap Sheet Request 46
   1G: Appointment Confirmation Letter/Intake Sheet 48
   1H: Client Information Sheet 49

This chapter represents an overview of immigration law, including immigration statuses, sources of legal authority, and the government agencies that enforce the immigration laws. Although this chapter will be too basic for the experienced immigration law practitioner, it represents a good starting point for both the criminal lawyer looking for orientation to the immigration system and the new immigration lawyer. In addition, this is an excellent source of orientation for new support staff and paralegals. At the conclusion of this chapter there is a section on tips and tools for the criminal–immigration law practice.

Who (or What) Is Your Client? An Introduction to Statuses

In representing a foreign-born criminal defendant, it is important to know, early on, your client's immigration status, as it will affect the immigration consequences of the criminal activity. In the immigration context, it is likewise key to an effective first-time consultation to understand the basis of the client's presence, or status, in the United States.

Accordingly, it is important to advise a potential client coming in for a first-time consultation (or the client's friends or family members, if the person is detained or living outside the United States) to bring in all immigration-related documents that will explain the person's presence in the United States, including, for example, the passport, resident card, work permit, Form I-94, and/or correspondence from the U.S. Department of Homeland Security (DHS). The person's status, or lack thereof—the means by which he or she is presently in the United States—is the foundation of the attorney's consultation and analysis. It is key for criminal lawyers and beginning immigration attorneys to understand that the *consequences of crime vary* based on a person's immigration status.

Some clients enter and exit the United States on visas without intending to remain in the country forever (nonimmigrants). Others reside here permanently (immigrants).[1] There are nonimmigrants who would like to become permanent residents, and permanent residents who aspire to become U.S. citizens. Some individuals do not have any desire to remain permanently in the United States, but would like to preserve their nonimmigrant visas, enabling them to come and go.

Some lawful permanent resident (LPR) clients (green-card holders) who fear deportation for crime may be American citizens through derivation and not even know it. As discussed later, an LPR whose parents are American citizens may be a citizen through derivation.

Thus, the starting point in representation is to understand the client's status or position in the eyes of immigration law. The lawyer's second question is what the client's hopes are for the future. The reader will bear in mind that there is the reality of what a client's status is as well as the client's aspiration—the status that he or she would like to acquire in the future. Both the reality and the aspiration are important in an attorney's case analysis. The discussion below represents a basic introduction to the different types of immigration statuses (or lack thereof) referred to in the Immigration and Nationality Act (INA).[2] These terms will be used in subsequent chapters.

Citizenship and Naturalization

The most commonly understood category of American citizen is a person born in the United States or one of its territories.[3] However, certain persons are "derivative" citizens, such as a permanent resident child whose parent(s) naturalize before he or she turns 18 years old, or have "acquired" citizenship, such as an individual born abroad of a U.S. citizen parent or parents. People can become American citizens through naturalization. And within the context of naturalization, certain persons have relaxed eligibility requirements, such as individuals who served in the U.S. armed forces during a period

---

[1] Although the term "immigrant" is often used colloquially to describe all noncitizens, the immigration laws distinguish between the concepts of permanent residents (immigrants) and temporary visitors (nonimmigrants).

[2] Immigration and Nationality Act of 1952 (INA), Pub. L. No. 82-414, 66 Stat. 163 (codified as amended at 8 USC §1101 *et seq.*).

[3] The Fourteenth Amendment to the U.S. Constitution states that all persons born or naturalized in the United States and subject to the jurisdiction thereof shall be citizens of the United States.

of hostilities. An American citizen is not, of course, subject to removal from the United States. The law of nationality and naturalization is found at Title III of the INA, §§301–61 [8 USC §§1401–1504].[4] A word of both caution and comfort: the subject of acquired and derivative citizenship is complicated. The laws change from time to time, but are not retroactive. Thus, different clients will be covered by different laws, depending on their age.

Chapter 1 of Title III in the INA covers acquisition of U.S. citizenship at birth. Chapter 2 of the same title covers the eligibility requirements for naturalization, and section 320 in Chapter 2 covers derivative citizenship. Again, under that section (and former section 321), clients whose parent or parents are U.S. citizens may have derived U.S. citizenship. Clients who have served in the armed forces may fall under relaxed rules of naturalization.[5] It may be important in certain cases to examine the client's background in analyzing potential immigration consequences.[6] This, in turn, requires instructing a client at the outset (in advance of the first consultation) to bring in the parents' naturalization certificates.

The Lawful Permanent Resident ("Green-Card" Holder)

A person with LPR status is allowed by law to live and work permanently in the United States.[7] In many respects, LPR status is one step shy of American citizenship. There are many methods for obtaining LPR status—common ones include relative or employer petitions, professional or investment visas, a grant of asylum, or some other designated legalization program. Some individuals are able to petition for themselves under a special immigrant or battered spouse/child provision in the INA.

An LPR is subject to removal from the United States for a violation of relevant immigration laws, regardless of the length of residency or the age at which permanent-resident status was attained. An LPR who immigrated to the United States at the age of 6 months who is convicted of a crime at age 60 can and will be removed, depending on the nature of the conviction. Conviction of a crime also can jeopardize an LPR's eligibility for naturalization. The grounds of deportability have expanded in recent years, while the eligibility requirements for waivers have become increasingly strict. Long-time permanent residents are increasingly taken into immigration custody, detained for extended periods, and removed from the United States on the basis of criminal convictions. Because an LPR will often have strong family ties and lengthy residence in the United States, it is especially crucial to give the immigration conse-

---

[4] Certain portions of the 1952 INA are codified in Title 8 of the United States Code (USC).

[5] For an in-depth discussion of naturalization and citizenship for people serving in the U.S. armed forces, see *Immigration Law & the Military*, 2nd Ed. (AILA 2015).

[6] For an in-depth discussion of naturalization and citizenship, see *AILA's Guide to U.S. Citizenship & Naturalization Law* (AILA 2014).

[7] INA §101(a)(20); 8 USC §1101(a)(20) (defining "lawfully admitted for permanent residence").

quences of criminal charges close attention in his or her case. Simply put, the stakes are high.

The Nonimmigrant Visa Holder

There are many kinds of nonimmigrant statuses. This book is about the immigration consequences of crime, and does not go into visa statuses in depth.[8] The nonimmigrant visa classification, defined at INA §101(a)(15) [8 USC §1101(a)(15)], includes visitors to the United States, foreign students, investors, businesspersons, professionals, athletes, entertainers, and religious workers—to name just a few. There also are nonimmigrant statuses for the victims of crime who are cooperating with law enforcement.[9] The length of time that a person is entitled to remain in the United States pursuant to a nonimmigrant visa is based on the status conferred. For example, tourist visas confer visitor-for-pleasure status and entitle the visitor to remain for up to six months. An investor or professional visa will allow admittance for two to three years at a time.

In the event of being convicted of a crime, individuals in nonimmigrant status may be removed from the United States. Even if a nonimmigrant convicted of a crime is not placed in removal proceedings (for whatever reason, including U.S. Department of Homeland Security's (DHS) failure to detect the crime), it will be difficult to travel in and out of the United States. A nonimmigrant convicted of a crime also jeopardizes his or her eligibility for lawful permanent residency. In most (though not all) cases, a nonimmigrant convicted of a significant crime will either be removed from the United States or be denied admission or an extension of status. There are waivers of inadmissibility for crime in the nonimmigrant category, which are discussed in chapter ten, relating to waivers and relief.

Persons from the Caribbean, Canada, and Mexico who do not need visas—tourists and temporary workers

Pursuant to regulation, every non–American citizen must have a valid, unexpired passport to enter the United States.[10] However, individuals of certain neighboring countries are allowed to enter the United States as tourists or temporary agricultural workers without a visa. The persons who can enter the United States without visas are set forth in Title 8 of the Code of Federal Regulations (CFR) at §§212.1(a) and 1212.1(a). Under

---

[8] The American Immigration Lawyers Association (AILA) publishes several excellent books by experienced practitioners that explain the visa statuses and application process. See *http://agora.aila.org* for additional information about AILA's publications and resources.

[9] Cooperating witness visas are discussed in chapter twelve.

[10] 8 Code of Federal Regulations (CFR) §§212.1, 1212.1. Certain Canadian citizens are exempt from the passport requirement if they are pre-cleared pursuant to a specific travel program. These persons will, however, have a NEXUS, Free and Secure Trade (FAST), or Secure Electronic Network for Travelers Rapid Inspection (SENTRI) card. *See* 22 CFR §41.2(a), 8 CFR §212.1. Canadian Indians have a status card issued by Indian and Northern Affairs Canada (INAC) and do not require a passport.

these code sections, Canadian citizens, as well as citizens of Bermuda, do not require a visa to enter the United States. Bahamian citizens (and British subjects resident in the Bahamas) do not need a visa if they are coming for tourism purposes and satisfy an immigration inspector that they are not inadmissible.[11] British subjects residing in the Turks and Caicos Islands, or Cayman Islands, require a passport but no visa. Also, certain temporary agricultural workers from islands in the Caribbean are not required to hold visas. Mexican nationals with a border crossing card are not required to have visas.[12]

The Visa Waiver Program (tourists without visas)

Under INA §217 [8 USC §1187], citizens of designated countries (primarily industrialized countries) are allowed to enter the United States for 90 days as tourists without a visa. These persons will have registered in advance through the Electronic System for Travel Authorization (ESTA).[13] The Visa Waiver Program (VWP) carries certain restrictions. Most notably, an individual who entered under the VWP has no right to a removal hearing before an immigration judge (IJ) if he or she becomes deportable for a crime (unless he or she claims a fear of persecution, thereby commencing an asylum claim).

It is important for the criminal defense attorney to be aware of a VWP entry; if an individual has entered this way, is convicted of a crime, and is detected by DHS, he or she will be detained and removed without administrative procedures or protection. Again, the only exception is if the individual has a fear of persecution in the home country. Such individual can receive an "asylum-only" hearing before an IJ. Although certainly not impossible, the asylum scenario is uncommon, because the visa-waiver countries are stable democracies. Except for those who claim asylum, a VWP entrant convicted of a crime will be arrested and summarily deported with little due process.

Other Protective Categories

Refugees and asylees

A refugee or asylee is an individual who is allowed to reside and work in the United States pursuant to a grant of protection against persecution in the native country. Refugees are admitted to the United States from outside the country pursuant to INA §207 [8 USC §1157]. Asylees apply for and receive asylum within the United States pursuant to procedures at INA §208 [8 USC §1158]. An IJ or an asylum officer can

---

[11] 8 CFR §212.1(a)(3).
[12] 8 CFR §§212.1(c), 1212.1(c); *see also* 8 CFR §§212.6, 1212.6.
[13] For information on the Electronic System for Travel Authorization, see *www.CBP.gov*.

grant asylum—both have jurisdiction. But an individual in immigration court proceedings will apply for asylum in front of an IJ.[14]

Asylum status is similar to refugee status, except that the former is granted within the United States, and the latter is granted outside the United States at a refugee office, normally housed within an American embassy abroad. To receive asylum or refugee status, an applicant must establish a well-founded fear of persecution according to the definition of "refugee" under INA §101(a)(42) [8 USC §1101(a)(42)]. The definition of refugee dictates that the harm or threat of harm be based on an enumerated ground, or category: race, religion, nationality, membership in a particular social group, or political opinion. Harm or the threat of harm that does not fall into an enumerated category will not qualify a person as a "refugee." Note that by law a person must apply for asylum within one year of the date of admission into the United States.[15] However, there are some exceptions to the one-year filing deadline.[16]

Asylum and extended family: An applicant for asylum may include the spouse and children in the application, and they receive asylum at the same time. If the family members were not included in the application, there is a procedure for bringing them in from outside the United States (or applying for family members in the United States), so that they also may become asylees.[17]

Persons in refugee or asylum status generally would like to become LPRs, and can apply for LPR status after one year in protected status. They are subject to removal from the United States for conviction of a crime, although there is a specific waiver available to refugees and asylees.[18]

Withholding of removal

Restriction on removal[19]—commonly referred to as withholding of removal—is a type of protection from persecution similar to asylum. However, withholding allows fewer benefits and carries a higher burden of proof. The burden of proof for asylum is a "well-founded fear,"[20] whereas the burden for withholding (if the applicant's fear of future threat to life or freedom is unrelated to past persecution) is that the applicant "more likely than not" will suffer harm.[21] A person who receives withholding is not

---

[14] See *AILA's Asylum Primer*, 7th Ed., to learn more about asylum and refugee law.

[15] INA §208(a)(2)(B); 8 USC §1158(a)(2)(B).

[16] INA §208(a)(2)(D); 8 USC §1158(a)(2)(D); 8 CFR §§208.4(a)(5), 1208.4(a)(5).

[17] 8 CFR §208.21.

[18] The waiver is discussed in chapter ten. AILA publishes several excellent books that explain the different waivers and application process. See *http://agora.aila.org* for additional information about AILA's publications.

[19] INA §241(b)(3); 8 USC §1231(b)(3).

[20] INA §101(a)(42)(A); 8 USC §1101(a)(42)(A).

[21] 8 CFR §§208.16(b)(1)(iii), (2), 1208.16(b)(1)(iii), (2).

eligible for residency status after one year. Nor is such a person eligible for travel permission. And a person with withholding may be removed in the future if conditions in the country of persecution change and there is no longer a danger of harm. A person who receives withholding actually is ordered deported; however, the deportation is "withheld." Experience shows that DHS often requires the withholding recipient to search for a third country to accept him or her; DHS also may require periodic reporting to an Enforcement and Removal Operations (ERO) office.

Withholding and extended family: A key distinction between withholding of removal and asylum is that family members are not included in a grant of withholding. Family members of a withholding recipient must apply with independent applications and be heard in front of an immigration court.

The reader may wonder why someone would request or receive withholding instead of asylum, since the latter is clearly a superior benefit. The answer is that some persons do not qualify for asylum, but will qualify for withholding. The two applications are considered together by an IJ. People who would like to receive asylum, but instead receive withholding, are persons who are applying for asylum outside the one-year filing deadline, who have been convicted of an aggravated felony, or who have committed a crime or some other act that is not a per se bar, but dictates denial in the exercise of discretion. These consequences are discussed further in chapter nine. In general, withholding is a tenuous status that does not offer security comparable to that of an asylum grant.

Protection under the Convention Against Torture

In the same general category of asylum and withholding is protection from removal under the Convention Against Torture (CAT). CAT protection is important in the criminal-alien context because a person who has a serious criminal conviction may still qualify for CAT relief where no other waiver or benefit is available. Deferral or withholding under the CAT is granted when the non–American citizen establishes a likelihood that he or she will be tortured by the government or an individual acting with the government's acquiescence. The CAT is an international treaty that is not encompassed within the INA. The United States is a signator, and its provisions for implementation in the United States are found at Title 8 of the CFR.[22] Unlike asylum and withholding, which require a finding of persecution based on an enumerated ground, CAT protection does not require that the torture be on account of a certain enumerated category (*e.g.*, on account of political opinion). The law simply protects against government-sponsored torture, regardless of the motive or reason. Like with-

---

[22] 8 CFR §§208.16(c), 208.17, 208.18, 1208.16(c), 1208.17, and 1208.18.

holding, a person who receives protection under the CAT receives an order of removal, but the removal is withheld or deferred.[23]

Temporary protected status

Temporary protected status (TPS) is perhaps best understood as a sort of temporary asylum, although the status is conferred on an entire nationality, not for reasons of political or other individualized persecution, but based on ongoing strife, civil war, or natural disaster in the home country. The U.S. attorney general designates certain nationalities for this status and sets an appropriate duration for the status—usually two-year increments.[24] For example, many persons from Honduras and Nicaragua who entered the United States before December 1999 currently are in TPS because of the lingering adverse effects of Hurricane Mitch. Likewise, many El Salvadorans are currently residing in the United States in TPS as a result of the 2001 earthquake. Haiti is currently designated for TPS status due to lingering effects from a devastating earthquake. Several African countries, such as Somalia, Sudan, and Sierra Leone, currently are designated for TPS status.[25]

TPS is not available to recent or incoming arrivals. TPS is for individuals from the particular country who were in the United States before the designation period, and the designation date will be based on the triggering event (*i.e.*, the earthquake, hurricane, or hostilities).

A person with TPS is allowed to live and work in the United States and may even travel outside the country with prior permission (an advance parole, discussed below). However, TPS is just that—temporary—and, short of special legislation, does not automatically lead to permanent resident status. A person with a felony conviction or two or more misdemeanors is not eligible for TPS.[26] The felony or two misdemeanor rule is without regard to the classification of crime; in other words, the felony or misdemeanor offense need not be a "crime involving moral turpitude."[27] A person in TPS who is convicted of crime may lose his or her status, and could be subject to removal from the United States.

Parole

Certain persons are physically present in the United States pursuant to parole. Technically, parole is not a "status" at all. Parole is a legal fiction—the body is physically

---

[23] 8 CFR §§1208.17(a) and (b)(2). Deferral under CAT is for individuals convicted of serious crime or national security risks. Withholding is for persons without a conviction for serious crime, or who are not a national security risk.

[24] *See* INA §244; 8 USC §1254a.

[25] For a list of countries designated for TPS: *www.uscis.gov/humanitarian/temporary-protected-status-deferred-enforced-departure/temporary-protected-status*.

[26] INA §244(c)(2)(B); 8 USC §1254a(c)(2)(B).

[27] See chapter six for an extensive discussion on crimes involving moral turpitude.

here, but there is no specific immigration status attached to the body. A person may be paroled into the United States from outside for a variety of reasons, including—but not limited to—humanitarian reasons or for law enforcement purposes (*i.e.*, witnesses or informants).[28] The agency within DHS that grants parole will depend on the legal basis for the parole. U.S. Customs and Border Protection (CBP) paroles people, as appropriate, if they are arriving at a port of entry. ERO, a detention and removal unit of U.S. Immigration and Customs Enforcement (ICE), can parole persons out of custody at a detention center. Special witness paroles are processed through ICE's Office of Investigations. U.S. Citizenship and Immigration Services (USCIS) headquarters (in conjunction with the secretary of DHS) has the ability to process applications for humanitarian parole for persons outside the United States who have an urgent need to come to the United States (for medical reasons, for example).

The above categories involve persons outside the United States who receive parole and come into this country. However, an individual already in the United States with a pending application for adjustment of status may request an advance parole in order to depart from the country temporarily and then re-enter to resume processing of the application.[29] Persons with TPS (discussed above) also may request an advance parole.[30] There are limited procedures for a "parole-in-place" for persons physically present within the United States. Most commonly, a parole-in-place procedure will apply to Cuban nationals, or cooperating witnesses.[31]

A person initially detained upon arrival in the United States may be paroled out of immigration custody to become a "parolee" from within the United States.[32] A parole document is issued to the parolee, usually a four-by-four white document with a photo attached, specifying the regulatory provision under which parole has been granted. A parole document is proof of permission to be in the United States. The holder is legally present in the country and may receive a work permit.

Persons in parole status who are subsequently convicted of crime and come to the attention of DHS may have their parole status revoked, and are subject to removal from the United States. In removal proceedings, they are entitled to very few rights or protections. An IJ has no jurisdiction to grant parole; it is granted through the appropriate agency within DHS.

Deferred action

Deferred action, like parole, is technically neither an immigrant nor a nonimmigrant status. It is a determination, made either on a case-by-case basis or for a specific na-

---

[28] INA §212(d)(5)(A); 8 USC §1182(d)(5)(A); 8 CFR §§212.14, 1212.14.
[29] 8 CFR §212.5(f).
[30] 8 CFR §244.15.
[31] See *Immigration Law & the Military*, 2nd Ed. (AILA 2015) for a discussion of parole-in-place for military members and their immediate family.
[32] 8 CFR §212.5.

tionality at a designated time [also called deferred enforced departure (DED)], to defer removal from the United States as a matter of discretion. For a period of time in the 1990s, deferred action was rarely utilized. It was a matter of prosecutorial discretion, without mention in the regulations. Initially, the ability to defer removal action against a noncitizen was found only in legacy Immigration and Naturalization Service's (INS) internal operating instructions (OIs). To be precise, INS OI 242.1(a)(22) was removed on June 24, 1996, but the practice of deferring removal proceedings, or removal following proceedings, continued.

Today, deferred action is in fact a widely used tool in connection with various benefits. It is still utilized in certain humanitarian cases, including the cases of certain battered or abused spouses and children, and victims of trafficking. Individuals applying for battered spouse, "U," or "T" benefits (these are statuses for cooperating victims of crime) receive deferred action while their applications are pending.[33] Deferred action is also utilized by DHS for persons whose "S"[34] cooperating witness applications are pending.

Deferred action cannot be granted by an IJ; the immigration court has no jurisdiction. In the case of someone facing removal, deferred action is granted by the ICE's ERO. When connected to an affirmative immigration benefit (such as a battered spouse or "V"[35] petition), deferred action is granted by USCIS. When an S cooperating witness application is pending, deferred action is granted by the Investigations component of ICE.[36]

Deferred action status is indicated in the form of a letter from DHS, an approval notice (Form I-797), or a work permit (employment authorization card) in the category of (c)(14). Deferred action is not a visa and does not give an individual authorization to travel—or even apply for travel permission vis à vis an advance parole.

An individual in deferred action status may be a candidate for permanent resident status, but conviction of a crime jeopardizes that status. If a removal order is not being enforced because deferred action has been granted, the discretionary decision not to execute a final order may be reversed as the result of a crime. Accordingly, an individual in deferred action status is on tenuous ground in the United States and should avoid a criminal conviction.

Deferred action for childhood arrivals: Another type of deferred action is deferred action for childhood arrivals (DACA). On June 15, 2012, DHS issued a directive announcing that it would consider deferred action for those who were brought to the United States before their 16th birthday and are either currently enrolled in school, have graduated from high school, or have earned a General Equivalency Diploma

---

[33] U and T status are discussed in chapter twelve.

[34] *See* INA §101(a)(15)(S); 8 USC §1101(a)(15)(S).

[35] *See* INA §101(a)(15)(V); 8 USC §1101(a)(15)(V).

[36] These agencies are discussed later in this chapter.

(GED). At the time of the application, the applicant must be at least 15 years of age and not over 30 years of age. This is a great opportunity for educated youths because it gives them a renewable two-year grant of deferred action, a work permit, and the ability to obtain a driver's license. Although deferred action is a discretionary decision, USCIS now considers applications if the applicant meets the criteria as set forth by the DHS directive.

On November 20, 2014, President Barack Obama announced an expansion of the existing DACA eligibilities. However, on February 16, 2015, a federal district judge in Brownsville, TX, issued a preliminary injunction pending review of the legality of the program.[37] As of the spring of 2015, it is unclear whether the new and expanded DACA program will go forward. Under the revised DACA program, deferred action will be granted for three years. The applicant must have been continuously present in the United States from January 1, 2010, as opposed to the previous requirement of continuous presence since June 15, 2007. The applicant is now able to apply at any age; previously, the applicant must have applied before his or her 30th birthday. All other criteria remain the same. The applicant must have been present in the United States before his or her 16th birthday and must be either currently enrolled in school, have graduated from high school, or have earned a GED. At the time of the application, the applicant must be at least 15 years of age.[38]

Order of supervision

An individual is placed on an order of supervision following the entry of an order of removal or deportation if he or she cannot be physically removed.[39] For example, persons who are stateless or citizens and nationals of Cuba cannot be removed, and are supervised pursuant to 8 CFR §241.5(a). Like deferred action, an order of supervision is issued by ICE's ERO; it cannot be granted by an IJ. Orders of supervision are sometimes used for cooperating witnesses with a final order of removal; their presence is required for purposes of cooperation and they may be waiting for S status or some other protection. An individual on an order of supervision is eligible for employment authorization. He or she can live and work in the United States, but is required to report to ICE as indicated on the particular order.

---

[37] *Texas v. United States*, 2015 U.S. Dist. LEXIS 18551 (S.D. Tex. Feb. 16, 2015). Judge Hanen's Memorandum Opinion and Order is available at *www.scribd.com/doc/255994067/Memorandum-Opinion-Texas-v-United-States*. His Order of Temporary Injunction is available at *www.scribd.com/doc/255992850/Order-of-Temporary-Injunction-Texas-v-United-States*. As a result, USCIS stopped accepting applications for the new extended DACA and the proposed deferred action for parents of U.S. citizens and lawful permanent residents (DAPA). However, USCIS does note the district court's temporary injunction does not affect the existing DACA. Read more at *http://cmsny.org/federal-court-halts-dapa-and-expanded-daca-programs/#ixzz3UVZLtiY5*.
[38] More information can be found online at USCIS's website (*www.uscis.gov*), ICE's website (*www.ice.gov*), or the DHS website (*www.dhs.gov*).
[39] 8 CFR §241.4 *et. seq.*

An order of supervision is prepared on paper with a photo attached along with other instructions and warnings to the holder. A person on an order of supervision is eligible for a work permit in the (c)(18) category. The duration of employment authorization, as reflected on the work permit, will usually correspond to the reporting period on the order of supervision.

An individual who is on an order of supervision already has been ordered removed, so the immigration situation cannot get much worse. Be advised, however, that ERO is likely to take an individual who is under its supervision back into immigration custody if he or she is convicted of an additional crime.

No Status: Present Without Inspection or Admission, or Overstay

Aside from myriad legal statuses, there are the "illegal" categories: persons who enter the United States surreptitiously by crossing the border by land or entering by the sea, as well as persons who enter legally but later fall out of status.

Prior to 1996, individuals who entered the United States without inspection were referred to as persons who entered without inspection (EWIs). They were charged as deportable persons under the INA, similar to persons who had been lawfully admitted but overstayed their time. Since legislative changes in 1996, persons who evade inspection are referred to by statute as "present in the United States without being admitted or paroled," or someone who "arrives at any time or place other than as designated by the Attorney General."[40] If detected, these persons are charged under INA §212(a) as if they were arriving at a port of entry as "applicants for admission."[41] At first glance, it may seem to a nonimmigration lawyer that these persons are not eligible for any form of relief from removal, but this is not always the case. Depending on the type of benefit they seek, and the years they have been physically present, these illegal entrants may be eligible for residency, TPS, asylum, or some other benefit. Again, it very much depends on the facts of the particular case.

Many persons find themselves in removal proceedings because they have become present in the United States unlawfully following a legal admission. A person can violate his or her nonimmigrant status in many ways, the most common being overstaying the time granted. An initial lawful admission and subsequent overstay, generally speaking, places a person in a better position than an EWI. The former has greater due process rights, such as a right to a hearing in front of an IJ (as opposed to expedited removal), a right to a bond hearing in front of a judge, and potential qualification for other benefits under the INA.

---

[40] INA §212(a)(6)(A); 8 USC §1182(a)(6)(A).
[41] INA §235(a); 8 USC §1225(a).

Other Useful Terms

Notice to Appear

The Notice to Appear (NTA) is immigration law's charging document. Like an indictment or information, this document commences removal proceedings before the immigration court. It contains factual allegations and charges of removability pursuant to the INA.

Form I-94

Form I-94 is the arrival-departure record created when foreign individuals enter the United States (with some exceptions, notably Canadian visitors entering at a land border). If entry was by air or sea after March 2013, the I-94 is kept in an electronic database accessible to the public at *https://i94.cbp.dhs.gov*. Otherwise, the I-94 is a little white card (about 4″ x 4″ in size) with an identifying number across the top, and spaces for the individual's name, address, date of birth, and country of birth.

The I-94, in its purest sense, is used for nonimmigrants arriving in the United States; it indicates date of entry and required date of departure. However, the I-94 also is used to create a parole document, show proof of asylum status, and temporary proof of lawful admission to the United States. In other words, the I-94 both indicates nonimmigrant status and can be used as proof of status beyond nonimmigrant status.

Visa

A nonimmigrant visa is like a large postage stamp affixed to a passport page to indicate that the holder is eligible for admission into the United States in that particular status. A visa may be issued for multiple entries for an extended period of time, or for one entry and a relatively short period of time. Normally, if a waiver is required in connection with a visa, or an issue of inadmissibility for crime is resolved at the consulate, a typed notation will be made on the visa to indicate to CBP inspectors at the port of entry that the ground of inadmissibility has been waived or otherwise resolved. The length of time given on a visa will not necessarily correspond to the length of stay authorized on the I-94. In the event that a visa holder does not depart the United States on or before the date on the I-94 card, the visa is automatically null and void—cancelled—and the individual must apply for a new visa at the U.S. consulate in his or her home country.

Employment Authorization Document

The employment authorization document (EAD) is a laminated work permit card with the individual's photo and date of birth. There are specific categories that qualify a person for a work permit. The categories, or classifications, are found at 8 CFR §274a.12. A prospective client should present the work permit to you for review, because the category listed on the face of the work permit is an indication of the person's status in the United States.

Authority over Immigration Law Enforcement: A Look at the Government Agencies

Authority over enforcement of the immigration laws used to be straightforward. The U.S. Department of Justice (DOJ) encompassed legacy INS and the Executive Office for Immigration Review (EOIR) (the immigration court system). The U.S. Department of State (DOS), through the U.S. embassies, issued visas to persons applying for entry abroad. However, jurisdiction over legacy INS was transferred to DHS in March 2003, and legacy INS was divided and distributed among agencies within DHS. EOIR remains under the attorney general's control within DOJ. DOS, through the American embassies, retains jurisdiction over the issuance of visas. However, DHS maintains an office in many American embassies—and certainly in various regions overseas—and is very much involved in the visa issuance process by virtue of its jurisdiction over waivers of inadmissibility that might be necessary in conjunction with visa issuance. This is discussed further below, as well as in chapter ten. The following is a discussion of the governmental structure.

The U.S. Department of Homeland Security: USCIS, ICE, and CBP

For purposes of enforcement of the immigration laws, DHS is divided into three agencies: USCIS, ICE, and CBP. Non–American citizens still have one alien-file (A-file) with DHS. The agencies are expected to share this primary file. Many of the agencies continue to be housed in the same office buildings, but the agencies are slowly becoming more independent, including moving their offices to different physical sites.

From a practitioner's perspective, the delineation between agencies makes representation of a non–American citizen more complicated and difficult. Often, the agencies do not communicate well, and there is a frequent problem with overlapping jurisdiction in an individual case. For example, which authority has the final word over a person who is both eligible for a benefit (*e.g.*, adjustment of status to permanent resident) *and* subject to detention and removal? Often, more than one component of DHS is responsible for an aspect of the case, yet each agency will point to the other as being required to act—in other words, passing responsibility to the other component.[42] In any event, the following agencies are entrusted with immigration law responsibilities within DHS:

- USCIS has jurisdiction over affirmative immigration benefits, including, but not limited to, work permits, visa applications, residency, and naturalization applications.[43]

---

[42] For organizational charts of U.S. Customs and Border Protection (CBP), U.S. Immigration and Customs Enforcement (ICE), and U.S. Citizenship and Immigration Services (USCIS), see Appendices 1B–1D.

[43] For more information about immigration benefits and services, see the USCIS website at *www.uscis.gov*.

- ICE is charged with the enforcement of the immigration and customs laws within the United States (as opposed to at the borders). This agency encompasses the former investigations, detention, and removal units of legacy INS. ICE's Office of Investigations is charged with investigating immigration law violations by both individuals and entities and can make immigration law arrests. The formal title is Homeland Security Investigations (HSI).
- ICE's ERO detains individuals pending removal. It also arrests persons with final orders of removal, executes removal orders, and has discretion to grant orders of supervision and deferred action.
- Housed within ICE's Office of the Principal Legal Advisor are the Offices of Chief Counsel (formerly, the offices of district counsel), the legal offices responsible for representing DHS before EOIR (the immigration courts).[44]
- U.S. Customs and Border Protection (CBP) is responsible for border and transportation security. The agency incorporates the former inspections unit of legacy INS, as well as the Border Patrol. CBP also includes the former Customs Service.[45]

> ➢ **Scenario**: Consider the following example: an attorney receives a frantic call from a recently convicted client's relative. The client has been taken into custody by immigration authorities. But who really has taken the convicted client into custody? Is it USCIS, ICE, or CBP? The answer is that either ICE or CBP could have taken the client into custody.

USCIS is in charge of services, such as granting residency, citizenship, and asylum status. Although the client may have gone to USCIS to pick up a work permit, for example, this agency does not have an enforcement component and has not arrested the client. However, the agencies are in communication with each other. The client picking up a work permit also may be deportable as a result of a conviction, and USCIS may alert enforcement.

Determining which agency within DHS has taken a client into custody can be a challenge. Both Border Patrol (CBP) and HSI (ICE) investigate immigration violations and receive tips from the public regarding undocumented individuals. CBP will detain persons at a port of entry. ICE arrests persons who have final orders of removal, but not usually before then. The following is a guide to locating your client:

An arrest at the border

CBP is in charge of the national border, whether at an airport, seaport, or land port. If an individual has been arrested at the time of entry into the United States, he or she is probably being held by CBP and may be detained at the port for several hours—even days. An individual who is subject to expedited removal[46] may be de-

---

[44] For more information about the enforcement units of ICE, see the ICE website at *www.ice.gov*.

[45] For more information regarding borders and inspections, see the CBP website at *www.cbp.gov*.

[46] See chapter three.

ported from the port without ever being transferred to a detention center. If a person requests asylum or is entitled to contest removal, he or she will be transferred to a detention center, where that person will be turned over to ERO, the detention component of ICE. ERO decides who will go into custody.

An arrest upon termination of sentence

A non–American citizen serving a sentence (or in pretrial detention) at a state or federal facility often comes to the attention of immigration authorities, who lodge a detainer and take custody of the non–American citizen upon his or her release. If the individual is serving a sentence, he or she may have been interviewed and issued a Notice to Appear, the immigration charging document, while incarcerated. An officer of ICE-HSI or ICE-ERO issues a charging document to a person detained in penal custody. If the individual has been detained for only a short period of time (*e.g.*, pretrial detention), the detainer and immigration arrest may come as an unpleasant surprise. The lodging of a detainer and subsequent arrest can be performed by several agencies, including Border Patrol (CBP), HSI (ICE), or—after the lodging of a detainer—by ICE-ERO. An individual who is picked up at a jail or prison may be taken to a government office, but will probably be transported directly to a detention center. Based on a policy announced in 2012, persons in penal custody are to be provided a copy of their detainer with appropriate contact information for inquiries.[47]

Arrest while out in the community

Many individuals are arrested by surprise while they are at liberty in the community; for example, at home, the worksite, or at the probation and parole office (the latter a logical favorite of ICE and CBP). Indeed, persons are often arrested at an immigration building, waiting for a naturalization or residency interview, or even while applying for asylum. If the client does not have a removal order, an arrest at the immigration building is being carried out by ICE-HSI. If it takes place out in the community, the arrest is being executed by HSI or Border Patrol (CBP).

The arrested individual will most likely be taken into a government office for questioning, fingerprinting, and other paperwork before being brought to the detention center. The attorney can call the local HSI and Border Patrol offices to locate the client and determine the nature of the arrest and charges. In such a situation, it may be possible to negotiate release (perhaps on bond) prior to transfer to a detention facility. If the person already is under a removal order entered by an IJ, the arrest is most likely being executed by a deportation officer of ICE, and he or she will be transported to the closest detention center, pending travel arrangements and deportation.

---

[47] ICE maintains a detainee locator system at *https://locator.ice.gov/odls/homePage.do*.

The U.S. Department of State

Both immigrant and nonimmigrant visas (with the exception of certain renewals) are issued by consular officers at U.S. embassies or consular posts abroad. Consulates fall under the jurisdiction of DOS and the secretary of state. Visa issuance falls under DOS's Bureau of Consular Affairs, Visa Services.

An individual with a conviction, be it in the United States or a foreign jurisdiction, applying for a visa abroad will be interviewed by a consular officer at an American embassy or consular post. A consular officer makes the determination whether to issue the visa; in other words, that officer determines the person's admissibility. However, if it is determined that a visa applicant requires a waiver because of a criminal conviction, the waiver application is forwarded to a USCIS regional office under the auspices of DHS, and the ultimate decision whether to grant a waiver (on which visa eligibility depends) will be made by an officer of DHS—not DOS. The two agencies do coordinate their procedures and work together: the consular officer will make a recommendation on the waiver to USCIS.

As discussed in chapter ten, nonimmigrant waivers are requested in connection with nonimmigrant visas. The consular office will make a recommendation to the designated DHS-USCIS office abroad for adjudication of a waiver.[48] Similarly, when an applicant for an immigrant visa requires a waiver, DHS makes the final decision, albeit in consultation with the consular office.[49] The Administrative Review Office (ARO) makes final decisions on nonimmigrant waivers. ARO is part of CBP. Immigrant visa waivers are decided by USCIS. The consulate forwards the waiver request to DHS for adjudication.

The Executive Office for Immigration Review

The EOIR—the immigration court system—is under the jurisdiction of the attorney general and within DOJ.

The EOIR comprises 59 immigration courts and more than 260 judges located across the country.[50] The IJs hear removal cases, decide issues of inadmissibility and deportability, and adjudicate applications for residency and waivers. In a sense, the IJs share jurisdiction with USCIS over many applications. Once an individual is in removal proceedings, authority over his or her application (for residency, asylum, or a waiver) rests with the IJ. If an individual is not in immigration custody, he or she will attend the immigration hearing at an immigration court having jurisdiction over the case. For persons who are detained, the detention centers generally house small immigration courts, or fall under the jurisdiction of an immigration court nearby.

---

[48] 22 CFR §40.301; 8 CFR §1212.4.

[49] Reference is made throughout 22 CFR's chapter 40 to the procedure of forwarding waivers of inadmissibility to the Department of Homeland Security (DHS) for decision in connection with immigrant visa applications.

[50] Statistics as of 2015. *See* Appendix 1A. For the most current list, see the Executive Office for Immigration Review's (EOIR) website at *www.usdoj.gov/eoir/sibpages/ICadr.htm*.

Thus, an individual who is detained in immigration custody will have a hearing at the detention center, or will be brought by detention officers to an immigration court nearby.

Institutional removal cases (brought under ICE's Institutional Removal Program (IRP), formerly the Institutional Hearing Program) are immigration court cases heard while the non–American citizen is serving a sentence in state or federal prison. ICE also refers to this program as the Criminal Alien Program (CAP). The government's goal in a CAP-IRP case is to resolve the deportation matter before a person finishes his or her criminal sentence, thus expediting deportation (or release) upon completion of the sentence. CAP-IRP cases are conducted in selected state, local, and federal jails and prisons. Not every prison facility has an IRP program. These hearings often take place by video.

The rules of procedure for the immigration courts may be found at 8 CFR Part 1003, subpart C. These rules include instructions on the commencement of proceedings, change of venue, custody determinations, motions, the filing of documents, and the general form of proceedings.[51]

The Board of Immigration Appeals

The Board of Immigration Appeals (BIA or Board) is the administrative appellate body charged with reviewing appealed IJ decisions. An individual who has been ordered removed (but not pursuant to expedited removal) has an automatic right to appeal to the BIA, and will not be deported during the appeal period. Although the BIA's primary function is appellate review of IJ decisions, the BIA has jurisdiction over USCIS's denial or revocation of visa petitions.[52] In addition, the BIA has jurisdiction over certain fines imposed on carriers; the denial of a waiver under INA §212(d)(3) if the application is made within the United States; and determinations of bond made by an IJ.[53] The BIA sits at Falls Church, VA, and is authorized for up to 15 members.[54]

On occasion, the BIA will hear oral argument. When the BIA issues a precedent decision, it is binding on both immigration judges and DHS adjudicators. As discussed below, a BIA decision may be certified to the attorney general. Most BIA decisions may be appealed to a federal court of appeals.

Pursuant to regulations promulgated in 2002, BIA cases generally are considered by one BIA member; only cases of a significant nature (*e.g.*, inconsistencies among judges, the need for precedent, etc.) will be heard by a three-member panel or en

---

[51] For more information on immigration court proceedings, see the latest edition of EOIR's *Immigration Judge Benchbook*, available at http://agora.aila.org.

[52] 8 CFR §103.3(a)(1)(ii); 8 CFR §1003.1(a)(7)(b)(5).

[53] 8 CFR §1003.1(a)(7)(b).

[54] 8 CFR §1003.1.

banc.[55] The BIA generally issues a decision based on the record as it was completed by the IJ. As of September 2002, the BIA no longer exercises de novo review of factual issues.[56] If new evidence or legal issues are raised at the appellate level, they will be either disregarded or the case will be remanded to the IJ (as deemed appropriate).

Upon the issuance of a final decision by the BIA, the immigration case is considered administratively final, and if the person has been ordered deported, removal is automatic. Although there is limited review in the federal courts, there is no automatic stay of deportation connected to federal judicial review.

Attorney General Review

When the BIA rules against an individual, he or she may be able to appeal to a U.S. federal court of appeals. The DHS trial attorneys (who constitute the Office of Chief Counsel, which is now a component of ICE) cannot appeal an adverse decision of the BIA to the federal courts. Traditionally, the trial attorneys—part of legacy INS—fell under the jurisdiction of DOJ, as does the BIA; thus, an appeal of an adverse BIA decision would have resulted in one segment of DOJ suing another segment. Instead, the trial attorneys' recourse was to seek certification from the attorney general. Today, conceivably, the Office of Chief Counsel could appeal an adverse decision of the BIA (the latter being part of DOJ). Still, both agencies are part of the executive branch, and the tradition continues that the Office of Chief Counsel does not appeal an adverse decision of the BIA to the federal courts, but may only seek certification to the attorney general.

Thus, a third tier of administrative appellate review is referral to the attorney general. This option is not available to the individual respondent, only upon request of the government. Specifically:

- the attorney general may become aware of a specific BIA decision and direct the BIA to refer the matter to him or her;
- the BIA itself may determine that a matter should be referred to the attorney general; or
- the secretary of DHS may refer a case to the attorney general for review.[57] It is a rare but significant occasion when the attorney general issues an immigration decision.

The Administrative Appeals Office

The Administrative Appeals Office (AAO) (formally known as the Administrative Appeals Unit) sits in Washington, D.C., and was previously part of legacy INS. Now a part of USCIS, the AAO (rather than the BIA) has jurisdiction over the denial of

---

[55] *See, generally,* 8 CFR §1003.1(e)(6).

[56] 8 CFR §1003.1(d)(3).

[57] This procedure is spelled out at 8 CFR §1003.1(h).

certain applications and waivers decided by the former associate commissioner of examinations.[58] The AAO has appellate jurisdiction over the majority of employment-based visa cases. For purposes of the discussion in this book, note that the AAO has jurisdiction in certain contexts over denials of adjustment of status, immigrant visas, and concurrently filed criminal-alien waivers. The particular applications and petitions over which the AAO has appellate jurisdiction are listed at 8 CFR §§103.3, 1103.3.

The AAO exercises appellate review authority over the denial of INA §212(h) waivers when the individual is applying for an immigrant visa abroad. The AAO exercises jurisdiction over the denial of the nonimmigrant INA §212(d)(3) waiver. (These waivers are discussed in detail in chapter ten.) When an individual is inadmissible because of a criminal record, and is applying for an immigrant visa at an American consulate abroad, the AAO has appellate jurisdiction over a decision to deny a waiver. When an individual is inadmissible and applies for a nonimmigrant visa, the AAO has ultimate jurisdiction. For applications filed with USCIS within the United States, the AAO reviews denials of adjustment of status under the Cuban Adjustment Act (including the denial of a §212(h) waiver filed in conjunction with a Cuban Adjustment Act application); applications for T and U nonimmigrant status; TPS applications;[59] and battered spouse petitions. These categories are discussed in greater detail throughout this book.

The Agencies at Work: Removal Proceedings

Notice to Appear

In removal proceedings before the immigration court, charges are brought on a notice to appear (NTA).[60] This charging document is often prepared by one of the law enforcement agencies within DHS. The component or agency of DHS that will prepare and issue the NTA depends on the legal posture of the individual (*i.e.*, where he or she was when arrested).

Additionally, the service and benefits agency, USCIS, may issue and serve NTAs upon denial of an affirmatively requested benefit. For example, suppose USCIS routinely uncovers a criminal record in the course of a naturalization application and interview; in such a case, USCIS has the authority to issue an NTA. Likewise, upon denying an application for adjustment of status, for example, USCIS can issue an

---

[58] 8 CFR §1103.3.

[59] If the basis upon which temporary protected status (TPS) is denied also forms a ground of deportability, a charging document commencing removal proceedings will be issued with the denial, and at that point, the applicant may renew the application in front of the immigration judge. In such a situation, there would be no right to appeal USCIS's denial of TPS to the Administrative Appeals Office (AAO). 8 CFR §§244.10(c), 1244.10(c).

[60] 8 CFR §§239.1, 1239.1. For a sample notice to appear (NTA), see Appendix 1E.

NTA. The large regional service centers, responsible for adjudicating many immigrant and nonimmigrant visa petitions, have the authority to issue NTAs, but as of this writing rarely do so. The asylum office can issue and serve an NTA, and a large percentage of the immigration courts' workload can be attributed to files referred to the courts for removal proceedings upon denial of an asylum application.[61]

> *Tip*: Not every agency employee is authorized to sign off on an NTA. If the NTA is issued by an unauthorized individual, there are grounds for dismissal of proceedings. For a list of individuals within DHS who are authorized to issue NTAs, see 8 CFR §239.1(a).

One significant aspect of the changes to the INA by the Illegal Immigration Reform and Immigrant Responsibility Act of 1996[62] is that an NTA may now be served by regular mail when personal service is not practicable.[63] If the NTA is served by regular mail, there is no way of proving or disproving whether the document was properly sent. Prior to April 1, 1997 (the effective date of IIRAIRA), service—if not personal—had to be by certified mail. Thus, it was easy to detect if a clerk had made an error in preparing and/or mailing the NTA. Today, DHS and EOIR rely on the U.S. Postal Service. There is a built-in presumption that the preparation, mailing, and delivery of the NTA (or court notices) have been handled properly. An individual who does not appear for a hearing will be deported in absentia.[64] Motions to reopen and other specific court procedures are beyond the scope of this book; generally, it is extremely difficult to reopen a case when the individual is ordered deported in absentia. The only exceptions for failure to appear in immigration court are a demonstration of no proper notice, serious illness or death of the respondent or an immediate family member, or other exceptional circumstances.[65]

> **Practice Pointer**: Counsel can stay current on removal proceedings—whether the NTA was filed, the next hearing date, even the name of the assigned judge—by dialing EOIR's automated system at (800) 898-7180.

---

[61] The Asylum Office does not call this procedure a "denial" of asylum, but a "referral." In effect, a "referral" of the asylum application to the immigration court in conjunction with issuance of an NTA means—of course—that the affirmative asylum application has been denied and is now within the jurisdiction of the immigration court.

[62] Illegal Immigration Reform and Immigrant Responsibility Act of 1996 (IIRAIRA), Division C of the Omnibus Appropriations Act of 1996 (H.R. 3610), Pub. L. No. 104-208, 110 Stat. 3009.

[63] INA §239(a)(1), 8 USC §1229(a)(1); *see* INA §239(c); 8 USC §1229(c).

[64] INA §240(b)(5)(A); 8 USC §1229(b)(5)(A).

[65] INA §240(b)(5); 8 USC §1229(b)(5); *see* 8 CFR §1003.23.

Course of Proceedings

Removal proceedings are administrative hearings conducted by IJs under the auspices of EOIR. The procedures governing the immigration courts are set forth at 8 CFR Parts 239, 1239, and 1240.

Immigration court proceedings are adversarial in nature, in the sense there is an independent judge, a prosecutor (chief counsel for DHS), and the non–American citizen (the respondent). The respondent has a right to counsel, but at no expense to the government.[66] Removal proceedings are conducted in formal courtroom settings (unless the hearings take place in a prison).[67] Instead of a court reporter, the record is kept by way of recording, controlled by the IJ. The immigration court provides interpreters at no expense to the respondent. Although removal proceedings are governed by relaxed rules of evidence (*e.g.*, hearsay is allowed), immigration hearings are essentially trials to the bench and, in certain cases, may go on for days as issues of removability and relief are litigated.

Regarding evidence, 8 CFR §1240.7 states:

(a) *Use of prior statements.* The IJ may receive in evidence any oral or written statement that is material and relevant to any issue in the case previously made by the respondent or any other person during any investigation, examination, hearing, or trial.

(b) *Testimony.* Testimony of witnesses appearing at the hearing shall be under oath or affirmation administered by the IJ.

(c) *Depositions.* The IJ may order the taking of depositions pursuant to §1003.35 of this chapter.

8 CFR §1240.9 states:

Contents of record. The hearing before the IJ, including the testimony, exhibits, applications, proffers, and requests, the IJ's decision, and all written orders, motions, appeals, briefs, and other papers filed in the proceedings shall constitute the record in the case. The hearing shall be recorded verbatim except for statements made off the record with the permission of the IJ. In his or her discretion, the IJ may exclude from the record any arguments made in connection with motions, applications, requests, or objections, but in such event the person affected may submit a brief.

In immigration court, the initial hearing is referred to as a "master calendar" hearing. As with an arraignment or calendar call, many non–American citizen respondents can be scheduled for a master hearing at the same time. At the master calendar

---

[66] 8 CFR §1240.3.

[67] The Institutional Removal Program (IRP), discussed above, involves hearings conducted in jails or prisons; there is no formal courtroom. Indeed, many such hearings take place by phone or video, and the respondent does not even see the judge.

hearing, a respondent is expected to plead to the charge(s) of removability on the NTA and, if appropriate, request relief—or state a defense—from removal. Often, a continuance is requested at the first master calendar hearing so that the respondent can locate an attorney, or because either side requires preparation time. It is not atypical for a master calendar hearing to be continued several times at the request of either party.[68]

A final merits hearing is referred to as an "individual" hearing, at which time the application for relief from removal is presented to the court and evidence, witnesses, etc., are presented.[69] An individual hearing also may be conducted to determine removability in those cases in which a respondent contests the charge of removability under the INA and, in turn, litigates the underlying charge(s). In years past, it was routine to admit the allegations, concede removability, and move on to the relief stage. It was comparatively easy to statutorily qualify to seek a waiver, so, why bicker about removability? However, since legislative changes in 1990 and 1996, fewer individuals are prima facie eligible for waivers. Today, it is extremely important to review and research the underlying charge of removability, because once established, there may be no relief from removal available. Notably, DHS's law enforcement agents (CBP and ICE) *do make mistakes*—the law can be complicated—and errors are found in the NTA. For this reason, it is worthwhile for defense counsel to earnestly review the allegations and charges for legal sufficiency, and not hesitate to contest removability when appropriate.

The Burden of Proof

If a non–American citizen in removal proceedings contests the charge of removability, a burden of proof is assigned to one of the parties. In removal proceedings, the government has the burden of establishing that a person is *deportable* by clear and convincing evidence.[70] In other words, where the charge of removal is under INA §237 (deportability), the burden lies with the Office of Chief Counsel for ICE. In contrast, a person in removal proceedings who is subject to and charged with grounds of *inadmissibility* under INA §212(a) carries the burden of proof. An applicant for admission must establish that he or she is clearly and beyond doubt entitled to be admitted and is not inadmissible; and a person already in the United States must establish by clear and convincing evidence that he or she is lawfully present pursuant to a prior admission.[71] Persons physically present after an EWI fall into this latter category.

---

[68] 8 CFR §1240.6.

[69] See chapter thirteen for presenting applications for relief.

[70] INA §240(c)(3); 8 USC §1229a(c)(3); *see* 8 CFR §1240.8.

[71] INA §240(c)(2); 8 USC §1229a(c)(2).

Applications for Relief

As stated above, if the IJ determines that the respondent is indeed removable as charged, the respondent may file an application for relief as a defense to removal. There are various forms of relief. The application generally will carry a government filing fee (exceptions are applications for asylum, withholding, or protection under the CAT) and will be supported by relevant evidence. Paying the filing fee is what triggers the biometrics process: all applicants for a benefit must be fingerprinted and photographed. However, paying the filing fee is somewhat complicated because the immigration courts do not have their own cashiers and cannot accept payments. Payments must be made to a USCIS cashier.[72]

Before filing with the court, all applications must be filed by mail with the appropriate USCIS regional service center or local USCIS office.[73] Better said, a *copy* of the application (with fee, as required) must be sent to the service center. Upon receiving the application, the service center generates a receipt for the filing fee, and about two weeks later, provides a notice to the applicant to appear for fingerprinting. Sending the application and fee to a USCIS service center triggers the appointment for the taking of the photograph and fingerprints (biometrics) of the respondent in anticipation of the court hearing.

By regulation, an IJ cannot grant any form of benefit until the biometrics have been completed by DHS.[74] This fee and biometric procedure is time consuming and a bit of a bureaucratic nightmare. At a minimum, this process adds at least two weeks to the preparation time of an application. (After the application is filed, a biometrics notice is not generated for approximately 14 to 30 days.) However, the immigration court will generally not accept the application until there is a receipt for the filing fee.[75] Thus, unlike other court systems, immigration applications and fees must be mailed away, and a receipt received, before presenting the application to the IJ.[76]

Appeal to the Board of Immigration Appeals

Following a decision from the IJ, either party to the proceedings (or both) may file an appeal to the BIA. A notice of appeal must be filed with (must arrive at) the BIA within 30 days of the IJ's decision. The appeal is filed on Form EOIR-29;[77] notice of appearance of counsel is filed with the appeal on Form EOIR-27. As of this writing,

---

[72] 8 CFR §§103.7(a)(1), 1103.7(a)(3).

[73] Regulations determine where an application is filed, and the instruction portion of the form will provide the correct office and address. See the USCIS website for locations and addresses of regional service centers and local USCIS offices (*www.uscis.gov*).

[74] 8 CFR §1003.47.

[75] 8 CFR §1003.24(c)(1).

[76] Preparation of applications, including fees and filing, is discussed at greater length in chapter ten.

[77] 8 CFR §1003.3(a)(1).

the filing fee is $110, unless a fee waiver is requested.[78] The check or money order is made out to the "United States Department of Justice." An appeal to the BIA of a decision of the IJ acts as an automatic stay of the removal order.[79] The non–American citizen cannot be removed while the appeal to the BIA is pending.

Unlike notices of appeal in other forums, such as federal court, a notice of appeal to the BIA must precisely state the basis for the appeal. The regulations dictate that a notice of appeal must specifically identify the findings of fact, the conclusions of law, or both that are being challenged.[80] A notice of appeal that does not specifically set forth the bases for the appeal is subject to dismissal.[81] It is important that counsel take the time to address specific issues, even citing to statute, regulation, and/or case law, if appropriate, when preparing the notice of appeal. Counsel also may request oral argument.[82]

Appeals will be considered by one member of the BIA,[83] unless counsel makes a specific request for three-member panel review. A panel will consider the appeal if counsel presents a compelling argument that at least one of the following criteria is present: (1) there is an inconsistency among the rulings of different judges; (2) there is a need to establish precedent; (3) the underlying decision is not in conformity with the law or applicable precedent; (4) the case or controversy presented is one of national import; (5) the factual determination of the judge is clearly erroneous; or (6) there is a need to reverse the decision of the judge.[84]

Appeals are filed directly with the BIA, as opposed to the local office of the IJ. Following is the address for filing appeals to the BIA:

Board of Immigration Appeals
Office of the Chief Clerk
5107 Leesburg Pike, Suite 2000
Falls Church, VA 22041
(hand delivery or express mail)
or

Board of Immigration Appeals
Office of the Chief Clerk
P.O. Box 8530
Falls Church, VA 22041[85]

---

[78] 8 CFR §§1003.3(a)(3), 1003.8, and 1103.7.

[79] 8 CFR §1003.6(a).

[80] 8 CFR §1003.3(b).

[81] 8 CFR §1003.1(d)(2)(i)(A).

[82] 8 CFR §1003.1(e)(7).

[83] 8 CFR §1003.1(e)(3).

[84] 8 CFR §1003.1(e)(6).

[85] See *Board of Immigration Appeals Practice Manual*, at App. A.

(nonexpress mail)

Phone number: (703) 605-1007

> **Practice Pointer**: It is highly recommended to file the appeal by overnight courier such as FedEx, UPS, or DHL, or, in the alternative, the U.S. Postal Service Express Mail. The 30-day deadline for a notice of appeal is statutory and is not easily forgiven or waived in the event that the appeal is filed late. This recommendation also holds true for the filing of briefs and motions with the BIA. It is further recommended that counsel include an additional copy of the first page of the appeal, brief, or any other motion or memorandum, with a self-addressed, stamped envelope, so that the BIA clerk can date stamp the extra copy and return to counsel as proof of filing.

The notice of appeal and all filings with the BIA must be accompanied by a certificate of service on opposing counsel—the Office of Chief Counsel that handled the matter before the IJ.[86]

After receiving the notice of appeal, the BIA clerk's office will receive the file from the immigration court. The clerk's office orders transcripts of the audiotapes taken during the immigration court proceedings. Upon completion of the transcripts (which can take anywhere from a few weeks—in cases in which the non–American citizen is detained—to several months), a briefing schedule and transcripts are mailed to the parties for preparation of briefs. A party is given 21 days to file an opening brief; the opposing party is given 21 days to respond. Either party may request one extension of the briefing schedule by filing a motion for extension of time in advance of the brief's due date.[87]

Clients frequently ask how long an appeal to the BIA will take. Processing time of an appeal will vary based on the nature of the case. In cases in which the non–American citizen is detained, the BIA will normally review the case and issue a decision within four to six months—perhaps even less. In a non-detained case, processing of an appeal may take six months to two years.

Travel While a BIA Appeal Is Pending

If an individual respondent (LPR or not) appeals a decision by an IJ ordering him or her deported and then travels outside the United States while the appeal is pending, the appeal is considered to be abandoned and the IJ's order of removal becomes final.[88] By traveling, the person executes the deportation order and essentially self-deports.

---

[86] 8 CFR §§1003.3(a), (c).

[87] 8 CFR §1003.3(c)(1).

[88] 8 CFR §1003.3(e).

Review in Federal Court

An individual respondent may appeal an adverse decision of the BIA to the U.S. court of appeals with jurisdiction over the area where the immigration court proceedings took place.[89] A petition for review must be filed with the circuit court of appeals within 30 days of the decision of the BIA.[90] Note that unlike an appeal to the BIA, a petition for review to the federal court of appeals carries no automatic stay of removal. The non–American citizen must move for a stay of the removal order.

Also, as noted above, the government or the BIA may request attorney general review.[91]

Federal Judicial Review

Congressional authority over laws governing the admission, presence, and expulsion of non–American citizens is absolute. This fundamental and complete authority is known as the plenary doctrine.[92] The U.S. Supreme Court has written that "over no conceivable subject is the legislative power of Congress more complete than it is over the admission of aliens."[93] In the same vein, complete authority to execute congressional intent lies with the executive branch and courts have very little authority to review the determinations of Congress and the president. Of course non–American citizens in the United States do have constitutional rights; however, the level of constitutional protections afforded non–American citizens depends very much on their legal status and physical situation.[94] For example, an individual physically inside the United States has greater constitutional rights than an individual seeking admission at a port of entry (border); the latter person, however, has greater rights than an individual seeking a visa at an American consulate in a foreign country. A non–American citizen physically within the United States has an expectation of equal protection and due process as guaranteed in the Fifth Amendment, and may challenge the constitu-

---

[89] INA §242(b); 8 USC §1252(b).

[90] INA §242(b)(1); 8 USC §1252(b)(1). For additional information on how to file a petition for review, see R. Pauw, *Litigating Immigration Cases in Federal Court* (AILA 3d Ed. 2013) and *AILA's Immigration Litigation Toolbox* (AILA 3d Ed. 2013), *available at* http://agora.aila.org or call (800) 982-2839.

[91] *See* 8 CFR §1003.1(h).

[92] *Chinese Exclusion Case*, or *Chae Chan Pin v. U.S.*, 130 U.S. 581 (1889).

[93] *INS v. Chadha*, 462 U.S. 919, 1000 (1983), *citing Kleindienst v. Mandel*, 408 U.S. 753, 766 (1972).

[94] *See, e.g., Yick Wo v. Hopkins*, 118 U.S. 356, 373–74 (1886) (the constitutional guarantee of equal protection under the law applies to aliens as well as citizens); *Plyler v. Doe*, 457 U.S. 202, 210 (1982) (aliens, even aliens whose presence in this country is unlawful, have long been recognized as "persons" for purposes of due process guarantees in the Fifth and Fourteenth Amendments); *Mathews v. Diaz*, 426 U.S. 67, 77 (1976) (the Fifth Amendment protects aliens from unlawful discrimination by the federal government); *Johnson v. Robison*, 415 U.S. 361, 364 (1974) (the Due Process Clause of the Fifth Amendment incorporates the guarantees of equal protection).

tionality of an immigration statute.[95] However, constitutional attacks on an immigration statute based on equal protection are reviewed under the minimal "rational basis test": classifications must be reasonable, not arbitrary, and must rest upon some ground or difference having a fair and substantial relation to the object of the legislation.[96] Certainly, Congress affords certain rights and benefits via statute, and the courts have jurisdiction to interpret the statutes. The courts interpret statutes de novo; however, the BIA, as the agency entrusted with interpreting immigration laws, is entitled to great deference in its interpretation of the INA.[97] Note that where the appeal issue rests on the proper interpretation of a federal or state criminal statute, the federal courts do not owe the BIA deference in their interpretation of the elements or proper classification of the crime.[98] For example, in analyzing whether a certain offense under a state statute qualifies as a "crime of violence" for purposes of the aggravated felony statute, a federal court will review both the state penal code and the federal code; in such a situation, no deference is accorded the BIA.

Over the years, Congress has struggled with the desired scope of judicial review over immigration decisions and actions, including review of removal orders as well as review of decisions on affirmative applications (*e.g.*, applications filed with USCIS), detention, and agency policies and procedure. Today, orders of removal issued by the BIA may be appealed by a petition for review in the appropriate court of appeals;[99] however, only issues of statutory interpretation (questions of law) and constitutional questions may be appealed in federal court.[100]

As discussed more fully below, discretionary determinations by the IJ or BIA to deny an application for a benefit are not subject to review.[101] Notably, the courts of appeals retain jurisdiction to review asylum claims.[102] Findings of fact, including adverse credibility findings, are reviewed under a "substantial evidence" standard of review: administrative findings of fact are conclusive unless any reasonable adjudicator would be compelled to conclude the contrary.[103] Decisions whether to grant or

---

[95] *Yeung v. Immigration and Naturalization Service,* 76 F.3d 337 (11th Cir. 1995).

[96] *Fernandez-Bernal v. Att'y Gen.,* 257 F.3d 1034, 1312 (11th Cir. 2001), *citing Stanton v. Stanton,* 421 U.S. 7, 14 (1975).

[97] *Nat'l Cable & Telecomm. Ass'n v. Brand X Internet Services,* 545 U.S. 967 (2005); *Chevron v. USA Inc. v. Natural Resources Defense Council,* 467 U.S. 837, 844 (1984).

[98] *Leocal v. Ashcroft,* 543 U.S. 1 (2004).

[99] Venue lies with the court of appeals for the judicial circuit in which the immigration judge completed the proceeding. INA §242(b)(2); 8 USC §1252(b)(2).

[100] INA §§242(a)(2), (b)(4); 8 USC §§1252(a)(2), (b)(4).

[101] INA §242(a)(2)(B); 8 USC §1252(a)(2)(B).

[102] INA §242(a)(2)(B)(ii); 8 USC §1252(a)(2)(B)(ii). Note that the federal courts cannot review decisions to pretermit an asylum application for failure to file within one year of admission or arrival in the United States. *See* INA §208(a)(3); 8 USC §1158(a)(3).

[103] INA §242(b)(4)(B); 8 USC §1252(b)(4)(B).

deny asylum in the exercise of discretion, and procedural matters regarding adjudication of the asylum claim, fall under an "abuse of discretion" standard of review.[104]

In some cases, clients will be seeking a visa and/or waiver from an American consulate abroad. A conviction, or admission of a crime, or even the suspicion of certain criminal activity, may result in denial of a visa by the consulate. This book also discusses waivers, such as those available under INA §§212(h) and 212(d)(3), that may be presented in conjunction with an application for an immigrant or nonimmigrant visa. If a waiver for crime is denied, it is denied by a DHS or USCIS office abroad rather than by DOS. As discussed above, a denial may be appealed to the AAO. However, there is no federal judicial review of an ultimate decision to deny a waiver. In addition, case law is clear that there is no judicial review over a consulate's decision to deny a visa, or over any other consular action in processing a visa application. This is described in case law as the doctrine of nonreviewability of consular action.[105]

> **Practice Pointer**: Issues of jurisdiction and the scope of review are complicated. Immigration law has its own set of rules when it comes to federal court review. An attorney considering filing for judicial review of an immigration decision may want to conduct independent research on the issues of jurisdiction, venue, scope and standard of review, and procedure.

The following is intended as an introductory and basic discussion only. Generally, review of detention issues rests with the federal district courts, whereas issues of law and constitutionality claims are reviewed at the courts of appeals in the context of a petition for review following an administrative removal order.

The REAL ID Act

The year 2005 marked the passage of the REAL ID Act—the legislation that now governs federal judicial review (at both the district and court of appeals levels) of immigration cases.[106] The REAL ID Act amended INA §242 by significantly limiting habeas corpus jurisdiction over immigration law issues, yet it increased the jurisdiction of the federal courts of appeals. Pursuant to REAL ID, judicial review of final orders of removal may only be had in the courts of appeals by means of a petition for review; the district courts no longer have habeas corpus authority over final removal orders. Thus, a final removal order, as well as a denial of protection under the CAT, may only be appealed to a court of appeals. Prior to REAL ID, immigration attorneys who believed the law was being misinterpreted or applied illegally could seek interim relief via habeas in the district courts, while the case-in-chief was still pending before

---

[104] INA §242(b)(4)(D); 8 USC §1252(b)(4)(D). *Zuh v. Mukasey*, 547 F.3d 504, 507 (4th Cir. 2008).

[105] *Lihua Jiang v. Hillary Clinton*, 08-CV-4477, 2011 U.S. Dist. LEXIS 136584 (E.D.N.Y. Nov. 23, 2011), citing *Al Makaaseb Gen. Trading Co., Inc. v. Christopher*, 94-CV-U79 (CSH). 1885 U.S. Dist. LEXIS 3057, 1995 WL 110117 (S.D.N.Y. Mar. 13, 1995).

[106] REAL ID Act of 2005, Pub. L. No. 109-13, div. B, 119 Stat. 231, 302–23.

the immigration court or BIA. Now, all issues must be litigated through the agencies (EOIR and BIA) before going into federal court. The REAL ID Act is retroactive, and calls for the transfer of habeas petitions pending on its enactment date from a district court to the appropriate court of appeals.[107]

Although it is frustrating to see habeas corpus relief eliminated, in REAL ID, Congress explicitly restored the scope of judicial review. Prior to REAL ID, there was disagreement among the district courts as to jurisdiction over even legal/statutory issues. Today, INA §242(a)(2)(D) [8 USC §1252(a)(2)(D)] reads that nothing in §242 (regarding judicial review of removal orders) or any other provision of the INA will preclude judicial review of final orders, unless such review is barred by some other provision of §242. The courts of appeals interpret this provision to mean that they are no longer jurisdictionally barred from directly reviewing (de novo) any removal order if the petition for review raises a question of law or a constitutional claim—even in a case involving a criminal record.[108] In the words of one court:

> In short, Congress repealed all jurisdictional bars to our direct review of final removal orders other than those remaining in 8 USC §1252 (in provisions other than (a)(2)(B) or (C)) following the amendment of that section by the REAL ID Act.[109]

Thus, whether a particular criminal offense qualifies as a removable offense under the INA is subject to the judicial review of the courts of appeals upon exhaustion of the administrative process (IJ and BIA).[110] Based on INA §242(a)(2)(D), federal courts of appeals exercise review over constitutional claims and/or questions of law, as opposed to discretionary or factual determinations.[111] Indeed, much of the analysis contained in this book comes from researching the federal courts of appeals' decisions regarding the proper classification of crimes and the availability of waivers under the INA.

Jurisdiction

No review of discretionary determinations

The federal courts do not have jurisdiction to review discretionary denials of applications, such as waivers, by either USCIS or EOIR.[112] In other words, if an IJ decides—based on the facts—that a waiver is not warranted, and the BIA affirms, there

---

[107] REAL ID Act, at §106(c), 119 Stat. 311.

[108] *See, e.g., Fernandez-Ruiz v. Gonzales*, 410 F.3d 585 (9th Cir. 2005), *adopted in relevant part en banc*, 466 F.3d 1121 (9th Cir. 2006); *Alvarez-Barajas v. Gonzales*, 418 F.3d 1050 (9th Cir. 2005); *Kamara v. U.S. Att'y Gen.*, 420 F.3d 202 (3d Cir. 2005).

[109] *Fenandez-Ruiz v. Gonzales*, 410 F.3d at 587.

[110] *Dulal-Whiteway v. DHS*, 501 F.3d 116 (2d Cir. 2007).

[111] *Jean-Pierre v. Att'y Gen.*, 500 F.3d 1315 (11th Cir. 2007).

[112] INA §242(a)(2)(B); 8 USC §1252(a)(2)(B).

is no review of that discretionary aspect of the denial. Only if an appeal is presented in terms of a violation of the law, including the Constitution, may a discretionary denial be appealed. Discretionary forms of relief are discussed further in chapter ten of this book, and include applications for adjustment of status (residency), relief under INA §212(h), §212(c), and §209(c), and cancellation of removal.

Again, a federal court cannot review an immigration court's decision that an individual does not *merit* relief in the exercise of discretion. However, courts may determine whether the law has been properly interpreted, including issues of removability and statutory eligibility for relief. And certainly the courts may interpret constitutional claims of due process and equal protection.

Petitions for Review to the Courts of Appeals

Judicial review of a final order of removal issued by the BIA is obtained through a petition for review filed with the court of appeals having jurisdiction over the place where the IJ issued the decision (not necessarily where the petitioner resides).[113] The petition for review must be filed not later than 30 days after the date of the order of removal.[114] The "respondent" is the U.S. attorney general.[115]

The filing of a petition for review does *not* stay removal of the petitioner.[116] ICE's ERO may act to deport the individual during the 30-day filing period (as well as while a petition for review is pending). A separate motion for a stay of removal is required, and experience teaches that stays are rarely granted. However, the court of appeals does not lose jurisdiction over the case by reason of the petitioner being physically removed, *provided* the petition for review was filed prior to the removal.[117]

Neither the statute nor the regulations contain specific instructions as to how a successful petitioner should be returned to the United States. However, in 2012, the Office of Principal Legal Advisor in coordination with ERO announced a new procedure and guidelines for returning someone to the United States after a successful petition for review.[118] In liaison with the American Immigration Lawyers Association (AILA), ICE has stated it will not return every successful litigant to the United States. It depends on the outcome of the judicial review; if the case is remanded for further

---

[113] INA §242(b)(2); 8 USC §1252(b)(2).

[114] INA §242(b)(1); 8 USC §1252(b)(1).

[115] INA §242(b)(3)(A); 8 USC §1252(b)(3)(A).

[116] INA §242(b)(3)(B); 8 USC §1252(b)(3)(B).

[117] *Bejar v. Ashcroft*, 324 F.3d 127 (3d Cir. 2003) (alien's removal from the United States does not divest a federal court of appeals from considering the claims raised in a petition for review; citing *Tapia-Garcia v. INS*, 237 F.3d 1216, 1217 (10th Cir. 2001)).

[118] The policy and procedure for return of non–American citizens who prevailed in a petition for review or motion to reopen may be found in ICE Policy Directive No. 11061.1 (*www.ice.gov*). Frequently Asked Questions (FAQs) about ICE Policy Directive Number 11061.1, "Facilitating the Return to the United States of Certain Lawfully Removed Aliens," are published on AILA InfoNet at Doc. No. 12042642 (*posted* Apr. 26, 2012).

findings, this may not be enough to justify return. The contact person at ICE is the public advocate.[119]

If the government is willing to cooperate with bringing a person back following a successful petition for review (or BIA motion to reopen or reconsider), the regulations do have several different mechanisms to accomplish the return. If an individual is a non-LPR who has prevailed on asylum, the return could be accomplished through a parole. An LPR should be able to return with resident card in hand, and an understanding that all hits are removed from the databases at the port of entry (or an advance approval from CBP that the individual will be allowed in to resume residency status). If the government is unwilling to cooperate in facilitating the successful petitioner's return, counsel may have to litigate in federal court by filing a motion to compel return, either in the court of appeals or a district court.

Pursuant to a final rule published on December 18, 2008, the filing of a petition for review of an administratively final removal order automatically terminates a grant of voluntary departure unless the individual departs the United States within 30 days of filing the petition.[120] This regulation was in response to a previous split among the circuit courts regarding whether a petition for review effectively stayed a grant of voluntary departure.

Finally, a petition for review may not be filed until the individual has exhausted all administrative remedies (*i.e.*, has appealed the decision through the BIA).[121]

Every court of appeals has its own rules of procedure regarding the filing of a petition for review. It is recommended that the practitioner contact the applicable court clerk, and/or review the court's website, to review the rules of the court prior to filing. A petition for review must be filed within 30 days. Accordingly, when in doubt as to which court has jurisdiction (it should be the court of appeals with jurisdiction over the location of the immigration court that heard the case—but even this can be confusing in remote areas where the IJ travels to the site or conducts a telephonic hearing), it may be prudent to file the petition for review in all potential jurisdictions to preserve the right to judicial review. The petition always can be transferred later.

Again, a petition for review will address issues of law and/or constitutional claims, but not findings of fact or discretionary denials of relief.

Petitions for Habeas Corpus to the Federal District Courts

The REAL ID Act sharply curtailed habeas corpus jurisdiction over immigration issues that arise during the course of removal proceedings. Before passage of the REAL ID Act, habeas was useful, in that issues such as the proper interpretation of a

---

[119] As of 2015, the public advocate, Andrew Lorenzen-Strait, Esq., may be reached at the following e-mail address: *EROPublicAdvocate@ice.dhs.gov*.

[120] 8 CFR §1240.26(i).

[121] INA §242(d)(1); 8 USC §1252(d)(1).

statutory definition leading to removability could be raised during administrative proceedings, contingent on a finding that exhaustion of administrative remedies was futile.

However, federal district courts do retain jurisdiction over *detention* issues that may arise during the course of a removal hearing. For example, if DHS (through ICE) takes the position that an individual is subject to mandatory detention, or otherwise refuses to release a non–American citizen, that determination may be challenged through habeas proceedings in federal court.

A petition for writ of habeas corpus is brought pursuant to 28 USC §2241. A petition for writ of habeas corpus will typically incorporate a complaint for declaratory and injunctive relief. After identifying the parties and citing the facts and applicable law, the petition will conclude with a request for relief (for example, release from custody), a legal conclusion (such as a declaration that a regulation is illegal), and may request attorneys' fees through the Equal Access to Justice Act.[122] In addition, a petition may be accompanied by a memorandum of law.

If the habeas action requests urgent relief (and release from unlawful custody would qualify as "urgent"), a motion for a temporary restraining order (TRO) pursuant to Federal Rule of Civil Procedure 65(b) should also be filed with the petition or shortly thereafter. In addition to the motion for TRO, counsel may want to request an emergency hearing for the purpose of oral argument. By moving for a TRO and emergency hearing, counsel can attempt to get the matter heard as soon as possible. Otherwise, the government may be allowed up to 60 days to respond,[123] lengthening the time of a client's incarceration. The federal court will then set a schedule for briefing and/or hearings. Ultimately, it is up to the court to determine the speed within which the case will be heard and to determine whether the matter has merit and should be considered expeditiously.

A petition for habeas corpus should cite any and all defendants by name, beginning with the secretary of DHS, and include the local DHS officials (for example, the director of detention and removal and the local officer-in-charge of the detention facility). A petition for habeas corpus must be formally served according to the Federal Rules of Civil Procedure (and applicable local court rules). Thus, the petition and a summons must be delivered to the U.S. Attorney's office for the district where the action arises; the court clerk must receive return service of process before the action is formally commenced. It is recommended that a professional process server be used to ensure compliance with the rules.[124]

---

[122] 5 USC §504 *et seq.*

[123] Fed. R. Civ. P. 12(a)(3).

[124] AILA publishes an excellent reference on federal (and other) court actions. For detailed information on the procedural and legal aspects of habeas corpus petitions, as well as petitions for review and other types of litigation, practitioners should consult AILA's *Immigration Litigation Toolbox* (3d Ed. 2013), available at http://agora.aila.org.

Tips and Tools of the Trade

The criminal-alien law practice is an interesting one that invites creativity in representation. Certain resources and tools will make the attorney more effective in representing the client. Tools include legal research methods as well as strategic resources.

At the outset, it is the author's recommendation that attorneys not rely solely on online resources, but keep certain books on their desks. These include hard copies of the Immigration and Nationality Act, Title 8 of the Code of Federal Regulations,[125] the Federal Criminal Code, and the attorney's own state criminal code. It is useful to have the Federal Sentencing Guidelines. Certainly, these books should be kept up to date.

In addition, attorneys may consider utilizing the following tools and strategies:

1. Federal Bureau of Investigation (FBI) rap sheet

A rap sheet will include a print-out of a client's arrest history and, in many instances, also gives the disposition of criminal arrests. This is the same information USCIS is seeking through the biometrics procedure. Practitioners should be mindful that the FBI, as a depository of information, is only as good as the entities sending in the arrest information. At times, the client will have an arrest or arrests that are not reflected on the rap sheet. Secondary sources, such as clerk of court websites, are recommended as a backup source of information. Practitioners also should be aware that, at times, the FBI's information or data is incorrect and the arrest(s) attributed to a client do not actually belong to the client. In such a situation, 28 CFR §16.34 discusses the procedure to make corrections.

28 CFR Part 16 governs the issuance of rap sheets to private individuals. The proper procedure for requesting a rap sheet is set forth at 28 CFR §16.30. Basically, a request for a rap sheet includes the following components:

- a cover letter requesting a rap sheet;[126]
- a completed fingerprint chart;
- a notarized authorization signed by the client[127] allowing the attorney to request and receive the results of the rap sheet; and
- a money order in the amount of $18, signed by the client, and made out to the U.S. Treasury.

A request for a rap sheet is mailed to:

---

[125] AILA publishes on an annual basis both the *Immigration and Nationality Act* and Title 8 of the *Code of Federal Regulations* available at *http://agora.aila.org*.

[126] A sample cover letter is included in Appendix 1F.

[127] A sample client authorization is also included in Appendix 1F.

FBI

CJIS Division

Attn: Summary Request

1000 Custer Hollow Road

Clarksburg, WV 26306

It takes several weeks, sometimes over a month, to receive the rap sheet.

2. Accurint

Accurint is a LEXIS-NEXIS product available through the LEXIS website. It is used by some offices within DHS, including the Offices of Chief Counsel as well as USCIS, as background investigation software. An Accurint search accesses several databases instantly, including but not limited to professional licenses, driver's license information, property ownership, voter registration, concealed firearm permits, liens and judgments, relatives and associates, etc. Accurint also has criminal records, although the records contained in a complete search are usually lacking information. A lengthier criminal record search is available, including actual record documents, but the information is not available immediately and there is additional expense.

Accurint is a highly recommended tool, though not because it is perfect—contrary to its name, its results are sometimes not accurate because its information is only as good as its sources. The system draws from government databases, so if the government source is not updated or is otherwise incorrect, the Accurint report will not be precise. This author recommends Accurint because DHS uses it to obtain background information. Prudent counsel should be aware of what DHS is looking at, and be prepared to resolve negative issues. Accurint is not expensive, and the typical general search is completed in minutes. By way of example, Accurint will show whether a client has registered to vote, has a concealed weapons permit, has tax liens, child support liens, or shares property with a spouse or partner. All of this information may be taken into account in the exercise of discretion in a discretionary waiver case. Of course, inaccurate information should be resolved in advance of a hearing or interview (or better yet, the filing of an application).

3. PACER

PACER stands for public access to court electronic records. PACER is a service of the U.S. judiciary and is managed by the Administrative Office of the U.S. Courts. It is a federal court system database and contains case files online. This service can be used to track the progress of cases, or to obtain documents from a case file, such as the indictment, jury instructions, plea agreement, motions, memoranda of law, and briefs. PACER searches involving access to actual court documents carry a nominal fee.[128]

> **Practice Pointer**: Presentation of a document printed from PACER should satisfy the requirements of 8 CFR §1003.41, proof of a conviction in immigration court. This becomes important for the practitioner when the non–American citizen has the burden of proof, including arriving aliens and in the context of discretionary relief.

4. FOIA requests

Most immigration law practitioners are familiar with the Freedom of Information Act (FOIA) as a method to obtain a copy of the immigration A-file from USCIS. When a case is pending in immigration court, counsel can request in a cover letter that the FOIA request receive expedited processing. A FOIA request is filed on Form G-639. The form provides the proper address for mailing. If USCIS determines that the request involves documents from another department, such as DOS, the request will be forwarded to the other agency. FOIA requests are helpful in obtaining documents from the A-file, and will often include government notes, actions, and observations about the case.

5. Polygraph examinations

A polygraph, referred to in the vernacular as a "lie detector test," may be a useful tool in various situations. A successful polygraph result can be persuasive for an adjustment of status or naturalization case with USCIS or in immigration court. As the title of this book implies, there can be immigration law consequences for alleged criminal activity even where the client is not convicted. An admission to the essential elements of a crime may result in a finding of inadmissibility, or may be the basis for a "reason to believe" someone has been involved in drug trafficking. An allegation of crime also may be used to support a finding of a lack of good moral character and, hence, a denial of naturalization. A successful polygraph examination can exonerate a client who faces adverse immigration consequences for alleged activity that falls short of a conviction. The attorney can take steps to ensure a successful polygraph result by meeting with the examiner in advance and summarizing the situation; the examination may take place in the attorney's office, thereby ensuring a relaxed environment for the client.

6. Westlaw, LEXIS, AILALink, AILA.org, and Fastcase

These resources provide access to federal and agency case law as well as statutes. Westlaw and LEXIS provide other states' criminal law statutes, which can be useful when a client has been convicted out-of-state. AILALink provides a host of online

---

[128] An attorney may sign up for PACER at *www.pacer.psc.uscourts.gov/pacerdesc.html*. Access to PACER is essential for a criminal-alien law practice.

resources, such as primary law sources, AILA publications (legal books), agency memoranda, policies, field manuals, Operations Instructions, and much more. AILA's website (*www.aila.org*) provides up-to-date information in all areas of immigration law, including important court decisions and agency announcements. Fastcase is an online database of case law that is accessible through *www.aila.org* and is free to members.

7. Psychological and medical evaluations

Depending on the facts and nature of the case, psychological (mental and emotional) evaluations from a licensed professional will establish key aspects of the case. If the client is a battered spouse, a good evaluation can establish this fact. If a client is seeking a waiver of inadmissibility before USCIS, the consulate, or in immigration court, a family member's illness may be an important equity. The same is true for a good medical evaluation that describes any physical illness.

8. Country-condition experts

Background country conditions are relevant in a variety of cases, including asylum and withholding, and waiver cases (to establish hardship to the respondent and/or family members). A good affidavit or live testimony from a professional in the particular country may carry a lot of weight. Local colleges and universities are the best source of country-condition information, but experts can come from other professions also. The use of expert testimony on background conditions is highly recommended.

9. Country-condition sources of information (websites)

The State Department maintains Country Condition Reports on human rights practices, background notes, even travel advisory publications. USCIS and the immigration courts will usually defer to DOS's opinions. Other good sources include Human Rights Watch and Amnesty International. A good Internet search engine, given a particular situation or fact pattern, will yield results from various reputable sources regarding conditions in the home country. Country-condition information is an essential component of a good waiver package and asylum/withholding/torture claim.

10. Confirmation-of-appointment letters

When a potential client makes an appointment by phone for a first-time consultation, a confirmation letter may be mailed, e-mailed, or faxed to clarify the address of the office and the documents the client should bring to the appointment. In this way, the client will know to bring along all conviction records and immigration documents, and the consultation will go more smoothly

11. Intake sheets

Many seasoned practitioners utilize intake sheets as a way of synthesizing the key facts for a first-time consultation and establishing a good background record for creation of a client file. The intake sheet is provided to the client while in the waiting room. Attorneys are encouraged to develop an intake sheet that fits their own practice and philosophy regarding important preliminary information.[129]

Sources of Legal Authority

The primary statutory authority for immigration law is the INA, found at Title 8 of the U.S. Code (USC). INA and USC citations are often cited together when referencing statutory provisions.

Title 8 of the Code of Federal Regulations (CFR) contains the regulations that implement the INA. Regulations for DHS appear in chapter I of 8 CFR and those for EOIR appear in chapter V of 8 CFR.

DOS has jurisdiction over individuals making applications for immigrant and nonimmigrant visas at U.S. embassies, so consuls must interpret immigration law. DOS publishes the *Foreign Affairs Manual* (FAM) online and it can be found on AILA's online research library, AILALink; DOS's foreign relations regulations are at Title 22 of the CFR.

Precedent decisions also have authority in immigration law. The BIA's precedent decisions are collected and published in bound volumes of *Administrative Decisions Under Immigration and Nationality Laws of the United States* (I&N Decisions, cited as I&N Dec.). Precedent decisions that are not yet contained within a bound volume, or slip opinions, are referred to as interim decisions and cited by reference to their Int. Dec. number.[130] The attorney general may also issue a precedent decision, in which case the I&N Dec. citation will include a reference to the "AG."

The federal courts have limited jurisdiction over immigration matters, but a circuit court decision has precedence in that circuit, and in any BIA case arising in that circuit.

Recent Legislation

- Immigration Act of 1990 (IMMACT90), Pub. L. No. 101-649, 104 Stat. 4978;
- Antiterrorism and Effective Death Penalty Act of 1996 (AEDPA), Pub. L. No. 104-132, 110 Stat. 1214;
- Illegal Immigration Reform and Immigrant Responsibility Act of 1996 (IIRAIRA), Pub. L. No. 104-208, div. C, 110 Stat. 3009, 3009-546 to 3009-724;
- Uniting and Strengthening America by Providing Appropriate Tools Required to Intercept and Obstruct Terrorism (USA PATRIOT Act) Act of 2001, Pub. L. No. 107-56, 115 Stat. 272; and
- REAL ID Act of 2005, Pub. L. No. 109-13, div. B, 119 Stat. 231, 302–23.

---

[129] *AILA's Immigration Practice Toolbox* houses numerous templates including intake sheets that can be tailored to suit your needs. Visit *http://agora.aila.org*.

[130] See *Board of Immigration Appeals Practice Manual* §1.4(d).

APPENDIX 1A

CONTACT INFORMATION FOR IMMIGRATION COURTS

Offices of Chief Counsel and Detention Centers

www.justice.gov/eoir/sibpages/ICadr.htm

www.ice.gov/contact/legal

www.ice.gov/detention-facilities/

APPENDIX 1B

STRUCTURE OF CBP

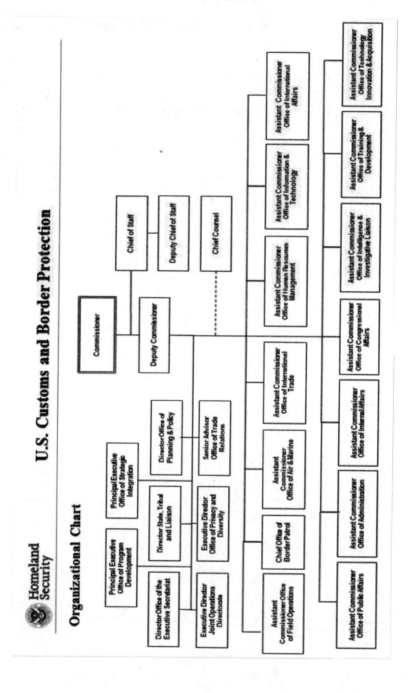

APPENDIX 1C

STRUCTURE OF ICE

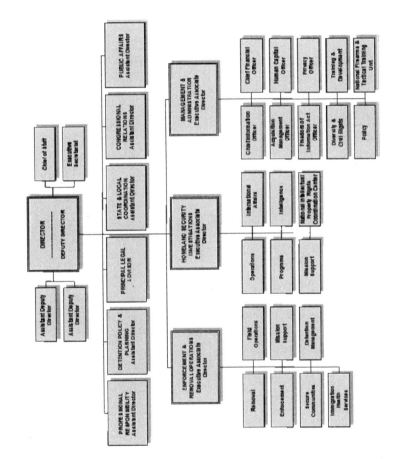

APPENDIX 1D
STRUCTURE OF USCIS

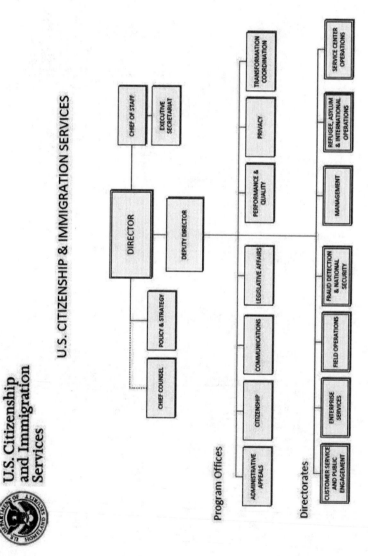

APPENDIX 1E

SAMPLE NOTICE TO APPEAR

U.S. Department of Justice
Immigration and Naturalization Service

Notice to Appear

In removal proceedings under section 240 of the Immigration and Nationality Act

File No: **A14 355**

In the Matter of:

Respondent: __Miguel__ currently residing at:

__Miami, Florida 33183__
(Number, street, city, state, and ZIP code) (Area code and phone number)

☐ 1. You are an arriving alien.

☐ 2. You are an alien present in the United States who has not been admitted or paroled.

☒ 3. You have been admitted to the United States, but are deportable for the reasons stated below.

The Service alleges that you:

1. You are not a citizen or national of the United States;

2. You are a native of **Uruguay** and a citizen of **Uruguay**;

3. You entered the United States at or near **New York, New York** on or about **August 29** as a **Lawful Permanent Resident**;

"Please see continuation sheet for additional allegations."

On the basis of the foregoing, it is charged that you are subject to removal from the United States pursuant to the following provision(s) of law:

Section 237(a)(2)(B)(i) of the Immigration and Nationality Act (Act), as amended, in that, at any time after admission, you have been convicted of a violation of (or a conspiracy or attempt to violate) any law or regulation or a State, the United States, or a foreign country relating to a controlled substance (as defined in Section 102 of the Controlled Substances Act, 21 U.S.C. 802), other than a single offense involving possession for one's own use of 20 grams or less of marijuana.

☐ This notice is being issued after an asylum officer has found that the respondent has demonstrated a credible fear of persecution.

☐ Section 235(b)(1) order was vacated pursuant to: ☐ 8 CFR 208.30(f)(2) ☐ 8 CFR 235.3(b)(5)(iv)

YOU ARE ORDERED to appear before an immigration judge of the United States Department of Justice at: _____

__333 South Miami Avenue, Suite 700, Miami, Florida 33130__
(Complete Address of Immigration Court, Including Room Number, if any)

on __September 27, 2007__ at __9:00am__ to show why you should not be removed from the United States based on charge(s) set forth above
  (Date)   (Time)

Elaine D. Watson
Elaine D. Watson, Section Chief, Naturalization
(Signature and Title of Issuing Officer)

Date: __May 8, 2007__

__Miami, Florida__
(City and State)

See reverse for important information

Form I-862 (Rev. 4-1-97)

U.S Department of Homeland Security
U.S. Citizenship and Immigration Services

Continuation Sheet for Notice to Appear

Respondent: Miguel

File no. A14 35

Allegations continued:

4. You were, on January 1989, convicted in the Circuit Court of Florida, in and for the County of Dade, for the offense of Possession of a Controlled Substance, to wit: Cocaine, in violation of Florida statute 893.13. Case # 88-41

Charges continued:

Signature: Elaine D. Watson

Title: SDAO

FORM I-831 (Rev 4-1-97)

2 of 3 Pages

Notice to Respondent

Warning: Any statement you make may be used against you in removal proceedings.

Alien Registration: This copy of the Notice to Appear served upon you is evidence of your alien registration while you are under removal proceedings. You are required to carry it with you at all times.

Representation: If you so choose, you may be represented in this proceeding, at no expense to the Government, by an attorney or other individual authorized and qualified to represent persons before the Executive Office for Immigration Review, pursuant to 8 CFR 3.16. Unless you so request, no hearing will be scheduled earlier than ten days from the date of this notice, to allow you sufficient time to secure counsel. A list of qualified attorneys and organizations who may be available to represent you at no cost will be provided with this Notice.

Conduct of the hearing: At the time of your hearing, you should bring with you any affidavits or other documents which you desire to have considered in connection with your case. If any document is in a foreign language, you must bring the original and a certified English translation of the document. If you wish to have the testimony of any witnesses considered, you should arrange to have such witnesses present at the hearing.

At your hearing, you will be given the opportunity to admit or deny any or all of the allegations in the Notice to Appear and that you are inadmissible or deportable on the charges contained in the Notice to Appear. You will have an opportunity to present evidence on your own behalf, to examine any evidence presented by the Government, to object, on proper legal grounds, to the receipt of evidence and to cross examine any witnesses presented by the Government.

You will be advised by the immigration judge before whom you appear, of any relief from removal for which you may appear eligible including the privilege of departing voluntarily. You will be given a reasonable opportunity to make any such application to the immigration judge.

Failure to appear: You are required to provide the INS, in writing, with your full mailing address and telephone number. You must notify the Immigration Court immediately by using Form EOIR-33 whenever you change your address or telephone number during the course of this proceeding. You will be provided with a copy of this form. Notices of hearing will be mailed to this address. If you do not submit Form EOIR-33 and do not otherwise provide an address at which you may be reached during proceedings, then the Government shall not be required to provide you with written notice of your hearing. If you fail to attend the hearing at the time and place designated on this notice, or any date and time later directed by the Immigration Court, a removal order may be made by the immigration judge in your absence, and you may be arrested and detained by the INS.

Request for Prompt Hearing

To expedite a determination in my case, I request an immediate hearing. I waive my right to have a 10-day period prior to appearing before an immigration judge.

_____
(Signature of Respondent)

Before:

Date: _____

_____
(Signature and Title of INS officer)

Certificate of Service

This Notice to Appear was served on the respondent by me or. _____, in the following manner and in compliance with section 239(a)(1)(F) of the Act:
(Date)

☐ in person   ☐ by certified mail, return receipt requested   ☒ by regular mail

☒ Attached is a list of organization and attorneys which provide free legal services.

☐ The alien was provided oral notice in the _____ language of the time and place of his or her hearing and of the consequences of failure to appear as provided in section 240(b)(7) of the Act.

_____   _Olga Domenech (BAO)_
(Signature of Respondent if Personally Served)   (Signature and Title of Officer)

Appendix 1F

FBI Rap Sheet Request

Date: _____

Federal Bureau of Investigations
CJIS Division
ATTN: SCU, Mod. D-2
1000 Custer Hollow Road
Clarksburg, WV 26306

Dear Sir or Madam:

By way of this letter, I am respectfully requesting that you issue a rap sheet based on the information contained on the attached fingerprint card (FD-258). Also, I have enclosed an authorization form signed by _____ allowing me to receive the rap sheet on his/her behalf.

If you have any questions or concerns, please do not hesitate to contact our office. I thank you for your time and attention.

Sincerely,

_____
Mary Kramer
Attorney at Law

Enclosures: fingerprint chart
$18.00 money order
Client authorization form

AUTHORIZATION FOR RELEASE OF INFORMATION

I, (client's name here), authorize the FBI to release the results of the fingerprint search of the Criminal Justice Information Service's Division's files to the following individual:

Individual: Attorney Mary Kramer
168 SE First St. Suite 802
Miami, FL 33131

I declare under penalty of perjury under the laws of the United States of America that the foregoing is true and correct, and that I am the person named above, and I understand that any falsification of this statement is punishable under the provisions of 18 USC §1001 by a fine of not more than $10,000 or by imprisonment of not more than five years or both, and that requesting or obtaining any record(s) under false pretenses is punishable under the provisions of 5 USC §522a(i)(3) by a fine of not more than $5,000.

(Client's) Signature: _____
(to be signed in front of notary)

Notarization
Subscribed and sworn to before me, this ___ day of _____, of the year _____.

Signature of Notary:

Expiration Date of Commission:

Notary Seal or Stamp

APPENDIX 1G

APPOINTMENT CONFIRMATION LETTER

[On Letterhead]
[date]
Dear [Sir or Madam}

Thank you for making an appointment with this office. You are scheduled for an appointment on (date of appointment) at (time of appointment). There is a consultation fee of _____.

Please note that it is very important that you bring to this appointment all immigration-related documents. This may include passports, residency cards, work permits, letters from the Department of Homeland Security, receipts, previously filed applications, etc. If you have immediate family members who are citizens and/or permanent residents, and their status may affect your case, bring copies of their documents, as well. If you are in removal proceedings in immigration court, bring the charging document, which is called a "Notice to Appear."

If you have a criminal arrest record, please bring the:

- arrest report or criminal complaint (prepared by police or law enforcement officials)
- criminal charging document (called an information or indictment)
- final judgment and sentence (the disposition from the court)

Online records from the Internet are not sufficient. Please go to the courthouse(s) where your case(s) was/were heard and speak to a clerk to obtain certified copies of these documents from your actual court file. If you do not have complete records, I cannot provide you with good, accurate advice. If you have a criminal record, but do not bring your complete records, I may choose not to see you. This is because I need to see the actual documents from your court file in order to understand your case.

We ask that you do not bring small children to the office. We are discussing important issues and children are a distraction.

This office is located in [name of city; description of location]. There is a parking lot adjacent to the building, as well as on the street behind the building. You should be prepared to pay parking costs.

If you have any questions, please call my office and request further information.

Sincerely,

[name and signature of attorney]

APPENDIX 1H

CLIENT INFORMATION SHEET

(The information contained herein is strictly confidential. This information is for the attorney's use only and will not be disclosed under any circumstances to outside persons or to the government.)

Date: _____

Name: _____

Address: _____   Phone Number(s) _____

_____   _____

_____   E-mail: _____

(Note: If the consultation is regarding someone else, who is not in the office at this moment because of personal reasons, please give their name in the line provided _____ and answer the following questions with their information, not yourself. If this consultation is for you, please answer the questions below with the information regarding yourself and your case).

Age: _____

Is this your first time in this office? ❑ Yes ❑ No

Who referred you to this office or how did you hear about us?

_____

_____

What is your nationality? _____

Are you a permanent resident (what category)? _____

_____

If you are not a permanent resident WHEN and HOW did you last enter the United States? _____

If you are not a permanent resident, have you applied for permanent resident status? ☐ Yes ☐ No

Are you in Immigration Court proceedings? ☐ Yes ☐ No

Do you have a criminal record? ☐ Yes ☐ No

Have you ever served in the Military? ☐ Yes ☐ No

Are either of your parents U.S. Citizens? ☐ Yes ☐ No

Please explain (specifically) your questions or situation that brings you here today.

_____
_____
_____
_____
_____
_____
_____

There is a _____ Consultation fee for the first-time consultation which must be paid by cash, credit card, or check (with proper identification, such as, social security card and/or driver's license).

Chapter Two

The Definition of "Conviction" According to Immigration Law

The Statutory Definition of "Conviction" 51
Proof of Convictions 81
Suspensions of Sentence 82
Appendices
  2A: Sample Motion to Vacate Plea, Judgment, and Sentence 84
  2B: Sample *Padilla* Motion to Vacate Plea, Judgment, and Sentence 90

The most remarkable thing about how the INA defines "conviction" is that it defines it at all. "Conviction" is a commonly used word among lawyers and laymen. The INA would have been perfectly comprehensible without a definition of "conviction," or at least no more ambiguous than with such a definition. And, indeed, the INA did not define "conviction" until the enactment of IIRIRA. By adding this definition, Congress must have intended it to displace any intuitive, popular, or common sense understanding.[1]

*****

Immigration law contains a unique definition of "conviction." Criminal law statutes at both state and federal levels contain various types of procedures, from deferred adjudications to sealings and vacaturs, which purport to avoid or eliminate a conviction for most purposes. However, immigration law, via statute and case law, takes an independent approach to the term "conviction," and hence, to the various types of adjudication procedures. As in other areas of immigration law, the evolving definition of "conviction" has become increasingly strict. This chapter discusses the immigration law perspective on the all-important question: is there a conviction?

The Statutory Definition of "Conviction"

Immigration and Nationality Act (INA) §101(a)(48) [8 USC §1101(a)(48)] defines "conviction" as follows:

(A) The term "conviction" means, with respect to an alien, a formal judgment of guilt of the alien entered by a court or, if adjudication of guilt has been withheld, where—

---

[1] *Renteria-Gonzales v. INS*, 310 F.3d 825, 833–34 (5th Cir. 2002).

(i) a judge or jury has found the alien guilty or the alien has entered a plea of guilty or nolo contendere or has admitted sufficient facts to warrant a finding of guilt, and

(ii) the judge has ordered some form of punishment, penalty, or restraint on the alien's liberty to be imposed.

(B) Any reference to a term of imprisonment or a sentence with respect to an offense is deemed to include the period of incarceration or confinement ordered by a court of law regardless of any suspension of the imposition or execution of that imprisonment or sentence in whole or in part.

The "Beyond a Reasonable Doubt" Standard and Municipal Court Proceedings

For the first prong of INA §101(a)(48) to be met, each element of the offense must be established beyond a reasonable doubt; in other words, the standard employed in the proceeding resulting in the conviction, in order to qualify it as a "conviction" for immigration purposes, must be the "beyond a reasonable doubt" standard.[2] In *Matter of Eslamizar*,[3] the respondent was found guilty of a "violation" (grand theft third degree)[4] under the lesser preponderance of the evidence standard in Oregon. This particular procedure allows a state prosecutor to elect to proceed in civil proceedings, in exchange for a possible monetary penalty rather than jail time. The Board of Immigration Appeals (BIA or Board) found that the "violation" under Oregon law did not constitute a "formal judgment of guilt of the alien entered by a court" in a criminal proceeding.

In *Matter of Cuellar-Gomez*,[5] the BIA reviewed a municipal court's adjudication of an ordinance violation and found the procedure to qualify as a "conviction." The case arose in Wichita and dealt with a Kansas state statute.[6] The respondent in this case argued against a finding of "conviction" because the proceedings did not allow for a jury trial or court-appointed counsel. However, the BIA noted that in misdemeanor prosecutions, there generally is not a right to a public defender. The Board further noted that a jury trial is available to the defendant in municipal court if the judge finds him guilty: there is a "second tier" whereby the defendant can seek review by jury trial. Noting that the standard of guilt is still beyond a reasonable doubt, the Board found that the Wichita proceedings satisfied the requirements of a "conviction."

---

[2] *Matter of Eslamizar*, 23 I&N Dec. 684 (BIA 2004).

[3] *Matter of Eslamizar*, 23 I&N Dec. 684 (BIA 2004).

[4] Or. Rev. Stat. §153.076.

[5] *Matter of Cuellar-Gomez*, 25 I&N Dec. 850, 852–55 (BIA 2012).

[6] Kan. Stat. Ann. §§12-4104(a)(5). The referenced statute has since been repealed.

The Third Circuit U.S. Court of Appeals questioned and criticized *Eslamizar* and *Cuellar-Gomez* in *Castillo v. Att'y General*,[7] wherein the non–American citizen was originally arrested for the criminal offense of shoplifting, but the New Jersey prosecutor elected to proceed in municipal court terming the offense "disorderly persons." This procedure does not entitle the accused to a trial by jury and does not result in a traditional conviction for any purpose under state law. The court noted that the Board's own precedent is inconsistent in regard to what qualifies as "genuine criminal proceedings" and that a municipal court could not deliver a "conviction" for immigration purposes.[8] The court remanded for the agency to explain and synchronize inconsistent criteria.

In contrast, the Ninth Circuit U.S. Court of Appeals, in an unpublished decision, did not object to the use of municipal court adjudications as "convictions."[9]

Court Martials

The BIA has held that a general court martial is a "genuine criminal proceeding" and qualifies as a conviction for immigration purposes.[10]

Finality

Prior to passage of the Illegal Immigration Reform and Immigrant Responsibility Act of 1996 (IIRAIRA),[11] case law was clear that a criminal conviction was not "final" for immigration purposes until all procedures for direct appeal were exhausted or waived; hence, a criminal conviction pending direct appeal in the criminal court system could not serve as the basis of a removal order.[12] Following IIRAIRA's definition of "conviction" at INA §101(a)(48), it is not clear whether a conviction pending direct appeal may support a finding of removability. In a 2009 decision by a sharply divided en banc Board, the BIA found that a criminal case that has been reopened for purposes of filing a direct appeal (*i.e.*, a late-reinstated direct appeal) did not justify reopening a removal order based on that conviction.[13] The motion to reopen was de-

---

[7] *Castillo v. Att'y Gen.*, 729 F.3d 296 (3d Cir. 2013).

[8] In so doing, the Third Circuit considered the following decisions, which it viewed as in conflict with *Cuellar-Gomez*: *Matter of Eslamizar,* 23 I&N Dec. 684 (BIA 2004), *Matter of Rivera-Valencia,* 24 I&N Dec. 484 (BIA 2008).

[9] *Ramos v. Holder*, 546 Fed.Appx 705 (9th Cir. Dec. 2, 2015).

[10] *Matter of Rivera-Valencia,* 24 I&N Dec. 484 (BIA 2008); *see also Matter of Chavez-Alvarez,* 26 I&N Dec. 274 (BIA 2014).

[11] Illegal Immigration Reform and Immigrant Responsibility Act of 1996 (IIRAIRA), Division C of the Omnibus Appropriations Act of 1996 (H.R. 3610), Pub. L. No. 104-208, 110 Stat. 3009.

[12] *Pino v. Landon,* 349 U.S. 901 (1955); *Matter of Punu,* 22 I&N Dec. 224 (BIA 1998); *Matter of Thomas,* 21 I&N Dec. 20 (BIA 1995) (conviction on direct appeal may not support finding of deportability, but may be considered as negative factor in the exercise of discretion); *Matter of Ozkok,* 19 I&N Dec. 546, 552 n.7 (BIA 1988).

[13] *Matter of Cardenas-Abreu,* 24 I&N Dec. 795 (BIA 2009), *vacated and remanded by, Cardenas Abreu v. Holder*, 378 Fed. Appx. 59, 2010 U.S. App. LEXIS 10498 (2d Cir. 2010).

nied, even though the state court conviction was no longer final. The Board specifically declined to consider whether a conviction on direct appeal that was not a "late-reinstated appeal," but rather, a direct appeal in the regular course of things while removal proceedings were pending (*i.e.*, not a motion to reopen a removal order) qualifies as a "conviction" for immigration purposes.[14]

Several circuit courts have ruled that, based on the language of INA §101(a)(48), finality of a conviction is no longer a requirement to support removability for the crime.[15]

Withholds or Deferrals of Adjudication

The INA's definition of conviction codified part of the BIA's decision in *Matter of Ozkok*.[16] In *Ozkok*, the individual pled guilty to possession of cocaine in Maryland. The adjudication of guilt was stayed and proceedings deferred while he completed three years of probation and 100 hours of community service. Under the Maryland statute, if the individual did not successfully complete probation, the judge was able to enter final judgment and proceed with a disposition without further proceedings on the issue of guilt or innocence. In this particular case, Ozkok successfully completed probation, and the discharge of probation represented the court's final action in the matter. Under the Maryland statute in effect at that time, "[d]ischarge of a person under this section shall be without judgment of conviction and is not a conviction for purposes of any disqualification or disability imposed by law because of conviction of a crime."[17] In a break from precedent, the BIA held that the Maryland action constituted a conviction for purposes of determining deportability for a controlled substance offense. INA §101(a)(48) was introduced in 1996 as part of IIRAIRA, and incorporates that part of the *Ozkok* decision that deals with withheld or deferred adjudications.

Shortly after the definition at §101(a)(48) was added to the INA, the BIA reaffirmed that state procedures for withholding or deferral of adjudication constitute convictions for immigration purposes even though the state court judge did not formally pronounce guilt.[18] The federal courts have generally approved of this interpretation of the statute. For example, in *Uritsky v. Gonzales*,[19] the Sixth Circuit U.S. Court of Appeals affirmed a decision of the BIA holding that a non–American citizen was "convicted" for purposes of removal where he had pled guilty to the charge of third-degree sexual conduct and had been designated as a "youthful trainee" under the Michigan Youthful Trainee Act

---

[14] *Matter of Cardenas-Abreu*, at 798–99.
[15] *Moosa v. INS*, 171 F.3d 994, 1009 (5th Cir. 1999); *Abiodun v. Gonzales*, 461 F.3d 1210 (10th Cir. 2006).
[16] *Matter of Ozkok*, 19 I&N Dec. 546 (BIA 1988).
[17] Md. Ann. Code art. 27, §641(c) (1982) (repealed in 2001).
[18] *Matter of Punu*, 22 I&N Dec. 224 (BIA 1998); *see also Matter of Salazar-Regino*, 23 I&N Dec. 223 (BIA 2002). Both of these cases involved deferred adjudications under Texas law.
[19] *Uritsky v. Gonzales*, 399 F.3d 728 (6th Cir. 2005).

(YTA).[20] Pursuant to the YTA, upon the plea of guilty, the defendant was sentenced to two years' probation, fines, and costs; the disposition included a statement that "no judgment of conviction is entered." Upon successful completion of the probation, proceedings are terminated with no final entry of an adjudication or conviction; however, a judge retains jurisdiction to revoke probation (and youthful trainee status) at any time and to enter an adjudication of guilt.[21] Based on the fact that the defendant must enter a plea of guilty or no contest, and a punishment follows, the Sixth Circuit found the YTA procedure to constitute a "conviction" for immigration purposes.

In *Gradiz v. Gonzales*,[22] the Fourth Circuit U.S. Court of Appeals upheld a finding by the BIA that a plea of no contest and deferral of proceedings pending successful completion of probation, with no subsequent adjudication and dismissal of proceedings, qualifies as a "conviction." The court clarified that a state's view that a certain procedure does not result in a "conviction" is not the determinative factor.[23]

However, *Crespo v. Holder*[24] illustrates why a careful review of the actual statutory section and the procedure that transpired in the particular criminal case is very important. In *Crespo,* the defendant/respondent pled not guilty. The criminal judge went on to "find sufficient facts" to justify a finding of guilt, but did not in fact find guilt. He then deferred adjudication. Following a year of probation, the case was dismissed. The circuit court overturned the BIA, stating that a "finding of sufficient facts to justify a finding of guilt" is not the same as finding guilt for §101(a)(48) purposes. Without a plea of guilt or no contest, and with no adjudication of guilt, the disposition did not qualify as a conviction.

A withhold with no penalty

A withhold of adjudication or deferred adjudication will meet the first prong of §101(a)(48) in that the defendant must either plead guilty or no contest. Prior to 2008, practitioners argued with success before immigration judges (IJs) and the BIA that a withhold of adjudication and court costs, with no fine, probation, imprisonment, or other punishment did not qualify as a "conviction" for immigration purposes. However, in February 2008, the BIA changed course and issued a decision in *Matter of Cabrera*[25] that held that the imposition of court costs in the context of a withhold of adjudication is sufficient to constitute "punishment" and qualifies as a conviction.

---

[20] Mich. Comp. Laws §§762.11–16.

[21] Mich. Comp. Laws §762.12.

[22] *Gradiz v. Gonzales*, 490 F.3d 1206 (10th Cir. 2007).

[23] *Gradiz v. Gonzales*, at 1208.

[24] *Crespo v. Holder*, 631 F.3d 130, 135 (4th Cir. 2011).

[25] *Matter of Cabrera*, 24 I&N Dec. 459 (BIA 2008).

Pretrial Intervention or Diversion

In comparison to the withhold or deferral of adjudication procedure, a pretrial intervention or diversion procedure does not result in a conviction for immigration purposes. Under pretrial diversion schemes, a defendant does not enter a plea, but is placed under some form of probation-type program—such as classes and/or reporting—while the criminal charges are held in abeyance. Upon successful completion of the program, the charges are dismissed.[26] Under pretrial diversion schemes, the defendant makes no formal admission of guilt on the record; thus, the first prong of INA §101(a)(48)(A) is not met.

Moreover, if the defendant in some fashion violates the program, he or she remains able to contest the charges (*i.e.*, go to trial). Diversionary programs vary from state to state, and fresh analysis in every case is recommended. Diversion should not be confused with deferred adjudication—the latter allows for an automatic entry of guilty upon violation of the program and/or conditions. Furthermore, diversion programs normally involve the agreement and interaction of the prosecutor's office and the defendant—and "bypass" the court. In comparison, deferrals of adjudication require the direct participation of the state court judge.

Although individual analysis is required in every case, the two keys to whether a "conviction" exists for immigration purposes are whether the disposition involves

(1) an admission or confession by the defendant, and

(2) some form of punishment.

Without these two components, the definition of "conviction" is not met.

Admissions to the prosecutor do not qualify

Many local prosecutors' offices will require, as a *quid pro quo* of diversion, that the defendant sign a statement admitting guilt. Assuming diversion or intervention is successfully satisfied, this statement will not be placed in the court file. This sort of written admission, if made between the parties outside the courtroom, does *not* qualify as an "admission" for purposes of INA §101(a)(48). It is not a part of the "record of conviction"; the record of conviction includes the indictment or information (*i.e.*, charges), the plea, and the final judgment and sentence.[27] This is well-settled law, embodied in the INA, the regulations, and administrative and federal-court case law.

---

[26] *See Paredes-Urrestarazu v. INS*, 36 F.3d 801 (9th Cir. 1994); *White v. INS*, 17 F.3d 475 (1st Cir. 1994); *Matter of Grullon*, 20 I&N Dec. 12 (BIA 1989). Although these cases precede the introduction of INA §101(a)(48), as well as Board of Immigration Appeals (BIA) cases decided thereafter, they remain good law today.

[27] *See* 8 CFR §1003.41; *Matter of Mena*, 17 I&N Dec. 38 (BIA 1979). A list of acceptable documents can be found under "Proof of Conviction," later in this chapter. For further discussion of what constitutes the "record of conviction," see chapters three and five (in the sections on "divisible statutes").

An ancillary document in the prosecutor's file does not suffice to meet the definition of "conviction" and is not admissible in immigration court to establish a "conviction." However, such an admission may be relevant in the context of an arriving alien charged with admission to the essential elements of a crime at a port of entry—*if* U.S. Customs and Border Protection (CBP) were to locate the document, which is highly unlikely.[28]

Expungements and Record Sealings

A conviction that has been expunged, dismissed, canceled, vacated, discharged, sealed, or otherwise removed pursuant to a post-conviction rehabilitative state procedure remains a conviction for immigration purposes pursuant to *Matter of Roldan*.[29]

Prior to the BIA's decision in *Roldan*, an expungement of a nondrug conviction eliminated the offense as a basis of deportability. Thus, when researching this issue, it is important *not to rely* on pre-*Roldan* cases. (For example, in *Matter of Ozkok*,[30] 11 years before *Roldan*, the BIA iterated its then-existing policy that an expunged nondrug offense did not support a finding of deportability).

Roldan involved a first-time offender who pled guilty to possession of a controlled substance, and whose conviction was subsequently vacated and the case dismissed upon termination of probation pursuant to §19-2604(1) of the Idaho Code. The BIA ruled that this individual had a final conviction for immigration purposes, notwithstanding the expunging procedure.

Based on INA §101(a)(48), combined with subsequent BIA case law interpreting the provision, expungements and sealings are not effective to prevent unfavorable immigration consequences, including inadmissibility and removability.

> ➢ *Tip*: U.S. Citizenship and Immigration Services (USCIS) routinely requires that records be *unsealed* so that adjudicators may review the documents. A failure to unseal records may lead to a denial of the benefit sought. Thus, as a practical matter, record sealing can be an impediment to successful resolution of an immigration application.

First offender/youthful offender provisions

As stated above, *Matter of Roldan* involved an individual whose record of conviction was expunged following successful completion of the Idaho first offender provision. Roldan's plea of guilty was vacated and the record expunged in a manner similar—although not identical—to federal first offender treatment.[31] In *Roldan*, the BIA announced that it would no longer recognize state *rehabilitative* actions in the context

---

[28] See chapter three.

[29] *Matter of Roldan*, 22 I&N Dec. 512 (BIA 1999).

[30] *Matter of Ozkok*, 19 I&N Dec. 546, 552 (BIA 1988).

[31] *See* 18 USC §3607(a) (the Federal First Offender Act (FFOA)).

of immigration proceedings or otherwise apply a first offender exception to the definition of "conviction."[32] Therefore, state first offender statutes that result in the vacatur and perhaps even expungement of a criminal judgment do not eliminate the "conviction" for immigration purposes. (But see the following discussion of the Ninth Circuit U.S. Court of Appeals' treatment of such cases.)

The Ninth Circuit's treatment of FFOA dispositions and their state counterparts

In *Lujan-Armendariz v. INS*,[33] the Ninth Circuit overruled in part the BIA's decision in *Matter of Roldan*. However, in 2011, the Ninth Circuit sitting en banc overruled *Lujan-Armendariz,* in the case of *Nunez-Reyes v. Holder*,[34] finding that equal protection does not require that state rehabilitative procedures be treated the same as expungements (for immigration purposes) under the Federal First Offender Act (FFOA). The decision in *Nunez-Reyes* applies prospectively only to convictions entered after July 14, 2011. Because the decision is prospective only, and also addresses in dicta federal first offender dispositions, the history of the Ninth Circuit's treatment of the definition of "conviction" in the context of first-time simple possession of a controlled substance is discussed below.

Lujan-Armendariz involved two separate individuals who petitioned the appellate court for review of the BIA's decisions that their first-time drug convictions, which had been vacated under state counterparts to the FFOA, were "convictions" for immigration purposes. Roldan was one of these individuals; as discussed above, he had been processed according to Idaho Code Ann. §19-2604(1), which reads:

Discharge of defendant—Amendment of judgment

If sentence has been imposed but suspended, or if sentence has been withheld, upon application of the defendant and upon satisfactory showing that the defendant has at all times complied with the terms and conditions upon which he was placed on probation, ... the court may, if convinced by the showing made that there is no longer cause for continuing the period of probation, and if it be compatible with the public interest, terminate the sentence or set aside the plea of guilty or conviction of the defendant .... The final dismissal of the case as herein provided shall have the effect of restoring the defendant to his civil rights.

The second petitioner, Lujan-Armendariz, had been convicted of a similar offense, and processed under Ariz. Rev. Stat. Ann. §13-907, which provides for the setting

---

[32] *Matter of Roldan*, 22 I&N Dec. 512 (BIA 1999).

[33] *Lujan-Armendariz v. INS*, 222 F.3d 728 (9th Cir. 2000), *overruled by Nunez-Reyes v. Holder*, 646 F.3d 684 (9th Cir. 2011).

[34] *Nunez-Reyes v. Holder*, 646 F.3d 684 (9th Cir. 2011).

aside of a judgment of a convicted person on discharge, with exceptions for certain offenses.[35]

The *Lujan-Armendariz* court concluded that an individual's first-time simple drug possession offense that is expunged by a state rehabilitative statute cannot be considered a "conviction" if first offender treatment would have been accorded under 18 USC §3607(a) in federal court proceedings. The FFOA allows for the dismissal and expungement of the case where the defendant is charged with first-time, simple possession of a controlled substance in federal court. After *Lujan-Armendariz*, the Ninth Circuit clarified its holding: the FFOA exception applies only to those individuals who would have been eligible for relief under the federal law and in fact have received relief under state law. In terms of the latter requirement, the individual must

---

[35] By way of comparison, 18 USC §3607, the FFOA, reads as follows:

Special probation and expungement procedures for drug possessors

(a) Pre-judgment probation.—If a person found guilty of an offense described in section 404 of the Controlled Substances Act (21 USC 844)—

(1) has not, prior to the commission of such offense, been convicted of violating a Federal or State law relating to controlled substances; and

(2) has not previously been the subject of a disposition under this subsection;

the court may, with the consent of such person, place him on probation for a term of not more than one year without entering a judgment of conviction. At any time before the expiration of the term of probation, if the person has not violated a condition of his probation, the court may, without entering a judgment of conviction, dismiss the proceedings against the person and discharge him from probation. At the expiration of the term of probation, if the person has not violated a condition of his probation, the court shall, without entering a judgment of conviction, dismiss the proceedings against the person and discharge him from probation. If the person violates a condition of his probation, the court shall proceed in accordance with the provisions of section 3565.

(b) Record of disposition.—A nonpublic record of a disposition under subsection (a), or a conviction that is the subject of an expungement order under subsection (c), shall be retained by the Department of Justice solely for the purpose of use by the courts in determining in any subsequent proceeding whether a person qualifies for the disposition provided in subsection (a) or the expungement provided in subsection (c). A disposition under subsection (a), or a conviction that is the subject of an expungement order under subsection (c) shall not be considered a conviction for the purpose of a disqualification or a disability imposed by law upon conviction of a crime, or for any other purpose.

(c) Expungement of record of disposition.—If the case against a person found guilty of an offense under section 404 of the Controlled Substances Act (21 USC 844) is the subject of a disposition under subsection (a), and the person was less than twenty-one years old at the time of the offense, the court shall enter an expungement order upon the application of such person. The expungement order shall direct that there be expunged from all official records, except the nonpublic records referred to in subsection (b), all references to his arrest for the offense, the institution of criminal proceedings against him, and the results thereof. The effect of the order shall be to restore such person, in the contemplation of the law, to the status he occupied before such arrest or institution of the criminal proceedings. A person concerning whom such an order has been entered shall not be held thereafter under any provision of law to be guilty of perjury, false swearing, or making a false statement by reason of his failure to recite or acknowledge such arrests or institution of criminal proceedings, or the results thereof, in response to an inquiry made of him for any purpose.

already have received a vacatur and expungement from the state court in order to avoid a finding of "conviction" in immigration proceedings.[36]

The other federal circuits

The Seventh Circuit U.S. Court of Appeals believes that a state counterpart to the FFOA results in a "conviction" for immigration purposes. In *Gill v. Ashcroft*,[37] the individual was arrested in Illinois for possession of cocaine. Gill pleaded guilty in state court, and was sentenced to "410 probation";[38] under this procedure, Gill completed a period of probation and the state court discharged the charges and dismissed proceedings against him. Under Illinois law, a discharge and dismissal of charges under this provision does not result in a conviction for purposes of disqualifications or disabilities imposed by state law for conviction of a crime.[39] This provision is thus comparable to the FFOA. The Seventh Circuit found that federal law (the INA) is not controlled by a state statute; under INA §101(a)(48)(A), Gill's disposition in Illinois—which required a plea before the state court—clearly qualified as a "conviction" for immigration law purposes.

The Third Circuit U.S. Court of Appeals also has held that a state disposition under a Pennsylvania statute similar to the FFOA is a conviction for immigration purposes. In *Acosta v. Ashcroft*,[40] the individual entered a plea of no contest to a charge of possession of a controlled substance (in this case, 0.36 grams of heroin). The state court did not enter a verdict; instead, Acosta was placed on one year of probation pursuant to §17 of the Pennsylvania Controlled Substance Act.[41] On completion of the program—and similar to disposition under the FFOA—the charges against Acosta were dismissed without any adjudication of guilt. The Third Circuit ruled that the disposition in Acosta's case qualified as a "conviction" for immigration purposes under INA §101(a)(48). The Third Circuit continues to apply this position.[42]

Similarly, the Fifth Circuit U.S. Court of Appeals has written that 18 USC §3607 has no "residual effect on the appropriate characterization of state-law deferred dispositions," and, therefore, a Texas dismissal and discharge of a first-time controlled substance violation remains a conviction.[43]

---

[36] *Chavez-Perez v. Ashcroft*, 386 F.3d 1284 (9th Cir. 2004).

[37] *Gill v. Ashcroft*, 335 F.3d 574 (7th Cir. 2003).

[38] Section "410 probation" is a reference to 720 Ill. Comp. Stat. 570/410(f).

[39] 720 Ill. Comp. Stat. 570/410(g).

[40] *Acosta v. Ashcroft*, 341 F.3d 218 (3d Cir. 2003).

[41] Pa. Stat. Ann. tit. 35, §780-117 (1995).

[42] *Richards v. Att'y Gen.*, 2005 U.S. App. LEXIS 20267, No. 05-1305; 05-3129 (3d Cir. 2005) (an unpublished decision); *Bamba v. Rile*, 366 F.3d 195 (3d Cir. 2004).

[43] *Madriz-Alvarado v. Ashcroft*, 383 F.3d 321 (5th Cir. 2004).

This is also the position of the U.S. Courts of Appeals for the First,[44] Second,[45] Tenth,[46] and Eleventh Circuits.[47] Thus, in all jurisdictions to have written on the matter, an individual who has been arrested and charged with first-time simple possession of a controlled substance, and subsequently processed under a state rehabilitative statute—resulting in no "conviction" vis-à-vis a set-aside of the initial verdict—is still "convicted" under the immigration law.

Based on *Nunez-Reyes v. Holder*,[48] the same is true now in the Ninth Circuit. However, for state simple-possession convictions entered prior to July 14, 2011, that are subsequently vacated and expunged pursuant to a rehabilitative procedure, the *Lujan-Armendariz* ruling applies and the disposition does not qualify as a "conviction" for immigration purposes.

> ➢ **Tip**: Consular posts acknowledge the *Lujan-Armendariz* holding for purposes of visa processing. The holding of *Lujan* and *Nunez-Reyes* and the issue of inadmissibility for simple possession of a controlled substance is covered in the *Foreign Affairs Manual*.[49]

Does an expungement under the FFOA result in a "conviction?"

The above discussion of both BIA and federal court case law involves state statutes that are counterparts of, and similar to, the FFOA. These cases specifically do not address whether a federal court disposition under the FFOA itself results in a "conviction" for immigration purposes. This question is pointedly not addressed by the BIA and the courts. Indeed, the BIA specifically recognizes in *Salazar-Regino*[50] that it does not reach—and has not had cause to consider—the impact of INA

---

[44] *Herrera-Inirio v. INS*, 208 F.3d 299, 304–05 (1st Cir. 2000).

[45] *U.S. v. Campbell*, 167 F.3d 94, 98 (2d Cir. 1999).

[46] *U.S. v. Zamudio*, 314 F.3d 517, 522 (10th Cir. 2002); *Corona-Garcia v. Gonzales*, 128 Fed. Appx. 77, 2005 U.S. App. LEXIS (10th Cir. 2005) (unpublished decision).

[47] *Ali v. Att'y Gen.*, 443 F.3d 804 (11th Cir. 2006); *Resendiz-Alcaraz v. Ashcroft*, 383 F.3d 1262 (11th Cir. 2004).

[48] *Nunez-Reyes v. Holder*, 646 F.3d 684 (9th Cir. 2011).

[49] 9 FAM 40.21(b) N4.1-6 a. (2) states:
(2) The Ninth Circuit Court of Appeals, however, disagreed with this holding, and in a series of cases determined that state judicial expungements will be considered effective for eliminating the conviction if the alien would have been eligible for relief under the Federal First Offender Act or similar statute (*see* 9 FAM 40. 21(b) N4.1-2, Federal First Offense Judicial Actions and State Equivalents). The Ninth Circuit subsequently overturned these decisions in the case Nunez-Reyes v. Holder, 646 F.3d 684 (July 14, 2011), and now follows the holding in Roldan. However, this decision did not have retroactive effect, so state judicial expungements that predate this decision can still be effective for immigration purposes in the Ninth Circuit. Because of the complexity of this issue, cases that involve claims for state judicial expungement relief, shall be submitted as an advisory opinion request to the Office of Legislation, Regulations and Advisory Opinions Division (CA/VO/L/A.)

[50] *Salazar-Regino*, 23 I&N Dec. 223 (BIA 2002).

§101(a)(48) on a "conviction" that has been vacated and expunged under the FFOA. Federal courts have specifically stated that whether an FFOA vacatur and expungement qualifies as a "conviction" for immigration purposes is an unresolved question.[51]

The reason that the BIA and the courts have avoided resolving this issue until there is a live case and controversy is that the question essentially pits two federal statutes against each other: 18 USC §3607 (the FFOA) versus INA §101(a)(48). The FFOA specifically states that upon successful completion of probation, the criminal proceeding against the person is dismissed, the record is expunged, and the person will not be held thereafter guilty of perjury or false statement by reason of his or her failure to acknowledge or recite that he or she was ever arrested. A beneficiary of an expungement under the FFOA may deny that the arrest ever occurred "for any purpose." These are strong, clear words. However, a procedure under the FFOA—which is essentially a "deferred" prosecution—does qualify as a "conviction" for immigration purposes.

> **Practice Pointer**: The effect of an expunged "conviction" under the FFOA in the removal context remains an issue subject to debate. The tone of the federal courts in dicta implies that—eventually—the courts (and perhaps the BIA) will find that a disposition under the FFOA does *not* result in a "conviction" for immigration purposes. However, at least one court has found that the INA's definition of "conviction" at INA §101(a)(48) trumps the FFOA because the former is specific to immigration law and was passed subsequent to the FFOA.[52] In the meantime, it is important that practitioners defending non–American citizens before the U.S. Department of Homeland Security (DHS) and in immigration court deny that an FFOA disposition qualifies as a "conviction" for immigration law purposes.

Pardons

Practitioners and the public alike are often disappointed to learn that a pardon is not a panacea in the immigration context. A pardon acts to eliminate a conviction as a ground of deportability in specific, limited instances. As ensuing chapters explain, grounds of removability are divided into inadmissibility (INA §212) and deportability (INA §237). A pardon will not cure a ground of inadmissibility under §212. A pardon does eliminate certain enumerated grounds of deportability under §237.

---

[51] *Wellington v. Holder,* 623 F.3d 115, 120 (2d Cir. 2010), *Acosta v. Ashcroft,* 341 F.3d 218, 224 n. 7 (3d Cir. 2003).

[52] *Danso v. Gonzales,* 489 F.3d 709 (5th Cir. 2007) (foreign expungement not effective to cure ground of deportation, even if similar to the FFOA).

A pardon does not eliminate the "conviction" itself. However, a pardon acts as a waiver—protects against removal—when a non–American citizen is charged as deportable under INA §§237(a)(2)(A)(i) and (ii), relating to crimes involving moral turpitude; (iii), relating to aggravated felonies; and (iv), relating to convictions for high-speed flight.[53]

A pardon does not eliminate the other criminal grounds of deportability, including, firearm offenses, controlled substance offenses, or crimes of domestic violence.[54] Where a certain criminal offense may trigger more than one ground of deportability, the pardon will not be effective unless both grounds are covered by the pardon provision. Perhaps the most common example would be a controlled-substance violation that qualifies as both an aggravated felony [(INA §237(a)(2)(A)(iii)] and a controlled substance offense [INA §237(a)(2)(B)]; the pardon will not be effective because it does not affect the second charge—deportability for a controlled-substance conviction.

The effect of a pardon on a ground of inadmissibility

Because pardons are not mentioned in INA §212(a), they are not effective to eliminate grounds of inadmissibility; §212(a) grounds apply to arriving aliens in removal proceedings, as well as to applicants for adjustment of status.[55] However, in the context of consular processing for a visa, the applicable regulation states that a visa applicant shall not be considered ineligible under INA §212(a)(2)(A)(i)(I), relating to crimes involving moral turpitude, on the basis of a conviction that has received a full and unconditional pardon.[56] This distinction is very interesting, and may be important strategically, as it places a visa applicant abroad in a potentially better situation than someone applying for residency from within the United States (assuming he or she has received a pardon). It is not clear why the U.S. Department of State (DOS), in its regulations, has chosen to give pardons full faith and credit in the context of INA §212(a)(2), but DHS, the Executive Office for Immigration Review (EOIR), and the federal courts do not honor pardons for persons within the United States facing issues of admissibility under the same section. Notably, the same regulatory section states that a pardon or clemency granted by a foreign state shall not serve to remove a ground of inadmissibility.[57]

---

[53] INA §237(a)(2)(A)(vi); 8 USC §1227(a)(2)(A)(vi).

[54] *Matter of Suh*, 23 I&N Dec. 626 (BIA 2003).

[55] *Aguilera-Montero v. Mukasey*, 548 F.3d 1248 (9th Cir. 2008); *Balogun v. Att'y Gen.*, 425 F.3d 1356, 1358 (11th Cir. 2005).

[56] 22 CFR §§40.21(a)(5), 40.22(c).

[57] 22 CFR §§40.21(a)(5), 40.22(c).

Pardon must be full and unconditional

The INA requires that the pardon be full and unconditional, issued by the president of the United States, or by the governor of the convicting state.[58] A pardon that is issued automatically according to a state statute passed by the legislature, or issued by a parole commission or parole board, or contingent on certain conditions, is not a "full and unconditional pardon" granted by an authority enumerated under the INA. Such a pardon will not effectively cure a ground of deportability.[59] Moreover, a pardon that involves limitations—for example, the right to carry a gun or some other limitation on civil rights—is not a "full and unconditional" pardon. The case law indicates that the BIA expects a pardon by either a governor or the president that has been issued based on discrete review of the individual's case and granted completely, without conditions or limitations.

Foreign pardons

The BIA and the federal courts generally have held that foreign pardons are ineffective to eliminate the non–American citizen's conviction for purposes of deportability.[60] The result may be different in the Ninth Circuit, which—by way of comparison—is willing to accept and honor a foreign expungement.[61] As stated above, in the context of visa processing abroad, DOS will not recognize a foreign pardon.[62]

Post-conviction Relief on the Merits: *Matter of Pickering*

Unlike the ameliorative procedures discussed above, a conviction that has been vacated on the merits—rather than sealed or expunged for rehabilitative purposes—is not a conviction for immigration purposes, according to the BIA in *Matter of Rodriguez-Ruiz*.[63] It has become common practice for individuals facing removal proceedings, or an impediment to residency or naturalization, to seek post-conviction relief through a vacation of the judgment. Seasoned immigration attorneys regularly suggest the possibility of vacating a conviction or convictions, and either handle the criminal matter themselves or refer the client to competent criminal defense counsel. For several years, *Matter of Rodriguez-Ruiz* has carried the day, and many clients have accomplished their immigration goals by having their criminal judgments reo-

---

[58] INA §237(a)(2)(A)(vi); 8 USC §1227(a)(2)(A)(vi).

[59] *Matter of Nolan*, 19 I&N Dec. 539 (BIA 1988).

[60] *See, e.g., Marino v. INS*, 537 F.2d 686, 691 (2d Cir. 1976) (citing *Matter of Adamo*, 10 I&N Dec. 593 (BIA 1964)); *see also Matter of Marino*, 15 I&N Dec. 284, 285 (BIA 1976) (citing *Palermo v. Smith*, 17 F.2d 534, 535 (2d Cir. 1975)).

[61] *Dillingham v. INS*, 267 F.3d 996 (9th Cir. 2001), *overruled by Nunez-Reyes v. Holder*, 646 F.3d 684 (9th Cir. 2011).

[62] *See* 22 CFR §§40.21(a)(5), 40.22(c).

[63] *Matter of Rodriguez-Ruiz*, 22 I&N Dec. 1378 (BIA 2000).

pened and vacated on account of a procedural or constitutional defect in the proceedings below.

The BIA limited the viability of post-conviction relief in 2003. In *Matter of Pickering*,[64] the BIA stated that if a court vacates an individual's conviction for reasons "solely related to rehabilitation or immigration hardships, rather than on the basis of a procedural or substantive defect" in proceedings below, the conviction is not eliminated for immigration purposes. A vacation of judgment must be grounded in a statute or the state or federal constitution, occurring to correct a violation or error of law.

There are two practical problems with the *Pickering* decision. First, the BIA unfortunately chose to write a precedent decision on this important issue where the underlying criminal case arose in Canada. The conviction in *Pickering* was quashed by a court in Ontario. This is a procedure not familiar to persons in the United States. Second, the decision simply is not clear in terms of its reach—which vacaturs will be honored by immigration courts, and which ones will not? And who has the burden of proof?

The BIA notes that in its decision to quash the conviction, the Ontario court did not reference a specific Canadian statute regarding vacaturs. The BIA further notes that the Ontario court appeared to rely solely on the individual's affidavit of immigration hardship for the vacatur (the petitioner could not obtain permanent resident status with the conviction on his record). Thus, should a case arise where a vacatur is obtained from a court within the United States—and the issue arises as to whether the vacatur is valid under the *Pickering* decision—there is no Canadian statute to compare and contrast with the relevant American legal provision. Moreover, with no Canadian provision cited, it is not clear that the Canadian law utilized in this matter allowed for a vacatur based solely on equities, or whether the Ontario statute *did* require a finding of error below. Set in a foreign country, with no statute cited and a skimpy set of facts, *Pickering* simply was not a good case on which to clarify the effect of a vacatur on immigration proceedings. Attorneys are left uncertain as to when a vacatur will effectively eliminate a conviction for immigration purposes.

Precisely because of the questions raised above, the BIA's decision in *Matter of Pickering* was reversed by the Sixth Circuit. The Sixth Circuit complained of a vague Canadian record as reiterated by the record of proceedings in immigration court.[65] The Sixth Circuit's decision clarified some of the key issues left unanswered by the BIA.

However, the principal import of the BIA's decision was reaffirmed: a vacatur must be based on a constitutional or statutory defect in the underlying criminal proceedings in order to effectively eliminate the conviction for immigration purposes.

---

[64] *Matter of Pickering*, 23 I&N Dec. 621 (BIA 2003), rev'd, *Pickering v. Gonzales,* 465 F.3d 263 (6th Cir. 2006).

[65] *Pickering v. Gonzales,* 465 F.3d 263 (6th Cir. 2006).

> **Practice Pointer**: It is highly recommended that anyone dealing with a *Pickering* issue read the federal court opinion hand-in-hand with the BIA's decision. The two decisions complement each other, resulting in a better understanding of the overall issue.

CASE STUDY: PICKERING v. GONZALES (Post-conviction relief)

In *Pickering v. Gonzales*, the Sixth Circuit made several important points. First, and perhaps most significantly, the court found that the burden of proof is on the government—not the respondent—to establish deportability. Thus, it was not Pickering's burden to show that the vacatur was valid, but the government's burden to show that it was not. Second, the court noted the record was unclear as to the legal bases for the vacatur. Third, because Pickering's motion cited to personal hardship and equity as grounds for vacating did not mean that the Canadian appeals court vacated for those same reasons; in other words, a defendant's motives cannot automatically be presumed to be the basis for a court's decision:

> The Petitioner, in his notice of appeal and affidavit, stated that he was appealing his conviction because of the bar it placed on his permanent immigration to the United States … . The BIA imparted the Petitioner's motivation for seeking to have the conviction quashed onto the Canadian court as its rationale for quashing the conviction … . However, the motive of the Petitioner in seeking to have his conviction quashed is of limited relevance to our inquiry. *See Sandoval v. INS*, 240 F.3d 577, 583 (7th Cir. 2001). Such motive is relevant only to the extent that the Canadian court relied upon it in quashing the conviction. As the record before us does not include a record of the hearing and is, therefore, incomplete, it is impossible to tell the extent to which the Canadian court relied upon Petitioner's motive, or even why the Canadian court acted in the manner it did.[66]

In his petition for review proceedings, the petitioner offered expert testimony that the only basis for a Canadian court to quash a conviction is under §24(a) of the Canadian Charter of Rights and Freedoms, for reasons related to a violation of rights granted Canadian citizens through the Charter. Thus, regardless of Pickering's stated motives, the court could only have quashed based on legal grounds involving a defect in the underlying proceedings.[67]

---

[66] *Pickering v. Gonzales*, at 267.
[67] *Pickering v. Gonzales*, at 268.

CH. 2 • THE DEFINITION OF "CONVICTION" ACCORDING TO IMMIGRATION LAW   67

The court found that it did not have the sua sponte authority to remand for expansion of the record where the issue is deportability. Noting that the evidence before the BIA at the time of its decision was insufficient to sustain a finding of deportability, the court simply reversed the final decision and remanded for an order terminating proceedings and quashing the order of deportation.[68]

In light of both the BIA's *Pickering* decision and the Sixth Circuit's subsequent reversal, there are two possible perspectives an immigration judge might adopt in analyzing a vacated conviction:

- The first view, which represents the positive perspective for defense attorneys, is that the determination of whether a vacatur is effective for immigration purposes depends on the statutory provision under which it was accomplished. If the provision calls for a vacatur of the judgment based on legal or substantive defect—for example, failure to advise of possible deportation—the judgment must be honored in subsequent immigration proceedings. If the criminal court judge's decision to vacate is based solely on equitable grounds, *e.g.*, to remove an impediment to obtaining residency, without reference to an error in proceedings below, the vacatur is not effective. Under this view, the defendant's personal motives are irrelevant. The language of the state statute controls.

- The second view of *Pickering* adopts the government's perspective. This view is that the BIA is indeed inviting an analysis of the defendant's personal motivations for seeking a vacation of judgment. Under this view, if the individual's primary goal is to vacate the judgment to obtain some immigration benefit, the vacatur is ineffective regardless of the underlying state statute and the relevant statutory criteria (*i.e.*, an identifiable defect or error). As discussed below, this particular area of the law is still developing.

The burden of proof in Pickering-*type cases*

According to several federal courts, including the Sixth Circuit in *Pickering*, the burden of proof is on the government to establish that a vacatur is *not* valid for immigration purposes.[69] The burden of establishing deportability in proceedings under INA §237(a) rests with the government, and this includes demonstrating the existence of a "conviction."[70] Certainly where the individual faces deportation under INA §237(a), it makes sense that the burden of proof rests with the government.[71] Where a

---

[68] *Pickering v. Gonzales*, at 270.

[69] *See, e.g., Barakat v. Holder*, 2010 U.S. App. LEXIS 19213 (6th Cir. 2010); *Nath v. Gonzales*, 467 F.3d 1185 (9th Cir. Ariz. 2006).

[70] *Pickering v. Gonzales*, 465 F.3d 263 (6th Cir. 2006) (citing *Cruz-Garza v. Ashcroft*, 396 F.3d 1125, 1130 (10th Cir. 2005) and *Matter of Kaneda*, 16 I&N Dec. 677, 680 (1977)).

[71] INA §240(c)(3); 8 USC §1229a(c)(3).

non–American citizen is charged under INA §212(a) as an arriving alien, it is not so clear. The INA states that applicants for admission have the burden of establishing admissibility.[72]

Unfortunately, the BIA has not resolved the issue of which party bears the burden of proof, even though it has had specific occasion to do so. In *Matter of Chavez-Martinez*,[73] the BIA acknowledged that there is a split among the federal circuits on the issue of burden of proof. This case involved a motion to reopen proceedings based on a vacated conviction; the BIA ruled that at this late stage, the party seeking to reopen has the burden of proving that the conviction was vacated on statutory or constitutional grounds. In a footnote, the BIA writes as follows regarding the burden of proof:

> We recognize that the respondent would be in a similar position in the context of determining his removability, but we express no opinion as to the proper result in such a case.[74]

Thus, the BIA implies that, even if not in a motion to reopen, the respondent would have the burden of showing a viable vacatur. In a decidedly sophomoric fashion, the BIA writes as follows, regarding justification for allocating the burden to the respondent:

> In this regard, we note that the respondent was a direct party to the criminal proceeding leading to the vacation of his conviction and is therefore in the best position to know why the conviction was vacated and to offer evidence related to the record of conviction.[75]

> ➢ **Practice Pointer**: Presentation of documents is one issue; where the government has a dated conviction, the non-detained respondent can logically be charged with presenting the vacatur order and (if applicable) the dismissal or reduction of charges. However, once the vacatur and final disposition are presented, practitioners should aggressively argue that the burden of persuasion lies with the government to establish that a vacatur is *not* valid for immigration purposes.

Motions to reopen

Where the vacatur of an underlying conviction becomes the basis for a motion to reopen removal proceedings—*i.e.*, the vacatur is subsequent to a final order of re-

---

[72] INA §240(c)(2); 8 USC §1229a(c)(2).

[73] *Matter of Chavez-Martinez*, 24 I&N Dec. 272 (BIA 2007).

[74] *Chavez-Martinez* at 274 n.1.

[75] *Chavez-Martinez* at 274. This author has never heard of the burden of proof being allocated based on which party should have the most knowledge of events; under this theory, criminal defendants should have to prove beyond a reasonable doubt that they are not guilty, since they must have been present "at the time."

moval—the federal courts are split on which party has the burden of proof.[76] As stated above, the BIA has ruled that the burden of proving that a vacatur is valid in a motion to reopen context lies with the respondent.[77]

In a particularly interesting decision, the Third Circuit found that the BIA abused its discretion by failing sua sponte to grant a motion to reopen that had been filed outside the statutory time limit, where the BIA had a pattern and practice of doing precisely that. The case cites to a long line of unpublished decisions of which the BIA reopened on its own accord because a conviction had been vacated after a final removal order.[78]

An even more challenging issue arises when the non–American citizen already has been physically removed. The few courts that have addressed this issue have disagreed in the final outcome. For example, the Ninth Circuit directed reopening of a removal order after the respondent's conviction had been vacated, even though the individual already had been physically deported. The Eleventh Circuit reached the opposite result.[79]

BIA decisions after Pickering

In an unpublished decision after *Pickering*, the BIA refused to honor a vacatur and ruled the individual remained "convicted" for purposes of removal proceedings. The individual in *Matter of Pacheco-Ventura*[80] was convicted of possession of drug paraphernalia. This conviction was subsequently "vacated and stricken" under Maryland law. Although the BIA does not specifically assign a burden of proof, the language strongly implies that the burden of showing that there is no "conviction" (because of the vacatur) lies with the respondent. This would contradict the INA, which states that in the case of *deportable* non–American citizens, the burden of establishing removability rests with DHS.[81] The BIA wrote:

> [T]he respondent has not presented evidence demonstrating whether his plea of guilty was vacated for reasons solely related to rehabilitation or immigration

---

[76] *See Rumierz v. Gonzales*, 456 F.3d 31 (1st Cir. 2006) (burden of proof in a motion to reopen is on respondent to establish vacatur based on legal or constitutional grounds; motion denied).

[77] *Matter of Chavez-Martinez*, 24 I&N Dec. 272 (BIA 2007).

[78] *Cruz v. Att'y Gen.*, 452 F.3d 240 (3d Cir. 2006).

[79] *Patel v. Att'y Gen.*, 334 F.3d 1259 (11th Cir. 2003) (vacation of a conviction not effective after removal order has been executed); *cf. Cardoso-Tlaseca v. Gonzales*, 460 F.3d 1102 (9th Cir. 2006) (BIA erred in denying motion to reopen—notwithstanding respondent's actual deportation from United States—where underlying conviction was vacated after final removal order; case remanded for determination of basis for vacatur).

[80] *Matter of Pacheco-Ventura*, A44 801 843, 2003 BIA LEXIS 14, 2003 WL 23508549 (BIA Dec. 29, 2003).

[81] INA §240(c)(3)(A); 8 USC §1229a(c)(3)(A).

hardships or on the basis of a procedural or substantive defect in the underlying criminal proceedings.[82]

In a 2006 case, *Matter of Adamiak*,[83] the BIA found that the respondent's vacatur effectively eliminated the conviction for immigration purposes where the underlying plea was defective because the court failed to advise the defendant of potential immigration consequences. Under Ohio Rev. Code Ann. §2943.031, a state judge must make certain advisements, including regarding adverse immigration consequences. The defendant was allowed to withdraw his guilty plea. The BIA found that the underlying plea contained a legal defect, and the subsequent vacatur was entitled to full faith and credit under 28 USC §1738.

The federal courts' approach to Pickering

The federal courts have deferred to the BIA's analysis in *Pickering*; however, the courts have approached the issue of proof and proper analysis of the record differently. It cannot be stressed enough that when it comes to *Pickering*-type issues, every individual case is unique and worth arguing. Although, generally, a "categorical approach" (a review limited to the statute itself) is adopted in immigration law, both the BIA and the courts have been willing to look to the underlying facts and circumstances—including ancillary documents—when reviewing the reasons behind a court-ordered vacatur.

> ➢ **Tip**: Hence, in every case, it is worth arguing that the conviction has been validly vacated based on substantive and procedural error below. And, where possible, the motion to vacate must be a collaborative effort between criminal and immigration attorneys, and the pleadings must be fashioned to focus on substantive and procedural legal defect, as opposed to immigration hardship.

Vacatur found effective in eliminating the conviction

As discussed at length above, the Sixth Circuit in *Pickering v. Gonzales* found that the Canadian quashing of a conviction could only be accomplished via a Canadian Charter provision grounded in the law and citizens' rights. Based on the only plausible statutory vehicle available (which was not a form of equity), the court reversed the BIA's conclusion based on the facts of the particular case.

In a more useful case from the Fifth Circuit, *Discipio v. Ashcroft*,[84] DHS agreed that a conviction was indeed properly vacated under *Pickering* and moved the court

---

[82] *Matter of Pacheco-Ventura*, A44 801 843, 2003 BIA LEXIS 14, 2003 WL 23508549 (BIA Dec. 29, 2003).
[83] *Matter of Adamiak*, 23 I&N Dec. 878 (BIA 2006).
[84] *Discipio v. Ashcroft*, 417 F.3d 448 (5th Cir. 2005).

of appeals to vacate its prior decision[85] and remand to the BIA so that DHS could move to dismiss removal proceedings. The court reiterated DHS's position that convictions vacated on the basis of procedural and substantive defects are not valid convictions for purposes of removal proceedings. Unfortunately, the decision does not discuss the underlying basis for the motion to vacate; thus, the reader is left unaware of what exactly constituted "substantive and procedural defect."

In *Cruz v. Att'y Gen.*,[86] the respondent moved to vacate his conviction based on ineffective assistance of counsel where his attorney did not request pretrial intervention (PTI). Although the state appeals court did find ineffective assistance of counsel, it declined to find prejudice because Cruz could not show that he would have been accepted into PTI even if his attorney had asked. Thus, the motion to vacate was actually denied. However, the ineffectiveness finding (combined with a change in prosecutors) prompted the state attorney to reconsider and amend the judgment, allowing Cruz into the PTI program. The conviction was withdrawn. When Cruz moved to reopen his removal order (he had, by this time, been ordered removed), the BIA denied the motion as out of time, and refused to reopen sua sponte. The Third Circuit reversed and remanded, finding that it appeared the vacatur was valid and that, as discussed above, the BIA departed from its general practice in other cases of sua sponte reopening upon vacation of the underlying criminal judgment.

Vacatur found ineffective for immigration purposes

After *Pickering v. Gonzales*, the Sixth Circuit again had occasion to analyze the impact of a vacated conviction on the determination of deportability. In *Sanusi v. Gonzales*,[87] the court found the government sustained its burden of proving that the conviction still existed, notwithstanding the grant of a writ of error *coram nobis* in Arkansas. The court distinguished the facts in *Sanusi* from those in *Pickering*: the former involved a writ that was essentially equitable in nature, utilized to secure relief from a judgment based on some fact not previously known, while the court in *Pickering* relied on the expert witness's testimony that the only vehicle for quashing the Canadian conviction was based on constitutional grounds. *Sanusi* highlights the importance of focusing on a state statute or rule of procedure that is based on legal or constitutional defect in drafting the motion to vacate. Effective drafting is discussed further below.

In *Saleh v. Gonzales*,[88] the respondent successfully amended nunc pro tunc his conviction from a felony theft offense to petty theft. Although the Second Circuit acknowledged that the burden of proof to establish a "conviction" is on the government, it noted that the criminal record did not identify any legal or statutory defect,

---

[85] *Discipio v. Ashcroft*, 369 F.3d 472 (5th Cir. 2001).

[86] *Cruz v. Att'y Gen.*, 452 F.3d 240 (3d Cir. 2006).

[87] *Sanusi v. Gonzales*, 474 F.3d 341 (6th Cir. 2007).

[88] *Saleh v. Gonzales*, 495 F.3d 17 (2d Cir. 2007).

and the respondent apparently admitted that the motion was for the purpose of avoiding immigration consequences. Thus the court of appeals upheld the removal order based on the BIA's *Matter of Pickering* analysis.

In *Renteria-Gonzalez v. INS*,[89] a case decided prior to *Pickering*, the Fifth Circuit held that a federal conviction vacated on purely equitable grounds, with jurisdiction premised on 28 USC §1331 and the All Writs Act, remains a "conviction" for immigration purposes. However, the decision diminishes in value as the court launches into a discussion of expungements, referring to case law on state court expungements (see discussion of the FFOA, above), and essentially muddles these two distinct legal animals.

In *Liberal de Araugo v. Ashcroft*,[90] the First Circuit considered a case in which multiple convictions were vacated. The individual in this case had been convicted of assault and battery with a deadly weapon—vacated—and multiple controlled-substance offenses—also vacated. The basis for the motion to vacate in state court was that the defendant, at the time of plea, was so addicted to both heroin and cocaine that the pleas were not knowing and intelligent. Notably, the BIA looked to the petitioner's affidavit in support of the motion to vacate in determining whether this was a valid vacatur under *Pickering*. The BIA found that it would need "more information" before it could ascertain the reason for vacating the convictions and determining that the vacaturs were not related to immigration purposes. The BIA continued by stating that none of the vacaturs was issued because the petitioner was "not factually guilty." Ultimately, the First Circuit found that it lacked jurisdiction to review the BIA's decision that the petitioner remained "convicted" for immigration law purposes and did not reach a decision on the validity of the vacaturs.

In a case that is equally disturbing (because the court allows for review of ancillary documents in ascertaining the nature of a vacatur), the Seventh Circuit in *Ali v. Ashcroft*[91] determined that the petitioner remained "convicted" of an aggravated felony even after his felony controlled-substance conviction was reduced to misdemeanor drug possession. This case received much press attention at a local level[92] because of the compelling humanitarian facts: Ali, a native of Afghanistan, immigrated to the United States in 1978 at the age of 3, became a lawful permanent resident in 1982, but had been convicted of receiving stolen property and distribution of THC (the active ingredient in marijuana). Since arriving in the United States, Ali had never re-

---

[89] *Renteria-Gonzalez v. INS*, 310 F.3d 825 (5th Cir. 2002), *reh'g en banc denied*, 322 F.3d 804 (5th Cir. 2003).

[90] *Liberal de Araugo v. Ashcroft*, 399 F.3d 84 (1st Cir. 2005).

[91] *Ali v. Ashcroft*, 395 F.3d 722 (7th Cir. 2005).

[92] B. Ingersoll, "Madison Man Loses Appeal to Avoid Deportation; Mirwais Ali Grew Up in Madison, But Could Be on His Way to Afghanistan," *Wis. St. J*, Jan. 23, 2005, at A1 (available at http://host.madison.com/news/madison-man-loses-appeal-to-avoid-deportation-mirwais-ali-grew/article_98ce2aae-fd99-5bbd-a6e9-8cffb65e0ea9.html).).

turned to Afghanistan and did not speak the language; both of his parents became American citizens. Equities notwithstanding, the court found that the reopening and reduction of the charge was accomplished purely for immigration purposes. The BIA and the court looked to the stipulated motion to amend conviction, signed by both the Wisconsin district attorney and petitioner's counsel. The motion stated that "by amending this felony conviction to that of a misdemeanor, the defendant would avert his pending deportation from the United States of America."[93] The court found it was "obvious" that the conviction was amended simply to avoid deportation.

Marya v. Gonzales[94] also involved an amendment, or modification, of the original conviction. In this Fourth Circuit case, the court found the petitioner remained convicted of a "crime of domestic violence" under INA §237(a)(2)(E), even though his original conviction for assault and battery of a family member[95] had been amended to simple assault. The court noted that the petitioner had not shown that the amendment of the original conviction was related to or called into question the "integrity of the merits of the original conviction." Thus, he remained convicted for immigration purposes.

The lesson of careful pleading within the motion to vacate is reiterated in another unpublished decision—the Third Circuit's *Myers v. McCormick*.[96] *Myers* involved a non–American citizen from Sierra Leone who entered the United States in 1978. Like the respondent in *Ali v. Ashcroft*, Myers entered the United States at a young age and faced deportation to a troubled country for relatively minor criminal activity (a theft offense and two convictions for of controlled substance possession). Unfortunately, the state court's order vacating the controlled-substance convictions expressly stated that the court "had considered the likelihood that Myers would be executed if deported." Myers even obtained an *amended* order from the state judge that refrained from referring to deportation. Nonetheless, the court of appeals found that:

> [T]he original order made clear that the court's grounds for vacating the conviction were not based on the merits, but rather was an attempt to prevent Myers's deportation. We review the amended order as suspect and we agree with Appellees that the absence of any discussion of reasoning or rationale in the amended order, the sole purpose of which was to clarify the prior order, indicates no change in the court's motivation for vacating the conviction.[97]

The court concluded by finding that Myers' 1992 conviction for cocaine possession, which was later vacated by the state court, remained a "conviction" for immigration purposes and upheld the order of removal to Sierra Leone.

---

[93] *Ali v. Ashcroft*, 395 F.3d 722, 729 (7th Cir. 2005).

[94] *Marya v. Gonzales*, 147 Fed. Appx. 336, 2005 U.S. LEXIS 16841, 2005 WL 1926376 (4th Cir. 2005) (citing *Yanez-Popp v. INS*, 998 F.2d 231, 235 (4th Cir. 1993)).

[95] Va. Code Ann. §18.2-57.2 (2004).

[96] *Myers v. McCormick*, 112 Fed. Appx. 149; 2004 U.S. App. LEXIS 21306, 2004 WL 2296506 (3d Cir. 2004).

[97] *Myers v. McCormick*, 112 Fed. Appx. at 152 (footnote omitted).

In an unpublished decision from the Eleventh Circuit, *Lawrence v. United States AG*,[98] the non–American citizen moved to vacate, and in court subsequently amended the marijuana charges (of which he had been convicted) to trespass. The immigration judge found that the substitution of possession of marijuana charges for two counts of trespass showed the vacatur was solely for immigration purposes. The Board of Immigration Appeals upheld the judge's decision, as did the Eleventh Circuit.

What stands out in all of the above-named federal cases is the lack of citation to a state statute authorizing the vacaturs. No reference is made by the federal courts to the specific rule of criminal procedure or other authority that authorized the vacatur; rather, the courts look to and analyze ancillary documents in the record to somehow divine the state court judges' reasons for granting the vacatur. Furthermore, it is not clear whether no reference is made because the motions to vacate were brought without statutory authority; because the parties did not raise the statutory authority before the federal courts; or that the federal courts simply did not find the statutory vehicle to be significant.

However, in every other area of immigration law—be it analyzing the definition of "moral turpitude" or defining "crime of violence"—the courts look to the state or federal criminal statute to define the immigration law consequences. This may be compared to the "categorical approach," discussed in various contexts throughout this book. The same type of approach (looking to the strict qualifications set forth in the statute) should apply in the *Pickering* context as courts evaluate the validity of a vacated criminal conviction. If the state or federal law statute (or rule of criminal procedure) under which the motion to vacate is brought—and on which the judgment is ultimately based—is premised on legal defect (procedural, constitutional, or statutory error), the discussion should end. There should be no review of the language in the motion, no review of the hearing's transcripts, no divination based on conversation in the record. It is the underlying statute or rule that should control.

> ➤ *Tip*: Two reminders on vacaturs: First, in the pleadings (*i.e.*, within the motion to vacate), counsel should refrain from mentioning immigration hardship, but instead identify specific procedural and/or substantive violations of state law that render the plea (or verdict) illegal. Such a basis will require a careful study of the original proceedings to ascertain any and all violations of the law unrelated to immigration hardship. Second, in arguing the validity of the vacatur to the IJ, BIA, or, ultimately, a federal court, the categorical approach must be promoted: that the BIA and federal court's review is limited to the elements of the statute under which the vacatur was ordered. If the statutory provision under which the motion to vacate is premised is based solely on legal defect, the "conviction" no longer exists for immigration purposes. The immigra-

---

[98] *Lawrence v. Att'y Gen.*, 457 Fed. Appx. 816 (11th Cir. 2012).

Vacatur ineffective for naturalization purposes

In *Phan v. Holder*,[99] the Fourth Circuit adopted the *Pickering* approach in the context of naturalization. The non–American citizen argued he was eligible to naturalize notwithstanding a conviction for an aggravated felony, because the conviction had been vacated under a rehabilitative statute. Applying *Pickering*, the court of appeals upheld U.S. Citizenship and Immigration Services's (USCIS) determination that the applicant remained convicted for naturalization purposes.[100]

Vacatur granted after removal order executed

In *Reyes-Torres v. Holder*,[101] the Ninth Circuit granted a petition for review for a non–American citizen, already physically removed from the United States, based on his successful vacatur of the conviction that formed the basis for his removal. In this case, the non–American citizen was convicted, ordered removed, vacated his conviction, and moved to reopen after his removal—based on the vacatur. The motion to reopen was filed before the 90-day statutory period for motions to reopen.[102] The BIA denied the motion to reopen, but the court of appeals reversed and remanded for further proceedings on the merits of the vacatur.[103]

Ineffective Assistance of Counsel

"It is our responsibility under the Constitution to ensure that no criminal defendant—whether a citizen or not—is left to the "mercies of incompetent counsel"…To satisfy this responsibility, we now hold that counsel must inform her client whether his plea carries a risk of deportation. Our longstanding Sixth Amendment precedents, the seriousness of deportation as a consequence of a criminal plea, and the concomitant impact of deportation on families living lawfully in this country demand no less."[104]

---

[99] *Phan v. Holder*, 667 F.3d 448 (4th Cir. 2012).

[100] A post–November 30, 1990, conviction for an aggravated felony is a bar to naturalization pursuant to 8 USC §1101(a)(13)(f); INA §101(a)(13)(f).

[101] *Reyes-Torres v. Holder*, 645 F.3d 1073 (9th Cir. 2011).

[102] For further discussion of the "post-departure bar" regulation and circuit court treatment of timely motions to reopen filed after removal, see *Perez Santana v. Holder*, 731 F.3d 50 (1st Cir. 2013).

[103] In a somewhat similar case, in *Pola v. U.S.*, 2015 U.S. 778 F.3d 525 (6th Cir. 2015, the Sixth Circuit U.S. Court of Appeals allowed to proceed a motion to vacate based on ineffective assistance of counsel (a Rule 2255 motion) notwithstanding the defendant's removal by ICE to Canada.

[104] *Padilla v. Kentucky*, 559 U.S. 356, 374 (2010).

CASE STUDY: PADILLA v. KENTUCKY (Ineffective assistance)

In *Padilla*, the Supreme Court ruled that the Sixth Amendment requires defense counsel to advise defendants of possible immigration consequences associated with a plea. Failure to provide such advice constitutes ineffective assistance of counsel. Notably, the Court rejected the analysis that immigration consequences of criminal convictions are collateral and counsel need not advise clients about them.

Significantly, *Padilla* has affected the plea bargain process for noncitizen defendants. Local prosecutors are generally inclined to reach plea agreements in the majority of cases, if only to avoid the time and expense of proceeding to trial. Criminal defense lawyers should no longer accept plea bargains that result in harsh immigration consequences, and local prosecutors will have to offer more favorable deals unless they want to go to trial. Criminal and immigration lawyers should cooperate in reaching the best possible outcome for their clients. Hopefully, better legal advice, more appropriate sentences, and less need to revisit old cases will be the fruits of *Padilla*.

Many motions to vacate convictions are now based on failure to advise of immigration consequences, pursuant to the *Padilla* precedent. However, in 2013, the Supreme Court ruled that the *Padilla* rule is not retroactive: it cannot be used to vacate decisions that became final prior to the decision.[105]

Post-conviction Relief Modifying the Sentence Imposed

Another type of post-conviction relief is modification of the sentence imposed, rather than vacation of the conviction itself. As addressed in the upcoming chapters, certain grounds of inadmissibility and deportability are premised on the length of the sentence imposed. For example, theft offenses and crimes of violence become "aggravated felonies" when the sentence of imprisonment imposed is one year or longer; mandatory detention for a crime involving moral turpitude is triggered by a one-year or longer sentence of imprisonment; and a waiver under INA §212(c) (repealed 1996) is not available to an individual who served five years or longer in prison for an aggravated felony offense. These are just a few examples. Many INA classifications of crime, as well as forms of relief (or consequences), turn on the length of sentence of imprisonment imposed. Accordingly, a post-conviction action to modify a sentence may obtain the desired result without an outright vacation of the conviction itself.[106]

---

[105] *Chaidez v. U.S.*, 133 S. Ct. 1103 (2013).
[106] *Matter of Song*, 23 I&N Dec. 173 (BIA 2001).

Post-conviction sentence modification is not subject to the same scrutiny as outlined in *Matter of Pickering*[107] for vacaturs of judgment. A criminal court's decision to modify or reduce a person's sentence nunc pro tunc is entitled to full faith and credit by the immigration court and is valid to ameliorate immigration law consequences without regard to the trial court's reasons for ordering the modification or reduction of sentence.[108]

Acts of Juvenile Delinquency

An adjudication of delinquency is not a "conviction" for immigration purposes.[109] This philosophy is based on the jurisprudence that juveniles, although charged with specific criminal acts, are adjudicated delinquent as opposed to convicted of specific criminal offenses. It is further noted that the burden of proof standard in juvenile proceedings is often *not* "beyond a reasonable doubt"; rather, some lower standard applies. Juvenile court proceedings are not criminal proceedings for immigration purposes.[110] Adjudications of delinquency in juvenile court are to be distinguished from youthful offender *sentencing*, wherein the disposition is in adult court, but certain unique sentencing standards apply (for example, special youth prisons or camps). A minor who is nonetheless prosecuted and convicted in adult court has a "conviction" for immigration purposes.[111] The best method for ascertaining the type of adjudication a client experienced and its impact under the immigration law is review of the state law combined with research on the statutory provision.

Although the precedent on juvenile delinquency adjudications is sound in the context of removal proceedings when an actual conviction is required to support a finding of either inadmissibility or deportability, the effect of a delinquency adjudication is not so clear in the context of immigration provisions when a final conviction is *not* required. Certain admissibility provisions [*e.g.*, INA §212(a)] do not require an actual conviction, but instead only an admission of guilt or—worse—a "reason to believe" that the applicant has been involved in criminal activity. For example, a person can be denied entry into the United States or adjustment of status to lawful permanent resident (LPR) based on an immigration officer's "reason to believe" that he or she has been involved in either drug trafficking or money laundering. These provisions, which are discussed in depth in chapter 5, do not require a conviction.

---

[107] *Matter of Pickering*, 23 I&N Dec. 621 (BIA 2003), *rev'd*, *Pickering v. Gonzales*, 465 F.3d 263 (6th Cir. 2006).

[108] *Matter of Cotas-Vargas*, 23 I&N Dec. 849 (BIA 2005).

[109] *Matter of Devison-Charles*, 22 I&N Dec. 1362 (BIA 2000); *Matter of De La Nues*, 18 I&N Dec. 140 (BIA 1981); *Matter of Ramirez-Rivero*, 18 I&N Dec. 135 (BIA 1981).

[110] *See Uritsky v. Gonzales*, 399 F.3d 728, 735 (6th Cir. 2005) (comparing juvenile delinquency proceedings with youthful offender proceedings; the former does not result in a "conviction" for immigration purposes, whereas the latter type of adjudication does result in a final "conviction").

[111] *Singh v. Att'y Gen.*, 561 F.3d 1275 (11th Cir. 2009).

It would appear axiomatic that because an individual does not have a "conviction" by reason of a delinquency adjudication, and therefore cannot be deported, he or she cannot be denied admission based on a "reason to believe" that criminal activity has occurred. However, this particular issue is not clarified by immigration case law. In practice, immigration adjudicators have been known to deny residency based on a "reason to believe" that the person has been involved in drug trafficking, for example, even though the applicant was adjudicated delinquent and not convicted of any offense. Conceivably, an LPR with an old delinquency adjudication could, upon returning to the United States from a trip abroad, be detained and removed based on the "reason to believe" provisions.[112] It is simply not clear that the juvenile delinquency precedent encompasses immigration provisions that do not turn on the existence of a "conviction."

In addition, and outside the context of the definition of "conviction," the BIA and the courts have considered juvenile delinquency convictions in adjudicating applications for discretionary relief, denying benefits based on the underlying activity as evidence of bad character.[113]

Jurisprudence outside the immigration law context may be helpful in arguing that a juvenile delinquency adjudication (or the underlying activity) cannot form the basis of a finding that someone is inadmissible. Completely aside from this factual denial, however, is the technical issue of whether a minor is able to form the mental intent to participate in crime—any crime, including drug trafficking. The jurisprudence behind juvenile statutes is the sound theory that minors, who are in the biological process of forming character, intellect, personality, and values, are unable to form the requisite mental intent to fully understand the criminality of their actions.

Scientific research shows that adolescents cannot "choose" to disobey laws in the same way that adults do. Research on teenage brains made possible by new technology shows that normal adolescent brains are immature—especially in the areas of the brain that "govern control of impulsivity, judgment, planning for the future, foresight of consequences, and other characteristics that make people morally culpable."[114] In other words, "basic anatomy makes juveniles more impetuous."[115]

The American Medical Association wrote recently in an amicus brief to the U.S. Supreme Court:

---

[112] *See* INA §§212(a)(2)(C), (I); 8 USC §§1182(a)(2)(C), (I).

[113] *See, e.g., Wallace v. Gonzales,* 463 F.3d 135 (2d Cir. 2006) (BIA did not abuse its discretion in considering underlying facts of juvenile delinquency adjudication as basis to deny adjustment of status).

[114] E. Hirsch, *et al.*, "'Raise the Age'—Return 17-Year-Olds to Juvenile Court," 80 *Wis. Law.* (June 2007) (citing National Institute of Mental Health, "Teenage Brain: A Work in Progress," NIH Publication No. 01-4929, Apr. 3, 2004.

[115] E. Hirsch, *et al., id.*

The adolescent's mind works different from ours. Parents know it. This court has said it. Legislatures have presumed it for decades or more. And now, new scientific evidence sheds light on the differences.[116]

Based on this anatomical perspective, treating juveniles differently from adults in the criminal justice system is not just good policy (*i.e.*, ameliorative or rehabilitative), but also scientifically appropriate.

The Supreme Court has indeed recognized a constitutional distinction between youths and adults in all areas of the law, civil and criminal. For example, in *Roper v. Simmons*,[117] the Court held that juveniles under the age of 18 are categorically different from adults and cannot be subjected to the death penalty. The Court cited three general differences between minors and adults:

- Lack of maturity and an underdeveloped sense of responsibility. Immature qualities result in impetuous and ill-considered actions and decisions.
- Juveniles are more vulnerable or susceptible to negative influences and pressures.
- The character of a juvenile is not as well formed as that of an adult. The personality traits of juveniles are more transitory, less fixed.[118]

In American society, most laws recognize 18 as the age at which people are old enough to make thoughtful choices and understand the significance of their actions. Minors cannot sign contracts, make wills, or serve on juries, and cannot smoke, drink alcohol, or (without parental consent) join the army, have an abortion, or even get a tattoo. Minors are not allowed to own a weapon. And they are not allowed to vote. These arguments, taken from criminal law and the field of psychology, may be helpful in convincing either the IJ or DHS that the acts of a juvenile should not be held against him or her in the immigration law context.

Other juvenile acts

In addition to jurisprudence on adjudications of delinquency, the INA states that an individual is not inadmissible for a crime involving moral turpitude committed when the alien was under 18 years of age, and the crime was committed (and the individual released from confinement) more than five years prior to the application for a visa, documentation, or admission.[119] Similarly, in the context of visa processing, an individual is not ineligible to receive a visa under INA §212(a)(2)(A)(i)(I) for one crime only, if the crime involving moral turpitude occurred prior to the applicant's

---

[116] AMA Amicus Brief, *Roper v. Simmons*, 543 U.S. 551 (2005).

[117] *Roper v. Simmons*, 543 U.S. 551 (2005).

[118] *See* E. Hirsch, *et al.*, "'Raise the Age'—Return 17-Year-Olds to Juvenile Court," 80 Wis. Law. (June 2007) (citing National Institute of Mental Health, "Teenage Brain: A Work in Progress," NIH Publication No. 01-4929, Apr. 3, 2004 (discussing *Roper* and *Bellotti v. Baird*, 443 U.S. 622, 634 (1979)).

[119] INA §212(a)(2)(A)(ii)(I).

15th birthday; or occurred between the applicant's 15th and 18th birthdays unless the crime involved violence and the individual was tried as an adult.[120] The exception for crimes involving moral turpitude committed under the age of 18 does not apply in the case of multiple crimes.[121]

Foreign Convictions

A foreign conviction is a "conviction" for immigration purposes. However, the reader will recall there is a distinction between having a conviction, and having a conviction for a crime that makes someone inadmissible or deportable (for example, a crime involving moral turpitude). The conviction must be for conduct that is deemed criminal by U.S. standards. In other words, the underlying criminal activity must be forbidden by U.S. law.[122] This precedent was recently reaffirmed by the BIA, in dicta, in a case dealing with the burden of proof in criminal proceedings.[123] The BIA will determine whether a foreign disposition constitutes a conviction for a crime involving moral turpitude or some other classification of crime by referring to its U.S. counterpart and considering both statutory and constitutional factors.[124]

For example, in *Matter of Ramirez-Rivero*,[125] the applicant had been convicted of a burglary in Cuba when he was 13 years old. Because a 13-year-old charged with burglary in the United States would have been adjudicated as a juvenile delinquent, the Cuban disposition was not considered a "conviction" under the purview of immigration law.

Certain grounds of inadmissibility or removability depend on the length of sentence imposed. When reviewing the consequences of a foreign conviction, the sentence imposed by the foreign jurisdiction does not govern. Rather, U.S. standards govern in determining whether an offense committed in a foreign country is a felony or a misdemeanor within the meaning of the INA.[126] More precisely, the foreign offense is examined in light of the maximum punishment imposable for an equivalent crime according to the U.S. Code or, if there is no federal counterpart, a comparable

---

[120] 22 CFR §40.21(a)(2).

[121] 22 CFR §40.21(a)(3).

[122] *Matter of McNaughton*, 16 I&N Dec. 569 (BIA 1978). *McNaughton* and other cases on "foreign convictions" were discussed and reaffirmed by the BIA in dicta in *Matter of Eslamizar*, 23 I&N Dec. 684, 689 (BIA 2004). *See also* 22 CFR §40.21(a)(1) (whether a crime involves moral turpitude for purposes of visa issuance/admissibility must be determined based on "moral standards generally prevailing in the United States.").

[123] *Matter of Eslamizar*, 23 I&N Dec. 684 (BIA 2004).

[124] *Matter of Dillingham*, 21 I&N Dec. 1001 (BIA 1997).

[125] *Matter of Ramirez-Rivero*, 18 I&N Dec. 135 (BIA 1981).

[126] *Matter of De La Nues*, 18 I&N Dec. 140 (BIA 1981) (citing *Soetarto v. INS*, 516 F.2d 778 (7th Cir. 1975), *Giammario v. Hurney*, 311 F.2d 285 (3d Cir. 1962), and *Matter of Scarpulla*, 15 I&N Dec. 139 (BIA 1974)).

offense in the District of Columbia Code.[127] A felony is an offense punishable by death or imprisonment for a term exceeding one year; any other offense is a misdemeanor.[128]

In *Matter of Adamo*,[129] the BIA held that the individual's Italian conviction for "aggravated embezzlement" did not qualify for the INA's petty-offense exception[130] because, under the District of Columbia Code, the comparable crime of "embezzlement by executors or other fiduciaries" was punishable by a possible sentence of 10 years in jail.

Finally, it is not necessary that a foreign jurisdiction's procedures comport with American standards of due process or constitutionality.[131] However, in the context of visa processing abroad, a conviction for a crime involving moral turpitude entered in absentia does not constitute a conviction within the meaning of INA §212a(2)(A)(i)(I).[132]

Proof of Convictions

The INA contains a list of the different types of documents that are acceptable in removal proceedings before an IJ to determine whether a conviction exists. INA §§240(c)(3)(B) and (C) [8 USC §§1229a(3)(B) and (C)] state as follows:

(B) Proof of convictions.—[A]ny of the following documents or records (or a certified copy of such an official document or record) shall constitute proof of a criminal conviction:

(i) An official record of judgment and conviction.

(ii) An official record of plea, verdict, and sentence.

(iii) A docket entry from court records that indicates the existence of the conviction.

(iv) Official minutes of a court proceeding or a transcript of a court hearing in which the court takes notice of the existence of the conviction.

(v) An abstract of a record of conviction prepared by the court in which the conviction was entered, or by a State official associated with the State's repository of criminal justice records, that indicates the charge or section of law violated, the disposition of the case, the existence and date of conviction, and the sentence.

---

[127] *Matter of De La Nues*, 18 I&N Dec. 140 (BIA 1981).

[128] *Matter of De La Nues*, 18 I&N Dec. 140 (BIA 1981).

[129] *Matter of Adamo*, 10 I&N Dec. 593 (BIA 1964).

[130] See chapter six.

[131] *U.S. v. Balsys*, 524 U.S. 666 (1998); *Matter of Linnas*, 19 I&N Dec. 302 (BIA 1985).

[132] 21 CFR §§40.21(a)(4), 40.22(b).

(vi) Any document or record prepared by, or under the direction of, the court in which the conviction was entered that indicates the existence of a conviction.

(vii) Any document of record attesting to the conviction that is maintained by an official of a State or Federal penal institution, which is the basis for that institution's authority to assume custody of the individual named in the record.

(C) Electronic Records.—In any proceeding under this Act, any record of conviction or abstract that has been submitted by electronic means to the Service from a State or court shall be admissible as evidence to prove a criminal conviction if it is—

(i) certified by a State official associated with the State's repository of criminal justice records as an official record from its repository or by a court official from the court in which the conviction was entered as an official record from its repository, and

(ii) certified in writing by a Service official as having been received electronically from the State's record repository or the court's record repository.

A certification under clause (i) may be by means of a computer-generated signature and statement of authenticity.

Suspensions of Sentence

It may seem that a discussion of sentence suspension may not naturally fall under the topic of "conviction"; however, the second paragraph of INA §101(a)(48) [8 USC §1101(a)(48)] addresses the immigration effects of a suspended sentence. Essentially, a suspension of the sentence imposed is not honored by immigration law. Under INA §101(a)(48)(B), a sentence that has been suspended in whole or in part is still considered to be the sentence imposed.[133]

It is important for criminal defense and immigration attorneys alike to be aware that a suspension of sentence is not effective in "reducing" the sentence, so to speak, for immigration law purposes. Several provisions within the INA, such as the definition of "aggravated felony," the grounds of removability and inadmissibility, and even the petty-offense exception, turn on the length of the sentence imposed (*e.g.*, a crime of violence is an "aggravated felony" when the sentence imposed can be at least one year of imprisonment).

---

[133] INA §101(a)(48)(B) states, "Any reference to a term of imprisonment or a sentence with respect to an offense is deemed to include the period of incarceration or confinement ordered by a court of law regardless of any suspension of the imposition or execution of that imprisonment or sentence in whole or in part."

Because of INA §101(a)(48)(B), the suspension of a sentence is not relevant for determining the sentence actually imposed for immigration purposes. The practical effects of this provision will be discussed in chapter five.

APPENDIX 2A

MOTION TO VACATE PLEA, JUDGMENT, AND SENTENCE

IN THE CIRCUIT COURT OF
THE 11TH JUDICIAL CIRCUIT
OF FLORIDA, IN AND FOR
DADE COUNTY, FLORIDA

CRIMINAL DIVISION

THE STATE OF FLORIDA,   CASE NO. [ ]
              JUDGE: [ ]
   Plaintiff,

vs.   **SWORN MOTION TO VACATE**
           PLEA, JUDGMENT AND SENTENCE
[NAME],

a.k.a. [NAME],

   Defendant.
_____/

Defendant, [NAME], a.k.a. [NAME], by and through undersigned counsel, files this Sworn Motion to Vacate Plea, Judgment and Sentence pursuant to F.R.C.P. 3.850 and, in support thereof, states as follows:

   1)   On [DATE], in the Circuit Court of the Eleventh Judicial Circuit of Florida in and for Dade County, Defendant entered a plea of guilty to the crimes of [CRIMES INVOLVING MORAL TURPITUDE].

   2)   Pursuant to this plea, adjudication was withheld, and Defendant was sentenced to one year of probation.

3) Florida Rule of Criminal Procedure 3.172(c)(8) states that before accepting a plea of guilty or nolo contendere, a trial judge **shall** warn a defendant as follows:

> that if he or she pleads guilty or nolo contendere the trial judge must inform him or her that, if he or she is not a United States citizen, the plea may subject him or her to deportation pursuant to the laws and regulations governing the United States Immigration and Naturalization Service. It shall not be necessary for the trial judge to inquire as to whether the defendant is a United States citizen, as this admonition shall be given to all defendants in all cases.

4) The deportation warning pursuant to F.R.C.P. 3.172(c)(8) became mandatory on January 1, 1989. See *In re: Amendments to Florida Rules of Criminal Procedure, 536 So.2d 992 (Fla. 1988)*.

5) Defendant is a native and citizen of [COUNTRY]. The Department of Homeland Security granted her Temporary Protected Status on [DATE].

6) At the time of her plea, Defendant was not advised of the possible immigration consequences as required by Rule 3.172(c)(8) Fla. R. Crim. P. The judge did not advise Defendant that if she was not a United States citizen, her plea could subject her to deportation under the laws of the Immigration and Nationality Act. *See* Exhibit 1, Transcript of Case No. [ ].

7) On or about [DATE], the Department of Homeland Security provided notice to Defendant indicating that based on said conviction, her lawful status in the United States as a beneficiary of Temporary Protected Status would be withdrawn pursuant to section 212(a)(2)(A)(i)(I) of the Immigration and Nationality Act, as amended, as an alien who has been convicted of, or who admits having committed, or who admits committing acts which constitute the essential elements of a crime in-

volving moral turpitude (other than a purely political offense) or an attempt or conspiracy to commit such a crime. *See* Exhibit 2, Notice To Appear.

8) Consequently, Defendant will be required to appear before an Immigration Judge and if she cannot defend herself from the charges subjecting her to removal from the United States or if she cannot submit any applications from relief from removal, she will be deported from this country. *See id.*

9) Prior to receiving notice from the Department of Homeland Security, Defendant was not aware that her earlier plea in criminal matters would result in immigration consequences.

10) Had Defendant been advised of immigration consequences as required by Rule 3.12(c)(8) prior to entering the plea, she would not have accepted a plea in this case. Thus, Defendant's plea was involuntary and obtained in violation of her procedural due process rights.

11) Defendant did not receive the mandatory immigration warnings from the Circuit Court judge. *See* Exh. 1. Specifically, after placing Defendant under oath, the judge did not address Defendant *personally* to inform her that the plea may subject her to deportation. *See id.* Although the judgment indicates that Defendant entered a plea of guilty, the record is void of evidence, such as a signature or written initials, that Defendant was personally informed, in a language she understood, of any type of warning actually pronounced by the judge. Therefore, there is no convincing evidence that Defendant at any time received proper warnings as required by law.

12) If Defendant's conviction in the instant case is vacated, she will not necessarily be subject to removal from the United States as she will be eligible to maintain Temporary Protected Status.

13) Based on the foregoing procedural defect in the underlying criminal proceedings, Defendant's plea, judgment and sentence should be vacated. Rule 3.172(c)(8) Fla. R. Crim. P.; *State v. Green*, 944 So. 2d 208 (Fla. 2006); *Peart v. State*, 756 So.2d 42 (Fla. 2000) (stating defendant is entitled to relief where failure to comply with Rule 3.172(c)(8) and resulting prejudice is shown); *See also State v. Lindo*, 863 So.2d 1237 (Fla. 4th DCA 2003) (stating defendant was entitled to relief under rule 3.172(c)(8) based on his testimony that he was never provided advice by the court or his attorney and that he was prejudiced by that lack of advice because he was facing deportation).

14) Defendant did not appeal from the [DATE], adjudication of guilt in this case and she has not filed any previous post-conviction motions.

WHEREFORE, for the above and foregoing, Defendant respectfully moves this Court to vacate the plea, judgment, and sentence in the above-styled cause.

Dated: _____ day of _____, 20_____.

Respectfully submitted,
[ATTORNEY NAME]
[ADDRESS]
[CITY, STATE ZIP]

By:_____
    [ATTORNEY NAME]
    Fla. Bar No. _____

Under penalty of perjury, I swear that I have read the foregoing Sworn Motion To Vacate Plea, Judgment, and Sentence in Case No. [XXXXXXX], in the Circuit Court of the Eleventh Judicial Circuit of Florida, in and for Dade County, Florida, and the facts stated therein are true.

_____   _____
[NAME]   [Date]

Sworn and subscribed before me this ____day of _____, 20_____.

_____
Notary Public

_____Identification Produced

       Type:_____
OR

_____Personally Known

CERTIFICATE OF SERVICE

    I HEREBY CERTIFY that a true and correct copy of the above and foregoing, was mailed by placing a true copy thereof enclosed in a sealed envelope, with postage thereon fully prepaid and depositing the same with the United States Postal Service for delivery to the person at the address set forth below.

State Attorney's Office
1350 NW 12th Ave.
Miami, FL 33136-2111

I declare under penalty of perjury that the foregoing is true and correct. Executed on this ____ day of _____, 20___.

By:_____
    [ATTORNEY NAME]
    [ADDRESS]
    [CITY, STATE ZIP]

APPENDIX 2B

Padilla Motion to Vacate Plea, Judgment, and Sentence

IN THE CIRCUIT COURT OF
THE 11TH JUDICIAL CIRCUIT
OF FLORIDA, IN AND FOR
DADE COUNTY, FLORIDA
CRIMINAL DIVISION

THE STATE OF FLORIDA,

    Plaintiff,

vs.

[NAME],

a.k.a., [NAME]

    Defendant.

_____/

CASE NO. [XXXXXX]
JUDGE: [XXXXXXX]

SWORN MOTION TO VACATE PLEA, JUDGMENT AND SENTENCE

Defendant, [NAME], a.k.a. [NAME], by and through undersigned counsel, files this Sworn Motion to Vacate Plea, Judgment and Sentence pursuant to F.R.C.P. 3.850 and, in support thereof, states as follows:

    1) On [DATE], in the Circuit Court of the Eleventh Judicial Circuit of Florida, in and for Dade County, Defendant entered a plea of guilty to the crimes of [AGGRAVATED FELONY].

    2) Pursuant to this plea, adjudication was withheld, and Defendant was sentenced to one year and one day of incarceration.

3) Florida Rule of Criminal Procedure 3.172(c)(8) states that before accepting a plea of guilty or nolo contendere, a trial judge **shall** warn a defendant as follows:

that if he or she pleads guilty or nolo contendere the trial judge must inform him or her that, if he or she is not a United State citizen, the plea may subject him or her to deportation pursuant to the laws and regulations governing the United States Immigration and Naturalization Service. It shall not be necessary for the trial judge to inquire as to whether the defendant is a United States citizen, as this admonition shall be given to all defendants in all cases.

4) The deportation warning pursuant to F.R.C.P. 3.172(c)(8) became mandatory on January 1, 1989. See *In re: Amendments to Florida Rules of Criminal Procedure, 536 So.2d 992 (Fla. 1988)*.

5) Defendant is a native and citizen of [COUNTRY]. The Department of Homeland Security granted her lawful permanent residency on [DATE].

6) Pursuant to Rule 3.172(c)(8) Fla. R. Crim. P., the judge did advise Defendant at the time of her plea that if she was not a United States citizen, her plea could subject her to deportation under the laws of the Immigration and Nationality Act. This was not prejudicial. *See* Exhibit 1, Transcript of Case No. [ ].

7) However, in contrast, the warning, both as written and as delivered to Defendant, was an inadequate representation of the actual consequence of Defendant's plea: certain deportation. Thus, the Florida colloquy served as an inadequate prophylactic measure to cure

constitutionally ineffective counsel, who also failed to properly assess and counsel Defendant regarding the obvious and certain consequences of her plea, as per *Padilla v. Kentucky*, 559 U.S. 356 (2010). *See Hernandez v. State,* 124 So. 3d 757 (Fla. 2012). Therefore, the Sixth Amendment violation remains clear.

8) On or about date, the Department of Homeland Security (DHS) served a Notice to Appear initiating Removal Proceedings against Defendant, and alleged her deportability based upon the instant convictions, considered "aggravated felonies" as "crime(s) of violence," pursuant to Immigration and Nationality Act ("INA") § 237(a)(2)(A)(iii). *See* Exhibit 2, Notice To Appear.

9) Consequently, Defendant will be required to appear before an Immigration Judge and if she cannot defend herself from the charges subjecting her to removal from the United States or if she cannot submit any applications from relief from removal, she will be deported from the United States. *See id.*

10) Prior to receiving notice from the Department of Homeland Security, Defendant was not aware that her earlier plea in criminal matters would result in immigration consequences, much less "aggravated felony" treatment that would mandate deportation and foreclose any availability for discretionary relief.

11) Defendant presents evidence of her eligibility to vacate her conviction pursuant to *Padilla v. Kentucky, supra*, because her prior counsel's performance was constitutionally deficient, by failing to properly advise Defendant of the obvious immigration consequences of a plea of guilty to the crimes of [AGGRAVATED FELONY]. Defendant was prejudiced by her attorney's deficient performance because this conviction made her deportation presumptively mandatory and served as a statutory bar to all forms of discretionary immigration relief at the time it was completed. Defendant's criminal attorney neither made proper determination of, nor conveyed to Defendant, these precise and obvious immigration consequences flowing from her conviction.

12) Had Defendant been advised of immigration consequences, as required under *Padilla v. Kentucky*, she would not have accepted a plea in this case. Thus, Defendant's plea was involuntary and obtained in violation of her procedural due process rights.

13) If Defendant's conviction in the instant case is vacated, she will not be subject to mandatory removal from the United States as she will be eligible to re-claim her lawful permanent resident status.

14) Defendant did not appeal from the [DATE], adjudication of guilt in this case and she has not filed any previous post-conviction motions.

WHEREFORE, for the above and foregoing, Defendant respectfully moves this Court to vacate the plea, judgment, and sentence in the above-styled cause.
Dated: _____ day of _____, 20____.

                                        Respectfully submitted,
                                        [ATTORNEY NAME]
                                        [ADDRESS]
                                        [CITY, STATE ZIP]

                                        By:_____
                                                  [ATTORNEY NAME]
                                                  Fla. Bar No. _____

Under penalty of perjury, I swear that I have read the foregoing Sworn Motion To Vacate Plea, Judgment, and Sentence in Case No. [XXXXXXX], in the Circuit Court of the Eleventh Judicial Circuit of Florida, in and for Dade County, Florida, and the facts stated therein are true.

_____   _____
[NAME]   [Date]

Sworn and subscribed before me this ____ day of _____,
20_____.

_____
Notary Public

_____ Identification Produced

       Type:_____
OR

_____ Personally Known

CERTIFICATE OF SERVICE

    I HEREBY CERTIFY that a true and correct copy of the above and foregoing, was mailed by placing a true copy thereof enclosed in a sealed envelope, with postage thereon fully prepaid and depositing the same with the United States Postal Service for delivery to the person at the address set forth below.

State Attorney's Office
1350 NW 12th Ave.
Miami, FL 33136-2111

I declare under penalty of perjury that the foregoing is true and correct. Executed on this _____ day of _____, 20___.

By:_____
    [ATTORNEY NAME]
    [ADDRESS]
    [CITY, STATE ZIP]

CHAPTER THREE

CONSEQUENCES OF CRIMINAL ACTIVITY: REMOVAL FROM THE UNITED STATES

Inadmissibility	98
Deportability	104
Expedited Removal of Certain Aggravated Felons	107
Detention	110
Re-entering After Removal: Criminal Prosecution and Reinstatement of Removal	111
How the Government Locates Your Client	115

Appendices

    3A: Sample Memorandum of Law in Support of Motion to Terminate 121

    3B: Sample Motion to Terminate Based on Improper Designation as Arriving Alien 128

The Immigration and Nationality Act (INA) contains two major sections that impose immigration law sanctions for crimes. INA §212(a) [8 USC §1182(a)] lists the grounds of *inadmissibility* for crimes. INA §237(a) [8 USC §1227(a)] lists the classes of non–American citizens *deportable* for crimes. Both of these sections fall under the larger canopy of *removability*: persons who can be *removed* from the United States for criminal activity. The concept of *removability* was introduced with the Illegal Immigration Reform and Immigrant Responsibility Act of 1996 (IIRAIRA).[1] A person who is inadmissible is subject to removal proceedings; likewise, a person who is deportable for a crime is subject to removal proceedings. However, as discussed below, the grounds of *inadmissibility* have application in many areas besides simply removal proceedings.

Recent years have seen significant litigation surrounding a seemingly simple term: *admission*. The term "admission" appears throughout the Immigration and Nationality Act. Whether an "admission" has occurred determines which chapter of removability applies: inadmissibility (§212(a)) or deportability (§237). In turn, which section applies may make the difference between mandatory detention, or liberty pending proceedings and in between expedited removal, or a full hearing before a neutral immigration judge; indeed, the question of whether an "admission" transpired will frequently determine whether a non–American citizen is even exposed to removal. At the same time, the factual question of an "admission" will determine whether an individual is eligible for relief: adjustment of status, cancellation of removal, or a §212(h) waiver. Only the asylum genre of relief does not ask whether there has been an admission. The amount of case law at both federal courts and the Board of Immigration

---

[1] Illegal Immigration Reform and Immigrant Responsibility Act of 1996 (IIRAIRA), Division C of the Omnibus Appropriations Act of 1996 (H.R. 3610), Pub. L. No. 104-208, 110 Stat. 3009.

Appeals (BIA) is frankly daunting, and the level of disagreement among judges is high. For decades, there was little controversy; the judiciary and the bar accepted the BIA's interpretation without a whimper. Today, defining the elusive term "admission" is both challenging and crucial in the practice of immigration law. As the reader will see, the discussion threads its way throughout the chapters of this book.

Inadmissibility

The Applications of INA §212(a)(2)(A)

Knocking at the door

INA §212(a) [8 USC §1182] lists all grounds (not just criminal grounds) for denying a person admission into the United States. INA §212(a)(2) covers the criminal grounds of inadmissibility. In theory, the term "admissibility" applies to persons seeking to enter the United States. However, there is more than just one door; a non–American citizen may be viewed as "seeking admission" in a variety of legal circumstances. For example, persons who are outside the United States and submit an application for an immigrant or nonimmigrant visa at an American embassy are subject to the grounds of inadmissibility at INA §212(a). Admissibility also applies to persons who have arrived at a port of entry, such as a seaport, airport, or land port, who seek to come into the United States. These may be individuals with temporary visas, lawful permanent residents (LPRs) returning from abroad, or persons with no documentation at all.

It is important to note that a long-time LPR returning from a trip outside the United States is potentially subject to the grounds of inadmissibility, just as is a person coming to this country for the very first time. Thus, the concept of "inadmissibility" refers to non–American citizens who are not in the United States, but seek to come in at any time.

Additionally, the grounds of inadmissibility contained at §212(a) apply in certain circumstances to persons who are already physically within the United States, but seek to "improve" their status; for example, by adjusting from nonimmigrant to immigrant (*i.e.*, LPR) status. Adjustment applicants, though already physically within the United States, are knocking at the door in the sense that they want to obtain a new status. In turn, an LPR may want to naturalize to U.S. citizenship; this requires "good moral character,"[2] whose definition references grounds of inadmissibility.

The categories of persons to whom inadmissibility may apply are summarized below. (Reference to chapter one of this book and the different statuses noted there may be helpful.)

---

[2] Defined at 8 U.S. Code (USC) §1101(f); Immigration and Nationality Act (INA) §101(f).

Applicants for admission

Perhaps the most fundamental application of §212(a) is the situation of a non–American citizen seeking admission at a port of entry, which can be an airport, seaport, land border, or pre-flight inspection (at an airport abroad). A non–American citizen, even one holding a valid nonimmigrant (*i.e.*, temporary) visa or other entry document, may be denied admission at a port on account of a criminal conviction, or suspected criminal *activity*. The exact grounds of inadmissibility are discussed in chapter nine of this book. The lesson here is that even a client with valid documents—for example, a client recently issued a visa by an American consul in his or her home country—is subject to renewed scrutiny at a port of entry. (For this reason, it is important to reveal potential grounds of inadmissibility at the consulate and seek a waiver, rather than hoping that criminal activity will simply not come to light during the admission process.)

When an LPR seeks admission

It is clear and understandable that a non–American citizen holding a nonimmigrant visa is potentially subject to charges of inadmissibility at a port of entry. It is harder to understand, however, that an individual who has lawful permanent resident status (a green card holder) may be subject to a finding of inadmissibility and placed in removal proceedings—charged under INA §212(a)—on return from what may only have been a brief trip abroad. There is a sentiment that an LPR who has resided lawfully in the United States for years and has strong ties to the community should not be viewed in the same light as a nonimmigrant visa holder (perhaps a tourist coming to the United States for the first time), but rather should have greater rights or protection.

This issue is important because the provisions of "deportability," which apply to persons who are deemed to be within the United States (and not seeking admission) are distinct from the provisions of "inadmissibility." More often than not, it is better to be subject to deportability under INA §237. An individual with a criminal record charged with "deportability" has a right to a bond hearing, for example, and INA §237 (relating to deportability) is not as broad-sweeping as INA §212(a) when it comes to actions that constitute a crime.

The *Fleuti* Doctrine

Prior to the passage of IIRAIRA, the INA distinguished LPRs arriving at a port of entry from a trip abroad from other non–American citizens (with a lesser status) for purposes of the question of admission. The pre-1996 INA contained a provision at §212(a)(13) [8 USC §1101(a)(13)] that defined "entry"; under this section, an LPR was not regarded as making an entry into the United States if he or she could show that the absence was not reasonably intended to constitute a break in residency status, or was not voluntary. Under U.S. Supreme Court precedent, *Rosenberg v. Fleuti*, this provision was interpreted to mean that an LPR does not effectuate an "entry" following a brief, casual, and innocent trip abroad.[3] Only return from a trip abroad that was meaningfully interruptive of permanent residence status in the United States would be viewed as a re-entry.

As a procedural matter, an LPR returning from a trip abroad who was charged in exclusion proceedings could file a motion to terminate the case in immigration court, arguing that his or her trip was "brief, casual and innocent." If the motion was granted, the legacy Immigration and Naturalization Service (INS) would have to re-charge the case in deportation proceedings; oftentimes, the criminal activity that formed the basis of exclusion proceedings could not be charged in deportation proceedings. This is because, again, the grounds under INA §212(a) are distinct from the grounds of deportability (prior to the 1996 legislation, under INA §241; after 1996, under INA §237).[4] The classifications of crime are discussed in chapters six, seven, and eight.

Thus, prior to the legislative changes of 1996, and based on the *Fleuti* doctrine, an LPR returning from a short trip outside the United States did not face grounds of inadmissibility (then referred to as "excludability"). Instead, a successful motion to terminate proceedings based on the *Fleuti* doctrine often resulted in an individual avoiding deportation altogether.

Today, an LPR who has a criminal conviction entered after April 1, 1997, and who travels abroad is deemed to be an arriving alien subject to inspection upon return, along with all other non–American citizens. In other words, a green card holder with a criminal conviction faces charges of inadmissibility upon return, just as does a nonimmigrant visa holder or someone with no visa at all. Such an individual does not lose his status immediately; a resident cannot be removed from a port of entry without consent. Rather, the re-entry is held in abeyance pending further inspection. This condition or status is perpetual until such time that a waiver is granted. If a waiver is required (because of a ground of inadmissibility), and the waiver is granted, the individual is re-admitted and returns to his permanent resident status (he is not "re-admitted" in terms of becoming a new permanent resident).

---

[3] *Rosenberg v. Fleuti*, 374 U.S. 449 (1963).

[4] By way of example, under INA §212(a) (inadmissibility grounds), a person who admits the commission of a crime can be removed from the United States; under INA §237(a) (the deportability grounds) an actual conviction is required. Under INA §212(a), an individual suspected of being involved in drug trafficking or money laundering can be removed from the United States; INA §237 requires an actual conviction. Also, although one offense of simple possession of less than 30 grams of marijuana is a basis for inadmissibility/excludability, it does not render someone subject to deportation. In addition, when charged as an arriving alien under INA §212(a), determinations of custody versus bond are determined by the U.S. Department of Homeland Security (DHS), U.S. Immigration and Customs Enforcement (ICE), or U.S. Customs and Border Protection (CBP)); where a person is charged as deportable under INA §237, jurisdiction over a bond hearing lies with the immigration judge (IJ). These are just a few of the more notable nuances between INA §212(a) consequences and INA §237 consequences. These distinctions are discussed in chapter nine.

Congress purposefully eliminated the *Fleuti* doctrine in passing IIRAIRA. Section 101(a)(13) of the INA was amended by §301 of IIRAIRA to read as follows:

(C) An alien lawfully admitted for permanent residence in the United States shall not be regarded as seeking an admission into the United States for purposes of the immigration laws unless the alien—

(i) has abandoned or relinquished that status,

(ii) has been absent from the United States for a continuous period in excess of 180 days,

(iii) has engaged in illegal activity after having departed the United States,

(iv) has departed from the United States while under legal process seeking removal of the alien from the United States, including removal proceedings under this Act and extradition proceedings,

(v) has committed an offense identified in section 212(a)(2), unless since such offense the alien has been granted relief under section 212(h) or 240A(a), or

(vi) is attempting to enter at a time or place other than as designated by immigration officers or has not been admitted to the United States after inspection and authorization by an immigration officer.

This statute, in the simplest of terms, means that an LPR with a criminal record may significantly jeopardize his or her legal position by traveling outside the United States. The *Fleuti* doctrine offered some protection by looking to the nature of the trip rather than to the existence of a criminal record. For those with post-April 1, 1997, convictions, this measure of protection no longer exists. Now, even a brief, casual, and innocent trip abroad exposes an LPR with a criminal record to removability and possible detention.

Supreme Court Finds IIRAIRA Amendment to §101(a)(13)(C) *Not* Retroactive

The *Fleuti* doctrine still survives for lawful permanent residents who were convicted prior to the effective date of IIRAIRA, April 1, 1997. In *Vartelas v. Holder*,[5] the Supreme Court found impermissible the retroactive application of the 1996 amendments to INA §101(a)(13)(C).

> ➢ **Tip**: An LPR with a criminal record may travel in and out of the United States several times, perhaps many times, without being stopped by Inspections (U.S. Customs and Border Protection (CBP)). These frequent admissions without incident may give the client a false sense of security. Every arrival at a border, every application for admission into the United States is a lottery; the 20th trip time may be the trip where a diligent officer catches the conviction record in the government's ever-

---

[5] *Vartelas v. Holder*, 132 S. Ct. 1479 (2012).

improving state-of-the-art computer database. It is important to advise clients that several trips in and out without incident are not a guarantee that no record exists in the system or that the client is immune from being detained for further inquiry.

BIA Speaks on the Burden of Proof. For lawful permanent residents with a post–April 1, 1997 conviction, the burden of proof rests with the U.S. Department of Homeland Security (DHS) (Immigration and Customs Enforcement (ICE) counsel) in immigration court proceedings to establish that a criterion of INA §101(a)(13)(C) exists. In *Matter of Rivens*,[6] the BIA considered the case of a returning LPR with a conviction for accessory after the fact to making materially false statements (18 USC §1001). DHS charged Rivens as an arriving alien on account of a conviction for a crime involving moral turpitude. Rivens contested the assertion that his offense qualified as a moral turpitude crime, and further argued that the burden of establishing its classification was with DHS. In other words, Rivens argued that he could not be treated as an inadmissible arriving alien unless DHS proved that the crime involved moral turpitude, thereby triggering application of INA §101(a)(13)(C)(v). The BIA agreed with the respondent, finding that in the case of a returning LPR, the burden of proof lies with the government to establish by clear and convincing evidence that the crime qualifies as a ground of inadmissibility.

Adjustment of status

Adjustment of status[7] refers to a *procedure* whereby someone applies to become a lawful permanent resident (green card holder) without leaving the United States. This procedure is utilized by many persons holding nonimmigrant visas, including those who are sponsored by a family member or by an employer, or who are eligible on some other basis, such as their professional skills or talents, or winning the visa lottery. Adjustment of status is also utilized by persons in asylum status, battered spouses, cooperating witnesses, and beneficiaries of country-specific legalization (amnesty) programs. Simply put, an individual who *on any basis* seeks to become an LPR without physically leaving the borders of the United States applies for "adjustment of status" with a U.S. Citizenship and Immigration Services (USCIS) office in this country.

A person who seeks to become an LPR through adjustment of status must establish that he or she is not *inadmissible*.[8] An adjustment applicant who falls under the purview of one or more of the grounds of inadmissibility enumerated in INA §212(a) will be denied adjustment of status, unless he or she qualifies for and receives a waiv-

---

[6] *Matter of Rivens*, 25 I&N Dec. 623 (2011).

[7] Adjustment of status is authorized by statute at INA §245 [8 USC §1255].

[8] An applicant for adjustment of status is assimilated to the position of someone applying to enter this country as a lawful permanent resident (LPR) and is subject to the grounds of inadmissibility in the same manner as a person seeking a visa or arriving at a port of entry. *Matter of Smith*, 11 I&N Dec. 325 (BIA 1965).

er.[9] Accordingly, notwithstanding the fact that he or she is physically present in the United States, the adjustment of status applicant is scrutinized for "admissibility" under INA §212(a). He or she is effectively placed in the position of "knocking at the door."

Visa applicants at American consular posts abroad

The counterpart to adjustment of status is consular processing. An individual who is physically present in a foreign country applies for a visa—nonimmigrant or immigrant (permanent)—at an American consulate (usually, but not necessarily, in his or her home country). A consulate may be housed within an American embassy, but some consular posts are outside the city in which the main American embassy is located. When an individual applies for an immigrant or nonimmigrant visa to come to the United States, the grounds of inadmissibility at INA §212(a) apply to him or her. An individual who falls under the purview of one or more of the grounds of inadmissibility will be denied the visa, unless he or she qualifies for and receives a waiver.

Change of status

A person who enters the United States in one nonimmigrant status, such as tourist status, and files an application to change status to another nonimmigrant classification, such as investor, business professional, athlete, or entertainer (to name just a few), must establish that he or she is not "inadmissible" under INA §212(a). A person who applies to change his or her status and is determined to be "inadmissible" may be denied the change of status, and could be placed in removal proceedings.

Parolees

As discussed in chapter one, a person who has been paroled into the United States is not considered to be in a specific legal status. The statute says that a person who is paroled into the United States will not be considered to have been admitted.[10] Although the person's body is physically present, the legal fiction is that he or she is still arriving at a port of entry. If DHS commences removal proceedings, a parolee will face charges of inadmissibility under INA §212(a) as if he or she were still knocking at the front door, hoping to come in.

Persons physically present in violation of the law

Persons who entered the United States surreptitiously—the most common examples are those who enter (cross the border) without inspection—are perpetually in a state of "knocking at the door." They are referred to by law as applicants for admission. An individual who is located in the United States after having evaded inspection (physically present without an admission or parole) and is placed in removal proceedings will be charged as inadmissible under INA §212(a). Note that this is a somewhat recent change in the law. Prior to IIRAIRA, persons who entered without inspection

---

[9] Waivers are discussed in chapter ten.
[10] INA §101(a)(13)(B); 8 USC §1101(a)(13)(B).

were treated as persons who had "entered" and were subject to grounds of *deportability*—the same as those who had been lawfully inspected and admitted. IIRAIRA substituted the term "admission" for "entry," and changed the law to the extent that those who enter by illegally crossing the border are subject to the removal provisions that apply to persons seeking admission.

Temporary protected status

An individual who applies for temporary protected status in the United States must establish that he or she is not inadmissible under INA §§212(a)(2)(A), (B), and (C) [8 USC §§1182(a)(2)(A), (B), and (C)].[11]

Naturalization and "good moral character"

The grounds of inadmissibility apply in the context of persons applying for U.S. citizenship. To be eligible for naturalization, an applicant must establish a certain period of good moral character (usually five years, but there are certain exceptions).[12] "Good moral character" is defined at INA §101(f) [8 USC §1101(f)]. The definition of good moral character specifically references INA §212(a)(2)(A), regarding inadmissibility for certain crimes. A person who is inadmissible because he or she committed a crime during the requisite period of time (*e.g.*, five years prior to the naturalization application) will not be able to establish "good moral character" and will be denied naturalization. Note that an individual who admits criminal activity but has not been convicted on a charge relating to that activity will be treated the same under the law as an individual who has a final conviction (because of the language of INA §212(a)(2)(A)(i)—"or who admits having committed…."). Furthermore, an individual who applies for naturalization and is denied on account of a crime involving moral turpitude may be referred for removal proceedings based on the criminal convictions.

Deportability

INA §237(a)

The grounds of deportation are found at INA §237(a) [8 USC §1227(a)], *General Classes of Deportable Aliens*. A person who is charged with deportability under §237(a) is placed in removal proceedings before an immigration judge (IJ) (if not subject to an expedited removal procedure).[13] Again, the grounds of deportation apply to a person who has been formally admitted into the United States in some status,

---

[11] *See* INA §§244(c)(2)(A)(iii)(I), (II); 8 USC §§1254a(c)(2)(A)(iii)(I), (II). A single offense of simple possession of marijuana is excused. INA §244(c)(2)(A)(iii)(II); 8 USC §1254a(c)(2)(A)(iii)(II).

[12] INA §316(a)(3); 8 USC §1427(a)(3).

[13] Expedited removal is a procedure whereby an individual who is not a permanent resident and who has been convicted of an aggravated felony offense may be ordered removed by a government officer without an adversarial-type hearing in front of an immigration judge (IJ). *See* INA §238; 8 USC §1228.

be it immigrant or nonimmigrant. Most of the criminal-related grounds of deportability are found at INA §237(a)(2) [8 USC §1227(a)(2)].

Deportability vs. Inadmissibility

As discussed above, the grounds of inadmissibility contained at INA §212(a) are applied in various legal settings beyond simply removal proceedings. Section 212(a) applies to various types of applications for immigration benefits, and can be the basis of charges in removal proceedings (when the person is an arriving alien, a parolee, or a person who is physically present after evading formal inspection). In comparison, the grounds of deportability at INA §237 [8 USC §1227] apply in the specific context of a person who has been admitted to the United States (usually lawfully so), and is later charged with being here in violation of the law. The grounds of deportation at §237 do *not* apply to persons who are applying for a visa at an American consulate abroad; they do *not* apply to a visa holder at the inspections counter of an international airport; and they do *not* apply to someone seeking adjustment of status. The grounds of deportability apply once an individual is placed in removal proceedings, and then only if they have been formally admitted into the United States.

The distinction between inadmissibility under §212(a) and deportability under §237(a) is important precisely because the listed grounds in each section *are* different. The consequences of a conviction for a person who has traveled outside the United States may vary from the consequences for a person with the same conviction who remains in the United States. Very often, the grounds of deportability pattern the grounds of inadmissibility. But not always; chapter nine of this book discusses the specific consequences of crimes, including inadmissibility and deportability. Sometimes, a person will be inadmissible for a crime, but not deportable. Other times, the reverse will be true. For example, simple personal possession of marijuana may make someone inadmissible, but not deportable—simply because of differences in sections 212(a) and 237(a). A firearms offense will make someone deportable (§237(a)), but not inadmissible (§212(a)).

It is because of this dichotomy that significant attention is given to an explanation of the different immigration statuses and legal procedures. A person's basis for being in the United States (the person's legal status or lack thereof) determines which section of the INA will apply if he or she is in removal proceedings. A client's goals or plans in terms of the immigration law will also determine which sections of law an attorney should be concerned with.

> **Example**: In the year 2008, Gloria Rodriguez, an LPR, seeks a consultation on naturalization to U.S. citizenship. In the attorney's waiting room, on her intake sheet, she writes: *I would like to become a U.S. citizen.* Gloria adjusted to permanent resident status in 1990. In 1995, she was arrested and ultimately received a withhold of adjudication for personal, simple possession of cocaine. The immigration attorney's analysis cannot be limited to whether Gloria is eligible for citizenship. He divides

his analysis into three categories, which he must now explain to the client:

(1) Is Gloria eligible for naturalization? Yes, she is. This analysis focuses on "good moral character," which is defined in large part by reference to INA §212(a). Gloria must show at least five years of good moral character. Gloria has been a lawful permanent resident for more than five years, and the most recent five years are coupled with "good moral character," *i.e.*, a clean record. The conviction falls outside this five-year time period.

(2) Is Gloria subject to deportation? Yes, she is. This portion of the analysis depends on INA §237. Gloria's conviction makes her amenable to removal proceedings. If she applies for citizenship, she will be placed in removal proceedings by USCIS.

(3) Once placed in removal, is Gloria eligible for a waiver? Fortunately, she is: she is eligible for a waiver under the pre-Antiterrorism and Effective Death Penalty Act of 1996 (AEDPA) INA §212(c) waiver.

So Gloria's dream of becoming a citizen—her purpose for being in the attorney's office—is muddled by issues that were not necessarily apparent to her.

And then there are the ancillary issues:

(4) Should Gloria travel? This question depends on Gloria's personal circumstances and is a decision she has to make, with guidance from the immigration attorney. Gloria can travel, but CBP Inspections will most likely detect the conviction in a database upon her return. Based on *Vartelas*,[14] because Gloria has a pre–April 1, 1997, conviction, the issue will become whether this trip was brief, casual, and innocent. If so, she is not subject to removal as an arriving alien and will not be charged with inadmissibility. However, the conviction will have come to light and she can be placed in removal proceedings after her entry. If placed in removal proceedings, she probably would not be detained, because she is not subject to mandatory detention[15] and it is a fairly minor conviction. However, if she is found to be inadmissible as an arriving alien, the immigration judge will not have jurisdiction over a bond.

(5) Can Gloria apply for a replacement green card? This question depends on INA §237. She can apply, but the biometrics procedure associated with the I-90 form to replace an expiring resident card will most likely reveal the

---

[14] *See Vartelas v. Holder*, 132 S. Ct. 1479 (2012), and the discussion of the *Fleuti* doctrine, above. This answer would change (and Gloria would be subject to the grounds of inadmissibility) if she had a post-April 1, 1997 conviction.

[15] Gloria is not subject to mandatory detention because it is assumed, with a 1995 conviction, that she was released from penal custody prior to October 8, 1998, the effective date for mandatory detention. This answer would change if she had been arrested and convicted after October 8, 1998.

conviction; USCIS will forward the file to ERO, and she will be placed in removal proceedings.

Of course in Gloria's situation, being placed in removal proceedings may be viewed as a welcome event, because she is eligible for a waiver. Removal proceedings give her the opportunity to resolve the matter of the criminal conviction by (hopefully) obtaining a waiver. She may then go on to apply for citizenship. In some jurisdictions—and by regulation—she can apply affirmatively for a §212(c) waiver, outside of the immigration court process, with USCIS. Affirmatively filing for a pre-AEDPA §212(c) waiver is discussed in chapter thirteen.

The point of this example is that an attorney's immigration-law analysis should take into consideration the client's goals, the possible risks of removal, the availability of a waiver or other relief from removal, and the likelihood of overall success. These answers require reference to both sections 212(a) and 237. A good consultation in Gloria's case will go far beyond the simple question: "Am I eligible for citizenship?"

Expedited Removal of Certain Aggravated Felons

Under INA §238(a) [8 USC §1228(a)], certain individuals who are convicted of aggravated felonies are not eligible for an immigration hearing before an independent judge. Removal without a hearing before an IJ is commonly referred to by DHS as "expedited removal"[16] or "administrative removal." (The use of these terms varies between jurisdictions.) When an individual is processed via expedited removal, he or she is deprived of the opportunity to apply for discretionary relief before an IJ (or any other officer). The only legal issue is whether the person's case meets the criteria for expedited removal. It is the government's choice whether to invoke expedited removal. In some jurisdictions, the authority is widely used to process and deport non–American citizens with criminal records; in other areas, expedited removal authority is generally not used. The trend, however, is that DHS will utilize expedited removal power to process "criminal aliens" more quickly.

An individual who is neither an LPR nor a conditional resident, and who has a final conviction for an aggravated felony, may be ordered removed by a designated officer. Pursuant to 8 CFR §§238.1(a), 1238.1(a), an officer of DHS[17] may determine whether the individual is indeed an aggravated felon and has never been admitted for

---

[16] In certain circumstances, nonimmigrants can be expeditiously removed at a port of entry if they are found inadmissible on noncriminal grounds. This is not the "expedited removal" discussed here. This discussion refers to administrative expedited removal of individuals deportable for criminal activity.

[17] The regulations have now been updated to reflect DHS titles.

lawful or conditional permanent residence. The statute and regulations contain a conclusive presumption of deportability.[18]

Upon determination of these facts, a Form I-851, Notice of Intent to Issue a Final Administrative Deportation Order, is issued to the non–American citizen. The individual has 10 calendar days within which to respond to the notice of intent; 13 days are allotted if the notice was mailed.[19] The written response is limited to rebutting: (1) that the conviction is final; (2) that the conviction is for an aggravated felony offense; or (3) that the person has not been admitted for permanent or conditional residence.[20] The response is not an opportunity to raise discretionary considerations; indeed, the entire process is based on the presumption that the individual is not eligible for any discretionary relief from removal.

According to regulations, the notice of intent must state the factual allegations and the conclusions of law (the legal basis for deportability as an aggravated felon).[21] The notice of intent will advise the individual of the right to counsel at no cost to the government, the right to request withholding of removal (based on a fear of persecution), and the right to examine the government's evidence.[22]

The fact that an individual may request the opportunity to review the government's evidence indicates that the evidence is *not* initially provided with the notice of intent. If the individual requests the opportunity to review the government's evidence, the government must provide it, and an additional 10 days (13 if mailed) must be given for the individual to furnish a final response.[23]

Following the response period, a designated DHS officer, other than the officer who issued the notice of intent, issues a final decision.[24] This deciding officer is the field director, chief patrol agent, or an individual designated for this function. A final determination of deportability must be based on clear, convincing, and unequivocal evidence of deportability.[25]

---

[18] INA §238(c); 8 USC §1228(c) ("An alien convicted of an aggravated felony shall be conclusively presumed to be deportable from the United States."); *see also* 8 CFR §§238.1(b)(1)(iv), 1238.1(b)(1)(iv).

[19] 8 CFR §§238.1(c)(1), 1238.1(c)(1).

[20] *See* 8 CFR §§238.1(c)(2)(i), 1238.1(c)(2)(i).

[21] 8 CFR §§238.1(b)(2)(i), 1238.1(b)(2)(i).

[22] 8 CFR §§238.1(b)(2)(i), 1238.1(b)(2)(i).

[23] 8 CFR §§238.1(c)(2)(ii), 1238.1(c)(2)(ii).

[24] *See* 8 CFR §§238.1(d), 1238.1(d).

[25] *See* 8 CFR §§238.1(d)(1), (2)(i), 1238.1(d)(1), (2)(i).

An individual ordered removed through the administrative removal process may file a petition for review to the federal courts of appeals within 14 days.[26] Neither the regulations nor the statute clarify what issues may be brought before the federal courts of appeals through a petition for review. Presumably, a petition for review would be limited to the fundamental statutory issue of whether the offense indeed qualifies as an aggravated felony under INA §101(a)(43). Again, there is no discretionary relief available in expedited removal proceedings.

At least two federal courts of appeals have upheld the constitutionality of the expedited removal process, finding that the federal courts have jurisdiction to review such orders for constitutional questions and errors of law; however, the courts cannot review the agency's underlying decision to utilize the procedure, or the ultimate decision to remove.[27]

In *Flores-Ledezma v. Gonzales*,[28] the U.S. Court of Appeals for the Fifth Circuit discussed expedited removal proceedings at length. *Flores-Ledezma* involved a non–American citizen with an aggravated felony conviction whose offense came to light when he applied for adjustment of status based on his marriage to an American citizen. Although Flores had an aggravated felony conviction (crime of violence),[29] the offense was waivable through INA §212(h). Rather than being granted adjustment of status, however, Flores received a Notice of Intent to Issue a Final Administrative Removal Order pursuant to INA §238(b). Flores's counsel formally requested—several times—that he be placed in general removal proceedings and allowed to proceed with adjustment of status before an IJ.

Nevertheless, within two months of receiving the notice, and five days after filing a petition for review,[30] Flores was physically removed to Mexico. Before the Fifth Circuit, Flores argued that expedited removal violates the Equal Protection Clause of the Fifth Amendment because, under the statute, the government has the discretion to choose *when* to utilize the procedure. This unfettered discretion, according to Flores, allows the government to discriminate between similarly situated classes of individuals. The court disagreed, finding that there is a rational basis to allow the government the ability to utilize expedited removal proceedings against certain non-LPRs with aggravated felony convictions.

---

[26] INA §238(b)(3); 8 USC §1228(b)(3); 8 CFR §§238.1(h), 1238.1(h). In *Flores-Ledezma v. Gonzales*, 415 F.3d 375 (5th Cir. 2005), the court found that the appeal period is 30 days, pursuant to INA §242(b)(1). *Flores-Ledezma* is discussed at length below.

[27] *Graham v. Mukasey*, 519 F.3d 546 (6th Cir. 2008); *Flores-Ledezma*, 415 F.3d at 375.

[28] *Flores-Ledezma*, 415 F.3d at 375.

[29] INA §101(a)(43)(F); 8 USC §1101(a)(43)(F).

[30] The petition for review went forward, although Mr. Flores had been removed from the United States.

Relief from Expedited Removal

There are several ways to either contest or avoid expedited removal. One is to argue that the offense is not an aggravated felony under INA §101(a)(43) [8 USC §1101(a)(43)]. If the deciding officer finds that there is a genuine issue as to deportability (such as whether the offense constitutes an aggravated felony), the officer may initiate traditional removal proceedings before the immigration court.[31] In addition, there may be rare situations in which an individual has a claim to LPR status; expedited removal applies only to non-LPRs. Another method of avoiding expedited removal is to request relief from removal in the form of withholding based on a fear of persecution.[32] Finally, and as discussed in greater detail in chapter ten, non-LPRs with aggravated felony convictions may be eligible for relief in the form of adjustment of status, perhaps (if appropriate) in conjunction with an INA §212(h) waiver.[33]

To be clear, neither the statute nor the regulations require that DHS give an individual subject to expedited removal the opportunity for full immigration court proceedings, even if he or she is eligible for adjustment of status. (The individual in *Flores-Ledezma* tried this approach and failed.) However, an individual eligible for adjustment may be able to advocate successfully for the opportunity to seek relief in full immigration court proceedings. The regulations imply that the DHS officer making a final decision always has the discretion to refer the case for full removal proceedings.[34]

Detention

Mandatory Detention

Mandatory detention is a law that requires that most non–American citizens with crimes be detained without bond in immigration custody during their removal hearings. It does not apply in all cases; but for persons released from jail or prison after October 1998 who are removable for crime, the likelihood is that mandatory detention (no release/no bond during removal proceedings) will apply. It depends on the underlying ground of removal that is triggered by the particular crime(s). Mandatory detention, because it can leave an individual detained for extremely long periods of times (years even), is perhaps the most important (and negative) consequence for counsel to consider. Given this importance, chapter four of this book has been devoted to a full discussion of mandatory detention issues.

---

[31] 8 CFR §§238.1(d)(2)(ii), 1238.1(d)(2)(ii). *See also Flores-Ledezma v. Gonzales*, (5th Cir. June 27, 2005), *published on* AILA InfoNet at Doc. No. 05072167 (*posted* July 21, 2005).

[32] INA §241(b)(3); 8 USC §1231(b)(3). Withholding of removal is discussed in chapter ten.

[33] *Matter of Kanga*, 22 I&N Dec. 1206 (BIA 2000); *Matter of Michel*, 21 I&N Dec. 1101 (BIA 1998); *Matter of Rainford*, 20 I&N Dec. 598 (BIA 1992).

[34] 8 CFR §§238.1(d)(2)(iii), (3), 1238.1(d)(2)(iii), (3).

Re-entering After Removal: Criminal Prosecution and Reinstatement of Removal

Re-entry of Removed Aliens[35]

Criminal prosecution for re-entry after deportation is a high priority for the U.S. Department of Justice (DOJ). In turn, much of immigration case law—interpreting the term "aggravated felony," for example—arises out of criminal cases prosecuting re-entry after deportation. INA §276 [8 USC §1326] provides for criminal penalties for any non–American citizen who, without first receiving permission of the attorney general (AG), enters or attempts to enter the United States after having been "denied admission, excluded, deported, or removed or [having] departed the United States while an order of exclusion, deportation, or removal is outstanding."[36] The maximum penalties increase from two years' imprisonment for individuals removed on non-criminal deportation grounds,[37] to 10 years for those with various criminal convictions that are not aggravated felonies,[38] to 20 years for individuals removed and who re-enter after an aggravated felony conviction.[39]

The government prosecutes these cases by introducing into evidence portions of the A-file, which documents the prior removal, by calling a witness from DHS to verify that records were searched and that permission to re-enter was not granted, and by calling a fingerprint expert who compares the print taken from the non–American citizen at the time of removal with a print taken from the defendant after the post–re-entry arrest and prior to the trial.

Challenging the underlying order

Where re-entry after deportation is criminally prosecuted, it is possible for the defendant to challenge the legality (constitutionality) of the underlying administrative proceeding.[40] However, in a criminal proceeding for re-entry after deportation, non–American citizens may successfully challenge the validity of the deportation order only by demonstrating that they exhausted all administrative remedies available at the time, that they were improperly deprived of judicial review, and finally, that the entry of an order was fundamentally unfair. The fundamental unfairness prong requires a

---

[35] This section on re-entry of removed aliens was contributed to the first edition of this book by criminal defense attorney Martin Roth of Miami. It has been added to and amended by author Mary Kramer in subsequent editions.

[36] INA §276(a)(1); 8 USC §1326(a)(1).

[37] INA §276(a); 8 USC §1326(a).

[38] INA §§276(b)(1) (three or more misdemeanors involving drugs or crimes against the person, or any felony), (3) (noncriminal aliens removed for security, espionage, or terrorism grounds), (4); 8 USC §1326(b)(1), (3), (4).

[39] INA §276(b)(2); 8 USC §1326(b)(2).

[40] *U.S. v. Mendoza-Lopez*, 481 U.S. 828, 837–38 (1987); *see U.S. v. Wilson*, 316 F.3d 506, 510 (4th Cir. 2003).

showing of (1) a defect and (2) prejudice suffered as a result of the defect.[41] Thus, if a defendant did not vigorously pursue a certain legal argument and appeal the IJ's order to the BIA, it is difficult (if not impossible) to argue unfairness in subsequent criminal proceedings. Furthermore, the defect must have been so unfair that the proceeding would have turned out differently except for the error.

For a discussion of scenarios in which the underlying order is collaterally attacked in a criminal prosecution for re-entry, see chapter ten.

> **Of interest**: The sentence for re-entry after removal is enhanced if deportation was for an aggravated felony or other crime. Thus, defendants can and will contest whether a certain offense falls within the aggravated felony definition, and the federal courts are left to analyze the criminal offense to determine its immigration consequences. Arguably, the outcome in a sentencing guidelines case is not as persuasive as an actual removal case that reaches the court of appeals on petition for review. Nevertheless, criminal sentencing cases do provide useful guidance in analyzing a crime, and are often considered binding until an actual removal case is decided.

Reinstatement of Removal

Pursuant to INA §241(a)(5) [8 USC §1231(a)(5)], a non–American citizen found to have illegally re-entered the United States after having been removed or having departed voluntarily under an order of removal is subject to having the prior order of removal reinstated from its original date. Reinstatement of a prior removal order applies to orders issued by an IJ in immigration court proceedings as well as to expedited (administrative) removal orders issued by a DHS officer (expedited removal is discussed above). The reinstatement law is particularly harsh as applied to persons who have been expeditiously removed either at the border, or by a DHS officer following conviction of a crime, because these individuals have never had the opportunity to seek relief before an IJ, under the auspices of full due process rights. The reinstatement provision reads as follows:

> If the Attorney General finds that an alien has reentered the United States illegally after having been removed or having departed voluntarily, under an order of removal, the prior order of removal is reinstated from its original date and is not subject to being reopened or reviewed, the alien is not eligible and may not apply for any relief under [the INA], and the alien shall be removed under the prior order at any time after the reentry.

---

[41] *U.S. v. Wilson,* 316 F.3d 506, 510 (4th Cir. 2003). *U.S. v. Garcia-Jurado,* 281 F. Supp 2d 498 (E.D.N.Y. 2003) (retroactive application of AEDPA that denied opportunity for an INA § 212(c) waiver represented fundamental error and prejudice, previous deportation order suppressed); *U.S. v. Diaz-Nin,* 221 F. Supp. 2d 584 (V.I. 2002) (same).

In other words, the individual will be summarily arrested and removed again, without a hearing before an IJ or the opportunity to reopen or petition for review of the prior order. IIRAIRA, which added INA §241, included this limitation on possible relief, such that a person who has re-entered illegally cannot apply for residency or any other benefit as a defense to reinstatement. The provision bars traditional relief, such as adjustment of status. One exception would be if the individual had a fear of persecution in his or her home country. In such a case, the person could request withholding of removal and be "referred" for proceedings before the IJ.[42] These proceedings would be limited to consideration of the application for withholding only.

INA §241(a)(5), by its limitation on relief, appears to nullify the concept of a *nunc pro tunc* application for permission to re-enter after deportation or removal (Form I-212).[43] The Ninth Circuit U.S. Court of Appeals, for a period of time, operated under the precedent that an I-212 application (permission to reapply for admission after deportation) which is filed prior to a reinstatement order prevents the reinstatement process. However, the Ninth Circuit reversed this precedent in deference to a subsequent BIA case which disagreed with the former's holding.[44]

Limited exception for certain nationality-based benefits

There is a further exception to INA §241(a)(5)'s bar to applying for relief following re-entry after removal. Persons applying for benefits under the Haitian Refugee and Immigrant Fairness Act (HRIFA)[45] are not subject to reinstatement of removal (until their application is heard) or barred from applying for this relief from removal.[46] Applicants for adjustment of status under §202 of the Nicaraguan Adjustment and Central American Relief Act (NACARA)[47] are similarly eligible to apply for the benefit notwithstanding a re-entry after deportation.[48] And applicants under §203 of NACARA[49] are not subject to reinstatement of removal or barred from seeking relief. NACARA §203 allows persons from El Salvador, Guatemala, and former Soviet-bloc countries to apply for the "old" suspension of deportation through special rule cancellation of removal.[50] Note that under NACARA §203, a qualifying non–American cit-

---

[42] 8 CFR §§241.8(e), 1241.8(e). These proceedings are commenced by using Form I-863. *See* 8 CFR §§208.2(c)(2), 1208.2(c)(2).

[43] Form I-212 and its viability / applicability are discussed in chapter thirteen.

[44] *Perez-Gonzalez v. Ashcroft,* 379 F.3d 783 (9th Cir. 2004), *abrogated by Gonzales v. DHS,* 508 F.3d 1227 (9th Cir. 2007).

[45] Haitian Refugee and Immigrant Fairness Act (HRIFA), Pub. L. No. 105-277, div. A, §101(h), tit. IX (secs. 901–04), 112 Stat. 2681, 2681-538 to 2681-542.

[46] 8 CFR §§241.8(d), 1241.8(d).

[47] Nicaraguan Adjustment and Central American Relief Act (NACARA), Pub. L. No. 105-100, tit. II, §202, 111 Stat. 2160, 2193–96 (1997).

[48] 8 CFR §§241.8(d), 1241.8(d).

[49] Pub. L. No. 105-100, tit. II, §203(b), 111 Stat. 2160, 2198–99 (1997).

[50] *See* 8 CFR §§240.66, 1240.66.

izen who is inadmissible for crime may qualify under the "10-year" suspension/cancellation rule and qualify for residency notwithstanding the conviction(s) *or* the unlawful re-entry. Persons with aggravated felonies are not eligible.[51] In addition, persons applying for adjustment of status through the 1986 legalization program (INA §245A) are not subject to reinstatement; although the 1986 amnesty cases are in large part completed, many individuals continue to apply for legalization based on certain class action lawsuits.[52]

> ***NACARA §203 Example***: Jorge Gonzalez is a native and citizen of El Salvador who was deported in 1987 and re-entered in 1988. He applied for asylum with legacy INS, and then for temporary protected status. In 1991 he was convicted of first-time simple possession of cocaine. For this offense, he is deportable and inadmissible. Gonzalez is eligible for special rule cancellation of removal under §203 of NACARA notwithstanding his controlled substance conviction (it is no longer considered an aggravated felony), and he is not subject to reinstatement of removal.

As a practical matter, the exceptions under HRIFA, NACARA §202, and the legalization (amnesty) programs are obsolete, since they carried deadlines for applying. The deadlines have long passed, but some applications are still pending. NACARA §203 has no deadline.

U.S. Supreme Court upholds retroactive application of §241(a)(5)

The reinstatement provision at INA §241(a)(5) was expanded by IIRAIRA, which went into effect April 1, 1997. For several years, the federal courts considered (and differed on) whether the reinstatement provision could be applied retroactively to persons who re-entered prior to April 1, 1997. The U.S. Supreme Court eventually granted certiorari to resolve a split in the circuits on the reach of §241(a)(5). In *Fernandez-Vargas v. Gonzales*,[53] the Supreme Court ruled that the reinstatement provision may be applied retroactively to persons who re-entered prior to the legislation's effective date. Thus, a person who was deported and re-entered unlawfully prior to April 1, 1997, is nonetheless subject to reinstatement. In somewhat harsh rhetoric, the Supreme Court reasoned that re-entry and presence in the United States after deportation is an ongoing violation—not a matter of the one point in time when the actual re-entry occurred. Because the illegal presence was perpetual, the statute was not, in fact, being applied retroactively; indeed, the Court noted that persons who entered prior to September 30, 1996, (IIRAIRA's enactment date) had a six-month grace pe-

---

[51] See the discussion of NACARA §203 in chapter ten.

[52] Lawsuits include *Catholic Social Services, Inc. v. Meese*, vacated sub nom. *Reno v. Catholic Social Services, Inc.*, 509 U.S. 43 (1993); *League of United Latin American Citizens v. INS*, vacated sub nom. *Reno v. Catholic Social Services, Inc.*, 509 U.S. 43 (1993); and *Zambrano v. INS*, vacated sub nom. *Immigration and Naturalization Service v. Zambrano*, 509 U.S. 918 (1993).

[53] *Fernandez-Vargas v. Gonzales*, 548 U.S. 30 (2006).

riod during which they were put on notice of a change in the law and had an opportunity to end the ongoing violation by returning to their home countries.[54] The Court further found that §241(a)(5)'s bar to all forms of relief from removal, including adjustment of status, could be applied retroactively without offending the Constitution.

As a result, DHS regularly picks up persons who re-entered after removal and deports them—sometimes on the basis of very old orders. These persons are not allowed to apply for relief from removal, and face a 10-year bar to re-entering lawfully again (*i.e.*, through a visa or Form I-212 process).[55]

> **Example**: Jean-Pierre is ordered deported (and is actually removed) in 1994. He returns to the United States without lawful inspection and admission in 1995. In 2000, he marries a U.S. citizen and she files a visa petition for him, along with an adjustment of status application. Jean-Pierre also files with his package Form I-212, requesting *nunc pro tunc* permission to apply for readmission after deportation.[56] When Jean-Pierre and his wife appear at the USCIS office for an interview, Jean-Pierre is taken into custody. In two weeks, he is deported; he gets no hearing. Jean-Pierre considers reapplying for an immigrant visa through the U.S. consulate. However, Jean-Pierre is barred for 10 years from re-entering the United States again—that is, he cannot ask for permission to reapply for at least 10 years.[57]

How the Government Locates Your Client

Immigration lawyers learn quickly how DHS locates clients with criminal convictions. Criminal defense attorneys, however, may not be aware of the nuances. As a practical matter, this information is useful in emphasizing to a client the significance of the consequences and where the risks actually materialize.

The Sure Ways

Serving time in state or federal detention, both pre– and post-trial

The levels of communication between ICE and county jails, state prisons, and the Federal Bureau of Prisons are stronger than ever before. When an individual is either awaiting trial (custody incident to arrest), or has been convicted, the institutions communicate to ICE that they have a foreign national in custody. When a non–American citizen is serving a prison sentence, ICE will lodge a detainer, and often

---

[54] *Fernandez-Vargas v. Gonzales*, 540 U.S. 30, at 45–46.

[55] INA §§212(a)(9)(C)(i), (ii); 8 USC §§1182(a)(9)(C)(i), (ii).

[56] For further information on Form I-212, which is permission to reapply after deportation, see chapters ten and thirteen.

[57] INA §212(a)(9)(C); 8 USC §1182(a)(9)(C); *see Matter of Torres-Garcia,* 23 I&N Dec. 866 (BIA 2006).

interview the person while in custody to obtain facts and information, and later serve a notice to appear (NTA). In 2008, ICE announced a new program known as the *Secure Communities Initiative,* which the government described as a comprehensive plan to identify and remove criminal aliens in federal, state, and local prisons and jails.[58] The program relied on integrated technology so that law enforcement entities are able to identify non–American citizens when they are arrested and initially detained, and to communicate with each other.

On November 20, 2014, however, the DHS Secretary dismantled Secure Communities, announcing that the program was largely a failure and had received widespread criticism. The program was replaced with a priorities based initiative: Priorities Enforcement Program, or "PEP." Persons being detained by local law enforcement will still be fingerprinted, and the biometrics information will interact with ICE databases. However, a detainer will not be automatically lodged. Rather, ICE on a case-by-case basis may send a notification of interest to the jail.[59]

Also encompassed within the Secure Communities program were initiatives to use video technology for immigration court hearings, instead of live appearances. And, another part of the program is a clemency of sorts: under Rapid Removal of Eligible Parolees Accepted for Transfer (REPAT), nonviolent criminal aliens serving state sentences may receive early parole and termination of their sentence in exchange for accepting a removal order. REPAT is currently utilized in New York and Arizona, but ICE would like to expand its reach to additional states. It is unclear whether these aspects of the program remain intact.

ICE's Institutional Removal Program involves immigration court hearings that take place while the individuals are still serving state or federal criminal sentences. Both ICE and the Executive Office for Immigration Review (EOIR) would like to expand the use of video hearings for this purpose.

It is not unheard of for a prison official to communicate with ICE if the institution is poised to release a non–American citizen and, for whatever reason, no detainer has yet been placed. In other words, the institution may become actively involved in making sure a non–American citizen is not released until ICE has been properly notified and given the opportunity to take the person into custody.

> **Tip**: In most cases, it is a good idea for several reasons to post criminal bail early on, even if there is an immigration "hold" or detainer. If a non–American citizen is arrested and held in advance of criminal trial, it may be strategically wise to post the bond, rather than delay in doing so because of a fear that DHS will lodge a detainer or has already lodged a detainer. Posting bail quickly (within a couple of days of incarceration) lessens the risk that DHS will be notified about the client by the local

---

[58] For historical information on Secure Communities, see *www.ice.gov/secure-communities*.

[59] For the November 20, 2014 memo, visit *DHS.gov*.

jailor. Even if an immigration detainer is lodged, defense counsel should consider advising the client to post the state bond. Posting the state bond means that the individual will go into the actual or constructive custody of DHS, at which time reasonable release terms can be negotiated with ICE. (Specifically, negotiations regarding release are made with the deportation unit of ICE within the detention center.) Or, DHS may decide against taking the individual into custody. DHS rarely considers lifting a detainer, or setting its own bond, until the body is in its custody, so negotiations with DHS to lift the detainer or set a bond in advance are usually futile. If the individual has not yet been convicted of a crime, he or she is probably bondable under immigration law. Counsel may contact the ICE officer that lodged the detainer, or determine which office has physical control over the A-file. Counsel can put together a short memorandum citing the statutory basis for eligibility for bond, as well as the facts and equities (with a focus on why the individual is unlikely to abscond and is not a danger to the community). Where possible, *hand deliver* or *courier* the request for bond, and then follow up with phone calls (or where available, e-mail) to the officer.

According to 8 CFR §287.7(d), a law enforcement agency may hold a non–American citizen for up to 48 hours, not including Saturdays, Sundays, and holidays, pursuant to an ICE detainer. By regulation, after the 48 hours, if ICE does not assume custody, the individual should be released. Recently, ICE revised the detainer form, and jails and prisons are under instructions to provide a copy of the detainer (with contact information for ICE) to the detainee.

The year 2014 (and the trend continues) saw many county jails, and even states, refuse to honor immigration detainers for even 48 hours because of the cost and resources involved. Local jails across the country might have a policy of not holding a person for ICE pick-up, and as a matter of strategy, it is worthwhile to check what the local jurisdiction's policy is before posting bail or negotiating a plea.

Filing an immigration application

Currently, background checks (through a biometrics procedure) are conducted for almost every immigration application. An applicant for an immigration benefit receives notice to report to a DHS substation for "biometrics," which includes fingerprinting and photos, as well as a name check. As a result, applying for naturalization and adjustment of status guarantees the bringing of old convictions to light and, if applicable, the commencement of adverse action (*i.e.*, removal proceedings and possible detention). For other kinds of applications, such as work permits, new resident cards, visa petitions, etc., the situation is not so clear. DHS requires biometrics processing for these applications; whether DHS will act on the information in a particular case is not clear. For example, an LPR who applies for an extension of his or her resident card must appear for biometric processing; however, many LPRs with criminal records are receiving extended resident cards without incident. It would appear that DHS does not have the time to take action against every non–American citizen with a criminal record, and certain cases are being set aside (perhaps with the information being filed away for action at a later date).

DHS advises that it performs background name checks on *all* applications; indeed, it checks on all the names that appear on the applications (*e.g.*, the petitioner in a visa petition). With regard to applications for work permits, resident card extensions, visa petitions, etc., it is impossible to know in any given case whether the background check will lead to an arrest and initiation of removal proceedings for a criminal conviction. DHS, and specifically ICE Investigations, is an agency with limited resources, and so it must prioritize which cases it will act on. Experience shows that ICE shifts its priorities from time to time, initiating task forces to focus on certain categories of persons, only to shift away from those groups a few months later. Certainly, individuals with criminal records, who are amenable to removal proceedings, are sometimes arrested while attending a work permit appointment. However, like resident cards, many work permits are issued through the mail by regional service centers. These applications have not thus far led to arrests.

In sum, background checks in connection with an application for naturalization will result in removal proceedings when an individual is removable for crime. Also, the adjustment of status process will focus on a criminal record and may result in removal proceedings. Other applications (*i.e.*, the biometrics process) may reveal a criminal record, but whether ICE decides to take action just depends and appears to be a question of luck as much as anything else. An individual with a criminal record is best advised to consult with experienced immigration counsel before applying for *any* benefit with USCIS.

Frequently, But Not Always

While reporting to a probation or parole officer

Probation and parole officers at both the state and federal levels are frequently in communication with DHS (ICE). Often, there are nationwide "sweeps" at state probation offices, such as in the case of child abusers and sex offenders, because of some new government priority. It is clear that if ICE makes an overture to a probation office for assistance, that assistance will be granted. What is not so clear is the reverse: do probation and parole officers feel obligated to investigate an individual's immigration status and contact DHS? Although the practice may vary from jurisdiction to jurisdiction, experience and observation teaches that it is within the probation or parole officer's *discretion* to report an individual under his or her supervision to ICE. At least in the federal parole system, officers often do not pursue an individual's immigration status or contact ICE at all. This is significant in light of the fact that all relevant immigration information is in the federal parole file (through the pretrial sentence investigation, or PSI).

When re-entering the United States after a trip abroad

This particular method is quickly moving up to "sure way" status, above. In the post-9/11 period, computer technology at the ports of entry has become increasingly sophisticated; officers are under instructions to check everyone. The larger question is whether arrest and conviction information has been entered into the government computer system. Most state court systems have internet-available records, and CBP officers utilize courthouse websites to access conviction records and justify detaining someone at the port.

Many LPRs with old convictions have traveled back and forth numerous times, and are now (for the first time and to their surprise) being identified by the computer database and being deferred for further inspection. The fact that an individual has previously traveled successfully, notwithstanding a criminal record, does not mean that the next time the conviction will not come to light. An individual with a recent conviction, especially an individual who served a sentence of imprisonment, is most certainly going to be delayed and questioned when returning via an airport or seaport from a trip abroad.

An individual whose entry brings up a "hit" at an airport will not necessarily be arrested at that time. CBP has certain choices available if an individual has a criminal record. CBP can detain the individual at a detention center, or expeditiously remove the individual (discussed earlier in this chapter). Often, CBP (Inspections) *defers* the inspection process; the individual's travel documents will be confiscated and he or she will be given an appointment to appear at a deferred inspection. At a deferred inspection, the criminal record and other aspects of the case will be examined. If appropriate, an NTA will be issued by the Office of Deferred Inspections and the person will be taken into custody at that time. An individual has a right to the presence of counsel at a deferred inspections appointment, but not to active representation.[60] It is very important that a non–American citizen with a criminal record whose inspection into the United States is scheduled for an appointment with Deferred Inspections attend the appointment with competent counsel.

Local Law Enforcement and the Enforcement of Immigration Laws

Local police

Since 9/11, there has been much policy discussion about the role of local law enforcement officers in enforcing the immigration laws. INA §287(g) [8 USC §1357(g)] authorizes state officers and employees to enforce immigration law if they first enter into an agreement with the U.S. AG to do so. While legacy INS was under DOJ, former AG John Ashcroft did take steps to deputize certain law enforcement officers (FBI and local police) to take action under the INA.[61] However, the number of law enforcement officers with power to enforce the INA is still small. According

---

[60] 8 CFR §§292.5(b), 1292.5(b).

[61] By way of example, in July 2002, DOJ and the state of Florida signed a memorandum of understanding authorizing 35 state and local law enforcement officers to work as part of a task force performing certain enforcement functions of immigration officers. "Memorandum of Understanding Authorizes Certain Florida Law Officers to Enforce Immigration Laws," *published on* AILA InfoNet at Doc. No. 02072605 (*posted* July 26, 2002).

to the ICE website, 34 law enforcement agencies in 17 states have requested memoranda of understanding and cross-training to allow their employees to act as DHS agents under ICE's ACCESS program.[62] (ACCESS stands for Agreements of Cooperation in Communities to Enhance Safety and Security.) The officers are essentially deputized and trained to enforce immigration laws, as if they were ICE agents themselves.[63] Even where state or local officers are not deputized to act as DHS agents, the agencies often work in concert on task forces in the various communities. The Obama administration has significantly scaled back implementation of §287(g).

---

[62] See *http://www.ice.gov/access/*.
[63] *Id.*

APPENDIX 3A

Memorandum of Law in Support of Motion to Terminate

UNITED STATES DEPARTMENT OF JUSTICE
EXECUTIVE OFFICE FOR IMMIGRATION REVIEW
OFFICE OF THE IMMIGRATION JUDGE
MIAMI, FLORIDA

IN THE MATTER OF :)	
)	
HERNAN MARTINEZ)	CASE NO. A 426 210 789
RESPONDENT)	Honorable Susan Ryan
IN REMOVAL PROCEEDINGS)	
_____/	

RESPONDENT'S SECOND MEMORANDUM OF LAW IN SUPPORT OF MOTION TO TERMINATE

STATEMENT OF THE CASE

This case was previously before Judge Ryan at the Krome Detention Center. On May 5, 2010, Judge Ryan asked the Undersigned to represent Respondent Hernan Martinez on a pro bono basis, and she agreed. Shortly thereafter, Mr. Martinez was paroled out of Krome. Counsel moved Judge Ryan to vacate all concessions and findings which occurred while Mr. Martinez was pro se and detained. On June 10, 2010, Judge Ryan issued an order changing venue, and vacating all prior concessions and findings, but not prior testimony.

The case is set for a conference / oral argument/ evidentiary hearing (if necessary) on May 3, 2011.

Respondent has several motions pending, all of which support and request termination of the proceedings:

1. Motion contesting "arriving alien" designation. Respondent stands by this motion and re-news said motion herein.

2. Respondent's denial of proper issuance and service of Notice to Appear. Respondent withdraws the portion of this motion that relates to his signature. However, Respondent stands by his argument that the failure to provide a title to the issuing officer of the NTA is a fatal flow which justifies rejection of the NTA and termination of proceedings.

3. Motion to dismiss charge. This motion is based on the fact that Mr. Martinez' conviction is not for a crime involving moral turpitude and he is not removable under either INA § 212(a)(2) or § 237(a)(2)(A) (the latter assuming this Court were to reject the "arriving alien" designation). Respondent stands by this motion.

This submission adopts by reference and incorporates herein the actual motions, previously filed on May 21, 2010. The instant writing is supplementary in nature.

Legal Discussion

A. The Department of Homeland Security did not properly prepare, hence issue, the NTA.

The Department does not contest that the issuing officer failed to provide his title on the NTA. The NTA has an illegible signature, and the printed portion of the name is also incomplete and somewhat illegible. There are other components missing or incomplete on this NTA.

Section 239(a)(B) of the INA states that an NTA must cite to a legal authority under which proceedings are conducted. Section 239(a)(G)(i) states that the NTA shall list a time and place of hearings. Eight CFR § 239.1(a) lists which officers / titles within the Department of Homeland Security may legally issue an NTA.

The Department submits one case for the proposition that these required components of the NTA are not justification to terminate the NTA. In *Kohli v. Gonzales*, 473 F.3d 1061, 1068 (9th Cir. 2007), the Court of Appeals for the Ninth Circuit did not find that the law required the name and title of the issuing officer; rather, the Court wrote that the petitioner failed to trace the inclusion on Form I862 of the name and title of the issuing officer directly to any statute or regulation. Thus it would seem that this particular argument, in that particular case, failed not because it was an incorrect argument, but because the petitioner failed in her burden of persuasion. The court went on to discuss the issue of prejudice, arguing that all required information was present on that NTA. No harm, no foul.

In this case, Respondent Martinez does point out for the Court that the statute and regulations contain certain parameters and procedures for proper issuance of a charging document. Without these rules and regulations, the system of justice that the immigration court operates in will slowly erode. The Court needs rules and regulations—required procedures—if the system is to operate smoothly. Failure to comply with the requirements for proper preparation and issuance of an NTA, and the argument that "who cares" if there's no prejudice, places all parties on an impermissible slippery slope.

Accordingly, Respondent Martinez respectfully submits that there is inherent per se prejudice when a DHS officer fails to comply with procedures. Every county, state, and federal court system produces charging documents that clearly state the head prosecutor or charging officer's name and title. These rules led credibility, consistency, and reliability to the system. Like the Fourth Amendment exclusionary rule, sometimes the only way the courts can ensure that everyone plays by the rules is to reject an otherwise valid document. The issuing officer in this case failed to provide his name, title, or even his agency. He also failed to provide the date and place of the next hearing, although clearly all agencies have the ability to access the EOIR scheduling system. The errors have now led to motions, reply motions, and hearings. *Foul.* There is a per se prejudice when a document which could have been correctly and lawfully prepared is instead prepared in violation of the law's designated procedures.

Eight CFR § 1240.1 gives the immigration judge authority to take any action consistent with applicable law and regulations as may be appropriate. The NTA violates the statute, as well as the regulations. The Respondent moves the Court to terminate proceedings because the NTA is not in compliance with the regulations.

B. Mr. Martinez' offense is not a crime involving moral turpitude because the Florida theft statute is divisible and neither the record of conviction nor the facts support a conclusion that he is guilty of a "taking."

Mr. Martinez is charged with inadmissibility for conviction of a crime involving moral turpitude. In his motion dated May 21, 2010, he moved to dismiss the charge and terminate proceedings because his conviction does not represent a crime involving moral turpitude. That motion addressed relevant case law, including but not limited to *Jaggernauth v. Attorney General,* 432 F.3d 1346 (11th Cir. 2005); *Wala v. Mukasey,* 511 F.3d 102 (2d Cir. 2007); *Matter of V-Z-S,* 22 I & N Dec. 1338, n. 12 (BIA 2000), citing: *Matter of Grazley,* 14 I & N Dec. 330 (BIA 1973). These decisions[64] stand for the proposition that a temporary taking or appropriation is not a generic theft offense which would qualify as a crime involving moral turpitude. In *Jaggernauth*, for example, the Court of Appeals for the Eleventh Circuit specifically found that the Florida theft statute is divisible and that an appropriation is not synonymous with taking.[65]

Because Fla. Stat. § 812.014 (the theft statute) is divisible, recourse is made to the record of conviction. Respondent through counsel has obtained and now attaches as an exhibit the Information (charging document). The Information does not clarify whether the State Attorneys Office charged a temporary or permanent taking or appropriation. If Mr. Martinez' offense involved a temporary taking, or an appropriation, the offense does not involve moral turpitude.

Also attached is the transcript of the plea hearing. It reflects several important points for this Court's consideration. One, Mr. Martinez did not plead guilty, but rather, no contest. It was called a "plea of convenience." Two, the State did not proffer any set of facts. The defense attorney vaguely stipulated that there was a factual basis, but did not stipulate to any particular version or document that would be indicative or representative of the factual basis. The Judge did not articulate any sort of factual summary of the offense or specify which portion of the divisible theft statute applies. Thus adopting a modified categorical approach, as required by Eleventh Circuit case law, the record of conviction in Mr. Martinez' case does not in fact specify which portion of the statute he was charged with or prosecuted under. A no contest plea which does not contain a specific factual summary does not resolve the inquiry because it is not an admission to any particular portion of the statute. Under these circumstances, it is impossible for the Immigration Court to determine which portion of the statute applies; thus the Court should assume the least culpable conduct proscribed by statute: a temporary appropriation.

Although Respondent respectfully submits that the Court's inquiry should end with a modified categorical approach, the facts of this case support a conclusion that it was an appropriation. By way of proffer,[66] the Court is advised that Mr. Martinez is innocent of theft. He was instructed by his employer to help another individual move some equipment from one area within an open storage lot to another area of the storage lot. He did so. He hooked up a trailer containing a tractor and a backhoe to his

---

[64] Case law is submitted with this filing.

[65] The Eleventh Circuit cited to *Jaggernauth* in its recent decision, *Accardo v. U.S. Atty General*, 634 F.3d 1363 (11th Cir. March 10, 2011), calling it a divisible statute and clarifying that where there is a divisible statute, recourse is made to the record of conviction via a modified categorical approach.

[66] Counsel's statements are not evidence. However, this version of events is borne out by the Information (charging document). The Respondent submits that the arrest report is not evidence of what occurred and should not be relied on as evidence in the removability phase. *Matter of Texeira*, 21 I & N Dec. 316 (BIA 1996). However, assuming arguendo that the Court does accept and consider the arrest report, its version is also consistent with Respondent's summary of events.

boss' truck. The trailer was in the front area of a lot of a storage facility / business. He moved the trailer with the equipment on top to another area of the same lot. He did not bring the equipment to the lot and was simply following orders. Again, Mr. Martinez did not transport the equipment to that lot. He did not steal. He had no idea as to the background of this equipment.

This conviction (which in the state system is not a "conviction" at all) really has no basis in fact, and is reflective of a low income, moderately educated, and humble man being herded through a system wherein no one stops to really listen or care. This conviction is now the subject of post-conviction relief pending before the state court of appeals.

C. Mr. Martinez is not properly classified as an "arriving alien" because he is not in the posture of seeking an admission; additionally, the evidence does not establish that he has "committed" a crime involving moral turpitude.

Generally speaking, a lawful permanent resident that departs on a brief trip outside the U.S. does not effect a departure and re-entry, such that he is seeking "admission" and is viewed as an arriving alien. A lawful permanent resident may only be charged as an arriving alien if he falls under certain scenarios, as set forth at INA § 101(a)(13). The Department bears the burden of proof and persuasion to show that Mr. Martinez' "committed" a crime, and that the crime involves moral turpitude. *Matter of Rivens,* 25 I & N Dec. 623 (BIA 2011).

In this case, the issue of whether Mr. Martinez (a returning lawful permanent resident) is properly classified as an "arriving alien" under INA § 101(a)(13)(C) is to a certain extent tied in with the moral turpitude issue. If the Court finds that this offense does not represent a crime involving moral turpitude (because it did not involve a permanent or even temporary "taking"), then he did not "commit" a crime involving moral turpitude for purposes of section 101(a)(13)(C)(v). End of inquiry. In such a circumstance, the Court's determination of moral turpitude also determines the arriving alien issue.

However, it is conceivable that the Court could find Respondent has a "conviction" for a crime involving moral turpitude, but is still not properly classified as an arriving alien. This is because it is possible, as a technical matter, for this Court to find he has a "conviction" for a crime involving moral turpitude (based on the withhold of adjudication) such that he is subject to removal, but at the same time, that there is no evidence he "committed" a crime involving moral turpitude. *See* INA § 101(a)(48)(A). "Conviction" and "commission" are not synonyms. The Court can find the former is established, without finding that proof of the latter exists.

As stated above, section 101(a)(13)(C) states that a lawful permanent resident does not "seek admission" unless one or more of six scenarios apply. In this case, the only relevant provision is subsection (v). Based on subsection (v), a lawful permanent resident is treated as someone seeking admission if he has "committed" an offense identified in section 212(a).

Mr. Martinez, a lawful permanent resident, returned to the United States on or about September 8, 2009. At that time, he had not yet been prosecuted. He did not have a conviction, and did not admit commission of a crime. He was paroled in, turned over to Miami Dade, and prosecuted.

As discussed above, Mr. Martinez pled no contest, did not admit to any factual basis for the plea, and received a withhold of adjudication. Where, in this record, is there an admission or proof of the "commission" of a crime? The answer is, there isn't. The evidence of a "conviction" is not the same as proof of the commission of a crime. Section 101(a)(13)(C)(v) states that an LPR who departs the U.S., having committed a crime involving moral turpitude, is seeking admission upon return. This is a separate issue from that of moral turpitude. Even if the Court finds that Mr. Martinez' conviction is for an offense that involves moral turpitude, it cannot find based on this record that he has admitted to the commission of a crime involving moral turpitude. The existence as a technical matter of a "conviction" does not automatically mean that the commission of a crime has also been established.

The point is, on September 8, 2009, when Mr. Martinez arrived at Miami International Airport, he should have been admitted as a permanent resident. There was no proof of the commission of a crime involving moral turpitude at that time. CBP is not allowed to hold a request for admission in abeyance to see if later down the line a factual basis to deny admission (in this case a "commission") is established.

Even today, there is still no proof of the commission of a crime. The subsequent fact of a "conviction" does not retroactively establish "commission" of a crime, because in this case the plea hearing's transcript makes clear that the no contest plea was a plea of convenience with no specified clear factual basis. [67] Thus the subsequent conviction only establishes (in this particular case) that Mr. Martinez entered a no contest plea of convenience and did not admit to any facts. As a technical matter, Mr. Martinez has a "conviction" for immigration purposes—and it may even be a "conviction" for a crime involving moral turpitude—but that does not mean for purposes of § 101(a)(13)(C)(v) that he has "committed" (or had "committed") a crime involving moral turpitude. Not when he sought admission. And not today. There is no evidence of the commission of a crime involving moral turpitude and Mr. Martinez does not admit the commission of a crime involving moral turpitude.

Under this set of circumstances, it was not legally appropriate for CBP to deny admission to Mr. Martinez and parole him in. Even if immigration law allows a sort of time warp, such that "commission" may be established retroactively by subsequent events, in this case there still has been no establishment of "commission" because a

---

[67] See pages 4 and 9 of the plea transcript.

convenience plea of no contest with no specification of an underlying set of facts does not equal proof of the commission of a crime (even though it does establish conviction). This is true even if the Court finds that the conviction qualifies as a crime involving moral turpitude (which, again, Respondent strongly states does not).

D. Respondent is eligible for a waiver under section 212(h) of the INA.

If the Court finds Mr. Martinez removable, he is eligible for a waiver under the Eleventh Circuit's decision in *Lanier v. Att'y Gen.*, 631 F.3d 1363 (11th Cir. 2011). The waiver is attached.

Conclusion

Respondent re-news his motions except for the objection based on signature. He moves the Court to either dismiss proceedings based on the defective NTA (which does not allow jurisdiction to vest); to dismiss proceedings because he is not properly charged as an arriving alien; and/or to dismiss the charge because is does not involve moral turpitude.

RESPECTFULLY SUBMITTED:

MARY KRAMER

ATTORNEY AT LAW

MARY E. KRAMER, P.A.

168 SE FIRST ST. SUITE 802

MIAMI FL 33131

(305) 374 2300

CERTIFICATE OF SERVICE

I certify that a true and correct copy of this filing was served by hand delivery on the Office of Chief Counsel ICE at 333 S. Miami Ave Miami FL 33130 on this 11th day of March, 2011.

_____/

APPENDIX 3B

MOTION TO TERMINATE BASED ON IMPROPER DESIGNATION AS ARRIVING ALIEN

UNITED STATES DEPARTMENT OF JUSTICE
EXECUTIVE OFFICE FOR IMMIGRATION REVIEW
OFFICE OF THE IMMIGRATION JUDGE
MIAMI, FLORIDA

IN THE MATTER OF:	)	
	)	
SMITH, SUSAN	)	CASE NO. A066 077 554
	)	Judge Esteban
RESPONDENT	)	
IN REMOVAL	)	
PROCEEDINGS	)	
_____	/	

MOTION TO TERMINATE REMOVAL PROCEEDINGS BASED ON IMPROPER DESIGNATION AS "ARRIVING ALIEN"

NOW COMES THE RESPONDENT, by and through Undersigned Counsel, and respectfully moves the Court to terminate removal proceedings under INA § 212(a) and as grounds therefore states:

1. The Respondent, Susan Smith, is scheduled for an initial master hearing on August 22, 2011.

2. Ms. Smith, a lawful permanent resident, is designated on the Notice to Appear as an arriving alien, and is charged under section 212(a) of the Immigration and Nationality Act ("INA").

3. Ms. Smith moves to terminate "212(a)" proceedings because under the law she is not in fact an alien seeking admission as that term is defined under INA § 101(a)(13)(C).

4. As brief background, Ms. Smith entered the United States lawfully in June of 1984 as a tourist. She adjusted status to LPR on October 8, 1985. She is married to a lawful permanent resident and is the mother of three U.S. citizen children. She is charged in removal proceedings as having one conviction for a crime involving moral turpitude. The NTA was issued by CBP on June 15, 2011. Ms. Smith was coming back to the United States from Colombia after a two-week trip; her mother was very ill and in fact died—to be with her mother, and attend the funeral, was the purpose of this brief, casual and innocent travel.

5. According to the NTA, Ms. Smith was convicted[68] on or about January 26, 1994, by virtue of a plea of guilty in Broward County for the offense of grand theft, under Fla. Stat. 812.014(2)(c). Ms. Smith concedes that she was convicted of this offense, but argues that (1) she is not an "arriving alien" seeking admission, and (2), this is not a crime involving moral turpitude.

Ms. Smith is not properly classified as an "arriving alien"

6. A returning lawful permanent resident does not seek admission under INA § 101(a)(13)(C) unless certain circumstances exist, as defined by that provision. For purposes of this case, the relevant provision is subsection 101(a)(13)(C)(v), which holds that an LPR will be considered to be "seeking admission" if she has committed an offense described at INA §212(a)(2). The burden of proof in this matter—to show Ms. Smith is properly designated as an "arriving alien"—rests with the Department of Homeland Security, and the standard of proof is clear and convincing. *See: Matter of Rivens,* 25 I&N Dec. 623 (BIA 2011).

---

[68] The disposition, following a guilty plea, was a withhold of adjudication.

7. Section 101(a)(13) of the statute was amended by § 301(a)(13) the Illegal Immigration Reform Act of 1996 (the "IIRAIRA"). Prior to the 1996 legislation, the statute defined "entry" (as compared with "admission") and held that an LPR was not regarded as making an entry into the United States following a brief and innocent departure. Pursuant to Supreme Court case law, an LPR did not effectuate an "entry" following a brief, casual and innocent trip abroad that was not meaningfully interruptive of permanent residence status in the United States. *Rosenberg v. Fleuti,* 374 U.S. 449 (1963). Under the pre-1996 *Fleuti* Doctrine, Ms. Smith is not chargeable under section 212(a) of the statute as an alien "seeking admission": she was out of the country approximately two weeks, the reason being that her parent was ill and died. The *Fleuti* doctrine applies to this case because Ms. Smith's conviction is a pre-1996[69] disposition: the IIRAIRA amendments to INA § 101(a)(13) do not apply to pre-IIRAIRA convictions. *Vartelas v. Holder,* 132 S. Ct. 1479 (2012).

Respondent's offense is not categorically a crime involving moral turpitude

8. As a discrete issue from the arriving alien designation, Ms. Smith respectfully states that her conviction for theft is not categorically a crime involving moral turpitude; put another way, she has not been convicted of a moral turpitude crime. under INA § 212(a)(2)(A).

9. If the Court looks to INA § 101(a)(13)(C)(v), it is significant that a "conviction" for a crime involving moral turpitude is *not* the key term; rather, it is "commission" of a crime involving moral turpitude that determines the LPR is seeking admission.

10. As stated above, the Department bears the burden of proof and persuasion that she has committed a crime involving moral turpitude. *See: Matter of Rivens, supra.*

11. The Eleventh Circuit Court of Appeals has ruled that the Florida theft statute at Fla. Sta. § 812.014 is in fact a divisible statute that describes temporary and permanent takings and /or appropriations. See: *Jaggernauth v. Attorney General,* 432

---

[69] *Vartelas v. Holder,* 132 S. Ct. 1479 (2012).

F.3d 1346 (11th Cir. 2005). In addition, other courts have found that there is a distinction between a temporary versus permanent taking. *See, e.g., Wala v. Mukasey,* 511 F.3d 102 (2d Cir. 2007); *Matter of V-Z-S,* 22 I & N Dec. 1338, n. 12 (BIA 2000), citing: *Matter of Grazley,* 14 I & N Dec. 330 (BIA 1973). These decisions stand for the proposition that a temporary taking or appropriation is not a generic "theft" offense that would qualify as a crime involving moral turpitude.

13. A review of Ms. Smith's Information (charging document) reflects that Broward County charged that she had the intent to either temporarily or permanently deprive Burdines of the right to property . . . or to appropriate the property to his own use. In other words, the Information does not delineate under which portion of the Florida statute. Moreover, the record of conviction does not indicate what portion of the divisible theft statute she pled to, or was adjudicated and sentenced under.

14. The record of conviction in this matter does not support a finding that Ms. Smith (1) was convicted of a crime involving moral turpitude (such that she is removable under INA § 212(a)(2)) or (2) that she committed a crime involving moral turpitude (such that she is properly charged as an arriving alien.

WHEREFORE, Respondent moves to terminate these proceedings in that she is not properly charged as an arriving alien, has not committed a crime involving moral turpitude, and is not removable for a moral turpitude conviction.

RESPECTFULLY SUBMITTED:

ILARIA CACOPARDO,
ATTORNEY AT LAW
MARY E. KRAMER, P.A.
168 SE FIRST ST. SUITE 802
MIAMI, FL 33131
(305) 374 2300

Certificate of Service

This motion was filed in Open Court and service provided at that time, August 22, 2011, Miami Florida.

_____/

Chapter Four

Consequences of Criminal Activity: Detention Inside the United States

Mandatory Detention 133
Other Detention Issues 153

Appendices

    4A: Custody Rule Invoked (Terminates the Transitional Period Custody Rules) 164

    4B: Section 309 of the IIRAIRA – the Transition Rule for 1996 Amendments to the INA .166

    4C: Section 303(b) of the IIRAIRA – Effective Date of INA §236(c) Mandatory Detention 169

    4D: Memorandum on INA §236(c)'s "Custody" Requirement and the Use of Alternatives to Detention to Meet the Statute's Requirements 171

    4E: Memorandum of Law in Support of Bond Motion – *Joseph* Motion Arguing Financial Loss to a Victim Did Not Exceed $10,000 for Purposes of INA §101(a)(43)(M) 176

> *Freedom from physical restraint has always been at the core of the liberty protected by the Due Process Clause from arbitrary governmental action. While ICE is entitled to carry out its duty to enforce the mandates of Congress, it must do so in a manner consistent with our constitutional values.*[1]

Mandatory Detention

In the vast majority of cases, the one consequence an individual client fears more than any other—usually more so than removal itself—is detention in an immigration facility. Deprivation of liberty via incarceration by U.S. Immigration and Customs Enforcement (ICE) is the worst immigration law consequence of criminal activity. Some individuals removable for criminal activity will be eligible for bond and successfully seek release. Other individuals may be statutorily eligible for release, but either will not receive a bond, or their release will otherwise be blocked by ICE's Office of Chief Counsel. Still others will be statutorily ineligible for bond and will be held under the law of mandatory detention. Mandatory detention is a provision of immigration law calling for continued custody while the removal hearing is pending: the person absolutely remains locked up until completion of the immigration court case. Because mandatory detention is such a serious consequence, and will apply to most individuals removable for crime based on recent convictions, it is critical that

---

[1] *Rodriguez v. Robbins*, 715 F.3d 1127 (9th Cir. 2013), *citing: Kansas v. Hendricks*, 521 U.S. 346, 356, 117 S. Ct. 2072, 138 L. Ed. 2d 501 (1997) (quoting *Foucha v. Louisiana*, 504 U.S. 71, 80 (1992)).

mandatory detention move to the top of the list of considered consequences in analyzing both the criminal and immigration law case. As counsel goes through a mental checklist during that first consultation (deportable for the offense? eligible for relief?), a major issue must be whether the client is subject to mandatory detention for crime.

The law of mandatory detention was introduced by the Illegal Immigration Reform and Immigrant Responsibility Act of 1996 (IIRAIRA).[2] Because the law represented a dramatic change in detention policy, and Congress realized that the necessary detention space would not be readily available, the law of mandatory detention was ushered in with a transition period of approximately two years. The transition period was governed by the Transition Period Custody Rules (TPCR),[3] invoked by Immigration and Naturalization Service (INS) Commissioner Doris Meissner, pursuant to authority delegated to her by the attorney general. During the transition period, the attorney general could release certain aliens who were lawfully admitted and who did not pose a security or flight risk, or those who were not lawfully admitted but who could not be removed because the designated country would not accept them. The TPCR expired on October 8, 1998, when Meissner notified Congress that the detention space was available and the mandatory rules could go into effect. The mandatory detention rules are not retroactive—they apply to persons released from state or federal custody *after* October 8, 1998.

The mandatory detention provisions are found at §236(c) of the Immigration and Nationality Act (INA) [8 USC §1226(c)], and state:

> (1) Custody.—The Attorney General shall take into custody any alien who—
>
>> (A) is inadmissible by reason of having committed any offense covered in section 212(a)(2),
>>
>> (B) is deportable by reason of having committed any offense covered in section 237(a)(2)(A)(ii), (A)(iii), (B), (C), or (D),
>>
>> (C) is deportable under section 237(a)(2)(A)(i) on the basis of an offense for which the alien has been sentenced to a term of imprisonment of at least 1 year, or
>>
>> (D) is inadmissible under section 212(a)(3)(B) or deportable under section 237(a)(4)(B),
>
> when the alien is released, without regard to whether the alien is released on parole, supervised release, or probation, and without regard to whether the alien may be arrested or imprisoned again for the same offense.

---

[2] Illegal Immigration Reform and Immigrant Responsibility Act of 1996 (IIRAIRA), Division C of the Omnibus Appropriations Act of 1996 (H.R. 3610), Pub. L. No. 104-208, 110 Stat. 3009.

[3] The rules regarding bond for individuals who fall under the Transition Period Custody Rules (TPCR) are found at 8 CFR §§236.1(c), 1236.1(c).

(2) Release.—The Attorney General may release an alien described in paragraph (1) only if the Attorney General decides pursuant to section 3521 of title 18, United States Code, that release of the alien from custody is necessary to provide protection to a witness, a potential witness, a person cooperating with an investigation into major criminal activity, or an immediate family member or close associate of a witness, potential witness, or person cooperating with such an investigation, and the alien satisfies the Attorney General that the alien will not pose a danger to the safety of other persons or of property and is likely to appear for any scheduled proceedings. A decision relating to such release shall take place in accordance with a procedure that considers the severity of the offense committed by the alien.

To understand the breadth of mandatory detention, it is important to recall the definitions of inadmissibility and deportability. Subsection (1), above, states that anyone charged with *inadmissibility* under INA §212(a) for a crime must be detained while removal proceedings are pending. This includes individuals arriving at a port of entry (arriving aliens) and individuals who are physically present, but subject to the grounds of inadmissibility (including persons who entered without inspection or who were paroled). Similarly, persons who face charges of *deportability* under INA §237(a) (*i.e.*, those persons who were admitted into the United States and are physically present in the United States) are also subject to mandatory detention *unless* they are removable for only one crime, involving moral turpitude, for which the sentence imposed was less than one year. Thus, there is a limited exception for persons who are deportable, as opposed to inadmissible: the former will not be detained without bond if they have only one conviction for a crime involving moral turpitude for which less than one year imprisonment was imposed.

> **Example**: Elizabeth is living in the United States pursuant to a lawful admission. She has one conviction only for a crime involving moral turpitude (fraud). Although the maximum penalty possible is five years' imprisonment, Bianca's sentence was 364 days in jail. Bianca is now in removal proceedings charged with deportability under INA §237(a)(2)(A)(i). However, she is not subject to mandatory detention.

Compare: Elizabeth has been residing in the United States as a lawful permanent resident (LPR); she does have the one conviction for fraud, for which she received 364 days in jail (same as above). She travels outside the United States, and upon arriving back at a port of entry, the conviction comes to light. U.S. Customs and Border Protection (CBP) issues a notice to appear (NTA) charging inadmissibility under INA §212(a)(2)(A)(i)(I). From the airport, CBP takes Bianca into custody and she is detained under the mandatory detention provisions.

Chapter six lists those offenses that render an individual subject to mandatory detention. Not every criminal offense that makes one deportable will lead to mandatory detention. For example, deportability for a domestic violence offense,[4] visa violation,[5] export violation,[6] or (as illustrated in Elizabeth's first case above) one crime involving moral turpitude[7] where the sentence of imprisonment imposed is less than one year is not a basis for mandatory detention.

Cooperating Witnesses

Mandatory detention is a harsh provision that *requires* the U.S. Department of Homeland Security (DHS) to detain those individuals described at INA §236(c). DHS has no discretion to release, for example, individuals who are seriously ill—even dying—who have outstanding personal equities or present other humanitarian factors. There is one class of persons potentially exempt: cooperating witnesses, their family members, and close associates. Very often, these are individuals with serious criminal records; however, they are cooperating with law enforcement—or have cooperated with law enforcement—and, thus, qualify for a reprieve from mandatory detention. Pursuant to INA §236(c)(2), set forth above, the attorney general may release an individual otherwise subject to mandatory detention if the individual is a cooperating witness pursuant to 18 USC §3521, which describes the witness protection program.

It is not clear from reading INA §236(c)(2) whether the non–American citizen actually must *be in* the witness protection program, or whether significant cooperation with law enforcement (and therefore incurring a risk of harm) is sufficient. In dicta, federal courts have stated that the exception refers to persons in the witness protection program. However, based on a plain reading of the statute, it can be argued that cooperating witnesses who are at risk as a result of their assistance to either state or federal law enforcement qualify for the exception. In addition, because the statute gives the release discretion to the attorney general, the immigration judge (IJ), as an agent of the U.S. Department of Justice (DOJ), as opposed to DHS, arguably has both the authority to decide the legal point and the discretion to order release.

Demore v. Kim

In 2003, the U.S. Supreme Court ruled that mandatory detention is constitutional. Its opinion in *Demore v. Kim*[8] addressed the constitutionality of mandatory detention of LPRs. This decision disappointed both LPRs and practitioners alike. On a positive note, the Court did reaffirm the federal courts' jurisdiction to review questions of statutory construction of the immigration law. Federal courts maintain subject-matter jurisdiction over detention issues, notwithstanding INA §242(a) [8 USC §1252(a)]. As stated in chapter one, INA §242(a) significantly limits judicial review of removal

---

[4] INA §237(a)(2)(E); 8 USC §1227(a)(2)(E).
[5] INA §237(a)(3)(B)(iii); 8 USC §1227(a)(3)(B)(iii).
[6] INA §237(a)(4)(A)(i); 8 USC §1227(a)(4)(A)(i).
[7] INA §237(a)(2)(A)(i)(I); 8 USC §1227(a)(2)(A)(i)(I).
[8] 538 U.S. 510 (2003).

issues, including final orders of removal, procedural determinations, and questions of law that may arise in the removal context. These issues may only be raised in the context of a petition for review to the court of appeals, after a final administrative order.[9] However, detention claims are independent of removal proceedings and are not barred by INA §242(b)(9) or any other provision of law.[10] The courts have held that, although there is no judicial review of the discretionary determination to release or hold in custody in a particular case, the law does not bar constitutional challenges to detention.[11]

Legal Challenges to Mandatory Detention Following *Demore*

In *Demore*, the individual was charged as an aggravated felon and did not have relief from removal available. Practitioners are encouraged to continue to challenge mandatory detention in those cases where the LPR client does have relief available. If presented with a more appealing set of facts, the Supreme Court may be willing to view mandatory detention as unconstitutional as it applies to LPRs with available relief.

In the class-action lawsuit *Rodriguez v. Robbins*,[12] the U.S. Court of Appeals for the Ninth Circuit affirmed the lower court's preliminary injunction that persons detained for more than six months pending removal proceedings were entitled to individualized bond hearings. As a result of the injunction, as of the spring of 2015, immigration detainees in the Ninth Circuit receive bond hearings after six months in mandatory detention.

Federal district courts have exercised jurisdiction over habeas petitions and ordered individualized bond hearings—notwithstanding the mandatory detention provisions—where the non–American citizen is held for an inordinate period of time. In *Ly v. Hansen*,[13] the U.S. Court of Appeals for the Sixth Circuit interpreted *Demore* to require that removal proceedings be concluded within a reasonable time. Incarceration for 18 months was found not reasonable, and thus, the non–American citizen in that case was entitled to an individualized bond hearing.

Other federal courts have also found prolonged detention unconstitutional, even though the non–American citizen was ostensibly subject to mandatory detention for crime.[14]

---

[9] INA §242(b)(9); 8 USC §1252(b)(9).

[10] *See, e.g., Aguilar v. ICE*, No. 07-1819, 2007 WL 4171244, slip. op. at 17–18 (1st Cir. Nov. 27, 2007) (citing *Hernandez v. Gonzales*, 424 F.3d 42 (1st Cir. 2005)).

[11] *See, e.g., Hussain v. Gonzales*, 492 F. Supp. 2d 1024, 1031 (E.D. Wis. 2007).

[12] *Rodriguez v. Robbins*, 715 F.3d 1127 (9th Cir. 2013).

[13] *Ly v. Hansen*, 351 F.3d 263 (6th Cir. 2003).

[14] *See, e.g., Madrane v. Hogan*, Civ. Action No. 1:05-CV-2228, 2007 WL 404032 (M.D. Pa. Feb. 1, 2007) (two-year detention unreasonable); *Tijani v. Willis*, 430 F.3d 1241 (9th Cir. 2005) (two years and four months' detention unreasonable); *Diomande v. Wrona*, No. 05-73290 (E.D. Mich. Dec. 12, 2005) (nearly two-year detention unreasonable).

In *Casas-Castrillon v. DHS*,[15] the LPR petitioner had been in custody for seven years during the pendency of removal proceedings; the case had been prolonged based on successful judicial review. Because he was from Colombia, the court noted that he could eventually be removed; thus, DHS had the authority to detain him. However, noting that seven years was an inordinate period of time, the court observed that continued detention of an LPR raises significant constitutional concerns. In so noting, the court of appeals pointed out that the Supreme Court, in *Demore v. Kim,* consistently opined that detention should be for a short duration of time, and that most cases would be concluded within a month and a half. The Ninth Circuit found that it would not reach the ultimate constitutional question regarding prolonged detention, because there is no evidence that Congress intended to authorize the long-term detention of aliens without some access to a bond hearing before an IJ.[16] Thus the court found that seven years' detention goes beyond Congress's intent in enacting §236(c). The case was remanded with instructions that the petitioner be provided a bond hearing.

In *Leslie v. Att'y Gen.*,[17] the Third Circuit U.S. Court of Appeals found that four years in ICE detention during removal proceedings was not reasonable and ordered an individualized bond hearing. Because of a combination of procedural delays and successful appeals, the respondent in *Leslie* remained in ICE custody. The Third Circuit found that the issue of detention was governed by INA §236(c) (pre-removal), as opposed to INA §241 (the post-removal period) and that the Supreme Court has not authorized a prolonged detention under either statute. The Third Circuit stated that what is "reasonable" must be based on a case-by-case individualized inquiry, and cited to its earlier decision in *Diop v. ICE/Homeland Security*,[18] to reiterate a two-part test for reasonableness: (1) whether detention has been unreasonably long; and (2) whether continued detention is necessary to serve the law's purpose.

Similarly, some courts have found that prolonged detention during the removal proceedings must be "reasonable" under the circumstances of the case. In *Alli v. Thomas*,[19] the district court found that prolonged detention would be examined for reasonableness, and the procedure would be administered by the district court. The following are the criteria for consideration:

- whether detention has continued beyond an average time;
- the probable extent of future removal proceedings;
- the likelihood that removal proceedings will actually end in removal; and

---

[15] *Casas-Castrillon v. DHS*, 535 F.3d 942 (9th Cir. 2008).
[16] *Casas-Castrillon v. DHS*, at 950.
[17] *Leslie v. Att'y Gen.*, 678 F.3d 265 (3d Cir. 2012).
[18] *Diop v. ICE/Homeland Security*, 656 F.3d 221, 231 (3d Cir. 2011).
[19] *Alli v. Thomas*, No. 4:09-CV-0698, 2009 US LEXIS 69413 (M.D. Pa. Aug. 10, 2009).

- the conduct of the non–American citizen and the government during the course of removal proceedings.[20]

In addition, and as discussed further below, some clients are not subject to "mandatory" detention because of the nature of their convictions, but are nonetheless detained by DHS. Practitioners should not hesitate to contest continued detention during removal proceedings whenever a meritorious legal argument can be made.

Bond Hearings Before the IJ

DHS makes an initial custody determination when the agency arrests and detains a non–American citizen. That decision is reflected within the NTA.[21] However, the individual—subject to jurisdictional rules discussed below—may request a custody (or bond) hearing before the IJ to contest DHS's initial determination.[22] The non–American citizen may want to contest the amount of bond set by DHS. More often, DHS has determined to hold an individual without bond, and for this reason, a hearing before an independent judge is requested. Where the individual is determined by DHS to be subject to mandatory detention, that determination may also be contested before an IJ in the context of a bond hearing.

Custody and bond hearings before the IJ are governed by 8 CFR §1003.19. The regulations state that custody and bond determinations made by the government pursuant to 8 CFR Parts 236, 1236 may be reviewed by an IJ pursuant to 8 CFR Parts 236, 1236.[23]

A request for bond hearing is made via written motion and delivered either to the detention facility where the individual is held or the office of the immigration court having administrative control over the file and/or place of custody. This motion, in the interests of expediency, may be skeletal in nature and followed by supplemental legal memoranda, or may include a complete legal argument in support of release. Certainly when the argument is that an individual is not properly classifiable as subject to mandatory detention, a memorandum of law—at some point—is in order.

> ➢ **Tip**: *Where to file the bond motion.* Increasingly, non–American citizens are detained and transferred to many detention centers (and jails) throughout the United States. It becomes difficult even to locate clients, much less pinpoint the immigration court with jurisdiction over the case. According to 8 CFR §1003.19(c)(3), the motion for bond hearing may be made with the Office of the Chief Immigration Judge for designation of the appropriate immigration court.

---

[20] *Alli v. Thomas*, No. 4:09-CV-0698, 2009 US LEXIS 69413, at 23–27.
[21] 8 CFR §§236.1(c)(8), 1236.1(c)(8); see Appendix 1E for a sample notice to appear (NTA).
[22] 8 CFR §§236.1(d)(1), 1236.1(d)(1).
[23] 8 CFR §1003.19(a).

Bond hearings are informal. The IJ has discretion to go "on the record" by audiotaping the proceedings. Often, the judge will opt not to go on the record. Furthermore, the record of bond hearing is to be kept separate and apart from the removal hearing in chief.[24] For example, if a document is submitted as evidence in the bond proceeding, and counsel would like to use the same document as evidence in the removal proceeding, the document must be reproduced and resubmitted. Cross-referencing evidence between the bond and removal proceedings is not appropriate because the two records are technically separate.

Either party may appeal the determination of the IJ with respect to custody to the Board of Immigration Appeals (BIA or Board).[25] (For a discussion of ICE counsel's automatic stay power, see below.) In the event of an appeal to the BIA, the judge prepares a memorandum of decision summarizing his or her findings and conclusions. There are no transcripts[26] or formal evidentiary record on appeal; the BIA will issue a briefing schedule and all parties are presumed to have a record of documentary evidence and recollection of what transpired at the hearing.

> **Bond Tip #1**: Where counsel has a good argument that the individual is not subject to mandatory detention, or should not be detained, it may be worthwhile to request redetermination of custody with the ICE Detention Office having jurisdiction over the detention facility in advance of a bond hearing before the IJ. Depending on the locale, an informal request for redetermination may result in faster consideration, and certainly gives the client the proverbial "two bites at the apple."

Numerical Limitations and Jurisdiction

There is no numerical limitation on the number of bond hearings a detained individual may request. Whenever a change in circumstances warrants renewed consideration of custody, either party may move for a bond hearing. After the initial bond redetermination, an individual's request for an additional bond hearing must be made in writing and shall be considered only if there is a "material change in circumstances."[27] Unlike removal proceedings-in-chief, an IJ does not lose jurisdiction over bond proceedings even if an appeal has been filed to the BIA over the *previous* custody determination.[28] In other words, if a bond appeal is pending before the BIA, yet there is a material change in circumstances warranting a renewed

---

[24] 8 CFR §1003.19(d).

[25] 8 CFR §§1003.19(c)(3), (f).

[26] If the bond hearing is taped at the discretion of the judge or at the request of one or both of the parties, it is not clear from the regulations whether transcripts will be prepared for appeal purposes at the Board of Immigration Appeals (BIA or Board) level. Presumably, a party must move the court to have transcripts prepared; in the alternative, counsel could have transcripts privately prepared and ask the BIA to accept the privately prepared transcripts into evidence.

[27] 8 CFR §1003.19(e).

[28] *Matter of Valles-Perez*, 21 I&N Dec. 769 (BIA 1997); *see also* 8 CFR §§236.1(d)(1), 1236.1(d)(1).

bond determination, either party may request a bond hearing before the IJ—notwithstanding the pending appeal at the BIA. A detained non–American citizen is free to request a bond redetermination at any time without a formal motion, without fee, and without regard to filing deadlines as long as the underlying deportation or removal proceedings are not yet final.[29]

Even after posting a bond and release from custody, a non–American citizen has seven days within which to move for a bond hearing and request amelioration of the terms of release.[30] This type of motion (after the respondent has been released from custody) will be filed with the immigration court after ICE has set bond. (One would not request a modification of bond from the judge after posting the bond that was set by the judge.) In some cases, after a judge has set a bond, ICE will unilaterally impose additional restrictions on liberty, such as electronic monitoring, periodic reporting, or curfew. These additional restrictions are part of new detention initiatives, and are discussed in more detail below. If ICE imposes additional restrictions on liberty that were not ordered by the judge in the context of the bond hearing, an individual may—within seven days of release—request a new bond hearing to request modification of the additional restrictions.[31]

> **Tip**: Carlota Rodriguez is arrested and taken into custody by ICE. She is charged as a deportable non–American citizen under INA §237. While in custody, Carlota files a motion with the IJ for a bond hearing. At the conclusion of the bond hearing, the judge sets a $5,000 bond, and the Office of Chief Counsel does not appeal. Carlota posts the $5,000 bond. However, before she is released from custody, Carlota is placed on the intensive supervision program. An electronic bracelet is affixed to her ankle, and she is given a curfew of 9:00 am to 6:00 pm. She must report weekly to the supervision office and will be subject to surprise home visits. Carlota does not like these additional restrictions on her liberty, and the judge was not advised that ICE would put her on intensive supervision. Within seven days of her release, Carlota files a second motion for a bond hearing to ameliorate the additional terms of her release; she asks the IJ to order that she be taken off intensive supervision.

Matter of Aguilar-Aquino

Regarding restrictions and conditions imposed in conjunction with bond, the BIA has ruled that the request for amelioration of additional restrictions must be requested by motion filed within seven days of release. In *Matter of Aguilar-Aquino*,[32] the

---

[29] *Matter of Valles-Perez*, 21 I&N Dec. 769; *see also Matter of Uluocha*, 20 I&N Dec. 133 (BIA 1989).
[30] 8 CFR §§236.1(d)(1), 1236.1(d)(1).
[31] 8 CFR §§236.1(d)(1), 1236.1(d)(1).
[32] *Matter of Aguilar-Aquino*, 24 I&N Dec. 747 (BIA 2009).

respondent was released directly from DHS custody without ever having a bond hearing in front of a judge. However, DHS released the respondent under an enhanced supervision program, including but not limited to curfew, reporting, and electronic monitoring. Approximately two and one-half months after his release, respondent filed a motion for amelioration of custody, arguing that he was still in "custody" by virtue of DHS's restrictions on liberty and the motion was therefore not tardy. The IJ assumed jurisdiction, ordered a monetary bond, and ruled that the enhanced supervision restrictions be eliminated upon posting of said bond. On appeal, the BIA found that the motion was tardy (outside the seven-day rule) because restrictions on liberty such as electronic monitoring did not constitute "custody" for purposes of 8 CFR §1236.1(d)(1). The "release from custody" pursuant to the seven-day rule was the time when DHS released him from the detention facility. The BIA specifically did not reach the issue of whether an IJ has authority to set conditions (or ameliorate conditions) beyond the fact of a monetary bond; in other words, the BIA declined to address whether a judge can either order, or ameliorate, intensive supervision-type restrictions on liberty.[33]

In only two circumstances will an IJ lose jurisdiction over bond proceedings. The first is when the non–American citizen in removal proceedings has been released from custody and seven days have elapsed since the release. The second is when a final administrative order of removal is issued and the case before the Executive Office for Immigration Review (EOIR) is thus concluded.

Matter of Joseph

Mandatory detention under INA §236(c) is based on the underlying ground of inadmissibility or deportability charged. If the ground is not correct, based on the underlying criminal offense, then mandatory detention does not properly apply, either.

Cases will arise in which the client is detained under mandatory detention and, in counsel's view, the underlying charge of inadmissibility or deportability (lodged in the NTA) is not legally sustainable. Normally, when a respondent denies removability, the issue is litigated through motions, at an individual hearing, or a combination of both. This process can take time. Custody situations, on the other hand, are urgent. Thus, cases will arise where counsel is faced with arguing the underlying ground of removability in the custody context (*i.e.*, the whole case) in an expedited manner because the question of bond depends on the fundamental issue of removability.

In *Matter of Joseph*,[34] the BIA discussed the situation in which an individual whom DHS has initially determined to hold without bond under INA §236(c) requests a bond hearing before a judge and argues that he or she is not, in fact, subject

---

[33] *Matter of Aguilar-Aquino*, 24 I&N Dec. 747, at 753.

[34] *Matter of Joseph*, 22 I&N Dec. 799 (BIA 1999).

to mandatory detention. The respondent was convicted in Maryland of "obstructing and hindering" a police officer and received a one-year sentence. Legacy INS took the respondent into custody, charging him as removable for an aggravated felony offense under INA §237(a)(2)(iii), as defined by §101(a)(43)(S) (obstruction of justice). In bond proceedings before the IJ, the issue was whether the respondent was deportable for an "aggravated felony" such that he fell under the mandatory detention provision. The IJ found that the Maryland offense was not an aggravated felony, and ordered the respondent's release. The BIA agreed. The BIA analyzed the Maryland statute and found that its provisions did not relate to the obstruction of justice-type offense envisioned at INA §101(a)(43)(S).[35] Finding that it was substantially unlikely that legacy INS would prevail on a charge of removability encompassed at §236(c), the BIA affirmed the determination that the respondent was not subject to mandatory detention.

Matter of Joseph is an important case because it affirms the principle that an IJ may hold a bond hearing even though DHS has classified an individual as subject to mandatory detention based on the underlying ground of removability. In *Joseph*, the government took the position that a judge did *not* have the authority to reconsider legacy INS's initial determination with regard to classification as mandatory detention. The BIA rejected this view:

> Although a conviction document may provide the Service with sufficient reason to believe that an alien is removable under one of the mandatory detention grounds for purposes of charging the alien and making an initial custody determination, neither the Immigration Judge nor the Board is bound by the Service's decisions in that regard when determining whether an alien is properly included within one of the regulatory provisions that would deprive the Immigration Judge and the Board of jurisdiction to redetermine the custody conditions imposed on the alien by the Service.

It bears repeating that mandatory detention is based on the ground of inadmissibility or deportability, as opposed to the specific criminal offense. In other words, a theft or drug conviction per se does not make someone subject to mandatory detention; it is the ground of deportability or inadmissibility implicated by the conviction that triggers mandatory detention. In a *Joseph* hearing, the IJ will consider whether the respondent's offense falls under the ground of removability charged (or, as discussed below, whether the respondent is properly classified as arriving versus admitted). The hearing will thus go to the very heart of the removal case itself. What's more, the U.S. Supreme Court has specifically upheld this approach (that a

---

[35] Specifically, the BIA found that the Maryland offense involved obstructing *one's own* arrest, rather than hindering or obstructing the investigation and arrest of another. The BIA wrote that INA §101(a)(43)(S) refers more to offenses that involve an intent to influence judicial or grand jury proceedings, rather than resisting arrest.

non–American citizen may request a *Joseph* hearing to contest the application of mandatory detention).[36]

Within this vein, the BIA set forth two different legal standards in *Joseph* to be applied in bond hearings, depending on the status or juncture of the removal case-in-chief.

1. Removability has been determined. Where removability has been determined (as in *Matter of Joseph*—the judge had already conducted the removal hearing), the judge's resolution of the removal case will be determinative. Thus, regardless of the requirement of separate bond and removal records, the judge may rely on his or her ultimate merits determination in deciding the bond case. An individual is not "properly included" in a mandatory detention category if the judge has already declined to sustain the pertinent charge of removability.

2. Removability has not been determined. In cases where the IJ has not yet determined whether the individual is removable as charged, the test is whether the government is "substantially unlikely" to prevail on the charge of removability as it pertains to INA §236(c). In other words, if the government is substantially unlikely to show that the respondent is removable as charged (as far as mandatory detention grounds are concerned), the judge may order the respondent released.

> **Bond Tip #2**: Certainly, a client desperately wants to be released from custody; however, counsel should not rush to a bond hearing unprepared, especially when the underlying issue is an important legal point—such as whether mandatory detention applies (in other words, a *Joseph* hearing that goes to the heart of removability). Where the case will be heavily contested by the parties, counsel should not hesitate to delay the hearing by two or three days—longer if necessary—to obtain important documentation, conduct appropriate research, and prepare quality legal argument. In the end, it is in the client's best interest to make sure the case is well prepared.

The significance of the burden of proof and persuasion in the context of a *Joseph* hearing is aptly illustrated in a recent decision on paraphernalia and personal possession of marijuana. In *Matter of Davey*,[37] the respondent was initially held by DHS in mandatory detention; the NTA alleged removability under INA §237(a)(2)(B). The respondent's crime? A conviction on two counts: one of simple possession of less than 30 grams of marijuana, the other possession of marijuana-related paraphernalia. The IJ found that DHS was unlikely to prevail in establishing deportability under INA §237(a)(2)(B) because the paraphernalia count was "related

---

[36] *Demore v. Kim*, 538 U.S. 510 (2003).
[37] *Matter of Davey*, 26 I&N Dec. 37 (BIA 2012).

to" a "single offense" for personal possession of less than 30 grams of marijuana. As such, according to the judge, the respondent was not deportable—or better said, DHS would not be able to meet its burden of establishing deportability (adopting a circumstance-specific approach). The BIA agreed with the IJ's decision, finding it substantially unlikely that DHS would prove the charge under INA §237(a)(2)(B). As such, the *Davey* decision is a great supplemental argument to *Joseph* in motions for custody redetermination.

Jurisdiction over Custody Issues

Arriving aliens

Although removal hearings are held in front of an IJ in an administrative court setting, not all respondents are eligible for a custody/bond hearing before an IJ. The IJ does not have jurisdiction over the custody determinations of "arriving aliens."[38] An "arriving alien" is an individual who is seeking admission at a port of entry. He or she will have been placed in proceedings by CBP. In addition, persons who have been paroled into the United States, whose parole is subsequently revoked, will be charged under INA §212(a) and treated as arriving aliens. They, too, are not entitled to a bond hearing before a judge.[39]

Where the non–American citizen is classified as an "arriving alien," authority over the custody determination lies with DHS. Initially, the custody determination (including a determination to set or deny bond) will be made by the arresting agency: ICE (in the case of a parolee) or CBP's Border Patrol (an alien arriving at a land border, or a parolee). Once the individual is in custody at a detention center, ICE's Office of Enforcement and Removal Operations (ERO) makes a custody determination. A request for release—and/or an argument that the individual is not subject to mandatory detention—is prepared and presented to the officer in charge, through the detention section of ICE. Thus, in a situation in which counsel believes the client is not subject to mandatory detention under INA §236(c), or otherwise should not be detained, the legal argument is presented to ICE and is not subject to review by the immigration court.

However, the regulations make clear that where an individual is classified by DHS in the NTA as an "arriving alien," and he or she does not agree with the "arriving alien" classification (based on the manner of entry into the United States), the individual may request a *Joseph*-type bond hearing to contest the classification.[40]

> ➢ **Compare**: Although persons who entered without inspection are charged in removal proceedings under INA §212(a) (grounds of inadmissibility), they are not "arriving aliens." They are persons who

---

[38] 8 CFR §1003.19(h)(2)(i)(B).
[39] 8 CFR §1003.19(h)(2)(i)(B).
[40] 8 CFR §§1003.19(h)(1)(ii) (for TPCR cases), (2)(ii) (for post-TPCR cases).

are present in the United States without being admitted or paroled.[41] These persons may seek a bond hearing in front of an IJ.[42]

Federal court review

Although neither the immigration court nor the BIA has jurisdiction over the custody determination of an "arriving alien," the federal courts may intervene pursuant to a petition for writ of habeas corpus when the continued detention is so long under the circumstances that it becomes an abuse of discretion. *Nadarajah v. Gonzales*[43] involved the case of a Sri Lankan national of Tamil ethnicity who was apprehended at the Mexican border in October 2001. His immigration case spanned several years, during which he remained detained. He won asylum in front of the IJ, and the BIA affirmed. DHS filed a motion to reopen for consideration of new evidence. The IJ denied reopening, but the BIA did reopen and remand. Asylum was again affirmed by both the IJ and the BIA, but the case was certified to the attorney general. By the time of certification, it was January 2006. The petitioner, although successful in his asylum application, was *still* detained by ICE authorities. ICE justified detention (in addition to contesting the asylum claim) based on its perspective that the petitioner was a member of the Tamil Tigers terrorist organization. In terms of custody, the IJ and BIA were without jurisdiction.

Although the district court denied the habeas petition, the U.S. Court of Appeals for the Ninth Circuit reversed, and ordered the petitioner's release pursuant to its authority at Fed. R. App. P. 23(b). The *Nadarajah* decision is significant on several scores. First, the Ninth Circuit reaffirmed jurisdiction over habeas corpus petitions involving detention. Second, the court found authority to order release based on Rule 23(b). Third, the court found that ICE cannot justify indefinite detention of an arriving alien based on suspicion of terrorism utilizing the general immigration detention provisions at INA §235(b) [8 USC §1225(b)] because the INA already contains specific provisions dealing with the detention of suspected terrorists [INA §507(b); 8 USC §1537(b)],[44] and these provisions (which require certification of continued detention to the attorney general in six-month increments) were not utilized

---

[41] *See* Appendix 1E, containing a sample NTA. There are three classifications of non–American citizens: arriving aliens, those present without admission or parole, and those who have been admitted. DHS checks a box at the top of the NTA to determine the classification.

[42] See 8 CFR §1003.19(2)(i) for a list of persons and cases over which the immigration judge (IJ) does not have jurisdiction in bond proceedings.

[43] *Nadarajah v. Gonzales*, 443 F.3d 1069 (9th Cir. 2006).

[44] For a case that indirectly disagrees with the analysis regarding suspicion of terrorism, see *Hussain v. Gonzales*, 492 F. Supp. 2d 1024 (E.D. Wis. 2007). In *Hussain*, the court did not specifically disagree with the *Nadarajah* decision, but did find that suspicion of terrorism justifies prolonged detention, even though the detainee is not specifically charged with suspicion of terrorism. *Id.* at 1034–35. The court did not mention INA §507(b).

in the petitioner's case. Fourth, relying on recent U.S. Supreme Court precedent,[45] the court found that petitioner's removal was not "reasonably foreseeable," and that the length of custody had become unreasonable:

> Applying the law to the facts of this case, we conclude that a writ of habeas corpus must issue and Nadarajah must be released from custody. The length of the detention in this case has been unreasonable. Nadarajah has established that there is no significant likelihood of removal in the reasonably foreseeable future. The government has failed to respond with sufficient evidence to rebut that showing.
>
> The nearly five-year detention in this case far exceeds both any period of confinement found reasonable by the Court, and the six-month period of presumptive reasonableness.[46]

Both before and after the *Nadarajah* decision, federal courts have been willing to entertain habeas petitions to consider whether the pre-order (pre-final removal order) detention is so long as to be unconstitutional.[47]

Deportable respondents and those who enter without inspection

Where the individual is charged as deportable under INA §237 [8 USC §1127] because he or she has already been admitted into the United States, the individual can request release, including bond, from the IJ in the context of a bond hearing. When an argument can be made that the individual is not subject to mandatory detention, the point may be litigated before the IJ.

In addition to individuals charged as deportable under INA §237, individuals who are physically present within the United States following an entry without inspection may request a full bond hearing before an IJ. [These persons are not "arriving aliens," even though they are charged with removability under INA §212(a) (inadmissibility).]

The "Release from Custody" Requirement

The mandatory detention provision cited in full above, states that a person will be taken into immigration custody upon release from state or federal custody. In other words, ICE will detain the person upon completion of the criminal sentence.

---

[45] *Zadvydas v. Davis*, 533 U.S. 678 (2001), and *Clark v. Martinez*, 543 U.S. 371 (2005), discuss continued detention after a removal order has been entered; these cases are discussed later in this book.

[46] *Nadarajah v. Gonzales*, 443 F.3d 1069 (9th Cir. 2006).

[47] *See, e.g., Madrane v. Hogan*, Civ. Action No. 1:05-CV-2228, 2007 WL 404032 (M.D. Pa. Feb. 1, 2007).

"When released" litigation[48]

A respondent who was not immediately detained following his criminal proceeding arguably should not be deemed to be subject to mandatory detention in the administrative immigration context. Under one reading of the statute, individuals who are not detained immediately upon concluding criminal custody are subject to discretionary detention and possible release under INA §236(a), 8 USC §1226(a), not mandatory detention under INA §236(c), 8 USC §1226(c).

However, the Board of Immigration Appeals held, in *Matter of Rojas*, that a noncitizen is subject to mandatory detention under INA §236(c), 8 USC §1226(c), even when DHS does not take the noncitizen into custody at the time of his or her release from incarceration.[49] Despite the holding of the BIA, the vast majority of federal district court decisions initially rejected *Matter of Rojas* as contrary to the unambiguous Congressional intent, as demonstrated by the statute's plain language and application of the canons of statutory construction.[50]

Three U.S. circuit courts of appeals, the Third, Fourth and Tenth, have held that the BIA's opinion in *Matter of Rojas* should receive deference.[51] After *Hosh* was decided, it was widely rejected by district courts outside of the U.S. Circuit Court of Appeals for the Fourth Circuit.[52] However, in *Sylvain,* the Third Circuit gave a much more reasoned decision, invoking *Chevron* for the principle of giving deference to an agency's reasonable interpretations of ambiguous statutes and detailing apparent ambiguity in the word "when" and the meaning of "when ... released," given the

---

[48] This section involving the "when released" provision of INA §236(c) and developing litigation was written by Attorney Sui Chung. The author thanks Ms. Chung for her contribution.

[49] *Matter of Rojas*, 23 I&N Dec. 117 (BIA 2001).

[50] *See, e.g. Charles v. Shanahan*, 2012 WL 4794313 at *6 (D.N.J. Oct. 9, 2012) ("This Court . . . holds that the plain language of §1226 unambiguously requires an alien to be detained immediately when released from criminal custody to be subject to mandatory detention. ... '[W]hen' means 'immediately'; it does not mean 'after.'") (citations omitted); *Scarlett v. ICE*, 632 F. Supp. 2d 214 (W.D.N.Y. 2009) at 219 ("[T]he clear language of the statute indicates that mandatory detention of aliens 'when' they are released requires that they be detained at the time of release. . . . [I]f Congress had intended for mandatory detention to apply any time after they were released, it could easily have used the language 'after the alien is released,' 'regardless of when the alien is released,' or other words to that effect.") (quoting *Quezada-Bucio v. Ridge*, 317 F. Supp. 2d 1221, 1224 (W.D. Wash. 2004)); *Bogarin-Flores v. Napolitano*, 2012 WL 3283287 at *3 (S.D. Cal. 2012) ("[A]liens who are not taken into custody immediately upon release from criminal custody are not subject to mandatory detention under §1226(c) for a variety of reasons ...").

[51] *See Sylvain v. Att'y Gen.*, 714 F.3d 150 (3d Cir. 2013); *Hosh v. Lucero*, 680 F.3d 375 (4th Cir. 2012); *Olmos v. Holder,* 2015 U.S. App. LEXIS 4778 (10th Cir. Mar. 24, 2015).

[52] *See e.g. Castaneda v. Souza*, No. 13-10874, at 12 (D.Mass. July 3, 2013) (noting that the "lack of analysis in *Hosh* is startling and likely the reason why the *Hosh* decision has had little impact as a persuasive precedent outside of the Fourth Circuit); *see also Davis v. Hendricks*, 2012 WL 6005713 *8 (D.N.J 2012) ("This Court notes that few (if any) courts outside the Fourth Circuit have been persuaded to follow *Hosh*"). *See also Bogarin-Flores*, 2012 WL 3283287 at *3 (noting the lack of "any independent reasoning or statutory construction" in the *Hosh* decision).

competing options of this being as a fixed event or a general time frame subsequent to release from criminal custody. Noting the precursor "shall take into custody" in §236(c), the court found the mandatory directive *to detain* should override the temporal ambiguity of *when to detain*, opining that "bureaucratic inaction—whether the result of inertia, oversight, or design—should not rob the public of statutory benefits.

Post-*Sylvain,* some district courts outside the Third and Fourth Circuits have continued to find that the "when ... released" language is an unambiguous congressional directive.[53] In their view, statutory interpretation must not render words superfluous within their context.[54] If the phrase "'when the alien is released' does not describe the class of aliens who are to be detained ... it would doom that clause to removable surplusage."[55] Because such a result is highly disfavored by traditional tools of statutory construction, this analysis suggests that the phrase "when the alien is released" must describe the group of aliens subject to mandatory detention."[56] Moreover, even assuming there is some ambiguity in the statute, it is arguable that the agency's interpretation of *Matter of Rojas* is unreasonable.[57]

However, in *Olmos v. Holder*,[58] the Tenth Circuit joined the Fourth and Third, noting that Congress requires the attorney general to impose mandatory detention for aliens convicted of certain crimes, even if the attorney general fails to fulfill this requirement in a timely manner. Thus, the Tenth Circuit views the "when ... released" language as a general principle that is not limited to the moment the defendant is released from custody, because the statutory requirement does not disappear. The requirement to detain remains, and the attorney general eventually would have to detain the alien under INA §236(c), whether immediately or upon detection of the immigrant at some point in the future. The Tenth Circuit further concluded that the canon of statutory interpretation dictating constitutional avoidance is inapplicable to the *Chevron* analysis of proper interpretation of the statute.

---

[53] *See Nieto Baquera v. Longshore*, 13-cv-00543 (D.Col. June 6, 2013) ("Here, the plain language of the statute requires immigration officials to detain an alien at the time the alien is released from custody in order for mandatory detention to apply. ... "When" connotes a temporal correlation between release and subsequent detention. The "when . . . released" phrase is a direction to the authorities that certain dangerous aliens should be continuously detained from the time of release from custody in qualifying criminal cases through their removal proceedings. That language means that this exception no longer applies to Mr. Nieto, given that ten years have lapsed since his "release.") "The most natural reading of the "when . . . released" provision is "immediately upon release." *Castaneda v. Souza*, No. 13-10874, at 12 (D.Mass. July 3, 2013) (noting that the "lack of analysis in *Hosh* is startling and likely the reason why the *Hosh* decision has had little impact as a persuasive precedent outside of the Fourth Circuit). *Id.* at 19.

[54] *See id.* at 13.

[55] *See id.*

[56] *See id.*

[57] *Louisaire v. Muller*, 758 F. Supp. 2d 229, 236 (S.D.N.Y. 2010).

[58] *Olmos v. Holder*, 2015 U.S. App. LEXIS 4778 (10th Cir. Mar. 24, 2015).

The First Circuit remains unsettled. In *Castaneda v. Souza*, the district court had found that "the most natural reading of the 'when ... released' provision is 'immediately upon release.'"[59] The court further noted that statutory interpretation must not render words superfluous within their context and that if the phrase "'when the alien is released' does not describe the class of aliens who are to be detained ... it would doom that clause to removable surplusage" in contradiction of principles of statutory interpretation.

The First Circuit initially agreed with the district court and held that the "when ... released" clause of INA §236(c) requires the government to take certain criminal aliens into immigration custody within a reasonable time after their release from criminal custody, and that the delay for the aliens in this case—a delay of "several years"—was not reasonable.[60] However, the court subsequently granted the motion of the Department of Justice to rehear *Casteneda* en banc, and withdrew its decision pending the resolution of rehearing.[61] As of the spring of 2015, the class action companion case, *Gordon, et. al. v. Holder*, also remains pending.

Does a sentence of imprisonment have to be imposed?

Another plain-reading interpretation of INA §236 is that an individual is not subject to mandatory detention if he or she is not sentenced to a term of imprisonment for the crime. In other words, if mandatory detention adheres to a person when he or she is released from custody, a person who is not sentenced to a period of custody cannot be subject to mandatory detention. Correct? Not quite. The BIA has recently taken a different approach.

ICE, and now the BIA, takes a cart-before-the-horse position: that custody at the time of initial arrest constitutes custody for purposes of INA §236(a). In *Matter of Kotliar*,[62] the BIA held that people who are not sentenced to any term of imprisonment for the crime may still be subject to mandatory detention based on the *custodial arrest* that preceded criminal court proceedings. Apparently, 10 minutes of detention in a police squad car would be sufficient physical restraint to trigger custody under this theory.

The BIA found support for this "custodial arrest = custody" position based on its dicta in *Matter of West*.[63] In *West*, the BIA stated in dicta that "released" can refer to release from physical custody following arrest. No further elaboration was provided, and there is no federal precedent precisely on point.

---

[59] *Castaneda v. Souza*, No. 13-10874, at 12 n. 4 (D. Mass. July 3, 2013).

[60] *Castaneda v. Souza*, 769 F.3d 32 (1st Cir. 2014).

[61] *Castaneda v. Souza,* No. 13-1994, Order of Court (1st Cir. January 23, 2015) (granting Appellees' motion for rehearing *en banc* and withdrawing decision).

[62] *Matter of Kotliar*, 24 I&N Dec. 124 (BIA 2007).

[63] *Matter of West*, 22 I&N Dec. 1405 (BIA 2000).

Attorneys should oppose this illogical interpretation of the law.[64] The proposition that a custodial arrest *in advance* of being tried and convicted for a crime can serve as the custody implicated by §236(c)(1)'s "when the alien is released" phrase is not logical in light of the language of the statute.

First, theoretically, mandatory detention is intended to keep incarcerated those persons who have been convicted of serious criminal activity; a person who is not even sentenced to serve time by a criminal court is probably not guilty of serious criminal activity. This philosophical position is sound based on the "when ... released" language chosen by Congress. The phrase becomes superfluous if Congress intended all persons convicted of crimes to be subject to mandatory detention, regardless of whether a sentence is imposed. (One may argue that Congress wanted to clarify that immigration custody should not take place until the penal sanction had been imposed. Yet it goes without saying that immigration proceedings do not commence until after state or federal custody is completed. In addition, the issue could be resolved with a simple sentence clarifying that, where a period of imprisonment is imposed as part of the sentence, immigration detention will commence upon completion of the criminal sentence.)

Second, the custodial arrest theory turns the statute on its head: a person cannot be subject to mandatory detention until he or she is removable on the basis of a conviction for a crime.[65] The custodial arrest comes before the conviction, not after. The logical sequence of mandatory detention is that first, the person is convicted (hence deportable or inadmissible); second, he or she is released from custody; third, he or she is picked up by DHS. A person does not take on the classification—or status—of being deportable until he or she has been convicted of crime. This classification must precede the release; the release from custody cannot precede the conviction.

Practitioners are encouraged to contest mandatory detention where the client was not sentenced to a period of imprisonment at all, and thus was never in custody following entry of a conviction that is a removable offense.

---

[64] This author used to lecture attorneys, as a matter of course, on the position that mandatory detention did not apply if a person was not sentenced to a period of incarceration for the crime. This position was based on two consecutive points: (1) a person is not subject to mandatory detention until he or she is actually convicted of a crime, and (2) is then released from custody. In other words, the individual must first be deportable or inadmissible for the crime, and *then* be released from custody. However, based on *Matter of Kotliar,* 24 I&N Dec. 124 (BIA 2007), it is clear the BIA disagrees with this interpretation of the law; certainly, the BIA's decision is subject to review in federal court.

[65] It should be noted that, presumably, some persons who do not have convictions but are charged with inadmissibility because of a "reason to believe" they have been involved in either drug trafficking or money laundering—or who admit the essential elements of a crime—could be held under mandatory detention. These nuances are discussed further in chapter eight.

Detention for Offense Not Charged on NTA

Matter of Kotliar, discussed above, stood for two propositions: First, custodial arrest (as well as other custody situations) can satisfy the "release" element of INA §236(c). Second, and just as troublesome from a strict construction standpoint, mandatory detention may be triggered based on a criminal offense for which the respondent *is not charged* in removal proceedings. In *Kotliar*, for the purposes of bond proceedings, ICE alleged that the respondent was removable for multiple crimes involving moral turpitude, but did not charge him as such. The BIA found that in the context of bond proceedings, a respondent may be held under mandatory detention even though the offense that triggers mandatory detention is not a ground of removability; it is not necessary that the charges be brought in the NTA in removal proceedings. According to the BIA, the respondent is advised in the context of bond proceedings of the criminal offenses that form the basis for §236(c) to apply; he or she does not need to be advised within the NTA. Thus, the BIA approached the issue as a question of advisal and fair notice, rather than adhering to the clear language of the statute, which requires that the person *be* inadmissible or deportable.

Matter of Kotliar is *not* a good decision; it is not based on sound reasoning that adheres to the plain language of INA §236. It simply does not make sense to impose mandatory detention on account of criminal offenses that are not alleged as the underlying bases for removal. Practitioners are encouraged to contest the holdings of *Kotliar* in federal court in habeas corpus proceedings.

After *Kotliar*, the BIA expanded on the theme of nonrelevant custodial situations (custody for situations that do not support removal proceedings) being sufficient to trigger mandatory detention. In *Matter of Saysana*,[66] the Board ruled that any non-DHS custody after October 8, 1998, is sufficient to trigger mandatory detention, including an arrest that does not lead to a conviction. In *Saysana*, the respondent was subject to removal for an aggravated felony offense (indecent assault and battery). The respondent was convicted in 1990, and sentenced to five years' imprisonment. Accordingly, he was released from criminal custody before the expiration of the TPCR. In 2005, the respondent was arrested for failure to register as a sex offender. This charge was later dismissed. The BIA ruled that any custody—even a dismissed charge—could trigger mandatory detention.

However, the First Circuit overruled *Saysana*.[67] In June 2010, the BIA overruled its decision in *Saysana*. In *Matter of Arreola*,[68] the Board ruled that the penal custody that triggers mandatory detention must be an offense directly tied to the basis for

---

[66] *Matter of Saysana*, 24 I&N Dec. 602 (BIA 2008).

[67] *Saysana v. Gillen*, 590 F.3d 7 (1st Cir. 2009).

[68] *Matter of Arreola*, 25 I&N Dec. 267 (BIA 2010).

detention as delineated by INA §236(c). The Board did not mention that it was modifying *Kotliar*.[69]

> **Notable**: In habeas corpus proceedings contesting mandatory detention, and challenging clear BIA precedent, the courts have held that exhaustion of administrative remedies is not a prerequisite to seeking judicial review because the agency has predetermined the issue before it. In such a case, administrative review would be "futile."[70] This means the detained individual may go directly from a determination by an IJ that there is no jurisdiction over bond to a habeas petition in federal court.

Releases on or Before October 8, 1998

Persons who were released from custody on or before October 8, 1998, are covered by the TPCR. In addition, the rules of custody and bond determinations for persons governed by the TPCR are spelled out in the regulations at 8 CFR §§236.1, 1236.1. Generally, individuals released from state or federal custody prior to October 8, 1998, who are now in removal proceedings, may be released on bond if they were lawfully admitted into the United States; *i.e.*, they are now in the *deportation* track under INA §237. Persons who are applicants for admission (arriving aliens) charged with being inadmissible under INA §212(a) are not eligible for release on bond unless they are returning LPRs.[71]

The discussion of mandatory detention and who is covered continues in chapters six, seven, and eight with the classifications of crimes and their corresponding consequences.

Other Detention Issues

Mandatory detention under INA §236(c) [8 USC §1226(c)] is the most drastic custody provision. However, what about those persons in removal proceedings who are not subject to mandatory detention, but nonetheless face detention in an immigration facility? In certain cases, ICE may desire to hold a person without bond even though the person does not fall under the purview of INA §236(c). This may be true when the individual's conviction, though pre-October 1998, is deemed serious, or there are other extenuating circumstances that in ICE's opinion—whether or not justified—merit custody without bond.

Whenever an individual is arrested by DHS, be it ICE or CBP, an initial custody determination, reflected on the NTA, must be made. Then, the individual may have

---

[69] *Matter of Kotliar*, 24 I&N Dec. 124 (BIA 2007).
[70] *See, e.g.*, *Hy v. Gillen*, 588 F. Supp. 2d at 125–26; *Garcia v. Shanahan*, 615 F. Supp. 2d 175, 179–180 (S.D.N.Y. 2009).
[71] *See* 8 CFR §§236.1(c)(2)(i), 1236.1(c)(2)(i).

an opportunity for a bond hearing before an IJ. In addition, the individual may be successful in having the initial custody determination reconsidered by the officer-in-charge of the detention facility, or the director of ERO. Following is a brief discussion of detention issues when the individual is not subject to mandatory detention but is detained nonetheless and would like to "get out."

Non–Mandatory Detention Cases: The Standard

When a client is not subject to mandatory detention, either because his or her case falls under the TPCR or because the ground of removability is not found at INA §236(c), the "traditional" bond standard applies. To be eligible for release, a non–American citizen must establish (by clear and convincing evidence) that he or she does not pose a danger to the safety of persons or property within the United States and is unlikely to abscond (*i.e.*, will report for any and all hearings and immigration-related appointments).[72] After October 8, 1998, a non–American citizen taken into custody who is not subject to mandatory detention and seeks a custody determination (bond hearing) before an IJ must post a minimum $1,500 bond.[73] Note that the field director for ICE is not required to set this minimum bond, but may release an individual on recognizance (for example, when ICE has sole jurisdiction, as with arriving aliens).

The automatic stay

Either party may appeal the IJ's bond determination to the BIA. Where DHS (the ICE Office of Chief Counsel) is the appealing party, it may want to stay the custody determination of the judge, thereby preventing release of the respondent during the course of the bond appeal. The regulations contain two separate provisions regarding stays. They are found at 8 CFR §1003.19(i). The first stay provision requires the government to *seek* an emergency stay from the BIA. The BIA may stay the IJ's custody determination in the exercise of its discretion.

However, the second stay provision is a powerful tool in DHS's arsenal: the automatic stay. Found at 8 CFR §1003.19(i)(2), the automatic stay provision allows the Office of Chief Counsel to *automatically* and *unilaterally* stay execution of the judge's bond decision and block the respondent's release from custody in conjunction with the bond appeal. The automatic stay has a history. This regulation is not supported by any statutory provision in the INA. It was inserted on an emergency basis on October 31, 2001[74] (45 days after the terrorist attacks of September 11, 2001), without traditional rule promulgation—including a public comment period—as required under the Administrative Procedure Act. Then–Attorney General John Ashcroft argued that the regulation was necessary to prevent the release of dangerous terrorists. However, the authority was abused. The Office of Chief Counsel routinely

---

[72] *Matter of Noble*, 21 I&N Dec. 672 (BIA 1997); 8 CFR §§236.1(c)(3), 1236.1(c)(3).

[73] INA §236(a)(2)(A); 8 USC §1226(a)(2)(A).

[74] 66 Fed. Reg. 54909 (Oct. 31, 2001).

utilized the automatic stay in all manner of cases that had nothing to do with terrorism or national security. The stay was even used when there was no criminal conviction, or only a minor conviction record. The automatic stay provision was amended by regulation (with traditional rule promulgation this time) on October 2, 2006[75]—perhaps in response to federal lawsuits, some of which resulted in a finding that the stay provision was unconstitutional.[76]

The provision now reads as follows:

Automatic stay in certain cases. In any case in which DHS has determined that an alien should not be released or has set a bond of $10,000 or more, any order of the immigration judge authorizing release (on bond or otherwise) shall be stayed upon DHS's filing of a notice of intent to appeal the custody redetermination (Form EOIR-43) with the immigration court within one business day of the order, and, except as otherwise provided in 8 CFR 1003.6(c), shall remain in abeyance pending decision of the appeal by the Board. The decision whether or not to file Form EOIR-43 is subject to the discretion of the Secretary [of Homeland Security].

The key change is the reference to 8 CFR §1003.6(c). Prior to October 2, 2006, the automatic stay allowed for indefinite detention. As a result of the amended rule, the automatic stay expires in 90 days if the bond appeal has not been decided by the BIA. However, extensions may be granted, by motion from DHS, and, in the discretion of the BIA, under 8 CFR §1003.19(i)(1). In this case, it is no longer a unilateral, automatic stay, but a stay imposed by the BIA at its discretion. Furthermore, if the non–American citizen detainee requests an extension of the briefing schedule for the bond appeal, the 90-day clock is tolled for the period of time that an extension is granted. The regulation at 8 CFR §1003.6 reads as follows:

(c) The following procedures shall be applicable with respect to custody appeals in which DHS has invoked an automatic stay pursuant to 8 CFR 1003.19(i)(2).

(1) The stay shall lapse if DHS fails to file a notice of appeal with the Board within ten business days of the issuance of the order of the immigration judge. DHS should identify the appeal as an automatic stay case. To preserve the automatic stay, the attorney for DHS shall file with the notice of appeal a certification by a senior legal official that—

(i) The official has approved the filing of the notice of appeal according to review procedures established by DHS; and

---

[75] 71 Fed. Reg. 5783 (Oct. 2, 2006) (final rule).

[76] The cases in which, prior to the amendment, the automatic stay at 8 CFR §1003.19(2)(i) was found to be unconstitutional include but are not limited to: *Zavala v. Ridge*, 310 F. Supp. 2d 1071 (N.D. Cal. 2004); *Ashley v. Ridge*, 288 F. Supp. 2d 662 (D.N.J. 2003); and *Uritzky v. Ridge*, 286 F. Supp. 2d 842 (E.D. Mich. 2003).

(ii) The official is satisfied that the contentions justifying the continued detention of the alien have evidentiary support, and the legal arguments are warranted by existing law or by a non-frivolous argument for the extension, modification, or reversal of existing precedent or the establishment of new precedent.

(2) The immigration judge shall prepare a written decision explaining the custody determination within five business days after the immigration judge is advised that DHS has filed a notice of appeal, or, with the approval of the Board in exigent circumstances, as soon as practicable thereafter (not to exceed five additional business days). The immigration court shall prepare and submit the record of proceedings without delay.

(3) The Board will track the progress of each custody appeal which is subject to an automatic stay in order to avoid unnecessary delays in completing the record for decision. Each order issued by the Board should identify the appeal as an automatic stay case. The Board shall notify the parties in a timely manner of the date the automatic stay is scheduled to expire.

(4) If the Board has not acted on the custody appeal, the automatic stay shall lapse 90 days after the filing of the notice of appeal. However, if the Board grants a motion by the alien for an enlargement of the 21-day briefing schedule provided in §1003.3(c), the Board's order shall also toll the 90-day period of the automatic stay for the same number of days.

(5) DHS may seek a discretionary stay pursuant to 8 CFR 1003.19(i)(1) to stay the immigration judge's order in the event the Board does not issue a decision on the custody appeal within the period of the automatic stay. DHS may submit a motion for discretionary stay at any time after the filing of its notice of appeal of the custody decision, and at a reasonable time before the expiration of the period of the automatic stay, and the motion may incorporate by reference the arguments presented in its brief in support of the need for continued detention of the alien during the pendency of the removal proceedings. If DHS has submitted such a motion and the Board is unable to resolve the custody appeal within the period of the automatic stay, the Board will issue an order granting or denying a motion for discretionary stay pending its decision on the custody appeal. The Board shall issue guidance to ensure prompt adjudication of motions for discretionary stays. If the Board fails to adjudicate a previously-filed stay motion by the end of the 90-day period, the stay will remain in effect (but not more than 30 days) during the time it takes for the Board to decide whether or not to grant a discretionary stay.

(d) If the Board authorizes an alien's release (on bond or otherwise), denies a motion for discretionary stay, or fails to act on such a motion before the automatic stay period expires, the alien's release shall be automatically stayed for five business days. If, within that five-day period, the Secretary of

Homeland Security or other designated official refers the custody case to the Attorney General pursuant to 8 CFR 1003.1(h)(1), the alien's release shall continue to be stayed pending the Attorney General's consideration of the case. The automatic stay will expire 15 business days after the case is referred to the Attorney General. DHS may submit a motion and proposed order for a discretionary stay in connection with referring the case to the Attorney General. For purposes of this paragraph and 8 CFR 1003.1(h)(1), decisions of the Board shall include those cases where the Board fails to act on a motion for discretionary stay. The Attorney General may order a discretionary stay pending the disposition of any custody case by the Attorney General or by the Board.

To sum up the automatic stay procedures after October 2, 2006: the automatic stay can only be utilized by the DHS Office of Chief Counsel if, at the time of arrest, ICE initially sets the bond at $10,000 or higher. If the initial bond at time of arrest was a lower amount, the automatic stay cannot be invoked. In addition, the notification of stay must be filed within one business day of the judge's decision, and the notice of appeal must then be filed within 10 business days. If the government does not follow up with a notice of appeal, the stay lapses. The stay expires after 90 days if the BIA has not made a decision; however, the BIA is instructed to carefully monitor and expedite adjudication of the appeal. The government may request a discretionary stay after 90 days, pursuant to 8 CFR §1003.19(i)(1).

The stay is also extinguished upon a final determination of the BIA in the bond case, with one important caveat: if the BIA's decision is unfavorable to the government, the stay remains in place for five additional days while the Office of Chief Counsel considers whether to seek attorney general review. If the bond case is certified to the attorney general, the stay remains in effect for 15 days, unless the attorney general specifically stays release.

Based on amended procedures, the Office of Chief Counsel must adhere to a set of criteria, and the determination to stay release must be agreed to by a senior legal official who has reviewed the stay in light of agency criteria. This certification must be included in the notice of appeal and stay.

Although certainly an improvement upon the previous system, the current stay authority still allows the government effectively to bypass the adversarial system of due process and trump both the judge's and the BIA's authority with regard to custody and bond. Although a 90-day limit is preferable to indefinite detention, three months is still a long time to be detained on noncriminal charges when an IJ has ordered release on bond. A BIA bond appeal may take months; attorney general review takes months longer. During the 90-day time period, the removal case-in-chief moves forward and will very often be decided. Thus, if the government is opposed to release of a respondent, bond proceedings before the judge and BIA remain a charade—the automatic stay provision still operates to keep a client detained throughout an entire removal case, despite the IJ's and/or BIA's decisions to the contrary.

Practitioners interested in contesting the automatic stay provision, notwithstanding the amended version of the rule, will want to consider the three-factor analysis set forth by the court in *Zavala v. Ridge*,[77] which is based on U.S. Supreme Court precedent,[78] to define the test of constitutionality:

(1) "the nature of the private interest affected by the government action"—the private interest at stake is an individual's interest in liberty versus the government's interest in keeping him or her detained.

(2) "the risk of an erroneous deprivation of the interest as a result of the procedures used and the probable value of additional or substitute safeguards"—Congress has already spoken at INA §236(c) as to who should be mandatorily detained; in addition, the stay will arise where an independent IJ has determined release appropriate based on the posting of a certain bond. Accordingly, the risk that the automatic stay will result in improper detention is high.

(3) "the government's interest in using its own procedures and the fiscal and administrative burdens by additional or substitute safeguards"—the government already has the ability to request an emergency stay from the BIA[79] and also has programs such as intensive supervision, including electronic monitoring (ankle bracelets), coupled with the financial bond, to ensure an individual's appearance.[80]

In light of the October 2006 modifications, the automatic stay is less troubling. (One need only ask the detained client how he or she feels about three more months in detention.) The question is more one of observation: it is unclear whether DHS continues to use (*i.e.*, abuse) the automatic stay in all sorts of cases, or whether—in light of the supervisory review requirements—its use is more tempered. This is a question that will be answered in time. If the individual case merits a habeas action, the automatic stay provision, even in its modified form, is still constitutionally suspect and worth challenging.[81]

Detention After a Removal Order

The INA requires the government to detain an individual who has been ordered removed.[82] The government "shall" remove an individual who has been ordered

---

[77] *Zavala v. Ridge*, 310 F. Supp. 2d 1071 (N.D. Cal. 2004).

[78] *Mathews v. Eldridge*, 424 U.S. 319, 335 (1976).

[79] The traditional emergency stay request is found at 8 CFR §1003.19(i)(1), and is accomplished via motion to the BIA, as opposed to a unilateral and automatic stay.

[80] *Zavala v. Ridge*, 310 F. Supp. 2d 1071 (N.D. Cal. 2004), at 1077–78.

[81] For sample habeas petitions and litigation reference in general, see *AILA's Immigration Litigation Toolbox* (4th Ed. 2013), available from AILA Publications, http://*agora.aila.org*, (800) 982-2839.

[82] INA §241(a)(2); 8 USC §1231(a)(2).

removed within 90 days: a period referred to by statute as "the removal period."[83] If the non–American citizen cannot be removed within 90 days, he or she is subject to supervision.[84]

Certain non–American citizens cannot be removed from the United States even after a final order of removal is entered against them.[85] These are the unremovables. They include, but are not limited to, most citizens of Cuba, and certain Jewish refugees from the former Soviet Union countries. Stateless persons can be removed only in certain situations. An IJ may order removal to their country of last residence; the country from which they came when it is a contiguous territory to the United States; or any country whose government will accept them.[86] For many years, the government continued to detain many "unremovable" individuals under the theory that they posed a threat to the community. In certain circumstances, procedures were put in place for a panel to interview indefinitely detained individuals and review whether they should be released. Some individuals, including many Cuban nationals, were detained for years after a final removal order—with no end in sight.

In *Zadvydas v. Davis*,[87] the U.S. Supreme Court ruled that indefinite detention of a non–American citizen who had been ordered removed was unconstitutional. The Court ruled that if removal is not reasonably foreseeable in the near future, detention beyond a six-month period is unconstitutional. The Court held that the burden is on the non–American citizen to show that there is no significant likelihood of removal in government to respond with evidence sufficient to rebut that showing.

The *Zadvydas* case involved petitioners who had been found deportable or removable under INA §237(a) [8 USC §1227(a)]—in other words, persons who had been admitted. It did not encompass arriving individuals, individuals paroled into the United States, or other detained non–American citizens found excludable or inadmissible under INA §212(a) [8 USC §1182(a)]. As a result, notwithstanding *Zadvydas*, many unremovable individuals continued in indefinite detention after 2001. However, in *Clark v. Martinez*,[88] the Supreme Court extended its ruling in *Zadvydas* to non–American citizens who had not been "admitted" upon arrival in the United States and were thus ordered removed under INA §212(a). Based on these decisions, absent a showing that it is likely the individual can and may be removed soon, a non–American citizen (admitted or not) may not be detained more than six months after the final removal order. These individuals, once released, may be

---

[83] INA §241(a)(1); 8 USC §1231(a)(1).
[84] INA §241(a)(3); 8 USC §1231(a)(3).
[85] *See* INA §241(b)(3); 8 USC §1231(b)(3).
[86] INA §241(b)(1); 8 USC §1231(b)(1).
[87] 533 U.S. 678 (2001).
[88] 543 U.S. 371 (2005).

monitored by ICE through orders of supervision.[89] Note that the six-month period begins to run from the day of the final removal order.

Several district courts have issued decisions post-removal order determining that the ongoing detention is unlawful. Some courts have focused on a bright-line six-month rule, and others have exercised broader criteria.[90] This discussion may be cross-referenced with the discussion of litigation post–*Demore v. Kim*[91] earlier in the chapter.

At least one court has found there is no cause of action under *Zavydas* until six months after the removal order, even if—during the course of proceedings—it appears highly unlikely that ICE will be able to remove the detainee.[92] Likewise, another court has found that the six-month period for purposes of a cause of action under *Zavydas* (the "presumptively reasonable period of detention") begins to accrue upon entry of a final administrative removal order. Moreover, even when an action becomes ripe (*i.e.*, after the six-month period), the non–American citizen has the burden to show there is no significant likelihood of removal in the foreseeable future. When ICE is taking active steps to find a third country to accept the detainee, and to obtain proper travel documents through diplomatic assistance, this burden cannot be met and detention remains lawful.[93]

Detention during judicial review of final removal order

As stated above, the law requires that following a final order of removal, the attorney general shall detain the non–American citizen; "under no circumstances during the removal period shall the Attorney General release" an individual found removable under INA §§212(a)(2) or 212(a)(3)(B), or deportable under §§237(a)(2) or 237(a)(4)(B).[94] Again, the period of time following an administratively final removal order is known as the "removal period." However, neither this provision, nor any other section of the law, specifically addresses whether a non–American citizen should be detained during the pendency of a petition for review.

In *Prieto-Romero v. Clark*,[95] the Ninth Circuit U.S. Court of Appeals ruled that the period of time that a petition for review is pending is not part of the "removal period," and release from custody is determined by the general rules at INA §236(a). The petitioner in *Prieto* was not subject to mandatory detention under INA §236(c);

---

[89] See chapter one for the definition of "order of supervision."

[90] *Tijani v. Willis*, 430 F.3d 1241 (9th Cir. 2005) (32 months); *Ly v. Hansen*, 351 F.3d 263 (6th Cir. 2003) (500 days); *Jeune v. Candemeres*, No. 13-22333-CIV-Altonaga/Simonton (S.D. Fla. Dec. 11, 2013).

[91] *Demore v. Kim*, 538 U.S. 510 (2003).

[92] *Khotesouvan v. Morones*, 386 F.3d 1298 (9th Cir. 2004).

[93] *Ali v. Barlow*, 446 F. Supp. 2d 604 (E.D. Va. 2006).

[94] INA §241(a)(2); 8 USC §1231(a)(2).

[95] *Prieto-Romero v. Clark*, 534 F.3d 1053 (9th Cir. 2008).

although he was removable for an aggravated felony, he had been released from penal custody prior to October 8, 1998. Upon entry of a final order of removal, he filed a petition for review, and also received a stay of removal.

The court found that he was entitled to an individualized bond determination as to whether he should be released pending a decision on the petition for review. The court of appeals noted, within this regard, that the attorney general's determination may be to continue with detention, and that would be constitutionally acceptable notwithstanding the fact that the petition for review had been pending for three years.[96] Section 236(a) continues to apply during the period of judicial review. The reader will note, in this case, that the petitioner received a stay of removal; the outcome could have been different (*i.e.,* deportation) if the stay was not in place.

Alternatives to detention

Over the past few years, ERO has experimented with alternative methods to detain individuals who are in removal proceedings but not subject to mandatory detention. As a result, many non–American citizens across the country who are not subject to mandatory detention and not detained in a facility are nevertheless supervised by ERO.

ERO has several methods of monitoring a person in removal proceedings:

- "Release on recognizance" involves regular reporting to an ERO office, but no bond. If ERO decides to impose a bond, the statute requires that the minimum bond set be $1,500.[97] This bond is forfeited if an individual does not report as required to ERO, to court, or for deportation.

- Electronic monitoring is part of a program whereby individuals in removal proceedings wear an ankle bracelet and/or report by telephone to a case manager between hearings. Although the electronic monitoring program was originally a pilot program, ICE introduced and implemented it nationwide.[98]

- The Intensive Supervision Appearance Program (ISAP) is a program, administered by a private contracting company hired by ICE, which closely monitors the movements of non–American citizens in removal proceedings in an effort to ensure their compliance with court dates and other immigration-related appointments. ISAP is not utilized in every city or region, but the program is quickly expanding. ISAP involves a combination of methods: electronic monitoring (an ankle bracelet), curfews, weekly or monthly reporting, surprise home visits, even assistance with translations and the local bus schedule. As an individual demonstrates compliance, the restrictions are eased—the bracelet comes off and the curfew is expanded.

---

[96] *Prieto-Romero v. Clark*, 534 F.3d 1053, at 1065.

[97] INA §236(a)(2)(A); 8 USC §1226(a)(2)(A).

[98] *See* www.ice.gov/doclib/foia/dro_policy_memos/dropolicymemoeligibilityfordroisapandemdprograms.pdf.

Increasingly, individuals with no criminal record, or a minor record, are placed under ISAP. The program is also utilized in connection with orders of supervision (following a removal order) and stays (for example, when a motion to reopen is pending).

Is ISAP good for the non–American citizen in removal proceedings? It depends on the case. If an individual has no criminal record (or a minor record), relief from removal available, and family support in the community, there really is no good reason to tether an electronic bracelet around his or her ankle and impose a curfew. It is an unnecessary and costly imposition. Certainly, this infringement on a person's liberty can be contested before the IJ in bond proceedings.[99] If an IJ orders release on bond and the bond is posted, arguably, ICE cannot or should not impose an additional burden. From this point of view, an individual who is not subject to mandatory detention should be released on a reasonable bond—or recognizance—with no other restraints on liberty (especially where the program is not utilized in all jurisdictions—an equal protection concern).

On the other hand, the availability of ISAP may be an extremely effective bargaining tool in a contested bond case. In other words, when the case involves some complicated issues and either the judge, ICE counsel, or both, hesitate to order release on bond, the added safeguard of ISAP lends itself to the argument that the client can and should be released pending removal proceedings. In both published and unpublished decisions, the BIA has found that the IJ may consider electronic monitoring (and, in the latter case, ISAP) in determining whether the non–American citizen should be released on bond.[100] From this point of view, ISAP is a positive development because defense counsel can argue that a monetary bond, coupled with ISAP, ensures a client's appearance and good behavior. Accordingly, as the argument goes, release from custody is justified.

These advanced tools and programs raise the question of whether an IJ has jurisdiction to order or ameliorate these conditions. There is also a legal question of whether intensive supervision qualifies as "custody" for purposes of mandatory detention under INA 236(c).

In *Matter of Garcia-Garcia*,[101] the BIA ruled that the IJ does have jurisdiction over the conditions of release and may order different forms of intensive supervision—or ameliorate said conditions—as part of the courts' jurisdiction over custody and release under INA §236(a)(2)(A).[102]

---

[99] See the earlier discussion of custody/bond hearings.
[100] *Matter of Khalifah*, 21 I&N Dec. 107 (BIA 1995).
[101] *Matter of Garcia-Garcia*, 25 I&N Dec. 93 (2009).
[102] See also 8 CFR §1236.1(d)(1).

For a discussion of whether intensive supervision meets the definition of "custody" for purposes of satisfying INA §236(c)'s mandatory detention requirement, see the position paper included as an appendix item to this chapter.

APPENDIX 4A

CUSTODY RULE INVOKED

(*Published on* AILA InfoNet at Doc. No. 96101590 (*posted* Oct. 15, 1996))

The Honorable Orrin G. Hatch
Chairman, Committee on the Judiciary
United States Senate
Washington, D.C. 20510

Dear Mr. Chairman:

Pursuant to authority delegated to me by the Attorney General, 28 C.F.R. Section 0.105, I am writing to provide you the notification regarding custody specified by section 303(b)(2) of the Illegal Immigration Reform and Immigrant Responsibility Act of 1996, Pub. L. No. 104-208 (1996 Act), and thereby to invoke the application, for the coming year, of the transition period custody rules provided by section 303(b)(3) of the 1996 Act.

I have made the statutory determination in recognition of the following facts: (1) that the notification must cover the entirety of the succeeding 1-year period yet must be provided no later than October 10, 1996; (2) that Immigration and Naturalization Service (INS) detention space is predominately used for the detention of criminal aliens, under the Administration's priorities and consistent with the statutory sections referred to in section 303(b)(2) of the 1996 Act, but must also be used to provide indispensable detention in connection with a wide variety of enforcement missions at the border and in the interior of the United States, including several responsibilities mandated by the Congress and monitored closely by your committee and the appropriations committees; (3) that the provisions of the Antiterrorism and Effective Death Penalty Act, Pub. L. No. 104-132, affecting criminal aliens have been subject to numerous court challenges, which make determination of the full detention and enforcement needs of the INS over the coming year difficult to predict, and that the comparable provisions of the 1996 Act are likely to be subject to similar challenges until definitive judicial rulings are obtained; (4) that additional requirements, of as yet uncertain impact, are imposed on INS to detain persons with final orders throughout the "removal period" under the new INA section 241(a), added by section 305 of the 1996 Act; and (5) that detention and enforcement requirements can change suddenly and dramatically based on factors outside the control of the Department of Justice or the INS, as in the case of a large-scale influx.

Therefore, based on the facts listed above, I hereby notify the Committee that there is insufficient detention space and Immigration and Naturalization Service personnel available to carry out section 236(c) of the Immigration and Nationality

Act, as amended by section 303(a) of the 1996 Act, or the amendments made by section 440(c) of Public Law 104-132, the Antiterrorism and Effective Death Penalty Act, throughout the coming year.

I assure you that the detention and removal of criminal aliens from the United States remain among my highest priorities and that the INS will administer the transition period custody rules provided by section 303(b)(3) of the 1996 Act in a manner that is fully consistent with these objectives.

Sincerely,

Doris Meissner
Commissioner

cc: The Honorable Joseph R. Biden, Jr.

APPENDIX 4B

SECTION 309 OF IIRAIRA

SEC. 309. EFFECTIVE DATES; TRANSITION.

(a) IN GENERAL.—Except as provided in this section and sections 303(b)(2), 306(c), 308(d)(2)(D), or 308(d)(5) of this division, this subtitle and the amendments made by this subtitle shall take effect on the first day of the first month beginning more than 180 days after the date of the enactment of this Act (in this title referred to as the "title III-A effective date").

(b) PROMULGATION OF REGULATIONS.—The Attorney General shall first promulgate regulations to carry out this subtitle by not later than 30 days before the title III-A effective date.

(c) TRANSITION FOR ALIENS IN PROCEEDINGS.—

(1) GENERAL RULE THAT NEW RULES DO NOT APPLY.— Subject to the succeeding provisions of this subsection, in the case of an alien who is in exclusion or deportation proceedings as of the title III-A effective date—

(A) the amendments made by this subtitle shall not apply, and

(B) the proceedings (including judicial review thereof) shall continue to be conducted without regard to such amendments.

(2) ATTORNEY GENERAL OPTION TO ELECT TO APPLY NEW PROCEDURES.—In a case described in paragraph (1) in which an evidentiary hearing under section 236 or 242 and 242B of the Immigration and Nationality Act has not commenced as of the title III-A effective date, the Attorney General may elect to proceed under chapter 4 of title II of such Act (as amended by this subtitle). The Attorney General shall provide notice of such election to the alien involved not later than 30 days before the date any evidentiary hearing is commenced. If the Attorney General makes such election, the notice of hearing provided to the alien under section 235 or 242(a) of such Act shall be valid as if provided under section 239 of such Act (as amended by this subtitle) to confer jurisdiction on the immigration judge.

(3) ATTORNEY GENERAL OPTION TO TERMINATE AND REINITIATE PROCEEDINGS.—In the case described in paragraph (1), the Attorney General may elect to terminate proceedings in which there has not been a final administrative decision and to reinitiate proceedings under chapter 4 of title II the Immigration and Nationality Act (as amended by this subtitle). Any determination in the terminated proceeding shall not be binding in the reinitiated proceeding.

(4) TRANSITIONAL CHANGES IN JUDICIAL REVIEW.—In the case described in paragraph (1) in which a final order of exclusion or deportation is entered more than 30 days after the date of the enactment of this Act, notwithstanding any provision of section 106 of the Immigration and Nationality Act (as in effect as of the date of the enactment of this Act) to the contrary—

(A) in the case of judicial review of a final order of exclusion, subsection (b) of such section shall not apply and the action for judicial review shall be governed by the provisions of subsections (a) and (c) of such in the same manner as they apply to judicial review of orders of deportation;

(B) a court may not order the taking of additional evidence under section 2347(c) of title 28, United States Code;

(C) the petition for judicial review must be filed not later than 30 days after the date of the final order of exclusion or deportation;

(D) the petition for review shall be filed with the court of appeals for the judicial circuit in which the administrative proceedings before the special inquiry officer or immigration judge were completed;

(E) there shall be no appeal of any discretionary decision under section 212(c), 212(h), 212(i), 244, or 245 of the Immigration and Nationality Act (as in effect as of the date of the enactment of this Act);

(F) service of the petition for review shall not stay the deportation of an alien pending the court's decision on the petition, unless the court orders otherwise; and

(G) there shall be no appeal permitted in the case of an alien who is inadmissible or deportable by reason of having committed a criminal offense covered in section 212(a)(2) or section 241(a)(2)(A)(iii), (B), (C), or (D) of the Immigration and Nationality Act (as in effect as of the date of the enactment of this Act), or any offense covered by section 241(a)(2)(A)(ii) of such Act (as in effect on such date) for which both predicate offenses are, without regard to their date of commission, otherwise covered by section 241(a)(2)(A)(i) of such Act (as so in effect).

(5) TRANSITIONAL RULE WITH REGARD TO SUSPENSION OF DEPORTATION.—Paragraphs (1) and (2) of section 240A(d) of the Immigration and Nationality Act (relating to continuous residence or physical presence) shall apply to notices to appear issued before, on, or after the date of the enactment of this Act.

(6) TRANSITION FOR CERTAIN FAMILY UNITY ALIENS.—The Attorney General may waive the application of section 212(a)(9) of the Immigration and Nationality Act, as inserted by section 301(b)(1) of this division, in the case of an alien who is provided benefits under the

provisions of section 301 of the Immigration Act of 1990 (relating to family unity).

(7) LIMITATION ON SUSPENSION OF DEPORTATION.—The Attorney General may not suspend the deportation and adjust the status under section 244 of the Immigration and Nationality Act of more than 4,000 aliens in any fiscal year (beginning after the date of the enactment of this Act). The previous sentence shall apply regardless of when an alien applied for such suspension and adjustment.

(d) TRANSITIONAL REFERENCES.—For purposes of carrying out the Immigration and Nationality Act, as amended by this subtitle—

(1) any reference in section 212(a)(1)(A) of such Act to the term "inadmissible" is deemed to include a reference to the term "excludable," and

(2) any reference in law to an order of removal shall be deemed to include a reference to an order of exclusion and deportation or an order of deportation.

(e) TRANSITION.—No period of time before the date of the enactment of this Act shall be included in the period of 1 year described in section 212(a)(6)(B)(i) of the Immigration and Nationality Act (as amended by section 301(c) of this division).

APPENDIX 4C

SECTION 303(b) OF IIRAIRA

(b) EFFECTIVE DATE.—

(1) IN GENERAL.—The amendment made by subsection (a) shall become effective on the title III-A effective date.

(2) NOTIFICATION REGARDING CUSTODY.—If the Attorney General, not later than 10 days after the date of the enactment of this Act, notifies in writing the Committees on the Judiciary of the House of Representatives and the Senate that there is insufficient detention space and Immigration and Naturalization Service personnel available to carry out section 236(c) of the Immigration and Nationality Act, as amended by subsection (a), or the amendments made by section 440(c) of Public Law 104-132, the provisions in paragraph (3) shall be in effect for a 1-year period beginning on the date of such notification, instead of such section or such amendments. The Attorney General may extend such 1-year period for an additional year if the Attorney General provides the same notice not later than 10 days before the end of the first 1-year period. After the end of such 1-year or 2-year periods, the provisions of such section 236(c) shall apply to individuals released after such periods.

(3) TRANSITION PERIOD CUSTODY RULES.—

(A) IN GENERAL.—During the period in which this paragraph is in effect pursuant to paragraph (2), the Attorney General shall take into custody any alien who—

(i) has been convicted of an aggravated felony (as defined under section 101(a)(43) of the Immigration and Nationality Act, as amended by section 321 of this division),

(ii) is inadmissible by reason of having committed any offense covered in section 212(a)(2) of such Act,

(iii) is deportable by reason of having committed any offense covered in section 241(a)(2)(A)(ii), (A)(iii), (B), (C), or (D) of such Act (before redesignation under this subtitle), or

(iv) is inadmissible under section 212(a)(3)(B) of such Act or deportable under section 241(a)(4)(B) of such Act (before redesignation under this subtitle),

when the alien is released, without regard to whether the alien is released on parole, supervised release, or probation, and without regard to whether the alien may be arrested or imprisoned again for the same offense.

(B) RELEASE.—The Attorney General may release the alien only if the alien is an alien described in subparagraph (A)(ii) or (A)(iii) and—

(i) the alien was lawfully admitted to the United States and satisfies the Attorney General that the alien will not pose a danger to the safety of other persons or of property and is likely to appear for any scheduled proceeding, or

(ii) the alien was not lawfully admitted to the United States, cannot be removed because the designated country of removal will not accept the alien, and satisfies the Attorney General that the alien will not pose a danger to the safety of other persons or of property and is likely to appear for any scheduled proceeding.

APPENDIX 4D

MEMORANDUM ON INA §236(c)'s "CUSTODY" REQUIREMENT AND THE USE OF ALTERNATIVES TO DETENTION TO MEET THE STATUTE'S REQUIREMENTS

Introduction:

This memorandum discusses whether the "custody" requirement of INA § 236(c) is satisfied by a combination of electronic monitoring, curfew and /or home confinement, and other aspects of intensive supervision. ICE may also comply with the Congressional mandate that certain criminal-aliens be in custody pending their removal proceedings through the significant restraints on an individual's liberty imposed *vis a vis* intensive supervision.

Discussion:

Section 236(c)

Section 236(c) of the INA is entitled "Detention of Criminal Aliens." However, the statutory language does not refer to "detention", but custody. The provision states that the Attorney General shall take into custody any alien who is inadmissible [for certain sections of law], or deportable [for certain sections of law] when the alien is released [from penal custody].

Defining "custody"

"Custody" and "detention" are not synonyms. The federal courts, in various contexts, have recognized that to be "in custody" is to suffer a severe restraint on individual liberty. This restraint must be one not shared by the public generally; however, custody need not be actual physical restraint or confinement.

For example, for purposes of bringing a federal habeas corpus claim under 28 USC § 2254, probation is sufficient restraint to satisfy the "in custody" requirement. *Olson v. Hart*, 965 F.2d 940 (10th Cir. 1993). Likewise, parole is a form of custody for purposes of habeas corpus proceedings. *Jones v. Cunningham*, 371 U.S. 236 (1963); *DePompei v. Ohio Adult Parole Authority*, 999 F.2d 138 (6th Cir.1993). A state court sentence requiring community service was deemed sufficient restriction on the individual's liberty to constitute "custody" for federal habeas corpus proceedings in *Barry v. Bergen County Probation Department*, 128 F.3d 152 (3^{d} Cir. 1997). Also, the Supreme Court has found that a detainer lodged on the basis of a sentence yet to be served meets the "in custody" requirement for purposes of a habeas petition. *Maleng, King County Prosecuting Attorney v. Cook*, 490 U.S. 488, 493 (1989).

In the habeas corpus context, the "custody" requirement is a jurisdictional prerequisite to a federal court considering a petition for writ of habeas corpus. *Fay v.*

Noia, 372 U.S. 391, 430 (1963). The restraints on liberty that are generally considered sufficient to meet the custody requirement are restraints on movement, including denying an alien entry into the U.S., a parolee or a convict's release on recognizance, mandatory attendance at rehabilitative sessions, or other rules that require physical presence at a given time or place or otherwise interfere with free movement. *Spano v. Hoffman,* No. 08-60238-CIV-Marra/Johnson, 2008 U.S. Dist. LEXIS 44251 (S.D. Fla May 28, 2008), *citing, Williamson v. Gregoire, 151 F.3d 1180, 1183* (9th Cir. 1998).

The habeas corpus context, however, is not the only legal context in which "custody" has been defined as encompassing both physical detention and situations of significant restraint on individual liberties. In reference to the federal escape statute at 18 USC § 751(a), the courts have held that escape or attempted escape may occur from a pre-release guidance center, work release program, or halfway house. For example, in *Perez-Calo v. United States,* 757 F. Supp. 1 (DC Puerto Rico 1991), the defendant "escaped" from a substance-abuse treatment halfway house which was ordered as part of his sentence. A halfway house providing treatment under the auspices of the penal custodian was deemed to constitute "custody." Likewise, in *United States v. Rudinsky,* 439 F.2d 1074 (6th Cir. 1971), the defendant was committed to a federal community treatment center where he was permitted to leave between 6:00 a.m. and 6:00 p.m. for the purpose of holding regular employment and eating his meals; he was prosecuted for escape when he failed to return at the prescribed time and did not inform anyone at the center of his whereabouts.

The dichotomy between detention and intensive forms of supervision both falling under the larger roof of "custody" is also illustrated in Florida's statute authorizing community control as a form of intensive probation. According to Fla. Stat. § 948.001(3), "community control" is a form of intensive, supervised custody in the community, including surveillance on weekends and holidays, administered by officers with restricted caseloads. Florida law explicitly states that community control provides "the courts and the Parole Commission an alternative, community-based method to punish an offender in lieu of incarceration." Fla. Stat. § 948.10(1). Thus by the terms of the statute, intensive probation through "community control" is a type of custody that is less than incarceration.

Criminal courts have also stressed that jail "credit" for time served in advance of a sentence is only available for time spent in actual detention, as opposed to while in alternative forms of custody, even though the latter may involve intensive supervision such as home confinement. *Paul v. Bragg,* EP-10-CV-470-KC (W.D. TX Aug. 1, 2011). Under federal law, the Federal Bureau of Prisons ("FBOP") may grant a defendant credit against a federal sentence for any qualifying period of pre-sentence custody. The relevant federal statute, 18 U.S.C. § 3585(b), states:

> (b) Credit for prior custody —A defendant shall be given credit toward the service of a term of imprisonment for any time he has spent in official detention prior to the date the sentence commences—
>
> (1) as a result of the offense for which the sentence was imposed; or

(2) as a result of any other charge for which the defendant was arrested after the commission of the offense for which the sentence was imposed;

that has not been credited against another sentence.

Section 3585(b) illustrates the central theme of this memorandum: that custody encompasses detention, but is a larger concept than detention.

The INA also illustrates the fact that custody is distinct from detention, in that the former encompasses the latter. As stated above, although INA § 236(c) is entitled "Detention of criminal aliens", the actual text instructs the Attorney General to "take into custody" any alien who meets the criteria; the actual text of the section does not utilize the term detention or incarceration. In comparison, INA §§ 241(a)(2) and (4) refer to "detention" of certain criminal aliens during the removal period and, where necessary, beyond said period.

Matter of Aguilar-Aquino

In *Matter of Aguilar-Aquino* 24 I & N Dec. 747 (BIA 2009), the Board of Immigration Appeals considered whether release on electronic monitoring and home confinement for 12 hours a day constitutes a form of "custody" for purposes of the seven day rule regarding motions for reconsideration of custody determination (i.e., "bond" hearings). In *Aguilar-Aquino*, the Board was not interpreting section 236(c). Rather, the Board was interpreting the seven-day rule for purpose of the regulation at 8 CFR § 1236.1(d)(1) and (2), which state that an immigration judge may order that an alien be "detain[ed] in custody", released, and set a bond. An alien who has already "been released from DHS custody", however, must request a bond hearing to seek amelioration of the terms of his or her released from custody before the Immigration Judge within seven days of release. The operative term in the *Aguilar-Aquino* analysis is the verb phrase "when released"; the "release" becomes the trigger for the seven-day clock.

In *Aguilar-Aquino*, the Board logically sought to set limits on the number of bond motions an alien in removal proceedings could file by interpreting the seven day rule to require a release from actual physical confinement. This interpretation is consistent with a reading of both subsections sections (d)(1) and (2) of the regulation, because subsection (d)(1) specifically references being *detained* in custody: the term detention is combined with the term custody to exemplify that custody in this particular regulation refers to actual detention.

The Board finds that for purposes of 8 CFR § 1236.1(d)(1) and bond hearings, the reference to seven days after release from custody is a reference to actual physical detention. In dicta, the Board writes that Congress did not intend the term "custody" in section 236 of the Act to be afforded the broad interpretation employed in the federal habeas corpus statute, where it is interpreted expansively to ensure that no person's imprisonment or detention is illegal. *Aguilar-Aquino* at 752. However, the Board's statement (which is not pertinent to the precise issue at hand), is inaccurate on two points: as stated above, the "in custody" requirement is a jurisdictional criteria—being in custody allows the federal courts to hear the petition;

moreover, as highlighted by the above mentioned cases and scores of others, the habeas statute has been used by countless defendants to address perceived legal violations who are not "prisoners" in detention, but rather, are suffering a restraint on individual liberty (i.e., probation, parole, community service, or a detainer).

In sum, *Aguilar-Aquino* poses no impediment to DHS' determination that the custody requirement of section 236(c) may be satisfied by restraints or conditions that are less than actual physical confinement.

Matter of Garcia-Garcia

In *Matter of Garcia-Garcia,* 25 I & N Dec. 93 (BIA 2009), the BIA considered a motion for custody determination filed within 7 days by an individual who was never detained at an ICE facility, but rather, was apprehended by ICE and placed on ISAP. Within 7 days, the respondent filed a motion for custody redetermination asking the IJ that he be allowed to post a monetary bond in lieu of electronic monitoring and reporting. Both the IJ and the BIA found that a judge has jurisdiction to consider the conditions imposed by ICE; in other words, the BIA found that it has authority to order—or ameliorate—terms of release such as ISAP conditions.

Policy Considerations

At the present time, the American taxpayer shoulders a tremendous financial burden in detaining individuals, including many lawful permanent residents, who are subject to removal for minor, non-violent crimes. It is estimated that the average cost of detention of an individual is $122 per day; at any given time there are over 34,000 non-American citizens detained by ICE, costing over $2 billion per year.[103] By some estimates, at least 40% of these individuals are non-criminal.

Clearly, in many cases incarceration is not necessary. By way of example, a returning lawful permanent resident with a conviction for simple possession of less than 30 grams of marijuana is subject to mandatory detention. A returning resident with one theft conviction, or two misdemeanor shoplifting offenses, will be held under mandatory detention. Many of these individuals have strong, long-term ties to the American community and are supporting families, including minor children. Very often, individuals detained as "mandatory" have relief from removal available to them. A lawful permanent resident with a minor conviction from the past is likely to receive cancellation of removal or other relief, but will lose anywhere from one to four months away from job, family, or other commitments in the process. Some detained individuals have serious illnesses or disabilities, yet section 236(c) does not contain exceptions for the seriously ill or disabled—adding another consequence (and

---

[103] 4 Dep't of Homeland Security, U.S. Immigration and Customs Enforcement Salaries and Expenses, Fiscal Year 2012 Congressional Budget Justification, p. 57, *available at www.dhs.gov/xlibrary/assets/ dhs-congressional-budget-justification-fy2012.pdf.*

financial burden) to a rigid interpretation of the "in custody" requirement. Detaining individuals with minor, old criminal convictions—and individuals who are in poor health or otherwise disabled—takes beds away from the more serious criminal-aliens. This situation in turn results in costly and sometimes confusing transfers of detainees across the country. Interpreting "custody" to include significant restraints on liberty through electronic monitoring, curfew, and supervision, alleviates many of the detention challenges that are facing DHS while simultaneously addressing the hardship suffered by non-violent individuals and their families.

As the Board acknowledged in *Aguilar-Aquino*, custody is not always detention, but detention is always custody. Section 236(c)'s language does not specifically call for physical detention, but references "taking into custody." The custody requirement may be lawfully satisfied by strict restrictions on liberty, including but not limited to electronic monitoring, curfews, reporting, and other forms of supervision.

DHS has consistently stressed to the public that alternatives to detention are a means of assuring an alien's presence at hearings and, if ordered, reporting for and complying with removal. In other words, ISAP and similar programs represent a risk assessment tool to ensure compliance, and are not intended to protect society from dangerous aliens. Admittedly, DHS has never presented alternatives to detention as a means of meeting the requirement of "custody" or otherwise falling under the auspices of INA § 236.

Conclusion

The author encourages ICE to adopt a legal position that the "custody" requirement of INA § 236(c) may be met by the tools currently available to the Department as alternatives to detention, including but not limited to, intensive supervision and electronic monitoring.

August 2012

APPENDIX 4E
MEMORANDUM IN SUPPORT OF BOND MOTION

DETAINED

Mary E. Kramer
Attorney at Law
Mary E. Kramer, P.A.
168 S.E. First Street, Suite 802
Miami, Florida 33131

UNITED STATES DEPARTMENT OF JUSTICE
EXECUTIVE OFFICE FOR IMMIGRATION REVIEW
ORLANDO IMMIGRATION COURT
ORLANDO, FLORIDA

IN THE MATTER OF:	)	
	)	
FLORES, LILLIAN	)	CASE No. 123 456 789
	)	
RESPONDENT	)	
IN REMOVAL PROCEEDINGS	)	
_____	)	

Immigration Judge: Judge Ortiz-Segura at 8:00 a.m. Next Hearing: October 1, 2014

<u>MEMORANDUM IN SUPPORT OF BOND MOTION</u>

MEMORANDUM IN SUPPORT OF BOND MOTION

The Respondent, Lillian Flores, by and through undersigned counsel, hereby submits this memorandum of law in support of her motion for a custody redetermination hearing.

I. Introduction

Section 236(c) of the Immigration and Nationality Act (INA) provides for mandatory detention for, inter alia, individuals deportable by reason of having committed any offense covered in INA § 237(a)(2)(A)(ii), (A)(iii), (B), (C), or (D). This Court has jurisdiction to determine whether a person is properly included within the mandatory detention provisions at INA § 236(c). 8 C.F.R. § 1003.19(h)(2)(ii). A person is properly included within INA § 236(c) unless the Department of Homeland Security (DHS) is substantially unlikely to prevail in its charges that she is removable on one of the grounds at INA § 236(c). *Matter of Joseph*, 22 I&N Dec. 799 (BIA 1999).

The Respondent has been charged with deportability pursuant to INA § 237(a)(2)(A)(iii) as having been convicted of an aggravated felony as defined in INA §§ 101(a)(43)(M) and (U) based on her convictions for conspiracy to commit fraud pursuant to 18 U.S.C. § 1349 and wire fraud pursuant to 18 U.S.C. § 1343. Section 101(a)(43)(M) defines an aggravated felony, in part, as "an offense that involves fraud or deceit in which the loss to the victim or victims exceeds $10,000." Section 101(a)(43)(U) defines an aggravated felony as "an attempt or conspiracy to commit an offense described" in INA § 101(a)(43).

DHS is substantially unlikely to prevail in establishing that the Respondent is removable pursuant to INA § 237(a)(2)(A)(iii) because the evidence filed in support of this charge is insufficient to establish that either of the Respondent's crimes were offenses "in which the loss to the victim or victims exceeds $10,000."

II. Loss Determination for Purposes of INA § 101(a)(43)(M)

The United States Supreme Court has called for a circumstance-specific approach to determine whether the monetary threshold for INA § 101(a)(43)(M)(i) is met. *Nijhawan v. Holder*, 557 U.S. 29, 40 (2009). Specifically, the Court has found that the monetary threshold applies to the specific circumstances surrounding an offender's commission of a fraud and deceit crime on a specific occasion. *Id.* In addition, for purposes of INA § 101(a)(43)(M)(i), the loss must be tied to the specific counts covered by the conviction. *Id.* at 42.

In determining the amount of loss, the Immigration Court must assess findings made at sentencing "with an eye to what losses are covered and to the burden of proof employed." *Id.* (quoting *Matter of Babaisakov*, 24 I & N Dec. 306, 219 (2007). An admission made during the criminal proceeding as to the amount of loss can only suffice for purposes of INA §101(a)(43)(M)(i) if the admission pertained to losses arising from the conduct in the particular charges or criminal counts covered by the conviction. *Matter of Babaisakov*, 24 I & N Dec. 306, 320 (BIA 2007).

While restitution orders may be considered in the Court's circumstance-specific inquiry into the monetary threshold, the amount of restitution ordered is not generally equivalent to the amount of loss. *See, e.g., Obasohan v. U.S. Atty. Gen.*, 479 F.3d 785, 790 (11th Cir. 2007). While a sentencing court in the criminal context may order restitution not only for *convicted* conduct but also for a broad range of "relevant conduct," the plain language of the INA requires that an alien have been *convicted of* an aggravated felony to be removable. The INA does not authorize removal on the basis of the "relevant conduct" that may be considered at sentencing. *Obasohan*, 479 F.3d at 790. Under the Federal Sentencing Guidelines, "relevant conduct" includes "all acts and omissions committed ... by the defendant ... during the commission of the offense of conviction ...", as well as "all harm that resulted from [those] acts and omissions[.]" U.S.S.G. § 1B1.3(a)(1), (a)(3). Relevant conduct for sentencing purposes, therefore, may include criminal conduct that was not charged. *Id.* (citing *United States v. Ignancio Munio,* 909 F.2d 436, 438-39 (11th Cir. 1990). Relevant conduct may also include acquitted conduct. *Id.* (citing *United States v. Watts,* 519 U.S. 148 (1997); *United States v. Averi,* 922 F.2d 765, 766 (11th Cir. 1991)). Thus, a restitution order which is based relevant conduct outside of the elements comprising the substantive criminal offense cannot be considered loss tethered to the conduct for which a defendant is convicted and is therefore insufficient to establish, by clear and convincing evidence, the amount of loss for purposes of INA § 101(a)(43)(M). *See Obasohan*, 479 F.3d at 791.

Further, references to loss within the sentencing-related material are likewise not a reliable measure of loss for purposes of INA § 101(a)(43)(M) because the definition of "loss" within the context of INA § 101(a)(43)(M) is considerably narrower than the definition of loss in the United States Sentencing Guidelines (U.S.S.G). While the plain language of INA § 101(a)(43)(M) does not contemplate the inclusion of potential rather than actual loss, section 2B1.1(b)(1)(H) of the U.S.S.G. defines loss within the sentencing context as including loss which is the reasonably foreseeable pecuniary harm that resulted from the offense as well as pecuniary harm that would have been impossible or unlikely to occur. U.S.S.G. § 2B1.1, comment. (n.3(A)(i)-(ii)).

III. The Respondent's convictions are not ones "in which loss to the victim or victims exceeds $10,000."

The Respondent was the sole proprietor of a small export-import company which dealt in computer parts. She took out a revolving line of credit through a broker, Ruben Grey, from New Nation Financial, whom she had known on a personal basis. The loan was backed by the Export-Import Bank. The loan issued by Mr. Grey was extended in order for borrowers sell items directly for export. The Respondent sold items to individuals in the United States who in turn, took the items to sell abroad. In May 2010, New Nation Financial closed her line of credit. In August 2010, the lender demanded payment in full of the outstanding balance. Her default on the loan was the result of her inability to pay after the lender abruptly closing her line of credit and requiring payment in full. The conduct for which the Respondent was convicted was related to the manner of securing the loan and selling the items, not to the default on the loan. The Respondent was not convicted for defaulting on a loan.

The elements of the crimes with which Ms. Flores was charged did not require that any loss amount be proven. Counts one and two of the criminal information, to which Ms. Flores pled guilty, state that Ms. Flores defaulted on her loan and that "as a result of" her default, the Export-Import Bank paid the lender $446,875.83. Nevertheless, the information does not allege a loss resulting from the offense conduct. The fact that Ms. Flores defaulted on the loan is not tethered to the specific conduct for which she was convicted. For this reason, the amount of the default cannot be properly considered the amount of loss resulting from her offenses. The default on her loan was the result of nonpayment, not the result of her offense conduct. The default on her loan was separate and apart from the conduct resulting in her convictions. *See Obasohan v. U.S. Att'y Gen.*, 479 F.3d at 791.

Further, in her criminal proceedings, the Respondent did not stipulate that the offense conduct for which she was convicted resulted in a loss exceeding $10,000 for purposes of INA § 101(a)(43)(M). Although her plea agreement contains a provision regarding loss defined in U.S.S.G. § 2B1.1(b)(H), this calculation of loss can include loss which is the reasonably foreseeable pecuniary harm that resulted from the offense as well as pecuniary harm that would have been impossible or unlikely to occur. U.S.S.G. § 2B1.1, comment. (n.3(A)(i)-(ii)). Importantly, the reference to loss in Ms. Flores' plea agreement does not constitute an admission by her that her convicted conduct resulted in an amount of loss exceeding $10,000 for purposes of INA § 101(a)(43)(M).

Although Ms. Flores was ordered to pay restitution, the restitution order in this case does not equate to the amount of loss resulting from the offense conduct underlying the Respondent's convictions for conspiracy and wire fraud. First, the restitution order is insufficient as a matter of law for the DHS to meet its burden to show that the Respondent's convictions constitute aggravated felonies because the restitution order includes "relevant conduct" which was not required to have been charged, proven, or admitted. Second, the sentencing judge made this restitution finding employing the preponderance of the evidence standard, rather than the beyond a reasonable doubt standard. Because the sentencing judge was entitled to base the Ms. Flores' restitution order on factual findings about "relevant conduct" made by a lower standard of proof, the amount of restitution ordered in Ms. Flores' case does not constitute clear and convincing evidence that the amount of loss exceeded $10,000 for purposes of INA § 101(a)(43)(M). *See Obasohan v. U.S. Att'y Gen.*, 479 F.3d 785, 791 (11th Cir. 2007).

IV. Conclusion

For the above reasons, DHS is substantially unlikely to prevail in demonstrating, by clear and convincing evidence that the Respondent has been convicted of an aggravated felony as defined in sections 101(a)(43)(M) and (U) of the INA. Accordingly, the Respondent is not subject to mandatory detention. *Matter of Joseph,* 22 I & N Dec. 799 (BIA 1999).

Respectfully Submitted,

Mary E. Kramer
Mary E. Kramer, P.A.
168 SE First Street, Suite 802
Miami, Florida 33131
(305) 374- 2300
Fax: (305) 374-3748
mary@marykramerlaw.com

Certificate of Service

I certify that a true and correct copy of this motion was served by _____ on the Office of Chief Counsel for ICE at 3535 Lawton Road, Suite 100, Orlando, Florida, on this ____ day of September 2014.

_____

CHAPTER FIVE

METHODOLOGY: CLASSIFYING CRIMES UNDER THE IMMIGRATION AND NATIONALITY ACT

Proper Classification of Crimes and the Methodology 181
Analyses and Terms 182
Divisibility after *Descamps*: Circuit Court Developments 197
Divisibility after *Descamps*: Board of Immigration Appeals 205
Chapter Review: A Review of Pertinent Terms 214
Appendices
    5A: Unpublished BIA Decision, *Matter of Forvilus*, Theft Not a CIMT 217
    5B: Unpublished IJ Decision Terminating Arriving Alien Status, Not a CIMT 226
    5C: Unpublished IJ Decision Finding 18 USC §1860 Not a CIMT 232
    5D: Immigration Attorney-Client Checklist for Analyzing a Case with a Crime 235

Proper Classification of Crimes and the Methodology

Prior to learning the actual classifications of crimes, it is fundamentally important to understand the methodology for determining whether a specific offense fits a certain ground of removability under the Immigration and Nationality Act (INA). It is a mistaken approach to automatically classify certain offenses as aggravated felonies, moral turpitude crimes, etc. Rather, a good immigration defense attorney will always begin with the criminal statute of conviction, review the elements, and consider challenging the U.S. Department of Homeland Security's (DHS) classification of the crime. Hence, this chapter discusses the methodology for doing so, including defining the various approaches.

Upon determination that there is a final conviction, the next step is to determine the proper classification of the crime, if any, under the INA. As stated in the introduction, this book does not attempt to list every possible crime and corresponding precedent (although many crimes and their case law treatment are cited herein); rather, the purpose of this book—and especially this chapter—is to teach the proper analysis so that the reader is prepared to conduct independent analysis of each client's case.

Understanding the analysis for determining the proper classification of a crime after a final conviction is fundamentally important for all criminal and immigration attorneys, regardless of the type of practice they have. A criminal defense lawyer representing a foreign-born defendant will want to understand how to analyze the criminal statute charged, recognize where there is divisibility, and mold a criminal record to avoid certain phrases and the more serious statutory elements. Indeed this discussion is relevant for criminal attorneys representing any client, foreign born or not, because of recidivist and enhancement schemes that may result in future punishment for past convictions. And immigration counsel representing a non-American citizen in removal proceedings must know how to ascertain the relevant elements of the criminal statute of conviction, and advocate for the proper approach in immigration court. For those immigration lawyers who rarely litigate, an understanding of how to properly analyze crime, classify a conviction, and advocate for a favorable reading of the statutes is important in representing clients before U.S. Citizenship and Immigration Services (USCIS) and the U.S. Department of State (DOS). USCIS and the consulates all adhere to a categorical approach to classifying crime, so crafting strong memoranda of eligibility are important even for those lawyers who may never see the inside of a courtroom.

The immigration statute contains two major classifications of crime: *crimes involving moral turpitude* and *aggravated felonies*. In previous editions, this book combined methodology, moral turpitude crimes, and aggravated felonies. In this sixth edition, however, methodology is a separate chapter, as are crimes involving moral turpitude and aggravated felonies.

In addition to categorizing crimes involving moral turpitude and aggravated felonies, the INA also has provisions addressing controlled substance offenses, money laundering, firearms offenses, crimes of domestic violence, alien smuggling, registration and visa/passport violations, and export law violations. Often, a specific crime will fall into more than one category, or classification.

Accordingly, with this new edition, classification of crimes is divided by chapters. This chapter discusses the methodology for classifying crimes, with an emphasis on recent case law defining the categorical and modified categorical approaches. Chapter six analyzes crimes involving moral turpitude. Chapter seven is devoted to the aggravated felony classification. Chapter eight goes into other classifications separate from moral turpitude and aggravated felony, including but not limited to controlled substance violations, money laundering, firearms, and domestic violence offenses.

With this foundation in place, chapter nine, in turn, discusses the consequences of specific criminal activity—inadmissibility (pursuant to INA §212) and deportability (pursuant to INA §237) being the main ones.

Analyses and Terms

By the end of this chapter, the reader should be fluent with the following terms:

- Categorical Approach
- Modified Categorical Approach
- Divisible
- Least Culpable Conduct (Minimal Conduct)
- Circumstance-Specific Approach
- Realistic Probability Test
- Element (alternative elements)
- Means
- Non-elemental Fact
- Missing Element Statute (Overly Broad)
- Alternative Statutory Phrase
- Alternative Statutory Provision
- Record of Conviction

U.S. Supreme Court Recalibrates the Categorical Approach: *Descamps v. U.S.*

In *Descamps v. U.S.*,[1] the U.S. Supreme Court made a strong statement about analyzing crimes according to a strict categorical approach. Following the Court's June 2013 decision, many practitioners mused that the Court told attorneys what they already knew: the decision simply serves to remind the courts of the correct method of reading and categorizing criminal statutes. However, this author disagrees that the Court's recalibrating of the categorical approach was simply a reaffirmation of what we already knew. The Board of Immigration Appeals (BIA or Board) and circuit courts of appeals had strayed so far from a strict categorical approach to analyzing statutes (with decisions like *Matter of Silva-Trevino*[2] and *U.S. v. Aguila-Montes de Oca*[3]) that *Descamps* feels like a whole new approach, and has certainly had the effect of a whole new approach. Scores of precedent decisions at administrative (BIA) and circuit court levels are no longer good law.

Unfortunately, post-*Descamps* cases from the circuit courts of appeals demonstrate that jurists still disagree on what is a divisible statute, such that the modified categorical approach applies. The significance of this discussion is that attorneys cannot rely solely on pre-*Descamps* case law when arguing a case, but must conduct fresh research based on *Descamps*' guidance. Moreover, it is vitally important to be cognizant of the emerging circuit court split on divisibility: the jurisdiction may very well determine the outcome of the case. This chapter begins with background on the categorical and modified categorical approach and explains the terms; the chapter then moves on to a discussion of *Descamps*.

Categorical Approach: An Elements Approach

Immigration law always has employed a categorical approach to determine the appropriate classification of a particular crime. The categorical approach seeks to answer the question, what was this person convicted of, as opposed to what did this person do? The categorical approach's analysis begins with viewing the actual elements of the criminal statute: the elements determine whether an offense fits within a certain category of crime. This means the statute of conviction is compared to the generic crime. The "generic crime" is determined based on the federal law counterpart, or the commonly understood definition of the generic offense, as determined by the federal law, the Model Penal Code, the 50 states' statutes, and common law.

It is an erroneous approach, in the context of determining removability, to consider the underlying circumstances of a crime, or what a statute's title or label "sounds like." Instead, a practitioner's first step in every new client's case should be

---

[1] *Descamps v. U.S.*, 133 S. Ct. 2276 (2013).

[2] *Matter of Silva-Trevino*, 24 I&N Dec. 687 (A.G. 2008).

[3] *U.S. v. Aguila Montes-de Oca*, 655 F.3d 915 (9th Cir. 2011), *abrogated by Descamps v. U.S.*, 133 S. Ct. 2276 (2013).

to refer to the actual language of the criminal statute involved. It is the penal statute—not the arrest report, and not the caption or title of a criminal code section—that controls the immigration law classification.

Taylor v. U.S.

Discussion of the categorical approach starts at the U.S. Supreme Court's decision in *Taylor v. U.S.*[4] For practitioners, step one before drafting a motion to dismiss a charge based on an improper removal classification always should be to review *Taylor*, and then *Descamps v. U.S.*[5] Neither *Taylor* nor *Descamps* was an immigration law case, but a criminal sentencing case. They concerned the application of the Armed Career Criminal Act (ACCA), a statute that prescribes enhanced penalties for certain firearms offenses where the offender has three prior convictions for "violent felonies" or "serious drug offenses."

The *Taylor* decision, routinely cited by federal courts and the BIA, specifically addressed whether burglary of a conveyance was properly categorized as a "burglary" offense for purposes of a federal sentencing statute based on the traditional, or generic, understanding of burglary: the unlawful entry into, or remaining in, a building, or structure, with the intent to commit a crime. The defendant had a prior Missouri state conviction for burglary; Missouri's statute encompassed burglaries not only of structures, but also conveyances. Taylor argued that because his state statute of conviction was broader than generic burglary, he did not have a prior violent felony and was not subject to a sentence enhancement.

The Supreme Court found that burglary of a vehicle did not fit within the traditional definition of burglary (because the traditional definition did not include conveyance, but only structure) and could not be categorized as a burglary offense for purposes of the sentencing statute. The Court noted that in categorizing an offense under the ACCA, the sentencing court looks not to the facts of the particular case, but to the state statute defining the crime of conviction.[6]

Taylor's categorical approach dictates that a determination of whether a prior offense qualifies as a violent felony must be limited to the elements of the criminal statute of the defendant's prior conviction, as opposed to a review of the factual circumstances involved. Thus the phrase "categorical approach" refers to the categorizing of crime in a generic sense (*i.e.*, fraud, theft, crime of violence) based on the elements of the criminal statute of conviction—without review of the underlying facts of the crime or the conviction record. The Supreme Court vacated and remanded for further proceedings as to under which portion of Missouri's burglary statute Taylor was convicted.

---

[4] *Taylor v. U.S.*, 495 U.S. 575 (1990).

[5] *Descamps v. U.S.*, 133 S. Ct. 2276 (2013).

[6] *Taylor v. U.S.*, 495 U.S. 575, at 599–600.

The Modified Categorical Approach: Divisible Statutes

An element of the crime is a fact that must be found beyond a reasonable doubt by a judge or unanimous jury in order to convict. Elements are most easily determined by looking at the statute's standard jury instructions. Some criminal statutes are divisible, which means that through the use of discrete alternative elements, the provision actually sets forth more than one type of criminal offense conduct. A divisible statute may encompass offenses or acts that implicate a certain immigration classification (*i.e.*, moral turpitude offense or aggravated felony) and acts that do not. In this situation, a strict categorical approach—limited to the elements of the statute—will not answer the immigration law inquiry.

When a statute is divisible, describing more than one offense through alternative elements, the next step is a modified categorical inquiry. The modified categorical approach is not distinct from the categorical approach. Rather, a modified approach is a subset, or tool, of the categorical approach. This "mechanism" allows the adjudicator to determine which portion or phrase of the statute (which offense conduct) was charged, prosecuted, and led to conviction. The modified categorical approach is not an opportunity to read "what happened" or consider the description of facts in a charging document, and then decide which part of the statute applied; rather, it is a mental "cut-and-paste" exercise in which the adjudicator ascertains which sentence or phrase was lifted from the criminal statute and prosecuted (leading to conviction) in the criminal case.

The record of conviction includes the charging document, plea bargain and colloquy or jury instructions, and sentence.[7] Circuit court case law may vary as to what is included in the record of conviction. Again, the modified categorical approach allows the adjudicator to look at the record to determine which part of the statute was charged; it is not an opportunity to consider factual circumstances.[8] In the criminal law context, courts often refer to the documents that may be referenced in determining which portion of the statute applies as "judicially noticeable documents."

In *Shepard v. U.S.*,[9] the Supreme Court identified the judicially noticeable documents as:

(1) charging documents;

(2) the terms of a written plea agreement;

(3) transcripts of a plea colloquy between a judge and the defendant in which the factual basis for the plea was confirmed by the defendant;

(4) jury instructions;

(5) any explicit factual finding by the trial judge to which the defendant assented;

---

[7] *Johnson v. U.S.*, 559 U.S. 133, 144 (2010).

[8] In *Johnson*, the U.S. Supreme Court referred to the "factual basis" of the record as meaning which "statutory phrase" was the basis for the conviction. *Id.*

[9] *Shepard v. U.S.*, 544 U.S. 13, 25 (2005).

(6) some comparable judicial record of this information.

The goal is to ascertain whether the charging document, plea records, and ultimate judgment identify which portion of the divisible criminal statute was charged, prosecuted, and ultimately disposed of. The reader will note, and must always remind the adjudicator, that at least in the deportability context,[10] individuals are removable for the crime of conviction, not the underlying activity.

> ➢ **Practice Pointer**: Portions of the pre-sentence investigation report, or PSI/PSR, may be acceptable as a record of conviction document for purposes of the modified categorical approach, if it contains facts that were stipulated to. It is important to contest all objectionable facts, even if they do not seem relevant to the ultimate sentence.

Missing Element Statutes

The background of *Descamps* was that certain courts, most notably the Ninth Circuit U.S. Court of Appeals, considered missing element statutes to qualify as divisible, resulting in recourse to the modified categorical approach—review of the criminal record documents to ascertain the offense conduct. The specific element is missing in the sense that the statute is so broad it could logically encompass the element (an example being a "weapons" offense, which may encompass a firearm) but not necessarily so. The BIA adopted this approach to divisibility in *Matter of Lanferman*,[11] finding that an overly broad statute qualified as divisible.

The expression, "missing element" statute, is a reference to a criminal statute that is not divisible per se, but does encompass more than one type of conduct by applying a phrase that naturally encompasses different acts. "Missing element" statutes have been described as criminal statutes that are missing one or more elements of the generic definition of the crime.[12]

Thus, there are two ways to describe or identify a "missing element" statute.

- The first is the per se missing element, meaning, the criminal statute does not contain an element of the generic definition of the crime.

- The second is a broad element, which means that an element utilized in the criminal statute encompasses—or is broader than—an element in the generic definition (the reader will remember that criminal statutes are compared to the

---

[10] As discussed throughout this book, the grounds of inadmissibility at Immigration & Nationality Act (INA) §212(a) contain certain grounds of removability that are not premised on a final conviction. However, a person who is present in the United States pursuant to a lawful admission is subject to grounds of deportability under INA §§237(a), and §237 requires a final conviction; this includes all aggravated felony grounds.

[11] *Matter of Lanferman*, 25 I&N Dec. 721 (BIA 2012), *withdrawn by Matter of Chairez*, 26 I&N Dec. 349 (BIA 2014).

[12] *U.S. v. Aguila-Montes de Oca*, 655 F.3d 915, 925 (9th Cir. 2011), *abrogated by Descamps v. U.S.*, 133 S. Ct. 2276 (2013).

generic definition of the crime, as determined by a combination of the federal criminal code, the majority of state codes, and the Model Penal Code).[13]

> **Examples**: An aggravated assault statute may reference the use of a "deadly weapon" without reference to a "firearm;" the word "weapon" may logically encompass firearms, tools, a blunt object, etc. Thus, although the criminal statute does not list all of the different items that may render the assault aggravated in nature, the word "weapon" by its very nature does—hence, the statute becomes divisible because it is missing a specific element but potentially covers said element based on normal usage of the key phrase.[14] Still, simply because a lay definition of "weapon" could encompass a firearm does not mean the missing element statute qualifies as a removable firearms offense. Rather, the trier of fact would still need to determine that the defendant used a firearm, and that this would satisfy the definition of "weapon" under the statute of conviction.

> Different states have different burglary statutes, and the reader must always recall that the title or caption of a criminal statute does not determine the classification of crime. For example, in *Taylor*, the Court wrote that the key elements of the generic definition of burglary are the "unlawful or unprivileged entry into, or remaining in, a building or structure, with intent to commit a crime." The Court held that this "generic" definition of burglary "ha[s] the basic elements of unlawful or unprivileged entry into, or remaining in, a building or structure, with intent to commit a crime."[15] If the state statute is missing the term "unlawful" or "unprivileged," it is missing an element of the generic crime.[16]

Pre-*Descamps*, some courts opined that a missing element statute, though not structurally a "divisible" statute, could have the same effect as a divisible statute because it contains a word or phrase that naturally encompasses a key element of the generic crime (hence, encompassing more than one type of offense or conduct), or is missing a key element of the generic crime altogether. Prior to *Descamps*, some courts would employ a modified categorical approach and look to the record of conviction documents where a statute was overly broad or was missing an element.

---

[13] *U.S. v. Taylor*, 459 U.S. 575, at 598.

[14] *U.S. v. Aguila Montes De Oca*, 655 F.3d 915, at 927.

[15] *U.S. v. Taylor*, 459 U.S. 575, at 599.

[16] This was the fact pattern in *U.S. v. Aguila Montes de Oca*, 655 F.3d 915 (9th Cir. 2011), which was overruled by *Descamps*.

Identifying the Minimal (Least Culpable) Conduct

Another important concept is the minimal, or least culpable, conduct described by a criminal statute. This is the default approach, and always applies in the categorical approach, and may apply in the modified categorical analysis. The least culpable conduct is the least serious—or most minor—conduct that is described in the criminal statute.

> ➤ **Example**: If a statutory provision contains three mental states, or *mens rea*, such as negligence, recklessness, and specific intent, the least culpable conduct is negligence. If a controlled-substance statute describes possession, possession with intent to distribute, and possession with intent to sell, the least culpable conduct is possession.

Where a statute is not divisible—and a strict categorical approach applies—the adjudicator is limited to the elements of the statute and must assume the defendant was convicted of the least culpable conduct described therein. Where a statute is divisible, but the record of conviction does not clarify which portion was charged, the adjudicator assumes the least culpable conduct described by statute. An example of a divisible statute wherein the record is not determinative would be where the prosecutor charges the entire criminal statute in a charging document, and the final judgment does not specify which element applied.

Thus, in the case of a divisible statute, where recourse to the record of conviction does *not* clarify which portion of the statute applies, the adjudicator assumes the least culpable conduct described by statute.[17]

> ➤ **Example**: Assume a criminal assault provision contains three subsections: one involving an intentional act and causation of harm; another describing a credible threat; and a third involving a touch or strike, with no causation of harm. Assume further that the record of conviction (for example, the charging document, plea colloquy, and judgment) does not pinpoint which of the three subsections was charged and pled to. In this situation, the immigration judge (IJ) should assume the least culpable conduct described in the statute (namely, a touch without causation of harm). Touching without causation of harm is not conduct involving moral turpitude. In such a circumstance—where the burden of proof lies with DHS—the government could not sustain its burden of proof.[18]

---

[17] *See, e.g., Partyka v. Att'y Gen.*, 417 F.3d 408 (3d Cir. 2005); *Dalton v. Ashcroft*, 257 F.3d 200 (2d Cir. 2001).

[18] *See, e.g., Matter of Sanudo,* 23 I&N Dec. 968, 975 (BIA 2006) ("[B]ecause the admissible portions of the respondent's conviction record do not reflect that he pled guilty to conduct encompassed with the 'crime of violence' definition, we agree with the Immigration Judge that the DHS has not satisfied its burden of proving by clear and convincing evidence that the respondent has been convicted of a crime of violence under 18 USC §16 or, by extension, a crime of domestic violence under section 237(a)(2)(E)(i) of the [INA].").

Non-elemental Facts and the Circumstance-Specific Approach

Other important terms of methodology include the non-elemental fact and the circumstance-specific approach. (The "non-elemental fact" phrase should not be confused with the term "missing element"; these two expressions apply in different contexts.) There are some instances in the INA where a provision of removability turns on a factual issue that will not be determined by the elements of the criminal statute; in this instance, a strict categorical approach does not apply.

The most common example of a non-elemental fact is the more than $10,000 dollar loss amount necessary for a crime to be an aggravated felony crime of fraud or deceit under INA §§101(a)(43)(M)(i). Other examples of immigration provisions dependent on non-elemental facts include:

- money laundering in excess of $10,000;
- whether an act is committed for commercial advantage; or
- whether the victim is a family member.

These may be "non-elemental facts" because the particular element that renders the conviction a removable offense[19] will oftentimes not be found within the four corners of the criminal statute.[20]

Whether an immigration ground, or classification, of removal depends on a non-elemental fact may not always be clear. In other words, there will be cases where DHS argues that a required fact for removability is a non-elemental factor and can be determined outside the statute or even the record of conviction, yet defense counsel will disagree and instead advocate for a categorical approach. Throughout this chapter, there is further discussion of non-elemental facts in the context of specific offenses. There are certain provisions wherein the BIA has been willing to go outside the categorical and modified categorical approaches, but circuit courts have rejected this larger view.

Thus, a reference to a modified categorical approach in this context implies that the adjudicator (IJ, BIA, or federal court) may look to the record of conviction to

---

[19] The reverse may also be true, in that establishing a non-elemental fact will remove the conviction from the ambit of a removable offense. The most common example is where the "recipient" of specified criminal activity is a family member. For example, INA §§101(a)(43)(N) and (P) define certain crimes of alien smuggling and passport fraud as aggravated felonies; however, if it is affirmatively shown that the person who was smuggled, or who received the passport, is the defendant's spouse, child, or parent, the conviction is excepted from the aggravated felony definition.

[20] To illustrate, INA §101(a)(43)(k)(ii) defines as an aggravated felony violation of 18 USC §§2421, 2422, or 2423 acts relating to transportation for the purposes of prostitution, if committed for commercial advantage; the BIA treats the factor of "commercial advantage" as a non-elemental fact. *Matter of Gertsenshteyn*, 24 I&N Dec. 111 (BIA 2007). In contrast, INA §237(a)(2)(C) makes it a removable offense to be convicted of any law relating to the purchase, sale, exchange, use, ownership, or possession of a destructive device or firearm. The element of "firearm" must be present in the criminal statute. Defense counsel would never concede that the element of a firearm may be determined by evidence outside of the criminal statute itself.

determine whether the required characteristic (*i.e.*, financial loss, commercial gain, age or gender of victim, etc.) is present in the conviction record.[21]

Still, an IJ or the BIA may want to go beyond a modified categorical approach and review other evidence outside the traditional record of conviction. Where removability turns on the existence of a non-elemental fact, the adjudicator may engage in an expanded evidentiary approach, or a "circumstance-specific approach," to determine whether the required fact exists. Again, defense counsel should be prepared to challenge this approach.[22]

Nijhawan v. Holder

The U.S. Supreme Court's 2009 decision in *Nijhawan v. Holder*[23] represents the best illustration of a "non-elemental fact" that dictates a circumstance-specific inquiry. The non-elemental fact determined in *Nijhawan* was the $10,000 loss to a victim provision contained in the aggravated felony definition at INA §101(a)(43)(M). This provision defines an aggravated felony to include a crime involving fraud or deceit where loss to a victim exceeds $10,000. The issue at hand involved what sort of evidence could be considered to determine whether the loss indeed exceeded the $10,000 mark.

Nijhawan was a lawful permanent resident (LPR) who had been indicted for mail fraud, wire fraud, bank fraud, and money laundering. He was eventually convicted by jury trial. The jury made no findings as to amount of loss. At the sentencing phase of the criminal trial, Nijhawan stipulated to a loss in excess of $100 million. Restitution was ordered in the amount of $683 million.[24]

In ordering the non–American citizen removed, the IJ had relied on a sentencing stipulation and restitution order to establish that the loss exceeded $10,000. The BIA and Third Circuit U.S. Court of Appeals upheld that decision. Throughout the appeal process, Nijhawan (the respondent before the court of appeals and Supreme Court) argued first for a strict categorical approach (that the statute of conviction must include the financial amount). The Supreme Court found this approach untenable, as criminal fraud provisions do not include a loss amount as an element of the offense. In the alternative, Nijhawan advocated for a limited modified categorical approach: that the loss must be determined by the jury verdict, or a judge-approved equivalent, that may include only the charging documents, jury instructions, any special jury

---

[21] *See, e.g., Conteh v. Gonzales*, 461 F.3d 45, 55 (1st Cir. 2006).

[22] In *Matter of Gertsenshteyn*, 24 I&N Dec. 111 (BIA 2007), the Second Circuit U.S. Court of Appeals vacated the BIA's decision and found that the element of "commercial advantage" may be determined solely from the traditional record of conviction. *Gertsenshteyn v. U.S. DOJ*, 544 F.3d 137 (2d Cir. 2008). The Supreme Court, in dicta, disagreed with the appeals court's approach and implied that the factor of "commercial advantage" requires a circumstance-specific approach. *See Nijhawan v. Holder*, 557 U.S. 29 (2009).

[23] *Nijhawan v. Holder*, 557 U.S. 29 (2009).

[24] *Nijhawan v. Holder*, 557 U.S. 29 (2009).

finding or judge-made findings, and the plea documents or plea colloquy. Prior to the Supreme Court's decision, there was a split among the circuits as to what documentation could be properly considered in determining loss.

The Court disagreed with the respondent, finding that neither the categorical nor modified categorical approach (limited to the record of conviction) could properly or fairly determine the amount of financial loss as required by INA §101(a)(43)(M). Instead, the Court concluded that the fraud and deceit provision calls for a "circumstance-specific" approach, wherein relevant evidence may be considered in determining the loss involved in a specific offense. The Court found nothing unfair in considering the respondent/defendant's own stipulation regarding loss produced for sentencing purposes, as well as the sentencing court's own restitution order. The Supreme Court does note that an individual, such as the respondent in *Nijhawan*, has the opportunity in immigration court to produce evidence to establish a loss lower than $10,000. The Court further notes that the amount of loss must be tied to the specific count or counts of the conviction.[25]

The burden of proof to establish a deportable offense rests with DHS counsel;[26] thus, the burden of establishing a non-elemental fact rests with them also.

> **Practice Pointer**: The concept of non-elemental fact is an important one to understand, and also for defense counsel to try and limit. Depending on the case, DHS may argue for an expanded modified categorical approach that considers evidence outside the record of conviction to determine removability—in other words, a circumstance-specific approach. In response, defense counsel always should argue for a strict categorical approach unless the specific removal provision clearly includes what will never be an element of a criminal statute. In such circumstances, stage two would be to advocate for a modified categorical approach that looks solely to the traditional record of conviction to identify the non-elemental factor. Counsel should concede to stage three, a circumstance-specific approach, only where precedential case law allows an expanded evidentiary inquiry (such as in the case of an aggravated felony crime of fraud or deceit).

The Realistic Probability Test: *Gonzales v. Duenas-Alvarez*

Back in 2007, the Supreme Court affirmed the applicability of the categorical approach to immigration law cases in *Gonzales v. Duenas-Alvarez*.[27] However, the Court also introduced the "realistic probability" test, which is a tedious and hard-to-grasp concept that requires a significant amount of legal research into applicable state law. This section explains the realistic probability test.

---

[25] *Nijhawan v. Holder*, 557 U.S. 29 (2009).

[26] INA §240(c)(3); 8 USC §1229a(c)(3).

[27] *Gonzales v. Duenas-Alvarez*, 549 U.S.183 (2007).

The realistic probability analysis arises where the non–American citizen argues that the statute of conviction is not a categorical match to the generic crime that forms the basis for a removal charge (*i.e.*, firearms offense, controlled substance violence, theft offense). Under this scenario, the non–American citizen would be arguing that the criminal statute is broader than the generic crime, or includes conduct that falls outside of the generic crime. The realistic probability test asks the respondent to prove that the criminal statute at issue has ever been used to prosecute the proposed conduct that makes it different from the generic crime: *show the adjudicator a real case, rather than a theoretical possibility, that the statute has been used to prosecute nonremovable conduct.*

The realistic probability test may arise in the context of a minimum conduct argument. Where a non–American citizen argues that minimum conduct described by the criminal statute does not qualify as a removable offense, the government (DHS) may respond that the proposed minimal conduct is hypothetical—not realistic—and would never be prosecuted under the statute. The burden falls on the non–American citizen to present a real-life example where the proposed minimum conduct was in fact prosecuted under this particular statute.

> **Practice Pointer**: To find a real-life example, look to case law and the client's own case. Also, survey colleagues or the public defender's office, and ask for an affidavit(s) that they have seen the statute charged in the manner argued (non-removable conduct). Also review the annotations that follow a criminal statute on LEXIS or Westlaw.

The issue in *Duenas-Alvarez* was whether an automobile theft statute, Cal. Veh. Code Ann. §10851(a), which includes temporary and permanent deprivations of a vehicle, as well as aiding and abetting the crime, could be generically categorized as a pure "theft offense" constituting an aggravated felony under INA §101(a)(43)(G).[28] Duenas-Alvarez argued that the California statute swept more broadly than the generic definition of theft. Consider the following juxtaposition:

> The **generic definition of theft** is the taking of property or an exercise of control over property without consent with the criminal intent to deprive the owner of rights and benefits of ownership, even if such deprivation was less than total or permanent.

> The **California vehicle theft statute** makes it an offense to (1) drive or take a vehicle not his or her own, without the consent of the owner, or (2) be a party or an accessory to, or an accomplice in, the driving or unauthorized taking or stealing.

---

[28] Cal. Veh. Code Ann. §10851(a) states: "Any person who drives or takes a vehicle not his or her own, without the consent of the owner thereof, and with intent either to permanently or temporarily deprive the owner thereof of his or her title to or possession of the vehicle, whether with or without intent to steal the vehicle, or any person who is a party or an accessory to or an accomplice in the driving or unauthorized taking or stealing, is guilty of a public offense."

Respondent Duenas-Alvarez argued that the language of the statute was broad enough to encompass traditional theft offenses (*i.e.*, a permanent or temporary taking of property without the owner's consent) as well as acts that were not generic thefts (such as an accessory or accomplice after the fact). California law defines "aiding and abetting" such that an aider and abettor is criminally responsible not only for the crime he intends, but also for any crime that "naturally and probably" results from his intended crime. This is called the "natural and probable consequences doctrine." Respondent Duenas-Alvarez argued that a person could potentially be prosecuted under the vehicle theft statute for a crime that had nothing to do with theft.

In the simplest of terms, according to Duenas-Alvarez, because the statute included this aiding and abetting phrase—and without an indication in the record of conviction as to which clause applied—the adjudicator should assume the least culpable conduct described by statute. Under this approach, and because the record was not clear, he could not be deportable for an aggravated felony offense. His view was supported by a Ninth Circuit decision that found that the relevant California Vehicle Code provision did sweep more broadly than generic theft, precisely because of the aiding and abetting clause.[29]

The Supreme Court disagreed with this strict categorical approach to interpreting the criminal statute and instead proposed a "realistic probability" test, which may be described as follows: To establish that the statute of conviction is not categorically a theft offense, the individual must provide the adjudicating court with a real case (including, if relevant, the non–American citizen's own case) where the California statute has been applied to prosecute a person for an offense that was *not* a generic theft crime.

In the absence of an actual case, as opposed to a theoretical example, wherein the criminal statute was used to prosecute an offense that did *not* qualify as a theft, the Court found that the California statute categorically described a theft offense, hence, an aggravated felony. Specifically, the Supreme Court found that aiding and abetting a theft offense qualifies as a theft crime for purposes of the aggravated felony definition at INA §§101(a)(43)(G).[30]

Fast-forward to 2015. Some courts and the BIA are using the realistic probability test to undermine the categorical approach. Circuit court and BIA application of the realistic probability test is discussed further, following the discussion of *Descamps*.

---

[29] *Penuliar v. Ashcroft,* 395 F.3d 1037 (2005).

[30] *Gonzales v. Duenas-Alvarez*, 549 U.S. at 183 (2007). Note that Justice Stevens filed an opinion concurring in part and dissenting in part, arguing that the case should be remanded to the court of appeals for a determination in the first instance as to whether the California law would ever be applied to a non-theft offense.

Re-emergence of the Categorical Approach

Moncrieffe v. Holder

Decided by the Supreme Court in April 2013, the precise issue in *Moncrieffe v. Holder*[31] was whether a Georgia controlled-substance conviction could qualify as an aggravated felony drug trafficking crime[32] where the state statute was not a categorical match to the federal Controlled Substances Act (CSA). As background, the federal code contains a provision for distribution of a small amount of marijuana without remuneration.[33] Under the federal law, distribution without remuneration of a small amount of marijuana is a misdemeanor offense, and does not meet the definition of aggravated felony drug trafficking crime at INA §101(a)(43)(B); 8 USC §1101(a)(43)(B).

Moncrieffe, a citizen of Jamaica, had been convicted of possession with intent to distribute about 1.5 grams of marijuana.[34] He was charged as an aggravated felon.[35] The Georgia Code, unlike the federal code, does not have an independent misdemeanor provision for distribution without remuneration of a small amount of marijuana. A review of Georgia case law showed that the state treated distribution without remuneration of marijuana as a felony. Moncrieffe argued the two codes did not fit, because his offense was akin to the federal non-drug trafficking misdemeanor. The Supreme Court agreed, finding that: (1) drug trafficking is a generic offense; and (2) the Georgia statute did not present a categorical match to the federal crime.[36] Without a categorical match, it could not be said that the state statute represented a federal felony drug trafficking crime.[37] According to the Court, the conviction did not necessarily involve facts that correspond to an offense punishable as a felony under the CSA. Assuming the least culpable conduct described by statute, the Court would proceed as if this was a misdemeanor offense, not a federal felony. From a categorical standpoint, according to the Court, Moncrieffe did not have an aggravated felony drug trafficking conviction.

Notably, the BIA, prior to *Moncrieffe*, had acknowledged the problem that some state statutes lack a distribution-without-remuneration provision and did not present a categorical match to the federal CSA. However, the BIA in a decision called *Matter*

---

[31] *Moncrieffe v. Holder*, 569 U.S. _, 133 S. Ct. 1678 (2013).

[32] INA §101(a)(43)(B); 8 USC §1101(a)(43)(B).

[33] 21 USC §841(b)(1)(D).

[34] Ga. Code Ann. §16-13-30(j)(1).

[35] The aggravated felony provision is INA §237(a)(2)(A)(iii) [8 USC §1227(a)(2)(A)(iii)] as it relates to INA §101(a)(43)(B) [8 USC §1101(a)(43)(B)].

[36] Cases to read in conjunction with *Moncrieffe* that require the state statute to present a categorical match to a federal felony based on the CSA include, *Lopez v. Gonzales*, 549 U.S. 47, 53–54 (2006) and *Carachuri-Rosendo v. Holder*, 130 S. Ct. 2577 (2010).

[37] *Moncrieffe v. Holder*, 133 S. Ct. 1678, at 1687.

of *Castro-Rodriguez*[38] placed the burden of proving a small amount without financial consideration on the noncitizen, as opposed to the DHS. Indeed, in as early as 2008, the BIA ruled that the amount of marijuana and the issue of remuneration are "non-elemental facts" that are adjudicated through a "circumstance-specific"[39] approach.[40] In comparison, the Supreme Court specifically rejected this "hypothetical felony" approach, and clarified that it is a categorical approach—as opposed to a circumstance-specific approach—that applies in the context of the aggravated felony drug-trafficking crime definition.[41]

On a practical level, practitioners whose clients appear to have a "trafficking" crime will want to review the state code to determine whether there is a provision for distribution of marijuana without remuneration. If yes, is the language close enough to the federal law? And if there is no such provision at all—as in the case with the Georgia Code—then it *cannot* be said that the client has been convicted of a federal felony drug trafficking crime.

> **Tip:** *Moncrieffe* is significant not only for the purposes of the aggravated felony drug trafficking conviction. The decision is literally an immigration law goldmine, in that it cites to a litany of important cases as it describes the evolution of the categorical approach in the immigration law context. There is good language and citations outside simply the trafficking context: it is the analysis that counts. Turn to *Moncrieffe* when drafting a motion or memorandum that seeks to articulate the categorical analysis.

Descamps v. U.S.

In 2012, the Supreme Court accepted certiorari in *Descamps v. U.S.*[42] to resolve a circuit split on whether a criminal statute that is missing an element of the generic crime—yet is broad enough to encompass the offense conduct—qualifies as divisible, such that an adjudicator may utilize a modified categorical approach to find the missing element in the conviction record. *Descamps* took aim at the Ninth Circuit's decision in *U.S. v. Aguila Montes de Oca*,[43] a sentencing guidelines case wherein the defendant's sentence would be enhanced if he had re-entered after deportation for an aggravated felony. Prior to *Aguila-Montes de Oca,* the Ninth Circuit took the

---

[38] *Matter of Castro-Rodriguez*, 25 I&N Dec. 698 (BIA 2012).

[39] The circumstance-specific approach is applied where the Immigration and Nationality Act includes within its definition, or classification, of aggravated felony a non-elemental fact—a fact that will never be included in the federal statute, such as financial loss to a victim. *Nijhawan v. Holder,* 557 U.S. 29 (2009).

[40] *Matter of Aruna,* 24 I&N Dec. 452 (BIA 2008).

[41] *Moncrieffe v. Holder*, 133 S. Ct. 1678, at 1688.

[42] *Descamps v. U.S.*, 133 S. Ct. 2276 (2013).

[43] *U.S. v. Aguila Montes de Oca*, 655 F.3d 915 (9th Cir. 2011), *abrogated by Descamps v. U.S.*, 133 S. Ct. 2276 (2013).

approach that if a statute was missing an element of the generic crime, the court should not revert to the modified categorical approach. The crime was, categorically, not of the purported classification. See *Navarro-Lopez v. Gonzales*.[44] However in 2011, a divided Ninth Circuit overruled *Navarro-Lopez* and held that where a statute is missing an element, the court may revert to a modified categorical approach and review the record of conviction to determine if that key element was in fact charged, pled to, or prosecuted to final conviction.

Similar to *Montes de Oca*, *Descamps* was a federal criminal sentencing case under the Armed Criminal Career Act (ACCA). The issue in *Descamps* was whether the defendant, who had been convicted under a federal firearm statute,[45] would have his sentence enhanced by virtue of three prior convictions for "a violent felony."[46] [Of note for immigration practitioners, the definition of "violent felony" is almost identical to the definition of "crime of violence" according to 18 USC §16, which, in turn, is used to define a "crime of violence" under the INA's aggravated felony definition.[47]]

In this case, the prior conviction at issue was burglary under Calif. Penal Code §459. This statute penalizes the entry into certain locations "with intent to commit grand or petit larceny or any felony is guilty of burglary." Missing from this provision is an unlawful entry—breaking and entering—a classic component of generic burglary. Certainly, unlawful entries could be penalized under §459, but the provision also could punish lawful entries, such as entering a store, wherein later a crime occurred. In the sentencing phase, the district court judge looked to the transcript of the plea hearing to ascertain that, in fact, Descamps had unlawfully entered a structure. Based on this review of the record (a modified categorical approach), the judge found Descamps' prior conviction to be a generic burglary, akin to a violent felony, and imposed the sentencing enhancement. The Ninth Circuit upheld the sentence.

The Supreme Court disagreed.

Divisibility

What is important about *Descamps* in the immigration law context is that the Supreme Court clarifies what is a divisible statute, justifying recourse to the record of conviction through a modified categorical approach. True divisibility occurs when a criminal statute lists "potential offense elements in the alternative," such as through punctuation or formatting.[48]

---

[44] *Navarro-Lopez v. Gonzales*, 503 F.3d 1063 (9th Cir. 2007) (en banc).
[45] 18 USC §922(g).
[46] 18 USC §924(e).
[47] INA §101(a)(43)(F); 8 USC §1101(a)(43)(F).
[48] *Descamps v. U.S.*, 133 S. Ct. 2276, at 2283.

The modified categorical approach is limited to a very "narrow range of cases" that offer alternative offenses; it is not an equal counterpart to the categorical approach, but a "tool" for implementing the overriding analysis, which is categorical.[49] This tool allows the adjudicator to review documents, such as the jury instructions, charging papers, plea, and judgment, in an attempt to identify which offense was charged and disposed of.[50] However, a statute that is missing an element altogether is not divisible, and the modified categorical approach cannot be used to look for the desired element.

Means vs. Elements

What does *Descamps* mean for immigration adjudications? The BIA traditionally has applied an elements-based test to classifying crimes in the aggravated felony, moral turpitude (and other) contexts, and at least has paid lip service to the idea that the underlying facts are not determinative.[51] However, in cases like *Matter of Silva-Trevino*,[52] and *Matter of Lanferman*,[53] the Board has pushed the proverbial envelope and stretched the concept, justifying a modified categorical approach to find the "missing element" or determine a "non-elemental fact." *Descamps* appears to abrogate these cases because the Court has clarified what qualifies as a divisible statute; and in the absence of divisibility, there is no recourse to the record of conviction—or any other evidence. The analysis on removability ends with the essential elements of the criminal statute. If based on the elements of the criminal statute, the crime of conviction is not a categorical match to the generic crime, then the offense cannot qualify as a removable offense—for example, an aggravated felony or moral turpitude crime.

Divisibility after *Descamps*: Circuit Court Developments

Since the *Descamps* decision, circuit courts of appeals have issued decisions in both the criminal and immigration law contexts interpreting the Supreme Court's decision and applying the categorical approach. The approaches adopted by the various courts have varied in terms of how they define divisibility. *Descamps* instructs that the categorical approach applies unless a statute is divisible, and a statute is divisible only when it sets forth necessary elements in the alternative. If the statute is divisible, encompassing more than one type of offense conduct, then the adjudicating court may look to the record of conviction in a modified categorical approach. The circuits appear to be split on defining a "necessary element."

---

[49] *Descamps v. U.S.*, 133 S. Ct. 2276, at 2283–84.

[50] *Descamps v. U.S.*, 133 S. Ct. 2276 (2013).

[51] *See, e.g., Matter of Short,* 20 I&N Dec. 136 (BIA 1989).

[52] *Matter of Silva-Trevino*, 24 I&N Dec. 687 (AG 2008). *Matter of Silva-Trevino* is discussed later in this chapter.

[53] *Matter of Lanferman*, 25 I&N Dec. 721 (BIA 2012), *withdrawn by Matter of Chairez I*, 26 I&N Dec. 349 (BIA 2014).

The issue comes down to the proper interpretation of a few select words and phrases in the *Descamps* decision. To set the context, the reader will consider the below excerpts from the Supreme Court's decision in *Descamps*. The Court distinguishes "means" from "elements." Means are a method of committing the crime and do not determine the proper classification of a crime (*i.e.*, crime of violence, firearm offense, etc.) The elements form the ingredients for the statutory definition of the offense, or define the essential offense conduct. The Court also criticizes the Ninth Circuit for allowing a list of possible means of committing the crime to serve as essential elements:

> If a sentencing court, as the Ninth Circuit holds, can compare each of those "implied ... means of commission" to the generic ACCA offense, then the categorical approach is at an end. At that point, the court is merely asking whether a particular set of facts leading to a conviction conforms to a generic ACCA offense. And that is what we have expressly and repeatedly forbidden. Courts may *modify* the categorical approach to accommodate alternative "statutory definitions." [T]o 'modify' means to change moderately or in minor fashion.[54] They may not, by pretending that every fact pattern is an "implied" statutory definition, convert that approach into its opposite.[55]

It is not clear what a "statutory definition" is. Is this a synonym for element? Then consider footnote 2. The Supreme Court addresses the dissent's concern that it is often difficult to distinguish between elements and means, and what's more, that prior Supreme Court decisions have found divisible statutes that in fact set forth alternative means.[56] In an attempt to respond to the dissent's concern, the majority opinion includes the following footnote, which appears to blur the distinction between elements and means:

> And if the dissent's real point is that distinguishing between "alternative elements" and "alternative means" is difficult, we can see no real-world reason to worry. Whatever a statute lists (whether elements or means), the documents we approved in *Taylor* and *Shepard*—*i.e.*, indictment, jury instructions, plea colloquy, and plea agreement—would reflect the crime's elements. So a court need not parse state law in the way the dissent suggests: When a state law is drafted in the alternative, the court merely resorts to the approved documents and compares the elements revealed there to those of the generic offense.

Because of perceived ambiguity in the *Descamps* decision (and footnote 2 is not the only contradictory language), some courts are still willing to find that punctuation, statutory phrasing, or reference to alternative statutory definitions,

---

[54] Internal citation here to *MCI Telecommunications Corp. v. American Telephone & Telegraph Co.*, 512 U.S. 218, 225 (1994).

[55] *Descamps v. U.S.*, 133 S. Ct. 2276, at 2291.

[56] Reference is made to the Supreme Court's decisions in *Taylor v. U.S.*, 495 U.S. 575 (1990), which involved a Michigan statute for burglary; *Shepard v. U.S.*, 544 U.S. 13 (2005) (Massachusetts' burglary statute); and *Johnson v. U.S.*, 559 U.S. 133 (2010) (Florida's simple battery statute).

render a statute divisible. For example, some appellate courts find that an overly broad statute can be divisible based on reference to other statutory provisions or regulations (such as statutory definition of "weapon," or controlled substance schedules). Still, other courts of appeals are remaining true to the *Descamps* decision and complying with a necessary alternative elements approach, as is the BIA, which applies *Chairez I*[57] in all jurisdictions outside of those circuits that have said otherwise. As of spring 2015, what noncitizens and their attorneys face is a set of complicated analyses based on a fluctuating and confusing discord among the circuits. Different circuits' approaches are discussed below.

Alternative Statutory Phrases: Tenth Circuit on Conspiracy Statute

U.S. v. Trent[58] out of the Tenth Circuit U.S. Court of Appeals was a criminal sentencing guidelines case. As background, under the Armed Criminal Career Act (ACCA), a defendant's sentence for a federal firearm offense will be increased if there are three previous convictions for violent felonies or serious drug offenses. The defendant in *Trent* suffered the enhanced penalty and appealed, among other issues, the sentencing portion of the case, arguing that his state conviction under Oklahoma's general conspiracy statute was not a "serious drug offense." Specifically, Trent argued that from a categorical approach, the conspiracy statute[59] could relate to conspiracy to commit *any* kind of crime, and was not a generic drug offense. However, the Tenth Circuit ruled that the conspiracy statute is divisible.

The appeals court notes that a conspiracy statute—like aiding and abetting and attempts—necessarily depends on alternative statutory provisions to illustrate the offense conduct: an example being conspiracy to commit burglary (reference to burglary statute) or assault with a weapon (reference to the statutory definition of "weapon").

The appeals court frames the issue as whether alternative statutory phrases can qualify as alternative elements for purposes of determining divisibility. Turning the chronological order of the categorical approach upside down, the court looks first to the charging document to determine whether it identifies the "alternative statutory phrase" (in Trent's case, delivery of methamphetamine), coins the alternative statutory phrase an "element," and finds divisibility. In other words, the Tenth Circuit allows the charging document to determine divisibility if the indictment or complaint "chooses" the alternative statutory phrase. The court essentially asks, *why quibble about means versus elements*? The appeals court notes, as an alternative analysis, that in the specific context of Oklahoma's conspiracy statute, state case law may be interpreted as requiring identification of the underlying crime—thereby making the underlying offense a required "element."

---

[57] *Matter of Chairez I*, 26 I&N Dec. 349 (BIA 2014).

[58] *U.S. v. Trent*, 767 F.3d 1046 (10th Cir. 2014).

[59] Okla. Stat. Ann. tit. 21 §421(A).

While it may be appropriate to look to the underlying crime in the context of inchoate crimes such as conspiracy, aiding and abetting, and attempts, it is not appropriate to do so for specific offenses, such as crimes of violence (assault, battery, burglary) or weapons offenses. Practitioners may want to distinguish *Trent* precisely because it involves a conspiracy statute. A close reading of *Trent* reflects that the court applies a *Lanferman*-type analysis, [60] citing heavily to pre-*Descamps* case law (including the overruled *Aguila-Montes de Oca* [61] analysis) and Justice Alito's *Descamps* dissent. Reliance on rejected case law and a dissenting opinion makes for a troubling foundation. The decision equates statutory phrasing with elements, something *Descamps* advises against.

Alternative Statutory Provisions: Ninth Circuit on Controlled-Substance Schedules

Trent cites to the Ninth Circuit's decision in *Coronado v. Holder*.[62] In *Coronado*, the court of appeals found that California's possession of a controlled substance[63] is divisible based on reference to a number of drug schedules and statutes that organize controlled substances into five different groups, and then lists the substances in the disjunctive. This act of referencing different schedules, according to the court, creates "several different crimes" that render the statute divisible. Looking to the charging document, the court of appeals found that the substance in question was methamphetamine and upheld the finding of removability.[64]

Alternative Statutory Provisions: Fifth Circuit on General Export Statute

The Fifth Circuit U.S. Court of Appeals also allows a modified categorical approach where the statute of conviction references other statutory provisions. In *Franco-Casasola v. Holder*,[65] the court of appeals considered whether a tremendously broad federal export violation could be construed as an aggravated felony firearm offense. Title 18 of the U.S. Code (USC) §554(a) prohibits the export of any merchandise, article, or object from the United States contrary to "any law or regulation." Nowhere does §554 mention firearms. Yet the noncitizen in *Franco-Casasola* was found removable for an aggravated felony firearms trafficking

---

[60] *Matter of Lanferman*, 25 I&N Dec. 721 (BIA 2012). *Matter of Chairez I*, 26 I&N Dec. 349 (BIA 2014), withdrew the BIA's decision in *Lanferman*, which set forth the Board's approach to divisibility prior to the *Descamps* decision.

[61] *U.S. v. Aguila Montes de Oca*, 655 F.3d 915 (9th Cir. 2011).

[62] *Coronado v. Holder*, 759 F.3d 977 (9th Cir. 2014).

[63] Calif. Health & Safety Code §11377(a).

[64] In finding that a statute's reference to a long schedule of different controlled substances makes a statute divisible, *Coronado* actually represents a stricter approach than that applied by the BIA. In *Matter of Ferreira*, 26 I&N Dec. 415 (BIA 2014), the Board refrained from finding that the Connecticut controlled-substance statute was divisible based on reference to schedules. Instead, the BIA remanded for a realistic probability analysis of whether the state ever prosecuted the drugs that were not found on the federal CSA.

[65] *Franco-Casasola v. Holder*, 773 F.3d 33 (5th Cir. 2014).

offense.⁶⁶ The court of appeals opined that a statute or conviction that depends on reference to other statutes and regulations to provide the specific elements of the offense charged is divisible. The Fifth Circuit justifies the finding of divisibility because the potential list of items is finite (though lengthy), and the prosecutor must select the relevant elements from the alternative statutes and regulations; in other words, the government must allege the specific items identified by the alternative statutory provision.

Facts-Based Approach: Third Circuit and Simple Assault

In *Marrero v. United States*,⁶⁷ the Third Circuit U.S. Court of Appeals determined that Pennsylvania's simple assault statute was divisible based on three distinct *mens rea*: intent, knowledge, or recklessness. *Marrero* was also a criminal case involving application of a sentence enhancement for a past record of three violent felonies; the defendant argued that his simple assault conviction did not arise from a divisible statute and it must be presumed he acted with the least culpable intent of recklessness. However, the appeals court disagreed and looked to the plea transcript to determine that Marrero choked his wife—acting with specific intent to cause harm. The court cited to *Nijhawan* for the proposition that sentencing courts could look to factual findings of a prior court to determine whether the act was a crime of violence.⁶⁸

> ➤ **Tip**: Because *Marrero* involved a sentencing enhancement for "violent felony," which depends largely on the notion of violence, immigration attorneys should advocate it is not applicable in the immigration context. In addition, it would appear that the *Marrero* court got the analysis wrong: looking to the factual description of a prior conviction to determine the ultimate punishment for a current offense.

Essential Elements Only: Ninth Circuit on Felony Gang Enhancement

In *Hernandez-Gonzalez v. Holder*,⁶⁹ the Ninth Circuit reversed and remanded a decision by the BIA that possession of a weapon combined with a felony enhancement⁷⁰ because the activity was gang related did not qualify as a crime involving moral turpitude. The Board and IJ had reasoned that any activity that was related to a gang was by its nature base, vile, and depraved.⁷¹ The court of appeals,

---

⁶⁶ INA §101(a)(43)(E).

⁶⁷ *Marrero v. U.S.*, 743 F.3d 389 (3d Cir. 2014).

⁶⁸ *Marrero v. U.S.*, 743 F.3d at 396–97.

⁶⁹ *Hernandez-Gonzalez v. Holder*, 778 F.3d 793 (9th Cir. 2015).

⁷⁰ Cal. Penal Code §§12020(a)(1), 186.22(b)(1). Of key importance, the elements of the sentence enhancement must be proved to the fact-finder beyond a reasonable doubt. *Hernandez-Gonzalez v. Holder*, 778 F.3d 793 (9th Cir. 2015).

⁷¹ In *Matter of Hernandez*, 26 I&N Dec. 397, at 401 (BIA 2014) the Board ruled that the California gang enhancement statute renders a crime a moral turpitude offense. The Board further noted that there

Continued

however, found this to be "no analysis at all" and instead reasoned that, under an elements-based approach, neither the underlying offense (in this case, possession of a weapon[72]) nor the sentence enhancement (promotion or furtherance of gang activity) included the moral turpitude elements of an intent to injure or harm, actual injury, or a special class of victim.[73] Of note, in *Hernandez-Gonzalez*, both the BIA and the court of appeals conducted a realistic probability analysis. The appeals court found that there is in fact a realistic probability—based on its survey of state cases—that California prosecutors use the enhancement provision to punish non-moral turpitude conduct.

Essential Elements Only: Ninth Circuit on Disjunctive Burglary Statute

In *Rendon v. Holder*,[74] the Ninth Circuit looked at an automobile burglary statute that penalized the entry into a locked vehicle with "intent to commit grand or petit larceny or any felony."[75] Pre-*Descamps*, the BIA had upheld a removal order finding this to be (1) a divisible statute that (2) required the modified categorical approach, and (3) qualified as an aggravated felony theft offense.[76] The Ninth Circuit reversed and remanded, noting that the automobile burglary statute is not a categorical match to the generic "theft" concept because it includes any felony; thus, it is overbroad. At the same time, according to the court's analysis, the language, "intent to commit grand or petit larceny or any felony," is representative of means, not alternative elements. How did the Ninth Circuit determine "larceny versus any felony" are means? A determination that a jury need not choose between the terms in order to convict:

> Any statutory phrase that — explicitly or implicitly — refers to multiple, alternative means of commission must still be regarded as indivisible if the jurors need not agree on which method of committing the offense the defendant used.[77]

Because jury unanimity is not required, the disjunctive phrase represents means, not elements, and the statute is not divisible. Recourse to the record of conviction is not permissible; rather, the least culpable conduct applies. The court determined the non–U.S. citizen was not convicted of a "theft" offense and reversed the decision of the BIA.

---

had been no "realistic probability" showing that the enhancement would be applied to non-moral turpitude conduct.

[72] The weapon was a "billy club."

[73] *Hernandez-Gonzalez*, 2015 U.S. LEXIS 2328, at 12–14.

[74] *Rendon v. Holder*, 764 F.3d 1077 (9th Cir. 2014).

[75] Cal. Penal Code §459.

[76] INA §101(a)(43)(G); 8 USC §1101(a)(43)(G).

[77] *Rendon v. Holder*, 764 F.3d 1077, at 1084.

Essential Elements Only: Fourth Circuit on Disjunctive Larceny Statute

In *Omargharib v. Holder*,[78] the Fourth Circuit U.S. Court of Appeals adopted a strict elements-based approach to divisibility in finding that Virginia's larceny statute[79] did not categorically describe an aggravated felony theft[80] offense. In Virginia, larceny is defined by the common law; the statutory code section is a penalty provision. State case law makes clear that larceny encompasses both fraud and theft crimes: larceny is the "wrongful or fraudulent taking of another's property without his permission and with the intent to permanently deprive the owner of property." DHS argued that the word "or" makes the statute divisible. The court of appeals disagreed. Noting that Virginia juries are not instructed to agree unanimously and beyond a reasonable doubt whether the larceny charge involved a wrongful or fraudulent taking, but rather need only agree on a taking "without the consent of the owner," the court found that the "or" distinguished means, not elements. The statute is not divisible, and is categorically *not* a "theft" offense.

Essential Elements Only: Eleventh Circuit Throwing a Deadly Missile

In *U.S. v. Estrella*,[81] the Eleventh Circuit U.S. Court of Appeals considered whether Florida's Throwing or Shooting a Deadly Missile statute[82] qualifies as a "crime of violence" for purposes of a sentence enhancement under the Armed Criminal Career Act (ACCA). A "crime of violence" has as an element of the use, attempted use, or threatened use of physical force against the person of another. The Sentencing Guidelines definition patterns the definition of crime of violence at 18 USC §16, which in turn is referenced at the aggravated felony definition at 8 USC §1101(a)(43)(F). This criminal statute punishes "wantonly or maliciously" throwing a missile, stone, or other hard substance into a building, vehicle or vessel—and the various types of vehicles and vessels are listed. The Eleventh Circuit summarized the concept of alternative "elements" as follows:

> [W]e should ask ourselves the following question when confronted with a statute that purports to list elements in the alternative: If a defendant charged with violating the statute went to trial, would the jurors typically be required to agree that their decision to convict is based on one of the alternative elements? If that is true, then the statute is divisible, and the sentencing court can turn to the modified categorical approach to determine which of the alternative elements formed the basis of the particular conviction underlying the proposed sentence enhancement. If not, then the statute is both overbroad and indivisible

---

[78] *Omargharib v. Holder*, 775 F.3d 192 (4th Cir. 2014).

[79] Va. Code Ann. §18.2-95.

[80] INA §101(a)(43)(G); 8 USC §1101(a)(43)(G).

[81] *U.S. v. Estrella*, 758 F.3d 1239 (11th Cir. 2014).

[82] Fla. Stat. §790.19.

and cannot serve as a predicate offense for purposes of a sentence enhancement.[83]

Once a court confirms that the statute of prior conviction is divisible, then—and only then—can it analyze the conviction under the modified categorical approach.[84]

The Eleventh Circuit then looked at the type-of-structure element, as well as the *mens rea* element. The court determined the statute to be divisible. The different types of structures (buildings, vehicles, trains, vessels) qualified as separate elements.[85] Having made that determination, the court found that the element of directing force toward an occupied vehicle would not meet the "crime of violence" definition. In terms of *mens rea*, the court found that wantonly or maliciously were distinct elements, and that "maliciously" would not satisfy the crime of violence definition because the definition included damage to property (not only persons). The court then adopted a modified categorical approach, reviewed the record of conviction documents, and ascertained that the record did not specify which of the alternative elements were prosecuted and pled to.

Because the "Shepard documents" did not reveal which portion of the statute Estrella was convicted of, the court assumed the least culpable conduct, and reversed the lower court's judgment as to the sentence enhancement.[86]

Conclusion: Know the Circuit

The above cases demonstrate that there is a split in the circuits regarding the definition of divisibility. There are others. As of February 2015, the Second,[87] Fourth[88] and Eleventh[89] Circuits have issued decisions clinging to a strict-elements based approach. The Tenth[90] and the Fifth[91] have issued decisions that identify a criminal statute that references other criminal provisions to qualify as divisible. The Ninth Circuit has issued decisions that go both ways on divisibility: reference to an alternative statutory provision makes a statute divisible,[92] but punctuation that reads in the disjunctive ("or") does not make the statute divisible.[93] Disappointingly, the

---

[83] *U.S. v. Estrella*, 758 F.3d. 1239, at 1246.

[84] *U.S. v. Estrella*, 758 F.3d 1239 (11th Cir. 2014).

[85] *U.S. v. Estrella*, 758 F.3d 1239, at 1249.

[86] *U.S. v. Estrella*, 758 F.3d 1239, at 1253.

[87] *Flores v. Holder*, 779 F.3d 159 (2d Cir. 2015).

[88] *Omargharib v. Holder*, 775 F.3d 192 (4th Cir. 2014).

[89] *U.S. v. Estrella*, 758 F.3d 1239, 1245–48 (11th Cir. 2014).

[90] *U.S. v. Trent*, 767 F.3d 1046 (10th Cir. 2014).

[91] *Franco-Casasola v. Holder*, 773 F.3d 33 (5th Cir. 2014).

[92] *Coronado v. Holder*, 759 F.3d 977 (9th Cir. 2014).

[93] *Rendon v. Holder*, 764 F.3d 1077, 1084–88 (9th Cir. 2014).

Third Circuit[94] has issued a decision that alternative phrasing (listing *mens rea* in the disjunctive) results in divisibility.

Divisibility after *Descamps*: Board of Immigration Appeals

Prior to the Supreme Court's decision in *Descamps,* the BIA had adopted an analysis similar to the Ninth Circuit's decision in *Aguila Montes de Oca,*[95] discussed above. In *Matter of Lanferman,*[96] the BIA instructed that an overly broad statute (missing an element of the generic crime) was divisible, and merited a modified categorical approach. In *Lanferman,* the BIA considered whether a New York menacing statute could qualify as a firearms offense, when an alternative statutory provision defined "weapon" to include (among other objects) a firearm. The Board found the missing element (the firearm) within the definition of "weapon," and using a modified categorical approach, determined the crime of conviction was a firearms offense. In *Matter of Chairez I,*[97] the Board acknowledges the Supreme Court's analysis in *Descamps* and withdraws from *Lanferman,* finding that a statute that is missing an essential element of the generic crime is categorically not a removable offense—in this case, an aggravated felony crime of violence.[98] However, the BIA does reaffirm the realistic probability test, and remands for further proceedings on whether the crime qualifies as a firearms offense.[99]

In *Matter of Chairez I*, Chairez had a 2012 conviction for discharging a firearm under section 76-10-508.1 of the Utah Code, for which he was sentenced to an indeterminate term of imprisonment not to exceed five years. For this offense, DHS charged him with removability under two grounds: aggravated felony crime of violence and a firearm offense. The Utah statute includes three subsections and reads as follows:

Felony discharge of a firearm—Penalties

(1) Except as [otherwise] provided . . . , a person who discharges a firearm is guilty of a third degree felony punishable by imprisonment for a term of not less than three years nor more than five years if:

(a) the actor discharges a firearm in the direction of any person or persons, knowing or having reason to believe that any person may be endangered by the discharge of the firearm;

---

[94] *U.S. v. Marrero*, 743 F.3d 389, 395–97 (3d Cir. 2014).

[95] *U.S. v. Aguila-Montes de Oca,* 655 F.3d 915, 925 (9th Cir. 2011), *abrogated by Descamps v. U.S.*, 133 S. Ct. 2276 (2013).

[96] *Matter of Lanferman*, 25 I&N Dec. 721 (BIA 2012).

[97] *Matter of Chairez I*, 26 I&N Dec. 349 (BIA 2014).

[98] INA §101(a)(43)(F); 8 USC §1101(a)(43)(F).

[99] INA §237(a)(2)(C); 8 USC §1227(a)(2)(C).

(b) the actor, with intent to intimidate or harass another or with intent to damage a habitable structure . . . , discharges a firearm in the direction of any person or habitable structure; or

(c) the actor, with intent to intimidate or harass another, discharges a firearm in the direction of any vehicle.

Like many provisions under the INA, an aggravated felony "crime of violence" is defined according to federal criminal law. The definition at 18 USC §16 defines a "crime of violence" as (a) an offense that has as an element the use, attempted use, or threatened use of physical force against the person or property of another, or (b) any other offense that is a felony and that, by its nature, involves a substantial risk that physical force against the person or property of another may be used in the course of committing the offense. A "crime of violence" involves the intentional, active-use-of-violent-physical-force.[100] In *Chairez I*, the BIA notes that based on case law, §16 envisions an intentional act: "use" requires "volition." [101]

The BIA finds that of the above three subsections, only (b) and (c) carry the specific mental intent to qualify as a crime of violence, which is, the deliberate use of violent physical force. In comparison, clause (a) is substantially different, in that "this section requires only that the accused 'know[] or hav[e] reason to believe' that discharge of the firearm may endanger a person; it does not require that the firearm be discharged for a particular purpose." The Board specifies that the phrase, "knowing or having reason to believe" at subsection (a) maybe established by intent, knowledge, or recklessness: recklessness is not the intentional use of violent physical force and does not meet the definition of "crime of violence."

The Board next turns to the question of whether the terms "intent, knowledge, or recklessness" are necessary alternative elements, or means. In proceedings below, the immigration judge found clause (a) divisible as to these three mental states. The Board, however, disagreed with the IJ's decision, in light of *Descamps,* noting that under Utah law, a jury is not required to unanimously decide on the particular mental state involved in a prosecution, but may convict based on either intent, knowledge, or recklessness. Accordingly, the *mens rea* are alternative means, not alternative elements, and section 76-10-508.1 is not a divisible statute. Assuming the least culpable conduct described by the entire statute—recklessness—section 76-10-508.1 does not qualify as a crime of violence.

However, Chairez was not so fortunate in the Board's second half of the analysis: removability for a firearms offense. Chairez, relying on *Moncrieffe*, argued that because Utah's firearms statutes did not contain an exception for antique firearms—as does the comparable federal statute—it is not a categorical match. The Board disagreed, finding that Chairez has the burden of establishing a realistic probability that section 76-10-508.1 had ever been used to prosecute discharging an antique

---

[100] *See Leocal v. Ashcroft,* 543 U.S. 1, 9 (2004); *U.S. v. Johnson,* 559 U.S. 133, 140 (2010).

[101] *Matter of Chairez I*, 26 I&N Dec. 349, at 351.

firearm. In the absence of a realistic probability, as opposed to a theoretical possibility, that either he or someone else had been prosecuted for use of an antique firearm, the Utah section qualifies categorically as a firearms offense under INA §237(a)(2)(C).

The Realistic Probability Test

So how is one to know whether a strict categorical approach applies, or the case reverts to a realistic probability test? The answer may lie in the parameters of *Chairez* itself. In terms of crime of violence and the search for *mens rea,* the statute listed different types of mental state: deliberate intent, knowledge, and recklessness. The task was determining whether a deliberating judge or jury need find, under Utah law, one or the other—or whether any was suitable to sustain a conviction. The point being: the statute laid out the words, and the BIA then distinguished means and elements, finding these words to be means—hence, no divisibility.

In comparison, types of firearms are not delineated in section 76-10-508.1. The terms are not there. The provision is potentially broad enough to encompass antiques, but the burden fell to the respondent to establish realistically that the provision would be used in an antique firearm case. In the absence of a specific example—a real case—the fact that the state statute varied from the federal law provision (because it did not contain a specific exception for antiques) did not mean it could not qualify categorically as a firearms offense.

Matter of Chairez II: **Alternative Statutory Phrases**

Matter of Chairez was initially decided in July 2014. DHS filed a motion for reconsideration. In February 2015, the BIA granted reconsideration and issued *Matter of Chairez II*[102] in which the BIA reconsidered in part its categorical analysis on the issue of aggravated felony for certain jurisdictions only. Noting the Tenth Circuit's decision in *U.S. v. Trent,*[103] the BIA found that an element need not be an item determined by a unanimous jury, but that alternative elements could be present in alternative statutory phrases:

> In *Trent,* the Tenth Circuit acknowledged that a statute is divisible under *Descamps* only if it is broken down into "alternative elements" or "potential offense elements," but it concluded that the *Descamps* Court did not understand the term "element" to mean only those facts about a crime that must be proved to a jury unanimously and beyond a reasonable doubt. Instead, the *Trent* court concluded that a statute is divisible within the meaning of *Descamps* whenever it employs "alternative statutory phrases."[104]

---

[102] *Matter of Chairez II*, 26 I&N Dec. 478 (BIA 2015).

[103] *U.S. v. Trent*, 767 F.3d 1046 (10th Cir. 2014). *Trent* is discussed earlier in this chapter.

[104] *U.S. v. Trent*, 767 F.3d 1046, at 1060–61, *citing Descamps v. U.S.*, 133 S. Ct. at 2285 n.2.

Applying *Descamps* consistently with *Trent*, we conclude that the offense defined by section 76-10-508.1(1)(a) of the Utah Code is divisible into three separate offenses with distinct mens rea, namely, intent, knowledge, and recklessness. And while the reckless discharge of a firearm is not a crime of violence [internal citation omitted] we conclude that the offense is a crime of violence under 18 U.S.C. § 16 when committed intentionally or knowingly.[105]

The Board then looked to the plea agreement, found reference to intentional discharge of a firearm, and sustained the aggravated felony charge. The matter was remanded for possible relief. In footnote 3 of *Chairez II*, the BIA delineates what the agency sees as the circuit split as of February 2015. The circuit split is discussed above, in this chapter, and the issue is whether alternative statutory phrases (in *Chairez*, the discrete *mens rea*) can qualify as elements for purposes of divisibility, notwithstanding that a jury need not agree unanimously on the *mens rea* in deciding to convict.

Matter of Silva-Trevino: Vacated in April 2015

On April 10, 2015, the attorney general (AG) vacated the decision in *Matter of Silva-Trevino*.[106] *Silva-Trevino* was a 2008 case decided by the AG, which set forth a multi-step analysis for analyzing crimes involving moral turpitude. At the time of its publication, it represented a significant new approach to classifying crimes. Since 2008, however, the majority of circuit courts of appeals had rejected the approaches contained therein. By the spring of 2015, only the Seventh Circuit had reviewed and explicitly upheld *Silva-Trevino*.[107] One other circuit reluctantly complied with the decision based on deference.[108]

In *Silva-Trevino,* the AG stated that the concept of "moral turpitude" is a non-elemental fact that will never be found within a criminal statute. Where a categorical and modified categorical approach do not determine that a particular offense involves moral turpitude, it is appropriate to revert to an expanded modified categorical approach—a circumstance-specific approach—that looks to any and all relevant evidence to determine whether moral turpitude attaches to the crime of conviction. If the non–American citizen were to assert that the statute encompasses non-moral turpitude conduct, he or she must satisfy a realistic probability test: that is, present a real case wherein the statute was used to prosecute and convict for an offense that does not involve moral turpitude. Because of these various steps, the BIA had referred to the *Silva-Trevino* methodology as a "hierarchical or sequential approach to consideration of the evidence."[109]

---

[105] *Matter of Chairez,* 26 I&N Dec. 478, 480–481 (BIA 2015).

[106] *Matter of Silva-Trevino*, 24 I&N Dec. 687 (AG 2008), *vacated at* 26 I&N Dec. 550 (AG 2015).

[107] *Cano-Oyarzabal v. Holder*, 774 F.3d 914 (7th Cir. 2014); *Sanchez v. Holder*, 757 F.3d 712 (7th Cir. 2014).

[108] *Bobadilla v. Holder,* 679 F.3d 1052 (8th Cir. 2012).

[109] *Matter of Ahortalejo-Guzman,* 25 I&N Dec. 465, 468 (BIA 2011).

Silva-Trevino involved an LPR who pled no contest to the criminal offense of "indecency with a child" under Title 5, §21.11(a)(1) of the Texas Penal Code. The statute criminalizes sexual contact with a child younger than 17 years old who is not the person's spouse, unless the perpetrator is not more than three years older than the victim and the victim is of the opposite sex. "Sexual contact" includes any touching—including touching through clothing—of the anus, breast, or any part of the genitals, if committed with the intention to arouse or gratify the sexual desire of any person. As such, the statute could be applied to a "consensual" statutory rape situation. In this case, the respondent was 64 years old at the time of the offense.[110]

In removal proceedings, the respondent conceded that his conviction was an aggravated felony,[111] but proposed that it was not a crime involving moral turpitude. Respondent applied for adjustment of status, arguing that this relief would act as a waiver of the aggravated felony ground. According to the respondent, the offense was not a crime involving moral turpitude; there was no ground of inadmissibility; hence, no need for any other waiver. Because of waiver eligibility (relief stage), it was important for the respondent in *Silva-Trevino* to prevail on the argument that his offense was not a crime involving moral turpitude. According to the respondent, the Texas statute did not require that the perpetrator act with knowledge that the individual with whom he has sexual contact is a child, and thus could encompass cases where the individual honestly and reasonably believes he is having sexual contact with a consenting adult; this situation would not be one involving moral turpitude.

The IJ disagreed with the respondent and found that statutory rape qualifies as a crime involving moral turpitude; he ordered respondent removed. On appeal, however, the BIA reversed the decision of the IJ, stating that it was "constrained" by Fifth Circuit law to consider the least culpable conduct described by statute and that not every crime potentially covered by the Texas statute would involve moral turpitude.[112] Complying with circuit law, the Board did not look beyond the record of conviction into the factual circumstances of the offense, but confined itself to a modified categorical approach. The case eventually went before the AG, who vacated the decision and remanded to the BIA with instructions to adopt a broad new evidentiary methodology—along with a new legal standard—to determine whether the offense in question involved moral turpitude.

The AG's Previous Methodology for Determining Moral Turpitude

In the 2008 decision, the AG stated at the outset that the categorical approach still applies in determining whether a crime involves moral turpitude. The first step, he wrote, is to look at the criminal law statute: the elements of the statute still control the

---

[110] *Matter of Silva-Trevino*, 24 I&N Dec. 687, at 690.

[111] The definition of aggravated felony includes sexual abuse of a minor. *See* INA §101(a)(43)(A).

[112] *Matter of Silva-Trevino*, 24 I&N Dec. 687, at 691.

outcome, not the actual circumstances underlying the offense.[113] However, the AG allowed a modified categorical approach where the elements of the statute were not clear as to whether moral turpitude was involved. If a modified categorical approach that looked to the record of conviction did not determine a moral turpitude factor, then the immigration judge was free to look at any and all relevant evidence to determine if the crime involved moral turpitude.

Realistic probability test

In the 2008 decision, the AG utilized the realistic probability test as the applicable standard for deciding whether a criminal statute categorically involves moral turpitude, or may be viewed as divisible, including conduct that does not involve moral turpitude. The AG states that in determining whether a statute could possibly be construed or applied to conduct that does not involve moral turpitude, the non–American citizen must point to a case (which might include his own) wherein the criminal statute was used to prosecute and convict someone for conduct that did not involve moral turpitude. Put another way, if the respondent's interpretation of the statute is that its elements may be read in such a fashion as to penalize an act that does not categorically involve moral turpitude (*i.e.*, categorically an act involving theft, fraud, intentional violence), he must present a case or cases in which the state courts did in fact apply the statute in this special (non-generic) manner.[114] In this way, the non–American citizen must establish a realistic probability that the statute could be applied to conduct that does not involve moral turpitude.

If the non–American citizen is able to point to a case wherein the statute was applied to non-moral turpitude conduct, the case is not yet over; rather, the inquiry moves to the second stage of inquiry.

> ➢ *Note*: In the 2008 *Silva-Trevino* decision, the AG acknowledges a state court case in which the Texas penal statute was used to prosecute an individual for an offense that did not involve moral turpitude. In the highlighted case, the defendant was led to believe that the victim he had sexual contact with was over 17; thus, he did not have knowledge that the victim was underage, but he was prosecuted and convicted anyway. The AG notes that a realistic probability exists that the statute could be applied to non-moral turpitude situations.[115] However, this does not end the inquiry, but only leads to step two of the analysis.

Moral Turpitude as a "Non-elemental Fact"

The AG's justification for consideration of evidence outside the record of conviction was that the concept of "moral turpitude" is a non-elemental fact. This

---

[113] *Matter of Silva-Trevino*, 24 I&N Dec. 687, at 697.

[114] *Matter of Silva-Trevino*, 24 I&N Dec. 687, at 697.

[115] *Matter of Silva-Trevino*, 24 I&N Dec. 687, at 708, *citing Johnson v. State,* 967 S.W. 2d 848, 849 (Tex. Crim. App. 1998) (en banc).

premise is subject to question. Moral turpitude has been adeptly defined by case law for decades within and outside the immigration law context. The challenge, where it arose, was in properly analyzing the criminal statute and record of conviction, not in defining moral turpitude itself.

The term "non-elemental fact" applies to specific definitions of the term "aggravated felony"—definitions that contain specific elements that are not ascertainable within the particular criminal statutes: amount of loss, age of the victim, etc. The broad concept of "moral turpitude" is not similar to a specific and identifiable element like financial loss or age of victim; the AG misapplied the concept, yet this was the foundational justification for his methodology.

After *Silva-Trevino*: The Federal Courts' Response

Five circuit courts of appeals have rejected the *Silva-Trevino* analysis. In 2014, the Fifth Circuit (where the case arose) rejected the *Silva-Trevino* methodology.[116] The court decided that moral turpitude is not a non-elemental fact meriting the circumstance-specific approach, but rather, the traditional categorical approach applies. The INA's specific definition of "conviction" limits the courts to the criminal statute's elements.

Long before the Fifth Circuit considered *Silva-Trevino*, other courts rejected the methodology, also finding that moral turpitude describes a generic concept. The Third Circuit, in *Jean-Louis v. Att'y Gen.*,[117] soundly criticized the AG's methodology, finding that the categorical and, if appropriate, strict modified categorical approach (limited to the record of conviction) applies in determining whether a conviction involves moral turpitude. The Third Circuit re-emphasized that it is the elements of the statute under which a non–American citizen is convicted that determine deportability, not the underlying crime that may have been committed.

Likewise, the Eleventh Circuit, in *Sanchez-Fajardo v. Att'y Gen.*,[118] found that the *Silva-Trevino* analysis is contrary to the "unambiguously expressed intent of Congress" that adjudicators employ a categorical and modified categorical approach in determining whether a crime involves moral turpitude.[119]

In *Prudencio v. Holder*,[120] the Fourth Circuit similarly rejected *Silva-Trevino*, holding that "the procedural framework established in *Silva-Trevino* was not an authorized exercise of the AG's authority." Furthermore, the court wrote:

> Although DHS is correct that the term "moral turpitude" is not usually an element of an offense and thus will not appear literally in the record

---

[116] *Trevino v. Holder*, 742 F.3d 197 (5th Cir. 2014).

[117] *Jean-Louis v. Att'y Gen.*, 582 F.3d 462 (3d Cir. 2009).

[118] *Sanchez-Fajardo v. Att'y Gen.*, 659 F.3d 1303 (11th Cir. 2011).

[119] *Sanchez-Fajardo v. Att'y Gen.*, 659 F.3d 1303, at 1310.

[120] *Prudencio v. Holder*, 669 F.3d 472 (4th Cir. 2012).

of conviction, courts nevertheless have been able to interpret this phrase for over a century, and a robust body of law has developed in this regard.[121]

Two courts of appeals agree with the *Silva-Trevino* methodology. These are the Eighth and the Seventh Circuit U.S. Courts of Appeals. Indeed, it might be said the Seventh Circuit spawned the AG's decision in a case called *Ali v. Mukasey*.[122] In *Ali*, the petitioner was convicted of conspiracy under 18 USC §§371; the underlying offenses of the conspiracy were 18 USC §§922 and 925, firearms licensing and trafficking violations. Likening the concept of "moral turpitude" to the non-elemental financial loss issue, the Seventh Circuit found it appropriate to consider all manner of documents (including the pre-sentence report) in determining that the offense involved the "intent to defraud the United States" portion of the conspiracy statute:

> [W]e now conclude that when deciding how to classify convictions under criteria that go beyond the criminal charge—such as the amount of the victim's loss, or whether the crime is one of "moral turpitude," the agency has the discretion to consider evidence beyond the charging papers and judgment of conviction.[123]

Seven months later, the AG—citing heavily to the *Ali* decision—issued his opinion in *Silva-Trevino*. In 2010, the Seventh Circuit endorsed the AG's analysis in *Mata-Guerrero v. Holder*.[124] As stated above, in 2014, the Seventh Circuit again affirmed the *Silva-Trevino* analysis.

In May 2012, in a case called *Bobadilla v. Holder*,[125] the Eighth Circuit issued a decision in favor of the *Silva-Trevino* methodology. In a somewhat interesting twist, the Eighth Circuit granted a petition for review and reversed an order of removal by the BIA, finding that the Board had erred in finding the Minnesota crime of providing a false name to a police officer[126] is categorically a crime involving moral turpitude. Instead, according to the court, the false-name statute could realistically include non-moral turpitude acts, and DHS should have been held to its burden of proving, based on any relevant evidence, whether the non–American citizen's crime involved moral turpitude. Although the individual in *Bobadilla* may have scored a victory, it was a loss for the defense bar and immigrant community, because the *Silva-Trevino*

---

[121] *Prudencio v. Holder*, 669 F.3d 472, at 482.

[122] *Ali v. Mukasey*, 521 F.3d 737 (7th Cir. 2008).

[123] *Ali v. Mukasey*, 521 F.3d 737, at 743.

[124] *Mata-Guerrero v. Holder*, 627 F.3d 256, 260–61 (7th Cir. 2010).

[125] *Bobadilla v. Holder*, 679 F.3d 1052 (8th Cir. 2012).

[126] Minn. Stat. §609.506(1) provides: "Whoever with intent to obstruct justice gives a fictitious name other than a nickname, or gives a false date of birth, or false or fraudulently altered identification card to a peace officer [as defined] when that officer makes inquiries incident to a lawful investigatory stop or lawful arrest, or inquiries incident to executing any other duty imposed by law, is guilty of a misdemeanor."

analysis will rarely work in the non–American citizen's favor. As of the spring of 2015, *Bobadilla* remains good law in the Eighth Circuit.

To recap, the Third, Fourth, Fifth, Ninth and Eleventh Circuits have rejected *Silva-Trevino*; the Seventh and Eighth Circuits support the AG's former analysis. For those practitioners representing individuals in one of the two undecided circuits—and in light of five circuits' rejection of *Silva-Trevino*—defense counsel may want to preserve for the record the argument that *Silva-Trevino* is an incorrect analysis and that a strict categorical approach should apply instead. In some limited cases, the third step (any and all relevant extrinsic evidence) may work in the respondent's favor.

BIA attempts to limit *Silva-Trevino*

Following the AG's 2008 order, BIA decisions seemed to clarify and narrow *Silva-Trevino*'s impact in terms of consideration of evidence to determine whether there is a conviction for a crime involving moral turpitude. Of course any precedent decision that specifically relied on *Silva-Trevino* and went beyond a categorical analysis to find moral turpitude is subject to fresh review and challenge.

Matter of Ahortalejo-Guzman[127] involved a Texas conviction of simple assault; DHS sought to establish that this was a case of domestic violence and introduced various types of evidence, such as the arrest report and even testimony of the respondent. The BIA, however, overruled the IJ's decision. The Board found that because, categorically, the statute did not describe a moral turpitude crime, it was improper to look at the arrest report and other forms of evidence:

> Where the record of conviction conclusively shows that a conviction does not involve family violence, the fact that other evidence outside of the record of conviction may indicate that the victim was part of the offender's family does not establish that the offender was *convicted* on that basis (*i.e.*, that such fact was found beyond a reasonable doubt for purposes of the guilty plea ...). [T]he third stage analysis outlined in *Matter of Silva-Trevino* is properly applied only where the record of conviction does not itself resolve the issue, that is, where the record does not conclusively demonstrate whether an alien was convicted of engaging in conduct that constitutes a crime involving moral turpitude.[128]

The Attorney General's 2015 vacatur

In the 2015 decision vacating *Silva-Trevino*, the AG acknowledges that five circuit courts of appeals had rejected the expanded evidentiary analysis. The AG acknowledges that an analysis of moral turpitude must focus on the actual statute of conviction, rather than conduct for which the respondent was not convicted. The AG notes in footnote 3 that the analysis regarding scienter and some form of reprehensible conduct equating with moral turpitude remains intact, and that

---

[127] *Matter of Ahortalejo-Guzman*, 25 I&N Dec. 465 (BIA 2011).

[128] *Matter of Silva-Trevino*, 25 I&N Dec. 465 at 468–69.

decisions of the BIA that were premised on *Silva-Trevino* because of the scienter combined with reprehensible conduct analysis remain valid. The AG remanded *Silva-Trevino* to the Board to consider and articulate the proper analysis for determining when a modified categorical approach may apply.[129]

Chapter Review: A Review of Pertinent Terms

Categorical Approach: an approach to analyzing statutes to determine the classification of the crime, based on the essential elements of the criminal statute, and comparing to the generic definition of the crime.[130]

Modified Categorical Approach: a subset, or tool, of the categorical approach that allows recourse to the record of conviction to determine the portion of the statute charged, where the criminal statute is divisible.[131]

Divisible Statute: a statute that sets forth necessary elements in the alternative such that the criminal statute encompasses more than one type of criminal conduct or offense.[132] For purposes of immigration law as well as criminal sentence enhancements, typically one offense will represent the generic crime that triggers the classification, while the other offense conduct will not.

Missing Element Statute: an overly broad statute that encompasses the generic crime, but is missing an essential element, thus also incorporates other offenses and is not a categorical match.[133]

Circumstance-Specific Approach: an analysis that allows the adjudicator to look to information outside of the criminal statute and the record of conviction to determine a certain qualifying criterion because the immigration law provision at issue requires determination of a factor that will never be a specific element of the crime. The classic example is the amount of financial loss to a victim, at INA § 101(a)(43)(M).[134]

Non-elemental Fact: a criterion required by the immigration law provision (such as loss) that will never be an element in the generic crime.[135]

---

[129] *Matter of Silva-Trevino*, 26 I&N Dec. 550, at 554 (AG 2015).

[130] *Descamps v. U.S.*, 133 S. Ct. 2276 (2013); *Taylor v. U.S.*, 495 U.S. 575 (1990).

[131] *Moncrieffe v. Holder*, 133 S. Ct. 1678 (2013); *Descamps v. U.S.*, 133 S. Ct. 2276 (2013).

[132] *Descamps v. U.S.*, 133 S. Ct. 2276 (2013); *U.S. v. Trent* 767 F.3d 1046 (10th Cir. 2014); *Matter of Chairez I*, 26 I&N Dec. 349 (BIA 2014).

[133] *U.S. v. Aguila Montes-de-Oca*, 655 F.3d 915 (9th Cir. 2011), *abrogated by Descamps v. U.S.*, 133 S. Ct. 2276 (2013); *Matter of Lanferman*, 25 I&N Dec. 721 (BIA 2012), *abrogated by Matter of Chairez I*, 26 I&N Dec. 349 (BIA 2014).

[134] *Nijhawan v. Holder*, 557 U.S. 29 (2009); also in certain circuits, *Matter of Silva-Trevino*, 24 I&N Dec. 687 (AG 2008).

[135] *Nijhawan v. Holder*, 557 U.S. 29 (2009); also in certain circuits, *Matter of Silva-Trevino*, 24 I&N Dec. 687 (AG 2008).

Realistic Probability Test: an analysis that sometimes is used with the categorical approach, which asks one of the parties to establish a realistic probability (as opposed to a theoretical, hypothetical possibility) that the criminal statute, although not a perfect categorical match, would be used to prosecute conduct outside of the generic crime.[136]

Least Culpable Conduct: a test or standard which dictates that the minimal conduct described by a criminal statute will be assumed to be the conduct of conviction where a categorical approach applies to a broad statute, or when notwithstanding the application of a modified categorical approach, the record does not reflect which portion of the statute was charged.[137]

Element: an essential aspect of the crime as reflected in the criminal statute that a jury must agree on beyond a reasonable doubt, either unanimously, or by a majority (as dictated by state rules).[138]

Means: a method of committing the crime that is described in the criminal statute, but is not a necessary element.[139]

Alternative Statutory Phrase: a word or term in a criminal statute that is set off from other terms by the disjunctive or formatting. Some courts have found that an alternative statutory phrase fits the definition of an element for purposes of determining divisibility. Other courts have rejected this approach and found that alternative statutory phrases are akin to means unless the prosecutor must prove one or the other, and a jury must decide between one or the other.[140]

Alternative Statutory Provision: an alternative statutory provision is a statutory provision that is referenced by the statute of conviction, such that some adjudicators will find that reference to an alternative or additional section of law (*i.e.*, the definition of "weapon") renders a statute divisible.[141]

Record of Conviction: these are the documents that an adjudicator may look to when the statute of conviction is divisible, as part of a modified categorical approach. There may be nuances as to what qualifies as a record document, but all jurisdictions agree that at least the record of conviction includes the charging document, the plea colloquy and plea agreement, the judgment and sentence. A record of conviction may also include a factual proffer, including perhaps a non-disputed fact in a PSI/PSR. The record of conviction will not include the arrest report unless the factual proffer or

---

[136] *Gonzales v. Duenas-Alvarez*, 549 U.S. 183 (2007).

[137] *Moncrieffe v. Holder*, 133 S. Ct. 1678 (2013); *Sanchez- Fajardo v. Holder*, 659 F.3d 1303 (11th Cir. 2011).

[138] *Descamps v. U.S.*, 133 S. Ct. 2276 (2013); *Matter of Chairez I*, 26 I&N Dec. 349 (BIA 2014).

[139] *Descamps v. U.S.*, 133 S. Ct. 2276 (2013); *Matter of Chairez I*, 26 I&N Dec. 349 (BIA 2014).

[140] *U.S. v. Trent*, 767 F.3d 1046 (10th Cir. 2014); *Matter of Chairez II*, 26 I&N Dec. 478 (BIA 2015).

[141] *Franco-Casasola v. Holder*, 773 F.3d 33 (5th Cir. 2014).

plea includes an explicit stipulation by the parties to the facts set forth in the arrest report.[142]

---

[142] *Shepard v. U.S.*, 544 U.S. 13, 26 (2005).

APPENDIX 5A

UNPUBLISHED BIA DECISION, *MATTER OF FORVILUS*

U.S. Department of Justice

Executive Office for Immigration Review

Board of Immigration Appeals
Office of the Clerk

5107 Leesburg Pike, Suite 2000
Falls Church, Virginia 20530

FORVILUS, DIEUVU
A071-552-965
C/O KROME SPC
18201 SW 12 STREET
MIAMI, FL 33194

DHS/ICE Office of Chief Counsel - KRO
18201 SW 12th St.
Miami, FL 33194

Name: FORVILUS, DIEUVU

A 071-552-965

Date of this notice: 1/28/2014

Enclosed is a copy of the Board's decision in the above-referenced case. This copy is being provided to you as a courtesy. Your attorney or representative has been served with this decision pursuant to 8 C.F.R. § 1292.5(a). If the attached decision orders that you be removed from the United States or affirms an Immigration Judge's decision ordering that you be removed, any petition for review of the attached decision must be filed with and received by the appropriate court of appeals within 30 days of the date of the decision.

Sincerely,

Donna Carr

Donna Carr
Chief Clerk

Enclosure

Panel Members:
Guendelsberger, John
Pauley, Roger
Greer, Anne J.

yungc
Userteam: Docket

Cite as: Dieuvu Forvilus, A071 552 965 (BIA Jan. 28, 2014)

U.S. Department of Justice
Executive Office for Immigration Review

Decision of the Board of Immigration Appeals

Falls Church, Virginia 20530

File: A071 552 965 – Miami, FL   Date: JAN 2 8 2014

In re: DIEUVU FORVILUS

IN REMOVAL PROCEEDINGS

APPEAL

ON BEHALF OF RESPONDENT: Patricia Elizee, Esquire

ON BEHALF OF DHS: Margarita I. Cimadevilla
Assistant Chief Counsel

CHARGE:

Notice: Sec. 212(a)(2)(A)(i)(I), I&N Act [8 U.S.C. § 1182(a)(2)(A)(i)(I)] - Crime involving moral turpitude

APPLICATION: Termination

The respondent appeals from an Immigration Judge's October 3, 2013, decision ordering him removed from the United States. The Department of Homeland Security ("DHS") opposes the appeal. The appeal will be sustained and the removal proceedings will be terminated.

The respondent is a native and citizen of Haiti and a lawful permanent resident ("LPR") of the United States. In 2010 the respondent was convicted in Florida of third-degree grand theft in violation of Fla. Stat. § 812.014. In 2013, after traveling abroad, the respondent presented himself for DHS inspection at the Miami International Airport port of entry, where he requested permission to reenter the United States as a returning LPR. Upon discovering the respondent's 2010 conviction, however, the DHS denied his request to reenter the United States and initiated the present removal proceedings. In a notice to appear filed in August 2013, the DHS charged the respondent with inadmissibility to the United States as an arriving alien convicted of a crime involving moral turpitude ("CIMT"). Sections 101(a)(13)(C)(v) and 212(a)(2)(A)(i)(I) of the Immigration and Nationality Act, 8 U.S.C. §§ 1101(a)(13)(C)(v), 1182(a)(2)(A)(i)(I).[1] The Immigration Judge sustained the charge and ordered the respondent removed. This timely appeal followed, in which the respondent argues that the offense defined by Fla. Stat. § 812.014 is not a CIMT. We review that legal question de novo. 8 C.F.R. § 1003.1(d)(3)(ii).

At all relevant times, Fla. Stat. § 812.014(1) has stated in relevant part that "[a] person commits theft if he or she knowingly obtains or uses, or endeavors to obtain or to use, the property of another with intent to, either temporarily or permanently: (a) Deprive the other person of a right to the property or a benefit from the property [or] (b) Appropriate the property

---

[1] As the respondent is a returning LPR, the DHS bears the burden of proving by clear and convincing evidence that he has committed an offense which renders him amenable to a charge of inadmissibility. *Matter of Rivens*, 25 I&N Dec. 623 (BIA 2011).

Cite as: Dieuvu Forvilus, A071 552 965 (BIA Jan. 28, 2014)

A071 552 965

to his or her own use or to the use of any person not entitled to the use of the property." The statute also provides: "It is grand theft in the third degree and a felony of the third degree . . . if the property stolen is . . . [v]alued at $300 or more, but less than $5,000 . . . ." Fla. Stat. § 812.014(2)(c).

The United States Court of Appeals for the Eleventh Circuit, in whose jurisdiction this case arises, has held that an offense is a CIMT if it "involves '[a]n act of baseness, vileness, or depravity in the private and social duties which a man owes to his fellow men, or to society in general, contrary to the accepted and customary rule of right and duty between man and man.'" *Cano v. U.S. Att'y Gen.*, 709 F.3d 1052, 1053 (11th Cir. 2013) (quoting *United States v. Gloria*, 494 F.2d 477, 481 (5th Cir. 1974)). To determine whether a crime qualifies as a CIMT in cases arising within the Eleventh Circuit, we apply the traditional "categorical approach," under which we focus upon the statutory definition of the crime rather than the facts underlying the particular offense. *Fajardo v. U.S. Att'y Gen.*, 659 F.3d 1303, 1305 (11th Cir. 2011). The categorical approach requires that "we analyze whether the least culpable conduct necessary to sustain a conviction under the statute meets the standard of a crime involving moral turpitude." *Cano v. U.S. Att'y Gen.*, *supra*, at 1053 n. 3 (quoting *Keungne v. U.S. Att'y Gen.*, 561 F.3d 1281, 1284 n. 3 (11th Cir. 2009)).

It is undisputed that Fla. Stat. § 812.014 does not define a categorical CIMT because the statute, by its terms, encompasses offenses in which only a temporary taking or appropriation of property is intended. Under this Board's precedents, temporary takings of property are not CIMTs. *E.g., Matter of Grazley*, 14 I&N Dec. 330, 333 (BIA 1973). As the "least culpable conduct" necessary to support a conviction for third-degree grand theft under Fla. Stat. § 812.014 does not involve moral turpitude, the DHS can carry its burden only if the statute is "divisible" vis-à-vis the CIMT concept, such that the Immigration Judge may consult the respondent's conviction record under the "modified categorical" approach with a view to determining whether his particular offense of conviction involved moral turpitude.

The Immigration Judge found that Fla. Stat. § 812.014 is divisible because it encompasses some turpitudinous offenses in which a permanent taking or appropriation of property is intended, as well as some non-turpitudinous offenses involving temporary takings or appropriations. Thus, he found it proper to consider the respondent's plea agreement and charging document which, taken together, show that he was convicted of unlawfully obtaining food stamps and cash assistance from the State of Florida (I.J. at 2-3). Based on that evidence, the Immigration Judge concluded that the DHS had carried its burden of proving that the respondent was convicted of third-degree grand theft involving the intent to permanently take or appropriate the victim's property, a CIMT.

On appeal, the respondent maintains that the Immigration Judge's divisibility analysis was erroneous in light of the Supreme Court's decision in *Descamps v. United States*, 133 S. Ct. 2276 (2013). We agree with the respondent.

In *Descamps*, the Supreme Court explained that the modified categorical approach operates narrowly, and applies only if: (1) the statute of conviction is divisible in the sense that it lists multiple discrete offenses as enumerated alternatives or defines a single offense by reference to

A071 552 965

disjunctive sets of "elements,"[2] more than one combination of which could support a conviction, and (2) some (but not all) of those listed offenses or combinations of disjunctive elements are a categorical match to the relevant generic standard. *Id.* at 2281, 2283. Thus, after *Descamps* the modified categorical approach does not apply merely because the elements of a crime can sometimes be proved by reference to conduct that fits the generic federal standard; according to the *Descamps* Court, such crimes are "overbroad" but not "divisible." *Id.* at 2285-86, 2290-92.[3]

The Immigration Judge found that Fla. Stat. § 812.014 was divisible vis-à-vis the CIMT concept because it covers either "permanent" or "temporary" takings. In light of *Descamps*, however, this disjunctive phrasing does not render the statute divisible so as to warrant a modified categorical inquiry. Permanent and temporary takings are alternative *means* of committing grand theft in Florida; however, the DHS—which bears the burden of proof—has identified no authority to suggest that they are alternative *elements* of grand theft about which Florida jurors must agree in order to convict. *See Descamps v. United States, supra,* at 2285 n. 2; *accord Schad v. Arizona,* 501 U.S. 624, 636 (1991) (plurality) ("[L]egislatures frequently enumerate alternative means of committing a crime without intending to define separate elements or separate crimes.").[4]

As the offense defined by Fla. Stat. § 812.014 is neither a categorical CIMT nor divisible vis-à-vis the CIMT concept under *Descamps*, we conclude that the removal charge must be dismissed. No other charges are pending against the respondent, moreover, and therefore the removal proceedings will be terminated.

ORDER: The appeal is sustained, the Immigration Judge's decision is vacated, and the removal proceedings are terminated.

FOR THE BOARD

---

[2] By "elements," we understand the *Descamps* Court to mean those facts about a crime which must be proved to a jury beyond a reasonable doubt *and* about which the jury must agree by whatever margin is required to convict in the relevant jurisdiction. *Id.* at 2288 (citing *Richardson v. United States,* 526 U.S. 813, 817 (1999)).

[3] The Eleventh Circuit has held that the requirements of the categorical and modified categorical approaches may not be relaxed in CIMT cases. *Fajardo v. U.S. Atty. Gen., supra.*

[4] In its appellate brief, the DHS argues that "*Descamps* is of no applicability to the instant inquiry," largely because this Board has previously found statutes resembling Fla. Stat. § 812.014 to be divisible. On the contrary, we view *Descamps* as authoritative intervening precedent as to the scope of the "divisibility" concept; thus, after *Descamps* a theft statute can be divisible in CIMT cases on the basis of the permanent-versus-temporary-taking dichotomy only if permanent and temporary takings are set forth by the convicting statute as alternative elements. Prior Board decisions embracing a more expansive understanding of divisibility are necessarily superseded to the extent they are inconsistent with *Descamps*.

Cite as: Dieuvu Forvilus, A071 552 965 (BIA Jan. 28, 2014)

UNITED STATES DEPARTMENT OF JUSTICE
EXECUTIVE OFFICE FOR IMMIGRATION REVIEW
IMMIGRATION COURT
KROME PROCESSING CENTER
MIAMI, FLORIDA

File: A071-552-965   October 3, 2013

In the Matter of

DIEUVU FORVILUS   )
)   IN REMOVAL PROCEEDINGS
)
RESPONDENT   )

CHARGE: Section 212(a)(2)(A)(i)(I) of the Immigration and Nationality Act (Act) – Convicted of a crime involving moral turpitude.

APPLICATION: Motion to terminate.

ON BEHALF OF RESPONDENT: PATRICIA ELIZEE

ON BEHALF OF DHS: GEORGINA PICOS

ORAL DECISION OF THE IMMIGRATION JUDGE

The respondent is a native and citizen of Haiti who, on or about September 10, 2002, was accorded the status of lawful permanent resident of the United States.

On or about February 3, 2010, respondent was convicted in the 19th Judicial Circuit Court in and for St. Lucie County, Florida, for the offense of grand theft in the third degree under Case No. 562004CF002333A and in violation of Florida Statute 812.014. For this offense, the respondent was sentenced to 22 days in jail and three years' probation, along with restitution ordered.

On or about April 29, 2013, the respondent arrived in Miami International Airport and applied for admission to the United States as a lawful permanent resident.

On or about August 1, 2013, the Department of Homeland Security (Department) issued a Notice to Appear charging the respondent with being removable pursuant to the aforementioned section of law. The document was filed with the Immigration Court on August 5, 2013, and the respondent, through counsel, admitted the truth of the allegations, but denied removability. And as a result, the respondent put filed a motion to terminate these proceedings on the basis that he is not removable for having been convicted of a crime involving moral turpitude; specifically, that the offense that he was convicted of is not a crime involving moral turpitude; that the Government has not met its burden of establishing removability; that the Court is limited as to what it can review; that because of the statute, because of the way the statute is written, that the Government cannot presume that the taking was of a permanent nature. And therefore, again, the Government has not met its burden.

The Court has taken into consideration the respondent's arguments, as well as the arguments presented by the Government's memorandum of law, and the Court finds that the respondent's conviction is a crime involving moral turpitude because there is a presumption that it is a permanent taking due to the items that were taken.

The conviction record is here. It is Exhibit 2. There is an amended information, which is part of the record, and it shows that the respondent endeavored to obtain, or did obtain, food stamps and excessive cash assistance which was the property of the Florida Department of Children and Families, value of $300 or more. The rest of that, it just mirrors the statute that it was the intent to permanently or temporarily deprive the owner of the right to the property or a benefit there from or to appropriate the property, the use of the taker. The statute involved is a divisible statute because it does punish conduct that is a crime involving moral turpitude, which would be the intentional, permanent taking of property, and it also punishes conduct that is not a crime involving moral turpitude, which would be the temporary taking or the temporary appropriation of the property. So I believe that under current case law, the Court is allowed to use a modified categorical approach. But that still limits what the Court can look at. And what it can look at is the criminal conviction, which shows that the items taken were cash, as well as food stamps.

There is a precedent Board decision which the Court finds is on point, and does not believe that it has been overturned. And that is Matter of Grazley, 14 I&N Dec. 330, 333 (BIA 1973). In that case, I believe the person was convicted of a theft under the Canadian statute, which pretty much had language that it was a temporary or absolute taking. And in that case, the items taken were cash and also some stamps. And in that decision, the Board said that "while we have no direct evidence as to what the respondent's intent was at the time he took the purse, we believe it is reasonable to assume, since cash was taken, that he took it with the intention of retaining it permanently." And here, we have cash and food stamps. Again, I believe it is on point.

There is also the case of Matter of Garcia-Madruga, 24 I&N Dec. 436 (BIA 2008), where they say a theft offense under Section 101(a)(43)(G) ordinarily requires a taking of or exercise of control over property without consent and with the criminal intent to deprive the owner of the rights and benefits thereof, even if such deprivation is less than total or permanent.

There is a recent Eleventh Circuit decision, Ramos v. United States Attorney General, 709 F.3d 1066 (11th Cir. 2013), holding that a conviction under a Georgia Statute, a statute that criminalizes shoplifting, is not categorically an aggravated felony under 101(a)(43)(G) of the Act because it included two disjunctive intent requirements, an intent to deprive and an intent to appropriate, and was divisible. And I believe where the statutory language itself demonstrates the visibility, it is not required of the respondent to provide case law to demonstrate a realistic probably that the statute could be used to prosecute conduct outside the scope of a certain offense or its generic definition. That case dealt with whether it was an aggravated felony under 101(a)(43)(G) of the Act. What we are dealing here is with a crime involving moral turpitude. Although, Georgia case did deal with the issue of theft. But I do not believe that case overruled <u>Matter of Grazley</u>, and since I believe that <u>Grazley</u> is still good law, I must follow it. I, therefore, find that it is a crime involving moral turpitude and that he is removable as charged. And consequently, the motion to terminate must be denied.

Now, as to relief from removal, the respondent has not submitted any application for relief other than this motion to terminate and, consequently, the Court has to issue the following order:

ORDER

IT IS HEREBY ORDERED that the respondent be removed from the United States to Haiti pursuant to the charge contained in the Notice to Appear.

ADAM OPACIUCH
Immigration Judge

CERTIFICATE PAGE

I hereby certify that the attached proceeding before JUDGE ADAM OPACIUCH, in the matter of:

DIEUVU FORVILUS

A071-552-965

MIAMI, FLORIDA

was held as herein appears, and that this is the original transcript thereof for the file of the Executive Office for Immigration Review.

JUDITH MOORE (Transcriber)

FREE STATE REPORTING, Inc.-2

OCTOBER 29, 2013
(Completion Date)

APPENDIX 5B

UNPUBLISHED IJ DECISION TERMINATING ARRIVING ALIEN STATUS, NOT A CIMT

UNITED STATES DEPARTMENT OF JUSTICE
EXECUTIVE OFFICE FOR IMMIGRATION REVIEW
IMMIGRATION COURT
MIAMI, FLORIDA

IN THE MATTER OF:

IN REMOVAL PROCEEDINGS

RESPONDENT

ON BEHALF OF RESPONDENT
Sheri A. Benchetrit, Esq.
Stok Folk + Kon
18851 NE 29th Avenue, Suite 1005
Aventura, Florida 33180

ON BEHALF OF DEPARTMENT
Y. Michelle Ramirez
Assistant Chief Counsel
Department of Homeland Security
333 South Miami Avenue, Suite 200
Miami, Florida 33130

WRITTEN DECISION AND ORDERS OF THE IMMIGRATION JUDGE

I. Background

_____ ('Respondent) is a native and citizen of Haiti. Respondent received Lawful Permanent Resident status on December 14, 2005. Exh. 1. On May 7, 2007, Respondent pled *nolo contendere* to and was convicted of one count of Grand Theft in the Third Degree under section 812.014 of the Florida Statutes. Exh. 2. For this offense, Respondent was sentenced to eighteen months probation. *Id.* On June 15, 2010, Respondent arrived at the Fort Lauderdale/Hollywood International Airport and requested admission into the United States as a returning lawful permanent resident. Exh. 1. The U.S. Department of Homeland Security (DHS) served Respondent with a Notice to Appear on October 25, 2010, charging him as inadmissible under section 212(a)(2)(A)(i)(I) of the Immigration and Nationality Act (Act) for having committed—or attempted or conspired to commit—a crime involving moral turpitude (CIMT): Grand Theft in the Third Degree. *Id.*

During his April 25, 2012 hearing, Respondent admitted all allegations contained in his Notice to Appear. He denied the charge of inadmissibility, arguing that his conviction for Grand Theft in the Third Degree under section 812.014 of the Florida Statutes was not a conviction for a CIMT and, therefore, that he was not inadmissible as charged. Respondent asked to brief the issue, and the Court provided Respondent with a May 25, 2012 deadline to submit his arguments. The Court also provided DHS with a June 25, 2012 deadline to file an answer. Respondent filed a Motion to Terminate and an accompanying brief on May 25, 2012. The Court issued a written order granting Respondent's motion and terminating proceedings on June 14, 2012, before DHS had filed a response to Respondent's motion. On June 18, 2012, DHS filed a Motion to Reconsider, citing its lack of an opportunity to respond and asking the Court to reconsider its grant of Respondent's Motion to Terminate.[1]

The Court issued its June 14, 2012 order granting Respondent's Motion to Terminate before DHS's June 25, 2012 deadline had passed and before DHS had filed a response to Respondent's motion. Therefore, the Court's June 14, 2012 order is vacated, and Respondent's Motion to Terminate shall be considered anew.

II. Discussion

After careful consideration, the Court has decided, once again, to grant Respondent's Motion to Terminate, as DHS has failed to prove that Respondent's conviction for Grand Theft in the Third Degree under section 812.014 of the Florida Statutes is a CIMT.

A. Burden of Proof

Respondent is charged under section 212(a)(2)(A)(i)(I) of the Act as an alien seeking admission into the United States. An alien seeking admission has the burden of proving "that [he or she] is clearly and beyond reasonable doubt entitled to be admitted and is not inadmissible under section 212." INA § 240(c)(2)(A). However, Respondent is a returning lawful permanent resident.[2] Before Respondent can be found removable, DHS must prove—by clear and convincing evidence—that Respondent is to be treated as an applicant for admission into the United States in the first place. See Matter of Rivens, 25 I&N Dec. 623, 625-26 (BIA 2011); see also INA § 101(a)(13)(C). DHS may meet its burden of proof by showing, among other things, that Respondent "has committed an offense identified in section 212(a)(2)." INA § 101(a)(13)(C)(v). In this case, therefore, DHS must establish by clear and convincing evidence that Respondent has committed a CIMT. See id. If DHS meets its burden, Respondent will necessarily also be found removable pursuant to section 212(a)(2)(A)(i)(I) of the Act. Conversely, if DHS fails to meet its burden, then Respondent cannot be found removable as an alien seeking admission.

B. Crimes Involving Moral Turpitude

The Board of Immigration Appeals has described a CIMT as a "nebulous concept, which refers generally to conduct that shocks the public conscience as being inherently base, vile, or depraved, contrary to the rules of morality and the duties owed between man and man, either one's fellow man or society in general." Matter of Perez-Contreras, 20 I&N Dec. 615, 617-18 (BIA 1992). A finding that a crime is a CIMT under the Act requires both some form of scienter and reprehensible conduct. Matter of Silva-Trevino,

---

[1] DHS's motion also acts as a response to Respondent's Motion to Terminate. Thus, DHS has now had an opportunity to respond.
[2] DHS does not contest this fact.

24 I&N Dec. 687, 689 n.1, 706 n.5 (BIA 2008), *overruled on other grounds by Fajardo v. U.S. Att'y. Gen.*, 659 F.3d 1303 (11th Cir. 2011).

In order to determine whether a crime involves moral turpitude, the Court must first engage in a "categorical" inquiry in which it looks to "the inherent nature of the offense, as defined in the relevant statute." *Fajardo*, 659 F.3d at 1305 (quoting *Itani v. Ashcroft*, 298 F.3d 1213, 1216 (11th Cir. 2002); *Matter of Velazquez-Herrera*, 24 I&N Dec. 503, 513 (BIA 2008)). "If the statutory definition of a crime encompasses some conduct that categorically would be grounds for removal as well as other conduct that would not, then the record of conviction—i.e., the charging document, plea, verdict, and sentence—may also be considered." *Fajardo*, 659 F.3d at 1305 (quoting *Jaggernauth v. U.S. Att'y Gen.*, 432 F.3d 1346, 1354-55 (11th Cir. 2005)). This second step is referred to as the "modified categorical approach." The Court is limited to the categorical and modified categorical approaches when determining whether a crime is a CIMT and may not look beyond the record of conviction. *Id.* at 1310-11. If the Court fails to reach a conclusion after employing both approaches, then DHS will have failed to meet its burden of proof.

In this case, DHS argues that Respondent's conviction for Grand Theft under section 812.014 of the Florida Statutes is a conviction for a CIMT. "It is well settled that theft or larceny offenses involve moral turpitude." *Matter of Jurado-Delgado*, 24 I&N Dec. 29, 33 (BIA 2006) (citing *Giammario v. Hurney*, 311 F.2d 285, 286 (3d Cir. 1962); *Matter of De La Nues*, 18 I&N Dec. 140, 145 (BIA 1981); *Matter of Westman*, 17 I&N Dec. 50, 51 (BIA 1979)). However, "[o]rdinarily, a conviction for theft is considered to involve moral turpitude only when a permanent taking is intended." *Matter of Grazley*, 14 I&N Dec. 330, 333 (BIA 1973). Section 812.014 of the Florida Statutes holds, in part, that

> (1) A person commits theft if he or she knowingly obtains or uses, or endeavors to obtain or to use, the property of another with intent to, either temporarily or permanently:
>
> (a) Deprive the other person of a right to the property or a benefit from the property.
>
> (b) Appropriate the property to his or her own use or to the use of any person not entitled to the use of the property.

FLA. STAT. § 812.014. Because section 812.014 proscribes both temporary and permanent takings, it "encompasses some conduct that categorically would be grounds for removal as well as other conduct that would not." *Fajardo*, 659 F.3d at 1305. Consequently, the statute is divisible, and the Court will look to Respondent's record of conviction for clarification as to whether Respondent's conviction is for a CIMT. *Id.*

Respondent's charging document states that he

unlawfully and knowingly obtain[ed] or endeavor[ed] to obtain the property of Sears, to-wit: two cameras and a memory card ... with the intent to either temporarily or permanently deprive Sears of the right to the property or a benefit from the property, or to appropriate the property to his own use or the use of any person not entitled to the use of the property.

Exh. 2. Because the charging document also includes both temporary and permanent takings, it provides no clarification. Respondent may have been convicted for a temporary taking, or he may have been convicted for a permanent taking. Respondent's record of conviction sheds no further light on the matter, and *Fajardo* limits the Court to the categorical and modified categorical approaches when determining whether a crime is a CIMT. 659 F.3d at 1310-11.

DHS argues that Respondent's specific conduct—that he attempted to steal two cameras and a memory card from a retail store—establish clearly that he committed Retail Theft, and, therefore, under *Matter of Jurado-Delgado*, 24 I&N Dec. 29 (BIA 2006),[3] a permanent taking on the part of Respondent can be presumed. DHS Motion to Reconsider/Reopen Removal Proceedings for Failure to Allow DHS to Respond (Jun. 18, 2012). However, Respondent was convicted of Grand Theft in the Third Degree, not Retail Theft. Florida has a separate statute prohibiting Retail Theft. *See* FLA. STAT. § 812.015 (explaining that a person commits Retail Theft, in part, by "taking possession of or carrying away of merchandise ... with intent to deprive the merchant of possession, use, benefit, or full retail value."); *see also Rimondi v. State*, 89 So.3d 1059, 1062 (Fla. Dist. Ct. App. 2012) (comparing Felony Retail Theft under section 812.015 with Grand Theft in the Third Degree under section 812.014). Further, Florida's Retail Theft statute, like the Retail Theft statute at issue in *Jurado Delgado*, is narrowly worded to cover only certain conduct.[4] *See* FLA. STAT. § 812.015. Florida's Grand Theft statute, on the other hand, is much more broadly worded.[5] *See* FLA. STAT. § 812.014. Thus, the Court does not consider *Jurado-Delgado* controlling.

Moreover, "the determination that a crime involves moral turpitude is made categorically based on the statutory definition or nature of the crime, *not* the specific conduct predicating a particular conviction." *Fajardo*, 659 F.3d at 1308 (quoting *Vuksanovic v. U.S. Att'y Gen.*, 439 F.3d 1308, 1311 (11th Cir. 2006)) (emphasis added) (internal quotation marks removed); *see also Itani v. Ashcroft*, 298 F.3d 1213, 1215-16 (11th Cir. 2002) ("Whether a crime involves the depravity or fraud necessary to be one of moral turpitude depends upon the inherent nature of the offense, as defined in the relevant statute, rather than the circumstances surrounding a defendant's particular conduct."). That Respondent attempted to steal two cameras and a memory card from a

---

[3] DHS actually cites "*Id.* at 33-34" for this proposition. However, given the parenthetical explanation provided after the citation and the fact that the case previously cited in the brief begins on page 949 of its volume, the Court assumes that DHS meant to cite *Jurado-Delagdo*.
[4] The Retail Theft statute at issue in *Jurado-Delgado* "requires proof that the person took merchandise offered for sale by a store without paying for it and with the intention of depriving the store owner of the goods." 24 I&N Dec. at 33.
[5] For example, Florida's Grand Theft statute includes the "temporarily or permanently" disjunction, *see* FLA. STAT. § 812.014, and Florida's Retail Theft statute does not. *See* FLA. STAT. § 812.015.

retail store makes no difference under section 812.014. He could have attempted to steal a purse from a pedestrian and still been convicted of the same crime. The object Respondent attempted to steal, as well as the victim of his crime, although given in Respondent's record of conviction, are circumstances behind his conviction which the Court may not reference in its determination of whether his crime involves moral turpitude. *Fajardo*, 659 F.3d at 1308. To hold otherwise would produce "the 'manifestly unjust' result of 'exclud[ing] one person and admit[ting] another where both were convicted of [the same crime].'" Id. (quoting *United States v. Uhl*, 210 F. 860, 863 (2d Cir. 1914)) (alterations in original).

Therefore, the Court holds that DHS has not proved by clear and convincing evidence that Respondent's conviction for Grand Theft in the Third Degree under section 812.014 of the Florida Statutes is a conviction for a CIMT under section 212(a)(2)(A)(i)(I) of the Act. Thus, DHS has failed to prove that Respondent is seeking admission into the United States as outlined in section 101(a)(13)(C) of the Act. Consequently, Respondent is not inadmissible as charged under section 212(a)(2)(A)(i)(I).

Therefore, the following orders shall enter:

ORDERS

IT IS HEREBY ORDERED that DHS's Motion to Reopen is **GRANTED**.

IT IS FURTHER ORDERED that the Immigration Court's June 14, 2012 written decision is **VACATED**.

IT IS FURTHER ORDERED that Respondent's Motion to Terminate is **GRANTED**, and current proceedings are **TERMINATED** without prejudice to either party.

IT IS FURTHER ORDERED that Respondent's master calendar hearing scheduled for September 19, 2012, is **CANCELLED**.

DATED this 14th day of August 2012.

Charles J. Sanders
Immigration Judge

cc: Respondent
Counsel for Respondent
Assistant Chief Counsel

Mailed out: 8/14/2012 By: ___

RE:

File:

```
                        CERTIFICATE OF SERVICE
THIS DOCUMENT WAS SERVED BY:  MAIL (M)     PERSONAL SERVICE (P)
TO: [ ] ALIEN  [ ] ALIEN c/o Custodial Officer  [ ] ALIEN's ATT/REP  [ ] DHS
DATE:                   BY:  COURT STAFF
    Attachments:  [ ] EOIR-33  [ ] EOIR-28  [ ] Legal Services List  [ ] Other
```

APPENDIX 5C

UNPUBLISHED IJ DECISION FINDING 18 USC §1860 NOT A CIMT

UNITED STATES DEPARTMENT OF JUSTICE
EXECUTIVE OFFICE FOR IMMIGRATION REVIEW
IMMIGRATION COURT
MIAMI, FLORIDA

In The Matter of)
)
)
) IN REMOVAL PROCEEDINGS
)
)
Respondent)
)

FINDINGS OF THE COURT

Respondent is charged with removability pursuant to Section 237 (a)(2)(A)(ii) of the Immigration and Nationality Act ("ACT") and with removability pursuant to Section 237 (a)(2)(A)(iii) of the Act. One of the grounds of removability is an October 30, 2008 conviction in the United States District Court for an offense relating to the prohibition of unlicensed money transmitting business in violation of 18 USC1960(a) and (b)(1)(A).

The Court has examined the conviction involving the October 30, 2008 conviction. An amended judgment from the United States District Court for the District of New Jersey on October 30, 2008 indicates that Respondent was convicted of operating a money transmitting business without a license under 18 U.S.C. § 1960 (a) and (b)(1)(A) and (2). The provisions under which Respondent was convicted are as follows:

Section 1960(a) states that "whoever knowingly conducts, controls, manages, supervises, directs, or owns all or part of an unlicensed money transmitting business shall be fined in accordance with this title or imprisoned not more than 5 years, or both."

Section 1960(b)(1)(A) defines the term "unlicensed money transmitting business" as "a money transmitting business which affects interstate or foreign commerce in any manner or degree and is operated without an appropriate money transmitting license in a state where such operation is punishable as a misdemeanor or a felony under state law, whether or not the defendant knew that the operation was required to be licensed or that the operation was so punishable."

Section 1960 (b)(2) states that "'money transmitting' includes transferring funds on behalf of the public by any and all means including but not limited to transfers within this country or to locations abroad by wire, check, draft, facsimile, or courier."

Analysis

In determining whether Respondent's crime is a crime involving moral turpitude ("CIMT,") the Department of Homeland Security ("DHS") argues that the modified categorical approach should be used so that the Court can consider the record of conviction. The plea agreement reveals that Respondent "believed the funds were proceeds of unlawful activity," which supports the DHS argument that Respondent committed a CIMT.

However, the Court cannot consider the plea agreement or any other information in the record of conviction because the Court cannot employ the modified categorical approach. The categorical approach must be used in this case because the elements of the sections of 18 U.S.C. § 1960 under which Respondent was convicted describe a categorically non-morally turpitudinous offense. See Matter of Silva-Trevino, 24 I&N Dec. 687 (A.G. 2008).

Under Silva-Trevino, the categorical approach still applies. The elements of the statute control the outcome if the offense under which Respondent was convicted is categorically non-morally turpitudinous. As stated in Silva-Trevino, the only reason to look beyond the statute of conviction "is to discern the nature of the underlying conviction where a mere examination of the statute itself does not yield the necessary information." See id. at 690. In this case, an examination of the relevant sections of 18 U.S.C. § 1960 is all that is necessary. While 18 U.S.C. § 1960 encompasses behavior that involves moral turpitude, the amended judgment delineated the specific sections of the statute that Respondent was convicted under, and these sections only include behavior that does not involve moral turpitude.

Respondent was convicted of a licensing offense for failing to license his money transmitting business. The BIA has consistently held that "violation[s] of statutes which merely license or regulate and impose criminal liability, without regard to evil intent, do not involve moral turpitude." Matter of G, 7 I&N Dec. 114, 118 (BIA 1956); See Matter of B, 6 I&N Dec.

98, 107 (BIA 1954) (holding that a respondent's failure to obtain a license to conduct a money lending business did not involve moral turpitude); *See also Matter of Serna*, 20 I&N Dec. 579, 583 (BIA 1992). The DHS has also conceded that "simply managing a business that transfers funds without the appropriate license is not turpitudinous." (DHS brief page 4).

Therefore, the Court can only look to the statute of conviction under the categorical inquiry. Under this approach, respondent's conviction of October 30, 2008 is not a crime involving moral turpitude.

Accordingly, the Court finds that respondent's conviction in the United States District Court for the District of New Jersey on October 30, 2008 for operating a money transmitting business without a license under 18 U.S.C. § 1960 (a) and (b)(1)(A) and (2) is not a conviction for a crime involving moral turpitude.

Dated: November 23, 2010

_____
Teofilo Chapa, Immigration Judge

CERTIFICATE OF SERVICE

Copies HAND DELIVERED on the 23 day of November, 2010 to:

___ Respondent; ___ Respondent's counsel; ___ Assistant Chief Counsel, Miami, Florida

_____
Teofilo Chapa, Immigration Judge

APPENDIX 5D

IMMIGRATION ATTORNEY/CLIENT CHECKLIST FOR ANALYZING A CASE WITH A CRIME

Name: Nationality:

   Age:

1. Is client in proceedings? Yes/No

   If not, what is purpose of visit?

   If yes, date of service of NTA:
   Date of next hearing:

2. Current immigration status in USA:

   LPR/nonimmigrant/other

3. Date of last admission into USA:

   Date of initial admission:

4. Criminal offense(s):

5. Date of commission of criminal offense(s):
       (Note: could be date of arrest, but not necessarily)

6. Date of conviction for crime(s) and sentence(s):

7. Immediate family members in USA and their immigration status:

SUMMARY CONCLUSIONS:

1. Is client deportable? Yes/No

   If yes, for what classification of crime?
   (*i.e.*, moral turpitude, aggravated felony, controlled substance, etc.)

2. Is client subject to mandatory detention? (mandatory detention applies to release from penal custody after October 8, 1998)   Yes/No

3. Is client eligible for relief? (*e.g.*, cancellation of removal; INA §212(h); adjustment of status, etc.)   Yes/No

SAMPLE COMPLETED CHECKLIST

Date: January 1, 2008

Name: Joseph Smith   **Nationality**: Liberian   **Age**:   32

1. Is client in proceedings?

   No. Client would like to apply for naturalization; also, resident card expires in one month.

2. Current status: LPR

3. Date of last admission: adjusted status on January 1, 2000

   Date of initial admission: B-2 tourist on January 1, 1998

4. Criminal offense?
   Simple battery
   Simple possession of cocaine
   Carrying a concealed firearm

5. Date of commission:

1- simple battery involving ex-wife on January 1, 2002

2- simple possession of cocaine on January 1, 2006

3- CCF on January 1, 2007

6. Date of conviction:

1- simple battery on January 15, 2002 (credit time served 2 days)

2- cocaine on January 15, 2006 (probation 3 years)

3- CCF on January 15, 2007 (credit time served 2 days and forfeiture of firearm)

7. Immediate family members in USA:

Client is divorced, but has U.S. citizen mother and two USC teenage children of whom he has custody because mother abandoned them.

Conclusions:

Client is deportable for possession of cocaine and CCF, but not simple battery.

Client is subject to mandatory detention based on the CCF; ICE will also take position that client is m.d. based on cocaine possession.

Client is eligible for cancellation of removal because, although he became an LPR on January 1, 2000, and cocaine offense occurred on January 1, 2006, his continuous lawful residence begins to accumulate in 1998 with the NIV admission. Thus he has eight years of lawful residence.

If client applies for a new resident card, there is a strong possibility he will be taken into custody on account of the biometrics procedure. However he would be eligible for relief and there is a good chance, based on the teenage daughters, he will prevail.

If client applies for naturalization, he will be placed in proceedings and may be detained either at the naturalization office or at the immigration courthouse.

However, if client receives a grant of cancellation, he will become eligible for naturalization on January 1, 2011 (five years from date of commission of possession of cocaine).

Advice: explain situation fully to client and let him decide whether he is ready for several weeks to months of detention, and possible deportation. Note that he should not travel outside USA, and may one day not be eligible for a driver's license or other government benefits because the card will have expired.

Other facts to cover in balancing the risks and benefits of applying for a new resident card:

Tax filing history
Medical issues in family
Employment history
Success of children in school, or special needs

CHAPTER SIX

CRIMES INVOLVING MORAL TURPITUDE

The Concept of Crimes Involving Moral Turpitude 239
Specific Offenses and Whether They Involve Moral Turpitude 245
Crimes of Violence 253

The Concept of Crimes Involving Moral Turpitude

There are references throughout the Immigration and Nationality Act (INA) to "crimes involving moral turpitude." Crimes involving moral turpitude may cause deportability, inadmissibility, and may potentially bar relief from removal and affirmative benefits such as residency; they also implicate "good moral character" for purposes of naturalization. The potential ramifications of committing, or being convicted of, a crime involving moral turpitude are discussed in chapter three, "Consequences." This chapter is all about defining the term.

In spite of its frequent usage throughout the INA, the term "moral turpitude" is not defined by statute; instead, the term is governed by case law. The moral turpitude analysis takes a categorical approach, as discussed in chapter two. (If the reader has not read chapter two, now is a good time to do so.)[1] Also, moral turpitude looks to the generic classification of the crime, which is determined based on a combination of the Model Penal Code, a survey of state statutes, and the federal code.

The phrase "moral turpitude" refers generally to acts that are inherently evil or wrong by any society's standards (*malum in se*), rather than acts that are regulated by society (*malum prohibitum*).[2] The Board of Immigration Appeals (BIA or Board) has held that moral turpitude refers generally to conduct that is inherently base, vile, or depraved, and contrary to the accepted rules of morality and the duties owed between persons, or to society in general.[3] For example, in a 2013 opinion decided just before *Descamps v. U.S.*,[4] the BIA ruled that sponsoring or exhibiting an animal in an

---

[1] A categorical approach means that it is the statute-of-conviction that controls the analysis, not the facts or circumstances of the client's offense conduct.

[2] Except in those situations where there is clear precedent on the exact same state or federal statute, determinations of whether a crime involves moral turpitude are made on a case-by-case basis; this means an attorney may make a good faith argument in any particular case that the statute-of-conviction is not a moral turpitude offense. Indeed, even where there is precedential case law on point, defense counsel should not hesitate to present a meritorious challenge to the precedent, if appropriate. This is particularly true in light of *Descamps v. U.S.*, 133 S. Ct. 2276 (2013), discussed in chapter five.

[3] *Matter of L–V–C–*, 22 I&N Dec. 594 (BIA 1999); *Matter of Tran*, 21 I&N Dec. 291 (BIA 1996); *Matter of Danesh*, 19 I&N Dec. 669 (BIA 1988).

[4] *Descamps v. U.S.*, 133 S. Ct. 2276 (2013).

animal fighting venture [5] is a crime involving moral turpitude. [6] Acts of moral turpitude are essentially those that are offensive to American ethics and accepted moral standards. [7] Crimes involving permanent deprivations, fraud or material misrepresentations, and serious acts of intentional violence are normally viewed as acts involving moral turpitude. Licensing and regulatory violations (*i.e.*, driving under the influence, simple possession, and firearms) are generally found not to involve moral turpitude.[8]

In light of the 2015 vacatur of *Matter of Silva-Trevino*, [9] practitioners will want to double-check the validity of any cases cited that rely on *Silva-Trevino*'s expanded evidentiary analysis (going to a modified categorical approach even though the statute is not divisible, or considering evidence outside the record of conviction). Of note, the attorney general's (AG) vacatur specifically upholds that part of *Silva-Trevino*'s analysis that finds that a crime involving reprehensible conduct combined with scienter is a moral turpitude offense. The AG also does not vacate or modify any other decision, but rather leaves reconsideration of moral turpitude decisions premised on *Silva-Trevino* to be handled on a case-by-case basis.[10]

Felonies and Misdemeanors

In determining whether an offense involves moral turpitude, it is a common mistake to consider the degree of punishment (*i.e.*, whether the crime is punished as a misdemeanor or felony). Attorneys frequently meet with clients who minimize or dismiss a criminal conviction's significance because it was "not a felony." However, neither the seriousness of a criminal offense nor the severity of the sentence imposed determines whether a crime involves moral turpitude.[11] Intentional theft of a 10-cent item is nonetheless theft and thus involves moral turpitude, notwithstanding the cost of the item or the minimal punishment imposed. Whether the offense can be excepted or waived under the immigration statute based on its minor nature is distinct from whether the act involves moral turpitude. Exceptions and waivers are discussed in subsequent chapters.

---

[5] 7 USC §2156(a)(1). Of interest, this is a federal offense. It is punishable as a misdemeanor, and the non–U.S. citizen in the *Ortega-Lopez* case received one year's probation.

[6] *Matter of Ortega-Lopez,* 26 I&N Dec. 99 (BIA 2013).

[7] *Castle v. INS*, 541 F.2d 1064, 1066 (4th Cir. 1976).

[8] *Matter of Tiwari,* 19 I&N Dec. 875 (BIA 1989). *But see Matter of Tobar-Lobo,* 24 I&N Dec. 143 (BIA 2007), in which the Board of Immigration Appeals (BIA or Board) found that the regulatory violation of failure to register as a sex offender under California law was a crime involving moral turpitude. As discussed in the dissent by Board Member Filppu, this decision represents a departure from longstanding BIA precedent regarding the nature of regulatory violations.

[9] *Matter of Silva-Trevino,* 24 I&N Dec. 687 (AG 2008), *vacated at* 26 I&N Dec. 550 (AG 2015).

[10] *Matter of Silva-Trevino,* 26 I&N Dec. 550, at 553, n. 3.

[11] *Matter of Serna*, 20 I&N Dec. 579, 581 (BIA 1992).

The elements of the criminal statute control

It is worthwhile in every new client's case to review the actual criminal statute involved, even if counsel feels a familiarity with the offense, perhaps from handling similar cases in the past. As discussed in the section on practice tools,[12] immigration practitioners should have on hand their state's criminal code and the U.S. Code volumes enumerating federal crimes. Ideally, the client will bring to the consultation arrest reports, charging documents, and final dispositions to assist the attorney in ascertaining the criminal code section under which the client was convicted. It is important to engage in an objective analysis of whether the elements necessary to obtain a conviction under the particular criminal statute render the offense a crime involving moral turpitude.[13]

Practitioners are cautioned to avoid hasty determinations and always to scrutinize the elements of the criminal law provision. It is decidedly incorrect to assess based on the title of the offense (the penal provision's caption) whether moral turpitude adheres, or by what the offense "sounds like."

The question of intent

In addition to the actual proscribed conduct, an offense involving moral turpitude will generally (although not always) include specific intent to do harm, or knowledge of the act's illegality. Evil intent is usually required for a crime to be classified as one involving moral turpitude.[14] Thus, the elements of *knowledge* or *specific intent* should be identified in determining whether an offense involves moral turpitude.[15] A long-standing test employed by the BIA is whether the act is accompanied by a vicious motive or a corrupt mind.[16] Still, an evil or specific intent alone does not transform an otherwise non-base, vile, or fraudulent offense into one involving moral turpitude; rather, it is the combination of a morally wrong act with the element of willfulness or specific intent that represents a crime involving moral turpitude.[17]

Where the criminal statute sets a mental state of recklessness, the analysis becomes more difficult. Statutes involving a standard of recklessness represent the quintessential "grey area." The BIA has held that moral turpitude can lie in criminally reckless conduct when there is a conscious disregard of a substantial and unjustifiable risk. Although there may not be a specific intent to cause a particular harm, the violator must show a willingness to commit the act in disregard of the perceived risk.[18]

---

[12] See chapter one's section, "Tips and Tools of the Trade."

[13] *Matter of Short*, 20 I&N Dec. 136 (BIA 1989).

[14] *Matter of Khourn*, 21 I&N Dec. 1041, 1046 (BIA 1997).

[15] *Matter of Silva-Trevino*, 24 I&N Dec. 687 (AG 2008)..

[16] *Matter of Franklin*, 20 I&N Dec. 867 (BIA 1994).

[17] *See, e.g., Nicanor-Romero v. Mukasey*, 523 F.3d 992, 999–1000 (9th Cir. 2008), citing *Grageda v. INS*, 12 F.3d 919, 922 (9th Cir. 1993).

[18] *Matter of Medina*, 15 I&N Dec. 611, 614 (BIA 1976). In *Medina*, the individual had been convicted of aggravated assault with a firearm under the Illinois Code.

> **Example**: Driving one's vehicle in a manner indicating a wanton or willful disregard for the lives or property of others while attempting to elude a pursuing police vehicle with lights on[19] has been found to be a crime involving moral turpitude based on the combination of elements. Although the state of mind is only "wanton and willful disregard," rather than a specific intent to do harm (or the causation of harm), the level of recklessness combined with knowledge that a police car with lights on is in pursuit elevates this offense to a moral turpitude crime.[20]

The Second Circuit U.S. Court of Appeals has stated that in the assault context, reckless conduct represents a moral turpitude crime only where there is the presence of aggravating facts, such as use of a dangerous weapon, combined with the actual causation of bodily injury.[21]

In *Idy v. Holder,* however, the First Circuit U.S. Court of Appeals upheld a BIA determination that New Hampshire's general reckless conduct statute involves moral turpitude.[22] Under this provision, a person is guilty of reckless conduct if he or she recklessly engages in conduct that places or may place another in danger of serious bodily injury. In turn, a person acts "recklessly" under New Hampshire law when he or she is aware of and consciously disregards a substantial and unjustifiable risk that harm will result from the conduct.

The First Circuit agreed with the BIA that the aggravating factor of serious bodily injury potentially resulting from the reckless conduct equals a moral turpitude crime. Although the First Circuit's ultimate conclusion—that an awareness that reckless conduct may result in bodily injury is an aggravating factor—may be sound, the analysis is seriously flawed. The First Circuit "defers" to the BIA's analysis of the state statute where no such deference is owed. The First Circuit also engages in a dramatic recitation of the underlying facts and circumstances of the offense, something that has no relevance to a categorical or even modified categorical approach. In doing so, the court did not refer to *Matter of Silva-Trevino,*[23] but does appear to adhere to the pre-vacatur *Silva-Trevino* approach to moral turpitude analysis.[24] Because consideration of evidence outside the record of conviction is no longer permissible, this precedent is subject to challenge.

---

[19] Wash. Rev. Code § 46.61.

[20] *Matter of Ruiz-Lopez,* 25 I&N Dec. 551, 556 (BIA 2011).

[21] *Gill v. INS,* 420 F.3d 82, 89 (2d Cir. 2005).

[22] *But see Idy v. Holder,* 674 F.3d 111 (1st Cir. 2012), discussing N.H. Rev. Stat. Ann. §631:3 (2011).

[23] *Matter of Silva-Trevino,* 24 I&N Dec. 687 (AG 2008). This case is discussed in detail in chapter five.

[24] There has been a seven-year caveat to the tenet that the moral turpitude analysis follows a categorical approach. In the U.S. Courts of Appeals for the Eighth and the Seventh Circuits, the two circuits that deferred to *Silva-Trevino,* the U.S. Department of Homeland Security (DHS) has enjoyed wide latitude in presenting all manner of evidence to establish a moral turpitude crime, and may succeed in arguing that a particular offense involves moral turpitude. Defense counsel practicing in these circuits will want to give fresh consideration to precedent case law that relied on *Silva-Trevino.*

Attempted reckless behavior, however, does not involve moral turpitude because it is legally incoherent (*i.e.*, impossible) that a person will attempt to act recklessly.[25] Attempted reckless endangerment is not a crime involving moral turpitude because this concept is "nonsensical."[26] In *Silva-Trevino,* the attorney general (AG) did not spend a lot of time on the concept of mental state, or *scienter*, but did state in dicta that recklessness was enough to qualify a crime as one involving moral turpitude.[27] The focus of the AG's decision was not, of course, the issue of recklessness; thus a criminal statute that references reckless behavior is subject to argument on the issue of moral turpitude.

CASE STUDY: MATTER OF MEDINA

Negligence vs. recklessness

In *Matter of Medina*,[28] the BIA defined "recklessness" as an actual awareness of the risk created by the criminal violator's action. *Medina* involved a violation of an Illinois assault statute that required a *mens rea* of recklessness; the BIA found that moral turpitude attached to this offense. The BIA adhered to this approach in cases decided in 2001 and 2012, finding that criminally reckless conduct is a crime involving moral turpitude if the offense involves a conscious disregard of a substantial and unjustifiable risk.[29] Federal circuit courts have approved this approach.[30]

In comparison, criminal negligence lacks this essential culpability requirement. For example, a negligent assault is unintentional, unwitting, and committed *without* contemplation of the risk of injury involved.[31] Thus, while the element of recklessness can connote moral turpitude (because, although the person acts without specific

---

[25] *Gill v. INS*, 420 F.3d 82 (2d Cir. 2005).

[26] *Knapik v. Ashcroft*, 384 F.3d 84 (3d Cir. 2004).

[27] *Matter of Silva-Trevino*, 24 I&N Dec. 687, n.4 (AG 2008).

[28] *Matter of Medina*, 15 I&N Dec. at 614.

[29] *Matter of Ruiz-Lopez*, 25 I&N Dec. 551, 553–54 (BIA 2011), *aff'd*, 682 F.3d 513 (6th Cir. 2012); *Matter of Leal*, 26 I&N. Dec. 20, 23 (BIA 2012), *aff'd*, 771 F.3d 1140 (9th Cir. 2014). Before relying on pre–June 2013 case law, consider whether *Descamps v. U.S.* changes the analysis and the existing precedent should be challenged. The same philosophy applies to the cases discussed in this very book: if a case cited was decided prior to June 2013, the reader should research any case history and give the issue fresh consideration under a strict categorical approach.

[30] *Partyka v. Att'y Gen.*, 417 F.3d 408, 416 (3d Cir. 2005); *Knapik v. Ashcroft*, 384 F.3d 84, 89 (3d Cir. 2004). *Partyka* involved aggravated assault on a police officer, a felony of the third degree in violation of N.J. Stat. Ann. §C:12-1b(5)(a); the court found that this offense was not a crime involving moral turpitude because the statute was divisible, the record of conviction did not specify which subsection the individual was charged under or convicted of, and the least culpable conduct described in the statute was negligence.

[31] *Partyka v. Att'y Gen.*, 417 F.3d 408, 414 (3d Cir. 2005).

intent to carry out a certain crime, the statute might include as an element a conscious disregard of a specific, reasonably foreseeable risk), the element of negligence does not imply moral turpitude, because it is committed without contemplation of the risk of injury involved.[32]

Certainly, the line between recklessness and negligence is a fine line; it is for this reason that careful review and consideration of the specific elements of the statutory offense is essential. The mental state of recklessness is discussed in greater detail, below, in the section covering crimes of violence.

Divisible statutes and the record of conviction

As stated in the previous chapter, a divisible statute contains discrete elements that are stated in the alternative: one or more of which describe acts of moral turpitude and others that do not. When the criminal statute involved is a "divisible" statute, reference is made to the individual's record of conviction to determine whether the activity of which he or she was convicted involves moral turpitude.[33] The documents that constitute the record of conviction are the indictment, plea, verdict, and sentence.[34] In some circumstances, the record of conviction may include the jury instructions (in cases where there is a plea). The record of conviction does not include the arrest report.[35] The U.S. Supreme Court has held that when the case involves a guilty plea, the record of conviction may include consideration of the "charging document, written plea agreement, transcript of plea colloquy, and any explicit factual finding by the trial judge to which the defendant assented."[36]

Aiding and abetting; accessories and conspiracy

Where the underlying or substantive crime involves moral turpitude, then a conviction for aiding in the commission of the crime or for otherwise acting as an accessory before the fact is also a conviction for a crime involving moral turpitude.[37] Conversely, the federal offense of accessory after the fact under 18 USC §3 where the underlying crime does not involve moral turpitude will not qualify as a moral

---

[32] *See Perez-Contreras*, 20 I&N Dec. 615, 618–19 (BIA 1992) (mere negligence cannot support a finding of moral turpitude; underlying offense was assault against a police officer).

[33] *Matter of V–Z–S–*, 22 I&N Dec. 1338 (BIA 2000).

[34] *Matter of Mena*, 17 I&N Dec. 38 (BIA 1979). For a list of acceptable documents to establish a conviction, see chapter 2.

[35] *See Matter of Teixeira*, 21 I&N Dec. 316, 319–20 (BIA 1996).

[36] *Shepard v. U.S.*, 544 U.S. 13, 26 (2005).

[37] *Matter of Short*, 20 I&N Dec. 136 (citing *Matter of F–*, 6 I&N Dec. 783 (BIA 1955)). Further, note that in the context of the aggravated felony definition at INA §101(a)(43)(G), the Supreme Court found that aiding and abetting a theft constitutes a theft offense. *Gonzales v. Duenas-Alvarez*, 549 U.S. 183 (2007).

turpitude offense.[38] A conspiracy offense is a crime involving moral turpitude if it contains the element of fraud, or the underlying substantive offense involves fraud.[39] Note that 18 USC §371, the federal conspiracy statute, is a divisible statute: the first phrase refers to a conspiracy to commit "any offense against the United States," and the second phrase refers to the intent to defraud. The initial phrase: "committing an offense against the United States," involves moral turpitude only if the underlying substantive offense is a crime involving moral turpitude.[40]

Specific Offenses and Whether They Involve Moral Turpitude

The vacatur of *Silva-Trevino*, combined with U.S. Supreme Court decisions in *Descamps*[41] and *Moncrieffe*,[42] mean that some precedent may no longer be good law. Attorneys should not hesitate to challenge precedent if the underlying legal analysis that led to a conclusion of moral turpitude is no longer sound or valid.

Theft and Larceny

Larceny crimes involve moral turpitude.[43] Theft offenses will involve moral turpitude only if the criminal statute describes a permanent taking or intent to permanently deprive.[44] The circuit courts of appeals and the BIA have held that crimes of theft involve moral turpitude only where a permanent taking is intended.[45] The difference between theft and larceny is that the latter involves a permanent taking. Under the common law, larceny is distinguishable from theft because the former includes "all takings with a criminal intent to deprive the owner of the rights and benefits of ownership."[46]

---

[38] *Matter of Rivens*, 25 I&N Dec. 623 (BIA 2011).

[39] *Matter of Flores*, 17 I&N Dec. 225 (BIA 1980), citing *Matter of McNaughton*, 16 I&N Dec. 569 (BIA 1978), *Matter of G–*, 7 I&N Dec. 114 (BIA 1956).

[40] *Id. See also Notash v. Gonzales*, 427 F.3d 693, 699 (9th Cir. 2005) (discussing *Matter of Flores*, 17 I&N Dec. 225 (BIA 1980), for the proposition that the first clause of 18 USC §371 does not involve moral turpitude).

[41] *Descamps v. U.S.*, 133 S. Ct. 2276 (2013).

[42] *Moncrieffe v. Holder*, 133 S.Ct. 1678 (2013).

[43] *Matter of Scarpulla*, 15 I&N Dec. 139 (BIA 1974) (involving a conviction in Italy for theft of 30 kilograms of olives).

[44] *Matter of De La Nues*, 18 I&N Dec. 140, 145 (BIA 1981); *Matter of Westman*, 17 I&N Dec. 50, 51 (BIA 1979).

[45] *See Alvarez-Reynaga v. Holder*, 596 F.3d 534, 537 (9th Cir. 2010); *Castillo-Cruz v. Holder*, 581 F.3d 1154, 1161 (9th Cir. 2009). *Matter of V–Z–S–*, 22 I&N Dec. 1338 n.12 (BIA 2000) (citing *Matter of Grazley*, 14 I&N Dec. 330 (BIA 1973)).

[46] *Matter of V–Z–S–*, 22 I&N Dec. 1338 (BIA 2000) (citing *U.S. v. Pittman*, 441 F.2d 1098, 1099 (9th Cir. 1971)).

In comparison, theft statutes may encompass both temporary and permanent takings, and situations that involve something less than a specific intent to deprive an owner of property.

> **Example**: Joyriding, failure to return a rental car, and similar situations that do not involve stealing with an intent to permanently deprive an owner of a property right, may not—depending on the statute at hand—involve moral turpitude.[47] Unauthorized use of a motor vehicle has been found not to be a crime involving moral turpitude.[48]

Again, reference to the statute, the record of conviction, and if appropriate other additional evidence is required to establish whether the offense involved a permanent taking, or something less than a "theft." The reader will note that some larceny and theft statutes encompass fraud; a taking through fraud will qualify as a crime involving moral turpitude.[49]

CASE STUDY: ALMANZA-ARENAS v. HOLDER

Almanza-Arenas v. Holder[50] is highlighted here because the case's development illustrates application of *Descamps*'[51] categorical approach. In a 2009 published decision, the BIA did not disturb an IJ's ruling that vehicle theft under California law[52] is a divisible statute, because it could include the act of joyriding, defined as a crime of general intent to temporarily use a vehicle without authorization.[53] Ultimately, the respondent was denied relief because, based on the analysis of *Silva-Trevino*,[54] the immigration judge (IJ) placed the burden on respondent to establish—in the context of relief from removal—that his particular offense did not involve the non–moral

---

[47] *Almanza-Arenas v. Holder*, 771 F.3d 1184 (9th Cir. 2014).

[48] *Ramirez v. Ashcroft*, 361 F. Supp. 2d 650 (S.D. Tex. 2005).

[49] *Mendez v. Mukasey*, 547 F.3d 345 (2d Cir. 2008) (defrauding public community under Connecticut's larceny statute is a crime involving moral turpitude because a permanent taking is involved).

[50] 771 F.3d 1184 (9th Cir. 2014).

[51] *Descamps v. U.S.*, 133 S. Ct. 2276 (2013).

[52] Cal. Veh. Code §10851.

[53] *Matter of Almanza*, 24 I&N Dec. 771, 772 and n.3 (BIA 2009). The reader will note this is the same statute that was the subject of the Supreme Court's decision regarding the aggravated felony definition of theft at INA §101(a)(43)(G). *Gonzales v. Duenas-Alvarez*, 549 U.S. 183 (2007). The Supreme Court found that aiding and abetting under the California statute qualified categorically as a generic theft offense for aggravated felony purposes. The Court specifically did not reach the issues of whether accessory after the fact or joyriding fall outside the generic theft definition. This was also the statute analyzed by the BIA in *Matter of V–Z–S–*, 22 I&N Dec. 1338 (BIA 2000), wherein the Board found that a conviction under §10851 of the California Vehicle Code qualified as a crime involving moral turpitude.

[54] *Matter of Silva-Trevino*, 24 I&N Dec. 687 (AG 2008).

turpitude portion of the statute.[55] Specifically, the IJ required respondent to submit the transcripts of his plea colloquy in criminal court; the respondent declined to do so, resulting in the denial of relief in the form of cancellation of removal.[56] In 2014, in light of *Descamps*, the Ninth Circuit U.S. Court of Appeals reversed the BIA's decision, finding that the criminal statute was not divisible, but was overbroad, and a modified categorical approach did not apply. The Ninth Circuit looked to state case law as well as California's jury instructions to ascertain that a jury need not decide whether the intent to take the vehicle was something temporary or permanent: the duration of deprivation was not an issue for the jury.[57]

Assuming a strict categorical approach, the minimum conduct described by §10851 of the California Vehicle Code was a temporary deprivation—hence, it is not a moral turpitude statute. *Almanza-Arenas* makes several good, discrete points: the case reaffirms that a temporary taking does not involve moral turpitude; it illustrates how to ascertain divisibility and emphasizes that without divisibility, a modified categorical approach does not apply; and the court advises that the categorical approach applies in the relief context also—notwithstanding the burden of proof.

Where cash is the object of the theft, it is a crime involving moral turpitude.[58] Robbery and conscious receipt of stolen property are crimes involving moral turpitude.[59] Possession of stolen property when one believes it probably was stolen involves moral turpitude.[60] Additionally, theft by deception is a crime involving moral turpitude.[61]

In a 2006 decision, *Matter of Jurado*,[62] the BIA held that retail theft involves moral turpitude. The respondent in *Jurado* had been convicted under 18 Pa. Const. Stat. §3929(a)(1). This statute provides that a person is guilty of retail theft if he or she "takes possession" of merchandise without paying the value thereof. The respondent argued that, because the conviction did not specify either permanent or temporary taking (in other words, because the statute was *not* divisible), it could not be inferred that the taking was intended to be permanent. The BIA rejected this argument and found that the "nature" of the offense is such that it is "reasonable to

---

[55] *Matter of Almanza*, 24 I&N Dec. 771, at 773.
[56] Cancellation of removal as a form of relief is discussed in chapter ten.
[57] *Almanza-Arenas v. Holder*, 771 F.3d 1184, at 1191–92 (9th Cir. 2014).
[58] *Matter of Grazley*, 14 I&N Dec. 330 (BIA 1973).
[59] *Matter of Gordon*, 20 I&N Dec. 52 (BIA 1989).
[60] *De Leon-Reynoso v. Ashcroft*, 293 F.3d 633 (3d Cir. 2002).
[61] *Nugent v. Ashcroft*, 367 F.3d 162 (3d Cir. 2004).
[62] *Matter of Jurado*, 24 I&N Dec. 29 (BIA 2006).

assume" that the intention was to permanently deprive the merchant of goods.[63] In light of *Descamps*, *Jurado* should be challenged and (in this author's opinion) is not good law.

A crime may qualify as an aggravated felony theft offense[64] yet not be a crime involving moral turpitude. This is because a non-permanent taking may qualify as an aggravated felony theft offense, but not a crime involving moral turpitude.[65] In the simplest of terms, in the context of a theft conviction, the aggravated felony classification is broader than the moral turpitude ground.

> **Scenario:** Andres is not a permanent resident,[66] but is applying for adjustment of status in front of the immigration judge. He has a conviction for vehicle theft and the charging document indicates joyriding, a temporary deprivation. His sentence was one year in jail, which was suspended for one year's probation. DHS charges removability for an aggravated felony and crime involving moral turpitude. Andres will argue: (1) he is not inadmissible for a crime involving moral turpitude because the statute of conviction envisions a temporary taking, and his conviction record establishes joyriding only; (2) although his conviction may be an aggravated felony theft offense, the aggravated felony charge is waived *vis à vis* the adjustment application and no independent waiver (*i.e.*, 212(h)) is required, hence no showing of extreme hardship to a qualifying family member is required.

Commercial burglary with an underlying intent to commit theft under Cal. Penal Code §459 was held not to be a crime involving moral turpitude where the statute did not contain the taking of property as an element.[67]

---

[63] *Matter of Jurado*, 24 I&N Dec. 29, at 32 (BIA 2006).

[64] INA §101(a)(43)(G).

[65] *Castillo-Cruz v. Holder*, 581 F.3d 1154, n. 8 (9th Cir. 2009) (conviction for receipt of stolen property only a moral turpitude crime if statute envisions an intention to permanently deprive owner of property); *Mendez v. Mukasey*, 547 F.3d 345, n. 6 (2d Cir. 2008), *citing Wala v. Mukasey*, 511 F.3d 102, 107 (2d Cir. 2007), and *Matter of V–Z–S–*, 22 I&N Dec. 1338, n. 12 (BIA 2000).

[66] The reader will note that under this scenario, the analysis would be the same if Andres is already a lawful permanent resident: adjustment of status, if available to him, cures the aggravated felony charge. *Matter of Kanga*, 22 I&N Dec. 1206 (BIA 2000); *Matter of Rainford*, 20 I&N Dec. 598 (BIA 1992). The key is that no independent extreme hardship waiver is necessary. Adjustment as a waiver available to an LPR is also significant because an aggravated felony conviction precludes eligibility for cancellation of removal. These waivers and forms of relief are discussed in chapter ten.

[67] *Hernandez Cruz v. Holder*, 651 F.3d 1094 (9th Cir. 2011).

Burglary

In the first decision to be decided after the AG's decision in *Silva-Trevino*,[68] the BIA found that burglary of an unoccupied dwelling is categorically a crime involving moral turpitude.[69] The decision in *Matter of Louissaint* reviewed Florida's burglary statute at Fla. Stat. §810.02(3)(a), which contains three elements: (1) knowing entry into a dwelling; (2) knowledge that such entry is without permission; and (3) criminal intent to commit an offense within the dwelling. The Board's decision found that the conscious and overt act of unlawfully entering or remaining in an occupied dwelling with the intent to commit a crime is inherently reprehensible conduct accompanied by some form of *scienter*, therefore, it is categorically a crime involving moral turpitude.[70]

The *Louissaint* decision is at odds with other decisions regarding burglary. Burglary statutes vastly differ from state to state. Depending on which state you are in, burglary is generally a breaking and entering, and may involve a vehicle or conveyance, a building, or a dwelling. Most courts (and the BIA) have found burglary to be a crime involving moral turpitude only if the underlying offense (*i.e.*, breaking and entering with the intention to commit a crime therein) is a moral turpitude offense.[71] In *Wala v. Mukasey*,[72] the Second Circuit determined that burglary with intent to commit larceny under Connecticut law[73] was not a crime involving moral turpitude where it was not clear from the record whether the underlying larceny offense involved a permanent or temporary taking, and the larceny statute was divisible.

Burglary is the type of offense that definitely invites nuanced research and innovative argument with every new client case, notwithstanding the BIA's decision in *Louissaint*. The premise that burglary can categorically be a crime involving moral turpitude, irrespective of the underlying offense, is weak and (especially in light of past case law) this decision deserves to be challenged. The first issue is whether Florida's burglary statute is divisible into conveyance, structure, and dwelling, or whether these are means of committing the crime. The second issue is whether even burglary of a dwelling requires an underlying intent to commit a crime that involves moral turpitude.[74]

---

[68] *Matter of Silva-Trevino*, 24 I&N Dec. 687 (AG 2008). *Silva-Trevino* is discussed at length in chapter five, "Methodology."

[69] *Matter of Louissaint*, 24 I&N Dec. 754 (BIA 2009).

[70] *Matter of Louissaint*, 24 I&N Dec. at 758.

[71] Compare *Matter of M–*, 2 I&N Dec. 721 (BIA, AG 1946), *distinguished by Matter of Louissaint*, 24 I&N Dec. 754 (BIA 2009).

[72] *Wala v. Mukasey*, 511 F.3d 102, 107 (2d Cir. 2007).

[73] Conn. Gen. Stat. §53a-103.

[74] Of note, *Louissaint* was decided prior to *Descamps*, and relied on *Silva-Trevino*—a case that was subsequently rejected in the Eleventh Circuit U.S. Court of Appeals. Post-*Descamps*, it will be interesting to see how the circuits view the myriad state burglary provisions.

Fraud

Fraud, as a general rule, involves moral turpitude.[75] For example, in *Matter of Bart*,[76] the BIA held that issuance of a bad check *where guilty knowledge was an element of the offense* constituted a crime involving moral turpitude. In its very next decision, *Matter of Balao*,[77] the BIA found no moral turpitude where the Pennsylvania crime of passing bad checks[78] did not include intent to defraud as an essential element of the crime. These decisions comport with *Matter of Zangwill*,[79] wherein the BIA found that the crime of issuing worthless checks under Fla. Stat. §948.01(3) is *not* a crime involving moral turpitude because intent to defraud is not an essential element of that offense.

The offenses of mail fraud under 18 USC §1341 and receipt of kickbacks on government contracts in violation of 41 USC §§51 and 54 were both found to be crimes involving moral turpitude in *Matter of Alarcon*.[80] And the knowing unlawful use, possession, or transfer of food stamps is a crime of moral turpitude because fraud is a fundamental component of the offense.[81]

The use of fraudulent credit cards in violation of 18 USC §§1341 and 1342 was found to be a crime involving moral turpitude in *Matter of Adetiba*.[82] In the same case, falsely representing a Social Security number in violation of 42 USC §408 and fraud and related activity in connection with access devices in violation of 18 USC §1029(a)(2)[83] were found to be crimes involving moral turpitude.[84]

---

[75] *Jordan v. DeGeorge*, 341 U.S. 223 (1951); *Notash v. Gonzales*, 427 F.3d 693, 698 (9th Cir. 2005); *Matter of Flores*, 17 I&N Dec. 225 (BIA 1980).

[76] *Matter of Bart*, 20 I&N Dec. 436 (BIA 1992).

[77] *Matter of Bart*, at 440.

[78] 18 Pa. Cons. Stat. §4105(a)(1).

[79] *Matter of Zangwill*, 18 I&N Dec. 22 (BIA 1981), *overruled in part on other grounds by Matter of Ozkok*, 19 I&N Dec. 546 (BIA 1988).

[80] *Matter of Alarcon*, 20 I&N Dec. 557 (BIA 1992).

[81] *Abdelqadar v. Gonzales*, 413 F.3d 668 (7th Cir. 2005). But compare the unpublished decision of *Diem Thi Huynh v. Holder*, No. 05-73446, 2009 U.S. App. LEXIS 7269 (9th Cir. Apr. 6, 2009) (the federal offense of 7 USC §2024(b) for knowing use, transfer, acquisition, alteration or possession of food stamps in any manner contrary to the law is not a crime involving moral turpitude because the statute does not require an intent to defraud).

[82] *Matter of Adetiba*, 20 I&N Dec. 506 (BIA 1992).

[83] 18 USC §1029 is entitled "Fraud and related activity in connection with access devices," and covers a litany of offenses relating to the production, use, and/or trafficking in counterfeit access devices, including telecommunication instruments that have been modified or altered to obtain unauthorized use of telecommunications services. The term "access device" means any card, plate, code, account number, electronic serial number, mobile ID number, personal ID number, or other telecommunications service or equipment that can be used to obtain money, goods, services, or other items of value, including the transfer of funds. This section, which is enforced primarily by the U.S. Secret Service, covers such crimes as organized credit card theft and fraud, and other forms of identity theft.

[84] *Matter of Adetiba*, 20 I&N Dec. 506 (BIA 1992).

In an interesting twist on the fraud issue, the BIA ruled in 2007 that trafficking in counterfeit goods in violation of 18 USC §2320 is a crime involving moral turpitude, even though the consumer may be aware that the merchandise is counterfeit (*i.e.*, the consumer is not deceived)—and indeed may prefer to pay a lower price in exchange for a counterfeit brand.[85]

Money laundering, because it involves dishonesty and deceit, is a crime involving moral turpitude.[86]

False Statements

A fraudulent statement or act is not the same as a false statement. A false statement must be made with a specific intent to deceive in order to involve moral turpitude. According to the BIA, a materially false statement necessarily involves the intent to deceive.[87] A conviction under 18 USC §1001 is a crime involving moral turpitude because the offense involves willfulness and materiality, even if the offense did not involve fraud.[88]

A false statement made in writing (although not under oath) that the individual knows is not true, and that is made with the intent to mislead a public servant, is a crime involving moral turpitude even though materiality is not an element of the offense.[89] A false statement involving use of another person's name and Social Security number in an application for a U.S. passport will be adjudicated as a crime involving moral turpitude.[90] Likewise, a false statement in a driver's license application is a crime involving moral turpitude.[91]

However, not every crime involving a false statement will involve moral turpitude. In *Notash v. Gonzales*,[92] the Ninth Circuit held that a violation of 18 USC §542 for attempted entry of goods by means of a false statement was not a crime involving moral turpitude where the statute was divisible (including both an intent to defraud as well as a false statement) and the record of conviction did not establish under which clause the petitioner was convicted. 18 USC §542 states:

> Whoever enters or introduces, or attempts to enter or introduce, into the commerce of the United States any imported merchandise by means of any fraudulent or false invoice, declaration, affidavit, letter, paper, or by means of any false statement, written or verbal, or by means of any false or fraudulent

---

[85] *Matter of Kochlani*, 24 I&N Dec. 128 (BIA 2007).

[86] *Matter of Tejwani*, 24 I&N Dec. 97 (BIA 2007).

[87] *Matter of Pinzon*, 26 I&N Dec. 189 (BIA 2013), *citing: U.S. v. Boffil-Rivera*, 607 F.3d 736, 741 (11th Cir. 2010).

[88] *Ghani and Anwer v. Holder*, 557 F.3d 836, 840 (7th Cir. 2009).

[89] *Matter of Jurado*, 24 I&N Dec. 29, 33 (BIA 2006).

[90] *Matter of Correa-Garces*, 20 I&N Dec. 451 (BIA 1992).

[91] *Zaitona v. INS*, 9 F.3d 432, 437 (6th Cir. 1993).

[92] *Notash v. Gonzales*, 427 F.3d 693 (9th Cir. 2005).

practice or appliance, or makes any false statement in any declaration without reasonable cause to believe the truth of such statement, or procures the making of any such false statement as to any matter material thereto without reasonable cause to believe the truth of such statement, whether or not the United States shall or may be deprived of any lawful duties; or

Whoever is guilty of any willful act or omission whereby the United States shall or may be deprived of any lawful duties accruing upon merchandise embraced or referred to in such invoice, declaration, affidavit, letter, paper, or statement, or affected by such act or omission—

Shall be fined for each offense under this title or imprisoned not more than two years, or both.

The court noted that not every clause of §542 requires knowledge that the statement is false. The first paragraph requires only that the defendant lack reasonable cause to believe the truth of the statement; the second paragraph contains no intent requirement whatsoever. Furthermore, applying a modified categorical approach and turning to the record of conviction, the court found no documents in the record that would pinpoint the exact portion of the statute that applied.[93]

Obstruction of Justice; Misprision

Obstruction of justice in violation of 720 Ill. Comp. Stat. 5/31-4(a) (formerly Ill. Rev. Stat. ch. 38 §31-4(a)) involves moral turpitude even though a specific intent to defraud is not an element of the offense.[94] A conviction under this statute requires the defendant "knowingly" to provide false information "with intent to prevent the apprehension or obstruct the prosecution or defense of any person." The defendant/respondent in *Padilla v. Gonzalez*[95] provided a false name to police on being pulled over for a traffic violation; he was driving with his license revoked.[96] The Seventh Circuit U.S. Court of Appeals found that intentionally deceiving an officer to conceal criminal activity involves moral turpitude.[97]

The Eleventh Circuit U.S. Court of Appeals and the BIA have found that misprision of felony involves moral turpitude.[98] Misprision of felony under 18 USC §4 is as follows:

---

[93] *Notash v. Gonzales*, 427 F.3d 693, at 699.

[94] *Padilla v. Gonzales*, 397 F.3d 1016 (7th Cir. 2005); *subsequent petition for review dismissed on jurisdictional grounds at* 470 F.3d 1209 (7th Cir. 2006).

[95] *Padilla v. Gonzales*, 397 F.3d 1016 (7th Cir. 2005).

[96] *Padilla v. Gonzales*, 397 F.3d 1016 (7th Cir. 2005).

[97] *Padilla v. Gonzales*, 397 F.3d 1016 (7th Cir. 2005). *Note*: Obstruction of justice is an aggravated felony under INA §101(a)(43)(S) *if* a term of imprisonment of at least one year is imposed.

[98] *Itani v. Ashcroft*, 298 F.3d 1213, 1215 (11th Cir. 2002); *Matter of Robles-Urrea*, 24 I&N Dec. 22 (BIA 2006).

Whoever, having knowledge of the actual commission of a felony cognizable by a court of the United States, conceals and does not as soon as possible make known the same to some judge or other person in civil or military authority under the United States, shall be fined under this title or imprisoned not more than three years, or both.

In comparison, the Ninth Circuit in *Robles-Urrea v. Holder*[99] changed course on its position regarding misprision, finding that 18 USC §4 is not categorically a crime involving moral turpitude and does not (contrary to the Eleventh Circuit's finding) involve fraud. The Ninth Circuit noted that being cognizant that a felony has occurred does not necessarily connote moral turpitude. Moreover, the court of appeals wrote that it would like to find that misprision is categorically not—ever—a moral turpitude crime but for the circuit's elimination of the missing element rule:

> We would formerly have found it unnecessary to consider the modified categorical approach, because misprision of a felony lacks the requisite element of depravity or fraud necessary to fulfill the generic definition of a crime involving moral turpitude. *See [Navarro-Lopez v. Gonzales,* 503 F.3d 1063, 1073 (9th Cir. 2007) *(en banc)]* (holding that the modified categorical analysis "only applies when the particular elements of the crime of conviction are broader than the generic crime"). Such a course is no longer available, however, after *United States v. Aguila-Montes de Oca*,[100] which overruled the missing-element rule. As interpreted by *Aguila-Montes de Oca*, "the modified categorical approach asks what facts the conviction 'necessarily rested' on in light of the [prosecutorial] theory of the case as revealed in the relevant [judicially noticeable] documents, and whether these facts satisfy the elements of the generic offense."[101]

Hence, the Ninth Circuit remanded for a modified categorical approach that considers, based on the record of conviction, whether the particular facts necessary to establish the conviction qualify as moral turpitude conduct.[102]

Crimes of Violence

Crimes of violence merit special attention because they may involve the elements of specific or evil intent or knowledge. Simple assault and battery offenses are

---

[99] *Robles-Urrea v. Holder,* 678 F.3d 702 (No. 06-71935, 9th Cir. 2012).

[100] *U.S. v. Aguila-Montes de Oca*, 655 F.3d 915 (9th Cir. 2011).

[101] *Robles-Urrea v. Holder,* 678 F.3d 702, 711–12 (9th Cir. 2012).

[102] *Robles-Urrea v. Holder,* at 712–13. *Note*: Misprision of felony is not an aggravated felony offense involving obstruction of justice under INA §101(a)(43)(S). *See Matter of Espinoza-Gonzalez,* 22 I&N Dec. 889 (BIA 1999).

generally not considered to be crimes involving moral turpitude.[103] Aggravated assault and assaults accompanied by the use of a weapon have generally been found to involve moral turpitude. In determining whether a violent offense involves moral turpitude, the BIA looks to whether the act is accompanied by a vicious motive or corrupt mind.[104] Generally, for a crime of violence to involve moral turpitude, the act must be accompanied by specific intent to do harm; *i.e.*, the conduct must be knowing and intentional.

As stated above, moral turpitude also may be present in criminally reckless conduct.[105] Where recklessness is defined as a conscious disregard of substantial and unjustifiable risk, crimes committed recklessly have been found, to express a sufficiently corrupt mental state to constitute a crime involving moral turpitude (where there are aggravating factors).[106] For example, in a 2015 case,[107] the BIA found that the Texas crime of "deadly conduct,"[108] which involves recklessly engaging in conduct that places another in imminent danger of serious bodily injury, is a crime involving moral turpitude.

In a March 2009 case,[109] the Eleventh Circuit found that Georgia's criminally reckless conduct statute[110] involves moral turpitude because the individual acts with a conscious disregard of a substantial and unjustifiable risk that his or her act or omission will cause harm or endanger safety; under the statute, the disregard constitutes a gross deviation from the standard of care that a reasonable person would exercise, and either causes bodily injury or endangers the bodily safety of another person.[111]

Crimes involving moral turpitude

The BIA and the federal courts have analyzed various crimes involving violence and concluded the following with respect to moral turpitude:

- Attempted murder is a crime involving moral turpitude.[112]
- Voluntary manslaughter is generally a crime involving moral turpitude.[113]

---

[103] *Matter of Sanudo*, 23 I&N Dec. 968, 971 (BIA 2006); *Matter of Fualaau*, 21 I&N Dec. 475 (BIA 1996); *Matter of Perez-Contreras*, 20 I&N Dec. 615 (BIA 1992) (citing *Matter of Short*, 20 I&N Dec. 136 (BIA 1989)).

[104] *Matter of Perez-Contreras*, 20 I&N Dec. 615 (BIA 1992) (citing *Okabe v. INS*, 671 F.2d 863 (5th Cir. 1982)).

[105] *Matter of Wojtkow*, 18 I&N Dec. 111 (BIA 1981); *Matter of Medina*, 15 I&N Dec. 611 (BIA 1976).

[106] *Gill v. INS*, 420 F.3d 82 (2d Cir. 2005).

[107] *Matter of Hernandez*, 26 I&N Dec. 464 (BIA 2015).

[108] Tex. Penal Code §22.05(a).

[109] *Keungne v. Att'y Gen.*, 561 F.3d 1281 (11th Cir. 2009).

[110] O.C.G.A. §16-5-60(b).

[111] *Keungne v. Att'y Gen.*, 561 F.3d at 1287.

[112] *Matter of Sanchez-Linn*, 20 I&N Dec. 362 (BIA 1991).

[113] *Matter of Sanchez-Linn*, 20 I&N Dec. 362 (BIA 1991).

- Assault with a deadly weapon (*e.g.*, aggravated assault) is a crime involving moral turpitude.[114] Similarly, assault without a deadly weapon but with intent to do great bodily harm is a crime involving moral turpitude.[115]

- Pursuant to *Matter of Ajami*,[116] aggravated stalking is a crime involving moral turpitude where there is a "credible threat to kill another or inflict physical injury on the victim."[117] The BIA noted that under the Michigan statute[118] at issue, the perpetrator must have: (1) acted willfully; (2) embarked on a course of conduct (as opposed to a single act); and (3) caused another to feel great fear.[119]

- Making terroristic threats (threatening a crime of violence) toward another with a reckless state of mind is a moral turpitude offense.[120]

- Crimes involving "threatening behavior" are generally found to be crimes involving moral turpitude. For example, usury by intimidation and threats of bodily harm are crimes involving moral turpitude,[121] as are threats to take property by force.[122] Furthermore, extortion (by sending threatening letters via mail with the intent to extort money) is a crime of violence.[123]

- Second-degree arson in Florida is a crime involving moral turpitude.[124]

- Failure to stop and render aid following a fatal car accident under Texas law is a crime involving moral turpitude.[125]

- Maliciously firing a weapon into an occupied dwelling is a crime involving moral turpitude.[126]

---

[114] *Matter of Medina*, 15 I&N Dec. 611 (BIA 1976).

[115] *Matter of P*, 3 I&N Dec. 5 (BIA 1947).

[116] *Matter of Ajami*, 22 I&N Dec. 949 (BIA 1999).

[117] *Matter of Ajami*, 22 I&N Dec. 949 (BIA 1999).

[118] Mich. Comp. Laws §§750.411i(1)(a)–(e).

[119] *Note*: Depending on the specific elements of the state statute, misdemeanor stalking or harassment is unlikely to be considered a crime of violence that involves moral turpitude. However, even misdemeanor stalking will fall under the "domestic violence" ground of deportability, discussed in chapter eight.

[120] *Avendano v. Holder*, 770 F.3d 731 (8th Cir. 2014).

[121] *Matter of B–*, 6 I&N Dec. 98 (BIA 1954).

[122] *Matter of C–*, 5 I&N Dec. 370 (BIA 1953).

[123] *Matter of G – T–*, 4 I&N Dec. 446 (BIA 1951). *Note*: A crime of violence may not involve moral turpitude but still qualify as an aggravated felony "crime of violence" under INA §101(a)(43)(F). These are two separate analyses.

[124] *Vuksanovic v. Att'y Gen.*, 439 F.3d 1308 (11th Cir. 2006).

[125] *Garcia-Maldonado v. Gonzales*, No. 05-60692 (5th Cir. June 29, 2007).

[126] *Recio-Prado v. Gonzales*, 456 F.3d 819 (8th Cir. 2006).

- Fleeing and eluding a police officer where knowledge of the officer's signal to stop is a crime involving moral turpitude.[127]

Crimes not involving moral turpitude

Attempted assault, when the underlying statute contains an element of recklessness (*e.g.*, attempted assault in the second degree in violation of N.Y. Penal Law §120.05(4), which proscribes "recklessly [causing] serious physical injury to another person by means of a deadly weapon or other dangerous instrument"), is not a crime involving moral turpitude. There is no "legal coherence" to the theory that an individual can *attempt* to commit a crime of *recklessness*.[128] A similar conclusion was reached by the Third Circuit U.S. Court of Appeals;[129] the court found that attempted reckless endangerment is not a crime involving moral turpitude because, categorically speaking, the concept makes no sense: attempt (which connotes a specific intent to do something) is inconsistent with recklessness (which, by definition, connotes acting without intent).[130]

Simple assault and battery against a household member, including a spouse, was found *not* to be a crime involving moral turpitude in *Matter of Sejas*,[131] where the Virginia statute[132] at issue did not require the actual infliction of physical injury and could include something as minimal as touching. The BIA distinguished this case from an earlier precedent decision in which moral turpitude was found where the offense involved the willful infliction of corporal injury on a family member, resulting in a traumatic condition.[133]

In *Partyka v. Att'y General*,[134] the Third Circuit found that aggravated assault on a law enforcement officer is not a crime involving moral turpitude. In *Partyka*, the New Jersey statute[135] was divisible, containing provisions that covered reckless conduct as well as mere negligence. Because the minimum (or least culpable) conduct possible under the statute (in this case, negligence) does not involve moral turpitude, the conviction was found not to involve moral turpitude. However, in a 2014 unpublished case arising in the Third Circuit,[136] the court found that assault in the third degree on

---

[127] *Cano-Oyarzabal v. Holder*, 774 F.3d 914 (7th Cir. 2014); *Ruiz-Lopez v. Holder*, 682 F.3d 513, 521 (6th Cir. 2012); *Godinez-Arroyo v. Mukasey*, 540 F.3d 848 (8th Cir. 2008).

[128] *See Gill v. INS*, 420 F.3d 82 (2d Cir. 2005).

[129] *Knapik v. Ashcroft*, 384 F.3d 84, 91–94 (3d Cir. 2004).

[130] Assault under Hawaii Revised Statutes §§702–710 through 712, is a crime involving moral turpitude where the statute calls for a reckless state of mind but only if the element of infliction of serious bodily injury is also charged. *Matter of Fualaau*, 21 I&N Dec. 475, 478 (BIA 1996).

[131] *Matter of Sejas*, 24 I&N Dec. 236 (BIA 2007).

[132] Va. Code Ann. §18.2-57.2.

[133] *Matter of Tran*, 21 I&N Dec. 291, 294 (BIA 1996) (dealing with a conviction under Cal. Penal Code §273.5(a)).

[134] *Partyka v. Att'y Gen.*, 417 F.3d 408 (3d Cir. 2005).

[135] N.J. Stat. Ann. §2C:12-1.b.(5)(a).

[136] *Salomon-Bajxac v. Att'y Gen.*, 558 Fed. Appx. 160, No. 13-3711 (3d Cir. Mar. 7, 2014).

a law enforcement officer is a moral turpitude crime, but the analysis was focused on the elements of assault, not the fact that an officer was the victim.

Leaving the scene of an accident with injuries under California law is not a crime involving moral turpitude under either a categorical or modified categorical approach.[137]

Not clear if moral turpitude exists

Categorizing battery or assault on a law enforcement officer as a crime of violence involving moral turpitude is subject to debate. In *Matter of Danesh*,[138] the BIA held that aggravated assault against a peace officer was a crime involving moral turpitude. However, simple battery or assault against a police officer is arguably not a crime involving moral turpitude; normally, state statutes simply enhance the sentence for simple battery or assault when the victim is a law enforcement officer. The sentence enhancement should not change the underlying nature of simple assault and battery as exempt from classification as a crime involving moral turpitude.

Involuntary manslaughter may be a crime involving moral turpitude, depending on the language of the specific state statute involved. The BIA has found involuntary manslaughter to constitute a crime involving moral turpitude even though the perpetrator may lack a specific intent to do harm, because of the element of "recklessness," which demonstrates a conscious disregard of a substantial and unjustifiable risk.[139] The BIA has acknowledged, at least in dicta, that "some" involuntary manslaughter offenses will involve moral turpitude, depending on the elements of the statutory offense.[140] In light of the Supreme Court's analysis in *Leocal v. Ashcroft*,[141] it is not clear at this time whether recklessness alone is enough to constitute a crime involving moral turpitude.[142]

Gang Enhancement

In *Matter of Hernandez*,[143] a conviction for malicious vandalism[144] with a gang enhancement,[145] which requires that the underlying offense be committed for the benefit of a criminal street gang with the specific intent to promote criminal conduct by gang members, was held to be categorically a crime involving moral turpitude.

---

[137] *Cerezo v. Mukasey*, 512 F.3d 1163 (9th Cir. 2008).

[138] *Matter of Danesh*, 19 I&N Dec. 669 (BIA 1988).

[139] *Matter of Franklin*, 20 I&N Dec. 867 (BIA 1994), *aff'd, Franklin v. INS*, 72 F.3d 571 (8th Cir. 1995).

[140] *Matter of Torres-Varela*, 23 I&N Dec. 78, 84 (BIA 2001).

[141] *Leocal v. Ashcroft*, 543 U.S. 1 (2004).

[142] For discussion of the *Leocal* decision, see chapter seven on aggravated felony crimes of violence.

[143] *Matter of Hernandez*, 26 I&N Dec. 397 (BIA 2014).

[144] Cal. Penal Code §594(a).

[145] Cal. Penal Code §186.22(d).

This decision should be challenged as an incorrect application of the categorical approach.

According to the decision, the non–American citizen was convicted of vandalism and received the gang enhancement because he admitted he wrote graffiti at the direction of a gang. In order for a gang enhancement to apply, a jury must find that the illegal act was committed in furtherance of gang activity. If it is so found, the gang enhancement qualifies (according to the BIA) as an independent enhanced offense.[146] Indeed, the finding of moral turpitude focused on the gang enhancement provision, not the underlying crime of malicious vandalism, and the BIA's decision focuses on the reprehensible nature of gangs in general. The Ninth Circuit rejected the BIA's decision in a similar case involving the gang enhancement—with coincidentally the name *Hernandez*—but with the underlying offense being possession of a deadly weapon. The BIA found that a broad sentence enhancement for gang-related activity could not categorically qualify as a crime involving moral turpitude.[147]

Failure to Register as a Sex Offender

In *Matter of Tobar-Lobo*,[148] the Board found that the regulatory violation of failure to register as a sex offender under California law is a crime involving moral turpitude because sex-related crimes are so serious in nature that failure to register poses a serious threat to society: "some obligations, once imparted by proper notification, are simply too important not to heed."[149]

Clearly, the problem with this analysis is that the "importance" of a regulation has never been the test of moral turpitude. State registration laws impose strict liability without regard to evil intent or even a specific underlying event of a depraved nature—address violations, tardiness, forgetfulness, etc., can result in a violation of the statute. In a significant dissent, Board Member Filppu criticizes the decision as representing a departure from longstanding Board precedent regarding the nature of regulatory violations. The Ninth Circuit has likewise soundly rejected the Board's analysis in *Tobar-Lobo,* finding that "it is the sexual offense which is reprehensible, not the failure to register."[150] As of the spring of 2015, every circuit court to review a sexual predator registration law involving the application of *Tobar-Lobo* has rejected

---

[146] *Matter of Hernandez*, 26 I&N Dec. at 399, *citing Matter of Martinez-Zapata*, 24 I&N Dec. 424, 426 (BIA 2007).

[147] *Hernandez-Gonzalez v. Holder,* 778 F.3d 793 (9th Cir. 2015).

[148] *Matter of Tobar-Lobo*, 24 I&N Dec. 143 (BIA 2007).

[149] *Matter of Tobar-Lobo*, at 146–47.

[150] *Plasencia-Ayala v. Mukasey*, 516 F.3d 738, 748 (9th Cir. 2008).

the Board's decision as an impermissible departure from the traditional moral turpitude criteria.[151]

Crimes Involving Children

In *Matter of Alfaro*,[152] the BIA applied the *Silva-Trevino* analysis to determine that unlawful sexual intercourse with a minor under Cal. Penal Code §261.5(d), essentially a statutory rape section, is a divisible statute and a conviction will be one that involves moral turpitude if the record shows the perpetrator knew the victim was under the age of 16. In so doing, the BIA disagreed with the Ninth Circuit's decision regarding the same statute.[153]

Intentional sexual conduct with a person the defendant knew or should have known was a minor is categorically a crime involving moral turpitude. Where "mistake of age" is not a defense—meaning, a defendant can be prosecuted and convicted even though he did not believe the victim was a minor—the statute does not categorically involve moral turpitude, and a modified categorical approach is employed to determine whether moral turpitude was involved in the particular offense.[154]

Sexual abuse of a minor was found, in dicta, to involve moral turpitude by the Seventh Circuit.[155]

Annoying or molesting a child under the age of 18 where such act is motivated by an unnatural or abnormal sexual interest in the victim, a second-degree misdemeanor under California law,[156] is not categorically a crime involving moral turpitude.[157] In this post–*Gonzales v. Duenas-Alvarez*[158] decision, the Ninth Circuit applied the realistic probability test to the criminal statute, and pinpointed an unpublished case in which the statute was applied to non-turpitudinous conduct to determine the statute was not necessarily a crime involving moral turpitude.

The BIA has found that possession of child pornography is morally reprehensible, intrinsically wrong, and hence involves moral turpitude.[159] The Ninth Circuit also has held that possession of child pornography involves moral turpitude.[160]

---

[151] *Totimeh v. Att'y Gen.*, 666 F.3d 109 (3d Cir. 2012); *Efagene v. Holder*, 642 F.3d 918 (10th Cir. 2011); *Plasencia-Ayala v. Mukasey*, 516 F.3d 738 (9th Cir. 2008), *overruled on other grounds by Marmolejo-Campos v. Holder*, 558 F.3d 903 (9th Cir. 2009).

[152] *Matter of Alfaro*, 25 I&N Dec. 417 (BIA 2011).

[153] *Quintero-Salazar v. Keisler*, 506 F.3d 688 (9th Cir. 2007).

[154] *Matter of Silva-Trevino*, 24 I&N Dec. 687, 708 (AG 2008).

[155] *Padilla v. Gonzales*, 397 F.3d 1016 (7th Cir. 2005).

[156] California Penal Code §647.6(a) (*Note*: this conviction was in 1990).

[157] *Nicanor-Romero v. Mukasey*, 523 F.3d 992, 1000 (9th Cir. 2008).

[158] *Gonzales v. Duenas-Alvarez*, 549 U.S. 183 (2007).

[159] *Matter of Olquin-Rufino*, 23 I&N Dec. 896, 898 (BIA 2006).

[160] *U.S. v. Santacruz*, 563 F.3d 894, 896 (9th Cir. 2009).

Driving Under the Influence

Over the past decade, the BIA has struggled with crimes involving driving under the influence (DUI). Operating-while-intoxicated offenses fall under the larger canopy of crimes of violence. It is recommended that fresh research be conducted every time a DUI case arises, because BIA precedent (and federal court) cases have been inconsistent on the issue of whether DUI is a crime involving moral turpitude. Reference to the specific elements of the statute is essential.

Simple DUI, with no aggravating factors, is not a crime involving moral turpitude.[161] Likewise, felony DUI (based on multiple simple DUI convictions) is not a crime involving moral turpitude.[162]

However, the BIA has found that a DUI offense, combined with some other aggravating factor that contains the element of knowledge, such as driving with a suspended license, may be considered a crime involving moral turpitude.[163] In *Matter of Lopez-Meza,* the BIA analyzed Arizona's aggravated DUI statute,[164] which criminalizes driving or maintaining physical control of a vehicle, while under the influence of intoxicating liquor or drugs, while the driver's license is suspended, canceled, revoked, or suspended as a result of a prior DUI offense, and the driver knows or should have known that the license was suspended or revoked. The BIA found that this offense qualifies as a moral turpitude crime because of the knowledge element attached to the fact of the suspended license, reasoning that this element adds the *mens rea.*

The Ninth Circuit has issued two decisions subsequent to *Lopez-Meza,* analyzing the same statute and addressing the validity of the Board's decision. Those decisions are in tension with one another. In *Hernandez-Martinez v. Ashcroft,*[165] the Ninth Circuit rejected the BIA's interpretation of the statute as articulated in *Lopez-Meza* because the BIA did not distinguish between driving a vehicle and maintaining physical control of a vehicle. The court of appeals found that maintaining physical control is not a crime involving moral turpitude.

However, *Marmolejo-Campos v. Holder*[166] upheld the BIA's determination that a conviction under the same statute did involve moral turpitude, based on the Board having examined the record of conviction and determining that both of the respondent's convictions arose out of incidents in which he was actually driving. The dissents in *Marmolejo-Campos*[167] present compelling arguments against the majority's ruling. The dissenting opinions correctly point out that neither simple DUI,

---

[161] *Matter of Torres-Varela,* 23 I&N Dec. 78 (BIA 2001).

[162] *Matter of Torres-Varela,* 23 I&N Dec. 78 (BIA 2001).

[163] *Matter of Lopez-Meza,* 22 I&N Dec. 1188 (BIA 1999).

[164] Ariz. Rev. Stat. §28-1383(A)(1).

[165] *Hernandez-Martinez v. Ashcroft,* 329 F.3d 1117 (9th Cir. 2003).

[166] *Marmolejo-Campos v. Holder,* 558 F.3d 903 (9th Cir. 2009).

[167] *Marmolejo-Campos,* 558 F.3d 903, at 918.

nor driving with a suspended license, is a crime involving moral turpitude. The dissenting opinions criticize the combination of two non–moral turpitude crimes through some "undefined synergism," harnessing the mental intent attached to driving with a suspended license to somehow include DUI, to create a hybrid moral-turpitude crime. In fact, the dissenting opinions make good sense and are well supported (hence, good reading).

When looking at DUI-type offenses, it is important to remember, as discussed above, that the element of negligence does not implicate moral turpitude. Likewise, the element of recklessness—standing alone—does not trigger a finding of moral turpitude. Only if the statute combines a recklessness act with the element of knowledge of risk can the offense be interpreted to involve moral turpitude. The ultimate outcome (*e.g.*, bodily injury) is *not* determinative of moral turpitude.

Controlled Substance Offenses

Generally speaking, simple possession (or better said, personal possession) of a controlled substance is not a crime involving moral turpitude if the statute is written as a regulatory provision (*i.e.*, without specific intent).[168] *Trafficking* in a controlled substance, however, is considered a crime involving moral turpitude.[169]

Firearms Offenses

Firearms offenses are regulatory in nature and do not, standing alone, involve moral turpitude.[170] Carrying a concealed firearm and improper registration of a firearm fall into this category. If an element of the charge involves a firearm—for example, a crime of violence involving the use of a firearm—the offense may be a crime involving moral turpitude. In other words, it is important to distinguish between a moral turpitude crime that happens to involve a firearm, such as aggravated assault or armed robbery, and a pure firearms offense. Additionally, firearms offenses are treated as a separate category, or classification, under the INA, as discussed in chapter seven, "Aggravated Felonies."

Immigration Law Violations

Immigration law violations generally fall under the canopy of regulatory offenses and—in the absence of fraud or evil intent—do not involve moral turpitude.[171] For example, a conviction for alien smuggling under INA §241(a)(13) was found *not* to be a crime involving moral turpitude in *Matter of Tiwari*.[172] Immigration violations,

---

[168] *Matter of Abreu-Semino*, 12 I&N Dec. 775 (BIA 1968).

[169] *Matter of Khourn*, 21 I&N Dec. 1041 (BIA 1997).

[170] *See Matter of Campos-Torres*, 22 I&N Dec. 1289 (BIA 2000).

[171] *Matter of Jimenez-Santillano*, 21 I&N Dec. 567 (BIA 1996); *Matter of Tiwari*, 19 I&N Dec. 875 (BIA 1989), *reconsideration denied*, 20 I&N Dec. 254 (BIA 1991).

[172] *Matter of Tiwari*, 19 I&N Dec. 875 (BIA 1989), *reconsideration denied*, 20 I&N Dec. 254 (BIA 1991).

such as visa fraud, registration, and reporting violations, are discussed in greater detail in chapter eight, "Crimes Beyond Moral Turpitude and Aggravated Felony."

CHAPTER SEVEN

AGGRAVATED FELONIES

The INA Definition of Aggravated Felony	263
The Definition of "Crime of Violence"	290
Contesting "Loss" Findings; Understanding "Relevant Conduct"	313
"Aggravated Felony"—Must It Be a Felony?	318
Attempts and Conspiracies	320

The INA Definition of Aggravated Felony

"Aggravated felony" is a term defined by statute at Immigration and Nationality Act (INA) §§101(a)(43)(A)–(U) [8 USC §§1101(a)(43)(A)–(U)]. Over the past 20 years, Congress has expanded the aggravated felony definition in every new piece of criminal-alien legislation. Pursuant to §322(c) of the Illegal Immigration Reform and Immigrant Responsibility Act of 1996 (IIRAIRA),[1] the definition of aggravated felony is retroactive (indefinitely), and includes acts that occurred prior to their inclusion in the aggravated felony definition. The final paragraph of INA §101(a)(43) states that the term "aggravated felony" applies to offenses under federal and state law, and "applies to such an offense in violation of the law of a foreign country for which the term of imprisonment was completed within the previous 15 years."

Today, the definition of aggravated felony includes numerous offenses. The list below represents the types of aggravated felony offenses under the INA, most of which are discussed in greater detail throughout the chapter. The list should not be relied on as the sole point of reference in a particular case.[2]

(A) Murder, rape, or sexual abuse of a minor;

(B) Illicit trafficking in a controlled substance;

(C) Illicit trafficking in firearms or destructive devices;

(D) Certain money laundering offenses involving funds in excess of $10,000;

(E) Enumerated federal offenses relating to explosive materials and certain firearms offenses;

(F) A crime of violence, where the term of imprisonment imposed is at least one year;

---

[1] Illegal Immigration Reform and Immigrant Responsibility Act of 1996 (IIRAIRA), Division C of the Omnibus Appropriations Act of 1996 (H.R. 3610), Pub. L. No. 104-208, 110 Stat. 3009.

[2] For the specific statutory language, refer to INA §101(a)(43); 8 USC §1101(a)(43).

(G) A theft, burglary,[3] or possession of stolen property offense where the term of imprisonment imposed is at least one year;

(H) Kidnapping offenses;

(I) Child pornography offenses;

(J) Certain racketeering and gambling offenses, where a term of imprisonment of at least one year may be imposed;

(K) Offenses relating to prostitution enterprises, peonage, and slavery;

(L) Federal offenses related to gathering and transmitting classified national defense information, including acts of sabotage and treason under the National Security Act;

(M) A crime involving fraud or deceit where loss to the victim(s) exceeds $10,000; or a crime of tax evasion in which the revenue loss to the government exceeds $10,000;

(N) Alien smuggling, including harboring, transporting, and concealing;

(O) Re-entry after deportation for an aggravated felony;

(P) Falsely making, forging, counterfeiting, mutilating, or altering a U.S. passport or instrument, for which the punishment imposed is at least one year (not including first offenses where the person assisted was the alien's spouse, child, or parent);

(Q) Failure to appear for service of sentence where the underlying offense is punishable by a term of imprisonment of at least five years;

(R) Offenses relating to commercial bribery, counterfeiting, forgery, or trafficking in vehicles whose vehicle identification numbers have been altered, where the imprisonment imposed is at least one year;

(S) Offenses relating to obstruction of justice, perjury, subornation of perjury, or bribery of a witness, where the term of imprisonment imposed is at least one year;

(T) An offense relating to failure to appear before a court on a felony charge where the term of imprisonment that may be imposed on the underlying charge is two years or more ("bail jumping"); and

(U) An attempt or conspiracy to commit an offense described above.

Note that certain state misdemeanors are now considered to be aggravated felonies based on case law. The U.S. Supreme Court has issued several decisions regarding

---

[3] Burglary of a conveyance (particularly, a vehicle) is not considered an aggravated felony because this is not a traditional "burglary" offense (where there is a threat to people); rather, it is akin to a breaking-and-entering offense. *Matter of Perez*, 22 I&N Dec. 1325 (BIA 2000); *Taylor v. U.S.*, 495 U.S. 575 (1990) (holding that burglary of a conveyance is not a burglary).

the aggravated felony definition.[4] These decisions are important not only for their holdings but because they discuss the proper analysis for determining whether a particular crime qualifies as an aggravated felony. The Supreme Court has sanctioned a categorical and modified categorical approach to determining whether an offense is an aggravated felony, including use of evidence beyond the statute and record of conviction where there is a non-elemental factor (such as monetary loss) and a "realistic probability" approach to determining the breadth of a statute. These concepts are discussed at length in chapter five, "Methodology."

Much of immigration case law comes not only from the removal context, but from sentencing guidelines cases, wherein defendants are prosecuted for re-entry after removal and face stiffer penalties because of re-entry after deportation for an aggravated felony offense. Sentencing guidelines cases may be of use in analyzing a crime; however, practitioners are cautioned to make note of the different statutes and standards, and not embrace a finding in the sentencing context if its premise is based on the guidelines rather than immigration case law and the INA itself.

The discussion below covers decisions of the federal courts and the Board of Immigration Appeals (BIA or Board) as they define the different offenses under the definition of "aggravated felony."

Murder

Section 101(a)(43)(A) classifies "murder" as an aggravated felony. Murder was included in the original definition of aggravated felony in 1988, when the term was first introduced in the statute. The Model Penal Code defines "murder" as a class of criminal homicide that is committed either (1) purposely or knowingly, or (2) recklessly under circumstances manifesting extreme indifference to the value of human life.[5] In *Matter of M–W–*,[6] the BIA found the respondent removable for the aggravated felony of murder where he had been convicted under Michigan law of second-degree murder arising in the context of a drunk-driving traffic accident. The mental state for conviction was recklessness, defined as a wanton and willful disregard that the behavior would result in great bodily harm or death. The BIA found that the concept of malice aforethought encompasses extreme reckless behavior. It is not necessary, according to the BIA, for a statute's elements to include an "intent to kill" in order to meet the definition of murder.[7] Of note, the BIA arrived at a generic definition of murder by looking at the common law definition and the federal statute, but specifically stated that because the INA provision does not reference a federal code provision, the federal definition is not determinative—but is a "significant point

---

[4] *Kawashima v. Holder*, 132 S. Ct. 1166 (2012); *Nijhawan v. Holder*, 557 U.S. 29 (2009); *Gonzales v. Duenas-Alvarez*, 549 U.S. 183 (2007); *Lopez v. Gonzales*, 549 U.S. 47 (2006); *Leocal v. Ashcroft*, 543 U.S. 1 (2004).

[5] Model Penal Code §210.2(1).

[6] *Matter of M–W–*, 25 I&N Dec. 748 (BIA 2012).

[7] *Matter of M–W–*, 25 I&N Dec. 748, at 758.

of reference."[8] In 2013, the Sixth Circuit U.S. Court of Appeals upheld the BIA's decision in an unpublished opinion.[9]

Sexual Abuse of a Minor[10]

The INA does not contain a definition for "sexual abuse of a minor." The BIA utilizes a federal standard as a guide to determine what constitutes sexual abuse of a minor: the provisions of 18 USC §3509(a).[11] According to this section:

> The term "sexual abuse" includes the employment, use, persuasion, inducement, enticement, or coercion of a child to engage in, or assist another person to engage in, sexually explicit conduct or the rape, molestation, prostitution, or other form of sexual exploitation of children, or incest, with children.[12]

The federal courts generally have agreed with the BIA's reliance on 18 USC §3509(a) to define the term.[13] Thus, both the BIA and the federal courts generally cast a very wide net in determining whether conduct qualifies as "sexual abuse of a minor."

- *Texas*: The BIA has found that indecency with a child by exposure under Texas law is an aggravated felony, because the crime requires a high degree of mental culpability: the perpetrator acts with knowledge, as well as the intent to gratify his or her sexual desires.[14]

- *North Carolina*: The Eleventh Circuit U.S. Court of Appeals interprets "sexual abuse of a minor" to mean "a perpetrator's physical or nonphysical misuse or maltreatment of a minor for a purpose associated with sexual gratification."[15] In line with this definition, the Eleventh Circuit ruled that taking indecent liberties with a child under the age of 16, according to North Carolina law, is an aggravated felony even though the statute does not require any physical contact.[16]

- *Colorado*: In 2006, the Tenth Circuit found that contributing to the delinquency of a minor under Colorado law qualifies as sexual abuse of a minor where the

---

[8] *Matter of M–W–*, 25 I&N Dec. 748, at 751.

[9] *Wadja v. Holder*, 727 F.3d 457 (6th Cir. 2013).

[10] For additional discussion of sexual abuse of a minor—specifically, a federal conviction for failure to register as a sex offender—see chapter eight.

[11] *Matter of Rodriguez-Rodriguez*, 22 I&N Dec. 991, 995 (BIA 1999).

[12] 18 USC §3509(a)(8).

[13] *Restrepo v. Att'y Gen.*, 617 F.3d 787 (3d Cir. 2010); *James v. Mukasey*, 522 F.3d 250 (2d Cir. 2008); *Gaiskov v. Holder*, 567 F.3d 832, 835 (7th Cir. 2009).

[14] *Matter of Rodriguez-Rodriguez*, 22 I&N Dec. 991 (BIA 1999), *clarified by Matter of Esquivel-Santana*, 26 I&N Dec. 469 (BIA 2015).

[15] *U.S. v. Padilla-Reyes*, 247 F.3d 1158, 1163 (11th Cir. 2001).

[16] *U.S. v. Ramirez-Garcia*, 646 F.3d 778 (11th Cir. 2011); *Bahar v. Ashcroft*, 264 F.3d 1309 (11th Cir. 2001).

charging document identified unlawful, nonconsensual contact to be the underlying offense.[17]

- *New York*: The Second Circuit U.S. Court of Appeals has held that the use of a child in a sexual performance under New York law constitutes the aggravated felony of sexual abuse of a minor.[18]

Statutory Rape–Type Cases

Several circuits have found that offenses involving consensual sex with a minor—commonly referred to as statutory rape—meet the definition of aggravated felony sexual abuse of a minor.[19] In contrast, the Ninth Circuit U.S. Court of Appeals has ruled that in order for a state statute to qualify as "sexual abuse of a minor," the section must necessarily include an element of abuse. A minor over the age of 14 who voluntarily engages in sexual activity is not necessarily a victim of sexual abuse.[20] According to the BIA, however, a conviction for consensual activity with a minor under Fla. Stat. §794.05 is an aggravated felony; this section criminalizes sexual activity by a person 24 years of age or older with a person who is 16 or 17 years of age.[21] The BIA considers a minor to be anyone under the age of 18, regardless of whether the relationship appears superficially consensual. The Ninth Circuit has since clarified that its disagreement with the BIA's approach is in the context of consensual statutory-rape statutes only.[22]

---

[17] *Vargas v. DHS*, 451 F.3d 1105 (10th Cir. 2006). According to the decision, contributing to the delinquency of a minor requires the identification of an underlying, or predicate, offense. In this case, the defendant was charged with four counts, three of which were ultimately dismissed, leaving only the "contributing to the delinquency of a minor" charge. The written decision does not clarify whether the underlying charge of unlawful sexual contact with a child was described within the count of conviction, or whether the court looked to dismissed counts within the information to determine the underlying illegal conduct. If the court's decision rested on a dismissed count, rather than a predicate offense identified within the actual count of conviction, then this author would argue it is an erroneous conclusion premised on a faulty analysis: to look at dismissed counts to arrive at a finding of removability is not allowable under a modified categorical approach.

[18] *Oouch v. Dept. of Homeland Security*, 633 F.3d 119 (2d Cir. 2010) (interpreting N.Y.P.L. §263.05).

[19] *Gaiskov v. Holder*, 567 F.3d 832, 836–37 (7th Cir. 2009) (holding that the crime of touching a minor with sexual intent constitutes sexual abuse of a minor); *Gattem v. Gonzales*, 412 F.3d 758, 765–67 (7th Cir. 2005) (holding that conviction for sexual solicitation, which did not require the defendant to physically touch the victim, qualified as a conviction for sexual abuse of a minor); *Bahar v. Ashcroft*, 264 F.3d 1309, 1310–13 (11th Cir. 2001) (*per curiam*) (holding that "taking indecent liberties" with a child under 16 for sexual gratification constitutes sexual abuse of a minor, even without physical contact); *Mugalli v. Ashcroft*, 258 F.3d 52 (2d Cir. 2001).

[20] *Estrada-Espinoza v. Mukasey*, 546 F.3d 1147 (9th Cir. 2008).

[21] *Matter of V–F–D–*, 23 I&N Dec. 859 (BIA 2006).

[22] *U.S. v. Medina-Villa*, 567 F.3d 507 (9th Cir. 2009) (expressly limiting the analysis in *Estrada-Espinoza v. Mukasey*, 546 F.3d 1147 (9th Cir. 2008), to statutory rape offenses).

CASE STUDY: MATTER OF ALFARO

Matter of Alfaro,[23] decided in 2011, involved a "statutory rape" offense wherein the respondent was 21 and the victim was 15. The BIA decided this case according to the *Silva-Trevino*[24] framework in the jurisdiction of the Ninth Circuit. The California statute in *Alfaro* did not contain an element of knowledge of the victim's age:

> Any person 21 years of age or older who engages in an act of unlawful sexual intercourse with a minor who is under 16 years of age is guilty of either a misdemeanor or a felony, and shall be punished by imprisonment in a county jail not exceeding one year, or by imprisonment in the state prison for two, three, or four years.[25]

Methodically proceeding under all three steps of the attorney general's *Silva-Trevino* analysis, the BIA found that the statute does not categorically define sexual abuse of a minor; there is a realistic probability that it could be used to prosecute persons who did not have knowledge of the age; and that the respondent's knowledge was subject to further evidentiary inquiry. The Board remanded to the immigration judge (IJ) for further proceedings to determine whether Alfaro knew his victim's age. Since *Alfaro*, the Ninth Circuit has rejected the *Silva-Trevino* analysis, so the case would not have been decided in the same way today.

BIA modifies approach in *Matter of Esquivel-Quintana*

In January 2015, the BIA introduced a slight modification to its strict approach to statutory rape cases in *Matter of Esquivel-Quintana*,[26] where the Board clarified that in the context of state statutory rape offenses, a statute that includes victims of 16- or 17-years old also must contain a meaningful age differential to constitute "sexual abuse of a minor." The Board emphasized that the holding is limited to sexual abuse statutes that may include 16- or 17-year-olds as victims and where lack of consent is not an element of the offense. The Board notes in *Esquivel-Quintana* that the Ninth Circuit disagrees with the "meaningful age difference" approach and holds that, by statute, the "victim" must be under the age of 16[27] and there must be more than a four-year age difference.[28] In comparison to the Ninth Circuit, the Seventh Circuit U.S.

---

[23] *Matter of Alfaro*, 25 I&N Dec. 417 (BIA 2011).

[24] *Matter of Silva-Trevino*, 24 I&N Dec. 687 (AG 2008). A full discussion of the facts and impact of this decision can be found in chapter five, "Methodology."

[25] Cal. Penal Code §261.5(d).

[26] *Matter of Esquivel-Quintana*, 26 I&N Dec. 469 (BIA 2015). The statute under review in *Esquivel-Quintana* was Cal. Penal Code §261.5(c).

[27] *Rivera-Cuartas v. Holder*, 605 F.3d 699, 701 (9th Cir. 2010).

[28] *Estrada-Espinoza v. Mukasey*, 546 F.3d 1147, 1159 (9th Cir. 2008).

Court of Appeals has deferred to the BIA's interpretation of INA §101(a)(43)(A) sexual abuse of a minor in the context of statutory rape cases.[29]

Drug Trafficking Crimes

INA §101(a)(43)(B) relates to controlled substance trafficking and defines aggravated felony using two phrases: "illicit trafficking," and a "federal drug trafficking crime":

> Illicit trafficking in a controlled substance (as defined in section 102 of the Controlled Substances Act), including a drug trafficking crime (as defined in section 924(c) of title 18, United States Code)[.]

A quick, plain reading of this section would indicate that only drug *trafficking* crimes qualify as aggravated felonies under this provision. However, INA §101(a)(43)(B)—as interpreted by the BIA and federal courts—may also encompass some recidivist simple possession offenses. Again, the section describes two categories of trafficking crimes, which are distinct concepts, but are overlapping (because illicit trafficking subsumes federal drug trafficking crime). The phrases are: *illicit* trafficking, and crimes that would be classified as felonies by the federal code—in other words, federal drug trafficking crimes. It is the latter provision that may include simple possession if charged according to a recidivist statute. However, to be a "federal felony drug trafficking crime," the state or foreign offense must be a categorical match to 18 USC §924(c).[30] The breadth and nuances of these provisions are discussed below.

Federal controlled-substance law

Any federal law violation involving the element of illicit trafficking (a commercial transaction) in a controlled substance as defined in §102 of the Controlled Substances Act (CSA)[31] is an aggravated felony.[32] The limited exception is distribution of a small amount of marijuana ("social sharing") without remuneration (discussed at some length below). Furthermore, INA §101(a)(43)(B) includes within the definition of aggravated felony any "drug trafficking crime" as defined in 18 USC §924(c). This phrase encompasses any felony[33] punishable under the CSA.

---

[29] *Velasco-Giron v. Holder*, 768 F.3d 723 (7th Cir. 2014).

[30] *Lopez v. Gonzales*, 549 U.S. 47, 60 (2006) (A conviction under state law constitutes a "felony punishable under the CSA" only if it proscribes conduct punishable as a felony under that federal law.)

[31] 21 USC §802(6).

[32] INA §101(a)(43)(B); 8 USC §1101(a)(43)(B).

[33] "Felony" is defined at 18 USC §3559(a) as an offense that carries a penalty of more than one year imprisonment. "Misdemeanor" is an offense that carries as a punishment one year or less imprisonment. Thus, a sentence of exactly one year, under the U.S. Code, is a misdemeanor. State codes do not necessarily follow this formula. Several states classify crimes as "misdemeanors" although they carry maximum sentences of more than one year in prison.

First-time simple possession not an aggravated felony—except for flunitrazepam

Federal law treats the first offense of simple possession of most controlled substances (*i.e.*, not involving trafficking) as a misdemeanor.[34] This means, for example, that a first offense of simple possession of cocaine or marijuana in the federal system is not an aggravated felony. The exception is flunitrazepam. First-time possession of flunitrazepam (marketed under the name Rohypnol and often referred to as the "date-rape drug"), is treated as a felony under the CSA,[35] and therefore qualifies as an aggravated felony under INA §101(a)(43)(B).[36]

Recidivist simple possession statutes

A second or subsequent offense for simple possession of a controlled substance in the federal judicial system may (and often is) punishable as a felony. Thus, a first-time straight (or simple) possession offense, without an element of sale or distribution, is not an aggravated felony drug trafficking crime. This is irrespective of amount. However, a subsequent simple possession charge may be prosecuted as a felony. Not all subsequent offenses will be charged, or successfully prosecuted, as felonies in the federal system. As discussed in greater detail in the section on simple possession, below, the federal statute at 21 USC §851 (on proceedings to establish prior convictions) requires that the prior conviction be final, and its existence must be specifically alleged in the charging document or through amendment. The defendant is entitled to a hearing on whether a legal, final conviction does indeed exist before he or she may be charged as a recidivist. In some cases, the U.S. Attorney may choose to charge the subsequent act as another misdemeanor, rather than as a recidivist felony offense.

State controlled-substance convictions

The challenge in determining whether a controlled substance conviction is an aggravated felony lies within the context of state convictions. A state offense that is classified as a felony and involves an element of trafficking (commercial trading or dealing) will be an aggravated felony under the illicit trafficking prong of INA §101(a)(43)(B). In addition, a state conviction will be an aggravated felony if it is a categorical match to a federal drug trafficking crime under the federal felony prong of INA §101(a)(43)(B). Also, a subsequent state offense for simple possession that is punished under a recidivist scheme might qualify as an aggravated felony drug trafficking crime. In either situation (illicit trafficking or federal felony), federal law determines whether the state controlled-substance offense qualifies as an aggravated felony: a defendant must actually be convicted of a crime that is punishable as a

---

[34] 21 USC §844(a).

[35] 21 USC §844(a).

[36] Until recently, first-time simple possession of crack cocaine (as compared to cocaine base) was treated as a felony. However, the Fair Sentencing Act of 2010 (Pub. L. No. 111-220) eliminated the five-year minimum mandatory sentence for possession of crack cocaine, and brought crack into par with other controlled substances for sentencing purposes.

felony under federal law.[37] Whether an offense qualifies as a federal felony drug trafficking crime is based on a categorical approach.

Misdemeanor trafficking?

In some circumstances, a controlled substance offense that is classified as a misdemeanor under state law can be an aggravated felony drug offense. This would occur under the second phrase of INA §101(a)(43)(B): the federal drug trafficking crime. In *Matter of Davis*,[38] the respondent was convicted of conspiracy to distribute a controlled substance, a misdemeanor, in the state of Maryland. The BIA found that, although classified by Maryland as a misdemeanor, the underlying conspiracy offense included the elements of delivery of a controlled substance—which would be punishable as a federal felony—and therefore qualified as an aggravated felony.

> [I]f the offense is not designated as a felony [under the convicting sovereign] it may nonetheless be a 'drug trafficking crime' (and therefore 'illicit trafficking' and an 'aggravated felony') if it is analogous to an offense punishable under one of the federal acts specified in 18 U.S.C. §924(c)(2) and the offense to which it is analogous is a 'felony' under federal law.[39]

Offenses involving the element of illicit trafficking

The BIA has held that an aggravated felony drug trafficking crime includes any state, federal, or qualified foreign felony conviction involving the unlawful trading or dealing of a controlled substance, as defined in §102 of the CSA.[40] Illicit trafficking means commercial dealing.[41] Thus, trafficking involves the aspects of commerce, trade, sale, and exchange of goods; this includes, most obviously, sale. It may involve delivery, importation, and manufacturing, as well as possession with intent to do any of the above, if there is an element of consideration. The substance must appear on the federal controlled substance list of schedules.[42] For a state offense to fall under the illicit trafficking prong, it must be classified as a felony by the state.[43]

---

[37] *Moncrieffe v. Holder*, 133 S. Ct. 1678 (2013); *Carachuri-Rosendo v. Holder*, 560 U.S. 563 (2010); *Lopez v. Gonzales*, 549 U.S. 47 (2006).

[38] *Matter of Davis*, 20 I&N Dec. 536 (BIA 1992), *modified on other grounds by Matter of Yanez-Garcia*, 23 I&N Dec. 390 (BIA 2002) (Note: *Yanez-Garcia* was overruled by the Supreme Court's decision in *Carachuri-Rosendo v. Holder*, 560 U.S. 563 (2010)).

[39] *Matter of Davis*, 20 I&N Dec. 536 at 543.

[40] *Matter of Davis*, 20 I&N Dec. 536 (BIA 1992), *overruled in part on other grounds by Matter of Yanez-Garcia*, 23 I&N Dec. 390 (BIA 2002) ((Note: *Yanez-Garcia* was overruled by the Supreme Court's decision in *Carachuri-Rosendo v. Holder*, 560 U.S. 563 (2010)).

[41] *Lopez v. Gonzales*, 549 U.S. 47, 53–54 (2006).

[42] *Matter of Sanchez-Cornejo*, 25 I&N Dec. 273, 274 (BIA 2010), *citing Matter of Davis*, 20 I&N Dec. 536, 541 (BIA 1992); *modified, Matter of Yanez*, 23 I&N Dec. 390 (2002).

[43] *Matter of Sanchez-Cornejo*, 25 I&N Dec. 273, 274 (BIA 2010).

Divisible statutes

State statutes may be divisible because they include acts of dealing, manufacturing, and delivery, as well as straight possession. In this circumstance, it is important to review the entire record of conviction to determine whether the client was charged with a trafficking-type offense, or simple possession.[44]

In *Matter of L–G–H–*,[45] the BIA found that Florida's controlled substance law was an example of a divisible statute. Fla. Stat. §893.13(1)(a)(1) includes the offenses of sale, purchase, manufacture, delivery, possession with intent to sell, possession with intent to purchase, possession with intent to manufacture, and possession with intent to deliver. Adopting a modified categorical approach, the BIA found that the information charged "sale" and that this was an illicit trafficking offense. The BIA observed that manufacture could be for personal marijuana use, and delivery may be without remuneration. These offenses would not meet the so-called "commercial transaction test." Of note, the BIA found that Fla. Stat. §893.13(1)(a)(1) did not qualify as a federal felony drug trafficking crime (the second prong of INA §101(a)(43)(B)) because the Florida statute is unique among state laws in that it does not contain a *mens rea* of knowledge of the illegal substance.[46] In comparison, 18 USC §924(c) does require knowledge. Nevertheless, according to the BIA, a *mens rea* of knowledge is not necessary to qualify under the illicit trafficking prong. The Board found the conviction to be an aggravated felony.

The BIA's decision in *Matter of L–G–H–* is in response to the Eleventh Circuit's decision in *Donawa v. Att'y Gen.*[47] In *Donawa*, the Eleventh Circuit applied a strict categorical approach in analyzing whether a conviction under Florida law was punishable as a federal felony and found it was not. The decision illustrates an excellent application of the categorical and modified categorical approach. The court reversed the finding of aggravated felony, but remanded because the BIA had not addressed in its decision the illicit trafficking prong of INA §101(a)(43)(B). Rather than take up the *Donawa* case, however, the BIA selected *L–G–H–*, a case involving a detained individual with a conviction record that denoted "sale." *L–G–H–* did not file an appeal to the Eleventh Circuit, thus the BIA's analysis has not yet been put to the test. There are several problems with the decision. The BIA finds that the terms sale, delivery, manufacture, etc., are distinct offenses and reverts to a modified categorical approach. However, these terms represent means, not elements, under Florida jury instructions. Therefore, a modified categorical approach should not be applied. Moreover, it is not clear that a court of appeals (or Supreme Court) would agree that the phrase "illicit trafficking" does not require the offense to be a

---

[44] *Matter of L–G–H–*, 26 I&N Dec. 365 (BIA 2014) (describing Florida's controlled substance statute as divisible and delineating the distinct terms).

[45] *Matter of L–G–H–*, 26 I&N Dec. 365 (BIA 2014).

[46] *Matter of L–G–H–*, at 367, *citing*: Donawa v. Att'y Gen., 735 F.3d 1275 (11th Cir. 2013).

[47] *Donawa v. Att'y Gen.*, 735 F.3d 1275 (11th Cir. 2013).

categorical match to 18 USC §924(c). If illicit trafficking must be a federal categorical match, then the Florida statute's omission of the *mens rea* of knowledge would eliminate the crime from the aggravated felony definition. As of spring 2015, it remains to be seen when *L–G–H–*'s analysis will be tested.

To sum up, a controlled substance conviction will be an aggravated felony illicit/trafficking crime under INA §101(a)(43)(B) if:

- it is a felony and contains the element of commercial dealing in a federally controlled substance; and/or
- it is punishable as a felony under the federal CSA (or a state counterpart).

Distribution Without Remuneration: *Moncrieffe v. Holder*[48]

Federal law contains an exception for distributing a small amount of marijuana for no remuneration: the CSA states that an individual who violates 21 USC §841(a) by distributing a small amount of marijuana for no remuneration will be punished under the misdemeanor provisions at 21 USC §844.[49] On April 2, 2012, the U.S. Supreme Court accepted certiorari in *Moncrieffe v. Holder* to resolve a split in the circuit courts of appeals as to whether a state statute that did not include a misdemeanor provision for non-remuneration distribution could ever be an aggravated felony drug trafficking crime. To understand the significance of *Moncrieffe,* it is helpful to know the issue in terms of the circuit split leading up to the Supreme Court.

In 2007, in a case called *Jeune v. Att'y Gen.*,[50] both the IJ and BIA had ordered the respondent removed for a "drug trafficking" aggravated felony crime, but the Third Circuit U.S. Court of Appeals disagreed. The respondent had been convicted of a violation of 35 Pa. Cons. Stat. §780-113(a)(30), entitled "manufacture, delivery, or possession of a controlled substance." This statute reads as follows:

§780-113. Prohibited acts; penalties

(a) The following acts and the causing thereof within the Commonwealth are hereby prohibited:

(30) Except as authorized by this act, the manufacture, delivery, or possession with intent to manufacture or deliver, a controlled substance by a person not registered under this act, or a practitioner not registered or licensed by the appropriate State board, or knowingly creating, delivering or possessing with intent to deliver, a counterfeit controlled substance.

Noting that the statute includes various acts, including manufacturing, delivery, and possession with intent to deliver, the court assumed the least culpable conduct (the "bare

---

[48] *Moncrieffe v. Holder*, 133 S. Ct. 1678 (2013).

[49] 21 USC §841(b)(1)(D).

[50] *Jeune v. Att'y Gen.*, 476 F.3d 199 (3d Cir. 2007).

minimum necessary to trigger" a conviction) described by the statute.[51] The minimum conduct envisioned by the statute, the court concluded, would be manufacturing for personal use (*e.g.,* growing marijuana plants for personal consumption). Noting that the Pennsylvania statute did not include the requirement of remuneration, and that growing marijuana for personal use would not constitute illicit trafficking, the Third Circuit declined to find that the conviction constituted an aggravated felony drug trafficking crime, thereby vacating the removal order.[52]

The issue was how to interpret a state controlled-substance statute that did not present a categorical match to the federal CSA because there was no misdemeanor treatment of distribution without remuneration of a small amount of marijuana. In the absence of a non-remuneration provision, many state statutes punish this conduct as a felony. Under a strict categorical/modified categorical approach, an IJ should not go behind the elements of the statute or record of conviction to determine whether the conduct involved distribution without remuneration. Yet, there was a split in the circuits as to whether strict adherence to a categorical approach should apply in this situation.

The Second Circuit, in *Martinez v. Mukasey*,[53] agreed with the Third Circuit, finding that where a state statute punishes both trafficking and non-remuneration crimes as felonies (or said another way, contains no exception for distribution without remuneration of marijuana) and the record of conviction does not specify the activity charged, the adjudicator should assume the least culpable conduct described by statute. The First[54] and Sixth[55] Circuit Courts of Appeals disagreed, however, finding that the misdemeanor classification is a "default punishment," rather than a stand-alone crime.[56] The amount of marijuana is not an element of the offense, but rather, a consideration at sentencing.[57] According to these courts, the sentencing provision is a "carve-out," or exception, that allows the criminal court to consider that the offense basically involved social sharing of marijuana in determining whether the conviction should not be punished with the five-year minimum mandatory sentence required for most federal controlled-substance violations. Accordingly, these courts (pre-*Moncrieffe*) required the respondent to prove that the offense conduct involved distribution of marijuana without remuneration in order to defeat the aggravated felony charge. They took a circumstance-specific approach to the issue, rather than a categorical view.

---

[51] *Jeune v. Att'y Gen.*, 476 F.3d 199 (3d Cir. 2007) (citing to *Partyka v. Att'y Gen.*, 417 F.3d 408, 411 (3d Cir. 2005)).

[52] The *Jeune* court relied heavily on its decision in *Garcia v. Att'y Gen.*, 462 F.3d 287 (3d Cir. 2006), which also contains a good analysis of divisible statutes and the record of conviction in the controlled substance context.

[53] *Martinez v. Mukasey*, 551 F.3d 113 (2d Cir. 2008).

[54] *Juice v. Mukasey*, 530 F.3d 30 (1st Cir. 2008).

[55] *Garcia v. Holder*, 638 F.3d 511 (6th Cir. 2011).

[56] *Moncrieffe v. Holder*, 662 F.3d 387 (5th Cir. 2011).

[57] *See* 21 USC §§841(b)(4), (b)(1)(D).

In 2012, before *Moncrieffe*, the BIA weighed in on the issue of distribution of a small amount of marijuana without remuneration in a case called *Matter of Castro-Rodriguez*.[58] The BIA found that an individual convicted of possession of marijuana with intent to distribute under state law had the burden of showing that the offense was not an aggravated felony because it was a small amount passed with no remuneration. The BIA further clarified that the issue of amount and remuneration may take into consideration evidence outside the record of conviction (a "circumstance specific" approach). In so doing, the BIA modified its previous decision in *Matter of Aruna*.[59]

CASE STUDY: MONCRIEFFE v. HOLDER (Categorical Approach)

On April 2, 2012, the Supreme Court accepted certiorari in *Moncrieffe v. Holder*. This case arose out of a Fifth Circuit U.S. Court of Appeals decision[60] in which the court agreed with the First and Sixth Circuits—that the burden of proof was on the non–American citizen to establish that his or her offense conduct involved the federal misdemeanor offense of distribution of a small amount of marijuana for no remuneration. The Supreme Court was obliged to consider a Georgia controlled-substance statute that contained no exception for distribution without remuneration of marijuana. The reader should be clear on the choice of analyses presented when juxtaposing the state and federal code provisions:

Choice #1: *Categorical.* Because the state statute is not an absolute match to the federal definition of a "drug trafficking crime," the courts assume the least culpable conduct, distribution without remuneration, with no further analysis. [Meaning, this sort of state statute will *never* be a drug trafficking crime where the controlled substance in question is marijuana.]

Choice #2: *Modified categorical approach.* The state statute is overly broad, but does this make it divisible? Under a modified categorical approach, the courts would look to the record of conviction to ascertain whether there was remuneration.

Choice #3: *Circumstance specific.* The burden falls on the respondent to establish that the offense conduct involved distribution without remuneration of a small amount of marijuana.

Moncrieffe's conviction could correspond to either the CSA felony or the CSA misdemeanor. Ambiguity on this point means that the conviction did not "necessarily" involve facts that correspond to an offense punishable as a felony under

---

[58] *Matter of Castro-Rodriguez*, 25 I&N Dec. 698 (BIA 2012).
[59] *Matter of Aruna*, 24 I&N Dec. 452 (BIA 2008).
[60] *Moncrieffe v. Holder*, 662 F.3d 387 (5th Cir. 2011).

the CSA. Under the categorical approach, then, Moncrieffe was not convicted of an aggravated felony.[61]

Moncrieffe applies a strict categorical approach to analyzing state statutes for possible aggravated felony classification. In the absence of a state statute that presents a categorical match to the federal CSA, the conviction cannot be an aggravated felony. The Court then presumed the least culpable conduct under the federal code, distribution without remuneration of marijuana—a misdemeanor. The larger importance of *Moncrieffe* is the Court's analysis and explanation of the categorical approach. This is not an analysis that only applies to controlled substance cases, but is applicable to classifying crimes under the INA in general (unless the ground takes a circumstance-specific approach because it contains a non-elemental fact). *Moncrieffe* and *Descamps*[62] complement each other as precedent on the categorical approach to analyzing crime.

Practitioners will note that distribution without remuneration only applies in the context of marijuana. The federal statute's exception refers to marijuana. Criminal courts have been unwilling to apply the non-remuneration exception for distribution of a small amount of controlled substance in the context of cocaine or other controlled substances. Criminal courts have noted that "distribution" of a controlled substance does not need to be for financial consideration and even social sharing of a controlled substance without sale qualifies as "delivery."[63]

CASE STUDY: MATTER OF FERREIRA (Realistic Probability)

Matter of Ferreira,[64] decided after both *Moncrieffe* and *Descamps*, addressed whether a state trafficking crime could qualify as an aggravated felony where the state controlled-substance schedule was not a precise match to the federal CSA. The respondent challenged whether his Connecticut conviction for sale of certain illegal drugs[65] qualified as an aggravated felony or controlled substance violation (under INA §237(a)(2)(B)), where the Connecticut schedule of controlled substances varied from the federal CSA[66] based on the state's inclusion of two drugs, benzylfentanyl and thenylfentanyl, not found in the federal controlled-substance schedules. The plea

---

[61] *Moncrieffe v. Holder*, 133 S. Ct. 1678, 1687 (2013).

[62] *Descamps v. United States*, 133 S. Ct. 2276 (2013).

[63] *U.S. v. Wallace*, 532 F.3d 126 (2d Cir. 2008).

[64] *Matter of Ferreira*, 26 I&N Dec. 415 (BIA 2014).

[65] Conn. Crim. Code §21a-277(a).

[66] 21 USC §802(6).

colloquy in this case did mention "narcotic," and on that basis, the IJ ordered removal. However, the BIA found that because the Connecticut statute was broader than the federal provision, the judge erred in proceeding to a modified categorical approach. Nevertheless, the BIA did remand to the IJ for a hearing for a realistic probability analysis. By 2014, the two drugs had been excluded from Connecticut's schedules. The purpose of remand was for the respondent to demonstrate a realistic probability that Connecticut used the statute to prosecute offenses involving the two obscure drugs.

The *Ferreira* decision is not the first time a non–American citizen has raised the issue of non-matching state controlled-substance schedules:

- In 1965, in *Matter of Paulus*,[67] the BIA upheld a special inquiry officer's decision to terminate deportation proceedings where the respondent was convicted for selling or delivering a narcotic drug, yet the record of conviction was silent as to the type of narcotic involved, and the California definition of narcotic drug was different from federal law.

- *Paulus* was applied with favor in *Ruiz-Vidal v. Gonzales*,[68] wherein the Ninth Circuit granted the non–American citizen's petition for review because the record did not establish that the substance involved in the California conviction for transportation of a controlled substance[69] was in fact on a federal schedule.

- However, in *Mellouli v. Holder*,[70] the Eighth Circuit U.S. Court of Appeals looked with disfavor on this approach and stated that *Paulus* (again, a 1965 case) had essentially been abrogated by statute (the aggravated felony definition), and although the BIA has not expressly overruled *Paulus*, it is no longer controlling authority. The *Mellouli* decision went before the Supreme Court in 2015.[71] *Mellouli* involves removability under INA §237(a)(2)(B) for the possession-of-a-controlled-substance ground of removability, rather than an aggravated felony charge, and is discussed in the next chapter in the section on controlled substance violations.

- In *Rojas v. AG of the United States*, the Third Circuit U.S. Court of Appeals issued a decision in contrast to *Mellouli,* finding that if the state controlled-substance schedule is broader than the federal, and the record of conviction is silent as to the drug, there can be no further inquiry.[72]

---

[67] *Matter of Paulus*, 11 I&N Dec. 274 (BIA 1965).
[68] *Ruiz-Vidal v. Gonzales*, 473 F.3d 1072 (9th Cir. 2007).
[69] Calif. Penal Code §11378.
[70] *Mellouli v. Holder*, 719 F.3d 995 (8th Cir. 2014).
[71] *Mellouli v. Holder*, 134 S. Ct. 2873 (2014).
[72] *Rojas v. Att'y Gen.*, 728 F.3d 203 (3d Cir. 2013). *Rojas* is also a simple possession case under INA §237(a)(2)(B) and is discussed in the next chapter.

Prescription Drugs

Whether a drug qualifies as a controlled substance is determined by the CSA, found at 21 USC §§801–904. Certainly, prescription drugs may in certain instances also be controlled substances, found on Schedules I through V, as listed at 21 USC §812. However, prescription drugs are not necessarily—or automatically—controlled substances. The Federal Food, Drug and Cosmetic Act (FDCA) at 21 USC §§201–399d regulates prescription drugs. In *Borrome v. Att'y Gen.*,[73] the Third Circuit found that, categorically, the FDCA is not a divisible statute, and, to the extent that it regulates the distribution of prescription drugs, a violation of the FDCA is not an aggravated felony drug trafficking crime, even if the underlying substances at issue also qualify as controlled substances under the CSA.

The respondent in *Borrome* was convicted under 21 USC §§331(t) and 353(e) for the illegal wholesale distribution of certain prescription drugs, including but not limited to Oxycontin, a substance under the CSA. Noting that sections 331(t) and 353(e) do not reference the term "controlled substance," and, further, that illegal distribution of prescription drugs is not punishable under the CSA, the court found that this offense was not a hypothetical federal felony. (The court also found that the petitioner's conviction did not qualify as a ground of removability under INA §237(a)(2)(B), which is discussed further in this chapter in the section on controlled substance violations.)

Purchase of a Controlled Substance

The above cases on trafficking raise the question of whether purchase of a small amount of a controlled substance—an amount indicative of personal use—can qualify as an aggravated felony drug trafficking crime. The theme of the above cases implies that a state misdemeanor conviction for purchase of a small amount of a controlled substance (an amount indicative of personal use only) cannot meet the definition of aggravated felony. However, ICE regularly charges "purchasing" crimes as aggravated felonies, equating "purchase" to illicit dealing. Certainly it does not seem fair that purchase of a small amount of marijuana, for example, should be dealt with more harshly than possession of marijuana. Case law is not clear on the matter.

In *Matter of L–G–*, the BIA opined in dicta contained within a footnote that purchase can be viewed as commercial trafficking because the act of purchasing facilitates the distribution.[74] The BIA cited to a criminal case called *U.S. v. Binkley*,[75] in which the Seventh Circuit U.S. Court of Appeals held that a customer purchasing drugs might be considered part of the drug trafficking conspiracy. The dissent in *Binkley* makes for outstanding reading and may serve as immigration counsel's template in challenging the

---

[73] *Borrome v. Att'y Gen.*, 687 F.3d 150 (3d Cir. 2012).

[74] *Matter of L–G–*, 21 I&N Dec. 89 (BIA 1995), *overruled in part by Matter of Yanez-Garcia*, 23 I&N Dec. 390 (2002) (Note that *Yanez-Garcia* was abrogated by the Supreme Court's decision in *Lopez v. Gonzales*, 549 U.S. 57, 60 (2006).

[75] *U.S. v. Binkley*, 903 F.2d 1130 (7th Cir. 1990).

proposition that "purchase" equates with "trafficking." In 2009, the Supreme Court rejected the *Binkley* holding and others like it in a case called *Abuelhawa v. U.S.*[76] The Court found that the individual buyer of a misdemeanor amount does not facilitate commercial distribution of a controlled substance when he utilizes a communications facility to purchase a controlled substance.[77] The *Abuelhawa* decision sets forth a strong analogy for arguing that the act of purchasing a small amount of a controlled substance for personal use is not distribution and does not qualify as aggravated felony drug trafficking.

In an unpublished decision from the Ninth Circuit, *U.S. v. Navarro-Coyazo*,[78] a criminal case involving a sentencing enhancement for deportation and re-entry after being convicted of an aggravated felony, the court found that purchasing a controlled substance under Cal. Health & Safety Code §11351 does not automatically qualify as a drug trafficking crime because the statute does not require proof of actual purchase; rather, a conviction may be premised on an offer or attempt to purchase. Unfortunately, the focus of this decision seems to be the fact that an offer to purchase does not require actual constructive possession of the controlled substance; the opinion does not turn on the nature of the purchase itself.

Decided in 2014, *Matter of L–G–H–*, discussed above, implies that purchase might not involve a commercial transaction because the decision focuses only on the term "sale." The statute includes several terms, among them "purchase." However, the Board expressly declines to address the statute's terms beyond "sale."[79]

State Simple-Possession Offenses: A Mixed Approach

Prior to December 2006, it was in the context of state simple possession offenses that defining "drug trafficking crime" was most challenging. Because INA §101(a)(43)(B) defines "drug trafficking crime" as any felony punishable under 18 USC §924(c)(2), the question became: whose felony—state or federal? This section describes the evolution of classifying state simple possession offenses.

To frame the question: if a controlled substance offense was classified and punished as a felony by state law, but qualified as a misdemeanor under the federal code, did it qualify as an aggravated felony for immigration law purposes by virtue of the state's categorization of the offense? Flipping the question presented the reverse issue: if the state classified and punished an offense as a misdemeanor, but under the federal code it was punishable as a felony, was the offense an aggravated felony based on the federal scheme? These issues—which, for over a decade, inspired much litigation at the BIA and the circuit courts—were ostensibly resolved in two Supreme Court decisions in 2006 and 2010. However, as illustrated by the cases discussed

---

[76] *Abuelhawa v. U.S.*, 129 U.S. 2102 (2009).

[77] Use of a communications facility to commit a felony is punishable by 21 USC §843(b).

[78] *U.S. v. Navarro-Coyazo*, 108 Fed. Appx. 490, 2004 U.S. App. LEXIS 18530, 2004 WL 1923588 (9th Cir. Wash. 2004).

[79] *Matter of L–G–H–*, 26 I&N Dec. 365, 374 (BIA 2014).

below, the door to controversy over when a second or subsequent state simple-possession offense qualifies as an aggravated felony is in fact not entirely closed.

Review of the litigation history surrounding application of INA §101(a)(43)(B) in the state simple possession context is instructive in understanding the categorical approach. The federal criminal code defines "felony" as any crime punishable by more than one year in prison. Up to and including one year is considered a misdemeanor.[80] State criminal codes do not necessarily follow this formula. It is possible for an offense to be called—or labeled—a "misdemeanor" by a particular state code, but remain punishable by more than one year in prison. Conversely, some state codes may label a certain offense a "felony," but not impose a punishment of more than one year.

The "hypothetical felony" approach

As stated above, a state offense will be an aggravated felony drug trafficking crime if the statute is a categorical match to the federal CSA. Until May 2002, the BIA defined "aggravated felony" in the context of state simple possession offenses by asking whether the crime *could be* punished as a felony under the federal law. Under this so-called hypothetical felony approach, first articulated in *Matter of L–G–*,[81] the BIA looked to the underlying offense conduct to determine whether the crime would be punished as a felony or a misdemeanor under federal law. The federal CSA punishes first-offense simple possession of a controlled substance (at the time, anything other than crack[82] or flunitrazepam) as a misdemeanor.[83] This includes situations involving a large amount of the drug. (The operative word is "simple" possession, rather than "personal" possession.)

The practical effect of the BIA's approach in *L–G–* was that first-offense simple possession of cocaine, marijuana, heroin, etc. (anything but flunitrazepam), was not an aggravated felony under the INA, even if it was classified as a felony by state law. This approach cut both ways. This was a good result for the first-time offender convicted of simple possession, but not necessarily for an individual convicted of multiple simple possession crimes.

The hypothetical felony approach did not acknowledge or honor the state's treatment of the offense, but turned the crime into a hypothetical federal offense. The justification for this approach was arguably sound: to avoid the vagaries of state law

---

[80] 18 USC §3559(a); *see U.S. v. Medina-Villa*, 567 F.3d 507 (9th Cir. 2009) (expressly limiting the analysis in *Estrada-Espinoza*, 546 F.3d 1147 (9th Cir. 2008) to statutory rape offenses).

[81] *Matter of L–G–*, 21 I&N Dec. 89 (BIA 1995), *overruled in part by Matter of Yanez-Garcia*, 23 I&N Dec. 390 (BIA 2002).

[82] Crack cocaine has since been removed from the list of controlled substances that are punished as a felony for the first-time offense. The Fair Sentencing Act of 2010 (Pub. L. No. 111-220) eliminated the five-year minimum mandatory sentence for possession of crack cocaine and brought crack cocaine into par with other controlled substances for sentencing purposes.

[83] 21 USC §844(a).

from ultimately imposing different immigration law penalties on persons guilty of essentially the same conduct.

Over time, several circuit courts of appeals disagreed with the BIA's approach in *L–G–*. In rejecting the BIA's decision in *L–G–*, these courts held instead that a state conviction classified or labeled as a felony by the state is an aggravated felony for sentencing guideline purposes, even if the offense would not have been punished as a felony under the federal code.[84] Notably, the criticism occurred not in the context of removal cases on appeal, but in criminal sentencing guidelines cases—specifically, federal criminal prosecutions for re-entry after removal. According to the *U.S. Sentencing Guideline Manual* §2L1.2, a non–American citizen convicted of unlawfully entering or remaining in the United States after deportation for a criminal conviction will have his or her sentence increased eight levels if the conviction was for an aggravated felony. In sentencing re-entry convictions, the federal district courts may apply a significant punishment enhancement irrespective of whether the defendant had actually been charged with and deported for an aggravated felony offense in prior removal proceedings. If the *sentencing* court determined the conduct to be an aggravated felony offense, the enhancement would apply. Furthermore, *in the sentencing context*, a state drug conviction constitutes a "drug trafficking crime" (and therefore an aggravated felony for immigration-law purposes) if (1) it is punishable under the CSA or other federal statute, and (2) it is a felony under federal or state law.[85]

The "guidelines" approach

In May 2002, the BIA issued two side-by-side decisions that changed its traditional approach to the drug trafficking crime analysis. These cases were *Matter of Yanez-Garcia*[86] and *Matter of Santos-Lopez*.[87] Notably, in these two decisions the BIA relied heavily on sentencing guidelines cases from the federal courts—as opposed to federal court appeals of actual removal cases. The BIA held that from those decisions forward, it would apply the law as set forth by the specific federal court of appeals in whose jurisdiction the case arose. In the event that the circuit court had not issued a precedent decision on the issue, it would follow the rule of the majority of circuits. Thus, the rule in removal cases involving a state conviction for first-time simple possession of a controlled substance became the "guidelines" approach: if state law classifies (or labels) the controlled substance offense as a felony, it is an aggravated felony, regardless of how the same offense would have been punished by federal law.

---

[84] See note 91 for circuit court decisions contrary to the BIA's approach.

[85] For a useful overview of the different approaches and a summary explanation of the guidelines approach, see *Liao v. Rabbett*, 398 F.3d 389, 392 (6th Cir. 2005). The circuits adopting the "guidelines" approach are listed in the text.

[86] *Matter of Yanez-Garcia*, 23 I&N Dec. 390 (BIA 2002).

[87] *Matter of Santos-Lopez*, 23 I&N Dec. 419 (BIA 2002).

Under *Yanez-Garcia*, the test for determining whether a state offense is a drug trafficking crime, and hence an aggravated felony, became:

(1) Is it conduct that is punishable by federal law?[88] (Note, as discussed below, that not *all* conceivable drug-related activity is covered by federal law.)

(2) Does it involve the element of trafficking?

—or—

(3) Is it classified as a felony by the state?

Under this test, if the offense involves an element of trafficking, it is an aggravated felony,[89] regardless of whether the state classifies it as a misdemeanor.[90] If the offense involves simple possession, but is classified as a felony by the state, it is an aggravated felony.

Dueling circuits

The *Yanez-Garcia* decision became the proverbial line in the sand; by the fall of 2006, six federal circuits[91] had issued decisions following the guidelines approach, ruling that a state felony offense for simple possession was an aggravated felony for immigration purposes. This determination was not necessarily bad for the non–American citizen. In these "guidelines" jurisdictions, a state misdemeanor controlled-substance violation—including a second or subsequent misdemeanor offense—was not an aggravated felony. This was useful to persons with multiple misdemeanor convictions, *e.g.*, personal possession of marijuana. On the other hand, first-offense simple possession of a controlled substance—where classified as a felony by the state—was an aggravated felony for immigration purposes, irrespective of the fact that the same conduct would be punished as a misdemeanor in the federal system.

---

[88] The three relevant federal statutes are the Controlled Substances Act (21 USC §801 *et seq.*), the Controlled Substances Import and Export Act (21 USC §951 *et seq.*), and the Maritime Drug Law Enforcement Act (46 USC app. §1901 *et seq.*). *See* 18 USC §924(c)(2).

[89] *But see Wilson v. Ashcroft*, 350 F.3d 377 (3d Cir. 2003), stating that distribution of a small amount of marijuana without remuneration is not treated as a drug trafficking crime by the federal code, and, therefore, a state conviction for distribution of small amounts of marijuana without remuneration is not an aggravated felony drug trafficking crime. Note this case arose in the context of expedited (administrative) removal (see chapter three); the petitioner was indeed physically removed. The court found his removal to be contrary to law because he was not properly classified as an aggravated felon.

[90] Three misdemeanor convictions, including two for sale or distribution of marijuana, under New York law were found to be aggravated felonies in *U.S. v. Simpson*, 319 F.3d 81 (2d Cir. 2002).

[91] Prior to December 2006, the following circuit courts of appeals defined "aggravated felony" to include controlled substance violations punishable as felonies by the state: First Circuit: *U.S. v. Restrepo-Aguilar*, 74 F.3d 361 (1st Cir. 1996); Fourth Circuit: *U.S. v. Amaya-Portillo*, 423 F.3d 427 (4th Cir. 2005); Fifth Circuit: *U.S. v. Hernandez-Avalos*, 251 F.3d 505 (5th Cir. 2001); Eighth Circuit: *Lopez v. Gonzales*, 417 F.3d 934 (8th Cir. 2005) and *U.S. v. Briones-Mata*, 116 F.3d 308 (8th Cir. 1997); Tenth Circuit: *U.S. v. Castro-Rocha*, 323 F.3d 846 (10th Cir. 2003); Eleventh Circuit: *U.S. v. Simon*, 168 F.3d 1271 (11th Cir. 1999).

Three federal circuits went with the "hypothetical felony" approach (also known as the L–G– approach), and issued decisions holding that in order to be an aggravated felony for immigration purposes, the conduct must be punishable as a felony under the federal criminal code.[92] In these circuits, first-offense simple possession of a controlled substance—though punishable as a felony by the state—did not automatically constitute an aggravated felony conviction. Of course, multiple state misdemeanors could result in classification as an aggravated felony in these circuits, as recidivist offenses are punishable as felonies by federal law.

Two federal circuits adopted a hybrid approach, interpreting "aggravated felony" according to the hypothetical (L–G–) felony approach for removal cases, and applying the state definition of "felony" for sentencing guidelines cases in the criminal-law context (i.e., in those cases in the sentencing phases of criminal prosecution for re-entry after removal).[93]

The Supreme Court's decision in Lopez v. Gonzales

In 2006, the Supreme Court resolved the circuit conflict and effectively overruled the BIA's decisions in *Matter of Yanez-Garcia* and *Matter of Santos-Lopez*. In *Lopez v. Gonzales*,[94] the Supreme Court held that a state offense constitutes a "felony punishable under the Controlled Substances Act" only if the proscribed conduct is punishable as a felony under the federal law. The fact that the state code may or may not label the offense a "felony" is not determinative. As stated in the section on federal controlled-substance law, above, first-time simple possession of a controlled substance (even a large amount) may be prosecuted and punished as a misdemeanor by 21 USC §844(a). The exception is simple possession of flunitrazepam (otherwise known as Rohypnol.) Accordingly, regardless of whether the state classifies the crime as a felony, first-time simple possession of a controlled substance is *not* an aggravated felony.

However, the *Lopez* decision left another question unanswered: whether a state conviction for second or subsequent (multiple) simple possession of a controlled substance is an "aggravated felony." Bearing in mind the *Lopez* court's phraseology, "punishable as a felony under the federal Controlled Substances Act," the question became whether a subsequent state conviction for simple possession of a controlled substance is necessarily an aggravated felony because it could be punished as such in the federal system. Following *Lopez,* two circuit courts of appeals found that a second or subsequent state conviction for simple possession of a controlled substance—even if classified as a misdemeanor by the state—qualified as a hypothetical federal felony

---

[92] Third Circuit: *Gerbier v. Holmes*, 280 F.3d 297 (3d Cir. 2002); Sixth Circuit: *U.S. v. Palacios-Suarez*, 418 F.3d 692 (6th Cir. 2005); Seventh Circuit: *Gonzalez-Gomez v. Achim*, 441 F.3d 532 (7th Cir. 2006).

[93] Second Circuit: *U.S. v. Pornes Garcia*, 171 F.3d 142 (2d Cir. 1999) and *Aguirre v. INS*, 79 F.3d 315 (2d Cir. 1996); Ninth Circuit: *U.S. v. Ibarra-Galindo*, 206 F.3d 1337 (9th Cir. 2000) and *Cazarez-Gutierrez v. Ashcroft*, 382 F.3d 905 (9th Cir. 2004).

[94] *Lopez v. Gonzales*, 549 U.S. 47 (2006).

and was therefore an aggravated felony.[95] These circuits reasoned that if the criminal conduct was punishable as a federal felony, it should be treated as an aggravated felony for immigration law purposes. The problem with this approach, however, is that it ignores the complex nature of successfully prosecuting a case as a felony under federal law.

The Federal Recidivist Statute

Under 21 USC §844(a), a person who violates the law by possessing a controlled substance (other than flunitrazepam) may be sentenced to a term of imprisonment of not more than one year—except that if he or she commits the offense after having a prior conviction for a controlled substance offense, the offense may be prosecuted as a felony. Thus, a second or subsequent offense may become a felony if the prosecutor elects to prosecute the case as a felony and can establish the recidivist elements. A careful reading of §844(a) is important for counsel seeking to defend against an aggravated felony designation for a subsequent state simple possession offense. The provision reads, in pertinent part:

> [It shall be unlawful for any person knowingly or intentionally to possess a controlled substance ...] Any person who violates this subsection may be sentenced to a term of imprisonment of not more than 1 year, and shall be fined a minimum of $1,000 or both, except that if he commits such offense after a prior conviction under this subchapter or subchapter II of the chapter, or a prior conviction for any drug, narcotic, or chemical, offense chargeable under the law of any State, *has become final*, he shall be sentenced to a term of imprisonment for not less than 15 days but not more than 2 years, and shall be fined a minimum of $2,500, except, further, that if he commits such offense after two or more prior convictions under this subchapter or subchapter II of the chapter, or two or more prior convictions for any drug, narcotic, or chemical offense chargeable under the law of any State, or a combination of two or more such offenses have become final, he shall be sentenced to a term of imprisonment for not less than 90 days but not more than 3 years ...

Dissecting the above provision, one ascertains that the prior conviction must in fact be final prior to commission of the subsequent simple possession crime. In addition, the prior conviction must fit within the federal definition of "narcotic drug," "marijuana," or "chemical" offense. In other words, the substance involved in the prior offense must fall into a federal definition; the state's labeling of a substance as, for example, a narcotic is not sufficient. The key to a successful immigration defense may lie in distinguishing the state substance from the federal definition or categories.[96]

---

[95] Fifth Circuit: *Carachuri-Rosendo v. Holder*, 570 F.3d 263 (5th Cir. 2009); Seventh Circuit: *Fernandez v. Mukasey*, 544 F.3d 862 (7th Cir. 2008).

[96] For an excellent law review article on recidivism, challenging the recidivist classification, and comparing state classifications of drugs to controlled substances under the federal code, see: S. French

Continued

The next step in the federal recidivist scheme is the procedure. Section 851 of title 21 sets forth the process for the U.S. Attorney to charge someone as a recidivist:

(a) Information filed by the United States Attorney

(1) No person who stands convicted of an offense under this part [21 USC §841 *et seq.*] shall be sentenced to increased punishment by reason of one or more prior convictions, unless before trial, or before entry of a plea of guilty, the United States attorney files an information with the court [(and serves a copy of such information on the person or counsel for the person) stating in writing the previous convictions to be relied upon ... .

The section goes on to allow the defendant to deny the allegation of the previous conviction, and/or to deny the validity of the previous conviction, through written response to the information.[97] The defendant is entitled to a hearing at which the U.S. Attorney bears the burden of proving the prior conviction(s) beyond a reasonable doubt. The defendant may respond with the defense that the conviction alleged in the information was obtained in violation of the Constitution of the United States; the defendant bears the burden of sustaining such a challenge by a preponderance of the evidence.[98]

Based on 21 USC §851, if a subsequent simple possession offense is to be punishable as a felony in the federal system, the prior conviction must be alleged and proven beyond a reasonable doubt. This statute thus holds the key: for a subsequent state conviction for simple possession to be considered "punishable as a felony," and therefore an aggravated felony, the state adjudication process must contain procedural safeguards equivalent to the enhancement provisions of federal law. In the absence of a recidivist statutory scheme similar to 21 USC §851, there is no "hypothetical federal felony."

The Supreme Court's decision in Carachuri-Rosendo

In 2010, the state of the law was that in two circuits—the Fifth and the Seventh—a second or subsequent offense for simple possession of a controlled substance was classified as an "aggravated felony" drug trafficking crime. In the other circuits, DHS was required to establish that the conviction mimicked the federal recidivist statute in that (1) there was a prior, final conviction for a controlled substance violation, and (2) the conviction under scrutiny had been prosecuted and ultimately enhanced as a recidivist crime.[99] Ultimately, in the case of *Carachuri-Rosendo v. Holder*,[100] the

---

Russell, "Rethinking Recidivist Enhancements: The Role of Prior Drug Convictions in Federal Sentencing," 43 *U.C. Davis L. Rev.* 1135 (April 2010).

[97] 21 USC §851(c).

[98] 21 USC §851(c)(2).

[99] *Matter of Carachuri-Rosendo*, 24 I&N Dec. 382 (BIA 2007).

[100] *Carachuri-Rosendo v. Holder*, 570 F.3d 263 (5th Cir. 2009).

Supreme Court ruled with the BIA and the majority of the federal circuits, thereby overturning the Fifth and the Seventh's rule. The *Carachuri-Rosendo* court wrote:

> [W]hen a defendant has been convicted of a simple possession offense that has not been enhanced based on the fact of a prior conviction, he has not been "convicted" under §1229b(a)(3) of a "felony punishable" as such "under the Controlled Substances Act," 18 USC §924(c)(2).[101]//
>
> > ➢ **Practice pointer**: State laws include a variety of penalty classifications and procedures for charging someone as a repeat offender subject to an enhanced punishment. Where DHS charges a simple possession crime as an aggravated felony, the practitioner will cling to the procedure set forth in the federal statute: (1) is there a prior, final conviction; (2) does the state law in question require the prosecutor to prove the existence of the prior conviction; (3) does state law allow for the defendant to challenge the validity of the underlying previous conviction? An automatic sentence enhancement triggered by a previous conviction that was not charged in the pleadings, nor subject to challenge by the defendant, would not suffice under the Supreme Court's analysis in *Carachuri-Rosendo*.

Based on *Carachuri-Rosendo,* to qualify as an aggravated felony drug trafficking crime, a state simple-possession conviction must have been prosecuted under a recidivist scheme similar to the federal system. In the absence of a record that establishes recidivist prosecution, the subsequent conviction will not be an aggravated felony. If the state code does not contain a recidivist provision (with elements that must be proven to a jury), state simple-possession convictions in that state will never be aggravated felonies. In spite of *Carachuri-Rosendo's* guidance, however, litigation continues, as discussed below.

The BIA's response to Carachuri-Rosendo

Matter of Cuellar-Gomez[102] represents the BIA's first recidivist analysis post-*Carachuri-Rosendo*. Careful reading of this decision illustrates myriad ways to contest an aggravated felony finding based on a state recidivist scheme that is dissimilar to the federal scheme. However, solid arguments based on a categorical approach did not work for Mr. Cuellar-Gomez.

> ➢ **Tip**: The final outcome is not positive, and it is this author's opinion that it is not a sound analysis, does not appear to comply with *Carachuri-Rosendo,* and should be challenged by defense counsel when and where similar situations arise.

Matter of Cuellar-Gomez involved a lawful permanent resident, charged with two separate offenses in 2008 of simple personal possession of marijuana. Ultimately, the

---

[101] *Carachuri-Rosendo v. Holder*, 560 U.S. 563, 582 (2010).

[102] *Matter of Cuellar-Gomez*, 25 I&N Dec. 850 (BIA 2012).

BIA ordered him removed as an aggravated felon with a "drug trafficking conviction." Bearing in mind that the issue is whether the subsequent simple possession conviction was charged under a recidivist scheme that patterns federal law, the Board's opinion includes a long and tedious analysis of whether a municipal ordinance violation qualifies as a "conviction" for purposes of recidivism. (For this reason, *Cuellar-Gomez* is also discussed in chapter three, "Convictions.")

The two offenses and their dispositions arose in Wichita, KS. The first offense was charged as a municipal ordinance violation in municipal court.[103] According to the BIA decision, under the municipal code, the accused did not have a right to court-appointed counsel, or the right to trial by jury. The violation was not of state law, but of the municipal code; it was charged as a misdemeanor. The second offense was charged as a felony in state court. The information (charging document) did allege the prior municipal violation. The BIA found that the municipal ordinance violation qualifies as a "conviction" under INA §101(a)(48)(A).[104] The BIA further found that the second conviction qualified as an aggravated felony drug trafficking crime because the state information charged the prior offense.

The Board's decision is alarming. Clearly, the Kansas scheme (or lack thereof) does not mimic the federal recidivist statute at 21 USC §851. Curiously, the Board relies more on its own decision in *Matter of Carachuri-Rosendo*,[105] rather than on the Supreme Court's subsequent precedent in *Carachuri-Rosendo v. Holder*.[106] The Board makes light of the Supreme Court's mandate with the following discussion:

> [T]he CSA requires that a defendant charged with recidivism must be served in advance with an 'enhancement information' specifying the prior convictions to be relied upon. 21 U.S.C. §851(a) (2006). Furthermore, a Federal drug defendant charged with recidivism has a right to challenge the validity of his prior convictions (provided they are reasonably recent) and to require the Government to come forward with proof of them. 21 U.S.C. §851(c). As we explained in *Matter of Carachuri-Rosendo*, 24 I&N Dec. at 391, these requirements provide defendants with 'notice and an opportunity to be heard on whether recidivist punishment is proper,' rights that we consider to be 'part and parcel of what it means for a crime to be a 'recidivist' offense.'
>
> Here, the charge set forth in the Complaint/Information, quoted above, provided the respondent with pretrial notice that the State government was seeking a recidivist enhancement against him and also identified the prior conviction with particularity. Furthermore, Kansas drug defendants who dispute the existence or validity of prior convictions have a right to challenge

---

[103] Section 5.26.010 of the Wichita, Kansas, Code of Ordinances. Provisions governing Kansas municipal courts are at K.S.A. §§12-4104 and 12-4106.

[104] For a discussion of the definition of "conviction," see chapter two.

[105] *Matter of Carachuri-Rosendo*, 24 I&N Dec. 382 (BIA 2007).

[106] *Carachuri-Rosendo v. Holder*, 560 U.S. 563 (2010).

the convictions and to require the government to prove those convictions to the sentencing judge. [Citations omitted]. The procedures specified [by the Kansas statute] are not as elaborate as those described in 21 U.S.C. §851, but they are sufficient to establish that the respondent had notice that he was facing a recidivist enhancement, as well as a meaningful opportunity to object to the propriety of such an enhancement and to put the government to its proof. [fn. 12]

[fn. 12:] We have not required an exact correspondence between State recidivism procedures and those prescribed by the CSA. *See Matter of Carachuri[-Rosendo]* ('It is not necessary . . . for the *structure* of the underlying State law to be comparable to the structure of the CSA. *Lopez v. Gonzales* [549 U.S. 47], requires a focus on a counterpart 'offense,' not a counterpart law.'). Moreover, State recidivism procedures need not 'categorically match' those required by 21 U.S.C. §851, because the categorical approach is concerned with establishing a correspondence between the 'elements' of State and Federal offenses.... .[107]

Is the Board complying with *Carachuri-Rosendo v. Holder*? The reader should consider the following:

Charging phase vs. sentencing phase

The Board does not refer to Kansas's recidivist procedural rule; it would appear that there is no state counterpart to 21 USC §851. Rather, according to the Board's decision, in Kansas the prior conviction may be contested in the sentencing phase only. There is a significant difference between the pretrial versus sentencing phase of a case. Under 21 USC §851, the federal prosecutor must raise the previous predicate offense in the charging document, prior to trial or entry of a guilty plea; and where the defendant contests the fact, the prosecutor must establish in a separate hearing the existence of a prior, final conviction for a federally controlled substance by evidence beyond a reasonable doubt. Where a defendant seeks to challenge the constitutionality of the predicate conviction, he or she may do so, to the judge—the defendant carries the burden of proving by a preponderance of the evidence that the conviction is legally defective. Finally, according to federal law, a defendant's right to contest the predicate conviction continues throughout criminal proceedings until sentencing.[108]

> **Practice Pointer**: Defense counsel should thus argue that Kansas criminal procedure—by allowing argument only at the time of sentencing, after the decision to plea or go to trial—is inferior to the federal protections built in at 21 USC §851.

---

[107] *Matter of Cuellar-Gomez*, 25 I&N Dec. 850, 863 (BIA 2012).
[108] 21 USC §851(2).

CH. 7 • AGGRAVATED FELONIES

Prosecutorial discretion

The Supreme Court in *Carachuri-Rosendo* mentioned several times the prosecutor's discretion to charge recidivist possession only in certain key cases.[109] Relying on *Lopez v. Gonzales,* the Court instructed that a petty simple drug possession offense is not typically thought of as an "aggravated felony" or as "illicit trafficking," because trafficking implies commercial dealing. According to the Supreme Court, "a reading of a statutory scheme that would apply an 'aggravated' or 'trafficking' label to a simple possession offense is, to say the least, counterintuitive and unorthodox."[110] The Supreme Court noted that the government could not point to "even a single eager United States Attorney" who would charge a minor personal possession case as a felony.[111] Neither DHS nor the BIA in *Cuellar-Gomez* could cite to a single federal case wherein a prosecutor utilized a municipal ordinance violation as the predicate offense in a recidivist prosecution. No internal policy memoranda—*i.e.,* the *U.S. Attorneys' Manual*—are cited for the proposition that such a disposition would ever be used in a federal case.

> ➤ **Practice Pointer**: Thus, defense counsel, in challenging an aggravated felony designation based on *Cuellar-Gomez,* may argue that the decision defies the guidance set forth by the Supreme Court in both *Lopez* and *Carachuri-Rosendo,* including the Court's repeated theme that the aggravated felony designation must be reserved for the most serious drug offenses.

Is there a "conviction"?

The BIA's position is that comparison of the federal and state recidivist statutes does not utilize a strict categorical approach. This author reads *Carachuri* to require that the underlying (or first) predicate conviction must be a categorical match to a federal scheme, which means that the underlying violation must represent a controlled substance offense under federal law; what's more, the "conviction" must qualify as such under the federal criminal code. It is far from clear that the disposition in *Cuellar-Gomez* represents a "conviction" under the federal definition for purposes of recidivist prosecution. As a starting point, the plain language of INA §§237(a)(2)(B)(i) and 212(a)(2)(A)(i)(II) require a violation of any law or regulation of a state, the United States, or a foreign country relating to a controlled substance. These provisions do not allow for municipal or county ordinance violations. By way of contrast, INA §237(a)(2)(E) (regarding domestic violence convictions) references the "domestic of family violence laws of the United States or any State, Indian tribal government, or unit of local government."

---

[109] *Carachuri-Rosendo,* 560 U.S. 563, 579–81 (2010).
[110] *Carachuri-Rosendo,* 560 U.S. 563, at 574.
[111] *Carachuri-Rosendo,* 560 U.S. 563, at 581.

In addition, according to the BIA's decision,[112] a defendant charged with simple possession under a municipal ordinance violation in Kansas does not have a right to a jury trial and will only receive court-appointed counsel if there is the possibility of jail time (a fact determined, apparently, after the initial bench trial—if the judge is inclined to impose jail time—then the matter must be sent to a higher court for trial). On the other hand, under the federal scheme, all persons convicted of crimes that qualify as "predicate" convictions for recidivism penalties under the CSA were entitled to an attorney and a jury trial, and the prosecution had to prove their guilt beyond a reasonable doubt.

The Board's conclusion in *Cuellar-Gomez* that this ordinance violation qualifies as a final "conviction" is of suspect legal merit because it does not have a federal categorical match. As of the spring of 2015, no federal court has looked at *Cuellar-Gomez* in the controlled substance context. However, in *Castillo v. A.G. United States*,[113] the Third Circuit questioned the Board's definition of a "conviction" as a "genuine criminal proceeding" in the context of shoplifting, and remanded for a more consistent definition; *Castillo* may be useful for contesting *Cuellar-Gomez*. In an unpublished decision, the Ninth Circuit did not criticize the Board's analysis of a "conviction."[114]

Attempts and Conspiracies

As discussed above, controlled substance cases based on an attempt or conspiracy conviction where the underlying felony offense involves the elements of unlawful trading or dealing are "illicit trafficking" crimes, and therefore, aggravated felonies. An attempt or conspiracy conviction where the underlying offense is not a felony may still be an "illicit trafficking" crime where the underlying offense contains the elements of unlawful trading or dealing (*i.e.*, sale, delivery, importation, etc.).[115]

The Definition of "Crime of Violence"

Section 101(a)(43)(F) of the INA includes within the definition of "aggravated felony" a crime of violence for which the term of imprisonment imposed is at least one year. "Crime of violence" is defined by 18 USC §16, which contains two separate provisions defining the term:

(a) an offense that has as an element the use, attempted use, or threatened use of physical force against the person or property of another, or

---

[112] Many of the referenced Kansas code sections have been repealed; thus, reference to the BIA's summary of the state law becomes necessary.

[113] *Castillo v. Att'y Gen.*, 729 F.3d 296 (3d Cir. 2013).

[114] *Ramos v. Holder*, 546 Fed. Appx. 705, 2013 U.S. App. LEXIS 23954, 2013 WL 6224635 (9th Cir. 2013).

[115] *Matter of Davis*, 20 I&N Dec. 536 (BIA 1992), *modified by Matter of Yanez-Garcia*, 23 I&N Dec. 390 (BIA 2002).

(b) any other offense that is a felony and that, by its nature, involves a substantial risk that physical force against the person or property of another may be used in the course of committing the offense.

Mens Rea: The Levels of Intent

In analyzing what qualifies as an aggravated felony crime of violence, a useful starting point is consideration of the *mens rea*, or mental state, required by the particular criminal statute at hand. A level of *mens rea* is an element of every crime. In turn, criminal statutes punish harmful acts based on the level of intent. A specific intent to cause harm through violent action will be punished more severely than harm that is caused by thoughtless or careless action, without intent to cause a specific result. The Model Penal Code[116] sets forth four levels of action, which it defines as types of culpability: (1) purposeful, (2) knowing, (3) reckless, and (4) negligent. For purposes of immigration law analysis, it is sufficient to consider three levels of *mens rea*: purposeful, reckless, and negligent. Immigration case law generally refers to one or more of these three levels of intent.

Negligence is the lowest tier and does not include a specific intent to cause harm, nor a conscious awareness of the potential harm; negligence occurs where an individual acts in a careless manner without regard to the risks involved, which results in harm to another. Criminal negligence requires a showing of "gross deviation from the standard of reasonable care."[117] An example of negligent conduct may be a person who drives on the wrong side of the road and accidentally strikes and injures another vehicle. Under the criminal laws, negligence is punishable because the person acted without regard to the significant possibility of harm occurring as a result of the conduct. Negligent conduct does not qualify as a "crime of violence" under 18 USC §16.

On the opposite end of the spectrum from negligence is purposeful action, or action with a specific intent to cause harm. For purposes of this discussion, a specific intent crime is one involving force directed at a victim or victims borne out of a desire to cause harm. According to the Model Penal Code, a person acts purposely when it is his or her conscious objective to engage in conduct that will cause a specific result.[118] An example of purposeful conduct is first-degree murder. Specific (purposeful) intent crimes of violence will meet the definition at 18 USC §§16(a) and (b).

In the middle of these two tiers, and the most difficult to classify, is recklessness. An individual acts in a criminally reckless manner when he or she engages in conduct that clearly poses a substantial and unjustifiable risk of harm.[119] Recklessness is

---

[116] Model Penal Code §2.02(2).

[117] J. Dressler, *Understanding Criminal Law*, ch. 5 (4th Ed. 2006).

[118] Model Penal Code §2.02(2)(a).

[119] Model Penal Code §2.02(2)(c).

distinguishable from negligence in that the person consciously engages in very risky behavior. In the words of the Ninth Circuit, to the extent recklessness differs from criminal negligence, the difference between them is that criminal negligence requires only a *failure to perceive* a risk, as compared to the recklessness requirement of an *awareness and conscious disregard* of the risk.[120] On the other hand, recklessness is distinguishable from specific intent in that the former conduct, although clearly dangerous, is not calculated to cause harm.

Certainly, negligence and recklessness are similar concepts—in some settings, they are interchangeable terms. Determining whether a criminal offense describing reckless behavior can qualify under 18 USC §16 as a "crime of violence" requires an extremely difficult analysis. Practitioners may find comfort in the fact that federal courts across the country have struggled with this exercise; hence, attorneys should not hesitate to put forth a well-thought-out argument that an offense encompassing reckless conduct is not a "crime of violence."

Generally speaking, reckless conduct will not qualify as a "crime of violence." As discussed below, and based on guidance from the Supreme Court, whether reckless conduct can qualify as an aggravated felony "crime of violence" depends on a secondary step in the analysis: whether the reckless conduct *also* involves the intentional use of force. Only where reckless conduct combines with the risk of intentional employment of physical force will the offense be properly classified as a "crime of violence."

> ➢ **Compare**: The breadth of "moral turpitude" stretches wider than the definition of "crime of violence." Case law teaches that a reckless act may involve moral turpitude based on the gross deviation of commonly accepted moral standards; in comparison, a reckless act that does not involve the intentional use of violent physical force will not qualify as a "crime of violence." In the simplest of terms, a crime may qualify as one involving moral turpitude, but not be an aggravated felony. Neither concept—moral turpitude or aggravated felony—is premised on the nature or degree of the harm itself.

The Supreme Court's interpretation of crime of violence

In *Leocal v. Ashcroft*,[121] the Supreme Court provided significant guidance in interpreting the phrase "crime of violence" for purposes of the aggravated felony definition. The Court considered the case of a lawful permanent resident (LPR) who was convicted in Florida of two counts of driving under the influence and causing serious bodily injury. The state statute under which he was convicted, Fla. Stat. §316.193, penalizes as a third-degree felony the operation of a motor vehicle while

---

[120] *Fernandez-Ruiz v. Gonzales*, 466 F.3d 1121 (9th Cir. 2006).

[121] *Leocal v. Ashcroft*, 543 U.S. 1 (2004).

under the influence, where it causes serious bodily injury to another. The statute reads, in pertinent part:

(3) Any person:

(a) Who is in violation of subsection (1) [DUI];

(b) Who operates a vehicle; and

(c) Who, by reason of such operation, causes or contributes to causing:

....

2. Serious bodily injury to another ... commits a felony of the third degree....

Although the statute requires proof of causation (driving under the influence leading to serious bodily injury), it does not dictate a particular mental state. The LPR in this case was placed in removal proceedings, charged as an aggravated felon for a "crime of violence" under INA §101(a)(43)(F). The Supreme Court analyzed both subsections of 18 USC §16 before reaching a conclusion that the offense did not meet the definition of "crime of violence." In terms of §16(a) ("an offense that has as an element the use, attempted use, or threatened use of physical force against the person or property of another"), the Court found that the "use of physical force" against the person or property of another naturally suggests a higher degree of intent than mere negligent or accidental conduct:

> The critical aspect of §16(a) is that a crime of violence is one involving the "'use ... of physical force against the person or property of another'." ... As we said in a similar context ..., "'use' requires active employment.... While one may, in theory, actively employ something in an accidental manner, it is much less natural to say that a person actively employs physical force against another person by accident. Thus, a person would "'use ... physical force against'" another when pushing him; however, we would not ordinarily say a person "'use[s] ... physical force'" against another by stumbling and falling into him.[122]

The Court further found that a DUI causing bodily injury did not fall under the definition at 18 USC §16(b) ("any other offense that is a felony and that, by its nature, involves a substantial risk that physical force against the person or property of another may be used in the course of committing the offense"). Noting that subsection (b) "sweeps more broadly," the Court found it nonetheless does not encompass all negligent conduct, such as negligent operation of a motor vehicle:

> The reckless disregard in §16 relates *not* to the general conduct or to the possibility that harm will result from a person's conduct, but to the risk that the use of physical force against another might be required in committing a crime. The classic example is burglary. A burglary would be covered under §16(b) *not*

---

[122] *Leocal v. Ashcroft*, 543 U.S. 1, at 7.

because the offense can be committed in a generally reckless way or because someone may be injured, but because burglary, by its nature, involves a substantial risk that the burglar will use force against a victim during the commission of the crime.[123]

In sum, the Court found that the "use ... of physical force" language in both parts of 18 USC §16 suggests a category of violent, active crimes that cannot be said to include DUI offenses naturally. These types of statutes do not require any mental state with respect to the use of force, and cover individuals who were "negligent or less."[124] The concept of the "use of force" requires active employment and naturally suggests a higher degree of intent than negligent or merely accidental conduct.

While *Leocal* was pending, the BIA reversed its longstanding position regarding statutes such as Florida's. Prior to 2002, the BIA had held that where an element of the offense involves the use of physical force against another, it may be deemed a crime of violence under §16(a).[125] In *Matter of Ramos*, the BIA held that DUI offenses must include a *mens rea* of at least recklessness to qualify as a crime of violence.[126] However, the BIA was bound to follow the case law of the individual circuits that held otherwise. These circuits included the Eleventh,[127] until that circuit's position was reversed by the Supreme Court in *Leocal*. The Court in *Leocal* reaffirmed decisions of other federal circuits, holding that DUI with bodily injury did not qualify as an aggravated felony "crime of violence."[128]

> ➤ *Note*: The Supreme Court's analysis reaches beyond the aggravated felony definition at INA §101(a)(43)(F) because the Court specifically employs the categorical approach. The Court's analysis illustrates how to dissect the specific elements of a criminal offense, identify the *mens rea*, and properly classify the crime within its generic category.

Recklessness and the use of force

Since *Leocal*, federal courts have issued decisions that hone in on the analysis and further explain the "use of force" requirement in the context of reckless conduct. These decisions reflect that "substantial risk" of physical force being used in the course of committing an offense, as that phrase is used in 18 USC 16(b), does not relate to the risk of physical injury that the conduct presents. Instead, 18 USC §16(b) refers to offenses that *by their nature* ignore the risk that the use of physical force

---

[123] *Leocal v. Ashcroft*, 543 U.S. 1, at 8 (footnote omitted).

[124] *Leocal v. Ashcroft*, 543 U.S. 1 (2004).

[125] *Matter of Puente-Salazar*, 22 I&N Dec. 1006 (BIA 1999).

[126] *Matter of Ramos*, 23 I&N Dec. 336 (BIA 2002).

[127] *Le v. Att'y Gen.*, 196 F.3d 1352 (11th Cir. 1999).

[128] *U.S. v. Vargas-Duran*, 319 F.3d 194 (5th Cir. 2003); *U.S. v. Trinidad-Aquino*, 259 F.3d 1140 (9th Cir. 2001); *Bazan-Reyes v. INS*, 256 F.3d 600 (7th Cir. 2001); *U.S. v. Chapa-Garza*, 243 F.3d 479 (5th Cir. 2001).

may well be *required* to commit the crime.[129] In other words, a crime of violence is an offense that presents a significant risk that the intentional use of force will arise in the course of committing the crime; burglary is a classic example because, in the course of breaking into a victim's home, there is a significant likelihood that violent force will be used against another person or property—even if causing this harm is not the core intent of the offender.

Since *Leocal*, the federal courts have consistently found that criminal acts involving reckless behavior will not meet the definition of "crime of violence" at 18 USC §16(b). For example, in *Jimenez-Gonzalez v. Mukasey*,[130] the Seventh Circuit U.S. Court of Appeals analyzed whether the crime of criminal recklessness under the Indiana Code[131] qualifies as an aggravated felony. The relevant statute states that "a person who recklessly, knowingly, or intentionally performs an act that creates a substantial risk of bodily injury to another person commits criminal recklessness."[132] According to the facts of the case, the petitioner admitted in his plea agreement to shooting a firearm from his truck into an apartment located in a residential neighborhood. He was sentenced to four years imprisonment. Review of the *Jimenez-Gonzalez* decision is strongly recommended for any practitioner dealing with a criminal statute with a *mens rea* of recklessness; the Seventh Circuit carefully analyzes reckless behavior in light of Supreme Court and other federal court precedent. The court places the focus squarely on the issue of the actor's intent, in light of *Leocal's* guidance that the use of force must be intentional (*i.e.*, purposeful): accidental and aggressive conduct (negligent or reckless behavior) does not qualify as a crime of violence under 18 USC §16(b). The petition for review was granted and the conviction was found not to be an aggravated felony.

Force versus contact

Another important aspect of the *Leocal* decision is the requirement that the force be violent in nature. As stated above, the term "crime of violence" suggests a category of violent acts. Not every form of physical contact will qualify as "force" for purposes of this analysis. For example, in *Larin-Ulloa v. Gonzales*,[133] the Fifth Circuit U.S. Court of Appeals considered the offense of aggravated battery under Kansas law, which provides as one definition of the crime:

---

[129] *U.S. v. Torres-Villalobos*, 487 F.3d 607, 616 (8th Cir. 2007) (under Minnesota law, a person can commit second-degree manslaughter without using force or risking the intentional use of force; a person can commit this crime by recklessly leaving a child alone with lit candles that later start a fire, by allowing a child to die of dehydration while in the person's car, or by storing explosives in an automobile).

[130] *Jimenez-Gonzalez v. Mukasey*, 548 F.3d 557 (7th Cir. 2008).

[131] Ind. Code §35-42-2-2(b)(1).

[132] Ind. Code §35-42-2-2(b)(1)..

[133] *Larin-Ulloa v. Gonzales*, 462 F.3d 456 (5th Cir. 2006).

intentionally causing physical contact with another person when done in a rude, insulting or angry manner with a deadly weapon, *or* in any manner whereby great bodily harm, disfigurement or death can be inflicted.[134]

The Fifth Circuit began its discussion as to whether this aggravated battery provision constitutes a crime of violence by noting that the statute is divisible in terms of the offenses it describes:

(1) intentionally causing physical contact with another in a rude, insulting or angry manner with a deadly weapon; and

(2) intentionally causing physical contact with another person in any manner whereby great bodily harm, disfigurement or death can be inflicted.

The court found that the first clause, causing physical contact with a deadly weapon, is a crime of violence because, although the circumstances will not always require the use of physical force, the prohibited conduct is by its very nature provocative and invites a response from the victim, hence creating a substantial risk that the confrontation will escalate to physical violence.[135] On the other hand, the second clause does not require the use of physical force in order to support a conviction. Rather, it requires only physical contact with the victim in a situation that might lead to great bodily harm, disfigurement, or death. The court noted that physical contact is not the equivalent of physical force. Moreover, the clause does not require that the physical contact be violent, harmful, offensive, or even nonconsensual.

Employing the modified categorical approach, the court turned to the record of conviction to determine whether qualifying documents specified which clause the defendant or respondent had been charged with and convicted of. However, the record of conviction did not reveal which clause applied. Thus, relying on the distinction between physical contact versus physical force, and noting a minimal risk that the risk of force was required to complete the crime, the court found that the aggravated felony charge could not be sustained.[136] This decision illustrates the difficult nature of the "crime of violence" analysis and highlights the importance of carefully delineating the particular elements of the offense to determine whether

(1) the use of intentional, violent force is required, or

(2) the risk of use of violent force is present and significant.

---

[134] Kan. Stat. Ann. §21-3414(a)(1)(C) (emphasis added).

[135] *Larin-Ulloa v. Gonzales*, 462 F.3d 456, 465–66 (5th Cir. 2006).

[136] *Larin-Ulloa v. Gonzales*, 462 F.3d 456, at 466 (5th Cir. 2006).

CASE STUDY: JOHNSON v. U.S.

In 2010, the Supreme Court issued another extremely important case in the context of defining crimes of violence, but this time in the context of a criminal law case. In *Johnson v. U.S.*,[137] the Supreme Court—as in *Leocal*—reviewed an Eleventh Circuit decision interpreting Florida law. The issue did not involve *mens rea* (negligence/recklessness, and crime of violence), but rather the concept of the active use of violent physical force. Specifically, the Supreme Court reviewed Florida's simple battery statute in the context of 18 USC §924(e) of the Armed Criminal Career Act, defining "violent felony." The defendant in this case pled guilty to a firearms violation under 18 USC §922(g)(1). The government sought an enhanced penalty under 18 USC §924(e), which allows for a sentence enhancement based on three prior convictions for a "violent felony." The definition of "violent felony" closely patterns the definition of "crime of violence" at 18 USC §16; thus, the Court's interpretation of violent felony was also extremely important in the aggravated felony crime of violence context.

A "violent felony" is defined as "any crime punishable by imprisonment for a term exceeding one year" that:

"(i) has as an element the use, attempted use, or threatened use of physical force against the person of another; or

"(ii) is burglary, arson, or extortion, involves use of explosives, or otherwise involves conduct that presents a serious potential risk of physical injury to another."[138]

Johnson did have prior convictions, but he argued that his conviction for simple, misdemeanor battery under Fla. Stat. §784.03 did not qualify as a violent felony. This section reads as follows:

(1)(a) The offense of battery occurs when a person:

1. Actually and intentionally touches or strikes another person against the will of the other; or

2. Intentionally causes bodily harm to another person.

The Court, noting that 18 USC §924(e) is similar to 18 USC §16, cited to *Leocal* in pointing out that the phrase "physical force" refers to violent physical force. To determine whether a criminal provision involves the active use of violent physical force, the Supreme Court relied on a categorical approach. The Court then found that Florida's battery statute is divisible, in that "touching" does not involve the active use

---

[137] *Johnson v. U.S.*, 559 U.S. 133 (2010).
[138] 18 USC

of violent physical force. The Court went on to endorse a modified categorical approach: where the statute is divisible in that it encompasses more than one generic crime, the adjudicator reverts to a modified categorical approach, which permits the court to determine which statutory phrase formed the basis of the conviction by reviewing the charging instrument, plea documents, findings of fact and conclusions of law from a bench trial, final judgment and sentence, and jury instructions.[139] The inquiry as to whether a certain crime meets the definition of violent felony (or crime of violence) ends with the modified categorical approach and does not take into account underlying circumstances. Finding that the simple battery conviction in Johnson's particular case did not establish a "violent felony," the Court remanded for resentencing.[140]

The *Johnson* case is useful for several distinct reasons. First, it means that simple battery statutes that include the element of "touch" or similar nonviolent or noncontact terms will not qualify as crimes of violence for purposes of the aggravated felony definition. Second, this important precedent carries over to the domestic violence deportation ground at INA §237(a)(2)(E) (discussed later in this chapter), which also depends on the definition of "crime of violence" at 18 USC §16. Third, *Johnson* reiterates what was said in *Leocal*: the concept of physical force envisions the active use of violent physical force; these six simple words should be the mantra echoing in the back of an attorney's mind while researching a criminal statute to determine whether it is an aggravated felony crime of violence. Fourth and finally, the Supreme Court's decision is a welcome confirmation that defining "aggravated felony" requires a categorical—and in the case of a divisible statute—modified categorical approach without regard to the underlying circumstances of the crime.

> ➢ **Of interest:** Justice Alito's dissenting opinion in *Descamps* calls into question whether the terms "touch" or "strike" represent elements, and

---

[139] *Johnson v. U.S.*, 559 U.S., *at* 144 (2010).

[140] The reader will note that this discussion on the aggravated felony "crime of violence" involves both criminal and immigration cases with overlapping concepts. The terms discussed include "crime of violence" under the INA; "violent felony" under the ACCA; and "crime of violence" for purposes of the U.S. Sentencing Guidelines (at 2L1.2(b)(1)(A)). These terms are not identical; their definitions are not the same. *See, e.g., U.S. v. Cortes-Salazar*, 682 F.3d 953 (11th Cir. 2012). Thus, in making a legal argument, counsel should be cautious in applying the precedent of one case (defining one of the terms) in another context (a similar term) without verifying that the comparison is in fact valid. In other words, a "crime of violence" for sentencing guidelines purposes may not be a "crime of violence" in the immigration law context. Counsel should also be wary of ICE counsel (or an immigration judge) relying on a criminal case to justify a finding of "aggravated felony" when in fact the precedent—although superficially similar—is in fact mismatched in the immigration context. The real key to all of this is that the categorical approach applies in analyzing statutes.

opines that these are means, resulting in an indivisible statute according to the majority's analysis.[141] Regardless of whether the statute is divisible, the thesis that a "touch" cannot meet the crime of violence definition remains constant.

Following the *Johnson* decision (but not mentioning *Johnson* at all), the Board ruled in *Matter of U. Singh*[142] that a stalking offense including harassing conduct qualifies as a crime of violence under 18 USC §16(b) because the crime involves a substantial risk that physical force will be used. Ironically, the Board seems to be concerned that the victim will utilize the violent physical force:

> [W]hen a person engages in stalking, there is a substantial risk that the individual being stalked will take exception and, as a result, cause the perpetrator to use force in self-defense or to further effectuate the harassment.[143]

In any event, the key aspect of *Singh* is that it focuses on subsection (b) of 18 USC §16's definition of crime of violence, which requires that the offense be a felony and further the risk that violence will be used in the course of committing the crime.

The Board's Analysis in Matter of *Chairez I* and *II*[144]

The *Matter of Chairez* decisions are discussed at length in chapter five on "Methodology." The respondent in *Chairez* had a Utah conviction for felony discharge of a firearm, and was charged with removability for an aggravated felony crime of violence and a firearms offense. In *Chairez I*, decided in 2014, the BIA found that the statute of conviction contained three mental states: intentional, knowing, and reckless discharge of a firearm. The Board further found that the statute was not divisible as to *mens rea*, but that these levels of intent represented means, not elements. Taking a categorical approach, and assuming the least culpable conduct of reckless, the Board found Chairez not to be deportable for an aggravated felony crime of violence because a reckless act does not involve the active use of violent physical force. According to the Board, a crime of violence must be with a deliberate purpose in mind and reckless conduct does not satisfy this standard.[145] In *Matter of Chairez II*, the Board did not overturn or modify its crime of violence analysis in terms of the mental state of reckless; the precedent that the deliberate use of violent physical force connotes something more than reckless behavior remains intact. Rather, in *Chairez II*, the BIA found that for purposes of a case within the Tenth Circuit, the statute is divisible as to the delineated mental states. Looking further through a modified

---

[141] *Descamps v. U.S.*, 133 S. Ct. 2276, 2298 (2013) (Alito, S., dissenting).

[142] *Matter of U. Singh*, 25 I&N Dec. 670 (BIA 2012).

[143] *Matter of U. Singh*, at 676, citing *Matter of Malta*, 23 I&N Dec. 656 (BIA 2004), *reversed by Malta-Espinoza v. Gonzales*, 478 F.3d 1080, 1083–84 (9th Cir. 2007).

[144] *Matter of Chairez I*, 26 I&N Dec. 349 (BIA 2014), vacated in part by *Matter of Chairez II*, 26 I&N Dec. 478 (BIA 2015).

[145] *Matter of Chairez I*, 26 I&N Dec. at 351 (BIA 2015).

categorical approach, the Board found that the plea agreement specified "knowing," thus making the respondent deportable for a crime involving the deliberate use of violent physical force.

Particular Offenses

Since the Supreme Court's decisions in *Leocal* and *Johnson*, courts have ruled that various offenses either are or are not crimes of violence that qualify as an aggravated felony under INA §101(a)(43)(F). Again, post-*Descamps*, fresh reading and research is of special import when considering the following precedents:

Not crimes of violence

- Assault and battery of a high and aggravated nature (South Carolina);[146]
- Resisting an executive officer (California);[147]
- Reckless assault on a police officer (Texas);[148]
- Reckless vehicular homicide (Tennessee);[149]
- Reckless domestic violence (Arizona);[150]
- Second-degree manslaughter (Minnesota);[151]
- Simple involuntary manslaughter (Virginia);[152]
- Reckless assault in the second degree (New York);[153]
- Unlawful driving or taking of a vehicle (California);[154]
- Simple (misdemeanor) assault (Pennsylvania);[155]
- Simple (misdemeanor) assault, including against a spouse (Texas);[156]

---

[146] *U.S. v. Montes-Flores*, 736 F.3d 357 (4th Cir. 2013). "ABHAN" is a common law offense composed of the elements of (1) an unlawful act of violent injury to another; and (2) circumstances of aggravation. The Fourth Circuit U.S. Court of Appeals found that these two indivisible elements did not trigger a modified categorical approach and the offense did not necessarily include the active use of violent physical force.

[147] *Flores-Lopez v. Holder*, 685 F. 3d 857 (9th Cir. 2012) (interpreting Cal. Penal Code §69).

[148] *U.S. v. Zuniga-Soto*, 527 F.3d 1110, 1124 (10th Cir. 2008) (Note this is a sentencing guidelines—not a removal—case).

[149] *U.S. v. Portela*, 469 F.3d 496, 499 (6th Cir. 2006) (Note this is a sentencing guidelines—not a removal—case).

[150] *Fernandez-Ruiz v. Gonzales*, 466 F.3d 1121, 1129–31 (9th Cir. 2006) (Note this is a sentencing guidelines—not a removal—case).

[151] *U.S. v. Torres-Villalobos*, 487 F.3d 607 (8th Cir. 2007) (interpreting Minn. Stat. §609.205).

[152] *Bejarano-Urrutia v. Gonzales*, 413 F.3d 444 (4th Cir. 2005) (interpreting Va. Code Ann. §18.2-36).

[153] *Garcia v. Gonzales*, 455 F.3d 465 (4th Cir. 2006) (interpreting N.Y. Penal Law §120.05(4)).

[154] *Penuliar v. Ashcroft*, 395 F.3d 1037 (9th Cir. 2005) (interpreting Cal. Veh. Code §10851(a)).

[155] *Popal v. Gonzales*, 416 F.3d 249 (3d Cir. 2005) (interpreting 18 Pa. Cons. Stat. §7201(a)).

[156] *U.S. v. Villegas-Hernandez*, 468 F.3d 874 (5th Cir. 2006) (interpreting Tex. Penal Code Ann. §22.01(a)).

- Vehicular homicide (New Jersey);[157]
- Reckless burning or exploding (Pennsylvania);[158]
- Possession of a firearm by a felon (federal offense);[159]
- Assault in the second degree (New York);[160]
- Second-degree sexual abuse (*i.e.*, nonconsensual sex) (Oregon).[161]

Crimes of violence

- Stalking based on harassing conduct (felony) (California);[162]
- Simple (misdemeanor) battery (Georgia);[163]
- Bodily injury to a child, where the record of conviction (the criminal information) specifies that the act was intentional under a divisible statute that includes negligent, reckless, and intentional acts or omissions (Texas);[164]
- Sexual battery (California);[165]
- Possession of a firearm, where intent to use is an element of the statute (New York);[166]
- Second-degree rape (Alabama);[167]
- Conspiracy to commit extortion (federal);[168]

---

[157] *Oyebanji v. Gonzales*, 418 F.3d 260 (3d Cir. 2005) (interpreting N.J. Stat. Ann. §2C:11-5(b)(1)).

[158] *Tran v. Gonzales*, 414 F.3d 464 (3d Cir. 2005) (interpreting 18 Pa. Cons. Stat. §3301).

[159] *U.S. v. Cornelius Johnson*, 399 F.3d 1297 (11th Cir. 2005) (interpreting 18 USC §922(g)(1)). Note that this case was not a removal matter, but a sentencing case. Note further that possession of a firearm by a felon, though not a "crime of violence," falls under the definition of aggravated felony at INA §101(a)(43)(E).

[160] *Garcia v. Gonzales*, 455 F.3d 465 (4th Cir. 2006).

[161] *U.S. v. Candelario*, 240 F.3d 1300 (11th Cir. 2001) (interpreting Or. Rev. Stat. §163.425). Note that this is a sentencing guidelines case, as opposed to a removal case. Note further that this decision is contrary to the result reached in *U.S. v. Ivory*, 475 F.3d 1232 (11th Cir. 2007).

[162] *Matter of U Singh*, 25 I&N Dec. 670 (BIA 2012) (interpreting Calif. Penal Code 646.9(b))

[163] *Hernandez v. Att'y Gen.*, 513 F.3d 1336 (11th Cir. 2008) (interpreting O.C.G.A. §16-5-23(a)(2)).

[164] *Perez-Munoz v. Keisler*, 507 F.3d 357 (5th Cir. 2007) (interpreting Tex. Penal Code §22.04(a)(3)).

[165] *U.S. v. Gonzalez-Jaquez*, 566 F.3d 1250, 1252–53 (10th Cir. 2009).

[166] *Henry v. ICE*, 493 F.3d 303 (3d Cir. 2007) (N.Y. Penal Code §265.03).

[167] *U.S. v. Ivory*, 475 F.3d 1232 (11th Cir. 2007) (interpreting Ala. Code §13A-6-62(a)). Note that this is a sentencing guidelines case, as opposed to a removal case. Note further this decision is contrary to the result reached in *U.S. v. Candelario*, 240 F.3d 1300 (11th Cir. 2001).

[168] *Strelchikov v. Att'y Gen.*, 242 Fed. Appx. 789, 2007 U.S. App. LEXIS 14321 (3d Cir. 2007) (interpreting 18 USC §1951(b)). Note that the respondent was found removable under INA §101(a)(43)(U), relating to conspiracy to commit an aggravated felony, as defined by INA §101(a)(43)(F).

- Aggravated criminal sexual abuse (Illinois);[169] and
- Hostage taking (federal).[170]

Divisible statute requiring a modified categorical approach

- Aggravated assault with a deadly weapon.[171]

CASE STUDY: MATTER OF BRIEVA-PEREZ

Following the *Leocal* decision, the BIA ruled in *Matter of Brieva-Perez*[172] that unauthorized use of a motor vehicle (akin to auto theft) under the Texas Penal Code is a "crime of violence" because the act of taking a vehicle involves a substantial risk that the use of force against person or property will be necessary in accomplishing the crime. The Board based its decision on Fifth Circuit case law that preceded *Leocal*.[173]

However, in the summer of 2009, the Sixth Circuit rejected the idea that auto theft qualifies as a "crime of violence" in *Von don Nguyen v. Holder*,[174] which interpreted unauthorized use of a vehicle under California law.[175] In so doing, the Sixth Circuit soundly defeats the Board's reasoning in *Brieva-Perez*. Quoting heavily from the Supreme Court's decision in *Leocal*, and applying a categorical approach to the California statute (which encompassed theft of various types of property, including but not limited to fruit, vegetables, livestock, money, labor, and real or personal property) the Sixth Circuit found as follows:

- The statutory elements make no mention of violent conduct;
- Although there is some chance that violent force may be used against an automobile to gain entry, or that the car may be damaged, it cannot be said that the risk is substantial;
- The proper inquiry is the risk associated with the proscribed conduct in the mainstream of prosecutions brought under the statute;
- In the ordinary case, the nature of the theft does not involve a substantial risk of the use of physical force.

---

[169] *Patel v. Ashcroft*, 401 F.3d 400 (6th Cir. 2005) (interpreting 720 Ill. Comp. Stat. 5/12-16).

[170] *Acero v. INS*, 2005 U.S. Dist. LEXIS 4440, 2005 WL 615744 (E.D.N.Y. Mar. 16, 2005).

[171] *U.S. v. Rede-Mendez*, 680 F.3d 552 (6th Cir. 2012).

[172] *Matter of Brieva-Perez*, 23 I&N Dec. 766 (BIA 2005) (interpreting Tex. Penal Code Ann. §31.07(a)).

[173] *U.S. v. Galvan-Rodriguez*, 169 F.3d 217 (5th Cir. 1999).

[174] *Von don Nguyen v. Holder*, 571 F.3d 524 (6th Cir. 2009).

[175] Cal. Penal Code §487 (note the petitioner's conviction was in 1990).

Contrasting theft and burglary (the latter offense being described by the Supreme Court as a crime of violence), the Sixth Circuit notes that entering a dwelling where people may be is not the same as taking an unoccupied car and driving away—which will almost never involve confrontation with the owner. Instead, the owner returns to an unoccupied parking spot.[176]

> ➢ *Consider*: The reader may wonder why arguing that theft is not an aggravated felony "crime of violence" under INA §101(a)(43)(F) was so important to Mr. Nguyen if theft is clearly an aggravated felony under INA §101(a)(43)(G). The answer lies with the BIA's decision in *Matter of Blake*,[177] which is discussed in chapter seven. *Blake* held that in order to qualify for a waiver under INA §212(c), the ground of deportability (usually, in this scenario, an aggravated felony offense) must have a corresponding ground of inadmissibility. The IJ and the BIA found in petitioner Nguyen's case that a §212(c) waiver was not available to him because, although the aggravated felony "theft" offense had a corresponding ground of inadmissibility at INA §212(a) (that being, presumably, a crime involving moral turpitude), there was no corresponding ground of inadmissibility for the aggravated felony "crime of violence" offense—hence he had no relief available from deportation. The issue of the aggravated felony ground of removability carried over into the relief phase and was of vital importance to defending against deportation. As discussed in the chapter on relief, the Supreme Court eventually overruled *Blake*.

The *Nguyen* decision is notable not only for its specific finding that theft of an automobile is not a crime of violence, but for the court's adherence to a categorical approach that considered the elements of the theft statute, combined with a stated unwillingness to consider the underlying circumstances of the actual offense. The court notes that the statute is ambiguous and, taking into account the "rule of lenity," determines that any doubt in interpreting the statute must be resolved in favor of the individual.[178]

> ➢ **Practice Pointer**: In terms of the definition of "crime of violence," practitioners will note that pre-*Descamps* precedent may no longer be good law; it is important to check the date of a particular decision and verify its validity if it is before June of 2013. In addition, both *Johnson* and *Leocal's* analyses require case-by-case consideration; it is vitally important to pull out the particular state code and consider the criminal

---

[176] *Von don Nguyen v. Holder*, 571 F.3d 524, at 534 (6th Cir. 2009).

[177] *Matter of Blake*, 23 I&N Dec. 722 (BIA 2005).

[178] *Von don Nguyen v. Holder*, 571 F.3d 524, at 527 (6th Cir. 2009).

statute at issue word by word, element by element, in determining whether a crime qualifies as a "crime of violence" under INA §101(a)(43)(F).

Firearms Offenses

Firearms offenses are a discrete ground of deportability under the INA, as discussed later in this chapter. However, certain firearms offenses are classified as aggravated felonies, making it possible for an individual with a firearms conviction to be deportable for both a firearms offense and an aggravated felony.

There are two separate provisions for firearms offenses under the definition of aggravated felony. One provision is broad; the other provision makes reference to specific federal criminal statutes. The first provision, found in INA §101(a)(43)(C) [8 USC §1101(a)(43)(C)], includes within the definition of "aggravated felony" any illicit trafficking in firearms or destructive devices (as those terms are defined by 18 USC §921) or in explosive materials (as defined by 18 USC 841(c)). "Trafficking" has been defined as trading, selling, or dealing—activity relating to a business or merchant nature. [179] Under this definition, a federal court has found that the unlicensed export of firearms in violation of 22 USC §2778 is an aggravated felony under INA §101(a)(43)(C), as opposed to a mere licensing offense. [180]

In a 2006 case, *Joseph v. Att'y Gen.*,[181] the Third Circuit found that a conviction under 18 USC §922(a)(3) did not constitute an aggravated felony firearms offense because the criminal statute did not include the element of trafficking. Section 922(a) deals with transportation of firearms. Applying a categorical approach, the court noted that the minimum conduct described by statute included a lawful purchase or possession of a firearm in one state, where the firearm is then transported across state lines. Such conduct, according to the court, did not involve trafficking.

The second provision governing firearms offenses as aggravated felonies, INA §101(a)(43)(E) [8 USC §1101(a)(43)(E)], includes within the definition of "aggravated felony" specified firearms or explosive materials offenses:

- Those that relate to the unlawful use of explosive material, pursuant to
  - 18 USC §§842(h), (i); or
  - 18 USC §§849(d)–(i).
- Those that relate to prohibited firearms offenses under
  - 18 USC §§922(g)(1)–(5);[182]

---

[179] *Kuhali v. Reno*, 266 F.3d 93, 107 (2d Cir. 2001), *citing Matter of Davis*, 20 I&N Dec. 536, 541 (BIA 1992) (borrowing the definition of illicit trafficking from the controlled substance aggravated felony context).

[180] *Kuhali v. Reno*, 266 F.3d 93, 107 (2d Cir. 2001), at 108.

[181] *Joseph v. Att'y Gen.*, 465 F.3d 123 (3d Cir. 2006).

[182] (g) It shall be unlawful for any person—

Continued

- 18 USC §922(j) (unlawful receipt of shipment of firearms);
- 18 USC §922(n) (possession of a firearm while under indictment for a felony);
- 18 USC §922(o) (unlawful possession or transfer of a machine gun);
- 18 USC §922(p) (sale, shipment, or possession of a firearm that has been altered to escape x-ray detection);
- 18 USC §922(r) (assembly of a prohibited semiautomatic gun or rifle from imported parts);
- 18 USC §924(b) (use of a firearm in the commission of a felony); or
- 18 USC §924(h) (transfer of a firearm knowing it will be used to commit a crime of violence).

- Those that violate Internal Revenue Code (IRC) §5861.[183]

---

(1) who has been convicted in any court of a crime punishable by imprisonment for a term exceeding one year;

(2) who is a fugitive from justice;

(3) who is an unlawful user of or addicted to a controlled substance ... ;

(4) who has been adjudicated as a mental defective or who has been committed to a mental institution;

(5) who, being an alien—(A) is illegally or unlawfully in the United States or (B)

... has been admitted to the United States under a nonimmigrant visa ...

to ship or transport in interstate or foreign commerce, or possess in or affecting commerce, any firearm or ammunition; or to receive any firearm or ammunition that has been shipped or transported in interstate or foreign commerce.

[183] Prohibited acts.

It shall be unlawful for any person—

(a) to engage in business as a manufacturer or importer of, or dealer in, firearms without having paid the special (occupational) tax required by section 5801 for his business or having registered as required by section 5802; or

(b) to receive or possess a firearm transferred to him in violation of the provisions of this chapter; or

(c) to receive or possess a firearm made in violation of the provisions of this chapter; or

(d) to receive or possess a firearm which is not registered to him the National Firearms Registration and Transfer Record; or

(e) to transfer a firearm in violation of the provisions of this chapter; or

(f) to make a firearm in violation of this chapter; or

(g) to obliterate, remove, change, or alter the serial number or other identification of a firearm required by this chapter; or

(h) to receive or possess a firearm having the serial number or other identification required by this chapter obliterated, removed, changed, or altered; or

(i) to receive or possess a firearm which is not identified by a serial number as required by this chapter; or

(j) to transport, deliver, or receive any firearm in interstate commerce which has not been registered as required by this chapter; or

Continued

Whether a state firearms offense is "described in" a federal statute

The provision at INA §101(a)(43)(E) is worded in terms of offenses "described in" the U.S. Code and the IRC. (The "described in" language is also used in other provisions of §101(a)(43) of the INA.) Some of the federal offenses listed are clearly quite serious; others, though, are fairly common (and not so serious) offenses under state law. After muddling through concepts like moral turpitude, it seems—at first glance—a relief to have specific federal code sections spelled out for the reader. However, the BIA has tinkered with the phrase "described in" to envelop comparable state statutes. Thus, an aggravated felony offense under INA §101(a)(43)(E) can include state statutes that pattern a comparable section of the federal code. In light of *Descamps,* it is not clear whether the Board's treatment of the "described by" phrase (which occurs at various points within the INA) is still appropriate.

In *Matter of Vasquez-Muniz,*[184] the BIA held that a state or foreign offense may be classified as an aggravated felony because it is "described in" a federal statute enumerated at INA §101(a)(43)(E), even though the state or foreign statute might not include the federal jurisdictional element of "affecting interstate commerce" (some action of crossing state lines necessary for the offense to fall under *federal* purview). *Vasquez-Muniz* essentially says that the BIA will look to the underlying criminal conduct—without regard to whether something happened "across state lines"—in determining whether the offense is an aggravated felony firearms offense. In so doing, the BIA effectively disregards specific federal statutes as being cited at INA §§101(a)(43)(C) and (E), and rather endorses a "sounds like" test. If the state conviction "sounds like" one of these federal offenses, it will be deemed an aggravated felony, and the fact that it is the interstate "connection" that makes a crime a federal offense is irrelevant. In *Matter of Vasquez-Muniz,* the individual's state crime of possession of a firearm by a felon in violation of Cal. Penal Code §12021(a)(1) was found to be an offense "described in" 18 USC §922(g)(1), and, hence, an aggravated felony.

CASE STUDY: BAUTISTA v. ATT'Y GEN.

In 2014, in a case called *Bautista v. Att'y Gen.,*[185] the Third Circuit rejected the Board's analysis in *Matter of Vasquez-Muniz. Bautista* involved a charge of removability under INA §101(a)(43)(E)(i), which references (in pertinent part) an offense described in 18 USC §844(i). The respondent in Bautista had a New York

---

(k) to receive or possess a firearm which has been imported or brought into the United States in violation of section 5844; or

(*l*) to make, or cause the making of, a false entry on any application, return, or record required by this chapter, knowing such entry to be false.

[184] *Matter of Vasquez-Muniz*, 23 I&N Dec. 207 (BIA 2002).

[185] *Bautista v. Att'y Gen.*, 744 F.3d 54 (3d Cir. 2014).

conviction for attempted arson in the third degree, for which he served a period of probation.[186] Relying on *Vasquez-Muniz*, the Board upheld the IJ's order of removal in a published decision in 2011.[187] The Third Circuit disagreed with the Board's analysis that the phrase "described in" utilized in various subsections throughout INA §101(a)(43) authorizes the immigration courts to order removal based on similar state statutes that do not contain the jurisdictional element. Rather, according to the Third Circuit, the jurisdictional component of interstate commerce is an essential element:

> [A] state arson conviction will only be "described in", and punishable under §844(i), if the state statute includes an element requiring that the object of the arson be actively used in interstate commerce.[188]

The Second Circuit looked at the exact same arson statute in *Torres v. Holder*,[189] and arrived at an opposite result, finding the statute to be ambiguous, and choosing to defer to the BIA's interpretation. The Fourth Circuit also has disagreed with the Third Circuit, on the basis of deference to the agency.[190]

Theft and Burglary Crimes

Section 101(a)(43)(G) [8 USC §1101(a)(43)(G)] includes within the definition of "aggravated felony" any crime of theft or burglary, including receipt of stolen property, where the sentence of imprisonment imposed is at least one year.

Aiding and abetting

In 2007, the Supreme Court issued an important decision in *Gonzales v. Duenas-Alvarez*,[191] finding that aiding and abetting the theft of a vehicle in violation of California law[192] is a "theft" crime for purposes of the aggravated felony definition at INA §101(a)(43)(G). The California statute states as follows:

> §10851. Unlawful driving or taking of vehicle without consent of owner
>
> (a) Any person who drives or takes a vehicle not his or her own, without the consent of the owner thereof, and with intent either to permanently or temporarily deprive the owner thereof of his or her title to or possession of the vehicle, whether with or without intent to steal the vehicle, or any person who is a party or an accessory to or an accomplice in the driving or unauthorized taking or stealing, is guilty of a public offense and, upon conviction thereof,

---

[186] N.Y. Penal Law §§110.00 and 150.10.

[187] *Matter of Bautista*, 25 I&N Dec. 616 (BIA 2011).

[188] *Bautista v. Att'y Gen.*, 744 F.3d at 66.

[189] *Torres v. Holder*, 764 F.3d 152 (2d Cir. 2014).

[190] *Espinal-Andrades v. Holder*, 777 F.3d 163 (4th Cir. 2015).

[191] *Gonzales v. Duenas-Alvarez*, 549 U.S. 183 (2007).

[192] Cal. Veh. Code §10851(a).

shall be punished by imprisonment in a county jail for not more than one year or in the state prison or by a fine of not more than five thousand dollars ($5,000), or by both the fine and imprisonment.

The Court noted that a generic definition of "theft" includes the taking of property or exercising control over property without the consent of the owner, whether the criminal intent is either permanent or temporary deprivation. The Court further found that most states have eliminated the distinction between principals versus aiders and abettors when it comes to punishment. Accordingly, one who aids and abets an offense that includes the generic elements of theft is guilty of the theft offense in the same manner as the principal.

Of note in this case, the Court specifically declined to find whether accessory-after-the-fact joyriding falls within the scope of generic "theft." The Court limited its decision to the simple conclusion that aiding and abetting theft qualifies as a "theft offense" for the purposes of INA §101(a)(43)(G).

Since the Supreme Court's decision, at least one appeals court has found, albeit in the sentencing context (for criminal prosecution of re-entry after removal), that joyriding in violation of Utah's criminal code is a "theft" offense. In *U.S. v. Elizalde-Altamirano*,[193] the defendant had been convicted of joyriding, which was a Class A misdemeanor, and received one year in prison, which was suspended. The court found, referring to *Duenas-Alvarez*, that even a temporary deprivation such as joyriding falls within the broad definition of theft; what's more, although the crime was classified as a misdemeanor, the defendant received a one-year sentence, and the suspension of his sentence was irrelevant under the immigration laws.[194]

The Supreme Court's decision in *Duenas-Alvarez* comports with BIA precedent. In *Matter of V–Z–S–*,[195] the BIA found that a conviction for unlawful driving and taking of a vehicle in violation of Cal. Veh. Code §10851 is a "theft offense" under INA §101(a)(43)(G).

In the summer of 2011, the Ninth Circuit reviewed an attempted commercial burglary conviction under Calif. Penal Code §459 and found the statute to be divisible because it encompasses entry into a building, vessel or structure with an intent to commit larceny, *or any felony* (emphasis added); case law indicates that the statute is utilized not only where the underlying crime is theft, but also for crimes such as vandalism and arson. Utilizing a modified categorical approach, the court found that the conviction did not support an attempted theft finding under INA §§101(a)(43)(G) and (U) because "simply entering a commercial building is not in

---

[193] *U.S. v. Elizalde-Altamirano*, 226 Fed. Appx. 846, 2007 U.S. App. LEXIS 14959, 2007 WL 1765521 (10th Cir. 2007).

[194] INA §101(a)(48)(B). See the discussion of suspension of sentence in chapter two.

[195] *Matter of V–Z–S–*, 22 I&N Dec. 1338 (BIA 2000).

itself a 'substantial step' supporting attempted theft liability."[196] The court noted that mere preparation to commit a crime, even if the intent is to purloin items within, does not constitute a substantial step toward theft.[197]

In an interesting case from the Eleventh Circuit, *Jaggernauth v. U.S. Att'y Gen.*,[198] the court found that Florida's theft statute[199] was divisible because it was written in the disjunctive, to include both "deprivations" and "appropriations," and that a temporary appropriation could not qualify as a "theft" offense. Applying a modified categorical approach, the court noted that the record of conviction did not specify which subsequent the non–American citizen was prosecuted under, thus, the aggravated felony charge should not have been sustained. In light of the "realistic probability" test set forth by the Supreme Court in *Duenas-Alvarez*, a practitioner seeking to rely on *Jaggernauth* may be required to submit a case or cases wherein the statute was utilized to prosecute an "appropriation" that fell short of the generic concept of "theft." The Eleventh Circuit upheld this precedent in 2013 in a case involving shoplifting of merchandise in Georgia; the court of appeals ruled that a temporary appropriation does not qualify as a "theft" offense for aggravated felony purposes.[200]

Burglary

State burglary statutes perhaps present the quintessential example of divisible statutes; the foundation case for the categorical approach, *U.S. v. Taylor*,[201] involved an analysis of burglary of a conveyance. The Supreme Court found that the nature of a conveyance or vehicle is distinct from a structure (or dwelling) and would not be encompassed within the definition of generic burglary. The Ninth Circuit's decision in *U.S. v. Aguila-Montes de Oca*[202] represents a pivotal decision in terms of the modified categorical approach, and involved California's burglary statute: the court of appeals found §959 of the California Penal Code to be divisible, and that reference to the record of conviction is required to determine if there was an unauthorized entry into a dwelling. The essential elements of a classical burglary are the unlawful or unauthorized entry into a structure with the intent to commit a crime. By comparison, trespass is an unauthorized entry or remaining, but without the intent to commit an underlying crime. Burglary of a structure, or dwelling, is also a distinct crime from burglary of a conveyance. Therefore, it is important to review the elements of the crime of conviction before conceding the burglary is a "burglary." The reader will

---

[196] *Hernandez-Cruz v. Holder*, 651 F.3d 1094 (9th Cir. 2011). (Note: the court of appeals further found that this conviction did not represent a crime involving moral turpitude.)

[197] *Hernandez-Cruz v. Holder*, 651 F.3d 1094 (9th Cir. 2011).

[198] *Jaggernauth v. Att'y Gen.*, 432 F.3d 1346 (11th Cir. 2005).

[199] Fla. Stat. §812.014.

[200] *Ramos v. Att'y Gen.*, 709 F.3d 1066 (11th Cir. 2013).

[201] *U.S. v. Taylor*, 495 U.S. 575 (1990).

[202] *U.S. v. Aguila Montes de Oca*, 655 F.3d 915, 946 (9th Cir. 2011).

also note that burglary is defined by some federal statute and case law as a "crime of violence."[203]

Possession of stolen property

Section 101(a)(43)(G) of the Act defines theft, including possession of stolen property, as an aggravated felony when the term of imprisonment is at least one year.

The BIA has found that attempted possession of stolen property is an aggravated felony. For example, attempted possession of stolen property under Nev. Rev. Stat. §§193.330 and 205.275 is a conviction for an attempted theft offense, hence an aggravated felony where a year or more imprisonment is imposed.[204] The phrase "receipt of stolen property" was intended "in a generic sense . . . to include the knowing receipt, possession, or retention of property from its rightful owner."[205] In the summer of 2009, the BIA issued a precedent decision that possession of stolen property in California, where the sentence of imprisonment exceeded one year, categorically qualifies as an aggravated felony theft offense.[206]

Likewise, aiding and abetting the concealment of stolen property (in other words, after the fact of the theft and the receipt) as a second degree principal under §496(a) of the California Penal Code falls within the generic definition of receipt of stolen property.[207]

Embezzlement

Generally speaking, embezzlement is a hybrid concept because it encompasses both theft and fraud and is characterized by an "inside job," meaning, someone in an employee or fiduciary position of trust takes from the employer or subject. The federal crime of embezzlement is found at 18 USC §656. The Third,[208] Ninth[209] and Second[210] Circuits have found that a violation of 18 USC §656 is not necessarily a crime involving fraud or deceit because the statute is divisible, including the intent to defraud and the intent to injure. "Injure," according to the Third Circuit, includes doing an injustice, harming, impairing, tarnishing, or inflicting material damage or loss upon."[211] The Second Circuit also has held that

---

[203] See "crime of violence" discussion earlier in this chapter, including the *Leocal v. Ashcroft* discussion.

[204] *Matter of Bahta*, 22 I&N Dec. 1381 (BIA 2000).

[205] *Matter of Bahta* (citing *Matter of Rodriguez-Carrillo*, 22 I&N Dec. 1031 (BIA 1999)).

[206] *Matter of Cardiel*, 25 I&N Dec. 12 (BIA 2009).

[207] *Matter of Cardiel*, 25 I&N Dec. 12 (BIA 2009).

[208] *Valansi v. Ashcroft*, 278 F.3d 203 (3d Cir. 2002).

[209] *Carlos-Blaza v. Holder*, 611 F.3d 583 (9th Cir. 2010).

[210] *Akinsade v. Holder*, 678 F.3d 138 (2d Cir. 2012).

[211] *Valansi v. Ashcroft*, 278 F.3d 203, 210 (3d Cir. 2002).

§656 is a divisible statute and the intent to injure does not satisfy the aggravated felony "fraud or deceit" definition at INA §101(a)(43)(M)(i).[212]

In comparison, the Eleventh Circuit has ruled that embezzlement qualifies as an aggravated felony crime of fraud and deceit.[213]

Alien Smuggling

INA §101(a)(43)(N) includes within the definition of "aggravated felony" a conviction for violation of INA §§274(a)(1)(A) or (2) [8 USC §§1324(a)(1)(A), (2)]. Sections 274(a)(1)(A) and (2) are broad sections relating to the bringing in or harboring, shielding, concealing, or transporting an undocumented alien within the United States. These provisions include aiding and abetting and apply regardless of the sentence imposed. However, there is an exception for a first-time offense involving the respondent's spouse, parent, or child (and no other individual).

Note that the conviction must be under INA §274(a); a conviction under a companion section at INA §275 [8 USC §1325] does not constitute an aggravated felony under INA §101(a)(43)(N).[214] However, a different provision—INA §101(a)(43)(O)—includes within the definition of "aggravated felony" a conviction under INA §§275 or 276 for an offense committed by an individual who has previously been deported for any aggravated felony.

Offenses That Depend on the Sentence Imposed

The following offenses are aggravated felonies under INA §101(a)(43) only if the sentence of imprisonment imposed is at least one year:

- Theft crimes,[215]
- Crimes of violence,[216]
- Passport-related crimes (falsely making, forging, counterfeiting, or altering),[217]
- Commercial bribery, counterfeiting, trafficking in vehicles with altered VINs,[218] and
- Obstruction of justice, perjury, subornation of perjury, or bribery of a witness.[219]

Commercial bribery; obstruction of justice

In *Matter of Gruenangerl*,[220] the BIA clarified that "commercial bribery" at INA §101(a)(43)(R) does not encompass bribery of public officials. In *Gruenangerl*, the

---

[212] *Akinsade v. Holder*, 678 F.3d 138 (2d Cir. 2012).

[213] *Moore v. Ashcroft*, 251 F.3d 919 (11th Cir. 2001).

[214] *Matter of Alvarado-Alvino*, 22 I&N Dec. 718 (BIA 1999).

[215] INA §101(a)(43)(G).

[216] INA §101(a)(43)(F).

[217] INA §101(a)(43)(P).

[218] INA §101(a)(43)(R).

[219] INA §101(a)(43)(S).

[220] *Matter of Gruenangerl*, 25 I&N Dec. 351(BIA 2010).

respondent was convicted of bribery of a public official under 18 USC §201(b)(1)(A). The BIA wrote that this particular aggravated felony definition does not have a general federal law definition because there is no specific federal offense of commercial bribery. The BIA instead defined "commercial bribery" by looking to *Black's Law Dictionary*, the Model Penal Code, and several state statutes. The Board's analysis dictates that commercial bribery involves improper pecuniary gain by someone in a fiduciary position in exchange for violating a trust or duty to a beneficiary.[221] The phrase does not encompass bribery of a public official. Interestingly, according to the facts, DHS also charged obstruction of justice under INA §101(a)(43)(S). This charge was not sustained by the IJ, but the government did not appeal.

Offenses That Depend on the Amount of Funds Involved

The following offenses are aggravated felonies under INA §101(a)(43) only if the amount of funds involved exceeds $10,000:

- Money laundering,[222]
- Crimes involving fraud or deceit,[223] and
- Tax evasion.[224]

The reference to loss of $10,000 in the provisions defining aggravated felony in terms of the amount of funds involved raises the issue of how to determine the amount of loss.

> **Tip**: DHS has the burden in removal proceedings of establishing deportability for an aggravated felony offense, including the amount of loss and the presence of a victim.[225] However, in the context of seeking relief—establishing eligibility for a certain waiver, affirmative applications like naturalization or adjustment, or a defense to removal—the burden of proof is on the respondent/applicant. Therefore, in the context of relief, the burden of establishing that the loss did not exceed $10,000 will fall on the non–American citizen.

CASE STUDY: KAWASHIMA v. HOLDER

Kawashima v. Holder[226] involved convictions for false statement in a tax return, and aiding and abetting false tax returns, under 26 USC §7206(1) and (2). The non–

---

[221] *Matter of Gruenangerl*, at 354.
[222] INA §101(a)(43)(D).
[223] INA §101(a)(43)(M)(i).
[224] INA §101(a)(43)(M)(ii).
[225] INA §240(c)(3)(A).
[226] *Kawashima v. Holder*, 132 S. Ct. 1166 (2012).

American citizens (husband and wife) argued against the aggravated felony designation because the terms "fraud" and "deceit" prescribed in INA §101(a)(43)(M)(i) are not specifically utilized in the criminal code section. What's more, they argued that since the aggravated felony definition at INA §101(a)(43)(M)(ii) deals specifically with tax evasion under 26 USC §7201—and evasion was distinct from false statement—Congress could not have intended that the false statement in a tax return offense be encompassed within the aggravated felony definition.

The Supreme Court disagreed, finding that the elements of 26 USC §7206(1) are the willful preparation of a material false statement signed under penalty of perjury. For this reason, according to the Court, fraud and deceit are inherent in the offense of submitting a false tax return, and the precise words need not be used. Moreover, the Court found that INA §§101(a)(43)(M)(i) and (ii) were not superfluous sections: it was reasonable that Congress would have a specific subsection dealing with general fraud crimes, and another subsection dealing with tax evasion.[227]

Contesting "Loss" Findings; Understanding "Relevant Conduct"

It is a common mistake to equate the restitution ordered as part of a criminal sentence with the financial loss to a victim in an aggravated felony fraud/deceit case. The "loss" stated in a criminal sentence may not be the actual loss for purposes of INA §101(a)(43)(M)(i). This is because, in the sentencing phase of a criminal case, the judge may order restitution based on a report by pretrial services (a Presentence Investigative Report, or PSI) whose aim it is to arrive at a fair sentence based on overall circumstances; neither restitution nor loss is an issue decided by a jury. The parties also may stipulate to a loss amount as a part of negotiating a proposed sentence. In either event, restitution and loss may be based on "relevant conduct." Simply put, it is absolutely essential that immigration practitioners understand the concept of "relevant conduct" as set forth in the Sentencing Guidelines before litigating an aggravated felony fraud case.

Relevant conduct, as defined by the Guidelines,[228] can include uncharged conduct, acquitted conduct, conduct described in dismissed counts, and conduct of co-conspirators. This means it may include conduct associated with the offense, but outside the count(s) of conviction.

In comparison, both the Supreme Court and the BIA have stated in crystal clear terms that the "loss to a victim" in the aggravated felony fraud definition must be

---

[227] *Kawashima v. Holder*, at 1175.

[228] USSG §1B1.3 (2011).

tethered to the count of conviction. This is what the Supreme Court said in Nijhawan:[229]

> [A]s the Government points out, the "loss" must "be tied to the specific counts covered by the conviction." Brief for Respondent 44; see, e.g., Alaka v. Attorney General of United States, 456 F.3d 88, 107 (3d Cir. 2006) (loss amount must be tethered to offense of conviction; amount cannot be based on acquitted or dismissed counts or general conduct); Knutsen v. Gonzales, 429 F.3d 733, 739–740 (7th Cir. 2005) (same).

This is what the BIA said in *Matter of Babaisakov*:

> We conclude that restitution orders can be sufficient evidence of loss to the victim in certain cases, but they must be assessed with an eye to what losses are covered and to the burden of proof employed.[230]

Immigration counsel will seldom want to concede that the amount of restitution is indicative of the "loss" (only if the amount is less than $10,000). Likewise, counsel should carefully review the record of conviction and other documents—and discuss the criminal case carefully with the client—to determine if the sentence's loss is actually the financial loss to a victim tethered directly to the count(s) of conviction. Again, loss in the sentencing context may be determined based on events that the non–American citizen was not convicted of, yet removability under INA §101(a)(43)(M)(i) does require that the loss be tied to the actual conviction.

CASE STUDY: SINGH v. ATT'Y GEN.

A good example of the above tenets is found in the Third Circuit's 2012 case, *Singh v. Att'y Gen.*,[231] which dissected the "loss to a victim" phrase of INA §101(a)(43)(M)(i). *Singh* involved a minority business' scheme to deceive the New Jersey Port Authority by receiving contracts intended for minority-owned subcontractors, and passing on the contracts to a different contractor, in exchange for a kickback. The problem for Singh, however, was that an undercover agent for the Port Authority orchestrated the entire scheme as part of a sting operation. Although the contractors' plan to fool the Port Authority was investigated, Singh (the minority contractor) was not ultimately prosecuted for the deceit, but rather, was criminally charged for failing to list the Port Authority's anticipated payments as an asset in

---

[229] *Nijhawan v. Holder*, 557 U.S. 29, 42 (2009).

[230] *Matter of Babaisakov*, 24 I&N Dec. 306, 319–320 (BIA 2007).

[231] *Singh v. Att'y Gen.*, 677 F.3d 503 (3d Cir. 2012).

unrelated, pending bankruptcy proceedings. By not listing the "account receivable," Singh committed perjury in the bankruptcy filing.[232]

Singh pled guilty and, ostensibly to avoid a sentence of incarceration (a negotiated *quid pro quo*), the parties stipulated in their plea agreement to a $54,000 loss amount. Significantly, at sentencing, the U.S. Attorney's Office agreed that, because bankruptcy proceedings were ongoing and the bankruptcy trustee would receive all entitled funds, the attempt to withhold assets would not affect the outcome of proceedings (in other words: no loss).

ICE commenced removal proceedings shortly after sentencing, relying on the $54,000 restitution order as proof of a loss. However, the Third Circuit disagreed, finding that §101(a)(43)(M)(i) requires an actual loss, not an intended or potential loss. Because the Port Authority's contract negotiations with Singh were all part of a sting operation, no funds were dispersed. Moreover, as stipulated to by the U.S. Attorney, the bankruptcy trustee's proceedings did not skip a beat—no resources were expended or lost by the failure to declare the [sting operation's] hypothetically forthcoming payment. Under these circumstances, ICE could not establish actual loss.[233]

Still, DHS argued that by federal statute, the restitution order is *ipso facto* evidence of a loss to a victim. The *Singh* court disagreed. Restitution is ordered pursuant to two federal statutes, the Mandatory Victim Restitution Act (MVRA)[234] and the Victim Witness Protection Act (VWPA).[235] It is the MVRA that applies most frequently to fraud and deceit cases, and both of these provisions require that the sentencing court identify a direct or proximate victim of harm before ordering restitution. However, there is in fact a third way to set restitution, outside of the statute, and that is pursuant to parties' agreement; in this context, restitution is not limited to the actual loss from the offense of conviction.[236] Moreover, according to the *Singh* decision, *Nijhawan* still clearly allows parties to a removal proceeding to

---

[232] To violate 18 USC §152(3), one must "knowingly and fraudulently make a false declaration . . . under penalty of perjury" in relation to a bankruptcy proceeding. The Third Circuit found this offense to necessarily involve deceit.

[233] The Ninth Circuit, in a case called *Kharana v. Gonzales*, 487 F.3d 1280, 1282 n.3 (9th Cir. 2007), found that a finding of removability under §101(a)(43)(M)(i) can be based on intended loss. Similarly, the BIA has held that §101(a)(43)(M)(i) may be based on a conspiracy charge with potential losses. *Matter of S–I–K–*, 24 I&N Dec. 324 (BIA 2007).

[234] 18 USC §3663A. Decisions since *Matter of S–I–K–* reflect that the issue of actual versus intended loss for purposes of §101(a)(43)(M) is an open one; certainly the plain language is clear: an offense "in which" the loss to a victim exceeds $10,000. A discussion of actual versus prospective loss and the viability of charging a noncitizen under both subsections (M) and (U) is left for another article, and another day.

[235] 18 USC §3663.

[236] *Singh v. Att'y Gen.*, 677 F.3d at 513.

relitigate the issue of loss.[237] In sum, there was no actual loss, because the Port Authority made no disbursements; there was no identifiable victim, either, because neither the trustee nor the creditors was harmed in any way. The stipulated restitution amount was a *quid pro quo* agreement between the parties in lieu of a long period of incarceration. The parties' agreement may have found justification in relevant conduct, but was part of a negotiated settlement, not payment for actual loss to a victim.

CASE STUDY: OBASOHAN v. ATT'Y GEN.

In *Obasohan v. U.S. Att'y Gen.*,[238] the respondent Obasohan was convicted of one count of conspiracy to produce, use, or traffic in counterfeit access devices, under 18 USC §1029(b)(2). This offense involved using a false driver's license to obtain a credit card in someone else's name. Obasohan received 41 months in prison and was ordered to pay restitution. The elements of the criminal statute clearly described an offense involving fraud or deceit; restitution was ordered in the amount of $37,000 to three different banks. However, as documented by the transcript of the plea colloquy, the specific count to which Obasohan pled did not in fact result in a loss to anyone; restitution was ordered based on other acts not charged in the one-count indictment: unrelated losses from the use of other fraudulent credit cards. Although the IJ (and the BIA) found that the restitution order could constitute proof of loss, the Eleventh Circuit disagreed. The appeals court noted that the criminal statute does not specify an amount of loss, or even require a loss as an element of the offense. Turning then to the record of conviction, the court observed that the indictment, plea, and judgment did not include an amount of loss. Indeed, during the plea hearing, it was clarified that no loss attached to the offense of conviction. Accordingly, the restitution order was not a reliable indicator of the amount of loss for purposes of determining whether the fraud crime met the aggravated felony definition.

Obasohan is one of several cases noted by the Supreme Court in explaining the difference among the federal circuits as the justification for granting certiorari in *Nijhawan v. Holder*.[239] After the Supreme Court's decision in *Nijhawan*, *Obasohan* has been modified in the sense that financial loss does not take a categorical (elements-based) approach; however, the analysis for determining loss and the principle that "loss" in the criminal context is not necessarily "loss" for aggravated felony purposes remains good law.

---

[237] *Singh v. Att'y Gen.*, 677 F.3d 503 (3d Cir. 2012).
[238] *Obasohan v. U.S. Att'y Gen.*, 479 F.3d 785 (11th Cir. 2007).
[239] *Nijhawan v. Holder*, 557 U.S. 29 (2009).

CASE STUDY: CONTEH v. GONZALES

In *Conteh v. Gonzales*,[240] the First Circuit U.S. Court of Appeals found that a jury did not have to find an individual guilty of a specified loss in order for an IJ to determine—based on the record of conviction—that the loss exceeded $10,000. In *Conteh*, the respondent was convicted of federal conspiracy to commit bank fraud. He was charged under INA §101(a)(43)(U) as removable for an aggravated felony offense: conspiracy to commit a fraud offense described in INA §101(a)(43)(M). Conteh argued that, under a strict categorical approach, he could not be removed because the conspiracy statute under which he was convicted [18 USC §371] did not specify an amount of loss, and the jury in its verdict did not specifically determine an amount of loss. The First Circuit disagreed with petitioner Conteh, finding that the IJ could consult the record of conviction under a modified categorical approach to determine the amount of loss. The First Circuit noted that the restitution order may (or may not) be conclusive as to the amount of loss: some restitution orders may be "artificially manipulated" to avoid immigration consequences, stating a loss below $10,000 that is in direct contradiction of the evidence.[241] The First Circuit further noted that the presentence "investigation report (PSI) is not a component of the record of conviction and should not be consulted to establish loss. The court specified that the record of conviction includes the plea, verdict, judgment, and sentence.[242]

The Supreme Court specifically mentions in *Nijhawan v. Holder* that the First Circuit is one of the circuits that have adopted a "fact based approach" to determining loss.[243] Although *Nijhawan* does not specifically mention the PSI, the decision does clarify that evidence from the sentencing phase of a criminal trial may properly be considered in determining the amount of financial loss for purposes of INA §101(a)(43)(M)(i).

Offenses That Depend on "Commercial Advantage"

Similar to the $10,000 loss requirement for crimes involving fraud or deceit, INA §101(a)(43)(K)(ii) includes within the definition of "aggravated felony" a violation of 18 USC §2422(a)—regarding transporting individuals for prostitution purposes across state lines—where the offense is committed for "commercial advantage." The criminal statute does not contain "commercial advantage" as an element of the

---

[240] *Conteh v. Gonzales*, 461 F.3d 45 (1st Cir. 2006).
[241] *Conteh v. Gonzales*, at 61.
[242] *Conteh v. Gonzales*, at 54.
[243] *Nijhawan*, 557 U.S. 29 (2009).

offense. In 2007, in *Matter of Gertsenshteyn*,[244] the BIA declined to apply a modified categorical approach to determining whether a respondent's offense under 18 USC §2422(a) was for commercial advantage. Noting that the traditional components of the record of conviction (indictment, plea, verdict, judgment) are unlikely to mention the issue of commercial advantage, the BIA stated as follows:

> In determining whether the offense was committed for 'commercial advantage,' it is certainly appropriate for an Immigration Judge to consider the record of conviction, but the inquiry is not restricted to the 'elements' needed for conviction. In addition, the Immigration Judge may consider the presentence report, the respondent's own admissions, and any other relevant evidence pertaining to aspects of the criminal conviction. Otherwise, section 101(a)(43)(K)(ii) of the Act would be rendered of little or no effect, because virtually no individual convicted under 18 U.S.C. §§2421, 2422, or 2423 could be ordered removed without examining the underlying nature of the offense to determine whether the crime was committed for a commercial advantage.[245]

The Second Circuit criticized the Board's decision in *Gertsenshteyn*, finding that the BIA improperly went beyond the record of conviction and looked to underlying factual circumstances in determining "commercial advantage." However, the Board's decision comports with the Supreme Court's approach in *Nijhawan*,[246] wherein the Court notes that nonelemental facts may be determined based on a liberal, modified categorical approach that takes into account information contained outside the traditional record of conviction.

"Aggravated Felony"—Must It Be a Felony?

Although the term "aggravated felony" certainly implies that any such offense must be a felony, the BIA and most federal courts have determined that state convictions classified as misdemeanors under state law may nonetheless, in certain circumstances, be considered aggravated felonies under the definition at INA §101(a)(43). If a state crime meets the definition of an aggravated felony offense in terms of its required conduct, and is punishable by more than one year in prison, it will likely be viewed as an aggravated felony—contingent on the other requirements of the particular provision being met (*i.e.*, term of imprisonment, amount of loss, or other specified characteristic).

Misdemeanor Crimes of Violence

In *Matter of Martin*,[247] the BIA held that the offense of third-degree assault in violation of Conn. Gen. Stat. §53a-61(a)(1) constitutes a crime of violence under INA

---

[244] *Matter of Gertsenshteyn*, 24 I&N Dec. 111 (BIA 2007).
[245] *Matter of Gertsenshteyn*, at 115–16 (footnote omitted).
[246] *Nijhawan v. Holder*, 557 U.S. 29 (U.S. 2009).
[247] *Matter of Martin*, 23 I&N Dec. 491 (BIA 2002).

§101(a)(43)(F), even though it is classified as a misdemeanor under Connecticut law. The BIA reasoned that the offense qualifies as a "crime of violence" under 18 USC §16(a). Although classified as a "misdemeanor" under Connecticut law, the individual was sentenced to one year in prison, thus qualifying the offense as an aggravated felony under the definition at INA §101(a)(43)(F).

In light of *Leocal*,[248] *Martin* is probably not good law today: its determination that third-degree assault is a crime of violence has been criticized by more than one federal court.[249] Nevertheless, the distinct point that an offense classified as a misdemeanor under state law can be an aggravated felony remains the prevailing view. This aspect of the decision illustrates the BIA's willingness to classify misdemeanors as aggravated felony offenses. Moreover, in light of the specific language at INA §101(a)(43)(F), it would appear this analysis is sound. Section 101(a)(43)(F) defines aggravated felony as a crime of violence under 18 USC §16. As discussed above, 18 USC §16 contains two subsections. Subsection (a) refers to misdemeanor acts of violence. Because the respondent's crime in *Martin*—at least according to the BIA's analysis—fell under the definition at 18 USC §16(a), and because he was sentenced to a term of imprisonment of exactly one year, his offense qualified as an aggravated felony.

Misdemeanor Sexual Abuse of a Minor[250]

Certainly in the area of sexual abuse of a minor, courts and the BIA are willing to find that misdemeanor offenses qualify as aggravated felonies under both INA §101(a)(43)(A) (sexual abuse of a minor) and INA §101(a)(43)(F) (crime of violence).

In *Matter of Small*,[251] the BIA found that the misdemeanor offense of sexual abuse of a minor qualifies as an aggravated felony under INA §101(a)(43)(A). In *Small*, the individual was convicted of sexual abuse in the second degree under N.Y. Penal Code §130.60(2). This offense is classified as a class A misdemeanor, punishable by imprisonment for one year or less. Quoting the Ninth Circuit's decision in *U.S. v. Robles-Rodriguez*,[252] the BIA noted, "'[A]n offense classified by state law as a misdemeanor can be an "aggravated felony" . . . if the offense otherwise conforms to the federal definition [of that term] found in 8 USC §1101(a)(43) . . . .'"[253] Again, in

---

[248] *Leocal v. Ashcroft*, 543 U.S. 1 (2004), *see* earlier discussion of crimes of violence.

[249] In *Chrzanoski v. Ashcroft*, 327 F.3d 188 (2d Cir. 2003), the Second Circuit found that Connecticut's statute defining intentional assault in the third degree does not expressly identify the use, attempted use, or threatened use of physical force as an element of the crime.

[250] The arrest, detention, and deportation of non–American citizens with convictions for child sexual abuse are priorities for DHS. "Operation Predator" is a national initiative to locate individuals who have been convicted of criminal offenses against children. *See* "DHS Implements 'Operation Predator'," published on AILA InfoNet at Doc. No. 03071146 (*posted* July 11, 2003).

[251] *Matter of Small*, 23 I&N Dec. 448 (BIA 2002).

[252] *U.S. v. Robles-Rodriguez*, 281 F.3d 900, 903 (9th Cir. 2002).

[253] *Matter of Small*, at 450; *see also U.S. v. Marin-Navarette*, 244 F.3d 1284 (11th Cir. 2001).

light of *Leocal's* scienter analysis, all types of offenses previously designated by precedent case law as "aggravated felonies" (especially those classified by a state as misdemeanors) can and should be re-examined.

The decision in *Santapaola v. Ashcroft*[254] involved a Connecticut misdemeanor offense of child abuse. In *Santapaola*, the court discussed at length the proposition that child victims are incapable of giving their consent to sexual activity and are often intimidated by the adult authority figure. The court noted that federal courts across the country have found a substantial risk that physical force will be used against a child to ensure compliance in the course of a sexual activity; thus, the offense is a crime of violence, and therefore, an aggravated felony.[255]

In *Gattem v. Gonzales*,[256] the Seventh Circuit agreed with the BIA that solicitation of a minor for sexual purposes, a class B misdemeanor under Illinois law, was an aggravated felony under INA §101(a)(43)(A). The court did not address the felony versus misdemeanor issue, but instead focused on the offense conduct. As a result, it is not clear how the court squared its finding that a misdemeanor could qualify as an aggravated felony.[257]

Attempts and Conspiracies

INA §101(a)(43)(U) [8 USC §1101(a)(43)(U)] is a catch-all provision that renders a conviction for an attempt or conspiracy to commit any of the offenses enumerated in INA §101(a)(43) an aggravated felony in its own right. In *Matter of Onyido*,[258] the individual was convicted of submitting a false claim with intent to defraud the Indiana Farmers Mutual Insurance Company, in violation of Ind. Code §35-43-5-4(10).[259] The factual scenario was that the individual submitted a false claim to his insurance company and agreed to settle for the amount of $15,000. When he arrived at the insurance office to collect his settlement, he was arrested; thus, the insurance company never actually paid out the funds. The individual was charged with a crime involving fraud or deceit under INA §101(a)(43)(M)(i)[260] and §101(a)(43)(U); he

---

[254] *Santapaola v. Ashcroft*, 249 F. Supp. 2d 181 (D. Conn. 2003).

[255] *Santapaola v. Ashcroft*, at 195–96.

[256] *Gattem v. Gonzales*, 412 F.3d 758 (7th Cir. 2005).

[257] This decision includes a well-written, scathing dissent by Justice Richard Posner, which argues that solicitation of a minor is essentially an attempt to abuse sexually, and therefore cannot be actual sexual abuse. Justice Posner also questions the majority's failure to reconcile the issue of how a second-degree misdemeanor can be an "aggravated felony" and invites the BIA to arrive at a universal definition based on federal law, perhaps setting the age of "minor" as 18 years.

[258] *Matter of Onyido*, 22 I&N Dec. 552 (BIA 1999).

[259] This provision states, in pertinent part, that "a person who knowingly and with intent to defraud, makes, utters, presents, or causes to be presented to an insurer, a claim statement that contains false, incomplete, or misleading information concerning the claim . . . commits fraud, a Class D Felony."

[260] A crime involving fraud or deceit where loss to the victim exceeds $10,000.

argued before the immigration court and the BIA that the insurance company suffered no actual loss—therefore, his offense did not qualify as an aggravated felony. The BIA analyzed the Indiana statute in question, which requires as an element a knowing intent to defraud, and noted that no actual loss need be suffered in order to sustain a conviction. The BIA found the fact that the individual did not actually obtain any money as a result of the attempted fraud to be of no consequence under INA §101(a)(43)(U). The Board applied a similar analysis to conspiracy in *Matter of S–I–K–*,[261] involving convictions for conspiracy to submit false statements in a health care benefit program, where the potential loss exceeded $10,000.

---

[261] *Matter of S–I–K–*, 24 I&N Dec. 324 (BIA 2007).

CHAPTER EIGHT

CLASSIFICATIONS BEYOND MORAL TURPITUDE AND AGGRAVATED FELONY

Controlled Substance Offenses 323
Firearms Offenses 333
Money Laundering 335
Crimes of Domestic Violence 336
Alien Smuggling 343
Crimes Involving Failure to Register; Visa and Passport Fraud 347
Export Law; National Security Violations 351
Public Safety and National Security 353
Failure to Register as a Sex Offender 354

Appendices
    8A: Sample Motion to Dismiss CIMT and RTB Charges 356
    8B: Unpublished BIA Decision on Drug Paraphernalia and *Pickering* Vacatur Standard ... 369

This chapter discusses criminal grounds of removability other than offenses involving moral turpitude and aggravated felony. This chapter deals with classification of crimes; the next chapter deals with consequences.

Controlled Substance Offenses

Certain controlled substance offenses qualify as crimes involving moral turpitude, aggravated felonies, or both. However, because the Immigration and Nationality Act (INA) contains specific provisions dealing with controlled substance offenses, such offenses are also independent grounds of inadmissibility (INA §212) and removability (INA §237). In addition, the law's treatment of controlled substances includes *regulatory* violations that may be neither crimes involving moral turpitude nor aggravated felonies. Finally, it is important to note that persons (and their family members) can be denied admission to the United States, or permanent resident status, based on a "reason to believe" that they have been involved in illicit trafficking. Thus, when talking about the controlled substance classification, it is important to remember that an individual may not have a final conviction—or even an arrest—on his or her record, yet nevertheless suffer adverse immigration consequences as a result of suspicion of illegal activity.

The Definition of "Controlled Substance Offense"

Under INA §212(a)(2)(A)(i)(II) [8 USC §1182(a)(2)(A)(i)(II)], an individual who has been convicted of or who *admits* having committed a "violation of any law or regulation of a State, the United States, or a foreign country relating to a controlled substance (as defined in section 102 of the Controlled Substances Act (21 USC §802)) is inadmissible." This means an individual applying for a visa or attempting to enter the United States may be denied the visa or admission. An individual who applies for permanent resident status may be denied such status, and an individual who is already a permanent resident, returning to the United States from a trip abroad, may be denied readmission. These consequences are discussed in chapter six.

In the same vein, an individual who has already been admitted to the United States in a lawful immigrant or nonimmigrant status may be placed in removal proceedings pursuant to INA §237(a)(2)(B) if he or she is *convicted* of a controlled substance violation (again, as defined under 21 USC §802). Once an individual is lawfully admitted to the United States, he or she must have a final conviction (as opposed to merely admitting to a §802 violation) to be removed. Moreover, as discussed in the next chapter, there is an exception to removability for a single offense of simple possession of 30 grams or less of marijuana.[1]

The *Descamps*[2] categorical methodology has an interesting effect in the controlled substance arena because most state schedules (if not all) will vary slightly from the federal Controlled Substance Act (CSA) lists. Decided in 2014, *Matter of Ferreira*[3] presented the purest of categorical approach issues: whether a controlled substance conviction in Connecticut for "sale of certain drugs" could qualify as an aggravated felony illicit trafficking crime, and/ or a controlled substance violation, when the Connecticut schedule of drugs differed from the federal CSA. The state schedule (at the time, in 2010) included two drugs ("obscure" opiate derivatives) not found on the federal CSA: *benzylfentanyl* and *thenylfentanyl*. In the absence of a precise categorical match, according to Ferreira, he was not deportable under either INA §237(a)(2)(A)(iii) (aggravated felony) or §237(a)(2)(B)—because both provisions reference the federal CSA. The immigration judge (IJ) disagreed, relying on the record of conviction to identify the nature of the substances involved, through a circumstance-specific approach. The Board of Immigration Appeals (BIA or Board) reversed and remanded, relying on *Moncrieffe*:[4] A state offense categorically matches a generic federal offense only if a conviction for the state offense "'necessarily' involved facts equating" to the generic federal offense. Upon administrative appeal, the BIA disagreed with the IJ, but added a realistic probability component to the analysis.

---

[1] Immigration and Nationality Act (INA) §237(a)(2)(B); 8 U.S. Code (USC) §1227(a)(2)(B).

[2] *Descamps v. U.S.*, 133 S. Ct. 2276 (2013). Discussion of the categorical approach is at chapter five.

[3] *Matter of Ferreira*, 26 I&N Dec. 415 (BIA 2014).

[4] *Moncrieffe v. Holder*, 133 S. Ct. 2276 (2013).

Drawing from the U.S. Supreme Court's decision in *Gonzales v. Duenas-Alvarez*,[5] and the Board's own decision in *Matter of Chairez I*,[6] the realistic probability test places the onus on the noncitizen to establish a realistic probability—as opposed to a hypothetical possibility—that the state would apply its statute to conduct that falls outside the generic definition of the crime. Hence, the BIA remanded Mr. Ferreira's case for further "fact-finding" proceedings, so he could show Connecticut actually prosecuted these obscure substances (which have since been removed from the state schedule).

In 2013, the Third Circuit U.S. Court of Appeals rejected the notion that a categorical or modified categorical approach applies in determining removability under INA §237(a)(2)(B). In *Rojas v. Att'y Gen.*,[7] the court of appeals analyzed the section's two parentheticals, "relating" to a controlled substance and "defined in" the federal CSA in the context of a paraphernalia conviction. According to the court, these phrases mean that neither a categorical nor a modified categorical approach applies; instead the court prescribed a circumstance-specific–type of approach (without coming right out and calling it that) wherein the Department of Homeland Security (DHS) has the burden of proving the substance involved and its inclusion in the federal CSA. Because in *Rojas* the record is silent, DHS failed in meeting its burden; the petition for review was granted.

In 2014, the same court of appeals applied a similar analysis to arrive at a different conclusion because (according to the court) the burden of proof rested with the respondent in the relief stage. In *Syblis v. Att'y Gen.*,[8] the Third Circuit denied the petition for review, finding that the respondent could not prove that his two convictions (according to the record, for simple possession of marijuana) did not involve substances on the federal CSA. Again, the court of appeals declined to apply a strict categorical approach and juxtapose the state and federal statutes—rather, the court found that the record was inconclusive as to the type of substance involved, and in light of the burden, denied relief.

A similar and potentially very important case was pending at the Supreme Court in the spring of 2015. In June 2014, the Court accepted certiorari in the case of *Mellouli v. Holder*, arising out of a decision of the Eighth Circuit U.S. Court of Appeals to deport Mellouli under INA §237(a)(2)(B). According to the facts, Mellouli was in possession of a few pills—stored in his sock—which were discovered while being booked into jail on unrelated charges. He ultimately pled to misdemeanor possession of drug paraphernalia (the sock), but neither the state statute nor the record of conviction identify the type of controlled substance involved. Again, the state schedule varies from the federal CSA. The issue from a categorical approach

---

[5] *Gonzales v. Duenas-Alvarez*, 549 U.S. 183 (2007).

[6] *Matter of Chairez I*, 26 I&N Dec. 349 (BIA 2014).

[7] *Rojas v. Att'y Gen.*, 728 F.3d 203 (3d Cir. 2013).

[8] *Syblis v. Att'y Gen.*, 763 F.3d 348 (3d Cir. 2014).|

would be whether a state statute of conviction must identify whether the "paraphernalia" (in this case, a sock) is related to a controlled substance on the federal list in order to support a charge of removability under INA §237(a)(2)(B). The issue from a modified categorical approach would be whether a federally controlled substance can be identified within the confines of the record of conviction. From a circumstance-specific approach, the Court would examine the nature of the substance using conviction documents outside the record.

Personal-use exception

For persons facing removal in the deportation track, INA §237(a)(2)(B) contains an exception for a single offense of simple possession less than 30 grams of marijuana. This exception does not exist at INA §212(a)(2)(A)(i)(II). This dichotomy is discussed in greater detail in the next chapter on "Consequences." *Matter of Dominguez-Rodriguez,*[9] decided in September 2014, addressed whether a categorical or circumstance-specific approach applies to the personal possession exception at INA §101(a)(43)(B). A Las Vegas court convicted Dominguez of possession of more than one ounce of marijuana. An ounce equals approximately 28.5 grams. Applying *Moncrieffe,*[10] the IJ ruled in favor of Dominguez, finding that the least culpable conduct described by statute would be less than 30 grams. To prove a larger amount, DHS must rely on the record of conviction, which in this case was silent to amount. The BIA disagreed, and reversed and remanded for a circumstance-specific inquiry utilizing all relevant evidence to determine the amount of marijuana involved. The BIA places the burden of proof by clear and convincing evidence on DHS, but rejects a modified categorical approach limited to the record of conviction and opts for a circumstance-specific inquiry.

Drugs, but Not Controlled Substances

It is important to note that many types of drugs are not controlled substances. A "controlled substance" is one listed in a schedule at 21 USC §802. Legend drugs, on the other hand, are drugs that are regulated by the U.S. Food and Drug Administration—such as prescription drugs—but are not "controlled" because they do not have narcotic or addictive effects. Currently, with widespread use of the Internet—along with enhanced computer databases to detect crime—defense attorneys frequently see import–export violations, criminal infringements on patents, illegal sale of legend drugs, and so on. These offenses involve, for example, unlicensed individuals violating patents and repackaging drugs, unlawfully importing them, and often selling them on the Internet. The violations (unlawful importation, license infringement, illegal sale, etc.) may fall into various classifications of crime, but if they do not involve "controlled substances," they are not "controlled-substance" violations under the INA.

---

[9] *Matter of Dominguez-Rodriguez*, 26 I&N Dec. 408 (BIA 2014).

[10] *Moncrieffe v. Holder*, 133 S. Ct. 1678 (2013).

Often, the terms "drug" and "controlled substance" are used interchangeably; but in fact, they are not synonymous. "Drug" is a much broader term. Illegal possession and importation of cancer drugs from Europe, for example, is certainly a crime, but it is not a "controlled substance" violation. Renaming, repackaging, and selling (in violation of a patent) a generic "Viagra" drug on eBay may be a type of theft—a fraud or a customs violation—but it is not a "controlled-substance" violation. In the new world of Internet sales of nutritional supplements and prescriptions for depression, sexual dysfunction, and even nasal congestion, it is important to remember that if an item is not listed on a federal schedule, it is not a controlled substance violation under the INA.

In *Borrome v. Att'y Gen.*,[11] the Third Circuit ruled that a conviction for violation of the Federal Food, Drug and Cosmetic Act (FDCA) at 21 USC §§201–399d does not qualify as a "controlled-substance violation" for purposes of INA §237(a)(2)(B) because—from a categorical standpoint—the FDCA does not reference controlled substances. This case involved the illegal distribution of several prescription drugs, some of which are controlled substances—such as Oxycontin. The circuit court noted that there is certainly an overlap between regulated prescription drugs and controlled substances, but clung to a strict categorical approach in its analysis that the CSA does not mimic the FDCA.

This case makes great reading for several key immigration law discussions, including application of the categorical approach and the hypothetical federal felony (which, the court explains, extends beyond state possession offenses, but can be used to mix-and-match different federal statutes); it also contains several memorable comments by the Third Circuit Court of Appeals. (As is discussed in the section on aggravated felonies in chapter seven, the court also found that petitioner's conviction was not an aggravated felony drug trafficking crime.) By way of example, the reader will consider the following passages wherein the court notes that §353(b)(1) of the FDCA does not provide a list of specific drugs subject to its prescription requirements and cannot categorically match—or qualify as "related to" the CSA:

> Whether a drug is a prescription drug by virtue of § 353(b)(1)(A) is a question of fact for the jury. See *U.S. v. Munoz*, 430 F.3d 1357, 1367 (11th Cir. 2005). The FDA does, however, publish in what is colloquially known as the "Orange Book" a list of what are prescription drugs by virtue of § 353(b)(1)(B) because they are "limited by an approved application under section 355 of [title 21] to use under ... professional supervision" ... .[12]
>
> The term "controlled substance" appears nowhere in §§ 331(t) and 353(e). A "controlled substance" is defined in the CSA to mean, "a drug or other substance, or immediate precursor, included in schedule I, II, III, IV, or V of part B of this subchapter." 21 U.S.C. § 802(6). A list of "controlled substances"

---

[11] *Borrome v. Att'y Gen.*, 687 F.3d 150 (3d Cir. 2012).
[12] *Borrome v. Att'y Gen.*, 687 F.3d 150, at 158.

is provided in 21 U.S.C. § 812 and supplemented by 21 C.F.R. §§ 1308.11-.15. The only way to discern an overlap between prescription drugs and controlled substances is to compare the list of prescription drugs in the FDA's Orange Book and the list of controlled substances in the CSA and its corresponding regulations ... .[13]

To repeat, §§ 331(t) and 353(e) do not use the term "controlled substance" nor do they list specific prescription drugs that are in fact controlled substances. To see the connection between prescription drugs and controlled substances, we must rummage through the 400-plus page "Prescription Drug Product List" in the FDA's Orange Book, see *Approved Drug Products with Therapeutic Equivalence Evaluations, supra* at 3-1 to 3-424, and then hunt for a match in the roughly 100 pages of schedules of controlled substances in the Code of Federal Regulations, *see* 21 C.F.R. §§1308.11-.15. Even if we complete this odyssey, the fruits of our labor are for naught. It is inconsequential under §§ 331(t) and 353(e)(2)(A) if the prescription drugs at issue are also controlled substances "(as defined in section 802 of Title 21)." Thus, the "relationship" between §§ 331(t) and 353(e)(2)(A) and "controlled substances" is a mere coincidence devoid of any legal significance under the FDCA.[14]

In terms of the "relating to" language at INA §237(a)(2)(B), the circuit court draws several interesting analogies (The sharp lawyer will want to use these in the context of other removal grounds.) The circuit court notes that if a truck driver for a pharmaceutical company fails to properly refrigerate or package his samples of Oxycontin while transporting them, and is prosecuted under the FDCA, his conviction does not "relate to" a controlled substance. Likewise, a person who is convicted of theft, or of dealing in stolen property, where the underlying item was Oxycontin, is not removable for a crime "relating to" a controlled substance. These are just a few pearls of wisdom from the court's discussion of what it means to "relate to" a controlled substance for purposes of INA §237(a)(2)(B).

Solicitation Offenses

Prior to *Descamps* and *Moncrieffe*, the BIA twice ruled that a conviction for solicitation under a general solicitation statute qualifies as a controlled substance offense where the underlying crime, as reflected in the record of conviction, is an offense relating to a controlled substance.[15] The offense of solicitation involves commanding, hiring, requesting, or encouraging another individual to commit a crime. It is a general, inchoate crime. In *Matter of Zorilla-Vidal*,[16] the respondent was

---

[13] *Borrome v. Att'y Gen.*, 687 F.3d 150.

[14] *Borrome v. Att'y Gen.*, 687 F.3d 150, at 162.

[15] *Matter of Zorilla-Vidal*, 24 I&N Dec. 768 (BIA 2009); *Matter of Beltran*, 20 I&N Dec. 521 (BIA 1992).

[16] *Matter of Zorilla-Vidal*, 24 I&N Dec. 768 (BIA 2009).

convicted of soliciting the delivery of cocaine. The Board notes that in the Ninth[17] and Sixth U.S. Circuit Courts of Appeals,[18] the courts have found that solicitation offenses—where the underlying offense involves a controlled substance—are not crimes relating to a controlled substance. In contrast, two courts of appeals have ruled in accordance with the Board's decision in *Matter of Beltran*.[19]

Paraphernalia

For many years, there was little case law on the classification and consequences of a conviction for an offense relating to drug paraphernalia. In the past several years, there have been many cases at both the administrative and circuit court levels (and now the Supreme Court) dealing with paraphernalia offenses and different issues, including:

- whether possession of paraphernalia "relates to" a controlled substance offense;
- whether one count of possession of marijuana combined with another count of possession of paraphernalia can be "rolled" into one offense (for purposes of either the removability ground or a waiver); and
- whether possession of certain types of paraphernalia can be distinguished from a federal law counterpart, hence be considered an offense not qualifying as a removal ground.

Certainly, possession of drug paraphernalia, standing alone, cannot be classified as a crime involving moral turpitude or as an aggravated felony (drug trafficking) offense. However, possession of paraphernalia may be a controlled-substance violation under INA §§212(a)(2)(A)(i)(II) and 237(a)(2)(B) because it "relates to" a controlled substance.[20] The more interesting question is: what is the analysis? A categorical comparison with the federal code; a modified categorical approach that looks for the type of substance within the parameters of the record of conviction documents; or a circumstance-specific approach that considers any and all relevant evidence.

The BIA has likened possession of paraphernalia to a regulatory violation. Violations of regulations relating to controlled substances may fall under this particular classification. In *Matter of Pacheco-Ventura*,[21] the BIA found that possession of drug paraphernalia in violation of Article 27, §287A of the Annotated Code of Maryland [now Md. Code Ann., Crim. Law §5-619] was a crime "relating

---

[17] *Coronado-Durazo v. INS*, 123 F.3d 1322, 1325 (9th Cir. 1997).

[18] *U.S. v. Dolt*, 27 F.3d 235 (6th Cir. 1994).

[19] *Matter of Beltran*, 20 I&N Dec. 521 (BIA 1992); *Mizrahi v. Gonzales*, 492 F.3d 156, 164–65 (2d Cir. 2007); *Peters v. Ashcroft*, 383 F.3d 302, 306–07 (5th Cir. 2004).

[20] *Matter of Martinez Espinoza*, 25 I&N Dec. 118, 120 (BIA 2009); *Barraza v. Mukasey*, 519 F.3d 388, 390–91 (7th Cir. 2008); *Alvarez Acosta v. Att'y Gen.*, 524 F.3d 1191, 1196 (11th Cir. 2008).

[21] *Matter of Pacheco-Ventura*, A44 801 843, 2003 BIA LEXIS 14, 2003 WL 23508549 (BIA Dec. 29, 2003). Because this is an unpublished decision, it is reproduced at Appendix 8B.

to" a controlled substance violation. The BIA cites to a Ninth Circuit case, *Luu-Le v. INS*,[22] and remarks that this is an issue of "first impression."

Prior to *Descamps* and *Moncrieffe*, every federal circuit court to rule on the issue found that possession of drug paraphernalia is a per se violation of a law "relating to a controlled substance."[23] Perhaps a more significant question is whether possession of marijuana paraphernalia can qualify for the exception for removability at INA 237(a)(2)(B) regarding less than 30 grams of marijuana. Yet another issue is whether possession of paraphernalia combined with one count of possession of marijuana can be considered "one offense" for purposes of the removability exception for possession of less than 30 grams of marijuana. And finally another twist on the two-counts-one-conviction issue is whether the two combined counts (possession of marijuana and possession of paraphernalia) may be viewed as rolled up into "one offense" for purposes of an INA §212(h) waiver.

In October 2012, the BIA issued an important decision, *Matter of Davey*,[24] that finally clarified whether a conviction on two counts—possession of marijuana and possession of paraphernalia for the purpose of marijuana use—could be considered a "single offense relating to" possession for one's own use of 30 grams of less of marijuana. The BIA correctly found that where an "offense" involves one count of paraphernalia and one count of possession of marijuana, this is "one offense" for purposes of removability. The context, notably, was a *Joseph* hearing[25] for custody redetermination. The BIA clarified that the correct analysis is a "circumstance-specific" approach that takes into consideration relevant issues outside the elements of the statute.

Again, the relevance of the *Davey* decision encompasses both removability and relief, discussed in the next two chapters: "Consequences" and "Waivers." Based on the *Davey* decision, attorneys can argue that one count of paraphernalia and one count of possession of marijuana is a "single offense." This is important for the INA §212(h) waiver. Again, more specificity is given to this topic in the next two chapters.

Possession must be accompanied by "intent to use"

Notably, the BIA in *Pacheco-Ventura* finds that possession of drug paraphernalia may be counted as a controlled substance violation "if that possession is accompanied by the use, or the intended use, of the drug paraphernalia for drug-related purposes."

---

[22] 224 F.3d 911 (9th Cir. 2000) (Arizona conviction for possession of drug paraphernalia is a conviction relating to a controlled substance).

[23] *Barma v. Holder*, 640 F.3d 749 (7th Cir. 2011); *Estrada v. Holder*, 560 F.3d 1039 (9th Cir. 2009); Alvarez *Acosta v. Att'y Gen.*, 524 F.3d 1191, 1196 (11th Cir. 2008); *Barraza v. Mukasey*, 519 F.3d 388, 390–91 (7th Cir. 2008).

[24] *Matter of Davey*, 26 I&N Dec. 37 (BIA 2012).

[25] The *Joseph* hearing (*Matter of Joseph*, 22 I&N Dec. 799 (BIA 1999)) is a custody redetermination (bond) hearing in which the underlying issue becomes removability. This is discussed in chapter four.

In this case, the record of conviction noted that the defendant had marijuana stuffed into a Visine eye-drop bottle. Based on the "accompanied by use" language, if the possession of paraphernalia was not accompanied by the indicia of use of a drug—for example, a companion charge for possession of marijuana, or other indication within the record of conviction that the defendant/respondent was poised to *use* drugs—the conviction would arguably not support a ground of deportability for a controlled substance violation.

In *Becker v. Gonzales*,[26] the respondent was found deportable for a controlled-substance violation under INA §237(a)(2)(B) on the basis of a conviction for possession of drug paraphernalia, a felony under Arizona law. However, in *Becker*, the respondent did not contest deportability on this basis, so whether possession of paraphernalia could be a deportable controlled-substance offense was not argued. The case dealt with the respondent's eligibility for relief on account of a previous aggravated felony conviction.[27]

> **Practice Pointer**: Practitioners should contest deportability where the item of paraphernalia has no federal counterpart under the U.S. criminal code, and read the *Mellouli* decision from the U.S. Supreme Court.[28]

Simulated or imitation controlled substances

Most states have laws criminalizing the distribution of "look-alike" or counterfeit controlled substances: imitation drugs sold as the real thing. The BIA has held that delivery of a simulated controlled substance is not a trafficking offense, and therefore not an aggravated felony, but is a violation of a law "relating to" a controlled substance for purposes of removability under INA §§212(a)(2)(A)(i)(II) and 237(a)(2)(B)(i).[29] The CSA does not penalize simulated controlled substances. Likewise, the Seventh Circuit U.S. Court of Appeals has found that distribution of a look-alike substance in violation of Illinois law is a removable offense under INA §212(a)(2)(A)(i)(II); the substance involved here was chocolates passed off as psilocybin, "the active ingredient in psychedelic mushrooms," for $20 to another nightclub patron (who was also an undercover police officer).[30]

"Reason to Believe"

Under INA §212(a)(2)(C) [8 USC §1182(a)(2)(C)], a non–American citizen who is inadmissible if a Department of State (DOS) consular officer or the AG [now DHS] *knows or has reason to believe* that the person—

---

[26] *Becker v. Gonzales*, 473 F.3d 1000 (9th Cir. 2007).

[27] See discussion on concurrent waivers in chapter ten.

[28] *Mellouli v. Holder*, docket no. 1034, was argued at the Supreme Court on January 14, 2015. The opinion had not been issued as of this writing.

[29] *Matter of Sanchez-Cornejo*, 25 I&N Dec. 273 (BIA 2010).

[30] *Desai v. Mukasey*, 520 F.3d 762 (7th Cir. 2008).

(i) is or has been an illicit trafficker in any controlled substance . . . or is or has been a knowing aider, abettor, assister, conspirator or colluder with others in the illicit trafficking in any such controlled substance or chemical, or endeavored to do so; or

(ii) is the spouse, son or daughter of any alien inadmissible under clause (i), [and] has, within the previous 5 years, obtained any financial or other benefits from the illicit activity of that alien, and knew or reasonably should have known that the financial or other benefit was the product of such illicit activity.

The "reason to believe" provision is under §212(a), relating to admissibility. It applies to persons who seek to enter the United States at a port of entry, or persons who are applying for permanent resident status. It does not apply to persons who are already here as LPRs—as long as they stay in the United States and do not travel (hence avoiding any potential grounds of inadmissibility when applying for admission upon return). This provision is used against almost any person who has been arrested for a controlled substance offense that carries an element of trafficking; indeed, it has been used by adjudicators to deny residency where the underlying charge or conviction was only personal possession. Its use is widespread across the country; its applicability varies from DHS office to office. For example, certain adjudicators will not allege "reason to believe" if the criminal charge was dismissed or a *nolle prosequi* entered by the state or federal prosecutor, but will pursue the ground if the individual went to jury trial and was acquitted. However, there is virtually no guidance or policy on how this particular charge should be used; thus, it is anyone's guess whether the "reason to believe" charge will be used against an individual at any given time.[31]

The second provision, relating to spouses, sons, and daughters, was added in 2000. The author has never seen it used, and suspects it is more widely utilized by consular officers in U.S. embassies as a justification for denying visas to the family members of drug traffickers or suspected drug traffickers. In today's immigration world, however, DHS is relying increasingly on a system of background checks for every benefit application; it may be that use of the second subsection of the "reason to believe" provision will become more prevalent in the future, as name checks reveal more about the history of an applicant's family.

Drug Abusers and Addicts

According to INA §237(a)(2)(B)(ii) [8 USC §1227(a)(2)(B)(ii)], an individual "who is, or at any time after admission has been, a drug abuser or addict is deportable" (subject to removal from the United States). This particular provision, utilizing the language "drug abusers and addicts," is a ground of deportation in

---

[31] The phrase "reason to believe" has been equated with the standard for "probable cause." *See U.S. v. Veal*, 453 F.3d 164, 167 n.3 (3d Cir. 2006); *see also Matter of A–H–*, 23 I&N Dec. 774, 789 (AG 2005).

removal proceedings. However, an individual who has used unlawful drugs also could be subject to §212 inadmissibility for admission of the essential elements of a crime involving a controlled substance.[32]

Firearms Offenses

Pursuant to INA §237(a)(2)(C) [8 USC §1227(a)(2)(C)], an individual who at any time after admission is convicted of violating any law of purchasing, selling, offering for sale, exchanging, using, owning, or possessing, etc., a weapon, firearm, or destructive device (as defined by 18 USC §921(a)) is deportable. A firearms conviction is not a basis for inadmissibility under INA §212(a) [8 USC §1182(a)].

"Firearm" and "Destructive Device" Defined

The term "firearm" is defined at 18 USC §921(a)(3) as follows:

(A) any weapon (including a starter gun) which will or is designed to or may readily be converted to expel a projectile by the action of an explosive; (B) the frame or receiver of any such weapon; (C) any firearm muffler or firearm silencer; or (D) any destructive device. Such term does not include an antique firearm.

The term "destructive device" is defined at 18 USC §921(a)(4) as follows:

(A) any explosive, incendiary or poison gas –

(i) bomb,

(ii) grenade,

(iii) rocket having a propellant charge of more than four ounces,

(iv) missile having an explosive or incendiary charge of more than one-quarter ounce,

(v) mine, or

(vi) device similar to any of the devices described in the preceding clauses;

(B) any type of weapon (other than a shotgun or a shotgun shell which the attorney general finds is generally recognized as particularly suitable for sporting purposes) by whatever name known which will, or which may be readily converted to, expel a projectile by the action of an explosive or other propellant, and which has any barrel with a bore of more than one-half inch in diameter; and

(C) any combination of parts either designed or intended for use in converting any device into any destructive device described in subparagraph (A) or (B) and from which a destructive device may be readily assembled.

---

[32] INA §212(a)(2)(A)(i)(II); 8 USC §1182(a)(2)(A)(i)(II).

The term "destructive device" shall not include any device which is neither designed nor redesigned for use as a weapon; any device, although originally designed for use as a weapon, which is redesigned for use as a signaling, pyrotechnic, line throwing, safety, or similar device; surplus ordnance sold, loaned, or given by the Secretary of the Army pursuant to the provisions of section 4684(2), 4685, or 4686 of title 10; or any other device which the Secretary of the Treasury finds is not likely to be used as a weapon, is an antique, or is a rifle which the owner intends to use solely for sporting, recreational or cultural purposes.

Firearms offenses are regulatory in nature, and do not fall under the category of crimes involving moral turpitude. It is a misplaced approach to consider whether the offense encompasses evil intent or even specific intent, because the INA imposes strict liability for any sort of firearms violation, regardless of severity. For example, in *Awad v. Gonzales*,[33] the non–American citizen was a sport hunter with a license to carry a rifle. He was stopped and cited by a Minnesota Department of Natural Resources officer for transporting a loaded gun in his vehicle, received a misdemeanor citation, and eventually paid a $100 fine. The Eighth Circuit U.S. Court of Appeals upheld the removal order, finding the minor nature of the offense was not relevant to deportability under INA §237(a)(2)(C). What's more, the court found that the recreational exception to the firearms ground relates only to destructive devices, and not all firearms—including the type involved in the particular case—qualified as destructive devices.

Firearm must be an element

Chapter five, "Methodology," discusses the *Chairez* decisions[34] at length. Based on *Chairez I*, the fact of a firearm is an essential element that must be present in the statute. Moreover, a state firearms offense must be a categorical match one in the federal code: Firearm is defined at 18 USC §921(a). *Chairez* rejected the pre-*Descamps* notion that an adjudicator may utilize a modified categorical approach to look for the presence of a firearm in the record of conviction when the statute is overly broad and does not specifically include firearm as an essential element. An overly broad statute (one that is missing the element) will fail as a firearms offense. This means that broad language such as "weapon" will not qualify as a firearm offense. In *Chairez* I, the respondent argued his state conviction for discharging a firearm (which included as an element use of a firearm) was not a categorical match to the federal statute because federal law contains an exception for antique firearms that the Utah law lacks. The BIA agreed that the state statute was not categorically a

---

[33] *Awad v. Gonzales*, 494 F.3d 723 (8th Cir. 2007).

[34] *Matter of Chairez I*, 26 I&N Dec. 349 (BIA 2014); *Matter of Chairez II*, 26 I&N Dec. 478 (BIA 2015).

firearm offense, but remanded for the respondent to show a realistic probability that Utah would ever prosecute use of an antique firearm.[35]

Firearms offense not a ground of inadmissibility

An important nuance in the area of firearms offenses is that they do not form a basis of inadmissibility, because the firearms ground is listed only in INA §237, referring to deportability. The distinction between admissibility and deportability, as well as other adverse consequences attached to a firearms offense, is discussed in the next chapter. However, it is an important issue that merits highlighted attention: a person will *not* be statutorily ineligible to receive a visa, enter the United States, or adjust status on the basis of a firearms charge because it is not a ground of inadmissibility under INA §212(a). A firearms conviction does not bar adjustment of status or a visa. (Note, however, that a firearms conviction, or any conviction, may lead to a discretionary denial of a benefit sought.)

No "Reason to Believe" or "Admission of the Essential Elements" Standards Apply

As discussed above, under certain immigration law provisions, an admission to the essential elements of a crime involving moral turpitude or a controlled-substance violation can lead to denial of a benefit even in the absence of a conviction. In comparison, the firearms section at INA §237(a)(2)(C) [8 USC §1227(a)(2)(C)] contains no such provisions. A final conviction is required to be deportable for a firearms offense.

Money Laundering

As discussed above in chapter seven, money laundering in the amount of $10,000 or more is an aggravated felony. (By federal law, the offense activity must involve at least $10,000 to constitute a crime.) However, prior to 2001, immigration law contained a loophole of sorts because—as an aggravated felony—a conviction for money laundering did not render a person inadmissible, only deportable. Money laundering is arguably a regulatory offense, not a crime involving moral turpitude. This distinction—the fact that a person could be deportable but not inadmissible for the crime of money laundering—resulted in a situation where money laundering was not an impediment to entry, visa application grants, adjustment or change of status, or naturalization. This loophole was changed in 2001 with passage of the USA PATRIOT Act.[36] Money laundering—a crime that has been getting greater attention in recent years because of drug trafficking, terrorism, and sophisticated crime

---

[35] *Matter of Chairez I*, 26 I&N Dec. 349, 356. In so doing, the BIA relied upon, but also clarified, its previous decision in *Matter of Mendez-Orellana*, 25 I&N Dec. 254, 255–56 (BIA 2010).

[36] Uniting and Strengthening America by Providing Appropriate Tools Required to Intercept and Obstruct Terrorism Act of 2001 (USA PATRIOT Act), Pub. L. No. 107-56, 115 Stat. 272.

networks—is now a ground of inadmissibility at INA §212(a). Specifically, INA §212(a)(2)(I) renders inadmissible any individual who

> (i) a consular officer or the attorney general knows, or has reason to believe, has engaged, is engaging, or seeks to enter the United States to engage in an offense which is described in section 1956 or 1957 of title 18, United States Code (relating to laundering of monetary instruments); or
>
> (ii) a consular officer or the attorney general knows is, or has been, a knowing aider, abettor, assister, conspirator, or colluder with others in an offense which is described in such section.

"Reason to Believe"

Note that the section on money laundering follows the pattern of the "reason to believe" language found in the controlled-substance trafficking section at INA §212(a)(2)(C), discussed above. No conviction is required to deny someone admission or permanent resident status if there is a "reason to believe" that the individual has been involved in—including aiding, abetting, assisting, conspiring in, or colluding in—money laundering under 18 USC §§1956 or 1957.[37]

The money laundering provision was introduced in 2001, and the author is unaware of any precedent cases in which the "reason to believe" section was used by DHS to deny admission to an individual. Consular officers adjudicating visa applications utilize the money laundering ground of inadmissibility more often than USCIS or the immigration courts. Many years after its inclusion in the INA, it is still difficult to gauge the impact of the money laundering inadmissibility provision. Attorneys interested in researching the ground of inadmissibility at INA §212(a)(2)(I) may want to access the Administrative Appeals Office (AAO) virtual library through LEXIS or Westlaw, as most money laundering cases are decided by the AAO. The AAO sometimes publishes decisions as precedent. Otherwise, unpublished decisions may provide a useful guide, as the agency relies on both BIA and circuit court precedent.

Crimes of Domestic Violence

In the past 20 years, the issue of domestic violence has received increased attention in immigration law. There are a significant number of benefits available to the victims of domestic violence, including both adults and children. More important for purposes of this discussion, domestic violence offenses form an independent basis for removal. It is important to take a close look at the actual provisions of law, because they encompass a variety of acts—not simply battery in a domestic setting. It

---

[37] The phrase "reason to believe" has been equated with the standard for "probable cause." *See U.S. v. Veal*, 453 F.3d 164,167 n.3 (3d Cir. 2006); *see also Matter of A–H–*, 23 I&N Dec. 774, 789 (AG 2005).

is furthermore important to note that there has been important case law that further refines, and narrows, the reach of this ground of deportability.

Offenses Included as Ground of Deportability

Under INA §237(a)(2)(E) [8 USC §1227(a)(2)(E)], an individual who at any time after admission is convicted of one or more of the following offenses is deportable:

- a crime of domestic violence;
- stalking;
- child abuse;
- child neglect; or
- child abandonment.

"Crime of Domestic Violence" Defined

Under INA §237(a)(2)(E), a "crime of domestic violence" is defined according to the federal definition of "crime of violence" at 18 USC §16. Section 16 also is used in determining aggravated felony crimes of violence, as discussed earlier in chapter seven. Accordingly, the Supreme Court's holding in *Leocal v. INS*,[38] discussed at length in chapter seven, applies here. Indeed, the discussion in chapter seven regarding the aggravated felony definition of "crime of violence" at INA §101(a)(43)(F) may be referenced at this juncture, as the analysis is the same. Of great importance is the Supreme Court's decision in the criminal sentencing case of *Johnson v. U.S.*,[39] which has had a substantial effect in the context of INA §237(a)(2)(E).

The issue in *Johnson* was whether a sentence enhancement for a previous conviction for a "violent felony" should apply in the defendant's case. The proposed "violent felony" in this case was a conviction for simple battery under Florida law. Noting that the battery statute was divisible, including "touch" or "strike," the Court found that a "touch" does not meet the definition of violent felony, which requires the:

- active use of
- violent
- physical force.

Although it is a criminal sentencing case, this precedent applies to INA §237(a)(2)(E). The text of the decision covers the fact that the government attempted to dissuade the Court in argument by explaining that an adverse decision would hinder attempts to deport non–American citizens for simple battery offenses in the domestic context. And the Court specifically rejected this particular plea; because the statute is divisible, courts will revert to the modified categorical approach and review

---

[38] *Leocal v. INS*, 543 U.S. 1 (2004).

[39] *Johnson v. U.S.*, 559 U.S. 133 (2010).

documents from the record of conviction to determine whether it was a "touch" or "strike."[40] Thus, by its very terms, *Johnson* applies to domestic violence cases in immigration court. Simple assault and battery statutes that do not encompass the active use of violent physical force, or are divisible—encompassing innocuous acts such as "touch"—will not meet the standard for "crime of violence" under 18 USC §16.

States have a variety of assault and battery provisions. Some have per se domestic violence provisions; other states simply highlight the case as "domestic" and may utilize certain sentencing tools, such as group therapy or counseling, as punishment. In light of the *Johnson* decision—and irrespective of a state's title or classification of a provision—misdemeanor assaults and batteries, and even aggravated assaults that involve only negligent or reckless conduct (without a specific intent), are *unlikely* to fall under this ground of removability because such offenses will not meet the federal definition of "crime of violence" at 18 USC §16.[41] Moreover, if the assault or battery statute is a divisible statute that includes subsections that both do and do not involve negligence, reference must be made to the record of conviction. If the record of conviction does not clarify which subsection applies to the particular defendant (respondent), it is assumed that the least culpable act applies.

Even before the Supreme Court's guidance in *Johnson,* the BIA, in *Matter of Sanudo,*[42] found that domestic battery in violation of the California Penal Code did not qualify as a crime of domestic violence because the statute's described offense conduct did not meet the federal definition of "crime of violence" at 18 USC §16. The BIA noted that the minimum conduct necessary to complete this offense was an intentional "touching" without the other's consent; one may be convicted without using violence, without injuring, or even intending to injure the victim. The charging document repeated the language of the statute: willful and unlawful use of force or violence against another. The BIA found that, without further specification in the record of conviction, it could not be said that this offense met the definition of a crime of violence for purposes of deportability under INA §237(a)(2)(E).

Many federal courts have likewise found that simple assault and battery statutes cannot meet the federal definition of "crime of violence," and therefore are not crimes of domestic violence for purposes of removability under the INA.[43] In the case of simple assault or battery, it is imperative that attorneys not concede deportability. In

---

[40] *Johnson v. U.S.*, 559 U.S. 133, at 144 (2010).

[41] *Johnson v. U.S.*, 559 U.S. 133, at 134–35 (2010).

[42] *Matter of Sanudo*, 23 I&N Dec. 968 (BIA 2006).

[43] *Fernandez-Ruiz v. Gonzales,* 466 F.3d 1121 (9th Cir. 2006); *Cisneros-Perez v. Gonzales,* 465 F.3d 386 (9th Cir. 2006); *Flores v. Ashcroft,* 350 F.3d 666 (7th Cir. 2003). A contrary result was reached in *U.S. v. Griffith,* 455 F.3d 1339 (11th Cir. 2006), in which the Eleventh Circuit U.S. Court of Appeals found that Georgia's simple assault statute could qualify as a crime of violence, albeit under a distinct federal statute, and in the criminal sentencing context—as opposed to removal. In light of *U.S. v. Johnson, Griffith* can no longer be relied on as binding precedent.

addition, if a statute is divisible (including acts that involve the intentional use of physical force, as well as acts that do not), it is incumbent on defense counsel to deny deportability.

As defined by INA §237(a)(2)(E), the crime of domestic violence encompasses many different situations; the specific offenses and corresponding relationships are delineated individually below for better understanding.

The Domestic Violence Victim

To come under the purview of INA §237(a)(2)(E), the act of domestic violence must be committed against:

- a current or former spouse;
- a person with whom the individual shares a child in common;
- a person with whom the individual is cohabitating or has cohabitated with as a spouse;
- a person similarly situated to the spouse of the individual under the domestic or family violence laws of the jurisdiction where the offense occurs; or
- any other person who is protected from that individual's acts under the domestic or family violence laws of the United States or any state, Indian tribal government, or unit of local government.

Defining the "victim"; applying the categorical approach

The "categorical approach," described in various contexts throughout this book, dictates that in determining whether a criminal offense falls under a ground of removability, the IJ and BIA confine their analysis to the specific language and elements of the penal statute at issue. Only if the statute is divisible may the IJ or BIA look to the record of conviction. Under a categorical approach, the determination of deportability must not be made based on the underlying factual circumstances as described through ancillary evidence, such as an arrest report or testimony. Applying the categorical approach to INA §237(a)(2)(E) means that unless the criminal statute is entitled "domestic violence" and/or penalizes acts directed at an enumerated victim (*i.e.*, spouse, cohabitant, relative, etc.), the offense is not a "crime of domestic violence" for purposes of the statute.

Following recent Supreme Court decisions (discussed in chapter five), it is not clear whether the BIA and the federal courts will view the issue of "domestic violence victim" as a nonelemental fact, an issue for a modified categorical approach, or an issue to be determined by a pure categorical standpoint. If the issue of the victim (*i.e.*, whether he or she is some sort of domestic relative) is a nonelemental offense, IJs may go behind the statute and record of conviction to determine the victim's relationship to the defendant. If the issue of the victim is to be ascertained through a modified categorical approach, judges may look to the record of conviction to determine the identity of the victim. If a pure categorical approach is followed, the judges may only look to the elements of the criminal statute to determine whether the offense is a domestic violence crime.

Under this latter approach, a crime of assault (even aggravated assault), kidnapping, false imprisonment, harassment, etc., would not qualify under INA §237(a)(2)(E) unless the criminal provision specifically referenced one of the enumerated persons. This is the approach taken by the Ninth Circuit U.S. Court of Appeals.[44] As further support for this categorical approach (that the criminal statute must specify the victim as an enumerated domestic relative), note that federal law also penalizes acts of domestic violence, stalking, and violation of protective orders.[45] And federal law specifies who the victim must be and lists certain domestic relations.

However, the categorical approach may not always work in the respondent's favor. In an unpublished decision, *Cesar v. Att'y Gen.*,[46] the Eleventh Circuit U.S. Court of Appeals referenced the categorical approach in finding that the respondent's niece could qualify as an enumerated victim of domestic violence because Florida law protects persons who reside or have resided with each other as a family. Interestingly, *Cesar* involved a conviction for simple misdemeanor assault under Fla. Stat. §784.011. Under the *Sanudo* approach, discussed above, this offense should not have qualified as a "crime of violence," but this argument was apparently not raised before the court.

Child Abuse

Section 237(a)(2)(E)(i) also encompasses crimes of child abuse. The BIA has held that the term "crime of child abuse" means any offense involving an intentional, knowing, reckless, *or* criminally negligent act or omission that qualifies as maltreatment, and harms a minor's mental or physical well-being.[47] In *Matter of Velasquez-Herrera*,[48] the non–American citizen had been convicted under a general assault provision that did not specify a child or minor victim. The BIA conceded that, categorically, this was not a child abuse crime. The BIA then employed a modified categorical approach to determine if the charge, or any other aspect of the record of conviction, identified a victim under the age of 18. In this particular case, through a series of post-conviction relief actions, the information had been amended to eliminate any reference to the victim's age. The BIA reluctantly sustained the respondent's appeal, finding that—even utilizing a categorical approach—it could not

---

[44] *Tokatly v. Ashcroft*, 371 F.3d 613, 622–23 (9th Cir. 2004) (The immigration judge erred in relying on testimonial evidence to determine that respondent's burglary and kidnapping convictions qualified as "crimes of domestic violence" where neither the criminal statute nor the record of conviction indicated the violence was "domestic.")

[45] 18 USC §§2261A, 2262, and 115. 18 USC §115(a) defines "immediate family member"; this definition is, in turn, referenced in the federal domestic violence crime sections.

[46] *Cesar v. Att'y Gen.*, No. 06-15140, 240 Fed. Appx. 856, 2007 WL 2068359 (11th Cir. 2007).

[47] *Matter of Velazquez-Herrera v. Holder*, 24 I&N Dec. 503 (BIA 2008).

[48] *Matter of Velasquez-Herrera v. Holder*, 24 I&N Dec. 503 (BIA 2008).

be determined that the victim was a minor. If the record of conviction in this case had identified the victim as a minor, a different decision would have been reached in this case and the charge would have likely been sustained. Thus the decision is important for two reasons: one, a modified categorical approach is employed in analyzing whether the offense is a crime of child abuse; two, the offense need not be a specific intent crime, but can include criminally negligent conduct that results in mental or emotional harm of a minor.

In a subsequent case from the Ninth Circuit, *Fregozo v. Holder*,[49] the court of appeals applied *Velazquez-Herrera* in determining that the crime of child endangerment in California[50] is not a crime of child abuse because the full range of conduct criminalized by the statute is broader than acts of child abuse. Potential harm to a child by creating a situation or environment where he or she may suffer harm is not sufficient to establish deportability; instead, there must be actual injury to sustain a finding of deportability for child abuse under INA §237(a)(2)(E)(i).

However, following the Ninth Circuit's decision in *Fregozo*,[51] the Board clarified its decision in *Velazquez-Herrera* in a case called *Matter of Soram*,[52] ruling that state laws penalizing child endangerment—without proof of actual injury or harm to the child—qualify as "child abuse" offenses for purposes of INA §237(a)(2)(E)(i). The criminal statute in *Soram* involved "knowingly or recklessly" permitting a child to be unreasonably placed in a situation that posed a threat of injury to the life or health of the child.[53]

In 2013, in a lengthy and well-thought out decision, the Tenth Circuit U.S. Court of Appeals criticized the Board's decision in *Soram*, finding instead that crimes with a mens rea of negligence, involving non-injurious endangerment, do not qualify as "child abuse" under INA §237(a)(2)(E). *Ibarra v. Holder*,[54] involved Colorado's child abuse statute[55] and specifically a provision that did not require injury and involved a mental state of negligence. This case is recommended reading for any ground of removability (not just child abuse) defined by a categorical approach, because the court of appeals highlights the categorical analysis with reliance on *Moncrieffe*. The court illustrates the process for arriving at a generic definition of the crime, and juxtaposing the state statute of conviction with the generic offense. In this particular case, the court of appeals notes there is no federal crime of child abuse (not involving sexual contact), and in the year 1996 when INA §237(a)(2)(E) was added to the INA, the majority of states required an intentional

---

[49] *Fregozo v. Holder*, 576 F.3d 1030 (9th Cir. 2009).

[50] Calif. Penal Code §273a(b).

[51] *Fregozo v. Holder*, 576 F.3d 1030 (9th Cir. 2009).

[52] *Matter of Soram*, 25 I&N Dec. 378 (BIA 2010).

[53] Colo. Rev. Stat. §18-6-401(7)(b)(I).

[54] *Ibarra v. Holder*, 736 F.3d 903 (10th Cir. 2013).

[55] Colo. Rev Stat. §18-6-401.

act causing injury in order to qualify as "child abuse." Colorado's statute is therefore overly broad and removability under INA §237(a)(2)(E) could not be sustained.[56]

The Second Circuit U.S. Court of Appeals has given *Chevron* deference to *Matter of Soram* and upheld removability under INA §237(a)(2)(E)(i) for a conviction under a New York child endangerment statute[57] despite the absence of the element of any injury to a child.[58]

Violations of Protection Orders

INA §237(a)(2)(E)(ii) states that a person who at any time after admission violates that portion of a protection order involving "protection against credible threats of violence, repeated harassment, or bodily injury to the person or persons for whom the protection order was issued" is deportable. "Protection order" is defined as any injunction, including temporary or final orders, issued by a civil or criminal court as a means of preventing violent or threatening acts of domestic violence. This section does not apply to violations of child support or child custody provisions.

In *Szalai v. Holder*,[59] the U.S. Ninth Circuit Court of Appeals found that a contempt order for violation of the "stay away" portion of a restraining order supports deportability under INA §237(a)(2)(E)(ii) even though there was no evidence of violence, harassment, or bodily injury in the underlying event. In this case, the respondent had approached his ex-wife's home (walking "halfway up the driveway") while dropping off their child.[60] The IJ terminated proceedings, finding that the state law in question[61] did not categorically involve violence, harassment, or bodily injury.

Applying a modified categorical approach, the BIA reversed, based on its review of a policeman's probable cause affidavit. Upon review in the court of appeals, the government conceded that the conduct embraced by the statute included activity that would not meet the parameters of INA §237(a)(2)(E)(ii); the parties' dispute involved whether the BIA improperly applied a modified categorical approach and considered evidence outside the elements of the statute. The court of appeals upheld the BIA's decision, albeit based on different evidence: the hearing transcript of the contempt hearing, and the petitioner's own admission. (What remains unclear to this author, after reading the *Szalai* decision, is how the "evidence" established violation of a protective order relating to harassment, violence, or bodily injury.)

---

[56] *Ibarra v. Holder*, 736 F.3d 903 (10th Cir. 2013).

[57] N.Y. Penal Law §260.10(1).

[58] *Florez v. Holder*, 779 F.3d 207 (2d Cir. 2015).

[59] *Szalai v. Holder*, 572 F.3d 975 (9th Cir. 2009).

[60] *Szalai v. Holder*, 572 F.3d 975, at 977.

[61] Oregon's Family Abuse Protection Act, Or. Rev. Stat. §§107.700–107.735.

In *Matter of Strydom*,[62] the BIA confirmed that making phone calls in violation of a "no-contact" provision qualifies as violation of a protection order, as long as that order was instituted to prevent violence, harassment, or bodily injury. Based on *Strydom,* there is no requirement that the perpetrator actually engage in acts of violence, bodily injury, or harassment, because a "stay-away" or "no-contact" order encompasses a prohibition against threats of such conduct.

Applies to convictions after September 30, 1996

The domestic violence and protection order sections were added to the grounds of deportability by IIRAIRA,[63] and are not retroactive. These grounds of deportation apply only to convictions (not simply acts or admissions of acts) for domestic violence or violations of protective orders occurring after September 30, 1996.[64]

Domestic Violence Offense as a Crime Involving Moral Turpitude

A crime of violence in a "domestic" context may be a crime involving moral turpitude. A crime of simple assault or battery in a domestic situation will probably *not* be considered to involve moral turpitude.[65] However, an offense involving bodily injury to a spouse, cohabitant, or child has regularly been found to involve moral turpitude.[66] After the U.S. Supreme Court's decision in *Leocal v. Ashcroft*,[67] it is not clear whether these "results-oriented" decisions remain viable; a negligent act resulting in bodily harm does not equal a "crime of violence." Accordingly, fresh research is recommended in every new client's case.

Alien Smuggling

Reference to "alien smuggling" is made throughout the INA. Alien smuggling is a crime under INA §274 [8 USC §1324]. Alien smuggling is a ground of inadmissibility,[68] a ground of deportability,[69] and an aggravated felony under INA §101(a)(43).[70] However, these subsections do not employ identical language; in other words, a smuggling offense may be a ground of inadmissibility but not qualify as an aggravated felony. Likewise, the admissibility and deportability grounds are different.

---

[62] *Matter of Strydom,* 25 I&N Dec. 507 (BIA 2011).

[63] IIRAIRA, §350(a), Pub. L. No. 104-208, div. C, 110 Stat. 3009, 3009-639 to 3009-640.

[64] IIRAIRA, at §350(b), 110 Stat. 3009-640.

[65] *See* the discussion of crimes involving moral turpitude earlier in chapter six.

[66] *See Matter of Deanda-Romo,* 23 I&N Dec. 597 (BIA 2003) (misdemeanor assault with bodily injury to a spouse under Texas law found to be a crime involving moral turpitude); *In Re Phong Nguyen Tran,* 21 I&N Dec. 291 (BIA 1996) (corporal injury to a spouse under California law found to be a crime involving moral turpitude).

[67] *Leocal v. Ashcroft,* 543 U.S. 1 (2004), discussed earlier in this chapter.

[68] INA §212(a)(6)(E); 8 USC §1182(a)(6)(E).

[69] INA §237(a)(1)(E); 8 USC §1227(a)(1)(E).

[70] INA §101(a)(43)(N); 8 USC §1101(a)(43)(N).

The inadmissibility section at §212(a)(6)(E)(i) refers to an individual who at any time knowingly has encouraged, induced, assisted, abetted, or aided any other alien to enter or try to enter the United States in violation of law. The deportability section at INA §237(a)(1)(E)(i) states that the smuggling must have occurred prior to or at the time of entry, or within five years of the date of entry. Both sections allow exceptions for the smuggling of immediate family members. Finally, the reader will note that alien smuggling is generally not considered to be a crime involving moral turpitude.[71]

In *Matter of Martinez-Serrano*,[72] the BIA found that a conviction under 18 USC §2(a) for aiding and abetting unlawful entry (under 8 USC §1325(a)(2)) qualifies as a crime of alien smuggling under INA §237(a)(2)(E). In this case, the IJ dismissed the charge because the plea agreement described a scenario wherein the respondent/defendant harbored persons *after* their entry into the United States. The BIA, however, sustained DHS's appeal, finding that INA §237(a)(2)(E)(i) encompasses a "broader array of conduct" than the simple act of transporting aliens into the United States. An individual may be guilty of smuggling even if he or she is not present at the point of illegal entry.[73]

As stated above, a criminal conviction for alien smuggling is not required for either inadmissibility or deportability; DHS can charge a person for the underlying activity of smuggling regardless of whether he or she has been or will be criminally charged.[74] In a case wherein the respondent did not have a criminal conviction, but was charged in removal proceedings as inadmissible for alien smuggling, the Ninth Circuit found that her mere presence in a vehicle with knowledge of a plan to smuggle two individuals in the trunk did not constitute alien smuggling under INA §212(a)(6)(E)(i).[75] Instead, this ground requires an affirmative act of assistance or encouragement in the smuggling activity. Put another way, knowledge that an illegal alien is being brought in by others does not amount to aiding and abetting or assisting in the illegal entry of an alien.[76]

However, a final conviction is necessary in order to fall under the definition of "aggravated felony." What this means, in practical terms, is that an individual who is criminally charged with alien smuggling and is able to avoid a final conviction—either through plea bargaining or successfully going to trial—may still face the adverse immigration consequences of inadmissibility and deportability for the suspected underlying activity. A dismissal of charges does not exonerate a person in the immigration law context.

---

[71] *Matter of Tiwari*, 19 I&N Dec. 875 (BIA 1989).

[72] *Matter of Martinez-Serrano*, 25 I&N Dec. 151 (BIA 2009).

[73] *Matter of Martinez-Serrano*, 25 I&N Dec. 151, at 154; citing *Hernandez-Guadarrama v. Ashcroft*, 394 F.3d 674, 679 (9th Cir. 2005).

[74] *Matter of Martinez-Serrano*, 25 I&N Dec. 151, at 155 (BIA 2009).

[75] *Altamirano v. Gonzales*, 427 F.3d 586, 595–96 (9th Cir. 2005).

[76] *Altamirano v. Gonzales*, 427 F.3d 586, at 595–96.

Limited Exceptions for Smuggling an Immediate Family Member

The aggravated felony ground at INA §101(a)(43)(N), relating to convictions for alien smuggling, contains an exception if the smuggling involved the individual's spouse, parent, or child (and no other individual). This exception for an immediate family member does not apply to general grounds of inadmissibility and deportability. However, there are some limited exceptions where the offense involves a family member.[77] Unless an exception applies, a non–American citizen will be inadmissible or deportable even though the person or persons "smuggled" were immediate family members and the smuggling was for the purpose of family reunification, as opposed to pecuniary gain.[78]

Moreover, there are waivers—in qualified cases—for both inadmissibility and deportability for alien smuggling where the person being smuggled was the smuggler's spouse, parent, son, or daughter (and no other individual).[79]

Alien Smuggling Defined

First and foremost, it is important to note that the activity defined as "alien smuggling" need not be for pecuniary gain. Second, the definition of "smuggling" is broad.

"Alien smuggling" is defined as knowingly encouraging, inducing, assisting, abetting, or aiding an alien (non–American citizen) to enter or to try to enter the United States in violation of the law.[80] Alien smuggling grounds are retroactive, and apply to acts of smuggling before, during, or after respective legislative effective dates.[81]

The Crime of Alien Smuggling

Alien smuggling is essentially an immigration law violation; thus, the criminal statute is found within the INA. Again, the statute paints with a broad brush over the proscribed activity that qualifies as "alien smuggling." INA §274 [8 USC §1324] is captioned "Bringing in and Harboring Certain Aliens," and includes:

(a) Criminal Penalty. —

---

[77] INA §§212(a)(6)(E)(ii), 237(a)(1)(E)(ii). The exception in both cases is for "qualified immigrants" under §301 of the Immigration Act of 1990 who were physically present in the United States on May 5, 1988, and are seeking admission based on a family-sponsored immigrant petition filed by an immediate relative or LPR.

[78] *See, e.g., Matter of Ortega-Cabrera*, 23 I&N Dec. 793 (BIA 2005) (applicant for cancellation of removal found inadmissible where he aided and abetted the illegal entry of his wife and child by paying a smuggler $850 a decade earlier).

[79] INA §§212(d)(11), 237(a)(1)(E)(iii).

[80] This language is found at the grounds of inadmissibility at INA §212(a)(6)(E), and deportability at INA §237(a)(1)(E).

[81] In addition to actual texts of statutory provisions, see *Matter of Valiente-Castaneda*, A29 203 237 2005 BIA LEXIS 25, 2006 WL 448266 (BIA Jan. 23, 2006).

(1)(A) Any person who—

(i) knowing that a person is an alien, brings to or attempts to bring to the United States in any manner whatsoever such person at a place other than a designated port of entry or place other than as designated by the Commissioner, regardless of whether such alien has received prior official authorization to come to, enter, or reside in the United States and regardless of any future official action which may be taken with respect to such alien;

(ii) knowing or in reckless disregard of the fact that an alien has come to, entered, or remains in the United States in violation of law, transports, or moves or attempts to transport or move such alien within the United States by means of transportation or otherwise, in furtherance of such violation of law;

(iii) knowing or in reckless disregard of the fact that an alien has come to, entered, or remains in the United States in violation of law, conceals, harbors, or shields from detection, or attempts to conceal, harbor, or shield from detection, such alien in any place, including any building or any means of transportation;

(iv) encourages or induces an alien to come to, enter, or reside in the United States, knowing or in reckless disregard of the fact that such coming to, entry, or residence is or will be in violation of law, shall be punished as provided in subparagraph (B); or

(v)(I) engages in any conspiracy to commit any of the preceding acts, or

(II) aids or abets the commission of any of the preceding acts

shall be punished....

Any conviction under this section, regardless of the sentence imposed, is an "aggravated felony" offense (again, unless the individual involved (the "smugglee") was an immediate family member).[82]

Although INA §274 does not require that the smuggling or related activity be performed for financial gain, the criminal sanction imposed is enhanced where the offense is committed for commercial advantage or private financial gain. An individual who smuggles persons into the United States for pecuniary benefit may be fined and/or imprisoned up to 10 years per alien smuggled (*i.e.*, per smugglee). Where bodily injury occurs, or the smuggled person's life is placed in jeopardy, the possible term of imprisonment goes up to 20 years. Where the act of smuggling results in death to the person being smuggled, the INA calls for any term of years up to life imprisonment.[83]

---

[82] INA §101(a)(43)(N).

[83] Criminal penalties for smuggling or harboring are at INA §274(a)(1)(B); 8 USC §1324(a)(1)(B).

Where an individual brings, or attempts to bring, an alien into the United States in violation of the law, but not for commercial or financial gain, the offense is punished as a misdemeanor (imprisonment for not more than one year).[84] Where an individual brings an alien to the United States in violation of the law with the intent or knowledge that the alien will commit an offense against the United States, he or she may be punished by imprisonment of more than one year.[85]

> *Note and compare*: Section 274 includes not only smuggling, but also transporting and harboring within the United States, which often will not involve an actual entry. Accordingly, an individual with a §274 conviction may be an aggravated felon for "harboring," but not be inadmissible under INA §212(a)(6)(E). In addition, smuggling is not a moral turpitude crime. Accordingly, this individual would be deportable, but not inadmissible, and could adjust status to waive the smuggling ground.[86]

Crimes Involving Failure to Register; Visa and Passport Fraud

The law under INA §262 [8 USC §1302] states that all non–American citizens in the United States over the age of 14 who have not been registered under INA §221(b), and who intend to remain in the United States for more than 30 days, must be registered and fingerprinted. These registration and fingerprinting provisions have not been implemented with all nationalities, but all non–American citizens who fall into the §262 category must now report address changes within 10 days.[87] An individual who willingly fails to comply with these requirements may be criminally prosecuted.[88] These laws were dormant for many years, but former Attorney General (AG) John Ashcroft made a point to enforce them. Former AG Alberto Gonzales appeared to be less stringent (though certain U.S. Citizenship and Immigration Services (USCIS) support centers will not grant a benefit until they see that a current AR-11 change of address form is on file). Upon conviction for violating a §262 registration requirement, an individual is subject to removal.[89] Failure to report an address change may lead to a misdemeanor conviction under INA §266(b), but even without such a conviction, it is nevertheless a ground of removal.[90]

---

[84] INA §274(a)(2)(A); 8 USC §1324(a)(2)(A).

[85] INA §274(a)(2)(B)(i); 8 USC §1324(a)(2)(B)(i).

[86] Adjustment of status as a waiver of aggravated felony and other offenses is discussed in chapter ten.

[87] INA §265; 8 USC §1305.

[88] INA §266; 8 USC §1306.

[89] INA §237(a)(3)(B); 8 USC §1227(a)(3)(B).

[90] INA §237(a)(3)(A); 8 USC §1227(a)(3)(A).

In the wake of the terrorist attacks of September 11, 2001, federal authorities increasingly prosecute crimes of visa and passport fraud, including smuggling-type enterprises. Operation Tarmac, for example, was a nationwide DHS investigation of undocumented workers at airports across the country. Individuals were arrested on charges of false Social Security cards and fake immigration papers. After being prosecuted, they were turned over to DHS authorities for removal proceedings. In many jurisdictions, it has become common practice—even a priority of many U.S. Attorney's' offices—to criminally prosecute asylum-seekers who arrive at airports with false documents (*i.e.*, photo-switched passports, false visas, etc.). Registration and visa and passport fraud offenses have become increasingly significant in both the criminal and immigration law fields.

Failure to Register

As stated above, non–American citizens are required to register under INA §262, which states:

(a) It shall be the duty of every alien now or hereafter in the United States who–

(1) is fourteen years of age or older,

(2) has not been registered and fingerprinted under section 221(b) of the Act or section 30 or 31 of the Alien Registration Act, 1940, and

(3) remains in the United States for thirty days or longer,

to apply for registration and to be fingerprinted before the expiration of such thirty days.

(b) It shall be the duty of every parent or legal guardian of any alien now or hereafter in the United States who–

(1) is less than fourteen years of age,

(2) has not been registered under section 221(b) of this Act or section 30 or 31 of the Alien Registration Act, 1940, and

(3) remains in the United States for thirty days or longer,

to apply for the registration of such alien before the expiration of such thirty days. . . .

(c) The attorney general may in his discretion and on the basis of reciprocity pursuant to such regulations as he may prescribe, waive the requirement of fingerprinting . . . .

As a practical matter, most nonimmigrants subject to the above provisions are not fingerprinted. "Registration" is accomplished through various approved applications and statuses.[91] Although the requirement that certain "aliens" register has been

---

[91] *See* 8 CFR §264.1.

largely ignored for many years, the former AG announced in 2002 that the rule regarding reporting one's address to the government, by filing the AR-11 address card,[92] would be enforced.[93]

Violations of the civil "reporting" requirement (registration and change of address) carry criminal penalties; in turn, a criminal conviction for violation of the registration rules may lead to additional immigration consequences. INA §266(a) [8 USC §1306(a)] states that an individual (or the parent or guardian, in the case of a minor) who willfully fails or refuses to be registered is guilty of a misdemeanor and will, if convicted, be fined as much as $1,000, or be imprisoned for up to six months, or both. Under INA §266(b) [8 USC 1306(b)], an individual who fails to notify the government of an address change is guilty of a misdemeanor, and can be fined as much as $200, and be imprisoned for up to six months. This provision also provides that an individual who fails to give written notice can be removed, even without going through the conviction and punishment provisions of §266. An individual who is convicted of these misdemeanors is subject to deportation as a result of the offense.[94]

Special registration, which is no longer in force, required biometrics (photos and fingerprinting), targeting predominantly Muslim men from certain Arab countries.[95] Failure to register under the terms of "special registration" led to criminal prosecution. Those who did not register during the applicable period remain subject to prosecution and/or removal under the INA.

Visa and Passport Fraud

Pursuant to INA §237(a)(3)(B)(iii), an individual who has been convicted under 18 USC §1546 is deportable. 18 USC §1546 governs those acts and elements that constitute fraud, such as knowingly making false documents, giving false attestation, appearing falsely in the name of another, etc.[96] Because it is largely DHS immigration

---

[92] Visit the USCIS website at *www.uscis.gov* to download the latest AR-11 form.

[93] *See* 67 Fed. Reg. 52583 (Aug. 12, 2002); *see also* INA §265; 8 USC §1305.

[94] *See* chapter nine.

[95] Certain individuals from designated Arab countries were fingerprinted pursuant to "special registration," but special registration is not discussed at length in this book. For information on special registration of certain Arab nationals, including *Federal Register* notices, DHS/DOJ memoranda, and forms and documents used by local offices, see *www.aila.org*. *See also* R. Deasy, "Special Registration: Foundation, Requirements, and Impact," *Homeland Security, Business Insecurity: Immigration Practice in Uncertain Times* 125 (2003).

[96] 18 USC §1546 states:

Fraud and misuse of visas, permits and other documents

(a) Whoever knowingly forges, counterfeits, alters, or falsely makes any immigrant or nonimmigrant visa, permit, border crossing card, alien registration receipt card, or other document prescribed by statute or regulation for entry into or as evidence of authorized stay or employment in the United States, or utters, uses, attempts to use, possesses, obtains, accepts, or receives any such visa, permit, border crossing card, alien registration receipt card, or other document prescribed by statute or regulation for entry into or as evidence of authorized stay or employment in the United

Continued

officers who investigate these offenses, it is unlikely the person will escape notice upon completion of his or her criminal sentence.

Visa fraud as a crime involving moral turpitude and an aggravated felony

Certain offenses under 18 USC §1546 may involve moral turpitude, but not necessarily. The BIA has refrained from finding that a conviction for visa fraud is necessarily a crime involving moral turpitude.[97] Whether a particular visa or documentation offense is also a crime involving moral turpitude must be determined on a case-by-case basis, depending on the specific statutory provision charged. The BIA recently reiterated, albeit in dicta, the principle that a violation of 18 USC §1546(a) is *not* a ground of inadmissibility (*i.e.*, not a crime involving moral turpitude) in the context of eligibility for an INA §212(c) waiver.[98] Therefore, counsel should strenuously oppose a charge of inadmissibility for a crime involving moral turpitude where the underlying conviction is based on 18 USC §1546.

If the term of imprisonment imposed is at least 12 months, conviction of a crime under 18 USC §1546(a) is an aggravated felony under INA §101(a)(43)(P) [8 USC §1101(a)(43)(P)].

States, knowing it to be forged, counterfeited, altered, or falsely made, or to have been procured by means of any false claim or statement, or to have been otherwise procured by fraud or unlawfully obtained; or

[is in possession of a template or other equipment for creating false documents described above], or

Whoever, when applying for an immigrant or nonimmigrant visa, permit, or other document required for entry into the United States, or for admission to the United States personates another, or falsely appears in the name of a deceased individual, or evades or attempts to evade the immigration laws by appearing under an assumed or fictitious name without disclosing his true identity, or sells or otherwise disposes of, or offers to sell or otherwise dispose of, or utters, such visa, permit, or other document, to any person not authorized by law to receive such document; or

Whoever knowingly makes under oath, or as permitted under penalty of perjury . . . knowingly subscribes as true, any false statement with respect to a material fact in any application, affidavit, or other document required by the immigration laws or regulations prescribed thereunder, or knowingly presents any such application, affidavit, or other document which contains any such false statement or which fails to contain any reasonable basis in law or fact—

[shall be fined or imprisoned . . .]

(b) Whoever uses—

    (1) an identification document, knowing (or having reason to know) that the document was not issued lawfully for the use of the possessor,

    (2) an identification document knowing (or having reason to know) that the document is false, or

    (3) a false attestation,

for the purpose of satisfying a requirement of section 274A(b) of the Immigration and Nationality Act shall be fined under this title, imprisoned not more than 5 years, or both.

[97] *See Matter of Jimenez-Santillano*, 21 I&N Dec. 567 (BIA 1996); *Matter of Wadud*, 19 I&N Dec. 182 (BIA 1984).

[98] *See Matter of Blake*, 23 I&N Dec. 722 (BIA 2005).

The full breadth of immigration consequences, and potential forms of relief, for a visa fraud conviction are discussed in the next two chapters.

Immigration document fraud

Section 274C of the INA [8 USC §1324c] contains primarily civil, but also criminal penalties for possessing, using, or making false immigration documents. This section also encompasses persons who assist in preparing and presenting fraudulent immigration applications.

Under INA §237(a)(3)(C) [8 USC §1227(a)(3)(C)], an individual who is the subject of a final order under §274C is deportable. A conviction under §274C is also a ground of inadmissibility.[99] The gamut of consequences from these grounds, as well as potential relief, is discussed in the next two chapters.

Passport fraud

A conviction under 18 USC §1542 for false statement in an application for a U.S. passport is a crime involving moral turpitude.[100] The BIA has also held that conviction for violation of 18 USC § 1001(a)(2), involving generally a false statement (in this case, an application for a passport) is a moral turpitude crime.[101]

A conviction under 18 USC §1543 for forgery or false use of a U.S. passport is an aggravated felony if the term of imprisonment imposed is at least 12 months.[102] There is an exception in the case of a first offense where the individual committed the act for the purpose of aiding or assisting a spouse, child, or parent.

It is not necessary to be convicted of passport fraud in order to suffer adverse immigration consequences. Both INA §212(a)(6)(C) [8 USC §1182(a)(6)(C)] and §237(a)(3)(D) [8 USC §1227(a)(2)(D)] refer to "falsely claiming citizenship" as a ground of inadmissibility and deportability, respectively.

Export Law; National Security Violations

Export Law Violations: A Matter of National Security

Terrorism, espionage, and other national security issues are certainly important topics in the post-9/11 world, but these issues are a book unto themselves, and do not technically fall under the definition of crimes and their immigration-law consequences. However, it is important to address certain violations of the export laws, because common export violations are dealt with in the same INA section as those regarding national security and terrorism.[103] The INA paints national security

---

[99] INA §212(a)(6)(F); 8 USC §1182(a)(6)(F).

[100] *Matter of Correa-Garces*, 20 I&N Dec. 451 (BIA 1992).

[101] *Matter of Pinzon*, 26 I&N Dec. 189 (BIA 2013).

[102] INA §101(a)(43)(P); 8 USC §1101(a)(43)(P).

[103] INA §237(a)(4)(A)(i); 8 USC §1227(a)(4)(A)(i).

issues with a broad brush. The result is that certain criminal offenses that in reality have little to do with national security, but do involve issues of international commerce and the regulations governing the export of technology, are given increased attention and scrutiny in the immigration context.

Export violations are regulatory in nature and do not implicate moral turpitude. The regulations regarding export are created by agencies within the executive branch, including the U.S. Department of Commerce and the U.S. Department of State. More specifically, the Bureau of Industry and Security within the Commerce Department is responsible for implementing and enforcing the export administration regulations (EAR). The actual regulations are found at Chapter 7 of Title 15 of the Code of Federal Regulations. The list of items that are regulated by the Commerce Department (the Commerce Control List) changes; accordingly, an item whose export at one time violated the law may, at a later date, be removed from the list. Some items are purely commercial, while others have a "dual use," which means they have both commercial, military, or proliferation uses.

The EAR does not relate only to items and technology: persons can also be included in the EAR on an Entity List as parties (usually companies or organizations) to whom export is restricted or requires a special license.[104] With regard to export violations, in terms of both inadmissibility and deportability, it is not necessary to have a final conviction: any "activity" may result in a finding of removability (or ineligibility for a visa or admission). Accordingly, a careful immigration practitioner dealing with an export-type case—in either a visa, adjustment of status, or removal case—will want to be familiar with the applicable rules and regulations regarding sensitive technology. A good starting point is the Commerce Department's Bureau of Industry and Technology's website,[105] which contains links to applicable regulations and other useful information.

Export violations are made an independent ground for deportation under INA §237(a)(4), *Security and related grounds*:

> (A) *In general.* —Any alien who has engaged, is engaged, or at any time after admission engages in—
>
> (i) any activity to violate any law of the United States relating to espionage or sabotage or to violate or evade any law prohibiting the export from the United States of goods, technology, or sensitive information,
>
> (ii) any other criminal activity which endangers public safety or national security, or
>
> (iii) any activity a purpose of which is the opposition to, or the control or overthrow of, the Government of the United States by force, violence, or other unlawful means,

---

[104] 15 CFR Part 744.

[105] *www.bis.doc.gov*.

is deportable.

To convey the significance with which immigration law views export violations, the subsequent provisions of INA §237(a)(4) are entitled (B) *Terrorist activities* and (C) *Foreign policy*. According to the INA, any alien whose presence or activities in the United States the secretary of state has grounds to believe would have potentially serious adverse foreign policy consequences is subject to deportation.[106]

In at least one case, the BIA found that the above provision does not require a showing that the conviction involved a threat to national security; in a petition for review, a reviewing federal court declined to review the BIA's decision based on a "void for vagueness" challenge.[107] Thus there is an issue as to whether the government needs to establish a link between national security and a violation of the export laws in order to establish deportability under this section.

Issues of national security and terrorism also implicate inadmissibility. The language of the inadmissibility provision in the INA[108] is similar, but not identical, to its counterpart at §237(a)(4), quoted above. The nuances between inadmissibility and deportability for export-related crimes are discussed in the next chapter.

Public Safety and National Security

Section 237(a)(4)(A)(iii) of the INA refers to any criminal activity that endangers public safety or national security. In *Matter of Tavarez-Peralta*,[109] the non–American citizen was convicted of 18 USC § 32(a)(5) for interfering with a police helicopter pilot's vision by shining a laser light from the ground into the moving helicopter. The Board adopted a "totality of the circumstances" approach that looks to the circumstances of the crime, including the extent and character of the potential harm and the facts and circumstances underlying the criminal activity. The Board also rejected the notion that INA §237(a)(4)(A)(ii) deals only with crimes involving the national security.[110] This particular ground of removability is rarely seen: it is buried between export violations and violent overthrow of the government—then followed by terrorism provisions. The BIA's decision in *Tavarez-Peralta* is disappointing because the Board does not take a categorical approach, but rather, delivers what sounds like a morality lecture on what "could have happened" if the helicopter had crashed over Philadelphia. The decision reads like a hypothetical facts-based scolding rather than one based on the elements of the offense, and is potentially very broad. Under this decision, minor crimes such as disturbing the peace, trespass, or criminal mischief could lead to removability under INA §237(a)(4)(A)(ii). Moreover, this

---

[106] INA §237(a)(4)(C); 8 USC §1227(a)(4)(C).
[107] *Beslic v. INS*, 265 F.3d 568 (7th Cir. 2001).
[108] INA §212(a)(3); 8 USC §1182(a)(3).
[109] *Matter of Tavarez-Peralta*, 26 I&N Dec. 171 (BIA 2013).
[110] *Matter of Tavarez-Peralta*, 26 I&N Dec. 171, at 176.

author agrees with the respondent in *Tavarez-Peralta* that the provision's placement in the national security/terrorist section does imply a more serious type of offense with national security implications. As of the spring of 2015, no court of appeals has looked at the *Tavarez-Peralta* precedent.

Failure to Register as a Sex Offender

The Adam Walsh Act

The Adam Walsh Child Protection and Safety Act of 2006 added an additional ground of deportability at INA §237(a)(2)(A)(v) [8 USC §1227(a)(2)(A)(v)] for persons convicted under 18 USC §2250 for failure to register as a sex offender.[111] This newly added section of the federal criminal code states:

(a) In general. Whoever—

(1) is required to register under the Sex Offender Registration and Notification Act [42 USC §16911 *et seq.*];

(2) (A) is a sex offender as defined for the purposes of the Sex Offender Registration and Notification Act by reason of a conviction under Federal law (including the Uniform Code of Military Justice [10 USC §801 et seq.]), the law of the District of Columbia, Indian tribal law, or the law of any territory or possession of the United States; or

(B) travels in interstate or foreign commerce, or enters or leaves, or resides in, Indian country; and

(3) knowingly fails to register or update a registration as required by the Sex Offender Registration and Notification Act;

shall be fined under this title or imprisoned not more than 10 years, or both.

(b) Affirmative defense. In a prosecution for a violation under subsection (a), it is an affirmative defense that—

(1) uncontrollable circumstances prevented the individual from complying;

(2) the individual did not contribute to the creation of such circumstances in reckless disregard of the requirement to comply; and

(3) the individual complied as soon as such circumstances ceased to exist.

(c) Crime of violence.

(1) In general. An individual described in subsection (a) who commits a crime of violence under Federal law (including the Uniform Code of Military Justice [10 USC §801 *et seq.*]), the law of the District of Columbia, Indian tribal law, or the law of any territory or possession of the United

---

[111] Adam Walsh Child Protection and Safety Act of 2006, Pub. L. No. 109-248, §401, 120 Stat. 587, 622.

States shall be imprisoned for not less than 5 years and not more than 30 years.

(2) Additional punishment. The punishment provided in paragraph (1) shall be in addition and consecutive to the punishment provided for the violation described in subsection (a).

In addition, as discussed earlier in chapter six, "Moral Turpitude," the BIA has found a state conviction for failure to register as a sex offender—where the individual was previously apprised of the obligation to register—is a crime involving moral turpitude, and therefore a removable offense.[112] Several circuit courts of appeals disagree with the Board's approach and instead have found that failure to register as a sexual offender is not a crime involving moral turpitude.[113] Of course the moral turpitude ground of removal is separate and apart from INA §237(a)(2)(A)(v), which requires a conviction under 18 USC §2250.

---

[112] *Matter of Tobar-Lobo*, 24 I&N Dec. 143 (BIA 2007).

[113] As of the spring of 2015, every circuit court of appeals to review a sexual offender registration law involving the application of *Tobar-Lobo* has rejected the Board's decision as an impermissible departure from the traditional moral turpitude criteria. *See Totimeh v. Att'y Gen.*, 666 F.3d 109 (3d Cir. 2012); *Efagene v. Holder*, 642 F.3d 918, 925 (10th Cir. 2011) ("Were moral turpitude to reach any breach of duty to society, or the failure to meet any obligation 'too important not to heed,' the words 'moral turpitude' would be rendered superfluous and a noncitizen would be removable if convicted of 'two or more crimes' of any kind."); *Plasencia-Ayala v. Mukasey*, 516 F.3d 738 (9th Cir. 2008), *overruled on other grounds by Marmolejo-Campos v. Holder*, 558 F.3d 903 (9th Cir. 2009).

APPENDIX 8A

RESPONDENT'S MOTION TO DISMISS CHARGES

UNITED STATES DEPARTMENT OF JUSTICE
EXECUTIVE OFFICE FOR IMMIGRATION REVIEW
IMMIGRATION COURT
MIAMI, FLORIDA

IN THE MATTER OF:)	
)	
JOSHUA GARCIA)	File No. A 123 456 789
)	
IN REMOVAL PROCEEDINGS)	
_____)	

Immigration Judge: Jessica Baez   Next Hearing: December 27, 2014 at 9:30 a.m.

RESPONDENT'S MOTION TO DISMISS CHARGES

RESPONDENT'S MOTION TO DISMISS CHARGES

Comes now the Respondent, Mr. Joshua Garcia, by and through undersigned counsel and respectfully moves[114] this Court to dismiss the following charges of removability lodged against him in the Notice to Appear ("NTA") dated August 15, 2013: section 212(a)(2)(A)(i)(I) of the Immigration and Nationality Act ("INA") and section 212(a)(2)(C) of the INA, and as grounds for the dismissal of these charges Mr. Garcia states the following:

I. **Mr. Garcia's convictions do not render him removable under INA § 212(a)(2)(A)(i)(I) as convictions for crimes involving moral turpitude.**

The Department of Homeland Security ("DHS") bears the burden to prove, by clear and convincing evidence, that Mr. Garcia, a returning lawful permanent resident, is removable as charged under INA § 212(a)(2)(A)(i)(I). *See* INA § 240(c)(3); 8 C.F.R. § 1240.8(a). *See Matter of Huang*, 19 I & N Dec. 749 (BIA 1988) (holding that where an applicant for admission has a colorable claim to returning resident status, the burden is on DHS to establish by clear and convincing evidence that the applicant should be deprived of his lawful permanent resident status).[115] Section 212(a)(2)(A)(i)(I) of the INA states that an alien convicted of, or who admits having committed, or who admits committing acts which constitute the essential elements of a crime involving moral turpitude ("CIMT") is inadmissible.

A. Legal Standard

The Eleventh Circuit has found that moral turpitude involves "an act of baseness, vileness, or depravity in the private and social duties which a man owes to his fellow men, or to society in general, contrary to the accepted and customary rule of right and duty between man and man." *Keungne v. United States Att'y Gen.*, 561 F.3d 1281, 1284 (11th Cir. 2009); *see also Matter of Serna*, 20 I & N Dec. 579 (BIA 1992). A crime involving moral turpitude is an act which is *per se* morally reprehensible and intrinsically wrong or *malum in se* accompanied by a motive or corrupt mind. *Matter of Serna*, 20 I & N Dec. at 579; *see also Matter of Flores*, 17 I & N Dec. 225 (BIA 1980).

---

[114] Respondent has also filed a Renewed Motion to Terminate Proceedings on the basis that he is not an arriving alien and thus improperly charged under section 212. The present motion is submitted in the alternative to that motion, should the Court find that Mr. Garcia is properly in 212 proceedings.

[115] Respondent in no way concedes that he is indeed properly classified as an applicant for admission; rather, as noted above, he submits this argument in the alternative to his Renewed Motion to Terminate Proceedings.

In order for a theft offense to involve moral turpitude, a permanent taking must be intended. *See, e.g., Matter of Grazley*, 14 I & N Dec. 330, 333 (BIA 1973). Accordingly, temporary takings are not CIMTs. *See id.* Drug possession offenses are generally not considered to be CIMTs. See *Matter of Abreu-Semino*, 12 I & N Dec. 775, 777 (BIA 1968) (holding that "crimes in which evil intent is not an element, no matter how serious the act or how harmful the consequences, do not involve moral turpitude").

The United States Supreme Court in *Descamps v. United States*, 133 S. Ct. 2276 (2013) held that the modified categorical approach is a tool that should be used only in a narrow range of cases. *Descamps*, 133 S. Ct. at 2283. Further, the modified categorical approach "retains the categorical approach's central feature: a focus on the elements, rather than facts, of a crime." *Id.* at 2285. Therefore, the modified categorical approach plays no role where statutes are not divisible; courts must focus solely on the statutory elements of a crime. The approach to statutory divisibility announced in *Descamps* applies in removal proceedings in the same manner as in criminal sentencing proceedings. *Matter of Chairez-Castrejon*, 26 I & N Dec. 349, 354 (BIA 2014).

B. Grand theft pursuant to Fla. Stat. § 812.014 is categorically not a CIMT

Mr. Garcia was convicted[116] of grand theft pursuant to Fla. Stat. § 812.014 (2000), which states in relevant part:

> A person commits theft if he or she knowingly obtains or uses, or endeavors to obtain or to use, the property of another with intent to, either temporarily or permanently: (a) Deprive the other person of a right to the property or a benefit from the property (b) Appropriate the property to his or her own use or to the use of any person not entitled to the use of the property.

The statute also provides: "It is grand theft in the third degree and a felony of the third degree... if the property stolen is . . . valued at $300 or more, but less than $5,000." Fla. Stat. § 812.014(2)(c)(1).

---

[116] Mr. Garcia pled nolo contendere to the charge, adjudication was withheld, and he was sentenced to two years' imprisonment, suspended, and probation/community control for two years.

Even though Mr. Garcia's statute of conviction penalizes takings intended to be either temporary or permanent, an examination of Florida case law regarding the statutory phrase, "either temporarily or permanently," reveals that the disjunctive language does not render the statute divisible. *See Daniels v. State*, 587 So. 2d 460 (Fla. 1991). In *Daniels v. State*, the Florida Supreme Court explains that the prosecution need not prove whether a taking is permanent or temporary in order to convict a defendant. *See Daniels v. State*, 587 So. 2d 460 (Fla. 1991). "[T]he specific intent necessary for theft is the intent to steal, not the intent to permanently deprive an owner of his property." *State v. Dunmann*, 425 So. 2d 166, 167 (Fla. 1983). *Daniels* provides a historical perspective on the Florida Legislature's 1977 inclusion of the phrase "either temporarily or permanently" in the state's theft statute. 587 So. 2d at 462-63. Prior to the 1977 amendment, Florida's statutory definition of "larceny" did not include the specific requirement that a taking be permanent. The element of permanent deprivation was supplied by case law. *Id.*; *see also*, *Groover v. State*, 82 Fla. 427, 429 (Fla. 1921) (holding "[t]he intention to steal, that is, feloniously to deprive the owner permanently of his property at the time of the taking, is an essential element in the crime of larceny") (emphasis added). In 1977, the Florida legislature amended chapter 812, replacing the word "larceny" with the word "theft." *Daniels*, 587 So. 2d at 462-63. The legislature also added the phrase "either temporarily or permanently" to underscore its intent that Florida's theft statute, unlike common law larceny, penalizes takings that are temporary as well as those that are permanent. *Id.* The 1977 amendment, therefore, effectively removed the requirement that the prosecution establish beyond a reasonable doubt that an offender has effectuated a permanent taking. *See id.* So long as the prosecution establishes the offender's intent was to deprive or appropriate someone's property, the permanent or temporary nature of the taking is no longer relevant. The *Daniels* court summarizes the legislative history of section 812.014 thus:

> [b]y adding the phrase 'either permanently or temporarily' to subsection 812.014(1), the legislature has expressed its intent in this area, and we hold that the specific intent to commit [theft] is the intent to steal, i.e., to deprive an owner of property either permanently or temporarily. Consequently, the disjunctive language "either temporarily or permanently" neither sets out elements of the offense in the alternative nor creates alternative crimes that must be proven beyond a reasonable doubt. As the Supreme Court of the United States explains, it is incorrect to assume that "any statutory alternatives are ipso facto independent crimes under state law." *Schad v. Arizona*, 501 U.S. 624, 635-36 (1991). "[L]egislatures frequently enumerate alternative

means of committing a crime without intending to define separate elements or separate crimes."

Id.

Thus, the statutory language regarding permanent or temporary intent describes alternate means of committing the crime rather than alternate elements. As such, the statute is not divisible between temporary and permanent intent. The modified categorical approach plays no role in the analysis of a conviction under Fla. Stat. § 812.014. *See Descamps*, 133 S. Ct. at 2285. Therefore, assuming the least culpable conduct, an intent to temporarily deprive or appropriate, Mr. Garcia respectfully submits that DHS has not met its burden to demonstrate that Fla. Stat. 812.014 is a CIMT under *Matter of Grazley*.

C. Neither cultivation of cannabis[117] pursuant to Fla. Stat. § 893.13(1)(a) nor renting a structure for distribution/manufacture of drugs pursuant to Fla. Stat. § 893.1351(1) constitutes a CIMT

Mr. Garcia's conviction for cultivation of cannabis is not a conviction for a CIMT because the statute does not require, as an element, that the conduct punished be accompanied by any specific mens rea relating to the conduct itself or to the illegal nature of the substance.[118] *See Donawa v. U.S. Att'y Gen.*, 735 F.3d 1275, 1281 (11th Cir. 2013) (finding "[a] person could be convicted under the Florida statute [893.13(1)(a)] without any knowledge of the nature of the substance in his possession."); *see also Matter of Serna*, 20 I & N Dec. at 579; *Matter of Flores*, 17 I & N Dec. 225 (BIA 1980). Mr. Garcia's conviction for renting a structure for distribution/manufacture of drugs pursuant to section 893.1351(1)[119] of the Florida

---

[117] This is the title of the offense for which Respondent received a withhold of adjudication. Mr. Garcia has never been involved in cultivation of controlled substances of any sort and does not concede (or admit) such conduct.

[118] Section 893.13(1)(a) (2010) states, in pertinent part: "a person may not sell, manufacture, or deliver, or possess with intent to sell, manufacture, or deliver, a controlled substance. . . ."

[119] Section 893.1351(1) of the Florida Statutes (2010) states in pertinent part:

> A person may not own, lease, or rent any place, structure, or part thereof, trailer, or other conveyance with the knowledge that the place, structure, trailer, or conveyance will be used for the purpose of trafficking in a controlled substance, as provided in s. 893.135; for the sale of a controlled substance, as provided in s. 893.13; or for the manufacture of a controlled substance intended for sale or distribution to another.

Statutes (2010) is likewise not a conviction for a CIMT because the conduct proscribed by the statute (owning, leasing, renting of a place, structure, trailer, or conveyance) simply is not morally reprehensible and intrinsically wrong or *malum in se*. *See id.* Accordingly, Mr. Garcia respectfully requests that the charge of inadmissibility pursuant to INA § 212(a)(2)(A)(i)(I) be dismissed.

II. **Neither Mr. Garcia's conviction for cultivation of cannabis pursuant to Fla. Stat. § 893.13(1)(a)(2), nor his conviction for renting a structure for distribution/manufacture of drugs pursuant to Fla. Stat. § 893.1351(1) support a charge under INA § 212(a)(2)(C).**

The Department of Homeland Security bears the burden to prove, by clear and convincing evidence, that Mr. Garcia, a lawful permanent resident, is removable as charged under INA § 212(a)(2)(C). *See* INA § 240(c)(3); 8 C.F.R. § 1240.8(a). *See* INA § 240(c)(3); 8 C.F.R. § 1240.8(a). *See Matter of Huang*, 19 I & N Dec. 749 (BIA 1988) (holding that where an applicant for admission has a colorable claim to returning resident status, the burden is on DHS to establish by clear and convincing evidence that the applicant should be deprived of his lawful permanent resident status).[120] Section 212(a)(2)(C) of the INA renders inadmissible any alien whom the Attorney General knows or has reason to believe is or has been an "illicit trafficker" in any controlled substance, or is or has been a knowing aider, abettor, assister, conspirator, or colluder with others in "illicit trafficking."

"Illicit trafficking," has been defined, in another context within the INA, to include a felony which involves "unlawful trading or dealing" in a controlled substance as defined by federal law. *See Matter of L-G-H-*, 26 I & N Dec. 365, 368 (BIA 2014). The viability of a charge of inadmissibility pursuant to INA § 212(a)(2)(C) necessarily hinges on whether the offense or incident involves "illicit trafficking," as that term has been defined for purposes of the INA.

A. **Cultivation of cannabis**

Mr. Garcia was convicted[121] of "cultivation of cannabis" pursuant to Fla. Stat. §§ 893.13(1)(a)(2) and 893.03(1)(c)(7). Section 893.13(1)(a) (2010) states, in pertinent part: "a person may not sell, manufacture, or deliver, or possess with intent to sell, manufacture, or deliver, a controlled substance. . . . The statute classifies an offense

---

[120] Again, Respondent in no way concedes that he is properly classified as an applicant for admission; rather, as noted above, he submits this argument in the alternative to his Renewed Motion to Terminate Proceedings.

[121] Mr. Garcia pled nolo contendere to the charge, adjudication was withheld, and he was sentenced to two years' imprisonment, suspended, and probation/community control for two years.

involving cannabis (marijuana) as a third degree felony. Fla. Stat. §§ 893.13(1)(a)(2); 893.03(1)(c)(7). The evidence submitted by DHS does not demonstrate by clear and convincing evidence that Mr. Garcia's conviction for "cultivation," i.e., manufacture, requires, as an element, "unlawful trading or dealing." *See Matter of L-G-H-*, 26 I & N Dec. at 368. Further, DHS has not presented evidence that the circumstances of Mr. Garcia's arrest indicate unlawful trading or dealing. Thus, the conviction cannot be a basis for inadmissibility under INA § 212(a)(2)(C), as that ground is predicated on a finding of "illicit trafficking."

B. Renting a structure for distribution/manufacture of drugs

Mr. Garcia was convicted[122] of renting a structure for distribution/manufacture of drugs pursuant to section 893.1351(1) of the Florida Statutes (2010), which states in pertinent part:

> A person may not own, lease, or rent any place, structure, or part thereof, trailer, or other conveyance with the knowledge that the place, structure, trailer, or conveyance will be used for the purpose of trafficking in a controlled substance, as provided in s. 893.135; for the sale of a controlled substance, as provided in s. 893.13; or for the manufacture of a controlled substance intended for sale or distribution to another.

1. The conduct penalized by this statute is not equivalent to the conduct described in INA § 212(a)(2)(C)

The conduct penalized by this statute is owning, leasing, or renting; whereas the conduct described in INA § 212(a)(2)(C) is: being or having been an illicit trafficker, or aiding, abetting, assisting, conspiring, or colluding in illicit trafficking. The act of renting a home to another is not equivalent to the aiding, abetting, assisting, conspiring or colluding encompassed by INA § 212(a)(2)(C). The mens rea requirement in Fla. Stat. § 893.1351(1) is knowledge that any of the following three activities is occurring on the premises: (1) Trafficking in a controlled substance, as provided in Fla. Stat. § 893.135; (2) sale of a controlled substance as provide in Fla. Stat. § 893.13; and (3) manufacture of a controlled substance intended for sale or distribution to another. The knowledge that one of those three activities is occurring on the premises does not turn a landlord or an owner into an illicit trafficker or an aider, abettor, assister, conspirator, or colluder with illicit traffickers. To link the

---

[122] Mr. Garcia pled nolo contendere to the charge, adjudication was withheld, and he was sentenced to two years' Imprisonment, suspended, and probation/community control for two years.

conduct punishable under Fla. Stat. § 893.1351(1) to the activities in INA § 212(a)(2)(C) is to erroneously extrapolate from the Florida statute's mens rea requirement a level of participation in the activities occurring on the premises that is neither present in the statute nor required for a conviction.

> **2. The underlying activities, by others, referenced in Fla. Stat. § 893.1351(1) do not all describe "illicit trafficking," thus the act of renting a structure with knowledge of those activities is not categorically "illicit trafficking" within the meaning of INA § 212(a)(2)(C).**

Even if the Court were to find such extrapolation appropriate, the underlying activities of which the defendant must be proven to have knowledge, required in Fla. Stat. § 893.1351(1), do not categorically constitute "illicit trafficking"; therefore the act of renting a structure with knowledge of those activities cannot be categorically deemed "illicit trafficking." In the following discussion of the underlying activities described in Fla. Stat. § 893.1351(1), it is important to keep in mind that the statute penalizes not the person who *actually* committed these activities, but a person who simply rented, leased, or owned a structure in which *other people* were engaged in those activities.

Because Fla. Stat. § 893.1351(1) incorporates by reference the Florida definition of "trafficking" at Fla. Stat. § 893.135, as well as the concept of "sale of a controlled substance" within Fla. Stat. § 893.13, these statutes must be analyzed to determine whether the elements required therein amount to "illicit trafficking" within the meaning of INA § 212(a)(2)(C). In addition, the phrase "manufacture of a controlled substance intended for sale or distribution to another" must be interpreted vis-à-vis the concept of "illicit trafficking."

> **a. Trafficking, as provided in Fla. Stat. § 893.135**

Section 893.135 of the Florida Statutes defines "trafficking" as knowingly selling, purchasing, manufacturing, delivering, or bringing into this state, or knowingly being in actual or constructive possession of a controlled substance. The Florida Standard Jury Instructions for this section reveal that a conviction under this statute can lie without the a jury having to determine beyond a reasonable doubt whether the underlying conduct was sale, purchase, manufacture, delivery, bringing into the state, or possession. *See, e.g.,* Fla. Std. Jury Instruction 25.9 – 25.13. Thus, a "trafficking" conviction can lie even where the underlying conduct involved no consideration. For example, a conviction might be based on conduct amounting to mere delivery without remuneration, or simple possession. These examples do not involve "unlawful trading or dealing." *See Matter of L-G-H-*, 26 I & N Dec. at 368. Since Fla. Stat. § 893.135 is not divisible based on the structure of the jury instructions, and the least culpable conduct for which a defendant can be convicted does not involve "unlawful trading or dealing," the Florida definition of "trafficking" under Fla. Stat. § 893.135 is not equivalent to "illicit trafficking" within the context of the INA. *See id.*

Even if the Court were to find that Fla. Stat. § 893.135 does involve "unlawful trading or dealing," because Mr. Garcia's statute of conviction, Fla. Stat. § 893.1351(1), is divisible regarding the activity occurring within the premises, the Court may consult the record of conviction in order to determine the statutory phrase which was the basis for the conviction. *See Descamps*, 133 S. Ct. at 2283-85. Regarding the mens rea portion of Fla. Stat. § 893.1351(1), the Information in Mr. Garcia's criminal case reads as follows: "with the knowledge that such place . . . would be used for the purpose of trafficking in a controlled substance or the manufacture of a controlled substance intended for sale or distribution to another... ." Thus, the record of conviction is inconclusive as to whether Mr. Garcia's conviction is based on the portion of Fla. Stat. § 893.1351(1) relating to knowledge regarding trafficking, or on the portion relating to knowledge regarding manufacture for sale or distribution. Further, DHS has not presented evidence that Mr. Garcia's conviction was based on the portion of the statute relating to knowledge of trafficking.

b. Sale of a controlled substance, as provided in 893.13

As discussed above, because Fla. Stat. § 893.1351(1) is divisible regarding the activity occurring within the premises, the Court may consult the record of conviction in order to determine the statutory phrase which was the basis for the conviction. *Id.* In this case, Mr. Garcia's Information indicates that his conviction was not based on the portion of Fla. Stat. § 893.1351(1) which requires knowledge that the premises would be used for sale of a controlled substance, as that portion of the Fla. Stat. § 893.1351(1) is not recited in the Information.

c. Manufacture of a controlled substance intended for sale or distribution to another

The portion of Fla. Stat. § 893.1351(1) regarding knowledge that the premises would be used for the manufacture of a controlled substance intended for sale or distribution to another is further divisible between manufacture for sale and manufacture for distribution. *See Descamps*, 133 S. Ct. at 2283-85. While the former may suggest commercial trading or dealing, the latter does not. Distribution does not require trading or dealing; accordingly knowledge that the premises would be used for the manufacture of a controlled substance intended for distribution does not amount to "illicit trafficking" as that phrase has been defined within the context of the INA. The Information in Mr. Garcia's case recites the statutory phrase as a whole:

"manufacture of a controlled substance intended for sale or distribution to another." Thus, the Information does not reveal whether the conviction is based on manufacture intended for sale or manufacture intended for distribution. "Distribution" need not involve commercial dealing (but can be, for example, for personal use or without remuneration). *Moncrieffe v. Holder,* 133 S. Ct. 1678 (2013); *Matter of L-G-H-, supra.*

d. Summary of argument regarding Fla. Stat. § 893.1351(1)

In summary, the Respondent presents two arguments regarding his conviction pursuant to Fla. Stat. § 893.1351(1). First, the conduct proscribed by the Florida statute is not equivalent to the conduct covered in INA § 212(a)(2)(C). Second, even if the Court were to consider the mere act of renting with the knowledge that one of the activities listed was taking place on the premises to be equivalent to the conduct described in INA § 212(a)(2)(C), Fla. Stat. § 893.1351(1) is divisible such that the record of conviction should be examined to determine under which portion of the statute Mr. Garcia was convicted. *See Descamps,* 133 S. Ct. at 2283-85. The record of conviction is inconclusive in this regard. Ambiguity on this point means that the conviction did not necessarily involve a portion of the statute which might involve unlawful trading or dealing. *See Moncrieffe v. Holder,* 133 S. Ct. 1678, 1687 (2013). As such, the Court must assume the least culpable conduct. Moreover, DHS has not presented any evidence that Mr. Garcia was convicted for renting a structure with knowledge of any activity described within Fla. Stat. § 893.1351(1) that amounts to "unlawful trading or dealing." DHS has not submitted evidence that the circumstances of Mr. Garcia's arrest involved "unlawful trading or dealing." Consequently, neither the conviction nor the circumstances of the arrest can be considered to involve "illicit trafficking" within the meaning of the INA. DHS has not met its burden to prove by clear and convincing evidence that Mr. Garcia's conviction pursuant to Fla. Stat. § 893.1351(1) supports a charge under INA § 212(a)(2)(C).

III. Conclusion

Having presented no evidence that Mr. Garcia's convictions involved any type of consideration indicative of unlawful trading or dealing, DHS has not met its burden of establishing by clear and convincing evidence that Mr. Garcia's convictions present a reason to believe that he has been involved in "illicit trafficking" of a controlled substance. Mr. Garcia respectfully requests that the charge of inadmissibility pursuant to INA § 212(a)(2)(C) be dismissed. Likewise, as outlined in the above discussion, Mr. Garcia's convictions do not constitute convictions for

CIMTs and he respectfully requests that the charge pursuant to INA § 212(a)(2)(A)(i)(I) be dismissed.[123]

WHEREFORE, the Respondent moves this Honorable Court to dismiss the charges of inadmissibility pursuant to INA § 212(a)(2)(A)(i)(I) and (a)(2)(C).

Respectfully Submitted,

Mary E. Kramer
Attorney at Law
Law Office of Mary Kramer, PA
168 SE First Street, Suite 802
Miami, Florida 33131
(305) 374- 2300
Fax: (305) 374-3748
mary@marykramerlaw.com

Certificate of Service

I certify that a true and correct copy of this motion was served by hand delivery on the Office of Chief Counsel for ICE at 333 S. Miami Avenue, Miami, Florida 33130 on this ____ day of December 2014.

_____
Mary Kramer, Attorney at Law

---

[123] Mr. Garcia also contests the charge of removability pursuant to INA § 212(a)(2)(A)(i)(II) regarding conviction for a controlled substance violation. He submits that none of his statutes of conviction describe controlled substance violations because they include a presumption of intent rather than a mere non-element of intent. Thus, due to the lower level of intent required by the Florida statutes, Mr. Garcia submits that *Matter of L-G-H-,* 26 I & N Dec. 365, 368 (BIA 2014) was wrongly decided because it is inappropriate to apply a circumstance-specific inquiry to statutes with a presumption of intent. Further, even under the circumstance-specific approach, the unique presumption of intent present in the Florida statutes cannot be equated to the level of intent present in statute where the statute must either prove and intent or where intent is irrelevant, i.e., not an element of the offense.

UNITED STATES DEPARTMENT OF JUSTICE
EXECUTIVE OFFICE FOR IMMIGRATION REVIEW
IMMIGRATION COURT
MIAMI, FLORIDA

IN THE MATTER OF:)
)
JOSHUA GARCIA) File No. A 123 456 789
)
IN REMOVAL PROCEEDINGS)
)

ORDER OF THE IMMIGRATION JUDGE

Upon consideration of the Respondent's Motion to Dismiss, it is HEREBY ORDERED that the motion be

☐ **GRANTED** ☐ **DENIED** because:

- ☐ DHS does not oppose the motion.
- ☐ The respondent does not oppose the motion.
- ☐ A response to the motion has not been filed with the court.
- ☐ Good cause has been established for the motion.
- ☐ The court agrees with the reasons stated in the opposition to the motion.
- ☐ The motion is untimely per _____.
- ☐ Other:

_____   _____
Date   Jessica Baez
                           Immigration Judge

Certificate of Service

This document was served by: [ ] Mail [ ] Personal Service
To: [ ] Alien [ ] Alien c/o Custodial Officer [ ] Alien's Atty / Rep [ ] DHS

Date: _____ By: Court Staff _____

APPENDIX 8B

UNPUBLISHED BIA DECISION ON DRUG PARAPHERNALIA AND *PICKERING* VACATUR STANDARD

In re: Pablo Antonio Pacheco-Ventura

In Removal Proceedings

File: A44 801 843 - Baltimore

INTERIM DECISION: [NO INTERIM-DECISION IN ORIGINAL]

DEPARTMENT OF JUSTICE,
BOARD OF IMMIGRATION APPEALS

December 29, 2003

COUNSEL:

On Behalf of Respondent: Maribel LaFontaine, Esquire

On Behalf of DHS: Christopher R. Coxe, Jr., Assistant District Counsel

OPINION:

In a decision dated December 18, 2002, an Immigration Judge found the respondent subject to removal under section 237(a)(2)(C) of the Immigration and Nationality Act, 8 U.S.C. §1227(a)(2)(C), as an alien convicted of a firearms offense, but not removable under section 237(a)(2)(B)(i) of the Act, 8 U.S.C. §1227(a)(2)(B)(i), as an alien convicted of a controlled substance offense. The Immigration Judge granted the respondent's application for cancellation of removal under section 240A(a) of the Act, 8 U.S.C. §1229b(a). The Department of Homeland Security (the "DHS," formerly the Immigration and Naturalization Service) appeals from an Immigration Judge's decision finding that the respondent had not been convicted of a crime relating to a controlled substance, and from the Immigration Judge's decision granting cancellation of removal. The appeal will be sustained and the respondent will be ordered removed from the United States.

The respondent is a 24-year-old native and citizen of El Salvador who was admitted to the United States on November 27, 1994, as a lawful permanent resident.

On August 20, 1999, the respondent was convicted of possession of drug paraphernalia in violation of Article 27, section 287A of the Annotated Code of Maryland, and fined $250 (Respondent's Exh. B). On December 23, 1999, the respondent was convicted in the State of Maryland of carrying a concealed weapon and sentenced to a 1-year suspended term of imprisonment and 1 year of probation (Respondent's Group Exh. A, Tab F.16).[124] On May 10, 2002, the respondent was convicted of carrying a handgun in violation of Article 27, 36B of the Annotated Code of Maryland, and resisting arrest in violation of the Common Law, and sentenced to serve 90 days for each offense, sentences to be served concurrently (Government's Exh. 2).

The Immigration Judge found that while the respondent is removable as one who has been convicted of a firearms offense, he did not find the respondent removable as one convicted of a controlled substance offense. The Immigration Judge noted that while the certified copy of the criminal citation provides that the respondent "did possess with intent to use drug paraphernalia to wit ez wider rolling papers and Visine bottle used to store and contain marijuana" and that the respondent "was observed in playground area smoking marijuana" this citation is not contained in the actual record of conviction (Respondent's Exh. B; I.J. at 6). The Immigration Judge noted that if he were to consider the citation, he must consider all of the facts contained within--including the allegation that the respondent was smoking marijuana. Even though the respondent denied smoking marijuana that day (Tr. at 45, 46), the Immigration Judge found that if the citation is to be believed, the respondent would not have possessed more than 30 grams and, thus, would fall within the exception to the provision (I.J. at 6). Finding that the available evidence indicates that the respondent's drug crime concerned "a single offense involving possession for one's own use of 30 grams or less of marijuana" the Immigration Judge concluded that the respondent was not removable under section 237(a)(2)(B)(i) of the Act.

We have considered the Immigration Judge's finding. Despite this, our review of the record of conviction reveals that the respondent's August 20, 1999, conviction for possession of drug paraphernalia in violation of Article 27, section 287A of the Annotated Code of Maryland makes him removable as charged as his crime is one "relating to" a controlled substance within the meaning of section 241(a)(2)(B)(i) of the Act.

The Anti-Drug Abuse Act of 1986 significantly broadened the types of drug offenses which render an alien deportable. *See Matter of Hernandez-Ponce*, 19 I&N Dec. 613 (BIA 1988). The words "relating to" in the phrase "convicted of a violation of ... any law ... relating to a controlled substance" has long been construed to have broad coverage. *Matter of Beltran*, 20 I. & N. Dec. 521 (BIA 1992). *See also Matter of Del Risco*, 20 I&N Dec. 109 (BIA 1989); *Matter of Hernandez-Ponce, supra*. We

---

[124] This conviction is not mentioned in either the Notice to Appear (Exh. 1) or the Additional Charges of Inadmissibility/Deportability (Exh. 1A).

determined that Congress intended to give inclusive meaning in the immigration laws to the phrase "relating to controlled substances." In addition, in our discussion of the phrase in the context of section 241(a)(11) of the Act, now section 237(a)(2)(B)(i) of the Act, we held that Congress meant to encompass inchoate or preparatory crimes such as attempt, conspiracy, and facilitation when the underlying substantive crime involves a drug offense. We further determined that if an offense involved aiding and abetting an offense that alone would constitute a ground of deportability under section 241(a)(11) of the Act, it is consistent with congressional intent to consider the conviction for aiding and abetting the commission of that crime to be a violation of a law "relating to a controlled substance." *Matter of Beltran, supra.*

We note, as did the Immigration Judge, that there is no applicable case law from the Fourth Circuit as to whether a conviction for possession of drug paraphernalia is a conviction of a controlled substance violation (I.J. at 6). By way of reference, the Ninth Circuit has indicated that the question whether possession of drug paraphernalia is to be construed as relating to a controlled substance is a question of first impression. S*ee Luu-Le v. INS*, 224 F.3d 911, 914 (9th Cir. 2000). The Ninth Circuit then determined that the alien's Arizona conviction for possession of drug paraphernalia was a conviction relating to a controlled substance. *Luu-Le v. INS, supra*, at 914–16.

We further note that the Arizona statute considered in *Luu-Le* provides in pertinent part:

> A. It is unlawful for any person to use, or to possess with intent to use, drug paraphernalia to plant, propagate, cultivate, grow, harvest, manufacture, compound, convert, produce, prepare, test, analyze, pack, repack, store, contain, conceal, inject, ingest, inhale or otherwise introduce in to the human body a drug in violation of this chapter.
>
> B. It is unlawful for any person to deliver, possess with intent to use, drug paraphernalia to plant, propagate, cultivate, grow, harvest, manufacture, compound, convert, produce, process, prepare, test, analyze, pack, repack, store, contain or conceal a controlled dangerous substance, inject, ingest, inhale or otherwise introduce into the human body a drug in violation of this chapter.

Ariz. Rev. Stat §§13-3415(a) and (B).

The Maryland statute before us provides:

> (c). It is unlawful for any person to use, or to possess with intent to use, drug paraphernalia to plant, propagate, cultivate, grow, harvest, manufacture, compound, convert, produce, process, prepare, test, analyze, pack, repack, store, contain, conceal a controlled dangerous substance in violation of this subheading.
>
> (d)(1) It is unlawful for any person to deliver or sell, possess with intent to deliver or sell, or manufacture with intent to deliver or sell drug paraphernalia, knowing, or under circumstances where one reasonably should know, that it will be used to plant, propagate, cultivate, grow, harvest, manufacture,

compound, convert, produce, process, prepare, test, analyze, pack, repack, store, contain, conceal, inject, ingest, inhale, or otherwise introduce into the human body a controlled dangerous substance in violation of this subheading.

MD Code. Art. 27 §§287A(c) and (d); repealed effective October 1, 2002; MD Crim Law §5-619, language derived without substantive change from former Art. 27, §287A.

Having compared the Maryland and Arizona statutes, we find that there are no material differences between the provisions. Both the Maryland and Arizona statutes criminalize the possession of drug paraphernalia if that possession is accompanied by the use, or the intended use of the drug paraphernalia for drug-related purposes.

We further find the Ninth Circuit's reasoning in Luu-Le to be a correct interpretation of the law, and we will apply that analysis in the case before us now. Consequently, we find that the Immigration Judge erred in his determination that the respondent is not removable from the United States under section 237(a)(2)(B)(i) of the Act.

In reaching this conclusion, we note that the respondent has presented evidence on appeal that on April 8, 2003, his possession of paraphernalia conviction was vacated and stricken, and that he should therefore be released from custody. We note that removal proceedings and bond proceedings are separate and apart. See Matter of Balderas, 20 I. & N. Dec. 389, 393 (BIA 1991). In addition, the respondent has not presented evidence demonstrating whether his plea of guilty was vacated for "reasons solely related to rehabilitation or immigration hardships" or "on the basis of a procedural or substantive defect in the underlying criminal proceedings." See Matter of Pickering, 23 I. & N. Dec. 621 (BIA 2003) (holding that the vacating of an alien's conviction for possession of a controlled substance by a Canadian court for the sole purpose of avoiding the bar to his acquisition of permanent residence did not eliminate the conviction for immigration purposes). He has also failed to show that the state court's order "falls within an exception to the general rule that convictions expunged under state law retain their immigration consequences." He has not shown that his conviction was vacated based upon a procedural or substantive defect. Inasmuch as the conviction record adequately demonstrates that the respondent has been convicted of an offense relating to a controlled substance, we find that the respondent is removable as charged.

We next address whether the respondent is eligible for cancellation of removal. Pursuant to section 240A(a) of the Act, the AG may cancel removal in the case of an alien who is inadmissible or deportable from the United States if the alien:

(1) has been an alien lawfully admitted for permanent residence for not less than 5 years.

(2) has resided in the United States continuously for 7 years after having been admitted in any status.

(3) has not been convicted of any aggravated felony.

Section 240A(a) of the Act further provides that:

For purposes of this section, any period of continuous residence or continuous physical presence in the United States shall be deemed to end when the alien is served a notice to appear under section 239(a) or when the alien has committed an offense referred to in section 212(a)(2) that renders the alien inadmissible to the United States under section 212(a)(2) or removable from the United States under section 237(a)(2) or 237(a)(4), whichever is earliest.

The respondent became a lawful permanent resident of the United States on November 27, 1994. On August 20, 1999, he was convicted of possession of drug paraphernalia rendering him removable from the United States under section 237(a)(2)(B)(i) of the Act. Inasmuch as the respondent's offense was committed less than 7 years from the date he commenced his period of continuous residence, he cannot satisfy the eligibility requirements for cancellation of removal set forth in section 240(A)(a)(1) of the Act, 8 U.S.C. §1229a(A)(a)(1). See also Matter of Perez, 22 I. & N. Dec. 689 (BIA 1999). Consequently, the DHS appeal will be sustained and the grant of cancellation of removal will be vacated.

Accordingly, the following orders are entered.

ORDER: The DHS' appeal is sustained and the Immigration Judge's decision is vacated.

FURTHER ORDER: The respondent's application for cancellation of removal under section 240A of the Act in denied.

FURTHER ORDER: The respondent shall be removed from the United States.

FOR THE BOARD

Board Member Lauri S. Filppu dissents without opinion

CHAPTER NINE

CONSEQUENCES OF SPECIFIC CRIMINAL ACTIVITY

Consequences of Crimes Involving Moral Turpitude 376
Consequences of an Aggravated Felony Conviction 390
Consequences of a Controlled Substance Conviction 394
Consequences of a Firearms Offense 401
Consequences for Money Laundering Offenses 405
Consequences of a Domestic Violence Conviction 410
Consequences of Alien Smuggling 415
Falsification of Documents, and Visa and Passport Fraud 419
Consequences of Export Law Violations 425
Appendix
    9A: Crimes and Possible Consequences Chart 429

Author's musings:

As a law student in 1986, I did a summer clinical program providing post-conviction type representation to federal detainees at Oxford prison in Wisconsin. I recall the first time a group of us eager young students entered the maximum security facility, and observed the guards, the uniforms, the rules, restrictions, and learned of various indignities like strip searches, open bathrooms, and lockdowns that the detainees endure. I recall a fellow student asking our professor: how do they stand it? Don't the conditions drive them crazy? Our professor answered, "Any inmate will tell you, it is not the rules or treatment that drives them crazy—it is quite simply the loss of liberty." This short statement has stuck in my mind, well, forever. It is the loss of liberty that really hurts.

How to Use this chapter: This chapter is organized according to the classification of the crime (as set forth in previous chapters), and lists the specific consequences that attach to that particular type of offense. Each crime classification is stated and the consequences examined under the following scheme: inadmissibility, which includes adjustment of status and visa eligibility; deportability/removability; mandatory detention; voluntary departure; asylum and withholding of removal consequences; and naturalization consequences (including revocation of naturalization). In this way, when a client is charged with—or convicted of—a certain type of crime, the practitioner can use this book to readily identify the potential consequences that attach to both the offense and that individual's posture. (A synopsis of the chapter—a table linking the different crimes to their different possible consequences based on the immigration status of the alien—can be found at the end of this chapter.)

The immigration consequences attached to a specific crime will depend on the posture of the client. "Posture" means both legal status in the United States as well as individual, personal goals. The consequences a lawful permanent resident (LPR) may face as a result of, for example, a theft conviction, will vary from those confronting a nonimmigrant investor or an asylee. A client who frequently travels abroad because of his or her employment will have different personal goals (and therefore face different consequences) than an individual who has no need or plans to travel outside the United States.

Above all, it is important to understand—and always consider—mandatory detention. No person wants to be detained, and in many circumstances, an individual's interest in liberty outweighs all other concerns. Today, thousands of non–American citizens are detained in immigration custody on account of past criminal activity, or mere *suspicion* of criminal activity. The offense need not be serious; yet the length of time in detention may be long. Because of the liberty interest, mandatory detention is perhaps today's most significant adverse immigration consequence of criminal activity.

Therefore, it is important to understand that potential removal from the United States is not the only consequence of crime. This chapter explores the specific consequences attached to certain offenses, recognizing that the consequences will vary based on the specific immigration status or posture of the client. An understanding of these consequences for different statuses is essential to providing comprehensive advice, as well as planning an effective criminal defense and immigration strategy for the particular case. It is also important for the reader to recall that foreign convictions may serve as the basis of removability in the same way as convictions from the United States.

Consequences of Crimes Involving Moral Turpitude

Inadmissibility, Including Adjustment of Status and Visa Eligibility

The definition of a crime involving moral turpitude is discussed in chapter six. Under Immigration and Nationality Act (INA) §212(a)(2)(A)(i)(I) [8 USC §1182(a)(2)(A)(i)(I)], an individual who has been convicted of, or admits having committed, a crime involving moral turpitude (other than a purely political offense) is inadmissible. This includes attempts to commit and conspiracies to commit such a crime. In practical terms, an individual not previously legally admitted who has been convicted of (or who admits to) a crime involving moral turpitude may be denied a visa at a U.S. consulate abroad, denied admission into the United States at a port of entry, denied temporary protected status, or placed in removal proceedings if he or she was paroled into the United States or entered without inspection.

Moreover, an individual who is physically present in the United States pursuant to a lawful admission (for example, as a tourist) and who applies for adjustment of status to permanent resident, but has been convicted of (or admits committing) a crime involving moral turpitude, may be *inadmissible* for the benefit and will be denied adjustment of status, unless (1) the offense falls under the petty-offense exception (discussed below), or (2) he or she qualifies for a waiver. The same applies for persons seeking to change status from one visa to another, and for individuals applying for naturalization.

The point is, it is possible to confront grounds of inadmissibility under INA §212(a) even though the individual is physically present in the United States pursuant to a lawful admission—and even though any grounds of removability in immigration court would be under INA §237.

Admission of the essential elements

The law states that a person who "admits the essential elements" of a crime involving moral turpitude is inadmissible.[1] This is so even though the person may not have a "conviction" of a crime (or even a formal arrest record). If a person making an application for admission into the United States, *e.g.*, at an airport, is interviewed by an inspections officer and admits to a crime of theft, for instance, he or she may be denied admission. Often, suspected criminal activity comes to the attention of the U.S. Department of Homeland Security (DHS) through computer checks of various databases accessed at ports of entry or during the adjustment of status process. Almost every application with the U.S. Citizenship and Immigration Services (USCIS) requires biometrics and security checks. In turn, law enforcement agencies and American consulates alike are able to place derogatory information into databases even though a subject has not been arrested or even questioned. These "hits" may cause an officer to question an individual, and the questioning may lead to an admission of crime.

However, early Board of Immigration Appeals (BIA or Board) case law does set forth some ground rules regarding inadmissibility based on an admission of criminal activity. In order to constitute an effective admission of a crime, the individual must:

(1) be provided a definition of the crime in understandable terms, and

(2) admit all essential elements of the crime.[2]

In addition, where a final conviction entered by a court does exist, the government cannot go behind the actual conviction and look at ancillary documents to determine that an individual is guilty of other offenses.[3] In other words, a pretrial confession to offenses other than that for which the person is ultimately convicted cannot subsequently be used against the person in the immigration context.

> **Tip**: Certain state prosecutors require a written admission of guilt prior to agreeing to a pretrial intervention or diversion program. Defense attorneys worry that the written admission in the prosecutor's file can be used against the client to establish inadmissibility via admission of the essential elements of a crime. To the extent possible, avoid written admissions. Where the written admission is cause for concern, review the *Matter of K* and *Matter of Medina-Lopez* decisions (cited in notes 2 and

---

[1] INA §212(a)(2)(A)(i); 8 USC §1182(a)(2)(A)(i).

[2] *Matter of K*, 9 I&N Dec. 715 (BIA 1962).

[3] *See Matter of Medina-Lopez*, 10 I&N Dec. 7 (BIA 1962).

3) for guidance. Are the specific elements of the crime laid out? Has the definition of the crime been explained? The case law on "admissions" involves admissions made to immigration officers, not ancillary documents from other sources. It can be argued, based on *Medina-Lopez*, that if the ultimate disposition was a dismissal of the charge, that dismissal should be binding. Finally, it is important to note that admission of the essential elements of a crime does not constitute a ground of deportability, as opposed to inadmissibility, and thus does not pose a problem for LPRs so long as they remain in the United States.[4]

Petty offense and youthful offender exceptions

The law contains several exceptions to inadmissibility based on a conviction or admission of a crime involving moral turpitude. The youthful offender exception applies to a person who was under 18 years of age at the time the crime was committed, and who was also under 18 at the time of release from confinement for the offense. This exception also requires that the offense have occurred more than five years prior to the date of application for admission.[5]

The petty offense exception states that an individual will not be deemed inadmissible for one crime involving moral turpitude if the maximum penalty for the offense does not exceed imprisonment for one year, and, if convicted of the crime, the individual was not sentenced to a term of imprisonment of more than six months.[6]

Political offense exception

Unlike the youthful offender and petty offense exceptions described above, the political offense exception is not written as a specific phrase or subsection in the law. Rather, the ground of inadmissibility for crime involving moral turpitude contains a short parenthetical that reads as follows:

> [an alien is inadmissible for] a crime involving moral turpitude (other than a purely political offense) or an attempt or conspiracy to commit such a crime ...[7]

The political offense exception has been incorporated in one form or another within the INA since 1952. In addition to the statute, the U.S. Department of State's (DOS) *Foreign Affairs Manual* (FAM) also addresses the political offense exception

---

[4] Note that there may be rare situations in which someone who has been admitted, and is thus subject to the grounds of deportability, could be charged as "inadmissible at the time of entry" based on a reason to believe that he or she had been involved in drug trafficking or money laundering. Persons who are subject to deportation because of a ground of inadmissibility applied at the time of entry are charged under INA §237(a)(1)(A). This would apply to a person who has (allegedly) been involved in illegal activity such as drug trafficking or money laundering, but was granted a visa, adjustment of status, or otherwise admitted into the United States, and the suspicion of the illegal activity arose later.

[5] INA § 212(a)(2)(A)(ii)(I); 8 USC §1182(a)(2)(A)(ii)(I).

[6] INA §212(a)(2)(A)(ii); 8 USC §1182(a)(2)(A)(ii).

[7] INA §212(a)(2)(A)(i)(I); 8 USC §1182(a)(2)(A)(i)(I).

at 22 CFR §40.21(a)(6). The political offense exception will apply in the context of foreign convictions or criminal conduct. There is a lengthy legal analysis involved in whether a crime merits the political offense exception, and there is significant crossover with asylum and criminal extradition law, because the concept is embraced in these contexts as well. In arguing for the political offense exception to inadmissibility, these other sources (extradition and asylum) are useful and interesting, but cannot be wholly relied upon because of the distinction between removal, asylum, and extradition proceedings.[8] The theory behind the political offense exception is generally that charges that are trumped up—fabricated—to effectuate persecution or other human rights violations should not be the basis of a finding of inadmissibility. An offshoot of this concept is that a prosecution is politically motivated where the punishment far exceeds the nature of the crime, or is enhanced for political reasons.

In *Matter of O'Cealleagh*,[9] the BIA held that in order to meet the exception for inadmissibility, the crime committed must have been "purely" political, meaning that it was carried out for purely political reasons or motives. The Board found that a conviction for aiding and abetting the murder of British policemen at a funeral in Northern Ireland was not "purely" political in nature, but instead carried out for reasons of revenge.

In *O'Cealleagh,* the BIA was hesitant to apply a broader interpretation to the political offense exception and specifically did not want to embrace either asylum or extradition law. However, the FAM, which governs the visa issuance process at U.S. consulates, appears to bridge that gap by expounding on various circumstances in which prosecution and/or conviction for alleged crime can qualify for the exception under INA §212(a)(2)(A)(i). In contrast to the BIA's limited approach, the FAM refers to the political offense exception in terms of fabricated charges, or charges predicated upon repressive measures against racial, religious, or political minorities.[10] Although the BIA discourages looking to human rights law, the FAM seems to invite this approach and attorneys should advocate for reliance on asylum law when arguing an exception to inadmissibility. There are circumstances when the nature of the prosecution or punishment implies that the criminal case is politically motivated by the foreign government; the BIA and federal courts should acknowledge this side of the political offense exception in removal proceedings.

---

[8] In *Matter of O'Cealleagh*, 23 I&N Dec. 976, 980 (BIA 2006), the BIA stated that it has "no occasion to explore the extent of portability of extradition principles to the 'purely political offense' language we must apply, except to note the very different purposes served by extradition and removal or exclusion proceedings." Later, the Board reaffirmed that extradition and deportation are distinct and separate. However, this author believes that to fully understand the concept of political crime and the political offense exception, it is useful to review all case law, regulations, and policy on the overall topic of persecution in the guise of prosecution.

[9] *Matter of O'Cealleagh*, 23 I&N Dec. 976, 980 (BIA 2006).

[10] 22 CFR §40.21(a)(6).

In the asylum context, criminal prosecution becomes persecution when the legal process is a mere pretext for improper, illegitimate, or invidious motives.[11] The analysis for political persecution is discussed in greater detail in the asylum / withholding section later in this chapter. Also closely associated with the political offense exception to inadmissibility is the concept of the "political crime" in the asylum and withholding contexts, and this theme is also covered in the asylum section of this chapter.

Deportability/Removability

An individual who has been admitted to the United States, either as an LPR or in some other status, and is convicted of a crime involving moral turpitude within five years after the date of admission is deportable if he or she is *convicted* of a crime for which a sentence of one year or longer may be imposed.[12] Breaking these elements down, a person who is already in the United States following a lawful admission becomes deportable for a crime involving moral turpitude if:

(1) the crime is *committed* within five years of the date of admission;

and

(2) it is an offense for which one year or longer *may* be imposed.

> **Tip: Travel warning.** In the context of a conviction for a crime involving moral turpitude, compare deportability with inadmissibility. An individual who is convicted of one offense, whether a misdemeanor or a felony, committed more than five years after the date of admission is not subject to *deportation* as long as he or she remains in the United States. Once this individual departs the United States, though, and then applies for re-entry, he or she is subject to the grounds of inadmissibility—unless the crime falls under the petty-offense exception—and will be found inadmissible and placed in removal proceedings.

Defining "admission"

The year 2011 brought important case law regarding the definition of "admission" for purposes of deportability for one crime involving moral turpitude committed with five years *of the date of admission.* This issue is important because of the myriad ways a person can be physically present within the United States. There are nonimmigrant visa admissions, paroles, and entries without inspection. Moreover, vis à vis adjustment of status to permanent residency (a process that takes place inside the United States), an individual becomes legal without leaving and coming back into the country; for many purposes, adjustment of status is a type of "admission" to permanent residency, even though it is not an "admission" in the context of entering the country with valid documents that are inspected and approved.

---

[11] *Lin v. INS,* 238 F.3d 239, 244 (3d Cir. 2001); *Abdel-Masieh v. INS,* 73 F.3d 579, 584 (5th Cir. 1996); *Chang v. INS,* 119 F.3d 1055, 1061 (3d Cir. 1997).

[12] INA §237(a)(2)(A)(i); 8 USC §1227(a)(2)(A)(i).

For decades, the BIA held fast to the position that adjustment of status is an "admission" for purposes of calculating the five-year window within which a crime is committed for deportability under INA §237(a)(2)(A)(i)(I).[13] However, the circuit courts of appeals started disagreeing with this perspective in domino-like fashion, finding instead that a lawful inspection and entry with a visa is the "admission"—not the later adjustment of status.[14] The courts' perspective was based in large part on the definition of "admission" at INA §101(a)(13)(A), which describes a lawful *entry* after inspection and admission. In *Matter of Alyazji*,[15] the Board modified its position on adjustment of status as an admission, holding that where there is an initial lawful admission (for example, with a nonimmigrant visa), and the non–American citizen subsequently adjusts status to LPR, the initial admission is the "date of admission" for purposes of triggering the five-year window for deportability. The Board would not and did not find that adjustment of status is not an admission; it held simply that for purposes of calculating the five-year time period within which commission of a crime may have occurred, a previous valid admission starts the clock. For persons who initially entered without inspection or parole, adjustment of status does trigger the five-year period.

Multiple criminal convictions

An individual who, *at any time after admission*, is convicted of two or more crimes involving moral turpitude—that do not arise out of a single scheme of criminal misconduct—is deportable, regardless of whether he or she was confined therefor and regardless of whether the convictions were obtained in a single trial.[16]

Whether two or more offenses are part of a "single scheme" becomes important because deportability for the offenses is implicated regardless of when they occurred. Effectively arguing that two convictions were for acts that were committed as part of the same scheme may make the difference in whether someone is subject to deportation or not. To be deportable for one crime, it must have occurred within the first five years of admission. Two or more crimes render an individual deportable if they were committed at any time.

The BIA has held in *Matter of Adetiba* that when an individual performs an act that, in and of itself, constitutes a complete, individual, and distinct crime, he or she becomes deportable for multiple crimes if he or she again commits such an act, even

---

[13] *Matter of Shanu*, 23 I&N Dec. 754 (BIA 2005) *vacated by Aremu v. DHS*, 450 F.3d 578 (4th Cir. 2006), *overruled in part by Matter of Alyazji*, 25 I&N Dec. 397 (BIA 2011).

[14] *Zhang v. Mukasey*, 509 F.3d 313, 315-316 (6th Cir. 2007); *Aremu v. DHS*, 450 F.3d 578 (4th Cir. 2006); *Lemus-Losa v. Holder*, 576 F.3d 752, 757 (7th Cir. 2009) (adjustment is not an admission, but may be construed as an admission for certain purposes); *Martinez v. Mukasey*, 519 F.3d 532 (5th Cir. 2008) (adjustment is not an "admission" for purposes of applying the 212(h) waiver's bar to certain permanent residents).

[15] 25 I&N Dec. 397 (BIA 2011).

[16] INA §237(a)(2)(A)(ii); 8 USC §1227(a)(2)(A)(ii).

though one may closely follow the other and may be quite similar in nature.[17] In *Matter of Adetiba*, the individual was convicted in a single trial of several, separate counts of credit card fraud. The BIA found that each act of using a fake credit card (each transaction) constituted a separate and independent crime, and thus, the crimes were not part of a single scheme. Accordingly, the individual was found deportable for multiple criminal convictions.

In 2011, the Board upheld its *Adetiba* analysis in a case called *Matter of Islam*,[18] which also involved a fact pattern of an individual using multiple credit cards at different stores within a few hours' time. The Board found that the use of multiple cards at different locations did not involve a "single scheme." The Board also stated that it would apply the *Adetiba* analysis in all circuits.[19]

In *Akindemowo v. INS*,[20] the U.S. Court of Appeals for the Fourth Circuit, in finding that multiple crimes did not arise out of a single scheme of criminal misconduct, laid down a test similar to that of the BIA in *Adetiba*. The court looked to the defendant's conviction for two separate offenses, the presence of separate and independent victims, the fact that the defendant wrote more than one (false) check, and the time in between the two offenses (giving the defendant the opportunity to reflect on his actions). The court found that these factors supported a finding of multiple crimes, even though the offenses occurred at the same shopping mall within a short time frame.

Similarly, an individual who was convicted on two counts of misuse/illegal purchase of food stamps was guilty of crimes involving moral turpitude not arising out of a single scheme where the purchases occurred two days apart and represented two different transactions.[21] And, where the defendant/respondent was convicted of three counts of bank fraud, each offense concluding on a different day over a three-month period—the dates of "conclusion" specifically identified in the indictment—the court found multiple crimes not arising out of a single scheme.[22]

Mandatory Detention

An individual in removal proceedings before the immigration court who is charged with *inadmissibility* for one or more crimes involving moral turpitude is subject to mandatory detention under INA §236(c)(1)(A) if he or she was released from

---

[17] *Matter of Adetiba*, 20 I&N Dec. 506 (BIA 1992).

[18] *Matter of Islam*, 25 I&N Dec. 637 (BIA 2011).

[19] *Matter of Islam*, 25 I&N Dec. 637, at 641.

[20] *Akindemowo v. INS*, 61 F.3d 282 (4th Cir. 1995).

[21] *Abdelqadar v. Gonzales*, 413 F.3d 668 (7th Cir. 2005).

[22] *Hyacinthe v. Att'y Gen.*, 215 Fed. Appx. 856, 2007 U.S. App. LEXIS 1685, 2007 WL 186512 (11th Cir. 2007).

custody after October 8, 1998.[23] Thus, individuals arriving at a port of entry (including LPRs), or individuals within the United States as parolees or persons who entered without inspection, who are placed in removal proceedings on account of a crime are subject to immigration detention without bond.

An individual in removal proceedings before the immigration court who is charged with *deportability* for a crime involving moral turpitude may be subject to mandatory detention. A person lawfully admitted to the United States who has *only one* conviction for a crime involving moral turpitude, for which he or she was sentenced to less than one year, will not be subject to mandatory detention[24]—he or she can request a bond and release from custody. However, a person in removal proceedings for a crime involving moral turpitude for which more than one year of imprisonment was imposed, or for multiple crimes, will be held under mandatory detention.[25] Remember, this discussion pertains to persons who were released from penal custody after October 8, 1998.

Voluntary Departure

Pre-commencement or early stage of removal proceedings

An individual removable for one or multiple crimes involving moral turpitude is still statutorily eligible for voluntary departure[26] from either DHS (voluntary departure requested in advance of removal proceedings) or from an immigration judge (IJ) at the commencement of removal proceedings (at the master calendar stage).[27] Administrative voluntary departure granted by DHS, as well as voluntary departure prior to the conclusion of removal proceedings, is a benefit available even if the non–American citizen has been convicted of a crime or crimes involving moral turpitude. Keep in mind that the individual must be otherwise eligible; for a discussion of the general requirements of voluntary departure, see the next chapter on waivers and relief. Also, voluntary departure is a benefit that may be denied in the exercise of discretion. Certainly, a conviction for a crime involving moral turpitude is an element for consideration in making this discretionary determination.

Voluntary departure at conclusion of removal proceedings

In comparison with voluntary departure at a preliminary stage, voluntary departure granted at the *conclusion* of removal proceedings before an IJ requires that the non–American citizen show at least five years of "good moral character" prior to the ap-

---

[23] October 8, 1998, was the last day Transition Period Custody Rules were in effect. *See* 8 CFR §236.1(c)(1)(i); Illegal Immigration Reform and Immigrant Responsibility Act of 1996 (IIRAIRA), Pub. L. No. 104-208, div. C, § 303(b), 110 Stat. 3009, 3009-585 to 3009-587.

[24] INA §236(c)(1)(C); 8 USC §1226(c)(1)(C).

[25] *See* INA §236(c)(1)(C); 8 USC §1226(c)(1)(C); *see also* INA §§237(a)(2)(A)(i)(II) (for crimes for which more than one year may be imposed), (ii) (multiple crimes).

[26] *See* INA §240B(a); 8 USC §1229c(a).

[27] *Matter of Arguelles-Campos*, 22 I&N Dec. 811 (BIA 1999).

plication for relief.[28] This requirement applies when voluntary departure is requested after more than one hearing; for example, at an individual hearing where voluntary departure is requested as the alternative relief.[29]

"Good moral character" is defined at INA §101(f). Section 101(f)(3) makes reference to acts "described in" INA §§212(a)(2)(A), (B), or (C), regardless of whether the person is inadmissible. Section 212(a)(2)(A)(i) refers to crimes involving moral turpitude. Thus, conviction for a crime or crimes involving moral turpitude committed during the five-year period immediately preceding application will bar a finding of good moral character unless the offense falls under the petty-offense exception at INA §212(a)(2)(A)(i).[30] A conviction for a crime involving moral turpitude committed *more than* five years prior to the application for voluntary departure would not bar a grant of this relief. Moreover, an individual who has been confined in jail or prison for a criminal offense or offenses for 180 days or more (the time is counted in the aggregate) during the five years immediately preceding the request for voluntary departure cannot establish "good moral character."[31] Finally, voluntary departure is a discretionary benefit, which means the application can be denied notwithstanding the date of an offense.[32]

Asylum, Withholding of Removal, and Convention Against Torture

Asylum

An asylum applicant may be denied asylum based on a conviction for a crime involving moral turpitude, including a serious nonpolitical crime committed outside the United States. The asylum provisions do not specifically refer to crimes involving moral turpitude or the grounds of inadmissibility at INA §212(a). However, according to asylum law, an individual who has been convicted of a "particularly serious crime" and who "constitutes a danger to the community" may not receive asylum.[33] Aggravated felonies are, by statute, "particularly serious." However, non-aggravated felonies may be considered particularly serious crimes.[34] Whether a crime involving moral turpitude is "particularly serious" is determined on a case-by-case basis.[35] Factors for consideration include the nature of the conviction based on the statutory elements, the underlying facts and circumstances of the offense, the sentence imposed,

---

[28] INA §240B(b)(1); 8 USC §1229c(b)(1); *Matter of Arguelles-Campos*, 22 I&N Dec. 811 (BIA 1999).

[29] For more on voluntary departure, see the discussion of statuses in chapter one, and see chapter ten on relief.

[30] See the discussion of the petty offense exception later in this chapter.

[31] INA §101(f)(7); 8 USC §1101(f)(7).

[32] For a general discussion of voluntary departure requirements following IIRAIRA, see *Matter of Arguelles-Campos*, 22 I&N Dec. 811 (BIA 1999).

[33] INA §208(b)(2)(A)(ii); 8 USC §1158(b)(2)(A)(ii).

[34] *Matter of M–H–*, 26 I&N Dec. 46 (BIA 2012).

[35] *Matter of Frentescu*, 18 I&N Dec. 244 (BIA 1982).

and whether the offense indicates the individual is a danger to the community.[36] An individual who has committed a serious nonpolitical crime outside of the United States is likewise barred from receiving asylum.[37]

Also, outside of the statutory bar (meaning, even if a crime is not deemed "particularly serious"), asylum is a discretionary benefit. Conviction for a crime involving moral turpitude will be considered by an IJ or asylum officer and may result in a denial of the application on discretionary grounds.[38]

Withholding of removal

A conviction for a crime involving moral turpitude is not a per se bar to withholding under either the INA or the Convention Against Torture (CAT). Depending on the specific case, an individual who has been convicted of a crime involving moral turpitude may be barred from seeking withholding of removal (restriction against removal) under INA §241(b)(3). This section states that an individual who has been convicted of a "particularly serious crime," and who is a "danger to the community of the United States," is barred.[39] As discussed in the next section, an aggravated felony offense wherein the sentence of imprisonment imposed[40] is at least five years is automatically considered to be a particularly serious crime. What constitutes a particularly serious crime in the context of a moral turpitude offense that does not qualify as an aggravated felony is decided on a case-by-case basis.[41] In addition, if there are serious reasons to believe that an individual has committed a serious nonpolitical offense outside the United States, that individual is barred from seeking withholding.[42]

Political offense exception

An individual is not barred from asylum or withholding (restriction) of removal for commission of a crime outside the United States that is political in nature. The statute only bars asylum and/or withholding for commission of a "serious nonpolitical

---

[36] *Matter of Frentescu*, 18 I&N Dec. 244 (BIA 1982).

[37] INA §208(b)(2)(A)(iii); 8 USC §1158(b)(2)(A)(iii).

[38] A determination of whether a crime is a "particularly serious crime" will depend upon the specific facts of the case. The BIA will consider such factors as the nature of the conviction, the circumstances and underlying facts, the sentence imposed, and—most importantly—whether the facts and circumstances of the offense indicate that the applicant is a danger to the community. *Matter of Frentescu*, 18 I&N Dec. 244 (BIA 1982) (burglary offense found not to be a particularly serious crime—asylum granted). In *Matter of Garcia-Garrocho*, 19 I&N Dec. 423 (BIA 1986), the BIA found that the burglary offense at issue (burglary of the first degree—a residential building), was a "particularly serious crime" and that the applicant was barred from both asylum and withholding.

[39] INA §241(b)(3)(B)(ii); 8 USC §1231(b)(3)(B)(ii).

[40] This aggravated felony bar also references multiple aggravated felonies where the aggregate sentences imposed are at least five years.

[41] *Matter of N–A–M–*, 24 I&N Dec. 336 (BIA 2007).

[42] INA §241(b)(3)(B)(iii); 8 USC §1231(b)(3)(B)(iii).

crime."[43] For certain cases, closely connected to the issue of whether a criminal act is political in nature will be the issue of whether the foreign government's prosecution is politically motivated persecution. The section above on inadmissibility discusses the exception to inadmissibility under INA §212(a)(2)(A) for crimes of moral turpitude that are "purely political." This is a slightly different concept from whether a criminal offense is a political crime, because the BIA in addressing the concept of inadmissibility has put great emphasis on the adjective "purely."[44]

In determining whether an offense committed outside the United States is a political crime such that the bar does not apply, the Supreme Court of the United States has endorsed decisions of the BIA that set forth the following test:

> In evaluating the political nature of a crime, we consider it important that the political aspect of the offense outweigh its common-law character. This would not be the case if the crime is grossly out of proportion to the political objective or if it involves acts of an atrocious nature.[45]

In dealing with a foreign conviction, it may be appropriate to argue that the prosecution was politically motivated persecution. Prosecution is considered a form of persecution when the prosecution is mere pretext for improper, illegitimate, or invidious political motives.[46] The United Nations High Commissioner for Refugees has published three factors to consider in determining whether a criminal prosecution in a foreign country may actually be persecution for invidious motives. The first is whether the accused received fair judicial process. The second is the nature of the underlying law the state is enforcing; does the law have political or discriminatory goals? The third is the context, or political environment, in which the prosecution occurs.[47]

Convention Against Torture

An individual convicted of a crime involving moral turpitude that is considered to be a "particularly serious crime" is likewise barred from applying for withholding of removal under the CAT. However, such an individual is eligible to apply for deferral under the CAT. These forms of relief are found in the regulations at 8 CFR §§208.16–208.18, 1208.16–1208.18, and are discussed in greater detail in the next chapter.

---

[43] For the asylum provision, *see* INA §208(b)(2)(A)(iii); 8 USC §1158(b)(2)(A)(iii). For the withholding (restriction) on removal provision, *see* INA §241(b)(3)(B)(iii); 8 USC §1231(b)(3)(B)(iii).

[44] *See Matter of O'Cealleagh,* 23 I&N Dec. 976 (BIA 2006).

[45] *INS v. Aguirre-Aguirre,* 526 U.S. 415, 422 (1999), *citing: Matter of McMullen,* 19 I&N Dec. 90, 97–98 (BIA 1984), *affirmed,* 788 F.2d 591 (9th Cir. 1986).

[46] *See Lin v. INS,* 238 F.3d 239, 244 (3d Cir. 2001); *Abdel-Masieh v. INS,* 73 F.3d 579, 584 (5th Cir. 1996); *Chang v. INS,* 119 F.3d 1055, 1061 (3d Cir. 1997).

[47] United Nations High Commissioner on Refugees, *Handbook on Procedures and Criteria for Determining Refugee Status under the 1951 Convention and the 1967 Protocol Relating to the Status of Refugees* (HCR/1P/4/Eng/Rev.2; published Jan. 1992, reissued Dec. 2011), pp. 57–59. Available at www.unhcr.org/43d58e13b4.html.

Naturalization

Naturalization eligibility is a complicated topic because there are different types, or categories, of applicants with distinct eligibility requirements. Generally speaking, a person who desires to apply for naturalization must have at least five years of lawful permanent residency.[48] However, a person married to and living with an American citizen spouse requires only three years of permanent residency.[49] Likewise, an individual who obtained resident status as the battered spouse of a U.S. citizen need only have three years of permanent residency.[50] (Other individuals, such as persons who have served or who are actively serving in the military,[51] have a shorter or no residency requirement.) For the most common categories—persons who require either three or five years of permanent residency—eligibility for naturalization requires that the person be of "good moral character" during the requisite time period.[52] A conviction for a crime involving moral turpitude during the three- or five-year time period will result in a finding that the person cannot establish good moral character and thus cannot naturalize.[53]

Note that an individual who admits the essential elements of a crime involving moral turpitude may be denied naturalization even though he or she has no conviction.[54] Similarly, even an arrest and charge that has been dismissed (by a prosecutor, judge, or jury) may lead to a denial if the offense was committed during the statutory period for which good moral character must be shown, if the USCIS naturalization unit finds, based on the arrest report or other evidence, that the applicant in fact committed an act that reflects poorly upon him or her.[55]

> ➢ Tip: If an individual with a conviction applies for naturalization, and he or she is removable under INA §237(a) on the basis of that conviction, the naturalization unit may (and usually will) issue a notice to appear (NTA), commencing removal proceedings against the individual.

> ➢ Tip: The naturalization unit will request the arrest report(s) even for offenses that have been dismissed. The client should be prepared to provide a statement explaining the circumstances leading up to the arrest, and evidence of innocence or extenuating circumstances.

---

[48] INA §316(a); 8 USC §1427(a).

[49] INA §319(a); 8 USC §1430(a).

[50] INA §319(a); 8 USC §1430(a).

[51] INA §328; 8 USC §1439.

[52] INA §316(a)(3); 8 USC §1427(a)(3).

[53] *See* INA §101(f); 8 USC §1101(f); *see also* 8 CFR §§316.10(a), (b). An individual who falls under the purview of the petty-offense exception (INA §212(a)(2)(A)(ii)(II)) will not be denied naturalization on account of a single crime of moral turpitude. 8 CFR §316.10(b)(2)(i).

[54] *See* 8 CFR §316.10(b)(2)(iv).

[55] 8 CFR §316.10(b)(3)(iii).

Revocation of naturalization (de-naturalization)

Naturalization to American citizen status normally insulates a foreign-born defendant from removal consequences for a crime. However, if an individual is convicted after the naturalization process for a crime or crimes that occurred prior to naturalization—and were not revealed during the citizenship process—he or she is subject to revocation of naturalization under INA §340 [8 USC §1451]. Under these provisions, it is not necessary that an individual have concealed or withheld information about criminal activity; "unlawful procurement" of citizenship relates simply to the fact that the individual was not statutorily eligible for naturalization based on relevant criminal activity occurring before the swearing-in ceremony that USCIS was not aware of. Revocation occurs when the district director of the USCIS office refers the case to the regional director, who upon review sends the matter to the appropriate U.S. Attorney's office. By regulation, DHS may administratively revoke within two years of naturalization.[56] However, at the present time revocation occurs where the U.S. Attorney's office files suit in federal district court. Under the statute at 8 USC §1451(a), the U.S. Attorney may move in district court to revoke and set aside a grant of citizenship on the ground that the naturalization was:

- illegally procured, or
- procured by concealment of a material fact, or
- procured by willful misrepresentation.

In *Kungys v. U.S.*,[57] the Supreme Court found that false testimony or concealment does not have to be about a material fact. A false statement simply has to cut off a relevant line of questioning. *Kungys* was a material misrepresentation and concealment case, not an illegal procurement case. In *Chaunt v. U.S.*,[58] the Supreme Court found that failure to reveal three minor arrests that occurred more than 10 years prior to naturalization did not rise to the level of clear and convincing evidence that naturalization was illegally procured. Under the concept of illegal procurement, there is no need to find fraud or misrepresentation: commission of a crime that negates a finding of "good moral character" under INA §101(f)[59] during the statutorily required period for naturalization will result in denaturalization even if there is no proof that the individual intended to mislead or conceal.[60] Once a district court becomes aware that citizenship was unlawfully procured because the person did not meet the re-

---

[56] 8 CFR §340.2.

[57] 485 U.S. 759 (1988).

[58] 364 U.S. 350 (1960).

[59] 8 USC §1101(f).

[60] *Fedorenko v. U.S.*, 449 U.S. 490 (1981) (a naturalized citizen's failure to comply with the statutory prerequisites for naturalization renders the certificate "illegally procured" and revocable); *U.S. v. Jean-Baptiste*, 395 F.3d 1190 (11th Cir. 2005).

quirements of "good moral character," revocation is required; the court has no discretion to decline revocation.[61]

Although it may seem unusual for DHS to become aware of a recently naturalized U.S. citizen having since been convicted of a crime for pre-naturalization activity, DHS does in fact often find out. The plethora of federal case law on denaturalization is evidence of this. In federal court, there is often a pre-sentence investigation report (PSI) wherein the parole office will contact DHS to confirm a foreign-born person's immigration status; during this inquiry, the fact of recent naturalization will come up and be discussed by the parties. The U.S. Attorney offices across the country also have assistant chief counsel from U.S. Immigration and Customs Enforcement (ICE) embedded and sharing immigration law knowledge on issues of cross-concern. As for state court proceedings, it may be more difficult for DHS to ascertain that pre-swearing-in criminal activity is being prosecuted; however, any time someone who is foreign born is processed for booking or detention, the Secure Communities database checks the status. An eager ICE agent may scrutinize the date of naturalization. And even a U.S. citizen's criminal conviction can come to light through routine security checks at a port of entry. The question is whether a U.S. Customs and Border Protection (CBP) officer will inquire further into the date of citizenship and the date of criminal activity.

Criminal prosecution for knowing illegal procurement of citizenship

An individual who knowingly procures citizenship through fraud or misrepresentation is also subject to criminal prosecution under 18 USC §1425. An individual who is convicted under 18 USC §1425 automatically loses his or her citizenship. Thus, while it is possible for naturalization to be revoked in a civil process based on illegal procurement, a knowing illegal procurement may also lead to criminal sanctions. The penalties for illegal procurement of citizenship are severe, including a maximum of 15 to 25 years' imprisonment and fines.

A defense attorney's obligations

Pursuant to *Padilla v. Kentucky*,[62] a defense attorney representing a foreign-born U.S. citizen may still have Sixth Amendment obligations. When a client is a U.S. citizen by naturalization, the criminal lawyer should inquire when citizenship was obtained. If the indictment or information implicates activity prior to swearing in, the prosecution (even without an eventual conviction) implicates revocation, criminal prosecution, and then removal proceedings. Even if a person is not convicted, the alleged activity could come to the attention of DHS; revocation could lead to removal based on fraud or misrepresentation. Successfully maneuvering around this Pandora's

---

[61] *U.S. v. Lekarczyk,* 354 F. Supp. 2d 883, 888 (W.D. 2005), citing *Fedorenko v. U.S.*, 449 U.S. 490, 517 (1981).

[62] *Padilla v. Kentucky*, 559 U.S. 356 (2010).

box requires a team of both defense and immigration counsel. Chapter eleven discusses possible resolutions.

Consequences of an Aggravated Felony Conviction

Inadmissibility, Including Adjustment of Status and Visa Eligibility

Conviction of an "aggravated felony" offense is *not*—repeat, *not*—a ground of inadmissibility under INA §212(a). Very often, an aggravated felony offense will fall into some other category, such as a crime involving moral turpitude or a controlled substance violation. But not always. (This dichotomy can sometimes be crucial when seeking a benefit or relief from removal.)

Because it is not a ground of inadmissibility, a conviction for an aggravated felony offense, standing alone, is not a basis to deny adjustment of status or a visa. However, an aggravated felony conviction may lead to a discretionary denial, or fall within some other classification of inadmissibility. Again, the nuance between inadmissibility and deportability—and the fact that aggravated felonies do not fall within the former category—can be important in the area of relief, as discussed in the next chapter.

Deportability/Removability

An individual who has been convicted of an aggravated felony offense at any time is subject to removal from the United States.[63]

Mandatory Detention

An individual who is released from penal custody after October 8, 1998, for an aggravated felony conviction is subject to mandatory detention.[64] He or she will be detained in immigration custody without bond while removal proceedings are pending.

Voluntary Departure

A non–American citizen who is deportable for an aggravated felony offense is not eligible for voluntary departure, either before removal proceedings are commenced, at the preliminary stage of proceedings, or at the conclusion of proceedings.[65]

The only exception would be for a non–American citizen classified as an arriving alien under 8 CFR §1.1(q), or someone who entered without inspection, who is charged with inadmissibility under INA §212(a), seeks voluntary departure at the conclusion of the proceedings, and whose aggravated felony conviction pre-dates

---

[63] INA §237(a)(2)(A)(iii); 8 USC §1227(a)(2)(A)(iii).

[64] *See* INA §236(c)(1)(B). October 8, 1998, was the last day Transition Period Custody Rules were in effect. *See* 8 CFR §236.1(c)(1)(i); Illegal Immigration Reform and Immigrant Responsibility Act of 1996 (IIRAIRA), Pub. L. No. 104-208, div. C, § 303(b), 110 Stat. 3009, 3009-585 to 3009-587.

[65] INA §§240B(a)(1), (b)(1)(C); 8 USC §§1229c(a)(1), (b)(1)(C).

November 29, 1990. Under the INA, voluntary departure is not available to an "arriving alien" at the pre-commencement or master calendar stage.[66]

Furthermore, an "arriving alien" may only seek voluntary departure at the conclusion of proceedings if he or she has been physically present in the United States for at least one year preceding service of the NTA.[67] Such persons would include parolees, who retain the status of "arriving aliens" no matter how long they have been in the United States. The immigration judge may permit such an individual to voluntarily depart at the conclusion of removal proceedings only if the immigration judge finds that "the alien is not deportable under [INA] §237(a)(2)(A)(iii) [for an aggravated felony conviction]...,"[68] but arriving aliens and persons who enter without inspection, having never been admitted, are charged under INA §212(a) as inadmissible, not as deportable under INA §237(a)(2)(A)(iii). Finally, voluntary departure requires a minimum of five years of "good moral character."[69] A person who has been convicted of an aggravated felony is permanently barred from establishing good moral character under INA §101(f)(8), but this provision was introduced by the Immigration Act of 1990 (IMMACT90)[70] and is not retroactive: it applies only to aggravated felony convictions entered on or after November 29, 1990.

Summary of caveat eligibility for individual with aggravated felony conviction seeking voluntary departure:

- Must be charged under INA §212(a) as an arriving alien or a person who entered without inspection;
- Must have been physically present at least one year prior to service of NTA;
- Aggravated felony conviction must pre-date November 29, 1990.

Asylum and Withholding of Removal

An individual who has been convicted of an aggravated felony offense is barred from receiving asylum.[71] INA §208(b)(2)(B)(i) mandates that "an alien who has been convicted of an aggravated felony *shall* be considered to have been convicted of a particularly serious crime," which would lead to a denial of asylum under INA §208(b)(2)(A)(ii) [8 USC §1158(b)(2)(A)(ii)]. The reader will note, in this regard, that the BIA has held that even if a conviction is *not* an aggravated felony, it may be

---

[66] INA §240B(a)(4); 8 USC §1229c(a)(4).

[67] INA §240B(b)(1)(A); 8 USC §1229c(b)(1)(A). For a full discussion of voluntary departure, see chapter ten's section on voluntary departure.

[68] INA §240B(a)(1); 8 USC §§1229c(a)(1).

[69] INA §240B(b)(1)(B); 8 USC §1229c(b)(1)(B).

[70] Immigration Act of 1990 (IMMACT90), Pub. L. No. 101-649, 104 Stat. 4978.

[71] INA §208(b)(2)(B)(i), 8 USC §1158(b)(2)(B)(i).

considered—after an evidentiary hearing—to be a particularly serious crime for purposes of asylum.[72]

An individual is barred from receiving withholding (or restriction) of removal if he or she has been convicted of a "particularly serious crime."[73] An individual who has been convicted of an aggravated felony or felonies, and has been *sentenced to* an aggregate term of imprisonment of at least five years,[74] will be considered to have committed a "particularly serious crime,"[75] and thus be precluded from seeking withholding of removal under INA §241(b)(3). Moreover, an individual who has been sentenced to less than five years for an aggravated felony offense may also be found to have committed a "particularly serious crime."[76] The language of the withholding provision is distinct from asylum, however, in that withholding refers to the fact that the non–American citizen, having been convicted by a final judgment of a particularly serious crime, is a danger to the U.S. community. What qualifies as a particularly serious crime, and the nuanced language between the asylum and withholding provisions, is discussed in the next chapter.

Accordingly, receiving a sentence of less than five years is not a guarantee that an aggravated felony conviction will not be viewed as "particularly serious." This is determined on a case-by-case basis utilizing criteria set forth in case law with a focus on danger to the community and specifically acts against a person.[77] In a decision combining several cases, *Matter of Y–L–, A–G–, R–S–R–*,[78] the attorney general (AG) held that drug trafficking crimes are presumed to be "particularly serious crimes" despite less-than-five-year sentences, unless the presumption may be overcome.[79] In this case, the AG classified all drug trafficking (with only minor exceptions) as categorically particularly serious. However, for the most part, case law does not categorically classify certain crimes as "particularly serious" (as it does, by comparison, in the aggravated felony "crime of violence" context); instead, BIA case law teaches that each case merits an independent review of the facts and circumstances.

---

[72] *Matter of N–A–M–*, 24 I&N Dec. 336 (BIA 2007).

[73] INA §241(b)(3)(B)(ii); 8 USC §1231(b)(3)(B)(ii).

[74] In other words, the particularly serious crime bar may be triggered by one aggravated felony offense with a sentence of imprisonment of at least five years, or multiple aggravated felony offenses whose sentences combined in the aggregate are at least five years imprisonment.

[75] See the final paragraph of INA §241(b)(3)(B) [8 USC §1231(b)(3)(B)], which defines "aggravated felony" for clause (ii).

[76] INA §241(b)(3)(B); 8 USC §1231(b)(3)(B).

[77] *Matter of N–A–M–*, 24 I&N Dec. 336 (BIA 2007); *Matter of L–S–*, 22 I&N Dec. 645 (BIA 1999).

[78] 23 I&N Dec. 270 (AG 2002).

[79] *See McNeil v. Att'y Gen.*, 238 Fed. Appx. 878, 2007 WL 2412165, 2007 U.S. App. LEXIS 20582 (3d Cir. Aug. 27, 2007). For further discussion of this case and persons who are barred from withholding based on an aggravated felony offense—including the reach of the five-year statutory language—see the next chapter, and the section on withholding of removal, later in this chapter.

The next chapter, on waivers and relief, contains examples of particularly serious crime determinations in the withholding section; again, these precedents do not purport to categorically declare certain offenses to be particularly serious without an independent review of the facts and circumstances.

Judicial review of the "particularly serious crime" determination

The federal courts are divided on whether they have jurisdiction to review the AG's (*i.e.*, the BIA's and/or the immigration court's) determination that an offense, including an aggravated felony offense, is a particularly serious crime for purposes of withholding. The Ninth Circuit has found that, because the BIA's determination of whether an offense constitutes a particularly serious crime is a question of "adjudication," it is akin to a discretionary determination over which the courts of appeals have no jurisdiction to review."[80] Likewise, the Seventh Circuit has held it will not review the merits of the Board's determination that an offense is particularly serious.[81] The Second Circuit disagrees, stating that the particularly serious crime determination is not a matter of discretion (in either the asylum or withholding context) and is therefore subject to judicial review.[82] The Third Circuit has also found it has jurisdiction to review the particularly serious crime determination.[83]

Political offense exception

A nonpolitical crime committed abroad prior to entering the United States may qualify as an aggravated felony and also be a bar to asylum and/or withholding.[84] For a discussion on whether a crime committed abroad qualifies for a political offense exception, see the discussion above in the moral turpitude section.

Convention Against Torture

The regulations that dictate eligibility for withholding under the CAT are similar to the language for withholding under the INA. An individual who has been convicted of an aggravated felony offense that is considered to be a particularly serious crime is barred from receiving withholding under the CAT.[85] An individual who is

---

[80] *Delgado v. Holder*, 563 F.3d 863, 870–72 (9th Cir. 2009).

[81] *Ali v. Achim*, 468 F.3d 462, 470 (7th Cir. 2006), *cert. dismissed*, 552 U.S. 1085 (2007).

[82] *Nethagani v. Mukasey*, 532 F.3d 150, 154–55 (2d Cir. 2008).

[83] *Alaka v. Att'y Gen.*, 456 F.3d 88, 94–101 (3d Cir. 2006).

[84] INA §§208(b)(2)(A)(iii), 241(b)(3)(B)(iii); 8 USC §§1158(b)(2)(A)(iii), §1231(b)(3)(B)(iii).

[85] 8 CFR §§208.16(d)(2), 1208.16(d)(2), state:

Mandatory Denials. Except as provided in paragraph (d)(3) of this section, an application for withholding of removal under section 241(b)(3) of the Act or under the Convention Against Torture shall be denied if the applicant falls within section 241(b)(3)(B) of the Act or, for applications for withholding of deportation adjudicated in proceedings commenced prior to April 1, 1997, within section 243(h)(2) of the Act as it appeared prior to that date. For purposes of section 241(b)(3)(B)(ii) of the Act, or section 243(h)(2)(B) of the Act as it appeared prior to April 1, 1997, an alien who has been convicted of a particularly serious crime shall be considered to constitute a danger to the community. If the evidence indicates the applicability of one or more of the grounds for denial of withholding

Continued

barred from receiving withholding under the CAT based on an aggravated felony conviction that is determined to be a "particularly serious crime" may nonetheless apply for deferral of removal under the CAT.[86]

Naturalization

As discussed above in the section on crimes involving moral turpitude, eligibility for naturalization generally requires five years of "good moral character." A person who has been convicted of an aggravated felony offense is *permanently barred* from establishing good moral character, and is thus permanently barred from becoming an American citizen.[87] However, this particular provision, introduced by IMMACT90, is not retroactive; it applies only to persons convicted of an aggravated felony offense *on or after* November 29, 1990.[88] An individual with an aggravated felony conviction pre-dating November 29, 1990, is not ineligible for naturalization on account of the offense.

> ➤ **Tip**: An individual with an aggravated felony conviction is amenable to removal proceedings. If he or she applies for naturalization, the naturalization unit may issue an NTA and commence removal proceedings. If the person is subject to mandatory detention on account of the conviction, he or she may be arrested at the naturalization office.

Revocation of naturalization (denaturalization)

A naturalized U.S. citizen who is convicted of an aggravated felony offense that occurred prior to naturalization and was not revealed during the citizenship process is subject to revocation of citizenship for illegal procurement.[89] If naturalization is knowingly illegally procured (via fraud or misrepresentation), the individual may be criminally prosecuted under 18 USC §1425. Under either scenario, the individual is then subject to removal proceedings. For a thorough discussion of denaturalization, see the section on moral turpitude and naturalization, above.

Consequences of a Controlled Substance Conviction

Inadmissibility, Including Adjustment of Status and Visa Eligibility

An individual who has been convicted of (or admits having committed the essential elements of) a crime—including a regulatory offense—relating to a controlled

---

enumerated in the Act, the applicant shall have the burden of proving by a preponderance of the evidence that such grounds do not apply.

[86] For further discussion, see chapter seven.

[87] INA §101(f)(8); 8 USC §1101(f)(8).

[88] *See* IMMACT90, §509.

[89] INA §340; 8 USC §1451; 8 CFR §340.2.

substance is inadmissible.[90] This includes violations of state, federal, or foreign laws.[91]

This means that he or she may be:

- denied a visa at an American consulate abroad;
- denied a change of status from one visa category to another;
- denied adjustment of status;
- denied naturalization; or
- placed in removal proceedings and charged with inadmissibility if arriving at a port of entry.

If the conviction is for a single offense of personal possession of 30 grams or less of marijuana, the individual may apply for a waiver.[92] However, beyond simple possession (less than 30 grams) of marijuana, there is absolutely no waiver for persons who would like to become LPRs but have a controlled substance violation.[93]

"Reason to believe"

It is important to remember that, in the context of inadmissibility (under INA §212(a)), an individual does not have to be convicted of a controlled substance offense in order to be considered inadmissible. If the government has "reason to believe" an individual has been involved in drug trafficking, that individual is considered inadmissible under INA §212(a)(2)(C). An individual's immediate family members may also be denied admission if there is "reason to believe" that they have obtained financial gain or any other benefit within the previous five years on account of the principal's drug trafficking activity.

> *Tip*: **Travel Warning.** Consider this scenario: Fabio Septimo, an LPR of the United States and a citizen of Colombia, is arrested on drug trafficking charges in 2003. This is the only time he has ever been arrested. His attorney, a famous criminal defense lawyer, takes the case to trial and the jury's verdict is "not guilty." As long as he remains in the Unit-

---

[90] INA §212(a)(2)(A)(i)(II); 8 USC §1182(a)(2)(A)(i)(II).

[91] INA §212(a)(2)(A)(i)(II); 8 USC §1182(a)(2)(A)(i)(II).

[92] INA §212(h); 8 USC §1182(h). For further discussion, see chapter ten.

[93] One small window of opportunity, or exception, may exist for persons who seek to adjust status or consular process for an immigrant or nonimmigrant visa at a consulate abroad, and who were adjudicated in the Ninth Circuit between 2000 and 2011. A discussion of the Ninth Circuit's treatment of first offense simple possession of a controlled substance is found at chapter two, "Convictions." The State Department may be the most generous in terms of inadmissibility in the visa application process. The relevant provision of the *Foreign Affairs Manual* is at 9 FAM 40.21(b) N4.1-6 Action After Conviction. It explains that for criminal cases arising in states within the Ninth Circuit Court of Appeals, a state disposition and subsequent expungement that patterns the Federal First Offender Act prior to July 14, 2011, will not form a ground of inadmissibility under INA §212(a)(2)(A)(i)(II).

ed States, Fabio is not subject to deportation, because he does not have a conviction for drug trafficking. He is "safe." However, Fabio travels to South America to visit his ailing mother and father. He is gone two days. Upon his return to the United States, Fabio is placed in removal proceedings and charged with "reason to believe" that he has been a drug trafficker. His wife and three daughters—traveling with him—are also charged. If the reason-to-believe charges are sustained, there is no waiver available to the Septimo family.

Deportability/Removability

An individual who has been convicted of a controlled substance violation is deportable pursuant to INA §237(a)(2)(B). The only exception is a single offense involving possession for one's own use of 30 grams or less of marijuana.[94]

The personal use exception

In *Matter of Moncada*,[95] the BIA found that personal possession of less than 30 grams of marijuana in a prison setting would not qualify for the exception because the enhancement for possession in a prison made the crime more serious. The Board noted in a footnote that it may well reach the same conclusion for possession of marijuana in or near a school.[96]

Does the personal use exception extend to paraphernalia?

Until recently, it was an unsettled area of the law as to whether a conviction possession of marijuana paraphernalia would qualify for this exception. As background, in *Matter of Martinez Espinoza*,[97] the Board found that the 212(h) waiver (discussed in the next chapter on waivers) may be used to waive both simple possession of less than 30 grams of marijuana or possession of marijuana paraphernalia, if it is clear that the possession of paraphernalia "relates to" simple possession for personal use of a small amount of marijuana. The question arises whether the *Espinoza* holding can be applied in the deportability context to qualify for the exception under INA §237(a)(2)(B): in other words, if simple possession for one's own use of less than 30 grams of marijuana is excepted, what about possession of marijuana paraphernalia? Efforts to make this argument met with mixed success.

Practitioners will note the language at INA §212(h), the waiver provision, utilizes the phrase "as it relates to" simple possession of marijuana; the deportability provision does not use this term. In *Barma v. Holder*,[98] the court of appeals reviewed a BIA decision finding that possession of marijuana paraphernalia did not qualify for

---

[94] INA §237(a)(2)(B)(i).
[95] *Matter of Moncada*, 24 I&N Dec. 62 (BIA 2007).
[96] *Matter of Moncada*, 24 I&N Dec. 62, at *n*. 3.
[97] 25 I&N Dec. 118 (BIA 2009).
[98] 640 F.3d 749 (7th Cir. 2011).

an exception under INA §237(a)(2)(B); the court of appeals did not reach this issue, because the petitioner was deportable on other grounds.

In an unpublished decision, the Tenth Circuit held that a conviction for one count of paraphernalia possession and one count of marijuana possession qualified as two convictions and therefore the individual did not have a "single offense" of simple possession of marijuana for one's own use.[99] The Tenth Circuit did not allow the exception at INA §237(a)(2)(B).

However, in October 2012, the BIA spoke on this important, recurring issue. In *Matter of Davey*,[100] the BIA considered a case involving one conviction for two offenses: possession of marijuana and possession of marijuana paraphernalia. The context was a custody redetermination (bond hearing); however, the BIA was clear that the decision should encompass deportability under INA §237(a)(2)(B) as well as a waiver under INA §212(h) (discussed in the next chapter). The BIA found that one criminal case resulting in a conviction for two distinct counts of possession of marijuana paraphernalia and possession of marijuana (less than 30 grams) where circumstances indicate the paraphernalia was connected to the use of marijuana would not support deportability under INA §237(a)(2)(B). Rather, the BIA placed emphasis on Congress's use of the phrase "single offense" and found the two counts are constituent parts of a single act and are "adjunct" to each other.[101] Again, adopting a circumstance specific rather than categorical approach, the BIA emphasized that the burden of proof is on DHS to establish that the marijuana paraphernalia was not part of a single offense, or incident, relating to personal possession or use of less than 30 grams of marijuana.

Compare deportability with inadmissibility

An individual who is *in* the United States following a lawful admission cannot be deported based on a "reason to believe" that he or she has been involved in drug trafficking, unless he or she was inadmissible at the time of entry. "Reason to believe" applies only in the context of inadmissibility (which would preclude an individual who is physically present in the United States from adjusting status to permanent residency if there was a "reason to believe" he or she had been involved in drug trafficking).

Deportation is also more flexible than inadmissibility because it contains an exception for personal possession of marijuana. INA §212(a), governing inadmissibility, contains no such exception.

---

[99] *Martinez-Mercado v. Holder*, 492 Fed. Appx. 890, 2012 WL 3055844, 2012 U.S.App.LEXIS (10th Cir. July 27, 2012).

[100] *Matter of Davey*, 26 I&N Dec. 37 (BIA 2012).

[101] *Matter of Davey*, 26 I&N Dec. 37, *at* 39, 40.

> **Tip: Travel Warning.** Consider this scenario: Joe Notbornhere, a U.S. LPR but a citizen of somewhere else, has one conviction (after October 8, 1998) for simple possession of 20 grams of marijuana. As long as he remains in the United States, he is not subject to deportation as a result of the conviction. However, if he travels outside the United States and makes application for re-entry, Joe is subject to the INA §212(a)(2)(A)(i)(II) grounds of inadmissibility (controlled substance offense) and can be placed in removal proceedings. If he was incarcerated as a result of the arrest or conviction, he is subject to mandatory detention in an immigration facility while removal proceedings are pending. And finally, assuming the offense occurred after April 1996, unless Joe has resided in the United States for several years, he may not be eligible for a waiver.[102] Thus, travel outside the United States could result in removal proceedings, mandatory detention, and a loss of permanent residency for Joe—all on account of simple possession of marijuana.

Mandatory Detention

An individual who is removable on the basis of a controlled substance violation (under INA §237(a)(2)(B)) and who was released from penal custody after October 8, 1998, is subject to mandatory detention without bond in an immigration facility while removal proceedings are pending.[103]

> **Tip:** An individual who is *inadmissible* under INA §212(a)(2)(A)(i)(II) for an admission to the essential elements of a controlled substance violation, and/or under the §212(a)(2)(C) "reason to believe" language, would be subject to mandatory detention under INA §236(c), but for an important caveat: if there is no conviction, there has been no custody, and thus no release from custody that would trigger mandatory detention. Therefore, it is arguable that admission of the essential elements of a drug trafficking crime (§212(a)(2)(A)(i)(II)) and "reason to believe" one has been a drug trafficker (§212(a)(2)(C)) cannot trigger mandatory detention.

Voluntary Departure

Pre-commencement or early stage of removal proceedings

An individual who is removable for a controlled substance offense is nonetheless eligible for pre-commencement (administrative) or early-stage voluntary departure,

---

[102] *See* chapter eight.

[103] INA §236(c)(1)(B); 8 USC §1226(c)(1)(B). October 8, 1998, was the last day Transition Period Custody Rules were in effect. See 8 CFR §236.1(c)(1)(i); Illegal Immigration Reform and Immigrant Responsibility Act of 1996 (IIRAIRA), Pub. L. No. 104-208, div. C, § 303(b), 110 Stat. 3009, 3009-585 to 3009-587.

assuming he or she is otherwise eligible for the benefit.[104] Note that an individual is not eligible if the controlled substance violation qualifies as an aggravated felony for which he or she is *deportable* (as opposed to inadmissible).[105] In addition, voluntary departure is a discretionary benefit that can be denied in consideration of the controlled substance offense.

Conclusion of Proceedings

In order to receive voluntary departure at the conclusion of removal proceedings, the respondent must have five years of "good moral character"[106] and cannot be deportable for an aggravated felony.[107] A controlled substance violation beyond one offense of simple possession of less than 30 grams of marijuana will negate a finding of good moral character.[108] If the controlled substance offense occurred more than five years prior to the application for voluntary departure, the individual would be eligible to seek voluntary departure (as long as the conviction does not also qualify as an aggravated felony *and* the person is not charged with deportability for it under §237(a)). Also note that an individual who has been confined for 180 days or more for a conviction or convictions (the time is counted in the aggregate) during the five-year period cannot establish good moral character.[109] Finally, voluntary departure is a discretionary benefit that can be denied in light of the controlled substance violation.

Asylum and Withholding of Removal

Conviction for a controlled substance offense is not a per se bar to either asylum or withholding of removal (under the INA or the CAT). An individual who has been convicted of a controlled substance offense will be denied asylum if the offense is considered to be (1) a "particularly serious crime," such that (2) the applicant is a "danger to the community of the United States."[110]

Whether a controlled substance offense is deemed "particularly serious" such that it makes the applicant a "danger to the community" is determined on a case-by-case basis. However, if the controlled substance violation qualifies as an aggravated felony,[111] it is an automatic bar.[112] In addition, asylum is a discretionary benefit, and a conviction for a controlled substance offense will be considered. The Asylum Office does a series of extensive background checks in the process of adjudicating asylum

---

[104] INA §240B(a)(1); 8 USC §1229c(a)(1).

[105] INA §240B(a)(1); 8 USC §1229c(a)(1).

[106] INA §240B(b)(1)(B); 8 USC §1229c(b)(1)(B).

[107] INA §240B(b)(1)(C); 8 USC §1229c(b)(1)(C).

[108] INA §101(f)(3); 8 USC §1101(f)(3).

[109] INA §101(f)(7); 8 USC §1101(f)(7).

[110] INA §208(b)(2)(A)(ii); 8 USC §1158(b)(2)(A)(ii); 8 CFR §§208.13(c)(1), (2), 1208.13(c)(1), (2).

[111] See the discussion on aggravated felonies in chapter seven.

[112] INA §208(b)(2)(B)(i); 8 USC §1158(b)(2)(B)(i).

applications. If there is "reason to believe" the individual has been involved in drug trafficking, the application may well be denied even though there is no final conviction. For example, if an individual has a law enforcement hit for suspected drug trafficking, the Asylum Office may deny asylum in the exercise of discretion.

> **Tip**: Asylum applications that contain controversial issues, such as suspected drug trafficking, may be referred to USCIS's Asylum Division Headquarters, in Washington, D.C., where they can remain pending for a very long time—sometimes years—pending higher review.

Similar to the asylum analysis, an individual who is inadmissible or deportable for a controlled substance offense will be barred from receiving withholding of removal under INA §241(b)(3) if the conviction is deemed to be (1) a "particularly serious crime" for which (2) the applicant is a "danger to the community of the United States."[113] The same standard applies for an individual seeking withholding under the CAT.[114] Again, whether a controlled substance violation is considered a particularly serious crime is determined on a case-by-case basis. An individual with a controlled substance offense is eligible to seek deferral under the CAT.[115]

Naturalization

An individual who has been convicted of a controlled substance violation, or is inadmissible for admitting the essential elements of a controlled substance crime, during the required statutory period of good moral character (three or five years)[116] is ineligible for naturalization.[117] There is an exception for one offense of personal possession of marijuana (involving 30 grams or less).[118]

Outside of the three- or five-year period, an individual is not statutorily ineligible due to a controlled substance offense that is *not* an aggravated felony. However, an individual with a controlled substance conviction beyond 30 grams of marijuana is deportable, regardless of when the conviction occurred. In such a case, the naturalization unit will issue an NTA, commencing removal proceedings, and the non–American citizen may be arrested and detained, even at the time of the naturalization interview.

Revocation of naturalization (denaturalization)

A naturalized U.S. citizen who is convicted of a controlled substance offense that occurred prior to naturalization and was not revealed during the citizenship process is

---

[113] INA §241(b)(3)(B)(ii); 8 USC §1231(b)(3)(B)(ii); 8 CFR §§208.16(d)(2), 1208.16(d)(2).

[114] 8 CFR §§208.16(d)(2), 1208.16(d)(2).

[115] 8 CFR §§208.17, 1208.17.

[116] INA §316(a)(3); 8 USC §1427(a)(3). See the discussion of naturalization requirements above in the section on crimes involving moral turpitude.

[117] INA §101(f)(3); 8 USC §1101(f)(3); 8 CFR §316.10(b)(2)(iii).

[118] 8 CFR §316.10(b)(2)(iii).

subject to revocation of citizenship for illegal procurement.[119] It is not clear whether a conviction for simple possession of marijuana would lead to revocation because this offense is not a basis for denial of naturalization.[120] If naturalization is *knowingly* illegally procured (via fraud or misrepresentation), the individual may be criminally prosecuted under 18 USC §1425. Under either scenario, the individual is then subject to removal proceedings. For a thorough discussion of denaturalization, see the section on moral turpitude and naturalization, above.

Consequences of a Firearms Offense

Inadmissibility, Including Adjustment of Status and Visa Eligibility

An individual who has been convicted of a firearms offense is *not* statutorily ineligible for a visa, entry into the United States, or adjustment of status. A firearms conviction is not a ground of inadmissibility at INA §212(a) [8 USC §1182(a)]. To the extent that adjustment of status is discretionary, however, it is possible that an adjustment applicant may be denied permanent resident status based on a firearms offense. Experience teaches that an individual is unlikely to be denied adjustment of status based on one minor firearms conviction, such as carrying a concealed weapon.

Deportability/Removability

An individual who has been convicted of a firearms offense is deportable and subject to removal from the United States.[121] As stated in the previous chapter, deportability for a "firearms offense" encompasses selling, exchanging, using, possessing, or purchasing a firearm or destructive device in violation of state or federal law. An individual is deportable for a firearms violation regardless of when the offense occurred or the conviction was entered. However, this provision does require a final conviction; an individual cannot be deported based on a "reason to believe" or an "admission to the essential elements." For example (and in comparison to certain other types of offenses), an arrest for a firearms offense that is ultimately dismissed cannot form the basis of deportability.

Cross-reference with the aggravated felony definition

One consequence of having a state firearms offense is that it may be considered an aggravated felony. As discussed throughout this book, the aggravated felony classification carries its own set of consequences.

Many state firearms offenses may be considered aggravated felonies based on the BIA's decision in *Matter of Vasquez-Muniz*.[122] *Vasquez-Muniz* holds that certain state

---

[119] INA §340; 8 USC § 1451; 8 CFR §340.2.

[120] 8 CFR §316.10(b)(2)(iii).

[121] INA §237(a)(2)(C); 8 USC §1227(a)(2)(C).

[122] 23 I&N Dec. 207 (BIA 2002).

firearms offenses are aggravated felonies if they are *described in* a federal law counterpart.[123] By way of example, the following offenses—which are traditionally penalized by state law and are relatively innocuous—may potentially[124] be viewed as aggravated felonies by DHS.[125]

U.S. Code Cite	(Summary) Name of Offense
18 USC §922(g)(1)	Possession of a firearm by a convicted felon
18 USC §922(g)(2)	Possession of a firearm by a fugitive from justice
18 USC §922(g)(3)	Possession of a firearm by unlawful user of controlled substances or an addict
18 USC §922(g)(4)	Possession of a firearm by an individual adjudicated to be mentally defective or committed to a mental institution
18 USC §922(g)(5)	Possession of a firearm by an illegal alien or an alien in nonimmigrant status
18 USC §922(j)	Receipt, possession, concealment, sale, barter, disposal of a stolen firearm (with knowledge that it is stolen)
18 USC §924(b)	Use of a firearm in the commission of a felony
18 USC §924(c)	Transfer of a firearm, knowing it will be used in the commission of a felony

> ➤ **Why it matters**: Once a firearms conviction also falls under the aggravated felony definition, relief may be more limited. For example, an LPR deportable for a firearms offense may be eligible to seek cancellation of removal[126] (if the residence and physical presence requirements are met). Cancellation is *not* available to a person convicted of an aggravated felony. The individual in *Vasquez-Muniz* (an LPR) was originally granted cancellation of removal, only to have it taken away when

---

[123] *See* INA §101(a)(43)(E); 8 USC §1101(a)(43)(E) (defining aggravated felony in terms of certain offenses "described in" federal statutes).

[124] The author strongly encourages counsel to contest the holding in *Vasquez-Muniz*; state firearms offenses lack the jurisdictional element of the item having been moved, transported, sold, etc. across state lines. Arguably, a federal firearms offense is indeed more serious precisely because of the interstate movement of the weapon. Furthermore, because INA §101(a)(43)(E) specifically references certain federal law provisions, whereas other aggravated felony provisions do not cite to specific statutes (but instead reference the *type* of crime, *i.e.*, theft), it is inconsistent to hold that a state offense can be "described in" a specific federal statute such that the aggravated felony provision is implicated.

[125] This is not an exhaustive list, but highlights some of the offenses found at INA §101(a)(43)(E) that, absent movement across state lines, are penalized by state law.

[126] Cancellation of removal is provided for by INA §240A(a) [8 USC §1229b(a)], and is discussed in chapter ten.

the BIA reconsidered its previous decision, ruled that state firearms offenses can be aggravated felonies, and vacated the grant of relief. In addition, an LPR deportable for multiple offenses, such as a firearms offense and a crime involving moral turpitude, may be eligible to seek relief concurrently: adjustment of status (to waive the firearms offense) and INA §212(h) (to waive the moral turpitude crime). However, if the firearm offense is also considered an aggravated felony, the §212(h) waiver may not be available in certain circuits, or if the client obtained residency through consular processing. Availability of a §212(h) waiver and adjustment are discussed in the next chapter. An individual with an aggravated felony offense is barred from receiving asylum, and may be barred from withholding of removal.

Mandatory Detention

Deportability for a firearms offense triggers mandatory detention. An individual who is removable on the basis of a firearms offense who is released from custody after October 8, 1998, will be held in immigration custody without bond while removal proceedings are pending.[127] This is true even if the offense is relatively minor in nature, such as carrying a concealed weapon, discharge of a firearm, or unlawful display of a firearm.

Voluntary Departure

Pre-commencement or early stage of removal proceedings

An individual who is deportable for a firearms offense is eligible for voluntary departure prior to commencement of proceedings or at the early stage of proceedings unless the offense also qualifies as an aggravated felony.[128] Voluntary departure is a discretionary benefit and, conceivably, a firearms offense could be the basis for a discretionary denial.

Conclusion of proceedings

Voluntary departure at the conclusion of removal proceedings requires five years of "good moral character,"[129] which is defined at INA §101(f). That definition references the grounds of inadmissibility at INA §212(a). Because it is a ground of deportability, not inadmissibility, conviction for a firearms offense is not implicated by the definition of "good moral character." Thus a firearms offense, even if committed during the five years immediately preceding the application, is not a statutory impediment to eligibility. This conclusion would change, however, if the offense also qualifies as an aggravated felony, which (if the person is charged with deportability under INA §237) is a bar to voluntary departure. In addition, voluntary departure is a discre-

---

[127] INA §236(c)(1)(B); 8 USC §1226(c)(1)(B).

[128] INA §240B(a); 8 USC §1229c(a).

[129] INA §240B(b)(1)(B); 8 USC §1229c(b)(1)(B).

tionary benefit that could be denied if the firearms offense is considered serious enough.

Asylum and Withholding of Removal

Deportability for a firearms offense is not a *per se* bar to asylum, withholding of removal under the INA, or withholding under the CAT. Asylum is a discretionary benefit, and if the firearms offense is deemed particularly serious, asylum could be denied.[130] If the firearms offense is also an aggravated felony, asylum is not available.[131] Withholding of removal under the INA and the CAT may be denied if the firearms offense is an aggravated felony, and the individual is considered a "danger to the community."[132]

Naturalization

Conviction for a firearms offense is not a bar to naturalization. A firearms offense does not implicate "good moral character" as required for naturalization.[133] However, if the firearms offense is also an aggravated felony, and the conviction was entered on or after November 29, 1990, naturalization will be denied because the person is permanently barred from establishing "good moral character."[134] Moreover, an individual who has a conviction for a firearms offense may be subject to removal (and mandatory detention), in which case the USCIS naturalization unit may (probably will) issue an NTA and commence removal proceedings. This is true even if the offense occurred many years in the past. An individual who is referred for removal proceedings will be denied naturalization based on the pending immigration court proceedings (although a firearms conviction is not a per se basis to deny naturalization, issuance of an NTA is).[135] Finally, an individual who has served 180 days or more in a penal institution during the required statutory period of "good moral character" (usually five years—three for persons married to and living with American citizens[136]) for any offense (including a firearms offense) cannot qualify for naturalization until five (or three) years have elapsed since release from penal custody.[137]

---

[130] INA §208(b)(2)(A)(ii); 8 USC §1158(b)(2)(A)(ii); 8 CFR §§208.13(c)(1), (2), 1208.13(c)(1), (2).

[131] INA §208(b)(2)(B)(i); 8 USC §§1158(b)(2)(B)(i); 8 CFR §§208.13(c)(1), (2)(i)(D), 1208.13(c)(1), (2)(i)(D).

[132] INA §241(b)(3)(B); 8 USC §1231(b)(3)(B); 8 CFR §§208.16(d)(2), 1208.16(d)(2).

[133] INA §316(a)(3); 8 USC §1427(a)(3). The term "good moral character" is defined at INA §101(f); 8 USC §1101(f).

[134] INA §101(f)(8); 8 USC §1101(f)(8).

[135] INA §318; 8 USC §1429.

[136] See the discussion of the required period of good moral character in the section on crimes involving moral turpitude, earlier in this chapter.

[137] 8 CFR §316.10(b)(2)(v).

Revocation of naturalization (denaturalization)

Again, a firearms offense is not a per se bar to naturalization because firearm convictions are not implicated at INA §101(f), the definition of good moral character. However, a firearms conviction is a relevant point for consideration in the naturalization process and may qualify as an aggravated felony. Accordingly conviction for a firearms offense where commission of the crime occurred prior to naturalization may lead to revocation of the benefit under INA § 340, and even criminal prosecution for illegal procurement under 18 USC §1425. For a more through discussion of revocation and criminal prosecution for illegal procurement, see the section earlier in this chapter on moral turpitude.

Consequences for Money Laundering Offenses

Inadmissibility, Including Adjustment of Status and Visa Eligibility

Money laundering is a distinct ground of inadmissibility under INA §212(a)(2)(I) [8 USC §1182(a)(2)(I)]. An actual conviction is not required. As cited in the previous chapter, the law states that if there is a "reason to believe" that a person has engaged, is engaging, or will engage in an offense under 18 USC §§1956 or 1957 (relating to money laundering), he or she will be found inadmissible. Likewise, if there is reason to believe an individual is an aider, abettor, conspirator, or colluder with others in the offense of money laundering, he or she will be denied admission and/or adjustment of status. The practical effect of this broad provision is that many individuals can be placed on "lookout" lists and denied visas and/or admission into the United States without a conviction, or even an arrest. Law enforcement agencies can dash a person's hope of getting a visa or becoming a permanent resident quickly and permanently. This section was added by the Uniting and Strengthening America by Providing Appropriate Tools Required to Intercept and Obstruct Terrorism (USA PATRIOT) Act,[138] which calls for a specific lookout list, the "Money Laundering Watchlist."[139] A person who is inadmissible based on either a money laundering conviction or a suspicion of involvement in money laundering:

- is permanently ineligible to receive an immigrant visa;
- is permanently ineligible to be admitted to the United States;
- is permanently ineligible to change status or adjust status; and
- can be placed in removal proceedings upon arrival at a U.S. port of entry.

To be clear, an individual (who is not already a permanent resident) who has a conviction for money laundering under 18 USC §§1956 or 1957 is permanently ineli-

---

[138] Uniting and Strengthening America by Providing Appropriate Tools Required to Intercept and Obstruct Terrorism (USA PATRIOT) Act of 2001, Pub. L. No. 107-56, 115 Stat. 272.

[139] *Id.* §1006(b), 115 Stat. 394.

gible for adjustment of status or issuance of an immigrant visa.[140] The same result holds true where there is a "reason to believe" that the adjustment or visa applicant has been, is, or will be involved in money laundering.

> **Arguable**: The reason that money laundering becomes a permanent bar to an immigrant visa or adjustment of status is that the INA §212(h) waiver does not appear to cover subsection (I) relating to money laundering. The waiver specifically states it covers inadmissibility under subsections (A), (B), (D) and (E). Money laundering is in some cases interpreted to be a crime involving moral turpitude.[141] If the offense is a crime involving moral turpitude, it is arguable that the §212(h) waiver should waive subsection (I), because of the fact that there is overlap between subsections (A) and (I).

> **Rare but possible**: An asylee seeking adjustment of status who is inadmissible under INA §212(a)(2)(I) for money laundering could apply for a waiver under INA §209(c), the refugee waiver.

> **Nonimmigrant visa**: An applicant for a nonimmigrant visa could seek a waiver of inadmissibility for money laundering utilizing the nonimmigrant waiver at INA §212(d)(3). Realistically, obtaining a nonimmigrant visa and waiver where there is a suspicion or conviction for money laundering (like a controlled substance trafficking issue) will be very difficult.

State money-laundering offenses

INA §212(a)(2)(I) specifically refers to money laundering, "which is described in" 18 USC §§1956 and 1957. It is not clear that a state offense for money laundering would apply.

Moral turpitude

A state money laundering offense may be construed as a crime involving moral turpitude, depending on the elements of the criminal statute (and if divisible, other evidence indicating the circumstances of the crime). The BIA has ruled that money laundering under the New York Penal Code is a crime involving moral turpitude because that statute specifically involved the knowing concealment of funds derived from illegal activity.[142]

Another relevant decision is *Matter of L–V–C–*,[143] in which the BIA found that a conviction for structuring currency transactions to avoid the reporting requirement

---

[140] INA §212(a)(2)(I); 8 USC §1182(a)(2)(I).
[141] *Smalley v. Ashcroft*, 354 F.3d 332 (5th Cir. 2003).
[142] *Matter of Tejwani*, 24 I&N Dec. 97 (BIA 2007).
[143] *Matter of L–V–C–*, 22 I&N Dec. 594 (BIA 1999).

under 31 USC §§5324(1) and (3) is not a crime involving moral turpitude. At least one federal court has found that money laundering under the federal statute is a crime involving moral turpitude.[144] Therefore, if the matter involves a state offense for money laundering—depending on the elements of the crime—it is arguable that the offense does not implicate inadmissibility.

> **Tip**: INA §212(a)(2)(I) was added by the USA PATRIOT Act, which is specifically intended to combat terrorism. Moreover, the section makes reference to federal money-laundering crimes. Accordingly, an individual who has a state conviction for money laundering is probably not inadmissible under §212(a)(2)(I), and this charge—whether made in the context of inadmissibility or deportability—should be contested.

Deportability/Removability

An individual who has been convicted of a crime "described in" 18 USC §§1956 or 1957 (involving money laundering), where the amount of the funds exceeds $10,000, is deportable for an aggravated felony.[145] The BIA has not ruled in a precedent decision on whether a state money-laundering conviction can be "described in" 18 USC §§1956 or 1957 (à la firearms convictions); thus, it remains to be seen whether a state money-laundering conviction can constitute an aggravated felony, and is thus a deportable offense. As stated in the section on inadmissibility, above, money laundering will in some circumstances be considered a crime involving moral turpitude. The most common example is the laundering of profits from drug trafficking, which the BIA has found to be a crime involving moral turpitude.[146]

Mandatory Detention

An individual who is charged with inadmissibility because of money laundering (including a "reason to believe" that he or she has engaged in money laundering) is subject to mandatory detention.[147] An individual who is deportable for the aggravated felony offense of money laundering is subject to mandatory detention.[148] For potential arguments that a state money-laundering conviction does not implicate mandatory detention, see the sections immediately above on inadmissibility and deportability.

---

[144] *Smalley v. Ashcroft*, 354 F.3d 332 (5th Cir. 2003). *See also Matter of Tejwani*, 24 I&N Dec. 97 (BIA 2007).

[145] INA §101(a)(43)(D) [8 USC §1101(a)(43)(D)] defines money laundering exceeding $10,000 as an aggravated felony. INA §237(a)(2)(A)(iii) [8 USC §1227(a)(2)(A)(iii)] states that an individual with an aggravated felony conviction is deportable.

[146] *Matter of Tejwani*, 24 I&N Dec. 97 (BIA 2007).

[147] INA §236(c)(1)(A); 8 USC §1226(c)(1)(A).

[148] INA §236(c)(1)(B); 8 USC §1226(c)(1)(B).

Voluntary Departure

Pre-commencement or early stage of removal proceedings

Voluntary departure in advance of removal proceedings or at the early stages of proceedings is not available to an arriving alien charged under INA §212(a) where proceedings are initiated at the time of arrival.[149]

An individual who is charged as an arriving alien under INA §212(a), but is issued an NTA at some point after arrival in the United States, is eligible for voluntary departure notwithstanding a charge under INA §212(a)(2)(I). By statute, pre-commencement voluntary departure is specifically not available to persons whose proceedings are commenced at the time of arrival in the United States. By the plain language of this provision, persons who are charged under INA §212(a) but were detected and issued an NTA sometime after arrival are eligible for the benefit. Similarly, an individual who entered the United States without inspection—though not an arriving alien—is charged under INA §212(a). This individual would also qualify for voluntary departure notwithstanding inadmissibility for a money laundering offense.

Note that a person who is charged as deportable for a crime involving moral turpitude under INA §237(a)(2)(A) on account of a money laundering conviction is eligible for pre-commencement or early stage voluntary departure notwithstanding the conviction.[150]

If the money laundering offense is also an aggravated felony under INA §101(a)(43)(D), voluntary departure is not available.[151]

Finally, voluntary departure at any stage of proceedings is discretionary,[152] and a conviction for money laundering could be the basis for denial of this benefit.

Conclusion of proceedings

A money laundering offense that is viewed as a crime involving moral turpitude will interrupt the five years of good moral character required for voluntary departure when the relief is requested at the conclusion of the proceedings.[153] A money laundering offense committed more than five years prior to the request for voluntary departure does not pose an impediment to establishing good moral character. In addition, an individual who has been confined for 180 days or longer in a penal institution for a criminal conviction or convictions (the time is counted in the aggregate) cannot establish good moral character.[154] Moreover, if a money laundering offense also qual-

---

[149] INA §240B(a)(4); 8 USC §1229c(a)(4).

[150] INA §240B(a)(1); 8 USC §1229c(a)(1). The effect of a conviction for a crime involving moral turpitude on eligibility for voluntary departure is discussed earlier in this chapter.

[151] INA §240B(a)(1); 8 USC §1229c(a)(1).

[152] INA §§240B(a)(1), (b)(1); 8 USC §1229c(a)(1), (b)(1).

[153] INA §240B(b)(1)(B); 8 USC §1229c(b)(1)(B).

[154] INA §101(f)(7); 8 USC §1101(f)(7).

ifies as an aggravated felony, it will pose a bar to voluntary departure.[155] Finally, voluntary departure is discretionary,[156] and a money laundering offense could result in a negative discretionary determination, regardless of when it was committed.

Asylum and Withholding of Removal

Inadmissibility for money laundering will lead to a denial of asylum if the adjudicator or judge determines the offense to be a "particularly serious crime."[157] There is some precedent that money laundering may be construed as a particularly serious crime;[158] this classification poses a bar to both asylum and withholding. If an individual is deportable as an aggravated felon based on a conviction under 18 USC §§1956 or 1957 (relating to money laundering over $10,000), he or she is barred from receiving asylum.[159]

A conviction for money laundering is not a per se bar (by statute or regulation) to withholding of removal under either the INA or the CAT. However, if the offense is considered to be (1) a "particularly serious crime" for which (2) the applicant is deemed a "danger to the United States community," the applicant will be denied withholding.[160] In an unpublished decision, the U.S. Court of Appeals for the Ninth Circuit found that money laundering was an aggravated felony and a particularly serious crime; the case did not mention the sentence imposed.[161]

Cross-reference to the section on aggravated felonies in this chapter is recommended, because federal money laundering convictions are likely to be aggravated felony offenses, for which specific statutory and regulatory language applies. An individual with a money laundering conviction remains eligible to seek deferral of removal under the CAT.

Naturalization

A conviction for money laundering is not a per se bar to naturalization. Inadmissibility for money laundering under INA §212(a)(2)(I) is *not* mentioned in the definition of "good moral character" required for naturalization.[162] However, an individual

---

[155] INA §240B(b)(1)(C); 8 USC §1229c(b)(1)(C).

[156] INA §240B(b)(1); 8 USC §1229c(b)(1).

[157] INA §208(b)(2)(A)(ii); 8 USC §1158(b)(2)(A)(ii).

[158] *Kenyeres v. Ashcroft,* 538 U.S. 1301 (2003).

[159] INA §208(b)(2)(B); 8 USC §1158(b)(2)(B).

[160] INA §241(b)(3)(B); 8 USC §1231(b)(3)(B); 8 CFR §§208.16(d)(2), 1208.16(d)(2).

[161] *Merlos v. INS,* 203 Fed Appx. 863, 2006 U.S. App. LEXIS 27247, 2006 WL 3147422 (9th Cir. 2006).

[162] INA §101(f) [8 USC §1101(f)] defines "good moral character." Subsection 8 refers to certain classes of people described at INA §212(a); this provision does not mention INA §212(a)(2)(I). This omission is probably an oversight in the drafting of the USA PATRIOT Act. It does open the door for persons with money laundering offenses to apply for naturalization in certain situations—an excellent form of relief (*see* chapter ten).

who has an aggravated felony conviction based on a money laundering offense[163] is permanently barred from naturalizing *if* the conviction was entered on or after November 29, 1990.[164] If the money laundering conviction qualifies as an aggravated felony offense, the USCIS naturalization unit may issue an NTA and commence removal proceedings.

Revocation of naturalization (denaturalization)

As discussed in the section on moral turpitude crimes, above, an individual who is convicted after naturalization for a crime that occurred prior to naturalization is subject to revocation of citizenship based on illegal procurement[165] and even criminal prosecution[166] if the status was knowingly illegally procured. Commission of a money laundering crime during the statutory period of required good moral character would lead to revocation if ascertained by DHS.

Consequences of a Domestic Violence Conviction

The Definition

"Domestic violence" offenses are defined in chapter eight. It is recommended that the reader review that definition before reading the following discussion, because the list of offenses that are considered to be domestic violence related is long. It encompasses many relationships (*i.e.*, victims), and various offenses such as stalking and violation of protective orders. Moreover, not every assault and battery, injunction violation, abuse charge, or similar case will qualify as a "domestic violence" offense triggering inadmissibility under INA §212(a)(2)(E).

Inadmissibility, Including Adjustment of Status and Visa Eligibility

A conviction for a crime involving domestic violence is not a per se ground of inadmissibility at INA §212(a). In other words, there is no counterpart at §212(a) to the domestic violence ground of deportability at INA §237(a)(2)(E). This can be an extremely important distinction, because certain offenses listed at §237(a)(2)(E) may not be crimes involving moral turpitude falling under §212(a), and thus will not trigger a finding of inadmissibility in any context.

Cross-reference to crimes involving moral turpitude

Depending on the elements of the particular offense (to be determined by the statute under which the individual has been convicted), a crime involving domestic vio-

---

[163] *See* INA §101(a)(43)(D).

[164] INA §101(f)(8) [8 USC §1101(f)(8)] states that a person who has been convicted of an aggravated felony is permanently barred from establishing "good moral character," which is required for naturalization. This provision was passed as part of IMMACT90, and does not apply to convictions entered prior to the date of enactment, November 29, 1990.

[165] INA §340; 8 USC §1451.

[166] 18 USC §1425.

lence may be a crime involving moral turpitude, thereby implicating inadmissibility under INA §212(a)(2). For example, domestic violence offenses that involve corporal injury or other aggravating circumstances—with a specific intent to do harm—may often be considered crimes involving moral turpitude.[167]

Simple battery or assault, however, is generally not considered to be a crime involving moral turpitude; thus, simple battery in a domestic violence context[168] may not be a crime involving moral turpitude. If an adjudicator or IJ *does* find that a simple battery/domestic violence-related offense is a crime involving moral turpitude, it may fall under the petty-offense exception to crimes involving moral turpitude.[169]

Violation of a protective order or injunction may be a crime involving moral turpitude, depending on the particular statute involved. It cannot be said often enough that the particular state statute involved must be reviewed and the specific elements considered in every case.

It is important to note that adjustment of status is discretionary; a crime of domestic violence may not be a ground of denial per se, but it may lead to a discretionary denial.

Deportability/Removability

An individual who is convicted of a crime of domestic violence *after* September 30, 1996, the effective date of the Illegal Immigration Reform and Immigrant Responsibility Act of 1996 (IIRAIRA),[170] is subject to deportation from the United States under INA §237(a)(2)(E) [8 USC §1227(a)(2)(E)]. ICE previously took the position that a simple assault and/or battery in a domestic violence context could be charged as a ground of deportability under §237(a)(2)(E). However, based on the U.S. Supreme Court's decision in *Leocal v. Ashcroft*,[171] and based on other case law (discussed in chapter eight),[172] this view has changed over recent years.

In *Johnson v. U.S.*,[173] the Supreme Court ruled that simple battery in Florida did not categorically qualify as a violent felony under the Armed Criminal Career Act because the statute is divisible, including the terms "touch or strike." The definition of violent felony is essentially the same as a crime of violence under 18 USC §16; thus the *Johnson* decision is very persuasive that a simple battery or assault that does not involve as elements the active use of violent physical force will not meet the defi-

---

[167] Misdemeanor assault with bodily injury under Texas law is a crime involving moral turpitude. *Matter of Deanda-Romo*, 23 I&N Dec. 597 (BIA 2003). Willful infliction of corporal injury on a spouse, cohabitant, or parent of the perpetrator's child in violation of Cal. Penal Code §273.5(a) constitutes a crime involving moral turpitude. *Matter of Phong Nguyen Tran*, 21 I&N Dec. 291 (BIA 1996).

[168] *See, e.g., Matter of Sanudo*, 23 I&N Dec. 968 (BIA 2006).

[169] *See* INA §212(a)(2)(A)(ii); 8 USC §1182(a)(2)(A)(ii), discussed earlier in this chapter.

[170] Pub. L. No. 104-208, div. C, 110 Stat. 3009, 3009-546 to 3009-724.

[171] *Leocal v. Ashcroft*, 543 U.S. 1 (2004).

[172] *See, e.g., Matter of Sanudo*, 23 I&N Dec. 968 (BIA 2006).

[173] *Johnson v. U.S.*, 559 U.S. 133 (2010).

nition of "crime of violence" for purposes of INA §237(a)(2)(E). Shortly after the Supreme Court's decision in *Johnson,* the BIA issued a decision acknowledging the Supreme Court's guidance regarding violent felony/crime of violence in a decision called *Matter of Velasquez.*[174] In this case, the BIA found that misdemeanor assault and battery on a family member under Virginia law[175] did not qualify categorically as a crime of active violent force, and remanded for further review under a modified categorical approach. Certainly, defense counsel should argue that a simple assault and battery may not support a charge under INA §237(a)(2)(E).

A "crime of domestic violence" means any crime of violence against a spouse, former spouse, roommate, or person with whom the individual shares a child in common.[176] "Crime of violence" is defined by 18 USC §16.[177] An act of domestic violence also includes stalking, child abuse, child neglect,[178] and violations of protective orders (temporary restraining orders (TROs) and injunctions).[179]

An IJ has the authority to "waive" the domestic violence ground of deportability where the non–American citizen with a conviction has in fact been the victim of domestic violence. Although the statute utilizes the term "waive," this is not a traditional waiver, but acts more as an exception to the removability ground—hence its inclusion here. INA §237(b)(7) [8 USC §1227(b)(7)] states as follows:

(A) In general—The Attorney General is not limited by the criminal court record and may waive the application of paragraph (2)(E)(i) (with respect to crimes of domestic violence and crimes of stalking) and (ii) in the case of an alien who has been battered or subjected to extreme cruelty and who is not and was not the primary perpetrator of violence in the relationship—

(i) upon a determination that—

(I) the alien was acting in self-defense;

(II) the alien was found to have violated a protection order intended to protect the alien; or

(III) the alien committed, was arrested for, was convicted of, or pled guilty to committing a crime—

(aa) that did not result in serious bodily injury; and

(bb) where there was a connection between the crime and the alien's having been battered or subjected to extreme cruelty.

---

[174] 25 I&N Dec. 278 (BIA 2010).

[175] Va. Code Ann. § 18.2-57.2(A).

[176] INA §237(a)(2)(E)(i); 8 USC §1227(a)(2)(E)(i).

[177] INA §237(a)(2)(E)(i); 8 USC §1227(a)(2)(E)(i)..

[178] INA §237(a)(2)(E)(i); 8 USC §1227(a)(2)(E)(i)..

[179] INA §237(a)(2)(E)(ii); 8 USC §1227(a)(2)(E)(ii). For further discussion of this classification, see chapter five.

(B) Credible evidence considered—In acting on applications under this paragraph, the Attorney General shall consider any credible evidence relevant to the application. The determination of what evidence is credible and the weight to be given that evidence shall be within the sole discretion of the Attorney General.

Again, although the provision is entitled "Waiver," it is not really a form of relief; rather, it is a determination that the ground of deportability should not be applied in the particular situation presented. The provision is very broad. It allows an IJ essentially to dismiss the charge if the non–American citizen can show that he or she was the victim of domestic violence, and essentially was arrested for an act of self-defense, or violated a protective order (an injunction or restraining order) that was entered for his or her own protection. In the alternative, the deportation ground may be waived if a connection can be shown between the offense conduct and the domestic violence, and the offense did not result in serious bodily injury.

Mandatory Detention

An individual who is deportable for a crime involving domestic violence—where there is no other ground of removability charged—is *not* subject to mandatory detention. INA §237(a)(2)(E), the ground of deportation relating to domestic violence, is not an enumerated offense at INA §236(c)(1)(B) (the mandatory detention provision). However, if a domestic violence crime also qualifies as an aggravated felony offense (because a sentence of one year or longer is imposed),[180] or is one of multiple convictions for which the person is deportable,[181] mandatory detention will be imposed.

Additionally, if a person has a domestic violence conviction that the government considers to be a crime involving moral turpitude—such that he or she is inadmissible under INA §212(a)(2)—the offense will trigger mandatory detention for an individual arriving at a U.S. port of entry following a trip abroad.[182]

> ➢ **Remember:** Mandatory detention applies to persons released from penal custody after October 8, 1998.

---

[180] INA §236(c)(1)(B); 8 USC §1226(c)(1)(B) (referencing INA §237(a)(2)(A)(iii)).

[181] INA §236(c)(1)(B); 8 USC §1226(c)(1)(B) (referencing INA §237(a)(2)(A)(ii)).

[182] INA §236(c)(1)(C); 8 USC §1226(c)(1)(C) (referencing INA §237(a)(2)(A)(i)). October 8, 1998, was the last day Transition Period Custody Rules were in effect. *See* 8 CFR §236.1(c)(1)(i); Illegal Immigration Reform and Immigrant Responsibility Act of 1996 (IIRAIRA), Pub. L. No. 104-208, div. C, § 303(b), 110 Stat. 3009, 3009-585 to 3009-587.

Voluntary Departure

Pre-commencement or early stage of removal proceedings

Deportability under INA §237(a)(2)(E) is not an impediment to voluntary departure.[183] However, this relief is discretionary, and a domestic violence offense could support a discretionary denial.

Conclusion of proceedings

A domestic violence charge under INA §237(a)(2)(E) is not a per se bar to voluntary departure at the conclusion of proceedings, even if the offense occurred within the required five-year period of "good moral character." This is because INA §237(a)(2)(E) is not cross-referenced at INA §101(f), the provision defining "good moral character."

As discussed immediately above and in the preceding chapter, a domestic violence offense will very often not qualify as a crime involving moral turpitude. However, if the domestic violence offense qualifies as a crime involving moral turpitude, and it occurred within the five-year period immediately preceding the application for voluntary departure, good moral character—and hence eligibility for voluntary departure—will be implicated. In analyzing eligibility, first determine whether the domestic violence offense qualifies as a "crime involving moral turpitude." Often, it will not.[184] If the crime is one involving moral turpitude, it will be difficult to establish "good moral character."[185] However, as the second part of your analysis, consider whether the offense falls within the petty-offense exception at INA §212(a)(2)(A)(ii). If it falls under this exception, good moral character can be established.[186]

If the offense is outside the five-year period, the respondent is statutorily eligible for voluntary departure notwithstanding the fact that the domestic violence offense qualifies as a crime involving moral turpitude. However, voluntary departure is a discretionary benefit that could be denied for an offense such as domestic violence.

Finally, note that an individual who has been confined for 180 days or longer in a penal institution for a criminal conviction or convictions (the time is counted in the aggregate) cannot establish "good moral character."[187]

Asylum and Withholding of Removal

Conviction of a domestic violence offense is not a per se bar to asylum. Asylum law says that persons who have been convicted of a "particularly serious crime,"

---

[183] *See* INA §240B(a)(1); 8 USC §1229c(a)(1).

[184] *See* chapter eight.

[185] INA §101(f)(3); 8 USC §1101(f)(3).

[186] For more on the petty-offense exception, see the section on crimes involving moral turpitude, earlier in this chapter.

[187] INA §101(f)(7); 8 USC §1101(f)(7).

within the United States or abroad, are barred from receiving asylum.[188] Whether an offense involving domestic violence constitutes a "particularly serious crime" is determined on a case-by-case basis. Asylum is a discretionary benefit,[189] and a conviction for a crime involving domestic violence can be considered and may result in a discretionary denial.

A conviction for a domestic violence offense is not a per se bar to withholding of removal under the INA or the CAT. Again, the issue becomes whether the offense involving domestic violence can be considered (1) a "particularly serious crime" for which (2) the applicant is a "danger to the United States community."[190] This analysis is made on a case-by-case basis. An individual who is deemed ineligible for withholding under either the INA or the CAT may still seek deferral of removal under the CAT.[191]

Naturalization

Having a conviction for a crime involving domestic violence during the required statutory period (usually five years) of "good moral character"[192] will most likely result in a denial of the application for citizenship. In addition, if an individual is considered deportable under INA §237(a)(2)(E), the USCIS naturalization unit will likely issue an NTA, commencing removal proceedings.

Revocation of naturalization (denaturalization)

As with any of the categories listed above, a consequence for failure to reveal criminal activity constituting domestic violence during the naturalization process could lead to revocation of naturalization[193] and even criminal prosecution for knowing illegal procurement.[194] For a complete discussion of post-naturalization convictions wherein the conduct preceded naturalization, see the moral turpitude section, above.

Consequences of Alien Smuggling

Inadmissibility, Including Adjustment of Status and Visa Eligibility

An individual who at any time has knowingly encouraged, assisted, abetted, or aided a non–American citizen to enter the United States in violation of the law is in-

---

[188] INA §208(b)(2)(A)(ii); 8 USC §1158(b)(2)(A)(ii).
[189] INA §208(b)(1)(A); 8 USC §1158(b)(1)(A).
[190] 8 CFR §§208.16(d), 1208.16(d).
[191] 8 CFR §§208.17, 1208.17.
[192] INA §316(a)(3); 8 USC §1427(a)(3).
[193] INA §340; 8 USC §1451.
[194] 18 USC §1425.

admissible,[195] regardless of whether he or she has been criminally convicted of smuggling or harboring. This means that the persons accused of smuggling may be denied a visa at an American consulate abroad, denied admission into the United States at a port of entry, and denied adjustment of status to permanent resident status within the United States. It is not necessary that the act of smuggling be for commercial advantage or for financial gain.

An individual, even a lawful permanent resident, who is stopped at the border under suspicion of alien smuggling will be placed in proceedings as an arriving alien under INA §212(a). This means that the burden of proof (clear and convincing) will rest with the non-American citizen to establish that he or she was not aiding and abetting an illegal entry.[196]

Deportability/Removability

An individual who—prior to the date of entry, at the time of any entry, or within five years of the date of any entry—has knowingly encouraged, induced, assisted, abetted, or aided any other alien (non–American citizen) to enter or try to enter the United States in violation of the law is deportable.[197] Defense attorneys will note that deportability under INA §237(a)(1)(E) does not require a final "conviction," although a conviction will lead to a per se finding of deportability. For plea strategies when faced with a smuggling charge, see chapter eleven, "Fashioning a Plea."

Cross-reference with the aggravated felony definition

Certain alien smuggling offenses will meet the definition of aggravated felony,[198] which is an independent classification that carries significant consequences. Some courts have found that a conviction for harboring an alien in violation of INA §274(a)(1)(A)(iii) [8 USC §1324(a)(1)(A)(iii)] is an aggravated felony crime of "smuggling" even though the offense conduct did not involve bringing a non-American citizen into the United States from outside the border.[199]

Mandatory Detention

An individual who is charged with either inadmissibility or deportability for alien smuggling is not subject to mandatory detention. However, an individual who has been convicted of smuggling or harboring, such that he or she falls under the definition of aggravated felony, is subject to mandatory detention.[200]

---

[195] INA §212(a)(6)(E); 8 USC §1182(a)(6)(E).

[196] *Altamirano v. Gonzales,* 427 F.3d 586, 591 (9th Cir. 2005); *Matter of Guzman-Martinez,* 25 I&N Dec. 845 (BIA 2012).

[197] INA §237(a)(1)(E); 8 USC §1227(a)(1)(E).

[198] INA §§101(a)(43)(N), (O); 8 USC §§1101(a)(43)(N), (O).

[199] *Patel v. Ashcroft,* 294 F.3d 465 (3d Cir. 2002).

[200] INA §236(c)(1)(B); 8 USC §1226(c)(1)(B).

Voluntary Departure

Pre-commencement or early stage of removal proceedings

An individual who is otherwise eligible for voluntary departure is not barred by virtue of an alien smuggling charge or conviction.[201] If the act of alien smuggling also qualifies as an aggravated felony conviction, the respondent will be barred from voluntary departure.

Conclusion of proceedings

A respondent who has knowingly encouraged, induced, assisted, abetted or aided an alien to enter the United States illegally is "described in" INA §212(a)(6)(E) (relating to alien smuggling) and thus will be unable to meet the definition of "good moral character"[202] necessary to qualify for voluntary departure, unless the act occurred outside the five-year window of required good moral character.[203] This is regardless of whether the respondent is charged as inadmissible or deportable in removal proceedings for smuggling, and regardless of whether the smuggling was for financial gain. Note further that an individual who has been confined for 180 days or longer in a penal institution for a criminal conviction or convictions (the time is counted in the aggregate) cannot establish "good moral character."[204]

If the act of smuggling occurred more than five years prior to the application for voluntary departure, the smuggling incident or conviction will not be a per se basis to deny voluntary departure; however, voluntary departure is a discretionary benefit[205] that could be denied based on the adverse nature of the smuggling incident. This will be decided on a case-by-case basis. In addition, if the smuggling offense resulted in a conviction that qualifies as an aggravated felony,[206] the respondent is barred from this relief.[207]

Asylum and Withholding of Removal

Suspicion of, or a conviction for, alien smuggling is not a *per se* bar to asylum or withholding. However, asylum is a discretionary benefit[208] that may be denied based on adverse information. In addition, where an individual has been *convicted* of a "particularly serious crime," such that he or she is a "danger to the United States community," asylum and/or withholding may be denied.[209]

---

[201] For a full discussion of the requirements for voluntary departure, see chapter ten.

[202] INA §101(f)(3); 8 USC §1101(f)(3).

[203] INA §240B(b)(1)(B); 8 USC §1229c(b)(1)(B).

[204] INA §101(f)(7); 8 USC §1101(f)(7).

[205] INA §240B(b)(1); 8 USC §1229c(b)(1).

[206] See INA §§101(a)(43)(N), (O); 8 USC §§1101(a)(43)(N), (O).

[207] See INA §240B(b)(1)(C); 8 USC §1229c(b)(1)(C).

[208] INA §208(b)(1)(A); 8 USC §1158(b)(1)(A).

[209] INA §208(b)(2)(A)(ii); 8 USC §1158(b)(2)(A)(ii).

An individual who has been convicted of alien smuggling or harboring under INA §274(a), such that the offense is classified as an aggravated felony, is barred from receiving asylum.[210] An individual who has been convicted of criminal alien smuggling or harboring, and is thus considered an aggravated felon, will be barred from seeking withholding under the INA and the CAT if the term of imprisonment imposed is at least five years.[211] Regardless of the sentence imposed, an individual may be denied withholding under the INA and CAT if he or she has been convicted of aggravated felony alien smuggling, and is deemed a danger to the U.S. community.[212] An individual who is barred from asylum and withholding under both the INA and the CAT based on a conviction for alien smuggling may still seek deferral of removal under the CAT.[213]

Naturalization

An individual who has encouraged, aided, induced, or abetted alien smuggling [such that he or she falls under the purview of INA §212(a)(6)(E)] is not eligible for naturalization if such act occurred during the required statutory period of "good moral character."[214] An individual who has a conviction for alien smuggling after November 29, 1990, that qualifies as an aggravated felony offense is permanently ineligible for naturalization.[215] The need to cross-reference alien smuggling and the aggravated felony definition is discussed, above.

An individual who is not ineligible to naturalize because the act of smuggling occurred outside the statutory period (for example, more than five years prior to the application for naturalization) may be referred for removal proceedings, depending on the facts of the case and when the "smuggling" occurred. If the act of smuggling involved encouragement, inducement, or assistance from within the United States (as opposed to actually bringing someone in at the time of entry), and was more than five years prior, the individual is not deportable under INA §237(a)(1)(E).

Revocation of naturalization (denaturalization)

A naturalized citizen faces the consequence of denaturalization if it comes to light that he or she was involved in alien smuggling prior to the naturalization ceremony and said conduct was not revealed during the naturalization process. Revocation of naturalization for illegal procurement authorized at INA §340, and criminal prosecution under 18 USC §1451(e) is possible for a willful and knowing misrepresentation

---

[210] INA §208(b)(2)(B)(i); 8 USC §1158(b)(2)(B)(i).

[211] INA §241(b)(3); 8 USC §1231(b)(3).

[212] INA §241(b)(3)(B)(ii); 8 USC §1231(b)(3)(B)(ii).

[213] 8 CFR §§208.17(a), 1208.17(a).

[214] INA §101(f)(3); 8 USC §1101(f)(3).

[215] *See* INA §101(a)(43)(N); 8 USC §1101(a)(43)(N). *See also Kai Tung Chang v. Gantner,* 464 F.3d 289 (2d Cir. 2006) (aggravated felony definition, amended to include conviction for alien smuggling, applies retroactively to pre-amendment aggravated felony offense and bars naturalization).

leading to illegal procurement. For a thorough discussion of revocation of naturalization, see the section on moral turpitude, above.

Falsification of Documents, and Visa and Passport Fraud

Inadmissibility, Including Adjustment of Status and Visa Eligibility

Immigration and registration violations do not logically fall under the canopy of immigration consequences of crime. However, civil registration and documentation violations are grouped together with criminal visa fraud and documentation violations at INA §237(a)(3) [8 USC §1227(a)(3)] and are thus included in the following discussion of criminal offenses involving visa and immigration documentation crimes.[216]

Visa fraud

A conviction for a crime involving visa fraud under 18 USC §1546 is not a per se ground of inadmissibility under INA §212(a). On the other hand, INA §237(a)(3)(C)(i) does make criminal and civil judgments for visa and document fraud grounds for deportation.

However, some visa offenses[217] may be crimes involving moral turpitude, and depending on the specific subsection charged, can lead to a finding of inadmissibility under §212(a)(2)(A).[218] The BIA has stated in several precedent decisions that a conviction under 18 USC §1546 does *not* form the basis of an independent ground of inadmissibility (as it forms a ground of deportability under INA §237), and is *not* automatically a crime involving moral turpitude.[219] [The Board's finding in *Matter of*

---

[216] In previous editions of this book, this section contained a brief discussion of the National Security Entry-Exit Registration Program, or NSEERS. An individual could face removal, and certainly be denied a visa, for failure to comply. The Obama Administration has largely dismantled the NSEERS program, and it would appear there are no penalties or consequences at this time—in any forum—for failing to register. For a summary of the NSSER's program, its impact, and current dormant status, the American Immigration Council's practice advisory, "DHS's NSEERS Program, While Inactive, Continues to Discriminate," *http://immigrationimpact.com/2012/06/28/dhss-nseers-program-while-inactive-continues-to-discriminate/#sthash.2PpHpCYG.dpuf*.

[217] Passport and visa offenses are found at 18 USC §§1541–47.

[218] A conviction under 18 USC §1546 for possession of an altered immigration document with knowledge that it was altered, but without use or proof of any intent to use it unlawfully, is not a conviction for a crime involving moral turpitude. *Matter of Serna*, 20 I&N Dec. 579 (BIA 1992), modified by *Matter of Khourn*, 21 I&N Dec. 1041 (BIA 1997).

[219] See *Matter of Jimenez-Santillano*, 21 I&N Dec. 567 (BIA 1996); *Matter of Wadud*, 19 I&N Dec. 182 (BIA 1984). In *Jimenez-Santillano*, the BIA states, "[N]o ground of inadmissibility enumerated in section 212(a) of the Act [is] comparable to 18 USC §1546...." Further in the decision, the BIA writes, "[T]hus if the respondent had departed from the United States following his conviction under 18 USC §1546(a) and completion of his sentence and thereafter sought reentry as a returning permanent resident, it appears that he would not have been inadmissible under section 212(a)(6)(C)(i) of the Act, notwithstanding his deportability for the 18 USC §1546(a) conviction. The same would be true if the re-

Continued

Jimenez-Santillano[220] was abrogated in large part by the Supreme Court's decision in *Judulang v. Holder*,[221] to the extent that it was a foundational case in the BIA's longstanding "comparable grounds" theory that a ground of deportability under §237 was not automatically a ground of inadmissibility under INA §212(a) for purposes of a waiver under INA §212(c) (repealed 1996); however, the decision is still useful to the extent that the BIA confirms that 18 USC §1546 is not automatically a crime involving moral turpitude or an inadmissible offense.]

Possession vs. use

The determination of whether a visa or passport offense involves moral turpitude must be made on a case-by-case basis, according to the specific statutory provision charged, and will turn on the element of fraud. Another way of looking at the element of fraud is whether the defendant/respondent was charged and convicted of mere possession of an altered document, or use (including an intent to use) the document. In *Omagah v. Ashcroft*,[222] the non–American citizen was convicted of conspiracy to obtain, possess, and use falsely made immigration documents under 8 USC §371; the conspiracy count specifically referenced 18 USC §1546. The court of appeals upheld the BIA's distinguishing treatment of possession versus use offenses under 18 USC §1546, and found that the non–American citizen's conviction for conspiracy to violate §1546 to be a crime involving moral turpitude.

[Note that even if a visa or passport offense is not a crime involving moral turpitude (or does not result in a criminal conviction at all) the *conduct* may lead to a charge of inadmissibility under INA §212(a) for immigration fraud or false claim to U.S. citizenship.[223]]

If, in a particular case, a client's conviction under 18 USC §1546 is viewed as a crime involving moral turpitude, or as a fraud against the government, the conviction may lead to a denial of adjustment of status or a visa. It is important to remember that adjustment of status is a discretionary benefit[224] that can be denied even if the applicant is not per se inadmissible.

---

spondent had been convicted in the United States of a 'firearms offense' …." *Jimenez-Santillano* is discussed in dicta and reaffirmed by the BIA in *Matter of Blake*, 23 I&N Dec. 722 (BIA 2005) (overruled by *Judulang v. Holder*, 132 S. Ct. 476 (2011)).

[220] *Matter of Jimenez-Santillano*, 21 I&N Dec. 567 (BIA 1996).

[221] *Judulang v. Holder*, 132 S. Ct. 476 (2011).

[222] *Omagah v. Ashcroft*, 288 F.3d 254 (5th Cir. 2002).

[223] INA §212(a)(6)(C)(i) [8 USC §1182(a)(6)(C)(i)] states that an individual who, by fraud or misrepresenting a material fact, seeks to procure or has procured a visa, documentation, or admission into the United States is inadmissible. Section 212(a)(6)(C)(ii)(I) states that any alien who falsely represents or has represented himself or herself as a citizen of the United States for any purpose or benefit under the INA or any other federal or state law is inadmissible. The provision on false claims to U.S. citizenship was added by IIRAIRA and applies only to representations made on or after September 30, 1996.

[224] INA §245(a); 8 USC §1255(a).

Civil or criminal document fraud violations under INA §274C

Section 274C of the INA [8 USC §1324c] contains primarily civil—but some criminal—penalties for the use, preparation, alteration, etc., of both immigration documents and immigration applications. This section relates to individuals who use fraudulent documents for themselves, and the persons who assist in providing and selling such documentation (including the preparation of fraudulent immigration applications). An individual who is the subject of a final order (civil or criminal) for violation of INA §274C is inadmissible under INA §212(a)(6)(F) [8 USC §1182(a)(6)(F)]. This means that a person with a final order under §274C may:

- be denied a visa at an American consulate abroad;
- be denied admission into the United States;
- be denied a change of status from one visa category to another;
- be denied adjustment of status;
- be denied naturalization;
- be placed in expedited removal proceedings and charged with inadmissibility if arriving at a port of entry.

Inadmissibility under INA §212(a)(6)(F) may be waived.[225]

Deportability/Removability

Registration and Visa Fraud

INA §237(a)(3)(B) [8 USC §1227(a)(3)(B)] renders deportable persons who have been convicted for failure to register or visa fraud. It states as follows (emphasis added):

(B) Failure to register and falsification of documents—Any alien who *at any time* has been convicted—

(i) under section 266(c) of this Act or under section 36(c) of the Alien Registration Act, 1940,

(ii) of a violation of, or attempt or conspiracy to violate, any provision of the Foreign Agents Registration Act of 1938 (22 U.S.C. 611 *et seq.*), or

(iii) of a violation of, or an attempt or a conspiracy to violate, section 1546 of title 18, United States Code (relating to fraud and misuse of visas, permits and other entry documents),

is deportable.

---

[225] *See* chapter ten.

Civil or criminal document fraud violations under INA §274C

An individual with a final order—either a civil order, or a criminal conviction—pursuant to INA §274C is deportable.[226] A waiver of this ground of deportability is available.[227]

Mandatory Detention

An individual who is deportable under INA §237(a)(3)(B), relating to registration and visa fraud violations, is *not* subject to mandatory detention *if* this is the only ground of deportation charged. INA §237(a)(2)(B) is not an enumerated offense at INA §236(c) (relating to mandatory detention).

There is a caveat. If (1) the government considers an individual's visa fraud conviction under 18 USC §1546 to be a crime involving moral turpitude and the person was sentenced to more than one year,[228] or (2) the individual has more than one such conviction, implicating deportability for multiple crimes under INA §237(a)(2)(A)(ii),[229] the individual will be subject to mandatory detention. If the government views the visa fraud conviction as a crime involving moral turpitude and the individual travels outside the United States, the client will become inadmissible under INA §212(a)(2)(A)(i)(I), and will be subject to mandatory detention (regardless of the length of sentence imposed, or the fact that it may be a single offense).[230] (For a discussion of whether an offense under 18 USC §1546 is an offense involving moral turpitude, see the discussion of visa offenses in chapter eight.) Finally, if the conviction under 18 USC §1546 is an aggravated felony because a term of 12 months or more of imprisonment was imposed,[231] the individual will be subject to mandatory detention.[232]

Neither registration violations (INA §§262, 264) nor civil or criminal document violations (INA §274C) implicate mandatory detention.

Voluntary Departure

Pre-commencement or preliminary stage of removal proceedings

A conviction under 18 USC §1546 or some other criminal or civil document-related offense does not pose a bar to voluntary departure. The only conceivable exception would be a conviction under 18 USC §1546 that also qualifies as an aggra-

---

[226] INA §237(a)(3)(C); 8 USC §1227(a)(3)(C).
[227] *See* chapter ten.
[228] INA §236(c)(1)(C); 8 USC §1226(c)(1)(C).
[229] INA §236(c)(1)(B); 8 USC §1226(c)(1)(B).
[230] INA §236(c)(1)(A); 8 USC §1226(c)(1)(A).
[231] INA §101(a)(43)(P); 8 USC §1101(a)(43)(P).
[232] INA §236(c)(1)(B); 8 USC §1226(c)(1)(B).

vated felony offense[233] because the elements of the crime involved fraud or deceit (*i.e.*, in the use of documents) and the loss to a victim exceeded $10,000.[234]

Voluntary departure is discretionary[235] and may be denied if the applicant has a conviction or civil judgment for visa fraud or other immigration documentation violation.

Conclusion of proceedings

Voluntary departure at the conclusion of proceedings requires a showing of "good moral character" for the five-year period immediately preceding the application for this relief.[236] A conviction for visa fraud under INA §1546, and a corresponding charge of deportability under INA §237(a)(3)(B), is not a per se bar to receiving voluntary departure. However, as discussed above, if the offense involved use of a fraudulent document, the conviction will be considered to involve "moral turpitude" and bar a finding of good moral character if committed within the five-year period.[237] Note that an individual who has been confined for 180 days or longer in a penal institution for a criminal conviction or convictions (the time is counted in the aggregate) cannot establish "good moral character."[238]

Voluntary departure is a discretionary benefit[239] that may be denied on account of a criminal or civil judgment for visa or other immigration related document fraud.

Asylum and Withholding of Removal

A conviction for a registration violation or a visa offense under 18 USC §1546 is not a per se bar to asylum. Indeed, in the context of asylum, it is unlikely that either a registration violation or a visa fraud conviction will result in a discretionary denial (*unless* the conviction under §1546 involved visa fraud for pecuniary benefit—as opposed to an individual's possession of a fraudulent document for his or her own purpose).[240] In addition, a civil order or criminal conviction for document fraud under INA §274C is neither a bar to asylum nor likely to result in a discretionary denial.

An individual who is inadmissible or deportable for a registration, visa, or passport offense is unlikely to be denied withholding of removal under either the INA or

---

[233] INA §240B(a)(1); 8 USC §1229c(a)(1).

[234] INA §101(a)(43)(M); 8 USC §1101(a)(43)(M).

[235] INA §240B(a)(1); 8 USC §1229c(a)(1).

[236] INA §240B(b)(1)(B); 8 USC §1229c(b)(1)(B).

[237] *Omagah v. Ashcroft*, 288 F.3d 254 (5th Cir. 2002).

[238] INA §101(f)(7); 8 USC §1101(f)(7).

[239] INA §240B(b)(1); 8 USC §1229c(b)(1).

[240] An individual's manner of entry is a proper and relevant discretionary factor to consider in adjudicating an asylum claim; the circumvention of orderly refugee procedures is only one factor for consideration, and standing alone, is insufficient to require unusual countervailing equities. *Matter of Pula*, 19 I&N Dec. 467 (BIA 1987).

the CAT, unless such an offense can be characterized as a "particularly serious crime."[241] The only instance in which a visa or passport crime could conceivably fall under this definition is if it were a federal offense involving widespread sale, manufacturing, or delivering of fraudulent visas and/or passports—in other words, a crime that goes beyond assisting oneself and instead extends to a business or trafficking in fraudulent documents. An individual with a registration, visa, or passport offense is eligible to apply for deferral of removal under the CAT.[242]

Naturalization

A conviction for visa fraud under 18 USC §1546 does not pose a statutory bar to naturalization unless it is determined to be a crime involving moral turpitude under INA §212(a)(2)(A)(i)(I).[243] This is determined on a case-by-case basis. However, an individual with a conviction for visa fraud under §1546 is amenable to removal proceedings because, as stated above, visa fraud is a ground of deportability at INA §237(a)(3)(C). Accordingly, although a naturalization applicant may be eligible to seek naturalization notwithstanding a §1546 conviction—especially where the conviction falls outside the three- or five-year window of required "good moral character"—this person will, as a matter of course, be referred for removal proceedings.

Likewise, a registration or address violation under INA §§262 or 265 does not pose a per se statutory bar to naturalization. In the past, a person who had not registered address changes with the government would be approved for naturalization in a "New York minute." This is unlikely to change in the near future.

> **Tip**: File the AR-11 address change form at the time of filing for naturalization.

A civil or criminal violation of document fraud under INA §274C does not pose a statutory (per se) bar to naturalization. Such a violation does not automatically implicate "good moral character," but it may be a crime involving moral turpitude. If an individual has such a conviction and has not been referred for removal proceedings (an unlikely scenario, since DHS prosecutes these types of cases), an application for naturalization would trigger referral of the case for removal proceedings.

Note that in all three of the above situations, if a waiver is granted in removal proceedings, the individual may proceed with an application for naturalization (especially if the requisite three or five years have passed since commission of the offense).

---

[241] *See* INA §241(b)(3)(B)(ii); 8 USC §1231(b)(3)(B)(ii).

[242] *See* 8 CFR §§208.17, 1208.17.

[243] INA §316(a); 8 USC §1427(a) (requiring good moral character, which, under INA §101(f)(3), is negated by crime involving moral turpitude under INA §212(a)(2)(A)(i)(I)).

Revocation of naturalization (denaturalization)

As stated throughout this chapter, an individual who naturalizes to American citizenship and is later convicted of a crime that preceded the naturalization date is subject to revocation of naturalization under INA §340, and even criminal prosecution under 18 USC §1425. For a complete discussion of denaturalization, see the section on moral turpitude above in this chapter.

Consequences of Export Law Violations

Inadmissibility, Including Adjustment of Status and Visa Eligibility

Section 212(a)(3)(A)(i) of the INA [8 USC §1182(a)(3)(A)(i)] states in pertinent part:

(A) In General.—Any alien who a consular officer or the Attorney General knows, or has reasonable ground to believe, seeks to enter the United States to engage solely, principally, or incidentally in—

(i) any activity

(I) to violate any law of the United States relating to espionage or sabotage or

(II) to violate or evade any law prohibiting the export from the United States of goods, technology, or sensitive information …

is inadmissible.

It is important to note that this provision is written in a prospective sense. It does not state that an individual with a conviction for an export violation is inadmissible; nor does it state that if there is reason to believe an individual has been involved in export violations, he or she is inadmissible. Rather, the provision states that if a person *seeks to enter* the United States to engage—either solely, principally, or incidentally—in an activity that violates or evades the laws relating to export from the United States of goods, technology, or sensitive information, he or she is inadmissible. Certainly, an individual might have a past conviction for violation of the export law, but have no intention of being involved in future activity. Thus, proof of past violations or even a conviction—where the applicant establishes that he or she will not engage in future activity—should not automatically be a basis to deny adjustment of status or a visa.[244]

Although a past export violation, with no evidence of a likelihood that it will occur in the future, is not a basis to deny adjustment, an individual with an export conviction who applies for adjustment may be referred for removal proceedings. In removal proceedings before a judge, adjustment of status would then become a form of

---

[244] *But see Beslic v. INS*, 265 F.3d 568, 570 (7th Cir. 2001) (court of appeals upheld BIA's divided opinion finding, in part, that a prior conviction for exporting defense articles gives "rise to a presumption" that the individual seeks to enter the country to engage in illegal export of technology).

relief from removal to cure the past export violation. This legal argument was discussed in dicta in *Zhan Gao v. Holder*,[245] wherein the non–American citizen argued before the IJ, BIA, and then the court of appeals that the ground of inadmissibility was phrased only prospectively. The discussion within *Zhan Gao* reflects that the IJ agreed that inadmissibility could only be premised on a future intention to violate the export law; apparently the BIA initially agreed, and then reversed course. Upon appeal, the court of appeals found it did not need to decide the issue of whether inadmissibility under INA §212(a)(3)(A)(i)(II) required a prospective intent to engage in export violations because the petitioner was removable on other grounds.[246]

If an individual falls under INA §212(a)(3)(A)(i)(II), he or she may be:

- denied a visa at an American consulate;
- denied admission into the United States at a port of entry;
- denied a change of status from one visa category to another;
- denied adjustment of status to permanent residency;
- denied temporary protected status;[247] and
- placed in removal proceedings if in the United States pursuant to parole status, or an entry without inspection.

Deportability/Removability

As noted in chapter eight, an individual who has engaged, is engaged, or at any time after admission engages in any activity to violate any law of the United States relating to the export from the United States of goods, technology, or sensitive information is deportable.[248] The deportability ground thus encompasses far more than the inadmissibility ground; the deportability ground reaches persons who have ever been involved in the violation of an export law relating to goods, technology, or sensitive information. Note that at least one court of appeals has found that in order for the court to find deportability under this section, the government need not establish that the exported items related to national security.[249]

Mandatory Detention

An individual who is inadmissible under INA §212(a)(3)(A)(i) (seeks to enter to engage in an activity in violation of the export laws) is not subject to mandatory deten-

---

[245] *Zhan Gao v. Holder*, 595 F.3d 549 (4th Cir. 2010).

[246] *Zhan Gao v. Holder*, 595 F.3d 549, at 558.

[247] 8 CFR §§244.3(c)(2), 1244.3(c)(2).

[248] INA §237(a)(4)(A)(i); 8 USC §1227(a)(4)(A)(i).

[249] *Beslic v. INS*, 265 F.3d 568, 570 (7th Cir. 2001).

tion. Similarly, an individual who is deportable under INA §237(a)(4)(A)(i) (has or is engaged in a violation of the export laws) is not subject to mandatory detention.[250]

Voluntary Departure

Pre-commencement or early stage of removal proceedings

An individual inadmissible based on the export ground of inadmissibility at INA §212(a)(3)(A) is not, by reason of the offense, ineligible for voluntary departure. However, note that an arriving alien placed in proceedings at the time of arrival is ineligible for pre-commencement/early stage voluntary departure.[251] A person who entered without inspection or an arriving alien who is placed in proceedings after arrival is eligible for voluntary departure notwithstanding a charge under INA §212(a)(3)(A).

An individual charged with deportability for an export violation under INA §237(a)(4)(B) is not ineligible for pre-commencement or early stage voluntary departure. However, voluntary departure is a discretionary benefit[252] that can be denied upon consideration of the facts and circumstances of the offense conduct.

Conclusion of proceedings

An individual charged with deportability under INA §237(a)(4) is not eligible for voluntary departure.[253] Note that this particular provision does not precisely comport with the phrase regarding voluntary departure eligibility at the pre-commencement or early stage of proceedings in INA §240B(a)(1). That subdivision reads that an individual deportable [for an aggravated felony] or under §237(a)(4)(B) is not eligible for voluntary departure. At INA §240B(b)(1)(C), on the other hand, the statute reads that an individual who is deportable [for an aggravated felony] or under §237(a)(4) is not eligible. Subsection (B) is not specified. Section 237(a)(4) is broadly entitled *Security and related grounds*. Subsection (A) refers to export violations; subsection (B) refers to terrorism. (There are also subsections (C), (D), and (E), relating to foreign policy concerns, Nazi persecution, and paramilitary participation). The fact that §240B(a) specifies only terrorism, yet subsection (b) draws in the entire breadth of §237(a)(4), leads one to believe that Congress may have made a scriber's error in drafting either subsection (a) or (b). In any event, note that the pre-commencement/early-stage voluntary departure provision is far more generous in regards to export violations; if voluntary departure is the ultimate desired benefit, it is important to request the relief at an early stage of immigration court proceedings. Requesting relief at the end, for example as an alternative form of relief, may result in a mandatory denial.

---

[250] *See* INA §236(c); 8 USC §1226(c).

[251] INA §240B(a)(4); 8 USC §1229c(a)(4).

[252] INA §240B(a)(1); 8 USC §1229c(a)(1).

[253] INA §240B(b)(1)(C); 8 USC §1229c(b)(1)(C).

Finally, note that voluntary departure is a discretionary benefit[254] that may be denied upon consideration of the offense activity.

Asylum and Withholding of Removal

A conviction for violation of the export laws, or a suspicion that a person will engage in violation of the export laws, is not an enumerated basis to deny or bar an application for asylum.[255] An individual who has been convicted of a particularly serious crime, and who is considered a danger to the community, is barred from receiving asylum; a serious export law violation could bring someone under the purview of this provision.[256]

In *Zhan Gao v. Holder*,[257] the Fourth Circuit Court of Appeals upheld a BIA determination that a conviction for exporting military equipment was a "particularly serious crime" even though the offense did not qualify as an aggravated felony.

An individual who is either inadmissible or deportable for an export violation is not per se barred from seeking withholding of removal under either the INA or the CAT. However, if the export violation truly does implicate national security interests, it may be deemed a "particularly serious crime" such that the applicant poses a "danger to the United States community."[258] An individual who is barred from seeking withholding under the statute or the CAT may request deferral of removal under the CAT.[259]

Naturalization

Violation of the export laws, or an established intent to violate the export laws, is not an enumerated basis on which to deny naturalization.[260] There is a catch-all provision in the regulations stating that an individual may be denied naturalization if during the relevant statutory period he or she "committed unlawful acts that adversely reflect upon the applicant's moral character."[261] It is important to note, however, that an individual who applies for naturalization, even if not technically denied naturalization because of an export law violation, may be considered deportable under INA §237(a)(4)(A)(i) for a violation of export laws; USCIS may issue an NTA, thereby commencing removal proceedings.

---

[254] INA §240B(b)(1); 8 USC §1229c(b)(1).

[255] INA §208(b)(2)(A) [8 USC §1158(b)(2)(A)] cites the categories of persons who are barred from receiving asylum.

[256] INA §208(b)(2)(A)(ii); 8 USC §1158(b)(2)(A)(ii).

[257] 595 F.3d 549 (4th Cir. 2010).

[258] INA §241(b)(3)(B); 8 USC §1231(b)(3)(B); 8 CFR §§208.16(d)(2), 1208.16(d)(2).

[259] 8 CFR §§208.17, 1208.17.

[260] 8 CFR §316.10 defines "good moral character" for purposes of naturalization.

[261] 8 CFR §316.10(b)(3)(iii).

APPENDIX 9A

CRIMES AND POSSIBLE CONSEQUENCES

CLASSIFICATION OF CRIME	INADMISSIBLE	DEPORTABLE	MANDATORY DETENTION[262]
One Crime Involving Moral Turpitude (CIMT)	Maybe. Yes, unless offense falls under petty-offense exception.	Maybe. Yes, if committed within five years of date of admission and is a crime for which a sentence of one year or longer may be imposed.	Maybe. If subject to deportability for only one CIMT, for which less than one year imprisonment imposed, *not* mandatory detention. If subject to inadmissibility as arriving alien or having entered without inspection, mandatory detention applies.
Multiple CIMTs	Yes	Yes	Yes
Aggravated Felony Offense	No; unless the offense falls into some other classification that forms the basis of a ground of inadmissibility; *i.e.*, CIMT or drug offense.	Yes	Yes
Controlled Substance Violation	Yes	Yes, except for one offense simple possession (30 grams or less of marijuana).	Yes
Firearms Offense	No, but may be a basis for discretionary denial.	Yes	Yes
Money Laundering	Yes. However, argue that ground of inadmissibility applies only if in violation of federal, not state, law.	Maybe. Money laundering is not a *per se* ground of deportation. It may, however, be an aggravated felony.	Yes

---

[262] Mandatory detention applies to releases from custody after October 8, 1998. October 8, 1998, was the last day Transition Period Custody Rules were in effect. *See* 8 CFR §236.1(c)(1)(i); Illegal Immigration Reform and Immigrant Responsibility Act of 1996 (IIRAIRA), Pub. L. No. 104-208, div. C, §303(b), 110 Stat. 3009, 3009-585 to 3009-587. For purposes of this chart, it is assumed that the release took place after October 8, 1998.

Classification of Crime	Inadmissible	Deportable	Mandatory Detention
Domestic Violence	No. Domestic violence is not a *per se* ground of inadmissibility; may be a CIMT.	Yes, if conviction entered on or after Sept. 30, 1996.	No, unless offense is also classified as a CIMT or aggravated felony.
Alien Smuggling	Yes	Yes	No, unless crime is also classified as an aggravated felony under INA §101(a)(43)(N).
Immigration Violations (registration), Visa and Passport Fraud	Maybe. Check federal statute and see details in chapter 6.	Yes	No, unless crime is also classified as a CIMT or aggravated felony.
Export Violations	Yes, if there is a reasonable ground to believe that the individual (prospectively) comes to the United States to engage in a violation or evasion of export laws. Past conviction may not form a ground of inadmissibility if it can be shown there is no future intent to do so.	Yes, for a conviction of export laws at any time.	No

CHAPTER TEN

IMMIGRATION DEFENSE: WAIVERS AND OTHER RELIEF

Adjustment of Status 432
Waivers Under INA §212(h) 441
INA §209(c) Waiver for Refugees and Asylees 459
Asylum and Withholding of Removal 462
Cancellation of Removal 467
The Waiver That Keeps Giving: INA §212(c) (repealed 1996) 476
Voluntary Departure 495
Is Your Client an American Citizen? An Introduction to Derivative and Acquired Citizenship . 499
Naturalization as a Defense to Deportation 504
Relief from Alien Smuggling Charges 507
Nonimmigrant Visa Waiver Under INA §212(d)(3) 510
Defending the Criminal Charge of Re-entry After Removal 515

Appendices
    10A: Sample Motion to Reopen Sua Sponte Based on New Case Law 519
    10B: Unpublished BIA Decision re: Sua Sponte Motion to Reopen for INA §212(c) After Removal Order, Conviction by Trial 524
    10C: Brief Excerpt: Particularly Serious Crime Analysis, Asylum Versus Withholding 526
    10D: Sample Motion to Pretermit Waiver Application Under INA §212(h) 529
    10E: Sample Memorandum in Support of INA §212(h) Eligibility 534
    10F: Unpublished BIA Decision re: Cancellation of Removal, Waiver of Inadmissibility Under INA §212(h) 540
    10G: Sample Motion to Terminate Removal Proceedings Under INA §237(a)(2)(A)(iii) ... 544
    10H: Sample Memorandum in Support of INA §240A(a) Eligibility for Cancellation of Removal 549
    10I: Sample Statement in Support of Naturalization Eligibility 556

This chapter discusses the various waivers and other relief provided in the Immigration and Nationality Act (INA) for persons convicted of criminal activity.

For criminal defense attorneys (or the immigration attorneys assisting them), an understanding of the different forms of relief and their eligibility criteria is key in representing someone charged with a criminal offense. The plea bargaining stage is ideally the time to start thinking about deportation defense. When it is not possible to avoid a conviction that leads to charges of removability (and it often will not be), the defense attorney works toward a different but valuable goal: ensuring that the individual is statutorily eligible to seek a waiver—or apply for some other form of defense—to avoid deportation, obtain residency, apply for citizenship, or whatever goal the client eventually may seek. Successful plea-bargaining often depends on knowledge of the different forms of relief.

For the immigration attorneys, eligibility criteria for certain applications are important not only in terms of relief from removal, but also for visa eligibility and adjustment of status. Statutory eligibility for waivers and other relief depends on a variety of factors, both legal and factual. It is not always the case that waivers are more readily available to lawful permanent residents (LPRs); there are provisions of the law that deal more harshly with green-card holders than persons who are seeking residency for the first time. Certain waivers and defenses are available to both permanent and non–permanent residents. Some waivers depend on the amount of time in the United States. Most waiver provisions contain "bars"—a factor that renders the person ineligible for the benefit sought.

This chapter discusses statutory eligibility criteria. Chapter thirteen sets forth practical suggestions for presenting a waiver application, including use of witnesses and supporting documentation.

Adjustment of Status

Adjustment of status is a procedure by which an individual applies for permanent resident status in the United States without leaving the United States (thereby avoiding processing at an American embassy abroad). In the previous chapter, adjustment of status was discussed as a benefit that may be jeopardized because of a criminal act or conviction. However, this chapter will explore adjustment of status as a possible cure for criminal activity. When adjustment of status acts as a waiver, it may require an additional waiver (INA §§212(h), 212(c), or 209(c)) or may serve independently as a cure without the need for an additional waiver application. An adjustment application, standing alone, can waive a criminal offense where the criminal activity or conviction is a ground of deportability under INA §237, but does not form the basis of a ground of inadmissibility under INA §212(a). This is another reason why it is important to understand the dichotomy between grounds of inadmissibility under §212(a) and deportability under §212(h), as explained in chapter three.

> *Example*: Grounds that exist at §237 but not §212(a) are firearm offenses, aggravated felonies, domestic violence offenses (including stalking and protective order violations) and visa fraud under 18 USC §1547. Some of these offenses, however, may qualify as crimes involving moral turpitude. These offenses are explained at chapters six, seven, and eight.

If all negative issues, including arrest record and other criminal activity, are revealed and considered by an immigration judge (IJ) or U.S. Citizenship and Immigration Services (USCIS) during the adjustment process, and the adjustment is granted, it acts as a waiver and shields against any future consideration of the crime as a ground of deportability.

An exception would be if the individual is subsequently charged in removal proceedings for multiple crimes involving moral turpitude; a waived offense can still serve as the predicate crime involving moral turpitude to combine with a second or subsequent offense.)[1] Thus, the crime cannot be raised at a subsequent time, such as following a brief trip abroad, in removal proceedings, or in the naturalization process.[2]

CASE STUDY: MATTER OF RAINFORD

The Board of Immigration Appeals (BIA or Board) stated in *Matter of Rainford*:

Accordingly, we hold that the conviction which renders the respondent deportable under section 241(a)(2)(C) of the Act [the precursor of INA §237] will not preclude a showing of admissibility for purposes of section 245(a) and that if granted adjustment of status to lawful permanent resident, the respondent will no longer be deportable on the basis of this prior conviction.[3]

By way of example, firearms offenses and aggravated felonies do not, standing alone, give rise to inadmissibility under INA §212(a); that is, they are not per se grounds of inadmissibility. Similarly, neither domestic violence nor visa violation convictions are specific grounds of inadmissibility. In *Matter of Azurin*, the BIA wrote:

We held in *Matter of Rainford*, 20 I&N Dec. 598 (BIA 1992), that a conviction for an offense that rendered the alien deportable did not preclude a showing of admissibility for purposes of an application for adjustment of status where there was no corresponding ground of inadmissibility for the crime in the statute. Therefore, the respondent does not need section 212(c) relief to waive either the firearms or aggravated felony charges in order to adjust his status.[4]

Unless these offenses also form some other ground of inadmissibility (for example, the offenses also qualify as crimes involving moral turpitude), a grant of adjustment of status waives the criminal offense and the person becomes an LPR. Where a

---

[1] *Matter of Balderas*, 20 I&N Dec. 389 (BIA 1991), stands for the proposition that, although an offense has been waived, this is not a permanent pardon or expungement, and the crime can still be used to support a finding of deportability for two crimes involving moral turpitude.

[2] U.S. Citizenship and Immigration Services (USCIS), a component of the Department of Homeland Security (DHS), adjudicates naturalization. There are instances when USCIS will disagree with the decision of an IJ and deny naturalization. This may be an invitation to litigate, and goes into principles of collateral estoppel, but is beyond the scope of this book.

[3] *Matter of Rainford*, 20 I&N Dec. 598, 602 (BIA 1992) (emphasis added).

[4] *Matter of Azurin*, 23 I&N Dec. 695 (BIA 2005).

criminal offense falls into more than one category,[5] (*e.g.*, both an aggravated felony and a crime involving moral turpitude), adjustment can waive the aggravated felony ground of deportability, while an additional, concurrent waiver (if available) cures the ground of inadmissibility.

INA §245(a) [8 U.S. Code (USC) §1255(a)], the governing provision for adjustment of status, states (footnote added):

(a) The status of an alien who was inspected and admitted or paroled into the United States or the status of any other alien having an approved petition for classification as a VAWA [Violence Against Women Act] self-petitioner may be adjusted by the Attorney General,[6] in his discretion and under such regulations as he may prescribe, to that of an alien lawfully admitted for permanent residence if

1) the alien makes an application for such adjustment,

2) the alien is eligible to receive an immigrant visa and is admissible to the United States for permanent residence, and

3) an immigrant visa is immediately available to him at the time his application is filed.

An individual who is physically present in the United States following a lawful inspection and admission or parole may apply for adjustment of status.[7] Unless the non–American citizen is applying based on a special provision or program, an unlawful entry (such as crossing the border) eliminates eligibility for adjustment (and the person must visa process abroad). Adjustment of status requires a foundational eligibility. An applicant must have an underlying basis for applying for adjustment of status, such as an approved relative or employment petition in the immediate relative category, or where there is a visa immediately available. Another basis may be asylee status. At times, Congress has passed special legislation to allow adjustment of status for certain nationalities or groups, such as the Cuban Adjustment Act or another refugee program. An application for adjustment of status, Form I-485, is filed with USCIS, unless the individual is in removal proceedings, in which case the IJ has jurisdiction over the application. It is in front of the IJ that adjustment of status may be

---

[5] *Matter of Azurin*, 23 I&N Dec. 695 (BIA 2005).

[6] Adjustment of status was previously performed by the legacy Immigration and Naturalization Service (legacy INS), under the auspices of the Department of Justice (DOJ) and the U.S. attorney general (AG). At present, when an individual files for adjustment of status affirmatively with an agency (*i.e.*, outside the context of removal proceedings), this function falls under DHS, specifically USCIS. Applications for adjustment of status filed during removal proceedings are adjudicated by IJs, who remain under the authority of the DOJ and the AG.

[7] In some cases, there is a special program (*e.g.*, based on nationality, persecution, or country conditions) that allows for adjustment of status without an initial, lawful admission or parole.

used as an effective waiver of deportability.[8] The specific requirements for adjustment of status are spelled out in the regulations at Code of Federal Regulations (CFR) title 8 §§245.1, 1245.1.

The operative words for purposes of this discussion are in phrase (2), above: the individual must be *admissible* to the United States. This is a reference to INA §212(a) [8 USC §1182(a)], which lists both criminal and noncriminal grounds of inadmissibility.

Available to Permanent and Non–Permanent Residents

Logically, it is the non–permanent resident who most often applies for adjustment of status. Again, if adjustment of status is granted to an individual who has a criminal conviction (assuming it is revealed to USCIS), the act of adjusting waives the offense as a future basis for deportation. However, LPRs can apply for adjustment of status, too, effectively readjusting their status to "square one."[9] In the case of an LPR who is facing removal proceedings for a crime, adjustment of status may serve as a waiver of deportation. Like non-LPRs, an LPR must have a basis to adjust: an approved and current relative petition, a similar employment-based petition, Cuban citizenship or nationality,[10] or some other foundation for adjustment of status. If an individual has already adjusted status based on a family petition, a new petition must be filed and be in an immediately available visa category. The details of this procedure are discussed further in chapter thirteen, on presenting applications for relief.

Discretionary Benefit

It is important to remember that adjustment of status is a discretionary benefit;[11] neither the IJ nor USCIS is *required* to grant adjustment—even if the criminal record does not per se form a ground of inadmissibility, or even if the applicant is eligible for a waiver. In other words, although a person may be statutorily eligible to apply for adjustment of status notwithstanding a criminal offense, an adjudicator or judge may deny the application for discretionary considerations.

> ➢ **Compare**: Unlike adjustment of status, issuance of an immigrant visa is not discretionary; if the immigrant visa applicant is statutorily qualified for the visa, a consular officer has no discretionary authority to deny.

---

[8] The general eligibility and procedural requirements for adjustment of status are complicated and beyond the scope of this book. For an overview of the requirements for adjustment of status, see chapter five, "Adjustment of Status," *Representing Clients in Immigration Court* (3rd Ed. AILA 2013).

[9] *Matter of Gabryelsky*, 20 I&N Dec. 750, n.2 (BIA 1993) (citing *Tibke v. INS*, 335 F.2d 42 (2d Cir. 1964) and *Matter of Parodi*, 17 I&N Dec. 608, 611 (BIA 1980)).

[10] Citizens and nationals of Cuba, and their spouses and minor children, are eligible for adjustment of status following admission or parole pursuant to the Cuban Adjustment Act of Nov. 2, 1966, Pub. L. No. 89-732, §1.

[11] Immigration and Nationality Act (INA) §245(a); 8 U.S. Code (USC) §1255(a).

Unfortunately, there is not a lot of case law on precisely what the "exercise of discretion" means in the context of adjustment of status, where there is no ground of inadmissibility based on crime (or some other bar). It is incoherent that an individual who is not per se inadmissible on account of crime can still be denied the benefit based on a finding that—because of the criminal conviction—the exercise of discretionary authority is not merited. This broad-brush approach to discretion undermines Congress's determinations that certain acts should result in a finding of inadmissibility, as set forth at INA §212(a), while others will not. It does not make sense that certain criminal offenses do not make someone inadmissible under INA §212(a), but an adjudicator or IJ is free to impose other, nonstatutory, grounds by the exercise of his or her broad discretion.

With this query in mind, it is the author's opinion that the "exercise of discretion" in the context of adjustment of status refers *not* to an IJ's authority to deny adjustment based on criminal activity (where that activity is not a per se bar under INA §212(a), or may be waived). Rather, it is this author's perspective—and a perspective practitioners are encouraged to advocate—that the phrase "in the exercise of discretion" in the context of adjustment of status (which is, after all, a procedural mechanism that enables the applicant to avoid consular processing) refers to a general review of the applicant's compliance with immigration law and procedure. Under this view, relevant considerations in the exercise of discretion might include a history of immigration law violations, misleading statements in a visa application, a preconceived intent to remain in the United States though admitted as a nonimmigrant, unauthorized employment, or some similar pattern of benign immigration violations that fall short of forming the basis of inadmissibility.[12]

In an early 2009 case, the BIA set forth relevant considerations regarding the exercise of discretion in an adjustment of status case. Although the BIA places the focus on family ties and immigration history (*i.e.*, compliance with or violation of immigration laws), the BIA quickly mentions in one short sentence, "a respondent's criminal history is an additional consideration."[13] This one sentence contradicts the author's view, but there is neither statutory nor regulatory authority for the BIA's view—beyond the statute's use of the word "discretion."

Jurisdiction

Pursuant to regulation, adjustment of status is not available to an "arriving alien" in immigration court proceedings.[14] IJs normally do not have jurisdiction to adjudi-

---

[12] *See, e.g.*, *Matter of Rafipour*, 16 I&N Dec. 470 (BIA 1978); *Matter of Blas*, 15 I&N Dec. 626 (BIA 1974; AG 1976); *Matter of Arai*, 13 I&N Dec. 494 (BIA 1970).

[13] *Matter of Hashmi*, 24 I&N Dec. 785, 793 (BIA 2009), citing *Abu-Khaliel v. Gonzales*, 436 F.3d 627, 634 (6th Cir. 2006). [Note that the *Abu-Khaliel* case does not, in fact, support the Board of Immigration Appeals' (BIA or Board) proposition that a criminal law violation is a relevant factor for consideration in in the exercise of discretion in an adjustment of status case.]

[14] 8 Code of Federal Regulations (CFR) §1245.2(a)(1)(ii).

cate an adjustment of status application if the person is designated "arriving alien." As discussed in chapter one, the term "arriving alien" refers to a non–American citizen who, as an applicant for admission, is paroled in for further processing; an arriving alien has not been lawfully admitted, and in fact has no real status.[15] In a sense, the physical presence of an arriving alien in the United States represents a legal fiction: in the Department of Homeland Security's (DHS) eyes, this person is still knocking at the door at a port of entry. An exception to this jurisdictional rule is intended a non–American citizen who applied for adjustment before USCIS, traveled outside the United States and re-entered pursuant to an advance parole,[16] and is subsequently placed in removal proceedings.[17] If an individual is paroled in to pursue adjustment before USCIS, and USCIS subsequently denies the application, that application may be renewed in front of the IJ.

Based on a significant 2011 BIA decision, *Matter of Arrabally and Yerrabelly*,[18] an advance parole that is granted because adjustment of status is pending does not trigger "unlawful presence" under INA §212(a)(9)(B);[19] however, it will still be considered a parole-arrival for purposes of designation in front of an IJ—resulting in charges under INA §212(a). In other words, although the judge would have jurisdiction over the adjustment of status application, the person's posture in terms of inadmissibility versus deportability may change (if the individual was previously in the United States pursuant to an admission, but then travels and re-enters with parole). *Matter of Arrabally* is a welcome decision from the perspective of the unlawful presence ground of inadmissibility, but it is not a panacea in terms of the notion of admission at INA §101(a)(13)(C).[20]

Although an IJ may not have jurisdiction over an arriving alien's adjustment application, this individual may proceed on adjustment before USCIS. If in removal

---

[15] 8 CFR §1.1(q); *Brito v. Mukasey*, 521 F.3d 160 (2d Cir. 2008); *Scheerer v. Att'y Gen.*, 513 F.3d 1244 (11th Cir. 2008).

[16] An individual with adjustment of status pending may apply for an advance parole, which is essentially a travel document, to allow him or her to travel outside the United States and then return to pursue the pending application. 8 CFR §212.5. Notwithstanding its availability, not all clients who are prima facie eligible for an advance parole should apply for one; there are risks involved in traveling. A person who is paroled back into the United States—if later placed in removal proceedings—will face grounds of inadmissibility rather than deportability. A person may be subject to mandatory detention. The nuances of advance parole go beyond the subject matter of this book; suffice it to say that the availability of advance parole does not mean it is a benefit every client should take advantage of.

[17] 8 CFR §1245.2(a)(1)(ii).

[18] *Matter of Arrabally and Yerrabelly*, 25 I&N Dec. 771 (BIA 2012).

[19] 8 USC §1182(a)(9)(B).

[20] The concepts of "arriving alien" and "admission" and how they impact removability are discussed in chapter three. The unlawful presence ground of inadmissibility is not a criminal ground and is beyond the scope of this book; however, for resources on adjustment of status and admissibility, including a discussion of unlawful presence, see *Representing Clients in Immigration Court* (3rd Ed. AILA 2013), and *The Waivers Book: Advanced Issues in Immigration Practice* (AILA 2011).

proceedings, an individual otherwise eligible for adjustment may seek termination of proceedings, administrative closure, or a continuance (*i.e.*, request that case be held in abeyance) while he or she pursues adjustment with USCIS. However, experience shows that attorneys for the Office of Chief Counsel may oppose termination or administrative closure of a court case if the individual has a criminal record.[21]

Aggravated Felony Offenses

Aggravated felonies are discussed in chapter seven. Aggravated felonies are certain crimes as defined at INA §101(a)(43) [8 USC §1101(a)(43)]. An "aggravated felony" is not a per se impediment to adjustment of status unless the offense forms some independent basis of inadmissibility. An aggravated felony conviction is a basis for deportability under INA §237(a)(2)(A)(iii); it is not a ground of inadmissibility at INA §212(a), which is the law that applies in the context of adjustment of status. An individual cannot be denied adjustment of status on the basis of an aggravated felony offense unless that offense is also, for example, a crime involving moral turpitude, a controlled-substance offense, or a money-laundering offense. This is a well-settled area of case law,[22] yet it is a nuance that is often overlooked by immigration law practitioners and judges, alike.

As a practical matter, many aggravated felony offenses will qualify as moral turpitude, controlled substance, or other crimes, but not all. The provisions of INA §101(a)(43) reflect that certain offenses do not implicate moral turpitude, but are regulatory in nature. Certainly, recourse to the specific state or federal statute is necessary in each case, but the following aggravated felony offenses arguably do not implicate moral turpitude: firearms offenses, certain passport or visa violations, failure to appear for service of sentence or court appearance ("bail jumping"), and trafficking in vehicles with altered vehicle identification numbers.

It is important to remember that in certain aggravated felony cases, adjustment of status may be the cure, standing alone, or in conjunction with another waiver application.

Firearms Offenses

A conviction for a firearms offense is not a ground of inadmissibility and therefore does not bar adjustment of status. An individual with a firearms offense who adjusts his or her status effectively obtains a waiver of the firearms offense; it cannot be used

---

[21] Adjustment of status procedures in general, and strategies for arriving alien cases in particular, are beyond the scope of this book. However, excellent tips and practice pointers, as well as a summary of recent case law, are available on the American Immigration Lawyers Association's website (*www.aila.org*) in various areas, including practice advisories and agency memoranda. See also previous footnote for references.

[22] *Matter of Torres-Varela*, 23 I&N Dec. 78 (BIA 2001); *Matter of Kanga*, 22 I&N Dec. 1206 (BIA 2000); *Matter of Michel*, 21 I&N Dec. 1101 (BIA 1998).

as a basis for future charges of deportability.[23] An individual who faces removal (*i.e.*, deportation) because of a firearms offense can seek to waive the ground of deportability through adjustment of status.

> ➢ **Example**: John Fromelsewhere is a non–permanent resident who just married his U.S.-citizen girlfriend. On the way home from work one day, he is stopped for speeding and voluntarily tells police he keeps a gun under the car mat. He does not have a concealed weapon permit. He is arrested and ultimately convicted for carrying a concealed firearm (CCF). The case is turned over to immigration agents, and Mr. Fromelsewhere is placed in removal proceedings. His wife files a visa petition for him as her spouse. Before the judge, Mr. Fromelsewhere applies for adjustment of status under INA §245(a), and is granted permanent residency. If granted, adjustment of status serves as a waiver of the CCF conviction; no independent waiver application is required. Note: if the firearms arrest takes place after October 8, 1998, and Mr. Fromelsewhere spends any time in police custody, he may be held by U.S. Immigration and Customs Enforcement (ICE) under the mandatory detention provisions pending completion of removal proceedings; be prepared to argue that custody incident to arrest—with no sentence of imprisonment—does not trigger mandatory detention.[24]

Domestic Violence Offenses

Like firearms offenses and aggravated felonies, deportability for domestic violence offenses under INA §237(a)(2)(E) does not have a statutory counterpart of inadmissibility at INA §212(a). Section 237(a)(2)(E) covers convictions for crimes involving domestic violence, stalking, violations of protective orders, and crimes against children. The domestic violence offenses listed at §237(a)(2)(E) are not per se grounds of inadmissibility and, therefore, do not pose an impediment to adjustment of status unless the underlying offense also qualifies as a crime involving moral turpitude. Whether an offense committed in a domestic violence setting can qualify as a crime involving moral turpitude is discussed in the chapters on classifications and consequences. Where a simple assault or battery, or violation of a protective order, does not qualify as a crime involving moral turpitude based on the essential elements of the statute, the act of adjusting status effectively waives the offense for purposes of deportability.[25] This is true whether the non–American citizen applicant is in removal proceedings, adjusting status before USCIS, or applying for a visa abroad.

Acts of child abuse or stalking may be crimes involving moral turpitude, depending on the elements of the particular criminal statute involved. These offenses are discussed

---

[23] *Matter of Rainford*, 20 I&N Dec. 598 (BIA 1992).

[24] See the discussion of mandatory detention in chapter four.

[25] *Matter of Rainford*, 20 I&N Dec. 598 (BIA 1992).

in chapter eight. Fresh research on the specific state offense is required in every individual case to determine whether a "domestic violence" offense also qualifies as a crime involving moral turpitude. A violation of a protective order is often civil in nature and definitely does not have a counterpart at §212(a). The point of this particular discussion is that, if a client is deportable under INA §237(a)(2)(E), adjustment of status can act as a waiver of deportability if the offense does not form the basis of a ground of inadmissibility at §212(a); again, the most common example of such a ground would be a crime involving moral turpitude.

Visa and Registration Offenses

A conviction under 18 USC §1546 for "fraud and misuse of visas, permits, and other documents" forms the basis of a charge of deportability under INA §237(a)(3)(B)(iii). However, the BIA has held that a conviction under this federal statute does not form the basis of a ground of inadmissibility, and has stated clearly that §237(a)(3)(B)(iii) has *no* statutory counterpart at INA §212(a).[26] Although it may seem that "visa fraud" can—at least in some instances—constitute a crime involving moral turpitude, the BIA has stated that §1546 is broader.[27] Thus, because a conviction under 18 USC §1546 may not automatically constitute a crime involving moral turpitude (or any other ground at §212(a)), a grant of adjustment of status in certain circumstances waives the offense as a basis for deportability.[28]

Similarly, a conviction for failure to register under INA §262 [8 USC §1302] is not a ground of inadmissibility and is waived through the adjustment of status process.

Export Violations

An individual who is deportable for a conviction based on violation of an export law[29] may be able to waive the ground of deportability through adjustment of status if he or she can overcome INA §212(a)(3)(A)(i)'s prospective inadmissibility by showing that there is no reasonable ground to believe that the individual seeks to enter the United States to commit a violation of the export laws. Whereas the deportability section, INA §237(a)(4)(A), refers to past violations and/or convictions of the export laws, inadmissibility under INA §212(a)(3)(A)(i) is written in a future tense. Arguably, an individual in removal proceedings based on an export law conviction can ap-

---

[26] *See Matter of Jimenez-Santillano*, 21 I&N Dec. 567 (BIA 1996). This decision was abrogated in part by the Supreme Court in *Judulang v. Holder*, 132 S. Ct. 476 (2011), which rejected *Matter of Blake*, 23 I&N Dec. 722 (BIA 2005) and its "comparable grounds" test in the 212(c) waiver context. There is still good language in *Jimenez-Santillano* that will be helpful in arguing adjustment-without-a-waiver eligibility for a 1546 conviction. Also see the discussion of 18 USC §1546 and visa fraud offenses in chapter eight.

[27] *Matter of Jimenez-Santillano*, 21 I&N Dec. 567 (BIA 1996).

[28] *Matter of Jimenez-Santillano*, 21 I&N Dec. 567 (BIA 1996).

[29] INA §237(a)(4)(A)(i); 8 USC §1227(a)(4)(A)(i).

ply for adjustment of status and grant of the application effectively waives deportability—a good thing, since there is no independent waiver of INA §237(a)(4)(A).

Export violations are regulatory in nature. The regulations regarding export are promulgated and enforced by agencies within the executive branch, normally the Commerce Department, but also State. The list of items that are regulated changes frequently based on a variety of fluid factors; items can be added and removed. Rarely will an export conviction involve the element of intent to defraud, steal, harm, or other terminology indicative of moral turpitude offense.[30] An actor might have knowledge of violating a regulation, but there is no underlying evil motive. Because a violation of the export laws is clearly regulatory in nature, and does not implicate moral turpitude, no other waiver is required in conjunction with the adjustment of status.

There is little case law on the issue of whether the future tense phrasing of INA §212(a)(3)(B) renders the provision sufficiently distinct from INA §237(a)(4)(A) to allow adjustment of status to waive deportability for an export conviction. In *Beslic v. INS*,[31] the court upheld a divided opinion of the BIA, finding, in part, that a prior conviction for exporting defense articles gives "rise to a presumption" that the individual seeks to enter the country to engage in illegal export of technology. However, in a subsequent unpublished decision, *Matter of Michel Vincent Diago*,[32] the BIA affirmed that an individual with a conviction for an export violation is not per se inadmissible under INA §212(a)(3)(A) because the "statute refers to the intent to engage in future prohibited conduct." The BIA did find that a past conviction might create a presumption that the individual seeks to enter to engage at least incidentally in an export violation. But the presumption may be overcome with evidence that the applicant does not in fact seek to engage in export violations. In *Diago*, the BIA found that the presumption was overcome based on the respondent's overwhelming record of lawful activity, his equities, and the fact he had no other criminal convictions. Hence, adjustment of status waived the ground of deportability without a separate waiver.

Waivers Under INA §212(h)

A waiver of inadmissibility under INA §212(h) is traditionally sought in conjunction with an application for adjustment of status, or in applying for an immigrant visa at a U.S. embassy abroad. This waiver is not available when applying for a nonimmigrant visa. INA §212(h) [8 USC §1182(h)] contains three waivers of inadmissibility—the 15-year waiver, the hardship waiver, and the battered spouse or child waiver. These three waivers can be used to ameliorate inadmissibility for crimes involving

---

[30] *See, e.g., Matter of Tiwari*, 19 I&N Dec. 875 (BIA 1989); *Matter of Jimenez-Santillano*, 21 I&N Dec. 567 (BIA 1996).

[31] *Beslic v. INS*, 265 F.3d 568, 570 (7th Cir. 2001).

[32] File No. A026 358 802, 2008 Immig. Rptr LEXIS 5675 (BIA 2008).

moral turpitude, prostitution, crimes that were not prosecuted because of immunity, and single offenses for simple possession of marijuana (an amount of 30 grams or less).

In terms of marijuana possession, the Seventh Circuit U.S. Court of Appeals has found that the waiver may be used to waive possession of marijuana paraphernalia, because items used to smoke marijuana "relate to" marijuana.[33] Likewise, the BIA has ruled that the waiver may be used to waive possession of marijuana paraphernalia (intended for one's own personal use),[34] as well as a case involving one incident that combines separate counts for possession of marijuana and possession of marijuana paraphernalia.[35] In the latter situation, the respondent would bear the burden of establishing that the two counts (possession of marijuana and possession of paraphernalia) involved a single incident and the amount in question was less than 30 grams.

INA §212(h) states as follows (footnotes added, and notations in brackets added for the convenience of the reader):

> The Attorney General[36] may, in his discretion, waive the application of subparagraphs (A)(i)(I), (B), (D), and (E) of subsection (a)(2) and subparagraph (A)(i)(II) of such subsection insofar as it relates to a single offense of simple possession of 30 grams or less of marijuana if—
>
> [The 15-Year Waiver]
>
> (1) (A) in the case of any immigrant it is established to the satisfaction of the Attorney General that—
>
>> (i) the alien is inadmissible only under subparagraph (D)(i) or (D)(ii)[37] of such subsection or the activities for which the alien is inadmissible occurred more than 15 years before the date of the alien's application for a visa, admission, or adjustment of status,
>>
>> (ii) the admission to the United States of such alien would not be contrary to the national welfare, safety, or security of the United States, and
>>
>> (iii) the alien has been rehabilitated; or
>
> [The Extreme Hardship Waiver]
>
>> (B) in the case of an immigrant who is the spouse, parent, son, or daughter of a citizen of the United States or an alien lawfully admitted for

---

[33] *Barraza v. Mukasey,* 519 F.3d 388 (7th Cir. 2008).

[34] *Matter of Martinez-Espinoza,* 25 I&N Dec. 118 (2009).

[35] *Matter of Davey,* 26 I&N Dec. 37, 39 (BIA 2012).

[36] DHS—not DOJ through the U.S. Attorney General (AG)—now has authority over affirmative applications for adjustment of status (applications filed with USCIS). IJs, who review waivers during removal proceedings, remain under the authority of DOJ and the AG.

[37] INA §§212(a)(2)(D)(i) and (ii) [8 USC §§1182(a)(2)(D)(i) and (ii)] relate to inadmissibility for prostitution and commercialized vice.

permanent residence if it is established to the satisfaction of the Attorney General that the alien's denial of admission would result in extreme hardship to the United States citizen or lawfully resident spouse, parent, son, or daughter of such alien; or

[The Battered Spouse and Child Waiver]

(C) the alien is a VAWA self-petitioner; and

(2) the Attorney General, in his discretion, and pursuant to such terms, conditions and procedures as he may by regulations prescribe, has consented to the alien's applying or reapplying for a visa, for admission to the United States, or adjustment of status.

No waiver shall be provided under the subsection in the case of an alien who has been convicted of (or who has admitted committing acts that constitute) murder or criminal acts involving torture, or an attempt or conspiracy to commit murder or a criminal act involving torture.

[Special Clause for LPRs]

No waiver shall be granted under this subsection in the case of an alien who has previously been admitted to the United States as an alien lawfully admitted for permanent residence if either since the date of such admission the alien has been convicted of an aggravated felony or the alien has not lawfully resided continuously in the United States for a period of not less than 7 years immediately preceding the date of initiation of proceedings to remove the alien from the United States. No court shall have jurisdiction to review a decision of the Attorney General to grant or deny a waiver under this subsection.

The 15-Year Waiver

The first waiver, under §212(h)(1)(A) [8 USC §1182(h)(1)(A)], is available to waive inadmissibility for prostitution-type offenses, or crimes involving moral turpitude that occurred more than 15 years prior to the date of the application for a visa, admission, or adjustment of status. Eligibility for this "15-year waiver" does *not* require a qualifying relative (an immediate family member) or a showing of extreme hardship. A successful applicant under this section will show that he or she is not a danger to the community and has been rehabilitated. The waiver is still discretionary. Practice pointers on how to present a waiver application are discussed in chapter thirteen.

The Extreme Hardship Waiver

The second waiver, under INA §212(h)(1)(B) [8 USC §1182(h)(1)(B)], is the most frequently used of the three waivers. Indeed, reference to the §212(h) waiver is generally a reference to this particular subsection. A waiver under INA §212(h)(1)(B) requires that the applicant have a "qualifying family member"—a U.S. citizen or LPR spouse, parent, son, or daughter. The successful applicant must show that the qualifying relative (*not the applicant* him- or herself) will suffer *extreme hardship* if the application is not granted. The extreme hardship question has two sides: first, how will the family be affected by the applicant's absence; or second, how will the family be affected if they relocate to the foreign country with the applicant. Extreme hardship is determined on a case-by-case basis and may involve myriad factors, including equities and hardships. Note that even if extreme hardship to a qualifying relative is established, the waiver is discretionary.

The Battered Spouse and Child Waiver

The third waiver, under INA §212(h)(1)(C) [8 USC §1182(h)(1)(C)], is a waiver for certain battered spouses and children of U.S. citizens and LPRs. The INA's general treatment of battered spouses and children is beyond the scope of this book; suffice to say that the spouses and children of American citizens and LPRs may qualify for distinct benefits under the INA, including residency petitions in which they effectively sponsor themselves. This third waiver under INA §212(h) is essentially a waiver for battered spouses and children, and does not require a "qualifying relative" or a showing of "extreme hardship."

Special Rules for Lawful Permanent Residents

LPRs with aggravated felony and other convictions

As stated above, some persons who already are LPRs will seek to re-adjust in removal proceedings as a form of relief, or defense, from removal. The Illegal Immigration Reform and Immigrant Responsibility Act of 1996 (IIRAIRA)[38] amended INA §212(h) to include a final paragraph regarding persons who are already LPRs and seek to utilize the waiver because of a crime. Typically, this scenario is relevant to LPRs returning to the United States from a trip abroad who are determined to be inadmissible for a crime, or LPRs who are detected within the United States and charged with deportability. In either scenario, the individual could be placed in removal proceedings before an IJ, but he or she may be eligible for a §212(h) waiver.

The amended version of §212(h) (cited above) states that an individual who has previously been admitted to the United States as an alien lawfully admitted for permanent residence and has been convicted of an aggravated felony is *ineligible* for this waiver if, either since the date of such admission, he or she has been convicted of an aggravated felony, or he or she has not lawfully resided continuously in the United States for a period of not less than seven years immediately preceding the date of initiation of removal proceedings.[39] Because of this amendment, a non–permanent resident applying for adjustment of status may actually be in a better litigation position than an LPR. Consider the following example:

---

[38] Illegal Immigration Reform and Immigrant Responsibility Act of 1996 (IIRAIRA), Division C of the Omnibus Appropriations Act of 1996 (H.R. 3610), Pub. L. No. 104-208, 110 Stat. 3009.

[39] Note: It is incongruent to discuss aggravated felonies, which are not a ground of inadmissibility, in a provision for a waiver of inadmissibility. Nonetheless, aggravated felonies are a classification that can be used in different contexts and applications in the INA.

> ***Example***: John and Joe are brothers. John has been an LPR of the United States for 10 years; he obtained residency through consular processing for an immigrant visa. Joe is an illegal alien; however, his fiancée is a U.S. citizen. In 2003, John and Joe are arrested together and charged with dealing in stolen property. They each make a plea bargain and are sentenced to a year and a day in jail. Upon completion of their jail terms, they are taken into immigration custody, charged as aggravated felons, and held without bond. John, who had resided lawfully in the United States for 10 years, is ordered removed; he has no relief available.[40] On the other hand, Joe—who married his U.S. citizen girlfriend while in jail—applies for adjustment of status based on a marriage petition in conjunction with an INA §212(h)(1)(B) waiver. Based on hardship factors and other humanitarian issues presented, Joe's waiver is approved. On the day that John is deported from the United States for the burglary, Joe is released from ICE custody and becomes an LPR.

Variation: Assume John (the LPR brother) became a permanent resident through adjustment of status, instead of consular processing. In all but two circuit courts of appeals, John would be eligible to apply for a §212(h) waiver in connection with a new application for adjustment of status. The circuit courts' treatment of "admission" for §212(h) purposes is discussed below.

Retroactivity of the amendment

The BIA has held that the amendment to INA §212(h) by IIRAIRA is retroactive and applies to individuals who were in proceedings as of the date IIRAIRA was enacted (September 30, 1996).[41] However, at least one circuit court of appeals has held that a waiver under §212(h) remains available to persons who were in proceedings as of the IIRAIRA effective date, and that service of an order to show cause (OSC) constitutes being placed "in proceedings."[42]

Important circuit case law: defining "admission"

The provision of §212(h) that disqualifies certain permanent residents convicted of crime refers to individuals who have been "admitted" to the United States as "aliens lawfully admitted for permanent residence." In 2008, the U.S. Fifth Circuit Court of Appeals ruled that adjustment of status does not qualify as an "admission" for this purpose; thus, someone who became an LPR through adjustment of status who is subsequently convicted of a crime involving moral turpitude committed within seven years of residency status, or of an aggravated felony offense, remains eligible to ap-

---

[40] But see *Martinez v. Mukasey*, 519 F.3d 532 (5th Cir. 2008), for an argument that §212(h) is available to lawful permanent residents (LPRs) who adjusted status; this argument is discussed below.

[41] *Matter of Yeung*, 21 I&N Dec. 610 (BIA 1996).

[42] *Quee de Cunningham v. Att'y Gen.*, 335 F. 3d 1262 (11th Cir. 2003). The *Cunningham* decision is discussed in greater depth in the INA §212(c) waiver section of this chapter.

ply for a waiver under INA §212(h).[43] Following the *Martinez v. Mukasey* decision, several other circuits followed suit.[44] These are extremely important decisions, and each is unique; however, the Eleventh Circuit U.S. Court of Appeals case involved an initial illegal entry without inspection, the others involved nonimmigrant visa admissions. An attorney representing an LPR through adjustment in removal proceedings, who seeks to cure removability through the §212(h) waiver, will thus pay careful attention to the following discussion, and carefully review this exciting precedent.

The analysis: understanding "admission"

An individual can become an LPR through either consular processing for an immigrant visa, or adjustment of status. In consular processing, an individual attends an immigrant visa interview at a U.S. consulate abroad and is approved for the immigrant visa (residency). However, he or she does not obtain residency until arrival and inspection at a U.S. port of entry, where there is additional scrutiny: the visa envelope is opened, and on review, the passport is stamped "admitted."

As discussed earlier in this chapter, adjustment of status is a mechanism under INA §245(a) that allows an individual who was lawfully admitted or paroled to change over to permanent residency status without leaving the United States. Although adjustment is most commonly utilized where an individual entered lawfully with a nonimmigrant visa, there are myriad examples whereby an individual who was not lawfully admitted or paroled may eventually adjust status.

In some cases, individuals who were never lawfully admitted might also adjust status in the United States and avoid consular processing. These may be individuals who qualified for INA §245(i), a provision that allows certain illegal entrants to pay a fine and adjust status; this provision expired on April 30, 2001, but persons who already had filed a petition and were "in the pipeline" are grandfathered in.[45] Section 245(i) is not the only example, however, of a person who was not admitted or paroled into the United States qualifying for adjustment of status. There are programs or statutes that are designed to allow certain nationalities to adjust status irrespective of an illegal admission. An example would be the 1997 Nicaraguan and Central American

---

[43] *Martinez v. Mukasey*, 519 F.3d 532, 544 (5th Cir. 2008).

[44] As of the spring of 2015, eight other circuits have joined the Fifth and ruled that adjustment of status does not qualify as an "admission" for purposes of INA §212(h)'s disqualification. *See Husic v. Holder*, 776 F.3d 59 (2d Cir. 2015); *Hanif v. Att'y Gen.*, 694 F.3d 479 (3d Cir. 2012); *Bracamontes v. Holder*, 675 F.3d 380 (4th Cir. 2012); *Stanovsek v. Holder*, 768 F.3d 515 (6th Cir. 2014); *Papazoglou v. Holder*, 725 F.3d 790 (7th Cir. 2013); *Negrete-Ramirez v. Holder*, 741 F.3d 1047 (9th Cir. 2014); *Medina-Rosales v. Holder*, 2015 U.S. App. LEXIS 2734, 2015 WL 756345 (10th Cir. 2015); *Lanier v. Att'y Gen*, 631 F.3d 1363 (11th Cir. 2011).

[45] Adjustment of status for noncriminals, and the waiver under INA §245(i) are beyond the scope of this book. For additional resources on adjustment of status, including §245(i) processing, see *Representing Clients in Immigration Court* (3rd Ed. AILA 2013), and *The Waivers Book: Advanced Issues in Immigration Practice* (AILA 2011).

Relief Act (NACARA).[46] Some relief in immigration court results in a type of adjustment of status: cancellation of removal (discussed below) is a form of adjustment.

Parole itself is not a lawful "admission"—yet many persons will qualify for adjustment based on a parole arrival. For example, certain special immigrants—such as juveniles or battered spouses—who entered illegally are assimilated to an arrival via parole (are assumed to have entered with parole) under the law, precisely so they can adjust status.

Thus, adjustment of status may be preceded by a nonimmigrant lawful admission (such as with a tourist or student visa); it may be accomplished via parole; or it may follow an illegal, surreptitious entry (entry without inspection) by an individual who qualifies under a §245(i) waiver or through another program allowed by statute.

The analysis: understanding the criminal bar's language

Section 212(h)'s bar to certain lawful permanent residents reads, in pertinent part:

> No waiver shall be granted under this subsection in the case of an alien *who has previously been admitted* to the United States *as an alien lawfully admitted for permanent residence* ... [emphasis added]

The language in italics demonstrates that there are two parts to this phrase. "Admitted" into the United States is not the lynchpin of the argument; rather, it is the act of being "admitted" *as* an "alien lawfully admitted for permanent residence." These terms are defined by statute:

INA §101(a)(13)(A) [8 USC § 1101(a)(13)]: the terms "admission" and "admitted" mean, with respect to an alien, the lawful *entry* of the alien *into* the United States *after inspection* and authorization by an immigrant officer. [Emphasis added]

INA §101(a)(20) [8 USC § 1101(a)(20)]: the term "lawfully admitted for permanent residence" means the status of having been lawfully accorded the privilege of residing permanently in the United States as an immigrant in accordance with the immigration laws, such status not having changed.

With the circuit courts being split nine to two on the issue, the BIA has held firm to its position that adjustment of status qualifies as an "admission." Finally, on May 12, 2015, the BIA acquiesced in *Matter of J–H–J–*,[47] finding that in light of overwhelming circuit authority, an individual who adjusted status to LPR (as opposed to someone who underwent consular processing for an immigrant visa), if otherwise

---

[46] Nicaraguan Adjustment and Central American Relief Act (NACARA), title II of Pub. L. No. 105-100 111 Stat. 2160, 2193 (1997).

[47] *Matter of J–H–J–*, 26 I&N Dec. 563 (BIA 2015).

qualified,[48] is eligible to seek a waiver under INA §212(h) because adjustment of status is not an "admission."

Matter of Alyazji[49]

At the same time the Eleventh Circuit was considering the definition of "admission" in the context of the INA §212(h) waiver in *Lanier*, the BIA was considering the term in the context of deportability under INA §237(a)(2)(A)(i): one crime involving moral turpitude within five years of "admission."[50] In *Alyazji*'s briefing, DHS took the position that adjustment of status is not an "admission," thereby agreeing to a certain extent with the respondent in that case. DHS proposed that the five-year "clock" could be set at the time of adjustment *only* where the non–American citizen did not have a previous lawful nonimmigrant admission.[51]

In *Alyazji*,[52] the BIA did not agree with the parties' joint view, and instead took a sterner approach, holding to its longstanding position that adjustment of status is a type of admission.[53] However, the BIA ruled that for purposes of deportability under INA §237(a)(2)(A)(i), there can be only one admission; therefore, a preceding nonimmigrant admission prior to adjustment serves as the "admission."

Matter of Alyazji represents a significant step by the Board in conceding that adjustment of status is not a traditional "admission." Interestingly, *Alyazji* was decided one day after *Lanier*, thus making February 2011 an important month in defining "admission." Language in *Alyazji* may prove useful in arguing eligibility for INA §212(h). The cases and the issues should be considered in concert when briefing §212(h) eligibility.[54]

The analysis: what about entry without inspection?

The fundamental aspect of the *Martinez–Lanier–Bracamontes* trilogy (these were the first three decisions) and of the cases that came after, is that adjustment of status does not meet the definition of the phrase: "admitted" as an alien "lawfully admitted

---

[48] Again, §212(h) does not waive all grounds of removability. It is not available for controlled substance offenses beyond one offense simple possession less than 30 grams of marijuana/paraphernalia; it does not waive firearm offenses; it does not waive murder.

[49] *Matter of Alyazji*, 25 I&N Dec. 397 (BIA 2011).

[50] Defining "admission" and the *Alyzaji* case are also discussed in chapter nine.

[51] The DHS brief in the *Alyazji* case may be found at *www.legalactioncenter.org/sites/default/files/docs/lac/DHS-SupplementalBrief-Alyazji-4-21-2010.pdf.*

[52] *Matter of Alyazji*, 25 I&N Dec. 397 (BIA 2011).

[53] *Matter of Koljenovic*, 25 I&N Dec. 219 (BIA 2010).

[54] *Matter of Paek,* 26 I&N Dec. 403 (BIA 2014) (An alien who was admitted to the United States at a port of entry as a conditional permanent resident pursuant to INA §216(a) [8 USC §1186a(a)] is an alien "lawfully admitted for permanent residence" who is barred from establishing eligibility for a waiver of inadmissibility under INA §212(h) [8 USC §1182(h)] if he or she was subsequently convicted of an aggravated felony.)

for permanent residence." Meeting this two-part definition is required if the bar is to click in. Even though someone may have initially entered without inspection, or via parole, does not change the fact that adjustment of status is not an "admission" to LPR status because it is not an entry following inspection.

The response: BIA

In May 2012, the Board issued a decision, *Matter of Rodriguez*,[55] that addressed the circuit split on defining the §212(h) bar for certain LPRs convicted of crime. The BIA stated that it respectfully disagreed with the circuit courts of appeal, but would apply their precedent in those [at the time, three] circuits. Of interest, the BIA notes that the issue of an initial illegal entry, or parole (in other words, a situation where there is no initial lawful admission) is not a key aspect of the courts' analyses and the precedent will be applied regardless of the initial manner of entry. In *Rodriguez*, which arose in the Fifth Circuit, the respondent had initially entered without inspection and later adjusted status. DHS urged that this factual distinction should be the basis for disregarding the *Martinez-Mukasey* precedent. The BIA disagreed with the government on this point:

> Although the respondent's case is factually distinguishable from *Martinez* because he was never "admitted" to the United States, the breadth of the Fifth Circuit's holding persuades us that this factual distinction does not justify a different legal outcome.[56]

Accordingly, notwithstanding the factual question of an initial entry without inspection (or some other type of entry that does not qualify as an admission), the ultimate precedent still applies: adjustment of status is not an "admission" as an "alien lawfully admitted for permanent residence." (The reader will note that Board Member Pauley dissented on precisely this point, finding that *Martinez* and *Bracamonte* should be limited to situations of a nonimmigrant admission prior to adjustment in those circuits.)

The next move: DHS argues subsequent re-entries are "admissions"

A developing tactic used by ICE prosecutors in the Eleventh Circuit is to identify a trip out of the United States *after* adjustment of status, and *after* commission of the crime, but prior to removal proceedings, and then to propose that the LPR was in fact "admitted" under INA §101(13)(C)(v). The underlying scenario, in other words, is that where the LPR traveled and re-entered after commission of the crime, but was nonetheless allowed in because the offense did not come to light, *i.e.*, U.S. Customs and Border Protection (CBP) did not see the arrest or conviction, or the offense had not yet been prosecuted. This argument is misplaced and erroneous for several reasons.

---

[55] *Matter of Rodriguez*, 25 I&N Dec. 784 (BIA 2012).

[56] *Matter of Rodriguez*, 25 I&N Dec. 784, at 787.

The *Martinez-Lanier* line of cases is based on two definitions: INA §101(a)(20), defining "lawfully admitted for permanent residence" and §101(a)(13)(A), defining "admission." DHS's argument that a subsequent trip and re-entry may be considered after the fact an "admission" focuses on the concept of "admission," but ignores INA §101(a)(20).

> **Practice Pointer**: An attorney facing a U.S. Immigration and Customs Enforcement (ICE) motion to pretermit may consider the following response arguments:[57]

✓ An individual can only have one admission or adjustment to LPR status, not multiple adjudications (the limited exceptions would be an individual in removal who re-adjusts as relief, or an individual who abandons residency at one time and then reapplies and is re-adjudicated).

✓ Section §101(a)(13)(C) is not the pivotal section in the 212(h) case law. It deals with when an LPR will be treated as "seeking an admission," in other words, when he or she is viewed as an "arriving alien" subject to grounds of inadmissibility. It is not a reference to adjudication to that of a permanent resident. Based on §101(a)(13)(C), the inspection and authorization of a suspect individual to enter is suspended pending review of possible grounds of removability, but the LPR is not re-adjudicated for residency status. Upon successful resolution, such an individual is not admitted in terms of a *new* residency status: he or she maintains her continuous ongoing status.

✓ The DHS argument disregards that INA § 101(a)(13)(C) is written in the present tense. The plain language does not allow an adjudicator to go back in time and decide that an "admission" took place, when in fact the LPR was *not* viewed as seeking admission (because the offense had not come to light) and he or she returned to the United States without an "admission." It is precisely because time-travel is a fiction not allowed in the practice of immigration law that the very first ground of deportability at INA §237(a)(1) is entitled "classes of deportable aliens," persons who were "at the time of entry or adjustment of status within one or more of the classes of aliens inadmissible by the law existing at such time is deportable." Congress, recognizing that turning the clock back to the day of arrival is not feasible, permits a ground of deportation for individuals who did in fact successfully enter but were perhaps inadmissible at that time. An LPR who fits this scenario is one who did success-

---

[57] The appendices to this chapter contain one unpublished BIA decision that ruled against DHS, finding that a person who adjusted status, and subsequently travels after commission of a crime, is not readmitted for purposes of INA §212(h).

fully enter, was not viewed as an arriving alien, and was not "admitted" as an alien lawfully admitted for permanent resident status.

LPRs with nonaggravated felony convictions

As of the spring of 2015, in cases arising within the First and Eighth U.S. Circuit Courts of Appeals, *Matter of Koljenovic*[58] governs applications for a §212(h) waiver, and an adjustment of status is considered an "admission" such that the applicant is barred by the criminal offense clause. The bar refers not only to aggravated felony convictions, but also any crime where the LPR respondent has not resided continuously in the United States for a period of no less than seven years immediately preceding the date of initiation of proceedings. An LPR who would like to apply for the §212(h) waiver must establish that he or she has:

> lawfully resided continuously in the United States for a period of not less than 7 years immediately preceding the date of initiation of proceedings to remove the alien from the United States.

Accordingly, this phrase, dissected, has two key elements: (1) a lawful and continuous residence in the United States for a period of at least seven years, and (2) the residence was prior to initiation of proceedings. Significantly, this phrase does not require seven years of lawful permanent residence (green-card status), only a lawful residence.[59]

Defining Lawful Continual Residence

Neither the statute nor the regulations define "lawful residence" for purposes of this particular §212(h) provision. Previously, this author has written that "lawfully residing" could refer to a variety of circumstances in which a non–American citizen is rightfully present, such as nonimmigrant visa status, temporary protected status (TPS), asylum-pending status, deferred action, etc. This view is based on the realization that immigration law contains a panoply of conditions or statuses that allow a person to reside in the United States "lawfully." However, in 2008, the BIA issued a precedent decision in *Matter of Rotimi*[60] that limited the immigration situations that would qualify as "lawfully residing," and specifically found that a pending application for a benefit, such as asylum or adjustment of status, would not qualify.

Although the *Rotimi* decision specifically declines to adopt a "comprehensive definition of this statutory language," the Board interprets "lawfully residing continuously" to require some sort of actual status, such as a nonimmigrant visa status.[61] The Second U.S. Circuit Court of Appeals subsequently upheld the *Rotimi* decision as a rational

---

[58] *Matter of Koljenovic*, 25 I&N Dec. 219 (BIA 2010).

[59] The BIA has affirmed this interpretation. *See* the unpublished BIA decision that is reprinted as Appendix 10B.

[60] *Matter of Rotimi*, 24 I&N Dec. 567 (BIA 2008).

[61] *Matter of Rotimi*, 24 I&N Dec. 567, at 575–76 (BIA 2008).

interpretation of the statute.[62] The *Rotimi* decision holds open the question of whether voluntary departure, deferred action, parole, or other immigration situations that do not qualify as formal status, but do represent an affirmative grant of the temporary right to remain in the United States, qualify as "lawful residence" for purposes of the §212(h) waiver.

Tolling of Seven-Year Period: Initiation of Removal Proceedings

The second important issue connected with INA §212(h)'s seven-year continuous residence requirement is tolling: the period of continuous lawful residence does not toll upon commission of the crime or entry of a conviction (which are the tolling points in other provisions under the INA, notably cancellation of removal under INA §240A(a)); rather, it is the initiation of removal proceedings before an IJ that stops the clock and tolls the accumulation of lawful residence. Pursuant to 8 CFR §1003.14(a), jurisdiction vests, and proceedings before an IJ commence, on the filing of a charging document with the immigration court. The charging document (a notice to appear, or NTA) must show service on the opposing party pursuant to 8 CFR §1003.32. In sum, proceedings are initiated for purposes of the §212(h) waiver's limitations when a charging document (usually an NTA) is filed with the immigration court, along with a legally sufficient certificate of service. Understanding these elements is key, because the requirements for a §212(h) waiver do differ from the other traditional waiver available in immigration court proceedings—cancellation of removal (which is discussed next). Consider the following examples, which highlight both the continuous lawful residence requirement and the tolling issue:

Arriving Aliens or Those Adjusting Status

As stated above, an INA §212(h) waiver cures grounds of inadmissibility. It may be used by persons who are already LPRs in removal proceedings only in certain circumstances. Aside from the discussion of the bar, above, the BIA has traditionally required that the §212(h) waiver be available to LPRs in the following circumstances only: (1) in conjunction with an application for adjustment of status, or (2) in proceedings when the individual is *arriving* at a port of entry and making application for admission.[63] In this second circumstance—an LPR placed in proceedings at a port of entry (hence an "arriving alien")—a simultaneous application for adjustment of status is not necessary.[64]

---

[62] *Rotimi v. Holder*, 577 F.3d 133 (2d Cir. 2009).

[63] *Matter of Balao*, 20 I&N Dec. 440 (BIA 1992) (citing *Matter of Parodi*, 17 I&N Dec. 608 (BIA 1980) and *Matter of Bernabella*, 13 I&N Dec. 42 (BIA 1968)).

[64] *Matter of Abosi*, 24 I&N Dec. 204 (BIA 2007).

Based on BIA precedent, an LPR charged with deportability under INA §237 (having been convicted of a crime but still within the United States) can file for a §212(h) waiver only with an application for adjustment of status.[65]

CASE STUDY: MATTER OF BUSTAMANTE

Ten-year cancellation is not an adjustment of status for §212(h) purposes: In *Matter of Bustamante*,[66] the non–American citizen had a conviction for simple possession of less than 30 grams of marijuana. He sought relief through cancellation of removal under INA §240A(b),[67] a type of adjustment for individuals in removal proceedings who have 10 or more years' continuous physical presence and who are not inadmissible for crime. To cure the marijuana conviction (a bar to cancellation), Bustamante argued that 10-year cancellation is a type of "adjustment" and he could therefore apply simultaneously for the §212(h) waiver to cure the marijuana offense. The BIA disagreed, finding that §212(h) cannot be used to waive a ground of ineligibility for cancellation of removal; it only waives a ground of inadmissibility. Put another way, the §212(h) waiver is only available in connection with adjustment of status or for arriving alien LPRs facing a ground of inadmissibility.

In addition, the ground of deportability under INA §237 must have a corresponding ground of inadmissibility at INA §212(a). In other words, the offense conduct that forms the basis of the ground of deportability would, hypothetically, also have to form the basis of a ground of inadmissibility. (The reader will note that a strict "comparable ground" test has been disavowed by the Supreme Court in the INA §212(c) context in *Judulang v. Holder*,[68] and this important precedent may carry over to the INA §212(h) context.)

Thus, an LPR who has traveled outside the United States and is placed in removal proceedings on return—charged with inadmissibility under §212(a)—can file for §212(h) relief without the necessity of an adjustment application.

Due to recent activity by the BIA and the Eleventh Circuit, an application for §212(h) from inside of U.S. borders is only available in conjunction with an application to adjust status. Thus, an LPR in the "deportation track" under §237 cannot file a "stand alone" waiver.[69]

---

[65] *See Matter of Rivas*, 26 I&N Dec. 130 (BIA 2013).
[66] *Matter of Bustamante*, 25 I&N Dec. 564 (BIA 2011).
[67] 8 USC §1229b(b).
[68] *Judulang v. Holder*, 132 S. Ct. 476 (2011).
[69] *See Matter of Rivas*, 26 I&N Dec. 130 (BIA 2013); *Poveda v. Atty. Gen.*, 692 F.3d 1168 (11th Cir. 2012).

For more than a decade, an LPR charged in removal proceedings under INA §237(a) did not require a new application for adjustment of status to accompany the INA §212(h) waiver within the Eleventh Circuit.[70] The Seventh Circuit U.S. Court of Appeals pointedly disagreed with the position of the Eleventh, finding that LPRs in proceedings under the deportation track at INA §237 are not eligible for a waiver unless they apply for adjustment of status or are applying on a *nunc pro tunc* basis.[71] In August 2012, in *Poveda v. Att'y Gen.*, the Eleventh Circuit changed course in a divided opinion, holding that an application for §212(h) relief requires an accompanying application for adjustment of status.[72]

BIA abandons Matter of Sanchez

For many years, pursuant to *Matter of Sanchez*,[73] the only situation in which an INA §212(h) waiver could be filed in §237 track (deportation) proceedings without an adjustment application was where the LPR had traveled after the conviction, but successfully re-entered, in which case the waiver was considered *nunc pro tunc* to cure the existing ground of inadmissibility at the time of last entry. In *Matter of Rivas,* the Board expressly rejected *Sanchez* and recognized *Poveda*[74] as the acceptable standard:

> We conclude that since the statute does not provide for a "stand alone" waiver under section 212(h) without an application for adjustment of status, granting a waiver *nunc pro tunc* would violate the plain language of the statute and the intent of Congress. See *Poveda v. U.S. Att'y Gen.*, 692 F.3d at 1177—78. Our precedent issued prior to the 1990 and 1996 amendments to section 212(h), including *Matter of Sanchez*, is therefore no longer valid. Section 212(h), as amended, does not permit an alien in the respondent's situation to apply for a waiver given his ineligibility for adjustment of status. Because the Immigration Judge erred in granting the respondent's request for a section 212(h) waiver *nunc pro tunc* without an application for adjustment of status, the DHS's ap-

---

[70] *Yeung v. INS*, 72 F.3d 843 (11th Cir. 1996). Author's note: The *Yeung* decision was based on the premise that it is a violation of equal protection to allow an LPR with a conviction, who by happenstance, has traveled to apply for a §212(h) waiver, while a similarly situated LPR who has not traveled is ineligible.

[71] *Klementanovsky v. Gonzales*, 501 F.3d 788 (7th Cir. 2007).

[72] *Poveda v. Att'y Gen.*, 692 F.3d 1168 (11th Cir. 2012).

[73] *Matter of Sanchez* 17 I&N Dec. 218 (BIA) (under *Sanchez,* a deportable non-American citizen had the option to apply for a *nunc pro tunc* §212(h) waiver as a standalone defense in a removal proceeding, and there was no need to apply for adjustment of status because the waiver was retroactive to the time of the prior admission).

[74] *Poveda v. Att'y Gen.*, 692 F.3d 1168 (11th Cir. 2012) (embracing the BIA's interpretation of §212(h) to be available to an alien within the U.S. so long as he applies for adjustment of status.)

peal will be sustained and the decision of the Immigration Judge will be vacated.[75]

The negative impact of this ruling is profound: Section 212(h) can no longer be used as a "stand alone" defense in removal proceedings when the respondent cannot apply for adjustment of status. Previously, when *Matter of Sanchez* was not expressly overturned, a deportable noncitizen had the option to apply for a *nunc pro tunc* §212(h) waiver as a "stand alone" defense in a removal proceeding, and there was no need to apply for adjustment of status because the waiver was retroactive to the time of the prior admission. *Matter of Rivas* expressly forecloses that option. Thus, an alien who is seeking a waiver from inside of U.S. borders needs to file an application for adjustment of status in conjunction with §212(h) application.

Limited Availability of INA §212(h) for Persons Convicted of Violent or Dangerous Crimes

The above discussion on the INA §212(h) waiver involves the statute as interpreted by the BIA. The INA at §212(h) was amended in 2003, not by Congress, but by the attorney general (AG). In an unusual—and *ultra vires*—fashion, then–AG John Ashcroft changed the requirements for a waiver under INA §212(h) via an amendment to the regulations. The regulation at 8 CFR §§212.7(d), 1212.7(d) now states:

> (d) *Criminal grounds of inadmissibility involving violent or dangerous crimes.* The Attorney General, in general, will not favorably exercise discretion under section 212(h)(2) of the Act (8 U.S.C. 1182(h)(2)) to consent to an application or reapplication for a visa, or admission to the United States, or adjustment of status, with respect to immigrant aliens who are inadmissible under section 212(a)(2) of the Act in cases involving violent or dangerous crimes, except in extraordinary circumstances, such as those involving national security or foreign policy considerations, or cases in which an alien clearly demonstrates that the denial of the application for adjustment of status or an immigrant visa or admission as an immigrant would result in exceptional and extremely unusual hardship. Moreover, depending on the gravity of the alien's underlying criminal offense, a showing of extraordinary circumstances might still be insufficient to warrant a favorable exercise of discretion under section 212(h)(2) of the Act.

The above regulatory section means that in cases involving a violent or dangerous crime, the §212(h) applicant must meet a series of requirements in order to receive this relief. First, to be eligible (according to statute), the applicant must show that he or she meets §212(h)(1)(A) (the 15-year waiver), (B) (the extreme hardship to a citizen or LPR family member waiver), or (C) (the battered spouse or child waiver). Second (under 8 CFR §§212.7(d), 1212.7(d)), to be eligible for a favorable exercise

---

[75] *Matter of Rivas*, 26 I&N Dec. 130 (BIA 2013).

of discretion, the applicant must show extraordinary circumstances, defined as those involving national security or foreign policy considerations, or exceptional and extremely unusual hardship. Notably, the language of this regulatory provision indicates that the exceptional and extremely unusual hardship can be either to the applicant or the relative(s); the provision does not state that the hardship must be attached to the spouse, parent, or child. Finally, depending on the gravity of the offense, the regulation indicates that a showing of extraordinary circumstances still may be not enough to justify a favorable exercise of discretion.

Neither "violent" nor "dangerous" is defined. Do these terms refer to the underlying criminal statute, the underlying facts of the offense, or both? The precedent case that inspired the regulation might provide guidance.

CASE STUDY: MATTER OF JEAN

The regulatory amendment cited above "codifies" the AG's decision in *Matter of Jean*.[76] *Matter of Jean* did not involve a waiver under INA §212(h), but an application for a waiver under INA §209(c) [8 USC §1159(c)]. A §209(c) waiver is available to refugees and asylees applying for adjustment of status, and is more generous than the §212(h) waiver because it does not require a showing of hardship to qualifying relatives. (It does not require a qualifying relative at all.)

However, the very same language used in *Matter of Jean* (in which the AG reversed a decision of the BIA and denied the §209(c) waiver as a matter of discretion) is now used in the new regulation. Thus, it would seem that *Matter of Jean* should provide guidance in analyzing the terms "violent" or "dangerous" crime or "exceptional and extremely unusual hardship." However, the case opinion provides no specific guidance on either standard. Counsel may glean some criteria based on the facts of the case itself.

The underlying offense in *Matter of Jean* involved the beating and shaking of a 19-month old baby to death—shocking facts. The respondent, a woman originally admitted as a refugee under INA §207, was eventually convicted of second-degree manslaughter under N.Y. Penal Law §125.15(1), and served nearly six years in prison. Thus, arguably, "violent" or "dangerous" must involve serious bodily harm (perhaps to the point of death or near death) to trigger the heightened standard of 8 CFR §§212.7(d), 1212.7(d).

---

[76] *Matter of Jean*, 23 I&N Dec. 373 (AG 2002). The author rejects the notion that the attorney general (AG) may codify his own decision via regulations; this heaps insult on injury. Nevertheless, at a USCIS-sponsored and led seminar in South Florida in June 2003, the amendment to INA §212(h) via the regulation at 8 CFR §§212.7, 1212.7 was presented as a "codification" of the AG's decision in *Matter of Jean*.

In addition, a significant prison term might be a prerequisite. Does the victim have to be defenseless? It must be noted that the definition of "crime of violence" at 18 USC §16 is *not* utilized by the AG in either *Matter of Jean* or the regulation; it follows that "violent" or "dangerous" crime is an act more extreme than that described at 18 USC §16.

Since the *Jean* decision, the following criminal offenses have been found to be violent crimes requiring the heightened standard:

- Recklessly causing serious injury;[77]
- Burglary;[78]
- Child molestation, lewd and lascivious acts on a child;[79] and
- Robbery.[80]

Again, it is important to note that each case—each offense—will present a unique set of circumstances and, often, a criminal statute of first impression in the waiver context. Unlike the aggravated felony definition, and case law classifying certain offenses as crimes involving moral turpitude, neither the waiver provision at 8 CFR §1212.7(d) nor the case law invites classifications of crimes as per se violent. The BIA and courts have not adopted a categorical approach to the term "violent crime"; thus, counsel may argue in the context of his or her particular case that an offense (*i.e.*, robbery) is not a violent crime based on the individual facts presented. In an unpublished decision, the Ninth Circuit U.S. Court of Appeals has stated that although the AG did not exceed his authority in promulgating a regulation that dictates a standard for adjudication of this discretionary waiver, IJs must engage in an individualized determination that the crime is violent and dangerous.[81] The Third Circuit U.S. Court of Appeals he has held likewise: the regulation is a constitutional exercise of the AG's powers, but the non–American citizen is entitled to an individualized hearing on whether the offense was indeed "violent and dangerous."[82]

As for the expression "exceptional and extremely unusual hardship," a review of the *Matter of Jean* decision yields no specific guidance. The respondent in this case lived in the United States with five children and her husband. The AG found these

---

[77] *Waldron v. Holder*, No. 11-1981, 2012 U.S. App. LEXIS 16277 (8th Cir. Aug. 6, 2012) (this case involved breaking a glass over another's head).

[78] *Perez Pimentel v. Mukasey*, 530 F.3d 321, 325–26 (5th Cir. 2008).

[79] *Mejia v. Gonzales*, 499 F.3d 991, 996 (9th Cir. 2007).

[80] *Samuels v. Chertoff*, 550 F.3d 252 (2d Cir. 2008).

[81] *Rivas-Gomez v. Gonzales*, 225 Fed. Appx. 680, U.S. App. LEXIS 7269, 2007 WL 851768 (9th Cir. 2007).

[82] *Togbah v. Ashcroft*, 104 Fed. Appx. 788; 2004 U.S. App. LEXIS 14149, 2004 WL 1530494 (3d Cir, 2004).

equities insufficient to merit discretionary relief when balanced against the adverse facts of the conviction:

> In my judgment, that balance will nearly always require the denial of a request for discretionary relief from removal where an alien's criminal conduct is as serious as that of the respondent. Congress has authorized the Attorney General under section 209(c) to waive an alien's inadmissibility, notwithstanding certain otherwise disqualifying convictions, "for humanitarian reasons, to assure family unity, or when it is otherwise in the public interest." Congress did not compel the Attorney General to do so. It would not be a prudent exercise of the discretion afforded to me by this provision to grant favorable adjustments of status to violent or dangerous individuals except in extraordinary circumstances, such as those involving national security or foreign policy considerations, or cases in which an alien clearly demonstrates that the denial of adjustment of status would result in exceptional and extremely unusual hardship. Moreover, depending on the gravity of the alien's underlying criminal offense, such a showing might still be insufficient. From its inception, the United States has always been a nation of immigrants; it is one of our greatest strengths. But aliens arriving at our shores must understand that residency in the United States is a privilege, not a right. For those aliens, like the respondent, who engage in violent criminal acts during their stay here, this country will not offer its embrace. The BIA's grant of lawful permanent residency is reversed.[83]

While the AG's words send a strong signal to adjudicators and IJs that discretionary waivers should almost never be granted in the case of violent crime, the decision offers little tangible legal analysis in determining its application. Practitioners have leeway in arguing, first, that their client's particular offense does not represent a violent crime, and second, what the appropriate criteria should be to establish exceptional hardship.

As the chief executive of the U.S. Department of Justice (DOJ), the AG oversees IJs and the BIA; arguably, he can provide guidance as to how discretion should be exercised. In this situation, however, the AG's expression of guidance, or policy, is published in a regulation; it has become law. The heightened standards effectively modify and expand the statute itself; the AG has *changed* what Congress legislated.

In the past few years, several non–American citizens have challenged the regulation on grounds that it is (1) *ultra vires* (it goes outside the scope of the statute), and (2) it is impermissibly vague, arbitrary, and capricious (it sets forth no specific definitions or guidance as to the additional terms).

Others have argued the regulation cannot lawfully be applied retroactively to cases arising before its promulgation. Thus far, these arguments have not been successful in the federal courts; the courts of appeals that have looked at the issue have found that

---

[83] *Matter of Jean*, 23 I&N Dec. 373, at 383 (AG 2002).

the regulation is a valid exercise of the AG's discretionary authority and is not unconstitutionally vague. Nor have the courts found its retroactive application to be unlawful.[84] In addition, the actual *Jean* decision was upheld by the Fifth Circuit U.S. Court of Appeals.[85]

INA §209(c) Waiver for Refugees and Asylees

Individuals who are admitted as refugees to or receive asylum in the United States are eligible to apply for adjustment of status after one year in such status.[86] A refugee or asylee who has been convicted of a crime may apply for a waiver in conjunction with the application for adjustment of status.[87] The waiver is found at INA §209(c) [8 USC §1159(c)] and states (footnotes added):

> (c) The provisions of paragraphs (4), (5), and (7)(A) of section 212(a) shall not be applicable to any alien seeking adjustment of status under this section, and the Secretary of Homeland Security or the Attorney General may waive any other provision of such section (other than paragraph (2)(C)[88] or subparagraph (A),[89] (B),[90] (C),[91] or (E)[92] of paragraph (3)) with respect to such an alien for humanitarian purposes, to assure family unity, or when it is otherwise in the public interest.[93]

---

[84] *Samuels v. Chertoff*, 550 F.3d 252, 258 (2d Cir. 2008); *Perez-Pimentel v. Mukasey*, 530 F.3d 321, 325–26 (5th Cir. 2008); *Mejia v. Gonzales*, 499 F.3d 991, 996 (9th Cir. 2007).

[85] *Jean v. Gonzales*, 452 F.3d 392 (5th Cir. 2006).

[86] Refugees and asylees are defined in chapter one. For additional information on refugee and asylee procedures, including applications for adjustment of status, see D. Collopy, *AILA's Asylum Primer* (AILA 7th Ed. 2015), available from AILA, *http://agora.aila.org*, (800) 982-2839.

[87] According to *Matter of D–K–*, 25 I&N Dec. 761 (BIA 2012), a refugee who has not yet adjusted status and is convicted of crime may be placed in removal proceedings and charged with deportability under INA §237; it is not necessary for DHS to first revoke refugee status, nor is the individual properly charged with inadmissibility under INA §212(a).

[88] Relating to controlled substance traffickers and their immediate family members, including those for whom there is a "reason to believe" that they have been involved in drug trafficking.

[89] Security and related grounds, including export violations.

[90] Terrorist activities.

[91] Foreign policy considerations.

[92] Participants in Nazi persecution or genocide.

[93] When Congress enacted the Refugee Act of 1980 (Pub. L. No. 96-212, 94 Stat. 109, 204(c)(3) (Mar. 17, 1980), it carved out a specific savings clause covering individuals who were paroled into the United States as refugees prior to 1980 and require a waiver of ground of inadmissibility in order to adjust their status to lawful permanent residents. This clause will potentially benefit persons paroled in from "communist" countries, for example, Cuban nationals and former Soviet-Bloc countries who need a waiver for a controlled substance violation that is not trafficking (but goes beyond simple possession of marijuana). The Savings Clause Waiver patterns the INA §209(c) waiver.

Compare with the INA §212(h) Waiver

The waiver at INA §209(c) is more generous than that afforded under INA §212(h) to other adjustment applicants. An individual in refugee or asylee status who applies for adjustment of status does not need to establish hardship to a qualifying relative, as is required at INA §212(h)(1)(B). Section 209(c) is available to waive money laundering, prostitution, alien smuggling convictions, and controlled substance offenses that do not involve drug trafficking, such as simple possession offenses (not only marijuana).

However, based on the AG's decision in *Matter of Jean*,[94] the exercise of favorable discretion in a case involving a violent or dangerous crime requires exceptional and extremely unusual hardship.

Use of INA §209(c) by Certain Lawful Permanent Residents to Avoid Removal

This author has previously opined that an LPR who obtains status initially as an asylee or refugee, and who subsequently commits a crime and is stripped of refugee status, reverts back to the underlying status.[95] According to 8 CFR §207.9, refugee status can *only* be terminated upon a finding that the individual did not qualify as a refugee at the time of admission (usually where the admission was perpetrated by fraud). There follows a procedure for revocation, including notice to the individual and a 30-day period of time to respond that refugee status should not be revoked. A finding of refugee status is a significant and fundamental acknowledgment by the U.S. government that an individual has a well-founded fear of being persecuted in his or her home country. As a refugee, the respondent should be able to reapply for adjustment of status and the INA §209(c) waiver. However, the BIA does not agree with this view, and instead has found that a person who adjusted as a refugee cannot subsequently utilize that same underlying status to readjust.[96]

The same issue applies to individuals who become LPRs after being granted asylee status under INA §208. However, under the regulation at 8 CFR §§208.24, and 1208.24, an asylee's status can be terminated if he or she has been convicted of a particularly serious crime and is a danger to the U.S. community. By statute, an aggravated felony qualifies as a particularly serious crime.[97] Thus, as for refugee status, there is a procedure for termination; unlike refugee status, asylee status can be terminated for conviction of a crime (rather than simply fraud at the time of admission).

---

[94] *Matter of Jean*, 23 I&N Dec. 373 (AG 2002).

[95] *But see* D. Collopy, *AILA's Asylum Primer* (AILA 7th Ed. 2015), available from AILA, http://agora.aila.org, (800) 982-2839.

[96] *Matter of C–J–H–*, 26 I&N Dec. 284 (BIA 2014).

[97] INA §208(b)(2)(B).

Note that an asylee can also have status terminated because of fraud in the initial application, as well as a change in country conditions.[98]

However, case law at the BIA and federal level has rejected the argument that an LPR who loses residency status based on crime reverts back to the foundational asylum or refugee status.

In *Matter of Smriko*,[99] the BIA found that an LPR who was originally admitted to the United States as a refugee was subject to removal proceedings based on convictions for crimes involving moral turpitude. This decision does not address whether the individual could reapply for adjustment of status and a waiver under INA §209(c), but it does note that the respondent is eligible to reapply for asylum and withholding if he continues to fear persecution. One strategy, in light of *Smriko*, would be to apply for adjustment of status with a §209(c) waiver, arguing that the individual continues to be a "refugee" as defined by INA §101(a)(42) until such time as the AG determines he or she no longer merits that status. Note, however, that the Seventh Circuit has specifically rejected this approach in *Gutnick v. Gonzales*,[100] where it reluctantly deferred to the government in holding that refugee status extinguishes upon the grant of adjustment of status, and the waiver under INA §209(c) is thus no longer available. This decision is internally inconsistent in that the IJ determined the respondent was still in danger of persecution—granting withholding of removal—and this finding was not disturbed by the BIA or court of appeals. It would seem that with the finding of persecution in place, there should be no inconsistency in finding that the individual is still a refugee, and thus eligible for the waiver.

The Third and Eighth Circuit U.S. Courts of Appeals have upheld the BIA's decision in *Matter of Smriko*. Likewise, several federal courts have found that an LPR in removal proceedings for crime cannot utilize the 209(c) waiver, even though residency was based on either refugee or asylum status.[101]

Based on *Smriko* and similar federal cases, the government is likely to object to an LPR's filing of a §209(c) waiver in removal proceedings, even with an application for adjustment, asserting that refugee status simply no longer exists. The government is inconsistent in its approach, however. In an unusual twist, DHS has taken the position that LPRs who adjusted from asylee or refugee status are subject to revocation of the underlying status if they travel to their home country (*i.e.*, the country of feared persecution).[102] Indeed, LPRs have been placed in removal proceedings following a trip

---

[98] 8 CFR §§208.24, 1208.24.

[99] *Matter of Smriko*, 23 I&N Dec. 836 (BIA 2005).

[100] *Gutnik v. Gonzales*, 469 F.3d 683 (7th Cir. 2006).

[101] *Robleto-Pastora v. Holder*, 567 F.3d 437, 447 (9th Cir. 2009); *Gutnik v. Gonzales*, 469 F.3d 683, 692 (7th Cir. 2006); *Kholyavskiy v. Mukasey*, 540 F.3d 555, 569 n.16 (7th Cir. 2008).

[102] The position that an LPR is subject to revocation and termination of the underlying asylee/refugee status as a result of returning to the country of persecution is enunciated by a USCIS Fact Sheet, "Traveling Outside the United States as an Asylum Applicant, an Asylee, or a Lawful Permanent Resident

Continued

to the native country, and have had the underlying status terminated. This procedure and policy is inconsistent with a position that the refugee/asylee status is extinguished upon the grant of adjustment.

Asylum and Withholding of Removal

An individual who fears persecution and has been convicted of a crime, either in the United States or abroad, may still be eligible to seek asylum. If an individual is found statutorily ineligible to seek asylum on account of a criminal conviction, he or she may proceed on an application for withholding of removal under the INA. Finally, an individual who fears torture on return to his or her home country may seek protection under the Convention Against Torture (CAT).[103] Protection from persecution is a lengthy and complicated topic that will not be covered in depth here; rather, the following discussion addresses an individual's eligibility for this relief when he or she has a criminal conviction (without addressing eligibility for relief irrespective of the crime).[104]

Asylum

Section 208 of the INA [8 USC §1158] states:

(a) Authority to apply for asylum.—

(1) *In general.*—Any alien who is physically present in the United States or who arrives in the United States ... irrespective of such alien's status, may apply for asylum in accordance with this section or, where applicable, section 235(b).

...

(b) Conditions for granting asylum.—

(1) In general.—

> (A) *Eligibility.*—The Secretary of Homeland Security or the Attorney General may grant asylum to an alien who has applied for asylum in accordance with the requirements and procedures established by the Secretary of Homeland Security or the Attorney General under this section if the Secretary of Homeland Security or the Attorney General determines

---

Who Obtained Such Status Based on Asylum Status" (revised Jan. 4, 2007), *published on* AILA InfoNet at Doc. No. 06122875 (*posted* Dec. 28, 2006).

[103] Convention Against Torture and Other Cruel, Inhuman or Degrading Treatment or Punishment (CAT), Dec. 10, 1984, 1465 U.N.T.S. 85 (entered into force June 26, 1987).

[104] For a detailed discussion on law and procedure in the areas of asylum and withholding, see D. Collopy, *AILA's Asylum Primer* (AILA 7th Ed. 2015), available from AILA, *http://agora.aila.org*, (800) 982-2839.

that such alien is a refugee within the meaning of section 101(a)(42)(A).[105]

Under §208 of the Act [8 USC §1158], an individual who has been convicted of a crime may in some cases still receive asylum, thereby defeating removal if he or she is in removal proceedings. The law states that an individual who has been convicted of a "particularly serious crime" and who "constitutes a danger to the community of the United States" as a result of that crime is barred from asylum.[106] An aggravated felony offense is per se a particularly serious crime.[107] An offense that is not an aggravated felony may nonetheless be considered a particularly serious crime.[108]

For non-aggravated felony offenses, the AG may designate by regulation offenses that are considered to be particularly serious. The regulations do not at this time contain a definition of "particularly serious crime." Thus, an individual who has been convicted of a non-aggravated felony offense may apply for asylum, and the IJ must determine based on certain criteria whether the crime qualifies as "particularly serious."

The BIA has set forth criteria for determining whether a crime is particularly serious.[109] The criteria include: (1) the nature of the conviction; (2) the circumstances and underlying facts of the conviction; (3) the type of sentence imposed; and (4) whether the type and circumstances of the crime indicate the applicant is a danger to the community.

In addition to statutory eligibility, asylum is a discretionary benefit[110] that can be denied based on a criminal conviction or suspected criminal activity. In the event of a finding of persecution, but a discretionary denial, the individual should be eligible for withholding, discussed immediately below.

Withholding of or Restriction on Removal Under the INA

Both asylum and withholding of removal provide protection for an individual who fears persecution. The distinction between withholding of removal and asylum is that withholding is *not* discretionary. If an individual establishes that he or she will be persecuted, withholding must be granted notwithstanding adverse discretionary considerations. Withholding carries a higher burden of proof in terms of establishing the

---

[105] INA §101(a)(42)(A) [8 USC §1101(a)(42)(A)] defines "refugee" as an individual who is unable or unwilling to return to a country because of persecution or a well-founded fear of persecution on account of race, religion, nationality, membership in a particular social group, or political opinion.

[106] INA §208(b)(2)(A)(ii); 8 USC §1108(b)(2)(A)(ii).

[107] INA §208(b)(2)(B)(i); 8 USC §1108(b)(2)(B)(i).

[108] *Nethagani v. Mukasey*, 532 F.3d 150, 156 (2d Cir. 2008).

[109] *Matter of Frentescu*, 18 I&N Dec. 244, 247 (BIA 1982), *modified in Matter of C–*, 20 I&N Dec. 529 (BIA 1992).

[110] INA §208(b)(1)(A); 8 USC §1108(b)(1)(A).

likelihood of persecution,[111] and withholding does not lead to LPR status (as asylum can). Thus, in most cases, asylum is not only a superior form of relief, it carries a lower evidentiary burden.

However, an individual with a criminal conviction may be denied asylum in the exercise of discretion, and an individual with an aggravated felony conviction[112] is definitively barred from receiving asylum. In this situation, an individual who fears persecution should apply for withholding of removal as an alternative to asylum. Withholding of, or restriction on, removal is found at INA §241(b)(3) [8 USC §1231(b)(3)], which states:

> (A) In general.— ... [T]he Attorney General may not remove an alien to a country if the Attorney General decides that the alien's life or freedom would be threatened in that country because of the alien's race, religion, nationality, membership in a particular social group, or political opinion.

Defining the "particularly serious crime"

Pursuant to INA §241(b)(3)(B)(ii) [8 USC §1231(b)(3)(B)(ii)], an individual who, having been convicted of a particularly serious crime, is a danger to the community of the United States cannot receive withholding. This is the same language utilized in the asylum bar. However, the application of the "particularly serious crime" prohibition is different in the context of withholding because an aggravated felony offense is not a per se bar to withholding. The withholding provision states that an individual who has been convicted of an aggravated felony—or felonies—for which an aggregate term of imprisonment of at least five years is imposed will be considered to have committed a particularly serious crime. This provision further states that the AG is not precluded from denying withholding even though an individual received a sentence of less than five years.[113]

In the combined cases of *Matter of Y–L, A–G–, & R–S–R–*,[114] the AG interpreted the above statutory phrase, regarding aggravated felony offenses for which a sentence of less than five years is imposed, in the context of drug trafficking offenses. The AG held that drug trafficking offenses are presumed to be per se particularly serious crimes, even if a sentence of less than five years is imposed, unless "extraordinary and compelling circumstances" are present. To overcome the presumption, the appli-

---

[111] *INS v. Cardoza-Fonseca*, 480 U.S. 421, at 423–24 (1987) (emphasis added). The Court explained, "In *INS v. Stevic*, 467 U.S. 407 (1984), we held that to qualify for this entitlement to withholding of deportation, an alien must demonstrate that 'it is *more likely than not* that the alien would be subject to persecution' in the country to which he would be returned .... Congress used different, broader language to define the term 'refugee' as used in §208(a) than it used to describe the class of aliens who have a right to withholding of deportation under §243(h)."

[112] *See* chapter seven.

[113] INA §241(b)(3)(B); 8 USC §241(b)(3).

[114] *Matter of Y–L, A–G–, & R–S–R–*, 23 I&N Dec. 270 (AG 2002).

cant must establish that he or she had a minor role in the offense, a small amount of drugs was involved, no violence was involved, the offense did not involve organized crime or terrorism, and no juveniles were harmed.[115]

In other types of offenses, the analysis for determining whether a non-aggravated felony offense is a particularly serious crime is similar to that utilized in the asylum context.[116] However, the two statutory provisions, asylum and withholding, are written differently because of the dangerousness language as well as the five-year sentence-served language. Defense counsel should argue that because Congress chose different phraseology, the bar to withholding is distinct and in fact higher than asylum. The two bars, in other words, are not precise counterparts.[117] Again, withholding of removal carries a "dangerousness" component, implying that the crime, to be particularly serious, must involve danger or harm to victims, normally persons. In a position contrary to the BIA, the Third Circuit has stated that for purposes of withholding, the crime must be an aggravated felony.[118] The BIA has stated that the determination of whether a non-aggravated felony offense (or an aggravated felony offense for which the term of imprisonment imposed was less than five years) is a particularly serious crime is made on a case-by-case basis, with a view of the individual facts of the case, including specific circumstances as well as the charges and sentence.[119] Moreover, an individual is entitled to a hearing on whether the crime is particularly serious.[120] By way of example, the following offenses have been discussed by the federal courts and BIA:

- Three convictions for driving under the influence (DUI) did not qualify as particularly serious crimes.[121]
- Sexual abuse of a minor held to be a particularly serious crime.[122]
- Reckless endangerment by shooting a pistol into air is particularly serious.[123]
- Menacing by use of a deadly weapon is a particularly serious crime.[124]

---

[115] *Matter of Y–L, A–G–, & R–S–R–*, 23 I&N Dec. 270 (AG 2002).

[116] *Matter of Frentescu,* 18 I&N Dec. 244 (BIA 1982).

[117] For an example of this argument, see the excerpt included as Appendix 10C.

[118] *Alaka v. Att'y Gen.*, 456 F.3d 88 (3d Cir. 2006).

[119] *Matter of N–A–M–*, 24 I&N Dec. 336 (BIA 2007).

[120] *Matter of G–G–S–*, 26 I&N Dec. 339 (BIA 2014).

[121] *Delgado v. Holder*, 563 F.3d 863 (9th Cir. 2009) (Note that the particularly serious crime analysis was made in the context of an application for asylum; the court found that it did not have jurisdiction to consider whether the AG was correct in finding a crime to be particularly serious in the withholding context, because this determination is entirely within the discretion of the AG.)

[122] *Lovan v. Holder*, 574 F.3d 990 (8th Cir. 2009).

[123] *Nethagani v. Mukasey,* 532 F.3d 150 (2d Cir. 2008).

[124] *Matter of N–A–M–*, 24 I&N Dec. 336 (BIA 2007).

- Violent destruction of property, assault on citizens, found to be particularly serious.[125]

The reader will note that the Third Circuit has ruled that an offense must be an aggravated felony in order to be a "particularly serious crime."[126] Most courts of appeals have found they do not have jurisdiction to question the BIA's determination that an offense is particularly serious, based on the fact that the BIA has set forth standards for review and it qualifies as a type of discretionary determination.[127]

Withholding and Deferral Under the Convention Against Torture

The Convention Against Torture (CAT) is a treaty governed by international law; its provisions are not found in the INA. The United States is a signatory, and the provisions are implemented via the regulations at 8 CFR §§208.16–18, 1208.16–18. The CAT provides protection to persons who face torture by their government, or a government actor, in the proposed country of removal. There are two forms of protection under the CAT: withholding of removal and deferral of removal. Both forms of relief require the applicant to establish that he or she would be tortured in the country of removal. Unlike asylum and withholding under the INA, protection under the CAT is available only where the entity inflicting the torture is the government, or a group or individual acting under the auspices of, and with the consent of, the government. In comparison, asylum and statutory withholding may be granted in cases where the persecutor is a group or individual outside of the government's control, or whom the government is unwilling to control.

Under 8 CFR §§208.16(c), 1208.16(c), an adjudicator is first to determine whether the applicant "more likely than not" would be tortured in the proposed country of removal. If it is determined that the individual has met this burden and does face torture, either withholding or deferral will be granted. An individual who has been convicted of a particularly serious crime will be denied withholding and instead granted deferral.

Deferral of removal under the CAT is thus the last chance for an individual with a serious criminal conviction who fears harm on return to his or her country to remain in the United States. Deferral of removal under the CAT is mandatory where the burden of proof has been met, regardless of the person's criminal record. However, although the individual will avoid deportation (and torture), deferral is not a panacea: a deferral recipient is not eligible to apply for permanent residency after one year (unlike someone granted asylum), and may be indefinitely detained by the government. Deferral status can be terminated, and the individual returned, if it is determined that conditions have changed and the protection is no longer necessary.[128]

---

[125] *INS v. Aguirre-Aguirre*, 526 U.S. 415 (1999) (This case addresses the meaning of a "nonpolitical crime.")

[126] *Alaka v. Att'y Gen.*, 456 F.3d 88, 104–05 (3d Cir. 2006).

[127] *See, e.g., Lovan v. Holder*, 574 F.3d 990 (8th Cir. 2009).

[128] 8 CFR §§208.17, 1208.17.

Cancellation of Removal

Cancellation of removal under INA §240A(a) [8 USC §1229b(a)] is the most common waiver for LPRs facing removal proceedings for a criminal conviction or convictions. It is not a waiver for nonimmigrants; it is available only to individuals lawfully admitted for permanent residence. Cancellation of removal of a permanent resident, discussed here, should not be confused with cancellation of removal of a non–permanent resident; the latter is *not* a criminal-alien waiver, but an application through which an undocumented individual, if successful, adjusts to LPR status based on 10 or more years of continuous physical presence in the United States.[129]

In a sense, LPR cancellation of removal is the replacement provision for the INA §212(c) waiver, discussed later. The waiver under INA §212(c) [8 USC §1182] was repealed by IIRAIRA; cancellation of removal instead was added to the statute. However, cancellation of removal is more limited in its availability.

INA §240A(a) [8 USC §1229b(a)] states:

(a) Cancellation of Removal for Certain Permanent Residents.—The Attorney General may cancel removal in the case of an alien who is inadmissible or deportable from the United States if the alien—

(1) has been an alien lawfully admitted for permanent residence for not less than 5 years,

(2) has resided in the United States continuously for 7 years after having been admitted in any status, and

(3) has not been convicted of any aggravated felony.

Continuous Residence Versus Lawful Permanent Resident Status

It is important to distinguish between the required seven years of continuous residence and the five years of permanent resident status. The seven years of continuous residence commences after any lawful admission and will normally (although not always) toll upon commission of the criminal act; as discussed below, where the criminal act does not toll the seven-year "clock," service of an NTA will. In comparison, the five years of lawful permanent resident status does not toll until the entry of a final administrative decision.[130]

Residence Cannot Be Imputed to Minor Children Living Abroad

The BIA has consistently ruled that a parent's lawful permanent resident status and residence in the United States cannot be imputed to an unemancipated minor for

---

[129] Cancellation of removal of a nonpermanent resident replaces the pre-IIRAIRA suspension of deportation law. Cancellation of removal of a non–permanent resident is found at INA §240A(b) [8 USC §1229b(b)].

[130] According to 8 CFR §1.1(p), permanent resident status does not terminate until the entry of a final administrative order of exclusion, deportation, or removal.

purposes of establishing the child's eligibility for cancellation of removal under INA §240A(a). [131]

Defining "Admission"

The period of seven years of continuous residence does not have to be a continuously *lawful* residence in the immigration context; as long as the initial admission was lawful (for example, entry with a tourist visa), the fact that the individual falls out of lawful status before becoming an LPR is not material.[132] Not every lawful entry will qualify as an admission. For example, in *Matter of Reza-Murillo*,[133] the Board found that the grant of family unity benefits (a benefit given while in the United States to the spouse or children of legalized aliens)[134] does not qualify as an "admission" to meet the seven-year residence requirement for cancellation purposes. The U.S. Ninth Circuit Court of Appeals, however, has held the opposite: acceptance into the family unity program qualifies as an "admission in any status" for purposes of cancellation of removal.[135] The Ninth Circuit has also found that parole into special immigrant juvenile status under INA §245(h)[136] qualifies as a lawful admission for cancellation purposes.[137] And, the Ninth Circuit holds that a parent or guardian's lawful residence may be imputed to a minor child.[138]

For the commission of a criminal offense to toll the accumulation of continuous residence, the crime must be one that makes the person inadmissible under INA §212(a) [8 USC §1182(a)]. An act that renders the person deportable under INA §237 [8 USC §1227] (the section on deportability), but not inadmissible under INA §212(a), does not toll continuous residence.[139] The most common example of this principle involves a firearms offense, which does not form a ground of inadmissibility, but does form the basis of deportability.

Accordingly, continuous residence does not toll for a firearms offense. Another example would involve deportability under INA §237(a)(2)(E), for a domestic violence-type offense, which includes violations of protective orders. Section

---

[131] *Matter of Montoya-Silva*, 26 I&N Dec. 123 (BIA 2013), *affirming Matter of Escobar*, 24 I&N Dec. 231 (BIA 2007); and *Matter of Ramirez-Vargas*, 24 I&N Dec. 599 (BIA 2008).

[132] *Matter of Blancas-Lara*, 23 I&N Dec. 458 (BIA 2002); *Matter of Perez*, 22 I&N Dec. 689 (BIA 1999).

[133] *Matter of Reza-Murillo*, 25 I&N Dec. 296 (BIA 2010).

[134] 8 CFR §236.12.

[135] *Garcia-Quintero v. Gonzales*, 455 F.3d 1006, 1009 (9th Cir. 2006).

[136] 8 USC §1255(h)(1). A special immigrant juvenile is a juvenile who files a self petition and is deemed abandoned or neglected in the United States, following a dependency adjudication by a state or county court. *See:* INA §101(a)(27)(J); 8 USC §1101(a)(27)(J).

[137] *Garcia v. Holder*, 659 F.3d 1261 (9th Cir. 2011).

[138] *Cuevas-Gaspar v. Gonzales*, 430 F.3d 1013, 1029 (9th Cir. 2005).

[139] *Matter of Campos-Torres*, 22 I&N Dec. 1289 (BIA 2000).

237(a)(2)(E) does not have a counterpart at §212(a); accordingly, if someone is deportable for an enumerated offense, but that crime does not form the underlying basis of a charge of inadmissibility (such as simple misdemeanor battery), the offense will not toll the time.

Yet another example is where an individual is deportable for two or more crimes involving moral turpitude, but the first crime falls under the petty-offense exception, thereby creating a situation where the first offense does not render the person inadmissible under INA §212(a)(2), and consequently does not stop the clock. This factual scenario was analyzed by the BIA in *Matter of Deanda-Romo*;[140] it sets forth a good example of the "stop time" rule.

In *Deanda-Romo*, the respondent was admitted to the United States as an LPR in January 1992. In September 1999, he was convicted under Texas law of two separate incidents of misdemeanor assault with bodily injury to his spouse. The first incident occurred on October 30, 1998, when the respondent had approximately six and a half years of continuous residency. The second incident occurred on June 20, 1999, when the respondent had approximately seven and a half years of continuous residency. He was charged in removal proceedings with deportability under INA §237(a)(2)(A)(ii) [8 USC §1227(a)(2)(A)(ii)] for multiple crimes of moral turpitude. The respondent requested relief in the form of cancellation of removal, but the IJ pretermitted, finding that he was statutorily ineligible for this relief because of the "stop-time" rule. The BIA disagreed, holding that the first incident, in October 1998, fell under the petty-offense exception at INA §212(a)(2)(A)(i)(II); standing alone, it did not render the respondent inadmissible under INA §212(a)(2). Accordingly, the accrual of continuous residency for purposes of cancellation of removal did not toll until commission of the second offense, when the respondent had more than seven years of residency in the United States.

Where the commission of a criminal act does not render the person inadmissible, and therefore does not toll continuous residence, it is service of the NTA on the individual that tolls the period of continuous residence. The rules regarding termination of continuous residence are spelled out in the statute at INA §240A(d) [8 USC §§1229b, (d)], which states (in pertinent part, with emphasis added):

(1) Termination of continuous period.—For purposes of this section, any period of continuous residence ... shall be deemed to end

(A) ... when the alien is served a notice to appear under section 239(a), or

(B) when the alien has committed an offense *referred to in section 212(a)(2)* that renders the alien inadmissible to the United States under section 212(a)(2) or removable from the United States under section 237(a)(2) or 237(a)(4), whichever is earliest.

---

[140] *Matter of Deanda-Romo*, 23 I&N Dec. 597 (BIA 2003).

The BIA has held that the "stop-time" rule under INA § 240A(d)(1) is retroactive and thus can be applied to criminal conduct occurring before April 1, 1997, the effective date of the 1996 Illegal Immigration Reform and Immigrant Responsibility Act (IIRAIRA).[141] However, in a recent decision the Seventh Circuit went the opposite way and held that the "stop-time" rule cannot be retroactively applied to criminal conduct predating April 1997.[142] The Seventh Circuit heavily relied on the Supreme Court's 2012 decision in *Vartelas v. Holder*, which held that IIRAIRA's new definition of "admission" as relating to LPRs with pre-IIRAIRA criminal conduct is not retroactive.[143] It is possible that the BIA may abrogate its prior precedent on the stop-time rule based on *Vartelas*. Even if this does not happen, other circuits may be persuaded by the Seventh Circuit's opinion.[144]

Offense need not be charged in removal proceedings to stop the time

In a 2007 decision, the BIA ruled that a respondent need not be charged and found inadmissible or deportable in removal proceedings for an offense to "stop the time" for cancellation purposes. In *Matter of Jurado-Delgado*,[145] the respondent was admitted to LPR status on September 5, 1985. In 1991, he was convicted of retail theft; in 1992, he was convicted of unsworn testimony to authorities; and in 1997, he was convicted of two additional crimes involving moral turpitude. In removal proceedings, the respondent was charged as removable only for the 1997 convictions. However, ICE took the position that the earlier 1991 and 1992 offenses for crimes involving moral turpitude tolled the time.

The IJ ruled that the respondent was eligible for cancellation because the offenses were not charged in removal proceedings; the BIA disagreed, finding that offenses can "be described at" INA §212(a)(2), and not necessarily charged in the NTA. The BIA found that the earlier offenses did indeed toll the time and the respondent was ineligible for cancellation of removal. In an unpublished decision, the court of appeals upheld the BIA's interpretation of the statute, affirming that an offense that is not charged in the NTA can nevertheless toll the time for cancellation purposes.[146] This combination of decisions is disappointing. The statute refers to offenses that render an individual inadmissible; if there is no litigation of inadmissibility, it is incongruent that the particular underlying offense should pose an impediment to relief.

---

[141] *Matter of Robles-Urrea*, 24 I&N Dec. 22 (BIA 2006).

[142] *Jeudy v. Holder*, 768 F.3d 595 (7th Cir. 2014).

[143] *Vartelas v. Holder,* 132 S. Ct. 1479 (2012).

[144] The Fourth Circuit U.S. Court of Appeals followed suit in *Jaghoori v. Holder*, 772 F.3d 764 (4th Cir. 2014).

[145] *Matter of Jurado-Delgado*, 24 I&N Dec. 29 (BIA 2006); *rev. den. Jurado-Delgado v. Att'y Gen.*, No. 06-4495/07-1924, 2009 U.S. App. LEXIS 742 (3d Cir., Jan. 15, 2009).

[146] *Jurado-Delgado v. Att'y Gen.,* No. 06-4495/07-1924, 2009 U.S. App. LEXIS 742 (3d Cir. Jan. 15, 2009).

Within the context of a full hearing on removability, there are legal goalposts that act as safeguards to ensure a just and accurate determination. These include, for example, the definition of "conviction," the burden of proof, and the proper classification of the crime based on a categorical approach. The *Jurado-Delgado* decision opens the door to abuse in that an individual may be found ineligible for relief based on a finding of inadmissibility, without a full hearing on all relevant legal issues. However, this situation (where an underlying offense is not charged in removal proceedings) is probably rare.

The Requirement of a Lawful Admission

Section 240A(a) of the INA has a criterion that the applicant be lawfully admitted for permanent residence. In *Matter of Koloamatangi*,[147] the BIA interpreted the adjective "lawfully" to require that the original admission to LPR status have been lawful. In other words, where an individual obtains residency through fraud or misrepresentation, the status is not lawful and the individual is not eligible for cancellation of removal. *Koloamatangi* involved an individual who obtained residency through marriage to a U.S. citizen while he was knowingly married to another woman. (It is not clear from the decision whether he later was convicted of crime, or whether the charge in removal proceedings stemmed from the original fraud/bigamy itself.)

The BIA cited a litany of INA §212(c) cases predating the Antiterrorism and Effective Death Penalty Act of 1996 (AEDPA),[148] in which the same philosophy regarding lawful admission to permanent residence was used to pretermit §212(c) waiver applications. The BIA ruled that Koloamatangi was not eligible for cancellation of removal under INA §240A(a) because he was never originally lawfully admitted to permanent resident status.

This problematic situation (is the client *really* an LPR?) may arise in various scenarios. For example, suppose the client was convicted of a crime prior to becoming an LPR, and did not admit the offense at the time of obtaining residency. Later, when he or she returns from a trip abroad, this earlier crime comes up in an inspections database, and the client is questioned regarding the conviction and whether it was admitted (and, if applicable, waived) during the residency process. A second example may involve a client with two or more crimes. The client is convicted of one offense before becoming an LPR, and is convicted of another after becoming an LPR. He or she is will be snagged at some point by DHS because of the second crime and placed in removal proceedings. During the removal case, the first conviction also comes to light, and the validity of the permanent residence status is called into question.

Finally, in a third scenario, the reason why LPR status is not legitimate may have nothing to do with crime, but rather be immigration-related; this would be the case, for

---

[147] *Matter of Koloamatangi*, 23 I&N Dec. 548 (BIA 2003).
[148] Antiterrorism and Effective Death Penalty Act of 1996 (AEDPA), Pub. L. No. 104-132, 110 Stat. 1214.

example, where an individual becomes an LPR through fraudulent means (*e.g.*, a non–bona fide marriage) and is later placed in removal proceedings on account of crime. Through a series of questions and investigation, the illegal nature of the grant of permanent resident status comes to light and results in a finding, essentially, that the individual never actually became a lawful permanent resident. ICE counsel may argue the client is ineligible for cancellation of removal.

> **Tip**: At the initial consultation, counsel should ask the client how he or she became a permanent resident, check the classification on the card, and conduct further investigation if appropriate.

This author does not agree with the BIA's decision in *Koloamatangi*, especially since cancellation of removal can also waive the fraud and misrepresentation grounds of removal. It is notable, however, that the BIA did allow the respondent in that case to apply for a waiver under INA §237(a)(1)(H)—which may be a viable option in other cases where the LPR is found not to be an LPR after all. Another option for the arriving foreign national or LPR may be concurrent waivers under INA §§212(h) and 212(i). In the end, the IJ may require readjustment to permanent resident status combined with the appropriate waiver.

Individuals Who Are Ineligible for Cancellation

Section 240A(a) of the INA [8 USC §1229b(a)] is broadly written to include all permanent residents (with the requisite years of residency) who are inadmissible or deportable, as long as they do not have aggravated felony convictions. However, INA §240A(c) [8 USC §1229b(c)] contains limits on this relief for certain categories of persons. The following individuals are not eligible for cancellation of removal:

- An individual who is inadmissible under INA §212(a)(3) or deportable under INA §237(a)(4) (relating to security grounds, including export violations);
- An individual who is described in INA §241(b)(3)(B)(i) (an individual who has ordered, incited, or assisted in the persecution of others); and
- An individual who has previously received relief from deportation or removal in the form of suspension of deportation, cancellation of removal, or a waiver under INA §212(c).

Combining waivers

The issue of combining other waivers with cancellation arises where cancellation may cure one or more grounds of removability, but not all, thereby not acting as complete relief. One example may be where the respondent has an aggravated felony offense that could be waived through a pre-AEDPA §212(c) waiver; another example may be where one offense occurred prior to the accumulation of seven years of ongoing residency, but this offense could be waived by §212(h).

In terms of combining cancellation with the §212(c) waiver, several courts of appeals have found that these forms of relief cannot be combined based on the language at INA §240A(c), cited immediately above, which holds that an individual who has "previously received" relief in the form of suspension, cancellation, or 212(c) is ineligible. Individuals have argued that applying for the §212(c) waiver in conjunction with cancellation does not qualify as "previously received," because the waivers are being requested simultaneously, as opposed to one being previously received. The courts have thus far rejected this argument.[149] However, the point is worth arguing, as demonstrated by the dissent in one recent case.[150]

A previous grant of a waiver under INA §212(h) is not specifically named as a barring element at INA §240A(c). However, as a practical matter, the combination of these two forms of relief will not work. If a waiver under INA §212(h) is sought to cure removability for an offense that precedes the accumulation of seven years' residence, the government and court are likely to take the position that the offense nonetheless tolls the time.

In *Matter of Bustamante*,[151] the BIA held that a waiver under INA §212(h) may not be stacked with cancellation of removal to overcome a ground of inadmissibility caused by a moral turpitude crime. Although the individual in this case sought cancellation of removal of a non-permanent resident under INA §240A(b) (10-year residency), the same theory would hold true in the LPR cancellation-of-removal context (§240A(a)) if it were sought to remove a crime that tolls continuous residency before the seven-year mark.

Special Rule for Battered Spouses

As noted earlier, the INA contains a provision for the cancellation of removal of non–permanent residents based on their length of continuous physical presence (at least 10 years) and other outstanding equities. Within the canopy of cancellation of removal for the non-permanent resident, which is not a criminal offense waiver, there is a special provision for the cancellation of removal and adjustment to permanent resident status of certain battered spouses and children.[152] This provision covers U.S. citizens' or LPRs' spouses and children who have been battered or subject to extreme cruelty in the relationship. Battered and abused spouses and children need establish only three years of continuous physical presence (as contrasted with 10 years for other individuals).

Moreover, there may be certain situations where an individual (a battered or abused spouse or child) who has been convicted of a crime can utilize this provision. According to INA §§240A(b)(2)(A) and (C) [8 USC §§1229a(b)(2)(A) and (C)], the spouse or child of an American citizen or LPR—physically present in the United States for at least three years—who has been battered or subject to extreme cruelty

---

[149] *Garcia Jimenez v. Gonzales*, 488 F.3d 1082 (9th Cir. 2007), *citing Munoz-Yepez v. Gonzales*, 465 F.3d 347 (8th Cir. 2006). *See also Peralta-Taveras v. Gonzales*, 488 F.3d 580 (2d Cir. 2007).

[150] *See* dissent in *Garcia-Jimenez*, 488 F.3d at 1087.

[151] *Matter of Bustamante*, 25 I&N Dec. 564 (BIA 2011).

[152] INA §240A(b)(2); 8 USC §1229b(b)(2).

may still receive cancellation of removal (and thereby adjustment of status to LPR), notwithstanding a criminal conviction, if there is a determination that the crime:

- Involved an act of self-defense;
- Involved the violation of a protection order that was issued for the protection of the applicant; or,
- The crime did not result in serious bodily injury and there was a connection between the crime and the applicant having been battered or subjected to extreme cruelty.

In making such a determination, the IJ must consider any credible evidence relevant to the application.[153]

Thus, INA §240A(b), which, again, is not specifically intended as a waiver for persons deportable for crime, may be utilized by an LPR or nonresident who faces removal for a crime if he or she has been subject to significant abuse, and where there exists a connection between the crime and the abusive relationship.

Special Rule Cancellation of Removal: NACARA §203

Prior to changes made by IIRAIRA, the INA contained a provision entitled "suspension of deportation."[154] This provision entitled a non–lawful permanent resident who had been physically present in the United States for at least seven years (coupled with good moral character) to apply for residency in front of an IJ. Suspension required a showing of extreme hardship to a qualifying immediate family member or to the applicant (or both). In addition, there was a "10-year suspension" available to persons deportable for crime. These persons could qualify if 10 years had passed since commission of the offense, contingent upon a showing of exceptional and extremely unusual hardship to a qualifying family member, or to the person him- or herself.

Suspension of deportation was repealed by IIRAIRA. However, Congress revived the core aspects of suspension of deportation for certain classes of persons by section 203 of NACARA.[155] This benefit is known as "special rule" cancellation of removal.

NACARA §203 is essentially a residency program for qualified individuals from the former Soviet Union, El Salvador, and Guatemala. Normally, this refugee-type program would not be included in a criminal immigration law discussion. However, the 10-year special rule cancellation of removal can be useful to the non-permanent resident who is deportable or inadmissible for crime and who is not otherwise eligible for adjustment. If an individual is eligible, 10-year cancellation is more generous than adjustment of status with an INA §212(h) waiver. This discussion does not cover

---

[153] INA §237(a)(7); 8 USC §1227(a)(7).

[154] Suspension was found at INA §244(a).

[155] NACARA, Pub. L. No. 105-100, tit. II, §203(b), 111 Stat. 2160, 2198–99 (1997).

special rule cancellation for non-criminals, but rather sets forth the basic requirements for qualified applicants removable for crime.

Eligibility requirements are set forth at 8 CFR §§240.66 and 1240.66. A qualified individual will either be Guatemalan, Salvadoran, or from a former Soviet-bloc country. A Guatemalan either must have entered the United States on or before October 1, 1990, be a registered "*ABC* class member,"[156] or have filed for asylum on or before April 1, 1990.[157] A Salvadoran must have entered the United States on or before September 19, 1990, filed an *ABC* or TPS registration by October 31, 1991, or filed for asylum on or before April 1, 1990.[158] A former Soviet bloc national must have entered the United States on or before December 31, 1990, and filed for asylum by December 31, 1991.[159]

A qualified individual who is inadmissible or deportable on criminal-related grounds is eligible for special rule cancellation of removal as long as he or she does not have an aggravated felony conviction.[160] This means that special rule cancellation of removal, if granted, waives—for example—a simple possession of cocaine conviction or other controlled substance offense that is not an aggravated felony.

However, to waive a criminal conviction, the qualified applicant must have at least 10 years of continuous physical presence immediately following the commission of an act or assumption of status constituting a ground of removal.[161] During these 10 years or more, the applicant must show good moral character.[162] Also, the applicant must show exceptional and extremely unusual hardship to a qualifying family member or to him- or herself in the event of deportation.[163] It is noted, within this regard, that the regulations contain a built-in presumption of extreme hardship for Guatemalans and Salvadorans.[164] Thus, two-thirds of the burden—so to speak— already has been met in establishing the exceptional hardship.

---

[156] *ABC* is a reference to *American Baptist Churches v. Thornburgh*, 760 F. Supp. 796 (N.D. Cal. 1991). "*ABC* class member" refers to: (1) any Guatemalan national who first entered the United States on or before October 1, 1990; and (2) any Salvadoran national who first entered the United States on or before September 19, 1990. "Registered *ABC* class member" means an *ABC* class member who: (1) in the case of an *ABC* class member who is a national of El Salvador, properly submitted an *ABC* registration form to USCIS on or before October 31, 1991, or applied for temporary protected status on or before October 31, 1991; or (2) in the case of an *ABC* class member who is a national of Guatemala, properly submitted an *ABC* registration form to USCIS on or before December 31, 1991. See 8 CFR §§240.60, 1240.60.

[157] *See* 8 CFR §§240.66(c), 1240.66(c) (referencing 8 CFR §§240.61, 1240.61).

[158] 8 CFR §§240.66(c), 1240.66(c).

[159] 8 CFR §§240.66(c), 1240.66(c).

[160] 8 CFR §§240.66(c)(1), 1240.66(c)(1).

[161] 8 CFR §§240.66(c)(2), 1240.66(c)(2).

[162] 8 CFR §§240.66(c)(3), 1240.66(c)(3). Good moral character is defined at INA §101(f).

[163] 8 CFR §§240.66(c)(4), 1240.66(c)(4).

[164] 8 CFR §§240.64(d), 1240.64(d).

> **Example**: Maria is a national of Guatemala who entered the United States without inspection in 1989, fleeing violence related to the civil war in that country. She applied for asylum in January 1990. The application was left pending and she received a work permit as an *ABC* class member. In the year 2000, she was convicted of simple possession of cocaine. In 2009, she applied for cancellation of removal under NACARA §203 with her local Asylum Office. The application is denied because she does not have "good moral character" because of that cocaine conviction. The Asylum Office issues an NTA placing her in removal proceedings. It is now 2012 and Maria is in front of the IJ. She reapplies for special rule cancellation of removal because 10 years have passed since commission of the crime of possession of cocaine. Maria establishes exceptional and unusual hardship to family members and is granted relief, becoming an LPR of the United States.

Finally, it is noted that applicants for special rule cancellation under NACARA §203 are not subject to reinstatement of removal if they have re-entered unlawfully following a prior deportation or exclusion from the United States.[165] However, the removal and re-entry would have to have taken place prior to the NACARA §203 eligibility date.

The Waiver That Keeps Giving: INA §212(c) (repealed 1996)

Overview of Eligibility Criteria for §212(c) Waiver

- Repealed as of April 1, 1997—with limited exceptions applies only to pre-April 1, 1997 convictions.
- For convictions after April 24, 1996 (and before April 1, 1997), only waives moral turpitude crimes.
- Applicant must have been lawfully (legally) admitted to LPR status. This is a waiver for lawful permanent residents—not nonimmigrants.
- Applicant will have at least seven years of continuous LPR status at the time of filing; accumulation of years does not toll until entry of final administrative order of removal.
- Cannot have served more than five years in prison for an aggravated felony or combination of aggravated felony convictions entered between November 29, 1990 and April 24, 1996.
- Cures all grounds of removability (inadmissibility and deportability) except INA §§212(a)(3)(A), (B), (C), (E). or (10)(C).
- Convictions may be by plea or verdict.

---

[165] 8 CFR §§241.8(d), 1241.8(d).

- Persons in exclusion proceedings, or deportation proceedings pre-April 24, 1996 (*e.g.*, have an old Order to Show Cause) are not affected by the AEDPA bar or the IIRAIRA repeal.

Introduction

Prior to IIRAIRA and the introduction of cancellation of removal (INA §240A(a)), the long-standing waiver for LPRs convicted of crime was Advance Permission to Return to Unrelinquished Domicile under INA §212(c) [8 USC §1182(c)].[166] This waiver was significantly restricted in April 1996 by AEDPA,[167] and then repealed altogether by IIRAIRA in September 1996.[168] This waiver for LPRs removable for crime was replaced with cancellation of removal, discussed above. However, the two forms of relief are distinct, as cancellation is more restrictive in eligibility criteria and the breadth of relief it offers. Persons with convictions that pre-date the restrictions and subsequent repeal may still take advantage of the more generous §212(c) waiver, as discussed in this section.

Following the 1996 legislation, the BIA struggled with whether the restrictions imposed by AEDPA were retroactive provisions. One question was whether the waiver was available to persons in proceedings pending on the April 24, 1996; a separate question was whether persons with pre-AEDPA convictions would be barred from the relief. In 2001, the Supreme Court ruled that a waiver under former §212(c) remains available to LPRs who were convicted prior to April 24, 1996.[169] The *St. Cyr* decision was not clear as to whether the retroactivity analysis only applied to pleas, or all types of convictions. In autumn 2004, DOJ [through its Executive Office for Immigration Review (EOIR)] published a long-awaited regulation implementing the Supreme Court's decision.[170] This rule restricted *St. Cyr* to convictions by plea, and also implemented a comparable grounds test, requiring that persons in deportation-track (INA §237) proceedings may only utilize the waiver if a comparable ground could be found in the section on inadmissibility (INA §212(a)).

In 2011, the Supreme Court issued a decision in *Judulang v. Holder*,[171] rejecting the BIA's comparable grounds rule and requiring the BIA to implement a rule that more soundly promoted the purpose of the law.

---

[166] Note the §212(c) waiver is available only to LPRs; it is not a nonimmigrant waiver.

[167] Anti-Terrorist and Effective Death Penalty Act (AEDPA), Pub. L. No. 104-132, §440(d), 110 Stat. 1214, 1277.

[168] IIRAIRA, Pub. L. No. 104-208, div. C, §304(b), 110 Stat. 3009, 3009-597.

[169] *INS v. St. Cyr*, 533 U.S. 289 (2001); *see also Matter of Abdelghany*, 26 I&N Dec. 254 (BIA 2014).

[170] 69 Fed. Reg. 57826 (Sept. 28, 2004).

[171] *Judulang v. Holder*, 132 S. Ct. 476, 490 (2011); this decision invalidated the BIA's precedents applying the statutory counterpart rule as "arbitrary" and "capricious," leaving to the BIA to "devise another, equally economical policy respecting eligibility for §212(c) relief."

In February 2014, the BIA issued a decision in *Matter of Abdelghany* [172] regarding eligibility for §212(c) relief and held that an LPR who has accrued the seven years of lawful unrelinquished domicile and is in deportation-track (§237) proceedings is eligible regardless of whether that ground has a corresponding counterpart in the inadmissibility track (§212(a)). The BIA expanded the waiver to include grounds that were never encompassed previously, including for example firearm offenses. The Board also eliminated any distinction between convictions via plea or trial. *Matter of Abdelghany* is an extremely significant decision. Following years of restrictions (through case law and regulation) on the waiver, the BIA opened up eligibility to a point it had never been before.

> ➢ **Troubling Question**: In the approximately 18 years that it took the BIA to hone in, refine, and properly interpret the 1996 legislation, how many long-time lawful permanent residents were uprooted from their homes, separated from their families, and wrongfully deported? The American Immigration Council has some excellent practice advisories on relief for persons who already were unlawfully removed.[173] Unfortunately, this type of litigation and procedures are neither established, nor—frankly—easy.

The INA §212(c) waiver is still an important form of relief today, and the jurisprudence that has followed in its wake since 1952 contains valuable guidance on equal protection, retroactivity, and rational basis analyses. Because of increasingly enhanced biometrics and security databases, many LPRs with old convictions (who have for years entered and exited the United States without their convictions being noticed) will finally be stopped by CBP on return from a trip abroad, or by USCIS in the process of applying for a replacement resident card or when applying for naturalization. These individuals are generally not subject to mandatory detention, and can still benefit from the INA §212(c) waiver. It is important to note that the §212(c) application, by regulation, may be filed both as a defense in immigration court and as an affirmative application with USCIS. An affirmative §212(c) application may be an effective tool in relieving a client from the concerns and burdens of an old conviction. For these reasons, the history of INA §212(c), as well as affirmative filings, are discussed below.

> ➢ **Comparing waivers**: Why is §212(c) a superior waiver to cancellation? Cancellation of removal is not available to someone with an aggravated felony offense; a waiver under §212(c) waives an aggravated felony offense. Cancellation carries tolling dates that effectively cut off the seven

---

[172] *Matter of Abdelghany*, 26 I&N Dec. 254 (BIA 2014).

[173] *See, e.g.*, "Implications of *Judulang v. Holder* for LPRs Seeking §212(c) Relief and for Other Individuals Challenging Arbitrary Agency Policies," *available at www.legalactioncenter.org/sites/default/files/Judulang-212-c-relief.pdf*.

years of an ongoing residence; §212(c) does not carry a tolling provision—the seven years of lawful permanent residence ends only upon a final administrative order of removal. Cancellation is not available to someone who received a waiver (cancellation or §212(c)) previously; a waiver under §212(c) may be granted more than once. In sum, a waiver under § 212(c) is more flexible in terms of qualifying criteria, and waives more crimes.

Advance Permission to Return to Unrelinquished Domicile

As initially implemented in 1952, the INA §212(c) waiver was envisioned as a waiver of crime for long-time permanent residents who were going to travel outside the United States, or had already travelled, and would face exclusion under INA §212(a) on account of crime. Until 1990, the waiver read as follows:

> [a]liens lawfully admitted for permanent residence who temporarily proceeded abroad voluntarily and not under an order of deportation, and who are returning to a lawful un-relinquished domicile of seven consecutive years, may be admitted in the discretion of the Attorney General without regard to [their excludability under section 212(a) of the Act].

The application Form I-191 was drafted (and still reads this way today) to allow an applicant to indicate proposed travel (hence, requesting "advance permission to return") or as someone facing exclusion upon application for re-entry. The waiver was not available to persons in deportation proceedings.[174]

Case Law Expands Eligibility to Those in Deportation Track

In the 1970s, the Second Circuit U.S. Court of Appeals ruled in *Francis v. INS*,[175] that it was a violation of equal protection to treat similarly situated LPRs in deportation proceedings differently from their counterparts in exclusion proceedings by restricting the waiver only to those individuals who faced exclusion. Put another way, it was a violation of equal protection and notions of fundamental fairness to make the waiver available based on the nuance of travel, rather than the underlying fact of a crime. The BIA ultimately agreed with the Second Circuit, in a case called *Matter of Silva*,[176] and opened the §212(c) waiver to LPRs in deportation proceedings, as long as the charge of deportability had a corresponding ground in exclusion. Based on case

---

[174] The provision at INA §212(c) [8 USC § 1182(c)] has remained constant for decades, although in the 1996 immigration legislation, reference to "admission" or "admissibility" was substituted for the term "exclusion." In comparison, the chapter encompassing grounds of "deportation" for persons physically present within the United States has changed through renumbering over the years. Formerly designated as §241 [8 USC §1251], grounds of deportation were redesignated in 1996 as §237 by §305(a)(2) of the IIRAIRA.

[175] *Francis v. INS*, 532 F.2d 268 (2d Cir. 1976).

[176] *Matter of Silva*, 16 I&N Dec. 626 (BIA 1976).

law, however, if the deportability ground did not have a close counterpart in exclusion, the waiver was not available.[177]

> **Still Good Guidance:** the *Francis/Silva* cases are instructive guidance for any attorney considering a due process/equal protection challenge to the limited availability of a waiver, relief or benefit when restrictions are based on irrelevant guidelines that to do not relate to the underlying purpose of the law.

The Immigration Act of 1990

In November of 1990, Congress passed the Immigration Act of 1990 (IMMACT90),[178] which included a limitation on the §212(c) waiver; persons who had been convicted of an aggravated felony for which they served more than five years in prison would be ineligible for this relief. In 1991, in a Miscellaneous Technical Corrections bill, Congress amended the bar to include a person who served five years or more in prison for an aggravated felony conviction or convictions—in the aggregate.[179] Initially, some courts held that this bar applied retroactively to convictions entered before November 29, 1990.[180] Subsequent case law and regulation clarified that the bar only applies to a conviction or convictions entered after November 29, 1990 and before April 24, 1996: if convictions are aggregated to arrive at the five years or more served, the convictions all had to occur after November 29, 1990.[181]

The Antiterrorism and Effective Death Penalty Act of 1996

Section 440(d) of AEDPA[182] limited the availability of INA §212(c) relief to individuals deportable for (1) only one crime involving moral turpitude, or (2) multiple crimes involving moral turpitude for which both crimes are covered by INA §241(a)(2)(A)(i) [INA §237(a)(2)(A)(i)]. The AEDPA version of §212(c) is important for persons who were convicted in between April 24, 1996, and April 1, 1997.

---

[177] *See, e.g: Matter of Jimenez-Santillano,* 21 I&N Dec. 567 (BIA 1996); *Matter of Esposito,* 21 I&N Dec. 1 (BIA 1995); *Matter of Hernandez-Casillas,* 20 I&N Dec. 262 (BIA 1990; AG 1991), aff'd, 983 F.2d 231 (5th Cir. 1993); *Matter of Wadud,* 19 I&N Dec. 182 (BIA 1984). This entire line of cases is now abrogated by the Supreme Court's decision in *Judulang* and the BIA's decision in *Matter of Abdelghany.*

[178] Immigration Act of 1990, Pub. L. No. 101-649, §511(a), 104 Stat. 4978, 5052 (effective Nov. 29, 1990) (IMMACT90), *as amended by* Miscellaneous and Technical Immigration and Naturalization Amendments of 1991, Pub. L. No. 102-232, §306(a)(10), 105 Stat. 1733, 1751 (effective as if included in IMMACT90).

[179] Immigration Act of 1990, Pub. L. No. 101-649, §511(a), 104 Stat. 4978, 5052, *id.*

[180] *See, e.g., Alexandre v. Att'y Gen.,* 452 F.3d 1204 (11th Cir. 2006).

[181] *Matter of Abdelghany,* 26 I&N Dec. 254, 272 (BIA 2014).

[182] Antiterrorism and Effective Death Penalty Act of 1996 (AEDPA), Pub. L. No. 104-132, 110 Stat. 1214.

As it was in existence for less than one year, it can be hard to find and is reproduced here:

> Aliens lawfully admitted for permanent residence who temporarily proceeded abroad voluntarily and not under an order of deportation, and who are returning to a lawful unrelinquished domicile of seven consecutive years, may be admitted in the discretion of the Attorney General without regard to the provisions of subsection (a) (other than paragraphs (3) and (9)(C)). Nothing contained in this subsection shall limit the authority of the Attorney General to exercise the discretion vested in him under section 211(b). This subsection shall not apply to an alien who is deportable by reason of having committed any criminal offense covered in section 241(a)(2)(A)(iii), (B), (C), or (D), or any offense covered by section 241(a)(2)(A)(ii) for which both predicate offenses are covered by section 241(a)(2)(A)(i).[183]

Section 212(c) was repealed in its entirety by §304(b) of IIRAIRA. The repeal became effective April 1, 1997.

The U.S. Supreme Court Decision: *INS v. St. Cyr*[184]

Initially, the AG (at this time representing both legacy INS and EOIR) took the position that both AEDPA's and IIRAIRA's amendments to INA §212(c) were retroactive. In *Matter of Soriano*,[185] the AG ruled that the bar to relief at §440(d) of AEDPA was completely retroactive, even reaching individuals who already were in proceedings before the immigration court or BIA (who perhaps had prevailed before an IJ and were before the BIA on an appeal from legacy INS). Based on this decision, thousands of individuals' applications for §212(c) relief were pretermitted. People were ordered deported and many were physically removed.

Across the country, many non–American citizens affected by the *Soriano* decision filed federal lawsuits arguing against the retroactive application of AEDPA §440(d). Some cases urged eligibility for those persons who either committed a crime or were convicted prior to April 24, 1996; others argued that those *already in proceedings* could not be barred retroactively from seeking this relief.[186]

In *INS v. St. Cyr*, the U.S. Supreme Court ruled that the amendments made to INA §212(c) by §440(d) of AEDPA could not be applied retroactively to persons who

---

[183] INA §241 was later redesignated as INA §237 by IIRAIRA §305(a)(2). References to §241 should be substituted with §237; the subsections remain the same.

[184] *INS v. St. Cyr*, 533 U.S. 289 (2001).

[185] *Matter of Soriano*, 21 I&N Dec. 516 (BIA 1996, AG 1997).

[186] *See* 66 Fed. Reg. 6436 (Jan. 22, 2001) (*Soriano* rule). This rule, promulgated by the then–attorney general, which overturned her own decision in *Matter of Soriano*, added 8 CFR §212.3(g), which explicitly states, "Relief for certain aliens who were in deportation proceedings before April 24, 1996. Section 440(d) of Antiterrorism and Effective Death Penalty Act of 1996 (AEDPA) shall not apply to any applicant for relief under this section whose deportation proceedings were commenced before the Immigration Court before April 24, 1996." This exception is discussed later in this chapter.

would have been eligible for the waiver at the time of entering a plea. (Note: the facts of this case, and thus its holding, were limited to those individuals who entered pleas, not those convicted by trial.) The facts of the case in *St. Cyr* were that the individual entered a plea; he did not go to trial. The Court reasoned that, theoretically speaking, a person relies on the availability of relief at the time of entering a plea, and should not be penalized by a retroactive change in the law.

The 2004 Regulation

The *St. Cyr* decision left DOJ with the task of writing a regulation that would implement the Supreme Court's decision. On September 28, 2004 (three years after the ruling), DOJ clarified the breadth of *St. Cyr* by codifying the decision.[187] The final rule amends 8 CFR Parts 1003, 212, 1212, and 1240. The final rule's commentary section contains a fascinating legal analysis of the history of INA §212(c) and the 1996 legislation, along with important precedent cases. The comment section is recommended reading for all immigration law practitioners: it is a bonanza of legal interpretations, references, and even (inadvertently) useful strategies. Key section topics include: eligibility cut-off dates; exclusion versus deportation proceedings; retroactivity of aggravated felony definition; plea versus trial convictions; deportation proceedings commenced prior to April 24, 1996, persons deported prior to *St. Cyr*, and re-entry of those persons.

Eligibility cut-off dates

Persons convicted by plea or trial prior to April 24, 1996, are eligible to apply for INA §212(c) relief under the pre-AEDPA version of the waiver provision. [Note that some circuits and now the BIA have found that an individual who was in deportation proceedings prior to April 24, 1996, may utilize the §212(c) waiver for post-1996 convictions; this is discussed further in a later section on "Persons in Deportation Proceedings on or Before April 26, 1996."] The pre-AEDPA version of §212(c) reads (footnotes added):

> Aliens lawfully admitted for permanent residence who temporarily proceeded abroad voluntarily and not under an order of deportation, and who are returning to a lawful unrelinquished domicile of seven consecutive years, may be admitted in the discretion of the Attorney General without regard to the provisions of subsection (a) (other than paragraphs (3)[188] and (9)(C)[189]). Nothing contained in this subsection shall limit the authority of the Attorney General to exercise the discretion vested in him under section 211(b). The first sentence of this subsection shall not apply to an alien who has been convicted of one or more

---

[187] 69 Fed. Reg. 57826 (Sept. 28, 2004).

[188] Security-related grounds.

[189] INA §212(a)(9)(C) is entitled "Aliens Unlawfully Present After Previous Immigration Violations" and renders inadmissible any alien who illegally enters or attempts to re-enter the United States after having been removed.

aggravated felonies and has served for such felony or felonies a term of imprisonment of at least 5 years.

> **Tip**: The final sentence, regarding serving more than five years in prison for an aggravated felony offense, was also modified by the final regulation and no longer applies to persons who were convicted prior to November 30, 1990.[190]

In most cases of §212(c) use, the operative date will be April 24, 1996. Persons convicted after that date will not be eligible.

However, certain persons who were convicted (via plea or by trial) of a crime or crimes involving moral turpitude after April 24, 1996, but before April 1, 1997, will be eligible to proceed on an application for §212(c) relief if they meet the other eligibility requirements. For persons who were convicted during this timeframe, it is the revised AEDPA version of §212(c)[191] that applies.[192] According to the narrow AEDPA version, an individual remains eligible to apply for §212(c) relief if he or she is deportable for only one crime involving moral turpitude *or* if deportable for multiple crimes involving moral turpitude as long as only one (or neither) of the offenses occurred within the first five years of admission. In terms of CIMTs, the bar applies to convictions which would both fall under the auspices of INA §237(a)(2)(A)(i): within five years of admission, possible penalty of one year or longer.

> **Example**: Mitchell Curley becomes an LPR on January 1, 1990. On January 1, 1994, he is convicted of a theft offense that carries a maximum sentence of five years, but is sentenced only to a period of probation. On January 1, 1997, Mr. Curley commits a second theft offense, and is again sentenced to a period of probation. On February 1, 1997, legacy INS puts Mr. Curley in deportation proceedings by filing an OSC with the immigration court. He is eligible to apply for §212(c) relief under the AEDPA version because he is deportable for two crimes involving moral turpitude, one of which occurred within five years of entry, but the second of which occurred outside five years of entry. Note that he also has seven years of LPR status and is otherwise eligible for the waiver.

---

[190] 8 CFR §1212.3(f)(4)(i).

[191] The AEDPA version of §212(c) is set forth earlier in the chapter under the heading "The 1996 Legislation."

[192] Prior to the AEDPA amendment, INA §212(c) could waive any criminal ground of inadmissibility (at that time, referred to as "excludability") under INA §212(a), as well as any *corresponding* ground of deportability under INA §241 (now §237). In general, the waiver cured grounds of inadmissibility and deportability for controlled substance offenses, crimes involving moral turpitude, and prostitution and commercialized vice. In the deportability context, §212(c) would waive the aggravated felony charge if the criminal conviction forming the basis of the aggravated felony charge also formed the basis of a charge under INA §212(a), such as controlled substance or a crime involving moral turpitude.

> **Compare and contrast**: Note that an LPR who is eligible for §212(c) relief under the AEDPA version might also be eligible for cancellation of removal under INA §240A(a). However, the cancellation of removal provision includes cut-off dates that toll required periods of continuous residence and LPR status. The AEDPA version of §212(c) does not contain tolling dates. Thus, an LPR who was deportable for only one crime involving moral turpitude, for example, where the plea agreement came before April 1, 1997, will be eligible for (AEDPA) §212(c) relief if placed in removal proceedings today. However, if the commission of the offense occurred prior to accumulating seven years of continuous residence following a lawful admission, he or she would not have the requisite years of continuous residency for purposes of relief under §240A(a).

> **Example**: Miguel Angelo is admitted for LPR status on January 1, 1995. He was admitted to the United States for the first time on an immigrant visa issued by the embassy in Brazil. On October 1, 1996, he pleads guilty to aggravated assault, a second-degree felony, and receives one year of probation. He does not come to the attention of ICE. However, in 2005, Miguel applies for naturalization, and the USCIS naturalization unit refers the file to ICE for initiation of removal proceedings. Miguel is not eligible for cancellation of removal because he did not accumulate seven years of continuous residence prior to committing the crime of aggravated assault. His time tolled within two years of lawful admission. In comparison, the seven years of unrelinquished domicile required for §212(c) relief does not toll until the entry of a final administrative decision, and Miguel is deportable for only one crime involving moral turpitude; thus, he is eligible to proceed on an application for §212(c) relief under the revised, AEDPA version.

Individuals in exclusion proceedings

As discussed in chapter three, removal proceedings encompass two distinct types of grounds: the grounds of inadmissibility are found at INA §212(a), while grounds of deportability are found at INA §237(a). Prior to IIRAIRA, which for purposes of ushering in the new "removal" proceedings became effective April 1, 1997, inadmissibility was referred to as "excludability." The grounds of exclusion under INA §212(a) were charged, not in removal, but rather in exclusion proceedings before an IJ. Looking quickly at the AEDPA version of INA §212(c),[193] one sees that the operative term is "deportability"; "excludability" is not mentioned. Accordingly, individuals who are excludable, *i.e.*, were in pre-IIRAIRA "exclusion" proceedings for crimes—even offenses that are classifiable as aggravated felonies or controlled sub-

---

[193] The AEDPA version of §212(c) is set forth above under the heading "The 1996 Law."

stance offenses—are eligible for §212(c) relief if they were placed in exclusion proceedings before April 1, 1997.

Admittedly, the number of LPRs who are still in exclusion proceedings today is limited; however, there may be old exclusion files that were administratively closed or otherwise not processed to conclusion. It may be worthwhile, depending on the circumstances of the particular case, to re-calendar the old exclusion proceeding rather than to see the matter go forward in a removal proceeding.

IIRAIRA definition of aggravated felony retroactive: the summer of 1996

In discussing effective dates for purposes of eligibility for the INA §212(c) waiver, one particularly frustrating problem arises in the case of persons who pleaded guilty during the "summer of '96" (between April 26, 1996, and September 30, 1996) to an offense that, at the time of plea, was not an aggravated felony, but [following IIRAIRA's amendments to the definition of aggravated felony (September 30, 1996)] became classifiable as an aggravated felony. These two issues—the definition of aggravated felony and eligibility for §212(c) relief—are interconnected because under the revised AEDPA version of §212(c), an individual deportable for an aggravated felony conviction is not eligible for the waiver, yet the *definition* of aggravated felony was not modified within AEDPA—it was modified four months later via IIRAIRA.

The precise issue, then, is whether an individual who pleaded during summer 1996 to a crime that was not then classified as an aggravated felony—so that he or she would have been eligible for a §212(c) waiver at the time of plea—may be legally barred from that relief where the offense was subsequently classified as an aggravated felony offense by IIRAIRA.

Based on the retroactivity analysis of the *St. Cyr* decision, many practitioners hoped that the same due process and reliance principles would apply to application of the revised definition of aggravated felony; in other words, that persons who pleaded prior to the crime becoming defined as an aggravated felony would be allowed to pursue §212(c) relief. No such luck. The final rule makes clear that IIRAIRA's amendments to the aggravated felony definition apply to convictions entered before, on, or after the enactment date.[194] The amended definition is completely retroactive.

The contrast in approaches is due to the fact that AEDPA §440(d) did not contain an effective date, but Congress did include an effective date when it amended the definition of aggravated felony in IIRAIRA. The revised definition applies to convictions entered before, on, or after the date of IIRAIRA's enactment.[195] As a result, an individual who pleaded to an offense between April 24, 1996, and September 29, 1996, which did not fit the definition of aggravated felony at the time but subsequent-

---

[194] 69 Fed. Reg. 57826, 57830–31 (Sept. 28, 2004). See chapter seven for discussion of the aggravated felony definition.

[195] IIRAIRA §321(b), 110 Stat. 3009-628.

ly became an aggravated felony offense, is not eligible for §212(c) relief.[196] The BIA and many federal courts (including the Supreme Court in *St. Cyr*) have found that because Congress clearly included a retroactive effective date in IIRAIRA, it is constitutionally permissible to apply the revised definition of "aggravated felony" to convictions entered prior to September 30, 1996.[197]

Following are the more common aggravated felony offenses redefined by IIRAIRA:[198]

- Money laundering offenses:[199] the amount of loss was lowered from $100,000 to $10,000.

- Crimes of violence:[200] sentence of imprisonment imposed was lowered from five years to one year.

- Certain racketeering and gambling offenses:[201] a provision that previously read "where a term of five years imprisonment or more may be imposed" was changed to "where a sentence of one year imprisonment or more may be imposed."

- Theft offenses:[202] sentence of imprisonment imposed was lowered from five years to one year.

- Crimes involving fraud or deceit; crimes involving tax evasion:[203] amount of loss was lowered from $200,000 to $10,000.

- Passport offenses (falsely making, altering, forging, or counterfeiting a passport in violation of 18 USC §1543):[204] sentence of imprisonment imposed was lowered from five years to one year.

- Offenses involving commercial bribery, counterfeiting, forgery, trafficking in vehicles:[205] the provision that previously read "for which a term of 5 years imprisonment or more may be imposed" was changed to "for which the term of imprisonment imposed is at least one year."

---

[196] 69 Fed. Reg. 57826, 57830 (Sept. 28, 2004).

[197] *INS v. St. Cyr*, 533 U.S. 289 (2001); *Seale v. INS*, 323 F.3d 150 (1st Cir. 2003); *Flores-Leon v. INS*, 272 F.3d 433 (7th Cir. 2001); *Mohammed v. Ashcroft*, 261 F.3d 1244 (11th Cir. 2001); *Matter of Truong*, 22 I&N Dec. 1090 (BIA 1999).

[198] IIRAIRA §321 amended the definition of aggravated felony.

[199] INA §101(a)(43)(D).

[200] INA §101(a)(43)(F).

[201] INA §101(a)(43)(J).

[202] INA §101(a)(43)(G).

[203] INA §101(a)(43)(M).

[204] INA §101(a)(43)(P).

[205] INA §101(a)(43)(R).

CH. 10 • IMMIGRATION DEFENSE: WAIVERS AND OTHER RELIEF

- Offenses involving obstruction of justice, perjury, bribery of a witness:[206] sentence of imprisonment imposed was lowered from five years to one year.

In addition to the modifications noted above, IIRAIRA also amended the definition of "aggravated felony" by adding rape and sexual abuse of a minor after murder at INA §101(a)(43)(A).

Persons convicted by trial

Following *St. Cyr*, DHS and EOIR promulgated regulations implementing the Supreme Court's decision. Prior to *St. Cyr*, the agencies had interpreted AEDPA §440(d) to be completely retroactive and many lawful permanent residents had their applications for waivers pretermitted or denied.[207] The Supreme Court ruled in 2001 that retroactive application violated principles of reliance; still, in 2004 the agencies limited *St. Cyr* to situations where the non-American citizen was convicted via a plea—reasoning that a person who entered a plea to avoid a five year prison sentence reasonably exercised reliance on the availability of the waiver. This interpretation of the *St. Cyr* decision set off a new series of litigation and a split in the circuits (based on a retroactivity analysis) as to whether an individual convicted by trial verdict was eligible to apply for the waiver.[208] In *Matter of Abdelghany*, the BIA—in addition to abandoning the comparable grounds test—held that a person was eligible for the waiver whether convicted by plea or by trial verdict.[209] The Board supported this decision by looking to the Supreme Court's opinions in three cases: *INS v. St. Cyr*; *Vartelas v. Holder*;[210] and *Judulang v. Holder*. In terms of the reliance issue, the Board looked heavily to Supreme Court guidance in *Vartelas*, which is discussed in chapter three's section on the 1996 legislative changes to the INA §101(a)(13) and the conditions under which a returning LPR with a pre-1996 conviction faces removal as an arriving alien.

Utilizing the waiver to cure post-1996 convictions (persons already in deportation proceedings)

In an interesting twist on the breadth of the §212(c) waiver, at least three circuits ruled that a person who was in deportation proceedings as of April 24, 1996, may utilize the waiver to cure post-AEDPA convictions. In *Enriquez-Gutierez v. Holder*,[211] the court of appeals found that an individual in deportation proceedings prior to the effective dates of IIRAIRA and AEDPA, subsequently convicted again of another

---

[206] INA §101(a)(43)(S).

[207] 8 CFR §1212.3(h).

[208] For readers interested in the retroactivity analysis and discussion of reasonable reliance, and the circuit split pre-*Abdelghany*, see the fifth edition of this book. Because of new case law precedent, the discussion of the circuit split has been removed from this sixth edition.

[209] *Matter of Abdelghany*, 26 I&N Dec. 254 (BIA 2014).

[210] *Vartelas v. Holder*, 132 S. Ct. 1479 (2012).

[211] *Enriquez-Gutierez v. Holder*, 612 F.3d 400 (5th Cir. 2010).

crime after 1996, could utilize the §212(c) waiver to waive the post-1996 crime by virtue of the transition rule at §309(c)(1)(A) of the IIRAIRA and the regulation at 8 CFR §1212.3(g). Both of these provisions state that the amendments to INA §212(c) shall not apply to individuals in proceedings before the effective dates. The Fifth Circuit relied on a similar conclusion reached by the Second Circuit in *Garcia-Padron v. Holder*.[212] The Ninth Circuit reached a similar conclusion in *Pasqua v. Holder*,[213] which involved proceedings commenced before April 1, 1997—the IIRAIRA effective date.

Thus, for individuals in deportation proceedings prior to April 24, 1996 (or before April 1, 1997), who are convicted while proceedings are pending, it is possible for the waiver to encompass the post-1996 convictions. In such an event, locating a pre-IIRAIRA order to show cause and/or detainer could be a vital coup in representing someone who is not eligible for cancellation of removal.

INA §212(c) Eligibility Criteria

An LPR who has held such status for at least seven years is eligible to apply for an INA §212(c) waiver.[214] Time spent in temporary resident status (the status given to legalization applicants pursuant to a 1986 amnesty) counts toward the seven years of required permanent residency status.[215]

Prior to 2012, via a case called *Matter of Blake*,[216] the BIA employed a strict "comparable grounds" test that required an actual equivalent charge between INA §237(a) and INA §212(a) in order to utilize the waiver in §237 proceedings. Based on *Blake*, many individuals with an aggravated felony conviction (among other grounds) could not take advantage of the §212(c) waiver because there was no "comparable ground" under INA §212(a). However, the Supreme Court rejected the "comparable grounds test" in *Judulang v. Holder*,[217] unanimously finding the agency's policy "arbitrary and capricious":

> We must reverse an agency policy when we cannot discern a reason for it. That is the trouble in this case. The BIA's comparable-grounds rule is unmoored from the purposes and concerns of the immigration laws. It allows an irrelevant comparison between statutory provisions to govern a matter of the utmost importance—whether lawful resident aliens with longstanding ties to this country

---

[212] *Garcia-Padron v. Holder*, 558 F.3d 196 (2d Cir. 2009).

[213] *Pascua v. Holder*, 641 F.3d 316 (9th Cir. 2011).

[214] 8 CFR §§212.3(f)(2), 1212.3(f)(2).

[215] 8 CFR §§212.3(f)(2), 1212.3(f)(2). "Temporary residency status" was granted pursuant to §210 of the Special Agricultural Workers Program (SAW) or pursuant the general amnesty at INA §245A [8 USC §1255a].

[216] *Matter of Blake*, 23 I&N Dec. 722 (BIA 2005); *rev'd and remanded*, *Blake v. Carbone*, 489 F.3d 88 (2d Cir. 2007).

[217] *Judulang v. Holder*, 132 S. Ct. 476 (2011).

may stay here. And contrary to the Government's protestations, it is not supported by text or practice or cost considerations.[218]

In *Matter of Abdelghany*,[219] the BIA fully implemented the *Judulang's* Court's mandate to reject the "comparable grounds test" and held that "a deportable lawful permanent resident cannot be declared ineligible for section 212(c) on the basis of mechanical distinctions arising from the structure of the immigration statute." The BIA held that otherwise qualified applicants may apply for section 212(c) relief in removal proceedings to waive *any* ground of deportability[220] arising from either a plea or trial verdict. Of course the criminal conviction must have been entered prior to April 24, 1996, with the exception of certain crimes involving moral turpitude.

Based on the Board's 2014 decision in *Matter of Abdelghany*, the waiver is available to cure all grounds of removability unless the applicant is inadmissible under INA §§212(a)(3)(A),(B), (C), (E), or (10)(C).

> **Of Interest**: The §212(c) waiver will now cure deportability for a firearms offense under INA §237(a)(2)(C). This was not possible before *Abdelghany*.

Persons who served five years in prison for aggravated felony

Pursuant to the Immigration Act of 1990 (IMMACT90),[221] individuals who served five years or more in prison for an aggravated felony or combination of aggravated felonies are ineligible for the waiver. Via case law, this bar was applied retroactively even to persons convicted prior to November 29, 1990 (IMMACT90's enactment date).[222] However, in light of *St. Cyr's* retroactivity analysis, DOJ included in the final §212(c) rule a provision that individuals convicted of an aggravated felony or felonies prior to November 29, 1990, would not face this five-year prison bar.[223] In other words, individuals convicted prior to IMMACT90 would not be barred from seeking §212(c) relief as a result of serving five or more years in prison.

For convictions after November 29, 1990, an individual who served five years or more in prison for an aggravated felony or felonies is not eligible for the §212(c) waiver, even if convicted by plea or verdict and having LPR status for seven years or longer.[224]

---

[218] *Judulang v. Holder*, 132 S. Ct. 476, at 489.

[219] *Matter of Abdelghany*, 26 I&N Dec. 254, at 259 (BIA 2014).

[220] *Unless* the applicant is subject to the grounds of inadmissibility under §§212(a)(3)(A), (B), or (E), or (10)(C) of the INA. *Matter of Abdelghany*, 26 I&N Dec. 254, at 266.

[221] Immigration Act of 1990 (IMMACT90), Pub. L. No. 101-649, §511(a), 104 Stat. 4978, 5052.

[222] *See, e.g., Samaniego-Meraz v. INS*, 53 F.3d 254 (9th Cir. 1995).

[223] 8 CFR §1212.3(f)(4)(ii); *see* 69 Fed. Reg. 57826, 57830–31 (Sept. 28, 2004).

[224] 8 CFR §1212.3(f)(4)(i).

Persons wrongfully removed prior to *St. Cyr, Judulang, or Abdelghany*

Scores of LPRs were prevented from seeking INA §212(c) relief and were actually deported prior to the Supreme Court's decision in *St. Cyr*. Indeed, some may have been wrongfully deported even after that decision, if they were appearing pro se and waiting for a final, clarifying rule from legacy INS. Many commentators to the proposed rule implementing *St. Cyr* argued that individuals who had been wrongfully deported because their §212(c) applications were pretermitted under pre–*St. Cyr* precedent should be readmitted or paroled into the United States to seek the waiver. Unfortunately, the very first section of the final regulation makes clear that individuals who had been deported would not be allowed to re-enter to seek relief.[225] The final rule includes 8 CFR §1003.44(k), which states:

> (k) *Limitations on eligibility under this section*. This section does not apply to:
>
> (1) Aliens who have departed the United States and are currently outside the United States;
>
> (2) Aliens issued a final order of deportation or removal who then illegally returned to the United States; or
>
> (3) Aliens who have not been admitted or paroled.

In the comments to the regulation, DOJ reasoned that these individuals could have pursued appeals through the BIA and federal court system in anticipation of a Supreme Court decision, but they chose not to. In addition, according to DOJ, Congress's intent in passing the AEDPA legislation was to see criminal aliens deported. Finally, DOJ notes that it is illegal to re-enter after deportation and that such persons face criminal prosecution as well as reinstatement of the prior deportation order.

None of these arguments holds up under close scrutiny. First, not all individuals had the financial ability to pursue appeals in the federal court system. Many were detained, causing great emotional and mental distress to themselves and their families. Second, the various federal circuits interpreted the law differently, and some federal courts had not ruled on the retroactivity of AEDPA §440(d). In these cases, especially without a stay, execution of the deportation order could go forward notwithstanding the pending litigation. Third, congressional intent in regard to criminal aliens is not relevant to the fact that the Supreme Court ruled that the government's retroactive application of the law was illegal. Finally, the fact that distinct provisions of the law criminalize re-entry after deportation does not affect DOJ's ability to approve a specific procedure for re-parole of aliens unlawfully deported.

Regardless of its faulty justification, the state of the law is that an LPR who should have been allowed to proceed on an application for §212(c) relief, but was wrongfully deported prior to the Supreme Court's decision in *St. Cyr*, is not eligible to return to the United States and apply for the waiver. Indeed, the language of INA §212(c) itself

---

[225] 69 Fed. Reg. 57826, 57827 (Sept. 28, 2004).

indicates the waiver is not available to waive INA §212(a)(9)(C), which is a ground of inadmissibility for being unlawfully present after previous immigration violations.

Now, history repeats itself with the *Judulang* and *Abdelghany* decisions. Without statistics, it is probably safe to say hundreds if not thousands of LPRs were removed because they were convicted by trial; yet today they would be eligible for the waiver. Unlike the agency response to *St. Cyr*, there has been no rule promulgated with a motion to reopen procedure or time period. Individuals who are in the United States and believe that they benefit from the *Abdelghany* decision may file motions to reopen, *sua sponte* if necessary. But there are no set procedures, and certainly no precedent for returning LPRs to the United States.

For individuals who already have been removed and are outside the United States, a motion to reopen arguing a combination of the illegality of the departure bar regulation and equitable tolling to either the IJ or BIA, with an eye on a petition for review, may be the best strategy. Again, the American Immigration Council may serve as a useful resource with practice advisories regarding these two emerging areas of litigation.

Re-entry after pretermission of §212(c) application and deportation

There is no lawful mechanism for a former LPR who was denied the opportunity to apply for INA §212(c) relief and deported to return to the United States and apply anew. Indeed, individuals who return illegally to the United States after deportation are subject to criminal prosecution under INA §276 [8 USC §1326]. Moreover, where a non–American citizen re-enters the United States illegally after removal, the outstanding removal order may be reinstated and the prior proceedings may not be reviewed or reopened.[226] Even if a former permanent resident enters legally (for example, with a nonimmigrant visa and an INA §212(d)(3) waiver[227] or via parole), the prior deportation/removal proceedings cannot—according to regulation—be reopened.[228] The so-called "re-entry bar" has been found to be *ultra vires* by several circuit courts of appeal in the context of a motion to reopen within the 90 day reopening period.[229] A motion to reopen in the case of an unlawfully pretermitted §212(c) waiver application would not be a traditional 90-day motion to reopen. However, a motion

---

[226] INA §241(a)(5); 8 USC §1231(a)(5).

[227] See discussion of nonimmigrant visa waivers under §212(d)(3) later in this chapter.

[228] 8 CFR §1003.2(d).

[229] The following circuits have found that the right to reopen within 90 days of a removal order (or 30 days in the case of a motion to reconsider) is a statutory right that cannot be voided by regulation, and adheres regardless of physical deportation from the country: *Marin-Rodriguez v. Holder*, 612 F.3d 591 (7th Cir. 2010*)*; *Contreras-Bocanegra v. Holder*, 629 F.3d 1170 (10th Cir. 2010); *Prestol Espinal v. Att'y Gen.*, 653 F.3d 213 (3d Cir. 2011*)*; *Coyt v. Holder*, 593 F.3d 902 (9th Cir. 2010*)*; *William v. Gonzales*, 499 F.3d 329 (4th Cir. 2007); *Jian Le Lin v. Att'y General*, 681 F.3d 1236 (11th Cir. 2012*)*; *Pruidze v. Att'y Gen.*, 632 F.3d. 234 (6th Cir. 2011).

could be brought *sua sponte* or DHS could be persuaded not to reinstate the removal order.

Criminal prosecution for re-entry and reinstatement of removal orders are discussed in chapter three. For purposes of the §212(c) discussion, however, it is notable that some federal courts have allowed collateral attack on the underlying deportation or removal order in criminal cases for re-entry after removal [8 USC §1326] where the individual was denied the opportunity to seek the waiver and thus wrongfully deported.[230]

It is important to note that in criminal re-entry cases where the defense is a collateral attack on the legality of the underlying removal proceeding, the courts do consider whether the §212(c) case is strong in terms of equities. Where the underlying application is not considered strong, and unlikely to have been granted, some courts are unwilling to find that a deportation hearing was fundamentally unfair because §212(c) relief was not made available to the individual under pre–*St. Cyr* law.[231] Other courts have required that the defendant establish a "reasonable likelihood" of prevailing on the 212(c) application, finding no prejudice where the record established that the defendant was unlikely to have received discretionary relief.[232]

Finally, although a successful collateral attack on the underlying removal/deportation proceedings based on unlawful deprivation of the opportunity to apply for §212(c) relief may result in dismissal of the criminal charge, it remains to be seen whether the lucky defendant could then go on to avoid reinstatement and apply for a waiver. One strategy may be to seek reopening before the BIA or IJ during the criminal case for illegal re-entry, based on a *sua sponte* motion. Again, as discussed above, the regulations do not allow the reopening of proceedings once a deportation or removal order has been executed.

Gabryelsky *filings: adjustment of status combined with INA §212(c)*

A firearms offense (and certain aggravated felonies) do not form the basis of inadmissibility, and therefore deportability based on the offense cannot be waived by INA §212(c). In cases involving such an offense, adjustment of status may serve as the "waiver."[233] In cases involving two or more offenses—one a ground of inadmissibility and another only of deportability—it is possible to combine a waiver under

---

[230] *U.S. v. Gill*, 748 F.3d 491 (2d Cir 2014); *U.S. v. Lopez*, 445 F.3d 90 (2d Cir. 2006); *U.S. v. Calderon*, 391 F.3d 370 (2d Cir. 2004); *U.S. v. Lepore*, 304 F. Supp. 2d 183 (D. Mass. 2004) (motion to dismiss criminal count of re-entry after deportation ultimately *denied* because §212(c) relief in all likelihood would not have been granted; court notes that deprivation of right to seek §212(c) can be a violation of due process, rendering proceedings fundamentally unfair).

[231] *U.S. v. Torres*, 383 F.3d 92 (3d Cir. 2004); *U.S. v. Lepore*, 304 F. Supp. 2d 183 (D. Mass. 2004).

[232] *U.S. v. Luna*, 436 F.3d 312 (1st Cir. 2006); *U.S. v. Mendoza-Mata*, 322 F.3d 829 (5th Cir. 2003).

[233] See discussion of adjustment of status in this chapter. *See also Matter of Rainford*, 20 I&N Dec. 598 (BIA 1992); *Matter of Gabryelsky*, 20 I&N Dec. 750 (BIA 1993); *Matter of Kanga*, 22 I&N Dec. 1206 (BIA 2000).

§212(c) with an application for adjustment of status before the IJ. In *Matter of Gabryelsky*,[234] the BIA ruled that an individual with a firearms offense and a controlled substance violation could apply concurrently for a waiver under §212(c) and adjustment of status. Through this procedure, §212(c) waives the ground of inadmissibility (in this case, the drug offense) and adjustment of status cures the firearms (deportability) offense. In 2003, the Second Circuit reaffirmed the viability of *Gabryelsky* filings (§212(c) combined with adjustment of status) in *Drax v. Reno*.[235] In 2005, the BIA followed suit (and put to rest DHS's ongoing argument that concurrent waivers under the *Gabryelsky* scheme were no longer available because of certain regulatory amendments) in *Matter of Azurin*.[236]

> **Example**: Juan Rodriguez, a citizen of Cuba, has been an LPR for 20 years. Rodriguez is convicted by plea in 1994 of possession with intent to distribute a controlled substance. In 1998, he is convicted of possession of a firearm by a convicted felon. Rodriguez is placed in removal proceedings (and held under the mandatory detention provisions) in the year 2000. He is charged with deportability for a controlled substance violation *and* for a firearms offense. In addition, both the 1994 and 1998 convictions are aggravated felonies (drug trafficking and possession of firearm by convicted felon). Before the IJ, Rodriguez files for adjustment of status under the Cuban Adjustment Act and a concurrent waiver under §212(c). A waiver under §212(c) remains available pursuant to *St. Cyr*; the §212(c) application waives deportability for the 1994 controlled substance/aggravated felony conviction. The adjustment of status application waives deportability for the firearms offense, which is both a firearms violation and an aggravated felony. The waiver is granted, and Rodriguez readjusts status to lawful permanent residency.

Combining INA §212(c) and Cancellation of Removal

This topic is also discussed in the section on cancellation of removal, above. As noted, a common question is whether an individual in removal proceedings on account of a pre-AEDPA (April 24, 1996) conviction as well as a post-AEDPA conviction may combine waivers under INA §212(c) and cancellation of removal under INA §240A(a). This issue has not been definitively addressed by the BIA, but has been discussed by federal courts of appeals. If the pre-AEDPA conviction is an aggravated felony, the courts have held that the two waivers cannot be combined because cancel-

---

[234] *Matter of Gabryelsky*, 20 I&N Dec. 750 (BIA 1993).

[235] *Drax v. Reno*, 338 F.3d 98 (2d Cir. 2003).

[236] *Matter of Azurin*, 23 I&N Dec. 695 (BIA 2005).

lation of removal is not available to a person who has been convicted of an aggravated felony.[237]

In most cases, an individual seeking combined waivers will have an aggravated felony conviction; after all, if the pre-AEDPA conviction were *not* an aggravated felony, cancellation of removal would effectively cure most pre-AEDPA convictions without the need of §212(c). However, there may be situations in which the pre-AEDPA conviction is not an aggravated felony, but the individual would benefit from the combined waivers.

Affirmative Applications for §212(c)

The INA §212(c) waiver is most frequently filed in removal proceedings before the immigration court. However, the regulations state that an application can be filed affirmatively with the district director of USCIS.[238] If an individual is in removal proceedings, only an IJ has jurisdiction over the application. But if an individual has a conviction record that renders him or her either inadmissible or deportable, he or she may choose to confront the situation affirmatively by preparing a waiver application and supporting evidentiary package and filing it with USCIS.

If the application is denied, the individual will be referred for removal proceedings (and ultimately be ordered removed), so there is a risk involved in bringing the conviction to light. (In removal proceedings, the client can renew the application before an IJ, thereby getting a "second bite at the apple.") Yet filing an affirmative application to waive an old conviction—especially when the case involves rehabilitation and significant personal equities—may be a wise course of action for a client who is afraid to travel outside the United States; fears renewing the resident card (and with it the driver's license); would like to, but cannot, naturalize; or is otherwise frequently worried about his or her immigration status.

With increasingly strict enforcement and enhanced technology, realistically, it is only a matter of time before DHS ferrets out most LPRs with an old conviction and places them in removal proceedings—possibly taking people into custody in the process—under tougher immigration policies. For this reason, it may be a wise strategy to file with USCIS in advance; it also takes the adversarial nature of court out of the application process. Of course, the overall facts of the case must be carefully evaluated before taking the significant step of bringing an old conviction out of the closet. Prudent counsel will carefully consider the favorable factors and equities in a person's life, including (but not limited to) family ties, rehabilitation, tax filing history, property ties, and community service. Where the client has a serious criminal record and limited equities, it may not be wise to file an affirmative application. In any

---

[237] *Garcia-Jimenez v. Gonzales*, 488 F.3d 1082, 1085–86 (9th Cir. 2007); *Peralta-Taveras v. Gonzales*, 488 F.3d 580 (2d Cir. 2007); *Rodriguez-Munoz v. Gonzales,* 419 F.3d 245 (3d Cir. 2005); *Arriola-Arenas v. Att'y Gen.,* 145 Fed. Appx. 757, 2005 WL 2012262 (3d Cir. Aug. 23, 2005).

[238] 8 CFR §212.3(a)(1).

event, the risks and benefits should be carefully explained to the client; no application comes with a guarantee. Careful counsel will note in the file that the client has been advised of and accepts the risk that the application may not be granted and instead may trigger removal proceedings.

Naturalization After a Waiver Under INA §212(c)

The §212(c) waiver can effectively cure an aggravated felony offense such that it no longer serves as a basis for removal. Clients who obtain such waivers often then ask if they can apply for naturalization. Under INA §101(f), an individual with an aggravated felony conviction entered after November 29, 1990 (the effective date of IMMACT90), is permanently barred from establishing the "good moral character" required for naturalization purposes. At least one court of appeals has ruled that the grant of a waiver does not eliminate the aggravated felony conviction for purposes of naturalization eligibility.[239]

Voluntary Departure

Voluntary departure is a benefit whereby the individual avoids an order of removal and is allowed to leave the United States at his or her own financial expense, and generally of his or her own accord (*i.e.*, based on one's own plans). In certain circumstances, voluntary departure is conducted "under safeguards" (with an agent observing or facilitating and confirming the departure) or even from a detention facility, whereby the individual is taken to the port of departure by ICE. Theoretically, an individual who departs according to all set requirements pursuant to a grant of voluntary departure leaves with a clean record and is free to return to the United States with proper admission documents. In comparison, removal (or departure) from the United States under an order of removal entails a bar to returning, the length of which depends on the reasons for removal.[240]

Voluntary departure is not a panacea. Sometimes, an individual is in removal proceedings for a minor reason—a minor, technical violation—and will be able to obtain a visa and return to the United States without much ado, based on the voluntary de-

---

[239] *Chan v. Gantner,* 464 F.3d 289 (2d Cir. 2006).

[240] INA §212(a)(9); 8 USC §1182(a)(9). An individual classified as an "arriving alien" who is ordered removed under either INA §235(b)(1) or INA §240 is inadmissible for five years. This classification corresponds to the previous "exclusion" cases (*i.e.*, persons ordered excluded, as opposed to deported) under the statutory scheme prior to April 1, 1997. Persons who are ordered removed under §240 as "deportable" aliens under INA §237, or persons who are ordered removed for charges under INA §212(a) who are not arriving aliens (*i.e.*, persons who entered without inspection), are inadmissible for 10 years. Persons who are removed for an aggravated felony conviction are permanently inadmissible. Note, however, that in reference to these bars, including aggravated felony convictions, the person may seek a combination of waivers to overcome inadmissibility, included permission to reapply (Form I-212) combined with a waiver such as those available under INA §§212(h), 212(d)(3), etc., as discussed further in this chapter and the next chapter.

parture order. In other cases, however, a grant of voluntary departure is not enough to resolve outstanding immigration issues, such as a long period of unlawful presence in the United States or a record of criminal or immigration law violations. Whether voluntary departure is a successful strategy depends on the facts of the case; in certain circumstances, voluntary departure will have significant negative consequences.

In some cases, voluntary departure is the only relief sought in proceedings. This situation will often arise when the person has a strong basis for returning immediately to the United States with a visa. In other cases, persons may request voluntary departure at the conclusion of proceedings as an alternative form of relief to the main waiver or benefit (e.g., asylum) requested. An individual who is removed from the United States (or departs under an order of removal) is barred from returning for five years if proceedings commenced on the individual's arrival in the United States; i.e., if he or she is classified as an "arriving alien."[241] An individual who is removed from the United States after being charged under INA §237(a) (the "deportability track") is barred from returning for 10 years.[242] An individual removed for an aggravated felony faces a lifetime bar.[243] Note that there is a waiver of these bars, entitled "consent to reapply for admission," discussed later in this chapter.[244]

In any event, there are many circumstances in which an individual may desire an order of voluntary departure rather than an order of removal. However, there are severe consequences for failing to depart on time under an order of voluntary departure. The consequences for failure to depart under an order of voluntary departure are in some ways more severe than failing to depart pursuant to an order of removal. It is extremely difficult to reopen a case when voluntary departure has been given and the recipient did not depart. An individual who remains in the United States and allows voluntary departure to expire is barred from applying for adjustment of status, cancellation of removal, registry, or a change of status for 10 years; for this reason (because relief is not available), these individuals will rarely see their court cases reopened.[245]

In the previous chapter, voluntary departure was discussed as a benefit that someone might or might not be eligible for, depending on the classification of the crime. This chapter will now review the specific requirements for voluntary departure.

Precommencement or preliminary stage of proceedings

Pursuant to INA §240B(a) [8 USC §1229c(a)], an individual can request voluntary departure from DHS agents in lieu of being placed in removal proceedings. In addi-

---

[241] INA §212(a)(9)(A)(i); 8 USC §1182(a)(9)(A)(i).

[242] INA §212(a)(9)(A)(ii); 8 USC §1182(a)(9)(A)(ii).

[243] INA §212(a)(9)(A)(ii); 8 USC §1182(a)(9)(A)(ii).

[244] INA §212(a)(9)(A)(iii); 8 USC §1182(a)(9)(A)(iii).

[245] Motions to reopen are beyond the scope of this book. For a good discussion of motions to reopen before the immigration court, see *Representing Clients in Immigration Court* (AILA 2013 Ed.), available from AILA, *http://agora.aila.org/*, (800) 982-2839.

tion, an individual can request voluntary departure from an IJ at the preliminary stages of the removal hearing (at the master calendar stage).[246] This precommencement/preliminary stage of voluntary departure is not available to an "arriving alien" (someone arriving at a port of entry who is placed in proceedings at that time.)[247] Note that an individual who is arriving at a port of entry and is facing removal from the United States may withdraw the application for admission;[248] this is the counterpart to voluntary departure for arriving aliens.

An individual with a criminal record is still eligible to seek voluntary departure; however, eligibility requires that he or she not be deportable for an aggravated felony offense or on national security grounds.[249] He or she cannot request any other form of relief, and must concede deportability and waive appeal.[250] Unlike an individual who applies for voluntary departure at the conclusion of proceedings, an individual applying for precommencement or preliminary stage voluntary departure need not show the financial ability to pay for his or her own passage.[251]

At this stage the individual may be granted up to 120 days to depart voluntarily.[252] If the IJ grants less than 120 days, but the individual desires more time, he or she can request an extension from Enforcement and Removal Operations (ERO), a unit of ICE. However, from any and all sources combined, the period for voluntary departure cannot exceed 120 days.[253] Furthermore, the IJ may, in the exercise of discretion, require the posting of a voluntary departure bond.[254] ERO may request inspection of the individual's passport.[255]

There is a definite "check-out" procedure; if it is not followed, compliance with voluntary departure will not be entered in the DHS computer system and the individual's case may appear in the data system as a removal (deportation). With the IJ's voluntary departure order in hand, the individual should report to the local ERO office within a few days of the judge's order. ERO will provide the person with a verification-of-departure form. This form should be handed in at the U.S. embassy in the person's home country or the country to which he or she departed. This form is then sent back to the United States as verification of the departure. An individual who de-

---

[246] 8 CFR §1240.26(b)(1)(i)(A).

[247] INA §240B(a)(4); 8 USC §1229c(a)(4).

[248] INA §240B(a)(4); 8 USC §1229c(a)(4).

[249] INA §240B(a)(1); 8 USC §1229c(a)(1).

[250] 8 CFR §§1240.26(b)(1)(i)(B)–(D); *Matter of Ocampo*, 22 I&N Dec. 1301 (BIA 2000).

[251] *Matter of Arguelles-Campos*, 22 I&N Dec. 811 (BIA 1999).

[252] INA §240B(a)(2)(A); 8 USC §1229c(a)(2)(A); 8 CFR §1240.26(e).

[253] *See* 8 CFR §§1240.26(f), (h).

[254] INA §240B(a)(3); 8 USC §1229c(a)(3).

[255] *See* 8 CFR §1240.26(b)(3)(i).

parts on voluntary departure is encouraged to independently retain proof of departure, such as the airline ticket and a stamp in the passport.

If a person fails to comply with the voluntary departure requirements, the order is converted to an order of removal, with all the contingent consequences. It cannot be stressed strongly enough that an individual should request voluntary departure only if he or she plans to depart the United States within the time allotted.

Voluntary Departure at Conclusion of Proceedings

The requirements for voluntary departure at the conclusion of removal proceedings are stricter. An individual seeking voluntary departure at the end of an individual hearing, generally as an alternative or second form of requested relief, must have been physically present in the United States for at least one year prior to service of the NTA.[256] An individual in removal proceedings charged under INA §212(a) may request voluntary departure, but only if the proceedings did not begin at the time of arrival in the United States, and he or she has been present for at least one year. An example of this would be someone who was paroled into the United States and subsequently placed in proceedings, or an individual who entered without inspection. Likewise, an individual charged under INA §237(a) is eligible for voluntary departure, but must have one year of physical presence.

Voluntary departure at this stage requires five years of "good moral character." Good moral character is a term defined at INA §101(f). The definition makes reference, among other things, to INA §212(a)(2): an individual who is inadmissible because he or she has been convicted of a crime involving moral turpitude or a controlled substance violation cannot show good moral character. There is an exception for an offense involving less than 30 grams of marijuana. Section 101(f) also dictates that a person whose income is derived from illegal gambling, who has been convicted of two or more gambling offenses, or has been involved in (or comes to the United States to engage in) prostitution or commercialized vice-type enterprises cannot show good moral character. Anyone involved in (or convicted of) any of these activities within the five-year statutory period would be ineligible for voluntary departure.

In addition, §101(f) states that an individual who has been convicted of an aggravated felony at any time is permanently barred from ever establishing good moral character, hence eligibility for voluntary departure. However, this aggravated felony bar was added to the definition of good moral character by IMMACT90 and does not apply to convictions for aggravated felonies entered before November 29, 1990.

When requested at the conclusion of proceedings, receiving voluntary departure requires the applicant to establish the financial means to depart (*i.e.*, buy a ticket) and present his or her passport.[257] There is a mandatory voluntary departure bond (to be

---

[256] INA §240B(b)(1)(A); 8 USC §1229c(b)(1)(A).

[257] *See* 8 CFR §§1240.26(c)(1)(iv), (2).

paid to ERO) to be set by the judge, but it will be no less than $500.[258] If the individual does not timely post this bond, the voluntary departure is automatically revoked and the order becomes one of removal.[259] At this stage, the individual may be granted up to 60 days to depart voluntarily.[260]

Voluntary departure at the conclusion of proceedings does not require conceding removability or forgoing other forms of relief. An individual may contest the charges of removability, and/or request a waiver, asylum, or some other benefit, as well as voluntary departure. If the primary form of relief is denied, the individual can file an appeal to the BIA without forfeiting the grant of voluntary departure (keeping in mind that the bond must be posted, notwithstanding the filing of an appeal). If the appeal is not sustained, the BIA routinely reinstates voluntary departure for 30 days.

As mentioned above in the discussion of precommencement/early stage voluntary departure, it is critically important that a voluntary departure recipient report to the local ERO office and present the IJ's order, so that the information may be entered into the DHS computer system and the verification form obtained. Then, the individual must report to an American embassy (or consulate, if there is a procedure available) to hand in the verification form. The U.S. embassy staff will note the appearance of the individual on the form and send the form back to the United States. And again, it is advisable to retain independent evidence—aside from this procedure—to serve as proof of timely departure.

Is Your Client an American Citizen?
An Introduction to Derivative and Acquired Citizenship

Derivative citizenship and acquired citizenship are phrases that refer to persons who are U.S. citizens through their parents. In every new case involving potential removal for crime, or some other consequence, it is important to review whether the client is actually an American citizen. Derivative and acquired citizenship is a complicated topic and outside the precise scope of this book. This discussion is intended as an introduction to the topic; if counsel has a client who may be a U.S. citizen through derivation or acquisition, it is recommended that additional sources be consulted.[261]

Whereas naturalization is a procedure by which an individual, according to the law, is able to apply and qualify for U.S. citizenship, derivative citizenship and acquired citizenship refer to those persons who are American citizens by operation of law. Strategically, naturalization can in some cases be a defense to deportation, as

---

[258] 8 CFR §1240.26(c)(3).

[259] 8 CFR §1240.26(c)(3).

[260] INA §240B(b)(2); 8 USC §1229c(b)(2); 8 CFR §1240.26(e).

[261] For additional discussion and charts on derivative citizenship, see *Kurzban's Immigration Law Sourcebook* (AILA 14th Ed. 2014), available from AILA, *http://agora.aila.org*, (800) 982-2839.

discussed below. In comparison, derivative and acquired citizenship do not involve an affirmative application, but will involve legal analysis and a review of relevant facts. Technically, derivative and acquired citizenship are not "relief" from deportation. But because the topic is so important in the representation of foreign-born individuals with criminal convictions, it must be included in any discussion of criminal-alien law.

Certain individuals charged with removability for a crime may actually be American citizens under the law, but either do not realize it or do not have a U.S. passport or certificate of citizenship to prove it. In the process of interviewing a foreign-born individual convicted of a crime, DHS agents, as a matter of course, cover the issue of possible American citizenship because this would avoid deportation altogether. It behooves defense counsel to be aware of the issue and also to cover the possibility of citizenship. Derivative and acquired citizenship are a complicated subject, perhaps the most complicated area of immigration and nationality law. However, it is important to investigate at the very outset of representation whether a client facing deportation, or worried about the consequences of a conviction, is in fact a U.S. citizen.

> **Tip**: When interviewing a client, ask about the parents and their immigration statuses immediately. If one or both of the parents are American citizens, it is a red flag to ask further questions about when and how the parent became an American citizen.

Watch for Effective Dates

Citizenship laws, like all other laws, are periodically changed by Congress. When reviewing whether an individual is an American citizen, the most recent version of the law may not be the law that covers the client; different effective dates apply. For this reason, a good derivative and acquired citizenship chart is useful.

Acquired Citizenship at Birth

Certain persons are American citizens at the time of birth. INA §301 [8 USC §1401] provides categorization for who is a national and citizen at birth. This section includes, in paraphrased fashion:

- A person born in the United States, including a member of an Indian, Eskimo, Aleutian, or other aboriginal tribe.
- A person born outside the United States and its outlying possessions of parents both of whom are U.S. citizens, and one of whom has had a residence in the United States prior to the birth of such person.
- A person born outside the United States and its outlying possessions of parents one of whom is a U.S. citizen who has been physically present in the United States or one of its outlying possessions for a continuous period of one year prior to the birth of such person, and the other of whom is a national, but not a citizen, of the United States.

- A person born in an outlying U.S. possession of parents one of whom is a citizen of the United States who has been physically present in the United States or its outlying possessions for a continuous period of one year at any time prior to the birth of such person.

- A person of unknown parentage found in the United States while under the age of five years, until it is shown, prior to his or her attaining the age of 21 years, that he or she was not born in the United States.

- A person born outside the geographical limits of the United States and its outlying possessions of parents one of whom is an alien, and the other a citizen of the United States who, prior to the birth of such person, was physically present in the United States or its outlying possessions for a period or periods totaling not less than five years, at least two of which were after attaining the age of 14 years.[262] Periods of honorable service in the armed forces of the United States, or employment with the U.S. government or with an international organization by such citizen parent, count toward the physical presence requirement.

- A person born before noon (EST) May 24, 1934, outside the United States of an alien father and a U.S. citizen mother who had residence in the United States prior to the birth of that person.

Derivative Citizenship After Birth

INA §320 [8 USC §1431] states (emphasis added):

(a) A child born outside the United States automatically becomes a citizen of the United States when *all* of the following conditions have been fulfilled:

> (1) At least one parent of the child is a citizen of the United States, whether by birth or naturalization.
>
> (2) The child is under the age of 18 years.
>
> (3) The child is residing in the United States in the legal and physical custody of the citizen parent pursuant to a lawful admission for permanent residence.

(b) Subsection (a) shall apply to a child adopted by a United States citizen parent if the child satisfies the requirements applicable to adopted children under section 101(b)(1).

Under §320, an individual who is born outside the United States but later becomes an LPR derives U.S. citizenship if one parent is a U.S. citizen, including by naturalization, prior to the child's 18th birthday, provided that the individual resided in the custody of the citizen parent.

---

[262] The Immigration Reform and Control Act of 1986, Pub. L. No. 99-603, §12, 100 Stat. 3359, shortened the required period of U.S. residence for the citizen parent from the previous 10 total/five post–age-14 years. The shorter period applies only to persons born on or after Nov. 14, 1986.

➤ **Example**: Troy Goodluck was born in the Bahamas. Troy was born out of wedlock and has never known his biological father. He and his mother immigrated to the United States (in other words, became LPRs) when he was a child. When Troy was 15 years old, his mother naturalized to American citizenship. Troy became an American citizen automatically when his mother naturalized.

Individual who turned 18 before February 27, 2001

Section 320, as cited above, was amended by the Child Citizenship Act of 2000 (CCA).[263] The version cited above applies to individuals who were under 18 years of age on February 27, 2001 (the effective date of the CCA). Individuals who turned 18 prior to February 27, 2001, are covered by the pre-CCA INA §§320[264] and 321.[265]

Essentially, the CCA eliminated the requirement that *both* parents become American citizens prior to the individual's 18th birthday. Under the CCA, only one parent

---

[263] Child Citizenship Act of 2000 (CCA), Pub. L. No. 106-395, 114 Stat. 1631.

[264] The pre-CCA version of INA §320 [8 USC §1431] read:

(a) A child born outside of the United States, one of whose parents at the time of the child's birth was an alien and the other of whose parents then was and never ceased to be a citizen of the United States, shall if such alien parent is naturalized, become a citizen of the United States, when—

(1) such naturalization takes place while such child is under the age of eighteen years; and

(2) such child is residing in the United States pursuant to a lawful admission for permanent residence at the time of naturalization or thereafter and begins to reside permanently in the United States while under the age of eighteen years.

(b) Subsection (a) of this section shall apply to an adopted child only if the child is residing in the United States at the time of naturalization of the adoptive parent, in the custody of his adoptive parents, pursuant to a lawful admission for permanent residents.

[265] INA §321 [8 USC §1432], before it was repealed by the CCA in 2000, read:

(a) A child born outside of the United States of alien parents, or of an alien parent and a citizen parent who has subsequently lost citizenship of the United States, becomes a citizen of the United States upon fulfillment of the following conditions:

(1) the naturalization of both parents; or

(2) the naturalization of the surviving parent if one of the parents is deceased; or

(3) the naturalization of the parent having legal custody of the child when there has been a legal separation of the parents or the naturalization of the mother if the child was born out of wedlock and the paternity of the child has not been established by legitimating; and if

(4) such naturalization takes place while such child is under the age of eighteen years; and

(5) such child is residing in the United States pursuant to a lawful admission for permanent residence at the time of the naturalization of the parent last naturalized under clause (1) of this subsection, or the parent naturalized under clause (2) or (3) of this subsection, or thereafter begins to reside permanently in the United States while under the age of eighteen years.

(b) Subsection (a) of this section shall apply to an adopted child only if the child is residing in the United States at the time of naturalization of such adoptive parent or parents, in the custody of his adoptive parent or parents, pursuant to a lawful admission for permanent residence.

need be or become an American citizen prior to the child's 18th birthday; however, the child must be in the legal and physical custody of the American parent. And the child must be an LPR.

> ➢ *Example*: Fanny Badluck is born in the Bahamas in 1970. At the time of her birth, her parents are married, but they divorce when she is two years old. She subsequently immigrates to the United States with her mother. Although Fanny grows up in her mother's household, there is no formal custody agreement. In 1986, when Fanny is 16, her mother naturalizes. In the year 2000, Fanny is convicted of money laundering in the amount of $11,000, and placed in removal proceedings. Is Fanny an American citizen? No. Fanny turned 18 in the year 1988, approximately two and a half years before the CCA. Although Fanny's mother naturalized when she was only 16, and she lived with her mother, there was never any formal, legal agreement giving custody to Fanny's mother, and her father remains a Bahamian citizen.

> ➢ *Compare*: Fanny Betterluck is born in the Bahamas in 1970 of parents who are married and remain married. The family immigrates together to the United States. Fanny's parents both naturalize when she is 16. In the year 2000, Fanny is convicted of money laundering. Fanny is not subject to removal proceedings because she became an American citizen by operation of law: when her parents both naturalized, she was under 18, and she was an LPR.

In a nutshell, for individuals who were over 18 years of age before February 27, 2001: Where the child was born in wedlock, both parents must have become U.S. citizens before the child turned 18. Where the child was born out of wedlock (and paternity is not established through legitimating), the mother must naturalize before the child turned 18. In the case of divorce or separation, the custodial parent (*pursuant to a legal custody agreement*) would have had to become a U.S. citizen before the child's 18th birthday. In the case of death, the surviving parent must have naturalized before the child turned 18. Remember, the client must become an LPR while under the age of 18 in order to acquire citizenship. Citizenship is not passed on through the parents if the child does not become an LPR while under the age of 18. Finally, if a child is under 18 years of age, but married, he or she is ineligible for the derivative citizenship.

Naturalization as a Defense to Deportation

Termination of Removal Proceedings for Naturalization

The regulation at 8 CFR §1239.2(f) allows an IJ to terminate removal proceedings so that an individual may proceed on a pending application for naturalization[266] where:

- He or she establishes prima facie eligibility for naturalization; and
- The matter involves exceptionally appealing or humanitarian factors.

Unfortunately, in *Matter of Acosta-Hidalgo*, a 2007 decision that basically emasculates this regulation, the BIA ruled that the IJ may not terminate until he or she receives an affirmative communication from USCIS that the individual is statutorily eligible to naturalize.[267] This precedent has been upheld as reasonable by the Ninth Circuit.[268]

Under the regulation, an individual in removal proceedings can file an application for naturalization (Form N-400) with USCIS and prepare a motion to terminate with the immigration court. Assuming, first and foremost (and in light of *Acosta-Hidalgo*) that the respondent can obtain the required consent from USCIS, the motion should highlight, and be supported by, evidence of compelling equities and humanitarian factors. (Note that not being eligible for any other relief may be a particularly compelling factor.)[269]

Bearing in mind that an individual with an aggravated felony conviction on or after November 30, 1990, is barred from establishing eligibility for naturalization,[270] whom does this regulation help? Termination for naturalization is a good option for individuals with old convictions that, although they may be eligible for relief in the form of an INA §212(c) waiver or cancellation of removal, do not want to—and should not have to—go through the aggravation of full-blown removal proceedings. Termination also may be a good option for an individual who is deportable for a firearms offense, but has not accumulated the seven years of continuous residence or five years of lawful permanent residence to be eligible for cancellation of removal.

---

[266] Under INA §318 [8 USC §1429], an individual who is in deportation or removal proceedings, or is under a final order of removal, cannot naturalize.

[267] *Matter of Acosta-Hidalgo*, 24 I&N Dec. 103 (BIA 2007).

[268] *Hernandez de Anderson v. Gonzales*, 497 F.3d 927 (9th Cir. 2007).

[269] For suggestions for preparation of a motion to terminate under 8 CFR §1239.2(f), see chapter ten.

[270] *See* INA §316(a)(3) [8 USC §1427(a)(3)] (requiring good moral character, which is negated by aggravated felony pursuant to INA §101(f)(8)). Remember, the aggravated felony bar was added to the definition of good moral character by IMMACT90 and does not apply to convictions for aggravated felonies entered before its effective date, November 29, 1990, so persons with convictions prior to that date can be helped.

Soldiers and Veterans

Sections 329 and 330 of the INA [8 USC §§1440, 1441] allow certain members and veterans of the U.S. armed forces to naturalize under relaxed residence requirements.

Under INA §328 [8 USC §1439], an individual who served honorably in the armed forces for a continuous period of three years may be naturalized without meeting the five-year residence requirement, or having resided in a particular state for three months, if the application is filed while the applicant is still in the service, or within six months of the honorable termination of such service. Under this section:

- No residence within a state is required;
- Pending deportation proceedings are not an impediment to naturalization if the applicant is actually in the armed forces;[271] and
- The individual must establish honorable discharge from service.

Section 328 refers to individuals who are currently in service, or have been discharged within the last six months. As a practical matter, §328 will rarely be relevant to an individual facing removal for a crime. The section that may be useful, however, is INA §329 [8 USC §1440]. Under §329, an individual who served honorably in the armed forces during a period of hostilities may be naturalized notwithstanding pending deportation proceedings, and need only establish good moral character during the one-year period preceding the filing of the application. The statutory section is broken down in the regulations at 8 CFR §§329.1, 329.2.[272]

---

[271] INA §328(b)(2).

[272] **Part 329**—Special Classes of Persons Who May be Naturalized: Naturalization Based Upon Active Duty Service in the United States Armed Forces During Specified Periods of Hostilities

§329.1 Definitions. As used in this part:

Honorable service and separation means service and separation from service which the executive department under which the applicant served determines to be honorable, including:

    (1) That such applicant had not been separated from service on account of alienage;

    (2) That such applicant was not a conscientious objector who performed no military, air or naval duty; and

    (3) That such applicant did not refuse to wear a military uniform.

Service in an active duty status in the Armed Forces of the United States means active service in the following organization:

    (1) United States Army, United States Navy, United States Marines, United States Air Force, United States Coast Guard; or

    (2) A National Guard unit during such time as the unit is Federally recognized as a reserve component of the Armed Forces of the United States and that unit is called for active duty.

World War I means the period beginning on April 6, 1917, and ending on November 11, 1918.

§329.2 Eligibility. To be eligible for naturalization under Section 329(a) of the Act, an applicant must establish that he or she:

(a) Has served honorably in an active duty status in the Armed Forces of the United States during:

Continued

Thus, under INA §329 [8 USC §1440], an individual who served in the armed forces during a period of war and is honorably discharged must be naturalized even though he or she is in removal proceedings, provided he or she can establish one year of good moral character immediately prior to filing the application (and is still a person of good moral character at the time of interview and swearing in). Note that an individual with an aggravated felony conviction entered after November 29, 1990, still will be barred from naturalizing under this section, pursuant to IMMACT90 §509.

> ➢ *Example*: Johnny Soldado, a citizen of Costa Rica, entered the United States as an LPR when he was a teenager in the early 1960s. He is drafted and serves in the Vietnam War. He is then honorably discharged. In 1989, Soldado is arrested and charged with trafficking in firearms. He goes to trial. The jury finds him guilty. Johnny Soldado serves six years. At first, he lives his life undetected by legacy INS officials; he is never arrested for criminal activity again. But in 2002, Soldado is returning from a trip to Costa Rica, and Inspections runs a record check in the computer. The conviction comes to light and Soldado is placed in removal proceedings, charged with deportability for a firearms conviction and an aggravated felony. In removal proceedings, Johnny Soldado is

---

(1) World War I;

(2) The period beginning on September 1, 1939 and ending on December 31, 1946;

(3) The period beginning on June 25, 1950 and ending on July 1, 1955;

(4) The period beginning on February 28, 1961 and ending on October 15, 1978; or

(5) Any other period as may be designated by the President in an Executive Order pursuant to Section 329(a) of the Act;

(b) If separated, has been separated honorably from service . . .

(c) Satisfies the permanent residence requirement in one of the following ways:

(1) Any time after enlistment or induction ... the applicant was lawfully admitted to the United States as a permanent resident; or

(2) At the time of enlistment or induction, the applicant was physically present in the geographical territory of the United States, the Canal Zone, American Samoa, Midway Island (prior to August 21, 1959), or Swain's Island, ... whether or not the applicant has been lawfully admitted to the United States as a permanent resident;

(d) Has been, for at least one year prior to filing the application for naturalization, and continues to be, of good moral character, attached to the principles of the Constitution of the United States, and favorably disposed toward the good order and happiness of the United States; and

(e) Has complied with all other requirements for naturalization as provided in part 316 of this chapter, except that:

(1) The applicant may be of any age;

(2) The applicant is not required to satisfy the residence requirements under § 316.2(a)(3) through (a)(6) of this chapter; and

(3) The applicant may be naturalized even if an outstanding notice to appear pursuant to 8 CFR part 239 ... exists.

not eligible for §212(c) relief because he served more than five years in prison. However, his attorney files an application for naturalization based on his honorable service during the Vietnam War. While the immigration court case is still pending, Johnny Soldado is successfully interviewed, attends a naturalization ceremony, and becomes an American citizen. The removal case is terminated.

Relief from Alien Smuggling Charges

Relief from Deportability and Inadmissibility, Absent a Conviction

Waiver for smuggling immediate family members

As stated in previous chapters, an individual may be considered inadmissible or deportable for alien smuggling even though he or she has not been criminally convicted of that offense.[273] An individual who is either inadmissible or deportable for smuggling may qualify for a waiver if the smuggling involved a spouse, parent, son, or daughter.[274] In addition, the waiver applicant (the smuggler) must be an LPR to qualify for a waiver. The waivers in both inadmissibility and deportability utilize basically the same language, and state (in summary fashion):

> The Attorney General may, in his discretion for humanitarian purposes, to assure family unity, or when it is otherwise in the public interest, [waive the charge of alien smuggling] in the case of an alien lawfully admitted for permanent residence....

Thus, absent a conviction, an individual who is found to be either inadmissible (implicating issuance of a visa, entry, of adjustment of status), or deportable (subject to removal) for alien smuggling may request a waiver of the charge based on the following criteria:

- The smuggler-applicant must be an LPR;
- The smuggling must have involved a spouse, parent, son, or daughter; and
- The waiver may be granted:
  - based on humanitarian grounds;
  - to ensure family unity; or
  - in the public interest.

---

[273] *See* INA §212(a)(6)(E) [8 USC §1182(a)(6)(E)] (inadmissibility); §237(a)(1)(E) [8 USC §1227(a)(1)(E)] (deportability).

[274] INA §212(d)(11) [8 USC §1182(d)(11)] (inadmissibility); §237(a)(1)(E)(iii) [8 USC §1227(a)(1)(E)(iii)] (deportability).

Cancellation of removal

When an LPR is charged with inadmissibility or deportability for alien smuggling, and the underlying activity did not involve an immediate family member, cancellation of removal under INA §240A(a) [8 USC §1229b(a)] may waive the ground if the applicant is otherwise eligible for this relief.[275] Note that cancellation is not available if the individual has been convicted of alien smuggling, because a conviction implicates an aggravated felony status,[276] and aggravated felons are barred from this relief.[277] Rather, cancellation is an option for individuals who are charged with smuggling a person or persons other than an immediate family member if the following criteria are met:

- The applicant has been an LPR for at least five years;[278]
- The applicant has resided in the United States for at least seven years following a lawful admission;[279] and
- He or she has not been convicted under 8 USC §1324(a) (relating to alien smuggling, the aggravated felony conviction).

Relief from a Conviction for Alien Smuggling (An Aggravated Felony)

Forms of relief for aggravated felons are discussed throughout this chapter. However, because an individual who has engaged in alien smuggling may be inadmissible and/or deportable—notwithstanding a waiver of the aggravated felony ground—an independent discussion of relief for alien smuggling, in particular, is helpful.

Adjustment of status

As discussed previously, an aggravated felony conviction may—in certain circumstances—be waived through adjustment of status. However, adjustment of status will not be an effective cure for the individual convicted of alien smuggling. This is because the individual will remain inadmissible under INA §212(a)(6)(E), and is thus ineligible for adjustment.

In this regard, it is important to remember that a conviction for alien smuggling is not an aggravated felony if the "smugglee" was an immediate family member and it was the first offense. The only conceivable situation where an LPR would need to and could effectively "waive" the aggravated felony ground through adjustment of status is where the conviction is for a second or subsequent offense, and involved only an immediate family member. In this rare situation (a second conviction for smuggling a spouse, parent, son, or daughter), adjustment of status combined with the INA

---

[275] INA §240A(a); 8 USC §1229b(a).

[276] INA §101(a)(43)(N); 8 USC §1101(a)(43)(N).

[277] INA §240A(a)(3); 8 USC §1229b(a)(3).

[278] INA §240A(a)(1); 8 USC §1229b(a)(1).

[279] INA §240A(a)(2); 8 USC §1229b(a)(2).

§212(d)(11) waiver for smuggling could waive deportability for the aggravated felony. If this unusual fact pattern does arise, it is important to note that both adjustment of status and the §212(d)(11) waiver are discretionary benefits that can be denied, for example, for a second conviction for the same unlawful activity.

INA §212(h) waiver

Alien smuggling is not a crime involving moral turpitude; it is an independent ground of inadmissibility. Therefore, a waiver under INA §212(h) does not cure a conviction for alien smuggling.

Cancellation of removal

Cancellation of removal does not resolve deportability for an aggravated felony/alien smuggling conviction. Although cancellation can waive inadmissibility and removability for alien smuggling when there is no conviction, cancellation is not available to an individual with an aggravated felony offense (see discussion above).

INA §212(c) waiver

An individual who entered a plea to alien smuggling prior to April 24, 1996, may seek a waiver under the now-repealed INA §212(c). A waiver under §212(c) is available to LPRs who have maintained a continuous, lawful domicile for at least seven years. An individual who is an aggravated felon based on an alien smuggling conviction (under 8 USC §1324), and who has served five years or more in prison for the aggravated felony or felonies, is ineligible for the §212(c) waiver.

Asylum and withholding of removal

An individual with an aggravated felony conviction for alien smuggling is barred from receiving asylum.[280] Additionally, an individual with an aggravated felony conviction for alien smuggling who has been sentenced to a term of five years or more is presumed to have been convicted of a "particularly serious crime" and is barred from withholding of removal under both the INA and the CAT. An individual with an aggravated felony/alien smuggling conviction who has been sentenced to less than five years in prison may request withholding, but might be denied if a finding is made that the conviction represents a "particularly serious crime" such that the applicant is a "danger to the United States community."[281] The last-chance form of relief for an individual with an aggravated felony/alien smuggling conviction may be deferral of removal under the CAT.[282] This form of relief is available even to persons convicted of an aggravated felony offense, and is without regard to the length of sentence imposed.

---

[280] INA §208(b)(2)(B); 8 USC §1158(b)(2)(B).

[281] INA §241(b)(3)(B); 8 USC §1231(b)(3)(B); 8 CFR §§208.16(d)(2), 1208.16(d)(2).

[282] 8 CFR §§208.17, 1208.17.

Naturalization

An individual with an aggravated felony conviction entered on or after November 29, 1990, is barred from receiving naturalization; thus, a conviction for alien smuggling (other than an immediate family member) after this date results in a permanent bar to naturalization. An individual with a conviction before November 29, 1990, may be eligible for naturalization; however, if he or she is amenable to removal proceedings under INA §237(a)(1)(E) [8 USC §1227(a)(1)(E)], the file could be referred to ICE for removal proceedings. If the file is referred for removal proceedings based on an old conviction, naturalization becomes a form of relief through a motion to terminate proceedings under 8 CFR §1239.2(f).

Nonimmigrant Visa Waiver Under INA §212(d)(3)

Introduction: "My son's been deported for an aggravated felony; can he ever come back?"

The foregoing discussion on relief and waivers focuses primarily on individuals who are physically present in the United States and face removal based on a criminal record, or are applicants for either adjustment of status or an immigrant visa and require a waiver because of criminal activity. This section presents an alternative strategy—a "fall-back" position—for entering (or returning to) the United States. An individual who has been removed from the United States on account of crime, or cannot qualify for permanent residency because of a criminal record, may find relief in the nonimmigrant visa waiver found at INA §212(d)(3) [8 USC §1182(d)(3)]. This valuable provision of the law allows a waiver of inadmissibility for individuals who seek to enter the United States as *nonimmigrants*. These are persons who are inadmissible because of a crime (or because of any other ground of inadmissibility, such as health-related grounds), and seek to enter the United States temporarily as tourists, business professionals, investors, students, entertainers, etc.

This waiver may be particularly useful to an individual who has been removed on account of a criminal conviction, and is thus inadmissible to the United States for five, 10, or 20 years, or—in the case of an aggravated felon—for life.[283] An individual who has been removed for a crime may nonetheless return to the United States as a nonimmigrant if a waiver is approved under INA §212(d)(3). Similarly, and regardless of whether he or she has been removed, an individual with a criminal record who does not qualify for an *immigrant* visa waiver under INA §212(h) (because he or she does not have the qualifying relative, or cannot meet the eligibility criteria) may qual-

---

[283] INA §§212(a)(9)(A), (B) [8 USC §§1182(a)(9)(A), (B)] render inadmissible individuals who have previously been removed from the United States. An individual who was ordered removed as an arriving alien is inadmissible for five years; an individual ordered deported under INA §237 is inadmissible for 10 years; an individual who is removed a second or subsequent time is inadmissible for 20 years; and an individual removed on account of an aggravated felony is permanently ineligible for admission.

ify for a *nonimmigrant* waiver under INA §212(d)(3). Thus, an individual who may never obtain (or regain) permanent resident status in the United States may be successful in visiting family and friends, attending an important conference, or even working and investing on an extended basis, through issuance of this waiver.

Jurisdiction

Applications at the consulate

There are two separate provisions at INA §212(d)(3)—a waiver at a consulate and a waiver at a port of entry. Most individuals who seek to enter the United States in a nonimmigrant visa category must apply for a visa at the American consul's office abroad (normally, but not always, in the individual's country of citizenship). Nonimmigrant visa categories are defined at INA §101(a)(15) [8 USC §1101(a)(15)]. An individual who is inadmissible on account of crime (or any other basis) who seeks to enter the United States with a visa applies for the INA §212(d)(3)(A)(i) waiver simultaneously while applying for a visa. The consul, however, does not make a decision on the waiver; the consul makes a recommendation, and then forwards the application to a DHS office abroad.[284] Thus, DHS (through USCIS) makes the final determination on whether to approve a nonimmigrant §212(d)(3) waiver.

Regulations implementing this statutory provision are at 8 CFR §§212.4(a), 1212.4(a). Counsel also should review 22 CFR §41.95.[285] According to the regulation, an approved waiver will state each ground of inadmissibility that is waived. The approval also will state the date of intended arrival for the applicant, and whether the authorization is valid for multiple entries or a specified number of entries. When multiple entries are authorized, the approval of the waiver must state (in regards to the initial entry only):

- The purpose of each stay;
- The number of entries authorized;
- Any conditions precedent to admission;
- The justification for exercising the authority at INA §212(d)(3); and
- That the authorization of the waiver is subject to revocation at any time.[286]

Furthermore, according to regulation,[287] the period authorized to use the waiver shall not exceed the time needed based on the underlying justification for the waiver. In no case shall the waiver or authorization's validity period exceed five years. And,

---

[284] *See* 22 CFR §§40.301(a)–(c). The various consular posts fall under the jurisdiction of regional offices, located in Bangkok, Mexico City, Rome, or the specified district office with jurisdiction over the consular post. *See* 8 CFR §§100.4(b)(33)–(37). Prior to creation of DHS, these offices were referred to as "INS officers-in-charge overseas."

[285] Title 22 of the CFR governs the State Department—hence, the U.S. embassies and consulate offices.

[286] 8 CFR §§212.4(c)(1), 1212.4(c)(1).

[287] 8 CFR §§212.4(c)(2), 1212.4(c)(2).

where only a single entry is authorized, the period of stay authorized at the port of entry shall not exceed six months. After five years, authorization for the waiver may not be revalidated—a new application must be filed and approved.

Applications at a port of entry

INA §212(d)(3)(A)(ii) addresses applications for a nonimmigrant visa waiver for individuals who are in possession of a visa or other valid entry document, and do not need to apply for a visa at an American consular post. Individuals who already possess valid entry documents (normally a visa) apply for waiver with DHS, specifically before CBP. Subsection (A)(ii) also applies to individuals who are eligible for admission without a visa based on their nationality.[288] (Note, however, that in terms of the visa waiver program (VWP), regulations require that an individual who has been removed and is inadmissible for crime apply for a visa at a consular post; individuals from VWP countries who have been deported and are inadmissible are not eligible to take advantage of the visa waiver program.[289]) A nonimmigrant who does not require an actual nonimmigrant visa affixed in the passport (and thereby avoids applying for a visa at a consular post), or already has a nonimmigrant visa, applies for an INA §212(d)(3) waiver at the intended port of entry.

The §212(d)(3)(A)(ii) waiver application can be presented (or sent) in advance of the arrival to the Inspections component of CBP (it might take several months to process). The procedure for waivers under INA §212(d)(3)(A)(ii) is set forth at 8 CFR §§212.4(b), 1212.4(b). This regulation provides detailed explanation of the required information and procedure.[290]

An individual who does not present the application in advance, but simply arrives at a port of entry and seeks admission, may apply for a waiver under INA §212(d)(3)(A)(ii), but risks being denied admission until such time that the waiver is approved. DHS does have the authority (although it is by no means required) to parole a prospective nonimmigrant into the United States, and defer the inspection, pending adjudication of the waiver.[291] In such a situation, if the §212(d)(3) waiver is denied following parole for deferred inspection, the individual has a right to renew the application in front of an IJ in removal proceedings.[292] If the deciding officer at the port of entry denies the waiver application, and the applicant *was not paroled into the United States*, an appeal of the denial may be taken to the BIA. There is a 15-day appeal period. In addition, if CBP places the individual in removal proceedings, the application may be renewed before the IJ.[293]

---

[288] 8 CFR §1212.1(a); *see* chapter one.

[289] 8 CFR §§217.2(b)(2), 217.4(a).

[290] The waiver application is discussed more fully in chapter thirteen.

[291] 8 CFR §§235.2(b)(2), 1235.2(b)(2).

[292] 8 CFR §§235.2(d), 1235.2(d); *see also Matter of Hranka*, 16 I&N Dec. 491 (BIA 1978).

[293] 8 CFR §§212.4(b), 1212.4(b).

> **Tip**: Counsel should not apply by ambush. An individual (and his or her attorney) who is aware of a relevant ground of inadmissibility should not simply arrive at a port of entry, make application for admission, and await a determination of inadmissibility. Rather, an application should be presented (or sent) in advance of the trip. The regulation states that, if an application is made "at the time of arrival" at the port of entry, "the applicant shall establish that he was not aware of the ground of inadmissibility and that it could not have been ascertained by the exercise of reasonable diligence."[294]

Following an admission (entry) into the United States, the 212(d)(3) waiver is not available on a *nunc pro tunc* basis in removal proceedings before an immigration judge.[295] This situation (which would involve deportability under INA §237) is distinguishable from the case where an individual arrives in the United States, makes application for admission, and is not admitted based on a ground of inadmissibility. In this latter situation, the individual may seek a waiver under §212(d)(3) by presentation of the application to DHS at the border, or with an IJ in the context of removal proceedings based on inadmissibility.[296]

Separate permission to re-enter after deportation or removal (Form I-212) not required

An individual who has been removed from the United States on a criminal-related ground of inadmissibility or deportability, and is subsequently granted a waiver under INA §212(d)(3), does not require a separate approval of Form I-212, Application for Permission to Reapply for Admission into the United States After Deportation or Removal.[297] Immigration attorneys regularly advise clients who have been ordered removed that they are barred from returning to the United States for a certain period of time—sometimes forever. That part of immigration law that does not allow an individual to return after removal is, in fact, a ground of inadmissibility at INA §212(a)(9) [8 USC §1182(a)(9)]. The §212(d)(3) waiver is a waiver of the grounds of inadmissibility under INA §212(a) for individuals who seek to enter as nonimmigrants. Accordingly, the provision waives application of INA §212(a)(9)(A), relating to "aliens previously removed." Separate permission to re-apply for admission is not required. (Conversely, where the only ground of inadmissibility is the fact of the re-

---

[294] 8 CFR §§212.4(b), 1212.4(b).

[295] *Borrego v. Mukasey*, 539 F.3d 689 (7th Cir. 2008), citing: *Matter of Fueyo*, 20 I&N Dec. 84 (BIA 1989).

[296] *Atunnise v. Mukasey*, 523 F.3d 830, 838–39 (7th Cir. 2008).

[297] *See, e.g.*, *Atunnise v. Mukasey*, 523 F.3d 830, at 838. Note that 8 CFR §§212.2 and 1212.2 govern consent to reapply for admission after deportation, removal, or departure. This regulation refers to application Form I-212, which may be filed according to different procedures based on the posture of the case and location of the applicant.

moval (INA §212(a)(9)(A) or (B)), an approved I-212 application for permission to reapply is all that is required; an independent §212(d)(3) waiver is not necessary.)

Does not waive security or terrorism grounds of inadmissibility

The waiver under INA §212(d)(3) is not available to persons who are inadmissible under INA §212(a)(3), which includes security, terrorist, and related grounds. With the exception of persons inadmissible for export violations, traditional crimes do not fall within the scope of §212(a)(3); that section discusses inadmissibility for national security-type reasons.

Factors for Consideration

A waiver under INA §212(d)(3) is discretionary. In *Matter of Hranka*,[298] the BIA set forth the criteria for considering a §212(d)(3) waiver. The BIA noted that there is no requirement that the applicant's reasons for wishing to enter the United States be "compelling." The BIA said that there are three factors for consideration:

(1) the risk of harm to society if the applicant is admitted;

(2) the seriousness of the applicant's immigration or criminal law violation; and

(3) the nature of the applicant's reasons for wishing to enter the United States.

In an interesting criminal sentencing appeal decision penned by now–Supreme Court Justice Sonia Sotomayor (while on the U.S. Court of Appeals for the Second Circuit), the court goes through the various factors for consideration in deciding a §212(d)(3) waiver, noting that the length of the sentence imposed is a significant factor for review.[299]

Experience teaches that the period of time that has elapsed since the criminal activity occurred is a key concern for both consular officers and DHS offices abroad as they adjudicate these waivers. Generally speaking—and unless there is an emergent, humanitarian situation—an individual who has been removed on account of a criminal conviction should wait at least three years before seeking a §212(d)(3) waiver.

A waiver can be granted for one entry only, or for multiple entries. The precise terms will be noted on the visa itself. Conditions, such as posting of bond, can be attached to issuance of the visa and approval of the waiver. Finally, it is important to note that processing times vary, and in the post–9/11 world, and with the transition from legacy INS to DHS, the processing times for §212(d)(3) waivers have increased significantly. It is prudent to advise a client that consideration of a waiver request could take several months, or up to one year.[300]

---

[298] *Matter of Hranka*, 16 I&N Dec. 491 (BIA 1978).

[299] *U.S. v. Hamdi*, 432 F.3d 115, 118–19 (2d Cir. 2005).

[300] For further detail on how to file this application, see chapter thirteen.

Defending the Criminal Charge of Re-entry After Removal[301]

A non–American citizen who has been physically removed from and re-enters the United States without permission from DHS is subject to criminal prosecution under 8 USC §1326. A removal order is not necessarily an order by an IJ in removal proceedings. A removal order for purposes of 8 USC §1326 may be an expedited removal order (from CBP at the border); an expedited administrative order entered by ICE (for non-LPRs convicted of an aggravated felony); a removal order of a VWP entrant under INA §217; a stipulated (voluntary) removal order; or a previously ordered reinstatement (*i.e.*, a re-entry after a previous reinstatement).

The initial criminal penalty for illegal re-entry following removal is a maximum of two years in prison and a fine.[302] However, the criminal penalty increases if the individual was deported for three or more misdemeanors or a felony to a maximum of 10 years' imprisonment.[303] Reentry following removal for an aggravated felony charge carries a maximum penalty of 20 years.[304] (Hence, much of immigration case law comes from the sentencing guidelines/re-entry context, wherein the defendant contests the aggravated felony classification.)

Some obvious defenses to a criminal charge of re-entry after removal under 8 USC §1326 are misidentification or establishing that the individual had been granted a waiver to re-enter. Realistically, these defenses are rarely available. If facts support these defenses, they should be utilized.

Statute of limitations issues can be very helpful in defending against a re-entry after removal charge. 18 USC §3283 contains a five-year statute of limitations that governs re-entry cases. If the individual re-enters and files an application with DHS—or otherwise puts DHS on notice that he or she is physically present in the United States (*e.g.*, providing a current address), the statute of limitations begins to run from the date of this filing. If five years have passed since the date of such a filing, and the individual is then arrested and charged with re-entry after removal, the statute has run and the case cannot be prosecuted. There are many examples of applications a person (even a person who entered illegally) might file. The most typical include an application for temporary protected status,[305] a family visa petition (where the subject is the beneficiary of a petition), or a work permit application.

Some non–American citizen defendants re-enter because they face death or serious bodily injury if they remain in their country of nationality. For example, a national of a country whose institutions are weakened by narcotics trafficking organizations

---

[301] This section on re-entry of removed aliens was originally contributed by attorney Martin Roth of Fort Lauderdale; it has been updated and revised by author Mary Kramer.

[302] 8 USC §§1326(a).

[303] 8 USC §1326(b)(1).

[304] 8 USC §1326(b)(2).

[305] This classification is described in chapter one.

is removed to his native country after serving a reduced sentence after cooperation. His cooperation in the United States has placed him in mortal danger back home, so he re-enters out of necessity. Under these facts, the affirmative defense known as "coercion and intimidation" or "duress" is available. *U.S. v. Lee*[306] provides that a coercion instruction is appropriate when there is evidence the defendant acted under threat of imminent physical harm without the opportunity to avoid the harm or summon protection from the authorities.

An individual who fears persecution in his or her native country may fill out an asylum application and request a "reasonable fear interview" with the Asylum Office. If that reasonable fear threshold is established, the individual can apply for asylum, or withholding, or protection under the CAT in front of the IJ in limited proceedings called "asylum only" proceedings.[307] Note that if the individual is subject to reinstatement, asylum is not available (only withholding under the statute or CAT).

Collaterally attacking the underlying removal order

The U.S. Supreme Court, in *U.S. v. Mendoza-Lopez*,[308] held that where a deportation determination made in an administrative proceeding is to play a critical role in the subsequent imposition of a criminal sanction, judicial review by an Article III court must be available at the subsequent proceeding unless the deportation order was already judicially reviewed or review was waived.[309] To the extent that 8 USC §1326 purports to prohibit contesting the validity of the underlying deportation order, the statute was ruled violative of constitutional due process.[310] Put another way, because a valid deportation order is an element of the criminal offense at 8 USC §1326, the defendant has the right to collaterally attack the validity of the underlying order. The *Mendoza-Lopez* ruling was subsequently codified at 8 USC §1326(d).

> ➤ **Practice Pointer**: This book can be helpful in preparing a collateral attack: these chapters analyze immigration law with a focus on classifying crimes pursuant to a categorical approach, eligibility for waivers, and defining "admission" for purposes of inadmissibility versus deportability. Criminal attorneys should review chapters three, five, and nine in considering potential collateral attacks based on changes in case law that render the underlying order illegal.

A successful collateral attack on the underlying removal order pursuant to 8 USC §1326(d) requires establishing all three of the following elements vis à vis a Rule 16 motion to dismiss:

---

[306] *U.S. v. Lee*, 694 F.2d 649 (11th Cir. 1983).

[307] 8 CFR §§208.2(c)(1)(v) and (2)(i).

[308] *U.S. v. Mendoza-Lopez*, 481 U.S. 828 (1987).

[309] *U.S. v. Mendoza-Lopez*, at 837–40.

[310] *U.S. v. Mendoza-Lopez*, at 837.

CH. 10 • IMMIGRATION DEFENSE: WAIVERS AND OTHER RELIEF 517

1) The defendant exhausted administrative remedies in proceedings before the EOIR (whatever the basis for the underlying attack, did defendant raise the issue before the IJ and the BIA?);

2) The defendant was denied judicial review in proceedings (includes cases where IJ and BIA erroneously pretermit relief); and

3) The proceedings were fundamentally unfair (a due process violation combined with prejudice).

Examples of potential collateral attacks include *in absentia* orders where the defendant/respondent did not receive proper notice.[311] Some defendants may have been removed in proceedings where they were denied the opportunity to seek INA §212(c) relief because of the unconstitutional retroactive application of AEDPA and IIRAIRA in proceedings prior to the decision in *INS v. St. Cyr*.[312] In such circumstances, a defendant in a re-entry case can collaterally attack the deportation order in a motion to dismiss before the district court presiding over the criminal case. Another example is when a defendant was ordered deported *in absentia* where the immigration court file shows lack of proper notice. Other ideas for a successful collateral attack may include a change (post-removal) in the interpretation of aggravated felony "drug trafficking" or "crime of violence," as discussed in chapter five, which render the decision to remove erroneous. The erroneous interpretation of the statute must be combined with exhaustion of administrative remedies. The individual would of course have to be either not deportable, or eligible for relief, in order to establish prejudice.

In handling re-entry prosecutions, criminal defense counsel are well-advised to obtain the entire DHS A-file, as well as the EOIR file (including the tapes of proceedings) and look for addresses on envelopes and notices (to determine proper notice); for a determination that a crime was an aggravated felony, where case law indicates said interpretation has since changed; and for discussion of waivers and a possible pretermission of a waiver that now, based on case law, was an erroneous pretermission. Reviewing the government files in a §1326 prosecution is an exercise in not knowing what one is looking for until it is found; the key to a successful collateral attack will arise through careful review of the underlying proceedings.

> ➢ *Potential strategy:* File a motion to reopen[313] and vacate with the IJ or BIA during the pendency of criminal proceedings to reopen and vacate the underlying order, based on an identified defect in service or an erroneous determination of removability, or improper pretermission of re-

---

[311] *U.S. v. Essam Helmi El Shami*, 434 F.3d 659 (4th Cir. 2005) (§1326 conviction dismissed on appeal finding *in absentia* deportation order not valid for failure to provide notice to last-known address in file).

[312] 533 U.S. 289 (2001).

[313] Motions to reopen are beyond the scope of this book; for an excellent resource on immigration court practice including motions to reopen, see *Representing Clients in Immigration Court* (AILA 3rd Ed. 2013).

lief. If there is manifest injustice or extraordinary circumstances inherent in the case, file the motion seeking *sua sponte* review. If re-entry occurs within 90 days of the removal order, a unilateral motion is feasible.[314]

The U.S. Sentencing Guidelines provide an advisory framework for determining the sentence after a plea or conviction. Section 2L1.2 of the guidelines applies to a re-entry offense. The range of imprisonment varies from zero to six months for a noncriminal first offender to 125 months for certain criminal aliens. Enhancements of sentence occur where the defendant previously has been convicted of a firearms, terrorism, child pornography, alien smuggling, controlled substance, or aggravated felony offense. Defendants who plead guilty and accept responsibility for their conduct can receive reductions under §3.E1.1 of the guidelines. Defendants who go to trial and testify falsely can receive a sentencing enhancement. These enhancement and reduction provisions encourage defendants to evaluate the strength of their potential defenses before proceeding to trial.

As a practical matter, noncriminal alien defendants who enter guilty pleas can typically be sentenced at the time they enter the plea and often receive sentences of time already served. Custody is then turned over to ICE.

Successfully defending a §1326 prosecution based on a collateral attack of the underlying removal order does not protect against reinstatement of removal under INA §241(a)(5) [8 USC §1231(a)(5)]. To avoid reinstatement, the individual would either have to reopen the underlying removal order, or successfully convince ICE that reinstatement is not appropriate based on the circumstances. If a district court or court of appeals has found the underlying order to be illegal, there is a good chance ICE will decline to reinstate if the individual is eligible for relief (or was a permanent resident). These issues must be developed on a case-by-case basis.

---

[314] Several circuits have found the regulation prohibiting motions to reopen following actual removal to be *ultra vires* if the motion is filed within 90 days of the order because the statute clearly allows for a motion to reopen within 90 days notwithstanding execution of the order. *Marin-Rodriguez v. Holder*, 612 F.3d 591 (7th Cir. 2010*)*; *Contreras-Bocanegra v. Holder*, 678 F. 3d 811 (10th Cir. 2012); *Prestol Espinal v. Att'y Gen.*, 653 F.3d 213 (3d Cir. 2011); *Coyt v. Holder*, 593 F.3d 902 (9th Cir.2010); *William v. Gonzales*, 499 F.3d 329 (4th Cir. 2007); *Jian Le Lin v. U.S. Att'y Gen.*, 681 F.3d 1236 (11th Cir. 2012); *Pruidze v. Att'y Gen.*, 632 F.3d 234 (6th Cir. 2011).

APPENDIX 10A

MOTION TO REOPEN SUA SPONTE BASED ON NEW CASE LAW

UNITED STATES DEPARTMENT OF JUSTICE
EXECUTIVE OFFICE FOR IMMIGRATION REVIEW
BOARD OF IMMIGRATION APPEALS
FALLS CHURCH, VIRGINIA

IN THE MATTER OF:)
)
SANCHEZ, DIEGO) CASE NO. A 123 456 789
RESPONDENT)
IN REMOVAL PROCEEDINGS)
_____/

MOTION TO REOPEN *SUA SPONTE*

REMOVAL PROCEEDINGS BASED ON NEW CASE LAW

INTRODUCTION

Pursuant to 8 C.F.R. § 1003.2 the Respondent moves this Board of Immigration Appeals ("BIA or Board") to reopen his removal proceedings *sua sponte* in light of the Supreme Court's decision in *Vartelas v. Holder,* 132 S.Ct. 1479 (2012), which applied the anti-retroactivity principle to the immigration law and thus supports the assertion that eliminating eligibility for a waiver of inadmissibility under former section 212(c) of the Immigration and Nationality Act ("INA") for those who were convicted after a jury trial was impermissibly retroactive.

Since the Supreme Court's issuance of *Vartelas* several Circuit Courts of Appeal, have held that lawful permanent residents who sustained convictions prior to the enactment of the Antiterrorism and Effective Death Penalty Act of 1996, Pub. L. No. 104-132, 110 Stat. 1214 (Apr. 24, 1996) ("AEDPA") and the Illegal Immigration Reform and Immigrant Responsibility Act of 1996, Div. C, Pub. L. No. 104-208, § 304(a)(3), 110 Stat. 3009-546, 3009-590, 3009-593 ("IIRIRA"), may be eligible for 212(c) relief regardless of whether the conviction was by plea or by jury trial. See *Cardenas-Delgado v. Holder,* 720 F.3d 1111 (9th Cir. 2013); *Carraza-De Salinas v. Holder,* 700 F.3d 768 (5th Cir. 2012); *Lovan v. Holder,* 574 F.3d 990, 996 (8th Cir. 2009); *Matter of Abdelghany,* 26 I&N Dec. at 268.

Moreover, in recent case law this Board has extended relief under former INA § 212(c) to individuals like Mr. Sanchez who were convicted pursuant to a jury trial. In *Matter of Abdelghany,* 26 I&N Dec. 254 (BIA 2014), this Board held that Supreme Court and circuit court precedent have superseded the regulatory prohibition against granting section 212(c) relief to aliens convicted after trial. This Board has instructed, "Immigration Judges nationwide should now treat deportable lawful permanent residents convicted after trial no differently for purposes of section 212(c) eligibility than deportable lawful permanent residents convicted by means of plea agreements." *Matter of Abdelghany,* 26 I&N Dec. at 268.

STANDARD FOR REOPENING SUA SPONTE

This Board has jurisdiction to reopen *sua sponte* this case pursuant to 8 CFR §1003.2(a); *see also Matter of J-J,* 21 I&N Dec. 976 (BIA 1997); *Matter of G-D-,* 22 I&N Dec. 1132 (BIA 1999) ; *Matter of X-G-W,* 22 I&N Dec. 71 (BIA 1998).

In *Matter of X-G-W* the Board illustrated the type of situation in which *sua sponte* action is appropriate. In the case the Board examined the impact of an amendment to the definition of the term of "refugee" set forth in § 101(a)(42) of the INA. The statutory revision was so profound that as a result the Respondent in that case acquired eligibility for relief by virtue of that particular change in the law. Similarly, in the present case the Respondent has acquired eligibility for relief because of a significant change in the law resulting from the Supreme Court's decision in *Vartelas*. Accordingly, new case law has emerged from this Board and from several federal courts so that the exercise of *sua sponte* authority to reopen is now warranted.

ARGUMENT

I. Pursuant to the Supreme Court's decision in *Vartelas v. Holder* which resulted in new case law from this Board and from several federal courts, the Respondent is eligible to apply for 212(c) relief notwithstanding the fact that he was convicted after trial.

On September 28, 2004, the Executive Office for Immigration Review promulgated a final rule codifying the eligibility standards for § 212(c) relief. *See* 8 C.F.R. § 1212.3(h). In promulgating this new rule, the Department formalized its litigation position that *St. Cyr* preserved § 212(c) relief only for noncitizens who plead guilty in reliance on the availability of such relief.

The Supreme Court's decision in *Vartelas v. Holder*, 132 S. Ct. 1479 (2012) rejects the line of thinking expressed in the new rule and repudiates 8 C.F.R. § 1212.3(h)'s preclusion of § 212(c) relief to noncitizens convicted at trial as inconsistent with the anti-retroactivity principle. "[T]his Court has not required a party challenging the application of a statute to show he relied on prior law in structuring his conduct." *Vartelas* at 1490. "The operative presumption, after all, is that Congress intends its laws to govern prospectively only." *Vartelas* at 1491. The Court goes on to quote *Landgraf v. USI Film Products*, 511 U.S. 244 (1944); *Hughes Aircraft Co. v. United States ex rel. Schumer*, 520 U.S. 939 (1997); *Ponnapula v. Ashcroft*, 373 F.3d 480 (3rd Cir. 2004); and *Olatunnji v. Ashcroft*, 387 F.3d (4th Cir. 2004) to explain the commonsense principle that "the presumption against retroactive application of statutes does not require a showing of detrimental reliance[.]"*Vartelas* at 1491.

Vartelas' mode of analysis and interpretation of the anti-retroactivity principle overrules all other inconsistent expressions of it, including the Department's regulation and the court of appeals contrary opinions. This Board has embraced the new state of the law in *Matter of Abdelghany* of Several Circuit Court of Appeals have held that lawful permanent residents who sustained convictions prior to 1996 may be eligible for 212(c) relief regardless of whether the conviction was by plea or by jury trial. It is now clear that § 1212.3(h) relies on an incorrect understanding of the anti-retroactivity principle, and thus it is invalid in all respects where it premises § 212(c) eligibility only if a plea agreement was made prior to April 1, 1997.

II. Mr. Sanchez' Statutory Eligibility for Relief Pursuant to Former INA §212(c)

As a result of *Vartelas* and *Matter of Abdelghany*, Mr. Sanchez is no longer statutorily ineligible for relief pursuant to former INA § 212(c). He was convicted by jury trial on March 12, 1987, prior to the repeal of 212(c). Further, Mr. Sanchez's conviction does not render him ineligible for 212(c) relief, notwithstanding the prior finding that it constitutes an aggravated felony because the conviction was entered before November 29, 1990. *See* 8 C.F.R. § 1212.3(f)(4)(ii). Finally, Mr. Sanchez has accrued well over the required seven consecutive years of unrelinquished domicile in the United States.

His testimony during his individual hearing will establish that he merits a former 212(c) waiver in the exercise of discretion. *See Matter of Marin*, 16 I&N Dec. 581 (BIA 1978). Mr. Sanchez will present evidence of extensive family ties in the United States and his continuous residence here since he was a small child. He will also demonstrate that he has a strong and long history of employment, owns property, and has business ties in this country. Further, he will present evidence that he has been genuinely rehabilitated from the activity that led to his criminal convictions and he will present evidence attesting to his good moral character.

Based on the changed case law discussed above as well as the substantial positive factors in Mr. Sanchez's life that will be presented at his individual hearing, Mr. Sanchez humbly submits to this Honorable Court that he merits, both statutorily and as a matter of discretion, relief from removal in the form of a waiver under former INA § 212(c).

In the present case, the Immigration Judge found the Respondent statutorily barred from obtaining a section 212(c) waiver because he was convicted after trial. This Board affirmed. The Supreme Court's decision in *Vartelas* has nullified the basis of this Board's decision. The contemporary understanding of the statutory text is now that § 212(c) is available to all noncitizens with seven years of lawful un-relinquished residency in removal proceedings who have been charged with any ground of inadmissibility or deportability (except those relating to national security and international child abduction) where the underlying basis of the charge rests on conduct committed prior to § 212(c)'s repeal. This Board has embraced this rule. Therefore, Counsel respectfully moves this Board to reopen Respondent's case to allow him to apply for § 212(c) relief.

CONCLUSION

The Respondent has acquired eligibility for 212(c) relief because of a significant change in the law resulting from the Supreme Court's decision in *Vartelas v. Holder*, 132 S. Ct. 1479 (2012). This Board has embraced the new change in the law as well as several federal courts. Therefore Counsel respectfully moves this Board to reopen and remand this case allowing the Respondent to apply for relief for which he is now eligible.

RESPECTFULLY SUBMITTED:

> MARY KRAMER
> ATTORNEY AT LAW
> MARY E. KRAMER, P.A.
> 168 SE FIRST ST. SUITE 802
> MIAMI, FL 33131
> (305) 374-2300

CERTIFICATE OF SERVICE

I certify that a true and correct copy of this motion was served in person on the Office of the Chief Counsel for DHS at 333 S. Miami Ave., Miami FL 33130 on this ___ day of _____, 2014.

_____/
Ilaria Cacopardo

APPENDIX 10B

UNPUBLISHED BIA DECISION RE: SUA SPONTE MOTION TO REOPEN FOR §212(c) AFTER REMOVAL ORDER, CONVICTION BY TRIAL

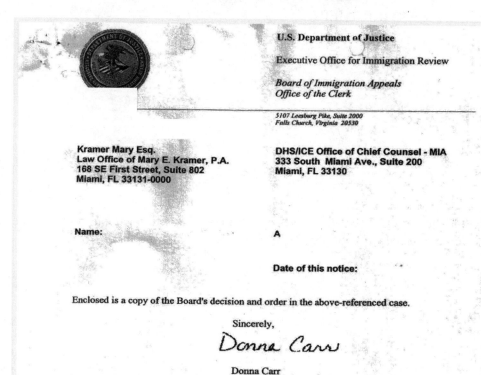

U.S. Department of Justice

Executive Office for Immigration Review

Board of Immigration Appeals
Office of the Clerk

5107 Leesburg Pike, Suite 2000
Falls Church, Virginia 20530

Kramer Mary Esq.
Law Office of Mary E. Kramer, P.A.
168 SE First Street, Suite 802
Miami, FL 33131-0000

DHS/ICE Office of Chief Counsel - MIA
333 South Miami Ave., Suite 200
Miami, FL 33130

Name:

A

Date of this notice:

Enclosed is a copy of the Board's decision and order in the above-referenced case.

Sincerely,

Donna Carr
Chief Clerk

Enclosure

Panel Members:
Holmes, David B.

williame
Userteam: Docket

U.S. Department of Justice
Executive Office for Immigration Review

Falls Church, Virginia 20530

Decision of the Board of Immigration Appeals

File: A— - Miami, FL   Date: MAY 27 2014

In re:

IN REMOVAL PROCEEDINGS

MOTION

ON BEHALF OF RESPONDENT: Mary Kramer, Esquire

APPLICATION: Reopening

ORDER:

The respondent has filed a motion to reopen his removal proceedings, requesting additional consideration of his application for a waiver of inadmissibility on the basis of a subsequent change in law. *See Vartelas v. Holder*, 132 S.Ct. 1479 (2012); *see also Matter of Abdelghany*, 26 I&N Dec. 254 (BIA 2014). The Department of Homeland Security has not responded to this motion. Given the particular circumstances present in this case, we will reopen and remand for a full hearing on the respondent's application. On remand, the Immigration Judge should hold a full evidentiary hearing and issue a new decision including a ruling as to whether the respondent merits relief in the exercise of discretion. In reopening and remanding, we intimate no opinion regarding the outcome of the respondent's application. Accordingly, the motion to reopen is hereby granted.

FURTHER ORDER: The record is remanded to the Immigration Judge for further proceedings consistent with the foregoing opinion and for the entry of a new decision.

_____
FOR THE BOARD

APPENDIX 10C

BRIEF EXCERPT – ADDRESSING DIFFERENCE IN "PARTICULARLY SERIOUS CRIME ANALYSIS" FROM ASYLUM TO WITHHOLDING

Brief Excerpt: Particularly Serious Crime Analysis, Asylum versus Withholding

C. The Court erred in finding that Mr. Putin was barred from asylum and withholding (restriction) of removal for commission of a particularly serious crime.

Respondent Putin received asylum from DHS in 2006. (Exh. 4-B) His case merits close attention and an adjudicator should pause before sending an asylum recipient back to the native country. In fact, but for the Court's finding that Mr. Putin is statutorily ineligible, the burden of proof would rest with the Department to show "fundamental" changed country conditions. 8 C.F.R. § 1208.13(b)(ii). The Court found Mr. Putin's offense to be a particularly serious crime without giving any consideration to mitigating factors. The Court's description of events does not take into account key testimony and documentary evidence and thus is an erroneous particularly serious crime analysis. The Board reviews the accuracy of the process and the ultimate conclusion *de novo*.

The Court applied the same analysis to both asylum and withholding and found Respondent Putin barred from both forms of protection. The Court found that because he is barred from asylum, Putin is barred from withholding. (I.J. at 71).

i. The particularly serious crime analysis differs from asylum to withholding

The particularly serious crime bar is not the same for both asylum and withholding. An alien who has been convicted by final judgment of a particularly serious crime may not receive asylum. Any aggravated felony, regardless of sentence, is a particularly serious crime. INA §§ 208(b)(2)(A)(ii) and (B)(i). In comparison, an alien who has been convicted by final judgment of a particularly serious crime and is therefore a danger to the community may not receive withholding (restriction on removal). INA § 241(b)(3)(B). An aggravated felony conviction for which a sentence of at least five years imprisonment is imposed is per se a particularly serious crime. Id.

Respondent is cognizant that the BIA does not treat the danger component as a separate necessary finding. Further, Respondent is aware that this Board has held that some crimes that are not aggravated felonies may qualify as particularly serious.

However, Respondent does urge that the Board consider what the nuanced terminology means. Surely, the words have meaning.

In *Matter of M-H-*, 26 I&N Dec. 46 (BIA 2012), the Board held that a particularly serious crime for withholding purposes need not be an aggravated felony. In so doing, the BIA disagreed with the Third Circuit Court of Appeals' decision in *Alaka v. A.G.*, 456 F.3d 88 (3d Cir. 2006). The *Alaka* court interpreted the final paragraph of INA § 241(b)(3), read in its entirety, to mean that a particularly serious crime must be an aggravated felony. The Eleventh Circuit apparently has not issued a precedent decision on this issue. With respect, the Respondent urges this Board to reverse its past precedent and find that to be barred under INA § 241(b)(3), a crime must qualify as an aggravated felony. Respondent reserves this issue, if necessary, for appeal purposes and would welcome oral argument from the Board on this point.

Bearing in mind that Board precedent for today does not require that a particularly serious crime in the withholding context be an aggravated felony, the Board must still presume that Congress chooses their words with purpose. The distinction in terminology between asylum and withholding indicates that the bar is set higher for withholding, which is to say, Congress intended that particularly serious crimes that by their nature pose an ongoing danger to the United States community trigger automatic denial.[315] And by way of illustration, Congress highlights that an aggravated felony with a significant sentence of imprisonment demonstrates their notion of what is a particularly serious crime. (Although, as discussed below, a crime with less than a five-year sentence might be a particularly serious crime—as determined on a case-by-case basis).

The Immigration Court erred in merging the standards because, in fact, a juxtaposition of the statutory provisions indicates that a particularly serious crime for withholding is more serious than in the context of asylum. The conclusion that the standards are different also makes sense overall in considering the nature of these two forms of relief. Asylum is discretionary. It is a superior benefit: an asylum recipient goes on to receive permanent resident status. Accordingly, a myriad of crimes might trigger the bar for asylum purposes. For restriction of removal, a person is actually ordered removed, but removal is withheld. Withholding is the bronze where the gold medal of asylum is not granted because of negative factors. Withholding is a very limited benefit, bestowed when the person does not merit asylum in the exercise of discretion, but nevertheless should not be removed to a country where he faces persecution. Based on the 2004 asylum grant, Mr. Putin does face persecution in Russia. 8 C.F.R. § 1208.16(b)(1)(i). The Department did not present any evidence whatsoever on country conditions—much less evidence that would establish a change in Russia.

Because these are two separate standards, and a particularly serious crime for withholding purposes is, well, *more* serious because of the danger component (illus-

---

[315] Of note, INA § 241(b)(3)(B)(ii) is phrased in the present tense: *is* a danger to the community.

trated by the example of an aggravated felony with a five year prison sentence), Respondent urges discrete consideration of the issue in the context of both forms of relief.

APPENDIX 10D

MOTION TO PRETERMIT WAIVER APPLICATION UNDER INA §212(h)

Susan Jenckins
Assistant Chief Counsel   NON-DETAINED
U.S. Department of Homeland Security
U.S. Immigration and Customs Enforcement
Philadelphia, PA 33140

UNITED STATES DEPARTMENT OF JUSTICE
EXECUTIVE OFFICE FOR IMMIGRATION REVIEW
IMMIGRATION COURT
PHILADELPHIA, PENNSYLVANIA

In the Matter of:)
)
Lawrence St. Louis   )   File No. A 303 765 900
)
In removal proceedings   )
)

Immigration Judge: Smith   Next Hearing: April 20, 2013

U.S. DEPARTMENT OF HOMELAND SECURITY'S MOTION TO PRETERMIT THE RESPONDENT'S WAIVER APPLICATION UNDER SECTION 212(h) OF THE INA AND FOR RELIEF UNDER SECTION 240A(a) OF THE INA

Because the respondent was admitted to the United States as an alien lawfully admitted for permanent residence and was thereafter convicted of an aggravated felony, he is ineligible for a waiver under section 212(h) of the Act ("§ 212(h) waiver"). Additionally, as an aggravated felon, he is ineligible for relief under Section 240A(a) of the INA. Therefore, the Department of Homeland Security ("Department") respectfully requests that the Immigration Judge pretermit the respondent's application for a waiver under section 212(h) and application for relief under section 240A(a) of the Immigration and Nationality Act ("INA").

Argument § 212(h) waiver

A section 212(h) waiver is unavailable to an "alien who has previously been admitted to the United States as an alien lawfully admitted for permanent residence" if such alien has, since that admission, been convicted of an aggravated felony. INA § 212(h). Per the decision of the Eleventh Circuit Court of Appeals in *Lanier v. U.S. Att'y. Gen.*, 631 F.3d 1363, 1367 (11th Cir. 2011), a section 212(h) waiver remains available to persons who adjusted to lawful permanent resident status while living in the United States. The Eleventh Circuit reasoned that "a person must have physically entered the United States, after inspection, as a lawful permanent resident in order to have "previously been admitted to the United States as an alien lawfully admitted for permanent residence." *Lanier*, 631 F.3d at 1366-7.

The respondent is a native and citizen of Haiti who was accorded lawful permanent resident ("LPR") status on or about May 31, 1988, under section 245 of the INA. Prior to becoming an LPR, the respondent was admitted on a B2 visitor's visa on September 22, 1986.

From 1993 to 1998, the respondent traveled abroad numerous times and each time he returned to the United States, he entered as an LPR. From August 1994 and continuing until December 31, 1995, the respondent along with his co-defendants engaged in a conspiracy to defraud the United States under 18 U.S.C. § 371. As part of that scheme, the respondent along with his co-defendants induced the victims into transferring large sums of money, in excess of $1 million, in exchange for fraudulently authenticated letters of credit. On or about May 26, 2000, the respondent was convicted under 18 U.S.C. § 371.

His crime is both a crime involving moral turpitude under section 212(a)(2)(A)(i)(I) of the INA and an aggravated felony under sections 101(a)(43)(M)(i) and 101(a)(43)(U) of the INA. After his conviction, the respondent continued his travels abroad. Each time the respondent returned to the United States, he was inspected and physically entered the United States as a lawful permanent resident.

Here, the respondent was previously admitted to the United States as an alien lawfully admitted for permanent residence following each trip abroad he took between July 19, 1993 and September 11, 1998. From August 1994 through December 31, 1995, however, the respondent committed the charge offense. As a result, when he sought admission on August 2, 1994, November 23, 1997, December 9, 1997, February 20, 1998, March 14, 1998, July 25, 1998, and September 11, 1998, he fell under the purview of INA § 101(a)(13)(C)(v). Following such admissions, the respondent was convicted on May 26, 2000, of the charged offense which the Department maintains constitutes both a crime involving moral turpitude and an aggravated felony.

Per section 212(h) of the INA and *Lanier*, because the respondent was previously admitted to the United States as an alien lawfully admitted for permanent residence and was thereafter convicted of an aggravated felony, he is ineligible for a § 212(h) waiver.

The respondent is statutorily ineligible for a section 212(h) waiver. Section 212(h) of the Act provides:

> No waiver shall be granted under this subsection in the case of an alien who has previously been admitted to the United States as an alien lawfully admitted for a permanent residence if... since the date of such admission the alien has been convicted of an aggravated felony.

INA § 212(h).

As previously noted the respondent was convicted of an aggravated felony. In *Lanier v. U.S. Att'y Gen.*, 631 F.3d 1363, 1367 (11th Cir. 2011), the Eleventh Circuit Court of Appeals determined that an alien's eligibility to seek a waiver is based on whether he has "previously been admitted to the United States as a lawful permanent resident." The *Lanier* Court note that the term "admitted" is defined as the "lawful [physical] entry of the alien into the United States after inspection and authorization by an immigration officer." *Lanier*, 631cF.3d at 1366 (citing INA § 101(a)(13)(A)). The *Lanier* Court ultimately concluded that because the alien had adjusted her status while in the United States, she was not subject to the aggravated felony bar of section 212(h) of the INA. *Lanier*, 631 F.3d at 1367.

The instant case is distinguishable from Lanier. Although the respondent adjusted his status in 1988 while residing the United States, he subsequently departed from and returned to the United States on a number of occasions. His foreign travels and subsequent admissions to the United States as an LPR from August 1994 when he began his turpitudinous criminal activity through December 1995 when he ceased this activity brought him under the purview of section 101(a)(13)(C)(v) of the INA.

An alien lawfully admitted for permanent residence in the United States in not deemed to be seeking an admission into the United States unless the alien "has committed an offense identified in section 212(a)(2) of [the INA], unless since such offense the alien has been granted relief under section 212(h) or 240A(a) of this title."

INA § 101(a)(13(C)(v); *see also Matter of Taveras*, 25 I&N Dec. 834, 835 (BIA 2012). The respondent participated in a scheme to defraud the United States from August 1994 through December 31, 1995. On May 26, 2000, he was convicted of conspiracy to defraud the United States under 18 U.S.C. § 371. In this case, the respondent and his co-defendants successfully induced victims to transfer funds in excess of $1 million in exchange for fraudulently authenticated letters of credit. *See* conviction records filed on July 17, 2012.

In short, between August 1994 and December 31, 1995, the respondent committed offenses identified in section 212(a)(2) of the Act. Between August 1994 and September 1998 (prior to his conviction), the respondent departed and re-entered the United States on at least seven occasions. He was inspected and admitted to the United States following each arrival. Each time he sought re-entry as a lawful permanent resident after one of his trips abroad, he was deemed to be seeking admission to the United States after a trip abroad, he was "admitted to the United States as a lawful permanent resident." *See Lanier*, 631 F.3 at 1366 (the term "admitted" is the "lawful entry of the alien into the United States after inspection and authorization by an immigration officer)(*citing Martinez v. Mukasey*, 519 F.3d 532, 544(5th Cir. 2008)("the plain language of § 212(h) reveals that "admitted", as employed in § 212(h), includes an alien's lawful entry into this country with permanent-resident status. Stated differently, for the section 212(h) bar to apply: when the alien is granted permission, after inspection, to enter the United States, he must then be admitted as an LPR."); *cf. Matter of Guzman*, 25 I&N Dec. 845, 848 (BIA 2012) ("When a lawful permanent resident voluntarily leaves the United States, he remains outside this country for immigration purposes until he completes the inspection process upon return. An alien does not meaningfully "enter" the United States simply by setting foot in a port of entry.") (*citing Matter of Patel*, 20 I&N Dec. 368 (BIA 1991)).

As such, he accomplished an "admission" to the United States. *See generally Matter of Quilantan*, 25 I&N Dec. 285, 290 (BIA 2010) (holding that an "admission" as defined in section 101(a)(13)(A) of the Act required procedural regularity rather that full compliance with substantive legal requirements).

Thus, the respondent committed an aggravated felony after having "previously been admitted to the United States as an alien lawfully admitted for permanent residence." He is thus ineligible for a section 212(h) waiver. *Lanier*, 631 F.3d qt 1366-7.

Argument § 240A(a) relief

As an aggravated felon, the respondent is ineligible for relief under section 240A(a) of the INA. An alien is prima facie eligible for this form of relief is the alien: (1) has been an alien lawfully admitted for permanent residence for no less than five years; (2) has continuously resided in the United States for seven years after having been admitted in any status; and (3) has not been convicted of an aggravated felony. See § 240A(a) of the INA.

After his conviction on May 6, 2000, the respondent was ordered to make restitution to one of the victims of $2000. The indictment, however, clearly established that the respondent, along with his co-defendants, engaged in fraud to "obtain millions of dollars in fees for procuring supposedly legitimate bank guarantees which had been actually fabricated by the defendants." Therefore, the respondent was convicted of an aggravated felony under section 101(a)(43)(M)(i) of the INA where the fraud or deceit in which the loss to the victim(s) exceeds $10,000.

The respondent is also an aggravated felon under section 101(a)(43)(U) of the INA as he was convicted of a conspiracy or attempt to commit an offense described in this paragraph 101(a)(43)(M). Therefore, even though he was only ordered to make restitution of $2000, his part in the conspiracy resulted in the loss of millions of dollars to the victim(s).

For example, under item 27 of the indictment, it can be seen that one victim, Mr. Kuti, wire-transferred over $10,000,000 in exchange for fraudulent letters of credit (for which respondent and others provided the telex facilities used to transmit some of the fraudulent letters of credit). Item 35 shows Mr. Kuti wire-transferring another $1,500,000 in exchange for fraudulently avalized AFE promissory notes (for which the respondent and others provided the telex facilities used to transmit the fraudulently avalized AFE promissory notes. For his direct participation and as a member of the conspiracy, the respondent is an aggravated felon under both sections 101(a)(43)(M)(i) and 101(a)(43)(U) of the INA. He is therefore ineligible for relief under section 240A(a) of the INA.

Based on the foregoing, the Department respectfully requests that the Immigration Court pretermit the respondent's waiver application under section 212(h) of the INA and pretermit any forthcoming application for relief under section 240A(a).

       Respectfully submitted,
       Susan Jenkins
       Assistant Chief Counsel

APPENDIX 10E

SAMPLE MEMORANDUM IN SUPPORT OF INA §212(h) ELIGIBILITY

UNITED STATES DEPARTMENT OF JUSTICE
EXECUTIVE OFFICE FOR IMMIGRATION REVIEW
OFFICE OF THE IMMIGRATION JUDGE
PHILADELPHIA IMMIGRATION COURT

IN THE MATTER OF :)
)
LAWRENCE ST. LOUIS) CASE NO. A303 765 900
RESPONDENT) Judge Smith
IN REMOVAL PROCEEDINGS)
_____/

MEMORANDUM OF LAW
IN SUPPORT OF 212(h) ELIGIBILITY

Statement of the Case

At a master hearing on July 19, 2012, the Immigration Court sustained the charge of removability under INA § 212(a)(2)(A)(i)(I). Respondent through Counsel filed an application for a waiver under INA § 212(h). On August 14, 2012, the Department filed a motion to pretermit relief. [316]

Question Presented

Whether Mr. St. Louis is eligible for a INA § 212(h) waiver notwithstanding an earlier entry (or entries) into the United States, prior to these proceedings, at which time his conviction did not come to light and he was not stopped or otherwise viewed as an arriving alien by Customs and Border Protection.

Answer

---

[316] Mr. St. Louis has not filed an application for cancellation of removal. Per Court order, that application is not due until October 17, 2012.

Mr. St. Louis is eligible to proceed on a INA § 212(h) waiver based on the Eleventh Circuit Court's decision in *Lanier v. Attorney General*, 631 F.3d 1363 (11th Cir. 2011) because there can be only one "admission as an alien lawfully admitted for permanent residence", which describes the act of acquiring or obtaining lawful permanent resident *status*. Moreover, where a potential ground of inadmissibility does not come to light at a port-of-entry and a returning lawful permanent resident is not treated or processed as an applicant for admission, no "admission" occurs.

Brief Facts

Mr. St. Louis is a citizen of Haiti. He is 59 years old. Mr. St. Louis is married to a U.S. citizen, has adult citizen children (from a previous marriage) and a teenage U.S. citizen son. Mr. St. Louis' mother is 93 years old and resides in Philadelphia also. Mr. St. Louis adjusted status to lawful permanent resident on May 31, 1988.

On May 30, 2000, Mr. St. Louis was convicted of one count of violation of 18 USC § 371, the federal conspiracy statute. He was sentenced to two years of probation. The judgment indicates zero loss. The judgment calls for $2,000 in restitution.

The Department's motion to pretermit § 212(h) relief is premised on the assertion that Mr. St. Louis has traveled outside and reentered the United States since commission of the criminal offense. The Department attaches to their motion a grid-like chart, or listing, of information. The Court is respectfully advised that Counsel for the Respondent cannot decipher—cannot understand—this document and therefore moves for either a more specific explanation from DHS, or in the alternative, that the document be disregarded by the Court. However, Mr. St. Louis, through Counsel, does state that he has traveled in and out of the United States since his conviction. He stipulates that he has indeed "reentered" the United States. With this factual premise in place, the Court may address the legal issues presented, as discussed below.

Discussion

A. *Lanier* refers to the acquisition of LPR status, not "re-admissions."

The Department seeks to pretermit based on previous trip(s) in-and-out of the United States, arguing that this constitutes an "admission" (notwithstanding the earlier adjustment of status to LPR) for purposes of the 212(h) bar. The Department misreads the decision in *Lanier*, as well as key statutory terms.

In *Lanier, supra,* as well as its predecessor *Martinez v. Mukasey,* 519 F.3d 532 (5th Cir. 2008), the courts reviewed section 212(h)'s statutory bar, and found that the bar for certain LPRs convicted of crime did not apply to persons who obtained lawful permanent resident status through adjustment of status because adjustment does not qualify as an "admission". In so doing, the courts looked not only to the term "admission", but the entire phrase: "lawfully admitted as an alien lawfully admitted for permanent residence status." As such, the courts were combining two statutory definitions, INA § 101(a)(13)(A) and § 101(a)(20).

Section 101(a)(13)(A) of the INA defines "admission" and "admitted" as the lawful entry of an alien into the United States after inspection and admission. In turn, section 101(a)(20) defines the term "lawfully admitted for permanent residence" as the status of having been accorded the privilege or residing permanently within the United States as an immigrant, *such status not having changed.*

Thus it is a mistaken approach to focus only on the term "admission" when reading *Lanier* and *Martinez*. These decisions deal with the entire concept established by combing the two definitions: that is, obtaining or acquiring the status of an LPR. Specifically, the Eleventh Circuit in *Lanier* wrote:

> Congress has defined the phrase "lawfully admitted for permanent residence" as a term of art meaning "the status of having been lawfully accorded the privilege of residing permanently in the United States as an immigrant in accordance with the immigration laws." INA § 101(a)(20), 8 U.S.C. § 1101(a)(20). This definition describes a particular immigration status, without any regard for how or when that status is **obtained**. Thus, this term of art encompasses all persons with lawful permanent resident status, including those who **obtained that status** prior to or at the time of their physical entry into the United States, as well as those who adjusted their status while already living in the United States. See *Martinez v. Mukasey*, 519 F.3d 532, 546 (5th Cir. 2008) (definition "encompass[es] both admission to the United States as a [lawful permanent resident] and post-entry adjustment to [lawful permanent resident] status"). (emphasis in bold added)

Lanier, 631 F.3d 1363, 1366 (11th Cir. 2011).

A review of these decisions reflects that the reference to admission is a reference to the act of acquiring or obtaining the status, and the method by which it is accomplished. This can happen only once, and is the time when a person obtains the status of LPR. [In some limited circumstances, a person might readjust status, such as when seeking relief in removal proceedings, but this example does not pertain to, nor change, this analysis.]

In comparison to the act of obtaining LPR status, INA § 101(a)(13)(C) refers to under what limited circumstances an LPR will be regarding as an arriving alien and be subject to scrutiny at a port-of-entry under INA § 212(a). *See, eg: Matter of Taveras*, 25 I & N Dec. 834,836 (BIA 2012) (the import of INA § 101(a)(13)(C) is that returning lawful permanent residents are not subject to "exclusion" proceedings unless an exception applies; the issue is the burden of proof and whether it lies with the government of the returning LPR). [317] This is a distinct, more limited analysis as

---

[317] The Department cites to *Taveras*—one sentence of the decision taken out of context—as supportive of their position; however, the reality is that *Taveras* clarifies that INA § 101(a)(13)(C) refers to the burden of proof and whether returning LPRs shall be exposed to grounds of inadmissibility, as opposed to deportability. It clarifies that the concept of "admissibility" and "admission" is distinct between INA § 101(a)(13)(C) and § 245(a).

it does not combine sections 101(a)(13) and 101(a)(20), but refers only to when someone seeks admission so that they can continue with their ongoing status. INA § 101(a)(13)(C) does not stand for the proposition that certain returning LPRs must reapply for, and re-acquire, permanent resident status. It refers to a process whereby, although already an LPR, the individual is subject to increased scrutiny because a condition may apply.[318]

By way of example, if a returning LPR is placed in proceedings under INA § 212(a), and applies for relief, and is granted relief, he does not become an LPR all over again; the immigration judge does not ordain such person an LPR as of the date of receiving relief. Rather, this person continues on in the same status he held prior to the initiation of proceedings. If this Court grants Mr. St. Louis a waiver, his green card will not be reprinted to say "LPR as of September 17, 2012." This acquisition of status occurred many years back.

For this reason—because an LPR does not reacquire status with every re-entry—Congress clarified that the term "application for admission" is a reference to the application for admission into the United States, and not to the application "for the issuance of an immigrant or nonimmigrant visa." *See:* INA § 101(a)(4).

The conclusion that the phrase "an alien admitted as an alien lawfully admitted for permanent resident status" is a reference to the one-time occasion of becoming a permanent resident is also bolstered by applicable regulations. Eight C.F.R. § 1.1(p) patterns the statute and defines the term "lawfully admitted for permanent residence" as the *status* of having been lawfully accorded the privilege of residing permanently in the United States as an immigrant in accordance with the immigration laws, **such status not having changed**. Such status terminates upon entry of a final administrative order of removal. *Id.* (emphasis in bold added) And, at 8 C.F.R. § 1.1(q), the regulation describes the term "arriving alien" as an applicant for admission coming or attempting to come into the United States at a port-of-entry.

Accordingly, the regulations bolster the statutory phrases and demonstrate that there is a distinction between an alien admitted as an alien lawfully admitted for permanent resident status, and any alien simply seeking admission. Again, INA § 101(a)(13)(C) simply determines when an LPR may be treated as an arriving alien; it is not a reference to re-obtaining, or reacquiring, the status. Yet this latter reference is the focal point of the 212(h) bar for certain permanent residents, and the courts' decisions in *Lanier* and *Mukasey*.

---

[318] The Supreme Court's decision in *Rosenberg v. Fleuti*, 374 U.S. 449 (1963) further illustrates the purpose of INA § 101(a)(13)(C), both pre-and post -1996. The issue in *Fleuti* was not whether a returning LPR is forced to re-process/reacquire/re-obtain permanent resident status because of a lengthy trip outside the United States; the issue in *Fleuti* (the import of then-section 101(a)(13)) was which returning LPRs were exposed to losing their residency at the border, through exclusion proceedings, rather than being allowed in for potential deportation proceedings.

Finally, BIA case law on admission further underscores the distinction between "admission" in certain portions of the statute, and the combined concept of "an alien admitted as an alien lawfully admitted for permanent resident status." The latter phrase is a reference to a precise moment in time, not to a constantly changing and arbitrary moment that depends on when and whether the LPR traveled and whether the LPR may have been inadmissible at the time he reentered the U.S. *See, e.g., Matter of Alyazji*, 25 I&N Dec. 397 (BIA 2011) (holding that for purposes of removability under Section 237(a)(2)(A)(i) there is only one "date of admission" that is relevant to measuring the statutory 5-year period in relation to a particular offense.)

B. The plain language of INA § 101(a)(13)(C) requires that the potential ground of inadmissibility be detected at the time of arrival, at the port-of-entry, in order for a returning LPR to be viewed as an arriving alien seeking admission.

The plain language of section 101(a)(13)(C) requires that the potential ground of inadmissibility be detected at the port-of-entry, not later. The provision is written in the present tense. Section 101(a)(13)(C) refers to persons who will be stopped at the border and viewed as arriving aliens because of a potential ground of inadmissibility. They are exposed to INA § 212(a) grounds. The key phrase is an LPR "shall not *be regarded* as seeking an admission into the United States for the purposes of the immigration laws . . ." Mr. St. Louis' previous trips, during which he re-entered the United States without ado, are over and complete and the potential issue of a conviction did not arise. That process is done. The plain language does not allow for retrospection. He was not "admitted" at that time, and he certainly was not "admitted as an alien lawfully admitted for permanent residence status."

Furthermore, for those LPRs who do "slip past", rather than time-travel back to that point in history, the statute gives us § 237(a)(1): inadmissibility at the time of "entry" or adjustment of status. And these persons are charged under INA § 237. Notably, INA § 237(a)(1)(A) does not refer to persons who were "inadmissible at the time of last *admission*"; rather, the ground of deportability utilizes the term "entry." This provision was amended with the IIRAIRA, and may be relied upon to express the intent of Congress in terms of the 1996 amendments.

C. The Department's view represents a violation of the Equal Protection Clauses of the Fourteenth Amendment.

Lastly, Mr. St. Louis maintains that the Department's position violates the equal protection clause of the 14th Amendment to the U.S. Constitution by treating disparately aliens who adjusted status and never left the U.S. and aliens who adjusted status and took a brief trip. *See Francis* v. *INS*, 532 F.2d 268 (2d Cir. 1976); *see also Matter of Silva*, 16 I&N Dec. 26 (1976). The DHS's position is also arbitrary, capricious and irrational. *See Judulang v. Holder*, 132 S. Ct. 476 (2011). While the Immigration Judge may not have jurisdiction to rule on Constitutional issues of first impression, the Court can certainly uphold important precedent of the Supreme Court and BIA. Mr. St. Louis asks this Court to reaffirm the constitutional principle of equal protection in light of precedent case law. Mr. St. Louis also preserves these arguments for purposes of federal court review, if necessary.

D. Mr. St. Louis does not have an aggravated felony offense and is therefore eligible for 212(h) and cancellation of removal.

Mr. St. Louis is clearly eligible for a waiver under INA § 212(h). Even if the Court agrees with the Department's view regarding "admission", and finds that a successful re-entry retroactively constitutes an "admission as an alien lawfully admitted for permanent resident status", Mr. St. Louis' conviction is not for an aggravated felony offense. There was no financial loss linked to his count of conviction, and restitution was ordered at only $2,000. Therefore, Mr. St. Louis requires only seven years of an ongoing lawful residence prior to the institution of removal proceedings. He became a resident in 1988, thus he has more than ample ongoing lawful residence.

Mr. St. Louis' application for cancellation of removal is not due until October 17, 2012. Counsel is meeting with her client to determine whether they will also file for this form of relief. Again, it is noted that the judgment does not support the proposition that Mr. St. Louis' conviction is an aggravated felony.

Conclusion

Mr. St. Louis acquired his LPR status through adjustment and is therefore eligible to proceed on an application for INA § 212(h). He reserves the right to file for cancellation of removal on or before the call up date of October 18, 2012.

RESPECTFULLY SUBMITTED:

MARY KRAMER
ATTORNEY AT LAW
MARY E. KRAMER, P.A.
168 SE FIRST ST. SUITE 802
MIAMI, FL 33131
(305) 374 2300
FAX: (305) 374 3748
mary@marykramerlaw.com

APPENDIX 10F

UNPUBLISHED BIA DECISION RE: CANCELLATION OF REMOVAL, WAIVER OF INADMISSIBILITY UNDER INA §212(h)

U.S. Department of Justice

Executive Office for Immigration Review

Board of Immigration Appeals
Office of the Clerk

5107 Leesburg Pike, Suite 2000
Falls Church, Virginia 20530

Kramer Mary Esq.
Law Office of Mary E. Kramer, P.A.
168 SE First Street, Suite 802
Miami, FL 33131-0000

DHS/ICE Office of Chief Counsel - MIA
333 South Miami Ave., Suite 200
Miami, FL 33130

Name:

A

Date of this notice: 2/9/2015

Enclosed is a copy of the Board's decision and order in the above-referenced case.

Sincerely,

Donna Carr

Donna Carr
Chief Clerk

Enclosure

Panel Members:
Creppy, Michael J.
Malphrus, Garry D.
Mann, Ana

Userteam: Docket

U.S. Department of Justice
Executive Office for Immigration Review

Falls Church, Virginia 20530

Decision of the Board of Immigration Appeals

File: A   – Miami, FL   Date: FEB - 9 2015

In re:

IN REMOVAL PROCEEDINGS

APPEAL

ON BEHALF OF RESPONDENT: Mary Kramer, Esquire

ON BEHALF OF DHS: Maria T. Armas
Assistant Chief Counsel

APPLICATION: Cancellation of removal; waiver of inadmissibility under section 212(h) of the Act

The respondent, a native and citizen of Haiti, appeals from the Immigration Judge's decision dated November 1, 2012, denying his application for cancellation of removal for certain permanent residents pursuant to section 240A(a) of the Immigration and Nationality Act, 8 U.S.C. § 1229b(a), and his application for a waiver of inadmissibility pursuant to section 212(h) of the Act, 8 U.S.C. § 1182(h). The Department of Homeland Security opposes the appeal. The appeal will be dismissed in part and sustained in part.

We review for clear error the findings of fact, including the determination of credibility, made by the Immigration Judge. 8 C.F.R. § 1003.1(d)(3)(i). We review de novo all other issues, including whether the parties have met the relevant burden of proof, and issues of discretion. 8 C.F.R. § 1003.1(d)(3)(ii). Because the respondent filed his applications for relief after May 11, 2005, they are governed by the provisions of the REAL ID Act. *See Matter of S-B-*, 24 I&N Dec. 42 (BIA 2006).

The respondent is not eligible for cancellation of removal under section 240A(a) of the Act because he has not met his burden of showing that he has not been convicted of an aggravated felony (I.J. at 3-4). *See* section 240A(a)(3) of the Act. The Immigration Judge determined that the respondent's conviction for conspiracy to defraud the United States in violation of 18 U.S.C. § 371 was for an aggravated felony as defined in sections 101(a)(43)(M)(i) and (U) of the Act (I.J. at 2-3). The respondent does not meaningfully dispute that he was convicted of an offense that involves fraud (I.J. at 3). He argues that the offense is not an aggravated felony because the record does not establish that the loss to the victim exceeds $10,000. *See* section 101(a)(43)(M)(i) of the Act (defining the term aggravated felony to include an offense that involves fraud or deceit in which the loss to the victim or victims exceeds $10,000). We do not agree.

For purposes of section 101(a)(43)(M)(i) of the Act, the amount of victim loss arising from an alien's offense is a fact which an Immigration Judge is permitted to find by means of a "circumstance-specific" inquiry. *See Nijhawan v. Holder*, 557 U.S. 29 (2009). Although the record reflects that the respondent was ordered to pay $2,000 in restitution following his

A.

conviction, this figure is not necessarily dispositive and the respondent has not provided any evidence that the amount of restitution was calculated based upon a determination of the loss to the victim (I.J. at 3; Exh. 2). *See Matter of Babaisakov*, 24 I&N Dec. 306, 319 (BIA 2007) (acknowledging that "restitution orders *can* be sufficient evidence of loss to the victim *in certain cases*") (emphasis added). The judgment, which is silent as to the total loss resulting from the respondent's offense, indicates that the respondent pled guilty to count 1 of the superseding indictment (I.J. at 3; Exh. 2). As discussed by the Immigration Judge, count 1 of the superseding indictment alleges an extensive scheme in which the victim was fraudulently induced to wire-transfer millions of dollars (I.J. at 3; Exh. 2).

We are not persuaded by the respondent's assertion that it was improper for the Immigration Judge to consider the actions of his co-conspirators in assessing the loss to the victim arising from his offense. When an alien is convicted of a joint fraud—either as an accessory or as a conspirator—the offense of conviction for purposes of section 101(a)(43)(M)(i) of the Act is the joint offense, and thus the relevant quantum of loss arising from such an offense will ordinarily be the whole loss caused by the joint conduct. *See, e.g., Khalayleh v. INS*, 287 F.3d 978, 979 (10th Cir. 2002). The offense of conviction was the entire scheme charged in count 1 of the superseding indictment and the loss to be measured is the loss resulting from that scheme.

We are also not persuaded by the respondent's claim that the Immigration Judge violated his due process rights by not holding an evidentiary hearing to determine the loss to the victim arising from his offense. The Immigration Judge considered all of the documentary evidence in the record relating to the respondent's conviction and the respondent has not identified any evidence that he was prevented from submitting or shown that such evidence would have affected the outcome of these proceedings. *See Tang v. U.S. Att'y Gen.*, 578 F.3d 1270, 1275 (11th Cir. 2009) ("To establish due process violations in removal proceedings, aliens must show that they were deprived of liberty without due process of law, and that the asserted errors caused them substantial prejudice.").

In light of the foregoing, we discern no clear error in the Immigration Judge's finding that the loss to the victim arising from the respondent's offense was greater than $10,000 (I.J. at 3). Because the respondent has been convicted of an aggravated felony, he is not eligible for cancellation of removal and his appeal will be dismissed with respect to that issue (I.J. at 3-4).

We disagree with the Immigration Judge's determination that the respondent's conviction renders him ineligible for a waiver of inadmissibility under section 212(h) of the Act (I.J. at 4). A waiver under that section is not available to an alien who has been convicted of an aggravated felony after having been previously admitted to the United States as an alien lawfully admitted for permanent residence. Section 212(h) of the Act. Although the respondent adjusted his status to that of a lawful permanent resident on or about May 31, 1988, this post-entry adjustment of status does not constitute an admission for purposes of section 212(h) of the Act. *See Lanier v. U.S. Att'y Gen.*, 631 F.3d 1363 (11th Cir. 2011); *see also Matter of E. W. Rodriguez*, 25 I&N Dec. 784 (BIA 2012). To the extent the Immigration Judge concluded that the respondent was admitted to the United States as an alien lawfully admitted for permanent residence because he departed and returned to the United States after he adjusted his status, the United States Court of Appeals for the Eleventh Circuit has held that "the statutory bar to [section 212(h)] relief does not apply to those persons who...adjusted to lawful permanent resident status while already living in the United States." *Lanier, supra,* at 1367. Because the respondent obtained lawful permanent resident status through adjustment of status, he is not statutorily precluded from seeking a section 212(h) waiver notwithstanding his conviction for an aggravated felony. Accordingly, the respondent's appeal will be sustained with respect to his application for a waiver under section 212(h) of the Act and the record will be remanded for the Immigration Judge for further consideration of the respondent's eligibility for such relief. On remand, the respondent bears the burden of demonstrating that the denial of his admission would result in extreme hardship to a qualifying United States citizen or lawful permanent resident relative and that he merits a favorable exercise of discretion. *See* section 240(c)(4)(A) of the Act, 8 U.S.C. § 1229a(c)(4)(A). The following orders will be entered.

ORDER: The respondent's appeal is dismissed with respect to his application for cancellation of removal.

FURTHER ORDER: The respondent's appeal is sustained with respect to his application for a waiver of inadmissibility under section 212(h) of the Act.

FURTHER ORDER: The record is remanded for further proceedings consistent with the foregoing opinion and for the entry of a new decision.

FOR THE BOARD

APPENDIX 10G

SAMPLE MOTION TO TERMINATE REMOVAL PROCEEDINGS

DETAINED

Mary E. Kramer
Attorney at Law
Mary E. Kramer, P.A.
168 S.E. First Street, Suite 802
Miami, Florida 33131

UNITED STATES DEPARTMENT OF JUSTICE
EXECUTIVE OFFICE FOR IMMIGRATION REVIEW
ORLANDO IMMIGRATION COURT
ORLANDO, FLORIDA

IN THE MATTER OF:)
)
MARIA RODRIGUEZ   )   CASE No. 123 456 789
)
RESPONDENT   )
IN REMOVAL PROCEEDINGS   )
_____)

Immigration Judge: Judge Ortiz-Segura   Next Hearing: October 1, 2014 at 8:00 a.m.

<u>RESPONDENT'S MOTION TO TERMINATE</u>

RESPONDENT'S MOTION TO TERMINATE

NOW COMES the Respondent, Maria Rodriguez, by and through undersigned counsel, and respectfully moves this Court to dismiss the charge of removability and terminate these removal proceedings and as grounds states the following:

1. Ms. Rodriguez is a lawful permanent resident.

2. On September 13, 2013, Ms. Rodriguez was convicted in the United States District Court, Southern District of Florida, of two offenses: conspiracy to commit fraud pursuant to 18 U.S.C. § 1349 and wire fraud pursuant to 18 U.S.C. § 1343.

3. On July 16, 2014, the Department of Homeland Security (DHS) served Ms. Rodriguez with a Notice to Appear charging her with removability pursuant to section 237(a)(2)(A)(iii) of the Immigration and Nationality Act (INA) as having been convicted of an aggravated felony as defined in INA § 101(a)(43)(U). On September 3, 2014, this charge was amended orally by DHS during a master calendar hearing to include an aggravated felony as defined in INA § 101(a)(43)(M). DHS has the burden to demonstrate, by clear and convincing evidence, that Ms. Rodriguez is removable as charged. See INA § 240(c)(3); 8 C.F.R. § 1240.8(a).

4. In this case, DHS has filed in support of the charge of removability: a judgment, an information, a certificate of trial attorney, and a waiver of indictment. The judgment submitted does not list an amount of loss.

5. Section 101(a)(43)(M)(i) of the INA defines an aggravated felony, in part, as "an offense that involves fraud or deceit in which the loss to the victim or victims exceeds $10,000." Ms. Rodriguez moves to dismiss the charge of removability and terminate these proceedings because neither of her offenses is ones "in which the loss to the victim or victims exceeds $10,000."

6. The United States Supreme Court has found that the monetary threshold applies to the specific circumstances surrounding an offender's commission of a fraud and deceit crime on a specific occasion. *Nijhawan v. Holder*, 557 U.S. 29, 40 (2009). In addition, for purposes of INA § 101(a)(43)(M)(i), the loss must be tied to the specific counts covered by the conviction. *Id.* at 42. Thus, in determining the amount of loss, the Immigration Court must assess findings made at sentencing "with an eye to what losses are covered and to the burden of proof employed." *Id.* (quoting *Matter of Babaisakov*, 24 I&N Dec.

306, 219 (2007). A defendant's admission during the criminal proceeding as to the amount of loss can only suffice for purposes of INA §101(a)(43)(M)(i) if the admission pertained to losses arising from the conduct in the particular charges or criminal counts covered by the conviction. *Matter of Babaisakov*, 24 I & N Dec. 306, 320 (BIA 2007).

7. Further, the definition of "loss" within the context of INA § 101(a)(43)(M) is considerably narrower than the definition of loss in the United States Sentencing Guidelines (U.S.S.G). While the plain language of INA § 101(a)(43)(M) does not contemplate the inclusion of potential rather than actual loss, section 2B1.1(b)(1)(H) of the U.S.S.G. defines loss within the sentencing context as including loss which is the reasonably foreseeable pecuniary harm that resulted from the offense as well as pecuniary harm that would have been impossible or unlikely to occur. U.S.S.G. § 2B1.1, comment. (n.3(A)(i)-(ii)).

8. While a sentencing court in the criminal context may order restitution not only for *convicted* conduct but also for a broad range of "relevant conduct," the plain language of the INA requires that an alien have been *convicted of* an aggravated felony to be removable. The INA does not authorize removal on the basis of the "relevant conduct" that may be considered at sentencing. *Obasohan v. U.S. Atty. Gen.*, 479 F.3d 785, 790 (11th Cir. 2007).

9. Under the Federal Sentencing Guidelines, "relevant conduct" includes "all acts and omissions committed ... by the defendant ... during the commission of the offense of conviction ...", as well as "all harm that resulted from [those] acts and omissions[.]" U.S.S.G. § 1B1.3(a)(1), (a)(3). Relevant conduct for sentencing purposes, therefore, may include criminal conduct that was not charged. *Id.* (citing *United States v. Ignancio Munio*, 909 F.2d 436, 438-39 (11th Cir. 1990). Relevant conduct may also include acquitted conduct. *Id.* (citing *United States v. Watts*, 519 U.S. 148 (1997); *United States v. Averi*, 922 F.2d 765, 766 (11th Cir. 1991)).

10. Thus, a restitution order which is based on additional or relevant conduct outside of the elements comprising the substantive criminal offense cannot be considered loss tethered to the convicted conduct and is therefore insufficient to establish, by clear and convincing evidence, the amount of loss for purposes of INA § 101(a)(43)(M). *See Obasohan v. U.S. Att'y Gen.*, 479 F.3d at 791 (11th Cir. 2007).

11. Ms. Rodriguez did not stipulate that the offense conduct for which she was convicted resulted in a loss exceeding $10,000 for purposes of INA § 101(a)(43)(M). Although her plea agreement contains a provision regarding loss defined in U.S.S.G. § 2B1.1(b)(H), this loss is not relevant to the instant

matter since U.S.S.G. calculation can include loss even where no actual loss occurred as well as pecuniary harm that would have been impossible or unlikely to occur. *See United States v. Menichino*, 989 F.2d at 442. Importantly, the reference to loss in Ms. Rodriguez's plea agreement is not an admission by her that her convicted conduct resulted in an amount of loss exceeding $10,000 for purposes of INA § 101(a)(43)(M). As noted above, Ms. Rodriguez's judgment does not include an amount of loss.

12. The elements of the crimes with which Ms. Rodriguez was charged did not require that any loss amount be proven. Counts one and two of the criminal information, to which Ms. Rodriguez pled guilty, state that Ms. Rodriguez defaulted on her loan and that "as a result of" her default, the Export-Import Bank paid the lender $446,875.83. Nevertheless, the information does not allege a loss resulting from the offense conduct. Therefore, the fact that Ms. Rodriguez defaulted on the loan is not tethered to the specific conduct for which she was convicted. For this reason, the amount of the default cannot be properly considered the amount of loss resulting from her offenses. In other words, her convictions were not ones "*in which* the loss to the victim or victims exceeds $10,000" because the default on her loan was separate and apart from the conduct resulting in her convictions. *See Obasohan v. U.S. Att'y Gen.*, 479 F.3d at 791. Ms. Rodriguez's default on her loan was the result of nonpayment, not the result of her offense conduct.

13. Although Ms. Rodriguez was ordered to pay restitution, the restitution order in this case does not equate to the amount of loss resulting from the offense conduct underlying Ms. Rodriguez's convictions for conspiracy and wire fraud. First, the restitution order is insufficient as a matter of law for the DHS to have met its burden to show that Ms. Rodriguez's convictions constitute aggravated felonies because the restitution order includes "relevant conduct" which was not required to have been charged, proven, or admitted. Second, sentencing judge made this restitution finding employing the preponderance of the evidence standard, rather than the beyond a reasonable doubt standard. Because the sentencing judge was entitled to base the Ms. Rodriguez's restitution order on factual findings about "relevant conduct" made by a lower standard of proof, the amount of restitution ordered in Ms. Rodriguez's case does not constitute clear and convincing evidence that the amount of loss exceeded $10,000 for purposes of INA § 101(a)(43)(M). *See Obasohan v. U.S. Att'y Gen.*, 479 F.3d 785, 791 (11th Cir. 2007).

14. Ms. Rodriguez was the sole proprietor of a small export-import company which dealt in computer parts. She took out a revolving line of credit through a broker, Carlos Smith, from New Continent Financial, whom she had known on a personal basis. The loan was backed by the Export-Import Bank. The loan issued by Mr. Smith was extended in order for borrowers sell items di-

rectly for export. Ms. Rodriguez sold items to individuals in the United States who in turn, took the items to sell abroad. In May 2010, New Continent Financial closed her line of credit. In August 2010, the lender demanded payment in full of the outstanding balance. Her default on the loan was the result of her inability to pay after the lender abruptly closing her line of credit and requiring payment in full.

15. The conduct for which Ms. Rodriguez was convicted was related to the manner of securing the loan and selling the items, not to the default on the loan. Importantly, Ms. Rodriguez was not convicted for defaulting on a loan. The default is tethered not to Ms. Rodriguez's offense conduct, but rather to her inability to pay back the loan when the lender called it in. As such, any monetary losses in this case are too attenuated from the conduct of which Ms. Rodriguez was convicted to render those convictions aggravated felonies as defined in INA § 101(a)(43)(M)(i). *See id.*

WHEREFORE, the Respondent requests that the Court grant this motion to dismiss the charge of removability under INA § 237(a)(2)(A)(iii) and terminate these removal proceedings.

Respectfully Submitted,

Mary E. Kramer
Mary E. Kramer, P.A.
168 SE First Street, Suite 802
Miami, Florida 33131
(305) 374- 2300
Fax: (305) 374-3748
mary@marykramerlaw.com

Certificate of Service

I certify that a true and correct copy of this motion was served by _____ on the Office of Chief Counsel for ICE at 3535 Lawton Road, Suite 100, Orlando, Florida, on this ____ day of September 2014.

_____

APPENDIX 10H

Sample Memorandum in Support of INA §240A(a) Eligibility for Cancellation of Removal

UNITED STATES DEPARTMENT OF JUSTICE
EXECUTIVE OFFICE FOR IMMIGRATION REVIEW
OFFICE OF THE IMMIGRATION JUDGE
MIAMI, FLORIDA

IN THE MATTER OF :)	
)	
HECTOR DIAZ)	CASE NO. A123 456 789
RESPONDENT)	Judge Williams
)	ACC: Sally Johnson
IN REMOVAL PROCEEDINGS)	Set for oral decision: 1/2/2012
_____ /	

MEMORANDUM OF LAW
IN SUPPORT OF STATUTORY ELIGIBILITY
FOR CANCELLATION OF REMOVAL

Statement of the Case / Introduction

On January 7, 2014, the Court held an individual relief hearing in this matter. The only issue that remains pending is whether the Respondent has an aggravated felony conviction such that he is not eligible for the relief sought. All parties agree that, assuming statutory eligibility under INA § 240A(a), relief should be granted in the exercise of discretion.

There have been numerous motions and memoranda filed in this case. Accordingly, this introduction will be brief. Other filings go over personal facts, and there was a full individual hearing with witnesses. This is a memorandum of law.

Mr. Diaz is a lawful permanent resident (since 1986). He is charged as an arriving alien. Mr. Diaz was originally charged with removability for two crimes. The first crime is a pre-1996 conviction for failure to return a rental car, which the DHS initially charged as a moral turpitude crime. Respondent contested. At the last hearing, DHS agreed to withdraw the moral turpitude charge. This leaves the controlled substance violation, under INA § 212(a)(2)(A)(i)(II), which the Court has sustained. Aggravated felony is not a charge of inadmissibility under INA § 212(a). Mr. Diaz is not charged with removability for an aggravated felony. The issue is whether, in the context of relief (cancellation), it is an aggravated felony that bars statutory eligibility.[319]

Questions Presented

I. Whether Respondent Diaz' conviction for violation of Fla. Stat. § 893.13(1) is a categorical match to a federal felony drug trafficking crime?

Brief Answer

II. No, for two discrete reasons. First, the Florida statute for distribution without remuneration of marijuana is not a categorical match to 21 USC § 841 because the federal provision references a "small amount" whereas the Florida statute specifies "20 grams"; and/or second, because Mr. Diaz' charging document is silent to the elements of remuneration and amount, the necessary factors for a federal felony are missing from his conviction record.

Facts

On or about February 2000,[320] Mr. Diaz was arrested in Tampa. The State charged him in a two-count Information. In the caption, count one is listed as "F.S. 893.13(1)(a)." In the text of count one, however, he is not charged under F.S. 893.13; rather, he is charged with the words "intent to sell or deliver" cannabis, as named or described in Section 893.03(1)(c).

Count two is possession of drug paraphernalia under Fla. Stat. § 893.03.

Count one of the Information states as follows:

Hector Diaz, on the 25th day of February, 2000, in the County of Hillsborough and State of Florida, did then and there knowingly, unlawfully, and feloniously

---

[319] Respondent also applied for a 212(h) waiver.

[320] Respondent acknowledges *Donawa v. U.S. Att'y General*, 735 F.3d 1275 (11th Cir. 2013). Mr. Diaz' case is not a *per se Donawa* matter, because *Donawa* involved convictions under Fla. Stat. 893.13 after a 2002 amendment to the statute that eliminated the intent (knowledge) requirement, removing it from the federal analogue's purview. Mr. Diaz' arrest and conviction precedes the Florida legislature's amendment; however, *Donawa* does contain very useful language, hence guidance.

possess with intent to sell or deliver a controlled substance, to wit: Cannabis, as named or described in Section 893.03(1)(c).

On or about November 20, 2000, Mr. Diaz pled no contest. On count one, he received a withhold of adjudication. On count two, he was adjudicated guilty. Mr. Diaz received 24 months' probation.

Legal Discussion

A. Fla. Stat. § 893.13 does not categorically describe a federal drug trafficking crime.

Section 101(a)(43)(B) of the INA defines an "aggravated felony as illicit trafficking in a controlled substance, including a drug trafficking crime" as defined in section 924(c) of title 18, United States Code. A state offense constitutes a "felony punishable under the Controlled Substance Act" only if the proscribed conduct is punishable as a felony under the federal law. *Lopez v. Gonzales,* 549 U.S. 47 (2006). This means that the state offense of conviction must meet the 'elements' of the generic federal offense, but the CSA must punish that offense as a felony. *Moncrieffe v. Holder,* 133 S. Ct. 1678, 1687 (2013);[321] *Donawa v. U.S. Att'y General,* 735 F.3d 1275 (11th Cir. 2013).

Federal law contains a provision at 21 USC § 841(b)(4) whereby a conviction for distribution of a "small amount" of marijuana will be punished as a misdemeanor, not a felony. In *Moncrieffe v. Holder, id.,* the non-citizen was convicted in George of possession of marijuana with intent to distribute. The immigration court ordered removal, finding this to be an aggravated felony drug trafficking crime. After affirmances below, the Supreme Court ultimately overruled this determination.

The High Court found that illicit trafficking in a controlled substance is a generic crime to which the categorical approach applies (as opposed to circumstance-specific). *Id, citing: Carachuri-Rosendo v. Holder,* 130 S. Ct. 2577, n. 11 (2010). The Court noted that federal law contains a misdemeanor provision for distribution of a small amount of marijuana without remuneration, at 21 USC § 841(b)(4). In order to qualify for misdemeanor treatment, the conviction must be for a "small amount" and "without remuneration."

The Georgia controlled substance statute does not contain a misdemeanor provision for distribution without remuneration. Thus it was impossible to tell whether Mr. Moncrieffe was convicted of a CSA felony or a CSA misdemeanor. *Moncrieffe,* at 1686-1687. Juxtaposing the state and federal statutes, categorically a conviction for

---

[321] The slim difference between a federal felony drug trafficking crime, and an illicit trafficking crime, is not relevant to this case because of the issue of remuneration. Without remuneration, there is neither a federal felony, nor a trafficking crime.

distribution of marijuana in Georgia could not ever qualify as an aggravated felony drug trafficking crime.

Unlike Georgia, Florida does contain a distribution-without-remuneration-of-marijuana misdemeanor provision. Mr. Diaz was convicted of a felony, so he was not charged under the misdemeanor provision. Still, the Florida statute is not a categorical match to the federal provision.

Fla. Stat. § 893.13(b)(3) states that "any person who delivers, without consideration, not more than 20 grams of cannabis, as defined in this chapter, commits a misdemeanor of the first degree . . ." In comparison, 21 USC § 841(b)(4) states that "notwithstanding paragraph (1)(D) of this subsection, any person who violates subsection (a) of this section by distributing a small amount of marihuana for no remuneration shall be treated as provided in section 844 . . ."

Thus the distinction rests in "small amount" (federal) versus "less than 20 grams" (state). This is in fact a major distinction. Federal case law states that the elements of "small amount" and "remuneration" are questions of fact, to be put to the jury, and will depend on the particular setting. *United States v. Lowe,* 143 F.Supp 2d (S.D.W.V. Nov. 28, 2000). "Small amount" is not defined in the statute, nor addressed in the legislative history of the CSA." Pre-*Apprendi,* Congress left small amount open for the courts to decide, indicating the determination should not be based purely on weight. *See: United States v. Damerville,* 27 F.3d 254, 258-259 (7th Cir. 1994). (Although the same amount might be considered 'small' when distributed in the general community, thirty-five balloons of marijuana, intended for use by three people, relative to the availability of drugs in a prison, is not, for penalty purposes, 'small.') Whether court or jury, "small amount" in the federal context is decided on a case-by-case basis that takes into account the setting, the amount, the number of social-sharers, etc. In contrast, Florida law sets the line of demarcation at 20 grams, period.

By way of additional comparison, for immigration purposes, 30 grams is the line of demarcation when considering what is a small amount. In *Moncrieffe,* the government quoted the BIA in arguing that 30 grams serves as a useful guidepost and should be the definition of "small." *Moncrieffe, supra,* at n. 7, *citing: Matter of Castro-Rodriguez,* 25 I & N Dec. 698, 699 n. 2 (BIA 2012).

Thus the distinction is potentially huge. The difference between the felony and state provisions means that a person prosecuted for distribution of less than 30, but more than 20 grams, in Florida is a felon, whereas if prosecuted in federal court, he could qualify for misdemeanor treatment. Under *Lopez, Carachuri,* and now *Moncrieffe,* this is an impermissible distinction for immigration law purposes, which pattern a federal paradigm.

Because the Florida controlled substance statute (as it relates to distribution of marijuana) is not a categorical match to the federal CSA, it cannot be said that Mr. Diaz has a federal felony drug trafficking conviction. Rather, the Immigration Court must assume the least culpable conduct described by the federal statute, which is a misdemeanor, and not an illicit trafficking crime. *Donawa, supra,* at 1280; *citing: Moncrieffe, supra,* at 1684.

B. Mr. Diaz' particular conviction does not contain the elements of a federal drug trafficking crime.

The Immigration Court need not reach the issue discussed in the section above, that is: that Florida's statute is not a categorical match to the federal CSA such that no marijuana distribution offense can ever be an aggravated felony drug trafficking crime. Rather, the Immigration Court can resolve this case specifically in the context of Mr. Diaz' conviction.

A close look at the Information and Judgment reflect that Mr. Diaz was not prosecuted for what qualifies as a federal felony trafficking crime.

In order for a state marijuana conviction to qualify as a felony punishable under the CSA, the offense must contain two elements: more than a small amount, and remuneration: "the fact of a conviction for possession with intent to distribute marijuana, standing alone, does not reveal whether either remuneration or more than a small amount of marijuana was involved." *Moncrieffe,* at 1686. *Also see: Matter of Flores-Aguirre,* 26 I & N Dec. 155 (BIA 2013).

Mr. Diaz was charged with intent to "sell or deliver"; no amount is listed; and, no remuneration is alleged. This Information fails to establish the essential elements of the generic federal felony:

> If a noncitizen's conviction for a marijuana distribution offense fails to establish that the offense involved either remuneration or more than a small amount of marijuana, the conviction is not for an aggravated felony under the INA. *Moncrieffe,* at 1693-1694.

In sum, the record of conviction does not establish an aggravated felony drug trafficking crime. Mr. Diaz is eligible for cancellation of removal.

C. The burden of proof in the relief context does not change the outcome of the Court's finding regarding the nature of the conviction.

Respondent is mindful that in the context of relief, he bears the burden of proving eligibility for relief. It is a low burden: preponderance of the evidence. 8 CFR § 1240.3. However, a burden of proof does not change the categorical analysis for looking at crime as defined by the Supreme Court. In other words, a straightforward categorical analysis of a criminal statute does not change over to circumstance-specific simply because the context is relief. If Florida's distribution of a controlled substance statute in general—or Mr. Diaz' conviction in particular—does not categorically describe a generic federal drug trafficking felony, a shifting burden of proof does not alter this fact. This point is illustrated in the conclusion of *Moncrieffe,* wherein the Supreme Court notes that the matter will be remanded for relief: the Court does not mention that the burden of proof in the relief stage may alter the analysis.

Conclusion

In finding that Mr. Diaz does not have an aggravated felony conviction, the Immigration Court may approach this case in two ways that are not mutually exclusive. First, the Court may find that categorically, across the board, a conviction for distribution of marijuana under Fla. Stat. 893.13 is never an aggravated felony drug trafficking crime because the Florida provision is too different from 21 USC § 841(b)(4) to qualify as a generic federal felony. Assuming the least culpable conduct described by the federal statute, all marijuana distribution convictions in Florida are for social sharing—a misdemeanor.

In addition to, or in the alternative, this Court may limit its finding to Mr. Diaz' specific record of conviction. This charging document lacks the essential elements of the generic crime: he was not specifically charged with remuneration (because of the "sell or distribute" phraseology) and there is no amount charged. In the absence of these clear elements, the Immigration Court must assume the least culpable conduct charged by the CSA: social sharing—a misdemeanor.

The context of relief does not alter the proper method of analyzing a criminal statute. Mr. Diaz has produced his record of conviction, and obviously it does not establish a federal drug trafficking crime.

Respondent asks that an order granting cancellation of removal be entered.

RESPECTFULLY SUBMITTED:

MARY KRAMER
ATTORNEY AT LAW
Mary E. Kramer, P.A.
168 SE First St. Suite 802
Miami, FL 33131
(305) 374 2300
fax: (305) 374 3748
mary@marykramerlaw.com

CERTIFICATE OF SERVICE

I certify that a true and correct copy of this motion was served by hand delivery to Attorney Benjamin Rosen Assistant Chief Counsel for DHS at 333 S. Miami Ave., Miami FL 33130 on this ___ day of February, 2014.

_____/

Index to Supporting Documents

CASELAW:

United States v. Damerville

United States v. Lowe

A. Information and Judgment for Case Number 00-00009999

B. 1999 version of the federal criminal code 21 USC § 841

C. 2001 version of Fla. Stat. § 893.13

APPENDIX 10I

SAMPLE STATEMENT IN SUPPORT OF NATURALIZATION ELIGIBILITY

UNITED STATES DEPARTMENT OF HOMELAND SECURITY
CITIZENSHIP AND IMMIGRATION SERVICES
MIAMI, FLORIDA

IN THE MATTER OF :   )
)
MATIAS RODRIGUEZ   )   Case No. A042 120 215
APPLICANT FOR   )
NATURALIZATION   )
_____/

Brief Statement in Support of Naturalization Eligibility

Introduction

Applicant Matias Rodriguez is scheduled for a preliminary naturalization interview on January 26, 2012. This memorandum is prepared for submission at the interview, to discuss statutory eligibility in light of Mr. Rodriguez' arrest record.

Facts

Mr. Rodriguez is a 44 year old citizen of Cuba who adjusted status as of May 21, 1995. He is married to a U.S. citizen and has one U.S. citizen child (as well as a teenage child in Cuba). He works as an independent electrical assistant.

The N-400 contains a supplement page that lists in a straightforward manner the dates of arrests and the nature of the charges, as well as the outcome. That list will not be repeated here; rather, the charges and their dispositions will be addressed in the legal discussion, below.

Suffice to say as a general summary that the Applicant has a dismissed arrest for obtaining property by fraud, relating to credit card abuse, in Bexar County, Texas. He has a 2002 arrest for Tampering with a government record (essentially possession of an I.D.) to which he originally pled; the plea was subsequently vacated and in 2011 he pled to a lower, Class B misdemeanor charge of interfering with the duties of a public servant. In 1998 and 1999, he had four arrests for violation of an injunction, obstruction w/o violence, and simple misdemeanor battery in Hillsborough County. The obstruction was immediately dismissed. Originally, he pled to simple battery, as well as the four injunction violations. However, all pleas were vacated and the charges dismissed.

This leaves Mr. Rodriguez with a conviction record for second degree misdemeanor "interference with a public servant." The offense conduct occurred in December 2002; the date of final disposition is September 16, 2011.

Legal Discussion

Eight CFR § 316.10 addresses the requirements of good moral character in the naturalization context. An individual who has a conviction for a crime involving moral turpitude within the statutory period[322] required for naturalization will not be approved. However, an offense that falls within section 212(a)'s petty offense exception does not normally pose a bar. Mr. Rodriguez does not have an offense that falls within the statutory five year period. His last arrest was in April of 2001, and he filed for naturalization on October 12, 2011.

In addition, a crime which constitutes an aggravated felony is a permanent bar to establishing good moral character. A review of his record reflects that he does not have an aggravated felony offense. The simple battery and domestic violence convictions were all vacated on legal, statutory grounds. (Discussed further, infra.) Even so, he did not receive (even in the original sentence) a year or more imprisonment as a sentence. In terms of the 2001 obtaining property by fraud / credit card abuse, it is Mr. Rodriguez' position that this offense was dismissed and does not constitute a "conviction" as that term is defined under INA § 101(a)(48). Moreover, the conviction records do not indicate a loss to a victim of $10,000 or more.

Thus it is clear that Mr. Rodriguez is eligible for naturalization in that he has five years of good moral character and does not have an aggravated felony conviction. The real issue in this case is whether CIS views him as amenable to removal proceedings such that an NTA would be issued commencing removal proceedings.

A review of the record reflects that Mr. Rodriguez is not subject to removal under INA § 237(a)(2). Most respectfully, it is requested that naturalization be approved.

A. **The Vacaturs of Pleas and Dismissal of Convictions were Obtained Based on Statutory and Constitutional Error in Proceedings Below and are Thus Valid for Immigration Law Purposes.**

---

[322] On the N400, counsel checked the "five year" period of classification; he may also qualify based on three year GMC, based on marriage. However, counsel is not clear on that point because the date of the spouse's citizenship is 2011. The legal issues presented by this case are not affected whether the period of GMC is five years or three years.

Mr. Rodriguez has available the motions to vacate for CIS' review. The Travis County plea was vacated based on constitutional and statutory defects in the plea, as was the Hillsborough County record. A plea which is vacated based on legal defect in the proceeding below is valid, and effectively vacates the "conviction", for immigration purposes. *Matter of Pickering,* 23 I & N Dec. 621 (BIA 2003). Specifically, in both Texas and Florida motions, counsel argued effectively that Mr. Rodriguez had not been sufficiently advised of the consequences of detention and deportation, thus the pleas were not voluntarily and knowingly made.

Mr. Rodriguez is thus not subject to removal on the basis of tampering with a government record (Travis County), because this plea was vacated, and the charge dismissed. Likewise, he has no conviction in Hillsborough County for battery or violation of an injunction, because following the vacatur, these charges were dismissed (and the files destroyed).

B. Obtaining Property by Fraud and Interfering with a Public Servant do not Support Removal Proceedings.

If Mr. Rodriguez has only one crime involving moral turpitude, committed more than five years after the date of admission, he is not amenable to removal. Again, he adjusted status on May 21, 1995 (after originally entering with a parole). Both the Texas cases occurred outside that five year window. Therefore, only if he has *two* convictions for crimes that involve *moral turpitude* is he subject to removal under INA § 237(a)(2).

i. Interference with Public Servant not a moral turpitude crime

In Travis County, Mr. Rodriguez (following a vacatur and dismissal of tampering with a government record), was charged and convicted of interference with an official in his duties, a Class B misdemeanor. The criminal statute is attached. Section 38.15 of the Texas Penal Code states, in pertinent part:

Sec. 38.15. INTERFERENCE WITH PUBLIC DUTIES. (a) A person commits an offense if the person with criminal negligence interrupts, disrupts, impedes, or otherwise interferes with:

> (1) a peace officer while the peace officer is performing a duty or exercising authority imposed or granted by law . . .

The state of mind, or mens rea, for this offense is negligence. The statute does not require as an element the specific intent to impede or obstruct. Without the elements of knowledge or specific intent, it cannot be said that this offense involves moral turpitude. See: *Matter of Franklin,* 20 I & N Dec. 867 (BIA 1994). Negligence is the lowest form of culpability, lower than even recklessness. See: *Matter of Medina,* 15 I & N Dec. 611, 615 (BIA 1976). Without an element of knowledge, courts have not been willing to find that obstruction offenses involve moral turpitude. See, e.g.: *Padilla v. Gonzalez,* 397 F.3d 1016 (7th Cir. 2005) (the knowing provision of false information to prevent apprehension or prosecution is a crime involving moral turpitude.)

ii. Interference with Public Servant a petty offense crime

Thus the conviction for interference with public duties is not a crime involving moral turpitude. Moreover, it would fall under the "petty offense exception", based on the maximum penalty possible and the fact that he did not receive a sentence of six months in jail. See: 8 CFR § 316.10(b)(2)(i). The Texas Penal Code states as follows regarding the penalty for a Class B misdemeanor:

§ 12.22. Class B Misdemeanor:

An individual adjudged guilty of a Class B misdemeanor shall be punished by:

(1) a fine not to exceed $2,000;

(2) confinement in jail for a term not to exceed 180 days; or both such fine and confinement.

iii. Credit Card Abuse disposition does not represent a "conviction"

The credit card abuse statute from Texas is also attached. It appears to be a fraud offense, committed with knowledge. However, this charge was dismissed. The record of conviction shows a period of deferred adjudication, including supervision, some sort of treatment, and 200 hours of community service. Nowhere does the conviction record reflect that Mr. Rodriguez entered a plea. Nowhere does the conviction record indicate that Mr. Rodriguez entered a plea of guilty or no contest. Thus although this record satisfies the "punishment" prong of INA § 101(a)(48), neither the plea nor adjudication prongs are present. The final document indicates an outright dismissal of charges—again, without a plea and without an adjudication. Under the circumstances, it cannot be said that this record represents a "conviction" for removal purposes under INA § 237(a)(2).

Conclusion

It is respectfully submitted that Mr. Rodriguez meets the statutory requirement of good moral character and he is therefore eligible for naturalization. He furthermore is not amenable to removal proceedings because he does not have a conviction for a crime involving moral turpitude committed within five years of admission, and he does not have two convictions for crimes involve moral turpitude committed at any time.

Mr. Rodriguez has strong family ties and sixteen years of residency status. He asks, with respect, that his application be granted.

RESPECTFULLY SUBMITTED:

[Signature]

MARY KRAMER
ATTORNEY AT LAW
MARY E. KRAMER, P.A.
168 SE FIRST ST. SUITE 802
MIAMI, FL 33131
(305) 374 2300
FAX: (305) 374 3748
mary@marykramerlaw.com

[Date]

Attachments:
Texas criminal statutes, as referenced, attached.

CHAPTER ELEVEN

FASHIONING A PLEA TO AVOID ADVERSE IMMIGRATION CONSEQUENCES

Avoiding Adverse Immigration Consequences	562
Avoiding a Conviction of a Crime Involving Moral Turpitude	566
Avoiding the Aggravated Felony Conviction	572
Avoiding Deportability for Domestic Violence Offenses	580
Creating Eligibility for Relief	581
Appendix	
11A: Sample Memorandum for Fashioning a Plea	588

One of the most rewarding aspects of a criminal-alien practice is collaborating with defense counsel on a pending criminal case. A criminal lawyer serves the criminal defendant best when working with an immigration attorney on potential immigration law issues. Collaboration may take many forms, including immigration advice on the potential consequences of a pending charge, alternatives to the charge (in anticipation of a plea), sentencing issues, and even post-conviction relief. In time, long-standing relationships between criminal and immigration lawyers form as colleagues learn with whom they work well as a team. Some attorneys practice both immigration and criminal defense; this chapter's discussion serves this dual practice well also. The point is, a defendant's interests are best served when defense counsel is cognizant of potential immigration law consequences attached to a charge, and works toward a positive immigration result alongside other case goals.

The U.S. Supreme Court's decision in *Padilla v. Kentucky*[1] is a mandate for criminal and immigration attorneys to work together to best serve the needs of the client-defendant. Collaboration may take the form of informal discussions, memoranda of law (and advice), meetings with prosecutors (to explain immigration concerns), affidavits for the court, and/or expert witness testimony at sentencing.

The preceding chapters discuss the definition of "conviction," the crimes that result in a conviction for immigration purposes, the consequences of a conviction, and eligibility for relief from a conviction. With this foundation in place, the following discussion takes the process back to square one and explores strategies in the plea bargaining process. In some criminal cases, it may be possible to avoid immigration consequences altogether. In other situations, through smart plea-bargaining, defense counsel can ensure that the client is eligible for a waiver or other relief.

---

[1] *Padilla v. Kentucky*, 559 U.S. 356 (2010).

To be sure, possibilities for successful plea-bargaining are endless. This book touches on some basic options, and attempts to teach awareness of basic concepts and methodology. Each criminal case involves a unique set of factual circumstances and varied criminal charges. Attorneys should exercise creativity in searching the state or federal statute for good immigration options, including negotiating alternative charges and lower sentences. Either way, the ideal point in time to consider immigration issues is at the commencement of the criminal case. If good immigration alternatives do not present themselves, a lawyer must be prepared to discuss the potential adverse immigration actions that may come of a plea or conviction honestly, and advise the client accordingly. This may mean advising a client to be prepared for deportation and to plan appropriately.

Avoiding Adverse Immigration Consequences

Avoiding adverse consequences altogether is of course the cherished prize. This may mean avoiding a final conviction, as that term is defined by immigration law; negotiating a charge down to a lesser offense; or keeping the sentence below the benchmark for inadmissibility or deportability.

The following discussion moves quickly and assumes knowledge of the terms, concepts, and statutory provisions discussed in the previous chapters. Where there is confusion or doubt as to a term, reference should be made to the earlier chapters.

Avoiding a Conviction Through Pretrial Diversion

As discussed in chapter two, a conviction exists for immigration purposes when there has been either a formal judgment of guilt entered by the court, a plea of guilty or no contest, or an admission to the offense, and the court has ordered some form of punishment, penalty, or restraint on the individual's liberty. Pretrial diversion schemes (such as pretrial intervention in Florida[2]) that do not require a formal plea before the court, and result in the ultimate dismissal of the charges, are effective in avoiding a conviction for immigration purposes.[3] In comparison, procedures whereby the individual enters a plea and is adjudicated, and the charges are later dismissed following successful completion of a rehabilitative program, are *not* effective.

> ➤ ***Compare pretrial diversion with deferred adjudications***: Deferred adjudications of guilt, unlike pretrial diversion procedures, are not effective to avoid a conviction. Under deferred adjudication procedures, such as withholding of adjudication, an individual enters a plea before the court. On successful completion of a probationary-type period or pro-

---

[2] Fla. St. §948.08.

[3] *Matter of Grullon*, 20 I&N Dec. 12 (BIA 1989). *Grullon* predates the definition of "conviction" at INA §101(a)(48) [8 USC §1101(a)(48)], as well as the BIA's decision in *Matter of Roldan*, 22 I&N Dec. 512 (BIA 1999). Nevertheless, *Grullon's* analysis of pretrial diversion schemes remains valid today.

gram, the charges are dismissed without the court ever entering a final adjudication. Outside the Ninth Circuit (see below), deferred adjudications are not effective to avoid a final "conviction" for immigration purposes.[4]

Beware of admissions to the crime

When advising a client regarding pretrial diversion, it is prudent to caution that an *admission* to the essential elements of the crime to U.S. Department of Homeland Security (DHS) officers may result in a finding of inadmissibility, notwithstanding dismissal of the charges. A client may be quizzed on the circumstances of the arrest in several scenarios, including arriving at a port of entry following a trip abroad (such as an airport or Deferred Inspections); at a U.S. consulate (in the context of applying for a visa); or at an immigration interview (for example, when applying for adjustment of status or naturalization). Thus, although pretrial diversion is an excellent option, it is not an all-encompassing protection; the client must be aware of the significance of admissions to crime.

Federal First Offender Act Treatment; 18 USC §3607

As discussed immediately below, state rehabilitative procedures that are modeled on the Federal First Offender Act (FFOA)[5] are not effective to eliminate a conviction for immigration purposes. However, what about dispositions under the FFOA itself? This legal question is undecided at both the administrative and federal court levels. The federal courts, attorney general, and the Board of Immigration Appeals (BIA or Board) have pointedly declined to determine whether the definition of "conviction" at Immigration and Nationality Act (INA) §101(a)(48) acts as a repeal of the FFOA for immigration purposes. Thus clients should be advised that an FFOA expungement or vacatur (it is not technically an expungement, but a vacation of the plea and dismissal of the charge) is a viable alternative to avoiding a conviction, but not a guarantee. If there is no better alternative, an FFOA procedure is the best option available to a non–American citizen defendant facing a charge of simple possession of a controlled substance in federal court. The following discussion summarizes the historical development of the issue.

In *Matter of Roldan*,[6] the BIA interpreted the impact of state rehabilitative programs in light of the definition of conviction at INA §101(a)(48). The BIA specifically left for another day the import of a disposition under the FFOA:

---

[4] *Matter of Salazar*, 23 I&N Dec. 223 (BIA 2002) (a non–American citizen whose adjudication of guilt is deferred under art. 42.12, §5(a) of the Texas Code of Criminal Procedure, following a plea of guilty to possession of a controlled substance, has a "conviction" for immigration purposes). *See Matter of Punu*, 22 I&N Dec. 224 (BIA 1998) (deferred adjudication under Texas law results in a "conviction").

[5] 18 USC §3607.

[6] *Matter of Roldan*, 22 I&N Dec. 512 (BIA 1999).

[W]e are presented here with an alien who has been accorded rehabilitative treatment under a state statute. We will leave the question of the effect to be given in immigration proceedings to first offender treatment accorded to an alien under 18 USC §3607 by a federal court to a case when that issue is directly presented.[7]

The attorney general has also avoided stating a position on whether the FFOA is partially repealed by INA §101(a)(48)(A)'s definition of conviction. The attorney general's most recent decision on the issue leaves open the question of whether controlled substance offenses processed and vacated under the FFOA result in a final "conviction" for immigration purposes.[8]

The federal courts have likewise avoided speaking directly to the effect of an FFOA procedure in the immigration context, but appear open to the theory that a dismissal of charges under the FFOA does *not* result in a conviction for immigration purposes.[9]

Keep the Case in Juvenile Court

Adjudications of juvenile delinquency are not considered criminal convictions under immigration law. It is essential to keep clients under the age of 18 in the juvenile court system if at all possible.[10] Note that juvenile court and adjudications of juvenile delinquency are not the equivalent of "youthful offender" *sentencing* schemes. An individual who is processed in adult court, but who is classified as a youthful offender for sentencing purposes, is still convicted under immigration law. Whether a state procedure qualifies as "juvenile delinquency" proceedings, such that the non–American citizen is not convicted for immigration purposes, is determined by comparison with the Federal Juvenile Delinquency Act (FJDA), found at 18 USC §§5031 and 5032.

> ➤ **Example**: In *Matter of Devison-Charles*,[11] the non–American citizen was adjudicated as a youthful offender under art. 720 of the New York Criminal Procedure Law. The BIA found that art. 720 corresponds to juvenile delinquency proceedings under 18 USC §5031 (FJDA), and that the individual did not have a conviction for immigration purposes.

---

[7] *Matter of Roldan*, 22 I&N Dec. 512, at n.9.

[8] *Matter of Marroquin-Garcia,* 23 I&N Dec. 705 (AG 2005; BIA 1997).

[9] *See, e.g.*, *Gill v. Ashcroft*, 335 F.3d 574, 578 (7th Cir. 2003) (INA §101(a)(48)(A) and 18 USC §3607 may coexist, "though the former reduces the domain of the latter"); *Acosta v. Ashcroft,* 341 F.3d 218, 227 (3d Cir. 2003); *Vasquez-Velezmoro v. INS,* 281 F.3d 693, 697–99 (8th Cir. 2002) ("For purposes of this opinion, we will assume that convictions expunged by the FFOA [Federal First Offender Act] are not convictions for immigration purposes.").

[10] *Matter of Devison-Charles*, 22 I&N Dec. 1362 (BIA 2000); *Matter of Devison* was affirmed in 2013 by *Matter of V-X-,* 26 I&N Dec. 147 (BIA 2013), in which BIA held that a "youthful trainee" status pursuant to Michigan law is a "conviction" because it is a sentencing provision, not a delinquency adjudication.

[11] *Matter of Devison-Charles*, 22 I&N Dec. 1362 (BIA 2000).

The BIA further noted that, based on New York law, the individual's resentencing under the youthful offender statute because of a violation of probation did not convert the youthful offender adjudication into a "conviction" under immigration law.

The Petty Offense Exception

If the offense charged involves the elements of intent to deprive, intent to defraud, or an act of intentional and serious violence, it is a crime involving moral turpitude. Under the petty offense exception,[12] an individual convicted of only one crime involving moral turpitude, for which the maximum sentence possible does not exceed one year, and who is not sentenced in excess of six months, is not inadmissible under INA §212(a)(2)(A)(i)(I) [8 USC §1182(a)(2)(A)(i)(I)].

> ➤ **Example**: Alexander Vavoom, a wealthy but eccentric investor residing in Central Florida on an E (investment) visa, is arrested and eventually convicted for stealing more than 50 buttons off girls' blouses at a local boutique. (His excuse is he likes to sew his own clothes, and cannot find the right buttons in the fabric stores.) The statute punishes petty theft by up to 364 days in jail, and Alexander is sentenced to only six months' probation and is credited time served (one afternoon). He has no other arrest record. Will Alexander lose his E visa or be denied readmission to the United States as a result of the conviction? No, because this offense falls under the petty-offense exception to inadmissibility. Is he deportable? No, because the maximum penalty possible is 364 days, and under INA §237, one conviction with a maximum sentence of under 365 days does not render an individual deportable.

> ➤ **Example**: Martin Trotsky is arrested and charged under 18 USC §1001, a felony encompassing materially false and fraudulent statements. The underlying criminal conduct involves the possession and use of a fraudulent resident card. Defense counsel negotiates a plea to 18 USC §1028(a)(4), unlawful possession of an identification document, and time served (60 days). Although the 18 USC §1028(a)(4) may also be interpreted as a crime involving moral turpitude due to its "intent to defraud" language, the plea deal calls for classification as a misdemeanor[13] and the offense thus falls under the petty offense exception.

Note that the petty-offense exception applies in the context of crimes involving moral turpitude. It does not apply to controlled substance offenses or other inadmissibility offenses. Note further that a sentence that is suspended is nonetheless the sen-

---

[12] INA §212(a)(2)(A)(ii)(II); 8 USC §1182(a)(2)(A)(ii)(II).
[13] 18 USC §1028(b)(6).

tence imposed under immigration law.[14] Finally, the petty-offense exception is only effective when the individual is inadmissible for *one* crime involving moral turpitude.

The petty-offense exception to inadmissibility applies in the contexts of adjustment of status, naturalization, and removal proceedings.

Section 237's version of the petty offense exception

The petty-offense exception described above applies in the context of inadmissibility under INA §212(a). A similar exception applies in cases involving deportability for a crime under INA §237(a)(2)(A)(i) [8 USC §1227(a)(2)(A)(i)]. An individual who has been admitted into the United States is not subject to deportation for a crime involving moral turpitude if there is only one conviction, and the maximum sentence possible does not exceed 364 days.

> **Compare**: In the context of inadmissibility, the petty offense exception applies if the maximum penalty possible for the crime does not *exceed* one year. For purposes of deportability, the exception applies as long as the maximum penalty possible is not one year or more.

Avoiding a Conviction of a Crime Involving Moral Turpitude

Why It Is Important (A Quick Rundown on Consequences)

Eligibility for permanent resident status

An individual who is not a lawful permanent resident (LPR), but who would like to adjust status to permanent residency or apply for an immigrant visa, will be considered inadmissible (ineligible) based on a conviction (or admission) of a crime involving moral turpitude. An individual who already has been admitted for lawful permanent residency may be denied re-entry to the United States based on a crime involving moral turpitude. And an LPR convicted of a crime involving moral turpitude within five years of admission may be subject to deportation.

Mandatory detention

An individual who is deportable (physically present within the United States, but placed in removal proceedings) with only one conviction for a crime involving moral turpitude is not subject to mandatory detention. Once there are multiple moral turpitude convictions, mandatory detention applies (for releases from custody after October 8, 1998). An individual arriving in the United States and charged with inadmissibility is subject to mandatory detention based on one crime involving moral turpitude (if released from penal custody after October 8, 1998).

---

[14] INA §101(a)(48)(B); 8 USC §1101(a)(48)(B).

Naturalization

An LPR who has been convicted of a crime involving moral turpitude within the statutory period required (usually five years; three years for persons married to and living with an American citizen) is ineligible for naturalization.

What Is "Moral Turpitude?"

The definition of a crime involving moral turpitude is discussed at length in chapter six of this book. Generally speaking, there are certain "red flags" when analyzing the elements of a criminal statute: moral turpitude crimes will involve specific or evil intent, knowledge, or willfulness. An intent to defraud involves moral turpitude. If the criminal activity involves harm to another human being, moral turpitude can even adhere where the offense involves criminally reckless conduct. Again, whether an offense involves moral turpitude is determined by the criminal statute involved. The analysis is based on the elements of the crime—not on the specific conduct or underlying activity of the particular case.

When working with a divisible statute that contains multiple *mens rea*, also advocate for a plea that references the least *scienter*.

Fraud crimes

Criminal charges involving fraud should be negotiated to (substituted with) offenses that do not involve a specific intent to defraud. For example, possession of an altered immigration document with knowledge that it was altered, but without its unlawful use, or proof of any intent to use it unlawfully, is not the basis of a conviction for a crime involving moral turpitude.[15]

A conviction for passing or using a worthless check where the statute does not contain the element of intent to defraud is not a crime involving moral turpitude.[16]

Theft offenses

Theft offenses may be crimes involving moral turpitude where a permanent taking is intended. For example, robbery and burglary are generally considered to involve moral turpitude; joyriding[17] and failure to return a rental car[18] may not be. In *Matter of Grazley*,[19] the BIA noted that theft is only a crime involving moral turpitude if a

---

[15] *Matter of Serna*, 20 I&N Dec. 579 (BIA 1992), *modified by Matter of Franklin*, 20 I&N Dec. 867 (BIA 1994).

[16] *Matter of Balao*, 20 I&N Dec. 440 (BIA 1992); *Matter of Zangwill*, 18 I&N Dec. 22 (BIA 1981), *overruled in part by Matter of Ozkok*, 19 I&N Dec. 546 (BIA 1988) (adjudication of guilt withheld qualifies as a "conviction"); *Matter of Stasinski*, 11 I&N Dec. 202 (BIA 1965).

[17] *Matter of P*, 2 I&N Dec. 887 (BIA 1947).

[18] *See, e.g., Matter of D*, 1 I&N Dec. 143 (BIA 1941).

[19] 14 I&N Dec. 330 (BIA 1973). *See also Matter of V–Z–S–*, 22 I&N Dec. 1338, 1350 (BIA 2000) (a temporary or less-than-permanent deprivation may qualify as a "theft" offense for purposes of the aggravated felony definition, but not be a crime involving moral turpitude. Unlawful driving and taking of

Continued

"permanent taking" is intended. Criminal charges of theft or an intent to deprive should be negotiated to (substituted with) offenses that do not involve a specific intent to permanently deprive. Where the criminal statute is divisible, defense counsel can mold the record to ensure that the non-moral turpitude provision (*i.e.*, temporary or less-than-permanent deprivation) is specified: for example, within the plea agreement, at the plea hearing, or within the final order, counsel can specify the subsections and words dealing with temporary appropriation.[20]

If possible, counsel should avoid pleas to theft or larceny and substitute with an entirely different sort of offense. For example, the offense of unauthorized use of a motor vehicle in violation of Tex. Penal Code §31.07 is not a crime involving moral turpitude.[21] (Note that this offense *is* an aggravated felony if a sentence of one year or more of imprisonment is imposed.)

Embezzlement

The embezzlement statute at 18 USC § 656 includes the terms: embezzle, abstract, purloin, or misapply. A possible option is to utilize the term abstract, purloin or misapply in the conviction record documents (charging document, plea, factual proffer) and delete and reference to fraudulent intent. (This will not be effective in the Eleventh Circuit, where the court of appeals has found that the provision per se involves fraud.)[22] Also, advocate for a charge, plea, and factual proffer specifying an intent to injure, rather than an intent to defraud.[23] Embezzlement is a hybrid of theft and fraud and therefore a dangerous offense of conviction all around: best to negotiate a plea to theft and advocate for a sentence of imprisonment of less than one year.

Burglary

Burglary offenses represent a good example of the need to pay close attention to the elements of the particular criminal statute involved. Some burglary offenses may involve moral turpitude while others may not. If the statute is divisible, the determination will be made based on the record of conviction (presenting an opportunity to tailor statements made in the plea process to avoid a determination of moral turpitude).

---

a vehicle under California law qualifies as an aggravated felony but not a crime involving moral turpitude).

[20] *See, e.g., Jaggernauth v. Att'y Gen.*, 432 F.3d 1346 (11th Cir. 2005), finding that Florida's theft statute is divisible where it contains two distinct provisions, one dealing with "appropriation," the other "deprivation."

[21] *Vo v. Gonzales*, 482 F.3d 363, 369 (5th Cir. 2007); *Matter of Brieva-Perez*, 23 I&N Dec. 766 (BIA 2005).

[22] *Moore v. Ashcroft*, 251 F.3d 919 (11th Cir. 2001).

[23] *See Valansi v. Ashcroft*, 278 F.3d 203 (3d Cir. 2002).

Working with a divisible statute: control the conviction record

The BIA has found that offenses involving, essentially, a breaking and entering or trespass may be deemed involving moral turpitude only if accompanied by the intent to commit a morally turpitudinous act after the entry.[24] In 2009, the BIA modified its position with respect to burglary of an occupied dwelling, finding that this offense is categorically a crime involving moral turpitude.[25] It is not clear whether state appeals courts would agree with this approach; moreover, the decision is limited to the factual scenario of an occupied dwelling. Where the state statute allows *any* crime to satisfy the intent element, the burglary offense will not be a crime involving moral turpitude if (1) no underlying offense is identified, or (2) the underlying offense does not represent a crime involving moral turpitude.[26] Defense counsel can control the conviction record by pointing out that the underlying crime did not involve moral turpitude within the plea bargain or at the plea hearing.

Alternative pleas

Burglary offenses may be negotiated down to trespass or criminal mischief. Avoid burglary of an occupied dwelling.

Crimes of violence

Crimes of violence, if the statute contains specific intent to cause bodily harm as an element of the offense, are crimes involving moral turpitude. In comparison, simple assaults and battery are not crimes involving moral turpitude.[27] This includes assaults involving negligent conduct, without the elements of recklessness or specific intent to do harm.[28]

DUIs (operating under the influence)

Simple driving under the influence (DUI) offenses that do not contain a specific intent to cause harm (such as bodily injury) are not crimes involving moral turpitude.[29]

Avoid Multiple Counts

An extremely important tip in fashioning a plea to avoid or ameliorate adverse immigration consequences is to avoid multiple counts where those multiple counts

---

[24] *Matter of M*, 2 I&N Dec. 721, 723 (BIA 1946), *distinguished by Matter of Louissaint*, 24 I&N Dec. 754 (BIA 2009).

[25] *Matter of Louissaint*, 24 I&N Dec. at 754 (BIA 2009).

[26] *Cuevas-Gaspar v. Gonzales*, 430 F.3d 1013, 1018–19 (9th Cir. 2005) (citing *Matter of M*, 2 I&N Dec. 721, 723 (BIA 1946), *distinguished by Matter of Louissaint*, 24 I&N Dec. 754 (BIA 2009)).

[27] *Matter of Perez-Contreras*, 20 I&N Dec. 615 (BIA 1992) (citing *Matter of Short*, 20 I&N Dec. 136 (BIA 1989)).

[28] *Id.*

[29] *Matter of Torres-Varela*, 23 I&N Dec. 78 (BIA 2001).

will be seen as distinct and separate offenses. Any conviction for a crime involving moral turpitude carries consequences; for multiple convictions, the consequences often will be worse. For example, a non–American citizen who has been convicted of only one crime of moral turpitude more than five years after the date of admission is not deportable (*i.e.*, subject to removal proceedings). In comparison, an individual who has been convicted of multiple crimes involving moral turpitude *at any time* is subject to removal proceedings. In addition, an individual physically within the United States (*i.e.*, not an arriving alien) who is placed in removal proceedings is not subject to mandatory detention for one conviction involving moral turpitude, but becomes so for multiple crimes involving moral turpitude. Also, the petty-offense exceptions (discussed above) apply only if the non–American citizen is inadmissible or deportable for a single crime involving moral turpitude.

When an individual is charged in an information or indictment with multiple counts of crimes involving moral turpitude, negotiate to a plea to one count only, possibly in exchange for a higher fine, or longer sentence. (However, keep it under one year.)

> ➢ *Example I*: The non–American citizen client is charged with several counts of criminal activity arising out of one incident; *i.e.*, grand theft auto, resisting arrest with violence, and aggravated battery. Negotiate a plea to one offense involving moral turpitude only (keeping the sentence below one year). If the offense occurred more than five years after the date of admission, the individual is not deportable.[30]

> ➢ *But compare*: In the process of negotiating a plea to only one crime involving moral turpitude, do not accept a sentence in excess of one year. If the choice comes down to multiple counts of moral turpitude crimes of violence—with concurrent sentences of less than one year—versus one crime of violence with a term of imprisonment of one year or longer, take the multiple-less-than-one-year counts deal.

> ➢ *Example II*: An individual is charged with three counts of credit card fraud; each count reflects a separate transaction in a different locale. Negotiate a plea to one count only, keeping the amount of loss below $10,000.

> ➢ *But compare*: If negotiating a plea to a single count, keep the amount of loss below $10,000. If the choice is between multiple counts—all below $10,000—or one count with the amount of loss over $10,000, go with the multiple counts below $10,000. (A conviction for a crime involving fraud where loss to the victim exceeds $10,000 is an aggravated felony.)

---

[30] INA §237(a)(2)(A)(i)(I); 8 USC §1227(a)(2)(A)(i)(I).

Summary Examples of Successful Plea Bargaining to Avoid a Crime Involving Moral Turpitude

- *Aggravated assault*: Negotiate a plea to simple assault or battery.

- *Aggravated driving or operating under the influence*: Negotiate an alternative plea to simple DUI (with no aggravating factors, such as suspended license or accident/bodily injury), or reckless driving.

- *Arson*: Negotiate an alternative plea of criminal mischief.

- *Burglary, including burglary of a conveyance*:[31] Negotiate an alternative plea of trespass or criminal mischief, or possession of burglary tools if intent or knowledge is absent from the statute. (Note: avoid trespass with a criminal *mens rea* to commit a crime involving moral turpitude after entry, and avoid a one-year term of imprisonment so as not to fall into the aggravated felony crime of violence range.)

- *Auto theft*: Negotiate a plea to unauthorized use of a motor vehicle. [Note: avoid a one-year or longer term of imprisonment, or the offense might be viewed as an aggravated felony crime of violence.]

    Or, negotiate an alternative plea to burglary of a conveyance (vehicle) if there is no underlying intent to commit a crime involving moral turpitude after entry. (Note: to avoid an aggravated felony charge, the sentence must be under one year imprisonment.[32])

    Or, negotiate a plea to possession of a vehicle with an altered vehicle identification number (VIN). Generally, there is no intent requirement to this latter offense. (Note: trafficking in motor vehicles where the VINs have been altered is an aggravated felony if the term of imprisonment imposed is at least one year.[33])

- *Aggravated fleeing and eluding*: negotiate a downgrade to simple fleeing and eluding; also negotiate a sentence of less than 365 days. Depending on the jurisdiction, simple fleeing and eluding may contain no intent requirement and usually encompasses only reckless conduct.

- *Aggravated stalking*: the BIA has found that aggravated stalking involves moral turpitude.[34] The Board implies that misdemeanor stalking is not a crime involving

---

[31] Burglary of a conveyance will only be a crime involving moral turpitude if an element of the offense is intent to commit a moral turpitudinous crime after entry. (See discussion on burglary earlier in this chapter). This is in comparison to burglary of an occupied dwelling, which the Board of Immigration Appeals (BIA) in 2009 found to categorically involve moral turpitude. *Matter of Louissaint*, 24 I&N Dec. 754 (BIA 2009).

[32] The U.S. Supreme Court has specifically stated that burglary can be an aggravated felony crime of violence. *Leocal v. Ashcroft*, 543 U.S. 1, 10 (2004). Thus, to avoid classification under INA §101(a)(43)(F), negotiate a plea to less than one year of imprisonment.

[33] INA §101(a)(43)(R); 8 USC §1101(a)(43)(R).

[34] *Matter of Ajami*, 22 I&N Dec. 949 (BIA 1999).

moral turpitude because it does not involve a credible threat to kill another or inflict physical injury.[35] In terms of stalking, state statutes will often be divisible. Fashion a charge that avoids a willful or intentional state of mind and credible threats of significant violence. Note that stalking may be a separate ground of deportability under INA §237(a)(2)(E), relating to crimes of domestic violence. However, depending on the particular client's case, it will be worthwhile to avoid the moral turpitude charge notwithstanding the distinct domestic violence ground: §237(a)(2)(E) is not a ground of inadmissibility, and is not a basis for mandatory detention.

- **Money laundering**: negotiate a plea to 18 USC §1960, prohibition against unlicensed money transmission business. This is a licensing statute, not a money-laundering statute.

Avoiding the Aggravated Felony Conviction

Why It Is Important (A Quick Rundown on Consequences)

Immigration law's "aggravated felony" classification is broad and contains many offenses. It is considered the worst category of immigration offense.

Limited eligibility for relief from removal and mandatory detention

An LPR who is deportable for an aggravated felony conviction entered after April 24, 1996, is ineligible for relief from removal.[36] Moreover, an individual who has been convicted of an aggravated felony and released from state or federal custody after October 8, 1998, is subject to mandatory detention, with no opportunity for bond during pending removal proceedings.

Barred from asylum

An individual who has been convicted of an aggravated felony offense is barred from receiving asylum, and may be denied withholding of removal under the INA and the Convention Against Torture.

No naturalization for convictions entered after November 29, 1990

Conviction of an aggravated felony offense on or after November 29, 1990, is a permanent bar to naturalization (American citizenship).

Avoiding an Aggravated Felony—Keep the Sentence Under One Year

The following offenses (under both state and federal law) are aggravated felonies if the term of imprisonment imposed is one year or more:

- Crimes of violence;

---

[35] *Id.* at 951–52. This case involved stalking under Michigan law; state statutes on stalking may vary.

[36] Antiterrorism and Effective Death Penalty Act of 1996 (AEDPA), Pub. L. No. 104-132, 110 Stat. 1214.

- Theft offenses and burglary offenses, including receipt of stolen property;
- Falsifying, forging, or counterfeiting a U.S. passport under 18 USC §1543;
- Offenses related to commercial bribery, counterfeiting, forgery, and trafficking in vehicles if the vehicle identification number has been altered; and
- Obstruction of justice, perjury, subornation of perjury, and bribery of a witness.

> ➢ *Example*: Juan Valencia, a native and citizen of Colombia, is arrested for grand theft auto. He decides to enter a plea. Juan's criminal attorney bargains for a sentence of "a year and a day" because under state rules, once the sentence goes over 365 days in jail, a defendant qualifies for good-time credit and will actually *serve* less time than 364 days. However, the plea bargain—arranged for the purpose of avoiding a few extra weeks in jail—results in an aggravated felony conviction for theft. Juan gets out of the county jail in less than one year but is taken into DHS custody, held for four months, and deported.

> ➢ *Post-Conviction Relief*: In *Matter of Song*,[37] a non–American citizen who had been ordered removed by the BIA for an aggravated felony offense returned to state court and successfully moved to vacate his sentence. The criminal court vacated the one-year prison sentence for theft and entered a revised sentence of 360 days. The individual's order of removal was subsequently reopened and vacated by the BIA.[38]

Remember that suspension of the term of imprisonment imposed is not effective in shortening the sentence; a suspension of sentence is irrelevant for immigration law purposes.[39]

Avoiding Loss to a Victim in Excess of $10,000

The following offenses are aggravated felonies if there is a loss to an identifiable victim or victims that *exceeds* $10,000:

- Money laundering;
- An offense involving fraud or deceit; and
- Tax evasion under Internal Revenue Code (IRC) §7201 (the loss in this instance being to the government).

---

[37] *Matter of Song*, 23 I&N Dec. 173 (BIA 2001).

[38] Note that post-conviction relief like that described in *Song* might not be effective if the non–American citizen already has been physically removed on account of the conviction. *See, e.g.*, *Patel v. Att'y Gen.*, 334 F.3d 1259 (11th Cir. 2003). *But see: Storey v. State*, 133 So.3d 528 (Fla. 2014) (petition for writ of mandamus granted; appeals court must consider motion to vacate plea on competency issues notwithstanding defendant's deportation).

[39] INA §101(a)(48)(B); 8 USC §1101(a)(48)(B).

> ***Proposed methods for avoiding loss to a victim***: Arrange for a civil settlement (noncriminal "restitution") outside of criminal court, contingent on "loss" being left out of (or modified in) the criminal court record and other documents (including the plea agreement, judgment, and presentence investigation report).

> Financial loss in the sentencing phase of a criminal proceeding may be based on "relevant conduct" under the Sentencing Guidelines;[40] relevant conduct is conduct outside the specific count of conviction.[41] If loss and/or restitution amounts are based on conduct not specifically tied to or included in the count of conviction, it is essential to clarify this point during the sentencing hearing and in sentencing related documents.

> Beware conspiracy charges under §371: Where the government charges conspiracy under 18 USC § 371, the defendant is potentially liable for the loss actually caused by co-defendants' actions. Counsel may avoid having a huge financial loss caused by co-defendants being attributed to the potential immigration client by requesting severance of defendants, a superseding information, and carefully specifying within the record of conviction a loss (less than $10,000) specifically attributable to the client. Defense counsel will also recall the loss must be tethered to the count(s) of conviction; restitution for relevant conduct may be set at a number above $10,000, but not be tied to the actual offense of conviction. This is acceptable in the immigration context if the distinction is carefully drawn and explained within the record of conviction.

Avoiding Crime of Violence by Pleading to a Non–Specific Intent Crime

A criminal charge or charges involving a specific intent to cause harm through violence should be negotiated to a lesser offense that does not involve a specific intent to do harm. Based on the U.S. Supreme Court's decision in *Leocal v. Ashcroft*,[42] an aggravated felony "crime of violence" is defined by 18 USC §16, and requires the intentional use of physical force against the person or property of another. An offense involving the elements of recklessness or negligence, without specific intent, is not an aggravated felony "crime of violence" under INA §101(a)(43)(F).

> ***Example***: Defendant (a non–American citizen) is involved in an automobile accident in which the other driver dies. The defendant is initially charged with driving under the influence and aggravated involuntary

---

[40] USSG § 1B1.3(a)(1); 18 USC § 3661.

[41] Cases that discuss the fact that "loss" in the criminal sentencing context is distinct from "loss" for purposes of INA § 101(a)(43)(M) include: *Nijhawan v. Holder,* 557 U.S. 29, 42 (2009) (loss must be tethered to count of conviction); *Obasohan v. Attorney General,* 479 F.3d 785, 789 (11th Cir. 2007); and *Matter of Babaisakov,* 24 I&N Dec. 306, 319 (BIA 2007).

[42] *Leocal v. Ashcroft,* 543 U.S. 1 (2004).

manslaughter. Defense counsel negotiates a plea to simple involuntary manslaughter, which penalizes the killing of a person as a proximate result of the defendant's *reckless* disregard for human life. This crime is not an aggravated felony "crime of violence" (and, arguably, is not a crime involving moral turpitude).[43]

Avoiding Alien Smuggling/Aggravated Felony Conviction

A conviction under 8 USC §§274(a)(1)(A) or (2) is an aggravated felony offense unless the individual smuggled was a spouse, child, or parent.[44] One alternative may be a plea to 8 USC §1325(a): entry of alien at improper time or place. As discussed in chapters eight and nine, an individual convicted under 8 USC §1325(a) may still be inadmissible or deportable for the underlying activity of alien smuggling, but will not suffer the adverse consequences attached to the aggravated felony definition—ineligibility for cancellation of removal (for permanent residents), mandatory detention, ineligibility for asylum, and ineligibility for naturalization.

Summary Examples of Effective Plea Bargaining to Avoid Aggravated Felony

- *Conspiracy to possess a controlled substance/drug-related conspiracies/aiding and abetting*: Negotiate an alternative plea to misprision of felony or accessory after the fact.

    - *Purpose*: The BIA has held that a conviction for misprision of a felony under 18 USC §4, where the underlying offense was a conspiracy to possess marijuana with intent to distribute, is not an aggravated felony under INA §101(a)(43)(S) (relating to obstruction of justice).[45] Moreover, a conviction for accessory after the fact to a drug trafficking crime under 18 USC §3 is not an aggravated felony "drug trafficking crime" or a "controlled substance violation."[46] Note, however, 18 USC §3 is a crime of "obstruction of justice"; therefore, if a year or more of imprisonment is imposed, it still becomes an aggravated felony under INA §101(a)(43)(S).

        > *Obstruction of justice vs. misprision*: Obstruction of justice is an aggravated felony under INA §101(a)(43)(S); however, the BIA has specifically held that misprision of a felony under 18 USC §4 is not an obstruction of justice offense.[47] Beware that misprision of felony has been

---

[43] This is the fact pattern in *Bejarano-Urrutia v. Gonzales*, 413 F.3d 444 (4th Cir. 2005); the analysis is premised on the *Leocal* decision. Decisions that have followed *Bejarano-Urrutia* (in terms of the "reckless" state of mind not reaching "crime of violence" definition) include *Oyebanji v. Gonzales*, 418 F.3d 260, n. 5 (3d Cir. 2005); *U.S. v. McMurray*, 653 F.3d 367, 374 (6th Cir. 2011); *U.S. v. Garcia*, 606 F.3d 1317, 1335 (11th Cir. 2011).

[44] INA §101(a)(43)(N); 8 USC §1101(a)(43)(N).

[45] *Matter of Espinoza-Gonzalez*, 22 I&N Dec. 889 (BIA 1999).

[46] *Matter of Batista-Hernandez*, 21 I&N Dec. 955 (BIA 1997).

[47] *Matter of Espinoza-Gonzalez*, 22 I&N Dec. 889 (BIA 1999).

found to be a crime involving moral turpitude. Accordingly, to avoid an aggravated felony conviction (which acts as a bar to almost all forms of relief), negotiate a charge of obstruction of justice down to misprision of felony. Misprision is a crime involving moral turpitude, making a client inadmissible and possibly deportable, but at least it is not an aggravated felony. A misprision conviction places the client in a better position for a waiver, and may result in no deportability at all.

> *Example*: Manuela has been an LPR for more than five years. She is arrested and charged with obstruction of justice and faces more than one year's imprisonment. The charge of obstruction is negotiated to misprision of felony. Manuela has no other criminal record. She receives one year in prison, but is not deportable: although misprision may be a crime involving moral turpitude,[48] the offense occurred outside the first five years of residency, so she is not deportable. Further, although obstruction of justice could be an aggravated felony for a one-year sentence or longer, misprision is not an aggravated felony.

- **Crime of violence**: (1) Negotiate a sentence of less than one year; (2) negotiate a plea to a non-intent crime that does not involve the intentional use of force or a substantial risk that force will be used.
  - *Purpose (1)*: A crime of violence where the sentence imposed is at least one year is an aggravated felony.[49]
  - *Purpose (2)*: An offense that is premised on reckless or negligent behavior without a specific intent to harm or use physical force, or a substantial risk that force will be used, is not a "crime of violence" under 18 USC §16. In *Leocal*,[50] the U.S. Supreme Court used the offense of burglary as an example of an offense that, by its very nature, involves a substantial risk that the burglar will use force against a victim in completing the crime.
    > *Examples*: Murder or manslaughter may be pled down to involuntary manslaughter or second-degree manslaughter.[51] Aggravated assaults may be pled down to simple assault.[52]

---

[48] There is a circuit split on whether misprision of felony involves moral turpitude. The Eleventh Circuit, in *Itani v. Ashcroft*, 298 F.3d 1213 (11th Cir. 2002), found that misprision is categorically a moral turpitude crime. However, the Ninth Circuit disagrees, finding in 2012 that a violation of 18 USC §4 is not categorically a moral turpitude offense; rather, the adjudicator must look to the underlying crime that has been concealed. *Robles-Urrea v. Holder*, 678 F.3d 702 (9th Cir. 2012).

[49] INA §101(a)(43)(F); 8 USC §1101(a)(43)(F).

[50] *Leocal v. Ashcroft*, 543 U.S. 1 (2004).

[51] *Bejarano-Urrutia v. Gonzales,* 413 F.3d 444 (4th Cir. 2005).

[52] *Garcia v. Gonzales,* 455 F.3d 465 (4th Cir. 2006).

- *Money laundering*: Negotiate an alternative plea of a currency reporting violation under Title 31 of the U.S. Code, such as structuring financial transactions or failure to file a currency report. (Reporting requirements are regulatory in nature; they are neither crimes involving moral turpitude nor aggravated felony crimes.)
  - *Purpose*: Money laundering in violation of the federal law is a ground of inadmissibility. Money laundering under federal or state law is an aggravated felony if the funds involved exceed $10,000. Title 31 offenses are neither crimes involving moral turpitude nor aggravated felony offenses, and do not constitute "money laundering" offenses for purposes of INA §212(a)(2)(I).

  Or, negotiate a plea to 18 USC §1960, Prohibition of unlicensed money transmitting business.
  - *Purpose:* This offense, which is a common negotiated plea in "money laundering" prosecutions, is not a money laundering offense and is regulatory in nature, hence does not implicate the aggravated felony ground and is also not a crime involving moral turpitude.

  Alternatively, negotiate a plea to misprision of a felony. For example, where the federal charge is under 18 USC §1956(h)—conspiracy to commit money laundering—negotiate a plea to misprision of felony under 18 USC §4.
  - *Purpose*: Money laundering is an aggravated felony.[53] Misprision is, according to case law,[54] a crime involving moral turpitude, but is not an aggravated felony offense. Depending on certain dates (*i.e.*, date of admission, date of commission of offense), the client may not be deportable at all. In addition, the client is more likely eligible for a waiver of removal when the offense is a moral turpitude crime, as opposed to an aggravated felony offense. Moreover, for persons facing deportability under INA §237, one conviction for a crime involving moral turpitude—where the sentence of imprisonment imposed is less than one year—is an exception to mandatory detention under INA §236(c).[55]

- *Controlled substance offenses involving trafficking component*: Negotiate an alternative plea to straight possession.
  - *Purpose*: as discussed in chapter five, first offense simple possession of a controlled substance is not an aggravated felony (unless the controlled substance is crack or *flunitrazepam*).

- *Firearm offenses as aggravated felonies*: Avoid the federal offenses listed at INA §101(a)(43)(E).
  - *Purpose*: All firearm offenses make an individual deportable under INA §237(a)(2)(C). However, certain firearm offenses (federal offenses and their

---

[53] INA §101(a)(43)(D); 8 USC §1101(a)(43)(D).

[54] *See* chapter eight.

[55] Mandatory detention is discussed in chapter four.

state counterparts) also qualify as aggravated felonies, thereby barring most relief. Defense counsel should double check a state firearms charge to ensure it does not have a federal counterpart listed at the aggravated felony definition at INA §101(a)(43)(E). One example is possession of a firearm with an altered serial or identification number. Although a fairly innocuous state charge, it is an aggravated felony offense at INA §101(a)(43)(E).[56] This charge should be negotiated to possession of a concealed firearm, period. Same for possession of a firearm by a convicted felon, which is an aggravated felony offense.[57] It, too, should be negotiated to carrying a concealed firearm, avoiding "by a convicted felon" element.

- **Sexual abuse of a minor**: Negotiate an alternative plea to contributing to the delinquency of a minor.
  - *Purpose*: Contributing to the delinquency of a minor is not an aggravated felony if "sexual abuse" is not an element of the crime; contributing to delinquency, arguably, is not a crime involving moral turpitude either.

Other alternative pleas:

  - Annoying or molesting children [under Cal. Penal Code §647.6][58]
  - Unlawful sexual contact in the third degree [under 11 Del. Code §767][59]
  - Child abuse statutes without an element of sexual contact
  - Statutory rape, depending on the elements of the statute and controlling case law in the jurisdiction.[60]

- **Tax evasion**: (1) Negotiate an alternative plea to failure to file a tax return; (2) negotiate an alternative plea to false statement in a tax return.
  - *Purpose (1):* Tax evasion and filing fraudulent tax returns are crimes involving moral turpitude and may be aggravated felonies. Ultimately, though, tax laws are regulatory in nature, and simply failing to file is neither an aggravated felony nor a crime involving moral turpitude.

---

[56] *See* 26 USC §5861(i).

[57] *See* 18 USC §922(g).

[58] *U.S. v. Pallares-Galan*, 359 F.3d 1088 (9th Cir. 2004).

[59] *Singh v. Ashcroft*, 383 F.3d 144 (3d Cir. 2004). Note: the Delaware statute did not specify an age of the victim, hence there was no requirement that the victim be a minor. Further, this statute did not describe rape.

[60] In *Estrada-Espinoza v. Mukasey*, 546 F.3d 1147 (9th Cir. 2008), the Ninth Circuit ruled that in order to qualify as an aggravated felony, a sex offense must involve "abuse"; consensual sex with an "older adolescent" is not necessarily abusive.

CH. 11 • FASHIONING A PLEA

- **Theft crime**: Negotiate a sentence of less than one year.
  - *Purpose*: A theft crime, if the punishment imposed is at least one year, is an aggravated felony.[61]
- **Fraud offense**: Utilize the divisible statute to the client's advantage.
  - *Purpose:* In cases in which the defendant is charged under a divisible statute, scrutinize the provisions of the applicable section and plead only to the portion that does not contain the element of fraud; take steps to ensure (in the plea agreement, on the record during the plea colloquy, and within the writing of the final judgment) that the record is clear that the defendant pleaded to the non-fraud provision.
    - ➤ *Example*: Defendant is charged in a two-count indictment of violation of 18 USC §2314—conspiracy to commit interstate transportation of stolen property. The defendant in this case burglarized a travel agency, stole blank airline tickets, created forged passenger tickets, and sold them to unwitting customers. 18 USC §2314 is a divisible statute. It reads:

      > Whoever transports, transmits, or transfers in interstate or foreign commerce any goods, wares, merchandise, securities or money, of the value of $5,000 or more, knowing the same to have been stolen, converted or taken by fraud; or

      > Whoever, having devised or intending to devise any scheme or artifice to defraud, or for obtaining money or property by means of false or fraudulent pretenses, representations, or promises, transports or causes to be transported, or induces any person or persons to travel in, or to be transported in interstate or foreign commerce in the execution or concealment of a scheme or artifice to defraud that person or persons of money or property having a value of $5,000 or more ...."

      The first paragraph, above, does not involve an intent to defraud or deceive and, thus, does not implicate the aggravated felony definition at INA §101(a)(43)(M); the second paragraph, however, would fall under the aggravated felony definition of a crime involving fraud or deceit. Defense counsel may enter a plea to the first paragraph only, and take steps to ensure the record is clear that this is the section to which the defendant is pleading. Under the categorical approach, it is the underlying language of the criminal statute—and not the circumstances of the offense—that controls for immigration law purposes.[62]

---

[61] INA §101(a)(43)(G); 8 USC §1101(a)(43)(G).

[62] This scenario is taken from *Omari v. Gonzales*, 419 F.3d 303 (5th Cir. 2005). The non–American citizen pleaded guilty to the first count of the indictment; the second count was dismissed. Because the statute was divisible, the court looked to the record of conviction, which includes the charging docu-

Continued

- ***The federal embezzlement statute***: For charges brought under 18 USC §656, entitled Theft, embezzlement, or misapplication by bank officer or employee, specify within the record of conviction documents (plea agreement, plea hearing, judgment) that the offense involved an intent to "injure" rather than "defraud." Two courts of appeal have found that 18 USC §656 is a divisible statute and where the intent is to injure, the conviction is not an aggravated felony fraud offense.[63] The embezzlement statute is also discussed earlier in this chapter in the section on moral turpitude.

  > ***A note about theft and fraud:*** Theft and fraud offenses are cousins, in the sense that the underlying offense conduct in the particular case may support either a theft or a fraud charge. In cases where the loss will exceed $10,000, opt for a theft charge, but negotiate a sentence of imprisonment for less than one year. When the prosecution (and other sentencing factors) dictates a sentence of imprisonment exceeding one year, perhaps a plea to fraud is a good option—*if* the loss to a victim as reflected in the record of conviction is under $10,000.

Avoiding Deportability for Domestic Violence Offenses

Bearing in mind the analysis set forth by the Supreme Court in *Leocal*,[64] deportability for a "domestic violence" offense may be avoided by pleading to simple battery or assault. These crimes, although they may occur in a domestic violence setting, will not meet the definition of "crime of violence" under 18 USC §16, which is referenced at INA §237(a)(2)(E). Thus, a charge of aggravated assault, or assault with intent to cause bodily harm, should be negotiated down to an assault offense that does not contain a specific intent to cause harm.

Similarly, stalking crimes can be negotiated down to misdemeanor simple stalking offenses with no *mens rea* or specific intent to cause harm. A state offense entitled "stalking" that does not contain as an element of the crime a specific, credible threat to do harm is arguably not "stalking" as envisioned under INA §237(a)(2)(E).[65]

---

ment, plea agreement, transcript of plea colloquy, and any explicit factual finding by the trial judge to which the defendant assented. The appeals court found that the indictment referred to "stolen" airline tickets, not fraudulently obtained ones, so that "nothing in the indictment indicates that Omari pleaded guilty to transporting fraudulently obtained goods." *Id.* at 308.

[63] *Valansi v. Ashcroft*, 278 F.3d 203 (3d Cir. 2002); *Akinsade v. Holder*, 678 F.3d 138 (2d Cir. 2012).

[64] *Leocal v. Ashcroft*, 543 U.S. 1 (2004).

[65] This is the author's theory; it has not been tested. In its favor, it is noted that under federal law, "stalking" includes as an element a specific intent to kill, injure, harass, or intimidate along with the commission or an attempt to commit an act of violence. Stalking is punishable as a felony. 18 USC §§2261A, 2262. Arguably, state misdemeanor stalking provisions that do not contain specific intent or attempt-to-do-harm elements do not fall under the general canopy of "stalking" crimes envisioned at INA §237(a)(2)(E). It is further noted that the federal criminal provisions were added by the Violence

Continued

➤ **Tip**: Negotiate an alternative plea to any assault offense that does not specify domestic violence (the categorical approach). At least one federal circuit has ruled that for a crime to qualify as a "crime of domestic violence" for purposes of INA §237(a)(2)(E), the offense must be entitled "domestic violence" and specify one of the enumerated domestic relationships. The immigration judge (IJ) and BIA may not look behind the record of conviction to determine the relationship between the offender and victim.[66]

Creating Eligibility for Relief

Realistically, it will often be impossible to avoid a final conviction for immigration purposes, or avoid pleading to an inadmissible or deportable offense. Very often, a non–American citizen client will end a criminal case facing some sort of immigration consequence as a result of the plea. Thus, fashioning a plea bargain so that the client is statutorily eligible for a waiver or other relief is a key aspect of a successful legal defense. Ideally, when the criminal case is finished, the statutory eligibility criteria for relief will fall into place in the immigration law context. The following discussion highlights benchmarks of eligibility for INA §212(h) relief and cancellation of removal. Citations are not given, as these forms of relief and statutory authority are fully discussed in chapter ten.

INA §212(h)

A waiver under INA §212(h) [8 USC §1182(h)] is a waiver of inadmissibility for use by persons applying for permanent residency, or persons who are already LPRs in removal proceedings. Following are some tips for creating §212(h) eligibility for clients with common convictions.

Less than 30 grams of marijuana

The §212(h) waiver is not available for controlled substance offenses beyond simple possession for personal use of marijuana. Clarify for the record in criminal court that the substance was marijuana and the amount involved was less than 30 grams.

Avoid the aggravated felony conviction

For LPRs in the First and Eighth Circuits, the §212(h) waiver is not available if the individual is convicted of an aggravated felony (see above discussion on avoiding the aggravated felony conviction).

Against Women Act [18 USC §2261 *et seq.*], which is the same law that amended the INA to include a provision of deportability for crimes of domestic violence, stalking, and violations of protective orders.

[66] *Tokatly v. Ashcroft*, 371 F. 3d 613, 622–23 (9th Cir. 2004); *see also Patao v. Gonzales*, 131 Fed. Appx. 516, U.S. App. LEXIS 8575, 2005 WL 1126984 (9th Cir. 2005).

> **Tip**: For nonpermanent residents applying for adjustment of status or an immigrant visa, an aggravated felony conviction is not a bar to §212(h).

Cancellation of Removal

Avoid offenses that toll the seven years of legal residence

Cancellation of removal requires at least seven years of residence following a lawful admission. An offense that is not a ground of inadmissibility under INA §212(a) does not toll the time. Accordingly, if the defendant/client has less than seven years of required residence and is charged with multiple offenses, attempt to pinpoint and plead to an offense that is not listed as an INA §212(a) ground of inadmissibility (and, thus, will not "stop the clock" on residency). Negotiate a plea to the offense that implicates deportability, but not inadmissibility. For example, consider the situation in which the defendant is charged with burglary of a residence and violation of a protective order. Burglary is a crime involving moral turpitude, but violation of the protective order implicates only deportability under INA §237(a)(2)(E). In this situation, attempt to negotiate a plea only to violation of the protective order, so that the plea does not trigger a finding of inadmissibility.

If a crime involving moral turpitude (such as theft) is charged along with a firearms offense (*e.g.*, carrying a concealed firearm), plead to the firearms offense, which does not form a ground of inadmissibility, in exchange for dismissal of the theft charge, to avoid a finding of inadmissibility. Eligibility for cancellation of removal relief will be preserved because the continuous residence is not tolled by commission of the offense. However, deportability for a firearms offense will trigger mandatory detention under INA §236(c). Though the client's eligibility for relief is preserved, he or she will be detained during the course of removal proceedings.

Avoid the aggravated felony conviction

Pursuant to INA §240A(a)(3), cancellation of removal is not available to persons convicted of aggravated felony offenses.

Withholding of Removal and Asylum

For asylum,[67] it is important to avoid an aggravated felony conviction.[68] A client who has an application for asylum pending, or who plans to seek asylum, will be barred from this relief if convicted of an aggravated felony offense.

For withholding of removal[69] (also called restriction on removal), it is important to avoid an aggravated felony conviction for which a sentence of imprisonment of at least five years has been imposed. Recalling the discussion of withholding at chapter ten, withholding is best described as a type of political asylum that carries a higher

---

[67] *See* INA §208; 8 USC §1158.

[68] See "Avoiding the Aggravated Felony Conviction" earlier in this chapter.

[69] *See* INA §241(b)(3); 8 USC §1231(b)(3).

standard of proof along with fewer benefits. Withholding is applied for with asylum, and as a lesser form of relief is granted to persons who do not merit asylum because of a criminal conviction, other negative discretionary factors, or an application filed outside the one-year deadline. The law says that a person who has been convicted of an aggravated felony offense (or offenses) and sentenced to five years or more in prison is ineligible for withholding.[70]

Naturalization eligibility

As stated in the section on naturalization (see chapter ten), an individual who has been convicted of an aggravated felony offense after November 29, 1990, is permanently barred from establishing the "good moral character" required for naturalization.[71] Thus it is important to avoid an aggravated felony conviction for the LPR client, not only because of waiver eligibility,[72] but also because of naturalization eligibility. Conceivably, a non–LPR client could become an LPR notwithstanding an aggravated felony conviction, because a non–LPR may be eligible to seek a waiver (depending on the type of offense);[73] however, this client would never become a U.S. citizen.

Creating a Good Record Through the Plea Agreement and Plea Colloquy

It is possible to create a record that will clarify certain issues down the road (in the immigration context) by purposefully inserting language into the plea agreement, or making statements during the plea hearing, or both. Clarifications—of the amount of loss, or lack thereof; a minor role in a conspiracy; lack of knowledge; mitigating circumstances; and outstanding equities—are helpful in fighting charges of removability, or in establishing eligibility for relief. Following are some examples.

- ***Domestic violence victims***: Where the defendant has been a victim of domestic violence, and the codefendant was his or her abuser, or the offense was related or linked to the domestic violence situation, *clarify these circumstances* on the record during the plea hearing.
    - *Purpose*: There are special provisions in the INA for providing benefits, and waiving criminal activity, where the non–American citizen has been the victim of domestic violence.

- ***Fraud crimes (insurance fraud, credit card fraud, Medicaid/Medicare fraud)***: Specify in the plea agreement and/or at the plea hearing that the amount involved was *less than $10,000* and/or that there was no identifiable victim.

---

[70] An aggravated felony conviction or convictions with a five-year sentence or longer in prison is deemed a "particularly serious crime." INA §241(3)(B).

[71] Good moral character is defined at INA §101(f); 8 USC §1101(f).

[72] See the discussion of cancellation of removal earlier in this chapter.

[73] *See, e.g., Matter of Kanga*, 22 I&N Dec. 1206 (BIA 2000).

- *Purpose:* A crime of fraud involving loss to a victim in excess of $10,000 is an aggravated felony under INA §101(a)(43)(M)(i) [8 USC §1101(a)(43)(M)(i)].

- **Controlled substance convictions/minor role**: Clarify that the client had a minor role, that there was no large-scale conspiracy, and that the offense was not related to organized crime, etc.
  - *Purpose:* Create eligibility for withholding of removal by establishing that the client was neither involved in a major crime organization nor played a principal role in trafficking.[74]
    - ➢ **Tip: Drugs versus controlled substances.** If the defendant is initially charged with offenses involving both controlled substances (*i.e.*, narcotics) and "legend" drugs (*i.e.*, pharmaceuticals), negotiate a plea that involves pleading to the "drug" offenses, but not the "controlled substance" offenses. Take steps to ensure that the record of conviction, including the transcript of the plea colloquy, will confirm that the "drugs" involved were controlled legend drugs but not controlled substances.

- **Possession of counterfeit currency or securities**: Specify in the plea agreement that the offense involved *possession only*—there was no "substantial step" toward use or cognizable attempt to use, and there was no loss to a victim.
  - *Purpose:* Avoid the element of "loss" to a "victim" by clarifying that there was no transfer of funds for consideration, and thereby avoid the aggravated felony crime of fraud or deceit at INA §101(a)(43)(M)(i) [8 USC §1101(a)(43)(M)(i)].

- **Weapons offenses, including aggravated assault**: In assaults or other offenses involving the use of a "deadly weapon," where the weapon was not a firearm or other traditional "weapon," specify that the instrument involved was, for example, a chair, a pool stick, or a high-heeled shoe.
  - *Purpose:* Let the record be clear when the offense involves a nontraditional weapon that could not have reasonably caused serious harm, in this way avoiding deportability for conviction of a "firearms offense."

Defense and immigration counsel must work as a team

The plea agreement and/or plea hearing may be a client's only chance to clarify certain issues in anticipation of immigration consequences. Opportunities are endless in utilizing the plea forum to fashion a record that is beneficial to future immigration proceedings. If the conduct involved self-defense or was provoked, that should be stated for the record. If there were extenuating circumstances, such as duress or undue influence, state it for the record. If there was a timely recantation or an attempt to repair the harm, it should be said for the record. If cooperation was significant, coun-

---

[74] *Matter of Y–L–, A–G–, R–S–R–*, 23 I&N Dec. 270 (AG 2002), *overruled in part on other grounds by Khouzam v. Gonzales*, 361 F.3d 161 (2d Cir. 2004). Also see the discussion of withholding of removal in chapter ten.

Plea Agreements to Avoid (Bad Plea Deals)

Every case involves its own set of facts. The following examples would vary in significance if the client has an additional criminal record. These hypotheticals are intended to point out pitfalls in the plea negotiation process. The point is, what looks like a good deal from a criminal defense perspective may have devastating consequences in the immigration law arena.

False statements and currency transactions

Client enters the United States with $50,000. He fails to declare it on the customs report. Client is charged with one count of violating 18 USC §1001 (false statement) and 31 USC §5316 (failure to report importation of more than $10,000). Attorney agrees to drop the 31 USC §5316 count and pleads to 18 USC §1001.

> Why is this not a good resolution? Title 31 USC §5316 is a regulatory offense that does not involve moral turpitude and is not an aggravated felony. In comparison, 18 USC §1001 appears to be a moral turpitude offense and could implicate removability for a crime involving moral turpitude and mandatory detention.

Possession, paraphernalia, and purchase

Client is charged with three counts: simple possession of less than 30 grams of marijuana, purchase of marijuana, and possession of drug paraphernalia. Defense attorney agrees to a deal entailing dropping the possession charge, in exchange for possession of paraphernalia and/or purchase.

> Why is this plea a bad idea? Simple possession of marijuana is not an aggravated felony. If the client is in the United States following a lawful admission, he or she will not be deportable for simple possession less than 30 grams. If the client is one day classified an "arriving alien" at a port of entry, the INA §212(h) waiver and/or cancellation of removal will waive simple possession. Likewise, a client who is not an LPR may seek a waiver of simple possession under INA §212(h).

However, possession of drug paraphernalia is a wild card. There is little case law analyzing the effects of this offense. An LPR client can seek a waiver for first offense possession of paraphernalia. However, a non–LPR is arguably not eligible for any waiver.

Purchase may be considered transactional; in other words, U.S. Citizenship and Immigration Services (USCIS), U.S. Immigration and Customs Enforcement (ICE), and/or an IJ may view "purchase" as an aspect of commerce, hence trafficking. This could put the client in aggravated felony land.

Because possession of paraphernalia is perhaps not waivable, and purchase may be viewed as trafficking, it is best for counsel to negotiate a plea to one count only, simple possession of less than 30 grams of marijuana.

Aggravated assault and probation only

Client is arrested for and quickly pleas to aggravated assault, thinking that a withholding of adjudication and probation only is a good deal. Defense attorney encourages client to accept withholding and probation only, without trying to negotiate the charged offense at all.

> Why is this a bad idea? A conviction for aggravated assault will most likely be a crime involving moral turpitude, possibly triggering deportability and definitely triggering inadmissibility. It may also qualify as a crime of "domestic violence" if the offense involved an enumerated victim.

Client will be ineligible for adjustment of status without a waiver.

Client will be ineligible for naturalization (if already an LPR) for a period of five years.

If an arriving alien, client will be subject to mandatory detention. Far better, if possible, would be to negotiate a plea to simple assault, perhaps in exchange for a short jail term. A few months in jail is arguably better than permanent deportation. Defense counsel should also keep in mind that avoiding time in a local jail does not prevent serving time in an immigration facility. The period of probation may turn into six months at an ICE detention center.

Multiple counts

Client is charged with three counts of credit card fraud arising at three different retail locations, on the same day. Defense counsel pleads to all three counts in exchange for probation only.

> Why is this a bad idea? Multiple counts trigger mandatory detention and deportability. The client also becomes inadmissible.

It is better for counsel to try to negotiate one count only—perhaps in exchange for a stiffer penalty—to avoid the multiple counts.

365 days in jail

Client is offered and accepts 365 days in jail for a crime involving theft or violence. Defense counsel recommends the deal because client will receive gain time/good time credit and actually serve less than the year; whereas if client receives less than 365 days in jail as a sentence, she will not be eligible for good time credit. Client accepts deal, hoping to shave a couple of weeks off her sentence.

> Why is this a bad idea? For crimes involving theft or violence (and other offenses also), a year or more jail sentence is the line of demarcation: the client has crossed over into aggravated felony land. It is difficult to qualify for a waiver; no naturalization; and mandatory detention.

It is far better for client to do a few extra days in jail, to probably avoid deportability and mandatory detention. If removable, client will be eligible for a waiver.

Five-year prison sentence

Client has an application for asylum pending but is arrested for a federal theft crime. Client faces five years or more in prison. Attorney accepts an offer from the U.S. Attorney's Office involving a recommended five-year sentence (for purposes of this hypothetical, it is acknowledged that ultimately the judge makes sentencing decisions.)

> Why is this a bad idea? A five-year sentence of imprisonment in connection with a theft offense will be an aggravated felony. The client will be ineligible for asylum and withholding of removal. Obviously, the crime was serious. It is best to work toward preserving eligibility at least for withholding.

Negotiate and work toward a stipulation to less than five years. Client will lose statutory eligibility for asylum, but can still apply for withhold of removal. Withholding will become unavailable, however, if client is sentenced to five years or longer in prison for a theft offense.

APPENDIX 11A
Sample Memorandum for Fashioning a Plea

LEGAL MEMORANDUM

TO: Criminal Attorney
CC: Client, Mrs. Arlette Pimiento
FROM: Mary Kramer and Maureen Contreni
RE: Analysis of the Immigration Consequences of the Criminal Charges Against Mrs. Pimiento
DATE: February 22, 2015

INTRODUCTION

Mrs. Arlette Pimiento was born in Panama and is a citizen of that country. She came to the United States on a tourist visa on March 13, 2009. She subsequently converted his tourist visa to a student visa and began attending the University of Miami to pursue a Master's degree. Mrs. Pimiento then obtained a visa to remain in the United States under the Optional Practical Training program.

On October 14, 2011, Mrs. Pimiento married a United States citizen, Mr. Michael Perez. Mrs. Pimiento applied for adjustment of status to a lawful permanent resident based on her marriage and was granted conditional permanent residence on June 26, 2012.[75] Mrs. Pimiento's conditional residence originally had an expiration date of June 26, 2014. Prior to that date, our office prepared an application to remove the conditions on his residence. As a result, the United States Citizenship and Immigration Services ("USCIS") extended Mrs. Pimiento's conditional resident status for one year until June 26, 2015. Notably, USCIS did not remove the conditions on Mrs. Pimiento's residence, likely due to the pending criminal charges against her.

---

[75] Lawful permanent residence on a conditional basis is afforded to individuals who acquire permanent residence based on a marriage of less than two years. The conditions on one's permanent residence can be removed after two years. During the 90-day period before the expiration of a person's conditional residence, she may apply jointly with her spouse to remove the conditions on her residence. If that application is granted, the conditions are removed on her lawful permanent residence.

In an Information dated June 3, 2013, Mrs. Pimiento was charged with eight counts of Unauthorized Use of Personal Identification pursuant to section 817.568(2)(a) of the Florida Statutes and one count of Dealing in Credit Cards of Another pursuant to section 817.60(5). The State of Florida charges that the purported offense conduct occurred on or about March 22, 2013.

We have looked at this case to determine whether Mrs. Pimiento is subject to being charged with removability (being placed in removal proceedings before an immigration judge). In so doing, we will explain the meaning of "conviction" for immigration purposes and whether a conviction for these charges would support grounds of removal.

This memorandum analyzes potential grounds of removability, and possible relief, and concludes with recommendations moving forward.

LEGAL QUESTIONS

1. What constitutes a "conviction" for immigration purposes?

2. Whether either of the criminal charges under Fla. Stat. § 817.568(2)(a) or §817.60(5) supports grounds of removability?

3. Whether Mrs. Pimiento would be eligible for any relief from removal?

ANSWERS

1. The Meaning of "Conviction" for Immigration Purposes

Section 101(a)(48)(A) of the Immigration and Nationality Act ("INA") defines a "conviction," with respect to an alien, as

> a formal judgment of guilt of the alien entered by a court or, if adjudication of guilt has been withheld, where (i) a judge or jury has found the alien guilty or the alien has entered a plea of guilty or nolo contendere or has admitted sufficient facts to warrant a finding of guilt, and (ii) the judge has ordered some form of punishment, penalty, or restraint on the alien's liberty to be imposed.

The imposition of probation is a form of "punishment" or "restraint." *Matter of Punu*, 21 I&N Dec. 224, 228 (BIA 1998). In addition, the imposition of court costs in the context of a withhold of adjudication also constitutes "punishment." *Matter of Cabrera*, 24 I&N Dec. 459 (BIA 2008).

Thus, even a plea of no contest followed by a withhold of adjudication will constitute a "conviction" for immigration purposes if court costs are imposed on the defendant.

Pre-trial intervention or diversion *with no plea and no admission of guilt*, in lieu of a plea, however do not constitute "convictions" for immigration purposes.

2. Mrs. Pimiento' Criminal Charges and Relevant Grounds of Removability

A. Florida Statutes §§ 817.568(2)(a) and 817.60(5)

Section 817.568(2)(a) of the Florida Statutes regarding Unauthorized Use of Personal Identification states:

> Any person who willfully and without authorization fraudulently uses, or possesses with intent to fraudulently use, personal identification information concerning an individual without first obtaining that individual's consent, commits the offense of fraudulent use of personal identification information, which is a felony of the third degree, punishable as provided in s. 775.082, s. 775.083, or s. 775.084.

Section 817.60(5) of the Florida Statutes regarding Dealing in Credit Cards of Another states:

> A person other than the issuer who, during any 12-month period, receives two or more credit cards issued in the name or names of different cardholders, which cards he or she has reason to know were taken or retained under circumstances which constitute credit card theft or a violation of this part, violates this subsection and is subject to the penalties set forth in s. 817.67(2).

For purposes of Fla. Stat. § 817.60(5), "credit card theft" is defined as taking a credit card from the person, possession, custody, or control of another without the cardholder's consent or, with knowledge that it has been so taken, receiving the credit card with intent to use it, to sell it, or to transfer it to a person other than the issuer or the cardholder. Fla. Stat. § 817.60(1).

B. Crimes Involving Moral Turpitude

Section 237(a)(2)(A)(i) of the INA concerns removability for people who have been convicted of a "crime involving moral turpitude" ("CIMT") committed within five years after the date of admission. Specifically, the section states:

> Any alien who – (I) is convicted of a crime involving moral turpitude committed within five years . . . after the date of admission, and (II) is convicted of a crime for which a sentence of one year or longer may be imposed, is deportable.

INA § 237(a)(2)(A)(i).

1. Definition of a "crime involving moral turpitude"

The Eleventh Circuit has found that moral turpitude involves "an act of baseness, vileness, or depravity in the private and social duties which a man owes to his fellow men, or to society in general, contrary to the accepted and customary rule of right and duty between man and man." *Keungne v. United States Att'y Gen.*, 561 F.3d 1281, 1284 (11th Cir. 2009); *see also Matter of Serna*, 20 I&N Dec. 579 (BIA 1992). A CIMT is an act which is *per se* morally reprehensible and intrinsically wrong or *malum in se* accompanied by a motive or corrupt mind. *Matter of Serna*, 20 I&N Dec. at 579; *see also Matter of Flores*, 17 I&N Dec. 225 (BIA 1980).

To determine whether a conviction for a particular crime constitutes a conviction of a CIMT, both the Eleventh Circuit Court of Appeals and the Board of Immigration Appeals (BIA)[76] have historically looked to "the inherent nature of the offense, as defined in the relevant statute, rather than the circumstances surrounding a defendant's particular conduct." *See Fajardo v. U.S. Att'y Gen.*, 659 F.3d 1303, 1305 (11th Cir. 2011); *Matter of Velazquez–Herrera*, 24 I&N Dec. 503, 513 (BIA 2008) This framework has come to be known as a categorical approach. *See Descamps v. United States*, 133 S. Ct. 2276 (2013) (defining the "categorical approach" as looking only to the statutory definitions of the prior offenses, and not to the particular facts underlying those convictions). If the statutory definition of a crime is divisible, in that it contains alternative elements, some which constitute CIMTs and some which do not, then the record of conviction—i.e., the charging document, plea, verdict, and sentence—may also be considered. *Id.*; *see also Fajardo* 659 F.3d at 1305; *Jaggernauth v. U.S. Att'y Gen.*, 432 F.3d 1346, 1354–55 (11th Cir. 2005). This has been called the modified categorical approach.

To reiterate, the analysis of whether a particular crime is a "crime involving moral turpitude" is based on the elements of the *statute* under which a person was convicted, *not* based on what happened during the incident.

2. Are either of the crimes with which Mrs. Pimiento is charged a CIMT?

Since Mrs. Pimiento was admitted as a conditional permanent resident on June 26, 2012, and the purported offense conduct was well within five years after the date of his admission, if either Fla. Stat. § 817.568(2)(a) or § 817.60(5) constitutes a CIMT, she would be subject to removability pursuant to INA § 237(a)(2)(A)(i) if she is convicted.

---

[76] The Board of Immigration Appeals ("BIA") is the highest administrative body for interpreting and applying immigration laws. The BIA has been given nationwide jurisdiction to hear appeals from certain decisions rendered by immigration judges and by district directors of the Department of Homeland Security (DHS) in a wide variety of proceedings in which the Government of the United States is one party and the other party is a noncitizen.

A. Unauthorized Use of Personal Identification pursuant to Fla. Stat. §817.568(2)(a)

The structure of the statutory language of Fla. Stat. § 817.568(2)(a), as well as the Florida Standard Jury instructions, are critical to analyzing whether a conviction under this statute constitutes a conviction for a CIMT.

The United States Supreme Court stated that "fraud has consistently been regarded as such a contaminating component in any crime that American courts have, without exception, included such crimes within the scope of moral turpitude." *Jordan v. DeGeorge*, 341 U.S. 223, 229 (1951). The Eleventh Circuit has likewise stated that in determining whether a conviction is a crime involving moral turpitude, an adjudicator must determine whether the crime "involves the depravity or fraud necessary to be one of moral turpitude . . . ." *Sanchez Fajardo*, 659 F.3d at 1308. The BIA has similarly stated that "[t]he phrase 'crime involving moral turpitude' has without exception been construed to embrace fraudulent conduct." *Matter of Flores*, 17 I&N Dec. 225, 228 (BIA 1980). The BIA has further stated "where fraud is inherent in an offense, it is not necessary that the statute prohibiting it include the usual phraseology concerning fraud in order for it to involve moral turpitude." *Id.* at 228; *see also Matter of Tejwani*, 24 I&N Dec. 97, 98 (BIA 2007).

Section 817.568(2)(a) of the Florida Statutes penalizes both "fraudulent use" and "possession with intent to fraudulently use." Based on the above-referenced case law, "fraudulent use," very likely constitutes a CIMT; however, "possession with intent to fraudulently use," is arguably[77] not a CIMT since the conduct involved is *possession*, not fraud itself. Because the statute penalizes both conduct that involves moral turpitude as well as conduct that does not, the issue of whether this statute is "divisible"[78] is paramount to the analysis of whether a conviction under Fla. Stat. § 817.568(2)(a) constitutes a conviction for a CIMT that triggers removability under INA § 237(a)(2)(a).

The fact that Fla. Stat. 817.568(2)(a) is written disjunctively does not necessarily make it a divisible statute. The Supreme Court's decision in *Descamps v. United States*, 133 S. Ct. 2276 (2013) has made clear that a disjunctive statute is not neces-

---

[77] If Mrs. Pimiento were convicted under this statute, we would present this argument; however, the matter is not settled and such argument may or may not be successful.

[78] The significance of a "divisible" statute is as follows: If a statute is divisible between elements which constitute removal offenses and elements which do not, an adjudicator is permitted to look at the record of conviction (i.e., the Information, Plea Agreement, or other judicially-approved documents, but *not* including the arrest report or criminal complaint) to determine on which prong of the statute the non-citizen's conviction was based. If the record of conviction indicates that she was convicted under the elements describing a removable offense, she will be deemed removable. If the record is ambiguous or if it indicates she was convicted under the prong of the statute that does not describe a removable offense, the non-citizen will be deemed not removable.

sarily equivalent to a divisible statute. A statute is divisible only if it involves alternative elements. This distinction is crucial. The jury instructions for Fla. Stat. § 817.568(2)(a) reveal that "fraudulent use" and "possession with intent to fraudulently use" are not alternative elements. Indeed, the crime is comprised of only two elements which the State must prove beyond a reasonable doubt: (1) (Defendant) willfully and without authorization [fraudulently used] [possessed with intent to fraudulently use] personal identification information concerning (victim); and (2) [He] [She] did so without first obtaining the consent of (victim). Fla. Std. Jury Instructions § 20.13 (2014). As a result, the State need not specifically prove beyond a reasonable doubt whether the offense conduct was *fraudulent use* or whether it was *possession with intent to fraudulently use* in order to get a conviction. Consequently, this statute is not divisible between "fraudulent use" and "possession with intent to fraudulently use" within the meaning of *Descamps*. The proper application of *Descamps* to this statute, within the context of a CIMT charge of removability, would not permit an Immigration Judge to look beyond the statutory language of Fla. Stat. § 817.568(2)(a) to determine whether Mrs. Pimiento was convicted of a CIMT.

Nevertheless, prior to the Supreme Court's decision in *Descamps*, many immigration prosecutors and judges viewed disjunctive statutes such as Fla. Stat. § 817.568(2)(a) as "divisible," thus justifying an examination of the record of conviction to determine the statutory phrase, or even the conduct, on which the individual's conviction was based. Although that approach has now been discredited, some prosecutors and judges continue to erroneously examine the record of conviction for statutes like Fla. Stat. § 817.568(2)(a). For this reason, I would recommend in an abundance of caution, that if Mrs. Pimiento were to plead to counts of Fla. Stat. § 817.568(2)(a), the information should be amended to describe the offense conduct such that it does not point to "fraudulent use" rather than "possession with intent to fraudulently use." Currently, each count under Fla. Stat. § 817.568(2)(a) charges that Mrs. Pimiento "did then and there willfully and without authorization fraudulently use, or possess with intent to fraudulently use, personal identification information, concerning an individual. . . ." That part is fine because it is ambiguous as to the portion of the statute underlying the charge. However, the portion following "to-wit," clearly indicates "fraudulent use" and should be amended to be ambiguous as to whether the conduct involved "fraudulent use" or "possession with intent to fraudulently use."

B. Dealing in Credit Cards of Another pursuant to Fla. Stat. § 817.60(5)

While there is no published case law indicating whether Fla. Stat. § 817.60(5) constitutes a crime involving moral turpitude, because Florida's Dealing in Credit Cards of Another statute requires the receipt of stolen credit cards receipt, case law on receipt of stolen property is instructive in this analysis.

Receipt of stolen property has been held to constitute a CIMT where the statute requires <u>knowledge</u> that the property is stolen. *See Matter of Salvail*, 17 I&N Dec. 19

(BIA 1979); *Matter of Z*, 7 I&N Dec. 253 (BIA 1956); *Matter of R*, 6 I&N Dec. 772 (BIA 1955). On the other hand, the BIA held in an old case that "where property is acquired without knowledge that it is stolen or without intent to deprive the rightful owner of his possession, the offense does not involve moral turpitude." *Matter of K-*, 2 I&N Dec. 90 (1944) (emphasis added). Although the case law is silent on whether a receipt of stolen property statute requiring a mens rea somewhere in between, such as the "reason to know" required by Fla. Stat. § 817.60(5), constitutes a CIMT, there is a strong argument that "reason to know" does not rise to the level of specific intent required for a finding of a CIMT. However, because there is no guarantee that such an argument would prevail, I would advise against Mrs. Pimiento pleading to this offense.

C. Aggravated Felony

Section 237(a)(2)(A)(iii) renders removable "any alien who is convicted of an aggravated felony at any time after admission[.]" Aggravated felonies are defined in section 101(a)(43) of the INA. Among the aggravated felonies listed in that section, the one which is pertinent to the charges against Mrs. Pimiento is "a theft offense (including receipt of stolen property) . . . for which the term of imprisonment [is] at least 1 year." The generic definition of a theft offense requires that the exercise of control over stolen property be "with the criminal intent to deprive the owner of rights and benefits of ownership, even if such deprivation is less than total or permanent." *Matter of Sierra*, 26 I&N Dec. 288, 291 (BIA 2014) (citing *Matter of Garcia-Madruga*, 24 I&N Dec 436, 438 (BIA 2008)).

In a case involving a California statute, the BIA held that receipt of stolen property is categorically a theft offense within the meaning of INA § 101(a)(43)(G). *See Matter of Cardiel*, 25 I&N Dec. 12 (BIA 2009). The California statute required that the offender receive the property "knowing" that it had been stolen or obtained by theft or extortion. *Id*. at 24-25. Subsequently, however, the BIA distinguished the California statute at issue in *Matter of Cardiel* from a Nevada statute in which a conviction will lie where the offender only has "reason to believe" that the property possessed was stolen. *See Matter of Sierra*, 26 I&N Dec. at 288. In *Matter of Sierra*, the BIA held that the mental state of "reason to believe" is insufficient to establish that the crime of attempted possession of stolen property is categorically an aggravated felony "theft offense (including receipt of stolen property)" within the meaning of INA § 101(a)(43)(G).

Mrs. Pimiento is charged with Dealing in Credit Cards pursuant to Fla. Stat. 817.60(5), a felony in the third degree. Fla. Stat. § 817.67(2). As such, it is punishable by a term of imprisonment "not exceeding 5 years." Fla. Stat. § 775.082(3)(e). The statute penalizes the receipt of stolen credit cards, and thus is akin to a receiving stolen property statute. Like the statute in *Matter of Sierra*, however, the mens rea required for a conviction under Fla. Stat. § 817.60(5) is "reason to know." *Compare* Fla. Stat. § 817.60(5) *with* Nev. Rev. Stat. Ann. § 205.275(1)(a)-(b) (stating that a person commits an offense involving possession of stolen property if he possesses it knowing that it is stolen property or under circumstances that should have caused a reasonable person to know that it was stolen"; *see also Crittenden v. State*, 137 So. 3d 1170, 1172 (3d Dist. Ct. Appeal of Fla. 2014) (equating "should have known" to "reason to know").

Therefore, Fla. Stat. § 817.60(5) is not categorically an aggravated felony as defined in INA § 101(a)(43)(G) because the required mens rea of "reason to know" is insufficient to establish a "theft offense (including receipt of stolen property)" within the meaning of INA § 101(a)(43)(G) and as interpreted by the BIA in *Matter of Sierra*. As such, if Mrs. Pimiento were convicted under this statute, we would use the above argument to fend off any charge by DHS that she is convicted of an aggravated felony. Keep in mind, however, as noted above a conviction under this statute would make her vulnerable to a CIMT ground of removability.

3. Relief from Removal - Would Mrs. Pimiento be eligible for a waiver of inadmissibility pursuant to INA § 212(h)?

A waiver of inadmissibility under section 212(h) of the INA may be available, in conjunction with adjustment of status, to individuals found to be removable from the United States. *See* 8 C.F.R. § 1182(h) (a waiver of inadmissibility is permitted where the "Attorney General . . . has consented to the alien's applying or reapplying for a visa, for admission to the United States, or adjustment of status); 8 C.F.R. § 1245.1(f) ("an application under this part shall be the sole method of requesting the exercise of discretion under sections 212(g), (h), (i), and (k) as they relate to the inadmissibility of an alien in the United States").

A 212(h) waiver to waive the application of INA § 212(a)(2)(A)(i)(I) (concerning a conviction for a crime involving moral turpitude) requires, in the case of an immigrant who is the spouse, parent, son, or daughter of a United States citizen or a lawful permanent resident, that the applicant establish that denial of admission would result in extreme hardship to the U.S. citizen or lawful permanent resident spouse, parent, son, or daughter of the applicant. This waiver is not available to individuals who have not "*lawfully resided continuously*"[79] in the United States for a period of not less than

---

[79] The phrase "lawfully resided continuously" has been construed by the BIA to mean "more than simple presence or residence." *Matter of Rotimi*, 24 I&N Dec. 567 (BIA 2008). The BIA has held that "for an alien's residence to be treated as 'lawful,' it must be authorized or in harmony with the law, which requires some formal action beyond a mere request for authorization or the existence of some impediment to actual physical removal." *Id.* at 574. Additionally, the BIA also referred to the definition of "residence" in INA § 101(a)(33) as the "place of general abode; the place of general abode of a person means his principal, actual dwelling place in fact, without regard to intent."

The phrase, however, does not require status as a lawful permanent resident. *Id.* at 570 (stating the applicant's failure to accrue 7 years of continuous residence as a lawful permanent resident is not

Continued

7 years." INA § 212(h)(2) (emphasis added). Nor is this waiver available to "an alien who has previously been admitted to the United States as an alien lawfully admitted for permanent residence if . . . since the date of such admission the alien has been convicted of an aggravated felony. . . ." *Id.* As noted above, Mrs. Pimiento is a conditional permanent resident, which is a form of permanent residence. Although she is unlikely to be barred from relief from removal under INA § 212(h) based on any assertion by DHS that she is an aggravated felon, *see supra* section C, Mrs. Pimiento has not accrued the necessary time in the United States to qualify for this relief for the following reason:

Mrs. Pimiento's period of lawful continuous residence commenced on March 13, 2009, when she was last admitted with an F-2 non-immigrant visa. Her residence in the United States since that time has been "lawful" within the meaning of *Matter of Rotimi*, in that it has been authorized and in harmony with the law. As a result, Mrs. Pimiento will not have accrued 7 years of lawful continuous residence until March 13, 2016. She does not yet, at the time of this writing, have the time necessary to pursue a waiver under INA § 212(h). The accrual of time for purposes of a 212(h) waiver is stopped by the issuance of a Notice to Appear, which is the document that the government files to initiates removal proceedings against a noncitizen.

At this time, Mrs. Pimiento is not in removal proceedings, so the time will continue to accrue. Provided he accrues the 7 years of lawful continuous residence since March 13, 2009, she appears to otherwise have a strong case for a waiver under INA § 212(h).

4. Summary and Recommendations

First, the term "conviction" has a particular meaning in the INA and includes nolo contendere pleas and withholds of adjudication. Therefore, avoiding a guilty plea is not enough to avoid adverse immigration consequences. It is critical to understand that even if Mrs. Pimiento pleads nolo contendere to a charge, such a plea will be a "conviction" for immigration purposes. The only exception to this rule is if the judge orders *no* form of punishment or penalty and *no* court costs or fines.

Second, if she is "convicted" of the charges currently pending against her, pursuant to Fla. Stat. §§ 817.568(2)(a) and 817.60(5), Mrs. Pimiento will be vulnerable to

---

decisive); *see also In re Carlos Rafael Castillo-Martinez*, 2005 WL 698343 (BIA February 16, 2005) (unpublished) ("We do not agree with the Immigration Judge's interpretation of the statute to conclude that the respondent was required to reside *as a lawful permanent resident* for the 7 years . . . ."). Rather, "lawfully resided continuously" requires only that the applicant demonstrate that she was residing in the United States in a lawful status. *See id.* Residence in the United States in non-immigrant status may be included in the period of lawful continuous residence, so long as the applicant did not breach that status and did not have a period in which she fell out of status. *See Matter of Rotimi* at 575; *In re Carlos Rafael Castillo-Martinez* at *1.

removal proceedings initiated under both INA § 237(a)(2)(A)(i) (crime involving moral turpitude within 5 years of admission) and § 237(a)(2)(A)(iii) (aggravated felony). It is likely that DHS would argue that both Fla. Stat. §§ 817.568(2)(a) and 817.60(5) constitute crimes involving moral turpitude. Though there are certainly arguments that can be made to counter that position, as described above, there is no guarantee that such arguments would be successful. Further, it is likely that DHS would argue that Fla. Stat. § 817.60(5) is an aggravated felony. Although that position is likely to fail based on recent case law, DHS could try to distinguish the Florida statute from the Nevada statue at issue in the recent case, *Matter of Sierra*.

Third, if Mrs. Pimiento were "convicted" under either of these statutes and if she were found removable by an Immigration Judge, she is not currently eligible for relief from removal. Mrs. Pimiento will accrue the 7 years of lawful continuous residence required for a waiver under INA § 212(h) on March 13, 2016 – so long as DHS does not issue a Notice to Appear (commencing removal proceedings) prior to that date.

My recommendations for Mrs. Pimiento are as follows:

1. Explore an alternate plea to a statute which fits the offense conduct but does not include an element of fraud. I am available to explore alternate pleas that do not involve intent to defraud.

2. Instead of making a plea, explore pre-trial intervention or diversion programs *with no plea and no admission of guilt*.

Sincerely,

Mary E. Kramer
Attorney at Law

Dated: February 22nd, 2015

CHAPTER TWELVE

VISAS FOR COOPERATING WITNESSES

"S" Status 600
"T" Status 609
"U" Status 614
Appendices
    12A: Sample Form I-854 625
    12B: Freedom of Information Act Request 631

Successful investigation and prosecution of crime depends in large part on informants and witnesses. If the cooperating informant or witness is a foreign national and the cooperation is significant and critical to the success of a case of major importance, immigration status may be available to the individual as an incentive for cooperation. At the same time, the informant or witness may him- or herself be a criminal defendant who eventually will be subject to removal on account of criminal activity. In such a case, negotiating for "S" status [which grants a witness nonimmigrant status[1] during the investigation and perhaps, ultimately, lawful permanent resident (LPR) status] is a key part of the plea package.

The "T"[2] and "U"[3] statuses have an underlying policy goal distinct from that of the "S" status. Although all three are intended to be law enforcement tools, a central policy goal behind the T, and particularly behind the U, is to improve rapport between law enforcement agencies and the immigrant communities that are targeted by criminals and to provide protection against removal for victims of certain crimes.[4] Unlike the S, the T and U are explicitly unavailable to participants in the underlying criminal activity, and practitioners should be mindful of this distinction in the negotiation context.[5] If the victim of criminal activity is also subject to criminal prosecution, then negotiating for immigration benefits is important. Sometimes the victim will not be guilty of any criminal conduct but will nonetheless be in the United States unlawfully. An attorney representing the interests of the victim should be aware of

---

[1] *See* INA §101(a)(15)(S); 8 USC §1101(a)(15)(S).

[2] *See* INA §101(a)(15)(T); 8 USC §1101(a)(15)(T).

[3] *See* INA §101(a)(15)(U); 8 USC §1101(a)(15)(U).

[4] *See* Trafficking Victims Protection Act of 2000 (TVPA), Pub. L. No. 106-386, div. A, 114 Stat. 1466, Sec. 102(a)(20); 72 Fed. Reg. 53014 (Sept. 17, 2007).

[5] 8 CFR §§214.11(c), 214.14(a)(14)(iii).

the immigration law provisions intended to provide safe haven and/or rewards as the quid pro quo of cooperation.

This chapter discusses the three cooperating witness categories—S, T, and U—that may represent the only hope for some non–American citizens to remain in the United States.

"S" Status

Often referred to as the "S visa," this benefit is more accurately described as a status under immigration law. As a corollary benefit of receiving classification in S status, the U.S. Department of State (DOS) may issue a visa in the passport for travel.

> **Tip**: The time to discuss S status is at the very beginning of the cooperation process. Along with a proffer and proposed immunity agreement, get S status on the table and obtain a commitment from law enforcement and the prosecutor to apply for *and actively pursue* S status for the client. If possible, this commitment should be put in writing, signed by both the law enforcement agency (LEA) and the prosecutor, and later incorporated into the plea agreement.

S status was introduced by legislation in 1994.[6] In theory, S status involves a two-part process, whereby nonimmigrant (temporary) status of up to three years is first granted while an investigation and prosecution are ongoing. If the investigation, or prosecution, or both are successfully completed partly because of the involvement of the witness, permanent resident status may be granted. In reality, law enforcement officials and prosecutors often are not willing to file for the nonimmigrant status until the investigation is either completed or well under way. If a criminal sentence of imprisonment is anticipated for the cooperating witness, the LEA will not ask even for non-immigrant S status until that sentence is close to completion.

An individual is sponsored for S status by the LEA, aided by the prosecutor. According to regulation, "law enforcement agency" also encompasses a federal or state court, or a U.S. Attorney's Office that is "directly in need of information to be provided by the alien witness or informant."[7] This status cannot be obtained by an affirmative application that a person can send in on his or her own. Moreover, immigration judges (IJs) have no jurisdiction to grant S status.

It is available to cooperating witnesses in both state and federal cases. However, there are only 200 numbers for S status available each year[8] to persons cooperating with criminal prosecutions, and 50 available for terrorist-type cases. (After the cap is

---

[6] Violent Crime Control and Law Enforcement Act of 1994, §130003(a), Pub. L. No. 103-322, 108 Stat. 1796.

[7] 8 CFR §214.2(t)(4).

[8] INA §214(k)(1); 8 USC §1184(k)(1).

reached, a waiting list is established for applicants in the backlog.) This small number underlies the fact that S status is reserved for high-profile cases that are extremely important.

The Statute

S status is set forth at INA §101(a)(15)(S) [8 USC §1101(a)(15)(S)], which includes within the definition of nonimmigrant:

(S) subject to section 212(k), an alien—

(i) who the Attorney General determines—

(I) is in possession of critical reliable information concerning a criminal organization or enterprise;

(II) is willing to supply or has supplied such information to Federal or State law enforcement authorities or a Federal or State court; and

(III) whose presence in the United States the Attorney General determines is essential to the success of an authorized criminal investigation or the successful prosecution of an individual involved in the criminal organization or enterprise; or

(ii) who the Secretary of State and the Attorney General jointly determine—

(I) is in possession of critical reliable information concerning a terrorist organization, enterprise, or operation;

(II) is willing to supply or has supplied such information to Federal law enforcement authorities or a Federal court;

(III) will be or has been placed in danger as a result of providing such information; and

(IV) is eligible to receive a reward under section 36(a) of the State Department Basic Authorities Act of 1956,

and, if the Attorney General (or with respect to clause (ii), the Secretary of State and the Attorney General jointly) considers it to be appropriate, the spouse, married and unmarried sons and daughters, and parents of an alien described in clause (i) or (ii) if accompanying, or following to join, the alien.

Thus, S status is available in both criminal– and terrorist-related investigations and prosecutions. If granted, it is also available to spouses, sons and daughters, and parents of the witness. The information provided must be reliable and critical to an investigation involving a criminal organization or enterprise, and the non–American citizen's presence in the United States must be *essential* to the success of the investigation or prosecution. Regarding terrorist investigations or prosecutions, the statute requires a showing that the individual has been placed in danger as a result of the cooperation.

Under INA §214(k) [8 USC §1184(k)], the initial period of nonimmigrant admission may not exceed three years. Status will be revoked if, after being granted S status, the individual is convicted of a felony offense. As a condition precedent to being granted S status, the individual must execute a form waiving his or her right to contest removal, except for an application for withholding of removal. An individual in U.S. Immigration and Customs Enforcement (ICE) custody, in removal proceedings, will more often than not be required to accept a removal order in order to receive first deferred action, and then S status.

The Regulations

There are references to S witnesses and informants throughout the Code of Federal Regulations (CFR). According to 8 CFR §214.2(t), a witness in criminal law proceedings receives S-5 status; a witness in a terrorist investigation receives S-6 status; and a family member of person in either S-5 or S-6 status receives S-7 status.

The application is the Form I-854. The application is prepared by the federal or state LEA, and it must identify the state or federal court in which the proceedings are pending and be signed by the prosecutor's office. The completed application is filed with the assistant attorney general, Criminal Division, U.S. Department of Justice (DOJ), who ultimately forwards the application to the appropriate authority within the U.S. Department of Homeland Security (DHS) if he or she recommends it for approval.[9] As a practical matter, the review and processing of Form I-854 (and similar cooperating witness applications) is handled by the Office of Enforcement Operations (OEO).[10] It is the role of the assistant attorney general to review the information and supporting documentation to determine completeness and accuracy. The assistant attorney general must consider the negative and favorable factors warranting an exercise of discretion on the individual's behalf.[11]

Often, the OEO will send the application back to the LEA, or request additional information, regarding negative information in the applicant's background (or any other questions about the case). This process can and usually does take a long time. There is no timeframe for processing these applications, and they can remain pending consideration for years. Where necessary, the assistant attorney general may submit the application for a recommendation by an advisory panel composed of representatives of DHS, the U.S. Marshals Service, the Federal Bureau of Investigation (FBI), the Drug Enforcement Administration, and DOS. The function of the advisory panel is to prioritize cases in light of the numerical limitation in order to determine which cases should be forwarded to DHS for final approval.[12]

Upon certification, the assistant attorney general must forward the approved Form I-854 to DHS with all supporting documents and a statement of all grounds of inad-

---

[9] 8 CFR §214.2(t)(4). Note that with the breakup of legacy Immigration and Naturalization Service (INS), it is not clear to whom the final application is forwarded for approval. The current regulations state that final approval is granted by the Commissioner of INS.

[10] The phone number for the Office of Enforcement Operations (OEO), an office within the Department of Justice, Criminal Division, is (202) 514-6809.

[11] 8 CFR §214.2(t)(4)(ii)(A).

[12] 8 CFR §214.2(t)(4)(ii)(B).

missibility that apply to the witness, the reasons that a waiver of inadmissibility should be granted, including national security interests, a detailed explanation of the nature of the cooperation and the government's need, the intended dates of stay in such status, and a statement that there is a number available for such status.[13]

Final approval of S nonimmigrant status rests with the appropriate immigration component of DHS.[14] In the event that the application is denied, the assistant attorney general may object within seven days. In the event of an objection, the matter is referred to the deputy attorney general for a final resolution. In no circumstances does the actual witness or the LEA have a right to appeal a decision to deny.[15]

Conditions of Status

Once granted S nonimmigrant status, the non–American citizen witness must report quarterly to the LEA and fulfill the terms of cooperation. He or she must notify the LEA of any changes in address or phone number. In turn, the LEA must report any *failures* to cooperate, or violations of status, to the assistant attorney general.[16]

The principal witness and derivatives in S status are employment authorized.[17] An individual in S status may *not* change status to another nonimmigrant classification; this includes derivatives.[18] This means, for example, that a spouse of a witness who is granted S status may not change status to E investor status, or obtain H-1B status as a professional in a specialty occupation. However, while the regulations prohibit change of status, there is nothing that prevents a spouse, son, daughter, or parent from applying for and obtaining a different visa abroad.[19] In addition, a witness and derivative family members who are in one particular nonimmigrant status may change status to S.[20]

As stated above, a condition for status as an S nonimmigrant is that the witness and derivative family members must waive their right to a removal hearing and the right to contest, other than on the basis of an application for withholding, a removal action.

---

[13] 8 CFR §214.2(t)(4)(ii)(C).

[14] 8 CFR §214.2(t)(4). Note that with the breakup of legacy Immigration and Naturalization Service, (INS) it is not clear to whom the final application is forwarded for approval. The current regulations state that final approval is granted by the commissioner of INS. Final regulations that reflect the transition from legacy INS to the Department of Homeland Security (DHS)—and designate the official responsible for final approval of an I-854—have not yet been published.

[15] 8 CFR §214.2(t)(5)(iii).

[16] 8 CFR §214.2(t)(7).

[17] 8 CFR §214.2(t)(10).

[18] 8 CFR §214.2(t)(12).

[19] Before a derivative family member applies for a visa abroad, it is prudent to review whether he or she is inadmissible for a reason to believe that he or she has benefited from drug trafficking. INA §212(a)(2)(C); 8 USC §1182(a)(2)(C). Family members are often put on lookout lists, or the surname raises a "hit."

[20] 8 CFR §214.2(t)(12)(ii).

This waiver is accomplished by executing Form I-854, which contains a clause to this effect.[21] The decision to remove an S nonimmigrant is made by the field director, presumably of the local ICE office. If an S nonimmigrant has the status revoked, he or she—and any derivatives—are eligible to apply for withholding of removal.[22] Withholding of removal is a type of asylum available to persons who are inadmissible because of crime, yet cannot be removed to the home country because of international asylum treaty obligations.[23] The principal witness has 10 days from receipt of the notice of revocation to file an application for withholding of removal.[24] Presumably, a derivative spouse or child also may apply for asylum. Based on these provisions, an S nonimmigrant who is removable for a crime, but may have some other form of relief available, is barred from seeking a waiver or adjustment of status and may only seek withholding.

Adjustment to Permanent Resident Status Under S

The overall scheme of S status is that the person is able to remain in the United States in nonimmigrant status while the investigation and prosecution is pending. Upon successful completion of the prosecution, the witness is essentially rewarded with permanent residency status. The same LEA that filed for nonimmigrant status may sponsor the witness and qualifying family members for adjustment of status.

The statute

According to INA §245(j) [8 USC §1255(j)]:

(1) If, in the opinion of the Attorney General—

> (A) a nonimmigrant admitted into the United States under 101(a)(15)(S)(i) has supplied information described in subclause (I) of such section; and
>
> (B) the provision of such information has substantially contributed to the success of an authorized criminal investigation or the prosecution of an individual described in subclause (III) of that section,

the Attorney General may adjust the status of the alien (and the spouse, married and unmarried sons and daughters, and parents of the alien if admitted under that section) to that of an alien lawfully admitted for permanent residence if the alien is not described in section 212(a)(3)(E).

(2) If, in the sole discretion of the Attorney General—

> (A) a nonimmigrant admitted into the United States under section 101(a)(15)(S)(ii) has supplied information described in subclause (I) of such section, and

---

[21] 8 CFR §§236.4(a), 1236.4(a).
[22] 8 CFR §§208.2(c)(1)(vi), 1208.2(c)(1)(vi).
[23] *See* chapter ten.
[24] 8 CFR §§236.4(d), 1236.4(d).

(B) the provision of such information has substantially contributed to—

(i) the prevention or frustration of an act of terrorism against a United States person or United States property, or

(ii) the success of an authorized criminal investigation of, or the prosecution of, an individual involved in such an act of terrorism, and

(C) the nonimmigrant receives an award under section 36(a) of the State Department Basic Authorities Act of 1956, the Attorney General may adjust the status of the alien (and the spouse, married and unmarried sons and daughters, and parents of the alien if admitted under such section) to that of an alien lawfully admitted for permanent residence if the alien is not described in section 212(a)(3)(E).

(3) Upon the approval of adjustment of status under paragraph (1) or (2), the Attorney General shall record the alien's lawful admission for permanent residence as of the date of such approval and the Secretary of State shall reduce by one the number of visas authorized to be used under sections 201(d) and 203(b)(4) for the fiscal year then current.

Thus, under the statute, the non–American citizen's efforts must have "substantially contributed" to the success of a criminal investigation or prosecution, or the frustration of a terrorist act. Additionally, the case must have ended successfully.

The regulations

The requirements and procedure for a cooperating witness adjusting to permanent residency are found at 8 CFR §§245.11, 1245.11. A procedure similar to applying for nonimmigrant status is utilized; the same I-854 form is used and the application must make its way up the same chain of command. The LEA must demonstrate the statutory requirement that the witness's efforts contributed substantially to the success of an investigation or prosecution. Even though a case is certified by the LEA and approved by the assistant attorney general, Criminal Division, the regulations state that an authoritative DHS position holder (formerly, the commissioner of legacy Immigration and Naturalization Service) makes the final decision and can effectively veto the Form I-854 application.[25]

Upon approval of the I-854, Form I-485, Application for Adjustment of Status, is prepared and filed locally at the U.S. Citizenship and Immigration Services (USCIS) office.[26]

Special requirements for family members

The regulations require that the principal witness and all derivative family members be approved for, and in, S nonimmigrant status to qualify for adjustment of sta-

---

[25] 8 CFR §§245.11, 1245.11(a)(4).
[26] 8 CFR §§245.11(d), 1245.11(d).

tus. The qualifying relationship must have existed at the time S nonimmigrant status was granted. And, the qualifying relationship must continue to exist at the time of applying for adjustment of status.[27] The application must be accompanied by:

- A complete copy, page-by-page, of the applicant's passport or a statement as to why he or she does not have a passport;
- If there is no passport, a list of all trips in and out of the United States while in S status; and
- Evidence of the qualifying relationship for derivative family members.

An adjustment of status application may be filed without regard to the availability of an immigrant visa number.[28] However, if residency status is to be approved and issued, there must be a visa number available in the employment-based category under INA §§201(d) and 203(b)(4). To date, there has never been a backlog for S adjustment applicants because of the unavailability of a visa number; but such a backlog is not impossible. In such circumstances, the applicant would be eligible to remain in the United States with a work permit pending final approval of residency status.

Miscellaneous Tips and Advice About S Status

S status is reserved for the most important investigations and prosecutions. However, it is not widely used by authorities. S status is a frustrating and difficult area of both immigration and criminal law practice. It requires good negotiating skills and polite tenacity on the part of counsel. S status can be promised to a client in order to obtain cooperation, but then never pursued in good faith by the LEA. It appears that this failure to follow through is, in large part, a result of the complicated procedures devised by DHS and the various LEAs. The bureaucracies have created much red tape when it comes to S status. Many agents simply want to avoid the tedious paperwork. In addition, prosecutors and agents may want to avoid the appearance of providing a benefit in exchange for testimony. This dynamic does not bode well for cross-examination.

In 2014, the South Florida Chapter of the American Immigration Lawyers Association (AILA) filed a Freedom of Information Act (FOIA) request with DHS asking for the exact numbers of persons who had received S nonimmigrant and immigrant status. The numbers were astonishingly low and demonstrate that DHS does not grant this benefit easily. For example, in the year 2010, only two nonimmigrant S status applications were granted. In 2013, 29 S nonimmigrant applications were approved. In fiscal year 2013, six persons were adjusted to permanent resident through S. The FOIA results do not indicate whether these numbers include dependent family members.[29]

---

[27] 8 CFR §§245.11(b), 1245.11(b).

[28] 8 CFR §§245.11(f), 1245.11(f).

[29] The FOIA request and results are included as an appendix item to this chapter.

Despite such challenges, counsel should obtain written and verbal commitment to the S process from both the LEA and the prosecutor. The commitment should be obtained in letters, the plea agreement, and at discussion meetings. Counsel should request nonimmigrant status in advance of testimony. LEAs often put off nonimmigrant status until testimony has been provided; counsel should point out that this is in contravention of the statutory and regulatory framework. Private attorneys should be aware that prosecutors are often hesitant to provide S status in advance of testimony, or make specific written agreements, because it may be used by the target's defense counsel on cross examination as a perceived benefit that potentially taints the witness's testimony. This is an inaccurate perception: S status is not a gift, but a mechanism to keep a witness safe and physically present, not unlike the witness protection program. And there are no guarantees it will be issued.

> ***Practice Pointer: Cooperating witnesses serving time in prison***: Another reality of the S program is that LEAs hesitate to make the application until a cooperating witness has finished his or her sentence of imprisonment. Waiting for a sentence to end is not required—or even envisioned—in the regulations; however, it appears to be an unofficial policy or practice of the government not to submit an application until the cooperating witness-applicant is done with his or her prison sentence. This delay can cause significant practical problems for the applicant. He or she may have a detainer, and go from Federal Bureau of Prisons custody or state custody into DHS custody. Moreover, the applicant's family members are not eligible for S status until the principal receives the status; family members will linger in the United States in deferred action status (if they're fortunate) or no status at all. Another practical concern is that the particular agent or prosecutor may not be in the same office—may have transferred, retired, or otherwise left the office they held during the prosecution—during the time the applicant is serving prison time. For these and other reasons, defense counsel should thus encourage prosecutors and the LEA to submit the application during the period of custody by pointing out the legal parameters of the program, as spelled out in the regulations.

Even if the commitment to apply for S status is in a plea agreement, a motion to compel compliance is not of much use if the agent is not 100 percent behind the application. (Who needs a disgruntled agent who has been ordered by a judge to file the application?) Thus, a positive relationship and good faith among the parties is crucial. And again, the LEA and prosecutor should be encouraged to submit the application as soon as possible.

The I-854 is not prepared by legal counsel. Because it involves significant paperwork and tedious technical requirements, in addition to a chain-of-command system, law enforcement agents may be slow both in preparation of the I-854 application and in subsequent lobbying for its approval. It is best to monitor the application's progress with frequent reminders to the agent and prosecutor. To the extent that the LEA allows it, assist in the preparation of the evidentiary package in support of the application, and compile necessary biographic data of the witness and family members. (Prepare Form G-325 for each applicant.) Ensure that translations are done for birth and marriage certificates, get photos, and be prepared to courier documents to their destination. Assistance in large and small ways will help the process go faster, and make the job easier for the assigned agent, thus increasing the likelihood of S status success. Prudent counsel, however, will advise clients that there are no guarantees; ultimately, the receipt of S status rests in the hands of the government, outside defense counsel's control.

> ➤ **Tip on Family Members**: The principal cooperating witness (the candidate for S status) is likely to have a serious criminal record and be ineligible for any other relief (except withholding of removal). However, if family members of the principal qualifying witness are eligible for other forms of nonimmigrant status, such as a student or professional visa, such status should be sought in lieu of depending on derivative S status. Defense counsel may want to refer a spouse and children to immigration law counsel for consultation regarding the availability of other visa classifications, so that the family does not depend solely on the goodwill of the law enforcement agent and prosecutor.

Counsel ought to advise clients that even where the LEA follows through, S status takes time, and how much time is impossible to say. (It could be several months to more than a year.) It will necessarily depend on the LEA—not the client or the attorney. Patience is required. While the I-854 is pending, the government has the ability to provide parole status or deferred action to the witness and family members. Deferred action is generally granted in one-year increments and forms the basis for employment authorization eligibility and (at least in most states) a driver's license.

However, counsel should not let the grant of deferred action or parole status take the focus from the ultimate goal of S status. Parole status or deferred action should be a stopgap measure to keep the individual and family members in the United States pending approval of the I-854; it should not be accepted as a substitute to vigorous pursuit of S status, if an application for S status has indeed been negotiated.

> ➤ **Tip**: For those cases that do not rise to the level of S importance, law enforcement can work with DHS (ICE) at either the federal or local level to obtain parole during the period of time the individual is working on a case. Parole can be issued based on "material witness" or "in the public interest" language. Parole allows the individual to re-enter the United States, remain here lawfully, and obtain employment authorization. Parole can also be issued to family members.[30]

---

[30] A parole can be issued in several categories under the general authority of 8 CFR §212.5. Specifically, 8 CFR §§212.5(d), 212.14 and 1212.14 allow DHS to authorize the parole of cooperating witnesses.

Continued

Finally, if S status is either denied or revoked, immigration law guarantees the individual's right to apply for withholding of removal (and asylum for family members).[31] The process requires that the client admit to inadmissibility. He or she will probably have been convicted of a crime, usually an aggravated felony. The government may want to sweep up and deport the client with little ado. However, the government cannot summarily remove the client without his or her opportunity to seek protection via withholding of removal from an IJ. Be prepared to invoke that right either by reopening the removal order, or seeking a reasonable fear interview under the asylum regulations at 8 CFR §208.2(c).

"T" Status

T status is for victims of human trafficking (commercial sex or forced labor) who cooperate or are willing to cooperate with law enforcement. The T category was created by legislation in the year 2000,[32] and is thus a relatively new area of the law. Like S status, T status begins with an initial four-year period of nonimmigrant status, and can lead to permanent resident status. As discussed below, a successful applicant for T status will be the victim of a severe form of trafficking who is willing to cooperate with law enforcement (or who is under the age of 18) and who will suffer extreme hardship involving unusual and severe harm in the event of removal.

The Statute

The statutory definition is found at INA §101(a)(15)(T) [8 USC §1101(a)(15)(T)]. This provision provides, in pertinent part, that an individual qualifies for T status if he or she meets the following criteria [*emphasis added*]:

- has been the victim of a *severe form of trafficking* in persons;
- is physically present in the United States, America Samoa, or the Commonwealth of the Northern Mariana Islands on account of such trafficking;
- has complied with any reasonable request for assistance in the investigation or prosecution of the trafficking **or** has not attained the age of 18 years;
- would suffer *extreme hardship* upon removal based on unusual and severe harm.

The Regulations

DHS regulations implementing T status are found at 8 CFR §214.11. In addition, regulations were published by DOS that implement the T visa category.[33] By regula-

---

Family members of cooperating witnesses may also be paroled into the United States. A grant of parole is usually valid for one year.

[31] 8 CFR §§208.2(c)(1)(vi), 1208.2(c)(1)(vi).

[32] Trafficking Victims Protection Act of 2000 (TVPA), Pub. L. No. 106-386, div. A, 114 Stat. 1464, 1466–91.

[33] 68 Fed. Reg. 37963 (June 26, 2003).

tion, an individual applying for T status must be physically present in the United States or a territory, be the victim of a severe form of trafficking and either be cooperating with law enforcement, or be able to establish extreme hardship in the event of removal. Note that an individual under the age of 18 is not expected to cooperate with law enforcement, but may do so at his or her discretion.[34]

"Severe form of trafficking" defined

According to 8 CFR §214.11(a):

Severe forms of trafficking in persons means sex trafficking in which a commercial sex act is induced by force, fraud, or coercion, or in which the person induced to perform such act has not attained 18 years of age; or the recruitment, harboring, transportation, provision, or obtaining of a person for labor or services, through the use of force, fraud, or coercion for the purpose of subjection to involuntary servitude, peonage, debt bondage, or slavery.

"Extreme hardship" defined

"Extreme hardship" is not based on current or future economic detriment or the lack of social or economic opportunities in the country of removal. Rather, criteria relevant to extreme hardship include, but are not limited to:

- The age and personal circumstances of the applicant;
- Serious physical or mental illness that necessitates attention in the United States;
- The nature and extent of the physical and psychological consequences of the trafficking;
- The impact of lack of access to U.S. courts and the criminal justice system;
- The expectation that the applicant will be punished in the home country based on laws, social practices, or customs that would essentially penalize the applicant for being a victim of trafficking;
- The likelihood of re-victimization;
- The likelihood that the trafficker or others acting on his or her behalf will punish the victim; and
- The applicant's safety based on the existence of civil unrest or armed conflict in the country, as determined by temporary protected status (TPS) designation.[35]

Application Procedure

An individual seeking T nonimmigrant status submits Form I-914, along with supporting documentation, by mail, to the Vermont Service Center (VSC) of USCIS. Only USCIS has jurisdiction over T status. Technical requirements for the application

---

[34] INA §101(a)(15)(T)(i)(III)(cc); 8 USC §1101(a)(15)(T)(i)(III)(cc).
[35] 8 CFR §214.11(i).

and supporting documentation are found at 8 CFR §214.11(d). The evidentiary package that accompanies the application must include proof that the individual is physically present in the United States because of having been trafficked; evidence that he or she has cooperated with law enforcement; and evidence that the individual would suffer extreme hardship involving unusual and severe harm if removed from the United States. An important aspect of T status is that, although an LEA certification is preferred, secondary evidence of cooperation may be submitted if the applicant does not have (or cannot get) the certification. The regulations state that "any credible evidence" relevant to the essential elements of T status may be submitted.[36] DHS will consider an LEA endorsement of the application as primary evidence that the applicant has been a victim of trafficking.[37] Thus, every effort should be made to obtain an LEA's endorsement of the application. The regulations state that a victim who has not made contact with law enforcement regarding the crime should contact either a local federal LEA (FBI, DHS, U.S. Attorney), or DOJ's Civil Rights Division, Trafficking in Persons Hotline at (888) 428-7581, to file a complaint and be referred to the appropriate LEA.[38]

Another way to establish that an applicant is a victim of a severe form of trafficking is by obtaining "continued presence," or CP, under 28 CFR §1100.35.[39] That is, even where no LEA is willing to provide an endorsement, it is enough to show that an LEA made a request to the DHS Office of International Affairs, Parole Humanitarian Affairs Branch, in Washington, DC. CP is particularly useful in those situations where the LEA wants to keep the victim around but is reluctant to assist overtly in the T visa process because such help might become an impeachment issue at trial. CP also carries the added bonus of creating eligibility for employment authorization and for a variety of public benefits similar to those available to refugees and asylees. ICE has a task force that deals with T applications, and most U.S. Attorneys' offices have a liaison attorney to deal with these cases.

> **Tip**: Homeland Security Investigations (HSI), a special division of ICE, will have an agent assigned to virtually all federal cases where trafficking or smuggling is involved. These agents are very familiar with both the LEA endorsement and the CP process. Where there are obviously severe forms of trafficking, HSI can be very helpful.

Finally, it should be noted that after submission of the application, a personal interview may be required.

---

[36] 8 CFR §214.11(d)(3).
[37] 8 CFR §214.11(f)(2).
[38] 8 CFR §214.11(f)(4).
[39] 8 CFR §214.11(f).

Effect of pending immigration proceedings

An individual in removal proceedings who would like to apply for T status may request that the proceedings be administratively closed; this used to require the consent of the DHS attorney, but the Board of Immigration Appeals (BIA or Board) has recently held that in certain circumstances the IJ may administratively close proceedings even over the objection of either party.[40] In the alternative, the applicant may request that proceedings be continued indefinitely pending a decision on the T application.[41]

Applicants with final orders of removal

T applicants with a final order of removal are not precluded from receiving T status because of that final order. If T status is approved by the VSC, the final order "shall be deemed cancelled by operation of law."[42] However, as a practical matter, many practitioners choose to seek joint motions to terminate in this context as lingering removal orders tend to create problems for clients who are seeking admission after travelling abroad, or when other government databases are not updated; it helps to have a termination order in hand.

Annual cap on number of admissions

The total number of principal applicants that may be granted T-1 status in any fiscal year is 5,000. Once the cap is reached, a waiting list will be established, and the applicant will receive notice of having been placed on the waiting list.[43]

Revocation of status

T nonimmigrant status can be revoked if the victim fails to provide cooperation or if the LEA withdraws its endorsement or disavows the statements made therein.[44]

Family Members

The principal applicant (victim) is issued T-1 status. An individual who has applied for or been granted T-1 status may apply for the admission of an immediate family member, including a spouse (T-2), child (T-3), or parent (T-4).[45] A parent may be a derivative beneficiary only if the T-1 principal is a child. The status is not accorded to family members automatically. A proposed derivative family member must establish that either he or she (the derivative) or the principal applicant (the victim) would suffer extreme hardship if not allowed to accompany or join the principal ap-

---

[40] *See Matter of Avetisyan*, 25 I&N Dec. 688 (BIA 2012).
[41] 8 CFR §214.11(d)(8).
[42] 8 CFR §214.11(d)(9).
[43] 8 CFR §214.11(m).
[44] 8 CFR §§214.11(s)(1)(iv), (v).
[45] 8 CFR §214.11(o).

plicant.⁴⁶ The extreme hardship must be substantially different than the hardship generally experienced by other residents of the home country who are not victims of a severe form of trafficking. USCIS will consider all credible evidence of extreme hardship, and the determination will be made on a case-by-case basis. Relevant factors may include, but are not limited to, financial support to the principal T applicant, the need for family support, or the risk of serious harm, particularly bodily harm, to immediate family members from the perpetrators of the trafficking.⁴⁷

Duration of nonimmigrant status and application for permanent residency

T nonimmigrant status is generally issued for four years. This status may be extended at the request of law enforcement.⁴⁸ T nonimmigrant victims and their qualifying relatives in T status can apply for adjustment of status to permanent residency. An individual must be in status in order to apply for adjustment of status; the now rare exception is for those who were granted T status prior to promulgation of the regulations, and is found at 8 CFR 245.23(a)(2)(i).

The regulations governing applications for adjustment of status are at 8 CFR §245.23. To qualify for adjustment of status, the T applicant must show:

- At least three years of continuous physical presence (an absence of more than 90 days, or absences totaling more than 120 days in the aggregate will interrupt continuous physical presence);
- Good moral character (an applicant under the age of 14 is presumed to have good moral character);
- Compliance with law enforcement's reasonable requests for assistance *or* a showing of extreme hardship involving unusual and severe harm upon removal from the United States.

To summarize, an applicant for permanent residency will either establish continued cooperation with law enforcement or, in the alternative, show that he or she would suffer extreme hardship involving unusual and severe harm upon removal. Extreme hardship cannot be established based on economic detriment or the lack (or disruption) of social or economic opportunities. Instead, relevant factors may include (but are not limited to) the applicant's physical or mental illness, the need for medical or psychological attention, the nature and extent of physical consequences from the trafficking, the need for access to the civil and criminal court system for redress, and the likelihood that the trafficker (the perpetrator) would inflict harm on the applicant in the native country.⁴⁹ The application for adjustment of status is discretionary. A denial may be appealed to the Administrative Appeals Office (AAO).⁵⁰ There is by

---

⁴⁶ 8 CFR §214.11(o)(1)(ii).

⁴⁷ 8 CFR §214.11(o)(5).

⁴⁸ 8 CFR §214.11(p)(1).

⁴⁹ 8 CFR §245.23(f)(2), which in turn refers to extreme hardship at 8 CFR §214.11(i).

⁵⁰ 8 CFR §245.23(i).

statute a cap of 5,000 adjustments per year in this category.⁵¹ Although the cap only applies to principals, not derivative family members, be mindful that T derivatives cannot adjust unless and until the principal adjusts. The regulations allow for a waiting list if the number is exhausted.⁵²

"U" Status

"U" status is a nonimmigrant visa classification that may lead to permanent resident status. It is important to understand the distinction between "U nonimmigrant status" and a "U visa." U nonimmigrant status is granted to persons already present in the United States, while a U visa is granted to someone who is abroad, seeking a visa through consular processing. Principal U applicants are victims of enumerated crimes who are helpful, or willing to be helpful, to law enforcement. The applicant must be in possession of information about the criminal activity of which he or she has been a victim. The criminal activity must have been in violation of U.S. law or have occurred in the United States or a territory or possession. The applicant must have suffered substantial physical or mental abuse as a result of having been the victim of the qualifying activity. Based on the statutory provisions, as well as the regulation, U status is a generous immigration classification that will apply to, and benefit, many individuals.

The regulations governing U nonimmigrant status are at 8 CFR §214.14. They went into effect on October 17, 2007. Prior to publication of this interim final rule, many persons applied for U status and received interim benefits, which included deferred action. Persons in deferred action status were encouraged to file the U application according to the interim rule within 180 days of its publication.

U status, like T, was passed as part of the Victims of Trafficking and Violence Protection Act of 2000,⁵³ specifically as part of the Battered Immigrant Women Protection Act of 2000.⁵⁴ According to the interim rule's preamble, Congress's purpose in enacting U status was to strengthen the ability of law enforcement agencies to investigate and prosecute cases of domestic violence, sexual assault, trafficking of aliens, and other crimes while affording protection to the victim/witness of such offenses.

U status may also be granted to certain family members of the principal victim/witness. If the principal is under 21 years of age, his or her spouse, children, unmarried siblings, and parents may qualify as derivatives for U status.⁵⁵ If the principal victim/witness is over 21 years of age, his or her spouse and children may qualify as derivatives.

---

[51] INA §245(*l*)(4).

[52] 8 CFR §245.23(*l*).

[53] Victims of Trafficking and Violence Protection Act of 2000, Pub. L. No. 106-386, 114 Stat. 1464.

[54] Pub. L. No. 106-386, §§1501–13, 114 Stat. 1464, 1518–37.

[55] INA §101(a)(15)(U)(ii)(II).

Applications for U status are filed with the VSC on Form I-918. Only USCIS has jurisdiction over U status; it is not a benefit one may seek in immigration court. There is a biometrics fee, but a fee waiver is available. An applicant who is inadmissible may file Form I-192 to apply for advance permission to enter as a nonimmigrant and seek the waiver found at INA §212(d)(14). Although the waiver is discretionary, it is theoretically available to waive all grounds apart from those found at INA §212(a)(3)(E) [participants in Nazi persecutions, genocide, torture or extrajudicial killings] where the applicant can show it is in the public or national interest. A requirement of U status is that the application be accompanied by a "certification" from a law enforcement entity (state or federal) verifying that the victim/applicant has been helpful, is being helpful, or is likely to be helpful in the investigation or prosecution of the qualifying criminal activity.[56] Additional requirements are discussed later in this chapter.

The Statute

According to INA §101(a)(15)(U) [8 USC §1101(a)(15)(U)], an individual files his or her own petition for status. Thus, the application is different from the Form I-854 application for S status, which is filed by a law enforcement entity. The criteria are as follows:

- The applicant has suffered substantial physical or mental abuse as a result of having been a victim of specified criminal activity;

- The applicant/victim (or if the victim is a child under the age of 16, the parent, guardian, or "next friend" of the victim) possesses information concerning specified criminal activity;

- The applicant/victim has been, is being, or is likely to be helpful to a federal or state law enforcement official, prosecutor, or judge in investigating or prosecuting the criminal activity; and

- The criminal activity violated the laws of the United States or its territories or possessions.

"Criminal activity" defined

An applicant for U status must be the victim of a criminal act *or similar activity* in violation of either state or federal law, involving rape, torture, trafficking, incest, domestic violence, sexual assault, abusive sexual contact, prostitution, sexual exploitation, female genital mutilation, being held hostage, peonage, involuntary servitude, slave trade, kidnapping, abduction, unlawful criminal restraint, false imprisonment, blackmail, extortion, manslaughter, murder, felonious assault, witness tampering, obstruction of justice, perjury, or attempt, conspiracy, or solicitation to commit any of the above mentioned crimes.[57] In 2013, the Violence Against Women Reauthorization Act (VAWA 2013) added two new qualifying crimes to the original statutory list for U

---

[56] INA §101(a)(15)(U)(i)(III).

[57] INA §101(a)(15)(U)(iii); 8 USC §1101(a)(15)(U)(iii).

nonimmigrant eligibility:[58] (1) stalking and (2) fraud in foreign labor contracting (as defined at §1351 of title 18 of the U.S. Code).

The Regulation

According to the regulation,[59] there are four qualifying criteria for U status.

1. The applicant must have suffered substantial physical or mental abuse as a result of having been a victim of qualifying criminal activity. The regulation specifically defines "victim."[60] A victim may be a direct victim of crime, or an indirect victim. An indirect victim is a qualifying family member (*e.g.*, spouse or child) of the direct victim who is now deceased on account of the crime (murder or manslaughter). An indirect victim may also arise where the crimes are witness tampering, obstruction of justice, and perjury, which are not crimes against a person.[61]

Substantial physical or mental abuse means injury or harm to the victim's physical person, or harm to or impairment of the emotional or psychological soundness of the victim.[62] The issue of harm will be determined on a case-by-case basis by a special unit at the VSC. USCIS will look to such factors as the nature of the injury inflicted or suffered; the severity of the perpetrator's conduct; the severity of the harm suffered; the duration of the infliction of harm; and the extent of permanent injuries or serious harm to appearance, health, and/or physical or mental soundness.

Note that an individual who is culpable for the actual criminal activity that is being investigated is excluded from being classified as a "victim"[63] and may not receive U status. This exclusion is not part of the statute, but has been added by USCIS in drafting the regulations. Note that this exclusion does not apply if the victim/applicant has a criminal record separate and apart from the criminal activity being investigated (that forms the basis for the U application: the "qualifying activity").

2. The applicant must be in possession of information about the criminal activity of which he or she has been a victim. According to 8 CFR §214.4(b)(2), "information" relates to knowledge of details and specific facts that will assist law enforcement in prosecution of the criminal activity. The information must be regarding the crime of which the applicant is a victim. The practitioner will note the regulation's use of the phrase "criminal activity." The regulations do not require that the witness/applicant be a victim of the specific crime or crimes charged (*i.e.*, the actual counts), but rather, be involved in the overall investigation of the larger offense activity.

---

[58] Violence Against Women Reauthorization Act of 2013 (VAWA 2013), Pub. L. No. 113-4, 127 Stat. 110.

[59] 8 CFR §214.14(b).

[60] 8 CFR §214.14(b)(1).

[61] 8 CFR §§214.14(a)(14)(i), (ii).

[62] 8 CFR §214.14(a)(8).

[63] 8 CFR §214.14(a)(14)(iii).

3. The applicant must be helping law enforcement by providing information and cooperation. A reasonable request may not be refused. The LEA must certify that the applicant has information and is being helpful to the investigation and prosecution of crime.[64] This certification is prepared on Form I-918, Supplement B, and must be signed within the six-month period of time preceding the filing of the application.[65] The requirement of a signed certification is a distinctive issue when comparing the U to T status; T status allows for secondary evidence where the applicant does not have a signed certification.

4. The final requirement is that the qualifying criminal activity be in violation of the laws of the United States or occur within the United States or its territories or possessions.[66] The regulations do not require that the criminal investigation result in actual prosecution in a court of law; nor do the regulations require a successful prosecution. In fact, not even an arrest is required. It is sufficient that the LEA certify the "investigation" of a qualifying criminal activity. The criminal activity must be similar to an enumerated crime (as listed in the statute) but need not be precisely one of the enumerated crimes.

Filing

As stated above, Form I-918 will be filed with the VSC. Qualifying family members are listed on Supplement A.[67] As previously noted, an essential aspect of the application is Supplement B, which is the U nonimmigrant status certification prepared by an LEA or other qualifying agency.[68] A qualifying agency may be law enforcement, prosecutor, or judge. The application must include evidence that the applicant is a victim of qualifying activity, has suffered substantial physical or mental abuse as a result of the crime, and is being helpful or will be helpful to law enforcement. The application must include the applicant/petitioner's statement regarding the crime and, specifically, the facts of the victimization.[69]

> **Tip**: Virtually all U applicants will need to file Form I-192 in order to waive at least one ground of inadmissibility, whether it is entry without inspection, overstaying a visa, working without authorization, or more serious criminal issues. Both the Form I-918 and the Form I-192 require a statement from the applicant, so why not address both issues in a single statement? Just be sure to clarify that the statement is made in support of both applications, and it is a good idea to use a separate heading addressing the waiver criteria and the public or national interest standard.

---

[64] 8 CFR §214.14(b)(3).
[65] 8 CFR §214.14(c)(2)(i).
[66] 8 CFR §214.14(b)(4).
[67] 8 CFR §214.14(c)(1).
[68] 8 CFR §214.14(c)(2)(i).
[69] 8 CFR §214.14(c)(2)(iii).

Form I-918 may be filed while the applicant/petitioner is in the United States or outside the country. Derivative family members residing outside the United States whose petitions are approved may be granted a U visa at a U.S. consulate abroad.

Once granted, an applicant in U status physically present in the United States will receive Form I-797 approval notice, as well as an I-94 ("arrival departure record") indicating U-1 nonimmigrant status. He or she is also eligible to seek employment authorization, or will receive it automatically if the applicant has indicated on the Form I-918 that employment authorization is desired. Although the holder of U status may travel abroad, it is generally discouraged unless there is an urgent need. Upon traveling, the victim/petitioner will need to apply for a U visa at an American consulate abroad, and the complexities of this endeavor are enough to warrant a separate treatise. The consular requirements vary wildly from country to country, and where there is significant consular delay, the traveler runs the risk of inadvertently being abroad for more than 90 days and thereby disrupting the continuous presence necessary for adjustment of status. In certain circumstances there is a waiver of the visa requirement.[70] When the application for U status is approved for an individual outside the United States, the applicant will receive a Form I-797 notice and the appropriate consulate will be notified through DOS.[71]

There is a cap. USCIS may grant U-1 nonimmigrant status to 10,000 applicants each year.[72] This number does not include derivative family members.

Qualifying family members

A derivative family member of a principal U applicant is referred to as a "qualifying family member" and includes the spouse or children of the principal, if he or she is over 21 years of age. In the case of a principal U applicant who is under the age of 21, a qualifying family member means the spouse, children, parents, or unmarried siblings under the age of 18.[73] This means that siblings of the principal under the age of 18 are also eligible for U nonimmigrant status. A qualifying family member may submit an application while the principal U applicant's own application is pending, or after the principal has been granted status.[74] The application is submitted on Form I-918, utilizing Supplement A. Notably, the qualifying relationship must exist at the time of filing and continue to exist at the time of adjudication. There are two exceptions. First, a child born to the principal applicant, after the principal receives U status, is eligible for nonimmigrant U status. Second, in the case of a sibling, where the principal was under 21 years of age and the sibling was under 18 at the time of filing,

---

[70] 8 CFR §212.1(g). The visa waiver request is filed on Form I-193.
[71] 8 CFR §§214.14(c)(5)(i)(A), (B).
[72] 8 CFR §214.14(d)(1).
[73] 8 CFR §214.14(a)(10).
[74] 8 CFR §214.14(f)(1).

the application for the sibling may still be approved notwithstanding reaching the age of 18. The sibling, however, must remain unmarried.[75]

Qualifying family members receive the following designation: U-2 (spouse), U-3 (child), U-4 (parent of U-1 principal), or U-5 (unmarried sibling under the age of 18).

Persons in removal proceedings

The regulatory provisions (there are several) that discuss pending removal cases and final orders of removal are somewhat unclear, as if DHS is torn between achieving prosecution and enforcement goals or effecting the congressional intent behind U status.

For those persons in pending proceedings, the U application may only be filed with USCIS; IJs do not have jurisdiction to adjudicate this application. Being in removal proceedings does not preclude an application for U status. Counsel for the U applicant in removal proceedings may request the consent of ICE chief counsel to file a joint motion to terminate proceedings before the BIA or the IJ.[76] Whether chief counsel will agree to terminate is in that office's sole prosecutorial discretion. The parties may also, according to the commentary, agree to an indefinite continuance of the proceedings pending adjudication of the U petition.

In *Matter of Sanchez-Sosa*,[77] the BIA set forth the test for an IJ to continue a case pending adjudication of a U petition. The Board wrote that in determining whether to continue a case before the immigration court, the judge will consider DHS's position, whether the petition is prima facie approvable, and the procedural history of the case. In *Sanchez-Sosa*, the Board discussed in depth the meaning of "prima facie" approvable: IJs will have to be well versed in U law, even though they do not have jurisdiction over the petition. In reading *Sanchez-Sosa*, it appears that the case had been pending several years for different reasons, and DHS was opposed to a continuance, claiming that the respondents had not exercised due diligence in pursuing U status, that there was inadequate evidence that it was even filed, and if so, that there was inadequate evidence that the U was prima facie approvable.[78] The case was remanded to the IJ to balance the competing issues as outlined by the Board. A review of the case reflects that a continuance was contested because of previous delays and a purported weak filing.

In this author's experience, in most cases the Office of Chief Counsel (OCC) will agree to continue a case pending U adjudication. And barring especially egregious factors, ICE chief counsel will agree to terminate or administratively close on a prima facie approval. ICE chief counsel will also communicate with ICE to request expedited processing for an individual who is detained in removal proceedings.

---

[75] 8 CFR §§214.14(f)(4)(i) and (ii).

[76] 8 CFR §§214.14(c)(1)(i), (f)(2)(i).

[77] *Matter of Sanchez-Sosa*, 25 I&N Dec. 807 (BIA 2012).

[78] *Matter of Sanchez-Sosa*, 25 I&N Dec. 807, at 809.

An individual who is already the subject of a final order of deportation, exclusion, or removal is still eligible for U status.[79] The regulation states that a person with a final order is not "precluded" from filing an application for U status; the filing of the application has no effect on ICE's authority to execute the order. The applicant should also seek a stay of deportation, according to the regulation, but may remain in detention.[80]

The regulation states that if USCIS approves U-1 status, the exclusion, deportation, or removal order issued by the "Secretary" (presumably referring to the Secretary of DHS, rather than an IJ) is deemed "cancelled by operation of law."[81] If the order of removal was issued by an IJ or the BIA, the applicant may seek reopening and cancellation of the order through a motion to reopen and terminate. ICE counsel may, in its discretion, join the motion to overcome regulatory bars (time and numerical limitations for motions). The regulation does not state that an IJ– or BIA-issued removal order is cancelled by operation of law; the regulation also does not state what a recipient of U status should do if OCC will not join in a joint motion. The implication from an overall reading of the regulatory provisions is that a person with a final removal order may apply for and receive U status without regard to the order, but again, the regulations are simply not clear on this point. Nevertheless, the USCIS service center that processes all U adjustment applications has stated in its stakeholder meetings that it is not necessary to obtain a termination order, and they have been routinely adjusting applicants with outstanding orders of removal. Moreover, some ICE OCC offices have taken the position that because holders of U status adjust under INA §245(m), which is a stand-alone provision separate from §245(a), and because USCIS has sole jurisdiction over U adjustment, termination of the order is not required for adjustment, and they refuse to join on that basis. As mentioned in the previous section about T status, lingering orders of removal may cause unnecessary headaches for LPRs returning from trips abroad or who are trying to clarify their status with other government entities or law enforcement. Thus, for strategic reasons, depending on the individual case, an attorney may seek reopening of a final removal order on the basis of a pending U application, or an approval of U status; however, reopening and vacating the removal order is not a requirement to receiving U status, and apparently, is not a requirement for adjustment of status in this context.

As stated above, the duration of U nonimmigrant status is four years; a qualifying family member's status will correspond to the principal U-1's time.[82] An extension may be requested if the initial time allowed was less than four years. An extension may also be requested by a qualifying family member if delays in consular processing result in a family member arriving later, such that the principal achieves three years

---

[79] 72 Fed. Reg. 53013, 53022 (Sept. 17, 2007).

[80] 8 CFR §214.14(c)(1)(ii).

[81] 8 CFR §214.14(c)(5)(i).

[82] 8 CFR §214.14(g)(1).

of nonimmigrant status before the derivative.[83] (Three years of status is required for the application for adjustment of status.)

Age-out protection

The VAWA 2013[84] finally introduced a long-sought procedural change and now provides relief to those qualifying children who aged out of derivative eligibility while their petitions for derivative U nonimmigrant status were pending.[85] Specifically, when a principal petitioner for U nonimmigrant status properly files his or her principal petition, the age of the qualifying family member is established upon the date on which the principal filed for his or her principal U nonimmigrant status. Thus, an unmarried qualifying family member "child" under 21 years of age who has a derivative petition properly filed by the principal will continue to be considered a "child" throughout the process, even if he or she turns 21 while the principal or derivative petition is still pending.[86]

VAWA 2013 also provides protection for derivative petitioners of a U principal petitioner who is under 21 years of age. If a U principal petitioner is under 21 years of age at the time he or she files the petition, unmarried siblings under 18 years of age at that time and parents will still be considered qualifying family members for derivative U status, even if at the time of the adjudication the principal is over 21 and even if the unmarried sibling is over 18.[87]

It is important to note that the changes introduced by VAWA 2013 are retroactive and, therefore, considered part of the original Victims of Trafficking and Violence Protection Act of 2000.

Nonimmigrant U status is automatically revoked if the beneficiary notifies USCIS that he or she will not be applying for admission to the United States.[88] Status may be revoked through a notice of intent to revoke where the certifying official withdraws the certification or disavows its contents.[89] Revocation by notice may also be based on error, fraud, or, for family members, a termination of the qualifying family rela-

---

[83] 8 CFR §214.14(g)(2).

[84] Pub. L. No. 113-4, 127 Stat. 110 (2013).

[85] VAWA 2013 amends INA §214(p) by adding a section (7)(A): "An unmarried alien who seeks to accompany, or follow to join, a parent granted status under section 101(a)(15)(U)(i), and who was under 21 years of age on the date on which such parent petitioned for such status, shall continue to be classified as a child for purposes of section 101(a)(15)(U)(ii), if the alien attains 21 years of age after such parent's petition was filed but while it was still pending."

[86] *See* USCIS Policy Memorandum, "Violence Against Women Reauthorization Act of 2013: Changes to U Nonimmigrant Status and Adjustment of Status Provisions" (June 15, 2014), *published on* AILA InfoNet at Doc. No. 14063041 (*posted* 6/30/14).

[87] *See* INA §§101(a)(15)(U)(ii)(I); 214(p)(7)(B).

[88] 8 CFR §214.14(h).

[89] 8 CFR §214.14(h)(2)(A).

tionship.[90] If the principal is revoked, the family member's status is also revoked.[91] The revocation may be appealed to the Administrative Appeals Office.[92]

Permanent Resident Status: A Change in Focus

U nonimmigrant status is generally issued for four years.[93] After three years, a victim/applicant may apply for LPR status.[94] Qualifying family members who were also admitted as U nonimmigrants are also eligible to apply for adjustment. Statutory authority for adjustment of status is found at INA §245(m).

The regulations regarding adjustment of status begin at 8 CFR §245.24. A review of the regulations indicates that adjustment of status is not an automatic benefit. Moreover, the emphasis at this stage is not on the applicant's victimization, but rather on his or her assistance to law enforcement in the investigation and prosecution of the underlying crime. Key provisions include an emphasis on continuous physical presence in U status; proof of actual assistance to law enforcement; and evidence in support of a favorable exercise of discretion based on humanitarian grounds, public interest, or to ensure family unity. Similar to the process of getting the underlying U nonimmigrant status, a certification from law enforcement is strongly recommended, but many practitioners successfully satisfy this requirement by including a simple sworn statement from the applicant stating that no further requests have been made and that the applicant would continue to comply with such requests if they were made.

The interim final rule also includes benefits for family members who are not yet in U nonimmigrant status. Procedures for these family members are discussed further, below.

The regulation states that an individual in U nonimmigrant status may apply for permanent residency after being continuously physically present for at least three years following admission in U status. Note than an absence exceeding 90 days, or aggregate absences of more than 180 days, will interrupt continuous physical presence.[95] There is an exception if the absence was necessary to assist law enforcement, and the LEA attests to such.[96] In addition to traditional adjustment of status information, such as proof of admission, the application for adjustment of status must be accompanied by:

- Evidence pertaining to any requests made to the non–American citizen by law enforcement for assistance in an investigation or prosecution of persons connected

---

[90] 8 CFR §§214.14(h)(2)(B)–(D).
[91] 8 CFR §214.14(h)(2)(E).
[92] 8 CFR §214.14(h)(3).
[93] INA §214(p)(6); 8 USC §1184(p)(6).
[94] INA §245(m)(1); 8 USC §1255(m)(1)(A).
[95] 8 CFR §245.24(a)(1).
[96] 8 CFR §245.24(d)(5)(iii).

with the qualifying criminal activity; this information may be provided in the form of a newly executed Form I-918, Supplement B, or some other document signed by law enforcement. If information from a law enforcement officer is not available, the applicant may submit a signed affidavit explaining why information directly from an LEA is not available, what efforts have been made to obtain corroboration, and whether law enforcement assistance was indeed requested from the applicant.[97]

- An affidavit attesting to continuous physical presence, along with other documentation establishing continuous physical presence;[98]
- Evidence establishing that "approval is warranted" based on discretion for humanitarian grounds, to ensure family unity; or otherwise in the public interest;[99]
- Evidence that discretion is warranted, including documentation to offset any negative factors (such as a criminal record).[100]

Of note, the applicant's affidavit regarding assistance should include specific information about law enforcement personnel involved in the underlying criminal case, the status of the criminal investigation or prosecution, information on any charges filed, and the outcome. If the prosecution was dropped, the affidavit should provide the reasons. Moreover, if an applicant does not submit evidence directly from the LEA regarding the ongoing assistance, DHS may refer to the original certification [Form I-918, Supplement B] and contact the original LEA directly.[101] If supporting documentation attesting to the applicant's amenability to cooperation is not produced, or if the LEA indicates that the applicant was *not* cooperative, the application for adjustment may be referred to DOJ to determine whether the applicant unreasonably refused to provide assistance in a criminal investigation or prosecution. DOJ has 90 days to submit a written determination to USCIS, although this time period may be extended by request.[102] This written determination regarding cooperation will in turn be taken into consideration by USCIS in adjudicating the application.

Some practitioners have difficulty adapting to the notion that the inadmissibility grounds of INA §212(a), apart from subsection (3)(E), simply do not apply in the U adjustment context.[103] This means that for all other grounds of inadmissibility, no waiver is necessary or available. All other factors will simply be taken into account in the in the agency's exercise of discretion. Therefore, in situations where significant

---

[97] 8 CFR §§245.24(d)(8), (e).
[98] 8 CFR §245.24(d)(9).
[99] 8 CFR §245.24(d)(10).
[100] 8 CFR §245.24(d)(11).
[101] 8 CFR §245.24(e)(3).
[102] 8 CFR §245.24(e)(4).
[103] INA § 245(m)(1); 8 USC § 1255(m)(1).

negative factors are present, an applicant would want to balance the equities by showing strong positive factors as well, but there is no waiver to be sought.

If an application for adjustment of status is denied, the applicant may appeal to the Administrative Appeals Office.[104]

Family Members Not Already in U Status

The regulations regarding residency for the family members of U applicants are at 8 CFR §245.24(g) and include family members both within and outside the United States. Statutory authority for family members is at INA §245(m)(3). These provisions are for family members who did not receive and have never held nonimmigrant U status.[105] According to the regulations, a principal U-1 applicant must file an immigrant petition on Form I-929. A "qualifying family member" includes the principal applicant's spouse, child, or—where the principal is a child—the parent.[106]

The I-929 petition for a family member who did not receive nonimmigrant U status must be accompanied by evidence establishing that the qualifying family member or the U-1 principal would suffer extreme hardship if the family member is not now able to remain or join the principal in the United States.[107] The regulations contain examples of what factors may qualify as extreme hardship.[108] Thus the U regulatory scheme clearly offers incentive for family members to seek U nonimmigrant status concurrently with the U-1 principal. If a family member seeks to join the principal at the residency stage, an extreme hardship requirement is imposed that does not exist at the nonimmigrant application phase. Family members may be within the United States (where they apply for adjustment of status concurrently with the petition), or may consular process from outside the United States upon approval of the petition.

Jurisdiction

The regulations state that USCIS has exclusive jurisdiction over adjustment of status applications filed under INA §245(m).[109] The regulation also states that the general adjustment procedures set forth at 8 CFR §§245.1 and 245.2 do not apply to U applications for adjustment under INA §245(m).[110]

---

[104] 8 CFR §245.24(f)(2).
[105] 8 CFR §245.24(g)(1).
[106] 8 CFR §245.24(a)(2).
[107] 8 CFR §245.24(h)(iv).
[108] 8 CFR §§245.24(h)(iv)(A)–(G).
[109] 8 CFR §245.24(k).
[110] 8 CFR §245.24(*l*).

APPENDIX 12A

FORM I-854, INTER-AGENCY ALIEN WITNESS AND INFORMANT RECORD

Department of Homeland Security
U.S. Citizenship and Immigration Services

OMB No. 1615-0046; Expires 05/31/2013
Form I-854, Inter-Agency Alien Witness and Informant Record

Part A. To be completed by Law Enforcement Agencies. *(See instructions for specific information.)*
Information must be Typed or Printed clearly.

1. Name of LEA/Requestor: _____

2. Requesting Agent: _____ Control Agent: _____

   Address: _____ Phone No.*(Including Area Code)*: _____

   _____ Fax No.*(Including Area Code)*: _____

Check if applicable:

3. ☐ Alien will be placed in danger in ☐ U.S. ☐ abroad as a result of providing information, etc.
   ☐ Alien poses no danger to people or property of the U.S.
   ☐ If the alien poses a danger, the danger posed by the alien is outweighed by the assistance the alien will furnish.
   ☐ Investigation. ☐ Prosecution. ☐ United States Attorney involvement.

4. Type of Request(s). *(Attach legal basis for request.)*
   ☐ S-5   ☐ S-6
   Consular post at which visa will be sought: _____
   ☐ Change of Status - If change of status is requested, current immigration status is _____
   ☐ Adjustment of Status *(Go to **Part F** after completing information in **items** 5, 6 and 7 below.)*
   ☐ Fees attached *(when applicable)* ☐ Security concerns. State special instructions regarding security precautions.

NOTE: Provide a clear statement of the operations that form the basis of the request (e.g., Grand Jury subpoena), the objective of the request and any bargain the requestor wishes to make or has made with the alien. Attach a complete criminal history, FBI No. and U.S. Social Security Number.

5. Alien's Name *(Last Name, First and Middle)*	Other Names Used		
Alien's Address *(Street Number and Name)*	A #		I-94 #
City	State or Province	Zip/Postal Code	Current Location of Alien
Marital Status	Date of Birth (mm/dd/yyyy)	Place of Birth *(City or Country)*	Citizenship/Nationality	Occupation

Date of Last Entry into U.S. *(mm/dd/yyyy)*:	☐ Form G-325 attached	☐ Form FD-258 attached	☐ Photos attached

6. On a separate application, provide all information requested in **item 5** above for each beneficiary who seeks derivative status - spouse, parents and all sons and daughters of the alien for whom an S classification is requested. *(Attach additional sheets of paper as necessary.)*

Form I-854 (Rev. 05/13/10)Y

7a. The following information must be provided for each alien named in items 5 and 6 above.

Has the alien, while outside of the United States, ever committed, ordered, incited, assisted, or otherwise participated in genocide, torture, or extrajudicial killing or participated in Nazi persecution?

☐ Yes   ☐ No   If yes please write a detailed statement below and attach any relevant documents. *(Attach additional sheets of paper as needed.)*

_____
_____
_____
_____
_____
_____
_____
_____

7b. For the above named alien, I request waiver(s) of the following grounds of inadmissibility. *(Check all possible grounds and attach all relevant documents establishing the ground(s) of inadmissibility and why you feel a waiver is appropriate for this alien. This information must be provided for each alien named in **items 5 and 6** above. Copy this check list of the grounds of inadmissibility for each derivative.)*

☐ Communicable disease
☐ Immigrant visa issued outside numerical limitation
☐ Crime involving moral turpitude
☐ International child abduction
☐ Multiple criminal convictions
☐ Engaged in unlawful commercialized vice
☐ Entrance predudicial to public
☐ Involved in espionage, sabotage or laws relating to technology
☐ Coming to overthrow the U.S. Government
☐ Foreign policy exclusion
☐ Unqualified physician
☐ Previously removed - aggravated felony
☐ Stowaway
☐ Nonimmigrant without a valid passport or visa
☐ Previously excluded and deported or removed
☐ Alien smuggler
☐ Physical/mental disorder (dangerous)
☐ Drug abuser or addict
☐ Convicted of law pertaining to controlled substances

☐ Controlled substance trafficker
☐ Prostitute and/or Procurer of Prostitution
☐ Exercised diplomatic immunity to avoid prosecution
☐ Unlawful activity related to National Security
☐ Terrorist activities
☐ Communist Party member
☐ Public charge
☐ Lacking labor certification
☐ Fraud/Misrepresentation
☐ Immigrant without a visa
☐ Draft evader-was immigrant when left U.S.
☐ Alien accompanying helpless inadmissible alien
☐ Violator of section 274C
☐ Ordered, incited, assisted or otherwise participated in the commission of the acts of torture or extra judicial killing.
☐ Engaged in conduct relating to severe violations of religious freedoms
☐ Weapons charges, domestic violence, and money laundering
☐ Other
☐ No waivers are requested/needed

Form I-854 (Rev. 05/13/10)Y Page 2

Part B. Certifications

1. Alien Certification. *(S classification request.)*

I certify under penalty of perjury that I have reviewed with the LEA all the information in **Part A**, disclosed all information to the best of my ability, and disclosed all reasons for which I may be removed from the United States; that I shall report at least every three months my whereabouts and activities as the above LEA shall require; that I understand I am subject to removal for any grounds of inadmissibility (conduct or condition) not disclosed at this time or for conduct committed after admission to the United States; that I shall abide by all conditions, limitations and restrictions imposed upon my entry; that the classification I seek is temporary and will terminate within three (3) years; that I am restricted by the terms of my admission to very specific means by which I will be able to remain permanently in the United States; that I will pay Social Security and all applicable taxes on all employment in the United States; and that I hereby waive my right to a removal hearing and to contest, other than on the basis of an application for withholding of removal, any action for deportation instituted against me.

Certification: I certify that I have read and understand all the questions and statements on this form. If I do not understand English, I further acknowledge that this has been read to me in a language I do understand. The answers I have furnished are true and correct to the best of my knowledge and belief.

_____   _____
Signature   Date *(mm/dd/yyyy)*

_____   _____   _____
LEA Witness   Title   Date *(mm/dd/yyyy)*

_____   _____   _____
Translator   Language Used   Date *(mm/dd/yyyy)*

2. LEA Certification.

I certify the above information is true and correct to the best of my knowledge; that I may make, have made, and will make no promises regarding the above alien's ability to adjust status or stay permanently in the United States other than those that comport with section 101(a)(15)(S) of the Act; that I will collect quarterly reports detailing the above alien's whereabouts and activities and forward required information to the Criminal Division; that I will immediately report to U.S. Immigration and Customs Enforcement, DHS if this alien fails to report quarterly or fails to comply or to cooperate with the terms and conditions of admission or if the alien commits any removable activity after the date of admission. I further certify that I assume complete law enforcement responsibility for control and continued stay in lawful status of the alien, including necessary monitoring, travel arrangements for arrival and departure, safety precautions and specified conditions of stay or departure; that I have provided a sworn declaration as to the basis of this application and checked all available database information on the above alien, and that I have carefully reviewed the above statements with the alien to ensure that all terms and conditions are understood.

☐ Translation. *(This serves to verify the alien's certification of translation. See **Page 2, Part B.1.** of this form.)*

_____   _____   _____
Signature of HQ Chief of LEA   Title of Certifier Date *(mm/dd/yyyy)*

_____   _____
Name of Agency Contact   Phone No. *(Including Area Code)*

Copyright ©2015. American Immigration Lawyers Association.

3. **For United States Attorney Use Only.** *(if applicable)*

Because the alien's presence is essential to the success of a Federal or State investigation or prosecution, the United States Attorney recommends the above request be granted and further certifies that there has not been and will not be any promises at all regarding the above alien's ability to adjust status or stay permanently in the United States, other than those that comport with section 101(a)(15)(S) of the Act.

_____   _____
Signature   Date *(mm/dd/yyyy)*

_____   _____
Office   Phone No.*(Including Area Code)*

4. **For U.S. Department of State/Rewards Committee - S6 Classification use only.**

After checking all information, the U.S. Department of State:

☐ Certifies the alien is eligible to receive an award under 22 U.S.C 2708(a).

☐ Certifies the alien is not eligible for such award.   Date *(mm/dd/yyyy)*

_____   _____   _____
Signature   Date *(mm/dd/yyyy)*   Phone No.*(Including Area Code)*

_____   _____
Title   Office

Part C. For Department of Justice, Criminal Division Use Only

After checking and evaluating all waiver and other information available, the Department of Homeland Security, U.S. Immigration and Customs Enforcement and Department of Justice, Criminal Division:

☐ Certify that, pursuant to section 101(a)(15)(S) of the Act and the request of the above LEA, the above alien is recommended for the S classification requested, that the above request(s) for waivers of inadmissibility appear to warrant approval, that all conditions and limitations of the request for classification are attached, that this request falls within the numerical limitation for an S visa and that, therefore, this request is forwarded to the Assistant Secretary of Immigration and Customs Enforcement for approval.

☐ Deny request.

_____   _____   _____
Signature   Date *(mm/dd/yyyy)*   Phone No.*(Including Area Code)*

_____   _____
Title   Office

Form I-854 (Rev. 05/13/10)Y Page 4

APPX. 12A • FORM I-854

Part D. For U.S. Immigration and Customs Enforcement Use Only

☐ Fee Received (If applicable). ☐ Request Denied. ☐ Request Granted

☐ Waiver(s) of Grounds of Inadmissibility.

Note all grounds waived and conditions attached thereto

_____ _____ _____
Signature   Date *(mm/dd/yyyy)* Phone No.*(Including Area Code)*

_____ _____
Title   Office

Part E. For U.S. Citizenship and Immigration Services Use Only

LEA Request: ☐ Granted. ☐ Forward to DOS/VO. ☐ Denied.

☐ Change of Classification Granted. ☐ Denied.

_____ _____ _____
Signature   Date *(mm/dd/yyyy)* Phone No.*(Including Area Code)*

_____ _____
Title   Office

Part F. For Department of State/Visa Office Use Only

☐ Forwarded to Consul by VO for Visa Approval. ☐ Not Forwarded.

_____ _____ _____
Signature   Date *(mm/dd/yyyy)* Phone No.*(Including Area Code)*

_____ _____
Title   Office

☐ Visa Granted.

☐ Visa Denied. Signature _____ Date *(mm/dd/yyyy)* _____

_____ _____
Title   Office

Form I-854 (Rev. 05/13/10)Y Page 5

Part G. Request to allow an S Nonimmigrant to file for adjustment of status to permanent resident.
(For Department of Justice, Criminal Division Use Only.)

(Please attach all relevant documentation establishing (1) the information certified below; (2) the recommendations and reasons for the certified recomendations.)

1. Name of LEA: _____ submitting request to allow an S nonimmigrant to file for adjustment of status.

   Date Submitted *(mm/dd/yyyy)* _____

2. **Criminal Division (Assistant Attorney General) Certifications.**

   I certify that (alien's name) _____ has -

   If S-5:
   ☐ Supplied the information that formed the basis of entry;

   ☐ The information substantially contributed to the success of an authorized criminal investigation or the prosecution of an individual as per terms of entry.

   If S-6:
   ☐ Supplied the information that formed the basis of entry;

   ☐ The information substantially contributed to the prevention or frustration of an act of terrorism against a U.S. person or property or the success of an authorized criminal investigaton of, or the prosecution of, an individual involved in such an act of terrorism.

   ☐ Has received a reward under section 36(a) of the State Department Basic Authorities Act of 1956;

   If S-5 or S-6:
   ☐ Has abided by all the terms, conditions and specific 22 U.S.C. 2708(a) limitations of the S classification.

   Other Comments:
   _____
   _____
   _____

   Signature _____ Date *(mm/dd/yyyy)* _____ Phone No. *(Including Area Code)* _____

   Title _____ Office _____

3. **For U.S. Citizenship and Immigration Services Use Only.**

   ☐ Adjustment.   ☐ Other Action.

   Signature _____ Date *(mm/dd/yyyy)* _____ Phone No. *(Including Area Code)* _____

   Title _____ Office _____

Form I-854 (Rev. 05/13/10)Y Page 6

APPENDIX 12B
FREEDOM OF INFORMATION ACT REQUEST

Southern Florida Chapter

South Florida Chapter
AMERICAN IMMIGRATION LAWYERS ASSOCIATION

July 1, 2013

PRESIDENT
Antonio G. Revilla III
Revilla Law Firm, P.A.
2250 SW 3rd Avenue, Suite 501
Miami, FL 33129
(305) 858-2323
arevilla@immigrationmiami.com

PRESIDENT-ELECT
Jacob Ratzan
jacob@ratzanlaw.com

1ST VICE PRESIDENT
Evan Shane
eshane@shanelaw.com

2ND VICE PRESIDENT
Andrea Martini
andrea@martini-legal.com

SECRETARY
Sui Chung
schung@lawgroupusa.com

TREASURER
Jeffrey A. Bernstein
jbmiamilaw@aol.com

BOARD OF DIRECTORS
Maggie Arias
Nicolas Olano
Roberto Ortiz
Jonathan Rose
Lizette Sierra
Michael Vastine
Matthew Weber
Xiomara M. Hernandez

FORMER PRESIDENTS
Karl Ann Fonte
John P. Pratt
Scott D. Devore
Stuart F. Karden
Linda Osberg-Braun
Lourdes Martinez Esquival
Anis Saleh
Jeffrey A. Devore
Maite Hoyos
Tim Murphy
Mary E. Kramer
Maria I. Casablanca
Michael D. Ray
Maya Chatterjea
Luis A. Cordero
Elaine F. Weiss
Tammy Fox-Isicoff
Mazen M. Sukkar
Larry S. Rifkin
Eugenio Hernandez
Sarah L. Tobocman
Barbara Warren
Joel Stewart
Michael Bander
David S. Berger
Michael Shane
Magda Montiel Davis
Phillip M. Zyne
Stephen E. Mander
Edward R. Shohat
Brian R. Hersh
Ira Kurzban
Michael Weiss
Donald Bierman
Oscar White
Neal Sonnet
Anastasios Notopoulus

FOUNDER
Charles B. Breslow
(1903-1978)

U.S. Immigration and Customs Enforcement
Freedom of Information Act Office
500 12th Street SW, Stop 5009
Washington, D.C. 20536-5009

RE: Request for Information pursuant to the Freedom of Information Act

Dear Sir or Madam:

The South Florida Chapter of the American Immigration Lawyers Association is comprised of over 650 attorneys. We are a voluntary bar association seeking to advance professionalism and knowledge of law among our members. We submit this request for the benefit of our members and the community.

Pursuant to the Freedom of Information Act, we are respectfully requesting statistics regarding "S" immigrant and nonimmigrant status. We are not requesting case specific information or names of particular individuals. We further note that this is non-classified information provided to Congress under INA § 214(k)(4).

Section 101(a)(15)(S) creates a nonimmigrant visa category for certain individuals who possess critical, reliable information and are working with law enforcement. Subsection (i) relates to approvals of status by the Attorney General and is limited to 200 persons per year. *See* INA § 214(k). Subsection (ii) relates to approvals by the Secretary of State and Attorney General, and is limited by statute to 50 approvals per year.

South Florida Chapter
AMERICAN IMMIGRATION LAWYERS ASSOCIATION

Please provide the following information with regard to principal "S" applicants only. We do not seek numbers regarding dependent family members.

(1) The number of "S" nonimmigrant applications submitted by law enforcement agencies, per year, since the 2007 fiscal year;

(2) The number of "S" nonimmigrant approvals, per year, since 2007, in both categories.

(3) The number of "S" nonimmigrant applications submitted by the Drug Enforcement Agency, per year, since 2007, and the number of approved applications from this group;

(4) The number of "S" nonimmigrant applications submitted by the Federal Bureau of Investigation, per year, since 2007, and the number of approved applications from this group;

(5) The number of "S" nonimmigrant applications submitted by Homeland Security Investigations, per year, since 2007, and the number of approved applications from this group.

(6) The number of "S" nonimmigrant applications submitted from some other federal LEA, other than DEA, FBI, or HSI, per year, since 2007, and the number of approved applications from this group.

(7) The number of "S" nonimmigrant applications submitted by a state entity, per year, since 2007, and the number of approved applications from this group.

(8) Based on the above statistics, please calculate and provide to AILA South Florida Chapter, the average processing time for an "S" nonimmigrant application.

In addition, section 245(j) of the INA allows for adjustment of status of "S" nonimmigrants to permanent residency.

South Florida Chapter
AMERICAN IMMIGRATION LAWYERS ASSOCIATION

(9) How many adjustment of status applications have been <u>submitted</u> for principal "S" applicants, per year, since the 2007 fiscal year? (We do not seek statistics on family members.)

(10) How many adjustment of status applications have been <u>approved</u> for principal "S" applicants, per year, since the year 2007. (We do not seek statistics on family members.)

Upon notification by the Department of Homeland Security, the AILA South Florida Chapter will be responsible for search, copying, and mailing fees associated with this request.

Thank you for your time and consideration given to this important matter.

Sincerely,

Antonio G. Revilla III, Esq.
President, AILA South Florida Chapter

U.S. Department of Homeland Security
National Records Center
P.O. Box 648010
Lee's Summit, MO 64064-8010

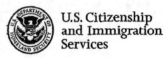

U.S. Citizenship
and Immigration
Services

January 21, 2014

COW2013000655

Antonio G. Revilla
AILA
2250 SW 3rd Ave., Suite 501
Miami, FL 33129

Dear Antonio G. Revilla:

This is in response to your Freedom of Information Act/Privacy Act (FOIA/PA) request which was initially submitted to Immigration and Customs Enforcement (ICE) and referred to our office (ICE referral number 2013FOIA25584) in which you seek data pertaining to S immigrant and nonimmigrant applications since the year 2007.

We have completed our search for records that are responsive to your request. The record consists of 3 pages of material and we have determined to release it in full.

Documents responsive to your request may contain discretionary releases of exempt information. If made, these releases are specifically identified in the responsive record. These discretionary releases do not waive our ability to invoke applicable FOIA exemptions for similar or related information in the future.

The National Records Center does not process petitions, applications or any other type of benefit under the Immigration and Nationality Act. If you have questions or wish to submit documentation relating to a matter pending with the bureau, you must address these issues with your nearest District Office.

All FOIA/PA related requests, including address changes, must be submitted in writing and be signed by the requester. Please include the control number listed above on all correspondence with this office. Requests may be mailed to the FOIA/PA Officer at the PO Box listed at the top of the letterhead, or sent by fax to (816) 350-5785. You may also submit FOIA/PA related requests to our e-mail address at uscis.foia@uscis.dhs.gov.

Sincerely,

Jill A. Eggleston
Director, FOIA Operations

www.uscis.gov

For **FY2007**:

In this year, the data collected only displays how many S-Visas were approved. The data does not display whether the individuals were principals or derivatives.

2007 Total S-Visa approvals: 44

For **FY2008**:

In this year, the data collected only displays how many S-Visas were approved. The data does not display whether the individuals were principals or derivatives.

The data does, however, display which Law Enforcement Agencies sponsored the S-Visa applicants.

Federal Bureau of Investigations (FBI): 7
Immigration and Customs Enforcement (ICE): 4
Drug Enforcement Agency (DEA): 7

2008 Total S-Visa approvals: 18

For **FY2009**:

Principal Approvals: 6

FBI: 1
ICE: 3
DEA: 2

For **FY2010**:

Principal Approvals: 2

FBI: 1
ICE: 1

For **FY2011**:

Principal Approvals: 62

FBI: 25
ICE: 17
DEA: 16
Internal Revenue Service (IRS): 1
Bureau of Alcohol, Tobacco, and Firearms (ATF): 2
U.S. Secret Service (USSS): 1

For **FY2012**:

Principal Approvals: 62

FBI: 24
ICE: 14
DEA: 20
IRS: 1
ATF: 2
State/Local: 1

For **FY2013**: 29

FBI: 6
ICE: 11
DEA: 12

S-Visa Adjustments by Year

FY2007 – 56
FY2008 – 39
FY2009 - 21
FY-2010- 46
FY-2011 – 54
FY2012 – 24
FY2013 – 6

Note: this information was collected for staffing purposes, not for official reporting.

Chapter Thirteen

Preparing and Presenting Applications That Waive a Criminal Conviction

Venues: Consulate, USCIS, ICE, and Immigration Court 640
The Universal List: Evidence in Support of a Waiver 644
Adjustment of Status 648
INA §212(h) Waivers—15-Year, Hardship, and Battered Spouse or Child 651
Refugee Waiver Under INA §209(c) 652
Waiver Under the Pre-AEDPA INA §212(c) (repealed in 1996) 654
Cancellation of Removal—INA §240A(a) 655
Special Rule Cancellation of Removal 656
Waiver Under INA §212(d)(3)(A) 657
Memoranda of Law and Witness Lists 659
Applications Filed After an Order of Removal 663

Appendix
    13A: Sample Respondent's Pretrial Statement 668

An intellectual man is a man who takes more words than necessary to tell more than he knows.

    —Dwight D. Eisenhower

    Good legal writing is a special talent. For some it's a gift—but for all lawyers, it is a skill that can be learned, developed, and nurtured for a lifetime. A persuasive legal writer will set forth key points and support for them in a concise yet creative manner. No one should have to read and re-read to understand the writer's message.

    The key to persuasive legal writing is to visualize one's reader, and bring the case to life for him or her with a clear explication of the facts combined with an accurate yet artful recitation of relevant law. Although as attorneys we will always rely on our own work—previous memoranda or motions in similar cases—unique, fresh thought is also required for each individual case; a reader's eye recognizes and quickly glosses over (or glazes over) cut-and-paste from a previous day, a previous client, last week's brief.

    Strong writing and presentation can make the difference in a winning application for relief or a waiver package before an embassy or U.S. Citizenship and Immigration Services (USCIS). Ultimately, every attorney will develop his or her own sense of style and philosophy when it comes to presenting a good memorandum or waiver package. This chapter offers some of the author's personal tips and strategies, but they are by no means the only way or even necessarily the best way, to an effective presentation.

This chapter provides practical advice and information on how to present the applications that waive a criminal conviction or convictions. This discussion may be basic for the experienced immigration law practitioner, but it is a good introduction for the beginning attorney, as well as for the criminal defense counsel who continues representation of the client through the course of immigration proceedings.

An individual with a criminal conviction may be seeking relief in several different venues. Waivers are filed with American consulates abroad, in front of USCIS, and in immigration court. Statutory requirements for the different forms of relief are discussed in detail in chapter ten. In comparison, this chapter is a nuts-and-bolts discussion of evidence and other basic filing requirements. Following coverage of venues, evidence, and the specific applications for relief, this chapter discusses legal memoranda, witnesses, and other litigation tips.

Because the criteria (and, hence, the types of evidence) used in waiver cases are similar (with a shifting focus on the priority of factors), this evidence discussion begins with a "universal list" of documents that should be considered for presentation—where available and relevant—in all types of discretionary relief cases. Following the universal evidence list is a discussion of the most frequently encountered applications—adjustment of status, the Immigration and Nationality Act (INA) §§212(h), 209(c), and 212(c) waivers, and cancellation of removal. If a certain type of evidence merits special focus, or there are distinct requirements, these nuances will be highlighted within the discussion of the specific application. Also discussed in this chapter are the Form I-212 application for permission to reapply for admission after removal, and the Form I-246 application for stay of deportation.

Venues: Consulate, USCIS, ICE, and Immigration Court

Waiver applications and other requests for discretionary relief may be heard in a variety of venues. Although the factors and relevant evidence, as determined by the regulations, case law, and facts of the particular case, are the same in all settings, there are nuances in *how* to present a waiver application in light of the setting.

An immigrant visa applicant who is physically abroad files a waiver with USCIS even though jurisdiction over the visa lies with the consulate. The consular officer may make a recommendation on the waiver, but it will ultimately be decided by USCIS. In other words, although the visa application falls under the broader jurisdiction of the U.S. Department of State (DOS), the discretionary waiver application is a component of the Department of Homeland Security (DHS). There are USCIS offices covering different regions abroad that adjudicate waivers for certain consulates within their designated area. In this situation, the applicant and family members probably will never have a meaningful face-to-face interview with the adjudicating officer. The attorney's written application, memoranda, and evidentiary package will present the relevant facts and law, and become the determining factor. Clearly, the attorney's creative presentation of the case is crucial: good, illustrative writing, legal analysis, and poignant documentation of hardship are a must. Specific examples of documentation are listed in the next section. The point is, for an application at the American consulate abroad, there is no testimony and no oral argument. Waivers will be decided based on paperwork alone.

An individual who is physically present in the United States, not in removal proceedings, and eligible for adjustment of status applies affirmatively for a waiver with either a regional service center or a local USCIS office. Regulations determine where an adjustment application is filed, and the instruction portion of the form will provide the correct office and address.[1] If the adjustment applicant has a conviction and requires a waiver, the waiver request accompanies the adjustment form. Note that INA §212(c) waivers, which are usually not filed in conjunction with affirmative adjustment applications, can be filed affirmatively with the local USCIS office.

Adjustment of status and waiver interviews at the local USCIS office are a step above (qualitatively speaking) the consulate scenario, but are still not evidentiary hearings. Again, testimony will not be taken during an interview at a local USCIS office (in the sense that there is no transcription). It is in the discretion of the interviewing officer whether to even informally discuss hardship, rehabilitation, and other important issues with the applicant and his or her family members. There will most likely be no formal record of an applicant's or family members' statements. A personal interview gives the chance to make a certain impression. This impression is formed in part by the attorney's statements and summary of the case; but again, although an officer may be swayed, no formal transcription of statements is made.

As is the case for the consulate venue, the evidentiary package, including detailed affidavits of affected family members and supporting memoranda of facts and law, are key to a successful waiver application in the context of an adjustment of status and waiver application filed with USCIS. The adjustment applicant and immediate family members who will attend the interview should nonetheless be prepared by counsel to offer a statement in support of the adjustment and/or waiver application, and answer possible, typical questions. Thus, in addition to preparing a compelling evidentiary package and legal memo, counsel should prepare clients to make a statement in support of the waiver and answer questions regarding the criminal activity as well as purported hardships and equities.

The waiver applicant in immigration court, in comparison with the above venues, is entitled to a full evidentiary hearing before an impartial judge. A waiver application will be filed in immigration court when the applicant is facing removal proceedings. Although certainly the documentary package filed in advance of the hearing is very important, a waiver case in immigration court involves oral testimony, and the judge's opportunity to meet the applicant and family members. Details of the case—including circumstances of the crime as well as personal equities—can be delved into.

---

[1] *See* 8 Code of Federal Regulations (CFR) §§103.2(a)(1), (6).

The applicant will testify in support of his or her application, and can have family members, friends, neighbors, and employers testify also. Indeed, expert witnesses, such as psychologists (testifying, *e.g.*, to psychological hardship to family members or the rehabilitation of the applicant), medical experts, experts on country conditions, and so on, can be called to testify in support of the application. For court cases, affidavits from persons of primary importance, such as the applicant, the spouse, children, and parents who are available to testify should probably not be submitted. Tactically, counsel risks the judge saying, "We do not need to hear from the respondent's mother because she submitted an affidavit." Furthermore, the written affidavit is only a potential source of conflict with oral testimony. The focus on oral testimony and, consequently, the advance preparation of witnesses is key in an immigration court setting.

Finally, certain applications for discretionary relief are filed (although rarely) with U.S. Immigration and Customs Enforcement (ICE) and U.S. Customs and Border Protection (CBP). Applications for a stay of deportation, voluntary departure, and deferred action are filed with ICE; an application for an INA §212(d)(3) waiver is filed with CBP (if the ground of inadmissibility is discovered on arrival at a port of entry).

Rules Regarding Biometrics Prior to Relief at Immigration Court

USCIS has been running biometric checks on all applicants for every type of benefit for several years now. The current fee is $85.[2]

In spring 2005, the requirement of a full background check through biometrics was applied (by regulation) to all applications presented to the immigration court.[3] Effective April 1, 2005, the regulations at 8 CFR Parts 1003, 208, and 1208 require that respondents in removal proceedings applying for most forms of relief (adjustment of status, waivers, cancellation of removal, asylum, etc.) present themselves for full biometrics: fingerprints, photos, and signature. If a respondent does not timely appear and provide biometric information, the application for relief may be deemed abandoned.[4] (There are exceptions for good cause shown.) In turn, USCIS runs full background checks, and the trial attorney (the assistant chief counsel of ICE) accesses the information in advance of the hearing. No application may be approved until background checks are complete. Where an individual is detained, DHS is responsible for obtaining biometrics information.[5]

> ➤ **Tip**: If the government is running a background check on the client, counsel should do the same. Private counsel can obtain fingerprints from the client and obtain a Federal Bureau of Investigation (FBI) "rap

---

[2] 8 CFR §103.7(b)(1).

[3] 70 Fed. Reg. 4743 (Jan. 31, 2005).

[4] 8 CFR §1003.47(c).

[5] 8 CFR §1003.47(d).

sheet" for a fee of $18. In this way, counsel has access to much (if not all—there are various types of background checks) of the information the government has. Counsel also can obtain a private background check through Accurint, a LEXIS-NEXIS product. For more information about investigative tools and techniques, see chapter 1.

> **Practice Pointer**: Counsel can avoid an erroneous finding that the application has been abandoned because of failure to provide biometrics. When a client presents him- or herself for printing and biometrics, the appointment notice is date-stamped. Counsel should advise the client to bring this date-stamped notice to court to establish that the client has complied with biometrics procedure.

In the past, fees for applications for relief were paid at the local USCIS cashier window and then the application was filed with the immigration court. Now, however, EOIR applications for waivers and other relief are mailed, along with the filing fee, to a USCIS regional service center.[6] The fee is collected and a receipt is mailed back to the client or the attorney. Several days to weeks later, the biometrics appointment for the particular application is mailed to the client or the attorney.

The biometrics process is imperfect and there is much room for error. Sometimes, appointments are not issued in time for the individual hearing. More frequently, biometrics "expire" (they are generally considered current for 18 months) and it can be difficult to get another appointment. Sometimes, the data obtained by USCIS are not properly entered into the system. Any error in the process can be interpreted as the individual's failure to comply with biometrics and result in the application being deemed abandoned. Some USCIS offices will resolve biometrics problems at an "InfoPass" appointment. InfoPass appointments are scheduled through the *https://infopass.uscis.gov* website, and are intended to allow checking on the status of a case or asking immigration-related questions.[7]

A biometrics "cover sheet" with mailing instructions is provided in open court by assistant chief counsel.[8] This instruction sheet is also available from the chief counsel's office. The cover sheet contains the address for the applicable service center, and it must accompany the application and fee.[9] Where the respondent is represented by counsel, the package must include a copy of the Form G-28, notice of appearance.

---

[6] For locations and addresses of regional service centers and local U.S. Citizenship and Immigration Services (USCIS) offices, see the USCIS website, *www.uscis.gov*.

[7] USCIS also has an online tool where you can submit a case status inquiry, *https://egov.uscis.gov/casestatus/landing.do*.

[8] The form is available at *www.uscis.gov/sites/default/files/files/article/PreOrderInstr.pdf*.

[9] Most applications have a requirement for an $85 biometrics fee. The exceptions are asylum/withholding (the I-589) and the INA §209(c) waiver (I-609).

The Universal List: Evidence in Support of a Waiver

The same basic themes run through all relief applications: the adjudicator, be it judge or officer, weighs the negative factors (the criminal offense and other negative issues of record) against the positive factors in the case. Relevant issues vary from case to case, but generally will include evidence of:

- Rehabilitation following commission of a crime;
- Strong family ties to the United States;
- Hardship to family members in the event of deportation (hardship may be financial, physical, or emotional);
- Significant medical issues, affecting either the applicant (client) or family members;
- Social, political, and economic conditions in the country of deportation;
- Solid employment history;
- Good tax filing record; and
- Contributions to the U.S. community (volunteer work and charity).

This universal list is not etched in granite. Every case is different, and counsel will determine strategically which issues and factors are most compelling for the particular client's case. A successful attorney will spend time talking personally with the client on different occasions to uncover relevant issues and "brainstorm" evidence. Although attorneys will utilize different practices, this author does not rely solely on support staff—and does not utilize a preprinted list—to cultivate relevant issues and delineate helpful documentation for a waiver case. Rather, because every client comes from a different situation and background, a list of evidence is generated through discussion (brainstorming) with the client about his or her personal life and background. Sample questions for this conversation might include:

- what led him or her to commit a crime (the circumstances);
- current personal relationships;
- employment history;
- education, including both educational background and academic goals;
- learning disabilities (of the client or a family member); and
- mental and physical health (of client and family members).

It should definitely include a discussion of the client's tax status (consistent and accurate tax returns are very important to both the immigration court and the Office of Chief Counsel). Another relevant topic of conversation is the situation in the home country; in addition to immediate and extended family ties in the United States, the attorney should know of the presence of family in the home country, and about those individuals' financial positions and living conditions.

For example, if a client's tax returns look dismal—or worse, suspicious—counsel may advise the client to correct them through filing amended returns, and not to present them unless required to do so. The following is presented as a guide to relevant points to cover in meeting and working with a client:

Evidence Relating to the Applicant

1. As discussed in chapter one, counsel should be sure to have complete conviction records. The burden of proving eligibility for a discretionary benefit, including waivers, rests with the applicant. Thus, USCIS requires that *certified* copies of the arrest report and final judgment with sentence be obtained by the applicant for affirmative adjustment of status. Often, USCIS will also request the charging document (*i.e.*, indictment or information). If a case is before the immigration court, the primary conviction records will most often be submitted by the office of chief counsel of ICE. However, if an individual has additional offenses that are not specifically charged, it is advisable to track down and present complete records to the court. If a document is no longer available because it has been lost, archived into a black hole, or otherwise destroyed, a letter from the clerk of courts and/or the police station verifying that the document is no longer available should be obtained. Records should be obtained for foreign convictions also.

> **Tip**: In an affirmative adjustment of status filing with USCIS, the office of adjudications will normally not track down records. The applicant for adjustment of status will be expected to account for every "hit" on the FBI record, or any other data source. For this reason, when there are multiple arrests, an attorney should consider obtaining an FBI rap sheet[10] before applying for adjustment—or at least before the final interview (to aid in obtaining a comprehensive list of arrests). If an applicant for adjustment does not provide records for each arrest (or a letter from the proper authority that no record is available), the adjustment application will be denied for "lack of prosecution."

2. Include any awards, certificates, and course diplomas earned while the client was in jail or prison (where relevant); disciplinary reports indicating good behavior; and letters or records from institutional officers and/or probation and parole officers, indicating good behavior and rehabilitation.

3. Elicit from the client his or her tax filing history (to show a good tax record). It is preferable to obtain a certified tax transcript from the Internal Revenue

---

[10] The Federal Bureau of Investigation (FBI) is a repository of information. An FBI rap sheet is usually an accurate list of arrests, but it is not perfect and counsel should never assume that it will provide a complete and accurate picture of the client's arrests [or the arrests of which the Department of Homeland Security (DHS) will be aware]. Experience shows that in rare instances, the FBI record will be affirmatively wrong, meaning it will assign criminal activity to the *wrong person*. In addition, some arrests will not show up on the FBI rap sheet. Finally, rap sheets often will not include disposition data; in other words, the arrest will be recorded, but the final disposition and sentence will not be indicated. Therefore, although ordering an FBI rap sheet is a prudent course of action, counsel should also utilize other sources of information such as clerk of court databases (which clerk of court will depend on the client's being forthcoming), and private databases.

Service (IRS), which can be ordered at any local IRS office. Recent-year filings can be obtained for free through the IRS website.[11]

4. Obtain a job letter to show gainful employment, if applicable.

5. Document evidence of charitable contributions or volunteer activity (service to the community).

6. Collect high school, post–high school course, and/or college diplomas, and any transcripts for ongoing coursework (if applicant is presently studying).

7. Prepare evidence of property ties, such as home ownership or business property owned.

8. Gather letters of recommendation if relevant and specific as to the applicant's character or good deeds. Letters of a generic nature are not useful. Letters or affidavits attesting to an applicant's good character should give the writer's name, immigration status, and address, but not phone numbers.

9. Detail special needs, such as medical or psychological, of the applicant. If the client has a compelling health situation, and records are not readily available or do not adequately explain the situation, the client should be referred for a professional evaluation.

> ➢ **Tip**: Medical or mental health evaluations can be difficult to obtain because they are not readily available, and may be financially prohibitive for the client. A good letter or evaluation is always the first and best choice to document a health situation. However if obtaining an evaluation is not feasible (or as supplementary evidence to the evaluation), the client can provide his or her prescriptions for medication. Then, through an Internet search or a good medical dictionary or encyclopedia, counsel can attach the written definition and usage of the medicine to a copy of the prescription(s).

10. Verify attendance and participation in Alcoholics Anonymous, Narcotics Anonymous, or other self-help groups, if relevant.

11. Prepare the applicant's own affidavit explaining the circumstances of his or her conviction, and indicate remorse and efforts toward rehabilitation. Be sure to highlight hardship to oneself and hardship to family members. *This should only be done when the case is not before the court.* For a case that will be heard in immigration court, there is no reason to attach the primary applicant/respondent's affidavit, because his or her testimony will be taken.

---

[11] Go to *www.irs.gov/Individuals/Get-Transcript*. There are instructions for obtaining older transcripts by mail order.

Evidence Relating to Family Members

1. Counsel should document the immigration status of all immediate family members legally present in the United States—spouse, children, parents, even siblings and grandchildren. Proof of citizenship can be U.S. passports, birth certificates, or naturalization certificates. For lawful permanent residents (LPRs), copy the LPR card or the residency stamp in the passport.

2. Gather health insurance documents for all family members (or at least children).

3. Evidence of child support for dependents who do not live in the applicant's household.

4. Highlight children's successes, such as good grades, certificates for good attendance, awards, and other certificates.

5. In the same vein, be sure to show evidence of learning disabilities or other academic problems that require special attention. This can take the form of evaluations, report cards, or letters from a school teacher, principal, or counselor.

6. Collect evidence of medical or emotional problems and/or other special needs of family members. This can take the form of medical records, a doctor's or therapist's letters or evaluations, or copies of prescriptions with accompanying explanations of the medication. Where a significant illness or disability does exist, consult the Internet or a good medical encyclopedia to provide a good definition of the condition.

7. Refine affidavits or letters from family members. These statements should be prepared in the individual's own words, but reviewed by counsel prior to submission. An outline of relevant factors may be provided by counsel as a guide, or counsel can interview the affiant personally and assist in preparing the statement. A family member's letter or affidavit should be *factual, detailed, and specific*—"He's a great Dad and I love him very much" is not as useful as:

> He helps me with my math homework and makes me dinner because Mom works at night. He taught me how to throw a curveball. He coaches the soccer team. He cooks spaghetti and meatballs, my favorite. There are some things I can only talk about with my Dad, and he is a good listener. I told him when the other kids in class were picking on me about my braces; I told him about my fear of taking tests. He always knows what to say and do to make me feel better about a situation.

As for an affidavit from a good friend:

> Marcus is my best friend. In 2003, after my divorce, Marcus came to the house to help me move out. He packed my possessions, moved them into the apartment, listened to my musings, and even lightened the day with jokes. That night, he took me out to Red Lobster. He paid. He listened to me analyze my failed marriage. He never criticized. When the bills were tight, he loaned me money. When my car broke down, he gave me his. The first Saturday that I had visitation with my two young girls, I felt so awkward. So

Marcus brought along his five-year-old daughter Jenny, and the two of them came along with my girls, and they really brightened the day. We went to the movies and out for ice cream. I feel like Marcus carried me through the most difficult period of my adult life. He is a very caring human being and outstanding, loyal friend.

8. Use evidence of country conditions when the country of removal is in dire straits or lacks basic facilities. Background country conditions are not just for asylum cases. When the waiver applicant and, by implication, his or her family, faces return to a country experiencing significant social, political, environmental, or economic problems, the information must be presented. Country condition information is easily obtainable through the Internet.[12] If the applicant has young children, focus on educational opportunities and the availability of health care. If the country has a poor women's rights record, including a history of harsh discrimination against women, this information should be emphasized.

9. Use photographs—*a picture paints a thousand words*. Both before the immigration court and USCIS (or an American consulate), counsel should not hesitate to begin the evidence package with school photos, family photos, and the like. Photographs make the case come alive. Photos should be clearly marked to show the names of people, the date, and the event. Do not overdo it. Fewer than 10 photos arranged as a collage on 8.5" x 11" paper should illustrate for the adjudicator that the case involves real people and real lives.

Adjustment of Status

Forms, Fees, and Attachments

An application for adjustment of status is filed on Form I-485. The filing fee is currently $985, with an additional fee of $85 for biometrics.[13] If the individual is qualifying for adjustment of status utilizing INA §245(i) [8 USC §1245(i)],[14] there is a supplemental form, the I-485A, and a fee (a fine) of $1,000. An application for adjustment of status must be accompanied by a biographic form, the G-325A,[15] which

---

[12] Excellent websites for country information are maintained by the U.S. Department of State at *www.state.gov/g/drl/hr/c1470.htm* and Amnesty International at *www.amnestyusa.org/annualreport*.

[13] 8 CFR §103.7(b)(1). Adjustment applicants under the age of 14 who are filing with a parent pay a filing fee of $635 and do not submit to biometrics. A child under the age of 14 who is not filing with at least one parent pays the fee of $985. Persons over 79 years old pay the full fee of $985 but do not pay for or submit to biometrics.

[14] Under INA §245(i), certain individuals who entered without inspection or as crewmen, or an individual in a preference category who is out of status, may apply for adjustment of status (avoiding consular processing) through payment of a fine of $1,000. Not everyone who would like to apply for adjustment of status is eligible under §245(i). This temporary provision of the law expired on April 30, 2001, and has not been renewed through legislation. The §245(i) mechanism is available to persons who filed a family petition or labor certification application on or before April 30, 2001.

[15] 8 CFR §245.2(a)(3)(i).

lists biographic data for the applicant. If an individual would like to apply for a work permit in conjunction with an application for adjustment of status, he or she should complete the work authorization application form, the I-765, and no filing fee is required, if submitted along with the I-485. Fees are paid by money order, cashier's check, or bank check, and are payable to the "U.S. Department of Homeland Security." An application for adjustment of status should be accompanied by two passport-style photos,[16] which can be attached to the G-325A biographic form. An adjustment application must be accompanied by the approved, underlying petition or be filed simultaneously with a petition (in the case of immediate relatives or an immediately available preference category). Adjustment applicants must have medical examinations, and the medical form (by an approved physician) should be filed with the application.

Where the adjustment of status is based on an already approved family– or employment-based petition, the approval notice should accompany the application. In certain cases, the Form I-130 (Petition for Alien Relative) or Form I-140 (Immigrant Petition for Alien Worker) petition can be filed concurrently with the adjustment application.[17] Certain adjustment of status applications do not depend on a petition; these include, but are not limited to, applications under the Cuban Adjustment Act, asylee and refugee adjustments, and nationality-based legalization programs. In certain circumstances (such as *all* family-based adjustments), an affidavit of financial support signed by the petitioner must accompany the application. An affidavit of support is not required in most employment-based cases, asylee and refugee cases, and in nationality-based, legalization-type adjustments. An affidavit of support is also not required in the case of a special immigrant self-petition (*e.g.*, a battered or abused spouse case).

When an individual is in removal proceedings, the application for adjustment of status is filed with the court (*after* sending the fee and a copy of the application to the designated USCIS service center, and obtaining a receipt, as discussed above). When the adjustment of status applicant is not in proceedings, the filing address varies according to the basis for filing and other factors. The correct address can be found at *www.uscis.gov/i-485-addresses*.

An in-depth discussion of adjustment of status is beyond the scope of this book. The focus here is on how to present an application for adjustment of status with an eye on waiving a criminal offense—again, often in conjunction with a waiver application.[18] In addition, the adjustment of status application form contains instructions

---

[16] Resident-type photos are the same as passport photos; the front-facing photo is utilized for all immigration applications.

[17] 8 CFR §245.2(a)(2)(i).

[18] For a more definitive discussion of adjustment of status, including the underlying statutory categories and their requirements, see "Adjustment of Status for Beginning Practitioners" in AILA's *Navigating the Fundamentals of Immigration Law* (updated annually). Also see the articles on adjustment of status

Continued

for different types of eligibility categories, and the regulations provide specific instructions at 8 CFR Parts 245 and 1245.

When Filing with the Court

The original adjustment application (Form I-485) *and a copy* of the Form G-325A are filed with the immigration court. A copy of the Form I-485 and the *original* Form G-325A are filed with the Office of Chief Counsel of ICE. A copy is retained for the client's file; it should be date-stamped to prove filing by both the court and DHS. (These documents can be mailed or sent by courier for persons living out of the local area). The application must contain a certificate of service establishing service on chief counsel. Review information on filing fees, above.

Adjustment Is Discretionary

Adjustment of status is in most, but not all, cases a discretionary form of relief. In family– and employment-based cases, adjustment of status is a discretionary benefit; the same holds true for adjustment under the Cuban Adjustment Act. However, certain applications for adjustment of status are not granted in the discretion of the government, but are mandatory if the statutory requirements are met. These include, but are not limited to, asylee and refugee adjustments under INA §209 [8 USC §1159], and certain nationality-based legalization programs such as §202 of the Nicaraguan Adjustment and Central American Relief Act,[19] and the Haitian Refugee Immigration Fairness Act of 1998.[20] Note that if a waiver is required to accompany the application for adjustment (such as an INA §209(c) waiver for asylees and refugees or an INA §212(h) waiver), approval of the waiver is a discretionary measure.

Where adjustment of status is *not* a discretionary benefit but "shall be" granted if the underlying requirements are met, it is not necessary to present equitable documentation in support of a favorable exercise of discretion. This situation would arise (albeit rarely) where the adjustment is waiving a firearms offense or an aggravated felony that is *not* also a ground of inadmissibility, *and* the adjustment of status is filed by an asylee, a refugee, or under a nationality-based legalization program that is not discretionary.

In most cases, however, adjustment of status is a discretionary benefit that can be denied based on a criminal record.[21] In these situations, the adjustment of status case takes on the characteristics of a waiver application and the favorable exercise of discretion must be earned.

---

in each annual edition of AILA's *Immigration Practice Pointers*. These publications are available for purchase at *agora.aila.org* and are available on AILALink.

[19] Pub. L. No. 105-100, tit. II, §202, 111 Stat. 2160, 2193–96 (1997).

[20] Pub. L. No. 105-277, div. A, §101(h), tit. IX (secs. 901–04), 112 Stat. 2681, 2681-538 to 2681-542.

[21] Chapter ten discusses the meaning of the term "discretion" in the context of adjustment of status.

INA §212(h) Waivers—15-Year, Hardship, and Battered Spouse or Child

Form and Fee

An application for waiver under INA §212(h) [8 USC §1182(h)] is filed on Form I-601. The waiver application normally will (but not always) accompany the adjustment application.[22] The waiver application can also be filed at the time of the interview with USCIS, in which case the fee will be paid at the local USCIS office's cashier window. As for immigration court cases, it is recommended that the waiver application be filed personally with the immigration court clerk, but it can be mailed in. There is a fee of $585,[23] (plus an $85 biometrics fee for those in proceedings), which can be paid by check or money order, payable to the "U.S. Department of Homeland Security."

A waiver application under INA §212(h)(1)(B) that is based on extreme hardship to a family member (as opposed to the 15-year waiver under §212(h)(1)(A)) must be accompanied by proof of a qualifying family member. This may be the parent's resident card or naturalization certificate, a child's U.S. birth certificate or resident card, or a spouse's resident card, birth certificate, naturalization certificate, or other evidentiary document. Of course, a U.S. passport is acceptable proof of citizenship in lieu of a naturalization certificate.

When Filing with the Immigration Court

If filed as a defense to removal before an immigration judge (IJ), I-601 is submitted according to the pre-order instructions (available at *www.uscis.gov/sites/default/files/files/article/PreOrderInstr.pdf*). The original I-601 is filed with the court, and a copy goes to the office of chief counsel. Counsel should retain a third copy, obviously, for the client's file, date stamped by both the court and chief counsel. The application must be accompanied by a certificate of service on chief counsel. Supporting documents should be fastened behind the application, via a two-hole punch and clip at the top, and indexed, paginated, and tabbed (according to local court rules, if applicable).

Emphasis on Hardship to Family Members

As discussed in chapter ten, the primary focus in an INA §212(h) waiver is hardship to family members—extreme hardship. Qualifying family members include a U.S. citizen or LPR spouse, parent, or child (including an unmarried adult son or daughter). Note that hardship to family members is not required if 15 years or more

---

[22] With USCIS, in the situation where inadmissibility is contested, the waiver application would not be filed until the adjudicator makes a finding of inadmissibility and it is determined that a waiver is necessary. Filing an I-601 waiver in advance of a finding where there is a contestable issue could be a tactical and legal error. In comparison, in front of the immigration court, it is a good idea to file the application for relief and clarify that the filing is in the alternative to legal arguments contesting removability

[23] 8 CFR §103.7(b)(1).

have passed since commission of the offense. On the other hand, in the case of a "violent or dangerous" crime, the regulation requires exceptional and extremely unusual hardship to a qualifying relative and/or the applicant.[24]

The documentation presented in a §212(h) case should emphasize medical, educational, economic, and emotional hardships. Also of significance are conditions in the home country. There is a tendency in these cases to stress economic hardship, because it will often be the most obvious issue. However, economic hardship, standing alone, will not carry the day. It is recommended that counsel dig deep to uncover educational issues for children—any disabilities or academic gifts—and juxtapose the resources available in the United States with the educational opportunities and resources available in the country of deportation. (This angle may not work if deportation is to Canada or another developed nation—unless there is a longstanding relationship with a psychologist or medical specialist that should not be interrupted.)

In addition, if a family member exhibits signs of extreme anxiety—even depression—at the prospect of deportation, get a thorough psychological evaluation that documents his or her emotional stress. Certainly, every possible piece of documentation in support of medical hardship must be presented; then, a nexus should be drawn between the medical hardship and the applicant's continued presence in the United States (health insurance is available through applicant's employment; applicant participates in the physical therapy sessions; applicant injects the insulin shots, etc.). Creativity and doggedness are required in showing extreme hardship, especially in working with U.S. consulates abroad. The consular officers and the USCIS offices abroad that determine these applications are not easily persuaded.

Discretion Must Be Warranted, Notwithstanding Hardship

Even though the primary emphasis in an INA §212(h) waiver is hardship to the qualifying relatives, the waiver can still be denied (although hardship is established) if the applicant does not merit a favorable exercise of discretion. For this reason, documents from the "universal list" that relate to the applicant are still necessary, just moved toward the back of the index. The §212(h) waiver can be thought of as a two-step process: first, extreme hardship to family must be established; and second, the applicant must establish that he or she merits a favorable exercise of discretion. This second step is accomplished through proof of rehabilitation, contributions to the community, a good employment record, etc. Health problems of the applicant also may be considered here.

Refugee Waiver Under INA §209(c)

Refugees and asylees who have been in the United States for one year or longer may file for adjustment of status by mailing the Form I-485 to either the Phoenix or

---

[24] 8 CFR §212.7(d).

Dallas lockbox.[25] If a refugee or asylee also requires an INA §209(c) waiver, it is filed on Form I-602. Note that there is *no fee* for the Form I-602 refugee waiver.

According to a 2005 USCIS memorandum from the acting director of domestic operations to all regional service centers, the applicant for a waiver of inadmissibility under INA §209(c) need not file the actual Form I-602.[26] According to the memorandum, the service center directors have the discretion to grant a waiver under INA §209(c) to waive the ground or grounds of inadmissibility where: (1) there are no negative factors in the case; and (2) sufficient information already is in the file. The memorandum notes that grounds of inadmissibility under INA §§212(a)(6)(A)(i)[27] and 212(a)(9)(B)[28] are the most typical grounds that may be waived without use of the actual form. In light of the fact that the I-602 is a relatively short application form and there is no fee required, it is recommended that the form be sent with the I-485 adjustment application in spite of USCIS's stated policy that the form is not required in every case. In this way, the record will be clear that a waiver was requested and granted in advance of the adjustment being approved.

For those cases involving negative factors, and especially when the ground of inadmissibility is based on crime, a quality waiver package with a memorandum is recommended. The "universal list," enumerated above, applies here. If the conviction is for a nonviolent crime, a focus on hardship to qualifying relatives is not required. If the conviction is for a violent crime, case law requires a showing of exceptional hardship.[29] Evidence should be indexed, but not tabbed on the side; use evidence stickers fastened directly on the document or separate documents with colored paper. (This is because the service centers, unlike IJs, often immediately discard tabs filed on the side.) If a §209 adjustment applicant has a criminal record and needs a waiver, the case will most likely be forwarded to the local USCIS office of adjudications for a personal interview (unless the matter falls under the petty-offense exception or is relatively minor). The evidence package can be updated at the time of the personal interview. If USCIS denies the adjustment and waiver because of the conviction, the applications can be renewed before an IJ.

---

[25] For further details, see the discussion on adjustment earlier in this chapter.

[26] USCIS Memorandum, M. Aytes, "Waivers under Section 209(c) of the INA" (Oct. 31, 2005), *published on* AILA InfoNet at Doc. No. 05110962 (*posted* Nov. 9, 2005). This memorandum is informative and it is recommended that the practitioner review it prior to filing a waiver request.

[27] Fraud or material misrepresentation at entry or in the application for a visa.

[28] Unlawful presence.

[29] See the discussion at chapter ten.

Waiver Under the Pre-AEDPA INA §212(c) (repealed in 1996)

Form and Fee

A waiver under INA §212(c) [8 USC §1182(c)] is filed on Form I-191 and carries a fee of $585[30] (plus an $85 biometrics fee for those in proceedings), which can be paid by check or money order to the "U.S. Department of Homeland Security." As noted in the section above on adjustment of status, fees for court cases must be sent by mail to USCIS. The immigration courts do not accept filing fees. If the application is being affirmatively filed (*i.e.*, with USCIS, and not the immigration court), the form instructions say the form must be mailed to one of the USCIS Texas Service Center facility:

> For U.S. Postal Service (USPS) deliveries, use:
> USCIS
> Texas Service Center
> P.O. Box 850965 Dallas, TX 75185
>
> For Express mail and courier deliveries, use:
> USCIS
> Texas Service Center
> 4141 N. St. Augustine Road
> Dallas, TX 75227

When Filing with the Immigration Court

When applying for an INA §212(c) waiver in removal proceedings, counsel should "fee in" the I-191 with USCIS (not the immigration court) according to the preorder instructions (available at *www.uscis.gov/sites/default/files/files/article/PreOrderInstr.pdf*.) File the original application with the immigration court, serve a copy on the office of chief counsel for ICE, and retain a copy for the client's file. Supporting documentation should be organized with an index and tabs, and attached directly to the application by two-hole punch. Follow any local rules for the filing of evidence (the type of tabs, pagination, etc.).

Emphasis on Unrelinquished Domicile; All Equities Are Relevant

An INA §212(c) waiver requires establishing a minimum of seven years' unrelinquished domicile in the United States. It is important to establish continuous domicile through tax records, property records, utility bills, driver's license records, etc. Where the applicant has not traveled frequently outside the United States, domicile should not be a major point of contention. However, if the applicant has spent a continuous period of six months or more outside of the United States at any one time, the gov-

---

[30] 8 CFR §103.7(b)(1).

ernment may allege abandonment, so it is incumbent on counsel to establish that the applicant maintained a lawful domicile in the United States.

Cannot have served five years in prison for an aggravated felony or felonies

As discussed in chapter ten, an applicant for an INA §212(c) waiver who has served five or more years in prison for an aggravated felony or felonies is ineligible for the waiver. The exception to this rule is if the conviction was entered before November 29, 1990. For convictions preceding this effective date of the Immigration Act of 1990,[31] the time spent in prison is not relevant to statutory eligibility. Where a client's period of time in incarceration approaches the five-year mark, counsel should be prepared to document the actual time spent in prison to establish statutory eligibility. (The client may possess his or her prison record; otherwise, contact the actual institution or the parole office to inquire as to where and how to request a record of time served.)

A balancing of the equities

In *Matter of Marin*,[32] the Board of Immigration Appeals (BIA) set forth the relevant factors for consideration in an INA §212(c) case. These include proof of rehabilitation, family ties, length of residency in the United States, service in the armed forces, property ties, employment history, a history of service to the community, etc. If the criminal offense was a serious crime, such as trafficking in a controlled substance, it is necessary to demonstrate unusual and outstanding equities.[33] The pretrial memorandum, and presentation of evidence, should focus on the standard involved in the particular case.

Cancellation of Removal—INA §240A(a)

Form and Fee

The application for cancellation of removal of a permanent resident is filed on Form EOIR-42A. Counsel should be sure that the right application form is in hand, since there are three cancellation-type applications that are similar in appearance. Look for the title "Application for Cancellation of Removal For Certain Permanent Residents" on the top of the form. (The other forms relate to nonpermanent residents and are not criminal waivers.) The filing fee is $100,[34] plus a biometrics fee of $85, which must be paid by cashier's check, money order, or bank check, by mail to USCIS (not the immigration court) according to the preorder instructions (available at

---

[31] Immigration Act of 1990, Pub. L. No. 101-649, 104 Stat. 4978.

[32] *Matter of Marin*, 16 I&N Dec. 581 (BIA 1978).

[33] *Matter of Buscemi*, 19 I&N Dec. 628 (BIA 1988), *clarified by Matter of Edwards*, 20 I&N Dec. 191 (BIA 1990) (holding that a clear showing of reformation is not an absolute prerequisite to a favorable exercise of discretion in every §212(c) application involving an alien with a criminal record; rehabilitation is a factor for consideration).

[34] 8 CFR §1103.7(b)(4)(i).

www.uscis.gov/sites/default/files/files/article/PreOrderInstr.pdf) before filing with the immigration court. The check may be made out to "U.S. Department of Homeland Security."

Filing with the Immigration Court

Unlike the other applications discussed above, an application for cancellation of removal is filed *only* with the court, because jurisdiction lies with the IJ in the course of removal proceedings. The original application is filed with the court, with proof of service on the Office of Chief Counsel for ICE. Counsel should, of course, retain a copy for the applicant's file.

Emphasis on Residency Requirements; All Equities Apply

There are two distinct "residency" requirements involved in cancellation of removal. First, the applicant must establish a continuous residence in the United States of at least seven years following a lawful admission. Second, the applicant must establish at least five years of LPR status. These two requirements are discussed in detail in chapter ten. For purposes of presenting an evidentiary package, counsel should recall that the minimum seven-year continuous residency tolls upon the commission of a criminal offense that is a ground of inadmissibility. Therefore, it is important to establish at least seven years of ongoing residence (following a lawful admission) prior to commission of the crime. An ongoing residence can be established in a variety of ways, including tax records, employment records, school records, utility bills, and the like.

A balancing of the equities

Upon establishing the residency requirements for cancellation, the IJ is charged with balancing the favorable factors of record against the negative factors, including the criminal conviction. The BIA has held in *Matter of C–V–T–*[35] that the same balancing test and factors delineated in *Matter of Marin*[36] for the INA §212(c) cases apply to cancellation of removal applications.

Special Rule Cancellation of Removal

Form and Fee

Special rule cancellation of removal is filed on Form I-881. It may be filed affirmatively with a regional service center (see the instructions on the form for the proper filing location) or with the immigration court in removal proceedings. The fee for an affirmative filing is $285 ($570 for a family). If filing with the immigration court, the fee is $165, plus the $85 biometrics fee,[37] mailed to USCIS (not the immigration

---

[35] *Matter of C–V–T–*, 22 I&N Dec. 7 (BIA 1998).

[36] *Matter of Marin*, 16 I&N Dec. 581 (BIA 1978).

[37] 8 CFR §103.7(b)(1). For further fee information, see the instructions to Form I-881.

court) according to the preorder instructions (available at *www.uscis.gov/sites/ default/files/files/article/PreOrderInstr.pdf*)

Supporting Documents

Special rule cancellation of removal in the criminal-alien context requires a showing of at least 10 years of physical presence in the United States, coupled with good moral character, since commission of the criminal act.[38] It is recommended that tax returns, job letters, driver's license records, bills, leases, and records of property ownership be submitted to establish the necessary physical residency. Special rule cancellation is only available to certain nationals who entered before a specific date and applied for asylum, temporary protected status, or *ABC* benefits.[39] In order to prevail, evidence must be submitted to establish exceptional and extremely unusual hardship to either a qualifying immediate family member or the applicant him- or herself.[40]

Waiver Under INA §212(d)(3)(A)

Form and Fee

Where the INA §212(d)(3)(A) waiver request is presented at a U.S. consulate office abroad, there is no actual form. Rather, the request is made in writing (with supporting documents). No fee is required.[41]

Where the §212(d)(3)(A) waiver request is presented at a port of entry, the form number is I-192, Application for Advance Permission to Enter as Nonimmigrant [Pursuant to Section 212(d)(3) of the Immigration and Nationality Act].[42] The form is filed in duplicate and has a fee of $585.[43]

Information Required

For applications filed with a consular office, the regulations set forth the criteria to be considered as follows:

- The reason(s) for inadmissibility, and each section of law under which the individual is inadmissible;
- Each intended date of arrival;
- The length of each proposed stay in the United States;
- The purpose of each stay;

---

[38] 8 CFR §§240.66(c), 1240.66(c).

[39] *See* chapter ten.

[40] 8 CFR §§240.66(c)(4), 1240.66(c)(4).

[41] 8 CFR §§212.4(a)(1), 1212.4(a)(1); 22 CFR §41.95.

[42] 8 CFR §§212.4(b), 1212.4(b).

[43] 8 CFR §103.7(b)(1). If applying with U.S. Customs and Border Protection (CBP): make the check or money order payable to U.S. Customs and Border Protection.

- The number of entries that the alien intends to make; and
- The justification for exercising authority under INA §212(d)(3)(B).[44]

It is recommended that an attorney's memorandum cover the above criteria, and contain supporting documentation as well.

For applications filed at a port of entry, the regulation requires a statement as to the following:

- The immigration law designation of each crime;
- The dates of commission and conviction of each crime; and
- The sentence and judgment of each crime.[45]

The regulation further states that the waiver application must be accompanied by relevant criminal records. If the waiver application is made at the time of arrival at a port of entry, the applicant must establish that he or she was not aware of the ground of inadmissibility and could not, through reasonable diligence, have ascertained the existence of the ground of inadmissibility. (If there is a criminal conviction, it is important to submit the application in advance of arrival, since one would be hard pressed to assert that one did not know about a conviction.)

It is recommended, when presenting §212(d)(3)(A) waiver requests, that relevant documents from the "universal" list be utilized. Because rehabilitation (*i.e.*, a clean record) over previous several years is key, it is important to document employment, residence, and good moral character through reference letters, employment letters, clearance letters, and the like. It is furthermore important to clarify the purpose and length of proposed travel.

Contacting LegalNet for Assistance When Consul Declines to Accept Waiver

According to 22 CFR §40.301(a), where a nonimmigrant visa applicant who is inadmissible requests a waiver under INA §212(d)(3)(A), the consular officer must transmit the request to DHS-CBP, specifically the Admissibility Review Office, or "ARO", with a recommendation. Experience shows that sometimes the consulate is either unfamiliar with the waiver procedure, or unwilling to accept and process the waiver. Yet 22 CFR §40.301 indicates that the consulate must process the waiver request by forwarding same to DHS-CBP. In the event that a consulate is unwilling to receive a waiver package—or seems unknowledgeable about the process and therefore declines—counsel may contact the State Department Advisory Opinions Office through Legal Net at *LegalNet@state.gov*. The consulate does not have the discretion to refuse an application for a waiver.

---

[44] 8 CFR §§212.4(a)(1), 1212.4(a)(1).
[45] 8 CFR §§212.4(b), 1212.4(b).

Memoranda of Law and Witness Lists

It is the author's opinion that waiver cases are, in many instances, won before an applicant ever steps into an adjudicator's office or the immigration courtroom. The critical aspect of high-quality representation (as opposed to a nonlawyer's typed-up form and photocopied paperwork) lies in the legal argument presented, including the artful presentation of compelling personal facts. For this reason, creative brainstorming of relevant documentation, combined with a well-written memorandum, is pivotal to a successful waiver application. This is where an attorney's skills will shine. Counsel should not leave preparation of pretrial memoranda to a paralegal or secretary. In addition, organizing one's case through preparation of evidence and writing a memorandum force the attorney to be aware of the specific details of the case in advance of the interview or hearing.

Before USCIS or American Consulate

The above heading is a bit of a misnomer. Persons who apply for adjustment of status and a waiver do so in front of the local USCIS office. Persons applying for an immigrant visa abroad physically present the applications to a consular officer in the U.S. embassy or consular post, but the waiver application is forwarded to (and decided by) a USCIS officer in a regional office. In cases of adjustment of status, the adjudicator will meet the applicant face-to-face, and probably also the spouse, but will not meet other family members—even though their hardships may be relevant to the case. In consulate filings, the ultimate adjudicator will never meet any of the individuals involved. In both cases, because of the limited interaction, counsel should prepare an evidentiary package and memorandum that literally leap off the page and touch the heart of the adjudicator. Specific, personal details (not, "I love my Dad") should be emphasized here (hence, the use of family photos). An illustration of relevant facts should be supported by relevant case law.

Counsel should put him- or herself in the shoes of the adjudicator: if he or she adjudicated hundreds of discretionary cases a month, what would catch the eye and capture the interest?

A well-written memorandum of facts and law is counsel's only forum before an officer—the only chance to get in front of the adjudicator and advocate for the cause. It is the author's advice to keep it short and to the point; make it well-written and *avoid boilerplate* legal argument. (The reader will recognize it as boilerplate, and will not be impressed.)

A supporting memorandum for USCIS can follow an informal, abbreviated legal brief format:

- A statement of the case or introduction.
- A statement of the facts, highlighting particularly important issues and citing to pieces of evidence that are tabbed as exhibits. If family members or friends have submitted letters or affidavits, cite to one or two key quotations, perhaps in an indented and justified fashion.

- A statement of relevant law. (Again, a memo should be short and to the point; boilerplate legal argument and regurgitating canned phrases from case law is not persuasive.) Where helpful, counsel can juxtapose the facts of a particular precedent case with the facts of the case at hand (for example, if the burden was met in X–Y–Z–, it is certainly met here).
- A conclusion.
    > Tip: As a practical matter, the application should go on top, with the legal memorandum directly below, and the tabbed evidence below the memorandum. This package can be two-hole punched and clipped on top, and also stapled in its entirety. In this way, the application will not become separated from the evidence and memorandum. (This is a common occurrence, unfortunately, with government agencies, where the package may be shipped from one place to another.)

Pretrial Statements to the Immigration Court

Some judges require a pretrial statement, and many local rules of the court require advanced submission of evidence and a witness list. The Executive Office for Immigration Review (EOIR)'s standard rules, including filing deadlines, are contained in the *Immigration Court Practice Manual*.[46]

There is a difference of opinion among immigration law practitioners as to whether a pretrial statement is a good strategy in immigration court cases. Some well-respected attorneys believe it is a misstep to advise ICE chief counsel of negative issues in advance—in other words, to give the case away (tip one's hat) in advance of the trial. There are judges who are not persuaded by an attorney's "testimonial" and will simply want to hear the case. Some attorneys believe a thorough and detailed index, or table of contents, describing the evidence may serve the purpose of a pretrial statement.

This author always prepares and files a short pretrial statement—even in the most noncontroversial cases—for several reasons. However, every attorney has a different approach and style, and each case presents a unique set of legal and factual circumstances. Professional strategies may vary.

First, a pretrial statement forces the attorney to learn the case (its issues and its drawbacks) in advance.

Second, most judges will appreciate a short recitation of the relevant facts and applicable law, including a list or chart of the crimes and their consequences, as well as relevant country condition facts. A pretrial statement can refer to the language of the hearing, and will note that biometrics are up-to-date. Providing these details is a common courtesy to the court.

---

[46] The rules of the immigration courts are available at *www.justice.gov/eoir/office-chief-immigration-judge-0*.

Third, via the pretrial statement, counsel is off to an early start convincing the judge with words (and supporting documentation) that the client merits a favorable exercise of discretion.

Fourth, pretrial statements offer an element of control. In the pretrial statement, counsel can bring forth negative information (and mitigating circumstances) in advance, thereby taking some of the pressure off the chief counsel's cross-examination and rebuttal argument. In the same way, legal issues can be raised and argued in the client's favor in writing, thereby minimizing or even avoiding oral argument in the courtroom. A pretrial statement puts counsel firmly in control of the direction of the case by laying out the parameters and covering relevant facts and legal issues in advance.

Again, a pretrial statement is not a requirement of EOIR rules; unless ordered by the court, it is in the discretion of the attorney. A pretrial statement can follow any format with which the attorney is comfortable (unless there are local court rules that dictate a specific format). The informal brief method, mentioned above, is appropriate for court, too.[47] The following is a roadmap of a pretrial statement:

- A statement of the case: The master calendar was heard on _____. At that time, the respondent admitted/conceded/denied the charges under _____. An application for relief was timely filed on _____. This matter is set for an individual hearing on the application for (cancellation of removal/adjustment of status/§212(h) waiver, etc.) on _____.
- A statement of the facts, including statutory eligibility for relief, equities, hardships, and, where relevant, adverse country conditions.
- A short statement of the law. Unless it is a complicated case with contested legal issues, or presents an unusual or novel question of law, it is this author's advice to keep the statement of the law short; the IJs know the basic law. Counsel will remember that the purpose of the pretrial statement is to give the court a general overview of the case in an easily readable fashion. The pretrial statement will often be read in chambers in a few minutes before court, or the afternoon before.
- Conclusion.

Witnesses

Witness list

As a separate document, or incorporated within the pretrial statement, a witness list is advisable (and it may be required by immigration court local rules). The witness list should cite the individual's name, immigration status, relationship to the respondent, and a very brief and general description of the testimony to be given.

---

[47] To avoid a client being cross-examined on the contents of the pretrial statement, the opening paragraph should include a disclaimer that the statement is submitted as counsel's opening remarks, and represent counsel's understanding of the case, but should not be viewed or received as "evidence."

Choosing witnesses

A variety of issues are relevant in choosing witnesses. First, the witnesses who testify in support of an application should be either close family members who are directly affected by the respondent's removal or close friends or colleagues who can impart unique and compelling information on behalf of the respondent. Second, chosen witnesses should be well-spoken (at least compared with other candidates) and have clean records themselves. (A character witness with a conviction record is not of much use to the case.) Avoid duplication of testimony; the court may not allow duplicative testimony, anyway. Counsel also should remember the importance of having individuals sitting in the courtroom—friends or relatives of the respondent—who are not going to testify, but want to be present and show their support. Individuals who attend the hearing and remain seated in the courtroom throughout the proceeding can be introduced to the IJ at the beginning of the hearing.

Working with witnesses

It is recommended that no one be allowed to testify in court unless counsel has met with him or her in advance.

Counsel must work with the witnesses to make sure they understand how to dress and present themselves. Counsel should practice the oath and explain sequestration. Counsel can go over questions with witnesses, both direct and cross, and ensure that the witness understands that different questions can be asked and that it is impossible to know with certainty what to expect.

Because of the rule of sequestration, counsel should attempt to bring witnesses together in one setting in advance of the hearing to go over relevant issues and possible testimony. In other words, in counsel's own office, the witnesses should be brought together for preparation, so that they can identify possible inconsistencies, and have knowledge of what the other witnesses will testify to. At this meeting, counsel should ensure that each witness (with the exception, perhaps, of small children) is aware of the client's criminal conduct and the reasons for removal proceedings. It is widely understood that if a close family member or character witness does not know that the respondent has been arrested and convicted of a criminal offense, rehabilitation cannot be shown (based on the theory that the respondent has not "come clean" with his or her closest supporters).

> Tip: Common witness traps to avoid:
>
> #1 "You mean he's never told you what he did? You don't even know why we're here?"
>
> #2 "You, Mr./Ms. Witness, have been arrested and done time for assault and battery?"

Details: The time and place of hearing, the need for an interpreter

Counsel should ascertain if a particular witness requires the assistance of an interpreter. The court will provide an interpreter free of charge, but the court administrator must be advised in advance. (This will not be an issue where the respondent speaks the same foreign language, and an interpreter has already been assigned for that purpose.) Counsel should ensure that witnesses know the location of the courtroom, the name of the judge, and the time of the hearing. Counsel should dissuade the principal respondent from playing chauffeur to a company of witnesses. The respondent needs to be focused on arriving at court on time without regard to the witnesses' arrivals.

Conclusion

Hearings will go more smoothly, and the applicant is more likely to prevail on the application for relief, where the evidence has been thoughtfully prepared and presented and all witnesses (especially the principal respondent) are ready to testify. A well-written pretrial statement with witness list, and tabbed, indexed documentary evidence are not guarantees of success, but certainly go a long way toward that goal. Again, it is an attorney's special skills, creativity, and knowledge that win the case, not the work of support staff. Criminal waiver cases are the most interesting type of immigration litigation; it is a rewarding opportunity to establish that the client may have erred, but has been duly punished and now merits a second chance. Advance preparation is what defines the successful immigration attorney.

Applications Filed After an Order of Removal

Stay of Deportation: Form I-246

An administrative application for a stay of deportation is filed on Form I-246 with the ICE Enforcement and Removal Operations (ERO) office having jurisdiction over the place where removal was ordered.[48] The I-246 form was recently revised. The form now has an expiration date of April 30, 2017.[49] If an individual is detained pending removal, the I-246 should be filed with the ERO office at the detention center. The I-246 carries a fee of $155.[50] Fee procedures may vary based on the jurisdiction. Upon payment, a receipt will then be affixed to the application and can be brought to the appropriate ERO location. Most ERO offices require that the stay request be filed in person.

The form's instructions state that the passport must be provided as well as a copy of the birth certificate. Practitioners should attach any and all relevant information in support of the stay request. The instructions highlight potentially relevant information.

A stay also may be requested from either the IJ or the BIA in conjunction with a motion to reopen.[51] In this case, Form I-246 is *not* utilized; rather, the request for a

---

[48] 8 CFR §241.6(a).

[49] The form can be found on *www.ice.gov/forms*.

[50] 8 CFR §103.7(b)(1). Payments can be made by cash, cashier's check, or money order and made out to the "Department of Homeland Security" or "Immigration and Customs Enforcement."

[51] 8 CFR §1003.23(b).

stay is in written form, as a motion. To clarify, the Form I-246 is an application form filed with DHS—not EOIR. EOIR and DHS have dual jurisdiction over stays. Depending on the case, counsel may want to file a written motion to the IJ or BIA (whichever has jurisdiction) and a Form I-246 application with ERO.

Criteria

There is no appeal from the denial of an administrative stay, and so there is no case law that provides guidance on adjudication criteria. The statute's only reference to the administrative stay is found at INA §241(c)(2)(B) [8 USC §1231(c)(2)(B)], but this subsection refers to stays in connection with arriving aliens at a port of entry. The regulation at 8 CFR §241.6(a) states that a stay is discretionary; it references criteria at 8 CFR §212.5 and INA §241(c). INA §241(c) states broadly that a stay may be granted when immediate removal is not "practical or proper." 8 CFR §212.5 is the section on DHS's parole authority. The criteria for parole authority (and, by reference, stay authority), is as follows:

- The presence of serious medical conditions;
- Women who are pregnant;
- Persons who are juveniles;
- Persons whose will serve as witnesses;
- Persons whose detention or removal is not in the public interest.

A stay may be requested in order to pursue a specific course of action, such as to file a motion to reopen, an immediate relative visa petition, or for post-conviction relief. A copy of the underlying motion to reopen, application, petition, motion for post-conviction relief, etc., should be attached to the stay application. If the stay is requested for personal, compelling reasons, certainly complete information should be provided. It is recommended that, rather than just dropping off the stay application, counsel request an appointment with the detention officer or a supervisor in order to discuss in more detail the reasons for the request. In the end, stays are discretionary and difficult to obtain. A thorough and well-reasoned package can make the difference in success.

Note that the filing of a stay request with ERO does not bring an automatic stay. A common complaint of immigration practitioners is that their clients are deported without the stay request being adjudicated, or even acknowledged. The instructions note that the filing of a stay does not stop execution of a removal order; unless and until there is a favorable adjudication, counsel should persist in taking whatever steps are appropriate to halt the removal.

Application for Permission to Reapply for Admission into the United States After Deportation or Removal

An application for consent to reapply for admission into the United States after deportation or removal is filed on Form I-212 and carries a fee of $585.[52] This form is filed when an individual applies for an immigrant visa at a consulate abroad. This form does not waive criminal grounds, but rather grants approval to re-enter the United States following removal. Depending on the case, it may be filed along with a waiver for inadmissibility based on crime.

As discussed below, the regulation at 8 CFR §212.2 contains several scenarios that dictate where to file the application, based on the posture and location of the applicant. For example, a client may already be abroad, having self-deported or been deported by DHS; still in the United States, but planning to depart and thereby self-deport; or already back in the United States, having re-entered without permission after deportation. The regulations and application form instructions also refer to certain persons who may apply at a port of entry,[53] but this type of application would be unusual.

The regulation at 8 CFR §212.2 is outdated and cannot be relied upon. The BIA recognized in 2006 that the regulation does not codify key changes in the INA as well as policies of DHS.[54] For example, DHS regularly reinstates a removal order for someone who enters after deportation (or refers the case for criminal prosecution). Therefore, permission to reapply in conjunction with adjustment of status in a nunc pro tunc fashion may not be inconceivable, but it will be rare. A person who enters or attempts to enter the United States without being admitted (in other words, without inspection) faces the so-called permanent bar to admissibility at INA §212(a)(9)(C)(i)(II). The permanent bar for entering or attempting to enter after a removal or deportation may be waived, in the discretion of DHS, only after 10 years have passed since the last departure.[55]

Persons arriving at a port of entry and requesting the waiver would most likely be expeditiously removed, be subject to reinstatement, or be criminally prosecuted. When reviewing 8 CFR §212.2, the practitioner should bear in mind that many of the described procedures will conflict with the immigration statute, criminal statutes, or other policies of DHS, and may not be realistic. An exception, of course, is for someone already abroad applying for a visa at a consulate abroad. In this scenario, the regulation remains current.

The regulation states that for persons who already have re-entered the United States after removal (without advance consent), the form may be filed with an appli-

---

[52] 8 CFR §103.7(b)(1). No biometric fee is required.
[53] 8 CFR §212.2(f).
[54] *See Matter of Torres-Garcia,* 23 I&N Dec. 866, 874 (BIA 2006).
[55] INA §212(a)(9)(C)(ii); 8 USC §1182(a)(9)(C)(ii).

cation for adjustment of status and requested on a nunc pro tunc basis (to retroactively approve of the re-entry).[56] If denied, it may be renewed in front of an IJ in removal proceedings. However, the BIA has ruled that nunc pro tunc approval of the Form I-212 is no longer available in conjunction with adjustment of status after an unlawful re-entry.[57] Indeed, the BIA ruled in *Matter of Torres-Garcia* that an individual who re-enters unlawfully after an order of removal is barred for 10 years from readmission; the I-212 waiver is not available until 10 years have passed from the reinstatement order. The circuit courts of appeal agree with the BIA that application for permission to re-enter after removal is not available on a nunc pro tunc basis to cure a subsequent re-entry; following an unlawful re-entry, the non–American citizen faces a permanent bar, and permission to reapply is available only after 10 years have passed.[58] In light of the ground of inadmissibility at INA §212(a)(9)(C)(i)(II), along with the reinstatement provision and possibility of criminal prosecution, the regulation's reference to a nunc pro tunc application for permission to reapply after admission (Form I-212) in conjunction with adjustment of status is obsolete.

An applicant for an immigrant visa who is already abroad files the application with the director for the USCIS office in the United States where removal proceedings took place, unless the applicant also requires an additional waiver of inadmissibility [such as those under INA §§212(g), (h), or (i)], in which case the Form I-212 is filed simultaneously with the waiver application at the consulate.[59] The consul forwards the application to a DHS office abroad for adjudication.[60] The regulations further state that an applicant may file the Form I-212 with the director having jurisdiction over the particular port of entry.[61] This would be the case where an applicant does not require a visa in order to enter, or already has a visa but did not obtain approval of the Form I-212 with the visa.

The regulations are ambiguous as to whether an applicant for a nonimmigrant visa should file either the Form I-212, or a waiver under INA §212(d)(3), or both.[62] Certainly, INA §212(d)(3) waives all grounds of inadmissibility (but for security-related), and thus waives INA §212(a)(9)(A). An additional I-212 should not also be required. This author's experience is that the §212(d)(3)(A) waiver successfully waives the prior removal order (and a criminal ground of inadmissibility) without the additional Form I-212. Confusingly, the regulations state that an applicant for a nonimmigrant visa who seeks readmission after deportation or removal may receive a

---

[56] 8 CFR §212.2(e).

[57] *Matter of Torres-Garcia*, 23 I&N Dec. 866 (BIA 2006).

[58] *Tenesaca Delgado v. Mukasey*, 516 F.3d 65 (2d Cir. 2008); *Gonzales v. DHS*, 508 F.3d 1227 (9th Cir. 2007).

[59] 8 CFR §212.2(d).

[60] 8 CFR §212.2(d).

[61] 8 CFR §212(f).

[62] 8 CFR §212.2(b).

grant only in accordance with INA §212(d)(3). However, the applicant "may" apply for such permission using Form I-212.[63] The language of the regulation implies that it is in the discretion of the consular officer to request a Form I-212 in addition to the §212(d)(3) waiver.

The exception is the K nonimmigrant visa (K-1, K-2, K-3, and K-4) for certain fiancé(e)s and spouses of American citizens. These nonimmigrant visa applicants must file Form I-212 to waive the existing removal order.[64] When the consular officer receives the Form I-212, he or she forwards it to the appropriate DHS office abroad for processing.[65]

Criteria

The factors to be considered in adjudicating an I-212 application include:

- The basis for the prior deportation order;
- Recency of deportation;
- Length of residence in the United States;
- The applicant's moral character;
- Respect for law and order;
- Evidence of reformation and rehabilitation;
- Family responsibilities;
- Any inadmissibility under other sections of law;
- Hardship involved to the applicant or others; and
- The need for the applicant's services in the United States.[66]

Accordingly, an evidentiary package should provide documentation covering these issues.

---

[63] 8 CFR §212.2(b).

[64] 8 CFR §212.2(c).

[65] 8 CFR §212.2(c).

[66] *Matter of Tin*, 14 I&N Dec. 371 (RC 1973).

APPENDIX 13A

RESPONDENT'S PRETRIAL STATEMENT

UNITED STATES DEPARTMENT OF JUSTICE
EXECUTIVE OFFICE FOR IMMIGRATION REVIEW
OFFICE OF THE IMMIGRATION JUDGE
MIAMI, FLORIDA

IN THE MATTER OF:)	
)	
ROSSI, Rosa)	CASE NO. A256 897 341
Respondent)	Judge Smith
IN REMOVAL PROCEEDINGS)	
_____/	

RESPONDENT'S PRETRIAL STATEMENT

Statement of the Case and Introductory Facts

This matter is set for an individual hearing on February 13, 2012 at 3:00 p.m. solely on the issue of manner of entry. Specifically, the Court has ordered the hearing to receive argument and take testimony on whether Ms. Rossi was lawfully admitted as a student, such that she should not be charged under INA § 212(a). The Court rightly stated at the last master (status conference) hearing that this fundamental issue should be addressed first and foremost.

Status of Case: Other Pending Issues and Applications

Respondent, through counsel, further notes the following for purposes of understanding the status or juncture of this case. Rosa Rossi is (was) a battered and abused spouse. Although now divorced, she was in an extremely abusive marriage to an American citizen, one Guido Bianchi. As is somewhat typical in this type of case, Ms. Rossi had a history of abusive relationships, including with her family in Jamaica. Ms. Rossi's ex-husband and she have two U.S. citizen minor children. He originally filed an I-130 on her behalf, which was approved by CIS in 2008; however, the I-485 was denied because Ms. Rossi could not convince CIS she had a lawful admission, and she is not 245(i) eligible.

Cancellation of Removal Application

Based on the abusive marriage, Ms. Rossi has filed for cancellation of removal under INA § 240A(b). Certainly, the criminal conviction (battery and grand theft) becomes an issue for cancellation eligibility. This memorandum addresses whether these convictions are moral turpitude crimes and takes the position that, in light of the Eleventh Circuit's recent decision in *Sanchez-Fajardo v. Att'y Gen.*, 659 F.3d 1303 (11th Cir. 2011), along with other recent appellate precedent, these offenses are not categorically moral turpitude crimes, although they certainly open the door to allegations of removability.

Respondent also believes that she may utilize and qualify for a waiver under INA § 237(a)(7), which is available in the cancellation context, because the crime was directly related to her own victimization. However, this particular legal issue will be addressed at a further date if the cancellation goes forward.

I-360 Petition Eligibility

In the meantime, the Court is advised that Counsel initially intended to file an I-360 petition for Ms. Rossi. However, Ms. Rossi was divorced before the I-360 could be filed. Counsel was operating under the erroneous assumption (based on the regulations, which unfortunately have *not* been updated in over 10 years) that the I-360 has to be filed while the marriage is in good standing. Recently, in consulting with Catholic Charities colleagues about the issue of I-360 eligibility, Counsel learned this week that in fact the statute allows for filing the I-360 up to within two years of the divorce, if it can be shown that the divorce was sought on account of the abuse. See: INA § 204(a)(1)(A)(iii) (II)(aa)(CC)(ccc). Ms. Rossi was divorced in November of 2010, and is thus eligible to file the I-360, which Counsel's office is doing now with a feeling of relief and also haste.

If the I-360 is approved, the admission issue essentially "goes away". A battered spouse is assimilated to a parole entry and can file for adjustment of status. A battered spouse can also file for adjustment and seek a § 212(h) waiver to "cure" the criminal offenses, if they are determined to be moral turpitude crimes. Thus in a separate but simultaneous filing, Counsel is seeking a continuance of this matter pending adjudication of the I-360, whose approval would also come with a grant of deferred action. **Because it is a discrete motion, a separate motion is being filed.** Counsel believes that in the interests of everyone's time and workload, this matter is best held in abeyance pending adjudication of the I-360, which Counsel observes as a meritorious petition which is likely to be granted.

Post-Conviction Relief

The Court is advised that the appeal of the motion to vacate denial (a *Padilla* motion) was unfortunately denied based on the retroactivity issue. Counsel believes that the criminal vacatur case is now on appeal to the Florida Supreme Court, as are other *Padilla* cases.

Manner of Admission

The issue of admission and proper classification under the INA was addressed in Respondent's Opening Pleadings dated June 21, 2011. Ms. Rossi is a native and citizen of Jamaica. She entered the U.S. in March of 1988 with a student visa to attend College. After a few months, she left school and returned to Jamaica (summer break) because she was unexpectedly pregnant and wanted to have the baby in Jamaica. She was supposed to return to school in August, but because of the birth, could not return until October. In October of 1988, she returned to the U.S. via a Bahamian Sea Escape ship (she flew to the Bahamas and then purchases passage on the cruise ship). She states that she showed her passport and I-20 to an inspector and she was admitted as a student; she does not recall whether anything was entered into a computer and she does not recall whether anything was stamped. She has since lost her passport. She has never again departed the United States.

Documentation was attached to the June 2011 filing to corroborate Respondent's claim. Additional documents are attached. She can also of course testify.

Legal Argument on Charges of Removability

Introductory Statement

Although this case is set for a hearing solely on the issue of manner of entry, Respondent, through Counsel, believes it is helpful to the Court to address the issue of moral turpitude. This memorandum is submitted to address primarily the issue of removability, which is a significant issue regardless of whether this case proceeds on the § 212(a) or § 237 track. (Again, however, it is noted that these issues need not be addressed now that it is determined Ms. Rossi can seek an I-360 petition and deferred action status as a battered spouse).

Respondent has been charged with removability under INA § 212(a)(2)(i)(I) as an alien convicted of multiple crimes involving moral turpitude on the basis of her theft and battery conviction. Again, this argument is submitted to briefly apprise the Court and the Department of the reasons why Respondent's convictions are not crimes involving moral turpitude.

Discussion

A) **Rosa Rossi's conviction for "grand theft" in violation of Florida Statute Section 812.014 is not a crime involving moral turpitude because the provision is a divisible statute; under the modified categorical approach it must be concluded that she did *not* intend to permanently deprive the alleged victim of any property.**

In order for a theft crime to qualify as a crime involving moral turpitude, the conduct requisite for the commission of the offense must include the intent to *permanently* deprive the victim of property. *See Matter of V-Z-S-*, 22 I&N Dec. 1338 (BIA

2000) (citing *Matter of Grazley*, 14 I&N Dec. 330 (BIA 1973)). When the elements of a statute encompass some conduct that would constitute a removable offense, and some that would not, that statute is considered divisible, and as a divisible statute it is subject to the "modified categorical approach." *Accardo v. U.S. Att'y Gen.*, 634 F.3d 1333 (11th Cir. 2011); *See also Jaggernauth v. United States Att'y Gen.*, 432 F.3d 1346, 1353 (11th Cir. 2005).

Under this approach, in order to determine which section of the statute the alien was convicted under, and hence whether she is in fact removable, a court should look to the "record of conviction," which includes the charging document, plea, verdict or judgment, and sentence." *Jaggernauth*, 432 F.3d at 1353.

In recent case law handed down by the Eleventh Circuit, the appeals court has unequivocally endorsed the modified categorical approach and effectively done away with the "realistic probability" test (a test which allowed an adjudicator to consider any additional evidence he or she determines necessary or appropriate to resolve the question of which conduct is applicable to a respondent when dealing with a divisible statute). *See: Sanchez-Fajardo v. Att'y Gen.*, 659 F.3d 1303 (11th Cir. 2011). (effectively disregarding *Matter of Silva-Trevino*, 24 I&N Dec. 687 (A.G. 2008)).

As this Court is aware, the categorical approach looks to the elements of the criminal statute to determine whether an offense involves moral turpitude. A divisible statute is a statute which, through formatting or punctuation, includes phrases which implicate moral turpitude, as well as phrases which do not. When a statute is "divisible", the courts revert to a modified categorical approach to determine which portion of the criminal statute applies to the particular respondent's case.

However, when an examination of the record of conviction under the modified categorical approach does not indicate under which section of the statute the respondent was convicted, it must be assumed that he was convicted under the section pertaining to the least culpable conduct. *See Sanchez-Fajardo, supra; Partyka v. Att'y Gen.*, 417 F.3d 408 (3d Cir. 2005).

It is well established that Florida's theft statute at Fla. Stat. § 812.014 is "divisible", as its language explicitly indicates that conviction under the statute may arise from an endeavor to deprive *or* appropriate the property of another *either* temporarily *or* permanently. *Jaggernauth*, 432 F.3d at 1346.

A review of Ms. Rossi's Information (charging document) does not indicate under which section of the Florida statute (with the intent to deprive *either* "temporarily" *or* "permanently") she was charged and ultimately convicted. Therefore, it must be concluded that she was convicted on the basis of having committed the "least culpable conduct" (i.e. an endeavor to appropriate or use the property of another *temporarily*). Thus, in light of this record of conviction, and given that a *temporary* taking of property is *not* a theft crime (and further that an appropriation is not a taking) Ms. Rossi's conviction for theft under Florida Statute § 812.014 is *not* a crime involving moral turpitude.

B) **Rosa Rossi's conviction for aggravated battery under Florida Statute § 784.045 is not a crime involving moral turpitude because her conviction must, under the modified categorical approach, be viewed as having been committed on the basis of a simple battery that involved a mere "touch" and the U.S. Supreme Court has ruled in** *Johnson v. United States* **that a mere "touch" can never constitute the violent force that would be necessary for a battery offense to involve moral turpitude.**

Crimes involving moral turpitude are generally said to be comprised of an "act of baseness, vileness, or depravity in the private and social duties which a man owes to his fellow men, or to society in general, contrary to the accepted and customary rule of right and duty between man and man.'" *Matter of Olquin*, 23 I&N Dec. 896, 896 (BIA 2006). In determining whether an offense of violence involves moral turpitude, the Board of Immigration Appeals (BIA) has looked to whether the act is accompanied by a "vicious motive" or "corrupt mind". *Matter of Sanudo*, 23 I&N Dec. 968, 971 (BIA 2006) (citing *Okabe v. INS*, 671 F.2d 863 (5th Cir. 1982).

Elements of violent offenses that have been deemed to be indicative of such vicious motive or corrupt mind have included: the knowing use or attempted use of deadly force as through the use of a deadly weapon; the *intentional* infliction of *serious* bodily injury; and the infliction of bodily harm upon a person whom society views as deserving of special protection, (i.e. a child, a domestic partner, or a peace officer). *See Matter of Sanudo*, 23 I&N Dec. 968, 971-72 (BIA 2006) (citing *Gonzales v. Barber*, 207 F.2d 398, 400 (9th Cir. 1953) (regarding the use of deadly force); *Nguyen v. Reno*, 211 F.3d 692, 695 (1st Cir. 2000); *Matter of P-*, 7 I&N Dec. 376, 377 (BIA 1956) (regarding intentional infliction of serious bodily injury); *Garcia v. Att'y Gen. of U.S.*, 329 F.3d 1217, 1222 (11th Cir. 2003); *Matter of Tran*, 21 I&N Dec. 291 (BIA 1996); *Matter of Danesh*, 19 I&N Dec. 669 (BIA 1988) (regarding infliction of bodily injury on those deserving special protection).

Lacking such elements indicative of vicious motive or corrupt mind, simple assault and battery are generally not considered to be crimes involving moral turpitude. *See Matter of Sanudo*, 23 I&N Dec. 968, 971 (BIA 2006); *Matter of Fualaau*, 21 I&N dec. 475 (BIA 1996); *Matter of Perez-Contreras*, 20 I&N Dec. 615 (BIA 1992) (citing *Matter of Short*, 20 I&N Dec. 136 (BIA 1989)).

In *Johnson v. United States*, 130 S. Ct. 1265 (2010), under an analysis mirroring the 'violent offense' moral turpitude analysis, the Supreme Court of the United States of America determined that Florida's battery statute does not categorically qualify as a "violent felony" under the Armed Career Criminal Act (ACCA) at 18 U.S.C. § 924(e)(1). For the purposes of the ACCA, a "violent felony" is defined as "any crime punishable by imprisonment for a term exceeding on year" that: (i) has as an element the use, attempted use, or threatened use of physical force against the person of another." 18 U.S.C. § 924(e)(2)(B). In their analysis of this section's "physical force" requirement, the Supreme Court concluded that "the phrase 'physical force' means *violent* force—that is, force capable of causing physical pain or injury to another person." *Johnson v. United States*, 130 S.Ct. 1265, 1271 (2010) (relying on *Leocal v. Ashcroft*, 543 U.S. 1 (2004); *Flores v. Ashcroft*, 350 F.3d 666,672 (CA7 2003)). The Court went on to characterize violent force as relating to force that is "extreme and sudden"; it is "furious; severe; vehement." *Id.*

In light of this analysis, the Court in *Johnson* determined that Florida's simple battery statute is not categorically a "violent felony" because it is a divisible statute:

(1)(a) The offense of battery occurs when a person:
1. Actually and intentionally touches or strikes another person against the will of the other; or
2. Intentionally causes bodily harm to another person. Fla. Stat. § 784.03 .

Thus, the offender may be convicted if she either strikes the victim, intentionally causes bodily harm to the victim, *or* merely touches the victim. Ultimately, the Court found that "touch" does not constitute the "violent force" required by a "violent felony."

Based on the conclusion that Florida's simply battery statute is not categorically a "violent felony" for the purposes of the ACCA, but is a divisible statute, the same conclusion must be reached that neither is Florida's simply battery statute categorically a crime involving moral turpitude. Indeed, under a nearly identical analysis, the Administrative Appeals Office (AAO) has determined this to be the case, finding that "simple battery" under Fla. Stat §784.03(1) is not categorically a crime involving moral turpitude. See *Matter of [redacted]*, 2008 Immig. Rptr. LEXIS 19895 (BIA 2008). In *Matter of [redacted]* the AAO held that Florida's simple battery statute is divisible and must be analyzed under the modified categorical approach. *Id* at 9-10. Furthermore, the AAO concluded that "an offense under §784.03(1)(a)(1) (encompassing "touch" or "strike") is not a crime involving moral turpitude." *Id.* In *Matter of [redacted]*, the AAO concluded that the applicant's conviction under §784.03(1)(a)(1) did not involve moral turpitude because since the applicant's conviction record did not specify whether his conduct was a "touch" or "strike", under the modified categorical approach the least culpable (i.e. non-morally turpitudinous) offense must be assumed.[67]

In *Sosa-Martinez v. U.S. Atty. Gen.*, 420 F.3d 1338 (11th Cir. 2005) (a case that preceded the Supreme Court's decision in *Johnson* by five years) the Eleventh Circuit held in a three page decision that *aggravated* battery as defined under Florida Statute § 784.045 *is* a crime involving moral turpitude. The Eleventh Circuit stated that they

---

[67] Recent case law handed down from the Eleventh Circuit indicates that this Circuit definitively endorses the modified categorical approach and has effectively done away with the "realistic probability" test (a test which allowed an adjudicator to consider any additional evidence he or she determines necessary or appropriate to resolve the question of which conduct is applicable to a respondent when dealing with a divisible statute). See *Sanchez-Fajardo v. Atty. Gen.*, Nos. -09-12962 (11th Cir. 2011) (effectively disregarding *Matter of Silva-Trevino*, 24 I&N Dec. 687 (A.G. 2008)).

were able to "*readily conclude* that *any* intentional battery that includes, as an element of the offense either (1) that it caused great bodily harm, permanent disability, or permanent disfigurement, or (2) involved the use of a deadly weapon constitutes a crime of moral turpitude." *Sosa-Martinez v. U.S. Atty. Gen.*, 420 F.3d 1338, 1342 (11th Cir. 2005) (emphasis added).

In other words, conviction under Florida's aggravated battery statute was considered to be a crime involving moral turpitude because the necessary elements of the statute were found to involve a 'corrupt mind' or 'vicious motive'. As evidenced by the Eleventh Circuit's *ready conclusion* that "*any* intentional battery" coupled with *either* of these elements will constitute a crime involving moral turpitude, this decision stands for the conclusion that aggravated battery in Florida is *categorically* a crime involving moral turpitude. This conclusion is wrong.

In *Sosa-Martinez* the Eleventh Circuit overlooked what the Supreme Court of the United States rightly recognized later in *Johnson v. United States*; namely that while either of the two forms of conduct described in Florida's *aggravated* battery statute may constitute a crime involving moral turpitude (as a crime of violence), the grounding offense for this crime (i.e. simple battery defined at Florida Statute § 784.03) is a divisible statute that includes conduct which *may* rise to the level of a crime involving moral turpitude *and* conduct with may *not* rise to the level of a crime involving moral turpitude.

An aggravated battery conviction in Florida requires that the offender: *first* commit a simple battery by intentionally (1) touching or striking another person, or (2) causing bodily harm to another person, and *second,* that in committing that battery, he or she (1) caused great bodily harm, permanent disability, or permanent disfigurement, or (2) used a deadly weapon. *See* Fla. Stat. § 784.045.

Thus in reality, Florida's aggravated battery statute *is itself* a divisible statute. Conviction requires proof beyond a reasonable doubt of two elements, the first of which must come from an element pertaining to "simple battery" (strike; intentionally cause bodily harm; or touch), the second of which must come from an element pertaining to "aggravated battery" (cause great bodily harm, permanent disability, or permanent disfigurement, or use a deadly weapon). But because one of the elements pertaining to "simple battery" *cannot* encompass a crime involving moral turpitude (*i.e.*, "touch"), any conviction for *aggravated battery* that includes the commission of a *simple battery* that was committed on the basis of a mere "touch", is *not* a crime involving moral turpitude.

As has been previously addressed, in the context of conviction, without an underlying simple battery, the greater offense of aggravated battery cannot itself exist, or even be said to have occurred. In *Sosa-Martinez*, the Eleventh Circuit held that the conduct elements of Florida's aggravated battery statute were clearly indicative of a "vicious motive" or "corrupt mind" and thus involved moral turpitude. Given that case law has clearly established that offense conduct such as: the knowing use or attempted use of deadly force as through the use of a deadly weapon; the *intentional* infliction of *serious* bodily injury; and or the infliction of bodily harm upon a person whom society views as deserving of special protection is particularly indicative of such "vicious motive" or "corrupt mind", it would appear on its face logical to conclude that the conduct elements of Florida's aggravated battery statute (namely the causation of great bodily harm, permanent disability, or permanent disfigurement, or use of a deadly weapon) fit this mold. Indeed, this would be the case when a Florida conviction for aggravated assault is based in a battery committed any *other* way than by a "touch", it *is not* the case when the underlying battery *has* been committed by a "touch".

The logical reality of this admittedly complex statutory analysis is that the simple act of a "touch" negates the possibility of "vicious motive" or "corrupt mind", yet "touch" may be an underlying element of Florida's aggravated battery statute. Indeed, under the legal definition of the term "touch" as set forth by the Supreme Court in *Johnson*, a "touch" can never constitute "violent force". As such, it is a legal and factual impossibility that by the mere act of a "touch" an offender could cause *great bodily harm, permanent disability, or permanent disfigurement*. But even while an offender may still engage in a mere "touch" through the *use of a deadly weapon*, this sort of conduct is *not* the sort of weapon-related conduct that case law has actually decided to be indicative of "vicious motive" or "corrupt mind".

Case law addressing morally turpitudinous weapon-related conduct in fact states that it is actually "the *knowing* use or attempted *use of deadly force*" as through the *use* of a deadly weapon that is indicative of such vicious motive or corrupt mind. *Matter of Sanudo*, 23 I&N Dec. 968, 971-72 (BIA 2006)(citing *Gonzales v. Barber*, 207 F.2d 398, 400 (9th Cir. 1953), *Matter of Medina*, 15 I&N Dec. 611, 614 (BIA 1976), see also *Sosa-Martinez v. U.S. Att'y Gen.*, 420 F.3d 1338, 1342 (11th Cir. 2005); *Yousefi v. U.S. INS*, 260 F.3d 318, 326-27 (4th Cir. 2001); *Pichardo v. INS*, 104 F.3d 756, 760 (5th Cir. 1997. Thus yet again, we must arrive at the conclusion that a mere "touch", an act that *by Supreme Court definition, cannot* be committed with "violent force", cannot involve moral turpitude regardless of whether it is committed via the softest fingertip *or* a "deadly" weapon.

In Ms. Rossi's case, her record of conviction states that she was charged with aggravated battery on the basis of having committed a simple battery in the form of *either* a "touch" *or* "strike" and that her "aggravated" battery conviction pertains to "use of a deadly weapon". Because Ms. Rossi's conviction record does not indicate whether the offense conduct of her underlying simple battery charged involved a touch *or* a strike, it must be assumed that she is guilty of the least culpable (i.e., non-morally turpitudinous) conduct, a "touch". This is possible because neither the battery nor aggravated battery statute require bodily harm, thus there is no indication a weapon was actually used.

In sum, given that Ms. Rossi's aggravated battery conviction is grounded upon a simple battery offense that could have been committed on the basis of a "touch", it must be concluded that her aggravated battery conviction did not involve moral turpitude.

Conclusion

Rosa Rossi's convictions for "grand theft" and "aggravated battery" do not categorically constitute crimes involving moral turpitude. Her conviction for grand theft did not involve moral turpitude because under the modified categorical approach it must be concluded that she acted without moral turpitude during the commission of the crime (i.e. *without* the intent to permanently deprive). Her conviction for aggravated battery did not involve moral turpitude either because, again, under the modified categorical approach, it must be concluded that she was convicted for the underlying offense of "simple battery" on the basis of having committed a "touch", which according to the Supreme Court's ruling in *Johnson v. United States* cannot involve moral turpitude and therefore negates the additional morally turpitudinous elements associated with "aggravated battery" as defined in Florida.

Additionally, the Respondent is eligible for a battered spouse petition under INA § 204 and will be filing this petition shortly. This matter should be held in abeyance pending adjudication of the petition; from this view, neither manner of entry nor removability need be decided.

In the alternative, Respondent is eligible for a waiver of her criminal convictions under INA § 237(a)(7)(a) and will proceed on her application for cancellation.

RESPECTFULLY SUBMITTED:

MARY KRAMER
ATTORNEY AT LAW
MARY E. KRAMER, P.A
168 S.E. FIRST ST. SUITE 802
MIAMI, FL 33131
(305) 374 2300
FAX: (305) 374 3748
mary@marykramerlaw.com

TABLE OF DECISIONS

A

Abdelghany, Matter of, 26 I&N Dec. 254 (BIA 2014) 477, 478, 480, 487, 489
Abdel-Masieh v. INS, 73 F.3d 579 (5th Cir. 1996) 380, 386
Abdelqadar v. Gonzales, 413 F.3d 668 (7th Cir. 2005) 250, 382
Abiodun v. Gonzales, 461 F.3d 1210 (10th Cir. 2006) 54
Abosi, Matter of, 24 I&N Dec. 204 (BIA 2007) 452
Abreu-Semino, Matter of, 12 I&N Dec. 775 (BIA 1968) 261
Abuelhawa v. United States, 129 U.S. 2102 (2009) 279
Abu-Khaliel v. Gonzales, 436 F.3d 627 (6th Cir. 2006) 436
Acero v. INS, 2005 U.S. Dist. LEXIS 4440, 2005 WL 615744 (E.D.N.Y. Mar. 16, 2005) 302
Acosta v. Ashcroft, 341 F.3d 218 (3d Cir. 2003) 60, 62, 564
Acosta-Hidalgo, Matter of, 24 I&N Dec. 103 (BIA 2007) 504
Adamiak, Matter of, 23 I&N Dec. 878 (BIA 2006) 70
Adamo, Matter of, 10 I&N Dec. 593 (BIA 1964) 64, 81
Adetiba, Matter of, 20 I&N Dec. 506 (BIA 1992) 250, 382
Aguila Montes-de Oca; United States v., 655 F.3d 915 (9th Cir. 2011) 183, 186, 187, 195, 200, 205, 214, 253, 309
Aguilar v. ICE, No. 07-1819 WL 4171244 (1st Cir. Nov. 27, 2007) 137
Aguilar-Aquino, Matter of, 24 I&N Dec. 747 (BIA 2009) 141, 142
Aguilera-Montero v. Mukasey, 548 F.3d 1248 (9th Cir. 2008) 63
Aguirre v. INS, 79 F.3d 315 (2d Cir. 1996) 283
Aguirre-Aguirre; INS v., 526 U.S. 415 (1999) 386, 466
A–H–, Matter of, 23 I&N Dec. 774 (AG 2005) 332, 336
Ahortalejo-Guzman, Matter of, 25 I&N Dec. 465 (BIA 2011) 208, 213
Ajami, Matter of, 22 I&N Dec. 949 (BIA 1999) 255, 571
Akindemowo v. INS, 61 F.3d 282 (4th Cir. 1995) 382
Akinsade v. Holder, 678 F.3d 138 (2d Cir. 2012) 310, 311, 580
Alaka v. Att'y Gen., 456 F.3d 88 (3d Cir. 2006) 393, 465, 466
Alarcon, Matter of, 20 I&N Dec. 557 (BIA 1992) 250
Alexandre v. Att'y Gen., 452 F.3d 1204 (11th Cir. 2006) 480
Alfaro, Matter of, 25 I&N Dec. 417 (BIA 2011) 259, 268
Ali v. Achim, 468 F.3d 462 (7th Cir. 2006), *cert. dismissed*, 552 U.S. 1085 (2007) 393
Ali v. Ashcroft, 395 F.3d 722 (7th Cir. 2005) 72, 73
Ali v. Barlow, 446 F. Supp. 2d 604 (E.D. Va. 2006) 160
Ali v. Mukasey, 521 F.3d 737 (7th Cir. 2008) 212
Ali v. Att'y Gen., 443 F.3d 804 (11th Cir. 2006) 61
Alli v. Thomas, No. 4:09-CV-0698, 2009 US LEXIS 69413 (M.D. Pa. Aug. 10, 2009) 138, 139
Al Makaaseb Gen. Trading Co. v. Christopher, 94-CV-U79 (CSH). 1885 U.S. Dist. LEXIS 3057, 1995 WL 110117 (S.D.N.Y. Mar. 13, 1995) 29
Almanza, Matter of, 24 I&N Dec. 771 (BIA 2009) 246, 247
Almanza-Arenas v. Holder, 771 F.3d 1184 (9th Cir. 2014) 246, 247
Altamirano v. Gonzales, 427 F.3d 586 (9th Cir. 2005) 344, 416
Alvarado-Alvino, Matter of, 22 I&N Dec. 718 (BIA 1999) 311
Alvarez Acosta v. U.S. Att'y Gen., 524 F.3d 1191 (11th Cir. 2008) 329, 330
Alvarez-Barajas v. Gonzales, 418 F.3d 1050 (9th Cir. 2005) 30

Alvarez-Reynaga v. Holder, 596 F.3d 534 (9th Cir. 2010) 245
Alyazji, Matter of, 25 I&N Dec. 397 (BIA 2011) 381, 448
Amaya-Portillo; United States v., 423 F.3d 427 (4th Cir. 2005) 282
American Baptist Churches v. Thornburgh, 760 F. Supp. 796 (N.D. Cal. 1991) 475
Arai, Matter of, 13 I&N Dec. 494 (BIA 1970) 436
Aremu v. DHS, 450 F.3d 578 (4th Cir. 2006) 381
Arguelles-Campos, Matter of, 22 I&N Dec. 811 (BIA 1999) 383, 384, 497
Arrabally & Yerrabelly, Matter of, 25 I&N Dec. 771 (BIA 2012) 437
Arreola, Matter of, 25 I&N Dec. 267 (BIA 2010) 152
Arriola-Arenas v. Att'y Gen., 145 Fed. Appx. 757, 2005 WL 2012262 (3d Cir. 2005) 494
Aruna, Matter of, 24 I&N Dec. 452 (BIA 2008) 195, 275
Ashley v. Ridge, 288 F. Supp. 2d 662 (D.N.J. 2003) 155
Atunnise v. Mukasey, 523 F.3d 830 (7th Cir. 2008) 513
Avendano v. Holder, 770 F.3d 731 (8th Cir. 2014) 255
Avetisyan, Matter of, 25 I&N Dec. 688 (BIA 2012) 612
Awad v. Gonzales, 494 F.3d 723 (8th Cir. 2007) 334
Azurin, Matter of, 23 I&N Dec. 695 (BIA 2005) 433, 434, 493

B

B–, Matter of, 6 I&N Dec. 98 (BIA 1954) 255
Babaisakov, Matter of, 24 I&N Dec. 306 (BIA 2007) 314, 574
Bahar v. Ashcroft, 264 F.3d 1309 (11th Cir. 2001) (*per curiam*) 266, 267
Bahta, Matter of, 22 I&N Dec. 1381 (BIA 2000) 310
Balao, Matter of, 20 I&N Dec. 440 (BIA 1992) 452, 567
Balderas, Matter of, 20 I&N Dec. 389 (BIA 1991) 433
Balogun v. Att'y Gen., 425 F.3d 1356 (11th Cir. 2005) 63
Balsys; United States v., 524 U.S. 666 (1998) 81
Bamba v. Rile, 366 F.3d 195 (3d Cir. 2004) 60
Barakat v. Holder, 2010 U.S. App. LEXIS 19213 (6th Cir. 2010) 67
Barma v. Holder, 640 F.3d 749 (7th Cir. 2011) 330, 396
Barraza v. Mukasey, 519 F.3d 388 (7th Cir. 2008) 329, 330, 442
Bart, Matter of, 20 I&N Dec. 436 (BIA 1992) 250
Batista-Hernandez, Matter of, 21 I&N Dec. 955 (BIA 1997) 575
Bautista, Matter of, 25 I&N Dec. 616 (BIA 2011) 307
Bautista v. Att'y Gen., 744 F.3d 54 (3d Cir. 2014) 306, 307
Bazan-Reyes v. INS, 256 F.3d 600 (7th Cir. 2001) 294
Becker v. Gonzales, 473 F.3d 1000 (9th Cir. 2007) 331
Bejar v. Ashcroft, 324 F.3d 127 (3d Cir. 2003) 31
Bejarano-Urrutia v. Gonzales, 413 F.3d 444 (4th Cir. 2005) 300, 575, 576
Bellotti v. Baird, 443 U.S. 622 (1979) 79
Beltran, Matter of, 20 I&N Dec. 521 (BIA 1992) 328, 329
Bernabella, Matter of, 13 I&N Dec. 42 (BIA 1968) 452
Beslic v. INS, 265 F.3d 568 (7th Cir. 2001) 353, 425, 426, 441
Binkley; United States v., 903 F.2d 1130 (7th Cir. 1990) 278
Blake, Matter of, 23 I&N Dec. 722 (BIA 2005), *rev'd & remanded*, Blake v. Carbone, 489 F.3d 88 (2d Cir. 2007) 303, 350, 420, 440, 488
Blancas-Lara, Matter of, 23 I&N Dec. 458 (BIA 2002) 468
Blas, Matter of, 15 I&N Dec. 626 (BIA 1974, AG 1976) 436
Bobadilla v. Holder, 679 F.3d 1052 (8th Cir. 2012) 208, 212

Boffil-Rivera; United States v., 607 F.3d 736 (11th Cir. 2010) 251
Bogarin-Flores v. Napolitano, 2012 WL 3283287 (S.D. Cal. 2012) 148
Borrego v. Mukasey, 539 F.3d 689 (7th Cir. 2008) 513
Borrome v. Att'y Gen., 687 F.3d 150 (3d Cir. 2012) 278, 327, 328
Bracamontes v. Holder, 675 F.3d 380 (4th Cir. 2012) 446
Brieva-Perez, Matter of, 23 I&N Dec. 766 (BIA 2005) 302, 568
Briones-Mata; United States v., 116 F.3d 308 (8th Cir. 1997) 282
Brito v. Mukasey, 521 F.3d 160 (2d Cir. 2008) 437
Buscemi, Matter of, 19 I&N Dec. 628 (BIA 1988) 655
Bustamante, Matter of, 25 I&N Dec. 564 (BIA 2011) 453, 473

C

C–, Matter of, 5 I&N Dec. 370 (BIA 1953) 255
C–, Matter of, 20 I&N Dec. 529 (BIA 1992) 463
Cabrera, Matter of, 24 I&N Dec. 459 (BIA 2008) 55
Calderon; United States v., 391 F.3d 370 (2d Cir. 2004) 492
Campbell; United States v., 167 F.3d 94 (2d Cir. 1999) 61
Campos-Torres, Matter of, 22 I&N Dec. 1289 (BIA 2000) 261, 468
Candelario; United States v., 240 F.3d 1300 (11th Cir. 2001) 301
Cano-Oyarzabal v. Holder, 774 F.3d 914 (7th Cir. 2014) 208, 256
Carachuri-Rosendo, Matter of, 24 I&N Dec. 382 (BIA 2007) 285, 287
Carachuri-Rosendo v. Holder, 560 U.S. 563 (2010) 194, 271, 286, 287, 289
Carachuri-Rosendo v. Holder, 570 F.3d 263 (5th Cir. 2009) 284, 285
Cardenas-Abreu, Matter of, 24 I&N Dec. 795 (BIA 2009) 53, 54
Cardenas-Abreu v. Holder, 378 Fed. Appx. 59, 2010 U.S. App. LEXIS 10498 (2d Cir. 2010) ... 53
Cardiel, Matter of, 25 I&N Dec. 12 (BIA 2009) 310
Cardoso-Tlaseca v. Gonzales, 460 F.3d 1102 (9th Cir. 2006) 69
Cardoza-Fonseca; INS v., 480 U.S. 421 (1987) 464
Carlos-Blaza v. Holder, 611 F.3d 583 (9th Cir. 2010) 310
Casas-Castrillon v. DHS, 535 F.3d 942 (9th Cir. 2008) 138
Castaneda v. Souza, No. 13-10874, 952 F. Supp. 2d 307 (D. Mass. July 3, 2013), *aff'd*, 769 F.3d
  32 (1st Cir. 2014), *withdrawn & reh'g granted*, No. 13-1994, 2015 U.S. App. LEXIS 5292
  (1st Cir. Jan. 23, 2015) 148, 149, 150
Castillo v. Att'y Gen., 729 F.3d 296 (3d Cir. 2013) 53, 290
Castillo-Cruz v. Holder, 581 F.3d 1154 (9th Cir. 2009) 245, 248
Castle v. INS, 541 F.2d 1064 (4th Cir. 1976) 240
Castro-Rocha; United States v., 323 F.3d 846 (10th Cir. 2003) 282
Castro-Rodriguez, Matter of, 25 I&N Dec. 698 (BIA 2012) 195, 275
Catholic Soc. Servs., Inc. v. Meese, vacated sub nom. Reno v. Catholic Soc. Servs., Inc., 509
  U.S. 43 (1993) 114
Cazarez-Gutierrez v. Ashcroft, 382 F.3d 905 (9th Cir. 2004) 283
Cerezo v. Mukasey, 512 F.3d 1163 (9th Cir. 2008) 257
Cesar v. Att'y Gen., No. 06-15140, 240 Fed. Appx. 856, 2007 WL 2068359 (11th Cir. 2007) .. 340
Chadha; INS v., 462 U.S. 919 (1983) 27
Chae Chan Pin v. United States, 130 U.S. 581 (1889) 27
Chaidez v. United States, 133 S. Ct. 1103 (2013) 76
Chairez, Matter of, 26 I&N Dec. 349 (BIA 2014) 186, 197, 199, 200, 205, 206, 214, 215, 299,
  325, 334, 335
Chairez, Matter of, 26 I&N Dec. 478 (BIA 2015) 207, 208, 215, 299, 334

Chan v. Gantner, 464 F.3d 289 (2d Cir. 2006) 495
Chang v. INS, 119 F.3d 1055 (3d Cir. 1997) 380, 386
Chapa-Garza; United States v., 243 F.3d 479 (5th Cir. 2001) 294
Charles v. Shanahan, 2012 WL 4794313 (D.N.J. Oct. 9, 2012) 148
Chavez-Alvarez, Matter of, 26 I&N Dec. 274 (BIA 2014) 53
Chavez-Martinez, Matter of, 24 I&N Dec. 272 (BIA 2007) 68, 69
Chavez-Perez v. Ashcroft, 386 F.3d 1284 (9th Cir. 2004) 60
Chevron v. USA Inc. v. Natural Res. Def. Council, 467 U.S. 837 (1984) 28
Chrzanoski v. Ashcroft, 327 F.3d 188 (2d Cir. 2003) 319
Cisneros-Perez v. Gonzales, 465 F.3d 386 (9th Cir. 2006) 338
C–J–H–, Matter of, 26 I&N Dec. 284 (BIA 2014) 460
Clark v. Martinez, 543 U.S. 371 (2005) 147
Conteh v. Gonzales, 461 F.3d 45 (1st Cir. 2006) 190, 317
Contreras-Bocanegra v. Holder, 629 F.3d 1170 (10th Cir. 2010) 491
Contreras-Bocanegra v. Holder, 678 F.3d 811 (10th Cir. 2012) 518
Coronado v. Holder, 759 F.3d 977 (9th Cir. 2014) 200, 204
Coronado-Durazo v. INS, 123 F.3d 1322 (9th Cir. 1997) 329
Corona-Garcia v. Gonzales, 128 Fed. Appx. 77, 2005 U.S. App. LEXIS (10th Cir. 2005)
    (unpublished) 61
Correa-Garces, Matter of, 20 I&N Dec. 451 (BIA 1992) 251, 351
Cortes-Salazar; United States v., 682 F.3d 953 (11th Cir. 2012) 298
Cotas-Vargas, Matter of, 23 I&N Dec. 849 (BIA 2005) 77
Coyt v. Holder, 593 F.3d 902 (9th Cir. 2010) 491, 518
Crespo v. Holder, 631 F.3d 130 (4th Cir. 2011) 55
Cruz v. Att'y Gen., 452 F.3d 240 (3d Cir. 2006) 69, 71
Cruz-Garza v. Ashcroft, 396 F.3d 1125 (10th Cir. 2005) 67
Cuellar-Gomez, Matter of, 25 I&N Dec. 850 (BIA 2012) 52, 286, 288
Cuevas-Gaspar v. Gonzales, 430 F.3d 1013 (9th Cir. 2005) 468, 569
C–V–T–, Matter of, 22 I&N Dec. 7 (BIA 1998) 656

D

D, Matter of, 1 I&N Dec. 143 (BIA 1941) 567
Dalton v. Ashcroft, 257 F.3d 200 (2d Cir. 2001) 188
Danesh, Matter of, 19 I&N Dec. 669 (BIA 1988) 239, 257
Danso v. Gonzales, 489 F.3d 709 (5th Cir. 2007) 62
Davey, Matter of, 26 I&N Dec. 37 (BIA 2012) 144, 330, 397, 442
Davis, Matter of, 20 I&N Dec. 536 (BIA 1992) 271, 290, 304
Davis v. Hendricks, 2012 WL 6005713 (D.N.J. 2012) 148
Deanda-Romo, Matter of, 23 I&N Dec. 597 (BIA 2003) 343, 411, 469
De La Nues, Matter of, 18 I&N Dec. 140 (BIA 1981) 77, 80, 81, 245
De Leon-Reynoso v. Ashcroft, 293 F.3d 633 (3d Cir. 2002) 247
Delgado v. Holder, 563 F.3d 863 (9th Cir. 2009) 393, 465
Demore v. Kim, 538 U.S. 510 (2003) 136, 144, 160
Desai v. Mukasey, 520 F.3d 762 (7th Cir. 2008) 331
Descamps v. United States, 133 S. Ct. 2276 (2013) .. 183, 184, 186, 195, 196, 197, 198, 205, 207,
    214, 215, 239, 245, 246, 247, 249, 276, 299, 324, 328
Devison-Charles, Matter of, 22 I&N Dec. 1362 (BIA 2000) 77, 564
Diaz-Nin; United States v., 221 F. Supp. 2d 584 (V.I. 2002) 112

Diem Thi Huynh v. Holder, No. 05-73446, 2009 U.S. App. LEXIS 7269 (9th Cir. Apr. 6, 2009) 250
Dillingham, Matter of, 21 I&N Dec. 1001 (BIA 1997) 80
Dillingham v. INS, 267 F.3d 996 (9th Cir. 2001) 64
Diomande v. Wrona, No. 05-73290 (E.D. Mich. Dec. 12, 2005) 137
Diop v. ICE/Homeland Sec., 656 F.3d 221 (3d Cir. 2011) 138
Discipio v. Ashcroft, 369 F.3d 472 (5th Cir. 2001) 71
Discipio v. Ashcroft, 417 F.3d 448 (5th Cir. 2005) 70
D–K–, Matter of, 25 I&N Dec. 761 (BIA 2012) 459
Dolt; United States v., 27 F.3d 235 (6th Cir. 1994) 329
Dominguez-Rodriguez, Matter of, 26 I&N Dec. 408 (BIA 2014) 326
Donawa v. Att'y Gen., 735 F.3d 1275 (11th Cir. 2013) 272
Drax v. Reno, 338 F.3d 98 (2d Cir. 2003) 493
Dulal-Whiteway v. DHS, 501 F.3d 116 (2d Cir. 2007) 30

E

Edwards, Matter of, 20 I&N Dec. 191 (BIA 1990) 655
Efagene v. Holder, 642 F.3d 918 (10th Cir. 2011) 259, 355
Elizalde-Altamirano; United States v., 226 Fed. Appx. 846, 2007 U.S. App. LEXIS 14959, 2007 WL 1765521 (10th Cir. 2007) 308
Enriquez-Gutierez v. Holder, 612 F.3d 400 (5th Cir. 2010) 487
Escobar, Matter of, 24 I&N Dec. 231 (BIA 2007) 468
Eslamizar, Matter of, 23 I&N Dec. 684 (BIA 2004) 52, 53, 80
Espinal-Andrades v. Holder, 777 F.3d 163 (4th Cir. 2015) 307
Espinoza-Gonzalez, Matter of, 22 I&N Dec. 889 (BIA 1999) 253, 575
Esposito, Matter of, 21 I&N Dec. 1 (BIA 1995) 480
Esquivel-Quintana, Matter of, 26 I&N Dec. 469 (BIA 2015) 268
Esquivel-Santana, Matter of, 26 I&N Dec. 469 (BIA 2015) 266
Essam Helmi El Shami; United States v., 434 F.3d 659 (4th Cir. 2005) 517
Estrada v. Holder, 560 F.3d 1039 (9th Cir. 2009) 330
Estrada-Espinoza v. Mukasey, 546 F.3d 1147 (9th Cir. 2008) 267, 268, 280, 578
Estrella; United States v., 758 F.3d 1239 (11th Cir. 2014) 203, 204

F

F–, Matter of, 6 I&N Dec. 783 (BIA 1955) 244
Fedorenko v. United States, 449 U.S. 490 (1981) 388, 389
Fernandez v. Mukasey, 544 F.3d 862 (7th Cir. 2008) 284
Fernandez-Bernal v. Att'y Gen., 257 F.3d 1034 (11th Cir. 2001) 28
Fernandez-Ruiz v. Gonzales, 410 F.3d 585 (9th Cir. 2005), *adopted en banc*, 466 F.3d 1121 (9th Cir. 2006) 30, 292, 300, 338
Fernandez-Vargas v. Gonzales, 548 U.S. 30 (2006) 114, 115
Ferreira, Matter of, 26 I&N Dec. 415 (BIA 2014) 200, 276, 324
Flores, Matter of, 17 I&N Dec. 225 (BIA 1980) 245, 250
Flores v. Holder, 779 F.3d 159 (2d Cir. 2015) 204
Flores-Ledezma v. Gonzales, 415 F.3d 375 (5th Cir. 2005) 109, 110
Flores-Leon v. INS, 272 F.3d 433 (7th Cir. 2001) 486
Flores-Lopez v. Holder, 685 F.3d 857 (9th Cir. 2012) 300

Florez v. Holder, 779 F.3d 207 (2d Cir. 2015) 342
Francis v. INS, 532 F.2d 268 (2d Cir. 1976) 479
Franco-Casasola v. Holder, 773 F.3d 33 (5th Cir. 2014) 200, 204, 215
Franklin, Matter of, 20 I&N Dec. 867 (BIA 1994), *aff'd*, Franklin v. INS, 72 F.3d 571 (8th Cir. 1995) 241, 257, 567
Fregozo v. Holder, 576 F.3d 1030 (9th Cir. 2009) 341
Frentescu, Matter of, 18 I&N Dec. 244 (BIA 1982) 384, 385, 463, 465
Fualaau, Matter of, 21 I&N Dec. 475 (BIA 1996) 254, 256
Fueyo, Matter of, 20 I&N Dec. 84 (BIA 1989) 513

G

G–, Matter of, 7 I&N Dec. 114 (BIA 1956) 245
Gabryelsky, Matter of, 20 I&N Dec. 750 (BIA 1993) 435, 492, 493
Gaiskov v. Holder, 567 F.3d 832 (7th Cir. 2009) 266, 267
Galvan-Rodriguez; United States v., 169 F.3d 217 (5th Cir. 1999) 302
Garcia; United States v., 606 F.3d 1317 (11th Cir. 2011) 575
Garcia v. Gonzales, 455 F.3d 465 (4th Cir. 2006) 300, 301, 576
Garcia v. Holder, 638 F.3d 511 (6th Cir. 2011) 274
Garcia v. Holder, 659 F.3d 1261 (9th Cir. 2011) 468
Garcia v. Shanahan, 615 F. Supp. 2d 175 (S.D.N.Y. 2009) 153
Garcia v. Att'y Gen., 462 F.3d 287 (3d Cir. 2006) 274
Garcia-Garcia, Matter of, 25 I&N Dec. 93 (BIA 2009) 162
Garcia-Jimenez v. Gonzales, 488 F.3d 1082 (9th Cir. 2007) 473, 494
Garcia-Jurado; United States v., 281 F. Supp 2d 498 (E.D.N.Y. 2003) 112
Garcia-Maldonado v. Gonzales, No. 05-60692 (5th Cir. June 29, 2007) 255
Garcia-Padron v. Holder, 558 F.3d 196 (2d Cir. 2009) 488
Garcia-Quintero v. Gonzales, 455 F.3d 1006 (9th Cir. 2006) 468
Gattem v. Gonzales, 412 F.3d 758 (7th Cir. 2005) 267, 320
Gerbier v. Holmes, 280 F.3d 297 (3d Cir. 2002) 283
Gertsenshteyn, Matter of, 24 I&N Dec. 111 (BIA 2007) 189, 190, 318
Gertsenshteyn v. United States DOJ, 544 F.3d 137 (2d Cir. 2008) 190
G–G–S–, Matter of, 26 I&N Dec. 339 (BIA 2014) 465
Ghani & Anwer v. Holder, 557 F.3d 836 (7th Cir. 2009) 251
Giammario v. Hurney, 311 F.2d 285 (3d Cir. 1962) 80
Gill v. Ashcroft, 335 F.3d 574 (7th Cir. 2003) 60, 564
Gill v. INS, 420 F.3d 82 (2d Cir. 2005) 242, 243, 254, 256
Gill; United States v., 748 F.3d 491 (2d Cir 2014) 492
Godinez-Arroyo v. Mukasey, 540 F.3d 848 (8th Cir. 2008) 256
Gonzales v. DHS, 508 F.3d 1227 (9th Cir. 2007) 113, 666
Gonzales v. Duenas-Alvarez, 549 U.S. 183 (2007) 191, 193, 215, 244, 246, 259, 265, 307, 325
Gonzalez-Gomez v. Achim, 441 F.3d 532 (7th Cir. 2006) 283
Gonzalez-Jaquez; United States v., 566 F.3d 1250 (10th Cir. 2009) 301
Gordon, Matter of, 20 I&N Dec. 52 (BIA 1989) 247
Gradiz v. Gonzales, 490 F.3d 1206 (10th Cir. 2007) 55
Grageda v. INS, 12 F.3d 919 (9th Cir. 1993) 241
Graham v. Mukasey, 519 F.3d 546 (6th Cir. 2008) 109
Grazley, Matter of, 14 I&N Dec. 330 (BIA 1973) 245, 247
Griffith; United States v., 455 F.3d 1339 (11th Cir. 2006) 338
Gruenangerl, Matter of, 25 I&N Dec. 351 (BIA 2010) 311, 312

Grullon, Matter of, 20 I&N Dec. 12 (BIA 1989) 56, 562
Gutnik v. Gonzales, 469 F.3d 683 (7th Cir. 2006) 461
Guzman-Martinez, Matter of, 25 I&N Dec. 845 (BIA 2012) 416

H

Hamdi; United States v., 432 F.3d 115 (2d Cir. 2005) 514
Hanif v. Att'y Gen., 694 F.3d 479 (3d Cir. 2012) 446
Hashmi, Matter of, 24 I&N Dec. 785 (BIA 2009) 436
Henry v. ICE, 493 F.3d 303 (3d Cir. 2007) 301
Hernandez, Matter of, 26 I&N Dec. 397 (BIA 2014) 201, 257, 258
Hernandez, Matter of, 26 I&N Dec. 464 (BIA 2015) 254
Hernandez v. Gonzales, 424 F.3d 42 (1st Cir. 2005) 138
Hernandez v. Att'y Gen., 513 F.3d 1336 (11th Cir. 2008) 301
Hernandez-Avalos; United States v., 251 F.3d 505 (5th Cir. 2001) 282
Hernandez-Casillas, Matter of, 20 I&N Dec. 262 (BIA 1990; AG 1991), *aff'd*, 983 F.2d 231 (5th Cir. 1993) 480
Hernandez-Cruz v. Holder, 651 F.3d 1094 (9th Cir. 2011) 248, 309
Hernandez de Anderson v. Gonzales, 497 F.3d 927 (9th Cir. 2007) 504
Hernandez-Gonzalez v. Holder, 778 F.3d 793 (9th Cir. 2015) 201, 202, 258
Hernandez-Guadarrama v. Ashcroft, 394 F.3d 674 (9th Cir. 2005) 344
Hernandez-Martinez v. Ashcroft, 329 F.3d 1117 (9th Cir. 2003) 260
Herrera-Inirio v. INS, 208 F.3d 299 (1st Cir. 2000) 61
Hosh v. Lucero, 680 F.3d 375 (4th Cir. 2012) 148, 149
Hranka, Matter of, 16 I&N Dec. 491 (BIA 1978) 512, 514
Husic v. Holder, 776 F.3d 59 (2d Cir. 2015) 446
Hussain v. Gonzales, 492 F. Supp. 2d 1024 (E.D. Wis. 2007) 137, 146
Hy v. Gillen, 588 F. Supp. 2d 122 (D. Mass. 2008) 153
Hyacinthe v. Att'y Gen., 215 Fed. Appx. 856, 2007 U.S. App. LEXIS 1685, 2007 WL 186512 (11th Cir. 2007) 382

I

Ibarra v. Holder, 736 F.3d 903 (10th Cir. 2013) 341, 342
Ibarra-Galindo; United States v., 206 F.3d 1337 (9th Cir. 2000) 283
Idy v. Holder, 674 F.3d 111 (1st Cir. 2012) 242
In re. *See name of party*
INS v. *See name of opposing party*
Islam, Matter of, 25 I&N Dec. 637 (BIA 2011) 382
Itani v. Ashcroft, 298 F.3d 1213 (11th Cir. 2002) 252, 576
Ivory; United States v., 475 F.3d 1232 (11th Cir. 2007) 301

J

Jaggernauth v. Att'y Gen., 432 F.3d 1346 (11th Cir. 2005) 309, 568
Jaghoori v. Holder, 772 F.3d 764 (4th Cir. 2014) 470
James v. Mukasey, 522 F.3d 250 (2d Cir. 2008) 266
Jean, Matter of, 23 I&N Dec. 373 (AG 2002) 456, 458, 460

Jean v. Gonzales, 452 F.3d 392 (5th Cir. 2006) 459
Jean-Baptiste; United States v., 395 F.3d 1190 (11th Cir. 2005) 388
Jean-Louis v. Att'y Gen., 582 F.3d 462 (3d Cir. 2009) 211
Jean-Pierre v. Att'y Gen., 500 F.3d 1315 (11th Cir. 2007) 30
Jeudy v. Holder, 768 F.3d 595 (7th Cir. 2014) 470
Jeune v. Candemeres, No. 13-22333-CIV-Altonaga/Simonton (S.D. Fla. Dec. 11, 2013) 160
Jeune v. Att'y Gen., 476 F.3d 199 (3d Cir. 2007) 273, 274
J–H–J–, Matter of, 26 I&N Dec. 563 (BIA 2015) 447
Jian Le Lin v. Att'y Gen., 681 F.3d 1236 (11th Cir. 2012) 491, 518
Jimenez-Gonzalez v. Mukasey, 548 F.3d 557 (7th Cir. 2008) 295
Jimenez-Santillano, Matter of, 21 I&N Dec. 567 (BIA 1996) 261, 350, 419, 420, 440, 441, 480
Johnson; United States v., 399 F.3d 1297 (11th Cir. 2005) 301
Johnson v. Robison, 415 U.S. 361 (1974) 27
Johnson v. State, 967 S.W. 2d 848 (Tex. Crim. App. 1998) (en banc) 210
Johnson v. United States, 559 U.S. 133 (2010) 185, 198, 206, 297, 298, 337, 338, 411
Jordan v. DeGeorge, 341 U.S. 223 (1951) 250
Joseph, Matter of, 22 I&N Dec. 799 (BIA 1999) 142, 330
Joseph v. Att'y Gen., 465 F.3d 123 (3d Cir. 2006) 304
Judulang v. Holder, 132 S. Ct. 476 (2011) 420, 440, 453, 477, 488, 489
Juice v. Mukasey, 530 F.3d 30 (1st Cir. 2008) 274
Jurado-Delgado, Matter of, 24 I&N Dec. 29 (BIA 2006), *rev. den.*, Jurado-Delgado v. Att'y
   Gen., No. 06-4495/07-1924, 2009 U.S. App. LEXIS 742 (3d Cir. Jan. 15, 2009) . 247, 248, 251, 470

K

K, Matter of, 9 I&N Dec. 715 (BIA 1962) 377
Kai Tung Chang v. Gantner, 464 F.3d 289 (2d Cir. 2006) 418
Kamara v. v. Att'y Gen., 420 F.3d 202 (3d Cir. 2005) 30
Kaneda, Matter of, 16 I&N Dec. 677 (BIA 1977) 67
Kanga, Matter of, 22 I&N Dec. 1206 (BIA 2000) 110, 248, 438, 492, 583
Kansas v. Hendricks, 521 U.S. 346, 356, 117 S. Ct. 2072, 138 L. Ed. 2d 501 (1997) 133
Kawashima v. Holder, 132 S. Ct. 1166 (2012) 265, 312, 313
Kenyeres v. Ashcroft, 538 U.S. 1301 (2003) 409
Keungne v. Att'y Gen., 561 F.3d 1281 (11th Cir. 2009) 254
Khalifah, Matter of, 21 I&N Dec. 107 (BIA 1995) 162
Kharana v. Gonzales, 487 F.3d 1280 (9th Cir. 2007) 315
Kholyavskiy v. Mukasey, 540 F.3d 555 (7th Cir. 2008) 461
Khotesouvan v. Morones, 386 F.3d 1298 (9th Cir. 2004) 160
Khourn, Matter of, 21 I&N Dec. 1041 (BIA 1997) 241, 261, 419
Khouzam v. Gonzales, 361 F.3d 161 (2d Cir. 2004) 584
Klementanovsky v. Gonzales, 501 F.3d 788 (7th Cir. 2007) 454
Knapik v. Ashcroft, 384 F.3d 84 (3d Cir. 2004) 243, 256
Kochlani, Matter of, 24 I&N Dec. 128 (BIA 2007) 251
Koljenovic, Matter of, 25 I&N Dec. 219 (BIA 2010) 448, 451
Koloamatangi, Matter of, 23 I&N Dec. 548 (BIA 2003) 471
Kotliar, Matter of, 24 I&N Dec. 124 (BIA 2007) 150, 151, 153
Kuhali v. Reno, 266 F.3d 93 (2d Cir. 2001) 304

L

Lanferman, Matter of, 25 I&N Dec. 721 (BIA 2012) 186, 197, 200, 205, 214
Lanier v. Att'y Gen., 631 F.3d 1363 (11th Cir. 2011) 446
Larin-Ulloa v. Gonzales, 462 F.3d 456 (5th Cir. 2006) 295, 296
Lawrence v. Att'y Gen., 457 Fed. Appx. 816 (11th Cir. 2012) 74
Le v. U.S. Att'y Gen., 196 F.3d 1352 (11th Cir. 1999) 294
League of United Latin Am. Citizens v. INS, 1988 U.S. Dist. LEXIS 12599 (C.D. Cal. July 15,
    1988), *vacated sub nom.* Reno v. Catholic Soc. Servs., Inc., 509 U.S. 43 (1993) 114
Leal, Matter of, 26 I&N. Dec. 20 (BIA 2012), *aff'd*, 771 F.3d 1140 (9th Cir. 2014) 243
Lee; United States v., 694 F.2d 649 (11th Cir. 1983) 516
Lekarczyk; United States v., 354 F. Supp. 2d 883 (W.D. 2005) 389
Lemus-Losa v. Holder, 576 F.3d 752 (7th Cir. 2009) 381
Leocal v. Ashcroft, 543 U.S. 1 (2004) ..28, 206, 257, 265, 292, 293, 294, 310, 319, 337, 343, 411,
    571, 574, 576, 580
Lepore; United States v., 304 F. Supp. 2d 183 (D. Mass. 2004) 492
Leslie v. Att'y Gen., 678 F.3d 265 (3d Cir. 2012) 138
L–G–, Matter of, 21 I&N Dec. 89 (BIA 1995) 278, 280
L–G–H–, Matter of, 26 I&N Dec. 365 (BIA 2014) 272, 279
Liao v. Rabbett, 398 F.3d 389 (6th Cir. 2005) 281
Liberal de Araugo v. Ashcroft, 399 F.3d 84 (1st Cir. 2005) 72
Lihua Jiang v. Hillary Clinton, 08-CV-4477, 2011 U.S. Dist. LEXIS 136584 (E.D.N.Y. Nov. 23,
    2011) 29
Lin v. INS, 238 F.3d 239 (3d Cir. 2001) 380, 386
Linnas, Matter of, 19 I&N Dec. 302 (BIA 1985) 81
Lopez v. Gonzales, 549 U.S. 47 (2006) 194, 265, 269, 271, 278, 283
Lopez v. Gonzales, 417 F.3d 934 (8th Cir. 2005) 282
Lopez; United States v., 445 F.3d 90 (2d Cir. 2006) 492
Lopez-Meza, Matter of, 22 I&N Dec. 1188 (BIA 1999) 260
Louisaire v. Muller, 758 F. Supp. 2d 229 (S.D.N.Y. 2010) 149
Louissaint, Matter of, 24 I&N Dec. 754 (BIA 2009) 249, 569, 571
Lovan v. Holder, 574 F.3d 990 (8th Cir. 2009) 465, 466
L–S–, Matter of, 22 I&N Dec. 645 (BIA 1999) 392
Lujan-Armendariz v. INS, 222 F.3d 728 (9th Cir. 2000) 58
Luna; United States v., 436 F.3d 312 (1st Cir. 2006) 492
Luu-Le v. INS, 224 F.3d 911 (9th Cir. 2000) 330
L–V–C–, Matter of, 22 I&N Dec. 594 (BIA 1999) 239, 406
Ly v. Hansen, 351 F.3d 263 (6th Cir. 2003) 137, 160

M

M–, Matter of, 2 I&N Dec. 721 (BIA, AG 1946) 249, 569
Madrane v. Hogan, No. Civ. Action 1:05-CV-2228, 2007 WL 404032 (M.D. Pa. Feb. 1,
    2007) 137, 147
Madriz-Alvarado v. Ashcroft, 383 F.3d 321 (5th Cir. 2004) 60
Malta, Matter of, 23 I&N Dec. 656 (BIA 2004) 299
Malta-Espinoza v. Gonzales, 478 F.3d 1080 (9th Cir. 2007) 299
Marin, Matter of, 16 I&N Dec. 581 (BIA 1978) 655, 656
Marin-Navarette; United States v., 244 F.3d 1284 (11th Cir. 2001) 319
Marino, Matter of, 15 I&N Dec. 284 (BIA 1976) 64

Marino v. INS, 537 F.2d 686 (2d Cir. 1976) 64
Marin-Rodriguez v. Holder, 612 F.3d 591 (7th Cir. 2010) 491, 518
Marmolejo-Campos v. Holder, 558 F.3d 903 (9th Cir. 2009) 259, 260, 355
Marrero v. United States, 743 F.3d 389 (3d Cir. 2014) 201, 205
Marroquin-Garcia, Matter of, 23 I&N Dec. 705 (AG 2005, BIA 1997) 564
Martin, Matter of, 23 I&N Dec. 491 (BIA 2002) 318
Martinez v. Mukasey, 519 F.3d 532 (5th Cir. 2008) 381, 445, 446
Martinez v. Mukasey, 551 F.3d 113 (2d Cir. 2008) 274
Martinez-Espinoza, Matter of, 25 I&N Dec. 118 (BIA 2009) 329, 396, 442
Martinez-Mercado v. Holder, 492 Fed. Appx. 890, 2012 WL 3055844, 2012 U.S. App. LEXIS
  (10th Cir. July 27, 2012) 397
Martinez-Serrano, Matter of, 25 I&N Dec. 151 (BIA 2009) 344
Martinez-Zapata, Matter of, 24 I&N Dec. 424 (BIA 2007) 258
Marya v. Gonzales, 147 Fed. Appx. 336, 2005 U.S. LEXIS 16841, 2005 WL 1926376 (4th Cir.
  2005) 73
Mata-Guerrero v. Holder, 627 F.3d 256 (7th Cir. 2010) 212
Mathews v. Diaz, 426 U.S. 67 (1976) 27
Mathews v. Eldridge, 424 U.S. 319 (1976) 158
Matter of. *See name of party*
MCI Telecomms. Corp. v. American Tel. & Tel. Co., 512 U. S. 218 (1994) 198
McMullen, Matter of, 19 I&N Dec. 90 (BIA 1984), *aff'd*, 788 F.2d 591 (9th Cir. 1986) 386
McMurray; United States v., 653 F.3d 367 (6th Cir. 2011) 575
McNaughton, Matter of, 16 I&N Dec. 569 (BIA 1978) 80, 245
McNeil v. Att'y Gen., 238 Fed. Appx. 878, 2007 WL 2412165, 2007 U.S. App. LEXIS 20582
  (3d Cir. Aug. 27, 2007) 392
Medina, Matter of, 15 I&N Dec. 611 (BIA 1976) 241, 243, 254, 255
Medina-Lopez, Matter of, 10 I&N Dec. 7 (BIA 1962) 377
Medina-Rosales v. Holder, 2015 U.S. App. LEXIS 2734, 2015 WL 756345 (10th Cir. 2015) ... 446
Medina-Villa; United States v., 567 F.3d 507 (9th Cir. 2009) 267, 280
Mejia v. Gonzales, 499 F.3d 991 (9th Cir. 2007) 457, 459
Mellouli v. Holder, 719 F.3d 995 (8th Cir. 2014), *cert. granted*, 134 S. Ct. 2873 (2014) .. 277, 331
Mena, Matter of, 17 I&N Dec. 38 (BIA 1979) 56, 244
Mendez v. Mukasey, 547 F.3d 345 (2d Cir. 2008) 246, 248
Mendez-Orellana, Matter of, 25 I&N Dec. 254 (BIA 2010) 335
Mendoza-Lopez; United States v., 481 U.S. 828 (1987) 111, 516
Mendoza-Mata; United States v., 322 F.3d 829 (5th Cir. 2003) 492
Merlos v. INS, 203 Fed Appx. 863, 2006 U.S. App. LEXIS 27247, 2006 WL 3147422 (9th Cir.
  2006) 409
M–H–, Matter of, 26 I&N Dec. 46 (BIA 2012) 384
Michel, Matter of, 21 I&N Dec. 1101 (BIA 1998) 110, 438
Mizrahi v. Gonzales, 492 F.3d 156 (2d Cir. 2007) 329
Mohammed v. Ashcroft, 261 F.3d 1244 (11th Cir. 2001) 486
Moncada, Matter of, 24 I&N Dec. 62 (BIA 2007) 396
Moncrieffe v. Holder, 569 U.S. __, 133 S. Ct. 1678 (2013) 194, 195, 214, 215, 245, 271, 273,
  324, 326, 328
Moncrieffe v. Holder, 662 F.3d 387 (5th Cir. 2011) 274, 275, 276
Montes-Flores; United States v., 736 F.3d 357 (4th Cir. 2013) 300
Montoya-Silva, Matter of, 26 I&N Dec. 123 (BIA 2013) 468
Moore v. Ashcroft, 251 F.3d 919 (11th Cir. 2001) 311, 568
Moosa v. INS, 171 F.3d 994 (5th Cir. 1999) 54
Mugalli v. Ashcroft, 258 F.3d 52 (2d Cir. 2001) 267

Munoz-Yepez v. Gonzales, 465 F.3d 347 (8th Cir. 2006) 473
M–W–, Matter of, 25 I&N Dec. 748 (BIA 2012) 265, 266
Myers v. McCormick, 112 Fed. Appx. 149, 2004 U.S. App. LEXIS 21306, 2004 WL 2296506 (3d Cir. 2004) 73

N

Nadarajah v. Gonzales, 443 F.3d 1069 (9th Cir. 2006) 146, 147
N–A–M–, Matter of, 24 I&N Dec. 336 (BIA 2007) 385, 392, 465
Nath v. Gonzales, 467 F.3d 1185 (9th Cir. Ariz. 2006) 67
National Cable & Telecomm. Ass'n v. Brand X Internet Servs., 545 U.S. 967 (2005) 28
Navarro-Coyazo; United States v., 108 Fed. Appx. 490, 2004 U.S. App. LEXIS 18530, 2004 WL 1923588 (9th Cir. Wash. 2004) 279
Navarro-Lopez v. Gonzales, 503 F.3d 1063 (9th Cir. 2007) (en banc) 196
Negrete-Ramirez v. Holder, 741 F.3d 1047 (9th Cir. 2014) 446
Nethagani v. Mukasey, 532 F.3d 150 (2d Cir. 2008) 393, 463, 465
Nicanor-Romero v. Mukasey, 523 F.3d 992 (9th Cir. 2008) 241, 259
Nieto Baquera v. Longshore, No. 13-cv-00543 (D.C. June 6, 2013) 149
Nijhawan v. Holder, 557 U.S. 29 (2009) 190, 191, 195, 214, 265, 314, 316, 317, 318, 574
Noble, Matter of, 21 I&N Dec. 672 (BIA 1997) 154
Nolan, Matter of, 19 I&N Dec. 539 (BIA 1988) 64
Notash v. Gonzales, 427 F.3d 693 (9th Cir. 2005) 245, 250, 251, 252
Nugent v. Ashcroft, 367 F.3d 162 (3d Cir. 2004) 247
Nunez-Reyes v. Holder, 646 F.3d 684 (9th Cir. 2011) 58, 61, 64

O

Obasohan v. Att'y Gen., 479 F.3d 785 (11th Cir. 2007) 316, 574
Ocampo, Matter of, 22 I&N Dec. 1301 (BIA 2000) 497
O'Cealleagh, Matter of, 23 I&N Dec. 976 (BIA 2006) 379, 386
Okabe v. INS, 671 F.2d 863 (5th Cir. 1982) 254
Olmos v. Holder, 2015 U.S. App. LEXIS 4778 (10th Cir. Mar. 24, 2015) 148, 149
Olquin-Rufino, Matter of, 23 I&N Dec. 896 (BIA 2006) 259
Omagah v. Ashcroft, 288 F.3d 254 (5th Cir. 2002) 420
Omargharib v. Holder, 775 F.3d 192 (4th Cir. 2014) 203, 204
Omari v. Gonzales, 419 F.3d 303 (5th Cir. 2005) 579
Onyido, Matter of, 22 I&N Dec. 552 (BIA 1999) 320
Oouch v. Department of Homeland Sec., 633 F.3d 119 (2d Cir. 2010) 267
Ortega-Cabrera, Matter of, 23 I&N Dec. 793 (BIA 2005) 345
Ortega-Lopez, Matter of, 26 I&N Dec. 99 (BIA 2013) 240
Oyebanji v. Gonzales, 418 F.3d 260 (3d Cir. 2005) 301, 575
Ozkok, Matter of, 19 I&N Dec. 546 (BIA 1988) 53, 54, 57, 250, 567

P

P, Matter of, 2 I&N Dec. 887 (BIA 1947) 567
P, Matter of, 3 I&N Dec. 5 (BIA 1947) 255

Pacheco-Ventura, Matter of, No. A44 801 843, 2003 BIA LEXIS 14, 2003 WL 23508549 (BIA Dec. 29, 2003) 69, 70, 329
Padilla v. Gonzales, 397 F.3d 1016 (7th Cir. 2005); *subsequent petition for review dismissed on jurisdictional grounds*, 470 F.3d 1209 (7th Cir. 2006) 252, 259
Padilla v. Kentucky, 559 U.S. 356 (2010) 75, 76, 389, 561
Padilla-Reyes; United States v., 247 F.3d 1158 (11th Cir. 2001) 266
Paek, Matter of, 26 I&N Dec. 403 (BIA 2014) 448
Palacios-Suarez; United States v., 418 F.3d 692 (6th Cir. 2005) 283
Palermo v. Smith, 17 F.2d 534 (2d Cir. 1975) 64
Pallares-Galan; United States v., 359 F.3d 1088 (9th Cir. 2004) 578
Papazoglou v. Holder, 725 F.3d 790 (7th Cir. 2013) 446
Paredes-Urrestarazu v. INS, 36 F.3d 801 (9th Cir. 1994) 56
Parodi, Matter of, 17 I&N Dec. 608 (BIA 1980) 435, 452
Partyka v. Att'y Gen., 417 F.3d 408 (3d Cir. 2005) 188, 243, 256, 274
Pascua v. Holder, 641 F.3d 316 (9th Cir. 2011) 488
Patao v. Gonzales, 131 Fed. Appx. 516, U.S. App. LEXIS 8575, 2005 WL 1126984 (9th Cir. 2005) 581
Patel v. Ashcroft, 294 F.3d 465 (3d Cir. 2002) 416
Patel v. Ashcroft, 401 F.3d 400 (6th Cir. 2005) 302
Patel v. Att'y Gen., 334 F.3d 1259 (11th Cir. 2003) 69, 573
Paulus, Matter of, 11 I&N Dec. 274 (BIA 1965) 277
Penuliar v. Ashcroft, 395 F.3d 1037 (9th Cir. 2005) 193, 300
Peralta-Taveras v. Gonzales, 488 F.3d 580 (2d Cir. 2007) 473, 494
Perez, Matter of, 22 I&N Dec. 689 (BIA 1999) 468
Perez, Matter of, 22 I&N Dec. 1325 (BIA 2000) 264
Perez-Contreras, Matter of, 20 I&N Dec. 615 (BIA 1992) 244, 254, 569
Perez-Gonzalez v. Ashcroft, 379 F.3d 783 (9th Cir. 2004) 113
Perez-Munoz v. Keisler, 507 F.3d 357 (5th Cir. 2007) 301
Perez-Pimentel v. Mukasey, 530 F.3d 321 (5th Cir. 2008) 457, 459
Perez Santana v. Holder, 731 F.3d 50 (1st Cir. 2013) 75
Peters v. Ashcroft, 383 F.3d 302 (5th Cir. 2004) 329
Phan v. Holder, 667 F.3d 448 (4th Cir. 2012) 75
Phong Nguyen Tran, Matter of, 21 I&N Dec. 291 (BIA 1996) 343, 411
Pickering, Matter of, 23 I&N Dec. 621 (BIA 2003), *rev'd*, Pickering v. Gonzales, 465 F.3d 263 (6th Cir. 2006) 65, 66, 67, 77
Pino v. Landon, 349 U.S. 901 (1955) 53
Pinzon, Matter of, 26 I&N Dec. 189 (BIA 2013) 251, 351
Pittman; United States v., 441 F.2d 1098 (9th Cir. 1971) 245
Plasencia-Ayala v. Mukasey, 516 F.3d 738 (9th Cir. 2008) 258, 259, 355
Plyler v. Doe, 457 U.S. 202 (1982) 27
Pola v. United States, 2015 U.S. 778 F.3d 525 (6th Cir. 2015) 75
Popal v. Gonzales, 416 F.3d 249 (3d Cir. 2005) 300
Pornes Garcia; United States v., 171 F.3d 142 (2d Cir. 1999) 283
Portela; United States v., 469 F.3d 496 (6th Cir. 2006) 300
Poveda v. Att'y Gen., 692 F.3d 1168 (11th Cir. 2012) 453, 454
Prestol Espinal v. U.S. Att'y Gen., 653 F.3d 213 (3d Cir. 2011) 491, 518
Prieto-Romero v. Clark, 534 F.3d 1053 (9th Cir. 2008) 160, 161
Prudencio v. Holder, 669 F.3d 472 (4th Cir. 2012) 211, 212
Pruidze v. Att'y Gen., 632 F.3d. 234 (6th Cir. 2011) 491, 518
Puente-Salazar, Matter of, 22 I&N Dec. 1006 (BIA 1999) 294
Pula, Matter of, 19 I&N Dec. 467 (BIA 1987) 423

Punu, Matter of, 22 I&N Dec. 224 (BIA 1998) 53, 54, 563

Q

Quee de Cunningham v. U.S. Att'y Gen., 335 F.3d 1262 (11th Cir. 2003) 445
Quezada-Bucio v. Ridge, 317 F. Supp. 2d 1221 (W.D. Wash. 2004) 148
Quintero-Salazar v. Keisler, 506 F.3d 688 (9th Cir. 2007) 259

R

Rafipour, Matter of, 16 I&N Dec. 470 (BIA 1978) 435
Rainford, Matter of, 20 I&N Dec. 598 (BIA 1992) 110, 248, 433, 439, 492
Ramirez v. Ashcroft, 361 F. Supp. 2d 650 (S.D. Tex. 2005) 246
Ramirez-Garcia; United States v., 646 F.3d 778 (11th Cir. 2011) 266
Ramirez-Rivero, Matter of, 18 I&N Dec. 135 (BIA 1981) 77, 80
Ramirez-Vargas, Matter of, 24 I&N Dec. 599 (BIA 2008) 468
Ramos, Matter of, 23 I&N Dec. 336 (BIA 2002) 294
Ramos v. Holder, 546 Fed. Appx. 705, 2013 U.S. App. LEXIS 23954, 2013 WL 6224635 (9th
 Cir. 2013) 53, 290
Ramos v. Att'y Gen., 709 F.3d 1066 (11th Cir. 2013) 309
Recio-Prado v. Gonzales, 456 F.3d 819 (8th Cir. 2006) 255
Rede-Mendez; United States v., 680 F.3d 552 (6th Cir. 2012) 302
Rendon v. Holder, 764 F.3d 1077 (9th Cir. 2014) 202, 204
Renteria-Gonzalez v. INS, 310 F.3d 825 (5th Cir. 2002), *reh'g en banc denied*, 322 F.3d 804
 (5th Cir. 2003) 72
Resendiz-Alcaraz v. Ashcroft, 383 F.3d 1262 (11th Cir. 2004) 61
Restrepo v. Att'y Gen., 617 F.3d 787 (3d Cir. 2010) 266
Restrepo-Aguilar; United States v., 74 F.3d 361 (1st Cir. 1996) 282
Reyes-Torres v. Holder, 645 F.3d 1073 (9th Cir. 2011) 75
Reza-Murillo, Matter of, 25 I&N Dec. 296 (BIA 2010) 468
Richards v. Att'y Gen., 2005 U.S. App. LEXIS 20267, No. 05-1305; 05-3129 (3d Cir. 2005) ...60
Rivas, Matter of, 26 I&N Dec. 130 (BIA 2013) 453, 455
Rivas-Gomez v. Gonzales, 225 Fed. Appx. 680, U.S. App. LEXIS 7269, 2007 WL 851768 (9th
 Cir. 2007) 457
Rivens, Matter of, 25 I&N Dec. 623 (BIA 2011) 102, 245
Rivera-Cuartas v. Holder, 605 F.3d 699 (9th Cir. 2010) 268
Rivera-Valencia, Matter of, 24 I&N Dec. 484 (BIA 2008) 53
Robles-Rodriguez; United States v., 281 F.3d 900 (9th Cir. 2002) 319
Robles-Urrea, Matter of, 24 I&N Dec. 22 (BIA 2006) 252, 470
Robles-Urrea v. Holder, 678 F.3d 702 (9th Cir. 2012) 253, 576
Robleto-Pastora v. Holder, 567 F.3d 437 (9th Cir. 2009) 461
Rodriguez, Matter of, 25 I&N Dec. 784 (BIA 2012) 449
Rodriguez v. Robbins, 715 F.3d 1127 (9th Cir. 2013) 133, 137
Rodriguez-Carrillo, Matter of, 22 I&N Dec. 1031 (BIA 1999) 310
Rodriguez-Munoz v. Gonzales, 419 F.3d 245 (3d Cir. 2005) 494
Rodriguez-Rodriguez, Matter of, 22 I&N Dec. 991 (BIA 1999) 266
Rodriguez-Ruiz, Matter of, 22 I&N Dec. 1378 (BIA 2000) 64
Rojas, Matter of, 23 I&N Dec. 117 (BIA 2001) 148
Rojas v. Att'y Gen., 728 F.3d 203 (3d Cir. 2013) 277, 325

Roldan, Matter of, 22 I&N Dec. 512 (BIA 1999) 57, 58, 562, 563, 564
Roper v. Simmons, 543 U.S. 551 (2005) 79
Rosenberg v. Fleuti, 374 U.S. 449 (1963) 100
Rotimi, Matter of, 24 I&N Dec. 567 (BIA 2008) 451
Rotimi v. Holder, 577 F.3d 133 (2d Cir. 2009) 452
Ruiz-Lopez, Matter of, 25 I&N Dec. 551 (BIA 2011), *aff'd*, 682 F.3d 513 (6th Cir. 2012) 242, 243, 256
Ruiz-Vidal v. Gonzales, 473 F.3d 1072 (9th Cir. 2007) 277
Rumierz v. Gonzales, 456 F.3d 31 (1st Cir. 2006) 69

S

St. Cyr; INS v., 533 U.S. 289 (2001) 477, 481, 486, 517
Salazar-Regino, Matter of, 23 I&N Dec. 223 (BIA 2002) 54, 61, 563
Saleh v. Gonzales, 495 F.3d 17 (2d Cir. 2007) 71
Salomon-Bajxac v. U.S. Att'y Gen., 558 Fed. Appx. 160 (3d Cir. 2014) 256
Samaniego-Meraz v. INS, 53 F.3d 254 (9th Cir. 1995) 489
Samuels v. Chertoff, 550 F.3d 252 (2d Cir. 2008) 4 .... 57, 459
Sanchez, Matter of, 17 I&N Dec. 218 (BIA) 454
Sanchez v. Holder, 757 F.3d 712 (7th Cir. 2014) 208
Sanchez-Cornejo, Matter of, 25 I&N Dec. 273 (BIA 2010) 271, 331
Sanchez-Fajardo v. Holder, 659 F.3d 1303 (11th Cir. 2011) 211, 215
Sanchez-Linn, Matter of, 20 I&N Dec. 362 (BIA 1991) 254
Sanchez-Sosa, Matter of, 25 I&N Dec. 807 (BIA 2012) 619
Sandoval v. INS, 240 F.3d 577 (7th Cir. 2001) 66
Santacruz; United States v., 563 F.3d 894 (9th Cir. 2009) 259
Santapaola v. Ashcroft, 249 F. Supp. 2d 181 (D. Conn. 2003) 320
Santos-Lopez, Matter of, 23 I&N Dec. 419 (BIA 2002) 281
Sanudo, Matter of, 23 I&N Dec. 968 (BIA 2006) 188, 254, 338, 411
Sanusi v. Gonzales, 474 F.3d 341 (6th Cir. 2007) 71
Saysana, Matter of, 24 I&N Dec. 602 (BIA 2008) 152
Saysana v. Gillen, 590 F.3d 7 (1st Cir. 2009) 152
Scarlett v. ICE, 632 F. Supp. 2d 214 (W.D.N.Y. 2009) 148
Scarpulla, Matter of, 15 I&N Dec. 139 (BIA 1974) 80, 245
Scheerer v. Att'y Gen., 513 F.3d 1244 (11th Cir. 2008) 437
Seale v. INS, 323 F.3d 150 (1st Cir. 2003) 486
Sejas, Matter of, 24 I&N Dec. 236 (BIA 2007) 256
Serna, Matter of, 20 I&N Dec. 579 (BIA 1992) 240, 419, 567
Shanu, Matter of, 23 I&N Dec. 754 (BIA 2005) 381
Shepard v. United States, 544 U.S. 13 (2005) 185, 198, 215, 244
Short, Matter of, 20 I&N Dec. 136 (BIA 1989) 197, 241, 244, 254, 569
S–I–K–, Matter of, 24 I&N Dec. 324 (BIA 2007) 315, 321
Silva, Matter of, 16 I&N Dec. 626 (BIA 1976) 479
Silva-Trevino, Matter of, 24 I&N Dec. 687 (AG 2008), *vacated*, 26 I&N Dec. 550 (AG 2015) 183, 197, 208, 209, 210, 213, 214, 240, 241, 242, 243, 246, 249, 259, 268
Simon; United States v., 168 F.3d 1271 (11th Cir. 1999) 282
Simpson; United States v., 319 F.3d 81 (2d Cir. 2002) 282
Singh, Matter of, 25 I&N Dec. 670 (BIA 2012) 299, 301
Singh v. Ashcroft, 383 F.3d 144 (3d Cir. 2004) 578
Singh v. Att'y Gen., 561 F.3d 1275 (11th Cir. 2009) 77

Singh v. Att'y Gen., 677 F.3d 503 (3d Cir. 2012) 314, 315, 316
Small, Matter of, 23 I&N Dec. 448 (BIA 2002) 319
Smalley v. Ashcroft, 354 F.3d 332 (5th Cir. 2003) 406, 407
Smith, Matter of, 11 I&N Dec. 325 (BIA 1965) 102
Smriko, Matter of, 23 I&N Dec. 836 (BIA 2005) 461
Soetarto v. INS, 516 F.2d 778 (7th Cir. 1975) 80
Song, Matter of, 23 I&N Dec. 173 (BIA 2001) 76, 573
Soram, Matter of, 25 I&N Dec. 378 (BIA 2010) 341
Soriano, Matter of, 21 I&N Dec. 516 (BIA 1996, AG 1997) 481
Stanovsek v. Holder, 768 F.3d 515 (6th Cir. 2014) 446
Stanton v. Stanton, 421 U.S. 7 (1975) 28
Stasinski, Matter of, 11 I&N Dec. 202 (BIA 1965) 567
Stevic; INS v., 467 U.S. 407 (1984) 464
Storey v. State, 133 So.3d 528 (Fla. 2014) 573
Strelchikov v. U.S. Att'y Gen., 242 Fed. Appx. 789, 2007 U.S. App. LEXIS 14321 (3d Cir.
    2007) 301
Strydom, Matter of, 25 I&N Dec. 507 (BIA 2011) 343
Suh, Matter of, 23 I&N Dec. 626 (BIA 2003) 63
Syblis v. Att'y Gen., 763 F.3d 348 (3d Cir. 2014) 325
Sylvain v. Att'y Gen., 714 F.3d 150 (3d Cir. 2013) 148
Szalai v. Holder, 572 F.3d 975 (9th Cir. 2009) 342

T

Tapia-Garcia v. INS, 237 F.3d 1216 (10th Cir. 2001) 31
Tavarez-Peralta, Matter of, 26 I&N Dec. 171 (BIA 2013) 352
Taylor v. United States, 495 U.S. 575 (1990) 184, 187, 198, 214, 264, 309
Teixeira, Matter of, 21 I&N Dec. 316 (BIA 1996) 244
Tejwani, Matter of, 24 I&N Dec. 97 (BIA 2007) 251, 406, 407
Tenesaca Delgado v. Mukasey, 516 F.3d 65 (2d Cir. 2008) 666
Texas v. United States, 2015 U.S. Dist. LEXIS 18551 (S.D. Tex. Feb. 16, 2015) 11
Thomas, Matter of, 21 I&N Dec. 20 (BIA 1995) 53
Tibke v. INS, 335 F.2d 42 (2d Cir. 1964) 435
Tijani v. Willis, 430 F.3d 1241 (9th Cir. 2005) 137, 160
Tin, Matter of, 14 I&N Dec. 371 (RC 1973) 667
Tiwari, Matter of, 19 I&N Dec. 875 (BIA 1989), *reconsideration denied*, 20 I&N Dec. 254 (BIA
    1991) 240, 261, 344, 441
Tobar-Lobo, Matter of, 24 I&N Dec. 143 (BIA 2007) 240, 258, 355
Togbah v. Ashcroft, 104 Fed. Appx. 788; 2004 U.S. App. LEXIS 14149, 2004 WL 1530494 (3d
    Cir. 2004) 457
Tokatly v. Ashcroft, 371 F.3d 613 (9th Cir. 2004) 340, 581
Torres v. Holder, 764 F.3d 152 (2d Cir. 2014) 307
Torres; United States v., 383 F.3d 92 (3d Cir. 2004) 492
Torres-Garcia, Matter of, 23 I&N Dec. 866 (BIA 2006) 115, 665, 666
Torres-Varela, Matter of, 23 I&N Dec. 78 (BIA 2001) 257, 260, 438, 569
Torres-Villalobos; United States v., 487 F.3d 607 (8th Cir. 2007) 295, 300
Totimeh v. Att'y Gen., 666 F.3d 109 (3d Cir. 2012) 259, 355
Tran, Matter of, 21 I&N Dec. 291 (BIA 1996) 239, 256
Tran v. Gonzales, 414 F.3d 464 (3d Cir. 2005) 301
Trent; United States v., 767 F.3d 1046 (10th Cir. 2014) 199, 204, 207, 214, 215

Trevino v. Holder, 742 F.3d 197 (5th Cir. 2014) 211
Trinidad-Aquino; United States v., 259 F.3d 1140 (9th Cir. 2001) 294
Truong, Matter of, 22 I&N Dec. 1090 (BIA 1999) 486

U

Uluocha, Matter of, 20 I&N Dec. 133 (BIA 1989) 141
United States v. *See name of opposing party*
Uritsky v. Gonzales, 399 F.3d 728 (6th Cir. 2005) 54, 77
Uritzky v. Ridge, 286 F. Supp. 2d 842 (E.D. Mich. 2003) 155

V

Valansi v. Ashcroft, 278 F.3d 203 (3d Cir. 2002) 310, 568, 580
Valiente-Castaneda, Matter of, No. A29 203 237 2005 BIA LEXIS 25, 2006 WL 448266 (BIA Jan. 23, 2006) 345
Valles-Perez, Matter of, 21 I&N Dec. 769 (BIA 1997) 139, 141
Vargas v. DHS, 451 F.3d 1105 (10th Cir. 2006) 267
Vargas-Duran; United States v., 319 F.3d 194 (5th Cir. 2003) 294
Vartelas v. Holder, 132 S. Ct. 1479 (2012) 101, 106, 470, 487
Vasquez-Muniz, Matter of, 23 I&N Dec. 207 (BIA 2002) 306, 402
Vasquez-Velezmoro v. INS, 281 F.3d 693 (8th Cir. 2002) 564
Veal; United States v., 453 F.3d 164 (3d Cir. 2006) 332, 336
Velasco-Giron v. Holder, 768 F.3d 723 (7th Cir. 2014) 269
Velazquez-Herrera v. Holder, 24 I&N Dec. 503 (BIA 2008) 340
V–F–D–, Matter of, 23 I&N Dec. 859 (BIA 2006) 267
Villegas-Hernandez; United States v., 468 F.3d 874 (5th Cir. 2006) 300
Vo v. Gonzales, 482 F.3d 363 (5th Cir. 2007) 568
Von don Nguyen v. Holder, 571 F.3d 524 (6th Cir. 2009) 302, 303
Vuksanovic v. Att'y Gen., 439 F.3d 1308 (11th Cir. 2006) 255
V–X–, Matter of, 26 I&N Dec. 147 (BIA 2013) 564
V–Z–S–, Matter of, 22 I&N Dec. 1338 (BIA 2000) 244, 245, 246, 308, 567

W

W–, Matter of, 22 I&N Dec. 1405 (BIA 2000) 150
Wadja v. Holder, 727 F.3d 457 (6th Cir. 2013) 266
Wadud, Matter of, 19 I&N Dec. 182 (BIA 1984) 350, 419, 480
Wala v. Mukasey, 511 F.3d 102 (2d Cir. 2007) 248, 249
Waldron v. Holder, No. 11-1981, 2012 U.S. App. LEXIS 16277 (8th Cir. Aug. 6, 2012) 457
Wallace v. Gonzales, 463 F.3d 135 (2d Cir. 2006) 78
Wallace; United States v., 532 F.3d 126 (2d Cir. 2008) 276
Wellington v. Holder, 623 F.3d 115 (2d Cir. 2010) 62
Westman, Matter of, 17 I&N Dec. 50 (BIA 1979) 245
White v. INS, 17 F.3d 475 (1st Cir. 1994) 56
William v. Gonzales, 499 F.3d 329 (4th Cir. 2007) 491, 518
Wilson v. Ashcroft, 350 F.3d 377 (3d Cir. 2003) 282
Wilson; United States v., 316 F.3d 506 (4th Cir. 2003) 111, 112

Wojtkow, Matter of, 18 I&N Dec. 111 (BIA 1981) 254

Y

Yanez-Garcia, Matter of, 23 I&N Dec. 390 (BIA 2002) 271, 278, 280, 281, 290
Yanez-Popp v. INS, 998 F.2d 231 (4th Cir. 1993) 73
Yeung, Matter of, 21 I&N Dec. 610 (BIA 1996) 445
Yeung v. INS, 72 F.3d 843 (11th Cir. 1996) 454
Yeung v. INS, 76 F.3d 337 (11th Cir. 1996) 28
Yick Wo v. Hopkins, 118 U.S. 356 (1886) 27
Y–L, Matter of, A–G–, & R–S–R–, 23 I&N Dec. 270 (AG 2002) 464, 465, 584

Z

Zadvydas v. Davis, 533 U.S. 678 (2001) 147
Zaitona v. INS, 9 F.3d 432 (6th Cir. 1993) 251
Zambrano v. INS, 509 U.S. 918 (1993) 114
Zamudio; United States v., 314 F.3d 517 (10th Cir. 2002) 61
Zangwill, Matter of, 18 I&N Dec. 22 (BIA 1981) 250, 567
Zavala v. Ridge, 310 F. Supp. 2d 1071 (N.D. Cal. 2004) 156, 158
Zhan Gao v. Holder, 595 F.3d 549 (4th Cir. 2010) 426, 428
Zhang v. Mukasey, 509 F.3d 313, 315-316 (6th Cir. 2007) 381
Zorilla-Vidal, Matter of, 24 I&N Dec. 768 (BIA 2009) 328
Zuh v. Mukasey, 547 F.3d 504 (4th Cir. 2008) 29
Zuniga-Soto; United States v., 527 F.3d 1110 (10th Cir. 2008) 300

SUBJECT-MATTER INDEX
IMMIGRATION CONSEQUENCES OF CRIMINAL ACTIVITY, SIXTH EDITION

A

AAO (Administrative Appeals Office)
overview, 19–20
T status, denial of, 613–614

Abuse. See Child abuse; Domestic violence

"Abuse of discretion"
standard of review, 29

ACCA (Armed Criminal Career Act of 1984)
classification of crimes, 184, 411

ACCESS (Agreements of Cooperation in Communities to Enhance Safety and Security)
immigration law enforcement, 120

Accurint
tool in criminal-alien law practice, 35, 643

Acquired citizenship
at birth, citizenship at, 500–501
effective dates, 500
relief under, 499–503

Adam Walsh Child Protection and Safety Act of 2006
failure to register as sex offender, 354–355

Addicts
controlled substance offenses, 332–333
ground for deportation, 332–333

Address, change of
registration requirement, 347–349

Adjustment of status
generally, 432–441
advance parole, 8
aggravated felony offenses, 390, 438
alien smuggling charges, 415–416, 508–509
arriving aliens, 452–455
defined, 102, 432
discretionary relief, 30–31, 435–436, 650
domestic violence offenses, 410–411, 439–440
employment, 649
entry without inspection, 448–449
export violations, 425–426, 440–441
failure to register, 419–421, 440
falsification of documents, 419–421
firearms offenses, 401, 438–439
forms, fees, and attachments, 648–650
ground of inadmissibility, 432–435
jurisdiction, 436–438
LPRs, 102–103, 435, 444–451
money laundering offenses, 405–407
moral turpitude, crimes of, 376–380
nonimmigrant visa holders, 102
Notice to Appear, 20–21
permanent and non-permanent residents, availability, 435
refugees, 650
registration offenses, 440
removal proceedings, 648–650
Section 212(c) waiver in conjunction with, 492–493
Section 212(h) waiver in conjunction with, 447–448
U status, 619–621
visa fraud, 419–420, 440

Administrative Appeals Office (AAO)
overview, 19–20
T status, denial of, 613–614

Administrative orders, challenge to
as defense to criminal charge of re-entry after removal, 515–516

Administrative Procedure Act of 1946
rulemaking procedure, 154

Admissions to prosecutor, required for diversion
advice to client about, 563
effect of, 56–57

Advance parole
adjustment of status, 8

Adverse immigration consequences, avoiding
federal first offender treatment, 563–564
juvenile delinquency, 564–565
methods to, 562–566

AEDPA. See Antiterrorism and Effective Death Penalty Act of 1996

petty-offense exception, 565–566
pretrial diversion, 562–563

AEDPA. See Antiterrorism and Effective Death Penalty Act of 1996

A-file
FOIA requests, 36
method of agencies locating client, 117

Africa
temporary protected status (TPS), 8

Agencies, government
locating clients with criminal convictions by, 115–120
overview, 14–20

Aggravated assault
moral turpitude, crimes of, 254, 256
pleas, 571, 586

Aggravated felonies. See also specific offenses
adjustment of status, 390, 438
alien smuggling, 264, 311, 343–344, 416, 508–510, 575
asylum and withholding of removal, 391–393, 572, 582–583
attempted possession of stolen property, 310
attempts, 320–321
bail jumping, 264
burglary, 264, 309–310
cancellation of removal, 582
child pornography, 264
classification of crimes, 263–321
commercial bribery, 264, 311–312, 486
consequences of conviction, 390–394, 429, 572–580
conspiracy, 264, 318–321
Convention Against Torture (CAT), 393–394
counterfeiting, 264, 311, 486
crimes of violence, 290–313, 318–320
definition of, 263–265, 486–487
denaturalization, 394
deportability or removability, 390, 397–398
drug trafficking crimes, 269–273
embezzlement, 310–311, 580
explosives, 263, 304
federal, state, and certain foreign convictions, 264

felony requirement, 318–320
firearms offenses, 301, 304–307, 401–403, 584
forgery, 264, 486
fraud, 264, 312
gambling, 264
judicial review of "particularly serious crime" determination, 393
kidnapping, 264
loss to victim in excess of $10,000, 573–574
LPRs and waivers, 444–445
mandatory detention, 390, 571–572
misdemeanors treated as, 318–320
modified categorical approach, 185–186
money laundering, 312, 335–336, 409
moral turpitude, crimes of, 254
murder, 263, 265–266
non-elemental facts, 192
not crimes of violence, 300–301
obstruction of justice, 264, 311
offenses that depend on amount of funds involved, 312–313
offenses that depend on "commercial advantage," 317–318
offenses that depend on sentence imposed, 311–312
pardons, 63
peonage, 264
perjury, 264, 311
personal use exception, 396–397
pleas to avoid, 581–582
political offense exception, 393
prostitution enterprises, 264, 317–318
racketeering, 264
rape, 263, 266–267
restitution, 314–316
Section 212(c) waiver, 485–487, 489
sentence for, 311–312, 586–587
    term of imprisonment, 572–573
slavery offenses, 264
statutory rape, 267–269
subornation of perjury, 264, 311
tax evasion, 264, 312–313
theft offenses, 248, 264, 307–311
U.S. instrument, falsely making, 264
voluntary departure, 390–391

Aggravated felons, expedited removal of
overview, 107–110
relief from, 110

Aggravated fleeing and eluding
pleas, 571

Aggravated stalking
moral turpitude, crimes of, 255
pleas, 571–572

Agreements of Cooperation in Communities to Enhance Safety and Security (ACCESS)
immigration law enforcement, 120

Aiding and abetting
classification of crime, 192
controlled substance offense, 575
moral turpitude, crimes of, 244–245

AILALink
tool in criminal-alien law practice, 36–37

AILA.org
tool in criminal-alien law practice, 36–37

Alien smuggling
adjustment of status, 415–416, 508–509
aggravated felony, 264, 311, 343–344, 416, 508–510, 575
asylum and withholding of removal, 417–418, 509
consequences of, 343–347, 415–419, 430
Convention Against Torture (CAT), 417–418
crime of, 345–347
defined, 345
denaturalization, 418–419
deportability or removability, 343–344, 416
  relief absent conviction, 507–508
immediate family member, exception for, 345, 507
inadmissibility
  adjustment of status, and visa eligibility, 415–416
  relief absent conviction, 507–508
mandatory detention, 416
moral turpitude, crimes of, 261–262
naturalization, 418–419, 510
pleas, 575
relief, 507–510
  aggravated felony, 508–510
  asylum and withholding of removal, 509
  cancellation of removal, 508–509
  deportability and inadmissibility, absent conviction, 507–508
  naturalization, 510
  Section 212(c) waiver, 509
  Section 212(h) waiver, 509
  waiver, 507–508
voluntary departure, 417

All Writs Act of 1789
conviction under, 72

American citizens
acquired citizenship. *See* Acquired citizenship
derivative citizenship. *See* Derivative citizenship
status of, 2–3

Amnesty programs
adjustment of status, 102. *See also* Adjustment of status
reinstatement of removal, 113–114

Anti-Drug Abuse Act of 1986
deportability, 370

Antiterrorism and Effective Death Penalty Act of 1996 (AEDPA)
key legislation, 38
lawful admission requirement, 471
motion to reopen, 520
retroactive application of, 482–488
Section 212(c) waiver, 106–107, 477, 480–482, 654–655

Appeals
AAO. *See* Administrative Appeals Office
Attorney General review, 19
BIA. *See* Board of Immigration Appeals
bond determination, 140
  automatic stay during, 154–158
federal judicial review, 27–33
Office of Chief Counsel, 19
petitions for review to Court of Appeals, 31–32
removal proceedings, 24–26
T status, denial of, 613–614

Applicants for admission
inadmissibility, 98–104

AR-11 Form
   change of address, 347
Arizona
   REPAT program, 116
Armed Criminal Career Act of 1984 (ACCA)
   classification of crimes, 184, 196, 199, 203, 411
   violent felonies, 297, 672
Arrest
   at border, 15–16
   upon termination of sentence, 16
   while out in community, 16
Arriving aliens
   adjustment of status, 452–455
   jurisdiction over custody issues, 145–146
   pleas, 584–585
   smuggling. *See* Alien smuggling
   voluntary departure, 495–496
Arson
   moral turpitude, crimes of, 255
   pleas, 571
Assault
   with deadly weapon, 254
   divisible statutes, 201
   on law enforcement officer, 256
   moral turpitude, crimes of, 256
   not crime of violence, 300
   pleas, 571
Asylum
   adjustment of status, 102. *See also* Adjustment of status
   aggravated felony conviction as bar to, 391–393, 572, 582–583
   alien smuggling charges, 417–418, 509
   controlled substance offenses and, 399–400
   Convention Against Torture (CAT) compared, 7–8
   defined, 5
   domestic violence offenses, 414–415
   entry without inspection, 12
   export violations, 428
   failure to register, 423–424
   family members and, 6
   filing fee exception, 24
   firearms offenses, 404
   immigration status, 5–8
   LPRs, 6
   money laundering, 409
   moral turpitude, 384–386
   Notice to Appear, 20–21
   "particularly serious crime" analysis, 526–528
   referral of petition, 21*n*61
   relief under, 462–463
   Section 209(c) waiver, 459–462
   standard of review, 28
   temporary protected status (TPS), 8
   visa fraud, 423–424
   Visa Waiver Program (VWP), 5
   withholding of removal distinguished, 6–7, 463–466
Athletes
   nonimmigrant visa holders, 4, 103
Attempt. *See also* **specific offenses**
   aggravated felony, 264, 320–321
   controlled substance cases, 290
Attempted murder
   moral turpitude, crimes of, 254
Attempted possession of stolen property
   aggravated felony, 310
Attorney General
   discretionary waivers, 457
   EOIR, 14
   invocation of custody rule, 164–165
   review, 19
   temporary protected status (TPS), 8
Attorneys
   classification of crimes, checklist, 235–238
   defense and immigration counsel, importance of working as team, 584–585
   Legal Net, 658
   notice of appearance of counsel, 24
   removal proceedings, right to, 22
   tools and strategies for criminal-alien law practice, 34–38
Authority over immigration law enforcement. *See* **Government agencies; specific agencies**
Automatic stay
   during appeal of bond hearing, 154–158
Automobiles. *See* **Vehicles**

Auto theft, 302–304
   as not crime of violence, 300
   pleas, 567

B

Background checks. See Biometrics and background checks

Bad checks, passing of
   moral turpitude, crimes of, 250

Bahamas
   tourists and temporary workers from, 5

Bail
   posting early in criminal process, importance of, 117

Bail jumping
   aggravated felony, 264

Battered child. See Child abuse

Battered Immigrant Women Protection Act of 2000
   U visa status, 614

Battered spouse
   adjustment of status, 102. *See also* Adjustment of status
   cancellation of removal, 473–474
   deferred action, 10
   review of petitions, 20
   waiver application, 443–444, 473–474, 651–652

Battery
   on law enforcement officer, 256
   moral turpitude, crimes of, 256
   pleas, 571
   sexual battery, 301

Bermuda
   tourists and temporary workers from, 5

Beyond reasonable doubt standard for conviction
   defined, 52–53

BIA. See Board of Immigration Appeals

Biographic form, G-325
   S status, 608

Biographic form, G-325A
   adjustment of status, 648–650

Biometrics and background checks
   convictions, 106–107
   fees, 24, 648–650, 656–657
   immigration applications requiring, 117, 642–643
   locating clients with criminal convictions, 117

Birth
   citizenship at, 500–503

Board of Immigration Appeals (BIA)
   attorney general review, 19
   divisible statutes, 205–214
   notice of appeal requirements, 24–25
   overview, 18–19
   removal proceedings, 24–26
   review after BIA appeal, 27, 31–32

Bonds, posting of
   agency arrests and detention, 139–145
   arriving aliens, 145–146
   automatic stay and, 154–158
   client held in detention, 117
   deportable respondents, 147
   entry without inspection, 147
   hearings before Immigration Judge on, 140, 153
   mandatory detention, 139–145
   memorandum in support of, 176–180
   voluntary departure, 497–499

Border
   arrest at, 15–16
   Customs and Border Protection (CBP), role of, 14–16

Bribery
   commercial, 264, 311–312, 486
   of witness, 264, 487

Burden of proof
   classification of crime, 191
   drug trafficking crimes, 275
   postconviction relief on merits (vacaturs), 67–68
   refugee or asylum status, withholding of removal, 6
   removal proceedings, 23

Bureau of Consular Affairs
   visa issuance, 17

Bureau of Industry and Security
export violations, 352

Burglary
aggravated felony, 264, 309–310
classification of crimes, 184
divisible statutes, 202
moral turpitude, crimes of, 249, 568
pleas, 568, 571

Business professionals
nonimmigrant visa holders, 4, 510

C

Canada
tourists and temporary workers without visas from, 4–5

Cancellation of removal
admission gained through fraud and, 471–472
aggravated felonies, 582
alien smuggling charges, 508–509
battered spouses, 473–474
continuous residence versus LPR status, 467
discretionary determination, 30–31
eligibility for relief and, 467
immigration court filings, 656
ineligible individuals, 472–473
memorandum in support of eligibility, 549–555
NACARA §203, 474–476
relief under, 467–476
Section 212(c) waiver, combined with, 467, 493–494
special rule, 474–476, 656–657

CAP (Criminal Alien Program)
generally, 18

Caribbean
tourists and temporary workers without visas from, 4–5

CAT. See Convention Against Torture

Categorical approach
classification of crimes, 183–186, 191, 194–196, 339–340
defined, 214

Cayman Islands
tourists and temporary workers from, 5

CBP. See Customs and Border Protection

CCA (Child Citizenship Act of 2000)
generally, 502–503

Change of address card
registration requirement, 347–349

Change of status
inadmissibility, 103

Child abuse
battered children
    cancellation of removal, 473–474
    deferred action, 10
    waiver application, 443, 651–652
crime of violence, 340–342, 412
moral turpitude, crimes of, 259
sexual abuse, 259, 266–267, 319–320, 578

Child born outside U.S.
derivative citizenship, 501–502

Child Citizenship Act of 2000 (CCA)
generally, 502–503

Child endangerment
deportability, 340–342

Childhood arrivals
deferred action for, 10–11

Child pornography
aggravated felony, 264
moral turpitude, crimes of, 259

CIMT (Crimes involving moral turpitude). See Moral turpitude, crimes of

Circumstance-specific approach
classification of crimes, 189–191
defined, 214

Citizenship. See Acquired citizenship; Derivative citizenship

Citizenship and Immigration Services (USCIS)
adjustment of status, 102, 649
applications for relief, removal proceedings, 24, 24n73
applications for waiver, 659–660
conviction records, requirement, 645–646
deferred action for childhood arrivals, 10–11
memoranda of law before, 659–660

overview, 14
parole, 9
structure of (chart), 42
visa applications, 14

Classification of crimes. *See also specific offenses*
alternative statutory phrases, 199–200, 207–208, 215
alternative statutory provisions, 200–201, 215
beyond moral turpitude and aggravated felonies, 323–355
burden of proof, 191
checklist, 235–238
definitions, 214–216
elements, 215
essential elements only, 201–204
facts-based approach, 201
under immigration law, 181–373
least culpable conduct, 215
means, 215
methodology, 181–216
   burden of proof, 191
   categorical approach, 183–186, 191, 194–196, 339–340
   circumstance-specific approach, 189–191
   minimal (or least culpable) conduct approach, 188
   modified categorical approach, 185–186, 191, 253, 339–340
   realistic probability test, 191–193, 259
moral turpitude, crimes of, 197, 239–262
non-elemental facts, 189–191, 214, 334–335
overview, 181–182
record of conviction, 215–216

Clients
background checks, running on, 642–643
confirmation-of-appointment letters, 37, 48
family members. *See* Family members
information sheet, 49–50
status of, defining, 1–12
tools and strategies for criminal-alien law practice, 34–38

Coercion and intimidation
as defense to criminal charge of re-entry after removal, 516

Collateral attack
removal proceedings, 516–518

Commerce Department
export violations, 352

Commercial bribery
aggravated felony, 264, 311–312, 486

Confirmation-of-appointment letters
as tool in criminal-alien law practice, 37, 48

Consequences of criminal act
generally, 429–430
aggravated felonies, 390–394, 429, 572–580
alien smuggling, 343–347, 415–419, 430
chart of, 429–430
controlled substance offenses, 394–401, 429
domestic violence, 410–415, 430
export violations, 425–428, 430
firearms offenses, 333–335, 401–405, 429
immigration law violations, 430
money laundering offenses, 405–410, 430
moral turpitude, crimes of, 376–390, 429
visa or passport fraud, 419–425, 430

Conspiracy
aggravated felony, 264, 318–321
divisible statutes, 199–200
drug-related, 575
drug trafficking, 290
moral turpitude, crimes of, 244–245

Consular office
waiver application, 511–512, 659–660

Continuous residence
LPR status distinguished, 451–452, 467

Contributing to delinquency of minor
pleas, 266–267, 578

Controlled substance offenses
aggravated felonies, 261, 270
asylum and withholding of removal, 399–400
consequences of, 394–401, 429
Convention Against Torture (CAT), 399–400
definition of, 323–331
denaturalization, 400–401
deportability or removability, 396

Controlled Substances Act of 1970

distribution without remuneration, 273–277
divisible statutes, 200
drug abusers and addicts, 332–333
drug paraphernalia, 329–330, 396–397
drugs but not controlled substances, 326–328
federal convictions, 269
federal recidivist statute, 284–290
inadmissibility
    adjustment of status, and visa eligibility, 394–396
        deportability compared to, 397–398
        removability and, as independent grounds for, 323
        waiver, 442
intent to use, 330–331
"look-alike" drugs, 331
mandatory detention, 398
moral turpitude, crimes of, 261, 323–331
naturalization, 400
Ninth Circuit variation on first offender or youthful offender provisions, 58–60
other federal circuits on first offender or youthful offender provisions, 60–61
pardons, 63
personal use exception, 326, 396–397
pleas, 575, 581, 583, 585
prescription drugs, 278
purchase of amount for personal use, 278–279
"reason to believe," 323, 331–332, 395–396
second or subsequent offense for simple possession, 285–290
simulated or imitation controlled substances, 331
solicitation offenses, 328–329
state convictions, 270–271, 279–284, 286–290
trafficking in, 271. *See also* Drug trafficking crimes
voluntary departure, 398–399

Controlled Substances Act of 1970

aggravated felonies, 269, 283, 286
cancellation of removal, eligibility for, 551
categorical approach under, 194
classification of crimes, 324

Convention Against Torture (CAT)

aggravated felonies, 393–394
alien smuggling, 417–418
asylum compared, 7–8
controlled substance offenses, 399–400
denaturalization, 394
domestic violence offenses, 414–415
filing fee exception, 24
firearms offenses, 404
money laundering, 409
moral turpitude, crimes of, 386
visa or passport fraud, 423–424
withholding of removal under, 7–8, 399–400, 404, 409, 414–415, 417–418, 423–424, 462, 466, 509

Conviction

admissions to prosecutor, required for diversion, effect of, 56–57
beyond reasonable doubt standard, 52–53
courts martial, 53
credit for time served, 172
defined, 51–83
diversion, 56–57
expungements, 57–62
FFOA expungements, 61–62
finality of, 53–54
first offender or youthful offender provisions, 57–61, 563–564
foreign convictions, 80–81
juvenile delinquency, acts of, 77–80
LPRs, 3
modification of sentence, postconviction relief, 76–77
Ninth Circuit variation on first offender or youthful offender provisions, 58–60
nonimmigrant visa holders, 4
other federal circuits on first offender or youthful offender provisions, 60–61
pardons, 62–64
postconviction relief on merits (vacaturs), 64–75, 84–96
pretrial intervention, 56–57
proof of convictions, 81–82
record sealings, 57–62
suspensions of sentence, 82
withholds or deferrals of adjudication, 54–55

SUBJECT-MATTER INDEX

Cooperating witnesses, visas for
generally, 599–600
FOIA requests, 631–637
mandatory detention, 136–137
S status, 600–609
    adjustment to permanent resident status, under S status, 604–606
    conditions of status, 603–604
    deferred action, 10
    family members, 605–606, 608
    I-854 form, 602–603, 625–630
    parole, 608
    regulations, 602–603
    statute, 601–602
    time to acquire, 608
    tips and advice on, 606–609
    written commitment, 607
T status, 609–614
    annual cap, 612
    application procedure, 610–612
    battered spouse, 10
    deferred action, 10
    extreme hardship, 610
    family members, 612–614
    final order of removal, 612
    nonimmigrant status, issuance of, 613–614
    pending immigration proceedings, 612
    permanent residency, 613–614
    regulations, 609–610
    review, 20
    revocation of status, 612
    "severe form of trafficking," defined, 610
    statute, 609
U status, 614–624
    adjustment of status, 619–621
    age-out protection, 621–622
    battered spouse, 10
    "criminal activity," defined, 615–616
    deferred action, 10
    family members, 618–619, 624
    filing, 617–618
    jurisdiction, 624
    permanent resident status, 622–624
    regulation, 616–622
    removal proceedings, persons in, 619–621
    review, 20
    statute, 615–616

Counterfeiting
aggravated felony, 264, 311, 486
currency or securities, pleas, 584
devices, 316–317
goods, 251

Country-condition experts
tool in criminal-alien law practice, 37

Country-condition sources of information (Websites)
tool in criminal-alien law practice, 37

Courts martial
conviction, 53

Credit card fraud
moral turpitude, crimes of, 250
pleas, 583–584

Crimes involving moral turpitude (CIMT). See Moral turpitude, crimes of

Crimes of violence. See Violence, crimes of

Crime victims. See also Cooperating witnesses, visas for
in crime of domestic violence, 339–340, 583
nonimmigrant visa holders, 4

Criminal activity. See also Classification of crimes
aggravated felons, expedited removal of, 107–110
    relief from, 110
Attorney General, invocation of custody rule, 164–165
deportability, 104–107
    for criminal record holders, 99
    distinguished from inadmissibility, 106
inadmissibility
    adjustment of status, 102–103
    change of status, 103
    for criminal record holders, 99
    entry without inspection, 103–104
    "good moral character," 104
    naturalization, 104
    parolees, 103
    temporary protected status, 104
    visa applicants at American embassies, 103

Criminal Alien Program (CAP)
   mandatory detention, 110, 133–153
   "release from custody," 147–151
Criminal Alien Program (CAP)
   generally, 18
Criminally reckless conduct
   crimes of violence, 254
   moral turpitude, crimes of, 254
Criminal mischief
   pleas, 569, 571
Cuban Adjustment Act of 1966
   adjustment of status, 434, 649–650
   review under, 20
   Section 212(c) waiver, 493
Cuban citizens and nationals. See also Cuban Adjustment Act of 1966
   order of supervision for, 11
   unremovable status of, 159
Currency reporting violations
   pleas, 585
Custody requirement
   memorandum on, 171–176
Custody rule. See Transition Period Custody Rules
Customs and Border Protection (CBP)
   application for waiver, 642
   deferred inspections, 119
   overview, 14–16
   parole, 9
   re-entry after trip abroad, procedures for, 118–119
   structure of (chart), 40

D

Deadly weapons
   pleas, 584
Deceit. See Fraud
Deferrals of adjudication
   comparison with pretrial diversion, 562–563
   defined, 54–55
Deferred action
   for childhood arrivals, 10–11
   criminal conviction, effect on, 10
   defined, 9–10

Deferred inspections
   clients with criminal records at, 119
Delinquency of minor
   pleas of contributing to, 266–267, 578
Denaturalization
   aggravated felonies, 394
   alien smuggling charges, 418–419
   controlled substance offenses, 400–401
   Convention Against Torture (CAT), 394
   domestic violence offenses, 415
   failure to register, 425
   falsification of documents, 425
   firearms offenses, 405
   money laundering, 410
   moral turpitude, crimes of, 388–389
   visa fraud, 425
Department of. See specific department
Deportability
   admission, defined, 380–381
   aggravated felonies, 390, 397–398
   aggravated felons, expedited removal of, 107–110
   alien smuggling, 343–344, 416
      relief absent conviction, 507–508
   burden of proof, 23
   child endangerment, 340–342
   controlled substance offenses, 396
      inadmissibility compared to, 397–398
   criminal activity, 104–107
      for criminal record holders, 99
      distinguished from inadmissibility, 106
   criminal record holders, 99
   domestic violence, 337, 411–413
   export violations, 351–353, 426
   failure to register, 421–422
   firearms offenses, 401–403
   grounds for LPRs, convictions, 4
   inadmissibility distinguished from, 106
   LPRs, convictions, 4
   money laundering, 407
   moral turpitude, crimes of, 380–382
   Notice of Intent, 108
   overview, 135
   pardons, 62–64
   protection orders, 342–343
   Section 212(c) waiver and, 106, 491–492
   stalking, 337

visa fraud, 421–422
Deportation
  Criminal Alien Program (CAP), 18
  in absentia, 21, 517
  naturalization as defense to, 504–507
  notice, 517
  permission to reapply for admission after deportation or removal, 665–667
  permission to re-enter after, Form I-212 not required, 513–514
  re-entry after removal, 111–112
  stay of, 663–664
  withholding of removal, 6–7
Depositions
  removal proceedings, 22
Derivative citizenship
  at birth, citizenship at, 501–503
  children born outside U.S., 501–502
  effective dates, 500
  LPRs, 2
  parents as citizens, 2–3
  relief under, 499–503
  requirements for, 2–3
Destructive devices. See also Explosives
  defined, 333–335
  trafficking in, 263, 304
Detainer
  persons in penal custody to be provided, 16
Detention, mandatory. See Mandatory detention
DHS. See Homeland Security, Department of
Discretionary determinations. See also specific applications and waivers
  adjustment of status, 30–31, 435–436, 650
  federal judicial review, 30–32, 137
Diversion
  pretrial, 56–57
Divisible statutes
  aggravated felonies, 302, 309, 579
  assault, 201
  BIA cases, 205–214
  burglary, 202
  Circuit Court cases, 197–205
  classification of crimes, 185–187, 196–197
  conspiracy, 199–200
  controlled substance offenses, 200

  defined, 214
  domestic violence, 337–339
  drug trafficking, 272–273
  export violations, 200–201
  firearms offenses, 301
  gang enhancement, 201–202
  larceny, 203
  moral turpitude, crimes of, 244, 256, 406–407, 567, 569
  realistic probability test and, 207
  throwing deadly missile, 203–204
DOJ. See Justice Department
Domestic violence. See also Battered spouse; Child abuse
  generally, 336–337
  adjustment of status, 410–411, 439–440
  asylum and withholding of removal, 414–415
  child abuse, 340–342
  consequences of, 410–415, 430
  Convention Against Torture (CAT), 414–415
  definition of crime of, 337–339, 410
  denaturalization, 415
  deportability or removability, 337, 411–413
  divisible statutes, 337–339
  "good moral character," 414
  inadmissibility, adjustment of status, and visa eligibility, 410–411
  mandatory detention, 413
  moral turpitude, crimes of, 255, 343, 410–411
  naturalization, 415
  offenses, 336–343
  pardons, 63
  pleas, 580–581, 583
  protection orders, 342–343
  reckless, 300
  stalking, including, 412
  victims, 339–340, 583
  voluntary departure, 414–415
DOS. See State Department
Driving under influence. See DUI (driving under influence) cases

Drug abusers or addicts. See Controlled substance offenses

Drug abusers or addicts. See Controlled substance offenses

Drug paraphernalia
BIA decision, 369–373
controlled substance offenses, 329–330, 396–397
pleas, 585

Drug trafficking crimes. See also Controlled substance offenses
aggravated felonies, 269–273
attempts, 290
burden of proof, 275
charging phase versus sentencing phase, 288
conspiracies, 290
federal law, 261, 269
felony classification, 279–284
misdemeanors, 271
pleas, 577
prosecutorial discretion, 289
"reason to believe," 331–332
state law, 279–284

DUI (driving under influence) cases
moral turpitude, crimes of, 260–261, 569
pleas, 569, 571

Duress
as affirmative defense to criminal charge of re-entry after removal, 516

E

EAR (Export Administration Regulations)
export violations, 352

Electronic monitoring. See also Intensive Supervision Appearance Program
alternative to detention, 141, 161, 174

Eligibility for relief
cancellation of removal and, 467
naturalization, 583
pleas, 581–587
agreement and colloquy, 583–585
Section 212(h) and, 581
withholding of removal and asylum, 582–583

El Salvador. See also Nicaraguan Adjustment and Central American Relief Act of 1997
reinstatement of removal, 113, 476

special rule cancellation of removal, 474–475
temporary protected status (TPS), 8

Embassies
abroad, forms of relief, 640–642, 658
memoranda of law before, 659–660
visa applicants at, 14, 17, 103
waiver applications, 640–642, 658

Embezzlement
aggravated felony, 310–311, 580

Employment
adjustment of status, 649
authorization document, 10, 13
deferred action, 10
EAD, 13
order of supervision, 11–12
temporary protected status (TPS), 8

Entertainers
nonimmigrant visa holders, 4, 510

Entry without inspection (EWI)
adjustment of status, 448–449
asylum, 12
bond hearing, 147
defined, 12
inadmissibility, 103–104
mandatory detention, 147
removal proceedings, 12

EOIR. See Executive Office for Immigration Review

EOIR-27 Form
notice of appearance of counsel, 24

EOIR-29 Form
appeal to BIA, 24

EOIR-42A Form
waiver application, 655

Equal Access to Justice Act of 1980
habeas corpus petitions, 33

Equities
cancellation of removal, 656
Section 212(c) waiver, 655

ERO. See Office of Enforcement and Removal Operations

Evidence. See also Burden of proof
removal proceedings, 22, 81–82
in support of waiver, 644–648

applicant, evidence relating to, 645–646
family members, evidence relating to, 647–648
before immigration court, 644–645

EWI. *See* **Entry without inspection**

Executive Office for Immigration Review (EOIR)
overview, 14, 17–18
rules of procedure, 18

Exhaustion of administrative remedies
habeas corpus petitions, 153

Expert witnesses
evidence from, 642

Explosives
aggravated felony, 263, 304
defined, 333–335
firearms offenses, 304–305

Export Administration Regulations (EAR)
export violations, 352

Export violations
adjustment of status, 425–426, 440–441
asylum and withholding of removal, 428
consequences of, 425–428, 430
deportability or removability, 351–353, 426
divisible statutes, 200–201
inadmissibility and visa eligibility, 352–353, 425–426
mandatory detention, 426–427
national security issues, 351–353, 426
naturalization, 428
voluntary departure, 427–428
withholding of removal, 428

Expungements
as convictions, 57–62
under FFOA, 61–62

Extortion
crime of violence, 301
moral turpitude, crimes of, 255

Extreme hardship
T status, visas for cooperating witnesses, 610
waiver applications, 442–444, 651–652

F

Failure to appear
on felony change, 264
for service of sentence, 264

Failure to register
adjustment of status, 419–421, 440
asylum and withholding of removal, 423–424
crimes involving, 347–351
denaturalization, 425
deportability or removability, 421–422
inadmissibility, adjustment of status, and visa eligibility, 419–421
mandatory detention, 422
naturalization, 424–425
visa fraud and, 349–351
voluntary departure, 422–423

Failure to register as sexual offender
Adam Walsh Act, 354–355
moral turpitude, crimes of, 258–259

Failure to stop and render aid after fatal car accident
moral turpitude, crimes of, 255

False statements
moral turpitude, crimes of, 251–252
pleas, 585

Falsification of documents
adjustment of status, 419–421
denaturalization, 425
mandatory detention, 422
naturalization, 424–425
visa fraud. *See* Visa or passport fraud
voluntary departure, 422–423

Family members
alien smuggling, exception for immediate family member, 345, 507
asylum and, 6
evidence in support, 647–648
hardship to, waiver application, 651–652
visas for cooperating witnesses
S status, 605–606, 608
T status, 612–614
U status, 618–619, 624
withholding of removal and, 7

Fastcase
tool in criminal-alien law practice, 36–37

Federal Bureau of Investigation (FBI) rap sheet
    request, 46–47
    tool in criminal-alien law practice, 34–35, 642–643, 645n10

Federal First Offender Act of 1984 (FFOA)
    adverse immigration consequences, avoiding, 563–564
    expungements, 61–62
    state counterparts to, 58–60

Federal Food, Drug and Cosmetic Act of 1938
    controlled substance violations, 327
    prescription drugs, 278

Federal judicial review
    arriving aliens, 145–146
    constitutionality, 137
    detention during review of final removal order, 160–161
    discretionary determinations, 30–32
    habeas corpus, 32–33, 153, 171–174
    jurisdiction, 27–33
    "particularly serious crime" determination, 464–466
    petitions for review to Court of Appeals, 31–32
    REAL ID Act, 29–30
    review after BIA appeal, 27

Federal Juvenile Delinquency Act of 1938
    pleas, 564

Federal Rules of Civil Procedure
    habeas petitions under, 33

Fees
    adjustment of status, 648–650
    application for relief from removal orders, 24
    BIA appeals, 24–25
    biometrics, 24
    removal proceedings, application for relief, 24–25

Felonies
    aggravated. *See* Aggravated felonies
    moral turpitude, crimes of, 240
    temporary protected status (TPS), 8

FFOA. *See* Federal First Offender Act of 1984

Filing fee. *See* Fees

Fingerprinting. *See* Biometrics and background checks

Firearms offenses
    adjustment of status, 401, 438–439
    as aggravated felonies, 301, 304–307, 401–403, 584
    asylum and withholding of removal, 404
    carrying concealed weapons, 261
    consequences of, 333–335, 401–405, 429
    Convention Against Torture (CAT), 404
    crime of violence, 263
    definition of firearm and destructive device, 333–335
    denaturalization, 405
    deportability or removability, 401–403
    divisible statutes, 301
    explosives, 304–305
    "good moral character," 404
    inadmissibility and visa eligibility, 335, 401
    mandatory detention, 403
    moral turpitude, crimes of, 261
    motion to terminate removal proceedings, 504
    naturalization, 404
    non-elemental facts, 192
    pardon, 63
    pleas, 577–578, 584
    possession by felon, 305
    "reason to believe," 335
    trafficking in firearms, 304–305
    voluntary departure, 403–404

First offender, youthful offender provisions
    convictions, 57–61, 563–564
    Ninth Circuit variation on, 58–60
    other federal circuits on, 60–61

Fleeing and eluding
    pleas, 571

Fleuti doctrine
    elimination of, 99–101

Florida
    immigration law enforcement, 119n61

FOIA requests. *See* Freedom of Information Act (FOIA) requests

Force, use of. *See* Violence, crimes of

Foreign convictions
 effect of, 80–81

Forgery
 aggravated felony, 264, 486

Former Soviet-bloc countries. See also **Nicaraguan Adjustment and Central American Relief Act of 1997**
 reinstatement of removal, 113, 476
 special rule cancellation of removal, 474–475

Forms. See specific Form

Fraud
 aggravated felony, 264, 312
 amount of funds involved, 312–313, 573
 crimes involving, 250–251, 312, 317
 pleas, 567, 579, 583–584
 visa fraud. See Visa or passport fraud

Freedom of Information Act (FOIA) requests
 A-file, obtaining, 36
 S status, 606
 tool in criminal-alien law practice, 36
 visas for cooperating witnesses, 631–637

G

G-325 Form
 S status, 608

G-325A Form
 adjustment of status, 648–650

G-639 Form
 FOIA requests, 36

Gambling
 aggravated felony, 264

Gang enhancement
 divisible statutes, 201–202
 moral turpitude, crimes of, 257–258

"Good moral character"
 alien smuggling, 417
 controlled substance offenses, 399
 domestic violence convictions, 414
 firearms offenses, 404
 money laundering, 408–409
 moral turpitude, crimes of, 383–384, 387
 naturalization, 104, 387, 400, 404, 409, 415, 418–419, 424
 visa or passport fraud, 423–425

Homeland Security, Department of (DHS)
 voluntary departure, 383–384, 403, 408–409, 414, 423, 498

Government agencies. See also specific agencies
 locating clients with criminal convictions by, 115–120
 overview, 14–20

"Green card" holder. See **Lawful permanent residents**

Guatemala. See also **Nicaraguan Adjustment and Central American Relief Act of 1997**
 reinstatement of removal, 113, 476
 special rule cancellation of removal, 474–476

H

Habeas corpus petitions
 exhaustion of administrative remedies, 153
 federal judicial review, 32–33, 153, 171–174
 mandatory detention, 153
 temporary restraining orders with, 33

Haitian Refugee and Immigrant Fairness Act of 1998 (HRIFA)
 adjustment of status, 650
 reinstatement of removal, 113

Harassment
 moral turpitude, crimes of, 255

Hardship
 extreme. See Extreme hardship
 to family members, waiver application, 651–652

Hearings
 bond hearings, 12, 139–145, 153
 removal proceedings. See Removal proceedings
 video, 116

Homeland Security, Department of (DHS)
 adjustment of status, 442n36
 admissions, making to officers of, 563
 deferred action, 10
 mandatory detention, 136
 order of supervision, 11–12
 overview, 14–16
 parole, 9

Honduras

waiver, 442*n*36

Honduras
temporary protected status (TPS), 8

Hostage taking
crime of violence, 302

HRIFA (Haitian Refugee and Immigrant Fairness Act of 1998)
adjustment of status, 650
reinstatement of removal, 113

Humanitarian efforts
deferred action, 10
parole, 8–9

Hurricane Mitch
temporary protected status (TPS), 8

I

I-94 card
defined, 13
initial client meeting, 2

I-130 Form
adjustment of status, 649

I-140 Form
adjustment of status, 649

I-191 Form
waiver application, 654

I-192 Form
Section 212(d)(3)(A) waiver, 657–658

I-212 Form
permission to reapply for admission after deportation or removal, 665–667
waiver application, 665–667

I-246 Form
stay of deportation, 663–664

I-485 Form
adjustment of status, 434, 605, 648–650
waiver application, 652–653

I-601 Form
waiver application, 651

I-602 Form
waiver application, 652–653

I-851 Form
Notice of Intent to Issue a Final Administrative Deportation Order, 108

I-854 Form
S status, 602–603, 625–630

I-918 Form
U status, 615, 617–618

I-929 Petition
U status, 624

ICE. See Immigration and Customs Enforcement

Illegal Immigration Reform and Immigrant Responsibility Act of 1996 (IIRAIRA)
aggravated felonies, 263, 444–445
applicants for admission, 104
convictions, 53–54
domestic violence and protection orders covered by, 343, 411
Fleuti doctrine eliminated by, 101
key legislation, 38
LPRs
    not retroactive for convictions prior to effective date, 101–102
    special waiver rules for, 485–487
Notice to Appear, 21
reinstatement after removal, 113–114
removability, concept introduced by, 97
Section 212(c), 477
Section 303(b), text of, 169–170
Section 309, text of, 166–168
suspension of deportation repealed by, 477
waiver applicability to LPRs, 444–445

Illegal procurement of citizenship
criminal prosecution for, 389

"Illegal status"
generally, 12

Immigration Act of 1990 (IMMACT90)
aggravated felonies, 489
good moral character requirement, 391, 498
key legislation, 38
naturalization, 506–507
Section 212(c) waiver, 480

Immigration and Customs Enforcement (ICE)
deferred action, 10
detention by, 115–117
institutional removal cases, 115–117
Institutional Removal Program, 18

local police, 119–120
order of supervision, 11–12
parole, 9
role of, 14–16
state or federal detention, individuals in, 115–117
structure of (chart), 41

Immigration and Nationality Act of 1952 (INA). See also specific Section
aggravated felonies, 263–265
classification of crimes, 181
convictions, 51–52, 56
custody requirement, memorandum on, 171–176
deportability, 23
derivative citizenship, 2–3
evidence at removal proceedings, 81–82
"good moral character," 104
inadmissibility, 97, 104
juvenile offenders and crimes of moral turpitude, 79–80
law of nationality and naturalization, 2–3
local police, 119–120
loss to victim, 313–317
mandatory detention, 134–135
nonimmigrant visa holders, 4–5
refugees, 5–6
reinstatement after removal, 113–114
relevant conduct, 313–314
status under, 3
Visa Waiver Program (VWP), 5

Immigration court. See also Executive Office for Immigration Review; specific types of proceedings
forms of relief, 642–643
pretrial statements to, 660–661, 668–676
Section 212(c) waiver, 654–655
Section 212(h) waiver, 651–652
witness list, 661–663

Immigration law violations
consequences of, 430

Immigration status
generally, 1–2
American citizen, 2–3
I-94 card, 13
"illegal" status, 12
lawful permanent resident, 3–4
nonimmigrant visa holder, 4–5
present without inspection or admission or overstay, 12
protective categories, 5–12

Imprisonment. See Sentence

INA. See Immigration and Nationality Act of 1952

Inadmissibility
adjustment of status, 102–103
alien smuggling
    adjustment of status, and visa eligibility, 415–416
    relief absent conviction, 507–508
applicants for admission, 98–104
burden of proof, 23
change of status, 103
controlled substance offenses
    adjustment of status, and visa eligibility, 394–396
    deportability compared to, 397–398
    removability and, as independent grounds for, 323
    waiver, 442
for criminal record holders, 99
deportability distinguished, 106
domestic violence, 410–411
entry without inspection, 103–104
export violations, 352–353, 425–426
failure to register, 419–421
firearms offenses, 335, 401
"good moral character," 104
ground of, adjustment of status, 432–435
LPRs, 98–102
money laundering, 405–407
moral turpitude, crimes of, 376–380
national security as grounds of, 514
naturalization, 104
pardons, 62–64
parolees, 103
persons physically present in violation of law, 103–104
petty offense exception, 380
protection orders, 342–343
scope of, 97–98, 134–135
Section 212(a)(2)(A), application of, 98–101
Section 212(c) waiver and, 491–492
temporary protected status, 104

Ineffective assistance of counsel
visa applicants at American embassies, 103
waiver of, 441–459, 540–543

Ineffective assistance of counsel
Padilla v. Kentucky (2010), 76

Infopass appointments
on case status, 643

Initial admission
seven years of continuous residence and, 468–471

INS, legacy
reorganization, 14

INS Operations Instruction (OI) 242.1(a)(22)
deferred action, 10

Inspection, evasion of
generally, 12

Institutional Removal Program (IRP)
generally, 18
prisoner removal, 116

Instrument, U.S., falsely making
aggravated felony, 264

Intake sheets
tool in criminal-alien law practice, 37–38

Intensive Supervision Appearance Program
alternative to detention, 161–162, 174

Intent. See also specific offenses
moral turpitude, crimes of, 241–244
non-specific intent crime, 574–575
recklessness. *See* Recklessness
violence, crimes of, 291–299

Interpreters
need for, 662–663

Intimidation
moral turpitude, crimes of, 255

Intoxication-related offenses. See DUI (driving under influence) cases

Investors
nonimmigrant visa holders, 4, 510

Involuntary manslaughter
moral turpitude, crimes of, 257
not crime of violence, 300

IRP (Institutional Removal Program)
generally, 18

ISAP (Intensive Supervision Appearance Program)
alternative to detention, 161–162, 174

J

Jewish refugees from former Soviet Union
unremovable status of, 159

Joyriding
intent, 246
pleas, 567
theft offense, 308

Judges. See Immigration court

Judicial review. See Federal judicial review

Jurisdiction
adjustment of status, 436–438
custody issues, 145–146
federal judicial review, 27–33
nonimmigrant visa waiver, 511–514
U status, 624

Justice Department (DOJ)
appeals, 19
overview, 14

Juvenile delinquency
adverse immigration consequences, avoiding, 564–565
convictions, effect of, 77–80
moral turpitude, crimes of, 79–80

K

Kickbacks on government contracts
moral turpitude, crimes of, 250

Kidnapping
aggravated felony, 264

K nonimmigrant visas
Form I-212 to waive existing removal order, 667

L

Larceny
divisible statutes, 203
moral turpitude, crimes of, 245–248

Law enforcement officer, assault or battery on
moral turpitude, crimes of, 256
not crime of violence, 300

Lawful admission

requirement for permanent residence, 471–472

Lawful permanent residents (LPRs)
adjustment of status, 102–103, 435, 444–451. *See also* Adjustment of status
citizenship by derivation, 2–3
continuous residence distinguished, 451–452, 467
criminal convictions, effect of, 3
defined, 3
inadmissibility, 98–102
lawful admission requirement, 471–472
moral turpitude, crimes of, 566
refugee or asylum status, 6
seeking admission, 98–102
status of, 3–4
U status, 622–624
waiver under Section 209(c), 460–462
waiver under Section 212(c), 485–487
waiver under Section 212(h)
    aggravated felony convictions, 444–445
    non-aggravated felony convictions, 451

Legal authority
sources of, 38

Legal Net
Section 212(d)(3)(B) waiver denials, contacting, 658

Legend drugs
offenses involving, 326, 584

Legislation
recent key pieces of, 38

Letters
confirmation-of-appointment, 37, 48

LEXIS
tool in criminal-alien law practice, 36–37, 643

Locating clients with criminal convictions
biometrics and background checks, 117
immigration application, filing of, 117–118
local police, 119–120
methods for, 115–120
probation or parole officers as source for, 118
re-entry after trip abroad, 118–119

serving time in state or federal detention, 115–117

Loss to victim
aggravated felonies, 313–317

LPRs. See Lawful permanent residents

M

Mail fraud
moral turpitude, crimes of, 250

Mail service
Notice to Appear, 21

Mandatory detention
generally, 110, 133–153
aggravated felony conviction and, 390, 571–572
alien smuggling, 416
alternatives to, 161–163
arriving aliens, 145–146, 584–585
bond hearings, 139–145
charge of inadmissibility for crime of moral turpitude and, 382–383
constitutionality of, 137
controlled substance offenses, 398
cooperating witnesses, release of, 136–137
deportable respondents and those who enter without inspection, 147
domestic violence, 413
entry without inspection, 147
export violations, 426–427
failure to register, 422
falsification of documents, 422
firearms offenses, 403
habeas corpus petitions, 153
invocation of custody rule, 164–165
legal challenges to, 137–139
money laundering, 407
moral turpitude, crimes of, 382–383, 566
non-mandatory detention cases, 154–158
overview, 110
policy considerations, 174–175
reasons to hold person without bond, 153–154
"release from custody," 147–151
releases on or before October 8, 1998, 153
Section 303(b) of IIRAIRA, text of, 169–170

Section 309 of IIRAIRA, text of, 166–168
Transition Period Custody Rules (TPCR),
  134, 383n23
    invocation of, by Attorney General,
    164–165
  visa fraud, 422
Mandatory Victim Restitution Act of 1966
  restitution, 315
Manslaughter
  moral turpitude, crimes of, 254
  not crime of violence, 300
Marijuana offenses. See Controlled substance
  offenses
"Master calendar" hearing
  defined, 23
Medicaid or Medicare fraud
  pleas, 583–584
Medical evaluations
  tool in criminal-alien law practice, 37
Memoranda of law
  in support of bond motion, 176–180
  in support of motion to terminate, 121–127
  USCIS or American Embassy, 659–660
  waiver applications, 659–663
Mens rea. See Intent
Mexico
  tourists and temporary workers without
    visas from, 4–5
Military service
  naturalization and, 3, 505–507
Minimal (or least culpable) conduct approach
  non-elemental facts, 189–191
Minors. See also Child abuse
  delinquency of, contributing to, pleas,
    266–267, 578
  sexual abuse of, 259, 263, 319–320, 578
Misdemeanors
  aggravated felonies, treated as, 318–320
  drug trafficking crimes, 271
  foreign convictions, 80–81
  moral turpitude, crimes of, 240
  not crime of violence, 300
  sexual abuse of minor, 319–320
  temporary protected status, 8
  violence, crimes of, 318–319

Misidentification
  defense of, 515
Misprision of felony
  moral turpitude, crimes of, 252–253
  pleas, 575–576
Missing element statutes
  classification of crimes, 186–187
  defined, 214
Modified categorical approach
  classification of crimes, 185–186, 191,
    253, 339–340
  defined, 214
Money laundering
  adjustment of status, 405–407
  aggravated felony, 312, 335–336, 409
  amount of funds involved, 573
  asylum and withholding of removal, 409
  consequences of, 405–410, 429
  Convention Against Torture (CAT), 409
  denaturalization, 410
  deportability or removability, 407
  "good moral character," 408–409
  inadmissibility, adjustment of status, and
    visa eligibility, 405–407
  mandatory detention, 407
  moral turpitude, crimes of, 251, 406–407
  naturalization, 409–410
  pleas, 572, 577
  "reason to believe," 336
  state offenses, 406–407
  voluntary departure, 408–409
Money transmitting, unlicensed
  moral turpitude, crimes of, 232–234
Moral turpitude, crimes of. See also specific
  offenses
  adjustment of status and inadmissibility,
    376–380
  admission of essential elements, 377–378
  aggravated assault, 254, 256
  aggravated felonies, 438
  aggravated stalking, 255
  alien smuggling, 261–262
  arson, 255
  assault, 256
  asylum and withholding of removal, 384–
    386
  attempted murder, 254

avoiding conviction for crime involving, 566–572
bad checks, passing of, 250
battery, 256
burglary, 249, 568
child pornography, 259
classification of crimes, 197, 239–262
consequences of, 376–390, 429
conspiracy, 244–245
Convention Against Torture (CAT), 386
credit card fraud, 250
criminally reckless conduct, 254
defined, 239, 567–569
denaturalization, 388–389
deportability or removability, 380–382
divisible statutes, 244, 256, 406–407, 567, 569
domestic violence offenses, 255, 343, 410–411
driving under influence, 260–261, 569
elements of criminal statute as controlling, 241
eligibility for LPR status, 566
false statements, 251–252
gang enhancement, 257–258
harassment, 255
intent, 241–244
intimidation, 255
involuntary manslaughter, 257
juvenile offenders, 79–80
kickbacks on government contracts, 250
larceny, 245–248
mail fraud, 250
mandatory detention, 382–383, 566
manslaughter, 254
methodology for determining, 209–210
misprision of felony, 252–253
money laundering, 251, 406–407
multiple criminal convictions, 381–382, 429
naturalization, 387–390, 567
negligence versus recklessness, 242–244
as non-elemental fact, 210–211
non-elemental facts, 197
obstruction of justice, 252–253
petty offense exception, 378, 411, 469
pleas, 566–572

political offense exception, 378–380, 385–386
possession of stolen property, 247
post-*Silva-Trevino* case law, 211–213
realistic probability test, 197, 210
recklessness, 242–244, 254, 256, 294–295, 567
robbery, 247
sexual offender, failure to register as, 258–259
specific offenses as crimes involving, 245–262, 567–569. *See also specific offenses*
stalking, 255
statutory rape, 259
theft, 226–231, 245–248, 356–358, 567–568
threats of bodily harm, 255
unlicensed money transmitting, 232–234
violence, crimes of, 253–262, 294–295, 569. *See also* Violence, crimes of
visa eligibility, inadmissibility, 419–420
voluntary departure, 383–384
voluntary manslaughter, 254
youthful offender exceptions, 378

Motion to pretermit
waiver application under Section 212(h), 529–533

Motion to reopen
new case law, based on, 519–525
postconviction relief on merits (vacaturs), 68–69, 84–96
removal proceedings, 68–69
sua sponte, 519–525

Motion to terminate
removal proceedings, 128–132, 504

Motor vehicles. See Vehicles

Multiple counts
pleas, 569–570, 586

Multiple criminal convictions
crimes involving moral turpitude, 381–382
moral turpitude, crimes of, 381–382, 429

Murder
aggravated felony, 263, 265–266
moral turpitude, attempted murder as crime of, 254

N

N-400 Form
naturalization, 504

NACARA. See Nicaraguan Adjustment and Central American Relief Act of 1997

Nationality-based legalization program. See specific groups

National security
crimes involving, 353–354
export violations, 351–353, 426
as grounds of inadmissibility, 514
Section 212(d)(3) waiver, 514

National Security Act of 1947
sabotage and treason under, 264

Naturalization
after Section 212(c) waiver, 495
aggravated felonies, 572
alien smuggling charges, 418–419, 510
controlled substance offenses, 400
as defense to deportation, 504–507
    termination of removal proceedings, 504
domestic violence offenses, 415
eligibility for relief, 583
export violations, 428
failure to register, 424–425
falsification of documents, 424–425
firearms offenses, 404
"good moral character." See "Good moral character"
inadmissibility, 104
military service and, 3, 505–507
money laundering, 409–410
moral turpitude, crimes of, 387–390, 567
Notice to Appear, 20–21
removal proceedings, 387
statement in support of eligibility, 556–560
termination of removal proceedings, 504
veterans and soldiers, 505–507
visa fraud, 424–425

Negligence versus recklessness
crimes of violence, 294–295
moral turpitude, crimes of, 242–244, 256

New York (state)
REPAT program, 116

Nicaragua
temporary protected status (TPS), 8

Nicaraguan Adjustment and Central American Relief Act of 1997 (NACARA)
adjustment of status, 446–447, 650
reinstatement of removal, 113
special rule cancellation of removal, 474–476

Ninth Circuit
first offender or youthful offender provisions, 58–60

Non-elemental facts. See Classification of crimes

Nonimmigrant visa holders
adjustment of status, 102. See also Adjustment of status
change of status, 103
criminal convictions, effect of, 4
defined, 4–5
status of, 2, 4–5
tourists and temporary workers from Caribbean, Canada, and Mexico, 4–5
Visa Waiver Program (VWP), 5

Nonimmigrant visa waiver (Section 212(d)(3)(B))
consulate applications, 511–512
factors to consider, 514
jurisdiction, 511–514
permission to re-enter after deportation, Form I-212 not required, 513–514
port of entry application, 512–513
relief under, 510–514
security or terrorism, as grounds of inadmissibility, 514

Non-mandatory detention cases
overview, 154–158

Nonreviewability of consular action
generally, 29

Notice of Appeal
Board of Immigration Appeals (BIA), 24–26

Notice of Intent
deportability, 108

Notice to Appear (NTA)
arrest upon termination of sentence, 16
asylum, 20–21

deferred inspections, 119
defined, 13
removal proceedings, 20–21, 387
sample, 43–45
state or federal detention, individuals in, 152–153

O

Obstruction of justice
aggravated felony, 264, 311
moral turpitude, crimes of, 252–253
pleas, 575–576

Office of Chief Counsel
burden of proof, 23
overview, 18

Office of Enforcement and Removal Operations (ERO)
custody determinations, 145
stay of deportation, 663–664
voluntary removal, 497

Operating vehicle under influence. See DUI (driving under influence) cases

Operation Tarmac
DHS investigation of undocumented workers at airports, 348

Order of supervision
defined, 11–12

Orders, administrative, challenges to
as defense to criminal charge of re-entry after removal, 515–516

Overstay
generally, 12

P

PACER (Public Access to Court Electronic Records)
tool in criminal-alien law practice, 35–36

Pardons
conviction, 62–64
foreign, 64
full and unconditional, 64

Parole
arriving aliens, 145
criminal conviction, effect on, 8–9

Customs and Border Protection (CBP), role of, 9
definition of, 8–9
document, 8–9

Parolees
inadmissibility, 103
locating clients with criminal convictions via, 118

Parole officers
locating clients with criminal convictions via, 118

Passport fraud. See Visa or passport fraud

Peonage
aggravated felony, 264

Perjury
aggravated felony, 264, 311
subornation of, 264, 311

Permanent residents. See Lawful permanent residents

Petitions for habeas corpus. See Habeas corpus petitions

Petitions for review to court of appeals
after BIA appeal, 31–32
removal proceedings, 32–33

Petty-offense exception
adverse immigration consequences, avoiding, 565–566
moral turpitude, crimes of, 378, 411, 469

Photographs. See Biometrics and background checks

Pleas
adverse immigration consequences, avoiding, 562–566
aggravated assault, 571, 586
aggravated felonies, to avoid, 572–580
aggravated fleeing and eluding, 571
aggravated stalking, 571–572
agreements to avoid, 583–585
arson, 571
assault, 571
auto theft, 567
bad deal pleas, 585–587
battery, 571
contributing to delinquency of minor, 266–267, 578
credit card fraud, 583–584

Political offense exception
    criminal mischief, 569, 571
    currency reporting violations, 585
    deadly weapons, 584
    domestic violence offenses, 580–581, 583
    driving under influence, 569, 571
    drug paraphernalia, 585
    drug trafficking crimes, 577
    eligibility for relief, creating, 581–587
        agreement and colloquy, 583–585
    false statements, 585
    fraud, 567, 579, 583–584
    misprision of felony, 575–576
    moral turpitude, to avoid, 566–572
    multiple counts, 569–570, 586
    obstruction of justice, 575–576
    rental cars, failure to return, 567
    sample memorandum, 588–597
    stalking, 571–572, 580
    statutory rape, 578
    tax evasion, 578
    theft, 567–568, 579
    trespass, 569
    violence, crimes of, 569, 576

Political offense exception
    aggravated felonies, 393
    moral turpitude, crimes of, 378–379, 385–386

Polygraph examinations
    tool in criminal-alien law practice, 36

Pornography, child. See Child pornography

Port of entry
    waiver application, 512–513

Possession of burglary tools
    pleas, 568, 571

Possession of stolen property
    aggravated felony, 310
    attempted, 310
    moral turpitude, crimes of, 247

Postconviction relief
    burden of proof, 67–68
    federal court approach, 70–75
    ineffective assistance of counsel, 75–76
    on merits (vacaturs), 64–75, 84–96
    modification of sentence, 76–77
    motion to reopen, 68–69
    motion to vacate, 84–96
    Pickering v. Gonzalez (2006), 66–67

    pleas, 573
    post-*Pickering* cases, 69–70
    vacatur found effective, 70–71
    vacatur found ineffective for immigration purposes, 71–75
    vacatur found ineffective for naturalization purposes, 75
    vacatur granted after removal order executed, 75

Pretrial detention
    arrest from, 16

Pretrial diversion programs
    avoiding conviction through, 562–563

Pretrial intervention
    effect of, 56–57

Pretrial statements to immigration court
    waiver application, 660–661
        sample, 668–676

Prior statements, use of
    removal proceedings, 22

Probation
    locating clients with criminal convictions on, 118

Professionals
    nonimmigrant visa holders, 4

Proof of convictions
    documents and electronic records, 81–82

Prostitution enterprises
    aggravated felony, 264, 317–318

Protection orders
    domestic violence, 342–343
    inadmissibility and deportability, 342–343

Protective categories
    deferred action, 10
    immigration status, 5–12
    order of supervision, 11–12
    parole, 8–9
    refugees and asylees, 5–8
    temporary protected status, 8

Psychological evaluations
    tool in criminal-alien law practice, 37, 646

Public Access to Court Electronic Records (PACER)
    tool in criminal-alien law practice, 35–36

Public safety
crimes involving, 353–354

R

Racketeering
aggravated felony, 264

Rape. See also **Statutory rape**
aggravated felony, 263, 266–267

Rapid REPAT (Removal of Eligible Parolees Accepted for Transfer)
prisoner removal program, 116

REAL ID Act of 2005
federal judicial review, 29–30
habeas corpus petitions, 32–33
key legislation, 38

Realistic probability test
classification of crimes, 191–193, 309
defined, 215
divisible statutes and, 207
moral turpitude, crimes of, 210

"Reason to believe"
controlled substance offenses, 323, 331–332, 395–396
firearms offenses, 335
money laundering, 336

Recidivism
possession of controlled substances, 284–290

Recklessness
crimes of violence, 254, 294–295, 576
moral turpitude, crimes of, 242–244, 254, 256, 294–295, 576

Record of case
for Board of Immigration Appeals (BIA), 25
removal proceedings, 22
through pleas agreement and colloquy, 583–585

Record sealing
as convictions, 57–62

Re-entry
after pretermission of §212(c) application and deportation, 491–492
after removal, 111–112
for aggravated felony, 264

criminal charge of, 515–518
locating client with criminal record at time of, 118–119
permission after deportation, when Form I-212 not required, 513–514

Referral
asylum petition, 21*n*61

Refugees
adjustment of status, 650
defined, 5
immigration status, 5–8
Section 209(c) waiver, 459–462, 652–653
withholding of removal, 6–7

Registration. See also **Failure to register**
aliens in United States, 347–351
special, 349

Reinstatement of removal
challenging underlying order, 111–112
nationality-based benefits, 113–114
overview, 112–115

"Release from custody" requirement
mandatory detention, 147–151

Release on recognizance
alternative to detention, 161

Relevant conduct
aggravated felonies, 313–314

Religious workers
nonimmigrant visa holders, 4

Removal proceedings
adjustment of status, 648–650
appeals, 18, 24–26
applications filed after order of removal, 663–667
applications for relief, 24
Board of Immigration Appeals (BIA), 24–26
burden of proof, 23
cancellation of removal. See **Cancellation of removal**
contents of record, 22
course of proceedings, 22–23
deferred action, 10
depositions, 22
detention after removal order, 158–163
entry without inspection, 12
evidence, 23, 81–82

Rental cars

filing fee, 24–25
final merits hearing, 23
individual hearings, 23
institutional removal cases, 18
judicial review, detention during, 160–161
legal sufficiency of charges, 23
LPR subject to, 3
"master calendar" hearing, 23
motion to reopen, 68–69
motion to terminate proceedings, 544–548
from naturalization, 387
nonimmigrant status, 4
Notice to Appear, 20–21
parole, 9
permission to reapply for admission after deportation or removal, 665–667
permission to re-enter after, Form I-212 not required, 513–514
record of case, 22
re-entry after, 111–112
    for aggravated felony, 264
    criminal charge of, 515–518
reinstatement of, 112–115
review after BIA appeal, 27, 31–32
stay of deportation, 663–664
stay of removal order, 25, 27, 31
travel during pending appeal to BIA, 26
unremovables, 159
U status, 619–621
Visa Waiver Program (VWP) restrictions, 5
voluntary departure compared, 496
withholding of removal. *See* Withholding of removal

Rental cars
failure to return, pleas, 567

REPAT (Removal of Eligible Parolees Accepted for Transfer)
prisoner removal program, 116

Restitution
for aggravated felonies, 314–316

Restriction on removal. See Withholding of removal

Robbery
moral turpitude, crimes of, 247

Rules of procedure
court of appeals, 32

EOIR, 18

S

Sabotage
under National Security Act, 264

Section 209(c)
asylees, 459–462
comparison to Section 212(h) waiver, 460
discretionary determination, 31
LPR use of, 460–462
refugees, 459–462, 652–653

Section 212(c)
adjustment of status, combined with, 492–493
advance permission to return to unrelinquished domicile, 479
AEDPA, 477, 480–482
affirmative applications for, 494–495
aggravated felonies, 485–487, 489, 655
alien smuggling charges, 509
applications for waiver, 654–655
cancellation of removal, combined with, 467, 493–494
defense to criminal charge of re-entry after removal, 517
deportation track, eligibility for persons in, 479–480
discretionary determination, 31
domicile, 655
eligibility criteria, 476–477, 488–492
IMMACT90, 480
immigration court filings, 654–655
inadmissibility or deportability, 491–492
naturalization after waiver, 495
1996 legislation, 477
overview, 477–479
persons convicted at trial, 487
persons physically deported prior to *St. Cyr,* 490–491
    re-entry after pretermission of §212(c) application and deportation, 491–492
post-1996 convictions, curing, 487–488
regulation post *St. Cyr* decision, 482–488
relief under, 476–495
Supreme Court decision, 477
2004 regulation, 482–488
    cut-off dates for eligibility, 482–484

IIRAIRA definition of aggravated felony retroactive, 486–487
individuals in exclusion proceedings, 484–485

Section 212(d)(3)(A)
waiver, 657–658

Section 212(d)(3)(B)
application, 658
nonimmigrant visa waiver, 510–514
consulate applications, 511–512
factors to consider, 514
jurisdiction, 511–514
permission to re-enter after deportation or removal, Form I-212 not required, 513–514
port of entry application, 512–513
relief under, 510–514
security or terrorism, as grounds of inadmissibility, 514

Section 212(h)
adjustment of status, waiver in conjunction with, 445–446
alien smuggling, 509
application, 651–652
arriving aliens, waiver, 452–455
Attorney General on, 455
battered spouse and child waiver, 443, 651–652
comparison to Section 209(c) waiver, 460
discretionary waivers, 31, 457
eligibility for relief and, 581
memorandum in support of waiver eligibility, 534–539
motion to pretermit waiver application, 529–533
special clause for LPRs, 443–451
violent or dangerous crime convictions, 455–459
waivers under, 651–652

Secure Communities Initiative (ICE)
prisoner removal program, 116

Security. See National security

Sentence
for aggravated felony, 311–312, 586–587
term of imprisonment, 572–573
need for imposition of, in case of mandatory detention, 150–151

non-criminal alien defendants, guilty pleas, 518
pleas, 572–573
postconviction relief modifying, 76–77
service of, failure to appear for, 264
suspension of, 82
termination of, arrest upon, 16
U.S. Sentencing Guidelines, 518

Service of process
Notice to Appear, 21

Sex offenders
failure to register, 258–259, 354–355

Sexual abuse. See also Rape
aggravated criminal, 301
battery, 301
of minor, 259, 263, 266–267, 319–320, 578
second degree, 301

Sexual offender, failure to register as
Adam Walsh Act, 354–355
moral turpitude, crimes of, 258–259

Slavery offenses
aggravated felony, 264

Smuggling of aliens. See Alien smuggling

Social security number
falsely representing, 251

Solicitation offenses
controlled substance offenses, 328–329

Somalia
temporary protected status (TPS), 8

Sources of legal authority
generally, 38

Special rule cancellation of removal
application, 474–476
NACARA, 474–476

Spouse, battered. See Battered spouse

S status, visas for cooperating witnesses. See Cooperating witnesses, visas for

***St. Cyr* decision**
AEDPA amendments, retroactive application of, 482–488

Stalking
deportability, 337
domestic violence including, 412
moral turpitude, crimes of, 255

State Department (DOS)
    pleas, 571–572, 580

State Department (DOS)
    application for waiver, 658
    overview, 14, 17
    pardons, 63

State laws
    drug possession offenses, 279–284
    money laundering, 406–407

Stateless individuals
    unremovable status of, 159

Statuses. *See* **Immigration status**

Statute of limitations
    as defense to criminal charge of re-entry after removal, 515

Statutory rape
    aggravated felony, 267–269
    classification of crime, 259
    moral turpitude, crimes of, 259
    pleas, 578

Stay of deportation
    applications filed after order of removal, 663–667
        criteria, 667
        Form I-246, 663–664
        permission to reapply for admission after deportation or removal, 665–667

Stay of removal
    BIA appeals, 25
    federal court of appeals review, 27, 32

Stolen property
    attempted possession of, 310
    interstate transportation of, 579
    possession of, 264, 310

Students
    nonimmigrant visa holders, 4, 510

Subornation of perjury
    aggravated felony, 264, 311

Supervision, intensive. *See* **Intensive Supervision Appearance Program**

Suspension of sentence
    conviction, effect of, 82. *See also* Consequences of criminal act

T

Taking of property
    theft offense, 192–193, 307–309. *See also* Theft

Tax evasion
    aggravated felony, 264, 312–313
    pleas, 578

Temporary protected status (TPS)
    advance parole, 8
    defined, 8
    felony convictions, effect on, 8
    immigration status, 8
    inadmissibility, 104
    review of denial, 20, 21n61

Temporary restraining orders
    with habeas corpus petitions, 33

Temporary workers without visas
    from Caribbean, Canada, and Mexico, 4–5

Termination of sentence
    arrest upon, 16

Terrorism
    anti-terrorism legislation. *See* Antiterrorism and Effective Death Penalty Act of 1996; USA PATRIOT Act
    as grounds of inadmissibility, 514

Testimony
    removal proceedings, 22

Theft
    aggravated felonies, 248, 264, 307–311
    classification of crimes, 192–193, 217–225
    joyriding, 308
    moral turpitude, crimes of, 226–231, 245–248, 356–368, 567–568
    pleas, 567–568, 579
    sentencing, 311
    vehicles, unauthorized use of, 302–304

Third country, acceptance by
    withholding of removal, 7

Threats of bodily harm
    moral turpitude, crimes of, 255

Throwing deadly missile
    divisible statutes, 203–204

Tolling
    seven-year period, 452, 582

Tools and strategies for criminal-alien law practice
generally, 34
Accurint, 35, 643
confirmation-of-appointment letters, 37, 48
country-condition experts, 37, 642
country-condition sources of information (websites), 37, 648
FBI rap sheet, 34–35, 46–47, 642–643, 645n10
FOIA requests, 36
intake sheets, 37–38
PACER, 35–36
polygraph examinations, 36
psychological and medical evaluations, 37, 646
Westlaw, LEXIS, AILALink, *AILA.org,* and Fastcase, 36–37

Torture Convention. See Convention Against Torture

Tourists
nonimmigrant visa holders, 5, 510
Visa Waiver Program (VWP), 5
without visas, 5

TPCR. See Transition Period Custody Rules

TPS. See Temporary protected status

Trafficking
in controlled substance, 263, 269–273, 575
counterfeit goods, 251
in firearms, 304–305
in vehicles, 264, 311
victims of
deferred action, 10
T status visas, 609–614

Transition Period Custody Rules (TPCR)
invocation of, by Attorney General, 164–165
mandatory detention, 134, 383n23
invocation of, by Attorney General, 164–165

Travel
advance parole, 9
controlled substance offenses, consequence of, 396
convictions, 100
deferred action, 10
during pending appeal to BIA, 26

S visas, 600
temporary protected status (TPS), 8
withholding of removal, 6–7

Treason
under National Security Act, 264

Trespass
pleas of, 569

T status, visas for cooperating witnesses. See Cooperating witnesses, visas for

Turks and Caicos Islands
tourists and temporary workers from, 5

U

Unlicensed money transmitting
moral turpitude, crimes of, 232–234

Unremovables
defined, 159

U.S. Customs and Border Protection. See Customs and Border Protection

U.S. Immigration and Customs Enforcement. See Immigration and Customs Enforcement

U.S. passport. See Visa or passport fraud

U.S. Sentencing Guidelines
re-entry offenses, 518

USA PATRIOT Act of 2001
key legislation, 38
money laundering under, 335, 405, 407

USCIS. See Citizenship and Immigration Services

Use of force. See Violence, crimes of

U status, visas for cooperating witnesses. See Cooperating witnesses, visas for

V

Vacaturs. See Postconviction relief

Vehicles
aiding and abetting in theft of, 307–309
auto theft, 302–304
as not crime of violence, 300
pleas, 567, 571
joyriding, 246, 308
rental car, failure to return, pleas, 567

Vehicular homicide

    trafficking in, 264, 311
    unauthorized use of, 302–304

Vehicular homicide
    not crime of violence, 300–301

Venues for waiver applications
    overview, 640–643

Veterans
    naturalization of, 505–507

Victims
    of crime as cooperating witnesses. *See* Cooperating witnesses, visas for
    of domestic violence, 339–340, 583

Victims of Trafficking and Violence Protection Act of 2000 (VTVPA)
    U visa status, 614

Victim Witness Protection Act of 1982
    restitution, 315

Violence, crimes of
    aggravated felonies, 263, 290–313
    arson, 255
    attempted murder, 254
    defined, 290–291
    extortion, 255
    firearms offenses, 263
    force
        active use of violent physical force, 297–300
        contact versus, 295–299
        recklessness, 295–299
    intent, 291–299
    involuntary manslaughter, 257
    manslaughter, 254
    mental state, 299–300
    misdemeanors, 318–319
    moral turpitude, crimes of, 253–262, 294–295, 569
    not crimes of violence, 300–301
    particular offenses, 301–302. *See also specific offenses*
    pleas, 569, 576
    recklessness, 254, 294–299, 576
    stalking, aggravated, 255
    threatening behavior, crimes involving, 255
    voluntary manslaughter, 254
    waiver under Section 212(h) and, 455–459

Violence Against Women Reauthorization Act of 2013
    U visa status, 615–616, 621–622

Visa
    defined, 13

Visa or passport fraud
    adjustment of status, 419–421, 440
    aggravated felonies, 264, 350–351
    asylum and withholding of removal, 423–424
    civil and criminal document fraud violations, 351
    consequences of, 419–425, 430
    Convention Against Torture (CAT), 423–424
    crimes of, 349–351, 422
    denaturalization, 425
    deportability or removability, 421–422
    failure to register, 347–351
    falsely making statements, 251, 264
    inadmissibility, adjustment of status, and visa eligibility, 419–421
    mandatory detention, 422
    moral turpitude, crimes of, 350–351, 419–420
    naturalization, 424–425
    possession versus use, 420
    voluntary departure, 422–423

Visa Waiver Program (VWP)
    criminal convictions, 5
    tourists without visas, 5

Voluntary departure
    generally, 495–499
    aggravated felonies, 390–391
    alien smuggling, 417
    applications for waiver, 642
    arriving aliens, 495
    bond, 497–499
    "check out" procedure, 496–498
    conclusion of proceedings, 498–499
    controlled substance offenses, 398–399
    domestic violence, 414–415
    export violations, 427–428
    failure to register, 422–423
    failure to timely depart, 496–498
    falsification of documents, 422–423
    firearms offenses, 403–404

"good moral character," 383–384, 403, 408–409, 414, 423, 498
money laundering, 408–409
moral turpitude, crimes of, 383–384
precommencement or preliminary stage of proceedings, 496–498
removal compared, 496
under safeguards, 495
use of, 495–496
visa or passport fraud, 422–423

Voluntary manslaughter
moral turpitude, crimes of, 254

V petition
deferred action, 10

VTVPA (Victims of Trafficking and Violence Protection Act of 2000)
U visa status, 614

VWP. See Visa Waiver Program

W

Waiver. See also specific Sections governing
applications for, 639–676
battered spouse and child, 443–444, 473–474, 651–652
combining waivers, 472–473
defense of, 515
discretionary determinations, no review of, 30–31
eligibility, 4
embassies, waiver applications, 640–642, 658
evidence in support of, 644–648
extreme hardship, 442–444
15-year waiver, 442, 651–652
Homeland Security, Department of, 442n36
inadmissibility, waiver of, 441–459, 540–543
LPRs and adjustment of status, 444–451
memorandum in support of waiver eligibility, 534–539
motion to pretermit waiver application, 529–533
pretrial statements to immigration court, 660–661
refugees and asylees, 459–462, 652–653

relief under, 431–432
Section 212(c), 476–495. *See also* Section 212(c)
Section 212(d)(3)(A), 657–658
Section 212(d)(3)(B), 510–514. *See also* Section 212(d)(3)(B)
Section 212(h), 441–459. *See also* Section 212(h)
smuggling immediate family members, 507

Weapons. See Firearms offenses

Westlaw
tool in criminal-alien law practice, 36–37

Withholding of removal
aggravated felony conviction and, 391–393, 582–583
alien smuggling charges, 417–418, 509
asylum distinguished, 6–7, 463–466
burden of proof, 6
controlled substance offenses and, 399–400
Convention Against Torture (CAT). *See* Convention Against Torture
deportation, 6–7
domestic violence offenses, 414–415
eligibility for relief, 582–583
export violations, 428
failure to register, 423–424
firearms offenses, 404
money laundering, 409
moral turpitude, crimes of, 385–386
"particularly serious crime" analysis, 526–528
periodic reporting requirement, 7
procedure, 6–7
refugees, 6–7
relief under, 462
third country, acceptance by, 7
travel, 6–7
visa fraud, 423–424

Withholds of adjudication
defined, 54–55
with no penalty, 55

Witnesses
bribery of, 264, 311
cooperating. *See also* Cooperating witnesses, visas for

Witness protection programs

    adjustment of status, 102. *See also* Adjustment of status
    release from detention of, 136
list, 661–663
parole, 8–9
waiver application, 659–663

Witness protection programs
cooperating witnesses, 136

Work permit
deferred action, 10
order of supervision, 11–12

Y

Youthful offenders. See also Juvenile delinquency
adverse immigration consequences, avoiding, 563–564
moral turpitude, exceptions to admissibility, 378